AF513322

R. Gupta's®

National Testing Agency (NTA)

UGC-NET/JRF

Junior Research Fellowship & Assistant Professor Eligibility Exam

Political Science

Previous Years' Papers

PAPER II

by

RPH Editorial Board

2027
EDITION

RAMESH PUBLISHING HOUSE, NEW DELHI

Published by

O.P. Gupta *for* Ramesh Publishing House

Admin. Office

12-H, New Daryaganj Road, Opp. Officers' Mess,
New Delhi-110002 ✆ 23275224, 23245124

E-mail: info@rameshpublishinghouse.com
For Online Shopping: www.rameshpublishinghouse.com

Showroom

• Balaji Market, Nai Sarak, Delhi-110006 ✆ 23282525 📱 9354373464
• 4457, Nai Sarak, Delhi-110006

Book Code: R-2775

ISBN: 978-93-5477-468-3

Price: ₹ 660

Printed at: Deepak Offset, Delhi

CONTENTS

UGC-NET/JRF—(PAPER-II) POLITICAL SCIENCE

Previous Years' Paper

National Testing Agency (NTA)

UGC-NET Junior Research Fellowship & Assistant Professor Eligibility Exam

POLITICAL SCIENCE, JANUARY-2026

(Exam held on 06-01-2026)

PAPER-II

1. The government set up a third committee on police reforms under the stewardship of a former Union Home Secretary, K. Padmanabhaiah in the year:

1. 2000
2. 1990
3. 2010
4. 1982

2. Match the List-I with List-II.

List-I (*Author*)	List-II (*Book*)
A. C.G. Hoag and G.H. Hallett	I. Proportional Representation
B. H. Sidgwick	II. Public Opinion and Popular Government
C. A.L. Lowell	III. Elements of Politics
D. J.A. Corry	IV. Democratic Government and Politics

Choose the *correct* answer from the options given below:

1. A-I, B-III, C-II, D-IV
2. A-IV, B-II, C-III, D-I
3. A-IV, B-III, C-I, D-II
4. A-IV, B-I, C-II, D-III

3. Match the List-I with List-II.

List-I (*Author*)	List-II (*Book*)
A. A.R. Ball	I. Modern Politics and Government
B. J.N. Bhagwati	II. Eco-Feminism
C. John Aart	III. Globalisation: A Critical Introduction
D. Vandana Shiva	IV. In Defense of Globalisation

Choose the *correct* answer from the options given below:

1. A-I, B-II, C-III, D-IV
2. A-II, B-III, C-IV, D-I
3. A-III, B-II, C-I, D-IV
4. A-I, B-IV, C-III, D-II

4. Arrange the following world events in descending order:

A. Japan invaded Manchuria
B. Mussolini seized power in Italy
C. Armenian genocide
D. Italy invaded Abyssinia (Ethiopia)
E. Battle of Stanlingard

Choose the *correct* answer from the options given below:

1. C, B, D, A, E
2. E, D, A, B, C
3. A, B, C, D, E
4. E, D, A, C, B

5. Dr. Rajendra Prasad was elected President of the Constituent Assembly on:

1. 11 December 1946
2. 29 December 1946
3. 13 October 1946
4. 15 September 1946

6. On which day, the Triple Entente formally condemned the Ottoman Empire for 'Crime against Humanity and Civilization in the backdrop of the Armenian Genocide'?

1. 17 November 1915
2. 13 December 1916
3. 13 March 1915
4. 24 May 1915

7. The National Democratic Alliance under Narendra Modi came to power for the second time in 2019, few important events of NDA's second term under Modi were:

A. The Muslim women Protection of Rights on Marriage Bill was passed in 2019.
B. The Transgender Persons (Protection of Rights) Act was passed in 2019.
C. In 2021, Amendments to the Protection of Animals from Sexual Offences Act were enacted.
D. The Jammu and Kashmir Re-organisation Act was passed in 2018.
E. The Central Government diluted Article 370 of the Constitution in 2022.

Choose the ***correct*** answer from the options given below:

1. A, B only 2. B, C, D only
3. A, B, C only 4. A, C, E only

8. In which year then Viceroy of India passed a resolution of local self-government which led the democratic forms of Municipal Governance in India?

1. 1882 2. 1879
3. 1877 4. 1885

9. Indira Gandhi broke the cycle of simultaneous poll of Lok-Sabha and State Assemblies on holding mid-term Lok-Sabha election in:

1. 1977 2. 1980
3. 1967 4. 1971

10. Arrange the following global regional organisations in ascending order as per their establishment:

A. Gulf Cooperation Council (GCC)
B. Latin American Integration Association (LAIA)
C. Benelux Economic Union (BEU)
D. Black Sea Economic Cooperation (BSEC)
E. Arab Maghreb Union (AMU)

Choose the ***correct*** answer from the options given below:

1. C, B, A, E, D 2. C, B, A, D, E
3. A, B, C, D, E 4. B, C, A, E, D

11. Identify the authoritarian regimes (countries) at the global level:

A. Italy B. Spain
C. India D. North Korea
E. Saudi Arabia

Choose the ***correct*** answer from the options given below:

1. A, B, E only 2. B, C, D only
3. D, E only 4. A, B, C, D only

12. The establishment of a Federal Railway Authority to look after the administration of railways was provided by the:

1. Charter Act of 1813
2. India Councils Act of 1909
3. Indian Councils Act of 1892
4. Government of India Act of 1935

13. Given below are two statements : one is labelled as Assertion (A) and the other is labelled as Reason (R).

Assertion (A): Sun Tzu's 'The Art of War' advocates attacking the opponents strategy and alliances and that would involve psychology and perception.

Reason (R): China is a Pacifist country and believes in peaceful mechanism to deal disputes with other countries.

In the light of the above statements, choose the *most appropriate* answer from the options given below:

1. Both (A) and (R) are correct and (R) is the correct explanation of (A)
2. Both (A) and (R) are correct, but (R) is NOT the correct explanation of (A)
3. (A) is correct, but (R) is not correct
4. (A) is not correct, but (R) is correct

14. Match the List-I with List-II.

List-I (*Treaty*)	List-II (*Year of Signing*)
A. Strategic Arms Limitation Treaty I (SALT I)	I. 2002
B. Intermediate Nuclear Forces (INF) Treaty	II. 1993
C. Strategic Arms Reduction Treaty II (START II)	III. 1987
D. Strategic Offensive Reduction Treaty (SORT)	IV. 1972

Choose the *correct* answer from the options given below:

1. A-III, B-IV, C-I, D-II
2. A-I, B-II, C-III, D-IV
3. A-I, B-III, C-I, D-IV
4. A-IV, B-III, C-II, D-I

15. Arrange the following major international initiatives on environment in descending order:

A. UN Convention of Law of the Sea (UNCLOS)
B. Convention on International Trade in Endangered Species (CITES)
C. UN Conference on the Human Environment (UNCHE)
D. World Meteorological Organization (WMO) established
E. Antarctic Treaty

Choose the *correct* answer from the options given below:

1. A, B, C, D, E 2. D, E, B, C, A
3. A, B, C, E, D 4. E, C, D, A, B

16. Arrange the following Vice-Presidents of India in descending order:

A. Krishna Kant
B. Gopal Swarup Pathak
C. B.D. Jatti
D. R. Venkatraman
E. Mohammed Hidaytullah

Choose the *correct* answer from the options given below:

1. B, C, D, E, A 2. A, B, C, D, E
3. A, D, E, C, B 4. A, C, D, B, E

17. Match the List-I with List-II.

List-I (*Bretton Woods Institutions*)	List-II (*Establishment Year*)
A. International Monetary Fund (IMF)	I. 1948
B. World Trade Organization (WTO)	II. 1947
C. International Bank for Reconstruction and Development (IBRD)	III. 1995
D. General Agreement on Tariffs and Trade (GATT)	IV. 1946

Choose the *correct* answer from the options given below:

1. A-I, B-II, C-III, D-IV
2. A-II, B-III, C-IV, D-I
3. A-IV, B-III, C-II, D-I
4. A-II, B-IV, C-I, D-III

18. Arrange the following UN Secretary Generals in descending order to hold the office at the UN:

A. Trygve Lie
B. Dag Hammarskjold
C. Boutros Boutros-Ghali
D. U. Thant
E. Kurt Waldheim

Choose the *correct* answer from the options given below:

1. A, B, C, D, E 2. A, D, B, C, E
3. B, A, D, E, C 4. C, E, D, B, A

19. Who termed Drafting Committee of the Constitution as Drifting Committee?

1. Naziruddin Ahmad
2. K.M. Munshi
3. Jawaharlal Nehru
4. Dr. Rajendra Prasad

20. The concept of "Deconstruction" is associated with:

1. Conservatism 2. Terrorism
3. Oligarchy 4. Post-Modernism

21. The first Administrative Reforms Commission was established in:

1. 21 May 1966
2. 5 January 1966
3. 9 January 1965
4. 17 March 1966

22. Who wrote the book "The India Way: Strategies for an Uncertain World"?

1. Sunil Khillani 2. S. Jaishankar
3. Raja Mohan 4. Sumit Ganguly

23. In which year Dr. Shyama Prasad Mukherjee was elected as a member of 'Bengal Legislative Council'?

1. 1933 2. 1931
3. 1929 4. 1927

24. Which British Prime Minister stated about Jallianwala Bagh massacre that "it was Unutterably Monstrous"?

1. Winston Churchill
2. Harold Macmillan
3. Sir Anthony Eden
4. William Ewart Gladstone

25. Arrange the following Chief Election Commissioners of India in ascending order as per their tenure:

A. M.S. Gill
B. T.S. Krishnamurthy
C. T. Swaminathan
D. R.V.S. Peri Sastri
E. S.L. Shakdhar

Choose the ***correct*** answer from the options given below:

1. C, E, D, B, A 2. E, C, A, B, D
3. D, B, A, C, E 4. C, E, D, A, B

26. Given below are two statements : one is labelled as Assertion (A) and the other is labelled as Reason (R).

Assertion (A): Pakistani Parliament has voted (November, 2025) to give its army chief new powers and lifetime immunity from arrest and persecution.

Reason (R): Judiciary is very weak in Pakistan.

In the light of the above statements, choose the ***most appropriate*** answer from the options given below:

1. Both (A) and (R) are correct and (R) is the correct explanation of (A)
2. Both (A) and (R) are correct, but (R) is NOT the correct explanation of (A)
3. (A) is correct, but (R) is not correct
4. (A) is not correct, but (R) is correct

27. Jawaharlal Nehru became the first Prime Minister of India in 1947. Events under Nehru's leadership includes:

A. The National Planning Commission appointed Nehru as it's Chairman in 1950.
B. Nehru visited China in 1958 and Signed the Panch-Sheel Treaty.
C. Nehru fought three general elections.
D. In 1952 the first of the five IIT's was set up.
E. India signed a treaty with Nepal in 1950.

Choose the ***correct*** answer from the options given below:

1. A, B, C, D only
2. A, C, D, E only
3. A, B, D, E only
4. B, C, D only

28. Match the List-I with List-II.

List-I (*Author*)	List-II (*Books*)
A. L. Woolf	I. The Tragedy of Great Power Politics
B. Hans Kohn	II. Essays on Nationalism
C. C.J.H. Hayes	III. Nationalism and Liberty
D. John Mearsheimer	IV. Imperialism and Civilisation

Choose the ***correct*** answer from the options given below:

1. A-IV, B-III, C-II, D-I
2. A-I, B-II, C-III, D-IV
3. A-III, B-IV, C-I, D-II
4. A-I, B-IV, C-III, D-II

29. In which year, Yazidi genocide was carried out by the Islamic State?

1. 2014
2. 2017
3. 2015
4. 2012

30. Australian House of Representatives has the strength of:

1. 177
2. 180
3. 150
4. 175

31. Which American President delivered following statement about India "I think it is really very sad that 600 million people have lost what they had since the mid-1940's. I hope that in time there could be a restoration of democratic processes as we know them in the U.S."?

1. Ronald Reagan
2. Gerald Ford
3. John F. Kennedy
4. George W. Bush

32. Match the List-I with List-II.

List-I (*Name of Committee's*)	List-II (*Year*)
A. Committee on Service Conditions of Municipal Employees	I. 1953-54
B. Rural-Urban Relationship Committee	II. 1963-66
C. National Commission on Urbanisation	III. 1965-68
D. Taxation Enquiry Commission	IV. 1985-88

Choose the ***correct*** answer from the options given below:

1. A-I, B-II, C-III, D-IV
2. A-IV, B-III, C-II, D-I
3. A-II, B-III, C-I, D-IV
4. A-III, B-II, C-IV, D-I

33. Which foreign country's Prime Minister abruptly announced his resignation while he was in Saudi Arabia on 4th November 2017?

1. Jordan
2. Lebanon
3. Kuwait
4. Syria

34. Arrange the following Constitutional Amendments in ascending order:

A. Incorporation of Goa, Daman and Diu in the Indian Union

B. Increased the retirement age of High Court Judges from 60 to 62 years

C. Included Sindhi as 15th Language in the Eighth Schedule

D. Incorporation of Dadra and Nagar Haveli in the Indian Union

E. Abolished the privy purse and privileges of the former rulers of the princely states.

Choose the ***correct*** answer from the options given below:

1. D, A, B, C, E
2. D, A, C, E, B
3. E, A, B, C, D
4. A, D, B, C, E

35. In which year, the Supreme Court of United States of America asserted the Power of Judicial Review?

1. 1803
2. 1805
3. 1811
4. 1809

36. Given below are two statements : one is labelled as Assertion (A) and the other is labelled as Reason (R).

Assertion (A): Ecofeminism has been a significant strand of feminist thought and activism since the term was coined by French Feminist Frencoise - d'Equbonne in the 1970s'.

Reason (R): Ecofeminists are accountable for climate change consequences.

In the light of the above statements, choose the ***most appropriate*** answer from the options given below:

1. Both (A) and (R) are correct and (R) is the correct explanation of (A)
2. Both (A) and (R) are correct, but (R) is NOT the correct explanation of (A)
3. (A) is correct, but (R) is not correct
4. (A) is not correct, but (R) is correct

37. The view that, the physical world and natural resources should be treated as subservient to human needs and interests refers to the idea of:

1. Anti-semiticism
2. Anthropo-centrism
3. Radical Feminism
4. Objective Punishment

38. Arrange the events related to the life of Vinayak Damodar Savarkar in ascending order.

A. Savarkar was arrested in London.
B. The Permanent Court of International Arbitration gave its decision on Savarkar Arbitration Case.
C. Savarkar was shifted to the Ratnagiri jail.
D. He's portrait was installed in the central hall of the Indian Parliament.
E. Savarkar passed away.

Choose the ***correct*** answer from the options given below:

1. A, B, C, D, E 2. B, D, A, C, E
3. A, B, C, E, D 4. D, B, A, C, E

39. Who proposed "truth" as an increduality towards metanarratives?

1. Jean Francois Lyotard
2. Niccolo Machiavelli
3. Richard Brown
4. Sarojini Naidu

40. Which Act led the foundation of a modern police bureaucracy in India?

1. Regulating Act of India, 1776
2. Govt. of India Act, 1935
3. Indian Council Act, 1861
4. British Indian Act, 1801

41. Match the List-I with List-II.

List-I (*Author*)	List-II (*Book*)
A. Andrew Heywood	I. Declaration of American Independence
B. David Held	II. Political Theory: An Introduction
C. Thomas Jefferson	III. Political Theory and the Modern State
D. John Locke	IV. Second Treatise of Civil Government

Choose the ***correct*** answer from the options given below:

1. A-II, B-III, C-I, D-IV
2. A-III, B-II, C-IV, D-I
3. A-I, B-II, C-III, D-IV
4. A-IV, B-III, C-II, D-I

42. Identify the characteristics of Parliamentary form of government.

A. Collective Responsibility
B. Dissolution of the Lower House
C. Leadership of the Prime Minister
D. President is the Real Boss.
E. President is directly elected by the People.

Choose the ***correct*** answer from the options given below:

1. B, C, D only
2. A, B, C only
3. A, B, C, D only
4. C, D, E only

43. Match the List-I with List-II.

List-I (*Regional Organization*)	List-II (*Number of Member Nations*)
A. Economic Cooperation Organization	I. 54
B. Council of Europe	II. 27
C. ASEAN Regional Forum	III. 47
D. African Union	IV. 10

Choose the ***correct*** answer from the options given below:

1. A-II, B-III, C-IV, D-I
2. A-I, B-II, C-III, D-IV
3. A-IV, B-II, C-III, D-I
4. A-IV, B-III, C-II, D-I

44. Arrange the following Chief Justices of India in Ascending order as per their tenure:

A. V.N. Khare B. B.N. Kirpal
C. M.H. Kania D. L.M. Sharma
E. A.M. Ahmadi

Choose the ***correct*** answer from the options given below:

1. A, B, C, D, E 2. C, D, E, A, B
3. B, C, D, A, E 4. C, D, E, B, A

45. Given below are two statements : one is labelled as Assertion (A) and the other is labelled as Reason (R).

Assertion (A): Swami Sahajanand Saraswati formed the Bihar Provincial Kisan Sabha in 1929 to mobilize peasant grievances against Zamindari attacks on their occupancy rights.

Reason (R): At Lucknow Session of the Congress in 1936, the All India Kisan Sabha was formed with Swami Sahajanand Saraswati as its president.

In the light of the above statements, choose the ***most appropriate*** answer from the options given below:

1. Both (A) and (R) are correct and (R) is the correct explanation of (A)
2. Both (A) and (R) are correct, but (R) is NOT the correct explanation of (A)
3. (A) is correct, but (R) is not correct
4. (A) is not correct, but (R) is correct

46. Narasimha Rao fought and won elections from:

1. Andhra Pradesh, Odisha and Maharashtra
2. West Bengal and Rajasthan
3. Assam and Kerala
4. Nagaland and Arunachal Pradesh

47. Identify the Deputy Speakers of the Central Legislative Assembly which was known as Deputy Presidents before independence:

A. Sachchidananda Sinha
B. H.S. Gour
C. Akhil Chandra Dutta
D. G.G. Swell
E. Godey Murahari

Choose the ***correct*** answer from the options given below:

1. A, B & C only
2. A, C, E only
3. B & E only
4. D & C only

48. In September 2000, the Government of India had set up a high level Committee on the Indian Diaspora under the Chairmanship of:

1. L.M. Singhvi 2. K. Natwar Singh
3. P. Chidambaram 4. Ranjan Gogoi

49. Match the List-I with List-II.

List-I (*Conference on the Environment*)	List-II (*Year*)
A. United Nations Conference on the Human Environment	I. 2009
B. Convention on International Trade in Endangered Species	II. 1992
C. UN Conference on Environment and Development	III. 1972
D. The UN Climate Change Conference	IV. 1973

Choose the ***correct*** answer from the options given below:

1. A-I, B-II, C-III, D-IV
2. A-IV, B-III, C-II, D-I
3. A-IV, B-III, C-I, D-II
4. A-III, B-IV, C-II, D-I

50. Arrange the Speakers of the Lok-Sabha in ascending order:

A. Baliram Bhagat
B. Neelam Sanjiva Reddy
C. K.S. Hegde
D. Gurdial Singh Dhillon
E. Rabi Ray

Choose the ***correct*** answer from the options given below:

1. D, A, E, B, C 2. A, B, C, D, E
3. B, D, A, C, E 4. C, A, B, D, E

51. Hannah Arendt in her essay "The Human Condition" identifies three levels of human activity: Labour, Work and Action.

A. 'Work' represents the activity of artists and craftsmen.
B. 'Action' is the highest activity which refers to public interaction between equal citizens
C. 'Action' belongs to the sphere of politics.
D. 'Action is the activity which denies freedom of thought'.
E. 'Labour' is the lowest level of activity in which man engages for the fulfillment of physical needs.

Choose the ***correct*** answer from the options given below:

1. A, B, D only
2. C, D, E only
3. D, E only
4. A, B, C, E only

52. Who is the final authority to determine a Bill as 'Money Bill'?

1. Attorney General of India
2. Chairman of the Law Commission of India
3. Speaker of the Lok Sabha
4. Chairman of the Rajya Sabha

53. Who was the first Non-Congress Chief Minister of Karnataka?

1. E.M.S. Namboodripad
2. Ram Krishna Hegde
3. H.D. Devagowda
4. S.R. Bommai

54. When Simon-de Beauvoir claims 'one is not born but rather becomes a woman', she identifies gender as:

1. An identity instituted through a stylized repetition of acts
2. Biological predetermined existence
3. An identity constituted through divine intervention in society
4. A concept constructed through gambling

55. Identify the post Cold War period events:

A. China-Vietnam war
B. Iran-Iraq war
C. Apartheid ends in South Africa
D. Taliban-II seized power in Afghanistan
E. Kargil War between India and Pakistan

Choose the ***correct*** answer from the options given below:

1. C, D, E only
2. A, B, C only
3. B, C, D, E only
4. B, D, C only

56. John Stuart Mill was a member of Parliament (Britain) during the period of:

1. 1851-1854 2. 1857-1860
3. 1861-1864 4. 1865-1868

57. Match the List-I with List-II.

List-I (***States***)	**List-II** (***Number of Seats in Rajya Sabha and Lok Sabha***)
A. West Bengal	I. 12 and 28
B. Tamil Nadu	II. 10 and 21
C. Odisha	III. 16 and 42
D. Karnataka	IV. 18 and 39

Choose the ***correct*** answer from the options given below:

1. A-I, B-II, C-III, D-IV
2. A-II, B-III, C-I, D-IV
3. A-III, B-IV, C-II, D-I
4. A-I, B-IV, C-III, D-II

58. Which of the following Constitutional Amendments empower women in India?

A. 69th B. 73rd
C. 74th D. 104th
E. 106th

Choose the ***correct*** answer from the options given below:

1. A, C, D only 2. A, B, C, D only
3. C, D, E only 4. B, C, E only

59. Given below are two statements : one is labelled as Assertion (A) and the other is labelled as Reason (R).

Assertion (A): Cold War started after the end of Second World War.

Reason (R): The entire world was largely divided into two blocks. The one was Capitalist led by the USA and the second was Communist led by the USSR during the Cold War era.

In the light of the above statements, choose the ***most appropriate*** answer from the options given below:

1. Both (A) and (R) are correct and (R) is the correct explanation of (A)
2. Both (A) and (R) are correct, but (R) is NOT the correct explanation of (A)
3. (A) is correct, but (R) is not correct
4. (A) is not correct, but (R) is correct

60. Given below are two statements : one is labelled as Assertion (A) and the other is labelled as Reason (R).

Assertion (A): In 1941, an Eastern Front opened up through the German invasion of Yugoslavia, Greece and the Soviet Union.

Reason (R): Nazi expansionism in Asia has been associated with the outbreak of the Second World War.

In the light of the above statements, choose the ***most appropriate*** answer from the options given below:

1. Both (A) and (R) are correct and (R) is the correct explanation of (A)
2. Both (A) and (R) are correct, but (R) is NOT the correct explanation of (A)
3. (A) is correct, but (R) is not correct
4. (A) is not correct, but (R) is correct

61. On which day, US president Woodrow Wilson issued the Fourteen Points?

1. 7 May 1918 2. 5 March 1918
3. 8 January 1918 4. 11 January 1919

62. The key Human Development Indicators are:

A. Leading a long and healthy life
B. Achieving equality for all animals and insects
C. Ensuring Human security
D. Acquiring good entertainments
E. Preserving resources for future generations

Choose the ***correct*** answer from the options given below:

1. A, B, C, D only
2. B, C, E, only
3. A, C, E only
4. C, D, B only

63. In which year, Vithalbhai Patel was elected to the Central Legislative Assembly?

1. 1927 2. 1921
3. 1923 4. 1924

64. Which university was the first to begin the protest against the imposition of Emergency (1975)?

1. University of Assam
2. University of Madras
3. University of Delhi
4. Delhi Technological University

65. Dr. Sachchidananda Sinha presided as the interim president during the inaugural meeting of the:

1. Constituent Assembly
2. Indian National Congress
3. Poona Sarvajanik Sabha
4. All India Women's Conference

66. Given below are two statements : one is labelled as Assertion (A) and the other is labelled as Reason (R).

Assertion (A): The Tashkent Declaration was signed by President Ayub Khan of Pakistan and Lal Bahadur Shastri Prime Minister of India on January 10, 1966.

Reason (R): The Tashkent Declaration was meant to form a framework for lasting peace between India and Pakistan.

In the light of the above statements, choose the ***most appropriate*** answer from the options given below:

1. Both (A) and (R) are correct and (R) is the correct explanation of (A)
2. Both (A) and (R) are correct, but (R) is NOT the correct explanation of (A)
3. (A) is correct, but (R) is not correct
4. (A) is not correct, but (R) is correct.

67. Given below are two statements : one is labelled as Assertion (A) and the other is labelled as Reason (R).

Assertion (A): The 'Axis' Alliance of Germany, Italy and Japan signed the Tripartite Pact in 1940.

Reason (R): The above mentioned Axis Alliance was meant for Global peace.

In the light of the above statements, choose the ***most appropriate*** answer from the options given below:

1. Both (A) and (R) are correct and (R) is the correct explanation of (A)
2. Both (A) and (R) are correct, but (R) is NOT the correct explanation of (A)
3. (A) is correct, but (R) is not correct
4. (A) is not correct, but (R) is correct

68. Given below are two statements : one is labelled as Assertion (A) and the other is labelled as Reason (R).

Assertion (A): British Viceroy Lord Curzon stated in 1901 that it would be madness for us to cross the Himalayas and occupy Tibet.

Reason (R): This British policy in a very big way helped the Chinese to re-establish their hold over Tibet during 1905-1911.

In the light of the above statements, choose the ***most appropriate*** answer from the options given below:

1. Both (A) and (R) are correct and (R) is the correct explanation of (A)
2. Both (A) and (R) are correct, but (R) is NOT the correct explanation of (A)
3. (A) is correct, but (R) is not correct
4. (A) is not correct, but (R) is correct

69. Arrange the following Chairman of Finance Commission appointed in descending order:

A. Mahavir Tyagi
B. J.M. Shelat
C. Y.B. Chavan
D. Brahamananda Reddy
E. A.K. Chanda

Choose the ***correct*** answer from the options given below:

1. A, E, D, B, C
2. A, B, C, D, E
3. B, C, D, E, A
4. C, B, D, A, E

70. On 2nd October 1959, who inaugurated Panchayat at Nagaur?

1. K.M. Munshi
2. Subhash Chandra Bose
3. Jawaharlal Nehru
4. Sucheta Kriplani

71. Bhikhu Parekh produced an in depth study of multiculturalism in his noted work:

1. Multicultural Citizenship: A liberal theory of minority rights
2. Justice and the Politics of Difference
3. In Defence of Globalization
4. Rethinking Multiculturalism: Cultural Diversity and Political Theory

72. Given below are two statements : one is labelled as Assertion (A) and the other is labelled as Reason (R).

Assertion (A): The term 'Third World' did not fall into the Capitalist so called 'First world' or the Communist 'Second World'.

Reason (R): The term 'Third World' has largely been emerging since the 1990's due to it's prejorative ideological implications.

In the light of the above statements, choose the ***most appropriate*** answer from the options given below:

1. Both (A) and (R) are correct and (R) is the correct explanation of (A)
2. Both (A) and (R) are correct, but (R) is NOT the correct explanation of (A)
3. (A) is correct, but (R) is not correct
4. (A) is not correct, but (R) is correct

73. The total number of the membership of the French Senate is:

1. 348 2. 327
3. 357 4. 388

74. Who defined politics as the "Authoritative Allocation of Values"?

1. J.S. Mill 2. Adam Smith
3. David Easton 4. John Locke

75. Who wrote that "Women should acquire human virtues by the same means as men, instead of being educated like a fanciful kind of half being"?

1. Karl Marx
2. Mary Wollstonecraft
3. Benjamin Franklin
4. Jean-Jacques Rousseau

76. The Peace of Westphalia was signed in:

1. October 1648 2. July 1648
3. September 1648 4. March 1649

77. Arrange the following UN events in descending order:

A. UN peace keepers sent to Cyprus
B. UN operation in Congo established
C. UN Development Programme (UNDP) founded
D. First UN Peacekeeping force sent to the Suez Canal
E. U. Thant appointed Secretary General of the United Nations

Choose the ***correct*** answer from the options given below:

1. C, A, B, E, D 2. A, B, C, D, E
3. B, C, D, E, A 4. C, A, E, B, D

78. Match the List-I with List-II.

List-I (*Articles of the Indian Constitution*)	List-II (*Subject Matter*)
A. 243 ZF	I. Constitution and Composition of Ward Committees
B. 243 ZD	II. Disqualifications for Members of Municipalities
C. 243 S	III. Continuance of existing Laws of Municipalities
D. 243 V	IV. Committee for District Planning

Choose the ***correct*** answer from the options given below:

1. A-III, B-IV, C-I, D-II
2. A-II, B-I, C-IV, D-III
3. A-I, B-II, C-III, D-IV
4. A-IV, B-III, C-II, D-I

79. A special committee under the chairmanship of H.N. Sanyal was appointed in 1961 to examine the:

1. Examine the appointment of Chief Justice of the Supreme Court
2. Examine the law related to the contempt of Courts
3. Look into certificate for appeal to the Supreme Court
4. Examine the concept of Public Interest Litigation

80. Match the List-I with List-II.

List-I (*Lokayukta and Uplokayukta Act*)	List-II (*Year of Enactment*)
A. Maharashtra	I. 1971
B. Uttar Pradesh	II. 1975
C. Himachal Pradesh	III. 1983
D. Punjab	IV. 1996

Choose the ***correct*** answer from the options given below:

1. A-IV, B-III, C-II, D-I
2. A-II, B-I, C-III, D-IV
3. A-III, B-II, C-I, D-IV
4. A-I, B-II, C-III, D-IV

81. The 'United Soverign Bengal' (1947) proposal was advocated by:

1. Chittranjan Das
2. Abul Hashim
3. Bhulabhai Desai
4. Sikandar Hayat Khan

82. Identify the Cold War events:

A. Korean war
B. Vietnam war
C. Cuban crisis
D. Bifurcation of Sudan
E. Russian invasion on Ukraine

Choose the ***correct*** answer from the options given below:

1. A & D only 2. A, B & C only
3. B & E only 4. C & D only

83. Consider the following events during Cold War period and arrange them in descending order:

A. Yuri Gagrin first person in space
B. Communist China joins the UN
C. Soviet invasion to Hungary
D. Six Day War
E. Apollo-11 lands on the moon

Choose the ***correct*** answer from the options given below:

1. A, B, C, D, E 2. B, C, A, E, D
3. C, A, E, D, B 4. B, E, D, A, C

84. In which Article of the American Constitution, a general outline about the Judiciary has been given?

1. Article 5 2. Article 4
3. Article 1 4. Article 3

85. Who wrote the book "A System Analysis of Political Life"?

1. Hannah Arendt 2. Thomas Hobbes
3. Jermy Bentham 4. David Easton

86. Arrange the correct sequence of Attorney Generals of India in the descending order of their tenure:

A. Ashok K. Desai B. K. Parasaran
C. Niren De D. L.N. Sinha
E. S.V. Gupte

Choose the ***correct*** answer from the options given below:

1. A, B, D, E, C 2. A, B, C, D, E
3. C, E, B, D, A 4. B, C, A, E, D

87. Match the List-I with List-II.

List-I (*Chief Justices of India*)	List-II (*Tenures*)
A. Altmas Kabir	I. April 2014-September 2014
B. R.M. Lodha	II. September 2012-July 2013
C. T.S. Thakur	III. January 2007-May 2010
D. K.G. Balakrishnan	IV. December 2015-January 2017

Choose the ***correct*** answer from the options given below:

1. A-I, B-II, C-III, D-IV
2. A-II, B-I, C-IV, D-III
3. A-III, B-I, C-II, D-IV
4. A-IV, B-III, C-II, D-I

88. Arrange the following events related to Swami Vivekananda in descending order.

A. Swami Vivekananda visited Japan for the first time
B. Swami Vivekananda visited United Kingdom

C. He founded the Vedanta Society in New York
D. He founded the Ramkrishna Mission
E. He delivered a lecture at the world Parliament of Religions at Chicago

Choose the *correct* answer from the options given below:

1. B, C, D, A, E
2. B, A, D, E, C
3. D, B, C, E, A
4. A, B, C, D, E

89. Match the List-I with List-II.

List-I (*Regional Organisations*)	List-II (*Year of Foundation*)
A. North American Free Trade Agreement	I. 1973
B. Association of South East Asian Nations	II. 1989
C. Asia Pacific Economic Cooperation	III. 1994
D. Organization for Security and Cooperation in Europe	IV. 1967

Choose the *correct* answer from the options given below:

1. A-I, B-II, C-III, D-IV
2. A-IV, B-III, C-I, D-II
3. A-III, B-IV, C-II, D-I
4. A-II, B-III, C-I, D-IV

90. Match the List-I with List-II.

List-I (*War/Revolutions*)	List-II (*Year*)
A. Falklands War	I. 1954-62
B. Soviet Invasion on Czechoslovakia	II. 1971
C. Emergence of Bangladesh	III. 1982
D. Algerian Revolution	IV. 1968

Choose the *correct* answer from the options given below:

1. A-I, B-II, C-III, D-IV
2. A-III, B-IV, C-II, D-I
3. A-II, B-I, C-IV, D-III
4. A-II, B-III, C-IV, D-I

Directions (Qs. No. 91 to 95): *Read the following passage and answer the question:*

East Timor (also known as Timor-Leste) was a Portuguese Colony for over 300 years. It was invaded in 1975 by Indonesian troops, following the precipitous departure of Portugal. This led to the development of one of the longest and bloodiest gureilla wars in history, in which about a third of East Timor's 6,50,000 inhabitants were killed through mass executions, bombings and above all starvation. Following the fall of the Indonesian dictator Suharto, the Government agreed to hold a referendum in 1999, in which 75 per cent of East Timorese voted for independence.

91. As per the passage East Timor was a Portuguese colony for:

1. Over 200 years
2. Over 300 years
3. Over 400 years
4. Over 500 years

92. As per the passage East Timor was invaded by Indonesian troops in ______.

1. 1975
2. 1965
3. 1985
4. 1995

93. As per the passage a referendum was held in East Timor in ______.

1. 2000
2. 1984
3. 1999
4. 1964

94. As per the passage how much percentage of East Timoreans voted for Independence?

1. 65%
2. 70%
3. 75%
4. 80%

95. As per the passage, approximately how many inhabitants of East Timor died in the mass executions, bombings and starvations?

1. 7,50,000
2. 8,50,000
3. 9,50,000
4. 2,17,000

Directions (Qs. No. 96 to 100): *Read the following passage and answer the question:*

In January 1957, the Government of India appointed a committee to examine the working of the community development programme (1952) and the Nation Extension Service (1953) and to suggest measures for their better working. The chairman of this committee was Balwant-Rai Mehta. The committee submitted it's report in November 1957 and recommended the establishment of the scheme of 'democratic decentralisation' which ultimately came to be known as Panchayat Raj. The specific recommendation made by it included establishment of a three-tier Panchayat Raj system, Gram Panchayat at the Village level, Panchayat Samriti at Block level and Zila Parishad at the District level.

96. As per the passage, the Balwant Rai Mehta committee recommended for the district level:

1. Zila Parishad
2. Zila Panchayat
3. Zila Samiti
4. Zila Sahakari Samiti

97. As per the passage, the Balwant Rai Mehta committee recommended the establishment of the scheme of:

1. 'Democratic Centralisation'
2. 'Democratic Decentralization'
3. 'Democratic Dictatorship'
4. 'Democratic Authoritarianship'

98. As per the passage, the Balwant Rai Mehta committee proposed establishment of a:

1. One-tier Panchayat Raj System
2. Two-tier Panchayat Raj System
3. Four-tier Panchayat Raj System
4. Three-tier Panchayat Raj System

99. As per the passage, when was the Balwant Rai Mehta committee appointed?

1. 1955
2. 1959
3. 1957
4. 1963

100. As per the passage, the Balwant Rai Mehta committee was appointed to examine the working of the _______.

1. Community Development Programme and the National Extension Service
2. Community Development Policy and the National Social Service
3. Community Drawback Programme and the National Social Security
4. Community Dairy Programme and the National Examination Service

ANSWERS

1	**2**	**3**	**4**	**5**	**6**	**7**	**8**	**9**	**10**
1	1	4	2	1	4	1	1	4	1
11	**12**	**13**	**14**	**15**	**16**	**17**	**18**	**19**	**20**
3	4	3	4	3	3	2	4	1	4
21	**22**	**23**	**24**	**25**	**26**	**27**	**28**	**29**	**30**
2	2	3	1	4	2	2	1	1	3
31	**32**	**33**	**34**	**35**	**36**	**37**	**38**	**39**	**40**
2	4	2	1	1	3	2	3	1	3
41	**42**	**43**	**44**	**45**	**46**	**47**	**48**	**49**	**50**
1	2	4	4	2	1	1	1	4	3
51	**52**	**53**	**54**	**55**	**56**	**57**	**58**	**59**	**60**
4	3	2	1	1	4	3	4	1	3
61	**62**	**63**	**64**	**65**	**66**	**67**	**68**	**69**	**70**
3	3	4	3	1	1	3	1	4	3

71	72	73	74	75	76	77	78	79	80
4	3	1	3	2	1	4	1	2	4
81	**82**	**83**	**84**	**85**	**86**	**87**	**88**	**89**	**90**
2	2	4	4	4	1	2	3	3	2
91	**92**	**93**	**94**	**95**	**96**	**97**	**98**	**99**	**100**
2	1	3	3	4	1	2	4	3	1

EXPLANATORY ANSWERS

1. The Government of India constituted the third major committee on police reforms under the chairmanship of former Union Home Secretary K. Padmanabhaiah in the year 2000. The committee was created to examine the functioning of the police system and to recommend reforms to improve professionalism, efficiency, accountability and public trust in policing. It reviewed issues such as modernization of police forces, training, autonomy of police leadership, better investigation systems, and improved relationship between police and citizens. The committee submitted a detailed report recommending administrative restructuring, improved working conditions for police personnel and insulation of policing from undue political interference. Therefore the year that correctly corresponds with the establishment of this committee is 2000.

2.
- **A — I:** C.G. Hoag and G.H. Hallett authored the work "Proportional Representation." The book discusses electoral systems and advocates proportional representation as a democratic method that ensures fair representation of political groups in legislatures. Their work became an important reference in the study of electoral reforms.
- **B — III:** H. Sidgwick wrote "Elements of Politics." This book is a classic work in political philosophy and examines the nature of the state, government authority, individual rights and the ethical basis of political institutions within modern political theory.
- **C — II:** A.L. Lowell authored "Public Opinion and Popular Government." The work studies the relationship between democratic governance and the influence of public opinion on political decision-making and constitutional functioning.
- **D — IV:** J.A. Corry wrote "Democratic Government and Politics." This text analyzes democratic institutions, constitutional structures and the working of modern political systems, making it a standard reference in political science.

3.
- **A — I:** A.R. Ball is the author of "Modern Politics and Government." The book explains the structure and functioning of political systems, political institutions, and the nature of democratic governance in modern states.
- **B — IV:** J.N. Bhagwati wrote "In Defense of Globalization." In this work he argues that globalization, when properly regulated, contributes to economic growth, poverty reduction and international cooperation.
- **C — III:** John Aart (referring to Jan Aart Scholte) authored "Globalisation: A Critical Introduction." The book critically examines the concept of globalization, its historical development, political implications and socio-economic impacts across the world.
- **D — II:** Vandana Shiva is associated with "Eco-Feminism." Her work connects environmental protection with feminist thought, arguing that ecological destruction and the oppression of women are interconnected in modern development models.

4. E. Battle of Stalingrad (1942–1943): This decisive battle of the Second World War took place between Nazi Germany and the Soviet Union. It is considered one of the turning points of the war because the German army suffered a major defeat.

D. Italy invaded Abyssinia (1935): Fascist Italy under Benito Mussolini invaded Ethiopia in 1935 in an attempt to build a colonial empire in Africa. The invasion demonstrated the aggressive expansionism of fascist regimes before World War II.

A. Japan invaded Manchuria (1931): Japan occupied the Chinese region of Manchuria after the Mukden Incident in 1931. This event marked the beginning of Japanese military expansion in East Asia.

B. Mussolini seized power in Italy (1922): Benito Mussolini came to power through the March on Rome in 1922, establishing the first fascist regime in Europe.

C. Armenian genocide (1915–1916): During the First World War, the Ottoman Empire carried out mass deportations and killings of Armenians. This event occurred earlier than all the other listed events, making it the last in descending order.

5. Dr. Rajendra Prasad was elected President of the Constituent Assembly of India on 11 December 1946. The Constituent Assembly had first convened on 9 December 1946, when Dr. Sachchidanand Sinha served as the temporary chairman. Two days later, the Assembly elected Dr. Rajendra Prasad as its permanent President. In this role he presided over the debates and proceedings that eventually led to the drafting and adoption of the Constitution of India. His leadership helped guide the Assembly through discussions on fundamental rights, federal structure, governance principles and constitutional provisions that shaped independent India.

6. The Triple Entente powers—Britain, France and Russia—issued a joint declaration on 24 May 1915 condemning the actions of the Ottoman Empire against the Armenian population during the First World War. In this declaration they described the mass killings and deportations of Armenians as "crimes against humanity and civilization." This statement is historically significant because it represented one of the earliest uses of such terminology in international diplomacy to condemn state-sponsored atrocities. The declaration warned Ottoman officials that members of the government responsible for the massacres would be held personally accountable by the Allied powers. This condemnation came at a time when large-scale deportations and killings of Armenians were taking place across the Ottoman territories, which later came to be known collectively as the Armenian Genocide. Therefore, the correct date associated with this formal denunciation by the Triple Entente is 24 May 1915.

7. A. Muslim Women (Protection of Rights on Marriage) Act, 2019: This law criminalised the practice of instant triple talaq (talaq-e-biddat) among Muslims in India. The Act was passed by Parliament in 2019 during the second term of the NDA government led by Narendra Modi.

B. Transgender Persons (Protection of Rights) Act, 2019: This legislation was enacted in 2019 to provide legal recognition and protection of rights for transgender persons. It prohibits discrimination in employment, education, healthcare and access to public services.

C. Amendments to Protection of Animals from Sexual Offences Act in 2021: No such law titled "Protection of Animals from Sexual Offences Act" was enacted in 2021. Therefore this statement does not correspond to an actual legislative development of the NDA's second term.

D. Jammu and Kashmir Re-organisation Act passed in 2018: The Act reorganising the state of Jammu and Kashmir into two Union Territories was passed in 2019, not 2018, making the statement incorrect.

E. Dilution of Article 370 in 2022: The constitutional provisions under Article 370 were effectively removed through a presidential order and parliamentary legislation in August 2019, not in 2022.

8. The landmark resolution on Local Self-Government in India was introduced in 1882 during the tenure of Viceroy Lord Ripon. This resolution encouraged the establishment and expansion of local bodies such as municipal committees and district boards with greater participation of elected non-official members. It aimed to decentralize administrative authority and involve local citizens in governance. The resolution emphasized training Indians in democratic administration and gave municipal institutions greater autonomy in local matters like sanitation, roads and public health. Because of its progressive emphasis on decentralisation and representative participation, Lord Ripon is often referred to as the "Father of Local Self-Government in India." Thus, the year associated with the introduction of democratic municipal governance through this resolution is 1882.

9. After independence, elections to the Lok Sabha and State Legislative Assemblies were generally conducted simultaneously. This cycle continued until political instability in the late 1960s. Prime Minister Indira Gandhi dissolved the Fourth Lok Sabha earlier than its normal term and called for mid-term general elections in 1971. This decision disrupted the earlier pattern of synchronized elections between Parliament and state assemblies. The mid-term election occurred because of political divisions within the ruling party and the need to seek a renewed mandate from the electorate. As a result, the cycle of simultaneous elections that had existed since the first general election in 1951–52 was broken, leading to different electoral schedules for the Lok Sabha and various state assemblies thereafter.

10. **C. Benelux Economic Union (BEU):** Established in 1958, the Benelux Economic Union brought together Belgium, the Netherlands and Luxembourg to promote economic integration, free movement of goods, labour and capital among the three countries.

B. Latin American Integration Association (LAIA): Formed in 1980, LAIA aimed to promote regional economic integration and trade liberalisation among Latin American countries, replacing the earlier Latin American Free Trade Association.

A. Gulf Cooperation Council (GCC): The GCC was established in 1981 by six Gulf countries—Saudi Arabia, Kuwait, Bahrain, Qatar, the United Arab Emirates and Oman—to strengthen political, economic and security cooperation in the Gulf region.

E. Arab Maghreb Union (AMU): Founded in 1989, this organisation seeks regional cooperation among North African states such as Algeria, Libya, Morocco, Mauritania and Tunisia.

D. Black Sea Economic Cooperation (BSEC): Created in 1992, BSEC promotes economic collaboration among countries surrounding the Black Sea region, including Turkey, Russia, Ukraine and several Southeast European and Caucasus states.

11. **D. North Korea:** North Korea is widely regarded as one of the most rigid authoritarian regimes in the world. Political power is concentrated in a single ruling party and the leadership of the Kim dynasty. Elections are not competitive, opposition parties are absent in practice, and the state maintains strict control over media, civil liberties and political activity.

E. Saudi Arabia: Saudi Arabia is an absolute monarchy where political authority is concentrated in the royal family. There are no national democratic elections for the head of state or legislature, and political parties are not permitted. Governance is based on hereditary rule and Islamic law with limited political participation by citizens.

Countries like Italy and Spain function today as democratic constitutional states, while India is a democratic republic with regular competitive elections. Hence the authoritarian regimes among the listed countries are North Korea and Saudi Arabia.

12. The Government of India Act of 1935 introduced extensive administrative reforms in British India. Among its various provisions was the establishment of a Federal Railway Authority to manage and administer railway operations. The purpose of creating this authority was to keep railway administration insulated from political interference and to ensure efficient management of railway finances and services across British India. The railways were considered a strategic and economically vital sector connecting different regions of the subcontinent, facilitating trade, mobility and administrative control. By creating an independent authority, the Act aimed to ensure technical and financial decisions could be taken with greater autonomy. Therefore, the establishment of a Federal Railway Authority was provided for under the Government of India Act of 1935.

13. The statement in Assertion (A) accurately reflects the strategic philosophy presented in Sun Tzu's "The Art of War." The text emphasizes that the most effective strategy is not merely battlefield combat but undermining the enemy's plans, alliances and morale through intelligence, deception, psychological influence and strategic perception. Sun Tzu argued that defeating the enemy without direct confrontation is the highest form of warfare, highlighting the importance of strategy and psychological advantage. However, the Reason (R) stating that China is a pacifist country that always prefers peaceful mechanisms for resolving disputes is not universally accurate. China has historically engaged in military conflicts and maintains a strong military posture along with territorial disputes. Therefore, the assertion is correct but the reason is incorrect.

14. A. **Strategic Arms Limitation Treaty I (SALT I) — 1972:** SALT I was signed between the United States and the Soviet Union in 1972 as part of efforts to control the nuclear arms race during the Cold War. It limited the number of strategic ballistic missile launchers possessed by both countries.

B. **Intermediate Nuclear Forces (INF) Treaty — 1987:** The INF Treaty was signed in 1987 and eliminated an entire class of nuclear missiles with ranges between 500 and 5,500 kilometres. It marked a major step in nuclear arms reduction.

C. **Strategic Arms Reduction Treaty II (START II) — 1993:** START II was signed in 1993 and aimed to further reduce the number of deployed strategic nuclear warheads possessed by the United States and Russia.

D. **Strategic Offensive Reduction Treaty (SORT) — 2002:** SORT, also known as the Moscow Treaty, was signed in 2002 and required the United States and Russia to significantly reduce their strategic nuclear warhead inventories.

15. A. **UN Convention on the Law of the Sea (UNCLOS):** UNCLOS was adopted in 1982 to establish legal frameworks governing oceans, maritime boundaries, navigation rights, resource management and marine environmental protection.

B. **Convention on International Trade in Endangered Species (CITES):** CITES was signed in 1973 to regulate international trade in endangered plants and animals to prevent species extinction.

C. **UN Conference on the Human Environment (UNCHE):** Held in 1972 in Stockholm, this conference marked the first major global meeting focused on environmental protection and sustainable development.

E. **Antarctic Treaty:** The Antarctic Treaty was signed in 1959, establishing Antarctica as a zone dedicated to peaceful scientific research and prohibiting military activity.

D. **World Meteorological Organization (WMO) established:** The WMO was formally established in 1950 as a specialized international organization responsible for coordinating global meteorological activities and climate observation.

16. A. **Krishna Kant:** Krishna Kant served as the Vice-President of India from 1997 to 2002. Since descending order requires the most recent office holder first, he appears at the beginning of the sequence among the given names.

D. **R. Venkataraman:** R. Venkataraman held the office of Vice-President from 1984 to 1987 before becoming the President of India. His tenure falls earlier than Krishna Kant but later than the others listed below.

E. **Mohammed Hidayatullah:** Mohammad Hidayatullah served as Vice-President between 1979 and 1984. He previously served as Chief Justice of India and also acted as President of India in an acting capacity earlier.

C. **B.D. Jatti:** B.D. Jatti served as Vice-President from 1974 to 1979. He also briefly served as Acting President after the death of President Fakhruddin Ali Ahmed in 1977.

B. **Gopal Swarup Pathak:** Gopal Swarup Pathak held the office of Vice-President from 1969 to 1974, making him the earliest among the listed Vice-Presidents. Thus he appears last in descending order of tenure.

17. A. **International Monetary Fund (IMF) — 1947:** The IMF was conceived at the Bretton Woods Conference in 1944 but began its formal financial operations in 1947 after the required number of member countries ratified the agreement and subscribed capital. Therefore the year considered for operational establishment is 1947.

B. **World Trade Organization (WTO) — 1995:** The WTO was established on 1 January 1995 through the Marrakesh Agreement. It replaced the earlier GATT framework and became the principal international institution governing global trade rules.

C. **International Bank for Reconstruction and Development (IBRD) — 1946:** The IBRD, commonly referred to as the World Bank's primary lending institution, was established in 1946 to finance post-war reconstruction and development projects, particularly in Europe and later in developing countries.

D. **General Agreement on Tariffs and Trade (GATT) — 1948:** The GATT agreement was signed in 1947 but came into force in 1948, marking the beginning of the multilateral trading system aimed at reducing tariffs and promoting international trade cooperation.

18. C. Boutros Boutros-Ghali: Boutros Boutros-Ghali served as UN Secretary-General from 1992 to 1996. Among the listed names, his tenure is the most recent, placing him first in descending order.

E. Kurt Waldheim: Kurt Waldheim held the office from 1972 to 1981, serving two terms and preceding Boutros-Ghali chronologically.

D. U Thant: U Thant served as Secretary-General from 1961 to 1971, leading the United Nations during critical Cold War crises such as the Cuban Missile Crisis.

B. Dag Hammarskjöld: Dag Hammarskjöld held the position from 1953 until 1961. His tenure ended after his death in a plane crash while undertaking a UN mission.

A. Trygve Lie: Trygve Lie was the first Secretary-General of the United Nations, serving from 1946 to 1952, making him the earliest among the listed names.

19. The member of the Constituent Assembly who famously described the Drafting Committee as the "Drifting Committee" was Naziruddin Ahmad. During the debates of the Constituent Assembly he criticised the Drafting Committee for making frequent amendments and revisions in the constitutional draft. He argued that the committee was continuously altering provisions and therefore jokingly referred to it as a drifting committee rather than a drafting committee. This remark was part of broader debates in the Assembly where members scrutinized the drafting process and suggested improvements to constitutional provisions before final adoption.

20. The concept of "Deconstruction" is most closely associated with post-modernist philosophy, particularly through the work of the French philosopher Jacques Derrida. Deconstruction is a method of critical analysis used to examine texts, ideas and philosophical traditions by revealing internal contradictions, hidden assumptions and multiple meanings within language. Instead of treating texts as having fixed or single interpretations, deconstruction argues that meaning is fluid and shaped by context, power structures and linguistic relationships. This approach became influential in literary theory, philosophy, cultural studies and social sciences, forming an important intellectual component of post-modern thought.

21. The First Administrative Reforms Commission (ARC) in India was constituted by the Government of India on 5 January 1966. The commission was established to examine the public administration system and recommend measures for improving efficiency, integrity and responsiveness of the administrative machinery. It was initially chaired by Morarji Desai, who later resigned after becoming Deputy Prime Minister, after which K. Hanumanthaiya became the chairman. The commission studied several aspects of governance including centre–state relations, financial administration, district administration, public sector undertakings and personnel management. It submitted numerous reports suggesting reforms to strengthen administrative accountability, decentralisation and modernization of government functioning in India.

22. The book "The India Way: Strategies for an Uncertain World" was written by Dr. S. Jaishankar, India's External Affairs Minister and a former diplomat. The book discusses India's foreign policy approach in the changing global geopolitical environment. It analyses India's diplomatic strategies, its relations with major powers, and the importance of strategic autonomy in international politics. The author draws upon historical experiences, diplomatic engagements and contemporary global challenges to explain how India should navigate an increasingly uncertain and multipolar world order. The work also highlights India's growing role in shaping international cooperation and global governance.

23. Dr. Shyama Prasad Mukherjee entered active legislative politics in 1929 when he was elected as a member of the Bengal Legislative Council representing the Calcutta University constituency. At that time he contested as a Congress candidate. His election marked the beginning of his formal participation in legislative and political affairs in British India. Soon after his election, the Indian National Congress adopted a policy of boycotting legislative councils, following which Mukherjee resigned his seat in accordance with the party decision. However, he later returned to the council after being re-elected as an independent candidate, continuing his involvement in provincial politics. This early political experience laid the foundation for his later prominent role in Indian politics, including his service in the Bengal government and later in the national cabinet after independence.

24. The British political leader who described the Jallianwala Bagh massacre of 1919 as "unutterably monstrous" was Winston Churchill, who was then serving as Secretary of State for War. During debates in the British Parliament regarding General Dyer's actions at Amritsar, Churchill strongly criticised the brutal firing on unarmed civilians. He condemned the massacre as a horrifying and unacceptable act that did not represent the principles of British governance. His speech reflected the serious controversy within Britain over the actions of General Dyer and the broader issue of colonial repression in India.

25. C. **T. Swaminathan:** T. Swaminathan served as Chief Election Commissioner of India from 1973 to 1977, making him the earliest among the listed individuals.

E. **S.L. Shakdhar:** S.L. Shakdhar held the office from 1977 to 1982, following T. Swaminathan.

D. **R.V.S. Peri Sastri:** R.V.S. Peri Sastri served as Chief Election Commissioner from 1986 to 1990, coming after S.L. Shakdhar.

A. **M.S. Gill:** M.S. Gill served as Chief Election Commissioner between 1996 and 2001, placing him later in chronological order.

B. **T.S. Krishnamurthy:** T.S. Krishnamurthy served as Chief Election Commissioner from 2004 to 2005, making him the most recent among the listed names, which places him last in ascending order of tenure.

26. The assertion is correct because in November 2025 Pakistan's Parliament approved a major constitutional change that expanded the powers of the army chief, created the position of a tri-service military head, and granted lifetime legal immunity from arrest and prosecution to the office-holder. So the factual core of statement (A) is correct. The reason is also broadly correct because Pakistan's judiciary has often been regarded as institutionally weaker than the military establishment, and these constitutional changes further reduced the effective independence of the top court in constitutional matters. However, this judicial weakness is not the direct explanation for why Parliament passed that measure. The more immediate explanation lies in the consolidation of military power, political control, and the formalization of an already dominant military role in the state structure. Therefore, both statements are correct, but the reason does not correctly explain the assertion.

27. A. **The National Planning Commission appointed Nehru as its Chairman in 1950:** The Planning Commission was established in 1950 and Prime Minister Jawaharlal Nehru served as its Chairman, guiding India's planned economic development.

C. **Nehru fought three general elections:** Jawaharlal Nehru led the Indian National Congress in the general elections of 1952, 1957 and 1962, winning all three and continuing as Prime Minister.

D. **In 1952 the first of the five IIT's was set up:** The first Indian Institute of Technology (IIT) was established at Kharagpur in 1951, and it began functioning during Nehru's early years of leadership as part of his emphasis on scientific and technical education.

E. **India signed a treaty with Nepal in 1950:** India and Nepal signed the Treaty of Peace and Friendship in 1950, establishing close diplomatic, economic and security relations between the two countries.

B. **Nehru visited China in 1958 and signed the Panchsheel Treaty:** The Panchsheel Agreement between India and China was signed in 1954, not 1958, therefore this statement is incorrect.

28. A. **L. Woolf — Imperialism and Civilisation:** Leonard Woolf wrote "Imperialism and Civilisation", a work that critically examined imperialism and its implications for international relations and colonial governance.

B. **Hans Kohn — Nationalism and Liberty:** Hans Kohn authored "Nationalism and Liberty," which analyzes the historical development and ideological foundations of nationalism.

C. **C.J.H. Hayes — Essays on Nationalism:** Carlton J. H. Hayes wrote "Essays on Nationalism," a collection exploring the evolution, forms and political significance of nationalist thought.

D. **John Mearsheimer — The Tragedy of Great Power Politics:** John J. Mearsheimer authored "The Tragedy of Great Power Politics," a key text in international relations presenting the theory of offensive realism and explaining the competitive behaviour of major powers.

29. The Yazidi genocide occurred in 2014 when the Islamic State (ISIS) launched attacks on the Yazidi minority community in northern Iraq, particularly in the Sinjar region. Thousands of Yazidis were killed, while many women and children were abducted, enslaved or forcibly displaced. The campaign involved mass killings, forced conversions, sexual slavery and destruction of communities. International organizations and several governments later recognized these actions as genocide due to the systematic attempt to destroy the Yazidi religious group. The events drew global attention to the humanitarian crisis in Iraq and led to international military and humanitarian responses.

30. The Australian House of Representatives, which is the lower house of the Federal Parliament of Australia, has a membership strength of 150 seats. Members are elected from single-member electoral divisions across Australia through preferential voting. The number of seats is periodically adjusted through redistributions based on population changes among the states and territories, but the commonly recognised strength has been 150 members for several years. The House of Representatives plays a central role in Australia's parliamentary system, as the government is formed by the political party or coalition that commands a majority in this chamber.

31. The statement referring to the loss of democratic processes by 600 million people was made during the period of the Emergency in India (1975–1977) when civil liberties were suspended and elections were postponed. At that time Gerald Ford was the President of the United States. He publicly expressed concern about the suspension of democratic institutions in India and remarked that it was unfortunate that such a large population had lost democratic freedoms that had existed since India's independence in the mid-1940s. The statement reflected Western criticism of the Emergency imposed by Prime Minister Indira Gandhi and highlighted the importance placed by the United States on democratic governance and electoral processes.

32. **A. Committee on Service Conditions of Municipal Employees — 1965–68:** This committee examined the working conditions, recruitment patterns, pay structures and administrative arrangements of municipal employees in India. It functioned during 1965–1968 and aimed to improve efficiency and professional standards in municipal administration.

B. Rural–Urban Relationship Committee — 1963–66: The Rural–Urban Relationship Committee studied the interaction between rural local bodies and urban local institutions. It examined economic, administrative and developmental linkages between villages and towns and worked during 1963–1966.

C. National Commission on Urbanisation — 1985–88: The National Commission on Urbanisation was established to study the growing process of urbanisation in India and recommend policies for planned urban development. It functioned between 1985–1988 and examined issues such as urban infrastructure, migration and regional planning.

D. Taxation Enquiry Commission — 1953–54: The Taxation Enquiry Commission was appointed to review the taxation system in India and recommend reforms for strengthening fiscal policy and revenue mobilisation. It functioned during 1953–1954, studying central, state and local taxation structures.

33. On 4 November 2017, Saad Hariri, the Prime Minister of Lebanon, unexpectedly announced his resignation while he was in Saudi Arabia. The announcement was made through a televised statement from Riyadh. In his speech he cited concerns about political instability and threats to his life. The sudden resignation created a major diplomatic and political controversy in the Middle East because many observers believed Hariri had been pressured while in Saudi Arabia. After international intervention and negotiations, Hariri later returned to Lebanon and eventually withdrew his resignation.

34. **D. Incorporation of Dadra and Nagar Haveli in the Indian Union:** This occurred through the 10th Constitutional Amendment (1961) which formally integrated the territory into India after its liberation from Portuguese control.

A. Incorporation of Goa, Daman and Diu in the Indian Union: This was carried out by the 12th Constitutional Amendment (1962) after the territories were liberated from Portuguese rule in 1961.

B. Increased retirement age of High Court Judges from 60 to 62 years: This change was introduced through the 15th Constitutional Amendment (1963) to strengthen judicial independence and experience within High Courts.

C. **Included Sindhi as the 15th language in the Eighth Schedule:** The 21st Constitutional Amendment (1967) added Sindhi to the list of recognised languages in the Constitution.

E. **Abolished the privy purse and privileges of former rulers:** This occurred through the 26th Constitutional Amendment (1971) which ended the special privileges and financial allowances given to former princely rulers.

35. The Supreme Court of the United States asserted the power of Judicial Review in 1803 in the landmark case Marbury v. Madison. In this case Chief Justice John Marshall declared that the judiciary had the authority to review acts of Congress and determine whether they were consistent with the Constitution. If a law was found to be unconstitutional, the Court could declare it invalid. This decision established the principle that the Constitution is the supreme law of the land and that the Supreme Court has the final authority to interpret it. The doctrine of judicial review later became a fundamental feature of constitutional systems across many democratic countries.

36. The term Ecofeminism was indeed coined in the 1970s by the French feminist Françoise d'Eaubonne. Ecofeminism links the domination of women with the exploitation of nature and argues that patriarchal systems promote both gender oppression and environmental destruction. Since its emergence in the 1970s, ecofeminism has become an important intellectual and activist strand within feminist and environmental movements. However, the reason statement claiming that ecofeminists are accountable for the consequences of climate change is incorrect. Ecofeminists actually criticize the social and economic systems responsible for environmental degradation and advocate ecological sustainability and gender justice. Therefore the assertion is correct but the reason is incorrect.

37. Anthropocentrism is a philosophical viewpoint that places human beings at the center of moral and environmental concern. According to this idea, the natural world and its resources are valuable primarily because they serve human needs and interests. Nature is therefore treated as subordinate to human welfare, development and economic progress. This perspective historically influenced industrial expansion and large-scale resource exploitation because environmental elements were considered instruments for human benefit. Anthropocentrism contrasts with ecocentric or biocentric philosophies which argue that nature and all living organisms possess intrinsic value independent of human use.

38. A. **Savarkar was arrested in London (1910):** Vinayak Damodar Savarkar was arrested in 1910 in London due to his revolutionary nationalist activities and alleged involvement in anti-colonial movements.

B. **Savarkar Arbitration Case decision (1911):** After Savarkar's attempted escape at Marseilles, an international dispute arose between Britain and France. The Permanent Court of Arbitration gave its decision in 1911 regarding his extradition.

C. **Shift to Ratnagiri jail (1921):** After long imprisonment in the Cellular Jail of the Andaman Islands, Savarkar was transferred to Ratnagiri prison in 1921 and later kept under restrictions there.

E. **Savarkar passed away (1966):** Savarkar died in 1966 after voluntarily undertaking a fast unto death, concluding a long and controversial political life.

D. **Portrait installed in Parliament (2003):** His portrait was installed in the Central Hall of the Indian Parliament in 2003, which is the most recent event among those listed.

39. The idea of "incredulity toward metanarratives" is associated with Jean-François Lyotard, a prominent philosopher of postmodernism. In his analysis of postmodern society, Lyotard argued that modernity relied on grand narratives such as progress, enlightenment or universal reason to legitimize knowledge and power. Postmodern thought, according to him, rejects these overarching explanations and instead recognizes multiple, localized and fragmented forms of knowledge. His argument challenged traditional philosophical assumptions about truth, objectivity and universal historical progress and became a central concept within postmodern theory.

40. The administrative reorganization undertaken by the British after the Revolt of 1857 led to several institutional reforms intended to strengthen colonial governance in India. During this phase, the British government introduced measures to centralize administration and establish structured bureaucratic institutions across the provinces.

The reforms of 1861 were particularly significant because they introduced a more organized framework for governance and administration, including the development of structured executive institutions at provincial and district levels. In this broader administrative restructuring, the policing system was reorganized into a hierarchical and bureaucratic structure with clear authority and supervision. A professional police organization headed by senior officers at provincial and district levels replaced earlier decentralized and irregular policing arrangements. These reforms laid the institutional groundwork for a modern, centralized police administration that later operated through the framework established by colonial legislation of the same period. Therefore, among the given options, the answer corresponding to this foundational administrative restructuring is Indian Council Act, 1861.

41. A. Andrew Heywood — Political Theory: An Introduction: Andrew Heywood is a prominent political theorist whose book "Political Theory: An Introduction" is widely used in political science for explaining core concepts such as liberty, equality, democracy, power and justice.

B. David Held — Political Theory and the Modern State: David Held authored "Political Theory and the Modern State," a work examining the development of modern political thought and the relationship between democracy, governance and the modern state.

C. Thomas Jefferson — Declaration of American Independence: Thomas Jefferson was the principal author of the Declaration of American Independence (1776), a historic document asserting the independence of the American colonies and articulating principles of natural rights and popular sovereignty.

D. John Locke — Second Treatise of Civil Government: John Locke wrote "Second Treatise of Civil Government," which presented ideas of natural rights, limited government and the social contract, influencing modern liberal democracy.

42. A. Collective Responsibility: In a parliamentary system, the Council of Ministers is collectively responsible to the legislature, especially the lower house. Loss of confidence requires the ministry to resign.

B. Dissolution of the Lower House: The lower house can be dissolved before completion of its term, usually on the advice of the Prime Minister, allowing fresh elections to resolve political deadlock.

C. Leadership of the Prime Minister: The Prime Minister is the real executive authority, leading the cabinet and coordinating government policies in a parliamentary system.

D. President is the Real Boss: In parliamentary systems the president or monarch is generally a nominal head, not the real executive authority.

E. President directly elected by the people: Direct election of the president is a feature of presidential systems, not parliamentary governments.

43. A. Economic Cooperation Organization — 10: The Economic Cooperation Organization (ECO) is a regional organization formed to promote economic cooperation among 10 member states primarily in Central and West Asia.

B. Council of Europe — 47: The Council of Europe is a major European organization focused on human rights, democracy and rule of law and currently includes 47 member states.

C. ASEAN Regional Forum — 27: The ASEAN Regional Forum (ARF) is a security dialogue forum involving 27 participating members, including ASEAN countries and their dialogue partners.

D. African Union — 54: The African Union is a continental organization with 54 member states working for political cooperation, economic integration and development across Africa.

44. C. M.H. Kania (1991): M.H. Kania served briefly as Chief Justice of India in 1991, making him the earliest among the listed names in chronological order.

D. L.M. Sharma (1992–1993): L.M. Sharma served as Chief Justice after Kania, placing him next in the ascending order of tenure.

E. A.M. Ahmadi (1994–1997): A.M. Ahmadi held the office during the mid-1990s, following L.M. Sharma.

B. B.N. Kirpal (2002): B.N. Kirpal served briefly as Chief Justice in 2002, making him later than Ahmadi.

A. V.N. Khare (2002–2004): V.N. Khare succeeded B.N. Kirpal and served until 2004, making him the most recent among the given names.

45. Swami Sahajanand Saraswati founded the Bihar Provincial Kisan Sabha in 1929 to mobilize peasants against the oppressive practices of zamindars and to defend tenant rights. This organization became an important platform for agrarian movements in Bihar and laid the groundwork for wider peasant mobilization in India. Later, in 1936 during the Lucknow session of the Indian National Congress, the All India Kisan Sabha (AIKS) was established with Swami Sahajanand Saraswati as its first president, bringing peasant movements under a national organization. Although both statements are historically correct, the formation of the All India Kisan Sabha in 1936 does not explain the earlier formation of the Bihar Provincial Kisan Sabha in 1929; it represents a later development in the expansion of the peasant movement.

46. P.V. Narasimha Rao, who later became the Prime Minister of India (1991-1996), had a long parliamentary career and contested elections from more than one state during different phases of his political life. He was primarily associated with Andhra Pradesh, from where he began his political career and served in the state legislature as well as the Lok Sabha. Later, during the 1991 general elections, when he was not initially a member of Parliament after becoming Prime Minister, he contested and won a Lok Sabha by-election from Nandyal in Andhra Pradesh. He also had political electoral connections with Odisha and Maharashtra, where he successfully contested parliamentary seats at different times. This reflects his national stature within the Congress Party and his ability to secure electoral victories beyond his home state. Therefore the correct option is Andhra Pradesh, Odisha and Maharashtra.

47. **A. Sachchidananda Sinha:** Sachchidananda Sinha served as a Deputy President of the Central Legislative Assembly, which was the title used before independence for what later became known as the Deputy Speaker.

B. H.S. Gour: H.S. Gour also served in the position equivalent to Deputy President of the Central Legislative Assembly, contributing to legislative proceedings during the late colonial period.

C. Akhil Chandra Dutta: Akhil Chandra Dutta held the office of Deputy President of the Central Legislative Assembly and participated in presiding over debates and legislative business.

D. G.G. Swell: G. G. Swell served as Deputy Speaker of the Lok Sabha after independence, not as Deputy President of the Central Legislative Assembly.

E. Godey Murahari: Godey Murahari served as Deputy Speaker of the Lok Sabha in independent India, not in the pre-independence Central Legislative Assembly.

48. In September 2000, the Government of India established a High Level Committee on the Indian Diaspora to study the status, problems and contributions of people of Indian origin living abroad. The committee was chaired by Dr. L. M. Singhvi, a distinguished jurist, diplomat and Member of Parliament. The committee examined the relationship between India and its overseas communities and suggested measures to strengthen cultural, economic and political links with the Indian diaspora. Its recommendations later led to initiatives such as the Pravasi Bharatiya Divas and policies aimed at improving engagement with overseas Indians.

49. **A. United Nations Conference on the Human Environment — 1972:** The Stockholm Conference of 1972 was the first major international conference focused on environmental protection and sustainable management of natural resources.

B. Convention on International Trade in Endangered Species — 1973: CITES was adopted in 1973 to regulate international trade in endangered species of plants and animals and to protect biodiversity.

C. UN Conference on Environment and Development — 1992: The Rio Earth Summit of 1992 addressed global environmental challenges and produced major agreements on climate change, biodiversity and sustainable development.

D. UN Climate Change Conference — 2009: The Copenhagen Climate Conference (2009) was an important global meeting aimed at negotiating international climate commitments and addressing global warming.

50. **B. Neelam Sanjiva Reddy:** Neelam Sanjiva Reddy served as Speaker of the Lok Sabha between 1967 and 1969 before later becoming President of India.

D. Gurdial Singh Dhillon: Gurdial Singh Dhillon served as Speaker of the Lok Sabha from 1969 to 1975, making him the earliest among the listed names.

A. Baliram Bhagat: Baliram Bhagat served as Speaker from 1976 to 1977, following Dhillon's tenure.

C. K.S. Hegde: K.S. Hegde served as Speaker from 1977 to 1980, placing him after the earlier Speakers.

E. Rabi Ray: Rabi Ray served as Speaker from 1989 to 1991, making him the most recent among the given names in chronological order.

51. A. 'Work' represents the activity of artists and craftsmen: In Hannah Arendt's framework in "The Human Condition", work refers to the creation of durable objects and artifacts that build the human world. Activities of craftsmen, builders and artists fall within this category because they produce lasting products beyond immediate survival needs.

B. 'Action' is the highest activity referring to public interaction between equal citizens: Arendt considered action the highest form of human activity because it occurs through interaction among individuals in the public sphere. It involves speech, participation and collective engagement among citizens.

C. 'Action' belongs to the sphere of politics: According to Arendt, action takes place in the political realm, where individuals appear before others as equals and engage in deliberation, debate and decision-making within public life.

E. 'Labour' is the lowest level of activity fulfilling physical needs: Labour refers to repetitive activities required for biological survival, such as food production and basic physical maintenance of life. Arendt placed it at the lowest level because it produces no permanent products and must be constantly repeated.

D. 'Action is the activity which denies freedom of thought': This statement contradicts Arendt's argument because she considered action to be the sphere where human freedom and plurality are expressed, not denied.

52. Under the Constitution of India, the authority to decide whether a Bill is a Money Bill rests solely with the Speaker of the Lok Sabha. Article 110 defines what constitutes a Money Bill, including matters related to taxation, borrowing of money by the government and expenditure from the Consolidated Fund of India. When a bill is introduced and there is doubt regarding its classification, the Speaker's decision is final and binding. This determination is crucial because Money Bills follow a special legislative procedure in which the Rajya Sabha has only limited powers, such as making recommendations but not rejecting or amending the bill.

53. Ram Krishna Hegde became the first non-Congress Chief Minister of Karnataka when he assumed office in 1983 representing the Janata Party. Before his tenure, the Indian National Congress had dominated politics in the state since independence. Hegde's leadership marked a significant political shift and introduced reforms in administrative transparency and decentralization. His government promoted policies like panchayat raj reforms, strengthening local self-government institutions in Karnataka. His tenure symbolized the rise of non-Congress regional political forces in several Indian states during the 1980s.

54. Simone de Beauvoir's famous statement "One is not born, but rather becomes, a woman" emphasizes that gender is not determined solely by biological factors but is shaped by social processes and cultural expectations. According to her analysis, society assigns roles, behaviours and norms to individuals, and through repeated performance of these roles individuals come to identify themselves as women or men. This idea influenced later feminist theories that describe gender as socially constructed through repeated actions and social practices rather than as a purely biological condition determined at birth.

55. C. Apartheid ends in South Africa: Apartheid officially ended in 1994, marking a major political transformation after the Cold War and establishing a democratic government under Nelson Mandela.

D. Taliban-II seized power in Afghanistan: The Taliban returned to power in Afghanistan in 2021, an event clearly occurring in the post–Cold War geopolitical period.

E. Kargil War between India and Pakistan: The Kargil conflict in 1999 occurred between India and Pakistan after the Cold War had ended and represents a significant regional military confrontation of the post–Cold War era.

A. China-Vietnam war: This war occurred in 1979, during the Cold War period.

B. Iran-Iraq war: The Iran-Iraq war took place between 1980 and 1988, also within the Cold War period.

56. John Stuart Mill, the influential British philosopher, economist and political thinker, served as a Member of the British Parliament from 1865 to 1868. He represented the Westminster constituency in the House of Commons. During his parliamentary tenure he advocated several progressive reforms including women's suffrage, expansion of representative government, protection of civil liberties and electoral reforms. Mill is especially remembered for presenting a petition in Parliament supporting women's right to vote and for attempting to amend the Reform Bill of 1867 to include women in the electoral franchise. His parliamentary career was relatively brief but historically significant because it reflected the practical application of his liberal political philosophy.

57. A. West Bengal — 16 and 42: West Bengal sends 16 members to the Rajya Sabha and 42 members to the Lok Sabha, reflecting its large population and representation in Parliament.

B. Tamil Nadu — 18 and 39: Tamil Nadu has 18 Rajya Sabha seats and 39 Lok Sabha seats, making it one of the states with substantial parliamentary representation.

C. Odisha — 10 and 21: Odisha is represented by 10 members in the Rajya Sabha and 21 members in the Lok Sabha.

D. Karnataka — 12 and 28: Karnataka has 12 members in the Rajya Sabha and 28 members in the Lok Sabha.

58. B. 73rd Constitutional Amendment: The 73rd Amendment (1992) introduced the Panchayati Raj system and provided reservation for women in rural local government institutions, ensuring their participation in grassroots governance.

C. 74th Constitutional Amendment: The 74th Amendment (1992) extended similar provisions for reservation of seats for women in urban local bodies, thereby promoting women's representation in municipal governance.

E. 106th Constitutional Amendment: The 106th Amendment (2023) provides reservation for women in the Lok Sabha and State Legislative Assemblies, strengthening women's representation in higher legislative institutions.

A. 69th Amendment: The 69th Amendment relates to the creation of the National Capital Territory of Delhi and does not specifically address women's empowerment.

D. 104th Amendment: The 104th Amendment primarily dealt with the extension of reservation for Scheduled Castes and Scheduled Tribes in legislatures, not specifically women.

59. The Cold War began after the end of the Second World War in 1945 when tensions emerged between the United States and the Soviet Union over ideological, political and military differences. The world gradually divided into two rival blocs: a capitalist bloc led by the United States and a communist bloc led by the Soviet Union. This division resulted in intense geopolitical rivalry, arms races, ideological competition and proxy conflicts across different regions of the world. The emergence of these two competing power blocs explains why the Cold War developed after World War II, making the reason statement an appropriate explanation of the assertion.

60. The assertion is correct because in 1941 Germany opened the Eastern Front of World War II when it launched military campaigns across Eastern and Southeastern Europe, including invasions of Yugoslavia, Greece and the Soviet Union (Operation Barbarossa). This expansion significantly widened the scope of the war in Europe. However, the reason statement is incorrect because Nazi expansionism was primarily centered in Europe, not Asia. The outbreak of the Second World War was largely associated with German aggression in Europe and Japanese expansionism in Asia, rather than Nazi expansionism in Asia. Therefore the assertion is correct while the reason is incorrect.

61. During the First World War, US President Woodrow Wilson presented the Fourteen Points to the United States Congress on 8 January 1918. These points outlined his vision for a just and lasting peace after the war. The proposals included principles such as open diplomacy, freedom of the seas, reduction of armaments, self-determination for nationalities and the establishment of an international organization to maintain peace, which later became the League of Nations. Wilson intended these principles to serve as the basis for the post-war settlement and to prevent future global conflicts by promoting cooperation and fairness among nations.

62. **A. Leading a long and healthy life:** One of the core components of human development is health, which is measured through indicators such as life expectancy and access to healthcare.

C. Ensuring Human security: Human development frameworks emphasize human security, including protection from poverty, violence and social vulnerability, allowing individuals to live safely and with dignity.

E. Preserving resources for future generations: Sustainable development is an important aspect of human development, focusing on environmental sustainability and preservation of resources so that future generations can also meet their needs.

B. Achieving equality for all animals and insects: This is not a human development indicator. Human development focuses on improving human well-being rather than animal equality.

D. Acquiring good entertainments: Entertainment is not considered a key human development indicator within the standard human development framework.

63. Vithalbhai Patel, an important nationalist leader and elder brother of Sardar Vallabhbhai Patel, was elected to the Central Legislative Assembly in 1924 under the constitutional framework created by the Government of India Act, 1919 (Montagu–Chelmsford Reforms). His entry into the Assembly represented the growing participation of Indian nationalist leaders in legislative institutions during the colonial period. Vithalbhai Patel was associated with the Swaraj Party, which aimed to enter legislatures and obstruct colonial policies from within the constitutional system. His parliamentary career became historically significant when, in 1925, he was elected as the President (equivalent to Speaker) of the Central Legislative Assembly, becoming the first Indian and the first elected person to hold that office. During his tenure he worked to strengthen parliamentary procedures, protect legislative autonomy and assert greater independence of the Assembly from executive control, thereby influencing the evolution of parliamentary traditions in India.

64. During the period of the Emergency declared in India in June 1975, democratic rights and political opposition were severely restricted. Among academic institutions, Delhi University became one of the earliest centres where resistance against Emergency policies began to emerge. Students and sections of the academic community expressed opposition to censorship, suppression of civil liberties and arrests of political activists. Although the Emergency period involved strict control over public dissent, universities remained important spaces where intellectual debate and political resistance gradually developed. Therefore the institution widely associated with the earliest protests in this context was the University of Delhi.

65. Dr. Sachchidananda Sinha presided as the interim (temporary) president of the Constituent Assembly of India during its first meeting on 9 December 1946. As the oldest member of the Assembly, he was invited to chair the inaugural session before a permanent president was elected. Two days later, on 11 December 1946, Dr. Rajendra Prasad was elected as the permanent President of the Constituent Assembly. The Assembly was responsible for drafting the Constitution of independent India, debating fundamental rights, governance structures and principles that would shape the future democratic framework of the country.

66. The Tashkent Declaration was signed on 10 January 1966 in Tashkent (then in the Soviet Union) by Prime Minister Lal Bahadur Shastri of India and President Ayub Khan of Pakistan after the Indo-Pakistan War of 1965. The agreement was mediated by Soviet Premier Alexei Kosygin and aimed to restore diplomatic and economic relations between the two countries and ensure withdrawal of forces to pre-war positions. The objective of the declaration was to establish a framework for peaceful relations and prevent further armed conflict between India and Pakistan. Thus the reason correctly explains the purpose behind the signing of the declaration.

67. The Tripartite Pact was signed on 27 September 1940 by Germany, Italy and Japan, formally establishing the Axis alliance during the Second World War. The agreement recognized the leadership of Germany and Italy in Europe and Japan in East Asia and aimed at mutual military cooperation, particularly against countries that might oppose their expansion. However, the alliance was not intended to promote global peace; instead it represented a strategic military partnership designed to expand territorial influence and challenge the Allied powers. Therefore the assertion is correct but the reason is incorrect.

68. In 1901, British Viceroy Lord Curzon expressed the view that it would be impractical and strategically unwise for Britain to cross the Himalayas and directly occupy Tibet. His statement reflected the British strategic doctrine of maintaining Tibet as a buffer zone rather than annexing it. The British government feared that a direct occupation would provoke rival powers and create administrative and military difficulties in such a remote region. Later British diplomatic policies, particularly the Anglo-Chinese Convention of 1906 and the Anglo-Russian Convention of 1907, formally acknowledged Chinese suzerainty over Tibet and committed Britain to non-interference in Tibetan internal affairs. Because Britain refrained from direct control and recognized Chinese authority, the Qing dynasty was able to strengthen and re-establish its control over Tibet during the period 1905–1911. Thus the reason correctly explains the strategic context behind Curzon's position.

69. **C. Y.B. Chavan:** Y.B. Chavan served as Chairman of the Eighth Finance Commission, appointed in 1982, making him the most recent among the listed names.

B. J.M. Shelat: J.M. Shelat chaired the Seventh Finance Commission, appointed in 1977, placing him after Chavan in descending chronological order.

D. Brahmananda Reddy: Brahmananda Reddy served as Chairman of the Sixth Finance Commission, appointed in 1972, earlier than Shelat but later than Tyagi and Chanda.

A. Mahavir Tyagi: Mahavir Tyagi chaired the Fifth Finance Commission, appointed in 1968, placing him next in descending order.

E. A.K. Chanda: A.K. Chanda served as Chairman of the Third Finance Commission, appointed in 1960, making him the earliest among the listed chairmen.

70. The modern Panchayati Raj system in India was formally inaugurated on 2 October 1959 at Nagaur in Rajasthan by Prime Minister Jawaharlal Nehru. This step followed the recommendations of the Balwantrai Mehta Committee (1957), which advocated democratic decentralization through a three-tier system of local self-government consisting of the Gram Panchayat, Panchayat Samiti and Zila Parishad. The inauguration at Nagaur symbolized the beginning of institutionalized rural self-government in independent India and reflected Nehru's vision of strengthening grassroots democracy and involving local communities in development planning and governance.

71. Bhikhu Parekh's most noted and detailed work on multiculturalism is "Rethinking Multiculturalism: Cultural Diversity and Political Theory." In this book, he examines how culturally diverse societies should respond to differences in identity, community values and political recognition. He argues that no society is culturally neutral and that political theory must seriously engage with pluralism and diversity. The book is regarded as one of the important modern works on multicultural political thought. Hence the correct option is the fourth one.

72. The term "Third World" was used during the Cold War for countries that did not belong either to the capitalist First World led by the United States or the communist Second World led by the Soviet Union. So the assertion is correct. However, the reason is incorrect because the term did not emerge in the 1990s; in fact, it had been in use much earlier, especially from the 1950s onward. It is true that by the 1990s the term increasingly came to be criticized for its negative or outdated implications, but that is not the origin of the term. Therefore, assertion is correct but reason is not correct.

73. The French Senate is the upper house of the French Parliament, and its total membership is 348. Senators are elected indirectly and represent territorial collectivities, overseas territories and French citizens living abroad. The chamber plays an important role in legislation, constitutional revision and parliamentary scrutiny. Although the National Assembly is the more powerful chamber in cases of disagreement, the Senate remains a permanent and significant institution in the French political system. Therefore, the correct total number is 348.

74. The famous definition of politics as the "authoritative allocation of values" was given by David Easton. He viewed politics as the process through which binding decisions are made for society regarding the distribution of values, benefits and burdens. This definition became highly influential in modern political science because it shifted attention from merely the study of the state to the broader functioning of the political system. Easton's systems approach helped political scientists understand how demands and supports from society are processed into decisions and policies. Hence the correct answer is David Easton.

75. The statement that "Women should acquire human virtues by the same means as men, instead of being educated like a fanciful kind of half being" was written by Mary Wollstonecraft. She was one of the earliest major feminist thinkers and strongly argued for equal education and rational development of women. In her work, especially A Vindication of the Rights of Woman, she criticized the social system that treated women as ornamental rather than rational human beings. Her writings laid a strong foundation for later feminist thought by demanding equality, dignity and intellectual freedom for women. Therefore, the correct option is Mary Wollstonecraft.

76. The Peace of Westphalia refers to a set of treaties signed in October 1648 in the cities of Münster and Osnabrück in the Holy Roman Empire. These treaties ended the Thirty Years' War (1618–1648) in Europe and also concluded the Eighty Years' War between Spain and the Dutch Republic. The agreements established the principle of state sovereignty, recognizing the authority of rulers over their territories and limiting external interference in domestic affairs. The Peace of Westphalia is often considered a foundational moment in the development of the modern international system, as it laid the groundwork for the concept of sovereign nation-states and diplomatic equality among states.

77. **C. UN Development Programme (UNDP) founded (1965):** The United Nations Development Programme (UNDP) was established in 1965 by merging the Expanded Programme of Technical Assistance and the UN Special Fund. It became the UN's principal global development network, making it the most recent event among the listed ones.

A. UN peacekeepers sent to Cyprus (1964): The United Nations Peacekeeping Force in Cyprus (UNFICYP) was created in 1964 to prevent further conflict between Greek Cypriot and Turkish Cypriot communities and maintain peace on the island.

E. U Thant appointed Secretary-General (1961): After the death of Dag Hammarskjöld, U Thant was appointed Acting Secretary-General in 1961 and later confirmed in the position, placing this event next in chronological order.

B. UN operation in Congo established (1960): The United Nations Operation in the Congo (ONUC) was launched in 1960 during the Congo Crisis to stabilize the newly independent state and facilitate the withdrawal of foreign troops.

D. First UN peacekeeping force sent to the Suez Canal (1956): The United Nations Emergency Force (UNEF I) was deployed in 1956 during the Suez Crisis, representing the first large-scale UN peacekeeping mission.

Thus, when arranged in descending order (most recent to earliest), the sequence becomes C, A, E, B, D.

78. **A. Article 243 ZF — Continuance of existing laws of Municipalities:** This provision ensures that existing municipal laws continue until they are amended or repealed to align with the constitutional provisions introduced through the 74th Constitutional Amendment.

B. Article 243 ZD — Committee for District Planning: This article provides for the creation of District Planning Committees, responsible for consolidating plans prepared by Panchayats and Municipalities within a district.

C. Article 243 S — Constitution and composition of Ward Committees: Article 243S deals with the formation and composition of Ward Committees in municipalities to strengthen local participation in governance.

D. Article 243 V — Disqualifications for Members of Municipalities: This article specifies the conditions under which a person may be disqualified from being chosen as or remaining a member of a municipal body.

79. In 1961, the Government of India appointed a special committee under the chairmanship of H. N. Sanyal to examine and review the existing legal framework concerning contempt of court.

The committee studied how the law operated in protecting the authority and dignity of courts while balancing the need for freedom of expression. Its recommendations formed the basis for reforms in the law relating to contempt of court, eventually leading to the enactment of the Contempt of Courts Act, 1971, which clarified and codified the principles governing civil and criminal contempt in India.

80. **A. Maharashtra — 1971:** Maharashtra enacted the Lokayukta and Uplokayukta Act in 1971, becoming one of the early states to create an anti-corruption ombudsman institution.

B. Uttar Pradesh — 1975: The Uttar Pradesh Lokayukta and Uplokayukta Act was enacted in 1975 to investigate allegations of corruption and maladministration against public officials.

C. Himachal Pradesh — 1983: Himachal Pradesh introduced its Lokayukta Act in 1983 to strengthen accountability in public administration.

D. Punjab — 1996: Punjab enacted its Lokayukta legislation in 1996, establishing an independent authority to investigate complaints against ministers and public servants.

81. The proposal for a "United Sovereign Bengal" in 1947 was advocated mainly by Abul Hashim, a prominent leader of the Bengal Provincial Muslim League, along with other leaders such as Huseyn Shaheed Suhrawardy. The idea aimed to prevent the partition of Bengal during the division of British India and instead create an independent, united Bengal state consisting of both Hindu-majority and Muslim-majority regions. Supporters believed that Bengal possessed a unique cultural and historical identity that justified a separate sovereign status rather than being divided between India and Pakistan. However, the proposal failed because it did not receive sufficient political support from the Indian National Congress, the Muslim League leadership at the all-India level, and sections of the Hindu leadership in Bengal.

82. **A. Korean War (1950–1953):** The Korean War was one of the earliest major Cold War conflicts, involving North Korea supported by communist allies and South Korea backed by the United States and United Nations forces.

B. Vietnam War (1955–1975): The Vietnam War represented a prolonged Cold War confrontation between communist North Vietnam and anti-communist South Vietnam supported by the United States and its allies.

C. Cuban Missile Crisis (1962): The Cuban Missile Crisis was a major Cold War confrontation between the United States and the Soviet Union over Soviet nuclear missiles stationed in Cuba, bringing the world close to nuclear war.

D. Bifurcation of Sudan: The division of Sudan into Sudan and South Sudan occurred in 2011, long after the Cold War had ended.

E. Russian invasion of Ukraine: The Russian invasion of Ukraine occurred in 2022, which is also outside the Cold War period.

83. **B. Communist China joins the UN (1971):** In 1971, the United Nations General Assembly adopted Resolution 2758 which recognized the People's Republic of China as the legitimate representative of China in the UN, replacing the Republic of China (Taiwan). This is the most recent event among the listed ones.

E. Apollo-11 lands on the Moon (1969): The Apollo-11 mission in July 1969 successfully landed astronauts Neil Armstrong and Buzz Aldrin on the Moon, marking a major achievement of the United States in the Cold War space race.

D. Six Day War (1967): The Six-Day War in 1967 occurred between Israel and the Arab states of Egypt, Syria and Jordan. It was a significant geopolitical event during the Cold War period.

A. Yuri Gagarin first person in space (1961): Soviet cosmonaut Yuri Gagarin became the first human in space on 12 April 1961, orbiting the Earth aboard Vostok-1 and demonstrating Soviet technological capability in the space race.

C. Soviet invasion of Hungary (1956): In 1956, the Soviet Union sent military forces into Hungary to suppress a national uprising against communist rule, making it the earliest event among the given list.

84. The general framework of the judiciary in the Constitution of the United States is outlined in Article III. This article establishes the Supreme Court of the United States and authorizes the creation of lower federal courts by Congress. It defines the jurisdiction of federal courts, including cases involving federal law, treaties, disputes between states and issues involving ambassadors. Article III also establishes the principle that federal judges hold office during good behaviour, ensuring judicial independence by protecting them from arbitrary removal.

85. The book "A Systems Analysis of Political Life" was written by David Easton, a leading political scientist known for developing the systems theory approach in political science. In this work he analyzed politics as a system in which inputs (demands and supports from society) are processed by political institutions and converted into outputs (decisions and policies). Easton's framework helped shift political science toward a more systematic and behavioural approach, emphasizing how political systems maintain stability and adapt to changing social pressures.

86. A. Ashok K. Desai (1996–1998): Ashok K. Desai served as Attorney General of India from 1996 to 1998, during the period of the United Front governments. Among the listed names, his tenure began the most recently, so he appears first in descending order.

B. K. Parasaran (1983–1989): K. Parasaran served as Attorney General from 1983 to 1989 under Prime Ministers Indira Gandhi and Rajiv Gandhi, placing him next in the sequence after Desai.

D. L.N. Sinha (1979–1983): L.N. Sinha served as Attorney General between 1979 and 1983, covering the period of the Janata Party government and the early years of Indira Gandhi's return to power.

E. S.V. Gupte (1977–1979): S.V. Gupte held the office of Attorney General from 1977 to 1979, during the Janata Party government led by Morarji Desai.

C. Niren De (1968–1977): Niren De served as Attorney General from 1968 to 1977, making him the earliest among the listed individuals and therefore the last in descending order of appointment.

87. A. Altamas Kabir — September 2012 - July 2013: Altamas Kabir served as the 39th Chief Justice of India during this period.

B. R.M. Lodha — April 2014 - September 2014: R.M. Lodha served as the 41st Chief Justice of India for a brief tenure in 2014.

C. T.S. Thakur — December 2015 - January 2017: T.S. Thakur served as the 43rd Chief Justice of India, overseeing several significant judicial developments.

D. K.G. Balakrishnan — January 2007 - May 2010: K.G. Balakrishnan served as the 37th Chief Justice of India, becoming the first Chief Justice from the Scheduled Caste community.

88. D. Founded the Ramakrishna Mission (1897): Swami Vivekananda founded the Ramakrishna Mission in 1897 in India to promote spiritual, educational and humanitarian work.

B. Visited the United Kingdom (1895): Vivekananda visited Britain in 1895, where he delivered lectures on Vedanta philosophy and gained many Western disciples.

C. Founded the Vedanta Society in New York (1894): The Vedanta Society of New York was established in 1894 to spread Vedantic philosophy in the United States.

E. Lecture at the Parliament of Religions in Chicago (1893): Swami Vivekananda delivered his famous speech beginning with "Sisters and Brothers of America" at the World Parliament of Religions in Chicago in 1893.

A. Visited Japan for the first time (1893): Vivekananda visited Japan in 1893 during his journey to the United States before attending the Chicago Parliament of Religions.

89. A. North American Free Trade Agreement — 1994: NAFTA came into force in 1994 between the United States, Canada and Mexico to promote free trade.

B. Association of South East Asian Nations — 1967: ASEAN was established in 1967 by five Southeast Asian countries to promote economic growth and regional stability.

C. Asia Pacific Economic Cooperation — 1989: APEC was founded in 1989 to enhance economic cooperation among Pacific Rim countries.

D. Organization for Security and Cooperation in Europe — 1973: The organization originated from the Conference on Security and Cooperation in Europe initiated in 1973, later evolving into the OSCE.

90. A. Falklands War — 1982: The Falklands War occurred in 1982 between the United Kingdom and Argentina over the Falkland Islands.

B. Soviet invasion of Czechoslovakia — 1968: Soviet forces invaded Czechoslovakia in 1968 to suppress the Prague Spring reforms.

C. Emergence of Bangladesh — 1971: Bangladesh became an independent nation in 1971 following the Indo-Pakistani War and the liberation movement.

D. Algerian Revolution — 1954–1962: The Algerian War of Independence lasted from 1954 to 1962, resulting in Algeria gaining independence from France.

91. The passage clearly states that East Timor (Timor-Leste) was a Portuguese colony for over 300 years before the events described later. Portuguese colonial control lasted several centuries until Portugal withdrew from the territory in the mid-1970s. Therefore, according to the information directly given in the passage, the correct option is Over 300 years.

92. The passage explicitly mentions that Indonesian troops invaded East Timor in 1975 after Portugal's rapid withdrawal from the colony. This invasion initiated a prolonged and violent conflict that resulted in guerrilla warfare and large-scale civilian suffering. Since the year 1975 is directly mentioned in the passage, this option correctly answers the question.

93. According to the passage, a referendum was held in East Timor in 1999 after the fall of Indonesian President Suharto. The Indonesian government agreed to allow the population to vote on their political future. This referendum ultimately led to the decision regarding independence.

94. The passage states that 75 percent of the East Timorese population voted in favour of independence in the referendum. This overwhelming majority demonstrated the desire of the people of East Timor to establish an independent nation separate from Indonesian control.

95. The passage mentions that about one-third of East Timor's population of 6,50,000 inhabitants died due to mass executions, bombings and starvation during the conflict. One-third of 6,50,000 equals approximately 2,16,667, which is closest to 2,17,000 among the given options. Hence, the correct answer is 2,17,000.

96. The passage clearly states that the Balwant Rai Mehta Committee recommended a three-tier Panchayati Raj system consisting of Gram Panchayat at the village level, Panchayat Samiti at the block level and Zila Parishad at the district level. Therefore, according to the passage, the institution recommended for the district level was the Zila Parishad.

97. The passage mentions that the Balwant Rai Mehta Committee recommended the establishment of the scheme of "democratic decentralisation." This concept meant transferring decision-making authority and administrative responsibility from the central and state governments to local institutions so that people could participate directly in governance and development at the grassroots level.

98. According to the passage, the committee specifically recommended the creation of a three-tier Panchayati Raj system. This structure included Gram Panchayat at the village level, Panchayat Samiti at the block level and Zila Parishad at the district level, thereby creating a hierarchical system of rural local governance.

99. The passage states that the Government of India appointed the Balwant Rai Mehta Committee in January 1957 to examine the functioning of the Community Development Programme and the National Extension Service. Therefore, the year mentioned in the passage for its appointment is 1957.

100. The passage explicitly mentions that the committee was appointed to examine the working of the Community Development Programme (1952) and the National Extension Service (1953) and suggest improvements for their better functioning. Hence, the correct answer is Community Development Programme and the National Extension Service.

Previous Years' Paper

National Testing Agency (NTA)

UGC-NET Junior Research Fellowship & Assistant Professor Eligibility Exam

POLITICAL SCIENCE, JUNE-2025

(Exam held on 26-06-2025)

PAPER-II

1. In which year, the Convention on the Elimination of All Forms of Discrimination Against Women, was adopted?

1. 1990
2. 1979
3. 1977
4. 1987

2. Who wrote the book 'Termites in the Trading System'?

1. Amartya Sen
2. Thomas Hobbes
3. Susan George
4. Jagdish Bhagwati

3. In which year, the United Nations General Assembly adopted the Millennium Development Goals?

1. 2007
2. 1993
3. 2000
4. 1997

4. In which year, U. Thant appointed as the Secretary-General of the United Nations?

1. 1959
2. 1961
3. 1963
4. 1967

5. In which year, Greece joined the European Community?

1. 1981
2. 1978
3. 1977
4. 1985

6. Which Russian Marxist was assassinated in Mexico in 1940?

1. Nikita Khruschev
2. Karl Marx
3. Joseph Stalin
4. Leon Trotsky

7. In which year, the referendum to leave European Union took place in Great Britain?

1. 2013
2. 2014
3. 2016
4. 2018

8. Who developed "a humanist critique of the Western Enlightenment that uncovered its links to colonialism and highlighted 'narrative of oppression', cultural and ideological biases that disempowered colonized peoples by representing them as the non-western other"?

1. Aristotle
2. Edward Said
3. Woodrow Wilson
4. Subash Chandra Bose

9. Who wrote the book 'The General Theory of Employment, Interest and Money'?

1. John Maynard Keynes
2. Milton Friedman
3. Raj Kumar Mittal
4. Thomas Hobbes

10. Who became the leading exponent of the 'Second Generation' of the Frankfurt School of Critical Theory?
1. Fredrick Hegel
2. Karl Marx
3. Validimir Lenin
4. Jurgen Habermas

11. Who argued that "property rights should be strictly upheld, provided that wealth has been justly acquired in the first place, or has been justly transferred from one person to another"?
1. Mahatma Gandhi
2. Antonio Gramsci
3. Robert Nozick
4. Thomas Hobbes

12. Who used the term 'Ecology' for the first time?
1. Dipankar Sengupta
2. Ernst Haeckel
3. Karl Marx
4. Adam Smith

13. Who wrote the book 'On Revolution'?
1. Hannah Arendt 2. Vladimir Lenin
3. Karl Marx 4. Edmund Burke

14. Who wrote the book 'A Vindication of the Rights of Women'?
1. Betty Friedan
2. Mary Woollstonecraft
3. Ana Ballesteros Peiro
4. Fatima Marsinni

15. Who wrote the book 'Development Administration: Concepts, Goals, Methods'?
1. George F. Gant
2. Sabu Thomas
3. Fred Riggs
4. Michel Crozier

16. In which year, Bali Terror Bombings took place?
1. 1999 2. 2002
3. 2005 4. 2007

17. Who stated 'War is merely a Continuation of Politics'?
1. Susan Sirk
2. John Locke
3. Carl Von Clausewitz
4. Adam Smith

18. PM Narendra Modi met Donald Trump, the newly elected President of the United States of America in Washington D.C. in:
1. December 2024
2. January 2025
3. April 2025
4. February 2025

19. China-Vietnam war took place in:
1. 1974 2. 1973
3. 1977 4. 1979

20. The book, 'Sexual Politics' is written by:
1. Rabindranath Tagore
2. Karl Marx
3. Kate Millett
4. Immanuel Kant

21. 'Samaj Samata Sangh' was founded by:
1. Jawaharlal Nehru
2. Pandita Ramabai
3. V.D. Savarkar
4. B.R. Ambedkar

22. The book, 'Six Glorious Epochs of Indian History' was written by:
1. Mahatma Gandhi
2. Karl Marx
3. Swami Vivekananda
4. V.D. Savarkar

23. The name 'Simone de Beauvoir' is associated with:
1. Radical Islamism
2. Feminism
3. Anarchism
4. Environmentalism

24. Arne Naess coined the term:

1. Deep Ecology
2. Homeostasis
3. Integral Humanism
4. Volksgeist

25. Pandita Ramabai was associated with:

1. Indian National Army
2. Mukti Mission
3. The Land Holder's Society
4. Dharma Sabha

26. The term 'The Washington Consensus' was coined by:

1. Hannah Arendt
2. Max Weber
3. Milton Friedman
4. John Williamson

27. Who stated, "There is nothing... absolute in management affairs. Seldom do we have to apply the same principle twice as in identical conditions; allowance must be made for different changing circumstances"?

1. Henri Fayol   2. Woodrow Wilson
3. Adam Smith   4. Tridiv Chakrabarty

28. Who wrote the book 'Roman Agrarian History and its Significance for Public and Private Law'?

1. Jawaharlal Nehru
2. Max Weber
3. Adam Smith
4. Woodrow Wilson

29. Who was the first speaker of the Lok Sabha?

1. K.S. Hegde
2. G.V. Mavalankar
3. M.A. Ayyangar
4. G.S. Dhillon

30. The G.V.K. Rao Committee was appointed by the Planning Commission to review the existing administrative arrangements for rural development in:

1. 1985   2. 1983
3. 1981   4. 1979

31. Which Article of the Indian Constitution vests legislative power in Parliament to make laws related to elections?

1. Article 267   2. Article 277
3. Article 285   4. Article 327

32. In which year, the BJP led National Democratic Alliance passed the Prevention of Terrorism Act?

1. 2007   2. 2005
3. 2002   4. 2001

33. In which year, PM Atal Bihari Vajpayee visited Lahore and inked 'Lahore Declaration' with Pakistani PM?

1. 2003   2. 1999
3. 1998   4. 2001

34. The National Commission for Women was set up in which year?

1. 1992   2. 1995
3. 1994   4. 1989

35. Who is the President of Pakistan?

1. Hina Rabbani Khar
2. Nawaz Sharif
3. Asif Aii Zardari
4. Bilawal Bhutto

36. Giorgia Meloni is the Prime Minister of:

1. France   2. Turkey
3. Spain   4. Italy

37. SAARC came into being in:

1. 1985   2. 1987
3. 1989   4. 1981

38. Article 370 was abrogated from the Indian Constitution in:

1. March 2017
2. August 2019
3. November 2017
4. July 2018

39. When was the G-20 Summit held in New Delhi, India?

1. March 2024
2. April 2023
3. September 2023
4. March 2023

40. Which river demarcates the border between Bangladesh and Myanmar?

1. Naf
2. Brahmaputra
3. Mekong
4. Indus

41. Arrange the following regional economic blocs as per their year of formation:

A. MERCOSUR
B. APEC
C. FTAA OR Free Trade area of the Americas
D. NAFTA
E. ASEAN

Choose the correct answer from the options given below:

1. B, E, A, D, C
2. B, E, A, C, D
3. E, B, A, D, C
4. E, A, B, C, D

42. Arrange the following subjects as inserted in the Constitution of India through amendments in chronological order:

A. Removed right to property from the list of Fundamental Rights.
B. Inserted a new chapter on the Fundamental Duties of Citizens
C. Formation of State of Meghalaya
D. Privy and privileges of the former rulers of Indian states were abolished
E. Union Territory of Arunachal Pradesh was conferred statehood

Choose the correct answer from the options given below:

1. D, C, B, E, A
2. C, D, B, A, E
3. C, E, D, A, B
4. D, B, A, E, C

43. Arrange the following subjects according to the year of its addition in the Constitution of India:

A. Santhali in Eighth Schedule
B. Twelfth Schedule
C. Tenth Schedule
D. Ninth Schedule
E. 'Forests' inserted in the Concurrent List.

Choose the correct answer from the options given below:

1. C, B, D, A, E
2. D, E, C, B, A
3. E, D, B, C, A
4. B, C, E, A, D

44. Arrange the following High Courts according to their year of establishment in chronological order:

A. Karnataka
B. Guwahati
C. Kerala
D. Punjab and Haryana
E. Sikkim

Choose the correct answer from the options given below:

1. C, D, A, E, B
2. A, B, C, D, E
3. E, C, B, A, D
4. D, B, A, E, C

45. Choose the correct sequence of articles mentioned in the Constitution of India in chronological order:

A. Council of ministers to aid and advice the President.
B. Appointment of Acting Chief Justice
C. Special address by the President in Parliament
D. Power of President to consult Supreme Court
E. Appointment of district judges

Choose the correct answer from the options given below:

1. C, A, B, E, D
2. A, C, D, E, B
3. A, C, B, D, E
4. C, A, D, B, E

46. Arrange the following in chronological order

A. Cuban Revolution
B. Russian Revolution
C. American Revolution
D. Nicaraguan Revolution
E. Tulip Revolution

Choose the correct answer from the options given below:

1. C, B, A, D, E
2. C, B, D, A, E
3. B, C, A, E, D
4. B, A, C, D, E

47. Arrange the following in chronological order according to their year of launch:

A. SVAMITVA
B. Swachh Bharat Mission
C. SVANidhi se Samriddhi
D. Inauguration of Kartavya Path
E. Namami Gange

Choose the correct answer from the options given below:

1. B, E, A, C, D
2. C, B, E, A, D
3. B, C, E, A, D
4. C, B, A, E, D

48. Arrange the following dignitaries with respect to rank, as appeared in the Table of Precedence:

A. Former Presidents
B. Speaker of Lok Sabha
C. Former Prime Ministers
D. Judges of Supreme Court
E. Solicitor General

Choose the correct answer from the options given below:

1. A, B, C, D, E
2. B, A, D, C, E
3. A, C, B, E, D
4. B, A, C, D, E

49. Arrange the following Acts/Codes in chronological order:

A. The Citizenship Act
B. Flag Code of India
C. Prevention of Insults to National Honour Act
D. State Emblem of India (Prohibition of Improper Use) Act
E. Emblems and Names (Prevention of Improper Use) Act

Choose the correct answer from the options given below:

1. A, B, E, D, C
2. E, C, A, D, B
3. A, E, B, C, D
4. E, A, C, B, D

50. Arrange the following acts/schemes in chronological order (as per year of inauguration/act passed) -

A. National Skill Development Mission
B. Pradhan Mantri Shram Yogi Maan-dhan Yojna
C. Minimum Wages Act
D. Mission Indradhanush
E. Ayushman Bharat Digital Mission

Choose the correct answer from the options given below:

1. C, A, D, E, B
2. C, D, A, B, E
3. D, A, B, E, C
4. D, C, E, B, A

51. Arrange the following in chronological order (as per year of inauguration/act passed):

A. Rastriya Gokul Mission
B. Rights of Persons with Disabilities Act
C. Pradhanmantri Jan Aushadhi Yojna

D. Food and Nutrition Board
E. National Co-operative Development Corporation

Choose the correct answer from the options given below:

1. D, E, B, A, C
2. D, B, E, C, A
3. E, D, C, A, B
4. E, C, D, A, B

52. Arrange the following former Vice-Presidents of India from their date of occupation of the Office as Vice President:

A. R. Venkataraman
B. Bhairon Singh Shekhawat
C. K.R. Narayanan
D. Krishan Kant
E. Varahagiri Venkata Giri

Choose the correct answer from the options given below:

1. E, A, D, C, B
2. A, E, C, B, D
3. E, A, C, D, B
4. A, C, E, B, D

53. Choose the sequence of articles mentioned in the Constitution of India in chronological order:

A. Abolition of Untouchability
B. Prohibition of employment of Children in Factories
C. Promotion of Co-operative Societies
D. Separation of Judiciary from Executive
E. Equal Justice and Free Legal Aid

Choose the correct answer from the options given below:

1. A, B, E, C, D
2. A, B, C, D, E
3. B, A, D, E, C
4. B, D, A, C, E

54. Arrange the following in chronological order:

A. Maastricht Treaty ratified
B. Chinese brutal military massacre in Tiananmen Square
C. Pinochet Coup in Chile
D. U.S. President Donald Trump and North Korea leader Kim Jong-un met at Singapore
E. Russian annexation of Crimea

Choose the correct answer from the options given below:

1. C, A, D, B, E
2. C, B, E, A, D
3. C, A, B, D, E
4. C, B, A, E, D

55. Arrange the following political parties in chronological order as per their year of formation:

A. Servant of the People (Ukraine)
B. Liberal Party of Canada (Canada)
C. Awami League (Bangladesh)
D. Democratic Party (USA)
E. Biju Janta Dal (India)

Choose the correct answer from the options given below:

1. D, B, E, C, A
2. B, C, A, D, E
3. B, D, C, A, E
4. D, B, C, E, A

56. Choose the correct Ministries/Departments under the jurisdiction of the Parliament's Committee on Home Affair:

A. Ministry of Home Affairs
B. Ministry of Law and Justice
C. Ministry of Space
D. Ministry of Defence
E. Ministry of Atomic Energy

Choose the correct answer from the options given below:

1. A, C, E Only
2. A, B Only
3. B, C, D, E Only
4. A, D, E Only

57. Under the rules of the Lok Sabha, choose the correct statements about Parliamentary Committees:

A. Every committee consisting of members of Parliament is a Parliamentary Committee.
B. It works under the direction of the Speaker/Chairman.
C. It is appointed or elected by the House or nominated by the Speaker/Chairman.
D. Presents its report to the President of India.
E. Has a Secretariat provided by the Lok Sabha/Rajya Sabha Secretariat.

Choose the correct answer from the options given below:

1. A, B, D, E Only
2. A, B, C, D Only
3. B, C, E Only
4. A, E, D Only

58. Which among the following President(s) of India died in office?

A. Neelam Sanjeeva Reddy
B. Dr. Zakir Hussain
C. V.V. Giri
D. Fakhruddin Ali Ahmad
E. B.D. Jatti

Choose the correct answer from the options given below:

1. A, C, D Only
2. B, D Only
3. B, D, E Only
4. B, C, D Only

59. Which of the following were written by Swami Vivekananda?

A. India and Her Problems
B. Modern India
C. The Evils of Adhikarvad
D. India in Transition
E. The Problem of Freedom

Choose the correct answer from the options given below:

1. A, B, C Only
2. B, C, D Only
3. A, D, E Only
4. B, D, E Only

60. Which of the following books are written by Noam Chomsky?

A. Syntactic Structures
B. American Power and the New Mandarins
C. New Military Humanism
D. The Tragedy of Great Power Politics
E. The Israel Lobby and US Foreign Policy

Choose the correct answer from the options given below:

1. A, B, C Only
2. C, D, E Only
3. B, C, D Only
4. A, D, E Only

61. Which of the following nuclear arms control agreements are correctly matched?

A. 1959 – Antarctic Treaty
B. 1963 – Partial Test Ban Treaty
C. 1968 – Nuclear Non-Proliferation Treaty
D. 1990 – Comprehensive Test Ban Treaty
E. 1982 – Anti-Ballistic missile Treaty

Choose the correct answer from the options given below:

1. A, C, D, E Only
2. A, B, C Only
3. C, D, E Only
4. B, C, D, E Only

62. Consider the facts about Afghanistan and choose the correct answers:

A. King Zahir Shah ruled Afghanistan for decades.
B. Mullah Muhammad Omar was the Supreme leader of the First Taliban government.
C. Indus River originates from Afghanistan.
D. Iraq shares land border with Afghanistan.
E. Soviet Union invaded Afghanistan in 1979.

Choose the correct answer from the options given below:

1. B, C, E Only
2. A, B, C Only
3. B, D, A Only
4. A, B, E Only

63. Consider the facts regarding Government of India Act 1935 and choose the correct answer:

A. Provided the establishment of a Federal Court.
B. Separated Burma from India.
C. Created two new provinces of Orissa and Sind.
D. Proposed the establishment of Chamber of Princes.
E. Introduced separate electorate for Muslims

Choose the correct answer from the options given below:

1. A, B, E Only
2. C, D, E Only
3. A, B, C Only
4. A, B, D, E Only

64. Choose the correct names of those who occupied the office of Comptroller and Auditor General(s) of India:

A. V. Narhari Rao
B. Ranjan Gogoi
C. Vinod Rai
D. J.M. Lyngdoh
E. Girish Chandra Murmu

Choose the correct answer from the options given below:

1. A, C, D Only
2. C, D, E Only
3. A, C, E Only
4. B, C, E Only

65. Consider the tenures of the Chief Justices of India and their tenures and choose the correct pairs:

A. Harilal J. Kania (1950-1951)
B. M. Patanjali Shastri (1951-1954)
C. Bhuvaneshwar Prasad Sinha (1959-1964)
D. K. Subba Rao (1970-1974)
E. M. Hidayatullah (1975-1978)

Choose the correct answer from the options given below:

1. A, B, C Only
2. B, C, E Only
3. A, B, C, D Only
4. C, D, E Only

66. Consider the following ideas associated with Douglas McGregor and choose the correct answer:

A. Theory X: The alternate assumptions of integration and self-control.
B. Theory Y: The coercive compulsions
C. Scanlon Plan
D. The Human side of the enterprise
E. Linking Pin Model

Choose the most appropriate answer from the options given below:

1. C, D, E Only
2. C, D Only
3. A, B, C, D Only
4. A, B, D Only

67. Choose the correct thinkers/ideas from below:

A. Henri Fayol: Management Process School
B. Max Weber: Legal Irrational Authority
C. Mary Parker Follett: Idea of Constructive Conflict
D. Elton Mayo: The Great Illumination Experiment
E. Chester Barnard: Spiritual Father of Social System School

Choose the correct answer from the options given below:

1. A, B, C, D Only
2. B, C, D, E
3. A, C, D, E Only
4. B, E Only

68. Abraham Maslow's theory of needs in the hierarchy consists:

A. Physiological needs
B. Esteem needs
C. Security needs
D. Self-actualisation needs
E. Spiritual needs

Choose the most appropriate answer from the options given below:

1. C, D, E Only
2. B, C, D, E Only
3. A, C, E Only
4. A, B, C, D Only

69. In the Preamble of Constitution of India, 'Justice' means:

A. Social Justice
B. Absolute Equality
C. Economic Justice
D. Political Justice
E. Military Justice

Choose the most appropriate answer from the options given below:

1. A, C, D Only
2. A, B, C Only
3. A, B, C, D Only
4. A, C, D, E Only

70. Fred Riggs developed the ideas of fused, prismatic and diffracted societies. The features of Prismatic Societies are:

A. Universalism
B. Ascriptive values
C. Selectivism
D. Attainment
E. Poly-functionalism

Choose the most appropriate answer from the options given below:

1. A, B Only
2. A, B, C Only
3. C, D, E Only
4. A, B, C, D

71. Rensis Likert considers 'Management Systems 1-4' as a model of management. These are:

A. Participative System
B. Consultative System
C. Benevolent-Authoritative
D. Exploitative-Authoritative
E. Maturity-Immaturity

Choose the most appropriate answer from the options given below:

1. A, B, E, D Only
2. B, C, D, E Only
3. A, C, D, E Only
4. A, B, C, D Only

72. The Preamble of the Constitution of India emphasises on:

A. Justice
B. Liberty
C. Equality
D. Monarchy
E. Fraternity

Choose the most appropriate answer from the options given below:

1. A, B, D Only
2. A, C, D Only
3. A, C, D, E Only
4. A, B, C, E Only

73. Choose the correct statements about the role/functions of the Parliament in India:

A. To Legislate.
B. To monitor the expenditure of public funds.
C. To hold the government accountable for its actions.
D. To keep a check on the opposition.
E. To be a forum for the expression of grievances.

Choose the most appropriate answer from the options given below:

1. A, C, D, E Only
2. A, C, D Only
3. D Only
4. A, B, C, E Only

74. According to Montevideo Convention on Rights and Duties of the State (1933), the state has four features:

A. A defined territory.
B. A permanent population.
C. An effective government.
D. The capacity to enter into relations with other states.
E. Freedom to form the Union.

Choose the most appropriate answer from the options given below:

1. A, B, C, D Only
2. B, C, D, E Only
3. A, C, D, E Only
4. A, B, D, E Only

75. Luther Gullick's four basis of departmentalisation are:

A. Purpose B. Process
C. Persons D. Place
E. Protest

Choose the most appropriate answer from the options given below:

1. A, B, C, E Only
2. B, D, E, C Only
3. A, B, C, D Only
4. D, A, E, B Only

76. Match the List-I with List-II:

List-I (Individual)	List-II (Positions Held)
A. K.P.S Menon	I. Chairman of the United Nations Commission on Korea
B. Justice Fazl Ali	II. Chairman of the Neutral Nations Repatriation Commission
C. General K.S. Thimayya	III. Chairman of the States Reorganisation Commission
D. Nalini Ranjan Sarkar	IV. The President of the Federation of Indian Chambers of Commerce and Industry

Choose the correct answer from the options given below:

1. A-I, B-III, C-II, D-IV
2. A-IV, B-II, C-III, D-I
3. A-II, B-IV, C-I, D-III
4. A-III, B-I, C-IV, D-II

77. Match the List-I with List-II:

List-I (High Court)	List-II (Year of Establishment)
A. Allahabad	I. 1916
B. Andhra Pradesh	II. 1862
C. Bombay	III. 1866
D. Patna	IV. 1954

Choose the correct answer from the options given below:

1. A-II, B-I, C-III, D-IV
2. A-III, B-IV, C-II, D-I
3. A-I, B-II, C-IV, D-III
4. A-IV, B-III, C-I, D-II

78. Match the List-I with List-II:

List-I (State)	List-II (Reserved Seats in Lok Sabha for Scheduled Tribes)
A. West Bengal	I. 4
B. Maharashtra	II. 3
C. Jharkhand	III. 2
D. Rajasthan	IV. 5

Choose the correct answer from the options given below:

1. A-III, B-I, C-IV, D-II
2. A-II, B-IV, C-I, D-III
3. A-IV, B-II, C-III, D-I
4. A-I, B-III, C-II, D-IV

79. Match the List-I with List-II:

List-I (Events)	List-II (Year)
A. Soviet Atomic Bomb Exploded	I. 1989
B. Soviet Invasion of Hungry	II. 1979
C. Islamic Revolution in Iran	III. 1949
D. Berlin Wall Falls	IV. 1956

Choose the correct answer from the options given below:

1. A-I, B-II, C-III, D-IV
2. A-IV, B-I, C-II, D-III
3. A-III, B-IV, C-II, D-I
4. A-II, B-III, C-I, D-IV

80. Match the List-I with List-II:

List-I (Act)	List-II (Year)
A. State of Mizoram Act	I. 2000
B. Goa, Daman and Diu Reorganisation Act	II. 1986
C. Bihar Reorganisation Act	III. 1966
D. Punjab Reorganisation Act	IV. 1987

Choose the correct answer from the options given below:

1. A-I, B-II, C-III, D-IV
2. A-IV, B-III, C-II, D-I
3. A-II, B-IV, C-I, D-III
4. A-III, B-I, C-IV, D-II

81. Match the List-I with List-II:

List-I (Event)	List-II (Year)
A. Battle of Stalingrad	I. 1942-1943
B. Munich Agreement	II. 1938
C. Armenian Genocide	III. 1915
D. European Union Created	IV. 1993

Choose the correct answer from the options given below:

1. A-I, B-II, C-III, D-IV
2. A-IV, B-III, C-II, D-I
3. A-III, B-IV, C-I, D-II
4. A-II, B-I, C-IV, D-III

82. Match the List-I with List-II:

List-I (Lok Sabha Speaker)	List-II (Tenure)
A. Rabi Ray	I. January 1985-December 1989
B. Dr. Balram Jakhar	II. December 1989-July 1991
C. Shivraj Patil	III. July 1991- May 1996
D. Meira Kumar	IV. June 2009- June 2014

Choose the correct answer from the options given below:

1. A-I, B-II, C-IV, D-III
2. A-III, B-IV, C-II, D-I
3. A-IV, B-III, C-I, D-II
4. A-II, B-I, C-III, D-IV

83. Match the List-I with List-II:

List-I (UN Peacekeeping Operations)	List-II (Year)
A. United Nations Truce Supervision Organisation	I. 2005
B. United Nations Mission in the Sudan Under Resolution 1590	II. 1948
C. United Nations Interim Force in Lebanon	III. 1964
D. United Nations Peacekeeping Force in Cyprus	IV. 1978

Choose the correct answer from the options given below:

1. A-II, B-I, C-IV, D-III
2. A-III, B-II, C-I, D-IV
3. A-IV, B-I, C-III, D-II
4. A-I B-IV, C-II, D-III

84. Match the List-I with List-II:

List-I (Finance Commission)	List-II (Year of Constitution)
A. The First Finance Commission	I. 1951
B. The Second Finance Commission	II. 1968
C. The Fifth Finance Commission	III. 1960
D. The Third Finance Commission	IV. 1956

Choose the correct answer from the options given below:

1. A-IV, B-III, C-I, D-II
2. A-II, B-I, C-III, D-IV
3. A-I, B-IV, C-II, D-III
4. A-III, B-II, C-IV, D-I

85. Match the List-I with List-II:

List-I (Human Rights Documents)	List-II (Year)
A. Convention on the Rights of the Child	I. 1990
B. Declaration on Torture	II. 1951
C. Vienna Convention on Human Rights	III. 1993
D. Genocide Convention	IV. 1975

Choose the correct answer from the options given below:

1. A-II, B-III, C-IV, D-I
2. A-I, B-IV, C-III, D-II
3. A-IV, B-I, C-II, D-III
4. A-III, B-II, C-I, D-IV

86. Match the List-I with List-II:

List-I (State)	List-II (Legislative Assembly Strength)
A. Andhra Pradesh	I. 182
B. Gujarat	II. 294
C. Mizoram	III. 175
D. West Bengal	IV. 40

Choose the correct answer from the options given below:

1. A-III, B-I, C-IV, D-II
2. A-II, B-IV, C-III, D-I
3. A-IV, B-III, C-I, D-II
4. A-I, B-II, C-III, D-IV

87. Match the List-I with List-II:

List-I (States)	List-II (Number of Lok Sabha Seats)
A. Assam	I. 28
B. Karnataka	II. 14
C. Odisha	III. 7
D. Delhi	IV. 21

Choose the correct answer from the options given below:

1. A-IV, B-III, C-I, D-II
2. A-I, B-II, C-III, D-IV
3. A-II, B-I, C-IV, D-III
4. A-III, B-IV, C-II, D-I

88. Match the List-I with List-II:

List-I (Chief Minister)	List-II (States)
A. Ram Krishna Hegde	I. Uttarakhand
B. Bhagat Singh Koshyari	II. Karnataka
C. Karpoori Thakur	III. Uttar Pradesh
D. Sucheta Kriplani	IV. Bihar

Choose the correct answer from the options given below:

1. A-I, B-II, C-III, D-IV
2. A-IV, B-III, C-I, D-II
3. A-III, B-IV, C-II, D-I
4. A-II, B-I, C-IV, D-III

89. Match the List-I with List-II:

List-I (Author)	List-II (Concepts)
A. Woodrow Wilson	I. Principles of Scientific Management
B. Frederick Taylor	II. Importance of Study of Administration as Science
C. Luther Gulick	III. Hierarchy of Needs
D. Abraham Maslow	IV. Structure based Principles of Organisation

Choose the correct answer from the options given below:

1. A-I, B-II, C-III, D-IV
2. A-II, B-I, C-IV, D-III
3. A-III, B-IV, C-II, D-I
4. A-IV, B-III, C-I, D-II

90. Match the List-I with List-II:

List-I (Author)	List-II (Books)
A. Dwight Waldo	I. Management Challenges for the 21st Century
B. Peter Drucker	II. The Study of Public Administration
C. Rensin Likert	III. The Motivation to Work
D. Frederick Herzberg	IV. The Human Organisation

Choose the correct answer from the options given below:

1. A-II, B-I, C-IV, D-III
2. A-III, B-IV, C-I, D-II
3. A-I, B-II, C-III, D-IV
4. A-IV, B-III, C-II, D-I

Directions (Qs. No. 91-95): *Read the following passage and answer the questions.*

Vinayak Damodar Savarkar is known to be an ardent nationalist, revolutionary, and a noted freedom fighter of India. He is regarded as the inspirational force behind the resurgence of Hindu nationalism in India. Veer Savarkar was kept as a prisoner at Andamans by the Britishers.

Savarkar's concept of Hindutva was comprehensive. For him, Hindutva implied not only the religious tenets of the Hindus, but also comprehended the cultural, social, political and linguistic aspects of their life. In his seminal work 'Hindutva' (1923), Savarkar asserted 'a Hindu means a person who regards this land of Bharatvarsha- from the Indus to the seas- as his fatherland as well as his Holyland, that is the cradle land of his religion'.

In his Presidential address to the Hindu Mahasabha at Ahmadabad (1937), Savarkar observed that the Hindus possess a common holyland. The Vedic Rishis are their common pride, their grammarians Panini and Patanjali, their poets Bhavabhooti and Kalidas, their heroes Shri Ram and Sri Krishna, Shivaji and Pratap, Guru Govind and Banda Bahadur are a common source of inspiration. Their prophets Buddha and Mahaveer, Kanad and Shankar, are held in common esteem... All tests whatsoever of a common country, race, religion, language that go to entitle a people to form a nation, entitle the Hindus with greater emphasis to that claim.

Savarkar was a powerful writer and orator. Some of his most important work includes, 'An Echo from Andamans'; 'Hindu Pad-Padshahi'; 'The Indian War of Independence'.

91. As per the passage, Vinayak Damodar Savarkar was kept in prison by the Britishers at:

1. Pune
2. Sabarmati
3. Andamans
4. Calcutta

92. As per the passage, the meeting of Hindu Mahasabha at Ahmadabad was held in:

1. 1930
2. 1937
3. 1940
4. 1943

93. As per the passage, the two grammarians of ancient India were:

1. Patanjali and Guru Govind
2. Shivaji and Bhavabhooti
3. Panini and Patanjali
4. Kalidas and Kanad

94. As per the passage, who is the author of Hindu Pad-Padshahi?

1. Banda Bahadur
2. Shankar
3. Vinayak Damodar Savarkar
4. Panini

95. Which among the following book is not written by Vinayak Damodar Savarkar?

1. Hindutva
2. A Nation in Making
3. An Echo from Andamans
4. The Indian War of Independence

Directions (Qs. No. 96-100): *Read the following paragraph and answer the questions.*

New patterns of interaction between governments and society can be observed in areas such as social welfare, environmental protection, education and physical planning. Development assistance to the Third World countries hi the post-Cold War era has been subject to the new politics of good-governance. In 1989, the concept of 'governance' was for the first time highlighted in a World Bank document on Sub-Saharan Africa. Four key dimensions identified in this context were- public sector management; accountability; legal framework for development; and information and transparency. The OECD linked development assistance with participatory development, human rights and democratization.

The 'good governance' paradigm has brought to surface the role of civil society in local collective social problem solving. Alexis De Tocqueville linked civil society to democracy in the mid 1800s. Robert Putnam, the neo-Tocquevillian, emphasized on social capital and observed that the propensity of individuals to join private, voluntary associations contributes to the effectiveness of democracy. Larry Diamond in his work 'Developing Democracy', emphasized that a healthy liberal democracy requires a public that is organized for democracy, socialized to its norms and values and committed not just to its myriad narrow interests but to larger, common civic ends. Such a civic public is only possible with a vibrant civil society.

96. As per the passage, which institution highlighted the concept of good governance first time?

1. IMF　　2. EU
3. World Bank　　4. ADB

97. As per the passage, which region was the focus of concept of governance in 1989?

1. South Asia
2. Europe
3. Sub-Saharan Africa
4. West Asia

98. As per the passage, which organization/ institution linked development assistance with human rights and democratization?

1. OECD　　2. SAARC
3. APEC　　4. QUAD

99. As per the passage, who linked civil society to democracy in the mid-1800s?

1. Thomas Hobbes
2. Alexis De Tocqueville
3. Larry Diamond
4. Robert Putnam

100. As per the passage, the work 'Developing Democracy' is associated with

1. John Locke　　2. J.S. Mill
3. Larry Diamond　　4. J. Bentham

ANSWERS

1	2	3	4	5	6	7	8	9	10
2	4	3	2	1	4	3	2	1	4
11	**12**	**13**	**14**	**15**	**16**	**17**	**18**	**19**	**20**
3	2	1	2	1	2,3	3	4	4	3
21	**22**	**23**	**24**	**25**	**26**	**27**	**28**	**29**	**30**
4	4	2	1	2	4	1	2	2	1
31	**32**	**33**	**34**	**35**	**36**	**37**	**38**	**39**	**40**
4	3	2	1	3	4	1	2	3	1

15

41	42	43	44	45	46	47	48	49	50
3	2	2	2	3	1	1	1	4	2
51	**52**	**53**	**54**	**55**	**56**	**57**	**58**	**59**	**60**
3	3	1	4	4	2	3	2	1	1
61	**62**	**63**	**64**	**65**	**66**	**67**	**68**	**69**	**70**
2	4	3	3	1	2	3	4	1	3
71	**72**	**73**	**74**	**75**	**76**	**77**	**78**	**79**	**80**
4	4	4	1	3	1	2	1	3	3
81	**82**	**83**	**84**	**85**	**86**	**87**	**88**	**89**	**90**
1	4	1	3	2	1	3	4	2	1
91	**92**	**93**	**94**	**95**	**96**	**97**	**98**	**99**	**100**
3	2	3	3	2	3	3	1	2	3

Explanatory Answers

1. The Convention on the Elimination of All Forms of Discrimination Against Women (CEDAW) was formally adopted by the United Nations General Assembly on 18 December 1979. It came into force on 3 September 1981, marking a major milestone in the advancement of women's rights worldwide. This convention serves as a comprehensive international bill of rights for women and aims to ensure gender equality by prohibiting discrimination in education, employment, health care, marriage, and political participation. It also mandates member states to submit periodic reports to the CEDAW Committee regarding measures taken to comply with the treaty's provisions.

2. The book "Termites in the Trading System: How Preferential Agreements Undermine Free Trade" was written by Jagdish Bhagwati, a renowned Indian-American economist and one of the leading advocates of multilateral free trade. In this book, Bhagwati compares the spread of preferential trade agreements (PTAs) and bilateral deals to "termites" slowly eating away the foundation of the multilateral trading system established under the World Trade Organization (WTO). He argues that such agreements create a confusing web of discriminatory rules and "spaghetti bowl" trade patterns that distort global commerce. Bhagwati emphasizes that genuine global welfare can only be achieved through a transparent, rule-based, and universal multilateral trade framework rather than a patchwork of exclusive regional blocs.

3. The Millennium Development Goals (MDGs) were adopted by the United Nations General Assembly in September 2000 during the Millennium Summit held in New York. A total of 189 UN member states endorsed the Millennium Declaration, leading to the formation of eight measurable goals to be achieved by 2015. These included reducing poverty and hunger, achieving universal primary education, promoting gender equality, reducing child and maternal mortality, combating major diseases, ensuring environmental sustainability, and fostering a global partnership for development. The MDGs became a global framework for coordinated international development efforts over the first 15 years of the 21st century.

4. U Thant, a Burmese diplomat, was appointed as the Acting Secretary-General of the United Nations in November 1961 following the sudden death of Dag Hammarskjöld. Later, he was formally elected as the third Secretary-General and served two full terms until 1971. U Thant played a vital role in mediating several global crises, notably the Cuban Missile Crisis (1962), and promoting peacekeeping and decolonization efforts during the Cold War. His tenure is remembered for strengthening the UN's peacekeeping functions and advocating for neutrality in global conflicts.

5. Greece officially joined the European Community (EC), now known as the European Union (EU), on 1 January 1981. This made Greece the 10th member state of the EC. The accession followed Greece's return to democracy in 1974 after years of military rule, and it symbolized the country's integration into the political and economic structures of Western Europe. Membership helped Greece modernize its economy, expand infrastructure, and stabilize its democratic institutions while gaining access to European markets and development funds.

6. The Russian revolutionary and Marxist theorist Leon Trotsky was assassinated in Mexico in August 1940. A key figure in the Bolshevik Revolution of 1917, Trotsky was the founder of the Red Army and a major rival of Joseph Stalin after Lenin's death. Exiled from the Soviet Union in 1929, Trotsky continued to oppose Stalin's authoritarian policies and formed the Fourth International to promote worldwide socialist revolution. He was murdered in Mexico City by Ramón Mercader, a Spanish communist agent working under Stalin's orders, using an ice axe — an event that symbolized Stalin's ruthless suppression of political dissent even beyond Soviet borders.

7. The referendum on the United Kingdom's membership in the European Union, popularly known as the Brexit referendum, was held on 23 June 2016. In this nationwide vote, citizens of Great Britain decided whether the UK should remain a member of or leave the EU. The result showed that 51.9% voted to leave, while 48.1% voted to remain, leading to one of the most significant political shifts in modern European history. The outcome triggered the formal withdrawal process under Article 50 of the Treaty on European Union, which ultimately resulted in the UK officially leaving the EU on 31 January 2020.

8. The person who developed a humanist critique of Western Enlightenment revealing its deep connections to colonialism and its "narratives of oppression" was Edward Said, a Palestinian-American scholar. His groundbreaking 1978 work "Orientalism" exposed how Western literature, art, and scholarship constructed the East (the "Orient") as exotic, backward, and inferior. Said argued that this portrayal served as a tool of imperial domination, shaping colonial policies and intellectual hierarchies. Through his critique, he laid the foundation for postcolonial theory, inspiring scholars to question Eurocentric worldviews and to highlight the voices and experiences of colonized peoples.

9. The book "The General Theory of Employment, Interest and Money" was written by John Maynard Keynes and published in 1936. This monumental work transformed modern economics by challenging classical theories that markets naturally achieve full employment. Keynes argued that aggregate demand—the total spending in an economy—determines overall economic activity and employment levels. During recessions, when private investment falls, he advocated for active government intervention through fiscal and monetary policies to boost demand and reduce unemployment. The "Keynesian Revolution" that followed laid the intellectual foundation for much of 20th-century economic policy worldwide.

10. The principal figure of the 'Second Generation' of the Frankfurt School of Critical Theory is Jürgen Habermas, a German philosopher and sociologist. Building on the ideas of first-generation theorists like Max Horkheimer, Theodor Adorno, and Herbert Marcuse, Habermas shifted focus from pessimism about mass culture to the possibilities of rational communication in modern society. His key contributions include the theory of communicative action, where he emphasized that social integration and understanding are achieved through free, rational dialogue rather than coercion or domination. He also developed the concept of the public sphere, advocating for democratic discourse as a means of achieving legitimacy and consensus in modern states.

11. The philosopher Robert Nozick, in his influential book "Anarchy, State, and Utopia" (1974), argued that property rights are inviolable, provided that wealth is justly acquired or justly transferred. According to Nozick's Entitlement Theory of Justice, any distribution of goods or wealth is just if it arises from voluntary exchanges or legitimate acquisition, without coercion or theft. He rejected redistributive taxation as a violation of individual rights, asserting that the state's role should be minimal—limited to protecting life, liberty, and property. His ideas form the cornerstone of libertarian political philosophy, standing in contrast to the egalitarian theories of John Rawls.

12. The term "Ecology" (Ökologie in German) was first introduced by Ernst Haeckel, a German biologist, in 1866. He derived the word from the Greek "oikos" (house) and "logos" (study), defining it as the scientific study of the relationships between organisms and their environment. Haeckel's concept laid the foundation for modern ecological science, emphasizing the interconnectedness of life and the environment. His broader biological works also contributed to evolutionary theory and popularized Darwin's ideas in continental Europe, linking biology with environmental awareness long before ecology became a major scientific discipline.

13. The book "On Revolution" was written by Hannah Arendt, a German-born political theorist, and first published in 1963. In this work, Arendt compares the American Revolution and the French Revolution, exploring why the former succeeded in founding lasting institutions of freedom while the latter descended into violence and terror. She argues that the true purpose of revolution is not social or economic change but the creation of political freedom and the establishment of a stable public realm where citizens can participate in self-governance. Arendt's analysis remains one of the most profound philosophical reflections on the meaning of modern revolutions.

14. The book "A Vindication of the Rights of Woman" was written by Mary Wollstonecraft in 1792 and is regarded as one of the earliest works of feminist philosophy. Wollstonecraft demanded equal education and rational treatment for women, arguing that women are not naturally inferior to men but appear so only because they lack access to proper education and opportunities. She emphasized that reason, virtue, and citizenship are not gendered attributes, and women should have the same moral and intellectual freedom as men. Her ideas laid the foundation for later feminist movements advocating for gender equality and women's rights.

15. The book "Development Administration: Concepts, Goals, Methods" was authored by George F. Gant in 1979. This work is considered a seminal contribution to the field of Public Administration, particularly in understanding the challenges of administrative systems in developing countries. Gant examined how administrative structures could be made more effective for achieving socio-economic development goals. He discussed the relationship between administration and development, focusing on issues such as capacity building, efficiency, planning, and innovation. His work helped shape the discipline of development administration, which seeks to apply administrative theory to the process of national development and modernization.

16. The Bali terror bombings occurred twice in Indonesia. The first bombing happened on 12 October 2002 in the Kuta tourist district, killing 202 people and injuring over 200. It involved coordinated explosions targeting nightclubs, carried out by Jemaah Islamiyah (JI), a Southeast Asian Islamist group linked to al-Qaeda. The second bombing took place on 1 October 2005, in Kuta and Jimbaran Beach, where suicide bombers detonated explosives in restaurants, killing 20 people and injuring more than 100. Both attacks severely affected Indonesia's tourism industry and highlighted the global reach of terrorism in the early 21st century.

17. The statement "War is merely a continuation of politics by other means" was made by Carl von Clausewitz, a Prussian general and military theorist, in his famous work "On War" (Vom Kriege) published posthumously in 1832. Clausewitz argued that war is not an isolated act but a political instrument used by states to achieve objectives when diplomacy fails. His theory established the foundation for modern military strategy by linking warfare directly to political purpose, emphasizing that every war must be understood within the context of the political aims it seeks to accomplish.

18. Prime Minister Narendra Modi met U.S. President Donald Trump in Washington, D.C., on February 13, 2025, for an official working visit that included bilateral talks and a joint press conference at the White House. Multiple contemporaneous reports and official readouts confirm the date and venue, including the White House briefing, Reuters coverage, PBS's live broadcast, and analyses by CSIS and CFR.

19. The China–Vietnam War occurred in February–March 1979. It began when China invaded northern Vietnam in retaliation for Vietnam's invasion of Cambodia, which had overthrown the China-backed Khmer Rouge regime. The brief but intense conflict lasted about three weeks, with heavy casualties on both sides. Although China declared victory and withdrew its forces, Vietnam maintained control over Cambodia, and relations between the two nations remained strained for years. The war marked one of the most significant regional conflicts in post-Vietnam War Southeast Asia.

20. The book "Sexual Politics" was written by Kate Millett and published in 1970. It became one of the foundational texts of second-wave feminism. Millett analyzed how literature, culture, and institutions perpetuate patriarchal power structures that oppress women. Using examples from male authors such as D. H. Lawrence, Norman Mailer, and Henry Miller, she argued that sexual relations are inherently political because they reflect power imbalances between men and women. Her book exposed the cultural mechanisms by which patriarchy maintains dominance and became a landmark in feminist literary criticism and gender studies.

21. The 'Samaj Samata Sangh' was founded by Dr. B.R. Ambedkar in 1924 to promote social equality and justice among oppressed communities in India. The organization aimed to eliminate caste-based discrimination and uplift marginalized sections through education, organization, and reform. It also served as a platform to mobilize people against untouchability and social exclusion. This initiative was one of the earliest organized movements led by Ambedkar that eventually paved the way for the Dalit movement and his later political and social reforms.

22. The book "Six Glorious Epochs of Indian History" was authored by Vinayak Damodar Savarkar (V. D. Savarkar). In this historical work, Savarkar presents a nationalist interpretation of India's past, identifying six defining eras that demonstrated the country's heroic resistance and resurgence against foreign invasions and oppression. Written from a perspective of cultural nationalism, the book seeks to inspire pride in India's civilizational endurance and valor. Savarkar's narrative blends historical analysis with ideological reflection, emphasizing the unity, courage, and resilience of the Indian people through centuries of struggle.

23. The name Simone de Beauvoir is closely associated with feminism, particularly through her groundbreaking book "The Second Sex" published in 1949. In this seminal work, she analyzed the social construction of women's roles and famously declared, "One is not born, but rather becomes, a woman." De Beauvoir explored how patriarchal societies define women as the "Other" in relation to men, thereby restricting their freedom and individuality. Her existentialist approach, influenced by Jean-Paul Sartre, laid the philosophical foundation for modern feminist thought, inspiring the second wave of feminism in the 20th century.

24. The term "Deep Ecology" was coined by the Norwegian philosopher Arne Naess in 1973. This concept represents an ecocentric philosophy that views all living beings—human and non-human—as having intrinsic value, independent of their utility to humans. Naess argued that environmental protection should not be motivated solely by human interests but by respect for the interconnectedness and equality of all forms of life. Deep Ecology thus calls for a profound shift in human consciousness and lifestyle to maintain ecological balance and harmony with nature, forming the moral and philosophical basis for many environmental movements worldwide.

25. Pandita Ramabai, an eminent 19th-century social reformer, scholar, and advocate for women's education, was associated with the Mukti Mission founded in 1898 at Kedgaon, near Pune. The mission was established to provide shelter, education, and vocational training to widows, destitute women, and orphaned girls, particularly those affected by famine and social discrimination. A convert to Christianity, Ramabai combined faith with social service, emphasizing compassion, literacy, and self-reliance among marginalized women. Her pioneering work in women's emancipation and education marked a significant step toward gender equality in colonial India.

26. The term "The Washington Consensus" was coined by John Williamson, a British economist, in 1989. It referred to a set of ten economic policy prescriptions promoted by institutions based in Washington, D.C., such as the International Monetary Fund (IMF), World Bank, and U.S. Treasury Department. These policies emphasized fiscal discipline, privatization, trade liberalization, deregulation, and market-oriented reforms as pathways for developing countries to achieve economic stability and growth. The Washington Consensus became a defining framework for global economic policy in the 1990s, though it was later criticized for promoting neoliberal agendas that overlooked social equity and local contexts.

27. The statement "There is nothing absolute in management affairs. Seldom do we have to apply the same principle twice as in identical conditions; allowance must be made for different changing circumstances" was made by Henri Fayol, a French industrialist and management theorist. Fayol is known as one of the founders of modern management theory, and he emphasized that managerial principles are flexible guidelines, not rigid rules. In his classic work "General and Industrial Management" (1916), he outlined 14 principles of management—such as unity of command, division of work, and scalar chain—stressing that effective management requires adaptation to context and the exercise of sound judgment.

28. The book "Roman Agrarian History and Its Significance for Public and Private Law" was written by Max Weber in 1891. This early scholarly work reflects Weber's deep interest in historical sociology and the interrelationship between economic systems and legal institutions. He examined how the agrarian structures of ancient Rome influenced its legal development and social organization. The book laid the groundwork for Weber's later theories on the sociology of law, authority, and economic behavior, eventually leading to his broader contributions in works like "The Protestant Ethic and the Spirit of Capitalism."

29. Ganesh Vasudev Mavalankar, popularly known as G. V. Mavalankar, was the first Speaker of the Lok Sabha of independent India. He served from 15 May 1952 until his death in 1956. Before that, he was also the Speaker of the Central Legislative Assembly (1946–1952). Known for his integrity, impartiality, and adherence to parliamentary norms, Mavalankar played a key role in establishing the traditions and procedures of the Indian Parliament in its formative years. His leadership helped shape the democratic legislative framework that continues to guide parliamentary functioning today.

30. The Planning Commission set up the G. V. K. Rao Committee in 1985 to review administrative arrangements for rural development and poverty-alleviation programmes. It found that a "programme-based" approach, run through parallel agencies, had weakened the regular administrative machinery and local institutions. Key recommendations included: restoring the District as the pivotal unit for planning and coordination; making the Zila Parishad the principal agency for rural development; strengthening Panchayati Raj Institutions with clear functions, finances, and functionaries; and integrating sectoral schemes under a unified district plan. These ideas strongly influenced later decentralization reforms and helped shape thinking that culminated in the 73rd Constitutional Amendment (1992).

31. Article 327 of the Indian Constitution empowers Parliament to make laws regarding elections to Parliament and State Legislatures, as well as matters relating to the delimitation of constituencies and other election procedures. This article provides the constitutional foundation for comprehensive election laws such as the Representation of the People Acts of 1950 and 1951. It works alongside Article 324, which vests the Election Commission of India with the power to supervise, direct, and control the conduct of elections, ensuring free and fair democratic processes across the nation.

32. The Prevention of Terrorism Act (POTA) was enacted in 2002 by the BJP-led National Democratic Alliance (NDA) government under Prime Minister Atal Bihari Vajpayee. It replaced the earlier Terrorist and Disruptive Activities (Prevention) Act (TADA), which had lapsed in 1995. POTA aimed to strengthen India's legal framework against terrorism following the 2001 Indian Parliament attack. The law provided enhanced powers for police investigations, preventive detention, and the interception of communications. However, it faced criticism for alleged misuse and human rights violations, leading to its repeal in 2004 by the succeeding UPA government.

33. Prime Minister Atal Bihari Vajpayee visited Lahore, Pakistan, from 19–21 February 1999, during which he and his Pakistani counterpart Nawaz Sharif signed the Lahore Declaration. This historic agreement aimed to promote peace and stability between the two nuclear-armed neighbours after the 1998 nuclear tests. The declaration emphasized mutual respect for sovereignty, the peaceful resolution of bilateral disputes (including Kashmir), and the strengthening of trade and cultural ties. Vajpayee's bus journey to Lahore symbolized a new hope for Indo-Pak friendship, though the optimism was later dampened by the Kargil conflict in the same year.

34. The National Commission for Women (NCW) was established in January 1992 under the National Commission for Women Act, 1990.

It serves as a statutory body to safeguard and promote the rights of women in India. The NCW's functions include reviewing constitutional and legal safeguards, recommending policy changes, investigating gender-based grievances, and creating awareness about women's rights. It acts as an advisory and monitoring body to ensure women's equality in social, political, and economic spheres. The first Chairperson of the NCW was Mrs. Jayanti Patnaik.

35. Asif Ali Zardari, a senior leader of the Pakistan Peoples Party (PPP) and husband of the late Prime Minister Benazir Bhutto, is the current President of Pakistan. He was elected for his second term on 9 March 2024 and formally assumed office on 10 March 2024. Zardari had earlier served as the 11th President of Pakistan from 2008 to 2013, becoming the first democratically elected president in the country's history to complete a full term. His political career has been marked by his role in promoting civilian democracy after years of military rule and by navigating complex power-sharing arrangements with other political parties. As President, he represents the federal unity of Pakistan and works within a parliamentary system where executive power rests primarily with the Prime Minister.

36. Giorgia Meloni has been the Prime Minister of Italy since 22 October 2022, leading a right-wing coalition government headed by her party, Fratelli d'Italia (Brothers of Italy). She is the first woman in Italian history to become Prime Minister. Meloni's leadership marked a significant political shift, as her party emerged from Italy's nationalist and conservative traditions. Her government focuses on issues such as immigration control, economic stability, family welfare, and national sovereignty within the European Union. Internationally, Meloni has maintained Italy's commitment to the EU and NATO while emphasizing Italy's independent voice in European affairs. Her rise to power reflects the changing dynamics of European politics, where populist and conservative movements have gained influence.

37. The South Asian Association for Regional Cooperation (SAARC) was formally established on 8 December 1985 with the signing of its Charter in Dhaka, Bangladesh. The founding members were India, Pakistan, Bangladesh, Sri Lanka, Nepal, Bhutan, and the Maldives, while Afghanistan joined later in 2007 as the eighth member. SAARC was created to promote regional cooperation, economic integration, cultural exchange, and collective self-reliance among South Asian countries. The SAARC Secretariat, located in Kathmandu, Nepal, began functioning in 1987. Over the years, SAARC has launched numerous initiatives in areas such as poverty alleviation, trade, agriculture, science, and technology. Despite its limited political integration due to regional tensions, it remains South Asia's foremost multilateral platform for dialogue and cooperation.

38. Article 370 of the Indian Constitution, which granted special autonomous status to the erstwhile State of Jammu and Kashmir, was abrogated on 5 August 2019 by the Government of India under Prime Minister Narendra Modi. This constitutional change was implemented through a Presidential Order (C.O. 272) and the passage of the Jammu and Kashmir Reorganisation Act, 2019, which bifurcated the state into two Union Territories — Jammu & Kashmir and Ladakh — effective from 31 October 2019. The abrogation removed the state's separate constitution and special privileges under Article 35A, bringing it fully under the jurisdiction of the Indian Constitution. This move marked a historic transformation in India's federal structure and national integration policy.

39. The G-20 Summit was held in New Delhi, India, on 9–10 September 2023 under India's presidency with the theme "Vasudhaiva Kutumbakam" — meaning "One Earth, One Family, One Future." The summit brought together the world's major economies, including the United States, China, Russia, Japan, and the European Union, to discuss global economic challenges, climate action, sustainable development, and digital transformation. A major outcome was the New Delhi Leaders' Declaration, adopted unanimously, highlighting global unity on key development issues. The summit also saw the inclusion of the African Union as a permanent member of the G-20, marking a significant milestone in global representation and cooperation.

40. The Naf River serves as the natural boundary between Bangladesh and Myanmar (Burma). Flowing between southern Bangladesh's Cox's Bazar District and Myanmar's Rakhine State, the river empties into the Bay of Bengal. It is strategically and humanitarianly significant, particularly because it forms part of the route taken by Rohingya refugees fleeing persecution in Myanmar to seek refuge in Bangladesh. The Naf River's width varies from about 1.6 km to 3 km, and it plays an important role in border security, trade, and regional geopolitics between the two neighboring countries.

41. To arrange these regional economic blocs by their year of formation:

E. **ASEAN :** Formed in 1967 (Bangkok Declaration, August 8, 1967).

B. **APEC :** Established in 1989 to promote trade and economic cooperation across the Asia-Pacific region.

A. **MERCOSUR :** Founded in 1991 under the Treaty of Asunción to integrate South American economies (Argentina, Brazil, Paraguay, Uruguay).

D. **NAFTA :** Signed in 1992 and implemented on 1 January 1994, linking the economies of the U.S., Canada, and Mexico.

C. **FTAA :** Proposed in 1994 at the Summit of the Americas (Miami) but never materialized.

Hence, the correct chronological sequence is: E, B, A, D, C.

42. Chronological order of constitutional changes and amendments:

C. **Formation of State of Meghalaya (1971):** Done through the North-Eastern Areas (Reorganisation) Act, 1971 (came into effect in 1972).

D. **Abolition of Privy purses and privileges (1971):** Through the 26th Amendment Act, 1971, ending special rights of former princely rulers.

B. **Fundamental Duties inserted (1976):** Added under 42nd Amendment Act, 1976, as Article 51A.

A. **Right to Property removed from Fundamental Rights (1978):** Via 44th Amendment Act, 1978, making it a constitutional/legal right under Article 300A.

E. **Arunachal Pradesh granted statehood (1987):** Through the 55th Amendment Act, 1986, effective 20 February 1987.

Thus, the order is: C, D, B, A, E.

43. Chronological order of their addition or inclusion in the Indian Constitution:

D. **Ninth Schedule (1951):** Inserted by the First Amendment Act, 1951 to protect land reform laws from judicial review.

E. **'Forests' inserted in the Concurrent List (1976):** Added through the 42nd Amendment Act, 1976, transferring it from the State List.

C. **Tenth Schedule (1985):** Added by the 52nd Amendment Act, 1985, providing provisions for disqualification due to defection (Anti-Defection Law).

B. **Twelfth Schedule (1992):** Added through the 74th Amendment Act, 1992, listing subjects under the powers of municipalities.

A. **Santhali in Eighth Schedule (2003):** Included by the 92nd Amendment Act, 2003, along with Bodo, Dogri, and Maithili.

Therefore, the correct chronological sequence is: D, E, C, B, A.

44. To arrange the given High Courts by their year of establishment in chronological order:

A. **Karnataka High Court (1884):** Originally known as the Mysore High Court, it came into existence during the princely state period and was reorganized as the High Court of Karnataka after 1973.

B. **Guwahati High Court (1948):** Established on 5 April 1948, it was originally known as the High Court of Assam and Nagaland, later renamed as the Guwahati High Court, having jurisdiction over several northeastern states.

C. **Kerala High Court (1956):** Constituted on 1 November 1956, following the reorganization of states, by merging Travancore-Cochin and Malabar regions.

D. **Punjab and Haryana High Court (1966):** Formed on 1 November 1966 after the reorganization of the erstwhile Punjab State, following the creation of Haryana and the transfer of certain territories to Himachal Pradesh.

E. **Sikkim High Court (1975):** Established on 26 May 1975, after Sikkim's merger with India as the 22nd state.

Hence, the chronological sequence is: A, B, C, D, E.

45. To verify and arrange the given constitutional provisions according to their Article numbers in the Constitution of India:

A. **Council of Ministers to aid and advise the President – Article 74:** This article provides that there shall be a Council of Ministers headed by the Prime Minister to aid and advise the President, who shall act in accordance with such advice, except in certain constitutional situations.

C. **Special address by the President in Parliament – Article 87:** It deals with the President's special address to both Houses of Parliament at the commencement of the first session each year and the first session after every general election to the Lok Sabha, outlining the government's policies and legislative agenda.

B. **Appointment of Acting Chief Justice – Article 126:** Under this article, when the office of the Chief Justice of India is vacant or he is temporarily unable to perform duties, the President may appoint the senior-most judge of the Supreme Court as the Acting Chief Justice.

D. **Power of President to consult Supreme Court – Article 143:** This provision empowers the President to seek the advisory opinion of the Supreme Court on any question of law or fact of public importance.

E. **Appointment of District Judges – Article 233:** It vests the Governor of a State, in consultation with the High Court, with the power to appoint district judges to the State's judiciary.

Hence, the correct chronological sequence is: A, C, B, D, E.

46. Chronological order of these major revolutions:

C. **American Revolution (1775–1783):** The 13 American colonies fought for and gained independence from British rule, leading to the creation of the United States of America.

B. **Russian Revolution (1917):** Overthrew Tsar Nicholas II and established Bolshevik rule under Vladimir Lenin, leading to the creation of the Soviet Union.

A. **Cuban Revolution (1953–1959):** Led by Fidel Castro, it overthrew the dictatorship of Fulgencio Batista and established a socialist state allied with the Soviet Union.

D. **Nicaraguan Revolution (1961–1990):** Centered on the Sandinista movement, it resulted in the overthrow of the Somoza regime in 1979 and introduced socialist-oriented governance.

E. **Tulip Revolution (2005):** A peaceful uprising in Kyrgyzstan, leading to the ousting of President Askar Akayev, part of a wave of "color revolutions" in post-Soviet states.

Thus, arranged by occurrence: C, B, A, D, E.

47. Chronological order based on the year of launch of major national initiatives:

B. **Swachh Bharat Mission (2014):** Launched on 2 October 2014 by Prime Minister Narendra Modi, aimed at achieving universal sanitation coverage, eliminating open defecation, and promoting cleanliness through public participation under the slogan "Clean India."

E. **Namami Gange (2014):** Announced soon after, in June 2014, as an integrated conservation and rejuvenation programme for the River Ganga. It is implemented by the National Mission for Clean Ganga (NMCG) under the Ministry of Jal Shakti.

A. **SVAMITVA Scheme (2020):** Launched on 24 April 2020, the scheme seeks to map rural inhabited lands using drone technology and issue ownership records (property cards) to village residents to promote clarity in land rights and rural planning.

C. **SVANidhi se Samriddhi (2021):** Initiated in March 2021 as a micro-credit and welfare linkage extension of the PM SVANidhi Scheme for street vendors, focusing on financial inclusion and access to social welfare schemes.

D. **Inauguration of Kartavya Path (2022):** On 8 September 2022, Prime Minister Narendra Modi inaugurated the redeveloped Central Vista Avenue (previously Rajpath) as Kartavya Path, symbolizing the shift from colonial legacy to national duty.

Thus, the correct order is: B, E, A, C , D.

48. According to the official Table of Precedence (issued by the Ministry of Home Affairs, Government of India), the dignitaries listed are ranked as follows:

A. **Former Presidents:** Placed at Rank 7, immediately below the Chief Justice of India and Speaker of the Lok Sabha. They are accorded very high ceremonial precedence due to having held the highest constitutional office.

B. **Speaker of Lok Sabha:** Placed at Rank 6, on par with the Chief Justice of India. The Speaker presides over the lower house of Parliament and holds one of the highest constitutional ranks.

C. **Former Prime Ministers:** Placed at Rank 8, immediately below Former Presidents, reflecting their past executive leadership.

D. **Judges of Supreme Court:** Placed at Rank 9, following the Former Prime Ministers, representing the senior-most judicial office after the Chief Justice.

E. **Solicitor General of India:** Placed much lower at Rank 23, as the third-ranking law officer of the Union Government after the Attorney General and Additional Solicitor General.

Hence, the correct sequence is A, B, C, D, E.

49. Chronological order of enactment or adoption of the given Acts and Codes:

E. **Emblems and Names (Prevention of Improper Use) Act – 1950:** Passed soon after Independence to prohibit misuse of national symbols, names, and emblems for commercial or professional gain without prior approval from the government.

A. **The Citizenship Act – 1955:** Enacted to define the acquisition, termination, and determination of Indian citizenship by birth, descent, registration, or naturalization.

C. **Prevention of Insults to National Honour Act – 1971:** Passed to protect national symbols such as the Flag, Anthem, and Constitution from insult or disrespect, prescribing punishments for violations.

B. **Flag Code of India – 2002:** Introduced to standardize the rules for display, hoisting, and use of the National Flag, consolidating various executive instructions into a single code.

D. **State Emblem of India (Prohibition of Improper Use) Act – 2005:** Enacted to prevent unauthorized or commercial use of the Lion Capital of Ashoka, the State Emblem of India, ensuring respect and proper usage.

Thus, the correct order is: E, A, C, B, D.

50. Chronological order according to year of enactment or inauguration:

C. **Minimum Wages Act – 1948:** Passed soon after independence, it aims to fix minimum wage rates for workers in scheduled employments to prevent exploitation and ensure fair pay.

D. **Mission Indradhanush – 2014:** Launched by the Ministry of Health and Family Welfare on 25 December 2014, to increase immunization coverage of children and pregnant women against vaccine-preventable diseases such as polio, TB, and hepatitis B.

A. **National Skill Development Mission – 2015:** Launched on 15 July 2015 to unify skill development efforts across sectors and promote employability through coordinated programs under the Ministry of Skill Development and Entrepreneurship.

B. **Pradhan Mantri Shram Yogi Maan-dhan Yojana – 2019:** Announced in February 2019, it provides pension benefits for unorganized-sector workers after the age of 60, ensuring old-age income security.

E. **Ayushman Bharat Digital Mission – 2021:** Inaugurated on 27 September 2021, it aims to create a digital health ecosystem by issuing unique health IDs and linking hospitals, doctors, and patients through interoperable digital platforms.

Hence, the correct chronological order is: C, D, A, B, E.

51. Chronological order according to their year of creation or launch:

E. **National Co-operative Development Corporation (NCDC) – 1963:** Established under the NCDC Act, 1962, it promotes and finances cooperative development programs for agriculture, dairy, and rural industries.

D. **Food and Nutrition Board – 1964:** Set up under the Ministry of Women and Child Development, it works to improve nutritional standards through nutrition education, training, and policy guidance.

C. **Pradhan Mantri Jan Aushadhi Yojana – 2008:** Launched to provide quality generic medicines at affordable prices through dedicated Jan Aushadhi Kendras across India.

A. **Rashtriya Gokul Mission – 2014 (launched Dec 2014, implemented 2015):** Introduced to conserve and develop indigenous cattle breeds, promoting milk productivity and genetic improvement programs.

B. **Rights of Persons with Disabilities Act – 2016:** Enacted on 27 December 2016, replacing the 1995 Act, it expanded recognized disabilities from 7 to 21 and strengthened rights and accessibility provisions.

Hence, the best-aligned sequence is E, D, C, A, B.

52. Chronological order by year of assuming office as Vice President of India:

E. Varahagiri Venkata Giri – Served as Vice President from 1967 to 1969, later became President of India (1969–1974).

A. R. Venkataraman – Held the Vice Presidency from 1984 to 1987, then became President (1987–1992).

C. K. R. Narayanan – Served as Vice President from 1992 to 1997, later the President (1997–2002).

D. Krishan Kant – Vice President from 1997 to 2002, passed away shortly before completing his term.

B. Bhairon Singh Shekhawat – Vice President from 2002 to 2007, known for his administrative experience and long tenure in Rajasthan politics.

Hence, the chronological order of their assumption of office is: E, A, C, D, B.

53. Chronological order:

- **Article 17 — Abolition of Untouchability (A):** Outlaws the practice of untouchability and makes its enforcement punishable, anchoring India's constitutional commitment to social equality.
- **Article 24 — Prohibition of employment of children in factories (B):** Forbids employing children below 14 years in factories, mines, or hazardous work, protecting child welfare.
- **Article 39A — Equal justice and free legal aid (E):** A Directive Principle (added by the 42nd Amendment, 1976) directing the State to ensure that justice is not denied due to economic or other disabilities.
- **Article 43B — Promotion of co-operative societies (C):** A Directive Principle (added by the 97th Amendment, 2011) to encourage voluntary, democratic, and professional co-operatives.
- **Article 50 — Separation of judiciary from executive (D):** A Directive Principle mandating institutional independence of the judiciary in public services.

Hence, the chronological order is: A, B, E, C, D.

54. Chronological order:

C. **Pinochet coup in Chile (1973):** Military overthrow of President Salvador Allende on 11 Sept 1973, ushering in Augusto Pinochet's dictatorship.

B. **Tiananmen Square crackdown (1989):** On 4 June 1989, the Chinese military suppressed pro-democracy protests in Beijing.

A. **Maastricht Treaty ratified / EU comes into force (1993):** The Treaty on European Union took effect on 1 Nov 1993, creating the EU and paving the way for the euro.

E. **Russian annexation of Crimea (2014):** In March 2014, Russia annexed Crimea from Ukraine after a disputed referendum.

D. **Trump–Kim summit, Singapore (2018):** First-ever meeting between a sitting U.S. president and a North Korean leader on 12 June 2018.

Hence, the chronological order is: C, B, A, E, D.

55. Chronological order:

D. **Democratic Party (USA), 1828:** Founded around Andrew Jackson; among the world's oldest active parties.

B. **Liberal Party of Canada, 1867:** Emerged at Confederation; Canada's long-standing centrist/liberal formation.

C. **Awami League (Bangladesh), 1949:** Led the Bengali nationalist movement; central to Bangladesh's independence under Sheikh Mujibur Rahman.

E. **Biju Janata Dal (India), 1997:** Odisha-based regional party founded by Naveen Patnaik, named after Biju Patnaik.

A. **Servant of the People (Ukraine), 2018:** Reformist party associated with Volodymyr Zelenskyy; rose rapidly to national power.

Hence, the chronological order is: D, B, C, E, A.

56. The Parliamentary Committee on Home Affairs examines the working of specific ministries that deal with internal administration and legal matters. Its jurisdiction covers:

A. Ministry of Home Affairs: Responsible for internal security, border management, police, disaster management, and Union Territories. This ministry forms the core subject of the committee's oversight.

B. Ministry of Law and Justice: Oversees legislative drafting, justice delivery, and legal reforms, closely linked to national security and governance mechanisms.

Other ministries like Space, Defence, and Atomic Energy fall under different committees (Science & Technology; Defence; and Energy respectively). Hence, the committee supervises A and B only.

57. Under the Rules of Procedure of the Lok Sabha, a Parliamentary Committee is defined by certain characteristics:

B. It works under the direction of the Speaker/Chairman: The presiding officers of each House exercise administrative and supervisory control over their respective committees.

C. It is appointed or elected by the House or nominated by the Speaker/Chairman: This ensures representation and proportional participation of political parties.

E. It has a Secretariat provided by the Lok Sabha/Rajya Sabha Secretariat: Dedicated staff and research support are provided to assist in committee functioning.

Statement A is incorrect because every group of MPs is not automatically a Parliamentary Committee—only those officially constituted for a defined purpose under House rules qualify. Statement D is also incorrect because reports are submitted to the respective House, not the President.

58. Among India's Presidents, two have died while in office:

B. Dr. Zakir Husain (1969): The third President of India and the first Muslim to hold the post, he passed away on 3 May 1969 while still serving. His death led to Vice President V. V. Giri acting as President.

D. Fakhruddin Ali Ahmed (1977): The fifth President of India, he died on 11 February 1977 during his term, leading to B. D. Jatti, the then Vice President, serving as Acting President.

The others listed—Neelam Sanjiva Reddy, V. V. Giri, and B. D. Jatti—completed their terms or served temporarily but did not die in office.

59. Checking options:

A. **India and Her Problems:** This is a compiled volume of Swami Vivekananda's speeches and writings on India's social regeneration (compiled by Swami Nirvedananda; Advaita Ashrama), widely circulated under Vivekananda's name.

B. **Modern India:** A short Advaita Ashrama booklet by Swami Vivekananda laying out his views on India's strengths, social reform, and nation-building. The publisher's catalog lists Vivekananda as author.

C. **The Evils of Adhikarvad:** An essay attributed to Vivekananda critiquing "adhikarvada" (privilege/authoritarianism) in India's social order; standard study materials on Vivekananda's social thought include it among his writings.

Not included:

D. **India in Transition** — authored by M.N. Roy (1922).

E. **The Problem of Freedom** — authored by M.N. Roy (1945).

Hence, only A, B, C are correct.

60. The following are among the major works written by Noam Chomsky, an American linguist, philosopher, and political analyst:

A. **Syntactic Structures (1957):** A seminal work that revolutionized linguistics by introducing transformational-generative grammar, reshaping the understanding of human language and cognition.

B. **American Power and the New Mandarins (1969):** A political critique of U.S. foreign policy during the Vietnam War, examining how intellectual elites justified imperialism.

C. **New Military Humanism: Lessons from Kosovo (1999):** Analyses NATO's intervention in the Balkans, arguing that humanitarian rhetoric often masks strategic interests.

The other two titles—The Tragedy of Great Power Politics (by John Mearsheimer) and The Israel Lobby and U.S. Foreign Policy (by John Mearsheimer and Stephen Walt)—were not written by Chomsky.

Hence, only A, B, C are correct.

61. Correctly matched nuclear arms control treaties and years are:

A. **1959 – Antarctic Treaty:** Signed in 1959, it demilitarized Antarctica, prohibiting any military activity or nuclear testing on the continent.

B. **1963 – Partial Test Ban Treaty (PTBT):** Signed by the U.S., U.K., and U.S.S.R., it banned nuclear tests in the atmosphere, underwater, and outer space, permitting only underground testing.

C. **1968 – Nuclear Non-Proliferation Treaty (NPT):** Entered into force in 1970, aiming to prevent the spread of nuclear weapons and promote peaceful nuclear cooperation.

The Comprehensive Test Ban Treaty (CTBT) was adopted in 1996, not 1990, and the Anti-Ballistic Missile (ABM) Treaty was signed in 1972, not 1982.

Hence, the correct set is A, B, C only.

62. Checking options:

A. **King Zahir Shah ruled Afghanistan for decades: Correct.** King Mohammad Zahir Shah ruled from 1933 to 1973, making him the last monarch of Afghanistan and one of the longest-reigning rulers in the country's modern history.

B. **Mullah Muhammad Omar was the Supreme Leader of the first Taliban government: Correct.** He founded the Taliban movement in 1994 and served as the Amir al-Mu'minin (Commander of the Faithful) from 1996 to 2001, during the first Taliban regime.

E. **Soviet Union invaded Afghanistan in 1979:** Correct. The Soviet invasion began on 24 December 1979, aiming to support the communist government in Kabul. It led to a decade-long conflict until Soviet withdrawal in 1989.

C. **Indus River originates from Afghanistan: Incorrect.** The Indus River originates in Tibet (China) near Lake Manasarovar, not in Afghanistan.

D. **Iraq shares land border with Afghanistan: Incorrect.** Afghanistan borders Iran, not Iraq.

Hence, the accurate combination is A, B, E.

63. Checking options:

A. **Provided the establishment of a Federal Court: Correct.** The Government of India Act, 1935 created a Federal Court, which was established in 1937 to resolve disputes between the provinces and the central government.

B. **Separated Burma from India: Correct.** The Act formally separated Burma (now Myanmar) from British India on 1 April 1937, making it a separate colony.

C. **Created two new provinces of Orissa and Sind: Correct.** The Act led to the creation of Orissa and Sind as separate provinces, reorganizing British Indian territories.

D. **Proposed the establishment of Chamber of Princes: Incorrect.** The Chamber of Princes was created earlier in 1921 under the Government of India Act, 1919, not 1935.

E. **Introduced separate electorate for Muslims: Incorrect** here; this was introduced earlier by the Indian Councils Act, 1909 (Morley-Minto Reforms).

Thus, correct provisions belong to A, B, C.

64. Checking options:

A. **V. Narahari Rao: Correct.** He was the first Comptroller and Auditor General (CAG) of India, serving from 1948 to 1954, responsible for establishing the constitutional framework of audit and accountability.

C. **Vinod Rai: Correct.** He served as CAG from 2008 to 2013, known for his bold audits of the 2G Spectrum and Coal allocation (Coalgate) scams that strengthened public accountability.

E. **Girish Chandra Murmu: Correct.** The current CAG of India, appointed in August 2020, and former first Lieutenant Governor of Jammu and Kashmir.

B. **Ranjan Gogoi: Incorrect.** He served as the 46th Chief Justice of India, not CAG.

D. **J.M. Lyngdoh: Incorrect.** He was the Chief Election Commissioner of India, not CAG.

Hence, the correct names are A, C, and E.

65. Checking options:

A. **Harilal J. Kania (1950–1951): Correct.** He was the first Chief Justice of India, serving from 26 January 1950 to 6 November 1951, after the Supreme Court of India was established following the enforcement of the Constitution.

B. **M. Patanjali Shastri (1951–1954): Correct.** He succeeded Justice Kania and served from 7 November 1951 to 3 January 1954, noted for strengthening the Court's constitutional interpretation framework.

C. **Bhuvaneshwar Prasad Sinha (1959–1964): Correct.** He was the sixth Chief Justice of India, serving from 1 October 1959 to 31 January 1964, recognized for his judgments upholding judicial independence.

D. **K. Subba Rao (1970–1974): Incorrect.** He served from 30 June 1966 to 11 April 1969, not during the 1970s.

E. **M. Hidayatullah (1975–1978): Incorrect.** He was CJI from 25 February 1968 to 16 December 1970.

Thus, only A, B, and C have correct tenures.

66. Checking options:

C. Scanlon Plan: Associated with Douglas McGregor, it is a gain-sharing incentive plan combining productivity improvement with employee participation, fostering cooperation between workers and management.

D. The Human Side of Enterprise (1960): McGregor's most influential book, where he formulated Theory X and Theory Y, highlighting two contrasting assumptions about human motivation at work.
Theory X assumes employees dislike work and need direction and control, while Theory Y views employees as self-motivated and capable of self-control when committed to objectives.

- The other items are incorrect:
- A and B misstate the content of Theory X and Y.
- E (Linking Pin Model) was proposed by Rensis Likert, not McGregor.

Hence, the correct ideas associated with McGregor are C and D only.

67. Checking options:

A. **Henri Fayol – Management Process School: Correct.** Fayol is the founder of the Administrative/Management Process School, identifying 14 principles of management and emphasizing planning, organizing, commanding, coordinating, and controlling.

C. **Mary Parker Follett – Idea of Constructive Conflict: Correct.** Follett introduced the concept of constructive conflict—a positive, integrative process that fosters creativity and cooperation within organizations.

D. **Elton Mayo – The Great Illumination Experiment: Correct.** Mayo led the Hawthorne Studies at Western Electric, beginning with the Illumination Experiments (1924–1927), which revealed the social and psychological dimensions of work productivity.

E. **Chester Barnard – Spiritual Father of the Social Systems School: Correct.** Barnard's book "The Functions of the Executive" (1938) emphasized the organization as a cooperative social system, forming the foundation of the Social Systems School.

B. **Max Weber – Legal Irrational Authority: Incorrect.** Weber defined Legal-Rational Authority, not "Legal Irrational."

Hence, the correct set is A, C, D, and E only.

68. Abraham Maslow's Hierarchy of Needs Theory (1943) presents five progressive levels of human motivation, each building upon the satisfaction of the previous one:

A. **Physiological Needs:** The most basic needs essential for survival—food, water, sleep, and shelter.

C. **Security (Safety) Needs:** The need for physical safety, stability, employment, and protection from harm.

B. **Esteem Needs:** Desire for respect, recognition, confidence, and self-worth—divided into self-esteem and esteem from others.

D. **Self-Actualisation Needs:** The highest level, where individuals seek personal growth, fulfillment, and realization of potential.

Maslow's original model does not include "Spiritual Needs" as a separate category; that was added in later extensions but not part of the classical hierarchy.

Hence, the correct combination is A, B, C, D.

69. In the Preamble of the Constitution of India, Justice encompasses three fundamental dimensions ensuring fairness and equality across all aspects of life:

A. **Social Justice:** Elimination of social inequalities, caste discrimination, and privileges based on birth, promoting equality of status.

C. **Economic Justice:** Equitable distribution of wealth, resources, and opportunities to reduce inequality and poverty.

D. **Political Justice:** Equal participation and representation in political processes, ensuring universal suffrage and equal access to public offices.

The Preamble does not refer to Absolute Equality or Military Justice; hence, only these three — social, economic, and political — constitute the meaning of justice.

70. In Fred W. Riggs's Prismatic Model of comparative public administration, a prismatic society represents a transitional stage between traditional (fused) and modern (diffracted) societies. Its characteristics include:

C. Selectivism: Decisions are based on personal connections and favoritism rather than universal rules.

D. Attainment: A partial shift from ascriptive (status-based) to achievement-based recognition; however, attainment remains inconsistent.

E. Poly-functionalism: Institutions and roles perform multiple overlapping functions — for example, the same office may handle political, religious, and administrative duties simultaneously.

Traits like Universalism and Attainment in full rational form belong to diffracted societies, while Ascriptive values characterize fused societies.

Therefore, prismatic societies display C, D, and E only.

71. Rensis Likert, a noted social psychologist, developed the Management Systems 1–4 model to describe four progressive styles of leadership and organizational management:

D. **Exploitative–Authoritative (System 1):** Characterized by fear, coercion, and top-down control; employees are rarely trusted or consulted.

C. **Benevolent–Authoritative (System 2):** A paternalistic style where authority remains centralized, but limited rewards and motivation are used to maintain control.

B. **Consultative System (System 3):** Managers seek subordinates' opinions before decision-making, promoting partial participation and improved morale.

A. **Participative System (System 4):** The most democratic form, encouraging full involvement, teamwork, and shared responsibility in decision-making.

The concept of E. Maturity–Immaturity belongs to Chris Argyris, not Likert. Hence, the correct systems are A, B, C, D only.

72. The Preamble of the Constitution of India expresses the guiding ideals and values upon which the Republic is founded. It emphasizes:

A. **Justice:** Social, economic, and political equality in all spheres of life.

B. **Liberty:** Freedom of thought, expression, belief, faith, and worship for all citizens.

C. **Equality:** Ensures equality of status and opportunity, eliminating discrimination based on birth, caste, religion, or gender.

E. **Fraternity:** Promotes the spirit of brotherhood and unity among citizens, safeguarding the dignity of the individual and the unity of the nation.

The term Monarchy (D) directly contradicts the Preamble's emphasis on a Sovereign, Socialist, Secular, Democratic Republic.

Therefore, the correct elements emphasized are A, B, C, and E.

73. The Parliament of India performs multiple essential roles in governance and accountability:

A. To legislate: Enacts laws on matters enumerated in the Union and Concurrent Lists, shaping national policy and governance.

B. To monitor expenditure of public funds: Through financial committees such as the Public Accounts Committee (PAC), Estimates Committee, and Committee on Public Undertakings, Parliament ensures financial oversight.

C. To hold the government accountable for its actions: Ministers are answerable to Parliament through questions, debates, motions, and no-confidence votes, ensuring responsible governance.

E. To be a forum for expression of grievances: Parliament allows members to raise public issues and citizen grievances through discussions, adjournment motions, and zero-hour interventions.

D. To keep a check on the opposition is incorrect, since Parliament's structure is designed for checks on the executive, not on opposition.

Hence, the correct set of parliamentary functions is A, B, C, and E only.

74. According to the Montevideo Convention on the Rights and Duties of States (1933), a state is considered a person of international law if it possesses four essential qualifications:

A. **A defined territory:** There must be a specific geographic area over which the state exercises sovereignty.
B. **A permanent population:** The state must have people who permanently reside within its territory.
C. **An effective government:** A functioning political authority capable of exercising control and maintaining order within its territory.
D. **The capacity to enter into relations with other states:** The ability to conduct foreign relations and be recognized diplomatically.

The fifth item, E. Freedom to form the Union, is not mentioned in the Convention. Thus, the four correct features are A, B, C, and D only.

75. Luther Gulick, a key figure in classical public administration, identified four bases of departmentalisation, which determine how governmental functions should be grouped:
A. **Purpose:** Departments organized by objectives or services, e.g., Ministry of Education or Ministry of Health.
B. **Process:** Grouped by the type of work or process involved, such as the Ministry of Law or Printing and Stationery.
C. **Persons:** Based on the clientele served, e.g., Department of Women and Child Development or Tribal Affairs.
D. **Place:** Organised by geographic or territorial divisions, such as regional or state-level departments.

The option E (Protest) has no connection with Gulick's administrative framework. Hence, the correct four bases are A, B, C, and D only.

76. Matching each personality with their corresponding position:
A. **K. P. S. Menon – I. Chairman of the United Nations Commission on Korea:** A senior Indian diplomat and independent India's first Foreign Secretary, he chaired the UN Commission on Korea in 1947–48.
B. **Justice Fazl Ali – III. Chairman of the States Reorganisation Commission:** Headed the States Reorganisation Commission (1953–55) that recommended reorganization of Indian states on linguistic lines.
C. **General K. S. Thimayya – II. Chairman of the Neutral Nations Repatriation Commission:** Commanded the Neutral Nations Repatriation Commission in Korea (1953–54) after the Korean War to supervise POW repatriation.
D. **Nalini Ranjan Sarkar – IV. President of the Federation of Indian Chambers of Commerce and Industry (FICCI):** A noted industrialist and politician, he served as FICCI President in 1934 and contributed to economic planning in colonial India.

Therefore, the correct matching is A–I, B–III, C–II, D–IV.

77. Matching options:
A. **Allahabad → 1866 (III):** The Allahabad High Court traces its origin to the Indian High Courts Act, 1861, and was constituted in 1866, replacing the Sadr courts of the North-Western Provinces.
B. **Andhra Pradesh → 1954 (IV):** Following the creation of the Andhra State (1953) from the Madras Presidency, the Andhra High Court was inaugurated on 5 July 1954 at Guntur (later shifting to Hyderabad on the formation of Andhra Pradesh in 1956).
C. **Bombay → 1862 (II):** One of the three charter High Courts (with Calcutta and Madras), the Bombay High Court was established on 14 August 1862 under the Indian High Courts Act, 1861.
D. **Patna → 1916 (I):** The Patna High Court came into being on 1 March 1916, after the separation of Bihar and Orissa from the Calcutta High Court's jurisdiction.

Therefore, the correct matching is A-III, B-IV, C-II, D-I.

78. Reserved Lok Sabha seats for Scheduled Tribes (STs) (based on Delimitation Commission data):
A. **West Bengal – III. 2 seats:** The state has two ST-reserved constituencies — Alipurduars and Jalpaiguri.
B. **Maharashtra – I. 4 seats:** The state has four constituencies reserved for Scheduled Tribes — Gadchiroli–Chimur, Nandurbar, Dindori, and Palghar.
C. **Jharkhand – IV. 5 seats:** Out of its 14 Lok Sabha seats, five are reserved for STs – Khunti, Lohardaga, Rajmahal, Singhbhum, and Dumka.
D. **Rajasthan – II. 3 seats:** The state has three ST-reserved constituencies — Banswara, Udaipur, and Dungarpur.

Hence, the correct mapping is A–III, B–I, C–IV, D–II.

79. Chronological matching of major 20th-century global events:

A. **Soviet Atomic Bomb Exploded – III. 1949:** The USSR successfully tested its first atomic bomb, "RDS-1," on 29 August 1949, marking the start of the nuclear arms race.

B. **Soviet Invasion of Hungary – IV. 1956:** The Soviet Union crushed the Hungarian Revolution of 1956 in November to maintain communist control in Eastern Europe.

C. **Islamic Revolution in Iran – II. 1979:** Led by Ayatollah Khomeini, the revolution overthrew Shah Mohammad Reza Pahlavi, establishing the Islamic Republic of Iran.

D. **Berlin Wall Falls – I. 1989:** On 9 November 1989, the Berlin Wall collapsed, symbolizing the end of the Cold War and the reunification of Germany.

Thus, the correct chronological association is A–III, B–IV, C–II, D–I.

80. Matching options:

A. **State of Mizoram Act—II (1986):** Parliament passed the State of Mizoram Act, 1986, paving the way for Mizoram's transition from Union Territory to statehood (statehood took effect on 20 Feb 1987, but the Act itself is 1986).

B. **Goa, Daman and Diu Reorganisation Act—IV (1987):** This Act granted statehood to Goa in 1987 and separated Daman & Diu as a Union Territory.

C. **Bihar Reorganisation Act — I (2000):** Enacted in 2000, this law created the new state of Jharkhand (effective 15 Nov 2000) by reorganising Bihar.

D. **Punjab Reorganisation Act—III (1966):** The 1966 Act bifurcated the erstwhile Punjab to create Haryana, designated Chandigarh as a Union Territory, and adjusted certain hill areas.

Thus, the correct chronological association is A-II, B-IV, C-I, D-III.

81. Matching options:

A. **Battle of Stalingrad—1942–1943 (I):** One of World War II's decisive battles between Nazi Germany and the Soviet Union, marking the turning point on the Eastern Front.

B. **Munich Agreement—1938 (II):** Signed in September 1938 by Germany, Italy, Britain, and France, permitting Hitler's annexation of the Sudetenland region of Czechoslovakia.

C. **Armenian Genocide—1915 (III):** Conducted by the Ottoman Empire during World War I, resulting in the mass killing and deportation of over a million Armenians.

D. **European Union Created—1993 (IV):** Formally established by the Maastricht Treaty, which came into force on 1 November 1993.

Thus, the correct order is A–I, B–II, C–III, D–IV.

82. Matching options:

A. **Rabi Ray—December 1989 – July 1991 (II):** Served as Speaker of the 9th Lok Sabha during the governments of V.P. Singh and Chandra Shekhar.

B. **Dr. Balram Jakhar—January 1985 – December 1989 (I):** Served as Speaker of the 8th Lok Sabha, the first to complete two full consecutive terms.

C. **Shivraj Patil—July 1991 – May 1996 (III):** Presided over the 10th Lok Sabha during the Narasimha Rao government.

D. **Meira Kumar—June 2009 – June 2014 (IV):** Served as Speaker of the 15th Lok Sabha, being the first woman to hold the position.

Hence, the correct matching is A–II, B–I, C–III, D–IV.

83. Matching options:

A. **United Nations Truce Supervision Organisation (UNTSO)—1948 (II):** Established in 1948, it was the first UN peacekeeping mission, created to monitor the ceasefire between Israel and its Arab neighbours following the Arab–Israeli War.

B. **United Nations Mission in the Sudan (UNMIS)—2005 (I):** Created by UN Security Council Resolution 1590 (2005) to support the implementation of the Comprehensive Peace Agreement between the Sudanese government and the SPLM/A.

C. **United Nations Interim Force in Lebanon (UNIFIL)—1978 (IV):** Established by Resolution 425 and 426 (1978) after Israel's invasion of Lebanon, to confirm Israeli withdrawal and restore peace.

D. **United Nations Peacekeeping Force in Cyprus (UNFICYP)—1964 (III):** Set up in 1964 to prevent further fighting between the Greek and Turkish communities on the island.

Hence, correct matching: A–II, B–I, C–IV, D–III.

84. Matching options:

A. **The First Finance Commission—1951 (I):** Constituted on 22 November 1951 under the chairmanship of K.C. Neogy, following Article 280 of the Constitution.

B. **The Second Finance Commission—1956 (IV):** Formed in 1956, chaired by K. Santhanam, to review financial relations between the Centre and States.

C. **The Fifth Finance Commission—1968 (II):** Established in 1968, chaired by Mahavir Tyagi, to recommend devolution of taxes and grants to states.

D. **The Third Finance Commission—1960 (III):** Constituted in 1960, headed by A.K. Chanda, continuing periodic fiscal review.

Hence, correct order: A–I, B–IV, C–II, D–III.

85. Matching options:

A. **Convention on the Rights of the Child—1990 (I):** Adopted by the UN General Assembly in 1989 and entered into force in 1990, it is the most widely ratified human rights treaty, protecting children's rights globally.

B. **Declaration on Torture—1975 (IV):** The UN Declaration on the Protection of All Persons from Being Subjected to Torture and Other Cruel, Inhuman or Degrading Treatment or Punishment was adopted in 1975.

C. **Vienna Convention on Human Rights—1993 (III):** Refers to the Vienna Declaration and Programme of Action, adopted at the World Conference on Human Rights (1993), reaffirming universal human rights.

D. **Genocide Convention—1951 (II):** The Convention on the Prevention and Punishment of the Crime of Genocide was adopted in 1948 and came into force in 1951.

Hence, correct order: A–I, B–IV, C–III, D–II.

86. Matching options:

A. **Andhra Pradesh—175 (III):** The Andhra Pradesh Legislative Assembly has 175 seats, as per the Delimitation of Parliamentary and Assembly Constituencies Order, 2008.

B. **Gujarat—182 (I):** The Gujarat Legislative Assembly consists of 182 members, representing its 182 constituencies.

C. **Mizoram—40 (IV):** The Mizoram Legislative Assembly has 40 seats, making it one of the smallest assemblies in India.

D. **West Bengal—294 (II):** The West Bengal Legislative Assembly comprises 294 elected members, making it one of the largest state assemblies in the country.

Hence, correct order: A–III, B–I, C–IV, D–II.

87. Matching options:

A. **Assam—14 (II):** The state of Assam sends 14 representatives to the Lok Sabha.

B. **Karnataka—28 (I):** Karnataka has 28 Lok Sabha constituencies, among the highest for a southern state.

C. **Odisha—21 (IV):** Odisha contributes 21 members to the Lok Sabha.

D. **Delhi—7 (III):** The National Capital Territory of Delhi has 7 parliamentary constituencies.

Hence, correct order: A–II, B–I, C–IV, D–III.

88. Matching options:

A. **Ram Krishna Hegde—Karnataka (II):** A prominent Janata Party leader, he served as Chief Minister of Karnataka (1983–1988), known for pioneering Panchayati Raj reforms.

B. **Bhagat Singh Koshyari—Uttarakhand (I):** Served as Chief Minister of Uttarakhand (2001–2002) and later as Governor of Maharashtra.

C. **Karpoori Thakur—Bihar (IV):** A socialist leader, he served twice as Chief Minister of Bihar (1970 and 1977–79), championing social justice and backward-class empowerment.

D. **Sucheta Kriplani—Uttar Pradesh (III):** India's first woman Chief Minister, she headed the Uttar Pradesh government (1963–1967).

Hence, correct order: A–II, B–I, C–IV, D–III.

89. Matching options:

A. **Woodrow Wilson—II. Importance of Study of Administration as Science:** In his 1887 essay "The Study of Administration," Wilson emphasized treating public administration as a distinct science, separate from politics, laying the foundation of modern administrative theory.

B. **Frederick Taylor—I. Principles of Scientific Management:** In his 1911 book "The Principles of Scientific Management," Taylor developed methods for improving efficiency, productivity, and time management through scientific analysis of work.

C. **Luther Gulick—IV. Structure-based Principles of Organisation:** Gulick, in his work "Papers on the Science of Administration," proposed the structural principles of management summarized as POSDCORB (Planning, Organizing, Staffing, Directing, Coordinating, Reporting, Budgeting).

D. **Abraham Maslow—III. Hierarchy of Needs:** Maslow's Need Hierarchy Theory (1943) explains human motivation through levels—physiological, safety, social, esteem, and self-actualization needs.

Hence, correct matching: A–II, B–I, C–IV, D–III.

90. Matching options:

A. **Dwight Waldo—II. The Study of Public Administration:** His 1948 work argued that administration is inherently value-laden and political, refuting the earlier notion of neutrality in public administration.

B. **Peter Drucker—I. Management Challenges for the 21st Century:** Published in 1999, Drucker analyzed future trends and emphasized knowledge management, innovation, and adaptability as core managerial challenges.

C. **Rensis Likert—IV. The Human Organisation:** In "The Human Organization" (1967), Likert elaborated on his Systems 1–4 model and emphasized participative management for better productivity.

D. **Frederick Herzberg—III. The Motivation to Work:** Co-authored with Mausner and Snyderman in 1959, this book introduced the Two-Factor Theory distinguishing hygiene factors and motivators in employee satisfaction.

Hence, correct order: A–II, B–I, C–IV, D–III.

91. Vinayak Damodar Savarkar was imprisoned by the British in the Cellular Jail at Andamans, known for its harsh treatment of freedom fighters. He spent several years there in solitary confinement, symbolizing the extreme sacrifices made by Indian revolutionaries for independence.

92. The Hindu Mahasabha meeting at Ahmedabad took place in 1937, where Savarkar delivered his Presidential Address articulating his vision of Hindutva as encompassing religion, culture, politics, and language within a unified national identity.

93. The passage identifies Panini and Patanjali as the two ancient grammarians of India, credited with shaping the Sanskrit grammatical tradition. Panini authored the Ashtadhyayi, while Patanjali composed the Mahabhashya, together forming the foundation of linguistic science in India.

94. The book 'Hindu Pad-Padshahi' was authored by Savarkar. It reflects his historical interpretation of Maratha supremacy under the Peshwas and his vision of political resurgence inspired by Hindu civilization and valor.

95. The book 'A Nation in Making' was written by Surendranath Banerjee, not Savarkar. Savarkar's key works include Hindutva (1923), The Indian War of Independence (1909), Hindu Pad-Padshahi, and An Echo from Andamans. Hence, A Nation in Making is not his work.

96. The passage states that the concept of "good governance" was first highlighted by the World Bank in a 1989 report on Sub-Saharan Africa. This report identified governance as a crucial factor in economic development and emphasized four pillars: public sector management, accountability, legal framework for development, and information transparency.

97. In 1989, the World Bank's report on Sub-Saharan Africa introduced the governance concept, focusing on how poor governance impeded development in the region. It became a landmark document linking governance quality with economic aid and policy reforms.

98. The Organisation for Economic Co-operation and Development (OECD) connected development assistance with participatory development, human rights, and democratization, marking a shift from purely economic aid to governance-based conditional assistance in international cooperation.

99. In the mid-19th century, Alexis De Tocqueville, in his classic work "Democracy in America" (1835–1840), analyzed how civil associations and voluntary organizations strengthened democracy by nurturing civic participation and social trust.

100. The book "Developing Democracy: Toward Consolidation" was authored by Larry Diamond, a political scientist who argued that a vibrant civil society and socialized democratic values are essential for sustaining liberal democracy in developing nations.

Previous Years' Paper

National Testing Agency (NTA)

UGC-NET Junior Research Fellowship & Assistant Professor Eligibility Exam

POLITICAL SCIENCE, JANUARY-2025

(Exam held on 06-01-2025)

PAPER-II

1. The Seventy Fourth Constitutional Amendment Act is intend for:

A. Rural Local Administration
B. Judicial Reforms
C. Urban Local Bodies Administration
D. Linguistic Administration

2. Arrange the following into chronological order:

(*a*) Charles I is forced to accept Petition of Right
(*b*) Falkland war is fought with Argentina
(*c*) King John I forced to sign Magna Carta
(*d*) Bill of Rights in Britain
(*e*) Act of Union United Kingdoms of England and Scotland

Choose the ***correct*** answer from the options given below:

A. (*a*), (*d*), (*c*), (*b*), (*e*)
B. (*c*), (*a*), (*e*), (*b*), (*d*)
C. (*a*), (*c*), (*e*), (*d*), (*b*)
D. (*c*), (*a*), (*d*), (*e*), (*b*)

3. Arrange the following constitutional amendments/provisions as per their inclusion in the chronological order:

(*a*) Special provisions with respect to Delhi
(*b*) Promotion of co-operative societies
(*c*) Privy purses abolished
(*d*) Representation for women in Legislature
(*e*) Total number of ministers in the Council of Ministers shall not exceed fifteen per cent of the strength of Lok-Sabha/ Legislative Assembly

Choose the ***correct*** answer from the options given below:

A. (*c*), (*a*), (*e*), (*b*), (*d*)
B. (*c*), (*e*), (*a*), (*b*), (*d*)
C. (*c*), (*a*), (*b*), (*d*), (*e*)
D. (*c*), (*e*), (*a*), (*d*), (*b*)

4. When the Legal Services Authorities Act, 1987 was amended in (to provide for the establishment of the permanent Lok-Adalats to the public utility services)?

A. 2006
B. 2002
C. 2005
D. 2007

5. Which Act provided that the term of the members of Rajya-Sabha shall be six years?

A. The Representation of the People Act (1951)
B. People Representation Act (1953)
C. Government of India Act (1935)
D. Government of India Act (1919)

6. Emergency powers relating to suspension of fundamental rights have been taken from:

A. Canadian Constitution
B. Australian Constitution
C. Weimer Constitution of Germany
D. French Constitution

7. Who suggested that bourgeois assumptions and values needed to be overthrown by the establishment of a rival 'proletarian hegemony' and 'the manufacture of consent'?

A. Anthony Giddens
B. John Stuart Mill
C. Antonio Gramsci
D. Ram Manohar Lohia

8. Who was a trenchant critique of Aryanism, Brahmanism and Hinduism?

A. Dayananda Saraswati
B. Swami Kripatri
C. E.V. Ramaswamy Naicker
D. Bal Gangadhar Tilak

9. Which of the following are not the part of the liberal democracy?

(*a*) Based on one-party system
(*b*) Based on formal legal rules
(*c*) Guarantee of civil liberties and individual rights
(*d*) A system of checks and balances
(*e*) State monopoly on the means of mass communication

Choose the ***correct*** answer from the options given below:

A. (*b*) and (*c*) only
B. (*a*) and (*e*) only
C. (*c*) and (*d*) only
D. (*b*), (*c*) and (*d*) only

10. Who is the proposed Secretary of State in the Donald Trump Administration II?

A. Ivanka Trump
B. Tulsi Gabbad
C. Mark Esper
D. Macro Rubio

11. Indian National Congress won how many seats in 2014 Lok-Sabha elections?

A. 53 B. 48
C. 49 D. 44

12. Arrange the following leader's assassination into chronological order:

(*a*) John F. Keneddy
(*b*) Zia-ur Rahman
(*c*) SWRD Bandarnaike
(*d*) Olof Palme
(*e*) Yitzhak Rabin

Choose the ***correct*** answer from the options given below:

A. (*a*), (*d*), (*c*), (*e*), (*b*)
B. (*a*), (*c*), (*d*), (*e*), (*b*)
C. (*c*), (*a*), (*b*), (*d*), (*e*)
D. (*c*), (*b*), (*a*), (*d*), (*e*)

13. Arrange the following countries into chronological order as per the year of admission in the United Nations:

(*a*) Pakistan (*b*) Myanmar
(*c*) Sri Lanka (*d*) India
(*e*) Israel

Choose the ***correct*** answer from the options given below:

A. (*a*), (*d*), (*b*), (*c*), (*e*)
B. (*d*), (*a*), (*c*), (*e*), (*b*)
C. (*d*), (*a*), (*b*), (*e*), (*c*)
D. (*a*), (*d*), (*c*), (*b*), (*e*)

14. Women's movement in the United States developed strong over the years. Some of its basic facts include:

(*a*) The Seneca Falls convention, held in 1848, marked the birth of the US women's rights movement.
(*b*) The Nineteenth Amendment of the US Constitution granted the vote to American women in 1920.
(*c*) The National Women's Suffrage Association was set up in 1869.
(*d*) A feminist writer Simon de Beauvoir published the book 'The Second Sex'.

(*e*) The history of black women in the US has been narrated first by Greta Thunberg.

Choose the ***correct*** answer from the options given below:

A. (*a*), (*b*), (*c*), (*d*) only
B. (*b*), (*c*), (*d*), (*e*) only
C. (*c*), (*d*), (*e*) only
D. (*a*), (*b*), (*e*) only

15. Match the List-I with List-II:

List-I (Treaties/Agreements)	List-II (Year)
(*a*) Antarctic Treaty	I. 1959
(*b*) Anti-Ballistic Missile Treaty (ABM)	II. 1972
(*c*) Outer Space Treaty	III. 1967
(*d*) Limited Test Ban Treaty	IV. 1963

Choose the ***correct*** answer from the options given below:

	(*a*)	(*b*)	(*c*)	(*d*)
A.	I	II	III	IV
B.	II	I	III	IV
C.	IV	III	I	II
D.	III	IV	II	I

16. Arrange the following international events in the chronological order:

(*a*) Fidel Castro assumed power in Cuba
(*b*) John F. Kennedy became 35th president of the United States of America
(*c*) Pope John XXIII implored the Kremlin not to start a nuclear war
(*d*) An American U-2 was shot down over Cuba
(*e*) Soviet leader Khrushchev announced that he has agreed to remove the Soviet missiles from Cuba

Choose the ***correct*** answer from the options given below:

A. (*a*), (*d*), (*b*), (*c*), (*e*)
B. (*e*), (*c*), (*d*), (*b*), (*a*)
C. (*a*), (*b*), (*c*), (*d*), (*e*)
D. (*b*), (*c*), (*d*), (*a*), (*e*)

17. Arrange the following initiatives/ establishments by United Nation in chronological order:

(*a*) UN Roll Back Malaria Initiative
(*b*) Universal Declaration on Human Genome and Human Rights
(*c*) Global Polio Eradication Initiative
(*d*) Establishment of University of Peace, Costa Rica
(*e*) Establishment of UN Forum on Forests

Choose the ***correct*** answer from the options given below:

A. (*c*), (*b*), (*a*), (*e*), (*d*)
B. (*c*), (*a*), (*b*), (*e*), (*d*)
C. (*d*), (*c*), (*b*), (*a*), (*e*)
D. (*d*), (*b*), (*c*), (*a*), (*e*)

18. Separate representation to the Muslim community was provided by:

A. Government of India Act - 1858
B. Indian Council Act - 1892
C. Indian Council Act - 1909
D. Indian Council Act - 1861

19. Which among the following was not a part of 'self respect movement' initiated by EV Ramaswami Naicker?

A. Dropping description of caste from the names
B. New interpretation to characters of Hindu mythology
C. Joining Congress to support national movement
D. Self respect weddings solemnized without Brahmin Priests

20. Which of the following pairs are *not* matched properly?

(*a*) First nuclear test/explosion by USA: 1945
(*b*) First nuclear test/explosion by USSR : 1949
(*c*) First nuclear test/explosion by France : 1965
(*d*) First nuclear test/explosion by China : 1974

(*e*) First nuclear test/explosion by India : 1974

Choose the ***correct*** answer from the options given below:

A. (*a*) and (*b*) only
B. (*b*) and (*e*) only
C. (*c*) and (*d*) only
D. (*a*) and (*e*) only

21. Consider the following statements regarding Representative Democracy and select the correct options.

(*a*) It offers a practicable form of democracy for large countries.
(*b*) It establishes a link between the government and the governed.
(*c*) It obliterates the distinction between the government and the people.
(*d*) It advocates a classless society.
(*e*) It's most common modern manifestation is the use of referendum.

Choose the ***correct*** answer from the options given below:

A. (*a*) and (*b*) only B. (*b*) and (*d*) only
C. (*c*) and (*d*) only D. (*d*) and (*e*) only

22. Identify the characteristic not associated with prismatic societies:

A. Selectivism B. Attainment
C. Universalism D. Poly-functionalism

23. Identify the characteristics of Presidential form of government:

(*a*) Separation of power
(*b*) Checks and balances
(*c*) Collective responsibility
(*d*) A nominal head
(*e*) Fusion of legislature and executive

Choose the ***correct*** answer from the options given below:

A. (*a*), (*b*), (*c*) only
B. (*a*), (*b*), (*c*), (*d*) only
C. (*a*), (*b*) only
D. (*a*), (*b*), (*c*), (*e*) only

24. South Africa held its First non-racial election in:

A. 1993 B. 1997
C. 1994 D. 1992

25. Who wrote the book 'The Death of Nature: Women, Ecology and the Scientific Revolution'?

A. Carolyn Merchant B. Judith Butler
C. Germaine Greer D. Savita Singh

26. Who is the first women Director-General of WTO?

A. Ngozi Okonj Iweala
B. Mike Moore Supachai
C. Peter Sutherland
D. Paskal Lamy

27. Identify the ***incorrect*** facts about GATT/ WTO:

(*a*) From 1948 to 1994 the GATT provided the rules for much of World Trade
(*b*) GATT was a provisional agreement and organization
(*c*) The WTO was created on 1 January 1995
(*d*) The first ministerial conference of WTO was held in 2009
(*e*) The WTO's 28th Ministerial Conference was held in Delhi in 2024

Choose the ***correct*** answer from the options given below:

A. (*a*) and (*b*) only B. (*b*) and (*c*) only
C. (*c*) and (*a*) only D. (*d*) and (*e*) only

28. Consider the statements regarding NAMAMI GANGE scheme and identify the ***incorrect*** options

(*a*) It is an Integrated Conservation Mission for rejuvenation of River Ganga.
(*b*) The programme was launched in 2006.
(*c*) This programme has budget outlay of ₹ 1000 crore.
(*d*) It has provisions for Sewerage Treatment infrastructure.

(*e*) It has provisions for industrial effluent monitoring.

Choose the *correct* answer from the options given below:

A. (*a*) and (*d*) only B. (*a*) and (*e*) only
C. (*b*) and (*c*) only D. (*d*) and (*e*) only

29. Which one of the following works were not authored by Sri Aurobindo Ghose?

A. Essays on the Gita
B. The Ideal of the Karmayogi
C. A System of National Education
D. The Discovery of India

30. Who asserted bureaucracy as an exploitative class instrument?

A. Frederick Herzberg
B. Karl Marx
C. B.R. Ambedkar
D. Fred Riggs

31. Allahabad High Court was established in:

A. 1861 B. 1863
C. 1869 D. 1866

32. Who of the following thinkers are not associated with the Realist school of International Relations?

(*a*) Stephen-Walt
(*b*) John Mearsheimer
(*c*) Kenneth Waltz
(*d*) Wodrow Wilson
(*e*) Immanuel Kant

Choose the *correct* answer from the options given below:

A. (*a*) and (*b*) only
B. (*b*) and (*c*) only
C. (*c*) and (*a*) only
D. (*d*) and (*e*) only

33. Protection of language, script or culture of minorities have been guaranteed through which Article of Indian Constitution?

A. Article 21 B. Article 29
C. Article 27 D. Article 23

34. Match the List-I with List-II:

List-I (Author)	List-II (Books)
(*a*) Thomas Hobbes	I. Critique of Pure Reason
(*b*) Immanual Kant	II. The Order of the Things: An Archaeology of the Human Science
(*c*) Michel Foucault	III. On Fire
(*d*) Naomi Klein	IV. Leviathan

Choose the *correct* answer from the options given below:

	(*a*)	(*b*)	(*c*)	(*d*)
A.	IV	I	II	III
B.	III	II	I	IV
C.	II	III	IV	I
D.	I	IV	III	II

35. Arrange the following into chronological order:

(*a*) Hammurabi established the legal code.
(*b*) Model Parliament of Edward I is convened
(*c*) Treaty of Westphalia enforced notion of sovereignty
(*d*) United Nations approval the Universal Declaration of Human Rights
(*e*) New Zealand became the first country to grant women the right to vote

Choose the *correct* answer from the options given below:

A. (*a*), (*b*), (*e*), (*c*), (*d*)
B. (*a*), (*b*), (*c*), (*e*), (*d*)
C. (*b*), (*a*), (*c*), (*d*), (*e*)
D. (*b*), (*a*), (*e*), (*c*), (*d*)

36. Match the List-I with List-II:

List-I (Scholar)	List-II (Work)
(*a*) Fred Riggs	I. The Practice of Management
(*b*) Yehezkel Dror	II. The Ecology of Public Administration

(*c*) Peter Drucker	III. The Eighteenth Brumarie of Louis Bonaparte
(*d*) Karl Marx	IV. Public Policy Making Re-examined

Choose the ***correct*** answer from the options given below:

	(*a*)	(*b*)	(*c*)	(*d*)
A.	II	IV	I	III
B.	III	I	IV	II
C.	I	II	III	IV
D.	IV	III	II	I

37. Identify true facts about Regional Organizations:

(*a*) East Asian Summit founded in 2005

(*b*) Shanghai Cooperation Organization founded in 2001

(*c*) Nordic Council founded in 1952

(*d*) ASEAN Regional Forum founded in 1994

(*e*) SAARC founded in 1987

Choose the ***correct*** answer from the options given below:

A. (*a*), (*e*) only
B. (*b*), (*c*), (*e*) only
C. (*e*), (*a*), (*b*) only
D. (*a*), (*b*), (*c*), (*d*) only

38. What is concept of 'Gangplank' in an organization?

A. A training tool
B. Budgeting software
C. Level jumping of hierarchy
D. An accounting agency

39. Match the List-I with List-II:

List-I (Author)	List-II (Book)
(*a*) Max Weber	I. Economy and Society
(*b*) Isaiah Berlin	II. Social Reform or Revolution
(*c*) Rosa Luxemburg	III. Capitalism and Freedom
(*d*) Milton Friedman	IV. Four Essays on Liberty

Choose the ***correct*** answer from the options given below:

	(*a*)	(*b*)	(*c*)	(*d*)
A.	IV	I	III	II
B.	I	IV	II	III
C.	III	II	IV	I
D.	II	III	I	IV

40. Arrange environmental events in chronological order:

(*a*) Minimata Convention on Mercury

(*b*) Publication of the Rio Declaration and Agenda 21

(*c*) Greenpeace founded

(*d*) Bhopal chemical plant disaster

(*e*) Chernobyl nuclear disaster

Choose the ***correct*** answer from the options given below:

A. (*a*), (*b*), (*c*), (*d*), (*e*)
B. (*b*), (*c*), (*d*), (*e*), (*a*)
C. (*c*), (*d*), (*e*), (*b*), (*a*)
D. (*d*), (*c*), (*e*), (*a*), (*b*)

41. Arrange the position of dignitaries as given in Table of Precedence (Higher to Lower position)

(*a*) Chief Election Commissioner

(*b*) Deputy Chairman, Rajya Sabha

(*c*) Attorney General of India

(*d*) Vice Chairperson, NITI Aayog

(*e*) Holders of Bharat Ratna decoration

Choose the ***correct*** answer from the options given below:

A. (*b*), (*a*), (*d*), (*e*), (*c*)
B. (*c*), (*a*), (*b*), (*d*), (*e*)
C. (*d*), (*e*), (*a*), (*b*), (*c*)
D. (*e*), (*b*), (*a*), (*c*), (*d*)

42. Identify the correct statements regarding the Ecologism:

(*a*) The term Ecology was first coined by Ernst Haeckel.

(*b*) It studies the relationship between living organism and their environment.

(*c*) It is a market centric approach.

(*d*) It believes humans are masters of nature.
(*e*) Rachel Carson was an environmental conservationist.

Choose the ***correct*** answer from the options given below:
A. (*a*), (*b*) and (*e*) only
B. (*b*) and (*c*) only
C. (*b*), (*c*) and (*e*) only
D. (*a*) and (*d*) only

43. Match the List-I with List-II:

List-I (Committee/ Act)	List-II (Outcome/ Recommendation)
(*a*) Pendleton Act	I. Increased Managerial Capacity in executive office of US President
(*b*) First Hoover Commission	II. Work environment and Productivity
(*c*) Hawthorne Studies	III. Russian Interference in US Election
(*d*) US Sentate Intelligence Committee Report on 2016 Presidential Election	IV. US Civil Service Commission

Choose the ***correct*** answer from the options given below:

	(*a*)	(*b*)	(*c*)	(*d*)
A.	IV	I	II	III
B.	III	II	I	IV
C.	I	II	III	IV
D.	II	I	IV	III

44. Arrange the following world's largest military spendor country (2023) in the ascending order:
(*a*) South Korea
(*b*) Ukraine
(*c*) USA
(*d*) China
(*e*) Russia

Choose the ***correct*** answer from the options given below:
A. (*c*), (*e*), (*d*), (*b*), (*a*)
B. (*e*), (*c*), (*d*), (*a*), (*b*)
C. (*a*), (*b*), (*e*), (*d*), (*c*)
D. (*b*), (*a*), (*d*), (*e*), (*c*)

45. The 52nd Constitution Amendment Act which provided for the disqualification of the members of parliament and the state legislators on the ground of defection from one political party to another was enacted in:
A. 1984 B. 1985
C. 1987 D. 1988

46. Which of the following terms are associated with conservatism?
(*a*) Tradition
(*b*) Social duty
(*c*) Change in order to conserve
(*d*) Revolution
(*e*) Gender equality

Choose the ***correct*** answer from the options given below:
A. (*a*), (*d*) and (*e*) only
B. (*b*), (*c*) and (*d*) only
C. (*c*), (*d*) and (*e*) only
D. (*a*), (*b*) and (*c*) only

47. Match the List-I with List-II:

List-I (Incident)	List-II (Year)
(*a*) First Visit by an Indian Prime Minister to China	I. 2008
(*b*) Soviet-Indian treaty of Peace, Friendship and Co-operation	II. 1971
(*c*) Indian Nuclear Test-2	III. 1954
(*d*) 26/11 Mumbai Terror Attack	IV. 1998

Choose the ***correct*** answer from the options given below:

	(*a*)	(*b*)	(*c*)	(*d*)
A.	III	II	IV	I
B.	II	III	IV	I
C.	I	II	III	IV
D.	IV	III	II	I

48. Russian Marxist thinker and ruler, Vladimir Ilyich Lenin died in:

A. 1921
B. 1924
C. 1919
D. 1927

49. Who among the following is the first to coin the term 'catch-all-party'?

A. C. Wright Mills B. William Gladstone
C. Otto Kirchheimer D. Bertrand Russel

50. Which of the following statements are correct?

(*a*) Radical feminists call for overturning of gender oppression.
(*b*) According to Marxism, Ideology is an instrument to legitimize the rule of the dominant class.
(*c*) According to Fascism, people should follow the dictates of their leader.
(*d*) J.S. Mill opposed the rights for women.
(*e*) To maintain the existing order, Karl Marx opposed any idea of revolution.

Choose the ***correct*** answer from the options given below:

A. (*a*), (*b*) and (*c*) only
B. (*b*), (*c*) and (*d*) only
C. (*c*), (*d*) and (*e*) only
D. (*a*), (*d*) and (*e*) only

51. Arrange the following terrorists attacks into chronological order:

(*a*) Moscow Theater Hostage Crisis
(*b*) Indian Parliament Attack
(*c*) Tokyo Subway Sarin Attack
(*d*) Camp Speicher Massacre
(*e*) Air India Flight-182 Bombing

Choose the ***correct*** answer from the options given below:

A. (*e*), (*c*), (*b*), (*a*), (*d*)
B. (*e*), (*b*), (*c*), (*d*), (*a*)
C. (*b*), (*e*), (*c*), (*a*), (*d*)
D. (*b*), (*c*), (*e*), (*a*), (*d*)

52. Match the List-I with List-II:

List-I (Ideology)	**List-II (Proponent)**
(*a*) Pluralism	I. Deen Dayal Upadhyay
(*b*) Utilitarianism	II. Auguste Comte
(*c*) Integral Humanism	III. Jeremy Bentham
(*d*) Positivism	IV. James Madison

Choose the ***correct*** answer from the options given below:

	(*a*)	(*b*)	(*c*)	(*d*)
A.	I	II	III	IV
B.	III	IV	II	I
C.	IV	III	I	II
D.	II	I	III	IV

53. Match the List-I with List-II:

List-I (SAARC Secretary General)	**List-II (Tenure)**
(*a*) Abul Ahsan	I. January 1, 1994 to December 31, 1995
(*b*) Yadav Kant Silwal	II. January 1, 1999 to January 10, 2002
(*c*) Nihal Rodrigo	III. January 16, 1987 to October 15, 1989
(*d*) Sheel Kant Sharma	IV. March 1, 2008 to February 2011

Choose the ***correct*** answer from the options given below:

	(*a*)	(*b*)	(*c*)	(*d*)
A.	I	III	IV	II
B.	II	IV	III	I
C.	I	III	IV	II
D.	III	I	II	IV

54. Who wrote the book 'The Human Condition'?

A. Hannah Arendt B. Max Weber
C. Herbert Simon D. Jagdish P. Bhagwati

55. Which of the following statements regarding the federal features of the Indian Constitution are correct?

(*a*) India is a Union of States.

(*b*) The Constitution is the supreme organic law of the land.

(*c*) The legislative powers are distributed between the center and the states.

(*d*) The residuary powers are reserved to the states.

(*e*) All states have equal representation in the Rajya Sabha.

Choose the ***correct*** answer from the options given below:

A. (*a*), (*b*) and (*d*) only
B. (*a*), (*b*) and (*c*) only
C. (*b*), (*c*) and (*d*) only
D. (*c*), (*d*) and (*e*) only

56. In which year, constructive programme was announced by Indian National Congress?

A. 1922 B. 1924
C. 1930 D. 1935

57. Donald Trump has become only the second American President to win non-consecutive terms after winning November 2024 election, who was the first President?

A. John Adams B. Grover Cleveland
C. Andrew Jackson D. Abraham Lincoln

58. Match the List-I with List-II:

List-I (Events)	List-II (Year)
(*a*) Dumbarton Oaks Conference	I. 1972
(*b*) UN Peace keeping Mission to Suez Canal	II. 1956
(*c*) Establishment of UN Development Programme	III. 1944
(*d*) Establishment of UN Environment Programme	IV. 1965

Choose the ***correct*** answer from the options given below:

	(*a*)	(*b*)	(*c*)	(*d*)
A.	II	III	I	IV
B.	IV	I	III	II
C.	I	IV	II	III
D.	III	II	IV	I

59. Arrange the following states in descending order as per their allocation of seats in Rajya Sabha.

(*a*) Karnataka (*b*) Assam
(*c*) Tamil Nadu (*d*) Kerala
(*e*) Bihar

Choose the ***correct*** answer from the options given below:

A. (*e*), (*c*), (*a*), (*b*), (*d*)
B. (*e*), (*a*), (*c*), (*d*), (*b*)
C. (*c*), (*e*), (*a*), (*d*), (*b*)
D. (*c*), (*a*), (*e*), (*b*), (*d*)

60. Match the List-I with List-II:

List-I (War and Crisis)	List-II (Year)
(*a*) Kosovo War	I. 2011
(*b*) Libyan Civil War	II. 2001
(*c*) US led invasion of Afghanistan	III. 1996
(*d*) Taliban I seized power in Afghanistan	IV. 1999

Choose the ***correct*** answer from the options given below:

	(*a*)	(*b*)	(*c*)	(*d*)
A.	I	IV	III	II
B.	II	III	IV	I
C.	III	II	I	IV
D.	IV	I	II	III

61. M.C. Rajah of Madras was the first elected president of:

A. All India Depressed Classes Association
B. All Assam Students Union
C. Indian National Congress
D. British Indian Association

62. Which of the following pairs are matched properly?

(*a*) Sustainable Development : Development that meets the needs of the present only.

(*b*) Patriarchy : The power relationship between men and women.

(*c*) Holism : The whole is more important than it's part

(*d*) Fascism : Support for freedom of expression

(*e*) Deep Ecology : Rejection of anthropocentricism

Choose the ***correct*** answer from the options given below:

A. (*a*), (*b*) and (*c*) only
B. (*b*), (*c*) and (*e*) only
C. (*c*), (*d*) and (*e*) only
D. (*a*), (*d*) and (*e*) only

63. Match the List-I with List-II:

List-I (Scholar)	List-II (Works)
(*a*) Dr. S. Jaishankar	I. A Theory of Human Motivation
(*b*) Herbert Simon	II. On Organizational Learning
(*c*) Abraham Maslow	III. The India Way
(*d*) Chris Argyris	IV. Administrative Behaviour

Choose the ***correct*** answer from the options given below:

	(*a*)	(*b*)	(*c*)	(*d*)
A.	I	II	III	IV
B.	IV	III	II	I
C.	II	I	IV	III
D.	III	IV	I	II

64. Identify the correct statements:

(*a*) Vinayak Damodar Savarkar argued that the revolt of 1857 was India's first war of independence.

(*b*) Jayaprakash Narayan advocated the notion of Sampoorna Kranti or total revolution.

(*c*) Bhimrao Ramji Ambedkar was a protagonist of social justice.

(*d*) Bal Gangadhar Tilak was the moderate leader.

(*e*) According to Rabindranath Tagore, the idea of hyper nationalism is inalienable with true freedom.

Choose the ***correct*** answer from the options given below:

A. (*a*), (*b*) and (*c*) only
B. (*b*), (*c*) and (*d*) only
C. (*c*), (*d*) and (*e*) only
D. (*b*), (*c*), (*d*) and (*e*) only

65. Identify the essential facts related to German philosopher George Friedrich Hegel.

(*a*) Hegel popularized the idea of climate change mitigation.

(*b*) Hegel's version of idealism is known as dialectical idealism.

(*c*) Hegel sought to describe the dialectical process in terms of thesis, antithesis and synthesis.

(*d*) Hegel authored the book 'Phenomenology of Spirit'.

(*e*) Karl Marx was highly influenced by Hegel.

Choose the ***correct*** answer from the options given below:

A. (*a*), (*b*), (*c*), (*e*) only
B. (*a*), (*c*), (*d*) only
C. (*a*), (*b*), (*e*) only
D. (*b*), (*c*), (*d*), (*e*) only

66. Giorgia Meloni is the PM of Italy. Meloni belongs to which Political party?

A. Conservative Party
B. Democratic Party
C. Brothers of Italy
D. Republican Party

67. Choose the correct pairs of Indian political thinkers and their views/works/ideas

(*a*) Kautilya : Dharamshastra

(*b*) Sri Aurobindo : Spiritual Nationalism

(*c*) Veer Savarkar : An Echo from Andamans

(*d*) Swami Vivekananda : Preface to Raja-Yoga

(*e*) Rabindranath Tagore : Tarana-e-Hind

Choose the *correct* answer from the options given below:

A. (*a*), (*b*), (*c*), (*d*) only
B. (*b*), (*c*), (*d*) only
C. (*b*), (*c*), (*d*), (*e*) only
D. (*a*), (*b*), (*c*), (*e*) only

68. Who wrote the book 'One-Dimensional Man'?

A. Muchkund Dubey B. Fareed Zakaria
C. Herbert Simon D. Herbert Marcuse

69. Minnowbrook Conference-I occurred in:

A. 1961 B. 1965
C. 1968 D. 1971

70. Which of the following are *not* matched correctly.

(*a*) Economic Nationalism : To foster the domestic economy through protectionism.
(*b*) Nativism : Voicing the needs of native inhabitants against those of immigrants.
(*c*) Colonialism : Practice of establishing control over a foreign territory
(*d*) Xenophobia : Demand for self-determination
(*e*) Universalism : Behaviour characterized by insularity and exclusivity.

Choose the *correct* answer from the options given below:

A. (*a*) and (*b*) only
B. (*b*) and (*c*) only
C. (*a*) and (*c*) only
D. (*d*) and (*e*) only

71. Who wrote the book "The Functions of the Executive"?

A. Chester Barnard B. Max Weber
C. Henri Fayol D. Sun Tzu

72. Who wrote the book "The Sociology of Religion"?

A. Max Weber
B. Ana Ballesteros Peiro
C. John Locke
D. Herbert Marcuse

73. Match the List-I with List-II:

List-I (SAARC Summits)	List-II (Date)
(*a*) Dhaka	I. 10-11 April, 1993
(*b*) New Delhi	II. 2-4 May, 1995
(*c*) Colombo	III. 2-6 January, 2004
(*d*) Islamabad	IV. 29-31 July, 1998

Choose the *correct* answer from the options given below:

	(*a*)	(*b*)	(*c*)	(*d*)
A.	II	I	III	IV
B.	I	II	IV	III
C.	III	IV	II	I
D.	IV	III	I	II

74. Which of the following are *not* the variables of input-output analysis of David Easton?

(*a*) Development
(*b*) Growth
(*c*) Demand
(*d*) Support
(*e*) Feedback

Choose the *correct* answer from the options given below:

A. (*c*) and (*d*) only
B. (*c*) and (*e*) only
C. (*d*) and (*e*) only
D. (*a*) and (*b*) only

75. Arrange the Directors- General of GATT/WTO as per their tenure in chronological order:

(*a*) Eric Wyndham White
(*b*) Olivier Long
(*c*) Arthur Dunkel
(*d*) Peter Sutherland
(*e*) Ngozi Okonjo

Choose the *correct* answer from the options given below:

A. (*a*), (*b*), (*c*), (*d*), (*e*)
B. (*b*), (*c*), (*d*), (*e*), (*a*)
C. (*c*), (*d*), (*e*), (*b*), (*a*)
D. (*d*), (*a*), (*b*), (*c*), (*e*)

76. Identify the essential facts about communism.

(*a*) Common Ownership
(*b*) Absolute Equality
(*c*) Classless Society
(*d*) Vanguard Party
(*e*) Dictatorship of the Priestly class

Choose the ***correct*** answer from the options given below:

A. (*a*), (*b*), (*c*), (*e*) only
B. (*a*), (*b*), (*c*), (*d*) only
C. (*a*), (*b*), (*d*), (*e*) only
D. (*b*), (*c*), (*d*), (*e*) only

77. Arrange the following states as per their year of formation in the chronological order:

(*a*) Manipur
(*b*) Sikkim
(*c*) Telangana
(*d*) Jharkhand
(*e*) Arunachal Pradesh

Choose the ***correct*** answer from the options given below:

A. (*a*), (*b*), (*c*), (*d*), (*e*)
B. (*b*), (*c*), (*d*), (*e*), (*a*)
C. (*a*), (*b*), (*e*), (*d*), (*c*)
D. (*c*), (*d*), (*e*), (*b*), (*a*)

78. Who wrote the book "The Law of Peoples"?

A. John Rawls B. John Locke
C. Edward Said D. Francis Fukuyama

79. Arrange the committees on Panchayati Raj in chronological order:

(*a*) Balwant Rai Mehta Committee
(*b*) GVK Rao Committee
(*c*) Ashok Mehta Committee
(*d*) LM Singhvi Committee
(*e*) PK Thungan Committee

Choose the ***correct*** answer from the options given below:

A. (*a*), (*b*), (*c*), (*d*), (*e*)
B. (*a*), (*c*), (*b*), (*d*), (*e*)
C. (*b*), (*c*), (*d*), (*e*), (*a*)
D. (*c*), (*b*), (*d*), (*e*), (*a*)

80. Ram Manohar Lohia advanced his theory of history through his famous work:

A. Wheel of History
B. An Introduction to the Principles of Morals and Legislation
C. Liberalism and the Limits of Justice
D. Eros and Civilization

81. The Book 'Sexual Politics' was written by:

A. Judith Butler B. Kate Millett
C. Pandita Ramabai D. Sister Nivedita

82. Match the List-I with List-II:

List-I (Events)	List-II (Year)
(*a*) Boxer Rebellion in China	I. 1910-1920
(*b*) Mexican Revolution	II. 1931
(*c*) Japan invaded Manchuria	III. 1936
(*d*) Germany Reoccupied the Rhineland	IV. 1900-1901

Choose the ***correct*** answer from the options given below:

	(*a*)	(*b*)	(*c*)	(*d*)
A.	I	II	III	IV
B.	IV	I	II	III
C.	III	II	I	IV
D.	II	III	IV	I

83. Who wrote the book "Poverty and un-British Rule in India"?

A. Khan Abdul Gaffar Khan
B. Bal Gangadhar Tilak
C. Dadabhai Naroji
D. Jawaharlal Nehru

84. Who wrote the book/article 'Civil Disobedience'?

A. Bell Hooks
B. James Tully
C. Herbert Marcuse
D. Henry David Thoreau

85. Who coined the term 'Possessive Individualism'?

A. Jean-Jacques Rousseau

B. John Rawls
C. C.B. Macpherson
D. Edmund Burke

86. Equality of opportunity in employment has been guaranteed through which article of Indian Constitution?

A. Article 13
B. Article 19
C. Article 16
D. Article 18

87. Which year 19th Chinese Communist Party (CCP) Conference held in Beijing?

A. 2013 B. 2017
C. 2015 D. 2019

88. Match the List-I with List-II:

List-I (Book)	List-II (Author)
(*a*) Asian Drama	I. Gunnar Myrdal
(*b*) The Indian Constitution: Cornerstone of a Nation	II. Norman D. Palmer
(*c*) The State and Poverty in India : The Politics of Reform	III. Atul Kohli
(*d*) The Indian Political System	IV. Granville Austin

Choose the ***correct*** answer from the options given below:

	(*a*)	(*b*)	(*c*)	(*d*)
A.	III	II	I	IV
B.	IV	I	II	III
C.	I	IV	III	II
D.	II	III	IV	I

89. Match the List-I with List-II:

List-I (Progress)	List-II (Year)
(*a*) Google launched	I. 1998
(*b*) Facebook launched	II. 2004
(*c*) Microsoft founded	III. 1975
(*d*) Apple Computers founded	IV. 1976

Choose the ***correct*** answer from the options given below:

	(*a*)	(*b*)	(*c*)	(*d*)
A.	II	I	III	IV
B.	I	II	III	IV
C.	I	II	IV	III
D.	II	I	IV	III

90. Concurrent List of the Indian Constitution have been borrowed form:

A. American Constitution
B. Irish Constitution
C. Canadian Constitution
D. Australian Constitution

Directions (Qs. No. 91-95): *Read the following passage and answer the questions.*

James Madison gave eloquent expression to the urgent need for popular information in a democracy. During colonial rule, the administrative culture had been basically inward-looking, people avoiding and secret practicing. The right to information of a product of both institutions and culture. Under popular pressure and contemporary democratization movement throughout the world, openness and transparency in governmental operations have become quite trendy in recent times. Right to information laws are being enacted in many countries. Sweden adopted freedom of the Press Act in 1766. United States passed the Freedom of Information Act, 1966. In France, freedom of information and accountability of public servants are an integral part of constitution rights. The freedom of information law in Japan came into effect in 2001, allowing access to administrative documents held by administrative agencies in electronic or printed form.

In Germany, the federal government passed a freedom of information law in 2005. Six Bundeslander (provincial governments) have also own separate law on the subject. The Supreme Court of India, in the State of Uttar Pradesh vs. Raj Narain case observed that the right to information is implied in the right to freedom of speech. In 1997, India set up a working Group on Right to Information and Promotion of Open and Transparent Government. In 2005, Right to Information Act was passed in India to provide citizen secure access to information under the control of public authorities, in order to promote transparency and accountability.

91. In Germany, Bundeslander is also known as:

A. Civil Society
B. Provincial Governments
C. High Courts
D. Election Commission

92. As per the passage, in which case, Supreme Court of India observed that the right to information is implied in the right to freedom of speech?

A. Raj Narain Case B. Golaknath Case
C. Re-berubari Case D. Navin Jindal Case

93. According to the passage, which country adopted the provisions related to Press information at the earliest?

A. USA B. Japan
C. India D. Sweden

94. As per the passage, which country made the freedom of information and accountability of public servants as in integral part of constitutional rights?

A. Britain B. Australia
C. France D. Germany

95. As per the passage, in which year, India passed the Right to Information Act?

A. 2000 B. 2005
C. 2010 D. 2015

Directions (Qs. No. 96-100): *Read the following passage and answer the questions.*

The post-independence land-reforms adopted broadly on the basis of the Kumarappa Committee. This Committee took, as its guiding principle, the elimination of exploitation and giving the land to the tiller. Bihar Pradesh Kisan Sabha (BPKS) was founded in 1929. It established a national presence in 1936 as the All India Kisan Sabha (AIKS). Swami Sahajanand Saraswati dominated the provincial organisations, and emerged as the foremost Kisan leader in India, and also headed BPKS in 1935. The formation of Congress Ministery in Bihar in 1937 accelerated the process of showdown between the two organizations Zamindars offered their help and co-operation in passing tenancy laws to improve the condition of the tenants. The post-colonial India including Bihar witnessed the emergence of the Congress as the dominant party in the political system. In 1952 elections, Jharkhand Party was the main opposition party inside the state legislature. The important consequences of the 1952 general elections in Bihar were the emergence of two regional political party, the Jharkhand Party and the Janta Party. The Janta Party was founded in 1950 by Raja Kamakhya Narayan Singh to built up a traditional opposition to Congress. Its political influence was confined mainly in south-Bihar. Until 1967, Bihar witnessed a one party dominance system i.e. the 'Congress system' as conceptualized by Rajni Kothari. Between 1967-69, elections witnessed a highly fractionalized multi-party system. The decline in the Congress electoral strength has benefitted socialists and communists on the one hand, and the Jan Sangha on the other hand.

96. As per the paragraph given, which party was the main opposition party inside the Bihar legislature?

A. All India Kisan Sabha
B. Bihar Pradesh Kisan Sabha
C. Jharkhand Party
D. Congress

97. As per the paragraph, the political influence of Janta Party was confined mainly in:

A. North Bihar B. Eastern Bihar
C. Western Bihar D. South Bihar

98. As per the passage, In which year, Janta Party was formed?

A. 1950 B. 1960

C. 1970 D. 1980

99. As per the paragraph, who headed Bihar Pradesh Kisan Sabha in 1935?

A. Rajendra Prasad

B. Swami Sahjanand Saraswati

C. Daroga Prasad Rai

D. Ram Jaipal Singh

100. As per the given passage, who conceptualized the 'Congress system' as one party dominance system?

A. Partho Ghosh

B. Bipin Chandra

C. Rajni Kothari

D. Rajendra Prasad

ANSWERS

1. (C): The Seventy-Fourth Constitutional Amendment Act, 1992, deals with the administration of Urban Local Bodies (ULBs) in India. It provides a constitutional status to municipalities and lays down the framework for their governance.

The Act introduced three types of municipalities:

- **Nagar Panchayats** (for transitional areas)
- **Municipal Councils** (for smaller urban areas)
- **Municipal Corporations** (for larger urban areas)

It also mandates regular elections, decentralization of power, and reservation of seats for SCs, STs, and women.

2. (D): Chronological order of the events:

(*c*) **King John I forced to sign Magna Carta (1215):** Magna Carta was a landmark document that limited the powers of the monarchy and laid the foundation for constitutional governance in England.

(*a*) **Charles I is forced to accept Petition of Right (1628):** The Petition of Right was presented to King Charles I by Parliament to limit the monarch's arbitrary powers, ensuring that taxation and imprisonment could not occur without Parliament's approval.

(*d*) **Bill of Rights in Britain (1689):** This document established parliamentary sovereignty, limited the powers of the monarchy, and affirmed rights such as free elections and freedom of speech within Parliament.

(*e*) **Act of Union (1707) – United Kingdoms of England and Scotland:** This Act created the United Kingdom of Great Britain by merging the Kingdom of England and the Kingdom of Scotland into a single sovereign state.

(*b*) **Falklands War is fought with Argentina (1982):** This war was fought between the United Kingdom and Argentina over the disputed Falkland Islands. The UK successfully retained control over the islands after a brief military conflict.

3. (A): Chronological order of the constitutional amendments/provisions:

(*c*) **Privy purses abolished (1971):** The 26th Amendment Act, 1971 abolished privy purses granted to rulers of princely states, thereby ending their financial privileges.

(*a*) **Special provisions with respect to Delhi (1991):** The 69th Amendment Act, 1991 granted Delhi the status of a National Capital Territory and provided it with a legislative assembly with limited powers.

(*e*) **Total number of ministers in the Council of Ministers shall not exceed fifteen per cent of the strength of Lok Sabha/Legislative Assembly (2003):** The 91st Amendment Act, 2003 introduced this provision to curb unnecessary expansion of the ministry.

(*b*) **Promotion of co-operative societies (2011):** The 97th Amendment Act, 2011 included provisions to promote cooperative societies and granted them constitutional status.

(*d*) **Representation for women in the Legislature (ongoing process):** Various bills, including the Women's Reservation Bill (2023), have aimed to provide 33% reservation for women in Parliament and state legislatures.

4. **(B):** The Legal Services Authorities Act, 1987 was amended in 2002 to provide for the establishment of permanent Lok Adalats for public utility services. This amendment allowed Lok Adalats to adjudicate disputes related to public utilities, such as transport, postal services, and telecommunication, ensuring quick and cost-effective justice.

5. **(A):** The Representation of the People Act, 1951, under Section 154, provided that the term of Rajya Sabha members would be six years, with one-third of members retiring every two years to ensure continuity in the house. This Act governs the elections and functioning of Parliament in India.

6. **(C):** The emergency powers relating to the suspension of fundamental rights in India were influenced by the Weimar Constitution of Germany (1919–1933). This constitution allowed the President of Germany to suspend civil liberties and rule by decree under Article 48 during emergencies. Similarly, Article 352, Article 356, and Article 360 of the Indian Constitution allow the suspension of fundamental rights during emergencies.

7. **(C):** Antonio Gramsci, an Italian Marxist thinker, argued that bourgeois assumptions and values needed to be overthrown by the establishment of a rival 'proletarian hegemony'. He introduced the concept of 'manufacture of consent', where the ruling class maintains dominance by shaping cultural norms and ideologies rather than relying solely on coercion. His ideas form the foundation of Cultural Marxism.

8. **(C):** E.V. Ramaswamy Naicker (Periyar) was a fierce critic of Aryanism, Brahmanism, and Hinduism. He led the Self-Respect Movement in Tamil Nadu and actively opposed the caste system and religious orthodoxy. He advocated for rationalism, social justice, and women's rights.

9. **(B):** The following are not part of a liberal democracy:

   (*a*) **Based on a one-party system:** Liberal democracies operate on multi-party systems to ensure political competition and representation.

   (*e*) **State monopoly on the means of mass communication:** In a liberal democracy, the media is independent, ensuring the free flow of information and preventing state-controlled propaganda.

10. **(D):** Marco Rubio is a Republican senator from Florida and has been proposed as the Secretary of State in a potential Donald Trump Administration II. He is a prominent figure in US politics, known for his foreign policy stance against China and Cuba and advocacy for conservative policies.

11. **(D):** In the 2014 Lok Sabha elections, the Indian National Congress (INC) won 44 seats out of 543. This was the worst performance in INC's history, as it failed to secure the required 10% of seats (55 seats) to claim the Leader of Opposition position in the Lok Sabha. The Bharatiya Janata Party (BJP) secured a landslide victory with 282 seats.

12. **(C):** Chronological order of assassinations:

    (*c*) **S.W.R.D. Bandaranaike (1959):** The Prime Minister of Ceylon (now Sri Lanka) was assassinated by a Buddhist monk due to political and religious conflicts.

    (*a*) **John F. Kennedy (1963):** The 35th President of the United States was assassinated in Dallas, Texas by Lee Harvey Oswald.

    (*b*) **Zia-ur-Rahman (1981):** The President of Bangladesh was assassinated by military officers during a coup.

    (*d*) **Olof Palme (1986):** The Swedish Prime Minister was assassinated while walking home from a cinema in Stockholm.

    (*e*) **Yitzhak Rabin (1995):** The Israeli Prime Minister was assassinated by a Jewish extremist opposing the Oslo Peace Accords.

13. **(C):** Chronological order of UN membership:

    (*d*) **India (1945):** A founding member of the United Nations, joining after its establishment.

(*a*) **Pakistan (1947):** Joined after gaining independence from British India.

(*b*) **Myanmar (1948):** Formerly Burma, it became independent and joined the UN.

(*e*) **Israel (1949):** Became a member after its establishment in 1948.

(*c*) **Sri Lanka (1955):** Formerly Ceylon, it joined the UN later.

14. (A):

(*a*) **Seneca Falls Convention (1848):** The first women's rights convention in the United States, advocating for gender equality.

(*b*) **Nineteenth Amendment (1920):** Granted American women the right to vote, a major victory for the suffrage movement.

(*c*) **National Women's Suffrage Association (1869):** Founded by Susan B. Anthony and Elizabeth Cady Stanton to promote women's voting rights.

(*d*) **Simone de Beauvoir published 'The Second Sex' (1949):** A foundational feminist text analyzing the oppression of women.

(*e*) Greta Thunberg narrating the history of black women in the US is incorrect, making it not a part of the correct answer.

15. (A): Match the treaties with their respective years:

(*a*) **Antarctic Treaty (1959):** Prohibits military activity and mineral mining in Antarctica.

(*b*) **Anti-Ballistic Missile Treaty (1972):** Signed between the USA and USSR to limit the use of missile defense systems.

(*c*) **Outer Space Treaty (1967):** Established that outer space should be free for all countries and not subject to national appropriation.

(*d*) **Limited Test Ban Treaty (1963):** Signed by the USA, USSR, and the UK to prohibit nuclear tests in the atmosphere, outer space, and underwater.

16. (C): Chronological order of events:

(*a*) **Fidel Castro assumed power in Cuba (1959):** Overthrew Fulgencio Batista and established a communist government.

(*b*) **John F. Kennedy became 35th US President (1961):** Elected as the youngest President at age 43.

(*c*) **Pope John XXIII implored the Kremlin not to start a nuclear war (1962):** Happened during the Cuban Missile Crisis.

(*d*) **An American U-2 was shot down over Cuba (1962):** This intensified tensions during the Cuban Missile Crisis.

(*e*) **Soviet leader Khrushchev announced the removal of Soviet missiles from Cuba (1962):** The crisis ended with the withdrawal of missiles, avoiding nuclear war.

17. (C): Chronological order of UN initiatives:

(*d*) **University for Peace, Costa Rica (1980):** Established to promote peace and security worldwide.

(*c*) **Global Polio Eradication Initiative (1988):** Launched to eliminate polio globally.

(*b*) **Universal Declaration on Human Genome and Human Rights (1997):** Adopted to regulate genetic research and prevent unethical practices.

(*a*) **UN Roll Back Malaria Initiative (1998):** Launched to combat malaria through global cooperation.

(*e*) **UN Forum on Forests (2000):** Established to promote sustainable forest management.

18. (C): The Indian Councils Act, 1909 (Morley-Minto Reforms) provided separate representation to Muslims in British India. It introduced:

- **Separate electorates for Muslims**, allowing them to vote for Muslim representatives.
- **Increased Indian participation** in legislative councils.
- The Act was intended to **divide Indian unity** by creating communal divisions.

19. (C): The Self-Respect Movement, led by E.V. Ramasamy (Periyar), aimed to eradicate caste discrimination and Brahmin dominance. It focused on:

- **Dropping caste names** to promote equality.
- **Reinterpreting Hindu mythology** to challenge Brahminical supremacy.
- **Self-respect marriages**, which were conducted without Brahmin priests.

Periyar opposed the Indian National Congress, viewing it as a Brahmin-dominated party, and did not support its nationalist movement.

20. (C):

(*a*) **First nuclear test by the USA (1945):** Correct, the Trinity test was conducted in New Mexico.

(*b*) **First nuclear test by the USSR (1949):** Correct, named RDS-1 or Joe-1.

(*c*) **First nuclear test by France (1965):** Incorrect (Correct year: 1960)

- France's first nuclear test, "Gerboise Bleue", was conducted in the Algerian Sahara in 1960.

(*d*) **First nuclear test by China (1974):** Incorrect (Correct year: 1964)

- China's first nuclear test, "596", was conducted in Lop Nur in 1964.

(*e*) **First nuclear test by India (1974):** Correct, known as Smiling Buddha, conducted at Pokhran.

21. (A):

(*a*) **It offers a practicable form of democracy for large countries:** Representative democracy is suitable for large countries where direct democracy is impractical due to vast populations and geographic size.

(*b*) **It establishes a link between the government and the governed:** Elected representatives serve as a bridge between the people and the government, making governance more accessible.

(*c*) **It obliterates the distinction between the government and the people (Incorrect):** Representative democracy does not eliminate this distinction, as elected officials make decisions on behalf of the people.

(*d*) **It advocates a classless society (Incorrect):** Representative democracy does not inherently aim for a classless society; it allows for political participation but does not necessarily remove social or economic classes.

(*e*) **Its most common modern manifestation is the use of referendum (Incorrect):** Referendums are more associated with direct democracy, not representative democracy.

22. (C): Prismatic societies, a concept developed by Fred Riggs, describe societies transitioning from traditional to modern structures. Their characteristics include:

- **Selectivism:** Decision-making based on personal preferences rather than universal rules.
- **Attainment:** Social status is often achieved rather than ascribed.
- **Poly-functionalism:** Institutions perform multiple overlapping functions.
- **Universalism (Incorrect):** Prismatic societies do not follow universalistic norms; instead, they rely on particularism and favouritism.

23. (C):

(*a*) **Separation of power:** The Presidential system strictly separates the executive, legislative, and judicial powers.

(*b*) **Checks and balances:** Each branch has mechanisms to limit the powers of the others, ensuring no single branch dominates.

(*c*) **Collective responsibility (Incorrect):** This is a feature of parliamentary systems, where the cabinet is collectively responsible to the legislature.

(*d*) **A nominal head (Incorrect):** In a presidential system, the President is the real executive head, not just a ceremonial figure.

(*e*) **Fusion of legislature and executive (Incorrect):** Presidential systems maintain a strict division between the two.

24. (C): South Africa's first non-racial elections were held in April 1994, marking the official end of apartheid. Nelson Mandela was elected as the first black President of South Africa, and the African National Congress (ANC) won a majority.

25. (A): Carolyn Merchant wrote "The Death of Nature: Women, Ecology, and the Scientific Revolution" (1980), which explores how the Scientific Revolution contributed to environmental degradation and the subjugation of women by portraying nature as a passive entity to be controlled.

26. (A): Ngozi Okonjo-Iweala became the first woman and first African Director-General of the World Trade Organization (WTO) in March 2021. She is a Nigerian economist and previously served as Finance Minister of Nigeria.

27. (D):

(*a*) **From 1948 to 1994, the GATT provided rules for much of world trade (Correct):** The General Agreement on Tariffs and Trade (GATT) governed international trade before the WTO.

(*b*) **GATT was a provisional agreement and organization (Correct):** It was an interim measure, not a permanent institution.

(*c*) **The WTO was created on 1 January 1995 (Correct):** The World Trade Organization (WTO) officially replaced GATT in 1995.

(*d*) **The first ministerial conference of WTO was held in 2009 (Incorrect):** The first WTO ministerial conference was held in Singapore (1996).

(*e*) **The WTO's 28th Ministerial Conference was held in Delhi in 2024 (Incorrect):** No such event has taken place in Delhi in 2024.

28. (C):

(*a*) **It is an Integrated Conservation Mission for rejuvenation of River Ganga (Correct):** Namami Gange was launched to restore the Ganga River ecosystem.

(*b*) **The programme was launched in 2006 (Incorrect):** It was launched in 2014 by the Government of India.

(*c*) **This programme has a budget outlay of ₹ 1000 crore (Incorrect):** The actual **budget was ₹ 20,000 crore.**

(*d*) **It has provisions for Sewerage Treatment Infrastructure (Correct):** Includes the construction of Sewage Treatment Plants (STPs).

(*e*) **It has provisions for industrial effluent monitoring (Correct):** The program monitors and regulates industrial waste discharge into the Ganga.

29. (D):

(*a*) **Essays on the Gita (Correct):** A philosophical interpretation of the Bhagavad Gita by Sri Aurobindo.

(*b*) **The Ideal of the Karmayogi (Correct):** Discusses the concept of Karma Yoga.

(*c*) **A System of National Education (Correct):** Aurobindo's ideas on education reform.

(*d*) **The Discovery of India (Incorrect):** This book was written by Jawaharlal Nehru, not Aurobindo.

30. (B): Karl Marx viewed bureaucracy as an instrument of class exploitation.

He argued that:

- Bureaucracy serves the interests of the ruling class.
- It acts as a mechanism for maintaining state power over the working class.
- Bureaucrats function as agents of the capitalist system, enforcing policies that favour the elite.

31. (D): The Allahabad High Court was established in 1866 under the Indian High Courts Act of 1861. It was originally called the High Court of Judicature for the North-Western Provinces and later renamed Allahabad High Court. It is one of the oldest high courts in India.

32. (D):

(*d*) **Woodrow Wilson (Incorrect for Realist School):** He was a liberal idealist, promoting international cooperation and organizations like the League of Nations.

(*e*) **Immanuel Kant (Incorrect for Realist School):** Kant was a liberal thinker who supported democratic peace theory and cooperation between nations.

(*a*) **Stephen Walt (Realist):** A defensive realist, known for his theory of balance of threat in international relations.

(*b*) **John Mearsheimer (Realist):** A structural realist (offensive realism), arguing that states seek power to ensure security.

(*c*) **Kenneth Waltz (Realist):** Developed neorealism (structural realism), emphasizing the anarchic nature of international relations.

33. (B): Article 29 of the Indian Constitution guarantees the protection of language, script, or culture of minorities. It ensures that any minority group, based on language or culture, has the right to conserve its heritage.

- **Article 21:** Right to life and personal liberty.

- **Article 27:** Prohibits the imposition of taxes for promoting any particular religion.
- **Article 23:** Prohibits human trafficking and forced labour.

34. (A):

(*a*) **Thomas Hobbes – Leviathan (IV):** A foundational work in political philosophy, advocating for a strong central authority.

(*b*) **Immanuel Kant – Critique of Pure Reason (I):** Discusses metaphysics, epistemology, and human understanding.

(*c*) **Michel Foucault – The Order of Things (II):** Explores the history of human sciences and discourse analysis.

(*d*) **Naomi Klein – On Fire (III):** A collection of essays on climate change and social justice.

35. (B): Chronological order of events:

(*a*) **Hammurabi established the legal code (c.1754 BCE):** One of the earliest written legal codes, defining justice in ancient Mesopotamia.

(*b*) **Model Parliament of Edward I convened (1295):** The first English Parliament with representation of commoners.

(*c*) **Treaty of Westphalia (1648):** Established the modern concept of state sovereignty.

(*e*) **New Zealand granted women the right to vote (1893):** The first country to grant universal suffrage.

(*d*) **Universal Declaration of Human Rights (1948):** A landmark UN resolution ensuring global human rights.

36. (A):

(*a*) **Fred Riggs – The Ecology of Public Administration (II):** Analyzes bureaucratic structures in developing nations.

(*b*) **Yehezkel Dror – Public Policy Making Re-examined (IV):** Focuses on decision-making and governance.

(*c*) **Peter Drucker – The Practice of Management (I):** A key text in business management and administration.

(*d*) **Karl Marx – The Eighteenth Brumaire of Louis Bonaparte (III):** Examines class struggle and political power.

37. (D):

(*a*) **East Asian Summit (2005):** A regional summit involving ASEAN and major powers.

(*b*) **Shanghai Cooperation Organization (2001):** A Eurasian political, economic, and security alliance.

(*c*) **Nordic Council (1952):** A regional organization for Nordic cooperation.

(*d*) **ASEAN Regional Forum (1994):** A security dialogue forum for the Asia-Pacific region.

(*e*) **SAARC (Incorrect - Founded in 1985, not 1987).**

38. (C): The "Gangplank" concept, introduced by Henri Fayol, allows direct communication between employees at different hierarchical levels to avoid delays and improve efficiency.

39. (B):

(*a*) **Max Weber – Economy and Society (I):** A key work in sociology and bureaucracy theory.

(*b*) **Isaiah Berlin – Four Essays on Liberty (IV):** Discusses freedom, pluralism, and liberal thought.

(*c*) **Rosa Luxemburg – Social Reform or Revolution (II):** Advocates revolution over gradual social change.

(*d*) **Milton Friedman – Capitalism and Freedom (III):** Promotes free-market policies and economic liberalism.

40. (C): Chronological order of environmental events:

(c) Greenpeace founded (1971): An international organization focused on environmental activism.

(*d*) **Bhopal disaster (1984):** A chemical gas leak in India, causing thousands of deaths.

(*e*) **Chernobyl nuclear disaster (1986):** The worst nuclear accident in history, affecting Ukraine and Europe.

(*b*) **Rio Declaration and Agenda 21 (1992):** Adopted at the Earth Summit, outlining sustainable development goals.

(*a*) **Minamata Convention on Mercury (2013):** A global treaty addressing mercury pollution.

41. (C): As per the Table of Precedence in India, the correct order from higher to lower position is:

(*d*) **Vice Chairperson, NITI Aayog:** Holds a high-ranking position in the planning body of India, functioning under the Prime Minister.

(*e*) **Holders of Bharat Ratna decoration:** Awardees of the highest civilian honour in India enjoy a high ceremonial rank.

(*a*) **Chief Election Commissioner:** Heads the Election Commission of India, ensuring free and fair elections.

(*b*) **Deputy Chairman, Rajya Sabha:** Presides over Rajya Sabha in the absence of the Chairman (Vice President of India).

(*c*) **Attorney General of India:** The highest law officer of the country but ranked lower than constitutional functionaries.

42. (A):

(*a*) **The term Ecology was first coined by Ernst Haeckel:** Haeckel introduced the term "Ökologie" in 1866 to describe relationships between organisms and their environment.

(*b*) **It studies the relationship between living organisms and their environment:** Ecology examines interactions between biotic and abiotic components.

(*e*) **Rachel Carson was an environmental conservationist:** Her book "Silent Spring" (1962) raised awareness about pesticide dangers, sparking the modern environmental movement.

(*c*) **It is a market-centric approach (Incorrect):** Ecologism rejects market-driven environmental policies, advocating sustainability.

(*d*) **It believes humans are masters of nature (Incorrect):** Ecologism views humans as part of nature, not its rulers.

43. (A):

(*a*) **Pendleton Act (IV):** Established the U.S. Civil Service Commission in 1883, replacing the spoils system with merit-based appointments.

(*b*) **First Hoover Commission (I):** Recommended reorganization of the executive branch to improve efficiency under U.S. President Truman (1947).

(*c*) **Hawthorne Studies (II):** Conducted in the 1920s-30s, explored work environment and productivity, leading to human relations theories.

(*d*) **U.S. Senate Intelligence Committee Report (III):** Investigated Russian interference in the 2016 U.S. elections.

44. (C)

45. (B): The 52nd Constitutional Amendment Act (1985) introduced the Anti-Defection Law, which:

- Disqualified MPs and MLAs switching parties after elections.
- Prevented defections due to monetary/political gains.
- Allowed disqualification by the Speaker (Lok Sabha) or Chairman (Rajya Sabha).

46. (D):

(*a*) **Tradition:** Conservatism preserves cultural values, customs, and religious institutions.

(*b*) **Social duty:** It emphasizes responsibility over individual rights, supporting a structured society.

(*c*) **Change in order to conserve:** Unlike radicalism, conservatism advocates gradual reform to maintain stability.

(*d*) **Revolution (Incorrect):** Conservatism opposes revolutionary change, favoring evolutionary progress.

(*e*) **Gender equality (Incorrect):** While modern conservatives may support equality, traditional conservatism often maintains gender roles.

47. (A):

(*a*) **First Visit by an Indian PM to China (III) – 1954:** Jawaharlal Nehru became the first Indian Prime Minister to visit China.

(*b*) **Soviet-Indian Treaty of Peace, Friendship and Cooperation (II) – 1971:** Signed between India and the USSR, ensuring Soviet support during the Bangladesh Liberation War.

(*c*) **Indian Nuclear Test-2 (IV) – 1998:** Also known as Pokhran-II, conducted under Atal Bihari Vajpayee.

(*d*) **26/11 Mumbai Terror Attack (I) – 2008:** Coordinated attacks by Pakistani-based militants, targeting Taj Hotel, CST station, and Nariman House.

48. **(B):** Vladimir Ilyich Lenin, the leader of the Bolshevik Revolution (1917) and founder of the Soviet Union (USSR), died in 1924 due to a stroke. His successor, Joseph Stalin, consolidated power after his death.

49. **(C):** Otto Kirchheimer, a German political scientist, coined the term "Catch-All Party" to describe:
- Broad-based political parties that appeal to diverse voter bases.
- Reducing ideological rigidity to attract more support.
- **Examples:** Congress (India), Democrats (USA), and CDU (Germany).

50. **(A):**

(*a*) **Radical feminists call for overturning of gender oppression:** Radical feminism challenges patriarchal structures, advocating overthrowing gender roles.

(*b*) **According to Marxism, ideology legitimizes the rule of the dominant class:** Karl Marx viewed ideology as a tool of the ruling class to maintain control over proletariat (working class).

(*c*) **According to Fascism, people should follow the dictates of their leader:** Fascism promotes absolute loyalty to the leader (e.g., Hitler, Mussolini).

(*d*) **J.S. Mill opposed the rights for women (Incorrect):** John Stuart Mill was an advocate for women's rights, supporting gender equality and suffrage.

(*e*) **To maintain the existing order, Karl Marx opposed any idea of revolution (Incorrect):** Marx actively promoted revolution to overthrow capitalism.

51. **(A):** Chronological order of terrorist attacks:

(*e*) **Air India Flight-182 Bombing (1985):** A terrorist bombing by Khalistani militants on an Air India flight travelling from Canada to India, killing 329 people.

(*c*) **Tokyo Subway Sarin Attack (1995):** Carried out by Aum Shinrikyo, a Japanese cult, releasing sarin gas in Tokyo subways, killing 13 and injuring thousands.

(*b*) **Indian Parliament Attack (2001):** Conducted by Pakistan-based terrorist groups Lashkar-e-Taiba and Jaish-e-Mohammed, attempting to storm the Indian Parliament.

(*a*) **Moscow Theater Hostage Crisis (2002):** Chechen rebels took 850 hostages at a theater in Moscow, leading to a Russian special forces raid that resulted in many casualties.

(*d*) **Camp Speicher Massacre (2014):** Conducted by ISIS in Iraq, killing 1,500 unarmed military cadets in the worst single massacre in the Iraq conflict.

52. **(C):**

(*a*) **Pluralism – James Madison (IV):** Madison's Federalist Papers supported pluralism, emphasizing multiple interest groups preventing government tyranny.

(*b*) **Utilitarianism – Jeremy Bentham (III):** A philosophy advocating the greatest happiness for the greatest number.

(*c*) **Integral Humanism – Deen Dayal Upadhyay (I):** Indian political philosophy integrating spiritual and economic well-being.

(*d*) **Positivism – Auguste Comte (II):** Comte founded positivism, stressing empirical knowledge and scientific approaches to society.

53. **(D):**

(*a*) **Abul Ahsan – January 16, 1987 to October 15, 1989 (III):** First SAARC Secretary-General from Bangladesh.

(*b*) **Yadav Kant Silwal – January 1, 1994 to December 31, 1995 (I):** A diplomat from Nepal serving SAARC.

(*c*) **Nihal Rodrigo – January 1, 1999 to January 10, 2002 (II):** From Sri Lanka, strengthening SAARC's role.

(*d*) **Sheel Kant Sharma – March 1, 2008 to February 2011 (IV):** Indian diplomat, promoting SAARC cooperation.

54. (A): "The Human Condition" (1958) by Hannah Arendt explores the political, philosophical, and social dimensions of human activity, distinguishing between labor, work, and action.

55. (B):

(*a*) **India is a Union of States:** The Indian Constitution describes India as a union, not a federation, ensuring indivisibility.

(*b*) **The Constitution is the supreme organic law of the land:** It overrides all laws and governs federal relations.

(*c*) **The legislative powers are distributed between the center and states:** Under Seventh Schedule, powers are divided into Union, State, and Concurrent Lists.

(*d*) **The residuary powers are reserved to the states (Incorrect):** In India, residuary powers rest with the center.

(*e*) **All states have equal representation in Rajya Sabha (Incorrect):** Representation varies based on state population.

56. (A): The Constructive Programme (1922) by Mahatma Gandhi focused on self-reliance, social reform, and economic independence through Khadi, village industries, and Harijan welfare.

57. (B): Grover Cleveland is the only U.S. President before Trump to serve non-consecutive terms:

- 22nd President (1885-1889)
- 24th President (1893-1897)

58. (D):

(*a*) **Dumbarton Oaks Conference (1944) – III:** Planned the formation of the United Nations (UN).

(*b*) **UN Peacekeeping Mission to Suez Canal (1956) – II:** First UN peacekeeping mission deployed to resolve the Suez Crisis.

(*c*) **Establishment of UN Development Programme (1965) – IV:** Created to promote global development.

(*d*) **Establishment of UN Environment Programme (1972) – I:** Set up after the Stockholm Conference to address environmental challenges.

59. (C): Descending order of Rajya Sabha seats allocation:

(*c*) Tamil Nadu (18 seats)

(*e*) Bihar (16 seats)

(*a*) Karnataka (12 seats)

(*d*) Kerala (9 seats)

(*b*) Assam (7 seats)

60. (D):

(*a*) **Kosovo War (1999) – IV:** NATO intervened in Serbia and Kosovo, leading to Kosovo's independence movement.

(*b*) **Libyan Civil War (2011) – I:** Resulted in the fall of Gaddafi's regime, leading to prolonged instability.

(*c*) **US-led invasion of Afghanistan (2001) – II:** Following 9/11 attacks, the U.S. launched the War on Terror.

(*d*) **Taliban I seized power in Afghanistan (1996) – III:** The Taliban captured Kabul, enforcing strict Sharia rule.

61. (A): M.C. Rajah, a social reformer from Madras, was the first elected president of the All India Depressed Classes Association. This association was established to protect the rights of Dalits and oppressed communities in colonial India. Rajah worked towards Dalit representation in politics and was a significant leader before the rise of Dr. B.R. Ambedkar.

62. (B):

(*b*) **Patriarchy – The power relationship between men and women:** Patriarchy describes a social system where men hold primary power, especially in politics, family, and economy.

(*c*) **Holism – The whole is more important than its part:** Holism asserts that a system must be viewed as a whole rather than as individual components.

(*e*) **Deep Ecology – Rejection of anthropocentrism:** Deep Ecology argues for an ecocentric approach, rejecting human-centered views of nature.

(*a*) **Sustainable Development (Incorrect):** Sustainable development means meeting present needs without compromising future generations, not just focusing on the present.

(*d*) **Fascism (Incorrect):** Fascism is authoritarian and suppresses freedom of expression.

63. **(D):**

(*a*) **Dr. S. Jaishankar – The India Way (III):** A book on India's foreign policy, written by India's External Affairs Minister.

(*b*) **Herbert Simon – Administrative Behaviour (IV):** A foundational work in decision-making theory and public administration.

(*c*) **Abraham Maslow – A Theory of Human Motivation (I):** Introduced Maslow's hierarchy of needs, explaining human motivation.

(*d*) **Chris Argyris – On Organizational Learning (II):** Focuses on organizational behaviour and learning processes.

64. **(A):**

(*a*) **V.D. Savarkar – 1857 as India's First War of Independence:** His book "The First War of Indian Independence" (1909) portrayed the 1857 Revolt as a nationalist uprising.

(*b*) **Jayaprakash Narayan – Sampoorna Kranti:** He called for Total Revolution in the 1970s against Indira Gandhi's rule, advocating political and social transformation.

(*c*) **B.R. Ambedkar – Protagonist of social justice:** Ambedkar led movements for Dalit rights, education, and constitutional reforms.

(*d*) **Bal Gangadhar Tilak was a moderate leader (Incorrect):** He was a hardcore nationalist, advocating Swaraj and mass protests.

(*e*) **Rabindranath Tagore viewed hyper-nationalism as a threat to true freedom (Incorrect):** He criticized excessive nationalism as restrictive.

65. **(D):**

(*b*) **Hegel's idealism – Dialectical Idealism:** He proposed that history progresses through thesis, antithesis, and synthesis.

(*c*) **Hegel's dialectical process:** His philosophy emphasized historical progress through contradictions.

(*d*) **Hegel – Author of Phenomenology of Spirit:** A key book in German idealism, exploring self-consciousness and reason.

(*e*) **Karl Marx's influence from Hegel:** Marx adopted Hegel's dialectics but applied it to class struggle, creating dialectical materialism.

(*a*) **Hegel popularized climate change mitigation (Incorrect):** Hegel's work focused on history, logic, and idealism, not environmental issues.

66. **(C):** Giorgia Meloni, the Prime Minister of Italy, is the leader of Brothers of Italy (Fratelli d'Italia), a right-wing nationalist party promoting sovereignty, conservative values, and strict immigration policies.

67. **(B):**

(*b*) **Sri Aurobindo – Spiritual Nationalism:** Aurobindo combined nationalism with spiritual revival, advocating India's independence as a divine mission.

(*c*) **Veer Savarkar – An Echo from Andamans:** A collection of Savarkar's nationalist writings from his imprisonment in Andaman jail.

(*d*) **Swami Vivekananda – Preface to Raja-Yoga:** His book discusses spiritual self-discipline and Vedantic philosophy.

(*a*) **Kautilya – Dharamshastra (Incorrect):** Kautilya (Chanakya) wrote Arthashastra, a treatise on politics, economy, and warfare.

(*e*) **Rabindranath Tagore – Tarana-e-Hind (Incorrect):** This patriotic song was written by Muhammad Iqbal, not Tagore.

68. **(D):** "One-Dimensional Man" (1964) by Herbert Marcuse critiques modern capitalist society and its role in technological domination, consumer culture, and suppressing critical thought.

69. **(C):** The Minnowbrook Conference-I (1968) was a major event in Public Administration, organized by Dwight Waldo to redefine New Public Administration (NPA) by emphasizing: • Equity and social justice. • Public participation. • Ethical governance.

70. **(D):**

(*d*) **Xenophobia – Demand for self-determination (Incorrect):** Xenophobia means fear or hatred of foreigners, not self-determination.

(*e*) **Universalism – Insularity and exclusivity (Incorrect):** Universalism promotes inclusivity and shared global values, opposite to insularity.

(*a*) **Economic Nationalism – Protectionism (Correct):** Advocates trade barriers, tariffs, and self-reliance to strengthen the domestic economy.

(*b*) **Nativism – Favoring native-born citizens (Correct):** Prioritizes the rights of native inhabitants over immigrants.

(*c*) **Colonialism – Control over foreign territories (Correct):** Involves political and economic domination over colonies.

71. (A): Chester Barnard wrote *The Functions of the Executive* (1938), a foundational work in **organizational theory**. He emphasized:

- Authority and communication in organizations
- The importance of informal organizations in decision-making
- The concept of the "zone of indifference", where subordinates accept authority

72. (A): Max Weber wrote *The Sociology of Religion*, which analyzed:

- The role of religion in shaping economic and social structures
- His famous theory of the "Protestant Ethic and the Spirit of Capitalism"
- The concept of charismatic, traditional, and rational-legal authority

73. (B):

(*a*) **Dhaka Summit – 10-11 April 1993 (I):** Focused on regional trade and economic cooperation.

(*b*) **New Delhi Summit – 2-4 May 1995 (II):** Addressed poverty alleviation and infrastructure.

(*c*) **Colombo Summit – 29-31 July 1998 (IV):** Promoted South Asian Free Trade Area (SAFTA).

(*d*) **Islamabad Summit – 2-6 January 2004 (III):** Focused on regional security and counterterrorism.

74. (D): David Easton's Input-Output Model explains how political systems function. The key variables are:

- **Input Variables:** Demands and support from society
- **Output Variables:** Decisions and policies
- **Feedback Mechanism:** Evaluates effectiveness

75. (A): Chronological order of Directors-General of GATT/WTO:

(*a*) **Eric Wyndham White (1948-1968):** The first Director-General of GATT.

(*b*) **Olivier Long (1968-1980):** Oversaw trade negotiations under GATT.

(*c*) **Arthur Dunkel (1980-1993):** Led the Uruguay Round, which led to WTO's creation.

(*d*) **Peter Sutherland (1993-1995):** The first Director-General of WTO.

(*e*) **Ngozi Okonjo-Iweala (2021–present):** First African and female WTO leader.

76. (B): Communism aims to abolish class structures and private property.

(*a*) **Common Ownership:** Abolishing private property in favor of state or collective ownership.

(*b*) **Absolute Equality:** Aims for equal distribution of wealth.

(*c*) **Classless Society:** Seeks to eliminate class struggles.

(*d*) **Vanguard Party:** A communist party leading the revolution (Lenin's concept).

(*e*) **Dictatorship of the Priestly class (Incorrect):** Communism rejects religious authority in governance.

77. (C): Chronological order of state formation in India:

(*a*) **Manipur (1972):** Became a full-fledged state along with Meghalaya and Tripura.

(*b*) **Sikkim (1975):** Merged into India via referendum.

(*e*) **Arunachal Pradesh (1987):** Upgraded from a Union Territory.

(*d*) **Jharkhand (2000):** Created from Bihar.

(*c*) **Telangana (2014):** The newest state, separated from Andhra Pradesh.

78. (A): John Rawls wrote *The Law of Peoples* (1999), expanding his theory of justice to international relations. He discussed:

- Justice among nations

- Human rights as universal values
- The concept of well-ordered societies

79. (B): Chronological order of Panchayati Raj Committees:

(*a*) **Balwant Rai Mehta Committee (1957):** Recommended a three-tier Panchayati Raj system.

(*c*) **Ashok Mehta Committee (1978):** Proposed a two-tier Panchayati Raj system and constitutional recognition.

(*b*) **GVK Rao Committee (1985):** Highlighted bureaucratic dominance over local governance.

(*d*) **LM Singhvi Committee (1986):** Suggested constitutional status for Panchayati Raj institutions.

(*e*) **PK Thungan Committee (1989):** Led to the 73rd Constitutional Amendment (1992).

80. (A): Ram Manohar Lohia's ***Wheel of History*** (1955) presents:

- A Marxist critique of history
- Analyzes cyclical patterns in history
- Advocates for socialist and egalitarian values

81. (B): Kate Millett wrote *Sexual Politics* (1970), a groundbreaking book in feminist literary criticism and political theory. It examined:

- The role of patriarchy in literature and society
- How male authors depict women as subordinate figures
- Radical feminism, advocating for women's liberation from male domination.

82. (B):

(*a*) **Boxer Rebellion in China (1900-1901) – IV:** A nationalist uprising against foreign influence and Christian missionaries.

(*b*) **Mexican Revolution (1910-1920) – I:** A major social and political upheaval that led to land reforms and a new constitution.

(*c*) **Japan invaded Manchuria (1931) – II:** The Japanese military occupation of Manchuria, marking the start of Japan's aggression in East Asia.

(*d*) **Germany reoccupied the Rhineland (1936) – III:** Hitler violated the Treaty of Versailles by moving German troops into the Rhineland, strengthening Nazi power.

83. (C): Dadabhai Naoroji, known as the "Grand Old Man of India," wrote this book in 1901, explaining:

- The Drain Theory, showing how British rule impoverished India
- The economic exploitation of India through unfair trade policies
- The need for self-governance to end economic suffering

84. (D): Henry David Thoreau wrote *Civil Disobedience* (1849) as a protest against unjust laws and government policies. His work influenced:

- Mahatma Gandhi's Satyagraha
- Martin Luther King Jr.'s nonviolent resistance
- The philosophy of peaceful protest against oppression

85. (C): C.B. Macpherson coined the term "Possessive Individualism" in his book *The Political Theory of Possessive Individualism* (1962). It describes:

- Capitalist ideology, where individuals are seen as self-interested property owners
- The idea that freedom means freedom from interference in economic activities
- A critique of liberal political thought

86. (C): Article 16 of the Indian Constitution guarantees equality of opportunity in employment by:

- Prohibiting discrimination in public employment based on religion, race, caste, sex, or place of birth
- Allowing reservation policies for underprivileged groups
- Ensuring merit-based employment in government services

87. (B): The 19th National Congress of the Communist Party of China (CCP) was held in Beijing in 2017. Key highlights:

- Xi Jinping consolidated power, removing term limits for the presidency
- The introduction of "Xi Jinping Thought on Socialism with Chinese Characteristics for a New Era"
- A focus on economic and military expansion

88. (C):

(*a*) **Asian Drama – Gunnar Myrdal (I):** A study on poverty and development in South Asia, critiquing economic policies.

(*b*) **The Indian Constitution: Cornerstone of a Nation – Granville Austin (IV):** A detailed analysis of the making of the Indian Constitution.

(*c*) **The State and Poverty in India – Atul Kohli (III):** Examines how state policies shape poverty and social inequality.

(*d*) **The Indian Political System – Norman D. Palmer (II):** A study of India's political framework and governance.

89. (B):

(*a*) **Google launched (1998) – I:** Founded by Larry Page and Sergey Brin.

(*b*) **Facebook launched (2004) – II:** Created by Mark Zuckerberg as a social networking platform.

(*c*) **Microsoft founded (1975) – III:** Established by Bill Gates and Paul Allen, revolutionizing software.

(*d*) **Apple Computers founded (1976) – IV:** Founded by Steve Jobs, Steve Wozniak, and Ronald Wayne.

90. (D): The Concurrent List in the Indian Constitution was borrowed from the Australian Constitution. It includes subjects where both the central and state governments can legislate, such as:

- Education,
- Marriage and divorce,
- Bankruptcy,
- Criminal law

If there is a conflict, the central law prevails (Article 254).

91. (B): In Germany, Bundesländer refers to the 16 federal states (provincial governments). These states have their own constitutions, parliaments, and administrative systems, operating under Germany's federal structure. Each Bundesland has authority over areas such as education, policing, and cultural affairs, while the federal government handles national and international matters.

92. (A): In State of Uttar Pradesh vs. Raj Narain (1975), the Supreme Court of India ruled that the Right to Information is implied within the Right to Freedom of Speech and Expression (Article 19(1)(a)).

This case was significant in establishing transparency in government functioning, laying the foundation for the Right to Information Act, 2005.

93. (D): Sweden was the earliest country to adopt provisions related to press freedom with its Freedom of the Press Act (1766).

This law:

- Guaranteed public access to official documents
- Limited government censorship
- Established the foundation for transparency and open governance

94. (C): France has freedom of information and accountability of public servants as a constitutional right.

French laws emphasize:

- Government transparency
- Access to public records
- Accountability of public officials

This framework aligns with democratic principles, ensuring that citizens can scrutinize government actions.

95. (B): The Right to Information (RTI) Act, 2005 was enacted in India to:

- Ensure transparency and accountability in public administration
- Provide citizens with access to government records
- Strengthen democratic governance

This Act replaced the Freedom of Information Act, 2002, making public authorities more answerable to citizens.

96. (C): In the 1952 Bihar legislative elections, the Jharkhand Party emerged as the main opposition party against the Congress. This party:

- Advocated for a separate Jharkhand state
- Represented tribal interests in Bihar
- Played a significant role in regional politics.

97. (D): The Janta Party (formed in 1950) had its political influence mainly in South Bihar. Its objectives included:

- Opposing Congress dominance
- Promoting traditional and regional interests
- Mobilizing landowners and conservative forces

98. (A): The Janta Party was founded in 1950 by Raja Kamakhya Narayan Singh to:

- Provide a right-wing alternative to the Congress
- Challenge land reforms and socialist policies
- Strengthen conservative political elements in Bihar

Its impact was primarily limited to regional politics.

99. (B): Swami Sahajanand Saraswati was the leader of Bihar Pradesh Kisan Sabha (BPKS) in 1935.

His contributions include:

- Advocating for peasant rights against Zamindars
- Leading agrarian movements for land reforms
- Founding the All India Kisan Sabha (AIKS) in 1936 to unite farmers at the national level

100. (C): Rajni Kothari, a political scientist, conceptualized the "Congress System" to describe:

- The one-party dominance of the Indian National Congress from 1952 to 1967.
- How Congress functioned as a broad coalition, accommodating diverse political groups.
- The gradual shift towards multi-party politics after 1967.

His analysis remains crucial in understanding India's post-independence political landscape.

Previous Years' Paper

National Testing Agency (NTA)

UGC-NET Junior Research Fellowship & Assistant Professor Eligibility Exam

Political Science, September-2024

(Exam held on 04-09-2024)

1. Who was the President of the Parliament of the World's Religions at Chicago in which Swami Vivekananda delivered his famous address?

A. Woodrow Wilson
B. Paul Deusen
C. John Henry' Barrows
D. Leo Tolstoy

2. Under which Prime-Minister, 73rd and 74th Constitution Amendment Act was passed?

A. V.P. Singh
B. Morarji Desai
C. Atal Bihari Vajpayee
D. P.V. Narasimha Rao

3. Find out the correct statements from the following:

(*a*) NITI Aayog like Planning Commission was also created by an executive resolution of the Government of India.

(*b*) The Consumer Protection Act, 2023 has repealed and replaced the earlier Consumer Protection Act, 1986.

(*c*) The earliest democratic institution in the world for the redressal of citizen's grievance is the Russian institution of Ombudsman.

(*d*) The First Administrative Reforms Commission (ARC) of India recommended the setting up of Lokpal and Loakyukta.

(*e*) The First ARC of India was headed by Morarji Desai.

Choose the ***correct*** answer from the options given below:

A. (*a*), (*b*), (*c*), (*e*) only
B. (*a*), (*c*), (*d*), (*e*) only
C. (*a*), (*d*), (*e*) only
D. (*b*), (*c*), (*d*), (*e*) only

4. Identify the correct statements:

(*a*) Eighth SAARC Summit held at New Delhi in 1995.

(*b*) 1989 was designated as SAARC year of Combating Drug Abuse and Drug Trafficking.

(*c*) There was an assassination attempt on US President Barack Obama while he was in office.

(*d*) Bilawal Bhutto Zardari became Prime Minister of Pakistan in March, 2024.

(*e*) The Agreement on SAARC Preferential Trading Arrangement was signed on 11 April, 1993.

Choose the ***correct*** answer from the options given below:

A. (*a*), (*b*), (*c*) only
B. (*b*), (*c*), (*d*) only
C. (*c*) and (*d*) only
D. (*a*), (*b*) and (*e*) only

5. Consider the Article 15 of Constitution of India:

The State shall not discriminate against any citizen on grounds only of:

(*a*) Religion
(*b*) Race
(*c*) Caste
(*d*) Sex
(*e*) Place of birth

Choose the ***correct*** answer from the options given below:

A. (*b*), (*c*) only
B. (*a*), (*c*), (*d*) only
C. (*b*), (*d*) only
D. (*a*), (*b*), (*c*), (*d*), (*e*)

6. Arrange the following Indian Constitutional Amendments in the chronological order:

(*a*) Amendment in the Preamble and addition of 'unity and integrity of the nation'.
(*b*) Maithili added as a language in the 8th Schedule of the Indian Constitution.
(*c*) Konkani added as a language in the 8th Schedule of the Indian Constitution.
(*d*) The Co-operative Societies inserted as Article 243 ZH.
(*e*) Women Reservation Act.

Choose the ***correct*** answer from the options given below:

A. (*a*), (*b*), (*c*), (*d*), (*e*)
B. (*b*), (*c*), (*a*), (*e*), (*d*)
C. (*c*), (*d*), (*e*), (*b*), (*a*)
D. (*a*), (*c*), (*b*), (*d*), (*e*)

7. Who was the Speaker of the Lok Sabha during Janata Party regime?

A. Baliram Bhagat
B. K.D. Hegde
C. Bal ram Jakhar
D. Shivraj Patil

8. Identify the incorrect statements:

(*a*) Jacques Derrida wrote the book 'Specters of Marx'.
(*b*) Deendayal Upadhyay opposed the idea of Integral Humanism.
(*c*) Federalism was borrowed by the framers of Indian Constitution from British Constitution.
(*d*) Asif Ali Zardari is the President of Pakistan.
(*e*) Panchayati Raj system in India provided 45% reservation for women.

Choose the ***correct*** answer from the options given below:

A. (*a*), (*b*), (*c*), (*d*) only
B. (*b*), (*c*), (*d*), (*e*) only
C. (*b*), (*c*), (*e*) only
D. (*a*), (*b*), (*c*), (*d*), (*e*)

9. Who wrote the book "Democracy, Bureaucracy and Hypocrisy"?

A. Fred Riggs
B. Dwight Waldoo
C. Renin Likert
D. Abraham Maslow

10. Identify the correct statements:

(*a*) Chinese Communist Party (CCP) is an example of a cadre based party.
(*b*) Otto Kirchheimer argues for a category of 'catch-all parties'.
(*c*) O. Kirchheimer puts the US Republican and Democratic parties in the category of catch-all parties.
(*d*) Anthony Downs portray politicians as power-seeking creatures who 'are willing' to adopt 'whatever' policies are likely to bring them electoral success.
(*e*) Thomas Jefferson was the principal author of UK Declaration of freedom.

Choose the ***correct*** answer from the options given below:

A. (*a*), (*b*), (*c*), (*e*) only
B. (*b*), (*c*), (*d*), (*e*) only
C. (*a*), (*b*), (*c*), (*d*) only
D. (*a*), (*b*), (*c*), (*d*), (*e*)

11. Choose the correct statements regarding elite theory:

(*a*) Robert Dahl advocated the Concept of polyrchial democracy.

(*b*) John Plamenatz argued that if the will of the people is a myth, then 'will of the minority' also belongs to the same category.

(*c*) Gaetano Mosca advocated the idea of elite theory in his classical work 'The Political Parties'.

(*d*) Robert Michels advocated the idea of 'Iron law of Oligarchy'.

(*e*) C. Right Mills advocated his idea of elite power in his book 'The Managerial Revolution'.

Choose the ***correct*** answer from the options given below:

A. (*a*), (*b*), (*c*) only
B. (*a*), (*b*), (*d*) only
C. (*a*), (*b*), (*c*), (*d*) only
D. (*a*), (*b*), (*c*), (*d*), (*e*)

12. Who proposed the 'Chaukhamba Model' of decentralization?

A. Ram Manohar Lohia
B. Jayaprakash Narayan
C. Jawaharlal Nehru
D. B.R. Ambedkar

13. Who was the first Chief Minister of Tamil Nadu?

A. J. Jayalalitha B. K. Kamraj
C. C.N. Annadurai D. K. Karunanidhi

14. Match the List-I with List-II.

List-I (Regional Organisation)	***List-II (Establishment Year)***
(*a*) North American Free Trade Agreement	I. 1991
(*b*) Asia Pacific Economic Cooperation	II. 1994
(*c*) Mercosur	III. 1993
(*d*) Free Trade Area of Americas	IV. 1989

Choose the ***correct*** answer from the options given below:

	(*a*)	(*b*)	(*c*)	(*d*)
A.	IV	II	III	I
B.	III	IV	I	II
C.	I	II	III	IV
D.	II	I	IV	III

15. Who coined the term 'Deep Ecology'?

A. Arne Naess B. Carolyn Merchant
C. Rachel Carson D. Murray Bookehin

16. Match the List-I with List-II:

List-I (President of India)	***List-II (Tenures)***
(*a*) Dr. Zakir Hussain	I. 25 July 1977 – 25 July 1982
(*b*) Fakhrudin Ali Ahmed	II. 13 May 1967 – 3 May 1969
(*c*) Neelam Sanjiva Reddy	III. 25 July 1987 – 25 July 1992
(*d*) R. Venkataraman	IV. 24 August 1974 – 11 February 1977

Choose the ***correct*** answer from the options given below:

	(*a*)	(*b*)	(*c*)	(*d*)
A.	I	II	III	IV
B.	IV	III	II	I
C.	II	IV	I	III
D.	III	I	IV	II

17. Choose the correct statements regarding political theorists:

(*a*) Mary Wollstonecraft emphasized the equal rights of women.

(*b*) Hannah Arendt examined the nature of both Nazism and Stalinism in 'The Origins of Totalitarianism'.

(*c*) Antonio Gramsei wrote the famous book 'On People's Democratic Dictatorship'.

(*d*) Franz Fanon wrote the famous book 'Black Skin White Masks'.

(*e*) In his famous book. 'Politics among Nations'. Aristotle advocated a system of mixed government.

Choose the ***correct*** answer from the options given below:

A. (*a*), (*b*), (*c*), (*d*), (*e*)
B. (*a*), (*b*), (*c*), (*e*) only
C. (*b*), (*c*), (*d*) only
D. (*a*), (*b*), (*d*) only

18. In which year, Swami Vivekananda founded the periodical 'Brahmayadin' to teach the Vedanta?

A. 1895 B. 1897
C. 1890 D. 1901

19. Who was the first Chief Election Commissioner of India?

A. S.P. Sen Verma
B. S.L. Shakdhar
C. Sukumar Sen
D. T.N. Seshan

20. Arrange the UN Secretary-General as per their tenures in the chronological order:

(*a*) Boutros Boutros-Ghali
(*b*) Ban-Ki-Moon
(*c*) U Thant
(*d*) Kofi A. Annan
(*e*) Kurt Waldheim

Choose the ***correct*** answer from the options given below:

A. (*c*), (*a*), (*e*), (*b*), (*d*)
B. (*a*), (*b*), (*c*), (*d*), (*e*)
C. (*c*), (*e*), (*a*), (*d*), (*b*)
D. (*e*), (*b*), (*c*), (*d*), (*a*)

21. Under which Article of the Indian Constitution, formation of the Finance Commission is laid down?

A. Article 269 B. Article 271
C. Article 280 D. Article 289

22. Which Chief Minister was removed first time in India by the use misuse of Article 356?

A. N.T. Rama Rao
B. E.M.S. Namboodripad
C. Ram Krishna Hegde
D. Bhagat Singh Koshyari

23. Who stated:

'Sri Aurobindo has appropriated Hegel's notion of an Absolute Spirit and employed it to radically restructure the architectonic framework of the ancient Hindu Vedanta system in contemporary' terms?

A. Mahatma Gandhi
B. Rabindranath Tagore
C. Swami Vivekananda
D. Steve Odin

24. Choose the correct statements regarding Constitution of India:

(*a*) The Governor is appointed by the Prime Minister.
(*b*) The Attorney general is appointed by the President.
(*c*) The Chairman of UPSC is appointed by the President.
(*d*) The Judges of the Supreme Court are appointed by the President.
(*e*) The Judges of the High Court are appointed by the Governor.

Choose the ***correct*** answer from the options given below:

A. (*b*), (*c*), (*d*), (*e*) only
B. (*b*), (*c*), (*d*) only
C. (*c*), (*d*), (*e*) only
D. (*a*), (*b*), (*d*), (*e*) only

25. Match the List-I with List-II:

List-I (Secretary General of SAARC)	***List-II (Tenures)***
(*a*) Abul Ahsan	I. January 16, 1987 - October 15, 1989
(*b*) Yadav Kant Silwal	II. January 1, 1994 - December 31, 1995
(*c*) Naeem U. Hasan	III. January 1, 1996 - December 31, 1998
(*d*) Sheel Kant Sharma	IV. March 1, 2008 - February 28, 2011

Choose the ***correct*** answer from the options given below:

	(*a*)	(*b*)	(*c*)	(*d*)
A.	IV	III	II	I
B.	I	II	III	IV
C.	III	I	II	IV
D.	II	IV	III	I

26. All Jammu Kashmir Muslim Conferene was formed in:

A. 1932 B. 1933
C. 1943 D. 1939

27. Arrange the following High Courts with their year of establishment in the chronological order.

(*a*) Manipur
(*b*) Gujarat
(*c*) Madhya Pradesh
(*d*) Rajasthan
(*e*) Sikkim

Choose the ***correct*** answer from the options given below:

A. (*a*), (*b*), (*c*), (*d*), (*e*)
B. (*d*), (*b*), (*a*), (*c*), (*e*)
C. (*e*), (*a*), (*b*), (*c*), (*d*)
D. (*d*), (*c*), (*b*), (*e*), (*a*)

28. Arrange the following Treaties and Agreements in the chronological order:

(*a*) India and Bangladesh signed the Farakka Treaty for sharing of the Ganga water.
(*b*) India and Pakistan signed the Shimla Agreement.
(*c*) India and Pakistan signed the Indus Water Treaty.
(*d*) Prime Minister Atal Bihari Vajpayee under took bus journey to Lahore and signed a declaration.
(*e*) India and Pakistan signed the Tashkent Agreement.

Choose the ***correct*** answer from the options given below:

A. (*a*), (*b*), (*c*), (*d*), (*e*)
B. (*c*), (*e*), (*b*), (*a*), (*d*)
C. (*c*), (*b*), (*a*), (*e*), (*d*)
D. (*e*), (*c*), (*b*), (*a*), (*d*)

29. Arrange the following Cases related to Indian Constitution in the chronological order:

(*a*) The Golaknath Case
(*b*) The Kesavananda Bharati Case
(*c*) The Minerva Mills Case
(*d*) The A.K. Gopalan Case
(*e*) The Indra Sawhney Case

Choose the ***correct*** answer from the options given below:

A. (*a*), (*b*), (*c*), (*d*), (*e*)
B. (*d*), (*a*), (*b*), (*c*), (*e*)
C. (*e*), (*a*), (*b*), (*d*), (*c*)
D. (*e*), (*c*), (*d*), (*b*), (*a*)

30. Which politician has become Chief Minister of two states?

A. N.D. Tiwari B. Sharad Pawar
C. Jyoti Basu D. Karpoori Thakur

31. After Jawaharlal Nehru, which one of the following leader became Prime Minister of India third time in row after completing two hill tenures?

A. Indira Gandhi
B. Dr. Manmohan Singh
C. Narendra Modi
D. Morarji Desai

32. Arrange the following Political Parties (as per their year of formation) in the chronological order:

(*a*) Janata Dal (U)
(*b*) All India Trinamool Congress
(*c*) Telugu Desam Party
(*d*) Asom Gana Parishad
(*e*) Dravida Munnetra Kazhagam

Choose the ***correct*** answer from the options given below:

A. (*a*), (*b*), (*c*), (*d*), (*e*)
B. (*b*), (*e*), (*c*), (*d*), (*a*)
C. (*e*), (*c*), (*d*), (*b*), (*a*)
D. (*d*), (*a*), (*b*), (*c*), (*e*)

33. 42nd Constitution Amendment Act was passed in India in:

A. 1974
B. 1973
C. 1976
D. 1979

34. Match the List-I with List-II:

List-I (Authors)	***List-II (Books)***
(*a*) David Apter	I. Comparative Politics : A Development Approach
(*b*) Walter Bagehot	II. An Introduction to Comparative Government
(*c*) Jean Blondel	III. English Constitution
(*d*) Almond and Powell	IV. The Politics of Modernisation

Choose the ***correct*** answer from the options given below:

	(*a*)	(*b*)	(*c*)	(*d*)
A.	I	II	III	IV
B.	II	I	IV	III
C.	III	IV	I	II
D.	IV	III	II	I

35. Which one of the following US President survived the American Congress impeachment proceedings by a single vote in 1868?

A. Andrew Johnson
B. Abraham Linchon
C. James Madison
D. Woodrow Wilson

36. Arrange the following Prime Minister of India in the chronological order as per their tenure:

(*a*) Chandra Shekhar
(*b*) H.D. Deve Gowda
(*c*) Vishwanath Pratap Singh
(*d*) Charan Singh
(*e*) Morarji Desai

Choose the ***correct*** answer from the options given below:

A. (*e*), (*d*), (*a*), (*b*), (*c*)
B. (*e*), (*d*), (*c*), (*a*), (*b*)
C. (*a*), (*b*), (*c*), (*d*), (*e*)
D. (*e*), (*c*), (*d*), (*b*), (*a*)

37. Pakistan exploded its first nuclear bomb at:

A. Abbotabad
B. Chagai
C. Dalbadin
D. Haripur

38. Arrange the following designated SAARC years in the chronological order:

(*a*) SAARC year of the Youth
(*b*) SAARC year of Girl-Child
(*c*) SAARC year of Environment
(*d*) SAARC year of Disabled Persons
(*e*) SAARC year of Poverty Eradication

Choose the ***correct*** answer from the options given below:

A. (*b*), (*d*), (*c*), (*e*), (*a*)
B. (*c*), (*a*), (*d*), (*e*), (*b*)
C. (*b*), (*c*), (*d*), (*a*), (*e*)
D. (*a*), (*b*), (*c*), (*d*), (*e*)

39. Match the List-I with List-II:

List-I (Author)	***List-II (Book)***
(*a*) George Soros	I. The Conscience of a Liberal
(*b*) Paul Krugman	II. Open Society
(*c*) Herman Daly	III. Decline of American Power
(*d*) Immanuel Wallerstein	IV. For the Common Good

Choose the ***correct*** answer from the options given below:

	(*a*)	(*b*)	(*c*)	(*d*)
A.	II	I	IV	III
B.	I	II	III	IV
C.	IV	III	II	I
D.	III	IV	I	II

40. Choose the incorrect answer related to the Indian Constitution:

(*a*) Provisions related to 'All India Services' are mentioned in Article 312.

(*b*) Provisions related to Administrative tribunals are mentioned in Article 342A.

(*c*) Provisions related to Inter-State council are mentioned in Article 244.

(*d*) Provisions related to facilities for instruction in mother-tongue at primary stage is not mentioned in Indian Constitution.

(*e*) Provisions related to languages are mentioned in Article 368.

Choose the ***correct*** answer from the options given below:

A. (*a*), (*b*), (*c*) only
B. (*a*), (*c*), (*d*), (*e*) only
C. (*b*), (*c*), (*d*), (*e*) only
D. (*a*), (*d*), (*e*) only

41. Who become first democratically elected woman Prime-Minister in Islamic world?

A. Sheikh Hasina Wazid
B. Hina Rabbani Khar
C. Khalida Zia
D. Benazir Bhutto

42. In which year, Planning Commission was converted into 'NITI Ayog"?

A. 2013 B. 2015
C. 2017 D. 2016

43. Arrange the following languages conferred with classical language status by Government of India in the chronological order:

(*a*) Kannada
(*b*) Odia
(*c*) Tamil
(*d*) Sanskrit
(*e*) Malayalam

Choose the ***correct*** answer from the options given below:

A. (*e*), (*d*), (*c*), (*b*), (*a*)
B. (*d*), (*c*), (*a*), (*e*), (*b*)
C. (*c*), (*d*), (*a*), (*e*), (*b*)
D. (*b*), (*a*), (*d*), (*e*), (*c*)

44. In which year, Jyotiba Phule started a girl's school at Poona?

A. 1850
B. 1851
C. 1950
D. 1852

45. Identify the correct statements regarding administrative ideas:

(*a*) Fred Riggs advocated the sala model of administration.

(*b*) Abraham Maslow advanced the idea of hierarchy of needs.

(*c*) Chester Barnard advanced the idea of Hawthorne effect.

(*d*) Max Weber gave the idea of legal-rational authority.

(*e*) Luther Gulick and Lyndall Urwick are associated with the concept of POSDCORB.

Choose the ***correct*** answer from the options given below:

A. (*a*), (*b*), (*c*), (*e*) only
B. (*b*), (*c*), (*e*) only
C. (*a*), (*b*), (*d*), (*e*) only
D. (*a*), (*b*), (*c*), (*d*), (*e*)

46. Which Indian President inaugurated newly restored Somnath Temple?

A. Rajendra Prasad
B. Giani Zail Singh
C. Neelam Sanjeeva Reddy
D. Radhakrishnan

47. 'Mook Nayak' newspaper was published by:

A. Mahatma Gandhi
B. Dr. B.R. Ambedkar
C. M.N. Roy
D. Gopal Krishna Gokhale

48. Who stated:

"There is nothing ______ absolute in management affairs. Seldom do we have to apply the same principle twice as in identical conditions; allowance must be made for different changing circumstances?

A. Max Weber B. Peter Drucker
C. Bertram Gross D. Henri Fayol

49. Fred Riggs developed ideal models to analyse the administrative systems of different countries. Choose the correct ones from the following.

(*a*) Fused (*b*) Focussed
(*c*) Prismatic (*d*) Rainbow
(*e*) Diffracted

Choose the ***correct*** answer from the options given below:

A. (*a*), (*b*), (*c*) only
B. (*a*), (*b*), (*c*), (*d*) only
C. (*a*), (*c*), (*e*) only
D. (*a*), (*b*), (*c*), (*d*), (*e*)

50. Which Naga queen responded to the call of Mahatma Gandhi and raised the banner of revolt against the British rule?

A. Kanaklata Baruah
B. Rani Gaidilieu
C. Chandraprava Saikaini
D. Lalnu Ropuiliani

51. In which year, Burma was bifurcated from British India?

A. 1915 B. 1917
C. 1923 D. 1937

52. "The state shall take steps to organize village Panchayats and endow them with high powers and authority as may be necessary to enable them to function as units of self-government" Which Article of the Indian Constitution mention it?

A. Article 40 B. Article 37
C. Article 33 D. Article 43

53. Choose the correct statements regarding political ideas:

(*a*) John Locke championed the cause of constitutional government.
(*b*) Montesquieu proposed a system of checks and balances in the form of separation of powers which became the important feature of British Constitution.
(*c*) Jeremy Bentham developed his idea of utilitarianism.
(*d*) J.S. Mill argued for broadening of popular participation with inclusion of women.
(*e*) Thomas Hobbes discussed the grounds of political obligation in his classical work 'Philosophy of Right'.

Choose the ***correct*** answer from the options given below:

A. (*b*), (*c*), (*d*), (*e*) only
B. (*a*), (*c*), (*d*) only
C. (*a*), (*b*), (*e*) only
D. (*a*), (*b*), (*c*), (*d*), (*e*)

54. Match the List-I with List-II:

List-I (Creation of States)	***List-II (Years of Creation)***
(*a*) Jharkhand	I. 2014
(*b*) Telangana	II. 1987
(*c*) Goa	III. 2000
(*d*) Sikkim	IV. 1975

Choose the ***correct*** answer from the options given below:

	(*a*)	(*b*)	(*c*)	(*d*)
A.	II	III	IV	I
B.	III	I	II	IV
C.	IV	II	I	III
D.	I	II	III	IV

55. Who conceived the notion of 'Linking Pin Model'?

A. Elton Mayo
B. Fred Riggs
C. Renin Likert
D. Woodrow Wilson

56. Which Article of the Indian Constitution makes special provision for the Administration of certain areas called 'Scheduled Areas'?

A. Article 249 B. Article 244 (1)
C. Article 253 D. Article 259

57. Identify the correct statements:

(*a*) A consensus on poverty eradication was adopted at the Seventh SAARC Summit.
(*b*) Giuseppe Mazzini wrote the book 'On Nationality'.
(*c*) V.D. Savarkar did not establish the Abhinav Bharat Society.
(*d*) Jurgen Habermas is the leading exponent of the 'Second Generation' of the Frankfurt School.
(*e*) India adopted planning process from United States of America.

Choose the ***correct*** answer from the options given below:

A. (*b*), (*c*), (*d*), (*e*) only
B. (*c*), (*e*) only
C. (*a*), (*b*), (*d*) only
D. (*a*), (*b*), (*c*), (*d*) only

58. Consider the following correct statements:

(*a*) Anthony Smith wrote the book 'The Ethnic Origins of Nations'.
(*b*) Ernest Gellner emphasised his idea of nationalism in book 'Nations and Nationalism.'
(*c*) Malcom X argued for rediscovery of Africa as a spiritual and cultural homeland.
(*d*) John Loke's idea of General Will was the seed from which nationalist doctrines sprang during the French Revolution of 1789.
(*e*) Eric Hobsbawn highlighted the idea of 'invented traditions.'

Choose the ***correct*** answer from the options given below:

A. (*a*), (*b*), (*d*), (*e*) only
B. (*b*), (*d*), (*e*) only
C. (*a*), (*b*), (*c*), (*d*), (*e*)
D. (*a*), (*b*), (*c*), (*e*) only

59. Choose the correct statements regarding Comparative Politics.

(*a*) In traditional approach, emphasis is on value-laden study of politics.
(*b*) Behavioural approach is one of the important traditional approach.
(*c*) David Easton is one of the leading theorist of Behaviouralism.
(*d*) David Easton's input-output analysis has three main variables in the form of demands, supports and feedbacks.
(*e*) 'Political assasination' is one of the important positive indices of political development.

Choose the ***correct*** answer from the options given below:

A. (*b*), (*c*), (*e*) only
B. (*a*), (*b*), (*c*), (*d*), (*e*)
C. (*a*), (*b*), (*c*), (*d*) only
D. (*a*), (*c*), (*d*) only

60. Match the List-I with List-II:

***List-I* (*Book*)**	***List-II* (*Author*)**
(*a*) A Theory of Justice	I. John Rawls
(*b*) Philosophy of Right	II. Jurgen Habermas
(*c*) Towards a Rational Society	III. Vladimir Ilyich Lenin
(*d*) State and Revolution	IV. Fridrich Hegal

Choose the ***correct*** answer from the options given below:

	(*a*)	(*b*)	(*c*)	(*d*)
A.	I	II	III	IV
B.	IV	III	II	I
C.	III	II	IV	I
D.	I	IV	II	III

61. In India, the Speaker of Lok Sabha appointed the Pataskar Committee in 1954 to examine the issue of:

A. Panchayati Raj
B. Fundamental Duties
C. Deligated Legislation
D. Money Bill

62. Who set up the 'Bahishkrit Hitakarini Sabha' in 1924?

A. V.D. Savarkar
B. Dada Bhai Naoroji
C. B.R. Ambedkar
D. Mahatma Gandhi

63. Who gave the notion of 'Radical Humanism'?

A. Mahatma Gandhi
B. Raja Rammohan Roy
C. Swami Vivekananda
D. M.N. Roy

64. Match the List-I with List-II:

List-I (Books)	*List-II (Authors)*
(*a*) Government by Committee	I. W.H. Morris Jones
(*b*) Parliament in India	II. Ramsey Muir
(*c*) How Britain is Governed	III. K.C. Wheare
(*d*) Musolini's Italy	IV. Herman Finer

Choose the ***correct*** answer from the options given below:

	(*a*)	(*b*)	(*c*)	(*d*)
A.	I	III	IV	II
B.	II	IV	III	I
C.	III	I	II	IV
D.	IV	II	I	III

65. Which American President got 'Nobel prize for Peace' for his efforts of mediation between Japan and Russia?

A. Ronald Reagan
B. John F. Kennedy
C. George W. Bush
D. Theodore Roosevelt

66. Who proposed the ideas of 'Pitribhu' (fatherland) and 'Punybhu' (holyland) in the classical text on the ideology of Hindutva?

A. M.N. Roy
B. Jai Prakash Narayan
C. Vinayak Damodar Savarkar
D. Mahatma Gandhi

67. Which one of the following organisation won the Nobel Peace Prize in 2017?

A. The International Campaign to abolish unclear weapons.
B. The International Campaign to counter-terrorism.
C. The International Campaign to safeguard environment.
D. The International Campaign to protect women and children.

68. Match the List-I with List-II:

List-I (Statewise membership in the Constitutional Assembly)	*List-II (Act on 31 December 1947)*
(*a*) Madras	I. 21
(*b*) Bombay	II. 49
(*c*) West Bengal	III. 55
(*d*) United Province	IV. 19

Choose the ***correct*** answer from the options given below:

	(*a*)	(*b*)	(*c*)	(*d*)
A.	II	I	IV	III
B.	III	IV	I	II
C.	IV	III	II	I
D.	I	IV	III	II

69. Match the List-I with List-II:

List-I (Events of the United Nations)	*List-II (Year)*
(*a*) Trygve Lie appointed Secretary General	I. 1964
(*b*) Kofi Annan appointed Secretary General	II. 1950

(*c*) U.N. Peace Keepers sent to Cyprus — III. 1946

(*d*) U.N. High Commissioner for Refugees established — IV. 1997

Choose the ***correct*** answer from the options given below:

	(*a*)	(*b*)	(*c*)	(*d*)
A.	IV	III	II	I
B.	I	IV	II	III
C.	II	I	III	IV
D.	III	IV	I	II

70. Match the List-I with List-II:

List-I (President's Rules States)	***List-II (Tenures)***
(*a*) Andhra Pradesh	I. 30.6.1981–13.1.1982
(*b*) Assam	II. 15.12.1992–3.12-1993
(*c*) Himachal Pradesh	III. 18.3.2016–6.5.2016
(*d*) Uttarakhand	IV. 18.1.1973–10.12.1973

Choose the ***correct*** answer from the options given below:

	(*a*)	(*b*)	(*c*)	(*d*)
A.	IV	I	II	III
B.	III	II	I	IV
C.	I	IV	III	II
D.	I	II	III	IV

71. Arrange the following events related to United Nations in the chronological order:

(*a*) UN peacekeepers sent to Cyprus.

(*b*) UN Peacekeeping Commission was established.

(*c*) First UN Peacekeeping Force sent to the Suez Canal.

(*d*) General Assembly adopts the Sustainable Development Goals (SDGs).

(*e*) UN High Commissioner for Refugees (UNHCR) established.

Choose the ***correct*** answer from the options given below:

A. (*e*), (*d*), (*c*), (*b*), (*a*)

B. (*b*), (*d*), (*a*), (*e*), (*c*)

C. (*e*), (*c*), (*a*), (*b*), (*d*)

D. (*c*), (*a*), (*d*), (*e*), (*b*)

72. Arrange the following Speakers of the Lok-Sabha as per their tenure in the chronological order:

(*a*) Ganesh Vasudev Mavalankar

(*b*) P.A. Sangma

(*c*) Om Birla

(*d*) Neelam Sanjiva Reddy

(*e*) Ms. Meira Kumar

Choose the ***correct*** answer from the options given below:

A. (*a*), (*b*), (*c*), (*d*), (*e*)

B. (*a*), (*d*), (*b*), (*e*), (*c*)

C. (*e*), (*a*), (*b*), (*c*), (*d*)

D. (*d*), (*a*), (*b*), (*e*), (*c*)

73. Arrange the following Commissions of India as per their year of formation in the chronological order:

(*a*) National Commission for Minorities

(*b*) National Commission for Schedule Castes

(*c*) Central Information Commission

(*d*) National Commission for Protection of Child Rights

(*e*) National Commission for Women

Choose the ***correct*** answer from the options given below:

A. (*e*), (*a*), (*b*), (*c*), (*d*)

B. (*e*), (*b*), (*a*), (*d*), (*c*)

C. (*a*), (*b*), (*c*), (*d*), (*e*)

D. (*c*), (*b*), (*a*), (*d*), (*e*)

74. Match the List-I with List-II.

List-I (International Human Right Documents)	***List-II (Enactment Years)***
(*a*) Convention Relating to the Status of Refugees	I. 1975

(*b*) Declaration on Torture		II. 1954
(*c*) Convention on the Rights of the Child		III. 1990
(*d*) Charter of Fundamental Rights of the European Union		IV. 2000

Choose the ***correct*** answer from the options given below:

	(*a*)	(*b*)	(*c*)	(*d*)
A.	II	I	III	IV
B.	IV	III	I	II
C.	III	IV	II	I
D.	I	II	IV	III

75. In which year, present Dalailama came to India?

A. 1959 B. 1960
C. 1961 D. 1963

76. Consider the following statements regarding judicial system and choose the correct answer:

(*a*) Supreme Court of Canada has three judges from the province of Quebec to ensure ethnic and religious balance.
(*b*) Some judges of the Federal Constitutional Court of Germany are elected by the Bundestag and Bundesrat.
(*c*) In United States, the judges are nominated by the House of Lords and ratified by the Senate.
(*d*) US Constitution of 1787 did not explicitly provide for judicial review.
(*e*) The power of judicial review originated in India in the leading case of Marbury Vs. Madison.

Choose the ***correct*** answer from the options given below:

A. (*a*), (*b*), (*c*), (*d*) only
B. (*b*), (*c*), (*d*), (*e*) only
C. (*a*), (*b*), (*d*) only
D. (*a*), (*c*), (*d*), (*e*) only

77. Arrange the Acts related to implementation of Directive Principle of State Policy in the chronological order:

(*a*) The Bonded Labour System Abolition Act
(*b*) The Child Labour Prohibition and Regulation Act
(*c*) The Trade Unions Act
(*d*) The Minimum Wages Act
(*e*) The Mines Act

Choose the ***correct*** answer from the options given below:

A. (*a*), (*b*), (*c*), (*d*), (*e*)
B. (*c*), (*e*), (*d*), (*b*), (*a*)
C. (*b*), (*e*), (*d*), (*c*), (*a*)
D. (*c*), (*d*), (*e*), (*a*), (*b*)

78. Read carefully the following statements regarding Fundamental duties in Indian Constitution and choose the incorrect answer:

(*a*) Fundamental duties were inserted by the 44th Constitution Amendment Act.
(*b*) Parliament cannot amend the fundamental duties.
(*c*) Fundamental duties can be enforced by writs.
(*d*) There are eleven fundamental duties in Article 51A.
(*e*) Promotion of international peace and securities in one of the important fundamental duty.

Choose the ***correct*** answer from the options given below:

A. (*b*), (*c*), (*d*) only
B. (*a*), (*b*), (*c*), (*e*) only
C. (*b*), (*d*), (*e*) only
D. (*a*), (*b*), (*c*), (*d*), (*e*)

79. In which year, Visvabharti was established by Rabindranath Tagore?

A. 1918 B. 1920
C. 1919 D. 1922

80. Who was the Chairman of 15th Finance Commission of India?

A. N.K. Singh
B. A.K. Chanda
C. Dr. Rajamannar
D. Montak Singh Ahluwalia

81. Choose the correct statements:

(*a*) UN declared 1975 as International Women's Year.
(*b*) B.N. Rau Committee prepared the first draft of the Hindu Code Bill.
(*c*) Kabir was a social reformer in ancient India.
(*d*) Sunderlal Bahuguna became popular in the Chipko-agitation.
(*e*) Subhash Chandra Bose formed Independent Labour Party in 1936.

Choose the ***correct*** answer from the options given below:

A. (*a*), (*b*), (*c*), (*d*) only
B. (*b*), (*c*), (*e*) only
C. (*a*), (*b*), (*d*) only
D. (*a*), (*b*), (*c*), (*d*), (*e*)

82. Match the List-I with List-II:

List-I (Legislatures)	***List-II (Country)***
(*a*) House of Representatives	I. United States of America
(*b*) National Assembly	II. Pakistan
(*c*) House of Commons	III. United Kingdom
(*d*) Knesset	IV. Israel

Choose the ***correct*** answer from the options given below:

	(*a*)	(*b*)	(*c*)	(*d*)
A.	IV	III	I	II
B.	II	I	IV	III
C.	I	II	III	IV
D.	II	I	III	IV

83. Identify the correct statements regarding Abraham Maslow's need of hierarchy.

(*a*) Esteem needs
(*b*) Self-actualisation
(*c*) Belonging needs
(*d*) Safety needs
(*e*) Entertaining needs

Choose the ***correct*** answer from the options given below:

A. (*a*), (*b*), (*c*), (*e*) only
B. (*c*), (*d*), (*e*) only
C. (*b*), (*d*), (*e*) only
D. (*a*), (*b*), (*c*), (*d*) only

84. Gabriel Almond classified the Pressure group into different categories. Find the correct ones:

(*a*) Associational groups
(*b*) Non-associational groups
(*c*) Institutional groups
(*d*) Anomic groups
(*e*) Non-anomic groups

Choose the ***correct*** answer from the options given below:

A. (*a*), (*b*), (*e*) only
B. (*a*), (*b*), (*c*), (*e*) only
C. (*a*), (*c*), (*d*), (*e*) only
D. (*a*), (*b*), (*c*), (*d*) only

85. Match the List-I with List-II:

List-I (Number of Women elected in Lok Sabha)	***List-II (Parliamentary Elections)***
(*a*) 22	I. Seventh (1980)
(*b*) 28	II. Fifth (1971)
(*c*) 28	III. Fifteenth (2009)
(*d*) 59	IV. Ninth (1989)

Choose the ***correct*** answer from the options given below:

	(*a*)	(*b*)	(*c*)	(*d*)
A.	I	III	II	IV
B.	II	I	IV	III
C.	IV	II	III	I
D.	III	IV	I	II

86. Arrange the following books in the chronological order (years of first publication)

(*a*) The End of History and the Last Man
(*b*) Man, the State and War
(*c*) Politics Among Nations: The Struggle for Power and Peace
(*d*) The Second Sex
(*e*) The Clash of Civilisations and the Remaking of World Order

Choose the ***correct*** answer from the options given below:

A. (*c*), (*b*), (*d*), (*a*), (*e*)
B. (*c*), (*d*), (*b*), (*e*), (*a*)
C. (*a*), (*b*), (*c*), (*d*), (*e*)
D. (*d*), (*c*), (*b*), (*e*), (*a*)

87. Democratic Party of the United States was established in:

A. 1779 B. 1803
C. 1828 D. 1901

88. Arrange the following events in the chronological order:

(*a*) Non Cooperation Movement
(*b*) Civil Disobedience Movement
(*c*) 'Purna Swaraj' accepted as Congress goal at the Lahore Congress
(*d*) Champaran Movement
(*e*) Peasant Movements in Kheda (Gujarat) and Worker's Movement in Ahmedabad

Choose the ***correct*** answer from the options given below:

A. (*b*), (*d*), (*a*), (*e*), (*c*)
B. (*a*), (*b*), (*c*), (*d*), (*e*)
C. (*e*), (*d*), (*a*), (*b*), (*c*)
D. (*d*), (*e*), (*a*), (*c*), (*b*)

89. Match the List-I with List-II:

List-I (Regional Organisation)	***List-II (Establishment year)***
(*a*) African Union	I. 1980
(*b*) Latin American Integration Association	II. 2005
(*c*) East Asia Summit	III. 2002
(*d*) Eurasian Economic Community	IV. 2000

Choose the ***correct*** answer from the options given below:

	(*a*)	(*b*)	(*c*)	(*d*)
A.	II	III	IV	I
B.	III	I	II	IV
C.	I	II	IV	III
D.	IV	II	I	III

90. Which American President had laid down "fourteen points" as the basis for peace after World War I?

A. Theodore Roosevelt
B. James Madison
C. Millard Fillmore
D. Woodrow Wilson

Directions (Qs. No. 91 to 95): *Read the following passage and answer the questions.*

To a large extent, British India and independent India helped China to re-establish and consolidate its hold on Tibet, particularly in view of Tibet having enjoyed de-facto independent status from 1913 to 1951. It must not be forgotten that India fecilitated the Tibetan delegation to proceed through India Peking to formally accept to be an autonomous part of China, even though the seventeen-point agreement signed in May 1951 has remained controversial, as something done under duress. India's large heartedness and its endeavours to befriend China did not end there. As a gesture of goodwill, the Panchsheel Agreement of 1954 was a classic example of India's one -sided generosity and diplomatic naivety, one that resulted in its giving away all rights and privileges and significantly, in ending india's presence in Tibet without the country gaining anything as a quid pro quo. Although at times, there has been friction on the border issue, the maturity and statesmanship of the leaders of both nations have ensured that there problems were resolved in a peaceful manner through dialogue and diplomatic exchange, as has been demonstrated during the recent stand-off at Doklam.

91. When was the Seventeen-point Agreement signed?

A. 1950 B. 1951
C. 1955 D. 1954

92. According to the passage, which one of the following helped China to consolidate its hold on Tibet?

A. Only British India
B. Only Independent India
C. Both British India and Independent India
D. Only Russia

93. Who facilitated the Tibetan delegation to proceed through India to Peking to formally accept to be an autonomous part of China?

A. Pakistan B. Bhutan
C. Myanmar D. British India

94. According to the passage, during which period Tibet enjoyed de-facto independent status?

A. 1913–1970 B. 1913–1951
C. 1952–1960 D. 1960–1990

95. In which year, Panchsheel Agreement was signed?

A. 1951 B. 1952
C. 1953 D. 1954

Directions (Qs. No. 96 to 100): *Read the following passage and answer the questions:*

The campaign for decentralization of authority has a long past. As history shows, sustained attempts were made to decentralize authority in India since the 1880s with the acceptance of Rippon resolution of 1882. One of the most clearly-stated justifications for Panchayati Raj Institutions (PRIs) was given by the report of the Ashok Mehta Committee. Another categorical statement regarding strengthening of local self-government was made by the report of the 1986 L.M. Singhvi Committee. Revitalisation of PRIs for Democracy and Development. What was strongly argued became a reality with the adoption of the 73rd Amendment Act in 1992, which not only constitutionalised local self government in India but also gave the long overdue constitutional recognition to PRIs. The legislative origins of the 73rd constitutional Amendment Act can be traced back to the constitutional 64th Amendment Bill, which was introduced in the Parliament in 1989. 73rd constitutional Amendment Act of 1992 introduced a three - tier structure of rural local level - gram Panchayats at the lowest level, panchayat samiti at the intermediate level and zilla parishad at the highest level.

96. According to the passage, which one of the following constitutional Act. constitutionalised local self-government in India?

A. 64th Constitution Amendment Act
B. 73rd Constitution Amendment Act
C. 80th Constitution Amendment Act
D. 93rd Constitution Amendment Act

97. Who brought out the report 'Revitalisation of PRIs for Democracy and Development'?

A. Ashok Mehta
B. L.M. Singhvi
C. Balwant Rai Mehta
D. Ashok Sen

98. Rippon Resolution was accepted in:

A. 1982
B. 1882
C. 1973
D. 1873

99. According to the paragraph. 73rd Constitutional Amendment Act introduced which kind of rural structure at the intermediate level?

A. Gram Panchayat
B. Panchayat Samiti
C. Zila Parishad
D. Town Planning Council

100. In which year, 64th Constitution Amendment Bill introduced in Parliament of India?

A. 1979 B. 1989
C. 1992 D. 1993

ANSWERS

1. **(C):** John Henry, Barrows was the President of the Parliament of the World's Religions during its first session held in Chicago in 1893. Swami Vivekananda delivered his famous address at this event, capturing international attention and promoting Hinduism and Indian spirituality to a Western audience. The Parliament was part of the larger World's Columbian Exposition and was significant for fostering interfaith dialogue.

2. **(D):** The 73rd and 74th Constitutional Amendment Acts, pivotal reforms for local governance in India, were passed under the Prime Ministership of P.V. Narasimha Rao. These acts, passed in 1992, aimed to strengthen the panchayati raj (local government) system throughout India, facilitating greater decentralization and empowerment at the village, block, and district levels.

3. **(C):** The correct statements are:

   (*a*) NITI Aayog, like its predecessor the Planning Commission, was established by an executive resolution of the Government of India, indicating continuity in this aspect of governance structure.

   (*d*) The First Administrative Reforms Commission (ARC) of India did indeed recommend the setting up of Lokpal and Lokayuktas to address corruption in public administration.

   (*e*) The First ARC was chaired by Morarji Desai, reflecting his commitment to administrative reforms.

   Statement (*b*) is incorrect as there is no Consumer Protection Act of 2023, and (*c*) is incorrect because the concept of the Ombudsman originated in Sweden, not Russia.

4. **(D):** The correct statements are:

   (*a*) The Eighth SAARC Summit was indeed held in New Delhi in 1995. This summit focused on increasing cooperation among member countries in South Asia.

   (*b*) 1989 was designated as the SAARC Year of Combating Drug Abuse and Drug Trafficking, marking a significant regional commitment to tackle these challenges.

   (*e*) The Agreement on SAARC Preferential Trading Arrangement was signed on 11 April 1993, facilitating preferential trade among the member nations, thus promoting regional economic cooperation.

5. **(D):** Article 15 of the Constitution of India prohibits discrimination by the state against any citizen on grounds only of religion, race, caste, sex, or place of birth. This article ensures equality before the law and embodies the principle of non-discrimination, which is fundamental to the Indian democratic ethos and legal framework.

6. **(D):** The correct chronological order of the Indian Constitutional Amendments related to the listed items is:

   (*a*) The 42nd Amendment in 1976 added the words "unity and integrity of the nation" to the Preamble.

   (*c*) The 71st Amendment in 1992 added Konkani to the 8th Schedule.

   (*b*) The 92nd Amendment in 2003 added Maithili, along with three other languages, to the 8th Schedule.

   (*d*) The 97th Amendment in 2011 added Article 243 ZH concerning the Co-operative Societies.

   (*e*) The Women Reservation Act, referred to, does not yet exist as a passed law, hence its position last reflects its non-enactment status.

7. (B): During the Janata Party regime, which was in power from 1977 to 1980 following the emergency period, K.D. Hegde served as the Speaker of the Lok Sabha. His tenure is noted for efforts towards maintaining parliamentary decorum and overseeing the transition period post-emergency.

8. (C): The incorrect statements are:

(*b*) Deendayal Upadhyay was the proponent, not the opponent, of Integral Humanism, which is a philosophy that was intended to guide the Bharatiya Jana Sangh with a focus on holistic human development.

(*c*) The concept of federalism in the Indian Constitution was inspired by the Constitution of the United States, not the British Constitution, as the UK operates a unitary system without a formal constitution that outlines a federal structure.

(*e*) The current provision for women's reservation in the Panchayati Raj system in India is 33%, not 45%, which is mandated by law to ensure increased participation of women in local governance.

9. (B): The book "Democracy, Bureaucracy and Hypocrisy" was written by Dwight Waldo, not Waldoo. This book critiques the functioning of democratic institutions and bureaucratic systems, illustrating the often hypocritical nature of administrative practices versus democratic ideals. Dwight Waldo is known for his contributions to the field of public administration and his critical examination of bureaucratic theories.

10. (C): The correct statements are:

(*a*) The Chinese Communist Party (CCP) is indeed a cadre-based party, where a small number of dedicated members control party operations and policymaking.

(*b*) Otto Kirchheimer conceptualized the idea of 'catch-all parties', which aim to attract a broad spectrum of voters, reducing ideological baggage to maximize appeal.

(*c*) Otto Kirchheimer's theory of catch-all parties includes larger contemporary parties like the US Republicans and Democrats as examples, which have broad, inclusive platforms designed to appeal to diverse voters.

(*d*) Anthony Downs portrayed politicians as fundamentally seeking power, willing to shift policies pragmatically to win elections, emphasizing the strategic nature of political behaviour.

11. (B): (*a*) Robert Dahl did advocate for the concept of polyarchal democracy, emphasizing multiple centers of power as a more realistic form of democratic governance than the traditional majority rule.

(*b*) John Plamenatz's critical reflections suggest that if the 'will of the people' is considered a myth, then so too should be the notion of a 'will of the minority,' challenging the simplistic views on political will and consent.

(*c*) Robert Michels formulated the 'Iron Law of Oligarchy,' which suggests that all forms of organization, regardless of how democratic they are at the start, will eventually and inevitably develop oligarchic tendencies.

12. (A): The 'Chaukhamba Model' of decentralization was proposed by Ram Manohar Lohia, which emphasizes governance through village councils, district councils, state assemblies, and the Parliament. Lohia's model advocates for a significant decentralization of power to ensure more effective governance and greater participation of the local populace in the democratic process.

13. (C): C.N. Annadurai was the first Chief Minister of Tamil Nadu following its renaming from Madras State in 1969. Annadurai's leadership was pivotal in the state's early years as he advocated for state rights and cultural revival, making significant contributions to the development of Tamil Nadu's political landscape.

14. (B): The correct matches for the establishment years of the regional organizations are:

(*a*) North American Free Trade Agreement (NAFTA) was established in 1993, matching with III.

(*b*) Asia Pacific Economic Cooperation (APEC) was established in 1989, matching with IV.

(*c*) Mercosur was established in 1991, matching with I.

(*d*) Free Trade Area of the Americas was proposed in 1994, matching with II, though it was not fully implemented.

15. (A): Arne Naess coined the term 'Deep Ecology' in 1973. His philosophy promotes an ecological and environmental perspective asserting that the living environment as a whole should be respected and regarded as having certain legal and moral rights. Deep Ecology emphasizes the intrinsic value of nature and its components, advocating for a radical restructuring of modern human societies to abide by these principles.

16. (C): The correct tenures of the Presidents of India are matched as follows:

(*a*) Dr. Zakir Hussain served as President from 13 May 1967 until his death on 3 May 1969, corresponding to II.

(*b*) Fakhruddin Ali Ahmed was President from 24 August 1974 to 11 February 1977, matching IV.

(*c*) Neelam Sanjiva Reddy's tenure was from 25 July 1977 to 25 July 1982, corresponding to I.

(*d*) R. Venkataraman served from 25 July 1987 to 25 July 1992, matching III.

17. (D): Mary Wollstonecraft is renowned for advocating the equal rights of women, particularly in her seminal work "A Vindication of the Rights of Woman". Hannah Arendt's "The Origins of Totalitarianism" does indeed examine both Nazism and Stalinism, providing a deep analysis of totalitarian regimes. Franz Fanon authored "Black Skin, White Masks", exploring the psychological effects of colonialism on the colonized. The incorrect statement is (*c*) as Antonio Gramsci did not write "On People's Democratic Dictatorship"; this work was written by Mao Zedong. Also, (*e*) is incorrect because "Politics Among Nations" was written by Hans Morgenthau, not Aristotle, and it discusses principles of political realism, not mixed government.

18. (A): Swami Vivekananda founded the periodical 'Brahmayadin' in the year 1895. The periodical served as a platform for teaching and spreading the ideas of Vedanta and Hindu philosophy, reflecting Vivekananda's efforts to interpret Hindu philosophical concepts to the broader public both in India and internationally.

19. (C): Sukumar Sen was the first Chief Election Commissioner of India. He served from 1950 to 1958, overseeing the first general elections in India, which were a monumental task given the size and diversity of the electorate. His contributions laid the foundation for the independent and authoritative functioning of the Election Commission in managing India's electoral processes.

20. (C): The chronological order of UN Secretary-Generals based on their tenures is:

(*c*) U Thant (1961-1971), followed by

(*e*) Kurt Waldheim (1972-1981), then

(*a*) Boutros Boutros-Ghali (1992-1996), followed by

(*d*) Kofi A. Annan (1997-2006), and finally

(*b*) Ban-Ki-moon (2007-2016).

This sequence reflects the correct historical progression of leadership within the United Nations.

21. (C): Under Article 280 of the Indian Constitution, the President is required to constitute a Finance Commission every five years, or at such earlier time as he considers necessary. This commission is tasked with reviewing financial relations between the central government and the states, including the distribution of net proceeds of taxes and the principles governing grants-in-aid to the states.

22. (B): E.M.S. Namboodripad, the Chief Minister of Kerala, was the first to be removed from office via the controversial use of Article 356 of the Indian Constitution. This occurred in 1959 when his communist government was dismissed by the central government, marking the beginning of what would be a long history of the contentious application of this constitutional provision, often criticized as a tool for the central government's overreach into state politics.

23. (D): Steve Odin stated that 'Sri Aurobindo has appropriated Hegel's notion of an Absolute Spirit and employed it to radically restructure the architectonic framework of the ancient Hindu Vedanta system in contemporary terms.' This reflects Sri Aurobindo's unique synthesis of Western philosophical concepts with traditional Indian spiritual ideas, aiming to present a modern interpretation of Vedantic teachings that addressed the challenges and needs of contemporary society.

24. (B): Correct statements regarding the appointments under the Constitution of India are:

(*b*) The Attorney General, the chief legal advisor to the Government of India, is appointed by the President.

(*c*) The Chairman of the Union Public Service Commission (UPSC) is also appointed by the President.

(*d*) The Judges of the Supreme Court are appointed by the President of India.

The incorrect statements are: (*a*) The Governor is not appointed by the Prime Minister but by the President of India. (*e*) The Judges of the High Court are appointed by the President, not the Governor.

25. (B): The correct matches for the Secretary Generals of SAARC with their tenures are:

(*a*) Abul Ahsan served from January 16, 1987, to October 15, 1989, corresponding to I.

(*b*) Yadav Kant Silwal's tenure was from January 1, 1994, to December 31, 1995, matching with II.

(*c*) Naeem U. Hasan served from January 1, 1996, to December 31, 1998, corresponding to III.

(*d*) Sheel Kant Sharma served from March 1, 2008, to February 28, 2011, matching with IV. These tenures reflect the chronological service periods of these key figures in the SAARC, which aims to promote economic and regional integration among its member states.

26. (A): The All Jammu Kashmir Muslim Conference was formed in the year 1932. This political organization was established to represent the interests of the Muslims in the princely state of Jammu and Kashmir. It played a crucial role in the political landscape of the region leading up to the partition of India in 1947.

27. (D): The chronological order of establishment for the High Courts is: Rajasthan (1949), Madhya Pradesh (1956), Gujarat (1960), Sikkim (1975), and Manipur (2013). This sequence reflects the expansion and evolution of judicial administration in India post-independence, with newer states and union territories establishing their high courts as their judicial needs grew.

28. (B): The chronological order of these treaties and agreements is:

(*c*) The Indus Water Treaty between India and Pakistani was signed in 1960, focusing on water distribution and management of the Indus river system.

(*e*) Tashkent Declaration, accord signed on January 10, 1966 by India's Prime Minister Lal Bahadur Shastri and Pakistan President Mohammad Ayub Khan.

(*b*) The Shimla Agreement, signed in 1972, aimed at normalizing relations post-1971 war.

(*a*) The Farakka Treaty with Bangladesh regarding the sharing of the Ganga waters was signed in 1974.

(*d*) The Lahore Declaration, marked by Prime Minister Atal Bihari Vajpayee's bus journey, was in 1999.

29. (B): The chronological order of these landmark Indian constitutional cases is: The A.K. Gopalan Case (1950) was one of the first major decisions by the Supreme Court on preventive detention. The Golaknath Case (1967) ruled that Parliament could not amend fundamental rights. The Kesavananda Bharati Case (1973) established the basic structure doctrine. The Minerva Mills Case (1980) further defined and reinforced the basic structure doctrine. Lastly, the Indra Sawhney Case (1992) dealt with reservations in government jobs and educational institutions.

30. (A): N.D. Tiwari is the politician who has served as the Chief Minister of two different states. He was the Chief Minister of Uttar Pradesh and later served as the Chief Minister of Uttarakhand. This unique political achievement highlights his long-standing influence and leadership within the Indian National Congress across different regional political landscapes.

31. (C): After Jawaharlal Nehru, Narendra Modi is the only other Prime Minister of India to have been elected for three consecutive terms, having completed his two full terms and currently serving the third. His leadership has been marked by significant policy reforms and initiatives aimed at economic growth, digital infrastructure, and international diplomacy.

32. (C): The chronological order of formation for the political parties listed is as follows: Dravida Munnetra Kazhagam (DMK) was established in 1949, focusing on the rights and interests of the Dravidian populations in Tamil Nadu. Telugu Desam Party (TDP) was founded in 1982 by N.T. Rama Rao, emphasizing regional pride and governance reforms in Andhra Pradesh. Asom Gana Parishad (AGP) formed in 1985, arising from the Assam Movement with a focus on regionalism and local governance. All India Trinamool Congress (AITC) was established in 1998 by Mamata Banerjee after splitting from the Indian National Congress, aiming to create political change in West Bengal. Finally, Janata Dal (United) (JD(U)) was formed in 2003 from a split in the Janata Dal, focusing on a mix of socialist and regional politics.

33. (C): The 42nd Amendment Act of 1976, often termed as the "Mini-Constitution," was passed during the Emergency period under Prime Minister Indira Gandhi. This amendment made significant changes to the Constitution, including the alteration of the Preamble and the curtailment of judicial review, which were later partially rectified by subsequent amendments following the Emergency.

34. (D): The correct matches for the authors and their respective books are:

(*a*) David Apter is known for his work "The Politics of Modernisation", which discusses how developing nations modernize through various political and social reforms.

(*b*) Walter Bagehot authored "The English Constitution", a seminal work analyzing the British constitutional system and its functions.

(*c*) Jean Blondel wrote "An Introduction to Comparative Government", offering a comprehensive overview of governmental systems worldwide.

(*d*) Almond and Powell are recognized for "Comparative Politics: A Development Approach", which provides a framework for analyzing political development and institutions across different countries.

35. (A): Andrew Johnson, the 17th President of the United States, narrowly survived impeachment proceedings in 1868 by just one vote in the Senate. The impeachment was primarily driven by his lenient policies towards the Southern states following the Civil War and his violation of the Tenure of Office Act, which led to political conflict with the Radical Republicans in Congress.

36. (B): The chronological order of these Prime Ministers of India based on their tenures is as follows: Morarji Desai served as the Prime Minister from 1977 to 1979, followed by Charan Singh from 1979 to 1980. Vishwanath Pratap Singh then took office from 1989 to 1990. Chandra Shekhar served briefly from 1990 to 1991, and H.D. Deve Gowda led from 1996 tc 1997. This order reflects the political transitions and instabilities of India during these years.

37. (B): Pakistan conducted its first nuclear test at Chagai, Balochistan, on May 28, 1998. This test was a response to India's nuclear tests earlier that month, marking Pakistan's entry into the group of countries with declared nuclear capabilities. The site at Chagai has since been synonymous with Pakistan's nuclear program.

38. (C): The designated SAARC years in chronological order are: SAARC Year of the Girl-Child was recognized in 1990, SAARC Year of Environment followed in 1992, then SAARC Year of Disabled Persons in 1993. SAARC Year of the Youth was designated in 1995, and lastly, SAARC Year of Poverty Eradication was marked in 1996.

These thematic years were established to focus regional efforts on significant social and environmental challenges within the South Asian Association for Regional Cooperation member countries.

39. (A): Matching the authors with their books, George Soros wrote "Open Society", advocating for liberal democratic governance and the protection of human rights. Paul Krugman authored "The Conscience of a Liberal", discussing income inequality and a vision for a more equitable economic policy. Herman Daly is known for "For the Common Good", emphasizing sustainable development and critiquing traditional economic growth models. Immanuel Wallerstein wrote "The Decline of American Power", analyzing the historical cycles of rise and decline in world systems, particularly focusing on the United States.

40. (C): The incorrect statements related to the Indian Constitution are:

(*b*) Administrative tribunals are actually mentioned in Article 323A and Article 323B, not 342A.

(*c*) The Inter-State Council is outlined in Article 263, not 244.

(*d*) Provisions related to facilities for instruction in mother-tongue at the primary stage are indeed mentioned in the Indian Constitution, specifically under Article 350A.

(*e*) Provisions related to languages are found in Articles 343 to 351, not Article 368, which deals with the procedure for amending the Constitution.

This correct identification of articles and their content is crucial for understanding the constitutional framework and governance of India.

41. (D): Benazir Bhutto became the first democratically elected woman prime minister in the Islamic world when she took office in Pakistan in 1988. Her election was a significant event, not only for Pakistan but also as a milestone for women in leadership roles in Muslim-majority countries. She served two non-consecutive terms, her first from 1988 to 1990 and the second from 1993 to 1996.

42. (B): The Planning Commission of India was converted into NITI Aayog (National Institution for Transforming India) in the year 2015. This transformation marked a significant shift from a centrally planned structure to a policy think tank aimed at fostering cooperative federalism through robust economic policymaking guided by the needs of the states.

43. (C): The Government of India conferred the status of classical languages to these languages in the following chronological order: Tamil was the first to be recognized in 2004, followed by Sanskrit in 2005. Kannada and Telugu were both accorded this status in 2008. Malayalam received the recognition in 2013, and Odia was the latest, being declared a classical language in 2014.

44. (B): Jyotiba Phule started a girls' school in Pune (Poona) in 1851. This was one of the earliest initiatives in India aimed at promoting education for girls, marking a significant step towards social reform in a society where education for women was not typically prioritized.

45. (C): Correct statements regarding administrative ideas include:

(*a*) Fred Riggs indeed advocated the sala model of administration, which describes a highly centralized administrative system often found in developing countries.

(*b*) Abraham Maslow is well-known for his hierarchy of needs theory, which outlines a five-tier model of human needs, ranging from physiological needs at the base to self-actualization at the top.

(*d*) Max Weber introduced the concept of legal-rational authority, a form of leadership that is grounded in rules and laws.

(*e*) Luther Gulick and Lyndall Urwick are associated with the concept of POSDCORB, an acronym for Planning, Organizing, Staffing, Directing, Coordinating, Reporting, and Budgeting, used in the field of management.

The incorrect statement is (*c*), as the Hawthorne effect, which describes changes in behaviour by the subjects of a study due to their awareness of being observed, was advanced by researchers at the Hawthorne plant of the Western Electric Company, not Chester Barnard.

46. (A): President Rajendra Prasad inaugurated the newly restored Somnath Temple on May 11, 1951. This event was significant as it marked the restoration of one of the most revered and historically significant temples in India, which had been repeatedly destroyed and rebuilt over the centuries. His participation underscored the importance of cultural heritage and religious continuity in post-independence India.

47. (B): 'Mook Nayak', meaning Leader of the Silent, was a newspaper published by Dr. B.R. Ambedkar. It was first issued in 1920 and served as a platform to advocate for the rights of the untouchables, challenging social discrimination and promoting the cause of Dalit empowerment. This publication was part of Ambedkar's broader efforts to address and rectify societal inequalities in India.

48. (D): Henri Fayol stated, "There is nothing absolute in management affairs. Seldom do we have to apply the same principle twice as in identical conditions; allowance must be made for different changing circumstances." Fayol, a French engineer and a key figure in the development of classical management theory, emphasized the flexibility required in management practices, acknowledging that managerial actions must adapt to varying organizational circumstances and contexts.

49. (C): Fred Riggs developed several models to analyze the administrative systems of different countries, among which the correct ones are: (*a*) Fused, (*c*) Prismatic, and (*e*) Diffracted. These models are part of Riggs' efforts to understand how administrative structures function under different societal contexts, especially in developing countries. The Fused model refers to a blending of traditional and modern administrative features, Prismatic describes societies in transition, and Diffracted represents highly differentiated and specialized administrative systems. The terms (*b*) Focused and (*d*) Rainbow are not part of Riggs' typology.

50. (B): Rani Gaidilieu was a Naga queen who responded to the call of Mahatma Gandhi and raised the banner of revolt against British rule. At the young age of 13, she joined the Heraka religious movement, which quickly turned into a political movement seeking to drive out British influence from Manipur and surrounding Naga areas. Her leadership and defiance made her a symbol of resistance and she was subsequently arrested in 1932, spending 14 years in prison for her actions.

51. (D): Burma was bifurcated from British India in the year 1937. This separation was formalized under the Government of Burma Act, 1935, which separated Burma Province from British India and established it as a separate colony under the direct governance of the British Crown. This move was part of the broader policy adjustments the British Empire was making in response to rising nationalist movements within its colonies.

52. (A): Article 40 of the Indian Constitution mentions that "The State shall take steps to organize village panchayats and endow them with such powers and authority as may be necessary to enable them to function as units of self-government." This directive principle of state policy underscores the commitment to strengthen grassroots democracy and promote decentralized governance through empowered local bodies.

53. (B): The correct statements regarding political ideas are:

(*a*) John Locke indeed championed the cause of constitutional government and was a proponent of the social contract theory.

(*c*) Jeremy Bentham developed his idea of utilitarianism, which posits that the best action is the one that maximizes utility, defined in terms of the well-being of sentient entities.

(*d*) J.S. Mill argued for the broadening of popular participation and was a strong advocate for the inclusion of women in the democratic process.

The incorrect statements are: (*b*) Montesquieu proposed a system of checks and balances through separation of powers, which became a key feature of the United States Constitution, not the British Constitution. (e) Thomas Hobbes discussed the grounds of political obligation in his work 'Leviathan', not 'Philosophy of Right', which was authored by Georg Wilhelm Friedrich Hegel.

54. (B): The correct years of creation for the states are:

(*a*) Jharkhand was created in the year 2000.

(*b*) Telangana was created in 2014, becoming the latest state formed in India.

(*c*) Goa was granted statehood in 1987.

(*d*) Sikkim was added as a state of India in 1975.

These dates reflect the periods during which significant regional and political changes led to the formation of these states, following demands for greater autonomy and recognition of distinct cultural identities.

55. (C): The 'Linking Pin Model' was conceived by Rensis Likert, not "Renin Likert". This model describes an organizational structure where every manager acts as a "linking pin" connecting the higher and lower levels of employees, facilitating communication and understanding across the organization. This model emphasizes the importance of inclusive management practices and the integration of various parts of an organization to enhance overall performance.

56. (B): Article 244 (1) of the Indian Constitution makes special provision for the administration and control of Scheduled Areas and Scheduled Tribes in any state except the states of Assam, Meghalaya, Tripura, and Mizoram. This article is part of the Constitution's framework to address the unique needs and protect the rights of indigenous communities by enabling specific governance mechanisms, such as the Fifth and Sixth Schedules, which outline the administration for these areas.

57. (C): The correct statements are:

(*a*) A consensus on poverty eradication was indeed adopted at the Seventh SAARC Summit, which reflects the regional commitment to tackle poverty as a unified agenda.

(*b*) Giuseppe Mazzini, a nationalist leader and philosopher, wrote extensively on nationalism, though not specifically titled 'On Nationality', his works heavily influenced the concept of nation-states in Europe.

(*d*) Jürgen Habermas is a leading exponent of the Second Generation of the Frankfurt School, known for his theories on communicative action and the public sphere.

The incorrect statement is (*c*) because V.D. Savarkar did indeed establish the Abhinav Bharat Society, an organization aimed at advocating for India's independence through revolutionary means.

58. (D): The correct statements are:

(*a*) Anthony Smith wrote 'The Ethnic Origins of Nations', where he discusses the role of ethnic groups in the formation of modern nations.

(*b*) Ernest Gellner's 'Nations and Nationalism' emphasizes how nationalism and the concept of nation-states emerged and their impact on societal structures.

(*c*) Malcom X was an advocate for Black nationalism and emphasized the importance of reconnecting African-Americans with their African heritage, viewing it as both a spiritual and cultural homeland.

(*e*) Eric Hobsbawm introduced the idea of 'invented traditions', which explores how many traditions that seem old are often quite recent in origin and sometimes invented for specific nationalistic or cultural purposes.

The incorrect statement is (*d*) as it was Rousseau, not John Locke, who developed the idea of the General Will, which influenced revolutionary ideas during the French Revolution.

59. (D): The correct statements regarding Comparative Politics are:

(*a*) The traditional approach in comparative politics often involves a value-laden study, focusing on normative and descriptive analysis of political systems.

(*c*) David Easton is a prominent theorist of Behaviouralism, known for his systemic approach to the study of political systems.

(*d*) David Easton's model of systems analysis in political science includes the three main variables of demands, supports, and feedbacks, providing a framework for understanding how political systems process inputs and produce outputs.

The incorrect statement is (*b*) because the behavioural approach is distinct from traditional approaches and is characterized by its emphasis on empirical, quantitative methods and the rejection of normative assertions.

60. (D): The correct matches for the books and their authors are:

(*a*) 'A Theory of Justice' was written by John Rawls, which is a seminal work in modern political philosophy and discusses theories of justice and fairness in a liberal society.

(*b*) 'Philosophy of Right' was authored by Friedrich Hegel, where he outlines his philosophy of law and ethics, including the role of the state.

(*c*) 'Towards a Rational Society' was written by Jürgen Habermas, who critiques modern society's failure to realize its potential for rationality in public discourse.

(*d*) 'State and Revolution' was penned by Vladimir Ilyich Lenin, discussing the role of the state and conditions for a proletarian revolution.

61. (C): In 1954, the Speaker of the Lok Sabha appointed the Pataskar Committee to examine the issue of delegated legislation. This committee was tasked with investigating the extent and effects of laws that allowed the executive to make decisions that would normally be the domain of the legislative branch, focusing on how such powers were granted and executed.

62. (C): Dr. B.R. Ambedkar set up the 'Bahishkrit Hitakarini Sabha' in 1924. This organization was established to promote the welfare of the outcasts—later known as Dalits—and improve their social status through various educational and socio-economic measures. It played a crucial role in advocating for the rights of the marginalized communities in India.

63. (D): M.N. Roy gave the notion of 'Radical Humanism', which he developed into a complete philosophical system. His ideology was built around human values and freedoms, distancing itself from traditional Marxist doctrine, and emphasized an intrinsic respect for all human beings while advocating for a radical restructuring of society through peaceful and democratic processes.

64. (C): The correct matches for the books and their authors are:

(*a*) 'Government by Committee' was written by K.C. Wheare, examining the use and implications of committees in governmental processes.

(*b*) 'Parliament in India' is authored by W.H. Morris-Jones, providing an in-depth look at the workings and structure of the Indian Parliament.

(*c*) 'How Britain is Governed' was written by Ramsey Muir, discussing the governance and political structures of Britain.

(*d*) 'Musolini's Italy' was penned by Herman Finer, detailing the governance, politics, and conditions under Mussolini's rule in Italy.

65. (D): President Theodore Roosevelt was awarded the Nobel Peace Prize in 1906 for his role in mediating the peace negotiations between Japan and Russia during the Russo-Japanese War. His mediation was instrumental in the signing of the Treaty of Portsmouth in 1905, which ended the conflict. Roosevelt's efforts were recognized as significant contributions to peace, making him the first American president to win a Nobel Prize.

66. (C): Vinayak Damodar Savarkar proposed the ideas of 'Pitribhu' (fatherland) and 'Punybhu' (holyland) in his classical text on the ideology of Hindutva. In his work, Savarkar conceptualizes Hindutva not just as a religious identity but as a cultural and nationalistic ideology, where 'Pitribhu' refers to the land of one's ancestors, and 'Punybhu' refers to the land where one's religion originated.

67. (A): The International Campaign to Abolish Nuclear Weapons (ICAN) won the Nobel Peace Prize in 2017. This coalition of non-governmental organizations in more than 100 countries was honored for its groundbreaking efforts to achieve a treaty-based prohibition on nuclear weapons, culminating in the United Nations Treaty on the Prohibition of Nuclear Weapons.

68. (A): The statewise membership in the Constitutional Assembly on 31 December 1947 for the states mentioned was as follows:

(*a*) Madras had 49 members,

(*b*) Bombay had 21 members,

(*c*) West Bengal had 19 members, and

(*d*) United Province (now Uttar Pradesh) had 55 members.

These numbers reflect the representation allotted based on factors including population and political significance at the time.

69. (D): The correct matches for events of the United Nations with their years are:

(*a*) Trygve Lie appointed Secretary General in 1946.

(*b*) Kofi Annan appointed Secretary General in 1997.

(*c*) U.N. Peace Keepers sent to Cyprus in 1964.

(*d*) U.N. High Commissioner for Refugees established in 1950.

These events mark significant milestones in the history of the United Nations, reflecting its evolving role in global governance and humanitarian efforts.

70. (A): The correct matches for the President's Rule in states with their tenures are:

(*a*) Andhra Pradesh had President's Rule from 18.1.1973 to 10.12.1973.

(*b*) Assam experienced President's Rule from 30.6.1981 to 13.1.1982.

(*c*) Himachal Pradesh was under President's Rule from 15.12.1992 to 3.12.1993.

(*d*) Uttarakhand was under President's Rule from 18.3.2016 to 6.5.2016.

These instances of President's Rule were invoked under Article 356 of the Indian Constitution when the state government could not be conducted in accordance with the constitutional provisions.

71. (C): The correct chronological order of these events related to the United Nations is as follows:

(*e*) The UN High Commissioner for Refugees (UNHCR) was established in 1950 to protect and support refugees at the request of a country or the UN itself.

(*c*) The first UN peacekeeping force was sent to the Suez Canal in 1956 during the Suez Crisis.

(*a*) UN peacekeepers were sent to Cyprus in 1964 to prevent further fighting between the Greek and Turkish Cypriots.

(*b*) The UN Peacekeeping Commission was established in 1948, designed to support the Security Council's decisions on peacekeeping missions.

(*d*) The General Assembly adopted the Sustainable Development Goals (SDGs) in 2015, which are a universal call to action to end poverty, protect the planet, and ensure that all people enjoy peace and prosperity by 2030.

72. **(B):** The chronological order of the Speakers of the Lok Sabha from earliest to latest is:

(*a*) Ganesh Vasudev Mavalankar served as the first Speaker from 1952 to 1956.

(*d*) Neelam Sanjiva Reddy served from 1967 to 1969 and then later became the President of India.

(*b*) P.A. Sangma served from 1996 to 1998 and was known for his role during the turbulent political times of the late 1990s.

(*e*) Ms. Meira Kumar served from 2009 to 2014 and was the first woman Speaker of the Lok Sabha.

(*c*) Om Birla has been serving since 2019 and continues to hold the position.

73. **(A):** The correct chronological order of the formation of these commissions in India is:

(*e*) National Commission for Women was established in 1992 to advise the government on all matters affecting the legal and constitutional rights of women.

(*a*) National Commission for Minorities was set up in 1993 to evaluate the progress of the development of minorities under the Union and States.

(*b*) National Commission for Scheduled Castes was formed in 2004, previously part of the National Commission for Scheduled Castes and Scheduled Tribes.

(*c*) Central Information Commission was established in 2005 under the Right to Information Act to act upon complaints from those individuals who have not been able to submit information requests due to a non-appointment of a Public Information Officer, among other duties.

(*d*) National Commission for Protection of Child Rights was set up in 2007 to ensure that all laws, policies, programs, and administrative mechanisms are in consonance with the Child Rights perspective as mandated by the Constitution of India and also the UN Convention on the Rights of the Child.

74. **(A):** The correct matches for the international human rights documents with their enactment years are:

(*a*) Convention Relating to the Status of Refugees was established in 1954.

(*b*) Declaration on Torture was recognized in 1975 as part of the broader efforts to combat torture globally.

(*c*) Convention on the Rights of the Child was adopted in 1990, which sets out the civil, political, economic, social, health, and cultural rights of children.

(*d*) Charter of Fundamental Rights of the European Union was proclaimed in 2000 and became legally binding on EU countries when the Treaty of Lisbon entered into force in December 2009.

75. **(A):** The current Dalai Lama, Tenzin Gyatso, came to India in 1959. He fled Tibet after a failed uprising against Chinese rule. His arrival in India marked the beginning of a significant exile community in India and he has since been based in Dharamsala, where the Central Tibetan Administration is also headquartered. His presence in India has been a cornerstone of the Tibetan exile community's efforts to preserve their cultural and religious identity.

76. (C): The correct statements are:

(*a*) The Supreme Court of Canada does indeed have three judges from the province of Quebec to ensure representation that reflects the civil law tradition unique to Quebec, which is different from the common law system in the rest of Canada.

(*b*) Some judges of the Federal Constitutional Court of Germany are elected by the Bundestag and some by the Bundesrat, demonstrating a shared responsibility between these federal bodies in judicial appointments.

(*d*) The US Constitution of 1787 did not explicitly provide for judicial review; this power was established by the Supreme Court in the landmark decision of Marbury vs. Madison in 1803.

The incorrect statements are: (*c*) In the United States, the judges of the Supreme Court are nominated by the President and confirmed by the Senate, not the House of Lords which is a British institution. (*e*) The power of judicial review originated in the United States in the case of Marbury vs. Madison, not in India.

77. (D): The correct chronological order of the Acts related to the implementation of the Directive Principles of State Policy is:

(*c*) The Trade Unions Act was enacted in 1926, fostering labour rights and unionization.

(*d*) The Minimum Wages Act, established in 1948, sets the minimum wages that must be paid to workers in certain types of employment.

(*e*) The Mines Act, coming into effect in 1952, aims to regulate the operation of mines and the safety of miners.

(*a*) The Bonded Labour System Abolition Act was passed in 1976, aimed at abolishing bonded labour practices.

(*b*) The Child Labour Prohibition and Regulation Act was enacted in 1986, designed to prohibit the engagement of children in certain employments and to regulate the conditions of work of children in certain other employments.

78. (B): The incorrect statements are:

(*a*) Fundamental duties were inserted by the 42nd Constitution Amendment Act of 1976, not the 44th.

(*b*) Parliament can amend the fundamental duties as they are part of the Constitution, and the Constitution can be amended by Parliament under Article 368.

(*c*) Fundamental duties are not enforceable by writs; they are intended as moral obligations that the citizens are expected to follow but are not enforceable through courts.

(*e*) Promotion of international peace and security is indeed one of the important fundamental duties listed under Article 51A.

The correct statement is (*d*) as there are indeed eleven fundamental duties listed under Article 51A of the Constitution.

79. (A): Visva-Bharati University was established by Rabindranath Tagore in 1918. It started as a school in Santiniketan, West Bengal, and later expanded into a university by 1921. Tagore founded it with the vision of bringing people from different backgrounds together to learn in a collaborative environment, blending educational philosophies from the East and the West.

80. (A): N.K. Singh was the Chairman of the 15th Finance Commission of India. His leadership was notable for addressing the fiscal needs of the Union and the States, ensuring the equitable distribution of resources in line with contemporary economic and political developments, and accommodating changes such as the introduction of the GST.

81. **(C):** The correct statements are:

(*a*) The UN declared 1975 as International Women's Year, which marked a significant global recognition of women's rights and issues. This year also witnessed the first World Conference on Women held in Mexico City.

(*b*) B.N. Rau Committee was indeed involved in preparing the initial draft of the Hindu Code Bill, which was a crucial step towards codifying and modernizing Hindu personal laws in India.

(*d*) Sunderlal Bahuguna became popular due to his role in the Chipko movement, an environmental campaign in India during the 1970s that advocated for the protection of trees and forests through the act of hugging trees to prevent them from being cut down.

The incorrect statements are: (*c*) Kabir was a social reformer in medieval India, not ancient India. His teachings challenged established norms and emphasized personal devotion to God beyond traditional religious practices. (*e*) Subhash Chandra Bose did not form the Independent Labour Party; it was formed by Dr. B.R. Ambedkar in 1936 to address the socio-political rights of the untouchables.

82. **(C):** The correct matches for legislatures and their corresponding countries are:

(*a*) House of Representatives is in the United States of America, reflecting the lower chamber of the U.S. Congress.

(*b*) National Assembly refers to Pakistan, representing the lower house of the country's parliament.

(*c*) House of Commons is located in the United Kingdom, as the lower house of the UK Parliament.

(*d*) Knesset is the national legislature of Israel, embodying its unicameral parliamentary system.

83. **(D):** The correct components of Abraham Maslow's hierarchy of needs are:

(*a*) Esteem needs, which involve the need for self-esteem, respect, and recognition from others.

(*b*) Self-actualization, which is the desire to achieve one's full potential and engage in creative or meaningful activities.

(*c*) Belonging needs, which encompass the desire for interpersonal relationships and being part of a group.

(*d*) Safety needs, which include security and protection from harm.

The incorrect statement is (e) "Entertaining needs," which is not part of Maslow's hierarchy.

84. **(D):** Gabriel Almond classified pressure groups into several categories, correctly including:

(*a*) Associational groups, which are formally organized groups with a specific interest or objective.

(*b*) Non-associational groups, which are more loosely organized and not formally structured.

(*c*) Institutional groups, which are based within established institutions like government or corporations.

(*d*) Anomic groups, which are spontaneously formed, often erupting in response to a particular event or issue.

The term (*e*) "Non-anomic groups" is not a category used by Almond in his classification.

85. **(B):** The correct sequence for the number of women elected in Lok Sabha during the specified parliamentary elections is:

(*a*) 22 women were elected in the Fifth Parliamentary Elections of 1971.

(*b*) 28 women were elected in the Seventh Parliamentary Elections of 1980.

(*c*) 28 women were elected in the Ninth Parliamentary Elections of 1989.

(*d*) 59 women were elected in the Fifteenth Parliamentary Elections of 2009, reflecting a gradual increase in the representation of women in India's parliamentary system over the years.

86. (*)

87. (C): The Democratic Party of the United States was established in 1828, making it one of the world's oldest active political parties. It was formed by supporters of Andrew Jackson, making it the party of the "common man" and emphasizing a populist approach to politics.

88. (D): The correct chronological order of these events in Indian independence movement is:

(*d*) Champaran Movement occurred in 1917, where Gandhi led farmers to protest against oppressive plantation systems.

(*e*) Peasant Movements in Kheda and Worker's Movement in Ahmedabad both took place around 1918, demonstrating early examples of non-cooperation with British authorities.

(*a*) Non-Cooperation Movement started in 1920, marking a significant nationwide campaign led by Gandhi to resist British rule.

(*c*) 'Purna Swaraj' was accepted as a goal by the Congress at the Lahore session in December 1929.

(*b*) Civil Disobedience Movement began in 1930, where Gandhi led the Salt March, a direct action campaign of tax resistance and nonviolent protest.

89. (B): The correct matches for the regional organizations and their establishment years are:

(*a*) African Union was established in 2002, making it match with III.

(*b*) Latin American Integration Association (ALADI) was established in 1980, corresponding to I.

(*c*) East Asia Summit was first held in 2005, making it align with II.

(*d*) Eurasian Economic Community was created in 2000, matching with IV.

90. (D): President Woodrow Wilson of the United States laid down the "Fourteen Points" in January 1918 as the basis for peace negotiations to end World War I. These points were designed to prevent international tensions from leading to war again and included proposals for openness in diplomacy, free trade, and the self-determination of peoples.

91. (B): The Seventeen-point Agreement was signed in May 1951. This agreement was between representatives of the Dalai Lama of Tibet and the government of the People's Republic of China. It formally incorporated Tibet within China on the condition that Tibet would be granted autonomy and the traditional authority of the Dalai Lamas would be maintained.

92. (C): According to the passage, both British India and Independent India helped China to consolidate its hold on Tibet. This assistance helped China re-establish and strengthen its control over Tibet, particularly during the period when Tibet enjoyed de-facto independent status from 1913 to 1951.

93. (D): British India facilitated the Tibetan delegation's travel through India to Peking (now Beijing) to formally accept Tibet as an autonomous part of China. This event is linked with the signing of the controversial Seventeen-point Agreement in 1951, which Tibetans claim was signed under duress.

94. (B): The passage indicates that Tibet enjoyed de-facto independent status from 1913 to 1951. This period refers to the time after the fall of the Qing dynasty and before the Seventeen-point Agreement, during which Tibet operated like an independent entity despite lacking broad international recognition.

95. (D): The Panchsheel Agreement, highlighting principles of peaceful coexistence, was signed in 1954 between India and China. This agreement is noted in the passage as an example of India's one-sided generosity, as it symbolically ended India's rights and privileges in Tibet without securing any reciprocal benefits.

96. (B): The 73rd Constitution Amendment Act, passed in 1992, is the legislative measure that constitutionalized local self-government in India. This act provided a constitutional status to the Panchayati Raj Institutions (PRIs), ensuring their creation across the country in a uniform manner and mandating their regular elections. It was a significant step in reinforcing the decentralization of authority to the grassroots level.

97. (B): The report titled 'Revitalisation of PRIs for Democracy and Development' was brought out by the L.M. Singhvi Committee in 1986. This committee made a strong case for strengthening local self-government through PRIs, emphasizing their role in fostering democracy and development at the grassroots level.

98. (B): The Ripon Resolution was accepted in 1882, named after Lord Ripon, the then Viceroy of India. It is historically significant as it marked the beginning of local self-government in India by promoting the creation of municipal institutions and thereby laying the foundation for democratic local governance.

99. (B): According to the 73rd Constitutional Amendment Act, the rural local governance structure introduced at the intermediate level is known as the Panchayat Samiti. This tier functions between the Gram Panchayat at the village level and the Zila Parishad at the district level, coordinating and integrating the work of several Gram Panchayats within its jurisdiction.

100. (B): The 64th Constitution Amendment Bill was introduced in the Parliament of India in 1989. Although it did not pass at that time, it laid the groundwork for the subsequent successful passage of the 73rd Constitution Amendment Act in 1992, which established a robust framework for Panchayati Raj Institutions across the country.

Previous Years' Paper

National Testing Agency (NTA)

UGC-NET Junior Research Fellowship & Assistant Professor Eligibility Exam

Political Science, December-2023

(Exam held on 11-12-2023)

PAPER-II

1. Which of the following is not a principle of Nozick's 'entitlement theory'?
   A. A principle of transfer-whatever is justly acquired can be freely transferred
   B. A principle of just initial acquisition- an account of how people come to initially own the things which can be transferred in accordance with (1)
   C. A principle of final acquisition- our account of how people come to finally own the things which have been transferred in accordance with (1)
   D. A principle of rectification of injustice- how to deal with holdings if they were unjustly acquired or transferred.

2. What is the main argument of philosophical anarchism?
   A. That no state should exist.
   B. That no state in fact has authority.
   C. That arguments for philosophical anarchism are opposed to liberal principles.
   D. That all states should exist in mutual cooperation and harmony.

3. Name the country that does not fall within the 'Asian Tiger' economies:
   A. South Korea
   B. Singapore
   C. Hong Kong
   D. Burma

4. Aristotle criticized popular rule on the ground that masses would resent the wealth of the few, and too easily, fall under the sway of the following:
   A. The King
   B. The leading citizens
   C. The demagogue
   D. None of the given options

5. Which of the following concepts are not related to John Rawls?
   A. Justice as Fairness
   B. Distributive Justice
   C. Class in itself
   D. Veil of ignorance

6. Who among the following thinkers is not associated with Feminist Theory?
   A. Susan Sontag B. Carole Pateman
   C. Martha Nussbaum D. Judith Butler

7. Which of the following is not, according to Bhikhu Parekh, a question usually ignored by Indian political thought?
   A. Modern Individual thinkers
   B. The nature of Indian state
   C. Social Justice
   D. Political Economy

8. Which of the following did not feature as a matter of debate between Mahatma Gandhi and Rabindra Nath Tagore?
   A. English Language

B. Nationalism
C. The spinning wheel
D. Freedom from colonial rule

9. Who of the following described Kabir as 'Muktidoot'?
A. Rabindra Nath Tagore
B. Mahatma Gandhi
C. Madan Mohan Malviya
D. Gopal Krishna Gokhale

10. Which of the following thinker is associated with 'syncretism'?
A. Abul Fazl
B. Kabir
C. Zia-ud-din Barani
D. Tulsidas

11. Who among the following has started the self-respect movement as part of social reform?
A. Mahatma Gandhi
B. Pandit Deen Dayal Upadhyay
C. E.V. Ramaswami Naicker
D. Swami Vivekananda

12. According to Manu, which of the following is not the foundation of diplomacy and statecraft?
A. Hostility
B. Neutrality
C. Subordinate Alliance
D. Contract

13. The book 'Capitalism, Socialism and Democracy' is authored by:
A. Joseph Schumpeter
B. Samuel Huntington
C. Andre Gunder Frank
D. Joseph Lapalombara

14. The theory that argues, "countries are more likely both to become democratic and to stay democratic as they develop economically", is known as:
A. Dependency theory
B. World systems theory
C. Classic modernization theory
D. Theory of underdevelopment

15. The process in which the dictatorial ruling elite introduces liberalizing reforms that ultimately lead to a democratic transition is known as:
A. Bottom-up democratic transition
B. Top-down democratic transition
C. First reverse wave
D. Second reverse wave

16. The present political regime in the Central Asia Republic of Tajikistan falls under which of the following category?
A. Monarchy
B. Military dictatorship
C. Democracy
D. Civilian dictatorship

17. Which event led George W. Bush to transform his foreign policy into one of global power projection and interventionism?
A. 26th November B. 11th September
C. 5th December D. 11th October

18. The true beginning of the modern state system marked the end of:
A. Fifty years war
B. Thirty years war
C. One hundred years war
D. Ten years war

19. Who found eight distinct meanings for the term "Balance of Power"?
A. Iris L. Claude, Jr
B. Ernst B. Haas
C. Richard Coleden
D. Alfred Vagdt

20. Who said that statesmen "think and act in terms of interest defined as power"?
A. Morgenthau
B. George F. Kennan
C. Harold Nicholson
D. Henry A. Kissinger

21. Which two countries' navies are jointly patrolling the Malacca Straits?
A. India-Japan
B. India-United States

C. India-Australia
D. India-Singapore

22. In which year did the UN climate change conference commonly known as Copenhagen summit hold?
A. 2009 B. 2006
C. 2010 D. 2012

23. Which year did Prime Minister Manmohan Singh visit China?
A. 2006 B. 2007
C. 2008 D. 2009

24. With which country India signed the declaration "to promote the building of a harmonius world of durable peace and common prosperity through developing the strategic and cooperative partnership for peace and prosperity"
A. United States B. China
C. United Kingdom D. Japan

25. Which one of the following is not the key element of direct democracy?
A. Referendum B. Recall
C. Filibustering D. Plebiscite

26. Who has stated that, religion is the real criterion of Manu's state-polity?
A. Nalini Sinha
B. Satyamitra Dubey
C. Mahendra Prasad Singh
D. Himanshu Roy

27. Which amendment overrode the Golaknath case decided in 1967?
A. Twenty third amendment
B. Twenty fourth amendment
C. Twenty fifth amendment
D. Twenty sixth amendment

28. Which of the subject is not the part of concurrent list?
A. Bankruptcy and insolvency
B. Prevention of cruelty to animals
C. Markets and fairs
D. Economic and social planning

29. B.R. Ambedkar demanded a separate electorate for the depressed classes in which of the following events?
A. First round table conference
B. Second round table conference
C. Third round table conference
D. Fourth round table conference

30. Linguistic Provinces Commission that was formed to advise Constituent Assembly was popularly known as:
A. Dar Commission
B. Menon Commission
C. Mukherjee Commission
D. Bose Commission

31. Satyashodhak samaj was founded by:
A. Ayyankalj B. Jyotiba Phule
C. B.R. Ambedkar D. Periyar

32. Under which of the following article of Indian constitution, the state legislature has power to make provision with respect to elections to such legislature?
A. Article 324 B. Article 326
C. Article 328 D. Article 352

33. Who among the following came out with an innovative idea of 'constructive conflict'?
A. Mary Parker Follett
B. Woodrow Wilson
C. Max Weber
D. Henry Fayol

34. Who introduced to organizations the concepts of the 40-hour week, time and motion studies and piece-rate compensation systems, as well as a 'fair day's work for a fair day's pay'?
A. Woodrow Wilson
B. Frederick Taylor
C. Max Weber
D. Elton Mayo

35. The paper entitled 'The study of administration', published in Political Science Quarterly in 1887, was written by:
A. Henry Fayol

B. Woodrow Wilson
C. Mary Parker Follett
D. Max Weber

36. Who wrote the book- Management: Tasks, Responsibilities, Practices?
A. John Dorr B. Peter Drucker
C. Gillian Tett D. Brene Brown

37. Mazdoor Kisan Shakti Sangathan (MKSS) pioneered which movement in India?
A. Namantar Andolan
B. Nirbhaya Movement
C. Jan Sunwai
D. None of the above

38. Citizens' charter was first articulated and implemented in UK as a national programme in which year?
A. 1989 B. 1991
C. 1993 D. 1998

39. Which one of the following is not a function of the estimates committee?
A. To suggest alternative policies in order to bring about efficiency and economy in administration
B. To examine whether the money is well laid out within the policy implied in the estimates
C. To examine the report of the CAG with a view to find out that the money voted by the Parliament has been utilized by the authority concerned.
D. To suggest the form in which estimates can be presented to Parliament

40. Which of the following is a right characteristic of the composition of the Public Accounts Committee?
A. Public Accounts Committee is composed of only Lok Sabha members.
B. Public Accounts Committee is an annually elected body in accordance with the principle of the proportional representation followed by single transferable vote system.
C. Public Accounts Committee is composed of 30 (Thirty) members.
D. No member can be re-elected to the Public Accounts Committee.

41. Which of the following statements explain Bhikhu Parekh's conception of human nature?
(*a*) All references to human nature should be subjected to the strictest scrutiny and viewed with a healthy dose of skepticism.
(*b*) Human beings are culturally embedded, in the sense that they are born into, raised in and deeply shaped by their cultural communities.
(*c*) Regardless of their different cultural contexts, human beings behave more or less in a uniform manner when it comes to critical matters.
(*d*) Although skin colour, gender, height and other physical features are universally shared, they are all differently conceptualized and acquire different meaning and significance in different societies.
(*e*) Skin colour is given a deep metaphysical meaning and made the basis of a differential distribution of power and status in all societies.
A. (*a*), (*b*) and (*c*) only
B. (*b*), (*c*) and (*d*) only
C. (*a*), (*b*) and (*d*) only
D. (*d*), (*e*) and (*b*) only

42. Which of the following arguments can we associate with 'right' wing political forces?
(*a*) To what extent are people poor because of their own choices as opposed to unequal opportunities?
(*b*) Are we helping the victims of unequal circumstances if we redistribute money to the poor?
(*c*) Has the welfare state helped the poor overcome their disadvantage and participate in society?

(*d*) Has the welfare state created a class of welfare dependants caught in a poverty trap?

(*e*) Are the sources of social ills like poverty, homelessness, high school drop-out rates, and so on so complex that state attempts to solve them will generally fail, and often worsen the problem?

A. (*a*), (*b*) and (*c*) only
B. (*a*), (*d*) and (*e*) only
C. (*a*), (*c*) and (*e*) only
D. (*a*), (*b*) and (*d*) only

43. Which of the following observations are correct about deliberative democracy?

(*a*) Deliberative democracy describes a normative ideal in which free and equal citizens publicly exchange reasons with one another.

(*b*) They do with a view to reaching a consensus about some issue or policy or about the principles underlying the system as a whole.

(*c*) The central claim is that a political decision or system is legitimate even if it cannot command free and reasoned agreement among equals

(*d*) Clearly this is a practical conception, which contemporary political life- with partisan rivalries and messy compromises often conforms to.

(*e*) Underlying the deliberative ideal is a powerful moral institution about the nature of truly democratic association

A. (*a*), (*b*) and (*e*) only
B. (*a*), (*b*) and (*c*) only
C. (*b*), (*c*) and (*d*) only
D. (*b*), (*d*) and (*e*) only

44. Which of the following aspects of Gandhi's theory of Satyagraha can help in the process of dialogue in plural societies threatened by mutual distrust?

(*a*) Attention to the preconditions of dialogue helps to establish the moral standing of the participants.

(*b*) Knowledge that our grasp over truth is partial inculcates self-restraint.

(*c*) The Satyagrahi is not responsible for creating and recreating dialogical space

(*d*) Commitment to non-violence dissipates feelings of alienation and otherness

(*e*) A readiness to compromise may negate the moral standing of participants

A. (*a*), (*b*) (*c*) and (*d*) only
B. (*a*), (*b*) and (*d*) only
C. (*b*), (*c*), (*d*) and (*e*) only
D. (*a*), (*c*), (*d*) and (*e*) only

45. Who among the following thinkers are associated with participatory democracy?

(*a*) Carole Pateman
(*b*) Ian Shapiro
(*c*) Benjamin Barber
(*d*) Jurgen Habermas
(*e*) C.B. Macpherson

A. (*a*), (*b*) and (*c*) only
B. (*a*), (*b*) and (*d*) only
C. (*a*), (*c*) and (*e*) only
D. (*a*), (*c*) and (*d*) only

46. What is correct about the qualification and appointment of the Governor?

(*a*) He is a citizen of India
(*b*) He has completed the age of 25 years
(*c*) He is appointed by the Prime Minister
(*d*) He holds the office of Governor for a term of 6 years.
(*e*) He resigns from his office, by writing under his hand addressed to the Prime Minister.

A. (*a*) only
B. (*a*) and (*b*) only
C. (*a*), (*b*) and (*d*) only
D. (*a*), (*b*) (*c*), (*d*), (*e*) only

47. Which of the following statements is not associated with Mahatma Gandhi?

(*a*) 'Non-violence is the law of our species as violence is the law of the brute'.

(*b*) 'A nation that is capable of limitless sacrifices is capable of rising to limitless height'.

(*c*) The injuction 'love your enemies' is not only the noblest idealism, it is also the most practical politics

(*d*) 'To be same in a world of mad men is itself a form of madness'

(*e*) 'My nationalism is intense internationalism'

A. (*a*), (*c*), (*d*), (*e*) only

B. (*a*), (*d*), (*e*) only

C. (*a*), (*b*), (*c*), (*e*) only

D. (*a*), (*b*), (*c*), (*d*), (*e*) only

48. What is true about the following statement related to Ram Manohar Lohia?

(*a*) He discusses seven types of revolution.

(*b*) He talks about 'Partyless Democracy'

(*c*) He is an author of the 'Aspects of socialist policy'

(*d*) He did not give the concept of 'Four-Pillar State'

(*e*) He said that 'the history of the growth of freedom is the history of the perfection of human relationship'

A. (*a*), (*b*), (*e*) only B. (*a*), (*c*), (*e*) only

C. (*b*), (*d*), (*e*) only D. (*b*), (*c*), (*d*) only

49. Who among the following vice-president of India later became the president of the country?

(*a*) Dr. Sarvapalli Radhakrishnan

(*b*) V.V. Giri

(*c*) Dr. Shankar Dayal Sharma

(*d*) B.D. Jatti

(*e*) R. Venkataraman

A. (*a*), (*b*) and (*e*) only

B. (*c*) and (*d*) only

C. (*a*), (*b*) and (*d*) only

D. (*a*), (*b*), (*c*) and (*e*) only

50. Find out the books written by Mahatma Gandhi given below

(*a*) Modern India

(*b*) Constructive Programme

(*c*) India's struggle for Independence

(*d*) Why socialism

(*e*) Hind Swaraj

A. (*a*) only B. (*d*) only

C. (*c*) only D. (*b*) and (*e*) only

51. Find out the correct definition of different scholars on party systems

(*a*) Modern democracy is a party democracy (Katz)

(*b*) Democracy is unthinkable save in terms of parties (Schumpeter)

(*c*) Parties are the core institutions of democratic politics (Lipset)

(*d*) The existence of political parties is often as a necessary condition for the existence of modern democracy (Robert Dahl)

A. (*a*), (*b*), (*c*), (*d*) only

B. (*b*) only

C. (*d*) only

D. (*a*) & (*c*) only

52. Find out the correct one with regard to "Failed state".

(*a*) Sierra Leone is a failed state.

(*b*) A failed state is unable to provide the functions that define them as states.

(*c*) A failed state is able to coerce the inhabitants.

(*d*) A failed state is able to successfully control the inhabitants.

A. (*c*) only B. (*d*) only

C. (*b*) & (*c*) only D. (*a*) & (*b*) only

53. Find out the correct one with regard to constructivist argument on democracy.

(*a*) Constructivist argument treats culture as something that is objective and inherited.

(*b*) Constructivist argument states that culture exists prior to, and remains unchanged by political interaction.

(*c*) Constructivist argument treats culture as something that is constructed or invented rather than inherited.

(*d*) Constructivist argument claims that culture has a causal effect.

A. (*a*), (*b*), (*c*) only

B. (*d*), (*c*), (*b*) only

C. (*c*) & (*d*) only
D. (*a*) & (*b*) only

54. Find out the correct one with regard to Atul Kohli's distinction between pro-market and pro-business state intervention in India in 1980s:
(*a*) Pro-business strategy mainly supports established producers
(*b*) Pro-business strategy supports new entrants and consumers
(*c*) Pro-market strategy supports established producers
(*d*) Pro-market strategy supports new entrants and consumers

A. (*b*) only B. (*c*) only
C. (*a*) & (*c*) only D. (*a*) & (*d*) only

55. Find out the correct one with regard to 108th Amendment Bill, 2008:
(*a*) Reservation of seats reserved for scheduled caste shall be for women shall cease to exit 15 years after the commencement of this Bill
(*b*) It seeks to reserve one-third of all seats for women in the Lok Sabha only
(*c*) One-third of the total number of seats reserved for scheduled castes shall be reserved for women of this group in legislative assemblies only
(*d*) Reserved seats may be allotted by rotation to different constituencies in the state or UTs

A. (*a*) & (*b*) only B. (*b*) only
C. (*a*) & (*d*) only D. (*c*) only

56. Choose the correct statements given below:
(*a*) India is amongst the first countries to establish diplomatic relations with EEC.
(*b*) The bilateral relationship was upgraded to strategic partnership in 2004
(*c*) The EU is also one of the largest sources of FDI for India
(*d*) The EU is a member of UN General Assembly.

A. (*a*), (*b*) & (*c*) B. (*b*), (*c*) & (*d*)
C. (*a*), (*c*) & (*d*) D. (*a*), (*b*) & (*d*)

57. Choose the correct statements given below:
(*a*) Conflict in society and politics is inevitable
(*b*) The usage of violence in conflicts cannot be eliminated by protests against such violence.
(*c*) Non-violent action can be categorized into three methods: protests and persuasion, non-cooperation and non-violent intervention
(*d*) Use of non-violent methods is a guarantee of success

A. (*b*), (*c*) & (*d*)
B. (*a*), (*c*) & (*d*)
C. (*a*), (*b*), (*c*) & (*d*)
D. (*a*), (*b*) & (*c*)

58. Find out the correct statements:
(*a*) On 1st April 1950, India was the first non-socialist bloc country to establish diplomatic relations with China
(*b*) Prime Minister Nehru never visited China during his premiership
(*c*) A phase of improvement in bilateral relations began in 1988.
(*d*) Rajiv Gandhi as the Prime Minister of India visited China in 1993

A. (*a*) & (*b*) B. (*a*) & (*c*)
C. (*c*) & (*d*) D. (*b*) & (*c*)

59. Choose the correct statement from the following:
(*a*) Under chapter-VII of the UN Charter, the Security Council can take action to maintain or restore international peace and security.
(*b*) Under Art. 41 sanction measures do not involve the use of armed force.
(*c*) Sanctions can be withdrawn by the UN General Assembly.
(*d*) Sanctions have been applied by the Security Council to support peaceful transitions, to deter non-constitutional changes etc.

A. (*a*), (*b*) & (*d*) only
B. (*b*), (*c*) & (*d*) only

C. (*c*), (*d*) & (*a*) only
D. (*a*), (*c*) & (*d*) only

60. Choose the correct statements from the following:
(*a*) Weapons of Mass Destruction, inter alia include atomic explosive Weapons.
(*b*) Biological weapons are not included under the category of Weapons of Mass Destruction
(*c*) Chemical Weapons Convention outlaws the Weapons of Mass Destruction.
(*d*) Chemical Weapons Convention entered into force in 1998.
A. (*a*) & (*b*) only B. (*c*) & (*d*) only
C. (*a*) & (*c*) only D. (*b*) & (*c*) only

61. 73rd constitution Amendment Act, 1992 has stipulated the following major provisions regarding Panchayat:
(*a*) A Gram Sabha may exercise such powers and perform such functions at the village level as the legislature of a state may by law, provide
(*b*) A Finance Commission to be constituted every fifth year by the Governor of a state to review the financial position of the Panchayat and to make recommendations to the Governor
(*c*) The legislature of a state cannot endow the Panchayat with any more powers and authority for their functioning as institutions of self-Government.
(*d*) An election to constitute a Panchayats shall be completed before the expiration of a period of six months from the date of its dissolution.
A. (*a*), (*b*) & (*c*) only
B. (*b*), (*c*) & (*d*) only
C. (*a*), (*b*), & (*d*) only
D. (*c*), (*b*) & (*d*) only

62. The concept of accountability has got the following characteristics:
(*a*) Accountability exists in a relationship when for the performance of functions an individual or a body is subject to another oversight, direction or request that the individual or the body should provide justification for their actions.
(*b*) There are various types of accountability like legal accountability, social accountability, political accountability and so on.
(*c*) Accountability can be found only in the institutions and processes of the developed countries.
(*d*) The effectiveness of public officials cannot be evaluated through the process of accountability.
A. (*a*), (*b*) & (*c*) only
B. (*a*), (*c*) & (*d*) only
C. (*b*) & (*c*) only
D. (*a*) & (*b*) only

63. Which of the following statements are correct in the arena of administrative theories:
(*a*) Ideal type bureaucracy was formulated by Max Weber.
(*b*) Frederick Taylor is considered as the father of Scientific Management Theory.
(*c*) Henry Fayol is considered to be the father of Human Relations Theory.
(*d*) The Hawthorne experiment is associated with Bureaucratic theory.
A. (*a*), (*c*) & (*d*) only
B. (*c*) & (*d*) only
C. (*a*) & (*b*) only
D. (*b*), (*c*) & (*d*) only

64. In his book Administration in Developing Countries: The Theory of Prismatic Society, Riggs mentioned the following points:
(*a*) The structures of a modern society are typically functionally specific.
(*b*) A structure is defined as any pattern of behaviour, which has become a standard feature of a social system
(*c*) Industria will move towards Agraria through the process of transition in the society.

(*d*) Although the "image" of Agraria resembles the 'model' of a fused society, the two constructions are by no means identical.

A. (*a*), (*b*) & (*d*) only
B. (*a*), (*b*) & (*c*) only
C. (*b*), (*c*) & (*d*) only
D. (*a*), (*c*) & (*d*) only

65. Which of the following statements is/are not correct regarding the ICT based e-governance?

(*a*) E-governance reduces the cost of government.
(*b*) E-governance reduces the transparency of government.
(*c*) E-governance increases citizen's input into government.
(*d*) E-governance increases bureaucratic red tapism.

A. (*a*), (*b*) & (*c*) only
B. (*b*) & (*d*) only
C. (*b*), (*c*) & (*d*) only
D. (*a*) & (*c*) only

66. Match List-I with List-II.

List-I	List-II
(*a*) Liberalism	I. Shared understanding and common meaning, based on shared history, culture or world-view
(*b*) Communitarianism	II. No need for member to share a common culture, history, world-view, language or value system
(*c*) Liberal Nationalism	III. Moral concern for one another as free and equal citizens
(*d*) Multi-culturalism/ Difference theory	IV. Shared nationality, based on a common history, language and culture

	(*a*)	(*b*)	(*c*)	(*d*)
A.	I	II	III	IV
B.	IV	III	II	I
C.	II	IV	I	III
D.	III	II	IV	I

67. Match List-I with List-II.

List-I	List-II
(*a*) Antonio Gramsci	I. On human conduct
(*b*) Robert Putnam	II. Prison notebooks
(*c*) Michael Qakeshott	III. The protestant ethics and the spirit of capitalism
(*d*) Max Weber	IV. Bowling Alone: The collapse and revival of American community

	(*a*)	(*b*)	(*c*)	(*d*)
A.	I	II	III	IV
B.	III	IV	II	I
C.	II	IV	I	III
D.	IV	III	I	II

68. Match List-I with List-II.

List-I (Books)	List-II (Writers)
(*a*) A plea for the Reconstruction of Indian Polity	I. V.D. Savarkar
(*b*) India of my Dreams	II. Ram Manohar Lohia
(*c*) The Indian War of independence of 1857	III. M.K. Gandhi
(*d*) Marx, Gandhi and Socialism	IV. Jayaprakash Narayan

	(*a*)	(*b*)	(*c*)	(*d*)
A.	I	III	II	IV
B.	IV	III	I	II
C.	I	II	IV	III
D.	IV	III	II	I

69. Match List-I with List-II.

List-I (Idea)	List-II (Thinker)
(*a*) Extremely Federal	I. Morris Jones
(*b*) Quasi Federal	II. Granville Austin
(*c*) Bargaining Federal	III. K.C. Wheare
(*d*) Cooperative Federal	IV. Paul Appleby

	(a)	(b)	(c)	(d)
A.	I	III	II	IV
B.	IV	III	II	I
C.	I	IV	II	III
D.	IV	III	I	II

70. Match List-I with List-II.

List-I (Electoral Systems Terminologies)	List-II (Meaning)
(*a*) Universal suffrage	I. An electoral system in which individuals cast a single vote for a candidate in a single-member district
(*b*) Majoritarian electoral systems	II. A form of majoritarian electoral systems that involves preferential voting
(*c*) Single-member district plurality system	III. The right to vote which is not restricted by race, gender, belief or social status.
(*d*) Alternative vote	IV. An electoral system in which the candidates or parties that receive the most votes win

	(a)	(b)	(c)	(d)
A.	III	IV	I	II
B.	I	II	III	IV
C.	IV	III	II	I
D.	II	I	III	IV

71. Match List-I with List-II.

List-I (Books)	List-II (Authors)
(*a*) The success of India's democracy	I. C.P. Bhambri
(*b*) Caste in Indian Politics	II. Atul Kohli
(*c*) Political process in India, 1947-1991	III. Rajni Kothari
(*d*) The oxford companion to politics in India	IV. Nirja Jayal and Pratap B. Mehta

	(a)	(b)	(c)	(d)
A.	I	II	III	IV
B.	IV	III	II	I
C.	II	III	I	IV
D.	III	IV	II	I

72. Match the following organization with the year it was established in.

List-I	List-II
(*a*) SCO	I. 1967
(*b*) BRIC	II. 2006
(*c*) ASEAN	III. 1957
(*d*) EEC	IV. 2001

	(a)	(b)	(c)	(d)
A.	III	I	II	IV
B.	IV	II	I	III
C.	I	II	III	IV
D.	II	III	IV	I

73. Match the past interventions with the year in which they took place.

List-I (Country)	List-II (Year)
(*a*) Iraq	I. 1991
(*b*) Darfur, Sudan	II. 2000
(*c*) Somalia	III. 2004
(*d*) Sierra Leone	IV. 1992

	(a)	(b)	(c)	(d)
A.	I	IV	III	II
B.	III	II	I	IV
C.	II	III	I	IV
D.	I	III	IV	II

74. Match List-I with List-II.

List-I	List-II
(*a*) Administration in developing countries: The theory of prismatic society	I. Herbert Simon
(*b*) Administrative behaviour	II. Gerald E. Caiden
(*c*) The dynamics of public administration: Guidelines to current transformations in theory and practice	III. Fred W. Riggs

(*d*) The human problem of an industrial civilization — IV. Elton Mayo

	(*a*)	(*b*)	(*c*)	(*d*)
A.	II	III	I	IV
B.	III	II	I	IV
C.	III	I	II	IV
D.	IV	III	II	I

75. Match List-I with List-II.

List-I	List-II
(*a*) Scientific management theory	I. Decision making process involves three phases–intelligence activity, design activity and choice activity
(*b*) New public management	II. The development of a true science of work, which in effect will benefit both the workers and manager alike
(*c*) Human relations theory	III. Government should be continuously engaged in improving quality of its programmes and services and therely adjusting with demands
(*d*) Rational decision-making theory	IV. Organization is to be viewed as a social system and informal elements play an important role in the overall organizational output.

	(*a*)	(*b*)	(*c*)	(*d*)
A.	II	III	IV	I
B.	III	II	IV	I
C.	III	IV	II	I
D.	I	III	II	IV

76. Arrange the following in their theoretical sequence, in keeping with the Marxist conception or the materialist conception of history

(*a*) The proletariat seizes political power and turns the means of production into state property.

(*b*) Finally the proletariat abolishes itself, abolishes all class distinctions and class antagonism and also abolishes the state as state

(*c*) While the capitalist mode of production more and more transforms the great majority of the population into proletarians, it creates a power that is forced to accomplish a revolution against capitalism

(*d*) The present structure of society is the creation of the current ruling class, the bourgeoisie

(*e*) Steam, machinery and the making of machines by machinery transformed the older manufacture, carried out under feudalism, into modern industry.

A. (*a*), (*b*), (*c*), (*d*), (*e*)
B. (*e*), (*d*), (*c*), (*a*), (*b*)
C. (*d*), (*a*), (*b*), (*c*), (*e*)
D. (*c*), (*a*), (*b*), (*e*), (*d*)

77. Arrange the following in a sequence that historically and conceptually presents the concepts of civil society.

(*a*) It can be understood as a collective entity that springs from society and exists for specific and limited purposes

(*b*) The concept was part of the economic and political liberalism that arose with John Locke and was celebrated by Scottish enlightenment.

(*c*) Civil society is one among many spheres of the larger society along with family, economy polities etc.

(*d*) The concept found a significant place in the writings of Hegel and Marx in the 19th century.

(*e*) The first articulation of the concept took place in the 17th and 18th centuries in Europe.

A. (*a*), (*b*), (*c*), (*d*), (*e*)
B. (*b*), (*d*), (*c*), (*e*), (*a*)
C. (*c*), (*a*), (*e*), (*b*), (*d*)
D. (*e*), (*b*), (*a*), (*c*), (*d*)

78. Arrange the organizations in chronology according to the year of their establishment:
(*a*) Tolstoy Farm
(*b*) Abhinav Bharat Society
(*c*) Ramkrishna Mission
(*d*) Sharda Sadan
(*e*) Bahishkrit Hitakarini Sabha
A. (*c*), (*d*), (*e*), (*b*), (*a*)
B. (*d*), (*a*), (*c*), (*b*), (*e*)
C. (*d*), (*c*), (*b*), (*a*), (*e*)
D. (*c*), (*d*), (*a*), (*b*), (*e*)

79. Arrange these life events of 'Aurobindo' in a chronological order
(*a*) Attended the Banaras session of the Congress
(*b*) Became the vice-principal of Baroda college
(*c*) Moved to England
(*d*) Arrested for the Alipore bomb case
(*e*) Cleared the ICS exam
A. (*c*), (*a*), (*d*), (*b*), (*e*)
B. (*e*), (*c*), (*a*), (*b*), (*d*)
C. (*a*), (*b*), (*e*), (*c*), (*d*)
D. (*c*), (*e*), (*b*), (*a*), (*d*)

80. Find out the different waves of democratic transition given below in ascending order:
(*a*) First reverse wave
(*b*) First waves of democratization
(*c*) Second wave of democratization
(*d*) Second reverse wave
(*e*) Third wave of democratization
A. (*a*), (*b*), (*c*), (*d*), (*e*)
B. (*b*), (*a*), (*c*), (*d*), (*e*)
C. (*e*), (*d*), (*c*), (*a*), (*b*)
D. (*c*), (*d*), (*e*), (*b*), (*a*)

81. Find out the agreements/accords signed between Indian government and its provincial regional organisations given below in ascending order:
(*a*) Assam Accord
(*b*) Anandpur Sahib Resolution
(*c*) Rajiv Gandhi-Longowal Accord
(*d*) Shillong Agreement
(*e*) Mizo Peace Accord
A. (*b*), (*d*), (*c*), (*a*), (*e*)
B. (*e*), (*a*), (*c*), (*b*), (*d*)
C. (*a*), (*b*), (*c*), (*d*), (*e*)
D. (*e*), (*d*), (*c*), (*b*), (*a*)

82. Arrange chronologically India's association with the following international organization:
(*a*) United Nations (*b*) G77
(*c*) NAM (*d*) G20
A. (*a*), (*b*), (*c*), (*d*)
B. (*a*), (*c*), (*b*), (*d*)
C. (*b*), (*a*), (*c*), (*d*)
D. (*d*), (*b*), (*a*), (*c*)

83. Arrange the following Director Generals of WTO who held office in ascending order:
(*a*) Mike Moore
(*b*) Pascal Lamy
(*c*) Supachai Panitchpakdi
(*d*) Roberto Azevedo
A. (*a*), (*c*), (*b*), (*d*)
B. (*a*), (*b*), (*d*), (*c*)
C. (*c*), (*b*), (*a*), (*d*)
D. (*d*), (*a*), (*b*), (*c*)

84. Arrange the following committees with regards to corruption and administrative reforms in India chronologically:
(*a*) Gorwala committee
(*b*) First Administrative Reforms Commission
(*c*) Vohra committee
(*d*) Shanthanam Committee
A. (*a*), (*b*), (*c*), (*d*)
B. (*b*), (*a*), (*c*), (*d*)
C. (*a*), (*d*), (*b*), (*c*)
D. (*b*), (*a*), (*d*), (*c*)

85. Arrange the following administrative thinkers/theorists chronologically
(*a*) F.W. Willoughby
(*b*) Max Weber
(*c*) David Easton
(*d*) Elton Mayo

A. (*a*), (*b*), (*c*), (*d*)
B. (*d*), (*c*), (*b*), (*a*)
C. (*b*), (*a*), (*d*), (*c*)
D. (*c*), (*b*), (*a*), (*d*)

86. Given below are two statements: one is labelled as Assertion (A) and the other is labelled as Reason (R).

Assertion (A): It is plausible to think that autonomy involves a kind of skill that individuals must develop, exercise and maintain. This ongoing process of planning and managing is not automatic but requires efforts and resources that are secured by social and material conditions provided by the state.

Reason (R): However, the commitment to individual autonomy cannot force the liberal state to provide the social and material conditions by which citizens could come to be autonomous. It must depend on the individuals to strive independently for achieving their autonomy.

In the light of the above statements, choose the most appropriate answer from the options given below:
A. Both (A) and (R) are correct and (R) is the correct explanation of (A)
B. Both (A) and (R) are correct, but (R) is not the correct explanation of (A)
C. (A) is correct, but (R) is not correct
D. (A) is not correct, but (R) is correct

87. Given below are two statements: one is labelled as Assertion (A) and the other is labelled as Reason (R).

Assertion (A): 'Ahimsa' was complementary to Gandhi's model of conflict resolution that was certainly the most original and creative model of social change and political action.

Reason (R): This was a theory of politics that gradually became the dominant ideology of a national political movement in which Gandhi reigned supreme.

In the light of the above statements, choose the most appropriate answer from the options given below:
A. Both (A) and (R) are correct and (R) is the correct explanation of (A)
B. Both (A) and (R) are correct, but (R) is not the correct explanation of (A)
C. (A) is correct, but (R) is not correct
D. (A) is not correct, but (R) is correct

88. Given below are two statements:

Statement I: The transformation of India's economy has not been as dramatic as that of post-communist countries in Eastern Europe.

Statement II: India has produced growth rates as high as those of China in 2010s.

In the light of the above statements, choose the most appropriate answer from the options given below:
A. Both Statement I and Statement II are correct
B. Both Statement I and statement II are incorrect
C. Statement I is correct, but statement II is incorrect
D. Statement I is incorrect, but statement II is correct

89. Given below are two statements: one is labelled as Assertion (A) and the other is labelled as Reason (R).

Assertion (A): India has historically been deemed a safe heaven for refugees

Reason (R): India has no refugee law and has not signed the 1951 Refugee Convention

In the light of the above statements, choose the most appropriate answer from the options given below
A. Both (A) and (R) are correct and (R) is the correct explanation of (A)
B. Both (A) and (R) are correct, but (R) is not the correct explanation of (A)

C. (A) is correct, but (R) is not correct
D. (A) is not correct, but (R) is correct

90. Given below are two statements: one is labelled as Assertion (A) and the other is labelled as Reason (R).

Assertion (A): Contracting out and public private partnerships are now part of the reality of public services and decision making in many countries.

Reason (R): There is a divorce between the complex reality of decision making associated with governance and the normative codes used to explain and justify government.

In the light of the above statements, choose the most appropriate answer from the options given below

A. Both (A) and (R) are correct and (R) is the correct explanation of (A)
B. Both (A) and (R) are correct but (R) is not the correct explanation of (A)
C. (A) is correct, but (R) is not correct
D. (A) is not correct, but (R) is correct

Directions (Qs. No. 91-95): *Read the following passage and answer the questions.*

What are the seed beds of civic virtue? There are a variety of aspects of liberal society that can be seen as inculcating CIVIC virtues, including the market, civic associations, and the family. Let me briefly look at each of these theorists of the 'New Right' often praise the market as a school of civic virtue. Many Thatcher/Reagan reforms of the 1980s aimed to extend the scope of markets in people's lives through free trade, deregulation, tax cuts, the weakening of trade unions, and reducing welfare benefits in part in order to teach people the virtues of initiative and self-reliance. Much of the recent right wing attack on the welfare state has been formulated precisely in terms of citizenship. The welfare state was said to promote passivity amongst the poor, creating a culture of dependency reducing citizens to passive dependants under bureaucratic tutelage. The market, by contrast, encourages people to be self-supporting. The new right believes that being self-supporting is not only an important civic virtue in itself, but also a precondition for being accepted as a full member of society. By failing to meet the obligation to support themselves, the long-term unemployed are a source of shame for society as well as themselves.

91. What is it that the 'New Right' does not associate with 'self-supporting' as a civic virtue?
A. Citizenship
B. Full membership of a society
C. Being a career oriented selfish person
D. Full filling the obligation to support oneself

92. How does the welfare state promote passivity in the poor?
A. Offering employment to the unworthy
B. Creating a culture of dependency
C. Giving free subsidies to the entire population
D. Incentivizing the habit of laziness

93. How does the market inculcate civic virtue according to New Right' theorists
A. By accelerating trade and commerce
B. By offering gainful employment
C. By encouraging to be self-supporting
D. By punishing those who are unemployed

94. Which of the aspects given below is not a direction favoured by Thatcher/Reagan reforms?
A. Deregulation
B. Tax cuts
C. Strong Trade unions
D. Reduced welfare benefits

95. Which is not a source of civic virtue among the following?
A. Army
B. Family
C. Civic associations
D. The market

Directions (Qs. No. 96-100): *Read the following passage and answer the questions.*

The group of twenty or G20 has of late emerged as a very premier forum for international cooperation. The significance of it arises from the fact that its members are the world's advanced and emerging economies. These G20 members altogether represents about 85% of the global GDP, 80% of global trade and two-thirds of the world's population. The G20 originated to overcome the financial crisis that occurred in 1990s in the emerging economies of Asia. This organization is broadly representative and inclusive as the G20 chair has been made rotational annually and a member from different regional grouping of countries is elected to its presidency. Since its beginning, India has actively participated in the G20 process. India is a major stakeholder and also interested in the stability of the world economy. Due to India's support during the Seoul summit development was included as an agenda item and the Seoul Development consensus also emerged. India's interest in G20 has imparted dimension and credibility to G20 deliberation. India's successful organization of G20 summit in New Delhi recently has again ignited hopes for the establishment of a framework for strong, sustainable and balanced growth and an alternative world order.

96. Which of the following is the reason for the formation of G20?
A. World financial crisis
B. Asian financial crisis
C. African financial crisis
D. European financial crisis

97. Why has India taken active interest in G20?
A. To not achieve its own economic stability
B. To endure world economic stability
C. To negotiate successfully its debt crisis
D. To not establish itself as a major economic power

98. Why G20 is considered a representative forum?
A. Chair is not rotational
B. Chair is rotational and from a different strategic grouping against China
C. Chair is rotational annually and from a different region.
D. Chair's term is limited to three years

99. Which of the following iis the objective of G20?
A. International cooperation
B. Regional cooperation
C. Sectoral cooperation
D. Cooperation with the powers on political matters

100. What is the significance of recently concluded G20 summit?
A. Consumers on a framework for sustainable balanced growth
B. Women led development process
C. Emergence of Global South as one voice
D. All of the above options

ANSWERS

1. (C): Robert Nozick's 'entitlement theory' is composed of three core principles, not including a "principle of final acquisition." The theory outlines the conditions under which a distribution is considered just: just initial acquisition, just transfer, and rectification of injustice. The principle of final acquisition does not exist within Nozick's framework; instead, the focus is on how holdings are initially acquired, transferred, and how injustices are corrected.

2. (B): Philosophical anarchism argues against the legitimacy of state authority, suggesting that no state has the moral justification for its rule or the authority over its citizens.

It does not claim that states should not exist but questions the basis of a state's authority and the moral obligations of individuals to obey such authority.

3. **(D):** Burma (Myanmar) is not considered part of the 'Asian Tiger' economies. The 'Asian Tigers' refer to Hong Kong, Singapore, South Korea, and Taiwan, known for their rapid industrialization and high growth rates from the 1960s to the 1990s. Burma, by contrast, has not experienced similar economic development patterns.

4. **(C):** Aristotle was concerned that the masses, if given power, would become susceptible to the influence of demagogues—charismatic leaders who appeal to emotions, fears, and prejudices rather than rational argument. He feared that these leaders could easily manipulate the masses, leading to instability and tyranny.

5. **(C):** "Class in itself" is a concept not related to John Rawls but to Karl Marx's theory of social classes and class consciousness. Rawls's work, including "Justice as Fairness," "Distributive Justice," and the "Veil of Ignorance," focuses on the principles of justice that would be chosen under conditions of fairness, without knowledge of one's own place in society.

6. **(A):** Susan Sontag, primarily known as a critic, writer, and filmmaker, is not typically associated with feminist theory in the same direct manner as the other options listed.

   While her work has intersected with feminist topics, the core of her intellectual contributions lies outside the traditional boundaries of feminist theory, unlike Carole Pateman, Martha Nussbaum, and Judith Butler, who have made significant contributions to feminist thought.

7. **(D):** Bhikhu Parekh notes that Indian political thought often overlooks questions related to political economy. While modern individual thinkers, the nature of the Indian state, and social justice have been subjects of consideration within Indian political discourse, Parekh highlights the relative neglect of political economy—a field that involves the study of how economic theories and principles affect political and social structures.

8. **(D):** The matter of "Freedom from colonial rule" was not a subject of debate between Mahatma Gandhi and Rabindranath Tagore. Both leaders, though differing in their approaches and philosophies, were committed to the cause of India's freedom from British colonial rule. Their debates were more focused on cultural and ideological issues such as the use of the English language, nationalism, and the spinning wheel, rather than the overarching goal of independence.

9. **(A):** Rabindranath Tagore described Kabir as 'Muktidoot,' which translates to 'messenger of liberation' or 'emancipator.' Tagore admired Kabir for his spiritual and social teachings, which transcended sectarian boundaries and aimed at universal human emancipation. Kabir's poetry and philosophy, emphasizing direct experience of the divine and social equality, greatly influenced Tagore's own views.

10. **(B):** Kabir is associated with 'syncretism'—the blending of different religious, cultural, or philosophical beliefs into a cohesive practice. Kabir, a 15th-century poet and saint, embodied syncretism in his life and teachings, drawing upon both Hindu and Muslim beliefs. His work reflects a convergence of the spiritual tenets of Hinduism and Islam, advocating a universal path to divine truth that transcended the sectarian divides of his time.

11. (C): E.V. Ramaswami Naicker, also known as Periyar, initiated the Self-Respect Movement as a part of social reform. The movement, started in the early 20th century, aimed at achieving a society where backward castes and classes would have equal human rights and would no longer be suppressed by the Brahminical caste system.

It emphasized self-respect as the key to emancipation and sought to end discrimination based on caste.

12. (D): According to Manu, 'Contract' is not listed as a foundation of diplomacy and statecraft. Ancient Indian political theory, as outlined by Manu, identified various strategies for statecraft and diplomacy, including hostility, neutrality, and subordinate alliances, but did not explicitly regard contracts in the modern sense as a foundation. Manu's treatise focuses on broader principles governing relationships between states rather than detailed legal agreements.

13. (A): "Capitalism, Socialism and Democracy" is a seminal work authored by Joseph Schumpeter. Published in 1942, Schumpeter's book analyzes the process of capitalism's evolution, its compatibility with democracy, and the potential for socialism to emerge as a viable alternative. Schumpeter is renowned for his theory of creative destruction, a concept he elaborates on within this work, exploring the dynamics of capitalist economies and their influence on social and political structures.

14. (C): The Classic Modernization theory posits that countries are more likely to democratize and maintain democratic institutions as they develop economically. This theory suggests a positive correlation between economic development and democratic governance, arguing that economic growth leads to social and political changes that foster the conditions necessary for democracy to flourish and be sustained.

15. (B): A 'Top-down democratic transition' describes the process whereby the dictatorial ruling elite initiates liberalizing reforms leading to a democratic transition. This model of democratization occurs when those in power, often from within the authoritarian regime, decide to implement changes that gradually introduce democratic elements into the political system. These reforms can stem from various motivations, including economic pressures, international influence, or the leadership's desire to legitimize their rule.

16. (D): Tajikistan's current political regime is best characterized as a Civilian dictatorship. It is a republic with a strong executive branch dominated by President Emomali Rahmon and his party.

Although there are elections, they are widely regarded as neither free nor fair, with the ruling party maintaining tight control over the political landscape, suppressing opposition and limiting political pluralism.

17. (B): The event of 11th September, specifically the September 11 attacks in 2001, led George W. Bush to transform his foreign policy into one of global power projection and interventionism.

In response to the attacks, the Bush administration launched the "War on Terror," which included the invasion of Afghanistan and Iraq, significantly shifting U.S. foreign policy towards active interventionism in international affairs.

18. (B): The true beginning of the modern state system is often marked by the end of the Thirty Years' War with the Peace of Westphalia in 1648.

This period established the principles of sovereignty and non-interference in the internal affairs of other states, laying the groundwork for the nation-state system as it is understood today.

19. (B): Ernst B. Haas found eight distinct meanings for the term "Balance of Power." His work in international relations theory and his analysis of the balance of power have contributed significantly to the understanding of this complex concept, which includes different interpretations related to power distribution among states, deterrence strategies, and mechanisms for maintaining international stability.

20. (A): Hans J. Morgenthau is the scholar who said that statesmen "think and act in terms of interest defined as power." This perspective is central to Morgenthau's theory of political realism, which posits that the actions of states in the international arena are driven by the pursuit of national interests, primarily defined in terms of power. Morgenthau's work has had a profound impact on the study of international relations and the development of realist theory.

21. (B): The navies of India and the United States are jointly patrolling the Malacca Straits. This collaboration reflects the strategic partnership between the two countries, aimed at ensuring maritime security and safe passage through one of the world's busiest shipping lanes, which is vital for international trade and energy transportation.

22. (A): The UN climate change conference, commonly known as the Copenhagen Summit, was held in 2009. This summit was a significant event in international efforts to address climate change, aiming to establish a global agreement to succeed the Kyoto Protocol. Despite high expectations, the conference faced challenges in reaching a binding agreement.

23. (C): Prime Minister Manmohan Singh visited China in 2008. This visit was part of the ongoing efforts to improve bilateral relations between India and China, addressing various issues including trade, border disputes, and regional security. Such visits are crucial in fostering dialogue and cooperation between the two nations.

24. (B): India signed the declaration with China "to promote the building of a harmonious world of durable peace and common prosperity through developing the strategic and cooperative partnership for peace and prosperity." This declaration signifies the mutual interest of both nations in enhancing their strategic partnership, focusing on peace, prosperity, and stability in the region and beyond.

25. (C): Filibustering is not a key element of direct democracy. Direct democracy involves citizens directly making decisions about laws and policies, typically through mechanisms like referendums, recalls, and plebiscites. Filibustering, on the other hand, is a legislative tactic used in some parliamentary or legislative bodies to extend debate or delay proceedings, and it does not involve direct decision-making by the general populace.

26. (B): Satyamitra Dubey has stated that religion is the great criterion of Manu's state-polity. Dubey's analysis of Manu's work highlights the profound influence of religious principles on the governance and social structure outlined in ancient Indian texts, where dharma (moral law) plays a central role in the organization and function of the state.

27. (B): The Twenty-fourth Amendment of the Indian Constitution, passed in 1971, overrode the Golaknath case decided in 1967. The Golaknath verdict held that Parliament could not amend Part III of the Constitution, which includes fundamental rights. The Twenty-fourth Amendment countered this by affirming Parliament's power to amend any part of the Constitution, including the fundamental rights, thus restoring the balance of power between the legislature and the judiciary.

28. **(C):** "Markets and fairs" is not part of the concurrent list in the Indian Constitution. The concurrent list contains subjects over which both the central and state governments have jurisdiction, such as bankruptcy and insolvency, prevention of cruelty to animals, and economic and social planning. However, markets and fairs are typically under the purview of state governments, falling outside the concurrent list's scope.

29. **(B):** B.R. Ambedkar demanded a separate electorate for the depressed classes during the Second Round Table Conference. His advocacy for separate electorates was aimed at ensuring adequate political representation for the depressed classes, distinct from the general electorate. This demand led to the signing of the Poona Pact in 1932, which provided reserved seats for the depressed classes in the general electorate instead of separate electorates.

30. **(A):** The Linguistic Provinces Commission formed to advise the Constituent Assembly was popularly known as the Dar Commission. This commission was tasked with examining the feasibility of reorganizing states on linguistic lines, a significant issue during India's post-independence period. The commission's recommendations played a crucial role in the eventual formation of states based on linguistic identities, shaping the country's federal structure.

31. **(B):** Satyashodhak Samaj was founded by Jyotiba Phule. Established in 1873, the society aimed to promote social equality and uplift the status of marginalized communities in India, including women, peasants, and the lower castes, challenging the prevailing caste system and the domination of the Brahminical order.

32. **(C):** Under Article 328 of the Indian Constitution, the state legislature has the power to make provision with respect to elections to such legislature. This article empowers state legislatures to legislate on the conduct of elections to the state legislatures, within the framework of the Constitution and subject to any laws that Parliament may enact.

33. **(A):** Mary Parker Follett came out with the innovative idea of 'constructive conflict'. Follett, a pioneering thinker in the field of organizational theory and behaviour, argued that conflict, when managed properly, could lead to creative and constructive outcomes rather than being detrimental to the organization. She emphasized the importance of integration and the constructive resolution of conflicts through understanding and mutual respect.

34. **(B):** Frederick Taylor introduced the concepts of the 40-hour workweek, time and motion studies, and piece-rate compensation systems, as well as the notion of 'a fair day's work for a fair day's pay' to organizations. Taylor is known as the father of scientific management and sought to improve industrial efficiency and labor productivity through systematic study and the application of scientific methods to work processes.

35. **(B):** "The Study of Administration", published in Political Science Quarterly in 1887, was written by Woodrow Wilson. This paper is considered a seminal work in

the field of public administration, marking the beginning of the study and systematic thought in public administration as a distinct field. Wilson's work laid the foundation for the development of public administration as an academic discipline and a profession.

36. (B): Peter Drucker wrote the book "Management: Tasks, Responsibilities, Practices." Drucker is widely recognized as the father of modern management for his extensive contributions to management theory and practice. His work covers a broad range of management topics, including leadership, innovation, and effective business practices, influencing generations of business leaders and scholars.

37. (C): Mazdoor Kisan Shakti Sangathan (MKSS) pioneered the Right to Information movement in India, which is closely associated with the practice of Jan Sunwai (public hearings). Through these public hearings, MKSS exposed corruption and advocated for transparency in governance, significantly contributing to the enactment of the Right to Information Act in 2005.

38. (B): The Citizens' Charter was first articulated and implemented in the UK as a national programme in 1991. The initiative aimed to improve public services by making them more responsive to the needs and preferences of citizens. It sought to set standards for service delivery, ensure transparency, and establish mechanisms for feedback and redressal.

39. (C): Examining the report of the Comptroller and Auditor General (CAG) with a view to finding out that the money voted by Parliament has been utilized by the authority concerned is not a function of the Estimates Committee. This task is primarily the responsibility of the Public Accounts Committee, which scrutinizes expenditure and audits government finances to ensure they are used effectively and for the intended purposes.

40. (B): The Public Accounts Committee (PAC) is an annually elected body in accordance with the principle of proportional representation followed by a single transferable vote system. This ensures that the composition of the PAC reflects the proportional strength of the different political parties in the Parliament, making it one of the most important committees for maintaining oversight of government expenditure and accountability.

41. (C): Bhikhu Parekh's conception of human nature emphasizes the cultural embeddedness of human beings and the variability of their understanding and experience across different societies. He advocates for a critical scrutiny of references to human nature, recognizing the deep impact of cultural contexts on individuals while also acknowledging the diverse conceptualizations of universal human characteristics like skin colour, gender, and physical features across different societies. This view contrasts with the idea that human behaviour is uniform across cultures or that skin colour invariably determines power and status universally.

42. (B): The arguments associated with 'right' wing political forces often emphasize individual responsibility over structural inequality, critique the welfare state for potentially creating dependency among its beneficiaries, and question the effectiveness of state intervention in addressing social issues like poverty, homelessness, and education. These perspectives include concerns about the consequences of redistributing wealth to the poor, the possibility of welfare policies trapping people in poverty, and a general skepticism about the state's ability to ameliorate complex social problems without unintended negative outcomes.

43. (A): Deliberative democracy is characterized by the normative ideal of free and equal citizens engaging in public reason exchange to reach consensus on policies or principles. It values the process of public deliberation where individuals reason together to make decisions that reflect collective interests and moral considerations, highlighting the moral intuition underlying truly democratic associations.

The central claim of deliberative democracy is the legitimacy derived from reasoned agreement among equals, rather than conformity to practical constraints of political life or the inevitability of partisan divisions and compromises.

44. (B): Gandhi's theory of Satyagraha, emphasizing non-violence and the recognition of the partial grasp over truth, can foster dialogue in plural societies marked by mutual distrust. Attention to dialogue's preconditions and the acknowledgment of our limited understanding encourage self-restraint and respect among participants. Commitment to non-violence also reduces alienation, facilitating a more inclusive and empathetic engagement. However, readiness to compromise, suggested as negating moral standing, is not part of this positive contribution to dialogue.

45. (C): Participatory democracy theorists like Carole Pateman, Benjamin Barber, and C.B. Macpherson argue for a political system where individuals have direct involvement in decision-making processes, emphasizing the importance of engagement and participation in democratic governance. Their work collectively advocates for expanding the role of citizens in the democratic process beyond traditional representative mechanisms, aiming to deepen democratic engagement and ensure that political decisions are more reflective of the public will and interests.

46. (A): The correct qualifications for the appointment of a Governor include that he or she must be a citizen of India. The age requirement is actually that he or she has completed the age of 35 years, not 25. Governors are appointed by the President of India, not the Prime Minister. The term of office for a Governor is five years, not six. A Governor resigns by writing under his hand addressed to the President, not the Prime Minister.

47. (*)

48. (B): Ram Manohar Lohia discusses seven revolutions in his works, is an author of "Aspects of Socialist Policy," and has indeed said, "the history of the growth of freedom is the history of the perfection of human relationships."

However, the concept of "Partyless Democracy" is more closely associated with Jayaprakash Narayan. Lohia did discuss various aspects of democracy and socialism, but "Partyless Democracy" as a specific term is not his. Additionally, Lohia is known for advocating a "Four-Pillar State," contradicting the claim in option (*d*).

49. (D): Dr. Sarvapalli Radhakrishnan, V.V. Giri, Dr. Shankar Dayal Sharma, and R. Venkataraman all served as Vice-Presidents of India before becoming the President of the country. B.D. Jatti, while serving as Vice-President, served as the Acting President but was never elected as the full President.

50. (D): Mahatma Gandhi wrote "Constructive Programme" and "Hind Swaraj." "Modern India" and "India's struggle for Independence" are not his works, and "Why Socialism" reflects a broader discourse on socialism not directly attributed to Gandhi. "Hind Swaraj" is a key text where Gandhi outlines his vision for India and critiques modern civilization, while "Constructive Programme" details his ideas for building the nation through positive action.

51. (D): The correct definitions of party systems by different scholars, according to the given options, include (*a*) "Modern democracy is a party democracy" by Katz and (*c*) "Parties are the core institutions of democratic politics" by Lipset. These statements emphasize the integral role of political parties in the functioning of modern democracies, highlighting their importance in structuring political debate, organizing electoral competition, and facilitating representation.

52. (D): The correct understanding of a "Failed state" includes (*a*) the example of Sierra Leone, often cited in discussions of state failure due to its historical struggles with civil war and governance challenges, and (*b*) the definition that a failed state is unable to provide the functions that define them as states, such as maintaining internal order, upholding the rule of law, and providing basic services to its citizens. This captures the essence of state failure, where the government's inability to perform its fundamental roles leads to significant instability and disorder.

53. (C): The constructivist argument on democracy, accurately represented by (*c*) "Constructivist argument treats culture as something that is constructed or invented rather than inherited" and (*d*) "Constructivist argument claims that culture has a causal effect," focuses on the idea that culture is not a fixed or immutable entity but is shaped by social interactions and political processes. Constructivists argue that political and social dynamics play a significant role in forming cultural identities and norms, which in turn can influence political structures and democratic practices.

54. (D): Atul Kohli's distinction between pro-market and pro-business state intervention in India in the 1980s is correctly described by (*a*) "Pro-business strategy mainly supports established producers," which highlights the government's focus on aiding existing businesses to enhance their productivity and competitiveness, and (*d*) "Pro-market strategy supports new entrants and consumers," reflecting policies aimed at liberalizing the economy to encourage competition and benefit consumers through better choices and lower prices.

55. (C): The correct aspects of the 108th Amendment Bill, 2008, are (*a*) "Reservation of seats reserved for scheduled caste shall be for women shall cease to exist 15 years after the commencement of this Bill," indicating a temporal limit on the reservation policy, and (*d*) "Reserved seats may be allotted by rotation to different constituencies in the state or UTs," which suggests a mechanism for implementing seat reservations across various electoral constituencies to ensure broad representation of women in legislative bodies.

56. (A): India was among the first countries to establish diplomatic relations with the European Economic Community (EEC), now the European Union (EU), highlighting the long-standing and evolving relationship between the two entities. The partnership was indeed upgraded to a strategic level in 2004, emphasizing a deeper commitment to collaboration across a range of sectors. Additionally, the EU is one of the largest sources of Foreign Direct Investment (FDI) for India, demonstrating the economic significance of this relationship. However, the EU, being a supranational entity, does not have membership in the UN General Assembly, which is reserved for sovereign states.

57. (D): Conflict in society and politics is recognized as inevitable due to the diverse interests and values present within any given community. The effectiveness of protests against violence is limited, and while they can raise awareness, they may not always succeed in eliminating the use of violence in conflicts. Non-violent action, which includes protests and persuasion, non-cooperation, and non-violent intervention, has been proven as a powerful method for social and political change. However, the use of non-violent methods is not a guarantee of success, as outcomes depend on various factors, including the strategies employed, the context of the conflict, and the responses of those in power.

58. (B): India established diplomatic relations with China on 1st April 1950, becoming the first non-socialist bloc country to do so. This move marked the beginning of a complex bilateral relationship. A significant improvement in bilateral relations began in 1988, indicating a shift towards engagement and dialogue after periods of tension. Prime Minister Nehru visited China in 1954, countering the claim that he never visited during his premiership. Rajiv Gandhi's visit to China took place in 1988, not 1993, marking the first visit by an Indian Prime Minister to China since Nehru's visit, aiming to normalize relations after the 1962 war.

59. (A): Under Chapter VII of the United Nations Charter, the Security Council has the authority to take measures to maintain or restore international peace and security. Article 41 specifies that the Council may decide what measures not involving the use of armed forces are to be employed to give effect to its decisions, which can include sanctions. However, sanctions are implemented and withdrawn at the discretion of the Security Council, not the UN General Assembly. Sanctions have been applied by the Security Council in various contexts to support peaceful transitions, deter unconstitutional changes, and address other security challenges, demonstrating their versatility as a tool for international governance.

60. (C): Weapons of Mass Destruction (WMD) encompass a broad range of weaponry, including atomic explosive weapons, highlighting the grave threat they pose to global security. The Chemical Weapons Convention (CWC), which entered into force in 1997, not 1998, aims to eliminate an entire category of WMD by prohibiting the development, production, acquisition, stockpiling, retention, transfer, or use of chemical weapons. Biological weapons, contrary to one of the statements, are indeed considered WMDs and are covered under their own treaty, the Biological Weapons Convention (BWC), demonstrating the international community's commitment to addressing the proliferation of these dangerous arms.

61. (C): The 73rd Constitutional Amendment Act of 1992 introduced significant provisions to empower the Panchayati Raj institutions in India, aiming to strengthen decentralization and local governance.

Key provisions include the empowerment of the Gram Sabha to exercise certain powers and perform functions at the village level as determined by state legislature laws (*a*), the mandate for a State Finance Commission to be constituted by the Governor every fifth year to review the financial position of Panchayats and make recommendations (*b*), and the requirement that elections to constitute a Panchayat must be completed before the expiration of six months from its dissolution (*d*).

Contrary to statement (*c*), the amendment enables state legislatures to endow Panchayats with necessary powers and authority for functioning as institutions of self-government, promoting autonomy and efficiency.

62. (D): Accountability is a fundamental concept in governance and public administration, characterized by oversight, direction, or request for justification of actions by an individual or body (*a*), and encompasses various types including legal, social, and political accountability (*b*).

It is a universal principle applicable not only in developed countries but across all nations, enabling the evaluation of public officials' effectiveness and enhancing transparency and responsibility in governance (contrary to statements (*c*) and (*d*)).

Accountability mechanisms are critical for ensuring that public officials and institutions are answerable for their actions and decisions, contributing to more effective and ethical governance.

63. (C): In administrative theories, Max Weber is renowned for formulating the ideal type bureaucracy, which describes a rational and highly structured organization designed to efficiently achieve goals (*a*). Frederick Taylor, recognized as the father of Scientific Management Theory, introduced principles to improve industrial productivity and efficiency through systematic study and design of work processes (*b*). Contrary to statement (*c*), Henry Fayol is known for his principles of management rather than being the father of Human Relations Theory, which is more closely associated with Elton Mayo, particularly through the Hawthorne Experiments (contradicting statement (*d*)) that emphasized the impact of social factors on productivity.

64. (A): Fred W. Riggs' work on prismatic societies in his book "Administration in Developing Countries: The Theory of Prismatic Society" explores the unique characteristics of societies transitioning from traditional to modern states. He highlights that modern societies feature functionally specific structures (*a*), defines a structure as any pattern of behaviour that becomes a standard feature of a social system (*b*), and contrasts the concept of Agraria and Industria, reflecting traditional and modern societal models, respectively, without suggesting a transition from Industria to Agraria (contrary to (*c*)).

Instead, Riggs discusses the complexities and challenges faced by transitional societies, or "prismatic" societies, navigating between these two models, and clarifies that Agraria and its "image" are not identical to a fused society model (*d*).

65. (B): ICT-based e-governance is designed to enhance the efficiency, transparency, and responsiveness of government operations. It aims to reduce the cost of government (*a*) by streamlining processes and making information and services more accessible to citizens. E-governance is expected to increase transparency (contrary to (*b*)) by making government actions and decisions more visible and understandable to the public.

It also seeks to increase citizen input into government (*c*), allowing for greater participation in governance processes. However, e-governance is sometimes critiqued for potentially increasing bureaucratic red tape (*d*), although its primary goals include reducing such inefficiencies. Statements (*b*) and (*d*) highlight common concerns or misconceptions about e-governance that may not accurately reflect its intended benefits and impacts.

66. (D): Liberalism is associated with moral concern for one another as free and equal citizens (III), reflecting its emphasis on individual rights and equality before the law. Communitarianism argues against the need for members to share a common culture, history, worldview, language, or value system (II), highlighting the importance of community values and social cohesion. Liberal Nationalism is based on shared nationality, which includes a common history, language, and culture (IV), emphasizing the role of national identity in liberal democratic frameworks. Multiculturalism/Difference theory advocates for the recognition of diverse cultures within a society, based on a shared understanding and common meaning that arises from a shared history, culture, or worldview (I), supporting the coexistence of multiple cultural identities.

67. (C): Antonio Gramsci is best known for his work "Prison Notebooks" (II), where he developed the concept of cultural hegemony. Robert Putnam authored "Bowling Alone: The Collapse and Revival of American Community" (IV), which discusses the decline of social capital in the United States. Michael Oakeshott, a philosopher known for his work on conservative ideology and political philosophy, wrote "On Human Conduct" (I). Max Weber is the author of "The Protestant Ethic and the Spirit of Capitalism" (III), a foundational text in sociology and economics that explores the relationship between religion and economic development.

68. (B): "A Plea for the Reconstruction of Indian Polity" is not listed among the provided options for matching with authors, leading to a focus on the remaining works. "India of My Dreams" is associated with M.K. Gandhi (III), who envisioned an India based on principles of non-violence and moral governance.

"The Indian War of Independence of 1857" was authored by V.D. Savarkar (I), providing a nationalist perspective on the 1857 uprising. "Mane Gandhi and Socialism" reflects the thoughts of Ram Manohar Lohia (II) on integrating Gandhian philosophy with socialist principles.

69. (D): The classification of federal systems into various types is associated with different scholars. Extremely Federal systems are discussed by Paul Appleby (IV), who explored the dynamics of federal governance. Quasi-Federal systems are described by K.C. Wheare (III), highlighting the blend of federal and unitary features in certain countries. Bargaining Federalism is attributed to Morris Jones (I), reflecting on the negotiation and compromise inherent in federal arrangements. Cooperative Federalism, discussed by Granville Austin (II), emphasizes collaboration among different levels of government within a federal system.

70. (A): Universal suffrage (III) refers to the right to vote without restrictions based on race, gender, belief, or social status, ensuring broad electoral participation. Majoritarian electoral systems (IV) involve electoral mechanisms where the candidates or parties that receive the most votes win, embodying the principle of majority rule. Single-member district plurality system (I) is an electoral system where individuals cast a single vote for a candidate in a single-member district, with the candidate receiving the most votes winning the seat. The Alternative vote (II) is a form of majoritarian electoral systems involving preferential voting, allowing voters to rank candidates in order of preference to ensure that elected officials have broad support.

71. (C): "The Success of India's Democracy" could be associated with the analytical and evaluative works on India's political system, possibly aligning with scholars like Atul Kohli who examines political dynamics and governance.

However, this specific title aligns more closely with authors engaged in comprehensive evaluations of India's democratic system, potentially including scholars like Nirja Jayal and Pratap B. Mehta who have edited volumes examining India's political structures and processes. "Caste in Indian Politics" is famously associated with Rajni Kothari, who has extensively analyzed the influence of caste in the Indian political landscape.

"Political Process in India, 1947-1991" would delve into the historical and political developments in post-independence India, a subject matter that might attract historians or political analysts examining the period's political dynamics. "The Oxford Companion to Politics in India" by Nirja Jayal and Pratap B. Mehta is a comprehensive reference work that offers in-depth insights into various aspects of Indian politics.

72. (B): The Shanghai Cooperation Organisation (SCO) was established in 2001, focusing on multilateral cooperation among its members in security, economy, and culture. BRIC is an acronym for the grouping of the world's leading emerging economies, namely Brazil, Russia, India and China. The grouping was formalised during the first meeting of BRIC foreign ministers in 2006. South Africa was invited to join BRIC in December 2010, after which the group adopted the acronym BRICS. ASEAN (Association of Southeast Asian Nations) was founded in 1967, aimed at promoting political and economic cooperation in Southeast Asia. The European Economic Community (EEC) was established in 1957, setting the foundation for what would become the European Union, focusing on economic integration among its member states.

73. (*):

74. (C): "Administration in Developing Countries: The Theory of Prismatic Society" is indeed authored by Fred W. Riggs (III), who introduced the concept of prismatic societies to describe the unique characteristics of developing countries' bureaucracies.

"Administrative Behaviour," a key text in understanding organizational decision-making and behaviour, is written by Herbert Simon (I), a pioneer in the field of administrative and organizational theory. "The Dynamics of Public Administration: Guidelines to Current Transformations in Theory and Practice" and "The Human Problem of an Industrial Civilization" are not directly associated with Gerald E. Caiden or Elton Mayo in the provided options, indicating a focus on the contributions of Riggs and Simon to administrative theory.

75. (A): Scientific management theory, attributed to Frederick W. Taylor, emphasizes the development of a true science of work to improve efficiency and productivity, benefiting both workers and managers (II). This approach marks a significant shift in management thinking towards optimizing work processes and labor management.

New public management (NPM) is characterized by a shift towards governance that mirrors private sector practices, aiming to enhance the quality of public service delivery and responsiveness of public services to citizen needs (III). The human relations theory, which emerged from the Hawthorne Experiments conducted by Elton Mayo, underscores the importance of social interactions, worker satisfaction, and the informal organization within workplaces (IV), focusing on the psychological and social aspects of work. Rational decision-making theory, often associated with Herbert Simon, outlines a systematic process of decision-making that includes stages of problem identification (intelligence), formulation of alternatives (design), and selection of a course of action (choice) (I), emphasizing a structured approach to decision-making within organizations.

76. (B): In the Marxist or materialist conception of history, the sequence starts with technological advancements under feudalism that lay the groundwork for modern industry (*e*). This economic transformation helps establish the bourgeoisie as the ruling class (*d*), fundamentally altering society's structure.

As capitalism develops, the majority are turned into proletarians (*c*), setting the stage for this class to eventually seize political power (*a*). The culmination of this process is the abolition of all classes, class antagonisms, and the state itself (*b*), representing the transition to a communist society.

77. (C): The historical and conceptual presentation of civil society begins with recognizing it as one among many spheres of the larger society (*c*), including the family, economy, and politics. This multifaceted view suggests that civil society is not a monolithic entity but part of a broader social fabric. The concept then evolves to be seen as a collective entity with specific and limited purposes (*a*), marking a shift towards understanding civil society as an organized domain of social action separate from the state and market. The first articulation of civil society in the 17th and 18th centuries in Europe (*e*) laid the groundwork for its development, influenced by economic and political liberalism, especially as articulated by John Locke and celebrated by the Scottish Enlightenment (*b*). By the 19th century, civil society found significant elaboration in the writings of Hegel and Marx (*d*), who explored its role and implications in the context of modern capitalist societies and their political economies.

78. (C): "Sharda Sadan" was established by Pandita Ramabai as a women's education and empowerment center in the late 19th century (*d*). "Ramkrishna Mission," founded by Swami Vivekananda, follows, dedicated to the spiritual, cultural, and social upliftment of society (*c*). "Abhinav Bharat Society," a secret society for independence activism, was founded by V.D. Savarkar (*b*). "Tolstoy Farm" was established by Gandhi in South Africa as a community living and non-violence practice center (*a*). "Bahishkrit Hitakarini Sabha" was founded by Dr. B.R. Ambedkar to promote the welfare of the socially marginalized (*e*).

79. (D): Aurobindo's life events in chronological order begin with his move to England for education (*c*), followed by clearing the ICS exam, a testament to his academic excellence (*e*). Rejecting the ICS position, he became the vice-principal of Baroda College, indicating his shift towards education and nationalism (*b*). His political activism is further evidenced by attending the Banaras session of the Congress (*a*), culminating in his arrest for the Alipore bomb case (*d*), highlighting his deep involvement in India's freedom struggle.

80. (B): The chronological order of democratic transitions starts with the "First wave of democratization," which began in the 19th century, marking the spread of democratic governance (*b*). The "First reverse wave" represents a period of retreat from these democratic gains (*a*). The "Second wave of democratization" followed World War II, as many countries underwent democratization (*c*). The "Second reverse wave" then saw some of these democracies revert to authoritarian rule (*d*). Finally, the "Third wave of democratization" began in the 1970s, significantly increasing the number of democratic states globally (*e*).

81. **(A):** The agreements/accords signed between the Indian government and its provincial regional organizations in ascending order start with the Anandpur Sahib Resolution, which was adopted by the Shiromani Akali Dal in 1973, outlining the demand for autonomy and rights for Punjab. The Shillong Agreement followed in 1975, involving the Government of India and the Naga National Council to settle Naga insurgency issues. Next is the Rajiv Gandhi-Longowal Accord (also known as the Punjab Accord), signed in 1985 to address demands and grievances in Punjab. The Assam Accord was signed in 1985 to conclude the Assam Movement, addressing issues of illegal immigration and cultural identity. Finally, the Mizo Peace Accord in 1986 ended insurgency in Mizoram and led to the establishment of peace and legislative autonomy.

82. **(B):** India's association with international organizations chronologically begins with its founding membership in the United Nations in 1945, right after gaining independence. This membership was significant for India's international engagement and diplomatic efforts. The Non-Aligned Movement (NAM) came next, with India being a founding member in 1961, emphasizing its stance of not aligning with any major power bloc during the Cold War. Then, India joined the Group of 77 (G77) in 1964, a coalition of developing nations advocating for economic interests. G2G, or Government to Government interactions, represent a broad category of bilateral engagements rather than a specific organization, thus not fitting into this chronological order.

83. **(A):** The Directors General of the World Trade Organization (WTO) who held office in ascending order begin with Mike Moore serving from 1999 to 2002, bringing his experience from New Zealand's political landscape to the global trade organization. Supachai Panitchpakdi took office next, serving from 2002 to 2005 and was notable for being the first WTO Director-General from Thailand. Pascal Lamy followed, serving from 2005 to 2013, with his tenure focusing on navigating the complexities of global trade negotiations. Roberto Azevedo then served from 2013 to 2020, leading the organization through numerous trade discussions and challenges.

84. **(C):** The sequence of committees regarding corruption and administrative reforms in India begins with the Gorwala Committee, established in 1951 to review public administration systems. The Santhanam Committee came next in 1964, specifically focusing on anti-corruption measures and practices within the government. The First Administrative Reforms Commission was constituted in 1966, aiming at a comprehensive review and recommendation for overhauling India's administrative systems. Lastly, the Vohra Committee was set up in 1993 to examine the issue of criminalization of politics and its nexus with the bureaucracy.

85. **(C):** Arranging the administrative thinkers/theorists chronologically, Max Weber's contributions to sociology and public administration, particularly his theory on bureaucracy, came in the early 20th century, influencing countless aspects of organizational theory. F.W. Willoughby, whose work around the same time period delved into government operations and public administration, provides foundational insights into the field. Elton Mayo's research, notably the Hawthorne Experiments conducted in the late 1920s and early 1930s, laid the groundwork for the human relations movement. David Easton, a political scientist known for his systems theory of political science, made significant contributions in the mid-20th century, further expanding the domain of administrative and political theory.

86. **(C):** Assertion (A) posits that autonomy is a skill that must be actively developed and maintained by individuals, which requires effort and resources often provided by social and material conditions facilitated by the state. This suggests an understanding of autonomy as not merely a matter of personal will but as something fostered by a conducive environment.

Reason (R) suggests that a commitment to individual autonomy does not obligate the liberal state to provide the necessary conditions for citizens to achieve autonomy, implying that individuals must independently strive for it. While (A) recognizes the role of the state in enabling autonomy, (R) seemingly absolves the state of responsibility in this regard. Therefore, (A) is correct in highlighting the complexity of achieving autonomy, while (R) incorrectly suggests that the state's role in facilitating this process is not necessary.

87. **(A):** Both Assertion (A) and Reason (R) are correct, and (R) provides a correct explanation for (A). Ahimsa, or non-violence, was indeed central to Gandhi's philosophy and methodology for social change and political action, complementing his model of conflict resolution. This approach was original and creative, significantly influencing India's struggle for independence. Reason (R) elucidates how Gandhi's political theory, characterized by non-violence, became the predominant ideology of the national movement, with Gandhi as a key figure. This connection between Gandhi's advocacy for Ahimsa and its adoption by the national movement provides a clear explanation for the assertion, making (R) an appropriate explanation for (A).

88. **(C):** Statement I is correct in observing that the economic transformation in India has not been as dramatic as that observed in post-communist countries in Eastern Europe, where the shift from state-run economies to market economies often involved significant and rapid changes to economic structures and policies.

Statement II, however, is incorrect; while India has experienced periods of high growth rates, particularly in the early 2010s, it has not consistently matched or sustained growth rates as high as those of China, which has been one of the world's fastest-growing economies for several decades.

89. **(B):** Both Assertion (A) and Reason (R) are correct, but (R) is not the correct explanation for (A). India has indeed been considered a safe haven for refugees due to its history of providing refuge to various groups fleeing persecution or conflict in neighboring countries.

This reputation stems from India's practice of offering shelter and assistance despite not having a specific refugee law and not signing the 1951 Refugee Convention. The lack of a formal refugee law or accession to the convention does not inherently explain India's actions as a host to refugees; instead, these actions reflect broader principles of humanitarianism and non-refoulement that have guided India's approach, even in the absence of formal legal commitments.

90. (B): Both Assertion (A) and Reason (R) are correct, but (R) is not the correct explanation for (A).

Assertion (A) accurately reflects the reality of modern public administration, where contracting out services to private entities and public-private partnerships have become common strategies to enhance efficiency, leverage expertise, and finance public services.

This trend marks a significant shift in how public services are delivered and decisions are made. Reason (R) addresses the gap between the complexity of contemporary governance, which includes such partnerships, and the traditional normative frameworks used to explain and justify government actions. While both statements are accurate, (R) addresses a broader issue of governance complexity and normative justification, which is not specifically an explanation for the rise of contracting out and public-private partnerships as outlined in (A).

91. (C): The 'New Right' does not associate being a career-oriented selfish person with 'self-supporting' as a civic virtue. Their emphasis on self-supporting is rooted in the belief that it teaches individuals the virtues of initiative and self-reliance, contrasting with a culture of dependency they attribute to the welfare state.

They argue that self-supporting individuals fulfill an obligation to themselves and society, contributing to their acceptance as full members of society. This perspective prioritizes self-reliance over dependency, not careerism or selfishness.

92. (B): The welfare state is said to promote passivity in the poor by creating a culture of dependency. According to critics from the 'New Right,' welfare benefits and support systems discourage individuals from seeking employment and becoming self-reliant, leading to a passive attitude towards work and life. This culture of dependency is viewed as reducing citizens to passive dependents under bureaucratic control, contrary to the virtues of initiative and self-reliance promoted by market forces.

93. (C): According to 'New Right' theorists, the market inculcates civic virtue by encouraging people to be self-supporting. This perspective holds that market-driven economies foster initiative, self-reliance, and personal responsibility, virtues deemed essential for active citizenship. By engaging in market activities, individuals learn to support themselves and contribute positively to society, thereby embodying important civic virtues.

94. (C): Among the directions favored by Thatcher/Reagan reforms, strong trade unions are not included. Instead, these reforms aimed at deregulation, tax cuts, and reducing welfare benefits, alongside weakening the power of trade unions. The goal was to extend the scope of markets, promote free trade, and encourage individual initiative and self-reliance by reducing state intervention and the influence of collective bargaining entities like trade unions.

95. (A): Among the options provided, the Army is not explicitly mentioned as a source of civic virtue in the passage. The passage highlights the market, civic associations, and the family as seedbeds of civic virtue within liberal society, emphasizing how these spheres contribute to fostering civic virtues such as initiative, self-reliance, and active citizenship. The Army, while it may instill certain virtues, is not discussed in this particular context.

96. (B): India actively participates in G20 to ensure world economic stability. Its involvement reflects its commitment to contributing to discussions and initiatives aimed at promoting global economic stability, growth, and development, showcasing its role as a responsible global player.

97. (B): India takes an active interest in G20 to ensure world economic stability. Its participation reflects its commitment to contributing to discussions and initiatives aimed at promoting global economic stability, growth, and development, showcasing its role as a responsible global player.

98. (C): G20 is considered a representative forum because the chair is rotational annually and from a different region. This ensures broad representation and inclusivity, allowing various regional groupings of countries to participate and contribute, enhancing the forum's legitimacy and effectiveness.

99. (A): The objective of G20 is international cooperation. It serves as a platform for member countries to engage in dialogue, coordinate policies, and collaborate on global economic issues such as financial stability, sustainable development, trade, and investment, aiming to address shared challenges and promote collective solutions.

100. (D): The recently concluded G20 summit holds significance for consumers on a framework for sustainable balanced growth, women-led development processes, and the emergence of the Global South as a unified voice. These outcomes reflect diverse priorities and objectives, promoting global economic stability, inclusivity, and cooperation.

Previous Years' Paper

National Testing Agency (NTA)

UGC-NET Junior Research Fellowship & Assistant Professor Eligibility Exam

Political Science, June-2023

(Exam held on 15-06-2023)

PAPER-II

1. Which of the following websites is a comprehensive website of Citizen Charters of Government of India?

A. www.goecharters.nic.in
B. www.goindiacharters.nic.in
C. www.goicharters.nic.in
D. www.echartersind.nic.in

2. Who amongst these is the proponent of the "process model" of social movements in comparative politics?

A. Peter Evans
B. Charles Tilly
C. Dough McAdams
D. Ralph A. Turner

3. Who among the following scholars gave the statement that, "In course of time, however (while Nehru was still alive), the Congress party ceased to be a movement and became a party and government"?

A. James Manor B. Morris Jones
C. Rajni Kothari D. Yogendra Yadav

4. Chronologically arrange the following books in order of its publication year.

(*a*) Liberty after Freedom
(*b*) Four Essays on Liberty
(*c*) The Constitution of Liberty
(*d*) Two Concepts of Liberty

Choose the correct answer from the options given below:

A. (*a*), (*b*), (*c*), (*d*) B. (*b*), (*c*), (*d*), (*a*)
C. (*c*), (*a*), (*b*), (*d*) D. (*d*), (*c*), (*b*), (*a*)

5. Which of the following statement represent the impact of globalisation on terrorism?

(*a*) Globalisation has permitted exchange of ideas and goods which is exploited by terrorist groups.
(*b*) The internet has allowed terrorists to recruit new followers.
(*c*) New technologies allow terrorists to operate in highly distributed network.
(*d*) Insurgent and terrorist groups in Iraq and Syria have not built sophisticated improvised explosive devices (IEDs) despite global access to resources.

Choose the most appropriate answer from the questions given below:

A. (*a*), (*b*), (*c*) & (*d*) only
B. (*b*) & (*c*) only
C. (*a*), (*b*), (*c*) only
D. (*a*), (*b*), (*d*) only

6. Arrange the following events of the U.S. constitutional development in ascending order:

(*a*) Establishment of the Federal Council of the U.S.A.
(*b*) Introducing the Articles of Confederation of the U.S.A.

(*c*) Addition of Bill of Rights in the U.S. Constitution.
(*d*) 14th Amendment to the U.S. Constitution that guarantees equal protection of laws.

Choose the correct answer from the options given below:
A. (*a*), (*c*), (*b*), (*d*) B. (*c*), (*a*), (*d*), (*b*)
C. (*b*), (*d*), (*c*), (*a*) D. (*b*), (*a*), (*c*), (*d*)

7. Given below are two statements:

Statement I: India's foreign remains pre-occupied with concerns about territorial integrity nationhood and independence of decision making.

Statement II: The structural logic of the global bipolar conflict gets reflected in the regional bipolar conflict between India and Pakistan.

In the light of the above statements, choose the most appropriate answer from the options given below:
A. Both Statement I and Statement II are correct
B. Both Statement I and Statement II are incorrect
C. Statement I is correct but Statement II is incorrect
D. Statement I is incorrect but Statement II is correct

8. Arrange the following political parties in a chronological order according to their year of formation:
(*a*) Samajwadi Party
(*b*) Bharatiya Janata Party
(*c*) CPI(M)
(*d*) Shiv Sena

Choose the correct answer from the options given below:
A. (*b*), (*c*), (*d*), (*a*)
B. (*d*), (*b*), (*a*), (*c*)
C. (*c*), (*d*), (*b*), (*a*)
D. (*c*), (*a*), (*b*), (*d*)

9. Which of the following statements is not correct regarding management according to Peter Drucker?
(*a*) Management is subjective
(*b*) Management has a specitic role to perform
(*c*) Management is designed for ordinary citizens too
(*d*) Management approves the mechanistic model of organizational management

Choose the correct answer from the options given below:
A. (*b*) and (*d*) only B. (*c*) and (*d*) only
C. (*a*) and (*b*) only D. (*a*) and (*d*) only

10. Which of the following statements given by Juan Linz and Alfred Stepan are true?
(*a*) Both civil society and political society are complementary to each other.
(*b*) The complimentarity is always recognized.
(*c*) Rule of law is condition for consolidation of democracy
(*d*) Modern consolidated democracies have pure market economies only.
(*e*) Modern democracies must have effective capacity to command, regulate and extract.

Choose the most appropriate answer from the questions given below:
A. (*a*), (*c*) and (*e*) only
B. (*a*) and (*b*) only
C. (*b*), (*c*) and (*e*) only
D. (*b*), (*c*) and (*d*) only

11. Which among the following statements is true about rise of alternative perspectives on Indian foreign policy?
(*a*) In the mid 1960s, the Swatantra party presented a classical conservative perspective on foreign policy.
(*b*) It was led by I.K. Gujral.
(*c*) The supporters were drawn from former bureaucrats, business community and members of princely families.

(*d*) They united in their opposition to Nehru's Fabian economics.

(*e*) They believed in the forces of the market and private enterprises.

Choose the most appropriate answer from the questions given below:

A. (*a*), (*b*), (*c*), (*d*) only
B. (*a*), (*c*), (*d*), (*e*) only
C. (*b*), (*c*), (*d*), (*e*) only
D. (*a*), (*b*), (*d*), (*e*) only

12. Who among the following has written the books 'Public Policy Making Reexamined' and 'Design for Policy Sciences'?

A. Horlod Lasswell B. Thomas R Dye
C. Rosolio Peter D. Yehezkel Dror

13. Who has stated that the idea of "praxis" is most clearly developed in a short eleven paragraphs or theses, that Marx had written to himself in 1845?

A. H.J. Laski B. B.R. Nelson
C. J. Wood D. R.E. Lenser

14. Which of these postulated the introduction of an elected President in the municipalities?

A. Lord Ripon's Resolution, 1882
B. Lord Mayo's Resolution, 1870
C. Bombay Municipal Corporation Act, 1888
D. Gujarat Municipalities Act, 1964

15. Who among the following thinkers said that, 'The communication of intangible facts, opinions, suggestions and suspicions that cannot pass through formal channels are communicated through informal channels'?

A. Hebert Simon B. Max Weber
C. Chris Argyris D. Chester Bernard

16. Who among the following thinkers holds the view that no citizen should be sufficiently opulent to be able to purchase another and none so poor as to be forced to sell himself?

A. Locke B. Burke
C. Rousseau D. Kant

17. Which of the following statements does NOT indicate deepening of democracy facilitated by gendering politics in India?

A. Women participating in politics as a community or group.
B. Articulation of political voice of women.
C. Women from upper caste carrying out a silent revolution.
D. Women getting involved in the public sphere.

18. According to Sri Aurobindo the task of "spiritual revolution" is based on:

A. Truth consciousness
B. Parliamentary democracy
C. Radical humanism
D. Individualism

19. Match List-I with List-II.

List-I (Thinker)	**List-II (Determinates of Foreign Policy)**
(*a*) K.J. Holsti	I. National role conceptions
(*b*) Jonathan Mercer	II. Emotion & Cognition-co-produce emotions
(*c*) Janice Gross Stein	III. Process of Political learning
(*d*) Arnold Wilfers	IV. National security as 'ambiguous symbol'

Choose the correct answer from the options given below:

	(*a*)	(*b*)	(*c*)	(*d*)
A.	I	II	III	IV
B.	II	III	IV	I
C.	III	IV	I	II
D.	IV	III	II	I

20. Who among the following thinkers is an advocate of cosmopolitan democracy?

A. Plato B. Hegel
C. Kant D. S.D. Lawrance

21. Limited franchise was introduced by which of these Acts?

A. Indian Council Act, 1892

B. Government of India Act, 1935
C. India Independence Act, 1947
D. None of these

22. Which among the following statements represent the principles of Just War?
(*a*) War as the last resort
(*b*) The purpose of war is revenge
(*c*) War must be declared on the basis of normally acceptable aims
(*d*) A wholesale invasion is a justifiable response to a border incursion

Choose the most appropriate answer from the questions given below:
A. (*a*), (*c*) and (*d*) only
B. (*a*), (*b*) and (*c*) only
C. (*a*) and (*c*) only
D. (*a*), (*c*), (*d*) and (*e*) only

23. Who among the following is the author of the critical scholarly memoir, "Envoy to Nehru"?
A. Escott Reid
B. Walter Crocker
C. Ramachandra Guha
D. Pratap Bhanu Mehta

24. Arrange the writings of Dr. B.R. Ambedkar in a chronological order:
(*a*) Annihilation of Caste
(*b*) Who were the Shudras?
(*c*) Future of Parliamentary Democracy
(*d*) The Untouchables

Choose the correct answer from the options given below:
A. (*a*), (*b*), (*c*) & (*d*)
B. (*b*), (*a*), (*d*) & (*c*)
C. (*a*), (*d*), (*b*) & (*c*)
D. (*a*), (*b*), (*d*) & (*c*)

25. Which of the following regimes of welfare states corresponds to Richard Tittmus's Institutional Redistribution Model in his three-fold classification of welfare state?
A. Anglo-Saxon Regime
B. Scandinavian social democratic regime
C. Conservative continental regime
D. Australian regime

26. Which among the following statements is *true* about JP Narayan's plan of reconstruction of Indian polity?
(*a*) He wanted to revive 'swaraj from below'.
(*b*) The basic unit of political organisation would be the gram panchayat.
(*c*) The gram sabha would act as the basis of grass roots democracy.
(*d*) This would also involves establishing an organic link amongst the different units of the panchayati raj.

Choose the correct answer from the options given below:
A. (*a*) and (*b*) only
B. (*b*) and (*c*) only
C. (*c*) and (*d*) only
D. (*a*), (*c*) and (*d*) only

27. Which of the two factors enhanced the growth rate of Indian economy in the 1980s as per Arvind Panagariya?
(*a*) Attitudinal change amongst the policy makers.
(*b*) Expert incentives for private companies.
(*c*) Political leadership was skeptical about import substitution industrialization.
(*d*) A more realistic exchange rate policy.

Choose the correct answer from the options given below:
A. (*b*) and (*d*) only
B. (*b*) and (*c*) only
C. (*d*) and (*c*) only
D. (*a*) and (*b*) only

28. Which of the following statements is are correct regarding Supreme Court of India?
(*a*) Under the Arbitration and Conciliation Act 1996, International Commercial Arbitration can also be initiated in the Supreme Court.
(*b*) The Supreme Court has special advisory Jurisdiction under Article 143.

(*c*) Article 32 of the Constitution gives an extensive original jurisdiction to the Supreme Court with regard to enforcement of Fundamental Rights.

Choose the correct answer from the options given below:
A. (*a*) and (*b*) only
B. (*b*) and (*c*) only
C. (*a*) and (*c*) only
D. (*a*), (*b*), (*c*) only

29. Given below are two statements: One is labelled as Assertion (A) and the other is labelled as Reason (R):

Assertion (A): Economic globalisation promotes prosperity and opportunity for all.

Reason (R): Economic globalisation promotes an open, market-based economy that brings social and political benefits.

In the light of the above statements, choose the correct answer from the options given below:
A. Both (A) and (R) are true, but (R) is the correct explanation of (A)
B. Both (A) and (R) are true, but (R) is not the correct explanation of (A)
C. (A) is true, but (R) is false
D. (A) is false, but (R) is true

30. Which among the following thinkers can be equated with the statement that, 'He proposes an ascetic communication, the purpose of which is to remove objects of desire'?
A. Karl Marx B. Plato
C. Glaucon D. Polybius

31. Who among the following scholars had levelled the criticism against J.S. Mill that, "we cannot separate two different compartments of individual conduct"?
A. Barker
B. C.E.M. Joad
C. L.T. Hobhouse
D. R.M. MacIver

32. Match List-I with List-II.

List-I	List-II
(*a*) Politics and Ethics of the Indian Constitution	I. B.L. Shankar and Valerian Rodrigues
(*b*) The Indian Parliament	II. K.C. Wheare
(*c*) Federal Government	III. Rajiv Bhargava
(*d*) Indian Constitution: Cornerstone of a Nation	IV. Granville Austin

Choose the correct answer from the options given below':

	(*a*)	(*b*)	(*c*)	(*d*)
A.	III	II	I	IV
B.	III	I	II	IV
C.	II	I	III	IV
D.	IV	III	II	I

33. Which among the following thinkers hold the view that, liberty is destroyed because the propertied classes possess the power to dominate others?
(*a*) Rousseau (*b*) Marx
(*c*) C. Locke (*d*) Engels

Choose the correct answer from the options given below:
A. (*b*), (*c*), (*d*) only
B. (*a*), (*b*), (*c*) only
C. (*a*), (*b*), (*d*) only
D. (*b*) and (*d*) only

34. Who is the author of the book Federation Versus Freedom?
A. Pandita Ramabai
B. M.N. Roy
C. Dr. B.R. Ambedkar
D. Ram Monohar Lohia

35. Frantz Fanon's book 'Black Skin, White Masks' includes following chapters:
(*a*) The Negro and language
(*b*) The Negro and culture
(*c*) The Negro and Psychopathology
(*d*) The Negro and Recognition

Choose the correct answer from the options given below:

A. (*a*), (*b*), (*c*) only
B. (*b*) and (*d*) only
C. (*a*) and (*c*) only
D. (*a*), (*c*), (*d*) only

36. Match List-I with List-II.

List-I (SGD goal number)	List-II (Goals)
(*a*) 5	I. Affordable and clean energy
(*b*) 7	II. Life on land
(*c*) 10	III. Gender equality
(*d*) 15	IV. Reduced inequalities

Choose the correct answer from the options given below:

	(*a*)	(*b*)	(*c*)	(*d*)
A.	I	II	III	IV
B.	II	I	IV	III
C.	III	I	IV	II
D.	I	III	II	IV

37. Who said, 'the truth is not that the spirit of conflict and conquest is at the origin and in the center of the western nationalism'?

A. Swami Vivekanand
B. Rabindranath Tagore
C. M.K. Gandhi
D. Dr. B.R Ambedkar

38. According to Kautilya, which among the following six methods of foreign policy is applied by the would-be conqueror to the element of his Circle of States?

(*a*) Making peace
(*b*) Remaining non-violent
(*c*) Staying quiet
(*d*) Seeking support

Choose the correct answer from the options given below:

A. (*a*), (*b*), (*c*), (*d*) only
B. (*a*), (*b*), (*c*) only
C. (*b*), (*c*), (*d*) only
D. (*a*), (*c*), (*d*) only

39. Which of the following principles are used to study the attitudes of people *i.e.* political culture in comparative politics?

(*a*) Riker's strategic principle
(*b*) Converse principle
(*c*) Robinson's principle
(*d*) Gallagher's least square index
(*e*) Rae's factionalization index

Choose the most appropriate answer from the questions given below:

A. (*b*) and (*c*) only B. (*c*) and (*e*) only
C. (*a*) and (*b*) only D. (*b*) and (*d*) only

40. Match List-I with List-II.

List-I	List-II
(*a*) Rational choice Theory of Public Administration	I. Emulates private sector practices
(*b*) New Public Administration	II. Encourages research in policy analysis
(*c*) New Public Management	III. Devices principles and laws of public administration
(*d*) Golden Era of Public Administration	IV. Focus of norms and client loyalty

Choose the correct answer from the options given below:

	(*a*)	(*b*)	(*c*)	(*d*)
A.	I	III	IV	II
B.	II	IV	I	III
C.	III	II	I	IV
D.	IV	III	II	I

41. Which of the following Commissions Committees recommended for the establishment of the Lokpal and Lokayukta for First time?

A. First Administrative Reforms Commission
B. Santhanam Committee
C. A.D. Gorwala Committee
D. IInd Pay Commission

42. Which of the following Laws/Rules are restricting the disclosure of official information to the people?
(*a*) Official Secrets Act, 1923
(*b*) Commission of Enquiry Act, 1952
(*c*) Indian Evidence Act, 1812
(*d*) Fifth Pay Commission

Choose the correct answer from the options given below:
A. (*a*), (*b*), (*c*), (*d*) only
B. (*a*), (*b*) and (*c*) only
C. (*b*), (*c*) and (*d*) only
D. (*a*), (*b*) and (*d*) only

43. "The logic of collective action" explaining the mobilization of interest groups in comparative political analysis is given by which of the following scholars?
A. Theda Scokpol
B. Marcur Olson
C. Nicolas Poulatzas
D. Paul Pierson

44. Who wrote the book 'State in capitalist society'?
A. Nicolas Poulantzas
B. Karl Marx
C. Rosa Luxemburg
D. Ralph Miliband

45. Who amongst these are meant to serve the shop floor according to Frederick Taylor's functional foremanship in his scientific management theory?
(*a*) Speed Boss
(*b*) Repair Boss
(*c*) Route clerk
(*d*) Time clerk
(*e*) Inspection foreman

Choose the correct answer from the options given below:
A. (*c*), (*d*) & (*e*) only
B. (*b*), (*d*) & (*a*) only
C. (*a*), (*b*) & (*e*) only
D. (*b*), (*a*) & (*c*) only

46. Which among the following statements are associated with Harold J. Laski?
(*a*) Every state is known by the rights that it maintains.
(*b*) We do not mean by the rights the grant of some historic conditions possessed in the childhood, but lost in the process of time.
(*c*) Rights in fact are those conditions of social life without which no man can seek in general to be him self at his best.
(*d*) Rights are the legal opportunities for a successful life.

Choose the correct answer from the options given below:
A. (*a*), (*b*), (*c*) only B. (*a*), (*c*), (*d*) only
C. (*a*) and (*c*) only D. (*b*) and (*c*) only

47. Given below are two statements: One is labelled as Assertion (A) and the other is labelled as Reason (R):

Assertion (A): A prismatic society has hetrogenous structures existing side by side and which are diametrically opposite to each other.

Reason (R): The social change in a prismatic society would be inconsistent, incomplete and unresponsive.

In the light of the above statements, choose the correct answer from the options given below.
A. Both (A) and (R) are true and (R) is the correct explanation of (A)
B. Both (A) and (R) are true and (R) is NOT the correct explanation of (A)
C. (A) is true, but (R) is false
D. (A) is false, but (R) is true

48. Given below are two statements:

Statement I: The socialist movement developed in France in the form of syndicalism.

Statement II: Syndicalism rejects the idea of class struggle.

In the light of the above statements, choose the most appropriate answer from the options given below:

A. Both Statement I and Statement II are correct

B. Both Statement I and Statement II are incorrect

C. Statement I is correct, but Statement II is incorrect

D. Statement I is incorrect, but Statement II is correct

49. If we consider the Gandhian idea of satyagraha as a dialogue, then which among the following statement is not true?

(*a*) The nature of Gandhi's truth facilitates dialogues.

(*b*) The nature of Gandhi's truth is antithetical to equality.

(*c*) In such a dialogue parties are constructed as the adversary.

(*d*) The quest for truth is a shared exercise.

Choose the correct answer from the options given below:

A. (*a*) and (*b*) only B. (*c*) and (*d*) only

C. (*b*) and (*c*) only D. (*a*) and (*d*) only

50. Match List-I with List-II

List-I (Books)	List-II (Authors)
(*a*) On Violence	I. Hannah Arendt
(*b*) Reason and Revolution	II. Herbert Marcuse
(*c*) Where do we go from here	III. Kirk Russell
(*d*) The Conservative Mind: From Burke to Elliot	IV. Martin Luther King

Choose the correct answer from the options given below:

	(*a*)	(*b*)	(*c*)	(*d*)
A.	I	II	IV	III
B.	III	IV	II	I
C.	I	II	III	IV
D.	IV	III	I	II

51. Place the following legislative acts in chronological orders:

(*a*) Right to Information Act

(*b*) Consumer Protection Act

(*c*) Right to Education Act

(*d*) Lokpal and Lokayukta Act

Choose the correct answer from the options given below:

A. (*b*), (*a*), (*d*), (*c*) B. (*a*), (*c*), (*d*), (*b*)

C. (*a*), (*b*), (*c*), (*d*) D. (*c*), (*a*), (*d*), (*b*)

52. Which of the following agreements does not outline country-specific emission targets but emphasises on climate change mitigation?

A. Kyoto Protocol

B. Law of Sea Treaty

C. Montreal Protocol

D. The Paris Agreement

53. Who among the following has defined deliberative democracy in terms of pluralistic association?

A. G.C. Sen B. A. Hanson

C. J. Cohen D. P Samuelson

54. Who among the following political thinkers reformulated the principle of realism by Hans J. Morgenthau from a feminist perspective?

A. Gunder Frank B. Janet Abu

C. Ann Tickner D. Hannes Peltonen

55. Which among the following rights is not group right, according to Will Kymlicka?

A. Self government rights

B. Polyethnic rights

C. Special representation rights

D. Right to speedy trial

56. Match List-I with List-II.

List-I (Books and Concepts)	List-II (Thinkers)
(*a*) Ethics of Care	I. Kate Millet
(*b*) Sexual Politics	II. Carol Gilligan
(*c*) Powers of Horror	III. Julia Kristeva
(*d*) Ecriture Feminine	IV. Helene Cexous

Choose the correct answer from the options given below:

	(a)	(b)	(c)	(d)
A.	I	II	III	IV
B.	IV	III	II	I
C.	II	I	III	IV
D.	II	IV	I	III

57. Who among following Prime ministers spoke about India's approach towards the US and Soviet Union drifting towards a cold War as

"They are our neighbors in Asia and inevitably we shall have to undertake many common tasks and have much to do with each other"

A. Jawaharlal Nehru
B. P.V. Narsimha Rao
C. Atal Bihari Vajpayee
D. Manmohan Singh

58. Arrange the following chapters of Leviathan in correct sequence:

(*a*) Of sense
(*b*) Of imagination
(*c*) Of reason and science
(*d*) Of speech

Choose the correct answer from the options given below':

A. (*a*), (*b*), (*d*), (*c*) B. (*d*), (*b*), (*c*), (*a*)
C. (*a*), (*c*), (*b*), (*d*) D. (*c*), (*d*), (*a*), (*b*)

59. Who has stated that, if life only were the object, slaves and brute animals might form a state?

A. Plato B. Aristotle
C. Confucius D. Hannah Aredent

60. Which of the following statements is are correct regarding parliamentary proceedings?

(*a*) Starred questions requires an oral answer and supplementary questions can follow.
(*b*) Short notice question is asked by giving a notice of less than 2 days.
(*c*) The Adjournment motion needs the support of 50 members to admit it.
(*d*) The Zero hour starts immediately after the question hour and lasts until the agenda for the day.

Choose the correct answer from the options given below:

A. (*a*), (*b*), (*c*) and (*d*) only
B. (*a*), (*c*) and (*d*) only
C. (*b*) and (*d*) only
D. (*a*), (*b*) and (*c*) only

61. The idealist school of thought in international relations proposed to replace 'balance of power' by:

A. Secret diplomacy
B. Disarmament
C. Autocratic rules
D. War

62. Who among the following thinkers proposal the concept of "Mental Revolution"?

A. FW Taylor B. Elton Mayo
C. Chester Barnard D. H. Simon

63. Match List-I with List-II.

List-I	List-II
(*a*) Rabindranath Tagore	I. True freedom
(*b*) J.P. Narayan	II. Chaukhamba Model
(*c*) Ram Manohar Lohia	III. Hindu Rashtra
(*d*) V.D. Savarkar	IV. Sampurna Kranti

Choose the correct answer from the options given below:

	(a)	(b)	(c)	(d)
A.	I	III	IV	II
B.	III	IV	II	I
C.	I	IV	II	III
D.	IV	I	III	II

64. Who among the following scholars has written the book "Remapping India: New states and their political origins"?

A. Ashutosh Varshney
B. Louisie Tillin
C. Paul Brass
D. Suhas Palshikar

65. Match List-I with List-II.

List-I (Concept/Theory)	List-II (Proponent)
(*a*) Critique of rational choice institutionalism's advocacy of universal generalizations	I. Campbell & Pederson
(*b*) Study of institutional change in skill regimes in Britain, Germany, Japan and the US	II. Scharph
(*c*) Origins of sociological institutionalism	III. Kathleen Theleen
(*d*) Discursive institutionalism	IV. Mever and Rowan

Choose the correct answer from the options given below:

	(*a*)	(*b*)	(*c*)	(*d*)
A.	II	IV	I	III
B.	III	IV	I	II
C.	II	III	IV	I
D.	I	II	III	IV

66. Which among the following constitutes membership criteria of the NAM?

(*a*) The country should support national independence movements.

(*b*) The country should be a member of multilateral military alliance concluded in the context of great power conflicts.

(*c*) The country should have adopted an independent policy based on co-existence of states

(*d*) If the country has granted military bases to a foreign power, the concession should be in the context of great power conflicts.

Choose the most appropriate answer from the questions given below:

A. (*a*) and (*b*) only
B. (*a*) and (*c*) only
C. (*a*) and (*d*) only
D. (*b*), (*c*) and (*d*) only

67. Arrange the following peacekeeping operations in chronological order:

(*a*) UNAMID in Darfur
(*b*) UNMISS in South Sudan
(*c*) UNAMIR in Rwanda
(*d*) UNPROFOR in former Yugoslavia

Choose the correct answer from the options given below:

A. (*a*), (*b*), (*c*) and (*d*)
B. (*b*), (*c*), (*a*) and (*d*)
C. (*d*), (*c*), (*a*) and (*b*)
D. (*c*), (*d*), (*b*) and (*a*)

68. Which among the following countries is not a member of NAM?

A. Burkina Faso B. Angola
C. Cameroon D. South Sudan

69. Arrange the following Committees/Commissions on local governments in chronological order:

(*a*) G.V.K. Rao Committee
(*b*) Ashok Mehta Committee
(*c*) Thungon Committee
(*d*) L.M. Singhvi Committee

Choose the correct answer from the options given below:

A. (*a*), (*d*), (*c*), (*b*) B. (*b*), (*a*), (*d*), (*c*)
C. (*a*), (*b*), (*c*), (*d*) D. (*a*), (*c*), (*d*), (*b*)

70. Arrange the following events conferences of public administration in chronological order:

(*a*) The Philadelphia Conference
(*b*) First Minnowbrook Conference
(*c*) Publication of book "Public Administration in a time of Turbulance" by Waldo
(*d*) Publication of "The Elements of Administration" by Urwick.

Choose the correct answer from the options given below:

A. (*b*), (*a*), (*c*), (*d*)
B. (*d*), (*b*), (*c*), (*a*)
C. (*a*), (*d*), (*c*), (*b*)
D. (*d*), (*a*), (*b*), (*c*)

71. Which of the following is not included in the list of India's initiatives in support of the US in strategic collaboration since 2001?

(*a*) India did not offer support for US anti terrorism mission in Afghanistan.

(*b*) India expressed opposition to President Bush's decision to withdraw from the ABM Treaty.

(*c*) India voted with the US at September 2005 International Atomic Energy Compliance Board of Governors meeting to declare that Iran was non-compliant of NPT.

Choose the most appropriate answer from the questions given below:

A. (*a*) only B. (*b*) only
C. (*c*) only D. (*a*) and (*b*) only

72. Which among the following sentences are associated with the notion of equality described by Amartya Sen?

(*a*) The basic capability, equality can be the sole guide to the moral good

(*b*) Morality is not concerned only with equality

(*c*) Basic capability, equality is a partial guide to the part of moral goodness that is associated with the idea of equality

(*d*) The index of basic capabilities like utility, can be used in many different ways

Choose the correct answer from the options given below:

A. (*b*) and (*d*) only
B. (*a*) and (*d*) only
C. (*a*), (*b*), (*c*) only
D. (*b*), (*c*), (*d*) only

73. Chronologically arrange the moments of crises of modern capitalism:

(*a*) U.S. sub-prime mortgage crisis

(*b*) Argentine economic crisis

(*c*) Dot com crisis in IT-related stocks

(*d*) Mexican economic crisis

Choose the correct answer from the options given below:

A. (*d*), (*b*), (*c*) & (*a*)
B. (*b*), (*d*), (*a*) & (*c*)
C. (*a*), (*b*), (*c*) & (*d*)
D. (*d*), (*b*), (*a*) & (*c*)

74. Rajiv Gandhi's participation at the Six Nation Five Continent Peace Initiative was a campaign:

A. to end nuclear testing.
B. for integration with Africans regional institutions.
C. for import substitution.
D. to end apartheid regime.

75. According to MP Follett, winch of the following is not a principle of organisation in achieving coordination?

A. Coordination as the reciprocal relation of all factors in a situation.
B. Coordination by indirect control.
C. Coordination in early stages.
D. Coordination as a continuing process.

76. Gramsci holds the view that:

(*a*) Progress is an ideology and becoming is a philosophical conception

(*b*) Becoming is a philosophical concept from which progress can be absent

(*c*) Progress depends on a specific mentality

(*d*) Progress and becoming were born at the same time

Choose the correct answer from the options given below:

A. (*a*), (*c*), (*d*) only
B. (*a*), (*b*), (*c*), (*d*) only
C. (*a*) and (*c*) only
D. (*b*) and (*d*) only

77. Which period of the evolution of public administration is referred as The Exploratory Period?

A. 1887-1910 B. 1910-1947
C. 1947-1970 D. 1970-1980

78. The justification for humanitarian intervention lies in:

(*a*) global interdependence
(*b*) national interest
(*c*) moral pluralism
(*d*) regional stability

Choose the most appropriate answer from the questions given below:

A. (*a*) and (*c*) only
B. (*b*) and (*c*) only
C. (*b*) and (*d*) only
D. (*a*) and (*d*) only

79. Who said, 'Radicalism thinks in terms neither of nation nor class, its concern is man; it concerns freedom as freedom of the individual'?

A. Sri Aurobindo
B. V.D. Savarkar
C. M.N. Roy
D. Deendayal Upadhyaya

80. Given below are two statements: One is labelled as Assertion (A) and the other is labelled as Reason (R):

Assertion (A): There is a significant ideological difference between political parties in a polarized multiparty system with a strong dose of dogmatic radicalism.

Reason (R): Political coalitions in polarized multiparty system are viable.

In the light of the above statements, choose the correct answer from the options given below:

A. Both (A) and (R) are true and (R) is the correct explanation of (A)
B. Both (A) and (R) are true and (R) is NOT the correct explanation of (A)
C. (A) is true, but (R) is false
D. (A) is false, but (B) is true

81. The Commission on the Status of Women was established vide resolution of the:

A. ECOSOC B. UNEP
C. WHO D. UNEF

82. Match List-I with List-II.

List-I (States/Union Territories)	List-II (Year of Establishment)
(*a*) Punjab	I. 1966
(*b*) Gujarat	II. 1960
(*c*) Ladakh	III. 2014
(*d*) Telangana	IV. 2019

Choose the correct answer from the options given below:

	(*a*)	(*b*)	(*c*)	(*d*)
A.	I	II	IV	III
B.	I	II	III	IV
C.	II	I	IV	III
D.	II	I	III	IV

83. NITI Aayog was established through the Cabinet Secretariat resolution dated:

A. 01-12-2014
B. 01-01-2015
C. 01-01-2016
D. 01-12-2016

84. Who among the following argued that, "when NGOs are tied up with social movements, they have occasionally changed their political agendas"?

A. Neera Chandhoke
B. Gurpreet Mahajan
C. Niraja Gopal Jayal
D. Manoranjan Mohanty

85. Which of the following statements is are correct regarding Central Information Commission (CIC)?

(*a*) CIC was constituted through an official gazzette notification under the provisions of the RTI Act 2005.
(*b*) When CIC was constituted initially, it has five commissions including Chief Information Commissioners.
(*c*) The Chief Information Commissioner holds office for a period of three years from the date on which he enters upon office.

Choose the correct answer from the options given below:

A. (*a*) and (*b*) only

B. (*a*) and (*c*) only

C. (*b*) and (*c*) only

D. (*a*), (*b*) and (*c*) only

86. Match List-I with List-II.

List-I	List-II
(*a*) Robert Cox	I. Impact of international regimes on cooperation
(*b*) Robert Keohane	II. Interaction between social forcess, forms of state and world orders
(*c*) Alexander Wendt	III. Constructivist idea of social structures
(*d*) Rob Walker	IV. Emphasis on continuity' and repetition in social structures

Choose the correct answer from the options given below:

	(*a*)	(*b*)	(*c*)	(*d*)
A.	II	I	III	IV
B.	I	II	III	IV
C.	III	IV	I	II
D.	II	I	IV	III

87. In which year did the amendment to the Constitution extend the Panchayati Raj provisions to the scheduled areas?

A. 1992 B. 1995

C. 1996 D. 1997

88. Which of the following statements have not been made by M.N. Srinivas regarding caste politics in India?

(*a*) There is horizontal solidarity of caste in India

(*b*) Modern technology created hurdles on the way to cast solidarity

(*c*) There was even vertical solidarity between castes

(*d*) There was competition amongst castes in political economic sphere

Choose the correct answer from the options given below:

A. (*a*) and (*b*) only

B. (*b*) and (*c*) only

C. (*b*), (*c*) and (*d*) only

D. (*a*), (*c*) and (*d*) only

89. Which of the following are the basic features of Eric Hobsbawm's theory of nationalism in Europe?

(*a*) There are three phases of nationalism that have shaped states in Western countries.

(*b*) He defines nationalism, for instance as reinventing traditions.

(*c*) He identifies petty bourgeoisie as a group that advocated separatist nationalism.

(*d*) He ignored the emergence of ethno-lingustic nationalism in East and West Europe.

Choose the correct answer from the options given below:

A. (*a*), (*b*), (*d*) only

B. (*b*) and (*d*) only

C. (*b*) and (*c*) only

D. (*a*), (*c*) and (*d*) only

90. Which among the following is not included in the right to life under Article 21 of the Indian Constitution as interpreted by the Supreme Court?

A. Right to suicide

B. Right to privacy

C. Right against public hanging

D. Right to good health

Directions (Qs. No. 91-95): *Read the following passage and answer the questions.*

It is interesting that John Stuart Mill's turn away from narrow utilitarianism began with his reading of the Romantic poets, Wordworth and Coleridge, who espoused in literature what Edmund Burke had espoused philosophically. They emphasised feeling and intuition rather than mere logic and rational categories of thought.

And it was this emphasis upon the emotional level human experience that attracted the young Mill who, as a young man, who overly exposed to the scientific and coldly rationalistic doctrine of utilitarianism, and whose upbringing in that doctrine had cut him off from much of what is genuinely human.

But Mill also had read de Tocqueville. And just as the Romantic poets taught Mill that utilitarian psychology was lacking terms, de Tocqueville pointed out to him its sociological inadequacies. Both demonstrated the need for a certain conservative perspective on humanity and society. Taken together, they emphasised along with Burke, emotional aspects of human behaviour and the need for human beings to be integrated into some strictly rational-individualistic perspective of classical liberalism.

What makes John Stuart Mill uniquely important in the development of liberal thought in his revision of the underlining assumptions of the classical doctrine. This de Tocqueville did not do: he was interested in critically analyzing a concrete example of liberal democracy, not in debating the validity of the liberal ideology as such. Mill, on the other hand, was precisely interested in the philosophical validity of liberalism. To his mind, the kinds of concrete reforms that de Tocqueville advocates in *'Democracy in America'* required a more fundamental reform of liberalism's basic philosophical assumptions.

91. Which one among the following clearly reflects in the writings of Tocqueville?
A. Debating the validity
B. Critically analysing
C. Philosophical validity of liberalism
D. Creating a pressure on Mill

92. Match List-I with List-II.

List-I	List-II
(*a*) Tocqueville	I. Rationalistic doctrine
(*b*) Young Mill	II. Democracy in America
(*c*) Edmund Burke	III. Espoused in literature
(*d*) Wordsworth	IV. Espoused Philosophically

Choose the correct answer from the options given below:

	(*a*)	(*b*)	(*c*)	(*d*)
A.	I	II	III	IV
B.	IV	III	II	I
C.	III	II	I	IV
D.	II	I	IV	III

93. Given below are two statements: One is labelled as Assertion (A) and the other is labelled as Reason (R):
Assertion (A): Young Mill was overly exposed to the scientific doctrine of Utilitarianism.
Reason (R): Utilitarian doctrine had cut him off from much of what is genuinely human.
In the light of the above statements, choose the correct answer from the options given below:
A. Both (A) and (R) are correct and (R) is the correct explanation of (A)
B. Both (A) and (R) are correct and (R) is NOT the correct explanation of (A)
C. (A) is correct, but (R) is not correct
D. (A) is not correct, but (R) is correct

94. Who among the following thinkers espoused feeling and intuition that influenced John Stuart Mill?
A. Locke B. Bentham
C. Wordsworth D. R.C. Smith

95. Given below are two statements:
Statement I: Romantic poets taught Mill that Utilitarian psychology lacks in human terms.
Statement II: Tocqueville pointed out scientific inadequacies of Utilitarian philosophy.
In the light of the above statements, choose the most appropriate answer from the options given below:
A. Both Statement I and Statement II are true
B. Both Statement I and Statement II are false

C. Statement I is true but Statement II is false
D. Statement I is false but Statement II is true

Directions (Qs. No. 96-100): *Read the following passage and answer the questions.*

Evaluating policy is a challenging experience that requires intricate knowledge and clever use of statistical and economic techniques. The confounding thing about policy change is that it neither happens over night nor in a setting where other environmental elements remain static. Consequently, figuring out the impact of a specific change on the observed outcome change becomes a serious metrological challenge. However several standard techniques have emerged to access the effectiveness of specific policy discussion. A broad discussion of a few of these approaches is helpful in understanding the logic of how to think about evaluating policy. Most famous techniques for policy impact measurement often referred to as "Gold Standard" in impact evaluation is Randomized Control Trails (RCT). Medicine and pharmaceutical research is the best example of RCT method. The standard metrological technique is to select a group of respondents on whom the drug is likely to work. The drug is then administered to a randomly selected subset of that group. The RCT approach here is to administer an intervention to a randomly selected group of recipients from amongst a group of potential beneficiaries to judge the effect of the intervention exactly. The RCT administrator can convince the policy maker to make his her choice of beneficiary units randomly rather than by aligning it to some other rule.

96. Given below are two statements:

Statement I: The confounding thing about policy change is that it happens neither over night nor in a setting where other environmental elements remain static.

Statement II: Figuring out the impact of a specific change on the observed outcome change becomes a serious metrological challenge.

In the light of the above statements, choose the most appropriate answer from the options given below:

A. Both Statement I and Statement II are correct
B. Both Statement I and Statement II are true
C. Statement I is true but Statement II is false
D. Statement I is false but Statement II is true

97. In which of the following field is 'The Randomized Control Trials' used mostly?

A. Space Research
B. Defence Research
C. Pharmaceutical Research
D. Oceanographic Research

98. The RCT approach is to administer an intervention to a ________ group of recipients from a large group of potential beneficiaries:

A. Specifically Selected
B. Randomly Selected
C. Qualified Selection
D. Pre determined Selection

99. Which of the following technique is considered as 'Gold Standard"?

A. Randomized sampling
B. Justified sampling
C. Randomized control trails
D. Snow ball method

100. Given below are two statements:

Statement I: The standard metrological is to select a group of respondents.

Statement II: In RCT Trails every individual participant in the trial differs from everyone else.

In the light of the above statements, choose the most appropriate answer from the options given below:

A. Both Statement I and Statement II are true
B. Both Statement I and Statement II are false
C. Statement I is true but Statement II is false
D. Statement I is false but Statement II is true

ANSWERS

1. (C): The Department of Administrative Reforms and Public Grievances (DARPG) launched a comprehensive website for Citizen's Charters in Government of India on May 31, 2002. The website is www.goicharters.nic.in. The Citizen's Charter is a voluntary declaration by service providers about their service standards, choice, accessibility, non-discrimination, transparency, and accountability. It was introduced in 1997 to improve the quality of public services. The charters must include service standards, grievance redressal mechanisms, and a provision for unbiased scrutiny by consumer/citizen groups.

2. (C): Doug McAdam has indeed refined the process model by highlighting the role of cultural framing, social networks, and movement organizations in shaping collective action. He has conducted in-depth case studies, often focusing on specific movements in the United States, to better understand the dynamics and factors influencing social and political mobilization. His work has been influential in advancing our understanding of how social movements emerge, evolve, and achieve their goals.

3. (C): The statement "In the course of time, however (while Nehru was still alive), the Congress party ceased to be a movement and became a party and government" is associated with the scholar Rajni Kothari. She was an Indian political scientist, made significant contributions to the understanding of Indian politics, particularly the evolution of the Congress party. In the early years of post-independence India, the Congress party, led by figures like Jawaharlal Nehru, played a pivotal role in the country's struggle for independence. During this period, the Congress was not just a political party but was also seen as a broader movement representing the aspirations of the Indian people. The statement encapsulates Kothari's perspective on the evolution of the Congress party from a movement during the independence struggle to a political party actively involved in governance after independence. It reflects his broader analysis of the changing dynamics of Indian politics during that period.

4. (D):

(*d*) "Two Concepts of Liberty" was the inaugural lecture delivered by the liberal philosopher Isaiah Berlin before the University of Oxford on 31 October 1958. It was subsequently published as a 57-page pamphlet by Oxford at the Clarendon Press.

(*c*) The Constitution of Liberty is a 1960 book by Friedrich Hayek that is considered a classic of economic philosophy. The book is a restatement of the basic principles of a philosophy of freedom. It is divided into three parts: The Value of Freedom, Freedom and the Law, and Freedom in the Welfare State. The book is considered a seminal text of modern liberalism and defends the principles of a free society. It also traces the origin, rise, and decline of the rule of law.

(*b*) Liberty is a revised and expanded edition of the book that Isaiah Berlin regarded as his most important—Four Essays on Liberty, a standard text of liberalism, constantly in demand and constantly discussed since it was first published in 1969.

(*a*) Liberty After Freedom: A History of Article 21, Due Process and the Constitution of India is a 2022 book by

Rohan J. Alva. The book explores the origins of the right to life and personal liberty, which is guaranteed by Article 21 of the Indian Constitution. It also examines how India's post-World War II Constitution was interpreted to protect liberty interests like privacy.

5. (C):

(*a*) Globalization has permitted the exchange of ideas and goods which is exploited by terrorist groups—Globalization has facilitated the movement of ideas, information, and goods across borders. Terrorist groups can take advantage of these global networks for communication, funding, and resource acquisition. This interconnectedness has allowed them to exploit the openness of global systems.

(*b*) The internet has allowed terrorists to recruit new followers—The internet, a key component of globalization, provides a platform for communication and recruitment. Terrorist groups can use online channels to spread their ideologies, recruit new members, and coordinate activities. The accessibility of the internet allows them to reach a global audience and attract individuals from different parts of the world.

(*c*) New technologies allow terrorists to operate in highly distributed networks—Advancements in technology have enabled terrorist groups to operate in decentralized and distributed networks. This makes it challenging for authorities to track and counteract their activities. The use of encrypted communication and sophisticated technologies enhances the agility and adaptability of terrorist organizations.

6. (D):

(*b*) The Articles of Confederation were adopted by the Continental Congress on November 15, 1777. This document served as the United States' first constitution. It was in force from March 1, 1781, until 1789 when the present-day Constitution went into effect.

(*a*) The federal government of the United States is the national government of the United States, a federal republic located primarily in North America. This was established in the year 1789. It composed of 50 states, five major self-governing territories, several island possessions, and the federal district and national capital of Washington, D.C., where most of the federal government is based.

(*c*) A joint House and Senate Conference Committee settled remaining disagreements in September. On October 2, 1789, President Washington sent copies of the 12 amendments adopted by Congress to the states. By December 15, 1791, three-fourths of the states had ratified 10 of these, now known as the "Bill of Rights."

(*d*) The 14th Amendment to the U.S. Constitution was adopted on July 9, 1868. The Equal Protection Clause is the first section of the 14th Amendment, and it guarantees equal protection under the law for all citizens. The 14th Amendment also grants citizenship to all people born or naturalized in the United States, including formerly enslaved people. It also extends the liberties and rights granted by the Bill of Rights to formerly enslaved people. The Equal Protection Clause targeted states because they were discriminating against newly freed slaves.

7. (A): Statement I: This statement is largely true. India's foreign policy has traditionally been focused on securing its borders, preserving its national identity, and maintaining autonomy in decision-making. This is evident in its focus on: India has faced numerous territorial disputes with its neighbors, particularly Pakistan and China. These disputes have shaped its foreign policy and its strategic alliances. India remains concerned about preserving its unique cultural and historical identity on the world stage. This is reflected in its emphasis on non-alignment and its resistance to external pressures. India aims to be a major player on the global stage and avoid being subservient to any other power. This is evident in its independent foreign policy choices and its reluctance to join military alliances.

Statement II: While the global bipolar conflict during the Cold War (between the US and the USSR) has largely ended, its impact on regional conflicts persists. The India-Pakistan conflict holds historical roots in the Cold War, with the USSR supporting India and the US supporting Pakistan. This legacy, combined with ongoing territorial disputes and ideological differences, creates a regional bipolar dynamic despite the global shift.

Therefore, both statements hold significant truth in understanding India's foreign policy and the regional context surrounding its relationship with Pakistan.

8.(C):

(*c*) The Communist Party of India (Marxist) (abbreviated as CPI(M)/CPIM/CPM) is a communist political party in India. It is the largest communist party in India in terms of membership and electoral seats, and one of the national parties of India. The party was founded through a splitting from CPI in 1964 and it quickly became the dominant fraction.

(*d*) Shiv Sena is a right-wing Marathi regionalist and Hindu ultranationalist political party in India founded in 1966 by Bal Thackeray. Currently led by Eknath Shinde, this party is the ruling party of the Indian state of Maharashtra since 2019. Shiv Sena's election symbol is the Bow and Arrow.

(*b*) BJP was formally established in 1980, following a split by dissidents within the Janata coalition, whose leaders wanted to prohibit elected BJS officials from participating in the RSS. Since 2014, it has been the ruling political party in India under the incumbent Prime Minister Narendra Modi. The BJP is aligned with right-wing politics, and its policies adhere to Hindutva, a Hindu nationalist ideology. It has close ideological and organizational links to the Rashtriya Swayamsevak Sangh (RSS) volunteer paramilitary organization.

(*a*) The Samajwadi Party founded on 4 October 1992 is a socialist political party in India. It was founded by formerly Janata Dal politicians Mulayam Singh Yadav, Beni Prasad Verma, Azam Khan and is headquartered in New Delhi. While the party is largely based in Uttar Pradesh, it has minor presence in other states as well.

9. (D):

(*a*) The statement "Management is subjective" conveys that managerial processes involve a significant degree of subjectivity, as decisions, interactions, and organizational approaches are influenced by individual perspectives, judgments, and values. The managerial role entails making subjective decisions based on an assessment of unique circumstances, and interpersonal relations within a team are inherently shaped by the manager's personal style. Moreover, organizational culture, a key aspect of management, reflects subjective choices made by leaders. In crafting strategic visions, managers draw upon their subjective understanding of the business environment, leading to diverse interpretations and implementations of management principles. This subjectivity acknowledges the complexity and human-centric nature of management, where leaders navigate through varying perspectives and adapt to the nuanced challenges presented by real-world scenarios.

(*d*) Peter Drucker, a renowned management thinker, rejected the notion of a mechanistic model of organizational management. Unlike traditional approaches that favored rigid structures and hierarchical control, Drucker emphasized a more dynamic and adaptive style of management. He believed that effective management should be responsive to the evolving complexities of the business environment. Drucker advocated for flexibility, innovation, and a focus on results rather than adherence to fixed procedures. In his view, successful management required a keen understanding of the external environment, a commitment to continuous learning and improvement, and the ability to adapt strategies and structures in response to changing conditions. Drucker's approach promoted a more organic and human-centric view of organizations, challenging the idea that management could be reduced to a mechanistic set of procedures and controls.

10. (A):

(*a*) **Both civil society and political society are complementary to each other:** This statement emphasizes the idea that civil society (non-governmental organizations, advocacy groups, etc.) and political society (governmental institutions and structures) are complementary and work together. It aligns with the notion that a well-functioning democracy involves a balance between these two sectors, as they contribute to the overall health and functioning of a democratic system.

(*c*) **Rule of law is a condition for the consolidation of democracy:** This statement highlights the significance of the rule of law in the consolidation of democracy. A strong rule of law ensures that there are consistent and fair legal frameworks, which is crucial for protecting individual rights and promoting the stability of democratic institutions.

(*e*) **Modern democracies must have an effective capacity to command, regulate, and extract:** This statement underscores the importance of the state's ability to govern effectively, regulate economic activities, and collect resources through taxation. It reflects the idea that a well-functioning democracy requires a capable and responsive state.

11. (B):

(*a*) **In the mid-1960s, the Swatantra party presented a classical conservative perspective on foreign policy:** The Swatantra Party, founded in 1959, indeed presented an alternative perspective on various issues, including foreign policy. It leaned towards classical liberal and conservative ideologies, advocating for a more market-oriented and less state-controlled approach.

(*c*) **The supporters were drawn from former bureaucrats, the business community, and members of princely families:** The Swatantra Party attracted support from diverse sections, including individuals with a background in bureaucracy, the business community, and those associated with princely families. This coalition reflected a shared interest in promoting economic liberalization and reducing state intervention.

(*d*) **They united in their opposition to Nehru's Fabian economics:** The Swatantra Party opposed the economic policies of Jawaharlal Nehru, which were influenced by Fabian socialism. They advocated for a shift towards more market-driven economic principles, emphasizing individual initiative and private enterprise.

(*e*) **They believed in the forces of the market and private enterprises:** The Swatantra Party was known for its pro-market stance, advocating for policies that promoted economic freedom, reduced government intervention, and supported the role of private enterprises in driving economic growth.

12. (D): Yehezkel Dror, an Israeli political scientist, is renowned for his significant contributions to policy sciences and public policy. In his book "Public Policy Making Reexamined," Dror delves into a critical examination of the processes involved in public policy formation. He explores the complexities, challenges, and dynamics inherent in the decision-making aspects of public policy. Additionally, his work "Design for Policy Sciences" reflects Dror's emphasis on developing frameworks and methodologies for the effective design of policies. Dror's insights often incorporate interdisciplinary perspectives, drawing from political science, sociology, and systems theory, offering a comprehensive and nuanced approach to understanding and shaping public policies. Through these works, he has left a lasting impact on the field of policy sciences, influencing scholars and policymakers alike in their understanding and practice of public policy.

13. (B): B.R. Nelson's works on Marx specifically pinpoint the eleven theses as the sole foundation for praxis, his comprehensive studies like "An Introduction to Marxism" delve into the concept's development within Marx's broader ideological framework, potentially offering an direct connection to the mentioned theses. In 1845, Karl Marx wrote 11 theses in Brussels, one of which is often quoted: "The philosophers have only interpreted the world in various ways; the point is to change it". In these theses, Marx formulated a conception of objectivity founded on praxis. Praxis is an ancient philosophy term, first introduced by Aristotle. It describes a kind of activity that is done in and for itself: the action itself is the goal.

14. (B): The process of introduction for an elected President in the municipalities was made in Lord Mayo's Resolution of 1870. Since then the current form and structure of municipal bodies followed is similar to Lord Ripon's Resolution adopted in 1882 on local self-governance. The 74th Constitutional Amendment Act of 1992 was introduced providing for the transfer of 18 different powers to urban local bodies, including the election of a mayor and to recognize them which included municipal corporations, Nagar Panchayat, Municipal Councils.

15. (D): "The communication of intangible facts, opinions, suggestions and suspicions that cannot pass through formal channels are communicated through informal channels," is most likely attributed to Chester Bernard. Bernard, a prominent organizational theorist, was one of the first to highlight the importance of informal channels in organizational communication. He emphasized that much of the crucial information flow within organizations happens through informal networks, gossip, and grapevines, bypassing formal communication channels. The phraseology of the statement closely aligns with Bernard's ideas about informal communication. He frequently referred to the transmission of "intangible facts," "opinions," and "suggestions" within organizations and recognized the role of informal channels in facilitating this exchange, especially when formal channels prove inadequate or cumbersome.

16. **(C):** The view that "no citizen should be sufficiently opulent to be able to purchase another and none so poor as to be forced to sell himself" is associated with Jean-Jacques Rousseau. Jean-Jacques Rousseau, an Enlightenment philosopher and political theorist, articulated his views on social contract and economic inequality in several key works. In "Discourse on the Origin and Basis of Inequality Among Men," Rousseau explores the idea that in the state of nature, individuals were free and equal, but with the advent of private property and societal structures, inequality emerged. Rousseau envisioned a social contract where individuals collectively agree to be governed by a general will, aiming to promote the common good. He believed that in a just society, no one should be so wealthy that they can essentially buy another person (enslave them), and conversely, no one should be so impoverished that they are compelled to sell themselves into a form of economic servitude.

17. **(C):** The concept of a "silent revolution" associated with women from upper castes may not necessarily indicate a deepening of democracy facilitated by gendering politics. It could be interpreted as a more subtle or gradual change, but it doesn't inherently reflect a transformation that contributes significantly to the deepening of democratic practices. The other options, on the other hand, generally align with the idea of increasing participation, articulation of political voice, and involvement in the public sphere, which are indicative of a potential deepening of democracy through the inclusion of diverse voices, including women's perspectives.

18. **(A):** Sri Aurobindo, a philosopher and spiritual teacher, advocated for a profound transformation in human consciousness, which he referred to as a "spiritual revolution." His philosophy is deeply rooted in the idea of evolving towards a higher state of consciousness, where individuals become attuned to spiritual truths and principles. This transformation, according to Sri Aurobindo, is not just a personal endeavor but also has implications for the collective evolution of society.

    The concept of "Truth consciousness" in Sri Aurobindo's teachings implies a state of awareness where individuals go beyond the limitations of the ego and intellect to connect with a universal and transcendent truth. This truth is not merely intellectual or conceptual but is experiential and transformative. It involves aligning one's life and actions with the deeper spiritual realities that underlie existence.

    Sri Aurobindo did not prescribe a political system like parliamentary democracy as the basis for his spiritual revolution. Instead, he emphasized the importance of individual transformation and the emergence of a higher, more conscious society. Radical humanism, in the context of Sri Aurobindo's philosophy, would likely be seen as an outcome of individuals awakening to their deeper spiritual nature, fostering a sense of unity and interconnectedness with all of humanity.

19. **(A)**

20. **(C):** The advocate of cosmopolitan democracy among the listed thinkers is Kant. Immanuel Kant, an Enlightenment philosopher,

advocated for cosmopolitan democracy, envisioning a world where democratic principles and individual rights transcend national boundaries. In his work "Perpetual Peace," Kant proposed the idea of a global federation of Free states, emphasizing universal moral and political principles. This cosmopolitan democracy would be rooted in the recognition of individuals as rational beings with inherent dignity, promoting a sense of global citizenship and moral obligations beyond national affiliations. Kant's vision seeks to establish lasting peace through democratic governance within states and cooperative efforts among nations, reflecting a commitment to justice, human rights, and a shared cosmopolitan identity that transcends geographic and cultural divides.

21. **(A):** The Indian Council Act of 1892, also known as the Second Morley-Minto Reforms, marked a significant development in the evolution of India's political landscape during the colonial era. The Act introduced a limited form of franchise, allowing a select number of Indians to participate in the legislative councils. However, this participation was constrained by various restrictions, including property qualifications and nominations from specific interest groups. While the Act aimed to provide a semblance of representative governance, the limited franchise fell short of true democratic inclusion, as the majority of the Indian population remained disenfranchised. This Act represented a step towards constitutional reforms but highlighted the ongoing struggle for broader political representation and enfranchisement in the years leading up to India's independence.

22. **(A):**

(*a*) **War as the last resort:** This aligns with Winch's emphasis on exhausting all peaceful possibilities before resorting to war. He believed war should be considered only when all other avenues have been exhausted.

(*c*) **War must be declared on the basis of normally acceptable aims:** This reflects Winch's insistence on adherence to international law and principles of justice in jus ad bellum (the right to go to war). He argued that war must be for a just cause, such as self-defense or preventing humanitarian atrocities.

(*d*) **A justified response to a border incursion:** While proportionality is crucial in Winch's view, he acknowledges that some level of force might be considered justified in response to a border violation, depending on the specific circumstances. He wouldn't necessarily advocate for a full-scale invasion as the first reaction, but a measured and appropriate response within the bounds of proportionality could be acceptable under certain conditions.

23. **(A):** Escott Reid is the author of the 1981 scholarly memoir Envoy to Nehru. Reid was the Canadian High Commissioner to India from 1952 to 1957. "Envoy to Nehru" is based on his personal experiences and observations during his time in India, offering insights into his interactions with Jawaharlal Nehru, the political landscape of the period, and India's relationship with Canada. The book provides a firsthand look at the challenges of building a democratic system from the ashes of colonialism. Reid describes the complexities of India's diverse population, the rise of regional and state-level politics, and Nehru's efforts to unite the nation. "Envoy to Nehru" remains a valuable historical document offering insights into Nehru, India's early democracy, and its complex position on the world stage during the Cold War.

24. (D):

(*a*) Annihilation of Caste is a 1936 political work by Bhimrao Ramji Ambedkar, also known as B.R. Ambedkar. The book is a detailed account of the harms caused by Hinduism's caste system and why it should be abolished. Ambedkar argues that caste has no scientific basis and that it is necessary to destroy the religious notions upon which it is founded. He also argues that social reform should take precedence over political and religious reform.

(*b*) Who Were the Shudras? Is a book by Bhimrao Ramji Ambedkar, published in 1946. The book discusses the origin of the Shudra Varna in the Indian caste system. Ambedkar argues that the Shudras were originally Aryans who were conquered by the Brahmins and forced into a subordinate position. He also challenges the Aryan race theory, which argues that the Aryans were a superior race that conquered the indigenous peoples of India. Who Were the Shudras? is a landmark work in the history of Indian social thought. The book helped to raise awareness of the plight of the Shudras and other lower castes in India. It also contributed to the development of the Dalit movement, which advocates for the rights of Dalits, a term that encompasses all of India's marginalized castes.

(*d*) The Untouchables: Who Were They? and why They Became Untouchables is a crucial work by Dr. Bhimrao Ramji Ambedkar, published in 1948. It delves into the complex origins and ongoing struggles of the Untouchables, also known as Dalits, within the Indian caste system. The book dismantles various myths used to justify the caste system and untouchability, including theories of race, origin, and occupation. Ambedkar argues that untouchability arose from social and economic factors, not inherent characteristics. The book also addresses the challenges of Dalit emancipation and explores potential avenues for social and political transformation. Ambedkar emphasizes the importance of education, self-organization, and political participation in dismantling the caste system and achieving equality.

(*c*) Future of Parliamentary Democracy is a work completed by Dr. Ambedkar in 1959. Dr. Ambedkar believed that political democracy cannot succeed without social and economic democracy. He also believed that people should strive for a social democracy based on equality, liberty, and fraternity. In a 1949 speech to the Constituent Assembly, Ambedkar said, "Political democracy cannot last unless there lies at the base of it social democracy".

25. (B): Richard Titmuss's three-fold classification of welfare states includes the Institutional Redistribution Model, which is associated with the Scandinavian social democratic regime. In this model, the welfare state is characterized by a strong emphasis on social equality and institutionalized mechanisms for the redistribution of wealth. The Scandinavian countries, such as Sweden, Norway, Denmark, and Finland, exemplify this model by implementing comprehensive social welfare policies. These policies aim to reduce social inequalities through progressive taxation, generous social benefits, and public services, ensuring a high level of social protection for citizens. The emphasis on institutionalized redistribution distinguishes the Scandinavian social democratic regime from other welfare state models, aligning with the principles of equality and social solidarity.

26. (D): Jayaprakash Narayan, popularly known as JP, was a prominent political leader and social reformer in India. His plan for the reconstruction of Indian polity reflected a commitment to decentralization and grassroots democracy. The key aspects of JP Narayan's plan include:

(*a*) **Reviving 'Swaraj from below':** JP Narayan advocated for the revitalization of self-rule or 'Swaraj' at the grassroots level. This concept aimed at empowering local communities and individuals, emphasizing participation in decision-making processes.

(*c*) **The gram sabha as the basis of grassroots democracy:** In JP Narayan's vision, the gram sabha, or village assembly, was envisioned as the basic unit of political organization. The gram sabha would serve as a forum for local residents to actively participate in decision-making, discuss community issues, and contribute to the governance of their village.

(*d*) **Establishing an organic link among Panchayati Raj units:** The Panchayati Raj system, with its emphasis on local self-governance, was a central component of JP Narayan's plan. He aimed to create an interconnected and organic link among different units of the Panchayati Raj, fostering collaboration and coordination for effective governance.

Overall, JP Narayan's plan for the reconstruction of Indian polity was rooted in the principles of decentralization, community participation, and empowerment at the grassroots level. His vision sought to strengthen local governance structures, giving people greater control over their destinies and promoting a more inclusive and participatory form of democracy.

27. (A): Arvind Panagariya points to two critical factors that contributed to the enhanced growth rate of the Indian economy in the 1980s:

(*b*) **Expert incentives for private companies:** The 1980s witnessed a shift towards economic liberalization policies that aimed at reducing government controls and promoting private sector participation. Incentives were provided to private companies to encourage investment, innovation, and entrepreneurship. This change in policy marked a departure from the earlier era of extensive state control and played a crucial role in fostering economic growth by leveraging the dynamism of the private sector.

(*d*) **A more realistic exchange rate policy:** The adoption of a more realistic exchange rate policy was instrumental in shaping India's economic landscape. A realistic exchange rate helped in promoting international trade by making Indian goods more competitive in the global market. This policy shift was aligned with a broader move towards economic openness, emphasizing the importance of trade and reducing reliance on protectionist measures. A realistic exchange rate policy contributed to a more efficient allocation of resources and facilitated economic growth through increased exports and imports.

These two factors, expert incentives for private companies and a realistic exchange rate policy, reflect a broader trend in the 1980s towards economic reforms and a departure from the import substitution industrialization (ISI) model. The reforms aimed at unlocking the potential of the private sector, encouraging global economic integration, and adopting more pragmatic economic policies, collectively contributing to the higher growth trajectory observed in that period.

28. (D):

(*a*) **Under the Arbitration and Conciliation Act 1996, International Commercial Arbitration can also be initiated in the Supreme Court:** This statement is accurate. While the Supreme Court of India has jurisdiction over appeals related to International Commercial Arbitration, it has the original jurisdiction to directly initiate such arbitrations. The correct understanding is that the Supreme Court can hear appeals arising from decisions of the High Courts or from orders of certain tribunals under the Arbitration and Conciliation Act.

(*b*) **The Supreme Court has special advisory Jurisdiction under Article 143:** This statement is correct. Article 143 of the Indian Constitution empowers the President of India to seek the Supreme Court's advice on any question of law or fact that is of public importance. The advisory jurisdiction allows the President to refer complex legal or constitutional questions to the Supreme Court for guidance.

(*c*) **Article 32 of the Constitution gives extensive original jurisdiction to the Supreme Court with regard to enforcement of Fundamental Rights:** This statement is also correct. Article 32 of the Indian Constitution confers original jurisdiction upon the Supreme Court for the enforcement of fundamental rights. Individuals can directly approach the Supreme Court by filing writ petitions under Article 32 to seek remedies for the violation of their fundamental rights. The Supreme Court, through this provision, acts as a guardian of fundamental rights and ensures their protection.

29. (A): Assertion (A) (Economic globalization promotes prosperity and opportunity for all) is true: While economic globalization has its critics and complexities, it has also led to increased trade and investment, which can foster economic growth and development. This can potentially translate to improved living standards and opportunities for many, particularly in developing countries.

Reason (R) (Economic globalization promotes an open, market-based economy that brings social and political benefits) is also true: Open markets and reduced trade barriers are generally associated with economic benefits. However, this reson fully capture the complexities of the relationship between globalization and social and political outcomes. While globalization might directly guarantee these benefits, it can create conditions conducive to their development, depending on how its effects are managed and distributed.

30. (B): In Plato's philosophical dialogues, especially in works like "Phaedo" and "The Republic," the concept of asceticism is tied to the pursuit of wisdom, virtue, and the transcendence of worldly desires. Plato's teacher, Socrates, is often depicted as living a simple and ascetic life, focusing on intellectual and moral development rather than material or sensual pursuits.

The idea behind asceticism in Plato's philosophy is rooted in the belief that excessive attachment to material possessions, bodily pleasures, and worldly distractions hinders the soul's quest for knowledge and the realization of higher truths. Plato envisions an ascetic life as a means of purifying the soul from the distractions and temptations of the physical world.

In "The Republic," Plato's character Socrates describes the philosopher as the one who seeks truth, justice, and the Forms—the ideal, abstract concepts of things. The philosopher, according to Plato, must detach from the material world and cultivate a life of contemplation and intellectual pursuits. This ascetic approach involves overcoming desires for wealth, fame, and bodily pleasures in favor of a higher, more transcendent understanding.

31. (A): The quote you provided highlights that the major criticism against J.S. Mill's defense of liberty comes from Sir Ernest Barker. Sir Ernest Barker, a political theorist and scholar, was critical of Mill's conception of liberty, especially in relation to individualism and utilitarian philosophy.

One key aspect of Mill's defense of liberty is his attempt to reconcile individual freedom with the greatest happiness principle of utilitarianism. While Mill expanded on Jeremy Bentham's utilitarianism and introduced the harm principle to protect individual freedoms, critics like Sir Ernest Barker questioned the coherence of Mill's synthesis.

Barker's criticism may involve questioning the practicality and consistency of Mill's approach, the potential conflicts between individual rights and the general welfare, or the broader implications of Mill's ideas for political theory and governance.

32. (B)

33. (C):

(*a*) **Rousseau's:** Rousseau social contract theory can also be interpreted as questioning liberty under concentrated power. He argues that individuals surrender some freedoms to the "general will" for collective benefit. However, if the propertied classes hold significant influence within this contract, their interests can disproportionately shape that "general will", effectively creating a system where they "dominate others" by limiting individual liberty through this supposedly collective voice.

(*b*) **Marx:** Karl Marx saw class conflict primarily driven by unequal ownership of the means of production. He argued that the capitalist class, by controlling property and resources, exercised power and exploited the working class, effectively limiting their liberty.

(*d*) **Engels:** Similar to Marx, Engels viewed property ownership as a tool of domination in the hands of the bourgeoisie. He believed that true liberty wouldn't exist until the capitalist system was dismantled and the means of production were collectivized.

34. (C): "Federation Versus Freedom" is a significant work authored by Dr. B.R. Ambedkar, the chief architect of the Indian Constitution. Published in 1955, the book delves into the complexities of federalism and its implications for India. Dr. Ambedkar critically examines the challenges and opportunities presented by the federal structure, discussing issues such as the distribution of powers between the center and states, the role of the President, and the potential threats to individual freedoms. Through meticulous analysis, Ambedkar addresses the balance between a strong, centralized government and the autonomy of individual states, offering insights into the intricate task of crafting a constitutional framework that ensures both unity and diversity in a vast and diverse nation like India. The book reflects Ambedkar's deep commitment to social justice, constitutional principles, and his visionary approach to nation-building.

35. (D):

(*a*) **The Negro and language:** In this chapter, Frantz Fanon explores the impact of language on the identity and consciousness of the Black individual. He delves into the linguistic aspects of colonization and how language contributes to the construction of racial and cultural identities.

(*c*) **The Negro and Psychopathology:** This chapter delves into the psychological effects of colonization and racism on the mental health and well-being of Black individuals. Fanon examines the ways in which racial prejudice and discrimination contribute to psychopathological conditions and explores the internalized effects of racism.

(*d*) **The Negro and Recognition:** This chapter addresses the theme of recognition and identity. Fanon discusses the struggle for recognition and the impact of social and cultural attitudes on the self-perception of Black individuals. It explores how identity is shaped through interactions with others and societal expectations.

These chapters collectively contribute to Fanon's broader exploration of the psychological, cultural, and social dimensions of racism and colonization in "Black Skin, White Masks." The book, written in the context of Fanon's own experiences and observations, remains a seminal work in postcolonial studies and critical race theory.

36. (C)

37. (B): Rabindranath Tagore, a prominent Indian poet, philosopher, and Nobel laureate, articulated a profound critique of Western nationalism in the early 20th century. In challenging the prevailing notions of nationalism, Tagore emphasized that the essence of Western nationalism was not rooted in a spirit of cooperation, unity, or shared humanity but, rather, in conflict and conquest. He contended that the aggressive and exclusionary nature of Western nationalism, marked by imperialistic tendencies, had adverse consequences for global harmony.

Tagore advocated for a more inclusive and spiritual understanding of nationalism that transcended narrow borders and celebrated the interconnectedness of all human beings. His critique reflected a broader call for a more humane and empathetic approach to nationhood, emphasizing the importance of cultural diversity and mutual respect for fostering a peaceful world.

38. (D): In Kautilya's Arthashastra, a classical treatise on statecraft and politics, the concept of "Mitra" (friend), "Amitya" (neutrals), and "Satru" (enemies) plays a crucial role in shaping foreign policy. The elements of the Circle of States, or neighboring states, are strategically approached using various methods:

(*a*) **Making peace:** Kautilya acknowledges the importance of establishing peaceful relations with neighboring states. Making peace involves negotiating treaties, alliances, and agreements to ensure stability and mutual benefit. It's a strategic move to avoid unnecessary conflicts that might weaken the state.

(*c*) **Staying quiet:** Staying quiet, in the context of foreign policy, can be interpreted as a form of strategic restraint. Kautilya suggests that sometimes it's prudent for a state to avoid unnecessary provocations or confrontations. By staying quiet, a state can focus on internal development and consolidate its strength.

(*d*) **Seeking support:** Kautilya emphasizes the significance of building alliances and seeking the support of other states. This involves diplomatic efforts to align with those who can contribute to the state's strategic interests. Seeking support can enhance a state's geopolitical position and provide additional resources or backing in times of need.

These methods reflect Kautilya's realpolitik approach, where foreign policy is seen as a pragmatic pursuit of the state's interests. The Arthashastra provides a comprehensive guide for rulers on how to navigate diplomatic relationships and geopolitical challenges to ensure the security and prosperity of the state.

39. (A):

(*b*) Converse principle acknowledges the limitations of human information processing in forming political attitudes. While it doesn't directly measure attitudes, understanding these limitations helps interpret how people form and hold their views, making it relevant to studying them.

(*c*) Robinson's principle emphasizes the crucial role of formal and informal institutions in shaping political culture. These institutions influence and reflect the dominant values, norms, and belief systems within a society, which in turn shape the attitudes of its members.

Therefore, both (*b*) and (*c*) offer valuable insights into understanding and comparing how people's attitudes are shaped and reflected within different political cultures.

40. (B)

41. (A): The First Administrative Reforms Commission (ARC) was constituted by the Government of India in 1966, and it was chaired by Morarji Desai. The commission was tasked with examining and making recommendations on the improvement and modernization of the administrative machinery of the government. In its interim report submitted in 1966, titled "Problems of Redressal of Citizen's Grievances," the ARC proposed significant reforms related to addressing citizen grievances and, notably, recommended the establishment of institutions like the Lokpal and Lokayukta. These bodies were envisioned as ombudsman institutions to investigate and redress complaints of corruption and maladministration at the central and state levels, respectively.

The recommendations of the First ARC laid the foundation for subsequent discussions and developments leading to the eventual establishment of the Lokpal and Lokayukta in India. These institutions play a crucial role in promoting transparency, accountability, and integrity in public administration by providing avenues for citizens to raise concerns about corruption and malpractices. The First ARC's contribution to the anti-corruption framework in India is significant, and its recommendations set the stage for subsequent legislative and administrative actions in this regard.

42. (B):

(*a*) **Official Secrets Act, 1923:** This law is specifically designed to prevent unauthorized disclosure of official information that could compromise national security. It restricts individuals from communicating, possessing, or publishing information that is considered to be sensitive or classified.

(*b*) **Commission of Enquiry Act, 1952:** This act primarily empowers the government to appoint commissions of inquiry to investigate specific matters of public importance. While it may deal with the investigation process, it doesn't inherently impose restrictions on the disclosure of official information.

(*c*) **Indian Evidence Act, 1872:** This act provides rules and regulations regarding the admissibility of evidence in legal proceedings. It doesn't directly pertain to restricting the disclosure of official information but rather focuses on the standards for presenting evidence in courts.

43. (B): Mancur Olson Jr. published The Logic of Collective Action: Public Goods and the Theory of Groups in 1965. The book is considered one of the most influential works in the study of public choice. It is a seminal work in political science that provides a theoretical framework for understanding the mobilization of interest groups. Olson argues that individuals have a tendency to free-ride on the efforts of others when it comes to collective action. He introduces the concept of "collective goods" and explains that rational individuals are less likely to participate in group activities when they can enjoy the benefits without actively contributing. Olson's analysis sheds light on the challenges faced by interest groups in organizing and mobilizing members to pursue common goals. The book has had a profound impact on the study of political science and collective action, influencing discussions on the dynamics of interest groups and their role in shaping political outcomes.

44. (D): "State in Capitalist Society," authored by Ralph Miliband, is a key work in Marxist political theory, published in 1969. Miliband critically examines the role of the state in a capitalist society, challenging conventional Marxist views on the state as a mere instrument of the ruling class. Instead, Miliband argues that the state has a relative autonomy and can exert influence over the capitalist class. He explores the ways in which the state apparatus, including its institutions and bureaucracy, may develop a certain degree of independence and serve as a mediator among competing interests within the capitalist system. Miliband's analysis contributes to a nuanced understanding of the complex relationship between the state and the capitalist class, offering insights into the mechanisms through which state power operates in a capitalist society.

45. (C): Frederick Taylor's scientific management theory, particularly the concept of functional foremanship, aimed at optimizing efficiency and productivity on the shop floor by dividing supervisory functions into specialized roles. Here's a more detailed explanation of each role mentioned:

(*a*) **Speed Boss:** This foreman's responsibility is to ensure that workers are operating at the most efficient speed. They focus on maximizing the output and productivity of each worker.

(*b*) **Repair Boss:** The Repair Boss is in charge of maintenance and repair work. Their role is crucial in ensuring that machinery and equipment are kept in good working condition to prevent disruptions in production.

(*e*) **Inspection Foreman:** This foreman oversees the quality control and inspection processes. They are responsible for ensuring that products meet the required quality standards before they leave the production line.

In summary, Taylor's functional foremanship aimed to increase efficiency by assigning specific tasks to specialized foremen, each focusing on a particular aspect of production. The roles mentioned cover aspects such as speed and efficiency, maintenance, and quality control, contributing to the overall goal of optimizing production processes in a scientific and systematic manner.

46. (A):

(*a*) "Every state is known by the rights that it maintains." - This statement emphasizes the idea that the character of a state can be understood and defined by the rights it upholds. The rights recognized and protected within a state contribute to its identity and values.

(*b*) "We do not mean by the rights the grant of some historic conditions possessed in childhood but lost in the process of time." - Laski is pointing out that when referring to rights, he is not talking about historical privileges that may have existed in the past but were gradually lost over time. Instead, he likely focuses on the contemporary and ongoing aspects of rights.

(*c*) "Rights in fact are those conditions of social life without which no man can seek, in general, to be himself at his best." - This statement suggests that, according to Laski, rights are essential conditions in social life. For an individual to reach their full potential or be the best version of themselves, certain rights and conditions in society must be present. It reflects a view that rights are not just legal concepts but integral to personal development and societal well-being.

Together, these statements underscore Laski's perspective on the significance of rights in shaping the character of a state, the contemporary nature of rights, and their crucial role in enabling individuals to thrive within society.

47. (A): Assertion (A): A prismatic society is a concept introduced by political scientist Fred Riggs to describe societies that exhibit characteristics of both traditional and modern forms of social organization. These characteristics tend to exist alongside each other and can be quite different in nature. For example, in a prismatic society, you might find traditional kinship-based networks operating alongside modern, bureaucratic institutions.

Reason (R): The coexistence of these diverse, often contrasting, structures can lead to inconsistent, incomplete, and unresponsive social change. Modernization efforts might be hampered by traditional practices, while traditional norms might be challenged by modern values. This creates a complex and sometimes contradictory dynamic that can hinder efficient and coherent social change.

48. (C): Statement I: This statement is correct. Syndicalism is a political and labor movement that originated in France in the late 19th century. It emphasizes the role of trade unions and worker solidarity in achieving social change. Syndicalists advocated for workers' control of the means of production and the abolishment of capitalism, often through direct action and general strikes.

Statement II: This statement is incorrect. Syndicalism is fundamentally based on the concept of class struggle. It views society as divided into two main classes: the working class (proletariat) and the owning class (bourgeoisie). Syndicalists believe that these classes have fundamentally opposed interests and that the working class must ultimately overthrow the capitalist system through revolutionary action.

Therefore, while Statement I correctly identifies the origin and core principles of syndicalism, Statement II misrepresents its essential focus on class struggle.

49. (C):

(*b*) **The nature of Gandhi's truth is antithetical to equality:** This statement is FALSE. On the contrary, Gandhi viewed truth as inseparable from equality and justice. He believed that seeking truth necessitates acknowledging and respecting the inherent dignity and equal worth of all human beings, regardless of their social standing or differences.

(*c*) **In such a dialogue parties are constructed as the adversary:** This statement is FALSE. While opposing viewpoints may exist, Satyagraha emphasizes empathy and understanding over antagonism. Participants engage in dialogue as fellow seekers of truth, aiming to bridge the gap between their positions through respectful communication and the potential for transformation.

50. (A)

51. (B):

(*a*) The Right to Information Act (RTI) was passed in 2005 to give Indian citizens the right to request information from public authorities. The act aims to make the government and its officials more accountable and responsible. The act gives citizens the same right to information as members of parliament and state legislatures. This means that information that can't be denied to parliament or a state legislature can't be denied to any person. The act empowers citizens to question the secrecy and abuse of power in governance. Information can include any material in any form, such as records, documents, memos, emails, opinions, advices, press releases, circulars, orders, logbooks, contracts, reports, papers, samples, models, and data material held in any electronic form.

(*c*) The Right of Children to Free and Compulsory Education Act, or Right to Education Act (RTE), was enacted by the Parliament of India on August 4, 2009. The act describes the importance of free and compulsory education for children between the ages of 6 and 14 in India. The 86th Constitutional Amendment (2002) inserted Article 21A in the Indian Constitution, which states that the State shall provide free and compulsory education to all children of 6 to 14 years.

(*d*) The Lokpal and Lokayuktas Act, 2013 is an anti-corruption law of the Indian Parliament. It establishes the Lokpal for the Union and Lokayukta for States to investigate corruption allegations against certain public officials. The President gave his assent to the act on January 1, 2014. The act allows citizens to file corruption complaints against the prime minister, other ministers, MPs, and group A, B, C, and D officers of the central government with the ombudsman.

(*b*) The Consumer Protection Act, 2019 (CPA) is a significant piece of legislation enacted in India to safeguard the interests of consumers and establish an efficient framework for addressing their grievances. The Act expands the definition of "consumer" to include any person who buys any goods or services for consideration. This means more individuals fall under the protection of the Act. The Consumer Protection Act, 2019 represents a significant advancement in consumer protection in India. By empowering consumers, promoting fair trade practices, and streamlining dispute resolution, it aims to create a more secure and just marketplace for all.

52. (D): The Paris Agreement, adopted in 2015 under the United Nations Framework Convention on Climate Change (UNFCCC), is a landmark international accord that focuses on global efforts to combat climate change. Unlike its predecessor, the Kyoto Protocol, the Paris Agreement employs a bottom-up approach, where each participating country voluntarily submits its own nationally determined contributions (NDCs) to address climate change mitigation. While the Kyoto Protocol set specific emission reduction targets for developed countries, the Paris Agreement emphasizes flexibility by allowing nations to determine their unique contributions based on their capacities and circumstances. The agreement's core aim is to limit global temperature increase to well below 2 degrees Celsius above pre-industrial levels, with efforts to pursue a more ambitious goal of limiting it to 1.5 degrees Celsius. The Paris Agreement underscores a cooperative and inclusive approach, recognizing the diverse responsibilities and capabilities of nations in addressing the complex challenges posed by climate change.

53. (C): J. Cohen, in the context of deliberative democracy, has defined it in terms of pluralistic association, emphasizing the idea that individuals participate in democratic deliberation not as isolated entities but as members of diverse and interconnected social groups. According to Cohen, the deliberative process should consider the plurality of perspectives and interests that arise from various social associations, ensuring that the discourse reflects the diversity of the society. This approach underscores the importance of recognizing and incorporating the multifaceted nature of individuals' identities and affiliations within the democratic deliberative framework, aiming for a more inclusive and representative decision-making process. Cohen's perspective on deliberative democracy aligns with the acknowledgment of pluralism and the intricate interplay of different social associations in shaping democratic discourse and decision outcomes.

54. (C): Ann Tickner, a prominent feminist international relations scholar, is known for her significant contributions to the field. In reformulating the principle of realism by Hans J. Morgenthau from a feminist perspective, Tickner challenges traditional realist assumptions that often neglect gender dynamics and the experiences of women in international relations. She argues that the traditional realist focus on power politics, military capabilities, and state-centric analysis tends to overlook the significance of gender as a critical factor in shaping global politics. Tickner advocates for a more inclusive and gender-sensitive approach to international relations that considers the experiences and perspectives of both men and women. By incorporating feminist insights into the realist framework, she highlights the interconnectedness of power and gender in shaping the international system, enriching the discourse with a more comprehensive understanding of global politics.

55. (D): Will Kymlicka, a political philosopher, is known for his work on multiculturalism and minority rights. According to Kymlicka, the right to a speedy trial is not categorized as a group right. Group rights, as conceptualized by Kymlicka, typically involve collective entitlements for cultural or national groups to protect and maintain their distinct identities within a broader society. In contrast, the right to a speedy trial is an individual right within the legal and justice framework, aimed at ensuring timely legal proceedings for individuals facing legal charges. Kymlicka's focus on group rights often centers around issues such as self-government rights, polyethnic rights, and special representation rights, which pertain to the collective rights of cultural or national groups rather than individual legal rights like the right to a speedy trial.

56. (C)

57. (A): Jawaharlal Nehru, India's first Prime Minister, expressed the sentiment about India's approach towards the United States and the Soviet Union during the Cold War era. Nehru emphasized the geographical proximity of India to both superpowers, referring to them as neighbors in Asia. His statement reflected a pragmatic understanding that, as a nation situated in a region where both superpowers had significant influence, India would inevitably engage in shared responsibilities and cooperation with both the United States and the Soviet Union. Nehru's approach was characterized by a commitment to non-alignment, advocating for India to maintain its independence and not align with any major power bloc during the Cold War. This stance aimed to safeguard India's sovereignty and pursue its own path in international relations amidst the ideological and geopolitical tensions of the Cold War.

58. (A):

(*a*) **Of Sense:** Hobbes begins by examining the fundamental role of sensory perception in human experience. He explores how our senses provide the raw material for all knowledge and understanding.

(*b*) **Of Imagination:** Building on the foundation of sense perception, Hobbes delves into the power of imagination. He explains how imagination enables us to retain and manipulate sensory impressions, create mental images, and anticipate future experiences.

(*d*) **Of Speech:** Hobbes then turns to language, which he views as a crucial tool for communication and reasoning. He discusses the nature of language, its origins, and its role in social interaction and the development of knowledge.

(*c*) **Of Reason and Science:** Finally, Hobbes examines the faculty of reason, which he regards as the highest human capability. He explores the nature of reasoning, its principles, and its application in various fields, including science, politics, and ethics.

59. (B): Aristotle, the ancient Greek philosopher, expressed the notion that if the sole purpose of communal living were the preservation of life, then it would be conceivable for a state to consist of both human slaves and brute animals. In his work "Politics," Aristotle delineated his views on the nature and purpose of political associations, arguing that human societies are not merely organized for survival but are more profoundly characterized by the pursuit of a common good and the development of virtues. While Aristotle acknowledged the necessity of basic needs for life, he believed that the true essence of a state lies in the pursuit of higher ideals, moral virtues, and the realization of a shared flourishing rather than a mere aggregation of individuals for survival.

60. (B):

(*a*) **Starred Questions:** In parliamentary proceedings, questions are categorized as starred and unstarred. Starred questions require an oral answer and can be followed by supplementary questions for further clarification.

(*c*) **Adjournment Motion:** The Adjournment motion is a parliamentary procedure that, if admitted, leads to the suspension of the business of the House to discuss a specific issue of urgent public importance. It requires the support of at least 50 members to be admitted.

(*d*) **Zero Hour:** The Zero Hour is a special hour in the parliamentary proceedings. It does not start immediately after the question hour. Instead, it usually begins at 12 noon, after the question hour, and provides Members of Parliament an opportunity to raise important matters that may not find a place in the regular agenda. It doesn't last until the agenda for the day but is fixed time duration.

61. (B): The idealist school of thought in international relations advocates for the replacement of the 'balance of power' paradigm with the concept of disarmament as a means to foster lasting peace and cooperation among nations. Idealists believe in the potential of diplomatic negotiations, international law, and the reduction of military capabilities to create a more harmonious global environment. In their vision, disarmament represents a proactive step towards preventing conflicts and mitigating the security dilemma that arises from nations building up military strength in response to perceived threats. By promoting mutual trust and cooperation, idealists argue that disarmament can pave the way for a world order characterized by peaceful resolution of disputes and collective security, challenging the traditional realist emphasis on power dynamics and strategic competition.

62. (A): In the industrial era, Frederick Winslow Taylor, the architect of Scientific Management, envisioned a paradigm shift. He called it the "Mental Revolution," an essential transformation in the mindsets of both managers and workers. For managers, it meant discarding the belief in workers' inherent laziness and embracing them as valuable partners in optimizing tasks. They were to transition from taskmasters to scientific analysts, designing optimal workflows and providing training for maximum efficiency. Workers, on the other hand, were encouraged to shed their distrust and resentment towards management. Taylor believed that by viewing managers as a resource for skill development and increased earnings, workers could shed the "soldier in the industrial army" mentality and actively contribute to organizational success. This radical shift in attitudes, a true "Mental Revolution," was Taylor's cornerstone for achieving unprecedented levels of efficiency and productivity through collaborative effort. It was a call for mutual respect, shared goals, and a win-win approach to the industrial landscape. While Taylor's methods faced controversy, the "Mental Revolution" concept undeniably left a lasting mark on management thinking, paving the way for future models emphasizing cooperation and human potential in the workplace.

63. (C)

64. (B): "Remapping India: New States and their Political Origins" by Louisie Tillin is a comprehensive exploration of the complex process of state formation in contemporary India. The book delves into the political dynamics that led to the creation of new states within the Indian federal structure, examining the historical, social, and political factors that shaped these transformations. Tillin scrutinizes the motivations behind demands for statehood, the strategies employed by regional movements, and the responses of the central government. Through detailed case studies, the author sheds light on the diverse experiences of states like Jharkhand, Chhattisgarh, and Uttarakhand, offering insights into the intricate interplay of identity politics, regional aspirations, and governance issues. "Remapping India" contributes to our understanding of the challenges and implications associated with the reconfiguration of political boundaries in the world's largest democracy.

65. (C)

66. (B): The membership criteria of NAM include:

(*a*) **Support for National Independence Movements:** NAM members are generally supportive of the right of nations to self-determination and independence. This criterion aligns with the movement's historical context, which emerged during the Cold War when many countries were seeking to assert their independence from colonial or imperial rule.

(*c*) **Adoption of an Independent Policy Based on Coexistence:** NAM countries are expected to pursue foreign policies that prioritize peaceful coexistence among nations. The movement promotes the idea that countries can maintain their sovereignty and pursue development goals without aligning with major power blocs or becoming entangled in their conflicts.

These criteria reflect the NAM's foundational principles of non-alignment, sovereignty, and cooperation. The movement seeks to provide member states with a platform to pursue their national interests without being drawn into the ideological or military conflicts of major powers. Therefore, a country meeting these criteria is likely to find alignment with the principles of the Non-Aligned Movement.

67. (C):

(*d*) The United Nations Protection Force (UNPROFOR) was established in 1992 to create conditions for peace and security in the former Yugoslavia. The UN Security Council Resolution 743 created UNPROFOR during the Croatian War of Independence. UNPROFOR's initial mandate was to ensure security and stable conditions for peace talks in three demilitarized "safe-haven" enclaves. The operational mandate of UNPROFOR extended to five republics of the former Yugoslavia: Croatia, Bosnia and Herzegovina, Macedonia, Montenegro, Serbia.

(*c*) The United Nations Assistance Mission for Rwanda (UNAMIR) was established in 1993 to help implement the Arusha Accords, which were signed to end the Rwandan Civil War. UNAMIR's main tasks were to:

- Ensure the security of Kigali, the capital city
- Monitor the ceasefire agreement
- Establish a demilitarized zone
- Monitor demobilization procedures

UNAMIR was a lightly armed force of about 2,500 troops. Some say that UNAMIR did not protect the majority of Rwandans, and that the killers did not see UNAMIR as a threat.

(*a*) The African Union-United Nations Hybrid Operation in Darfur (UNAMID) was a joint peacekeeping mission between the United Nations (UN) and the African Union (AU). The UN Security Council approved UNAMID on July 31, 2007 to bring stability to the Darfur region of Sudan. UNAMID was the world's largest peacekeeping mission for a long time, with a peak deployment of nearly 23,500 troops in 2011. The mission's mandate ended in 2020 after more than 13 years of operation.

(*b*) The United Nations Mission in South Sudan (UNMISS) is a peacekeeping mission that was established in 2011 to support the new government and protect civilians. The UNMISS headquarters is located in Juba. The UNMISS's mandate includes:

- Supporting the government of South Sudan in conflict prevention, mitigation, and resolution
- Protecting civilians
- Supporting peace consolidation
- Fostering longer-term state building and economic development

The UNMISS has nearly 20,000 peace-keepers. According to a 2019 report, the UNMISS has protected more than 200,000 civilians from violence.

68. (D): South Sudan is not a member of the Non-Aligned Movement (NAM). The Non-

Aligned Movement is a group of states that are not aligned with any major power bloc and seek to maintain their sovereignty and independence. While Burkina Faso, Angola, and Cameroon are associated with the NAM, South Sudan, a relatively new country that gained independence in 2011, has not joined the movement. The decision to join or not join international organizations, including the NAM, is typically based on a country's foreign policy priorities and its assessment of how such memberships align with its national interests and objectives. It's advisable to verify the current status, as international relations may evolve over time.

69. (B):

(*b*) **The Ashok Mehta Committee** was established in 1977 to examine the state of Panchayati Raj institutions in India. The committee was chaired by Ashok Mehta and submitted its report in August 1978. The committee made 132 recommendations to strengthen the declining Panchayati Raj system. The committee also provided a framework for states to develop their own Panchayat System. This resulted in many states having a working Panchayat system before the 73rd Constitutional Amendment.

(*a*) **The G.V.K. Rao Committee** was appointed in 1985 to review administrative arrangements in rural areas. The committee's goal was to improve the administrative, educational, and public health departments in rural areas. The committee recommended that the district be the basic unit of planning and that regular elections be held. The committee also suggested appointing a District Development Commissioner to serve as the CEO of the Zilla Parishad. The committee concluded that the developmental process had become increasingly bureaucratized and divorced from the Panchayati Raj. The committee made recommendations to strengthen and revitalize the Panchayati Raj system.

(*d*) **The L.M. Singhvi Committee** is a committee related to Panchayati Raj. The Government of India appointed the committee in 1986 to recommend steps to revitalize the Panchayati Raj systems for democracy and development. The committee recommended providing more financial resources and constitutional status to the panchayats to strengthen them.

(*c*) **The Thungon Committee** was established in 1988 to examine the political and administrative structure of districts and district planning. The committee recommended constitutional recognition for local government bodies and strengthening the Panchayati Raj system. The committee also recommended a constitutional amendment to provide for periodic elections to local government institutions, and enlistment of appropriate functions to them, along with funds. The committee was appointed during the time of Rajiv Gandhi. Prem Khandu Thungan was the Chief Minister of Arunachal Pradesh from 1975 to 1979.

70. (D):

(*d*) **The Elements of Administration** by Lyndall Fownes Urwick (1891-1983) was first published in 1944. The book was published by Harper and Brothers in New York, and is 118 pages long. A second edition was published in 1961 by Pitman. The Elements of Administration is about industrial management. Urwick also proposed 10 principles of organization, including the principle of definition.

(*a*) **The Philadelphia Conference,** also known as the Constitutional Convention, was held from May 25 to September 17, 1787. The convention's purpose was to address issues with governing the United States, which had been operating under the Articles of Confederation.

(*b*) **The first Minnowbrook Conference,** also known as Minnowbrook I, took place in 1968 at Syracuse University's conference center. The conference was commissioned to address the social unrest of the 1960s. The conference was led by Dwight Waldo and played a key role in shaping the field of public administration. The Minnowbrook Conference is a significant academic conference in public administration in the United States. It takes place every 20 years and is the result of the social disturbances of the late 1960s and early 1970s.

(*c*) **Public Administration in a Time of Turbulence** by Dwight Waldo was first published in 1971. The book examined the challenges facing public administration in an era of rapid social and technological change. Waldo argued that traditional approaches to public administration were no longer adequate, and that the field needed to adapt to the new realities of the time.

71. (C): The correct statement is "India did not offer support for the US anti-terrorism mission in Afghanistan." Since the early 2000s, India has consistently supported the United States in various strategic collaborations. India did express opposition to President Bush's decision to withdraw from the Anti-Ballistic Missile (ABM) Treaty, signaling a willingness to engage in dialogue on global security issues. However, the statement about India voting with the US at the September 2005 International Atomic Energy Compliance Board of Governors meeting to declare that Iran was non-compliant with the Nuclear Non-Proliferation Treaty (NPT) is not accurate. In reality, India has traditionally maintained a nuanced stance on Iran's nuclear program, often emphasizing diplomatic solutions and advocating for the peaceful use of nuclear energy. Therefore, "C only," correctly identifies the statement not included in India's initiatives in support of the US since 2001.

72. (D):

(*b*) **"Morality is not concerned only with equality.":** This statement suggests that Sen acknowledges the complexity of moral considerations and argues against reducing morality solely to concerns of material or economic equality. He emphasizes a broader understanding of morality that encompasses various dimensions beyond just economic factors.

(*c*) **"Basic capability, equality is a partial guide to the part of moral goodness that is associated with the idea of equality.":** Sen's notion of "basic capability" refers to individuals having the capabilities or capacities to achieve valuable functioning's. While economic resources are crucial, Sen contends that focusing on basic capabilities is a more encompassing approach to equality. This statement underscores that equality in basic capabilities is a key aspect of moral goodness related to the broader idea of equality.

(*d*) **"The index of basic capabilities like utility can be used in many different ways.":** Sen's emphasis on basic capabilities as an index goes beyond a narrow utilitarian perspective. He suggests that measuring equality in terms of basic capabilities allows for a more nuanced and flexible understanding of well-being. This aligns with his capability approach, which asserts that individuals should have the freedom to choose and achieve valuable functioning's based on their capabilities.

Sen's approach to equality extends beyond mere material equality and emphasizes the importance of basic capabilities as a key aspect of moral goodness. This perspective allows for a richer understanding of equality that considers the diverse dimensions of human well-being.

73. (A):

(*d*) **The Mexican peso crisis,** also known as the Tequila Crisis, began on December 20, 1994 and ended on January 3, 1995. The crisis was caused by the Mexican government's surprise devaluation of the peso against the U.S. dollar. The crisis was one of the first international financial crises caused by capital flight. The crisis was caused by a combination of domestic and international economic factors, as well as political forces. The Mexican government had been using a crawling peg exchange rate policy that allowed the peso to depreciate gradually.

(*b*) **Argentina's economic crisis** in 2001 was a political, economic, social, and institutional crisis. It was triggered by a run on the banking system, when people realized that the system didn't have enough dollars to cover all deposits. The crisis led to a partial deposit freeze, a partial default on public debt, and the end of a decade-long currency board. The crisis caused a collapse in output, high unemployment, and political and social turmoil. On December 26, 2001, Argentina defaulted on $93 billion of its external debt. The crisis is sometimes known as the Argentinazo, and was fueled by a revolt under the slogan "All of them must go!".

(*c*) **The dot-com bubble,** also known as the internet bubble, was a period from 1995 to 2000 when investors pumped money into internet startups. The bubble burst in 2000, causing a stock market crash. By October 2002, stocks had lost 75% of their value. The bubble couldn't sustain itself forever. Several factors, including rising interest rates, a saturated market, and the realization of many startups' unsustainable business models, triggered the bubble's burst in 2000. The NASDAQ Composite Index, which heavily weights technology stocks, plummeted from its peak of 5,048 in March 2000 to 1,139 in October 2002, a decline of over 75%.

(*a*) **The US subprime mortgage crisis** was a financial crisis that lasted from 2007–2010. It was a major contributor to the 2008 financial crisis and the Great Recession. The crisis led to a severe economic recession, with many businesses going bankrupt and millions of people losing their jobs. The crisis was caused by years of expanded mortgage access, which drove up housing demand and prices. This led to a real estate bubble. When the housing bubble burst, many borrowers were unable to pay back their loans. The dramatic increase in foreclosures caused many financial institutions to collapse. Some lenders or mortgage brokers may have given the impression that there was no risk to these mortgages and the costs weren't that high. However, many borrowers simply took on mortgages they couldn't afford.

74. (A): Rajiv Gandhi's participation in the Six Nation Five Continent Peace Initiative in 1988 was a campaign to end nuclear testing. The Six Nation Five Continent Initiative was formed by Prime Minister Indira Gandhi to bring together the heads of government from Argentina, Greece, Mexico, Sweden, Tanzania, and India.

The initiative aimed to put international pressure on the superpowers to reduce the number of weapons and eliminate nuclear weapons. In 1988, Prime Minister Rajiv Gandhi proposed an Action Plan for a nuclear weapon free and non-violent world order. The Action Plan envisioned a binding commitment by all nations to the elimination of nuclear weapons in stages by 2010.

In his speech at the opening session of the Six-Nation Five Continent Peace Initiative in Stockholm in 1988, Gandhi said that the cornering of resources for weaponry must be transmuted into the sharing of resources for global development.

75. (B): M.P. Follett, a pioneering thinker in the field of management and organizational theory, asserted that coordination is best achieved through direct and reciprocal relationships among all factors in a situation.

She advocated for coordination as a dynamic and continuous process, challenging the notion of indirect control mechanisms. According to Follett, relying on indirect control, where coordination is enforced through hierarchical authority or strict rules, undermines the potential for effective collaboration.

Instead, she emphasized the importance of coordination as a reciprocal relation among all elements involved, occurring at the early stages of decision-making, and as an ongoing and evolving process within the organization.

For Follett, achieving coordination is intrinsically tied to fostering understanding and collaboration among individuals and groups within an organization.

76. (B):

(*a*) **Progress is an ideology:** Gramsci believed that progress is not a universal or objective concept but rather a political and ideological construct used by dominant groups to justify their power and maintain the status quo.

(*b*) **Becoming is a philosophical concept:** Gramsci viewed becoming as an ongoing process of transformation, creation, and change, encompassing all aspects of human life and history.

(*c*) **Progress depends on a specific mentality:** For Gramsci, achieving meaningful progress requires fostering a critical consciousness that challenges dominant ideologies and promotes social change.

(*d*) **Progress and becoming are not necessarily linked:** While progress can emerge within the process of becoming, it's not a guaranteed outcome. Becoming is a more fundamental concept that encompasses both progress and regression, depending on the specific historical and social context.

77. (A): The Exploratory Period in the evolution of public administration spans from 1887 to 1910, characterized by significant intellectual exploration and the establishment of foundational principles. This period marked the early development of public administration as a distinct field of study. Pioneers like Woodrow Wilson, Frank Goodnow, and Leonard White focused on establishing its theoretical foundations, drawing inspiration from political science, history, and management principles. They explored concepts like efficiency, meritocracy, and professionalism, laying the groundwork for future advancements. During this era, scholars and practitioners were actively engaged in defining and refining the field of public administration. The focus was on understanding the emerging challenges of governance in the context of industrialization, urbanization, and societal complexities.

Influential works, such as Woodrow Wilson's essay on "The Study of Administration" in 1887, marked a turning point by advocating for a more scientific and specialized approach to public administration. Scholars explored the relationship between politics and administration, debated the merits of the spoils system, and sought ways to enhance efficiency and expertise in public service. This period laid the groundwork for subsequent developments, setting the stage for the progressive evolution of public administration theories and practices in the years to come.

78. (D):

(*a*) **Global interdependence:** This concept can justify humanitarian intervention because the interconnectedness of the world means suffering in one corner can affect others. Intervention may be seen as a duty to address global problems like human rights abuses and humanitarian disasters.

(*d*) **Regional stability:** Similarly, humanitarian intervention can be justified to maintain regional stability. Large-scale humanitarian crises can spill over into neighboring countries, leading to increased migration, conflict, and security threats. Intervention might be seen as necessary to prevent regional destabilization.

Therefore, the justification for humanitarian intervention primarily lies in addressing global problems and maintaining regional stability through considerations of global interdependence and avoiding interventions solely based on national interest.

79. (C): M. N. Roy, an Indian revolutionary philosopher and politician, played a crucial role in the Indian independence movement and left an enduring legacy as the founder of Radical Humanism. This philosophical framework, which he developed, placed a profound emphasis on individual freedom and human values, transcending traditional nationalist and class-based ideologies. The quoted statement encapsulates the essence of Roy's Radical Humanism, highlighting its departure from narrow affiliations with nation or class. Instead, the philosophy centers on the broader concern for humanity, advocating for freedom as a fundamental right of the individual. M. N. Roy's vision sought to reconcile the pursuit of personal freedom with the broader quest for human liberation, making him a notable figure in the intellectual landscape of India's struggle for independence.

80. (C): Assertion (A), stating a significant ideological difference between parties in a polarized multiparty system with strong dogmatic radicalism, rings true. Imagine a starkly divided spectrum: on one end, fervent nationalists clinging to tradition, and on the other, progressive champions of radical social change. Each clings to its uncompromising dogma, creating an ideological chasm almost impossible to bridge.

However, Reason (R), claiming viability for political coalitions within such a system, stumbles. The very factors that lead to polarization – entrenched convictions, zero-tolerance for compromise, and distrust towards the opposite pole – actively work against successful coalitions. Imagine trying to negotiate a budget between these diametrically opposed groups. Every concession feels like capitulation, every compromise a betrayal of core principles. This constant tug-of-war breeds instability and ultimately hampers the formation of lasting coalitions.

So, while the assertion about ideological divergence in a polarized system holds firm, the claim of viable coalitions crumbles under closer scrutiny. The dogmatic conviction and uncompromising nature of such environments work against, not for, stable alliances.

81. **(A):** The Economic and Social Council (ECOSOC) stands as the principal body within the United Nations system responsible for coordinating global economic and social issues. Established in 1945 under the UN Charter, ECOSOC plays a pivotal role in promoting international cooperation for sustainable development. It oversees and coordinates the work of various UN specialized agencies, functional commissions, and regional commissions, ensuring coherence and collaboration across diverse realms such as economic development, social progress, environmental sustainability, and human rights. ECOSOC serves as a platform for member states to discuss and address critical global challenges, fostering dialogue and collaboration among nations. Notably, it emphasizes the achievement of the Sustainable Development Goals (SDGs) and endeavors to create a more equitable and inclusive world by addressing issues like poverty, gender equality, and human rights through its coordination of UN programs and initiatives.

82. **(A)**

83. **(B):** NITI Aayog, established on January 1, 2015, represents a crucial institutional shift in India's approach to economic planning and development. Formed to replace the Planning Commission, NITI Aayog operates as a policy think tank and a platform for fostering cooperative federalism and participative governance. Unlike its predecessor, NITI Aayog adopts a more flexible and collaborative approach, emphasizing the involvement of states in the policy-making process. The institution aims to catalyze sustainable development by formulating strategic and innovative policies, promoting economic growth, and addressing key social challenges. Through its emphasis on cooperative federalism, NITI Aayog seeks to engage states as equal partners in the nation's development journey, reflecting a dynamic and responsive approach to India's evolving economic landscape.

84. **(A):** Neera Chandhoke, a prominent political scientist, has extensively studied the role of non-governmental organizations (NGOs) and their relationship with social movements. She argues that when NGOs become entwined with social movements, there is a dynamic interplay that may lead to shifts in their political agendas. The collaboration between NGOs and social movements can influence the priorities and goals of both entities. Chandhoke's perspective underscores the transformative potential that arises when NGOs actively engage with grassroots movements, suggesting that the collective activism and shared objectives within social movements can influence the strategies and priorities of NGOs, leading to an evolution in their political agendas. This nuanced understanding highlights the reciprocal relationship between NGOs and social movements in shaping political discourse and action.

85. **(D):**

(*a*) **CIC was constituted through an official gazette notification under the provisions of the RTI Act 2005:** This statement is correct. The Central Information Commission was established on October 12, 2005, as per the provisions of the Right to Information Act, 2005. The official notification was published in the Gazette of India on October 13, 2005.

(*b*) **When CIC was constituted initially, it has five commissions including Chief Information Commissioners:** This statement is correct. Initially, the CIC had five Information Commissioner, along with the Chief Information Commissioner. The number of Information Commissioners was later increased to ten through an amendment to the RTI Act in 2005.

(*c*) **The Chief Information Commissioner holds office for a period of three years from the date on which he enters upon office:** This statement is correct. The Chief Information Commissioner holds office for a term of five years, with the possibility of reappointment for a single term.

86. (A)

87. (C): The Panchayats (Extension to Scheduled Areas) Act (PESA) was enacted on December 24, 1996, to extend the provisions of Part IX of the Indian Constitution to Scheduled Areas, with necessary modifications and exceptions.

This legislation aims to empower tribal communities by granting them self-rule in regions identified under the Fifth Schedule of the Constitution. PESA recognizes the distinctive socio-cultural practices of tribal populations and provides for local self-governance through traditional systems.

The act enhances the autonomy of local bodies in these areas, fostering community development. The Panchayati Raj, a three-tiered system, aligns with the broader objective of promoting local self-governance in districts, zones, and villages, contributing to the overall development of rural communities.

88. (C):

(*b*) **Modern technology created hurdles on the way to cast solidarity:** While acknowledging the impact of urbanization and modernization on traditional caste structures, Srinivas didn't specifically pinpoint modern technology as a major hurdle for caste solidarity. He focused more on broader societal changes and economic factors.

(*c*) **There was even vertical solidarity between castes:** Srinivas recognized instances of alliances and cooperation between different castes for achieving common goals or political advantages. He called this phenomenon "segmental mobilization" and highlighted its role in Indian politics.

(*d*) **There was competition amongst castes in political economic sphere:** Srinivas extensively documented the competition among castes for political and economic resources. He saw this competition as a key driver of political mobilization and social change in post-independence India.

89. (C): Eric Hobsbawm's theory of nationalism in Europe, particularly outlined in his work "Nations and Nationalism since 1780," includes the following key features:

(*b*) **He defines nationalism, for instance, as reinventing traditions:** Hobsbawm argues that nations often construct or reinvent traditions to create a sense of continuity and shared identity. He emphasizes that many nationalist practices, symbols, and rituals are modern inventions designed to foster a sense of historical continuity and unity among diverse groups.

(*c*) **He identifies petty bourgeoisie as a group that advocated separatist nationalism:** Hobsbawm highlights the role of the petty bourgeoisie, particularly the educated and upwardly mobile middle class, in advocating for and championing separatist nationalism. This class often seeks to establish its cultural and political dominance through the promotion of distinct national identities.

Hobsbawm's theory is known for its focus on the constructed nature of national identity, the role of invented traditions, and the involvement of specific social classes, such as the petty bourgeoisie, in shaping and promoting nationalist movements. The theory doesn't ignore the emergence of ethno-linguistic nationalism; instead, it offers insights into the socio-economic factors influencing the development of nationalist sentiments in Europe.

90. (A): The right to life under Article 21 of the Indian Constitution, as interpreted by the Supreme Court, encompasses several dimensions aimed at safeguarding the dignity and well-being of individuals. While it includes the right to privacy, protection from public hanging, and the right to good health, the right to suicide is not recognized as part of this constitutional provision. The Supreme Court has consistently held that the right to life is a fundamental right, and the state has a duty to protect and preserve it. Suicide, in this context, is viewed as a tragic and unfortunate event that goes against the spirit of life preservation. The Court's interpretation underscores the importance of life and its inherent value, and it does not extend to include a right to intentionally end one's own life.

91. (B): In the given passage, the reference to Tocqueville's approach suggests that he was more inclined toward a practical and concrete analysis of liberal democracy. The phrase "critically analyzing a concrete example of liberal democracy" indicates that Tocqueville was interested in studying the functioning and implications of liberal democratic principles in real-world scenarios, particularly in America as depicted in his work 'Democracy in America.' Unlike John Stuart Mill, who, according to the passage, delved into the philosophical validity of liberalism, Tocqueville's focus was on the practical aspects and the actual workings of liberal democracy. While Mill sought to reassess and revise the underlying assumptions of classical liberalism on a philosophical level, Tocqueville's contribution lay more in the empirical observation and analysis of democratic societies.

92. (D)

93. (B): The assertion (A) states that young Mill was overly exposed to the scientific doctrine of Utilitarianism, which is correct based on the information provided in the passage. John Stuart Mill, as a young man, was extensively influenced by the utilitarian philosophy, which emphasized the maximization of happiness as a guiding principle for ethical decision-making.

The reason (R) states that the utilitarian doctrine had cut him off from much of what is genuinely human. This reason is also correct based on the passage, as it suggests that Mill's immersion in utilitarianism had its consequences, potentially leading to a certain detachment from aspects of human experience that go beyond strict utilitarian calculations, such as emotional and intuitive dimensions.

However, while both (A) and (R) are correct statements, (R) does not provide a direct or explanatory link to why young Mill was exposed to utilitarianism in the first place. It describes an outcome rather than explaining the cause. Therefore, option (B) is the correct answer: Both (A) and (R) are correct, but (R) is NOT the correct explanation of (A).

94. (C): The passage highlights that John Stuart Mill's turn away from narrow utilitarianism was influenced by the Romantic poets, specifically Wordsworth. Wordsworth, along with Coleridge, advocated in literature what Edmund Burke had espoused philosophically, emphasizing feeling and intuition over mere logic and rational categories of thought. For Mill, who had been overly exposed to the scientific and coldly rationalistic doctrine of utilitarianism during his upbringing, the emphasis on the emotional aspects of human experience by Wordsworth and the Romantic poets played a pivotal role in shaping his intellectual trajectory. The infusion of feeling and intuition into Mill's thinking signaled a departure from the rigid utilitarian framework and contributed to a more nuanced understanding of human nature and values.

95. (C): Statement I is accurate based on the passage, which emphasizes that the Romantic poets, particularly Wordsworth, imparted to John Stuart Mill the notion that Utilitarian psychology lacked depth in terms of human experience, as it overly relied on cold rationality. This aligns with the idea that feeling and intuitions were crucial aspects neglected by strict utilitarian calculations.

However, Statement II is incorrect in attributing the pointing out of scientific inadequacies of Utilitarian philosophy to Tocqueville. The passage does not specify Tocqueville as critiquing Utilitarian philosophy from a scientific perspective. Rather, it suggests that Tocqueville, like the Romantic poets, contributed by highlighting sociological inadequacies in Utilitarian thought. Therefore, the correct interpretation is that Tocqueville's critique was more sociological than scientific.

96. (A): Statement I correctly highlight the nuanced nature of policy change, emphasizing that it doesn't occur suddenly ("overnight") and typically takes place in dynamic settings where other environmental elements are not static. This recognition of the temporal and contextual aspects of policy change underscores the complexity involved in understanding its dynamics.

Statement II complements Statement I by addressing the inherent difficulty in evaluating the impact of a specific policy change on observed outcomes. The term "metrological" refers to measurement-related challenges, indicating that accurately assessing the effects of a policy change requires intricate measurement techniques. The passage acknowledges the intricate knowledge and clever use of statistical and economic techniques needed for effective policy evaluation. It underscores the methodological challenges policymakers face in determining the actual impact of a policy shift.

Both statements align with the passage's broader discussion on the challenges and intricacies of policy evaluation, emphasizing the temporal and measurement-related complexities associated with understanding the effects of policy changes.

97. (C): Randomized Control Trials (RCTs) are primarily employed in pharmaceutical research. In this field, RCTs are considered the "Gold Standard" for impact evaluation. The methodology involves selecting a group of respondents, such as patients, who are potential beneficiaries of a particular drug or intervention. The key feature is the random assignment of individuals to either receive the drug or intervention (treatment group) or not receive it (control group). This randomization helps control for confounding variables, ensuring that any observed differences in outcomes can be more confidently attributed to the intervention. Pharmaceutical researchers use RCTs to rigorously assess the effectiveness and safety of new drugs, therapies, or medical interventions, providing robust evidence for decision-making in the healthcare industry.

98. (B): In the context of Randomized Control Trials (RCTs), the term "randomly selected" is significant because it denotes a crucial principle in experimental design. When conducting an RCT, researchers aim to minimize selection bias and ensure that the treatment group and the control group are comparable in all aspects except for the intervention being studied. The random selection process involves assigning individuals from the larger pool of potential beneficiaries to either the treatment or control group using a random and unbiased method, such as a random number generator or drawing lots. This randomness helps control for any pre-existing differences between individuals and ensures that any observed differences in outcomes can be attributed to the intervention rather than systematic differences in the characteristics of the groups. The emphasis on random selection is a key strength of RCTs, contributing to their credibility as a robust method for evaluating the causal impact of interventions in various fields, including pharmaceutical research, social sciences, and policy evaluation.

99. (C): Randomized Control Trails (RCTs) are widely regarded as the "Gold Standard" in impact evaluation. This experimental methodology involves randomly assigning individuals from a larger pool to either a treatment group, which receives the intervention, or a control group, which does not. The randomization helps ensure that any observed differences in outcomes can be confidently attributed to the intervention itself, as opposed to pre-existing differences between the groups. RCTs are particularly valued for their ability to control for confounding variables and provide rigorous evidence of causation. This approach is extensively used in fields such as pharmaceutical research, social sciences, and policy evaluation, offering a robust and scientifically rigorous way to assess the effectiveness of interventions and contribute valuable insights to decision-making processes.

100. (C): Statement I is accurate as it points out that the standard metrological technique in the context of Randomized Control Trials (RCTs) involves selecting a group of respondents. This aligns with the fundamental principle of RCTs, where researchers choose a sample from the larger population and randomly assign individuals to either the treatment or control group.

However, Statement II is not accurate. In RCTs, the objective is not to ensure that every individual participant in the trial differs from everyone else. Instead, the emphasis is on the random assignment of individuals to different groups to control for potential confounding variables. The randomization process ensures that any observed differences in outcomes between the treatment and control groups are more likely attributable to the intervention itself rather than pre-existing differences between participants.

While Statement I correctly reflects the methodology, Statement II misrepresents the purpose of randomization in RCTs, leading to the conclusion that Statement I is true, but Statement II is false.

Previous Years' Paper (Solved)

National Testing Agency (NTA)

UGC-NET Junior Research Fellowship & Assistant Professor Eligibility Exam

POLITICAL SCIENCE, March–2023

(Exam held on 06-03-2023)

PAPER-II

1. 'A democracy is more than a form of government, it is a mode of associated living', who said this?

A. Jawaharlal Nehru B. John Locke
C. John Dewey D. Gandhi

2. Sophie or Sophia is a character in which of the following books?

A. Republic
B. A Vindication of the rights of women
C. The Archaeology of knowledge
D. The human condition

3. Who among the following has used the terms internal restriction and external restriction in the discourse of multiculturalism?

A. Bhikhu Parekh
B. Will Kymlicka
C. Okin
D. B. Berry

4. For whom among the following M.B. Foster has stated that his political thought represents more of a Pagan revival than a Protestant religion?

A. Machiavelli B. Hobbes
C. Bentham D. J.S. Mill

5. "Our souls have been corrupted in proportion to the advancement of our sciences and our arts towards perfection". It is mentioned in:

A. Discourse on the Science and Arts
B. Revolt against Reason
C. The Wealth of Nation
D. The Theory of Moral Sentiments

6. Which one of the following is not Aristotle's work?

A. Politics B. Nicomachean
C. Eudemian Ethics D. Apology

7. Which one of the following is perfect, eternal and fixed according to Plato?

A. Matter B. Ideas
C. Raw Material D. Darkness

8. The 'Analects' is related to:

A. Nicomachus B. Plato
C. Confucius D. Chou dynasty

9. When and at which place in South Africa the Indians assembled, demonstrated and took the oath of passive resistance?

A. September 1906, Johannesburg
B. October 1906, Natal
C. September 1905, Pretoria
D. October 1905, Pietermaritzburg

10. Who among the following launched the 'Self-Respect Movement' in 1925?

A. Dr. B.R. Ambedkar
B. Mahatma Phule
C. E.V. Ramaswami Naicker
D. J.P. Narayan

11. Who among the following categorized laws into two types : the Shariat and the Zawabit?

A. Dara Shukoh B. Basava
C. Abul Fazl D. Zia Barani

12. When did M.N. Roy dismantle his Radical Democratic Party?

A. 1940 B. 1945
C. 1948 D. 1950

13. Why Robert Nozick agrees with anarchist assertions regarding the position of State? Pick the incorrect argument
A. It is intrinsically immoral
B. It maintains monopoly on the use of force
C. It violates individual rights
D. It's motive is welfare of citizens

14. Which of the following statements is not correct regarding Union Public Service Commission (UPSC)?
A. The President of India can remove the Chairman of UPSC.
B. In case of removal of Chairman, the President has to refer the matter to the Supreme Court for an enquiry
C. An Individual Ministry or Department has no power to reject the advice of the UPSC
D. The State Governments can ask the UPSC to conduct the examinations for concerned state

15. Which of the following statements is correct regarding the vote value of a member of Parliament in presidential election?
A. Vote Value of MP

$$= \frac{\text{Total value of votes of all MLAs of all States \& UTs}}{\text{Total Members of Parliament}}$$

B. Vote Value of MP

$$= \frac{\text{Total value of votes of all MLAs of all States \& UTs}}{\text{Total Number of elected Members of Parliament}}$$

C. Vote Value of MP

$$= \frac{\text{Total value of votes of all voters of the country}}{\text{Total Members of Parliament}}$$

D. Vote Value of MP

$$= \frac{\text{Total value of votes of all MLAs of all State \& UTs}}{\text{Total Members of Lok Sabha}}$$

16. Which one of the following fundamental duty is inserted by 86th Constitutional Amendment in Article 51-A?
A. To strive towards excellence in all spheres of individual and collective activity
B. To provide opportunities for education by the parents to their child
C. To develop the scientific temper, humanism and spirit of inquiry and reform
D. Respect to the National Flag and Symbols

17. Which are the six minority religious communities notified by the National Commission for Minorities (NCM) setup by the Union Government under the National Commission for Minorities Act 1992?
A. Muslims, Christians, Sikhs, Buddhists, Zorastrians, Sindhis
B. Muslims, Christians, Sikhs, Buddhists, Sindhis, Bahais
C. Muslims, Christians, Sikhs, Sindhis, Bahais, Jews
D. Muslims, Christians, Sikhs, Buddhists, Zorastrians and Jains

18. Who among the following conducts the elections at Polling Station?
A. Polling Agent B. Presiding Officer
C. Returning Officer D. Revenue Officer

19. Who among the following is pioneer of Public Interest Litigation?
A. Justice S.N. Benarji
B. Justice P.N. Bhagwati
C. Justice Hingorani
D. Justice Ranjan Gogoi

20. Who among the following contributed to the framing of National Rural Employment Guarantee Act?
A. Jean Drieze B. Aruna Roy
C. Medha Patkar D. Baba Amte

21. Which one of the following is not a principle among the originally framed six principles of 'Citizen's Charter Movement'?
A. Choice B. Value
C. Accountability D. Quantity

22. Which of the following amendment is related to 'anti-defection'?
A. 51st Amendment
B. 52nd Amendment
C. 53rd Amendment
D. 59th Amendment

23. The four Ps in the 4 Ps theory of departmentalization as advocated by Luthur Gullick are ....
A. Purpose, Persons, Place, Process
B. Persons, Place, Process and Programmes
C. Process, People, Policies and Perception
D. People, Public, Problems and Perception

24. According to Follett the difference between 'power' and 'authority' is ....
A. Power exists when orders are obeyed irrespective of resistance, authority exists when orders obeyed voluntarily
B. Power can never be delegated, authority can be delegated.
C. Authority exists when orders are obeyed irrespective of resistance, power exists when orders obeyed by force.
D. Authority can never be delegated, power can always be delegated

25. The literature on New Public Administration lays emphasis on ....
A. Relevance, Relatedness, Moral Values and Equity
B. Relevance, Values, Ethics and Change
C. Values, Ethics, Relatedness and Self Reliance
D. Relevance, Values, Equity and Change

26. Which is the fifth stage of Policy Cycle according to Harold Lasswell?
A. Promotion B. Invocation
C. Application D. Intelligence

27. Which of the following Ministry is associated with Swachh Survekshan?
A. Ministry of Water and Sanitation
B. Ministry of Housing and Urban Affairs
C. Ministry of Rural Development
D. Ministry of Finance

28. Which of the following is the first state to bring Social Audit Law?
A. Andhra Pradesh B. Meghalaya
C. Tripura D. Chhattisgarh

29. Which of the following Ministry/Aayog is associated with Good Governance Index?
A. Ministry of Personnel Public Grievances and Pensions
B. Ministry of Rural Development
C. Ministry of Housing and Urban Affairs
D. NITI Aayog

30. Which of the following Act is also known as 'Hyde Act'?
A. U.S.-India Economic Co-operation Act
B. U.S.-India Peaceful Atomic Energy Co-operation Act
C. U.S.-India Trade Co-operation Act
D. U.S.-India Arms Trade Act

31. Which of the following are principles of Panchsheel?
(*a*) Mutual respect for each other's territorial integrity and sovereignty
(*b*) Mutual Non-aggression
(*c*) Interference in each other's affairs
(*d*) Equality and co-operation for mutual benefit
(*e*) Equal Existence

Choose the ***most appropriate*** answer from the options given below:
A. (*a*), (*b*), (*c*) only
B. (*a*), (*b*), (*d*) only
C. (*b*), (*c*), (*d*) only
D. (*c*), (*d*), (*e*) only

32. When did a Female Police Personnel from India took part in "first-ever peace keeping operations"?
A. January 2007 B. February 2008
C. January 2006 D. February 2009

33. The 'extended neighbourhood' has become conceptual umbrella for Indian foreign policy. Which of the option given below does not come under purview of India's 'extended neighbourhood'?

A. Suez Canal
B. South China Sea
C. Eastern Africa
D. The Asia Pacific

34. The foreign minister of India, S. Jaishankar has summerised India's approach to multilateral action as anchored in five 'S's. Choose the wrong option
A. Samman (Respect)
B. Samanjasya (Harmony)
C. Samvad (Dialogue)
D. Samriddi (Prosperity)

35. In which conference the decision to set up World Bank was taken?
A. New York B. Bretton Woods
C. Massacusetts D. Paris

36. In which year was the United Nations set up?
A. 1944 B. 1945
C. 1946 D. 1950

37. Who coined the term 'containment'?
A. George Kennan
B. Alfred Sauvy
C. George Marshal
D. John Marshal

38. Who categorized India as "a responsible state with advanced nuclear technology"?
A. President George W. Bush
B. President Bill Clinton
C. President Jimmy Carter
D. President Barrack Obama

39. Which of the following statements are true in Ecological Approach?
(*a*) The term 'ecology' has Greek roots.
(*b*) Ernst Haeckel coined the term 'ecology'.
(*c*) Andrew Dobson makes a distinction between environmentalism and ecologism.
(*d*) Green ideology debate is a 16th century debate.

Choose the ***most appropriate*** answer from the options given below:
A. (*a*), (*b*), (*c*) only B. (*b*), (*c*) only
C. (*c*), (*d*) only D. (*a*), (*d*) only

40. Who among the following believes that the superstructure is relatively autonomous?
(*a*) Louis Althusser
(*b*) Gramsci
(*c*) Poulantazas
(*d*) Mao Zedang

Choose the ***most appropriate*** answer from the options given below:
A. (*a*) and (*b*) only
B. (*c*) and (*a*) only
C. (*b*), (*c*) and (*d*) only
D. (*b*) only

41. Which of the following statements are correct in terms of Machiavelli's 'The Prince'?
(*a*) The book has been written with democratic spirit.
(*b*) Dual morality has been established in this book.
(*c*) The book is famous for anti secular approach.
(*d*) The book has supported a citizen army.

Choose the ***most appropriate*** answer from the options given below:
A. (*b*) and (*d*) only
B. (*a*) and (*c*) only
C. (*c*) and (*d*) only
D. (*b*) and (*c*) only

42. Which of the following sentences are correct in regards to John Locke?
(*a*) He subscribes empiricism
(*b*) He has written 'Essay Concerning Human Understanding'.
(*c*) He believes in limited state.
(*d*) He is the propounder of popular sovereignty

Choose the ***most appropriate*** answer from the options given below:
A. (*a*), (*b*), (*c*) only B. (*c*), (*d*) only
C. (*a*), (*d*) only D. (*b*), (*c*) only

43. Which of the following are correct in reference to Tagore's Philosophy?
(*a*) Tagore was an exponent of 'true freedom'.
(*b*) Tagore appeared to be a seeker of eternal truth.

(*c*) Tagore supported creative unity amongst diversity.

(*d*) Tagore supported aggressive nationalism.

Choose the ***most appropriate*** answer from the options given below:

A. (*a*), (*b*), (*c*) only
B. (*a*), (*b*), (*d*) only
C. (*b*), (*c*), (*d*) only
D. (*a*), (*b*), (*c*), (*d*)

44. What is the purpose of Danda Niti according to Kautilya?

(*a*) Acquisition of unacquired
(*b*) Preservation of the acquired
(*c*) Maintenance of law and order within the state
(*d*) Augmentation of the preserved
(*e*) Fair distribution of the augmented

Choose the ***most appropriate*** answer from the options given below:

A. (*a*), (*b*), (*c*), (*d*) only
B. (*b*), (*c*), (*d*), (*e*) only
C. (*a*), (*c*), (*d*), (*e*) only
D. (*a*), (*b*), (*d*), (*e*) only

45. Which of the following are functions of a political system?

(*a*) Political Socialisation
(*b*) Political Decay
(*c*) Political Recruitment
(*d*) Political Revolutions

Choose the ***most appropriate*** answer from the options given below:

A. (*a*) and (*b*) only
B. (*b*) and (*c*) only
C. (*a*) and (*c*) only
D. (*b*) and (*d*) only

46. Which of the below mentioned factors lead to revolution in a political system?

(*a*) Severe class divisions
(*b*) Role of intellectuals in mass mobilisation
(*c*) Social disequilibrium
(*d*) Strong desire for peace
(*e*) Incremental changes

Choose the ***most appropriate*** answer from the options given below:

A. (*a*), (*b*) and (*e*) only
B. (*b*), (*c*) and (*d*) only
C. (*a*), (*b*) and (*c*) only
D. (*a*), (*b*), (*c*), (*d*) and (*e*)

47. Which of the following statements is/are correct regarding the powers of Speaker of Lok Sabha?

(*a*) The Anti Defection Law is applicable on the Speaker in case he decides to quit his own party.
(*b*) The Speaker can not preside while a resolution for his removal from office is under consideration.
(*c*) Speaker can vote in the house on any matters of his removal from the office.

Choose the ***most appropriate*** answer from the options given below:

A. (*a*), (*b*) and (*c*)
B. (*b*) and (*c*) only
C. (*a*) and (*c*) only
D. (*a*) and (*b*) only

48. Which of the following statements are correct regarding preamble of the Indian Constitution?

(*a*) In the Berubari Case, Supreme Court said that the preamble is not part of the Constitution.
(*b*) In the Keshavananda Bharati Case, the Supreme Court said that preamble is the part of the Constitution.
(*c*) In L.I.C. of India Case, Supreme Court said that preamble is not part of the Constitution.

Choose the ***most appropriate*** answer from the options given below:

A. (*a*), (*b*) and (*c*)
B. (*b*) and (*c*) only
C. (*a*) and (*b*) only
D. (*a*) and (*c*) only

49. Which of the following are strengths of Globalization?

(*a*) Promotes free trade of goods and services among the nations.

(*b*) Strengthens the market economies of the developing world.

(*c*) Promotes socio-economic interactions between the countries.

(*d*) Increases economic disparities between rich and poor.

(*e*) It does not promote human and cultural interaction between the nations.

Choose the ***most appropriate*** answer from the options given below:

A. (*a*), (*b*) and (*c*) only
B. (*b*), (*c*) and (*d*) only
C. (*c*), (*d*) and (*e*) only
D. (*a*), (*d*) and (*e*) only

50. According to the Article 26 of the Constitution of India, every religious denomination shall have the right:

(*a*) to establish and maintain institutions for religious and charitable purpose.

(*b*) to manage its own affairs in matters of religion.

(*c*) to own and acquire movable property.

(*d*) to manage social affairs.

(*e*) to own and acquire immovable property.

Choose the ***most appropriate*** answer from the options given below:

A. (*a*), (*b*), (*c*), (*d*) only
B. (*b*), (*c*), (*d*), (*e*) only
C. (*a*), (*b*), (*c*), (*e*) only
D. (*a*), (*c*), (*d*), (*e*) only

51. Which of the following is correct regarding the classical theory of administration?

(*a*) It played a notable role in rationalizing and even stimulating production.

(*b*) It formulated a set of concepts in administration.

(*c*) It was the first to propound the idea that administration is a separate activity.

Choose the ***most appropriate*** answer from the options given below:

A. (*a*) and (*b*) only
B. (*b*) and (*c*) only
C. (*a*) and (*c*) only
D. (*a*), (*b*) and (*c*)

52. According to Ferral Heady, the comparative public administration addresses which of the following concerns?

(*a*) The search of theory

(*b*) The urge of practical application

(*c*) Contribution to the border field of comparative politics

(*d*) The comparative analysis of ongoing problems of Public Administration

Choose the ***most appropriate*** answer from the options given below:

A. (*a*), (*b*), (*c*) and (*d*)
B. (*a*), (*b*) and (*c*) only
C. (*b*), (*c*) and (*d*) only
D. (*a*), (*c*) and (*d*) only

53. Which is/are not true about Public Interest Litigation (PIL)?

(*a*) Only registered Civil Society Organisation can file a PIL.

(*b*) PIL can be filed in Supreme Court, under Article 32.

(*c*) PIL can be filed in High Courts under Article 226.

(*d*) There is no court fees for filing PIL.

Choose the ***most appropriate*** answer from the options given below:

A. (*b*) and (*c*) only
B. (*a*) only
C. (*d*) only
D. (*a*) and (*d*) only

54. Which of the following is/are true about amendment of RTI Act in 2019?

(*a*) From a fixed term of five years, now the Commissioner holds office at the pleasure of Government.

(*b*) Now, there can be more than 10 Central Information Commissioners.

(*c*) Now, the salaries and allowances of Commissioner are also decided by the Government.

(*d*) Now, the age of retirement of Chief Information Commissioner will be 62 years.

Choose the ***most appropriate*** answer from the options given below:

A. (*c*) only B. (*a*) and (*b*) only
C. (*a*) and (*c*) only D. (*a*) and (*d*) only

55. What are the core values of Indian Foreign Policy?

(*a*) Blend of idealism and realism
(*b*) Value of tolerance
(*c*) Anti-imperialism and anti-colonialism
(*d*) Territorial expansion
(*e*) Neighbourhood first diplomacy

Choose the ***most appropriate*** answer from the options given below:

A. (*a*), (*b*), (*c*) only B. (*a*), (*b*), (*d*) only
C. (*b*), (*c*), (*d*) only D. (*a*), (*b*), (*d*), (*e*) only

56. Which of the following are not the features of Cold War?

(*a*) There was nuclear arms race.
(*b*) There was a propaganda war.
(*c*) There was economic blockade against the non-aligned countries.
(*d*) The third world countries were directly involved in it.

Choose the ***most appropriate*** answer from the options given below:

A. (*a*) and (*b*) only B. (*b*) and (*c*) only
C. (*c*) and (*d*) only D. (*b*) and (*d*) only

57. Given below are two statements : One is labelled as Assertion (A) and the other is labelled as Reason (R).

Assertion (A) : Ever since the end of World War II, international environment has been dominated by the American relations with the Soviet Union characterized as Cold War.

Reason (R) : The Cold War coloured not only American and American aligned nations' relations with the Soviet Union and the latter's allies but relations of the U.S. and its allies with other non-aligned nations, as well.

In the light of the above statements, choose the correct answer from the options given below:

A. Both (A) and (R) are true and (R) is the correct explanation of (A)
B. Both (A) and (R) are true but (R) is NOT the correct explanation of (A)
C. (A) is true, but (R) is false
D. (A) is false, but (R) is true

58. Given below are two statements : One is labelled as Assertion (A) and the other is labelled as Reason (R).

Assertion (A) : In our time, history is that which transforms documents in to monuments.

Reason (R) : The archaeology of knowledge discovers the intrinsic description of the monuments.

In the light of the above statements, choose the most appropriate answer from the options given below:

A. Both (A) and (R) are correct and (R) is the correct explanation of (A)
B. Both (A) and (R) are correct but (R) is NOT the correct explanation of (A)
C. (A) is correct, but (R) is not correct
D. (A) is not correct, but (R) is correct

59. Given below are two statements : One is labelled as Assertion (A) and the other is labelled as Reason (R).

Assertion (A) : Inner contradictions of capitalism will destroy capitalism.

Reason (R) : Exploitation of surplus value is the biggest contradiction of capitalism.

In the light of the above statements, choose the correct answer from the options given below:

A. Both (A) and (R) are true and (R) is the correct explanation of (A)
B. Both (A) and (R) are true but (R) is NOT the correct explanation of (A)
C. (A) is true, but (R) is false
D. (A) is false, but (R) is true

60. Given below are two statements : One is labelled as Assertion (A) and the other is labelled as Reason (R).

Assertion (A) : Economically, the framework of the 'Sarvodaya' order would seek to establish a balanced and equitable economic setup in the country.

Reason (R) : J.P. (Jai Prakash) was sure to afford the first place to agricultural activities in the economic life of the people.

In the light of the above statements, choose the most appropriate answer from the options given below:

A. Both (A) and (R) are correct and (R) is the correct explanation of (A)
B. Both (A) and (R) are correct but (R) is NOT the correct explanation of (A)
C. (A) is correct, but (R) is not correct
D. (A) is not correct, but (R) is correct

61. Given below are two statements : One is labelled as Assertion (A) and the other is labelled as Reason (R).

Assertion (A) : Political culture is a set of beliefs and sentiments about politics as embodied in the verbal and non-verbal behaviour of the people.

Reason (R) : The typological and morphological models of political culture denote that there can be as many political cultures as the dynamics of political development in political systems.

In the light of the above statements, choose the most appropriate answer from the options given below:

A. Both (A) and (R) are correct and (R) is the correct explanation of (A)
B. Both (A) and (R) are correct but (R) is NOT the correct explanation of (A)
C. (A) is correct, but (R) is not correct
D. (A) is not correct, but (R) is correct

62. Given below are two statements : One is labelled as Assertion (A) and the other is labelled as Reason (R).

Assertion (A) : Robert Dahl has suggested for cross cultural studies in Public Administration.

Reason (R) : He believed that the Public Administration can escape the effects of political, cultural and environmental system in which it develops.

In the light of the above statements, choose the most appropriate answer from the options given below:

A. Both (A) and (R) are correct and (R) is the correct explanation of (A)
B. Both (A) and (R) are correct but (R) is NOT the correct explanation of (A)
C. (A) is correct, but (R) is not correct
D. (A) is not correct, but (R) is correct

63. Given below are two statements :

Statement (I) : Rights essentially belong to the sphere of conflicting claims between individual and the state.

Statement (II) : Any political theory which holds that an individual cannot have certain rights 'against the state' is no theory of rights.

In the light of the above statements, choose the correct answer from the options given below:

A. Both Statement (I) and Statement (II) are true
B. Both Statement (I) and Statement (II) are false
C. Statement (I) is true but Statement (II) is false
D. Statement (I) is false but Statement (II) is true

64. Given below are two statements :

Statement (I) : Problems of global environmental change could not have existed without modern technologies and population densities.

Statement (II) : Problems of climate change are difficult to address, because they involve both intra and inter-generational collective action problems.

In the light of the above statements, choose the correct answer from the options given below:

A. Both Statement (I) and Statement (II) are true

B. Both Statement (I) and Statement (II) are false

C. Statement (I) is true, but Statement (II) is false

D. Statement (I) is false, but Statement (II) is true

65. Given below are two statements:

Statement (I) : Nehru favoured a socialistic pattern of society.

Statement (II) : Nehru's commitment to civil liberties prevented him from accepting the idea of 'dictatorship of the proletariat'.

In the light of the above statements, choose the correct answer from the options given below:

A. Both Statement (I) and Statement (II) are true

B. Both Statement (I) and Statement (II) are false

C. Statement (I) is true, but Statement (II) is false

D. Statement (I) is false, but Statement (II) is true

66. Given below are two statements :

Statement (I) : Party system provides normal means of fighting political battles.

Statement (II) : One of the aims of the party system is to replace the traditional elites with new elites.

In the light of the above statements, choose the most appropriate answer from the options given below:

A. Both Statement (I) and Statement (II) are correct

B. Both Statement (I) and Statement (II) are incorrect

C. Statement (I) is correct, but Statement (II) is incorrect

D. Statement (I) is incorrect, but Statement (II) is correct

67. Given below are two statements:

Statement (I) : Exit poll is a post-election poll which is conducted when an elector walks out after casting his/her vote.

Statement (II) : Opinion poll, is a kind of research survey which is conducted to find out the public opinion after elections.

In the light of the above statements, choose the correct answer from the options given below:

A. Both Statement (I) and Statement (II) are true

B. Both Statement (I) and Statement (II) are false

C. Statement (I) is true, but Statement (II) is false

D. Statement (I) is false, but Statement (II) is true

68. Given below are two statements : Consider the following statements regarding the Vice President of India.

Statement (I) : He serves for a five year term. But can continue to be in office, irrespective of the expiry of the term, until the successor assumes office.

Statement (II) : The constitution is silent on who performs the duties of the Vice-President, when a vacancy occurs in the office before expiry of his term.

In the light of the above statements, choose the most appropriate answer from the options given below:

A. Both Statement (I) and Statement (II) are correct

B. Both Statement (I) and Statement (II) are incorrect

C. Statement (I) is correct, but Statement (II) is incorrect

D. Statement (I) is incorrect, but Statement (II) is collect

69. Given below are two statements:

Statement (I) : The policy agenda is the sum of all political demands that a number of individuals or groups have tried to get onto policy agenda.

Statement (II) : The policy agenda is composed of the demands that policy makers have agreed to consider.

In the light of the above statements, choose the most appropriate answer from the options given below:

A. Both Statement (I) and Statement (II) are correct

B. Both Statement (I) and Statement (II) are incorrect

C. Statement (I) is correct, but Statement (II) is incorrect

D. Statement (I) is incorrect, but Statement (II) is correct

70. Given below are two statements:

Statement (I) : Both IMF and IBRD have headquarters in Washington.

Statement (II) : India's vote share in IMF is 10%.

In the light of the above statements, choose the most appropriate answer from the options given below:

A. Both Statement (I) and Statement (II) are correct

B. Both Statement (I) and Statement (II) are incorrect

C. Statement (I) is correct, but Statement (II) is incorrect

D. Statement (I) is incorrect, but Statement (II) is correct

71. Match List-I with List-II:

List-I (Books)	List-II (Authors)
(*a*) Between Past and Future	I. Isaiah Berlin
(*b*) Vico and Herder : Two studies in the history of ideas	II. Hannah Arendt
(*c*) The voice of liberal learning	III. Michael J. Sandel
(*d*) The Tyranny of Merit	IV. Michael Oakeshott

Choose the ***correct*** answer from the options given below:

	(*a*)	(*b*)	(*c*)	(*d*)
A.	I	II	III	IV
B.	II	I	IV	III
C.	IV	III	II	I
D.	III	II	I	IV

72. Match List-I with List-II:

List-I (Concepts)	List-II (Thinker)
(*a*) Virtue is knowledge	I. Machiavelli
(*b*) Success is virtue	II. Plato
(*c*) Knowledge is power	III. Foucault
(*d*) Power is production of intended effects	IV. Russell

Choose the ***correct*** answer from the options given below:

	(*a*)	(*b*)	(*c*)	(*d*)
A.	IV	III	I	II
B.	II	I	III	IV
C.	III	II	IV	I
D.	I	II	III	IV

73. Match List-I with List-II:

List-I (Events)	List-II (Years)
(*a*) Surat split	I. 1927
(*b*) Quit India Movement	II. 1919-21
(*c*) Non-Cooperation Movement	III. 1942
(*d*) Mahad Satyagrah	IV. 1907

Choose the ***correct*** answer from the options given below:

	(*a*)	(*b*)	(*c*)	(*d*)
A.	I	II	III	IV
B.	IV	III	II	I
C.	II	I	III	IV
D.	IV	I	III	II

74. Match List-I with List-II:

List-I (Books)	List-II (Authors)
(*a*) Political change in underdeveloped countries : Nationalism and Communism	I. David E. Apter
(*b*) Political Development	II. S.N. Eisenstadt
(*c*) The Politics of Modernisation	III. C.H. Dodd
(*d*) Tradition, Change and Modernity	IV. John H. Kautsky

Choose the ***correct*** answer from the options given below:

	(*a*)	(*b*)	(*c*)	(*d*)
A.	IV	II	I	III
B.	III	I	II	IV
C.	I	IV	III	II
D.	IV	III	I	II

75. Match List-I with List-II:

List-I (Schedule)	List-II (Descriptions)
(*a*) Fourth Schedule	I. Allocation of seats in Rajya Sabha
(*b*) Tenth Schedule	II. Provisions relating to defection
(*c*) Seventh Schedule	III. Division of powers between Centre and States
(*d*) Sixth Schedule	IV. Administration of tribal areas in some States

Choose the ***correct*** answer from the options given below:

	(*a*)	(*b*)	(*c*)	(*d*)
A.	I	II	IV	III
B.	I	II	III	IV
C.	II	I	IV	III
D.	II	I	III	IV

76. Match List-I with List-II:

List-I (Regional Political Parties)	List-II (Founder Leaders)
(*a*) DMK	I. M.G. Ramachandran
(*b*) AIDMK	II. N.T. Ramarao
(*c*) TDP	III. C.N. Annadurai
(*d*) PDP	IV. Mufti Mohammad Sayeed

Choose the ***correct*** answer from the options given below:

	(*a*)	(*b*)	(*c*)	(*d*)
A.	I	II	III	IV
B.	IV	I	III	II
C.	III	I	II	IV
D.	II	I	IV	III

77. Match List-I with List-II:

List-I (Concept)	List-II (Thinker)
(*a*) Distinction between obedience and acceptance	I. H. Simon
(*b*) Distinction between economic man and administrative man	II. Chester Barnard
(*c*) Distinction between charishmatic leader and legal-rational authority	III. F.W. Taylor
(*d*) Distinction between principles and mechanics of management	IV. Max Weber

Choose the ***correct*** answer from the options given below:

	(*a*)	(*b*)	(*c*)	(*d*)
A.	I	III	II	IV
B.	II	III	IV	I
C.	II	I	IV	III
D.	I	III	IV	II

78. Match List-I with List-II:

List-I (Scheme)	List-II (Ministry)
(*a*) UJJAWALA	I. Ministry of Power
(*b*) Saubhagyam Yojana	II. Ministry of Finance
(*c*) Atal Pension Yojana	III. Ministry of Women and Child Development
(*d*) National Social Assistance Programme	IV. Ministry of Rural Development

Choose the ***correct*** answer from the options given below:

	(*a*)	(*b*)	(*c*)	(*d*)
A.	II	III	I	IV
B.	I	III	IV	II
C.	III	I	IV	II
D.	III	I	II	IV

79. Match List-I with List-II:

List-I	List-II
(*a*) Indian Peace Keeping Force in Sri Lanka	I. Indira Gandhi
(*b*) Shimla Agreement	II. Rajiv Gandhi
(*c*) Lahore Declaration	III. Atal Bihari Vajpayee
(*d*) Act East Policy	IV. Narendra Modi

Choose the ***correct*** answer from the options given below:

	(*a*)	(*b*)	(*c*)	(*d*)
A.	II	I	III	IV
B.	I	II	IV	III
C.	IV	III	II	I
D.	III	IV	I	II

80. Match List-I with List-II:

List-I (Year)	List-II (Summit)
(*a*) 1955	I. Bandung Summit
(*b*) 1961	II. Belgrade Summit
(*c*) 1983	III. New Delhi Summit
(*d*) 1998	IV. Durban Summit

Choose the ***correct*** answer from the options given below:

	(*a*)	(*b*)	(*c*)	(*d*)
A.	II	III	IV	I
B.	III	I	II	IV
C.	I	II	III	IV
D.	IV	II	I	III

81. Arrange the concepts in chronological order according to evolution:
(*a*) Legal Sovereignty
(*b*) Popular Sovereignty
(*c*) Political Sovereignty
(*d*) Theory of Plural Sovereignty

Choose the ***most appropriate*** answer from the options given below:
A. (*a*), (*d*), (*c*), (*b*) B. (*a*), (*b*), (*d*), (*c*)
C. (*a*), (*c*), (*b*), (*d*) D. (*d*), (*b*), (*a*), (*c*)

82. Arrange the following books according to their publication year in chronological order:
(*a*) The Archaeology of Knowledge
(*b*) The Human Condition
(*c*) Spheres of Justice
(*d*) After Virtue

Choose the ***most appropriate*** answer from the options given below:
A. (*b*), (*a*), (*d*), (*c*) B. (*a*), (*b*), (*c*), (*d*)
C. (*d*), (*a*), (*b*), (*c*) D. (*c*), (*d*), (*a*), (*b*)

83. Arrange the following concepts in chronological order according to their evolution:
(*a*) Sampurna Kranti
(*b*) The Saptang theory of State
(*c*) Radical Humanism
(*d*) Satyagrah

Choose the ***most appropriate*** answer from the options given below:
A. (*b*), (*c*), (*d*), (*a*) B. (*a*), (*d*), (*c*), (*b*)
C. (*d*), (*a*), (*b*), (*c*) D. (*a*), (*c*), (*d*), (*b*)

84. Chronologically arrange the features of constitutionalism as they developed over period of time:
(*a*) Checks and Balances
(*b*) Codification of Law
(*c*) Political Separatism
(*d*) Constitutional Monarchy

Choose the ***most appropriate*** answer from the options given below:

A. (*c*), (*b*), (*a*), (*d*) B. (*a*), (*b*), (*c*), (*d*)

C. (*b*), (*c*), (*a*), (*d*) D. (*c*), (*b*), (*d*), (*a*)

85. Arrange the following directive principles of state policy in a sequential order as mentioned in the Constitution of India:

(*a*) Equal pay for equal work for men and women

(*b*) To secure a uniform civil code throughout the country for all citizen

(*c*) To promote equal justice and to provide free legal aid to the poor

(*d*) Separate the judiciary from the executive in the public services

Choose the ***most appropriate*** answer from the options given below:

A. (*a*), (*b*), (*c*) and (*d*)

B. (*a*), (*c*), (*b*) and (*d*)

C. (*c*), (*a*), (*b*) and (*d*)

D. (*d*), (*b*), (*c*) and (*a*)

86. Arrange the following movements in chronological order:

(*a*) Chipko Movement

(*b*) Jal Satyagrah

(*c*) Appiko Movement

(*d*) Jan Lokpal Movement

(*e*) Narmada Bachao Andolan

Choose the ***most appropriate*** answer from the options given below:

A. (*b*), (*c*), (*d*), (*e*), (*a*) B. (*a*), (*c*), (*e*), (*d*), (*b*)

C. (*d*), (*c*), (*a*), (*e*), (*b*) D. (*c*), (*a*), (*d*), (*b*), (*e*)

87. Arrange the following experiments of Elton Mayo in chronological order.

(*a*) Relay Assembly Test Room Experiment

(*b*) Illumination Experiment

(*c*) Mass Interview Programme

(*d*) Bank Wiring Experiment

Choose the ***most appropriate*** answer from the options given below:

A. (*c*), (*a*), (*b*) and (*d*) B. (*b*), (*a*), (*c*) and (*d*)

C. (*c*), (*b*), (*a*) and (*d*) D. (*d*), (*a*), (*c*) and (*b*)

88. Arrange the following Anti-Corruption measures taken by Government of India in chronological order

(*a*) Ratification of the United Nations Convention Against Corruption (UNCAC)

(*b*) Black Money (Undisclosed foreign income and assets) and Imposition of Tax Act

(*c*) The Prevention of Money Laundering Act

(*d*) The Benami Transactions (Prohibition) Act

Choose the ***most appropriate*** answer from the options given below:

A. (*d*), (*a*), (*b*), (*c*) B. (*d*), (*c*), (*a*), (*b*)

C. (*d*), (*c*), (*b*), (*a*) D. (*d*), (*b*), (*c*), (*a*)

89. List chronologically the joint exercises conducted by Indian Air Force:

(*a*) Indradhanush-IV (*b*) Desert Eagle-II

(*c*) Table Top (*d*) Samvedna

Choose the ***most appropriate*** answer from the options given below:

A. (*a*), (*b*), (*c*) and (*d*)

B. (*b*), (*c*), (*d*) and (*a*)

C. (*c*), (*d*), (*a*) and (*b*)

D. (*d*), (*a*), (*b*) and (*c*)

90. Arrange the following BRICS summit in a chronological order:

(*a*) Ufa, Russia

(*b*) Johannesberg, South Africa

(*c*) Durban, South Africa

(*d*) Beijing Virtual Summit

Choose the ***most appropriate*** answer from the options given below:

A. (*c*), (*a*), (*b*) and (*d*)

B. (*b*), (*c*), (*a*) and (*d*)

C. (*a*), (*b*), (*c*) and (*d*)

D. (*d*), (*b*), (*a*) and (*c*)

Directions (Qs. No. 91-95): *Read the passage and answer the questions:*

Authoritarianism is characterized by highly concentrated and centralized power maintained through political repression and exclusion of political challenges. It uses political parties and mass organization to mobilize people for the attainment of the goals of the regime. Authoritarianism demands unquestioning obedience to authority believing it is important for maintaining social order and preventing disruption. Several typologies have been developed to describe their morphological variations. Authoritarian regimes can be autocratic or oligarchic in nature, based on party, leader or military rule. Authoritarian governments often lack free and competitive, direct or indirect election of leaders' or both. They also check civil liberties such as freedom of speech and expression. Authoritarian state may include nominally democratic institutions such as political parties, parliaments and elections designed to legitimize dictatorship through deceptive and uncompetitive elections.

91. Which of the following is not a characteristic of an authoritarian regime?

A. Nominally democratic institutions
B. Uncompetitive election of leadership
C. Mobilisation of people for attainment of regime's goals
D. Use of mass organization to strengthen democracy

92. Given below are two statements:

Statement (I) : Authoritarianism demands unquestioning obedience to authority.

Statement (II) : Authoritarian governments often lack free and competitive election of leaders.

In the light of the above statements, choose the correct answer from the options given below:

A. Both Statement (I) and Statement (II) are true
B. Both Statement (I) and Statement (II) are false
C. Statement (I) is true, but Statement (II) is false
D. Statement (I) is false, but Statement (II) is true

93. Why authoritarian regimes command unreasoned acceptance of their political authority?

A. To strengthen democratic ideals
B. For enhancing civil liberties
C. For constitutional governance
D. For preventing political disruption

94. Authoritarian regimes legitimise their dictatorship through which of the below methods?

(*a*) Through periodic fair elections.
(*b*) Through competitive election of leaders.
(*c*) Through deceptive and indirect elections.
(*d*) Through blocking opportunities to potential challenges

Choose the ***most appropriate*** answer from the options given below:

A. (*a*) and (*b*) only B. (*b*) and (*c*) only
C. (*c*) and (*d*) only D. (*a*) and (*d*) only

95. What remains the status of civil liberties in authoritarian regimes?

A. Remain as freely available as in democratic regimes
B. Their status remains unchanged
C. They are respected more
D. All the above are false

Directions (Qs. No. 96-100): *Read the passage and answer the questions:*

Public Administration is a discipline in transition. In fact, it has always been in continuous movement, but not always in the same direction. Contrary to the heavy, formal, and inflexible image of bureaucracies, public sector bodies in America, Europe, and elsewhere have been in a rapidly intensifying transition since the early 1990s. During the last century, Public Administration underwent significant changes resulting from crisis, as well as breakthroughs in an ultra dynamic environment. Some 30 years ago, Waldo (1968) noted that these ongoing transformations reflected an identity crisis of a science in formation. They also signaled a struggle for the recognition and legitimacy of Public Administration as an art, a body of knowledge and a profession (Lynn. 1996). It seems that today, at the beginning of the 21st century, the formation of Public Administration is still unfinished business, it is a subject for debate among academics and practitioners across the world who seek higher and more extensive scientific recognition, more accurate self-definition, and better applicability of the field to rapid changes in modern life. This process presents new challenges for Public Administration. Perhaps, the most important is to integrate more widely existing knowledge of the social sciences with efficient public action and with quality governmental cooperation. In the coming years Public Administration will be evaluated by higher stands of theory cohesiveness and by more comprehensive performance indicators rooted in a variety of scientific fields.

To talk of the 'Public' of 'Administration', and of the integration of the two constructs into a useful terrain for study involves promises as well as difficulties. But consensus does exist on at least one issue : the public needs a better bureaucracy. The public also expects good and skillful administrators, familiar with the mysteries of quality services and effective management. Only they can produce better 'public goods' and deliver them to all sectors of society with minimum time and cost. This is a revised version of the ideal type of Public Administration system applicable to modern times.

The role of the state and its relationship to bureaucracy and to citizens are undergoing substantial transformation, not only in the minds of the people but also in scientific thinking. In a rapidly changing environment, Public Administration has a major function and new aims that must be clearly recognized.

96. What is the main reason for a major role of Public Administration in future?

A. Scientific thinking among people
B. Citizens are static
C. Citizens are more active due to political complexity
D. Fall of relation between state and citizen

97. Who among the following has identified the transition of Public Administration to a profession?

A. Dwight Waldo B. Woodrow Wilson
C. Lynn D. F.M. Marx

98. Which among the following statements are not related to the transition of the discipline of Public Administration?

A. Accurate self-definition
B. Changes in the modern life
C. Extensive scientific recognition
D. Economic and Financial Crisis of the Markets

99. Given below are two statements: One is labelled as Assertion (A) and the other is labelled as Reason (R).

Assertion (A) : In future, Public Administration will be assessed with scientific tools viz. performance indicators and high standards of theory.

Reason (R) : The impact of public choice and NPM is more on the present day Administration.

In the light of the above statements, choose the most appropriate answer from the options given below:

A. Both (A) and (R) are correct and (R) is the correct explanation of (A)
B. Both (A) and (R) are correct but (R) is NOT the correct explanation of (A)
C. (A) is correct but (R) is not correct
D. (A) is not correct but (R) is correct

100. Identify the correct option among the following statements related to the discipline of Public Administration.

(*a*) Public expects good and skillful administrator
(*b*) Public expects quality of services
(*c*) Public expects effective management of institution
(*d*) Public wants to continue with the present model of bureaucracy

Choose the ***most appropriate*** answer from the options given below:

A. (*a*), (*b*) and (*c*) only
B. (*a*), (*b*) and (*d*) only
C. (*a*), (*c*) and (*d*) only
D. (*b*), (*c*) and (*d*) only

ANSWERS

1. **(C):** The statement "A democracy is more than a form of government; it is a mode of associated living" is attributed to John Dewey, an American philosopher, psychologist, and educational reformer. Dewey is well-known for his work in epistemology, ethics, and educational theory. His emphasis on democracy was not simply about a form of governance but extended into a way of life, a set of cultural practices, and a form of social organization. He believed that democracy was not just a mechanism for electing officials, but rather, it was a way of life that encouraged active participation and mutual respect among citizens. Dewey's idea of democracy emphasized the need for education, not just in a formal sense but also as a lifelong process of cultivating virtues, social skills, and intellectual habits that make democratic life possible. His views on democracy were elaborated in his works like "Democracy and Education," where he explored these themes in great detail. For Dewey, a truly democratic society would be one where every institution, be it in the private or public sphere, is geared towards enabling its members to fully participate in social, political, and economic life.

2. **(B):** Sophie or Sophia is a character in "A Vindication of the Rights of Woman," written by Mary Wollstonecraft. In this work, Wollstonecraft addresses various issues related to women's rights and presents her arguments for the educational equality of women. She adopts a philosophical approach to challenge the social norms that were keeping women subjugated. The character of Sophia is used to exemplify the kind of rational, educated woman that Wollstonecraft argues should be more common if society were structured in a fairer way. The book is considered a cornerstone text of feminist philosophy and was revolutionary for its time. It laid the groundwork for future discussions on gender equality and served as an intellectual foundation for the feminist movements that followed.

3. **(B):** The terms "internal restrictions" and "external protections" are used by Canadian philosopher Will Kymlicka in the discourse on multiculturalism. Kymlicka uses these terms to describe the ways in which minority cultures can be protected or restricted within a majority culture. "Internal restrictions" refer to limitations that a cultural community might place on its own members in the name of cultural preservation. "External protections," on the other hand, refer to safeguards against the larger society's ability to impose its culture on the minority. Kymlicka argues that while external protections are often justifiable to protect minority cultures, internal restrictions can conflict with principles of individual freedom and equality. His work has had a significant influence on the debate over multiculturalism, and he has published extensively on the subject.

4. **(A):** M.B. Foster stated that the political thought of Niccolò Machiavelli represents more of a "Pagan revival" than a Protestant religion. Machiavelli's most famous work, "The Prince," is often seen as a practical guide to political power, which diverges from moral or religious principles. While Machiavelli lived in a time when the Protestant Reformation was beginning to gain traction, his own views leaned more towards a secular or "pagan" understanding of politics, focused on the harsh realities of power and the need for pragmatism. He emphasized that effective rulers might have to engage in actions that are not morally virtuous to maintain power or achieve political objectives. Foster's characterization underlines the departure that Machiavelli's

political philosophy represents from the religious and moralistic political theories that preceded him.

5. **(A):** The statement "Our souls have been corrupted in proportion to the advancement of our sciences and our arts towards perfection" is found in Jean-Jacques Rousseau's "Discourse on the Sciences and Arts," also known as the "First Discourse." Rousseau argues that the progress in sciences and arts has not led to moral or social improvement. In fact, he contends that such advancements have led to moral decay and social inequality. Rousseau's discourse was a radical critique of Enlightenment optimism about the progress of knowledge. He believed that the advancement of arts and sciences led to the decline of virtue, as these pursuits encouraged vanity, luxury, and idleness rather than promoting genuine moral character. This work set the stage for Rousseau's later works, where he continued to explore the complexities and contradictions of civilization and its impact on human happiness and morality.

6. **(D):** The work "Apology" is not authored by Aristotle; it is a dialogue by Plato. The "Apology" is Plato's account of the trial of Socrates, his mentor. In it, Socrates defends himself against the charges of corrupting the youth and not believing in the gods of Athens. Unlike Aristotle, who wrote extensively on ethics, politics, metaphysics, and other subjects in a systematic manner, Socrates' teachings are presented through Plato's dialogues. Aristotle's "Politics," "Nicomachean Ethics," and "Eudemian Ethics" are foundational works in Western philosophy, examining subjects such as the ideal state, virtue ethics, and human happiness. These works have had a lasting impact on the Western intellectual tradition, influencing thinkers and scholars for centuries to come.

7. **(B):** According to Plato, Ideas (or Forms) are perfect, eternal, and fixed. Plato's theory of Forms is a pivotal aspect of his philosophy, presented in dialogues such as "The Republic." Forms are abstract, idealized concepts that exist in a realm separate from the physical world. They are the "true" reality, in contrast to the ever-changing, imperfect world that we experience through our senses. For Plato, Forms are the benchmarks against which everything in the material world is measured and understood. They are immutable and exist outside of time and space. This Platonic philosophy has been extremely influential in various fields, including philosophy, metaphysics, and even theology.

8. **(C):** The "Analects" is related to Confucius, the ancient Chinese philosopher and teacher. The Analects is a collection of sayings and ideas attributed to Confucius and his disciples, and it serves as the foundational text of Confucianism. Confucius lived during the Zhou dynasty, but his teachings gained greater prominence in later periods. The Analects focuses on ethics, proper personal conduct, and the ideal social order. It has had a profound influence on Chinese culture, philosophy, and governance for over two millennia. The text covers diverse topics, from politics and ethics to education and social harmony, presenting a comprehensive view of a well-ordered society.

9. **(A):** In September 1906, in Johannesburg, South Africa, Indians assembled, demonstrated, and took the oath of passive resistance against the newly enacted Asiatic Registration Act, also known as the Black Act. This moment was a seminal event in the anti-colonial struggles and marked the beginning of Mahatma Gandhi's Satyagraha movement. Gandhi, who was then a young lawyer in South Africa, led this resistance. The campaign involved civil disobedience and nonviolent protest against discriminatory

laws. It laid the groundwork for Gandhi's later involvement in India's struggle for independence and also had a lasting impact on civil rights movements globally.

10. (C): The Self-Respect Movement was launched in 1925 by E.V. Ramaswami Naicker, commonly known as Periyar. The movement was primarily based in the southern state of Tamil Nadu in India and aimed to achieve a society where backward castes have equal human rights, and it encouraged backward castes to have self-respect in the context of a caste-based society that considered them to be a lower end of the hierarchy. The movement was anti-Brahmin in nature and aimed to oppose the Brahminical dominance in Tamil Nadu. It also sought to challenge and break down the social inequalities perpetuated by a rigid caste hierarchy. The Self-Respect Movement was a socio-political movement that had a profound impact on Tamil society and politics. It laid the ideological groundwork for Dravidian parties that have governed Tamil Nadu for many years.

11. (D): The categorization of laws into two types: the Shariat and the Zawabit, is attributed to Zia Barani, a 14th-century Muslim historian and political thinker in India during the Delhi Sultanate. Shariat refers to Islamic law, a set of religious principles and guidelines that govern various aspects of life, including social, economic, and spiritual matters. On the other hand, Zawabit are state laws, which could be framed considering the socio-political circumstances, and which may or may not strictly conform to Islamic teachings. This distinction is noteworthy because it reflects an early attempt to reconcile religious law with the practical needs of governance, a challenge that has persisted in various forms across Muslim-majority countries. The dual structure aimed to respect Islamic jurisprudence while acknowledging the necessity for the state to pass laws addressing issues specific to its temporal governance.

12. (C): M.N. Roy dismantled his Radical Democratic Party in 1948. M.N. Roy was a prominent Indian revolutionary, philosopher, and political theorist who initially started his political career with communist ideologies but later veered towards radical humanism. The Radical Democratic Party was an attempt to provide a political platform for his ideas, which combined elements of Marxism with a strong emphasis on democratic principles. However, disenchanted with the practical inefficacy of party politics to bring about ideological change, Roy disbanded the party. His subsequent work focused more on intellectual and philosophical activism, particularly advancing his concept of "Radical Humanism," which called for a new social order based on the principles of individual freedom and democratic governance.

13. (D): The incorrect argument about why Robert Nozick agrees with anarchist assertions regarding the state is that "Its motive is the welfare of citizens." Nozick, a prominent American political philosopher, is known for his libertarian views, especially as presented in his book "Anarchy, State, and Utopia." He argues against the notion of a welfare state and asserts that the minimal state is the most extensive state that can be justified. He believes that the state maintains a monopoly on the use of force and can violate individual rights, but he doesn't assert that the state is intrinsically immoral or that its primary motive is the welfare of its citizens. In fact, Nozick contends that a minimal state, focused solely on the enforcement of contracts and protection against force, theft, and fraud, could emerge without violating individual rights.

14. (D): The incorrect statement regarding the Union Public Service Commission (UPSC) is that "The State Governments can ask the UPSC to conduct the examinations for concerned state." UPSC is a central agency that conducts examinations for recruitment to various posts under the Union Government of India. State governments have their own Public Service Commissions (PSCs) for this purpose. However, if requested by two or more states, the UPSC can assist in conducting joint examinations for services benefitting more than one state, but this is a far cry from individual state governments asking the UPSC to conduct their exams.

15. (B): The correct formula for calculating the vote value of a Member of Parliament (MP) in a presidential election in India is:

Vote Value of MP

$$= \frac{\text{Total value of votes of all MLAs of all States \& UTs}}{\text{Total Number of elected Members of Parliament}}$$

This formula is part of the electoral process for the President of India, which is an indirect election involving an Electoral College composed of elected members of both houses of Parliament and elected members of Legislative Assemblies of States and Union Territories. The formula aims to balance the voting power between the states and the union, ensuring a broad-based consensus for the presidential candidate. It's worth noting that the vote value for MPs is uniform, whereas the vote value for MLAs varies from state to state based on the population.

16. (B): The 86th Constitutional Amendment in 2002 inserted a new Fundamental Duty into Article 51-A of the Indian Constitution. This duty mandates parents or guardians to provide opportunities for education to their child or ward between the age of six and fourteen years. This amendment was closely linked to the introduction of the Right to Education Act, which sought to provide free and compulsory education to all children in this age group. The introduction of this duty highlighted the state's commitment to enhancing educational standards and making parents and guardians accountable for their child's education.

17. (D): The National Commission for Minorities (NCM), set up by the Union Government under the National Commission for Minorities Act of 1992, has notified six religious communities as minorities: Muslims, Christians, Sikhs, Buddhists, Zoroastrians (Parsis), and Jains. These communities are accorded minority status on the basis of their representation in the population, which allows them to avail certain protections, scholarships, and benefits under various government schemes designed to uplift minority communities.

18. (B): The Presiding Officer conducts the elections at the Polling Station. This individual is responsible for ensuring that the voting process is carried out in a smooth and lawful manner. Duties include verifying the identity of voters, ensuring the proper functioning of the Electronic Voting Machines (EVMs), and overseeing the sealing and safe transportation of EVMs to the counting centers. The role of the Presiding Officer is crucial for maintaining the integrity of the electoral process, as they are the highest authority at the polling station during the time of voting.

19. (B): Justice P.N. Bhagwati is widely considered the pioneer of Public Interest Litigation (PIL) in India. Under his tenure, the Indian judiciary underwent significant changes, especially with regard to its approach to human rights and social justice. He introduced the concept of PIL to the Indian legal system, enabling individuals and organizations to approach the court on behalf of those who are unable to do so themselves. This was a revolutionary step in making justice more accessible to the Indian populace. Under PIL, formal procedures were relaxed, and the focus shifted towards delivering speedy justice to those whose rights were being violated.

20. (A): Jean Drieze, a Belgian-born Indian economist, was instrumental in framing the National Rural Employment Guarantee Act (NREGA), now known as the Mahatma Gandhi National Rural Employment Guarantee Act (MGNREGA). Drieze is renowned for his work in developmental economics, focusing on issues like hunger, famine, and public welfare. The Act guarantees a minimum of 100 days of wage employment in a financial year to rural households whose adult members volunteer to do unskilled manual work. This groundbreaking initiative aimed to reduce rural poverty and offer a safety net to rural households by providing them with job opportunities.

21. (D): Among the options given, "Quantity" is not one of the originally framed six principles of the Citizen's Charter Movement. The Citizen's Charter is a tool for promoting quality, choice, and accountability in the delivery of public services. The six principles are: choice, value for money, standards, transparency, accountability, and redress. These principles guide how public services should interact with citizens, promising not just high-quality service but also avenues for redress in case of failure. The idea is to make public services more citizen-centric. "Quantity" does not directly capture the essence of what the charter aims to achieve, which is more about the quality and accountability of services rather than the sheer volume of services provided.

22. (B): The 52nd Amendment to the Indian Constitution is related to 'anti-defection.' This amendment was enacted in 1985 and led to the insertion of the Tenth Schedule in the Constitution. The schedule lays down the process by which legislators may be disqualified on grounds of defection. The aim is to bring stability to the structure of political parties and ensure that candidates are loyal to party ideologies and directives. Anti-defection laws are meant to curb the 'Aaya Ram Gaya Ram' phenomenon, where legislators switch loyalties for personal or political gains. However, the law has also been criticized for limiting the individual agency of elected representatives by binding them strictly to party lines.

23. (A): Luther Gullick, an expert on Public Administration theory, posited that departments in any organization could be divided based on 4Ps: Purpose, Process, Persons, and Place. This theory is a tool for understanding how work can be classified in an organization. "Purpose" refers to the objective that a department aims to achieve. "Process" relates to the type of work or activities being carried out. "Persons" indicate the people or clientele the department is expected to serve, and "Place" refers to the geographical area the department is responsible for. This model aims to make the functioning of organizations, particularly in the public sector, more efficient and streamlined.

24. (*)

25. (D): The literature on New Public Administration (NPA) lays emphasis on Relevance, Values, Equity, and Change. NPA emerged in the 1960s and 1970s as a critique of traditional models of public administration. While traditional models focused on neutrality, efficiency, and process-oriented rationality, NPA advocated for a more value-laden, equitable, and socially relevant approach to public administration. It considers public administration not merely as a means of implementing laws but as an active instrument for social change. By emphasizing relevance, it insists on the need for public administration to address the real-world issues affecting society. By stressing values and equity, it promotes a more ethical and fair distribution of resources. Lastly, by focusing on change, it encourages constant adaptation and evolution to better serve the public interest.

26. (C): The fifth stage of the Policy Cycle according to Harold Lasswell is "Application." Harold Lasswell, an influential figure in the field of policy sciences, outlined a seven-stage process for policy-making: Intelligence, Recommendation, Prescription, Invocation, Application, Appraisal, and Termination. In the "Application" stage, the policy that has been decided upon is implemented. It is the stage where plans and strategies are put into action, often requiring the coordination of various governmental agencies and departments. The success of a policy largely depends on this stage as it tests the practicability of the policy measures. Effective application often necessitates adjustments and adaptations to the original plan, underscoring the dynamic and evolving nature of policy-making.

27. (B): The Swachh Survekshan is associated with the Ministry of Housing and Urban Affairs in India. This annual survey aims to rank cities based on cleanliness and other aspects of urban sanitation. The initiative was launched to assess the progress of the Swachh Bharat Mission, which aims to make India open defecation free and improve cleanliness. The Swachh Survekshan not only serves as a performance indicator but also promotes competition among cities to improve sanitation standards. It evaluates various parameters such as solid waste management, sanitation strategies, citizen feedback, and independent observations to rank cities.

28. (B): Meghalaya is the first state in India to bring Social Audit Law. Social auditing is a way for organizations and governments to measure and understand the effectiveness of their social and ethical goals. In 2017, Meghalaya passed the "Community Led Initiatives for Rural Development (CLIRDAP) Act," which institutionalized social audits for all developmental programs in the state. This was a groundbreaking step for transparency and accountability, allowing communities to actively engage with and evaluate the success of various schemes. Meghalaya's pioneering legislation serves as a model for other states to follow in making governance more accountable to the people.

29. (A): The Good Governance Index is associated with the Ministry of Personnel, Public Grievances and Pensions. Launched in 2019, the index aims to assess the status of governance across Indian states and Union Territories. It provides actionable insights for improving governance and serves as a tool for promoting healthy competition among states. The index takes into account various sectors like commerce and industries, human resource development, public health, and public infrastructure. The composite index offers an overall governance score based on a wide array of indicators, thereby providing a comprehensive view of governance quality at the state and Union Territory levels.

30. (B): The U.S.-India Peaceful Atomic Energy Co-operation Act is also known as the Hyde Act. Named after Congressman Henry J. Hyde, the act was signed into law by President George W. Bush in 2006. It serves as the U.S. domestic law framework to facilitate the Indo-U.S. Civil Nuclear Agreement. The Hyde Act allows the United States to engage in civilian nuclear trade with India even though India is not a signatory to the Non-Proliferation Treaty. This legislation marked a significant departure from earlier U.S. policy and has been both praised for strengthening U.S.-India relations and criticized for potentially undermining international non-proliferation efforts.

31. (B): The principles of Panchsheel include mutual respect for each other's territorial integrity and sovereignty, mutual non-aggression, and equality and co-operation for mutual benefit. These principles were first formally agreed upon between India and China in 1954, but they have been regarded as general guiding principles for international relations. They do not include "interference in each other's affairs" or "equal existence" in their original formulation. Panchsheel was initially seen as a framework for peaceful co-existence between different nations, especially those with differing political systems. However, despite its initial promise, Panchsheel couldn't prevent tensions and conflicts, such as the Sino-Indian war of 1962, but it remains a concept that is invoked from time to time in discussions on diplomatic relations.

32. (A): The first-ever deployment of Female Police Personnel from India in UN peacekeeping operations occurred in January 2007. An all-female Formed Police Unit from India was deployed in Liberia under the United Nations Mission in Liberia (UNMIL). This deployment was a landmark in the history of female participation in UN peacekeeping missions, highlighting the role that women can play in maintaining peace and security. Their presence had a significant impact, serving as role models and contributing to a more gender-balanced approach to peacekeeping. The unit was involved in a range of policing duties and earned high praise for their service, setting a precedent for the increased involvement of women in peacekeeping operations.

33. (C): The term 'extended neighbourhood' in Indian foreign policy encompasses a wider geographical area that goes beyond the immediate neighbours. This includes regions like the Suez Canal, South China Sea, and the Asia-Pacific. Eastern Africa is not traditionally considered as part of India's 'extended neighbourhood.' While India has strong historical and cultural ties with countries in Eastern Africa, and there is ongoing diplomatic and economic engagement, it does not fall under the purview of the 'extended neighbourhood' concept that is more oriented towards strategic and security concerns, particularly in the maritime domain.

34. (B): India's approach to multilateral action, as outlined by Foreign Minister S. Jaishankar, is anchored in the five 'S's: Samman (Respect), Samvad (Dialogue), Sahyog (Cooperation), Shanti (Peace), and Samriddhi (Prosperity). These principles encapsulate India's philosophy of fostering a harmonious and mutually beneficial international order. 'Samanjasya' (Harmony) is not included in this list. These principles underpin India's active participation in various multilateral fora, from the United Nations to regional organizations like SAARC and ASEAN, and encapsulate India's aspirations to be a responsible stakeholder in the international system, dedicated to peaceful coexistence and mutual prosperity.

35. (B): The decision to set up the World Bank was taken at the Bretton Woods Conference held in July 1944 in Bretton Woods, New Hampshire, USA. The conference was attended by representatives from 44 countries and led to the establishment of the Bretton Woods system, the International Monetary Fund (IMF), and the International Bank for Reconstruction and Development (IBRD), which is part of today's World Bank Group. The primary focus of the World Bank initially was to provide loans for the reconstruction of war-torn Europe. However, its mandate has evolved over time, and it now primarily focuses on poverty reduction and development.

36. (B): The United Nations (UN) was officially established on October 24, 1945, after the conclusion of World War II. The foundational charter was initially signed by 51 member states. The main objective of setting up the UN was to prevent future international conflicts and facilitate cooperation among nations. Over the years, the UN has diversified its role to include peacekeeping, promoting human rights, fostering social and economic development, and coordinating humanitarian aid during disasters. October 24 is celebrated as United Nations Day to commemorate the establishment of this vital international body. The UN's establishment was an outcome of the failures of the League of Nations and the devastating consequences of World War II. It aimed to provide a platform for dialogue and collective action to prevent conflicts and promote global welfare.

37. (A): The term 'containment' was coined by George F. Kennan, who was an American diplomat and historian. He initially proposed the idea in an anonymous article in the journal "Foreign Affairs" in 1947 under the pseudonym "X". The containment policy aimed to restrict the spread of communism globally and was primarily targeted at the Soviet Union. Kennan's idea of containment significantly influenced American foreign policy during the Cold War era. It led to a variety of strategies to counter the spread of communism, including economic aid, diplomatic alliances, and military interventions. The concept of containment remains influential in discussions about international relations and strategic studies.

38. (A): President George W. Bush categorized India as "a responsible state with advanced nuclear technology" during the U.S.-India Civil Nuclear Agreement, also known as the 123 Agreement. This was a significant departure from the traditional U.S. policy, which had been skeptical of India's nuclear program, especially since India is not a signatory to the Nuclear Non-Proliferation Treaty (NPT). The statement was groundbreaking as it recognized India's nuclear capabilities while implying a level of trust in India's responsible conduct. The deal permitted India access to U.S. civil nuclear technology and marked a new era in U.S.-India relations, focusing on strategic and economic partnership.

39. (A): In the Ecological Approach, it's true that the term 'ecology' has Greek roots, Ernst Haeckel coined the term 'ecology,' and Andrew Dobson makes a distinction between environmentalism and ecologism. The term 'ecology' originates from the Greek words 'oikos,' meaning home, and 'logos,' meaning study. Ernst Haeckel, a German biologist, first coined the term 'ecology' in the late 19th century. Andrew Dobson, a political theorist, distinguishes between 'environmentalism,' which he sees as a reformist approach that works within existing political systems, and 'ecologism,' which he considers a radical approach demanding a new kind of political thinking. The green ideology debate is not a 16th-century debate but rather a more modern one, evolving in the late 20th century along with increasing awareness of environmental degradation.

40. (C)

41. (A)

42. (A): John Locke is an empiricist, meaning he believes that knowledge comes primarily from sensory experience. His work "An Essay Concerning Human Understanding" is a seminal text that lays down the principles of empiricism. Locke also believes in a limited state, advocating a system where the powers of the government are checked by laws and balanced by the will of the governed. Furthermore, Locke is considered a propounder of the concept of popular sovereignty, which asserts that the authority of the state is created and sustained by the will of its people. Locke's ideas had a significant influence on modern political thought and inspired many democratic systems.

43. (A): Rabindranath Tagore, a polymath and a Nobel laureate in Literature, was indeed an exponent of 'true freedom,' which for him was not just political freedom but a deeper, inner liberation. He appeared to be a seeker of eternal truths, a pursuit reflected in his vast array of writings, including poems, songs, and essays. Tagore also supported the idea of creative unity amidst diversity, evident in his criticisms of nationalism that sought to homogenize and decimate the local cultures. He felt that such nationalism could become a threat to human freedom and the pursuit of truth. He didn't support aggressive nationalism, making him distinct from other contemporary freedom fighters of India.

44. (D): According to Kautilya's "Arthashastra," Danda Niti, or the law of punishment, serves multiple functions: the acquisition of the unacquired, preservation of the acquired, and the augmentation of the preserved. It does not explicitly talk about the fair distribution of the augmented or maintenance of law and order within the state as its primary goals. Rather, it focuses on expansionist policies, retaining territories, and increasing wealth. Kautilya's pragmatism in statecraft is similar to Machiavellian ideas but rooted in the socio-political context of ancient India. His work has been considered an important treatise on governance and a guide for rulers for centuries.

45. (C): The functions of a political system include political socialization and political recruitment. Political socialization is the lifelong process by which people form their political beliefs and values. This includes the family, education system, peer groups, and the media. Political recruitment refers to the ways in which individuals are selected for involvement in politics. Political decay and political revolutions are not functions of a political system but rather outcomes or states that a political system may experience. Decay implies the deterioration or malfunction of the institutions that make up the political system, while revolutions are drastic changes that may happen within a political system.

46. (C): Factors like severe class divisions, the role of intellectuals in mass mobilization, and social disequilibrium are key contributors to revolutions in a political system. Severe class divisions create a strong undercurrent of discontent and can result in social and economic instability, providing fertile ground for revolution. Intellectuals often play a vital role in articulating grievances, formulating ideologies, and mobilizing support for revolutionary changes. Social disequilibrium, like rapid modernization without corresponding social and economic reforms, can also precipitate revolutions. A strong desire for peace and incremental changes, on the other hand, are usually associated with stability rather than revolutionary change.

47. (B): The Speaker of the Lok Sabha in India wields significant powers and privileges, but there are certain limitations. First, the Speaker cannot preside over a meeting in which a resolution for his/her removal is under consideration. Second, the Speaker can vote in the house but only in the case of a tie, and this vote is known as a casting vote. The Speaker is not subject to the Anti-Defection Law if he/she decides to quit his/her party after being elected as the Speaker, making statement (a) incorrect.

48. (C): In the Berubari Union Case (1960), the Supreme Court held that the preamble is not a part of the Constitution and, therefore, cannot be amended. However, this position was overturned in the landmark Keshavananda Bharati Case (1973), where the Supreme Court stated that the preamble is indeed part of the Constitution and subject to amendment, but the basic structure laid out in the preamble cannot be altered. The statement about the L.I.C. of India Case stating the preamble is not a part of the Constitution is incorrect.

49. (A)

50. (C): According to Article 26 of the Indian Constitution, every religious denomination or any section thereof shall have the right:

- to establish and maintain institutions for religious and charitable purposes

- to manage its own affairs in matters of religion
- to own and acquire movable and immovable property; and
- to administer such property in accordance with law.

51. (D): Classical theory in Public Administration was one of the earliest approaches to study the subject, and it had a significant impact on the field. This theory played a crucial role in rationalizing and stimulating production. This was done by focusing on efficiency and effectiveness in administrative practices, mainly through the concept of a division of labor. The theory also established a set of concepts that still serve as the foundation for many administrative practices, such as hierarchy and authority, unity of command, and specialization of jobs. Classical theory was also the first to propose that administration is a distinct activity separate from politics, law, and other forms of societal functions. Thus, all the statements are correct.

52. (A): Ferral Heady, an authority in the field of Comparative Public Administration, points out that the discipline addresses multiple concerns. First, it aims at theory-building by comparing different administrative systems and practices. Second, the discipline seeks practical application, intending to solve real-world administrative problems. Third, it contributes to the broader field of comparative politics by analyzing how public administration interacts with political systems. Lastly, the discipline also involves the comparative analysis of ongoing issues and challenges in public administration.

53. (D): Public Interest Litigation (PIL) in India is a significant legal innovation to ensure access to justice for all.

- Not only registered Civil Society Organizations but any citizen can file a PIL.
- It can be filed under Article 32 of the Constitution in the Supreme Court and under Article 226 in High Courts
- Although PILs usually come with relaxed procedural requirements, it's not accurate to say there is no court fee for filing a PIL; fees may be nominal but still exist.

54. (C): The Right to Information (RTI) Act of 2019 brought significant changes to the original law. The fixed term of five years for the Commissioner was changed, and now they hold office at the pleasure of the Government. This alteration raised concerns about the autonomy of the Information Commission. Additionally, the salaries and allowances of the Commissioner are now decided by the Government, which also stirred debates about the institution's independence.

55. (A): The core values of Indian Foreign Policy encompass a blend of idealism and realism. Idealism can be seen in India's anti-imperialistic stances and its leading role in the Non-Aligned Movement. Realism is evidenced by its strategic alliances and partnerships based on national interest. The value of tolerance is another core value, reflective of India's pluralistic society and its approach to international relations. Anti-imperialism and anti-colonialism have been strong pillars of Indian foreign policy, rooted in its own colonial past. Territorial expansion, however, has never been a core value of India's foreign policy.

56. (C): The Cold War, primarily between the United States and the Soviet Union, was marked by a nuclear arms race and a war of ideologies, often manifested through propaganda. These factors contributed to a tense international environment but didn't involve economic blockades against non-aligned countries or direct involvement from third-world countries. Non-aligned nations like India chose not to side explicitly with either of the Cold War superpowers, and these countries were generally not subject to economic blockades specifically due to Cold War tensions.

57. **(A):** The end of World War II marked the beginning of the Cold War era, characterized by the conflict and tension between the United States and the Soviet Union. This period had a ripple effect that influenced not just the relations between these superpowers but also impacted their relations with non-aligned nations. Policies like containment and alliances like NATO and the Warsaw Pact were part of a global strategy that even non-aligned nations could not entirely escape from. Therefore, both Assertion (A) and Reason (R) are true, and (R) is the correct explanation for (A).

58. **(A):** The statement "In our time, history is that which transforms documents into monuments" refers to the way historical narratives are crafted, often taking specific documents or pieces of evidence and elevating their importance to create a 'monumental' narrative. The "archaeology of knowledge" involves sifting through these narratives to uncover inherent systems of thought or discourse. Both statements encapsulate a Foucauldian view of knowledge and history, where the former transforms documents into significant monuments and the latter scrutinizes these transformations. Therefore, both (A) and (R) are correct, and (R) offers a proper explanation for (A).

59. **(A):** The assertion that the inner contradictions of capitalism will destroy capitalism is a concept primarily associated with Marxist theory. Marx believed that capitalism sowed the seeds of its downfall by exploiting labor for surplus value, leading to crises of overproduction and eventually revolution. The exploitation of surplus value is indeed considered the most significant contradiction within the capitalist mode of production according to Marxist thought. Hence, both Assertion (A) and Reason (R) are true, and (R) is the correct explanation for (A).

60. **(B):** The term 'Sarvodaya' refers to 'universal uplift' or 'progress for all,' which aims to establish a balanced and equitable economic setup. This was also an aim of Jai Prakash Narayan, popularly known as JP. He focused on agriculture as the core of economic life and believed that equitable growth could only be achieved by prioritizing agriculture. While both statements are true, JP's focus on agriculture doesn't serve as a direct explanation for the establishment of a balanced and equitable economic setup, as Sarvodaya encompasses more than just agricultural development. Hence, both (A) and (R) are true, but (R) is not the correct explanation of (A).

61. **(B):** Political culture refers to the set of attitudes, beliefs, and sentiments which give order and meaning to a political process and provide the underlying assumptions and rules that govern behaviour in the political system. It encompasses both verbal and non-verbal behaviours and is often shaped by historical, cultural, and social contexts. Reason (R) highlights that there can be different types of political cultures based on the dynamics of political development, which is a correct statement but not a direct explanation of what constitutes political culture as mentioned in Assertion (A). Typological and morphological models explore the diversity of political cultures but do not define what political culture is. Therefore, both statements are correct, but (R) is not a correct explanation of (A).

62. **(C):** Robert Dahl did indeed advocate for comparative studies in Public Administration, emphasizing that the discipline could benefit from analyzing different cultures and political settings. However, he did not believe that public administration could escape the effects of its political, cultural, or environmental system. In fact, his argument for comparative studies was partly because these factors deeply influence Public Administration. Therefore, Assertion (A) is correct, but Reason (R) is incorrect.

63. **(A):** Rights are inherently a matter of conflict between individuals and the state. They define what individuals can do without interference from the government and also what the state is obligated to do for its citizens. Statement (II) posits that any theory that denies individuals certain rights 'against the state' is not a genuine theory of rights, which aligns with the core principle of rights acting as safeguards against unwarranted state interference. Therefore, both statements are true.

64. **(A):** Statement (I) suggests that issues like global environmental change could not exist without modern technologies and high population densities, which is accurate. Industrialization and technological advancements have significantly contributed to climate change, pollution, and other environmental issues. Statement (II) observes that problems like climate change are complicated due to both intra and inter-generational collective action problems, which is also true. The effects of climate change will be felt both now and by future generations, and this makes collective action both urgent and problematic. Thus, both statements are true.

65. **(A):** Jawaharlal Nehru, India's first Prime Minister, was indeed in favour of a socialistic pattern of society. He advocated for a state-led model of development, where the government played a decisive role in economic planning and policy. However, unlike orthodox socialism, he did not support the 'dictatorship of the proletariat,' an essential component of Marxist theory. His commitment to democratic ideals and civil liberties prevented him from embracing such an authoritarian approach to governance. Thus, both statements are true.

66. **(A):** Both Statement (I) and Statement (II) are correct. The party system is indeed a normal means of fighting political battles. Through organized parties, different groups and individuals can voice their political demands, contribute to policy-making, and compete for power. Political parties bring order and predictability to electoral competition, enabling voters to make informed choices. Statement (II) is also correct as one of the implicit aims of a party system can be to replace traditional elites with new ones. This happens through democratic processes where parties that represent marginalized or newer social groups can gain power, thereby changing the traditional power structures. In various democracies, for example, the rise of labor or peasant parties has often replaced or at least challenged the dominance of traditional elites.

67. **(C):** Statement (I) is true, while Statement (II) is false. Exit polls are indeed conducted after an individual has cast their vote in an election. These polls aim to predict the outcome of the election based on a sample of voters and are generally very accurate. On the other hand, an opinion poll is usually conducted before elections, not after, to gauge public opinion on various candidates and issues. These polls help in understanding the mood of the electorate and can often guide electoral strategies for political parties.

68. **(A):** Both statements are correct. The Vice President of India serves for a five-year term but can continue to be in office until a successor assumes office, ensuring a seamless transition of responsibilities. Statement (II) is also accurate. The Indian Constitution is silent on who performs the duties of the Vice-President when a vacancy occurs before the expiry of the term, creating a constitutional ambiguity that would likely require judicial clarification or a constitutional amendment to resolve.

69. (D): Statement (I) is incorrect, while Statement (II) is correct. The policy agenda isn't the sum of all political demands that individuals or groups have tried to get onto it. It's rather composed of the demands that policymakers have agreed to consider. This is because not every demand made by the public or interest groups makes it to the stage where it is seriously considered by lawmakers. Items that enter the policy agenda have crossed a crucial threshold; they are issues that have garnered enough attention and support to warrant serious consideration for legislative action.

70. (C): Statement (I) is correct. Both the International Monetary Fund (IMF) and the International Bank for Reconstruction and Development (IBRD, part of the World Bank Group) have their headquarters in Washington, D.C. This has been the case since these institutions were founded in the mid-20th century. Statement (II) is incorrect. India's vote share in the IMF is not 10%; as of my last update in January 2022, it was approximately 2.6%. Voting power in the IMF is determined by a country's quota, which is broadly based on its relative size in the global economy. Developed countries like the United States and members of the European Union have a more significant share of the votes.

71. (B): The correct matching of authors and books is:

- Hannah Arendt wrote "Between Past and Future".
- Isaiah Berlin penned "Vico and Herder: Two Studies in the History of Ideas".
- Michael Oakeshott is the author of "The Voice of Liberal Learning".
- Michael J. Sandel wrote "The Tyranny of Merit".

Each of these works represents a significant contribution to the world of philosophy, political theory, or social criticism. Hannah Arendt, for instance, is known for her profound explorations of totalitarianism, authority, and the human condition. Isaiah Berlin's works frequently delve into the intellectual history, especially the ideas of Counter-Enlightenment thinkers like Vico and Herder. Michael Oakeshott is known for his conservative political philosophy and his focus on liberal learning as a means of human enrichment. Michael J. Sandel's "The Tyranny of Merit" is a recent critique of meritocracy, questioning the fairness and ethical soundness of a system that rewards talent and hard work but often disregards luck and social circumstance.

72. (B): Plato said that "Virtue is knowledge," Machiavelli posited that "Success is virtue," and Foucault famously declared that "Knowledge is power." Lastly, the concept "Power is the production of intended effects" is not directly attributed to a specific thinker among the options.

These concepts each epitomize the essence of their respective thinker's philosophies. Plato's assertion resides in his idea of an enlightened ruler educated in the virtues and the Forms. Machiavelli's view on success and virtue reflects his pragmatic and at times cynical perspective on political power. Foucault's concept of knowledge being power is central to his theories on the structures of societal control and surveillance.

73. (B): The Surat split occurred in 1907, the Quit India Movement was in 1942, the Non-Cooperation Movement took place between 1919-1921, and the Mahad Satyagrah happened in 1927.

- The Surat split was a significant event in the Indian National Congress between the extremists and moderates.
- The Quit India Movement was a significant push for independence, led mainly by Gandhi, during WWII.
- The Non-Cooperation Movement was an earlier attempt to resist British rule by boycotting British goods and institutions.
- Mahad Satyagrah was a significant event led by B.R. Ambedkar for Dalit rights to access public water.

74. (D)

75. (B): The correct matching of Schedules and their Descriptions are:

- The Fourth Schedule in the Indian Constitution deals with the allocation of seats in the Rajya Sabha.
- The Tenth Schedule contains provisions related to defection, which means changing parties after being elected.
- The Seventh Schedule provides for the division of powers between the Centre and the States in the form of Union, State, and Concurrent Lists.
- The Sixth Schedule pertains to the administration of tribal areas in some States.

76. (C): The correct matching of Regional Political Parties and their Founder leaders are:

- The Dravida Munnetra Kazhagam (DMK) was founded by C.N. Annadurai in 1949 as a breakaway faction from the Dravidar Kazhagam.
- The All India Anna Dravida Munnetra Kazhagam (AIADMK) was founded by M.G. Ramachandran, popularly known as MGR, in 1972 after he split from DMK.
- The Telugu Desam Party (TDP) was founded by N.T. Ramarao in 1982.
- The Jammu and Kashmir Peoples Democratic Party (PDP) was founded by Mufti Mohammad Sayeed in 1998.

77. (C): The correct matching of Concept and their Thinker are:

- The concept of "Distinction between obedience and acceptance" was advanced by Chester Barnard in his work on organizational theory.
- Herbert Simon distinguished between "economic man and administrative man," explaining that in administration, rationality is bounded by limitations like time, information, and cognitive abilities.
- Max Weber introduced the "Distinction between charismatic leader and legal-rational authority," explaining different types of legitimate rule in his theory of bureaucracy.
- F.W. Taylor, the father of Scientific Management, discussed the "Distinction between principles and mechanics of management" emphasizing efficiency and productivity.

78. (D): The correct matching of Scheme and their Ministry are:

- The Ujjwala Scheme, aimed at providing free LPG connections to poor families, comes under the Ministry of Women and Child Development.
- The Saubhagyam Yojana, aimed at electrifying all villages, comes under the Ministry of Power.
- The Atal Pension Yojana, a social security scheme, comes under the Ministry of Finance.

- The National Social Assistance Programme, aimed at public assistance to its citizens, comes under the Ministry of Rural Development.

79. (A): The Indian Peace Keeping Force in Sri Lanka was deployed during the tenure of Prime Minister Rajiv Gandhi. The Shimla Agreement, aimed at normalizing relations between India and Pakistan after the 1971 war, was signed during Indira Gandhi's time. The Lahore Declaration, a bilateral agreement and governance treaty between India and Pakistan, was initiated by Atal Bihari Vajpayee. The Act East Policy, aimed at improving relations with ASEAN countries, was initiated under Narendra Modi's government.

80. (C): The Bandung Summit, also known as the first Afro-Asian conference, took place in 1955. It was a significant step towards the Non-Aligned Movement. The Belgrade Summit in 1961 marked the official establishment of the Non-Aligned Movement. The New Delhi Summit in 1983 was important as it reviewed the role of the movement in a changing world, especially in the context of the Cold War. The Durban Summit in 1998 was notable as it addressed issues like economic cooperation among developing countries.

81. (C): Concepts in chronological order according to evolution are:

- Legal Sovereignty was perhaps the first concept to be developed in the context of the modern state system. Rooted in the Treaty of Westphalia (1648), it emphasized that the highest legal authority within a territory is the state itself.
- Political Sovereignty came next, which delved deeper into the actual exercise of power and authority, taking into account both legal norms and political realities.
- Popular Sovereignty emerged with the Enlightenment and democratic revolutions, asserting that the ultimate source of authority in a state rests with the people.
- Theory of Plural Sovereignty came into prominence in the 20th century, challenging the monolithic concept of sovereignty by acknowledging multiple sites of power, such as interest groups, corporations, and transnational bodies.

82. (A): Books according to their publication year are:

- "The Human Condition" by Hannah Arendt was published in 1958 and explores the concepts of labor, work, and action as they relate to human existence.
- "The Archaeology of Knowledge" by Michel Foucault, published in 1969, delves into the complexities of historical knowledge and epistemology.
- "After Virtue" by Alasdair MacIntyre was published in 1981 and deals with the decline of moral language.
- "Spheres of Justice" by Michael Walzer came out in 1983 and presents a liberal egalitarian theory of justice.

83. (A): Concepts in chronological order according to their evolution are:

- The Saptang theory of State is the oldest concept and finds its roots in ancient Indian political thought, specifically in Arthashastra by Chanakya.
- Radical Humanism, a 20th-century concept, was introduced by M.N. Roy as a philosophy that seeks to create a new human being devoid of prejudice.
- Satyagraha is an early 20th-century concept developed by Mahatma Gandhi and used most prominently in the Indian independence struggle against British rule.
- Sampurna Kranti (Total Revolution) is a concept introduced by Jayaprakash Narayan in the 1970s as a call for revolution across various aspects of society and governance.

84. (D): Features of constitutionalism as they developed over period of time:

- Political Separatism can be traced back to medieval Europe, where the church and state were separate entities.
- Codification of Law became prominent in the early modern period, particularly with the advent of nation-states.
- Constitutional Monarchy, where a monarch is guided by a constitution, became prevalent by the late 17th and early 18th centuries, particularly in Britain.
- The idea of Checks and Balances, especially in the context of Montesquieu's work in the mid-18th century, was institutionalized by the United States through its Constitution in 1787.

85. (B): According to the Indian Constitution, the Directive Principles of State Policy are enumerated from Articles 36 to 51. Equal pay for equal work for men and women is listed under Article 39(d), promoting equal justice and free legal aid to the poor falls under Article 39A, the uniform civil code is covered by Article 44, and separating the judiciary from the executive is Article 50. This arrangement mirrors their sequence in the Indian Constitution and indicates a varied approach to social justice, incorporating economic, judicial, and civil aspects.

86. (B): Movements in chronological order are:

- The Chipko Movement began in 1973 in the state of Uttarakhand, India, as a forest conservation movement where people hugged the trees to prevent them from being cut.
- The Appiko Movement was inspired by Chipko and started in Karnataka in 1983 to protect the forests of the Western Ghats.
- The Narmada Bachao Andolan started in 1985 to protest the dams being built on the Narmada River.
- The Jan Lokpal Movement led by Anna Hazare gained momentum in 2011, advocating for the passing of the Lokpal Bill.
- The Jal Satyagrah started in 2012 in the state of Madhya Pradesh to protest against the increasing water level in the Omkareshwar Dam.

87. (B): Elton Mayo conducted a series of experiments at the Hawthorne plant of the Western Electric Company in Chicago.

- The first was the Illumination Experiment (1924-1927), aimed at understanding the impact of lighting conditions on worker productivity.
- Next came the Relay Assembly Test Room Experiment (1927-1932), which studied the effect of various conditions on a group of female workers.
- This was followed by the Mass Interview Programme (1928-1930), which involved interviewing workers to understand their grievances and needs.
- The last was the Bank Wiring Experiment (1931-1932), which focused on the social environment affecting productivity.

88. (B): Anti-Corruption measures taken by Government of India in chronological order are:

- The Benami Transactions (Prohibition) Act was first enacted in 1988, targeting transactions where properties were held by one person but paid for by another, generally to evade taxes or hide black money.
- The Prevention of Money Laundering Act came into force in 2002, providing measures to combat money laundering.
- India Ratified the United Nations Convention Against Corruption (UNCAC) in 2011, affirming its commitment to fight corruption on an international scale.

- The Black Money (Undisclosed Foreign Income and Assets) and Imposition of Tax Act was enacted in 2015, targeting undisclosed income and assets held abroad.

89. (A): The joint exercises conducted by the Indian Air Force can be ordered as follows:

- Indradhanush-IV (2015), a joint exercise with the Royal Air Force of the United Kingdom, aimed to enhance operational coordination.
- Desert Eagle-II (2016) is a bilateral exercise with the United Arab Emirates Air Force.
- Table Top (2017) is a trilateral exercise involving the air forces of the United States, Japan, and India.
- Samvedna (2018) was the first exercise of the South Asian Regional nations spearheaded by the Indian Air Force for Humanitarian Assistance and Disaster Relief.

90. (A): The chronological order of the BRICS (Brazil, Russia, India, China, and South Africa) summits is as follows:

- Durban, South Africa (2013), focused on the creation of the New Development Bank.
- Ufa, Russia (2015) saw the formalization of the New Development Bank.
- Johannesburg, South Africa (2018) focused on inclusive growth and shared prosperity.
- The Beijing Virtual Summit (2020) due to the COVID-19 pandemic, emphasized cooperation in public health and economic recovery.

91. (D)	**92. (A)**	**93. (D)**
94. (C)	**95. (D)**	**96. (A)**
97. (C)	**98. (D)**	**99. (A)**
100. (A)		

Previous Years' Paper (Solved)

National Testing Agency (NTA)

UGC-NET Junior Research Fellowship & Assistant Professor Eligibility Exam

POLITICAL SCIENCE, June–2022

(Online exam held on 11-10-2022)

PAPER-II

Note: *This paper contains* ***hundred (100)*** *objective type questions of* ***two (2)*** *marks each.* ***All*** *questions are* ***compulsory***.

1. Which of the following characterises Rational choice Institutionalism, as a new institution approach in comparative politics?

(*a*) It explains interest based motivations of political actors

(*b*) It explains resolution of collective action dilemma

(*c*) It explains cultural construction of interest and institutions

(*d*) It follows a deductive approach

Choose the *most appropriate* answer from the options given below:

A. (*a*), (*b*) and (*c*) only

B. (*a*), (*b*) and (*d*) only

C. (*a*) and (*b*) only

D. (*b*) and (*c*) only

2. Which of the following Schemes is/are launched by the current Central Government?

(*a*) Pradhan Mantri Awas Yojna.

(*b*) Kisan Nyay Yojna.

(*c*) Pradhan Mantri Gareeb Kalyan Yojna.

(*d*) Meri Policy Mere Haath

Choose the *correct answer* from the options given below:

A. (*a*), (*b*), (*d*) only B. (*a*), (*b*), (*c*) only

C. (*a*), (*c*), (*d*) only D. (*a*), (*c*) only

3. Peaceful Nuclear Explosion (PNE) was a policy of the Government under:

A. A.B. Vajpayee B. Indira Gandhi

C. Narasimha Rao D. Narendra Modi

4. Who among the following authored 'Black Skin, White Mask?'

A. Hannah Arendt B. Frantz Fanon

C. Mary Wollston Craft D. Marcus Graveg

5. Given below are two statements: One is labelled as Assertion A and the other is labelled as Reason (R).

Assertion (A) : "Until Philosophers are kings and princes of the world have the spirit and powers of Philosophy, cities will never have rest from their evils.

Reason (R) : The republic aimed at the representation of human life in a state perfected by justice and governed according to the idea of good.

In the light of the above statements, choose the *most appropriate* answer from the options given below:

A. Both (A) and (R) are correct and (R) is the correct explanation of (A)

B. Both (A) and (R) are correct but (R) is not the correct explanation of (A)

C. (A) is correct but (R) is not correct

D. (A) is not correct but (R) is correct

6. Who among the following looks at revolution as a 'Sweeping fundamental change in the predominant myth of Social order'?

A. Newmann B. S.P. Huntington

C. T.S. Kuhn D. G.S. Pete

7. The first Lokpal bill was introduced in Parliament.

A. 1971 B. 1967
C. 1968 D. 1969

8. No money bill can be introduced in the legislative Assembly without the recommendation of the _______.

A. Speaker B. Governor
C. Chief Minister D. Finance Minister

9. Arrange the following regional political parties in chronological order, as per their date of establishment.

(*a*) DMK
(*b*) Shiromani Akali Dal
(*c*) TDP
(*d*) Biju Janata Dal

Choose the *correct answer* from the options given below:

A. (*b*), (*a*), (*c*), (*d*) B. (*a*), (*b*), (*c*), (*d*)
C. (*a*), (*b*), (*d*), (*c*) D. (*d*), (*a*), (*b*), (*c*)

10. In which case the Supreme Court of India ruled that the provision of Judicial review comes under an essential feature of the Indian Constitution:

A. S.R. Bommai case
B. Golaknath case
C. Minerva Mills case
D. Indira Sahani case

11. Who amongst the following is the editor of the book "The Indian Paradox"?

A. Rajeev Bhargava
B. Myron Weiner
C. Subhash Kashyap
D. Granville Austin

12. What is common in the election symbols of the Samajwadi Party, Telugu Desam Party and Manipur People's Party?

A. Leaf B. Cycle
C. Lantern D. Flower

13. Arrange the following according to chronological order.

(*a*) Kyoto Protocol
(*b*) International Covenant on Economic, Social and Cultural Rights.
(*c*) UN Conference on Environment in Rio de Janeiro.
(*d*) UN Declarations of Human Rights.

Choose the *correct answer* from the options given below:

A. (*a*), (*c*), (*b*), (*d*) B. (*d*), (*b*), (*c*), (*a*)
C. (*d*), (*c*), (*a*), (*b*) D. (*b*), (*c*), (*a*), (*d*)

14. What is not included in 'Five E' approach in Policy analysis?

A. Effectiveness
B. Efficiency
C. Ethical Consideration
D. Evidences

15. Given below are two statements: One is labelled as Assertion (A) and the other is labelled as Reason (R).

Assertion (A) : A student of Comparative politics should study the behaviours of voters.

Reason (R) : A student of comparative politics has to deal with the entire political systems.

In the light of the above statements, choose the *most appropriate* answer from the options given below:

A. Both (A) and (R) are correct and (R) is the correct explanation of (A)
B. Both (A) and (R) are correct but (R) is not the correct explanation of (A)
C. (A) is correct but (R) is not correct
D. (A) is not correct but (R) is correct

16. Which of the following is correctly matched?

(*a*) Sexual Politics – Kate Millett
(*b*) Second Sex – Shulamith Firestone
(*c*) The Feminine Mystique – Betty Friedan
(*d*) The Dialectic of Sex – Nicholson

Choose the *most appropriate* answer from the options given below:

A. (*a*) and (*b*) only
B. (*b*) and (*c*) only
C. (*a*) and (*c*) only
D. (*a*), (*b*), (*c*), (*d*) only

17. Who wrote the book "The Rise of the Plebians"?

A. Amartya Sen
B. Partha Chatterjee
C. Christophe Jafferlot and Sanjay Kumar
D. Suhas Palshikar

18. Arrange the following according to the chronological orders.

(*a*) Lahore Declaration
(*b*) Tashkent Agreement
(*c*) Indo-US Civil Nuclear Co-operation Agreement
(*d*) Indo-Soviet Treaty of Peace, Friendship and Co-operations.

Choose the *correct answer* from the options given below:

A. (*d*), (*c*), (*b*), (*a*) B. (*b*), (*d*), (*a*), (*c*)
C. (*a*), (*c*), (*b*), (*d*) D. (*d*), (*a*), (*b*), (*c*)

19. Which of the following is correctly matched

(*a*) Civil liability of Nuclear Damages Act – 2010
(*b*) India – US ten year frame work Agreement for Defence Co-operation – 2015
(*c*) Defence Technology and Trade Initiative – 2020
(*d*) Basic Exchange Co-operations Agreement – 2019

Choose the *most appropriate* answer from the options given below:

A. (*a*) and (*b*) only B. (*b*) and (*c*) only
C. (*b*) and (*d*) only D. (*a*) and (*d*) only

20. Who among the following defined socialism as a chameleon, which changes its colour according to the environment?

A. C.E.M. Joad B. Emile
C. Ramsay Muir D. Hugham

21. Which of the following is/are correct:

(*a*) Structural approach focuses on economy and efficiency.
(*b*) Human Relation approach deals with the relationship among the people working in organisation.
(*c*) Behavioural approach emphasises on the study of the development aspect of the administration.
(*d*) Political economy approach emphasises on the application of economic methods and models of political problem

Choose the *correct answer* from the options given below:

A. (*a*), (*b*), (*d*) only B. (*b*), (*c*), (*d*) only
C. (*a*), (*b*) only D. (*c*), (*d*) only

22. UNO proclaimed International Yoga Day through the Resolutions 69/131 in the year

A. 2015 B. 2014
C. 2016 D. 2017

23. Who among the following coined the term 'ecology' in 1866?

A. Ernst Heackel B. F. Riggs
C. R.A. Dahl D. Houghton Miffin

24. Which of the following have caused the growth of Co-operative federalism in India?

(*a*) Union – State collaboration in economic matters
(*b*) Union – State legislative relations
(*c*) Compulsion of developmental finance
(*d*) Dynamics of electoral politics

Choose the *most appropriate* answer from the options given below:

A. (*a*), (*c*) only B. (*a*), (*d*) only
C. (*b*), (*c*) only D. (*b*), (*d*) only

25. Match List-I with List-II:

List-I (Theory/Concept)	**List-II (Thinker)**
(*a*) Constructive Conflict	(*i*) Frederic Herzberg
(*b*) Acceptance Theory of authority and Zonal Indifference	(*ii*) Abraham Maslow
(*c*) Hierarchy of Needs	(*iii*) Chester I. Barnard
(*d*) Hygiene-Motivation theory	(*iv*) Mary Parker Follett

Choose the *correct answer* from the options given below:

	(*a*)	(*b*)	(*c*)	(*d*)
A.	(*iv*)	(*iii*)	(*i*)	(*ii*)
B.	(*iv*)	(*iii*)	(*ii*)	(*i*)
C.	(*iv*)	(*ii*)	(*iii*)	(*i*)
D.	(*iv*)	(*i*)	(*ii*)	(*iii*)

26. Which of the following is correctly matched.
(*a*) SAARC – Kathmandu
(*b*) Act East Policy – Narasimha Rao
(*c*) Neighbourhood first policy – Narendra Modi
(*d*) Asian Infrastructure Investment Bank – Kualalampur

Choose the *most appropriate* answer from the options given below:
A. (*c*) and (*d*) only B. (*a*) and (*c*) only
C. (*b*) and (*c*) only D. (*a*) and (*d*) only

27. Who has written the book 'Gender in International Relations'?
A. Ann Tickner B. Cynthia Enloe
C. Arundhati Roy D. Hillary Clinton

28. Match List-I with List-II:

List-I (Place)	**List-II (Jansunwai)**
(*a*) Kot Kirana	(*i*) IVth Jan Sunwai
(*b*) Bhim	(*ii*) Ist Jan Sunwai
(*c*) Vijapura	(*iii*) IInd Jan Sunwai
(*d*) Jawaja	(*iv*) IIIrd Jan Sunwai

Choose the *correct answer* from the options given below:

	(*a*)	(*b*)	(*c*)	(*d*)
A.	(*ii*)	(*iii*)	(*i*)	(*iv*)
B.	(*i*)	(*ii*)	(*iii*)	(*iv*)
C.	(*ii*)	(*iii*)	(*iv*)	(*i*)
D.	(*iii*)	(*iv*)	(*i*)	(*ii*)

29. Kautilya's theory of Rajamandala belongs to:
A. Social structure
B. The economy
C. Foreign policy and inter-state relation
D. Structure of Dharma

30. Which among the following is incorrect about Vice-President of India: While he discharges the functions of the President?
A. He will perform the duties of the office of Chairman of the Council of States
B. He will not perform the duties of the office of Chairman of the Council of States
C. He will not be entitled to any salary or allowances payable to the Chairman of the Council of States
D. He will not hold any office of profit

31. In which of the following books of 'Politics' Aristotle justifies slavery?
A. Book-1 B. Book-4
C. Book-6 D. Book-7

32. Who describes process of Modernisation as a 'Multi-faceted process involving change in all areas of human thought and activity'?
A. Huntington
B. S.M. Lipset
C. Rustow and Wand
D. David Easton

33. Who talked about 'Synthetic Universalism'?
A. M.N. Roy
B. Vinoba Bhave
C. M.K. Gandhi
D. Rabindranath Tagore

34. Which of the following is correctly matched
(*a*) War on Terrorism – USA
(*b*) Maritime Silk Road – India
(*c*) Viktor Yanukovych – Ukraine
(*d*) Line of Control – China

Choose the *correct answer* from the options given below:
A. (*a*) and (*d*) only
B. (*a*) and (*c*) only
C. (*b*) and (*c*) only
D. (*c*) and (*d*) only

35. Given below are two statements:

Statement I : Karl Marx agreed with Hegel that history unfolded itself according to a dialectical plan. But according to Marx the ideas were the result of material conditions.

Statement II : Dialectical materialism believes in the inseparability of matter and motion.

In the light of the above statements, choose the *most appropriate* answer from the options given below:
A. Both Statement I and Statement II are correct
B. Both Statement I and Statement II are incorrect

C. Statement I is correct but Statement II is incorrect
D. Statement I is incorrect but Statement II is correct

36. Para Diplomacy is/was part of India's Foreign Policy under:
A. P.V. Narasimha Rao
B. Rajiv Gandhi
C. Dr. Man Mohan Singh
D. Narendra Modi

37. Match List-I with List-II:

List-I (Thinker)	List-II (Idea)
(*a*) Hobbes	(*i*) Proportional Representation
(*b*) Locke	(*ii*) Popular Sovereignty
(*c*) Rousseau	(*iii*) Constitutional rule
(*d*) John Stuart Mill	(*iv*) Absolutism

Choose the *correct answer* from the options given below:

	(*a*)	(*b*)	(*c*)	(*d*)
A.	(*i*)	(*ii*)	(*iii*)	(*iv*)
B.	(*iv*)	(*iii*)	(*ii*)	(*i*)
C.	(*ii*)	(*i*)	(*iii*)	(*iv*)
D.	(*iii*)	(*ii*)	(*i*)	(*iv*)

38. Arrange in order:
The Right to Freedom of Religion as enshrined in the Constitution of India.
(*a*) Freedom to manage religious affairs
(*b*) Freedom as to payment of taxes for promotion of any particular religion.
(*c*) Freedom of conscience and free profession, practice and propogation of religion.
(*d*) Freedom as to attendance at religious instruction or religious worship in certain educational institutions.

Choose the *correct answer* from the options given below:
A. (*c*), (*a*), (*b*), (*d*) B. (*b*), (*a*), (*d*), (*c*)
C. (*a*), (*b*), (*c*), (*d*) D. (*b*), (*a*), (*c*), (*d*)

39. Which of the following is correctly matched
(*a*) Doklam – Trijunction
(*b*) Easter day Terror Attack – Sri Lanka
(*c*) Ukraine – NATO
(*d*) Iraq – GCC

Choose the *correct answer* from the options given below:
A. (*a*) and (*d*) only B. (*a*) and (*b*) only
C. (*b*) and (*c*) only D. (*a*) and (*d*) only

40. Arrange the following conventings on rights in Chronological order.
(*a*) The International Covenant on Civil and Political Rights.
(*b*) The Convention on the Elimination of All forms of Discrimination Against Women.
(*c*) The American Convention on Human Rights.
(*d*) The Universal Declaration of Human Rights.

Choose the *correct answer* from the options given below:
A. (*a*), (*b*), (*c*), (*d*) B. (*d*), (*a*), (*c*), (*b*)
C. (*c*), (*d*), (*b*), (*a*) D. (*b*), (*a*), (*d*), (*c*)

41. The United Kingdom (UK) voted for Brexit in:
A. 2017 B. 2019
C. 2016 D. 2020

42. Which among the following instruments of Direct Democracy are functional in Switzerland?
(*a*) Landszemeinde (*b*) Referendum
(*c*) Initiative (*d*) Recall

Choose the *most appropriate* answer from the options given below:
A. (*a*), (*b*), (*c*) only B. (*a*), (*c*), (*d*) only
C. (*b*), (*c*), (*d*) only D. (*a*), (*b*), (*c*), (*d*)

43. What is the effects of globalization on food security?
A. Wealthy countries subsidies and trade barrier make it difficult for developing countries to take advantage of the potential of globalization for advancing food security.
B. World Trade Organisation rules do not cover agriculture, so globalisation really has no bearing on food Security.

C. Supermarket are so far the only way in which food and agriculture have experienced a globalization.

D. Developing countries need to create publicly owned food reserves in order to realise the potential benefit.

44. Who among the following is the author of the book 'Introduction to the study of Law of the constitution'?

A. A.V. Dicey

B. Jermy Waldron

C. Stephen M. Griffin

D. Gordon Scoll

45. Consider the following regarding citizenship:

(*a*) A citizen is known by the rights, he is allowed to exercise

(*b*) A person living in the state territory is a citizen of state

(*c*) Citizenship can be granted through process of naturalization.

(*d*) If one is born in the territory of a state, he will be recognized as a citizen

Choose the *correct answer* from the options given below:

A. (*a*), (*b*), (*c*) only B. (*b*), (*c*), (*d*) only

C. (*a*), (*c*), (*d*) only D. (*a*), (*b*), (*d*) only

46. Match List-I with List-II:

List-I (Women Group)	List-II (Place)
(*a*) Forum Against oppression of Women	(*i*) Delhi
(*b*) Saheli	(*ii*) Mumbai
(*c*) Stree Shakti Sangthan	(*iii*) Bangalore
(*d*) Vimochana	(*iv*) Hyderabad

Choose the *correct answer* from the options given below:

	(*a*)	(*b*)	(*c*)	(*d*)
A.	(*i*)	(*ii*)	(*iv*)	(*iii*)
B.	(*ii*)	(*iii*)	(*i*)	(*iv*)
C.	(*iv*)	(*i*)	(*ii*)	(*iii*)
D.	(*ii*)	(*i*)	(*iv*)	(*iii*)

47. Who wrote the paper entitled. "A Discourse on the Moral Effects of the Arts and Science"?

A. Dante Alighieri

B. St. Thomas Acquinas

C. John Locke

D. Jean Jacques Rousseau

48. What is the correct sequencing of these movements in India?

(*a*) Quit India Movement

(*b*) Non Co-operation Movement

(*c*) Civil Disobedience Movement

(*d*) Total Revolution Movement

Choose the *correct answer* from the options given below:

A. (*b*), (*c*), (*a*), (*d*) B. (*d*), (*c*), (*a*), (*b*)

C. (*b*), (*c*), (*d*), (*a*) D. (*d*), (*b*), (*c*), (*a*)

49. In the event of the dissolution of a Panchayat before the completion of its time period, the Panchayat constituted thereafter shall perform:

A. For the remaining period

B. For the entire five year

C. As decided by Gram Sabha

D. As decided by Gram Pradhan

50. Which of the following is not true about Peter Drucker?

A. He authored the book titled "The Effective Executive"

B. He coined the term 'Knowledge workers'

C. He coined the term 'MBO'

D. He coined the term 'SMART'.

51. Given below are two statements:

Statement I : John Stuart Mill divided all actions of the individuals into two categories viz., self regarding actions and other regarding actions.

Statement II : John Stuart Mill says "Liberty consists in not doing what one desires".

In the light of the above statements, choose the *most appropriate* answer from the options given below :

A. Both Statement I and Statement II are correct

B. Both Statement I and Statement II are incorrect

C. Statement I is correct but Statement II is incorrect
D. Statement I is incorrect but Statement II is correct

52. Which of the following is not an essential condition of democracy?
A. Liberty
B. Equality
C. Independence of Judiciary
D. Committed Judiciary

53. Arab Spring began in which country?
A. Libya B. Syria
C. Egypt D. Tunisia

54. Types of policies proposed by Theodore J. Lowi:
(*a*) Distributive, Redistributive.
(*b*) Regulatory, Constituent.
(*c*) Substantive, Procedural.
(*d*) Distributive, Substantive.
(*e*) Constituent, Procedural.

Choose the *correct answer* from the options given below:
A. (*a*) and (*b*) only B. (*b*) and (*c*) only
C. (*c*) and (*d*) only D. (*d*) and (*e*) only

55. Article 169 of the constitution makes the provision for the abolition or creation of:
A. Legislative Councils in state
B. Specifies the number of seats for the Rajya Sabha
C. All India Services
D. None of the above

56. Who has coined the Word 'Soft Powers'?
A. Hans J. Morgenthau B. Joseph S. Nye
C. Robert Jervis D. Ann Tickner

57. Which of the following are related to electoral reform in India?
(*a*) Dinesh Goswami Committee
(*b*) Indrajit Gupta Committee
(*c*) Tarkunde Committee
(*d*) Santhanam Committee

Choose the *correct answer* from the options given below:
A. (*a*), (*b*) only B. (*b*), (*c*) only
C. (*a*), (*b*), (*c*) only D. (*a*), (*b*), (*c*), (*d*)

58. Consider the following statements regarding John Rawls's theory of justice?
(*a*) Justice is the first virtue of Social institutions.
(*b*) Justice is the first virtue of State institutions
(*c*) In a just society the rights Secured by justice are not subject of political bargaining.
(*d*) In a just society the rights secured by justice are not subject to social obligation.

Choose the *correct answer* from the options given below:
A. (*a*), (*b*) only B. (*b*), (*c*) only
C. (*a*), (*c*) only D. (*a*), (*b*), (*c*), (*d*)

59. Match List-I with List-II:

List-I (Books)	**List-II (Writers)**
(*a*) Tragedy of Great Power Politics	(*i*) Zakaria
(*b*) Politics among Nations	(*ii*) Waltz
(*c*) Theory of International Politics	(*iii*) Morgenthau
(*d*) From Wealth to Power	(*iv*) Mearsheimer

Choose the *correct answer* from the options given below:

	(*a*)	(*b*)	(*c*)	(*d*)
A.	(*iv*)	(*iii*)	(*ii*)	(*i*)
B.	(*iii*)	(*i*)	(*iv*)	(*ii*)
C.	(*iii*)	(*ii*)	(*i*)	(*iv*)
D.	(*i*)	(*ii*)	(*iv*)	(*iii*)

60. Which of the following is correctly matched.
(*a*) Cold War – Bipolar
(*b*) Berlin Crisis – 1955
(*c*) Cuban Missile Crisis – 1962
(*d*) Marshal Plan – Japan

Choose the *correct answer* from the options given below:
A. (*a*) and (*d*) only
B. (*b*) and (*d*) only
C. (*a*) and (*c*) only
D. (*c*) and (*d*) only

61. Match List-I with List-II:

List-I (Author)	List-II (Book)
(*a*) D.D. Raphael	(*i*) Elements of Social Justice
(*b*) Ernest Barker	(*ii*) Problems of Political Philosophy
(*c*) L.T. Hobhouse	(*iii*) Principles of Social and Political Theory
(*d*) F.A Hayek	(*iv*) Constitution of Liberty

Choose the *correct answer* from the options given below:

	(*a*)	(*b*)	(*c*)	(*d*)
A.	(*ii*)	(*iii*)	(*i*)	(*iv*)
B.	(*iii*)	(*ii*)	(*iv*)	(*i*)
C.	(*i*)	(*ii*)	(*iii*)	(*iv*)
D.	(*iv*)	(*i*)	(*iii*)	(*ii*)

62. What is Government 2.0?

A. Its NDA in its II term
B. It refers to Government policies that aim to harness interactive Internet tools to create an open source computing platform.
C. It refers to Metaverse Virtual Reality world
D. It refers to the Government of Nations emerged after II World War

63. Who among the following was the Chairman of the Advisory Committee of the Constituent Assembly?

A. Rajendra Prasad
B. Jawaharlal Nehru
C. Vallabhbhai Patel
D. Maulana Abul Kalam Azad

64. 'It is getting harder to run a constitution than to frame one'? Who made this statement?

A. L.D. White B. Ronald Reagan
C. Woodrow Wilson D. Margret Thatcher

65. Which of the following is correctly matched.

(*a*) Hydropower Diplomacy – India-Nepal
(*b*) Basic Group – China
(*c*) Group of 77 – USA
(*d*) BIMSTEC – Pakistan

Choose the *most appropriate* answer from the options given below:

A. (*a*) and (*d*) only B. (*a*) and (*b*) only
C. (*c*) and (*d*) only D. (*b*) and (*d*) only

66. While Justifying the slavery Aristotle says:

(*a*) "From the hour of birth some men are marked out for subjection and others for rule"
(*b*) That man of "Capacity, foresight, self-reliance and the life of virtue are intended by nature to work with their mind
(*c*) That they have capacity to discharge intelligently their own duties only.
(*d*) That they are machine without having any capacity to employ reason.

Choose the *correct answer* from the options given below:

A. (*b*), (*c*), (*d*) only B. (*d*), (*c*), (*a*) only
C. (*a*), (*b*), (*c*) only D. (*d*), (*b*), (*a*) only

67. Given below are two statements: One is labelled as Assertion (A) and the other is labelled as Reason (R).

Assertion (A) : Pressure groups are involved in politics and policy making process in India through direct and indirect means.

Reason (R) : They aspire to come to power to achieve their goals.

In the light of the above statements, choose the *correct answer* from the options given below:

A. Both (A) and (R) are true and (R) is the correct explanation of (A)
B. Both (A) and (R) are true but (R) is not the correct explanation of (A)
C. (A) is true but (R) is false
D. (A) is false but (R) is true

68. Which among the following is not included in classification of Interest groups given by Gabriel Almond?

A. Non Institutional Interest groups
B. Non Associational Interest groups
C. Anomic Interest groups
D. Associational Interest groups

69. Given below are two statements: One is labelled as Assertion (A) and the other is labelled as Reason (R).

Assertion (A) : India has a hybrid system of government.

Reason (R) : The hybrid system combines two classical models: the British tradition and American principles.

In the light of the above statements, choose the *correct answer* from the options given below:

A. Both (A) and (R) are correct and (R) is the correct explanation of (A)
B. Both (A) and (R) are correct but (R) is not the correct explanation of (A)
C. (A) is correct but (R) is not correct
D. (A) is not correct but (R) is correct

70. 'Open Door' Policy was associated with:

A. Mikhail Gorbachev
B. Ho Chi Minh
C. Schwarzes
D. Deng Xiaoping

71. Project Mausam is a policy linked with:

A. Environment protection
B. Climate change
C. Indian Ocean region
D. Bay of Bengal

72. Which of the following report is published by NITI AAYOG?

A. National Multidimensional Poverty Index
B. Economic Survey
C. Unemployment Rate
D. National Sample Survey

73. Arrange the following Schemes by order of the launching year:

(*a*) Demonetization
(*b*) Goods and Services Tax Act
(*c*) Pradhan Mantri Jandhan Yojna
(*d*) Beti Bachao, Beti Padhao

Choose the *correct answer* from the options given below:

A. (*a*), (*b*), (*c*), (*d*) B. (*a*), (*b*), (*d*), (*c*)
C. (*d*), (*a*), (*b*), (*c*) D. (*c*), (*d*), (*a*), (*b*)

74. The Saptang Theory of State Comprises:

(*a*) Swamy, Amatya
(*b*) Janpada/Rashtra, Mitra
(*c*) Durga, Kosa, Danda
(*d*) Adhyakshas, Ayamukham

Choose the *correct answer* from the options given below:

A. (*a*), (*b*), (*c*) and (*d*)
B. (*c*), (*d*), (*a*) only
C. (*b*), (*c*), (*d*) only
D. (*a*), (*b*), (*c*) only

75. Match List-I with List-II:

List-I (Trade Union)	List-II (Party/Organisation Affiliations)
(*a*) All India Central Council of Trade Union	(*i*) Dravida Munnetra Kazhagam
(*b*) Bharatiya Majdoor Sangh	(*ii*) Communist Party of India (ML)
(*c*) Indian National Trade Union Congress	(*iii*) Indian National Congress
(*d*) Labour Progressive Federation	(*iv*) Rashtriya Swayam-sevak Sangh

Choose the *correct answer* from the options given below:

	(*a*)	(*b*)	(*c*)	(*d*)
A.	(*iv*)	(*i*)	(*ii*)	(*iii*)
B.	(*i*)	(*ii*)	(*iii*)	(*iv*)
C.	(*ii*)	(*iv*)	(*iii*)	(*i*)
D.	(*ii*)	(*iii*)	(*iv*)	(*i*)

76. Which of the following book is/are authored by Max Weber:

(*a*) The theory of Social and Economic Organisation
(*b*) The theory of Administration of the State
(*c*) Economy and Society
(*d*) The Elements of Administration

Choose the *most appropriate* answer from the options given below:

A. (*a*) only B. (*a*) and (*b*) only
C. (*a*) and (*d*) only D. (*a*) and (*c*) only

77. A Civil Society eco system usually includes within its ambit:

(*a*) Non Profit Organisation
(*b*) Online groups
(*c*) Religious Leaders
(*d*) Legislature

Choose the *most appropriate* answer from the options given below:

A. (*a*), (*b*), (*d*) only B. (*a*), (*b*) only
C. (*a*), (*b*), (*c*) only D. (*a*) only

78. Match List-I with List-II:

List-I (Theory/concepts)	**List-II (Thinkers)**
(*a*) Integral Humanism	(*i*) M.N. Roy
(*b*) Total Revolution	(*ii*) Deen Dayal Upadhyaya
(*c*) Radical Humanism	(*iii*) Periyar
(*d*) Self Respect Movement	(*iv*) Jaya Prakash Narayan

Choose the *correct answer* from the options given below:

	(*a*)	(*b*)	(*c*)	(*d*)
A.	(*iii*)	(*i*)	(*ii*)	(*iv*)
B.	(*ii*)	(*iv*)	(*i*)	(*iii*)
C.	(*i*)	(*ii*)	(*iv*)	(*iii*)
D.	(*iv*)	(*i*)	(*ii*)	(*iii*)

79. Dr. B.R. Ambedkar's paper 'Small Holdings in India and their Remedies' is related to:

A. Indian Agrarian system
B. Indian Political system
C. Indian Education system
D. Indian Culture only

80. Who among the following proposed the concept of Constitutional Ombudsman in Parliament in India?

A. Dr. L.M. Singhvi B. Ashok Kumar Sen
C. Shanti Bhushan D. Aruna Roy

81. When and who launched 'Self-Respect movement'?

A. 1940, M.K. Gandhi
B. 1932, J.L. Nehru
C. 1925, Periyar
D. 1920, Tilak

82. Given below are two statements:

Statement I : U.N. has defined 12 Pillars of good governance.

Statement II : SDG 14 is directly linked to improvement in governance.

In the light of the above statements, choose the *correct answer* from the options given below:

A. Both Statement I and Statement II are true
B. Both Statement I and Statement II are false
C. Statement I is true but Statement II is false
D. Statement I is false but Statement II is true

83. Which of the following book is not written by Michael Oakeshott?

A. Experience and its modes
B. Rationalism in Politics
C. The History of England
D. Introduction to Leviathan

84. Who among the following identified two types of inequality: natural inequality and conventional inequality?

A. Thomas Hobbes
B. John Locke
C. J.J. Rousseau
D. Montesquieu

85. Which of the following is/are not a characteristic of the modernisation process according to Huntington:

(*a*) It's a revolutionary process
(*b*) It's a reversible process
(*c*) It's a homogenising process
(*d*) It's a complex process

Choose the *most appropriate* answer from the options given below:

A. (*a*), (*c*) only B. (*b*) only
C. (*a*), (*b*) only D. (*a*) only

86. When was the Hegal's book 'Philosophy of Right' published?

A. 1820 B. 1821
C. 1827 D. 1837

87. Arrange the following thinkers in chronologic order of their birth year:

(*a*) Chester Barnard (*b*) M.P. Follet
(*c*) Henri Fayol (*d*) Dwight Waldo

Choose the *correct answer* from the options given below:

A. (*b*), (*c*), (*d*), (*a*)
B. (*c*), (*b*), (*a*), (*d*)
C. (*c*), (*d*), (*b*), (*a*)
D. (*a*), (*b*), (*c*), (*d*)

88. Match List-I with List-II:

List-I (Books)	**List-II (Authors)**
(*a*) Political Parties	(*i*) C. Wright Mills
(*b*) Ruling Class	(*ii*) Robert Michels
(*c*) The Power Elite	(*iii*) Gaetano Mosca
(*d*) The Mind and Society	(*iv*) Vilfredo Pareto

Choose the *correct answer* from the options given below:

	(*a*)	(*b*)	(*c*)	(*d*)
A.	(*ii*)	(*i*)	(*iii*)	(*iv*)
B.	(*ii*)	(*iv*)	(*iii*)	(*i*)
C.	(*ii*)	(*iii*)	(*iv*)	(*i*)
D.	(*ii*)	(*iii*)	(*i*)	(*iv*)

89. Which among the following ideas are part of Cultural Revolution.

(*a*) Children are the masters of new society.
(*b*) Only the poor peasants can and must be the basic force to be relied upon the land reforms.
(*c*) Under feudal domination marriage is barbaric and inhuman institution.
(*d*) The women are reserve for home making.

Choose the *most appropriate* answer from the options given below:

A. (*a*), (*b*), (*c*) only B. (*a*), (*c*), (*d*) only
C. (*b*), (*c*), (*d*) only D. (*a*), (*b*), (*c*), (*d*)

90. Which of the following statements are incorrect with regard to Jayaprakash Narayan:

(*a*) He believed in Guarantee of full individual and civil liberty.
(*b*) He believed in Cooperative farms run by Village Panchayats.
(*c*) A true nationalist desires to build on old foundation.
(*d*) He regarded that Swarajya was not only a right but a 'Dharma'.
(*e*) J.P. was a Sarvodayi leader

Choose the *correct answer* from the options given below:

A. (*a*), (*b*) only B. (*c*), (*d*) only
C. (*b*), (*d*) only D. (*d*), (*e*) only

Directions (Qs. No. 91-95): *Read the passage and answer the questions:*

The theme of the World Economic Forum's Annual Meeting 2019, held in Davos was Globalization 4.0. Globalization 1.0 started in 1820 and ended at the starting of World War-I. Globalization 2.0 began after World War-II and ended around 1990. These two are called old globalization. Old globalization was especially beneficial to today's rich nations. The G7 saw rapid growth of their exports, income, and industry compared to today's poor nations during old globalisation. This led to what Kenneth Pomeranz, a historian, calls the Great Divergence. Globalization 3.0 was termed as new globalization.

This 'new globalization', or Globalization 3.0, had dramatically different effects on world income (GDP) shares. In just 20 years, the G7 share of world GDP plummeted to 50%, and its share of trade to 32%. This trend, which might be called the 'Great Convergence', is surely the dominant economic fact of the last 20 or 30 years.

What happened to the landscape of global manufacturing? The G7 nations lost share gradually between 1970 and 1990, followed by an accelerated decline from 1990. To where did manufacturing go? Just six developing nations—which we might call the 'Rapidly Industrializing 6', or I-6 for short-accounted for almost all of it. The I-6 are China, Korea, India, Poland, Indonesia and Thailand. It gained almost 16 percentage points of world manufacturing in just 20 years.

Globalization 4.0 is driven by cutting edge new technology like AI, Cloud Computing etc.

These technologies shrink distances, open up borders and minds and bring people all across the globe closer together. These technologies are changing the nature of work where no physical presence of workers will be required. Such workers are termed as telemigrant — persons who live in another developing country while working for a company located in a developed country.

91. The term Great Divergence is related to:

(*a*) Globalization 1.0

(*b*) Globalization 2.0

(*c*) Globalization 3.0

(*d*) Globalization 4.0

Choose the *correct answer* from the options given below:

A. (*c*) only B. (*a*), (*b*) only

C. (*d*) only D. (*b*), (*c*) only

92. Given below are two statements:

Statement I : Globalization 2.0 began after World War-I and ended around 1990

Statement II : Globalization 2.0 saw the establishment of UN-IMF and World bank

In the light of the above statements, choose the *correct answer* from the options given below:

A. Both Statement I and Statement II are true

B. Both Statement I and Statement II are false

C. Statement I is true but Statement II is false

D. Statement I is false but Statement II is true

93. The annual meeting 2019 of World Economic Forum was held in which of the following countries?

A. USA B. Britain

C. Switzerland D. Australia

94. The term 'Telemigrants' is related to globalisation:

A. 1.0 B. 2.0

C. 3.0 D. 4.0

95. Match List-I with List-II:

List-I	List-II
(*a*) 16	(*i*) Italy
(*b*) Globalization 3.0	(*ii*) Globalization 4.0
(*c*) G7	(*iii*) China
(*d*) Emergence of Remote working	(*iv*) New globalization

Choose the *correct answer* from the options given below:

	(*a*)	(*b*)	(*c*)	(*d*)
A.	(*iii*)	(*ii*)	(*i*)	(*iv*)
B.	(*i*)	(*iv*)	(*iii*)	(*ii*)
C.	(*iii*)	(*iv*)	(*i*)	(*ii*)
D.	(*i*)	(*ii*)	(*iv*)	(*iii*)

Directions (Qs. No. 96-100): *Read the passage and answer the questions:*

Good governance has 8 major characteristics. It is participatory, consensus oriented, accountable, transparent, responsive, effective and efficient, equitable and inclusive and follows the rule of law. It assures that corruption is minimized, the views of minorities are taken into account and that the voices of the most vulnerable in society are heard in decision-making. It is also responsive to the present and future needs of society.

Participation by both men and women is a key cornerstone of good governance. Participation could be either direct or through legitimate intermediate institutions or representatives. It is important to point out that representative democracy does not necessarily mean that the concerns of the most vulnerable in society would be taken into consideration in decision making. Participation needs to be informed and organized. This means freedom of association and expression on the one hand and an organized civil society on the other hand.

Good governance requires fair legal frameworks that are enforced impartially. It also requires full protection of human rights, particularly those of minorities. Impartial enforcement of laws requires an independent judiciary and an impartial and incorruptible police force.

Transparency means that decisions taken and their enforcement are done in a manner that follows rules and regulations. It also means that information is freely available and directly accessible to those who will be affected by such decisions and their enforcement. It also means that enough information is provided and that it is provided in easily understandable forms and media.

Good governance requires that institutions and processes try to serve all stakeholders within a reasonable time-frame. There are several actors and as many view points in a given society. Good governance requires mediation of the different interests in society to reach a broad consenses in society on what is in the best interest of the whole community and how this can be achieved. It also requires a broad and long-term perspective on what is needed for sustainable human development and how to achieve the goals of such development. This can only result from and understanding of the historical, cultural and social contexts of a given society or community.

A society's well being depends on ensuring that all its members feel that they have a stake in it and do not feel excluded from the mainstream of society. This requires all groups, particularly the most vulnerable, have opportunities to improve or maintain their well being.

Good governance means that processes and institutions produce results that meet the needs of society while making the best use of resources at their disposal. The concept of efficiency in the context of good governance also covers the sustainable use of natural resources and the protection of the environment.

96. Identify the major characteriste of Good Governance.

(*a*) Inclusiveness

(*b*) Transparent and responsive

(*c*) Elite-Centric

(*d*) Concentrates on present needs of the society only

Choose the *correct answer* from the options given below:

A. (*a*), (*b*), (*c*) only B. (*b*), (*c*) only

C. (*a*), (*b*), (*d*) only D. (*a*), (*b*) only

97. Transparency can't be explained as:

A. Restricted access to information

B. Decision as per rules and regulations

C. Incorruptable police force

D. Mediation of different interest in society

98. Which among the following is not related to the concept of efficiency in the context of good governance?

A. Protection of environment

B. Sustainable use of natural resources

C. Exclusions from the mainstream of the society

D. Understanding the contexts of society

99. Given below are two statements: One is labelled as Assertion (A) and the other is labelled as Reason (R).

Assertion (A) : Participation needs to be informed and organised.

Reason (R) : Representative democracy does not mean that the most vulnerable in the society will be part of decision making.

In the light of the above statements, choose the *correct answer* from the options given below:

A. Both (A) and (R) are true and (R) is the correct explanation of (A)

B. Both (A) and (R) are true but (R) is not the correct explanation of (A)

C. (A) is true but (R) is false

D. (A) is false but (R) is true

100. Which among the following characteristics is/are related to Good Governance:

(*a*) Fair legal frameworks

(*b*) Impartiality

(*c*) Protection of Minorities

(*d*) Centralised judiciary system.

Choose the *correct answer* from the options given below:

A. (*a*), (*c*), (*d*) only

B. (*b*), (*c*), (*d*) only

C. (*a*), (*b*), (*c*) only

D. (*a*), (*b*), (*c*), (*d*)

ANSWERS

1. **(B):** Rational Choice Institutionalism (RCI) is a theoretical approach to the study of institutions arguing that actors use institutions to maximize their utility, and that institutions affect rational individual behaviour. Rational Choice Institutionalism arose initially from the study of congressional behaviour in the U.S. in the late 1970s. Influential early RCI scholarship was done by political economists at California Institute of Technology, University of Rochester, and Washington University. It employs analytical tools borrowed from neo-classical economics to explain how institutions are created, the behaviour of political actors within it, and the outcome of strategic interaction. It follows a deductive approach.

2. **(C):** Except Kisan Nyay Yojana rest all schemes are launched by the current Central Government. The Kisan Nyay Yojana was launched by the Chhattisgarh Government on May 21, 2020, the death anniversary of former Prime Minister Rajiv Gandhi. This scheme encourages farmers to produce more crops and help them get the right price.

3. **(B):** On 18 May 1974 Indira Gandhi gave the go-ahead for India's first nuclear test in Pokhran in the Rajasthan desert. This explosion was labelled by the Indian government as a 'Peaceful Nuclear Explosion' (PNE). This could have been construed as major shift in Indian foreign policy, but it was "not even acknowledged as an act of foreign policy".

4. **(B):** Black Skin, White Masks is a 1952 book by philosopher Frantz Fanon. The book is written in the style of auto ethnography, in which Fanon shares his own experiences while presenting a historical critique of the effects of racism and dehumanization, inherent in situations of colonial domination, on the human psyche. There is a double process that is economic and internalized through the epidermalization of inferiority.

   The violent overtones in Fanon can be broken down into two categories: The violence of the colonizer through annihilation of body, psyche, culture, along with the demarcation of space. And secondly the violence of the colonized as an attempt to retrieve dignity, sense of self, and history through anti-colonial struggle.

5. **(B)**

6. **(A): Siegfried Newmann** defined revolution as "a sweeping fundamental change in political organization, social structure, economic property control and the predominant myth of a social order (thereby) indicating a major break in the continuity of development."

7. **(C):** The term "Lokpal" was coined by Dr. L.M. Singhvi in 1963. The concept of a constitutional ombudsman was first proposed in parliament by Law Minister Ashoke Kumar Sen in the early 1960s. The first Jan Lokpal Bill was proposed by Adv Shanti Bhushan in 1968 and passed in the 4th Lok Sabha in 1969, but did not pass through the Rajya Sabha. Subsequently, 'lokpal bills' were introduced in 1971, 1977, 1985, again by Ashoke Kumar Sen, while serving as Law Minister in the Rajiv Gandhi cabinet, and again in 1989, 1996, 1998, 2001, 2005 and in 2008, yet they were never passed. Forty five years after its first introduction and after ten failed attempts, the Lokpal Bill was finally enacted in India on 18 December 2013 after the tenth attempt. President gave his assent to Lokpal and Lokayuktas Act on 1 January, 2014.

8. **(B):** No money bill can be introduced without the governor's recommendation. Such a bill is a government bill and can be introduced

only by a minister. It can be introduced only in legislative assembly. The bill if passed goes to the legislative council.

9. (A): The Shiromani Akali Dal (SAD) is a centre-right Sikh-centric state political party in Punjab. The party is the second-oldest in India, after Congress, being founded in 1920.

The Dravida Munnetra Kazhagam (DMK) is a political party based in the state of Tamil Nadu. The DMK was founded in 1949 by the former chief minister of Tamil Nadu C. N. Annadurai (Anna) as a breakaway faction from the Dravidar Kazhagam headed by E.V. Ramasami (Periyar).

The Telugu Desam Party (TDP) is an Indian regional political party with great influence in the state of Andhra Pradesh and Telangana. It is founded by the former chief minister of Andhra Pradesh N. T. Rama Rao (N.T.R.) in 1982.

The Biju Janata Dal (BJD) is a regional political party in the Indian state of Odisha founded and led by Naveen Patnaik, the current Chief Minister of Odisha. It was founded in 1997.

10. (C) **11. (*)** **12. (B)**

13. (B): The Universal Declaration of Human Rights (UDHR) is an international document adopted by the United Nations General Assembly in 1948 that enshrines the rights and freedoms of all human beings.

The International Covenant on Economic, Social and Cultural Rights (ICESCR) is a multilateral treaty adopted by the United Nations General Assembly (GA) in 1966, and came into force from 3 January, 1976.

The United Nations Conference on Environment and Development (UNCED), also known as the 'Earth Summit', was held in Rio de Janeiro, Brazil, from 3-14 June, 1992.

Kyoto Protocol was an international treaty that extended the 1992 United Nations Framework Convention on Climate Change that commits state parties to reduce greenhouse gas emissions. The objective of the Kyoto Protocol is to reduce carbon dioxide emissions and the presence of greenhouse gases (GHG) in the atmosphere. The lessening of the number of emissions by industrialized nations was the essential belief of this agreement. The Kyoto Protocol was adopted on 11 December 1997, entered into force on 16 February 2005, and currently, there are 192 parties associated with it.

14. (D): When public policy is to be analyzed, two main aspects of the policy demands particular attention. Those two aspects are the "effects" of the policy and "implementation". The effects part helps gauge the effectiveness of the policy in terms of addressing the problem it intended to address. Since many policies are brought about with good intentions and on paper seem effective but fail to address the problems, due to deficiencies within the implementation phase of the policies. The 5-E approach of policy analysis is one of the basic models of analyzing public policies and within this approach the policies are measured up to five benchmarks; Effectiveness, Efficiency, Ethical Considerations, Evaluation of Alternatives and Establishment of Recommendations.

15. (A) **16. (B)**

17. (C): Rise of the Plebeians: The Changing Face of the Indian Legislative Assemblies was authored by Christophe Jaffrelot and Sanjay Kumar. This book is highly recommended to readers interested in the current dynamics of Indian politics, specifically with regard to the rise of 'the plebeians' to power, offering clear historical insights on some of the major Indian states and central issues concerning Indian politics.

18. (B): (*i*) Tashkent Agreement took place in the year 1966.

(*ii*) Indo-Soviet Friendship Treaty took place in the year 1971.

(*iii*) In 1999, India and Pakistan signed the Lahore Declaration.

(*iv*) Indo-US Nuclear Treaty took place in the year 2005.

19. (A): The Civil Liability for Nuclear Damage Act, 2010 aims to cater to the civil requirements for victims of those who were affected due to nuclear disasters. This act ensures apt compensation as a helping hand for the victims.

India-US ten year frameworks Agreement for Defence Co-operation came into force in 2015. This agreement reflects the need for Defence agreements between both the nations and the strengthening of Defence capabilities. A joint production of next-generation protective ensembles and mobile electric hybrid power sources, cooperation in the development of jet engines, aircraft carrier designs and construction, are also constituent concerns of the Framework Agreement. Most significant of all is the notion of 'Make in India', which encapsulates the din and intends to make it get executed through the American Defence conglomerates setting factory and shop in India.

20. (C): Ramsay Muir writes, "Socialism is a chameleon-like creed. It changes its colour according to its environments. For the street comer and the club room, it wears the flaming scarlet of class war; for the intellectuals it is red shot with tawny; for the sentimentalists, it becomes a delicate rose pink, and in clerical circles it assumes a virgin white just touched with a faint flush of generous aspiration."

21. (A)

22. (B): Yoga is an ancient physical, mental and spiritual practice that originated in India. The word 'yoga' derives from Sanskrit and means to join or to unite, symbolizing the union of body and consciousness. Today it is practiced in various forms around the world and continues to grow in popularity.

Recognizing its universal appeal, on 11 December 2014, the United Nations proclaimed 21 June as the International Day of Yoga by resolution 69/131. The International Day of Yoga aims to raise awareness worldwide of the many benefits of practicing yoga.

The draft resolution establishing the International Day of Yoga was proposed by India and endorsed by a record 175 member states. The proposal was first introduced by Prime Minister Narendra Modi in his address during the opening of the 69th session of the General Assembly, in which he said: "Yoga is an invaluable gift from our ancient tradition. Yoga embodies unity of mind and body, thought and action ... a holistic approach [that] is valuable to our health and our well-being. Yoga is not just about exercise; it is a way to discover the sense of oneness with you, the world and the nature."

23. (A): The word "ecology" was coined by the German scientist Ernst Haeckel in 1866. Ernst Heinrich Philipp August Haeckel was a German zoologist. He also coined the terms like phylum, phylogeny, and Protista.

24. (A): The growth of Cooperative federalism in India is due to Union-State collaboration in economic matters and legislative relations. In Cooperative federalism the Centre and states share a horizontal relationship, where they "cooperate" in the larger public interest. It is an important tool to enable states' participation in the formulation and implementation of national policies. Union and the states are constitutionally obliged to cooperate with each other on the matters specified in Schedule VII of the constitution.

25. (B)

26. (B): SAARC was founded by seven states in 1985. In 2005, Afghanistan requested its accession to SAARC and formally applied for membership in the same year. This organization was formed in Dhaka on

December 8, 1985, and its secretariat is based in Kathmandu, Nepal. SAARC comprises of 8 member states and 9 observer states.

Neighbourhood First Policy of India, a core component of India's foreign policy, focuses on peaceful relations and collaborative synergetic co-development with its South Asian neighbours of the Indian subcontinent encompassing a diverse range of topics, such as economic, technology, research and education, connectivity (digital, surface and air transport, energy grid connectivity, logistic chains, etc), space program, defence security, environment and climate challenge. It was conceived by Narendra Modi as his priority, in early days of which then Foreign Minister Sushma Swaraj played an important role, was taken forward by former Foreign Secretaries and next Foreign Minister S. Jaishankar, all of these were supported by the important roles played by NSA, Ajit Doval, and several successive Foreign Secretaries.

27. (A): In Gender in International Relations, **J. Ann Tickner** extends and applies a variety of contemporary feminist perspectives to the phenomena of international relations. These new ways of seeing suggest constructive criticisms of realist, liberal, and Marxist theories, and in particular reveal gender differences and inequalities in the historical construction of state identities and citizen responsibilities. Tickner explores economic and environmental concerns, asking what difference it makes when gender relations are introduced into the analysis. She demonstrates how a feminist perspective on international relations changes and expands our view of the global system. Having introduced a gendered perspective on international relations, the author links it to recent critiques of realism and neorealism, which she claims are inadequate for explaining international politics today. In addition, the book explores the ways in which the world economy has differentially rewarded men and women, and re-examines the gender implications of modern mankind's domination over nature. This review of gender differences in political, military, economic, and ecological relations offers a new view of the insecurities faced by women and men in world politics. Tickner's feminist reconceptualization of security deepens and recasts recent theoretical efforts in international relations to construct more adequate security arrangements, both comprehensive and common.

28. (C)

29. (C): The Rajamandala (or Raja-mandala meaning "circle of kings") was formulated by the Indian author Chanakya (Kautilya) in his work on politics, the Arthashastra . It describes circles of friendly and enemy states surrounding the king's (raja) state. Also known as Mandala theory of foreign policy or Mandala theory, the theory has been called as one of Kautilya's most important postulations regarding foreign policy.

30. (B): The Vice-President of India is the second-highest constitutional office in India, after the President. **Article 63** of Indian Constitution states that there shall be a Vice-President of India. The Vice President shall act as President in the absence of the President due to death, resignation, impeachment, or other situations. The Vice President of India is also ex-officio Chairperson of the Rajya Sabha. While he discharges the functions of the President he will not perform the duties of the office of Chairman of the Council of States.

Article 66 of the Indian Constitution states the manner of election of the Vice-President. The Vice-President is elected indirectly by members of an electoral college consisting of the members of both Houses of Parliament in accordance with the system of Proportional Representation by means of the Single transferable vote and the voting is by secret ballot.

31. (A): Aristotle is one of the greatest philosophers, and his moral and political philosophy remains especially influential. But he also believed that, for some people, being enslaved was just and even beneficial for them.

In *Politics 1,* Aristotle uses the method of his biological investigations and nine principles regarding causation and the working of nature known from his physics, psychology, and biology to demonstrate that the barbarians are natural slaves. His procedure is in line with his general way of thinking.

32. (A): Political modernisation stands for the transformation of the political culture in response to the changes in social and physical environment. Huntington describes modernisation as, "a multi-faceted process involving change in all areas of human thought and activity". Modernisation is a process which affects men of all levels. It brings changes which are psychological, social, political, economic, cultural, intellectual and demographic.

Characteristics of Political Modernisation:

1. Application of technology and mechanisation
2. Industrialisation
3. Urbanisation
4. Increase national income and per capita income
5. Growth of literacy
6. Political mobilisation
7. Mass-media
8. Social mobility
9. National identity

Agents of Modernisation:

1. Colonialism
2. Elite
3. Military Leaders
4. Political Parties
5. Bureaucracy

33. (D): Rabindranath Tagore talked about 'Nationalism and Synthetic Universalism'. For Tagore Nationalism was a great menace. He talks about why he withdrew his support from the National movement as the Indian political parties who earlier had few grievances against the colonial power started asking for autonomy. They lacked any real program or constructive measures, they just wanted higher representation. India does not need begging; it needs constructive growth from within. He also criticized the extremists in the Indian National congress who are blindly following the revolution and adopting violent measures for their nation but in reality, ignoring the real sufferings of its own people. He calls the youth to control its temperament before it is too late. The Indians still ride on their high horses by calling their rigid social organization its glory but it will cause a state of paralysis for India. They criticize the educated classes for their inability to solve the problem in our social structure. Their social structure is perfect and that is why they only work towards political ends and not social.

The Idea of Nationalism breeds separatism. Tagore rejected the idea of a Nation and called for the federation of man. He believed in the cosmopolitan world where people will iron out their differences and follow the path of humanity which is their true higher self. He firmly believes that there is a harmony of completeness in humanity. There will be a world where the downtrodden will not suffer anymore and all will gain freedom with unity. For Tagore *"when a man does not realize his kinship with the world, he lives in a prison house whose walls are alien to him."*

34. (B): War on terrorism, term used to describe the American-led global counterterrorism campaign launched in response to the terrorist attacks of September 11, 2001. In its scope, expenditure, and impact on international relations, the war on terrorism was comparable to the Cold War; it was intended to represent a new phase in global political relations and has had important consequences for security, human rights, international law, cooperation, and governance.

Viktor Fedorovych Yanukovych is a former politician who served as the fourth president of Ukraine from 2010 until he was removed from office in the Revolution of Dignity in 2014, after a long series of protests in support of closer ties with the European Union by diverse civil-society groups in response to his rejection of the Ukrainian-European Association Agreement. From 2006 to 2007 he was the prime minister of Ukraine; he also served in this post from November 2002 to January 2005, with a short interruption in December 2004. He currently lives in exile in Russia, where he has lived since his removal from office in 2014.

35. (A)

36. (D): Para diplomacy as it is conducted by sub-state governments introduces the idea of decentralisation of political power to make regional governments prominent actors in the international sphere.

While the Modi government can be credited for bringing paradiplomacy to the centre-stage of Indian policy-making, the idea of international relations being forged at the subnational level is not a new one. With the growing policymaking capacity of sub-state entities paradiplomacy can be employed by states, provinces and even cities both in federal as well as unitary states for solving diplomatic issues.

37. (B)

38. (A): Right to Freedom of Religion: The Constitution of India guarantees the right to freedom of religion to not only individuals but also religious groups in India. This is enshrined in Articles 25 to 28.

Article 25 (Freedom of conscience and free profession, practice, and propagation of religion)

Article 26 (Freedom to manage religious affairs)

Article 27 (Freedom as to payment of taxes for promotion of any particular religion)

Article 28 (Freedom as to attendance at religious instruction or religious worship in certain educational institutions)

39. (B): Doklam is an area disputed between China and Bhutan located near their tri-junction with India. Unlike China and Bhutan, India does not claim Doklam but supports Bhutan's claim.

On 21 April, 2019, Easter Sunday, three churches in Sri Lanka and three luxury hotels in the commercial capital, Colombo, were targeted in a series of coordinated Islamist terrorist suicide bombings. Later that day, there were smaller explosions at a housing complex in Dematagoda and a guest house in Dehiwala. A total of 269 people were killed, including at least 45 foreign nationals, three police officers, and eight bombers and at least 500 were injured.

40. (B)

41. (C): 'Brexit' is the name given to the United Kingdom's departure from the European Union. It is a combination of 'Britain' and 'exit'.

On 23 June, 2016, the UK held a referendum on its membership of the EU. The question facing voters was: 'Should the United Kingdom remain a member of the European Union or leave the European Union?' 51.89% of voters voted to leave the EU. The UK left the EU on 31 January, 2020.

42. (D) **43. (A)**

44. (A): A.V. Dicey wrote the book, 'Introduction to the Study of the Law of the Constitution' which was published in 1885 in which he identified the term 'Rule of Law'.

45. (C): A citizen is a participatory member of a political community. Citizenship is gained by meeting the legal requirements of a national, state, or local government. A nation grants certain rights and privileges to its citizens. In return, citizens are expected to obey their country's laws and defend it against its enemies.

The value of citizenship varies from nation to nation. In some countries, citizenship can mean a citizen has the right to vote, the right to hold government offices, and the right to collect unemployment insurance payments. Living in a country does not mean that a person is necessarily a citizen of that country. Citizens of one country who live in a foreign country are known as aliens. Their rights and duties are determined by political treaties and by the laws of the country in which they stay.

The principal grounds for acquiring citizenship (apart from international transactions such as transfer of territory or option) are birth within a certain territory, descent from a citizen parent, marriage to a citizen, and naturalization. There are two main systems used to determine citizenship as of the time of birth: jus soli, whereby citizenship is acquired by birth within the territory of the state, regardless of parental citizenship; and jus sanguinis, whereby a person, wherever born, is a citizen of the state if, at the time of his or her birth, his or her parent is one.

46. (D)

47. (D): The important works of Rousseau:

1. A discourse on the Moral Effects of the Arts and Sciences (1751).
2. Discourse on the Origin and Basis of Inequality among Men (1755).
3. Political Economy (article 1755)
4. The Nouville Heloise (1760)
5. Emile (1762)
6. Social Contract (1762)

48. (A): The JP movement also known as Bihar Movement was a political movement initiated by students in the Indian state of Bihar in 1974 and led by the veteran Gandhian socialist Jayaprakash Narayan, popularly known as JP, against misrule and corruption in the state government. It later turned against Prime Minister Indira Gandhi's government in the central government. It was also called Sampoorna Kranti (Total Revolution Movement) and JP Movement.

Quit India Movement:

- In August 1942, Gandhiji started the 'Quit India Movement' and decided to launch a mass civil disobedience movement 'Do or Die' call to force the British to leave India.
- Also known as India August Movement or Bharat Chodo Andolan was launched at the Bombay session of the All India Congress Committee (AICC) by Mahatma Gandhi on August 8, 1942.

Civil Disobedience Movement:

- It was launched in March 1930 under the leadership of Gandhi.
- It began with the famous Dandi March of Gandhi.
- Dandi March from his Ashram at Sabarmati in Ahmedabad.
- Lord Irwin was viceroy during the launch of the Civil Disobedience Movement.
- Sarojini Naidu was among the leaders who accompanied Mahatma Gandhi during the Dandi March.
- Salt March is also known as Salt Satyagraha, Dandi March or Civil Disobedience Movement

Non-Cooperation Movement:

- The Non-Cooperation Movement led by Mahatma Gandhi was the first nationwide mass protest in the history of Indian Independence.
- The non-cooperation movement by Gandhiji was followed from September 1920 to February 1922.

49. (A): Article 243E:

1. Every Panchayat, unless sooner dissolved under any law for the time being in force, shall continue for five years from the date appointed for its first meeting and no longer.
2. No amendment of any law for the time being in force shall have the effect of causing dissolution of a Panchayat at any level, which is functioning immediately before such amendment, till the expiration of its duration specified in clause (1).
3. An election to constitute a Panchayat shall be completed—
   (*a*) before the expiry of its duration specified in clause (1);
   (*b*) before the expiration of a period of six months from the date of its dissolution: Provided that where the remainder of the period for which the dissolved Panchayat would have continued is less than six months, it shall not be necessary to hold any election under this clause for constituting the Panchayat for such period.
4. A Panchayat constituted upon the dissolution of a Panchayat before the expiration of its duration shall continue only for the remainder of the period for which the dissolved Panchayat would have continued under clause (1) had it not been so dissolved.

50. (D): SMART is a mnemonic acronym, giving criteria to guide in the setting of goals and objectives that are assumed to give better results, for example in project management, employee-performance management and personal development. The term was first proposed by George T. Doran in the November 1981 issue of Management Review. He suggested that goals should be SMART (Specific, Measurable, Assignable, Realistic and Time-related). Since then, other variations of the acronym have been used, a commonly used version includes the alternative words: attainable, relevant, and timely. Additional letters have been added by some authors.

Those who support the use of SMART objectives suggest they provide a clear road map for both the person setting the goal and the person evaluating their progress (e.g. employee and employer, or athlete and coach). The person setting the goal is said to gain a clear understanding of what needs to be delivered and the person evaluating can then assess the outcome based on defined criteria. SMART criteria are commonly associated with Duckers' management by objectives (MBO) concept.

51. (C): John Stuart Mill made a clear distinction between self-regarding and other-regarding actions. He argued that the individual is free to engage in self-regarding actions even when society considers those actions to be improper. However, a sanction may be imposed when such actions impinge upon the freedom of others.

Societal attitudes towards pornography are a good illustration of Mill's distinction between self-regarding actions and other-regarding actions. Whereas graphic images of pornographic acts undoubtedly have the capacity to offend, access to such material in the private realm does not directly impact upon others provided it does not cause actions that threaten other people's liberty. John Stuart Mill also put forward the renowned liberal argument that "the only purpose for which power can be rightly exercised over any member of a civilised community, against his will, is to prevent harm to others. His own good, either physical or moral, is not a sufficient warrant." This is a key point of departure between liberals and anarchists in terms of the libertarian side of the political spectrum.

52. (D): Committed Judiciary refers to the judiciary which is committed to uphold the policies of the government in power by interpreting the laws and the Constitution in a way palatable to the Government in power. If the judiciary is committed the 'independence of the judiciary' and the 'system of checks and balances,' which are essential features of the Constitution, will be in peril and constitutional democracy will be reduced to the tyranny of the majority.

The committed judiciary will also destroy the federal fabric which is internal part of basic structure of the Constitution. There would be a mutual distrust among the states of the Union of India. There are many disputes between the states and it has become a natural tendency to not trust the central government because they might sense that the ruling party at the Centre favours states where, too, it is in power.

53. (D): Arab Spring, wave of pro-democracy protests and uprisings that took place in the Middle East and North Africa beginning in 2010 and 2011, challenging some of the region's entrenched authoritarian regimes. The wave began when protests in Tunisia and Egypt toppled their regimes in quick succession, inspiring similar attempts in other Arab countries. Not every country saw success in the protest movement, however, and demonstrators expressing their political and economic grievances were often met with violent crackdowns by their countries' security forces.

The first demonstrations took place in central Tunisia in December 2010, catalyzed by the self-immolation of Mohamed Bouazizi, a 26-year-old street vendor protesting his treatment by local officials. A protest movement, dubbed the "Jasmine Revolution" in the media, quickly spread through the country. The Tunisian government attempted to end the unrest by using violence against street demonstrations and by offering political and economic concessions. However, protests soon overwhelmed the country's security forces, compelling President Zine al-Abidine Ben Ali to step down and flee the country on January 14, 2011. In October 2011, Tunisians participated in a free election to choose members of a council tasked with drafting a new constitution. A democratically chosen president and prime minister took office in December 2011, and a new constitution was promulgated in January 2014. In October–November 2019, Tunisia became the first country of the Arab Spring protests to undergo a peaceful transfer of power from one democratically elected government to another.

54. (A)

55. (A): Article 169-Abolition or creation of Legislative Councils in States:

1. Notwithstanding anything in Article 168, Parliament may by law provide for the abolition of the Legislative Council of a State having such a Council or for the creation of such a Council in a State having no such Council, if the Legislative Assembly of the State passes a resolution to that effect by a majority of the total membership of the Assembly and by a majority of not less than two thirds of the members of the Assembly present and voting.
2. Any law referred to in clause (1) shall contain such provisions for the amendment of this Constitution as may be necessary to give effect to the provisions of the law and may also contain such supplemental, incidental and consequential provisions as Parliament may deem necessary.
3. No such law as aforesaid shall be deemed to be an amendment of this Constitution for the purposes of Article 368.

56. (B): In politics (and particularly in international politics), soft power is the ability to co-opt rather than coerce (contrast hard power). In other words, soft power involves shaping the preferences of others through appeal and attraction. A defining feature of soft power is that it is non-coercive; the currency of soft power includes culture, political values, and foreign policies. In 2012, Joseph Nye of Harvard University explained that with soft power, "the best propaganda is not propaganda", further explaining that during the Information Age, "credibility is the scarcest resource".

Nye popularised the term in his 1990 book, *Bound to Lead: The Changing Nature of American Power*. In this book he wrote: "when one country gets other countries to want what it wants might be called co-optive or soft power in contrast with the hard or command power of ordering others to do what it wants". He further developed the concept in his 2004 book, *Soft Power: The Means to Success in World Politics*.

57. (C): Various committees and commissions have examined India's electoral system in detail. They have analyzed the working of election machinery as well as election process and suggested reforms.

Some of the Committees are:

(*a*) Tarkunde Committee – It was appointed in 1974 by Jaya Prakash Narayan (JP). It was during his "Total Revolution" movement. This was an unofficial committee and it submitted its report in 1975.

(*b*) Dinesh Goswami Committee on Electoral Reforms (1990).

(*c*) Vohra Committee on the Nexus between Crime and Politics (1993).

(*d*) Indrajit Gupta Committee on State Funding of Elections (1998) – It upheld the reasoning for introduction of state funding of elections. It also said that state funding of elections is in public interest and constitutionally and legally justified.

(*e*) Law Commission of India Report on Reform of the Electoral Laws (1999).

(*f*) National Commission to Review the Working of the Constitution (2000-2002) – It was headed by M. N. Venkatachaliah.

(*g*) Election Commission of India Report on Proposed Electoral Reforms (2004).

(*h*) Second Administrative Reforms Commission of India Report on Ethics in Governance (2007) – It was headed by Veerappa Moily.

(*i*) Tankha Committee – It was appointed in 2010. It was to look into the whole gamut of the election laws and electoral reforms.

58. (C): John Rawls's theory of justice is a sound theory which says that a well-ordered society needed a concept of justice as a basic requirement and that such a concept could be developed by rational individuals behind a 'veil of ignorance' about their own position, and that it would involve, primarily, equal right to basic liberties for all, and secondly that social and economic inequalities should derive from equal opportunities and in the end should benefit the least advantaged.

To provide a justification for political liberalism Rawls made an attempt to work out a theory of justice that would be appropriate for a 'well-ordered society'. To Rawls a well-ordered society or a good society should have two major aspects:

1. A society "as one designed to advance the good of its members and effectively regulated by a public conception of justice"
2. "... it is a society in which everyone accepts and knows that the others accept the same principle of justice and the basic social institutions satisfy and are known to satisfy these principles."

59. (A)

60. (C): Bipolarity was viewed both as an empirical condition and as a central explanatory concept, albeit contested, during the Cold War (1945–1989), when two superpowers dominated the international system. The United States and the Union of Soviet Socialist Republics (USSR) confronted each other as military and ideological rivals heading competing alliance systems—the North Atlantic Treaty Organization (NATO), founded in 1949, and the Warsaw Pact established in 1955. Nuclear weaponry added a new wrinkle to the global superpower competition, particularly after the Soviet Union broke the American nuclear monopoly in 1949.

The Cuban Missile Crisis of October 1962 was a direct and dangerous confrontation between the United States and the Soviet Union during the Cold War and was the moment when the two superpowers came closest to nuclear conflict. The crisis was unique in a number of ways, featuring calculations and miscalculations as well as direct and secret communications and miscommunications between the two sides. The dramatic crisis was also characterized by the fact that it was primarily played out at the White House and the Kremlin level with relatively little input from the respective bureaucracies typically involved in the foreign policy process.

61. **(A)**

62. **(B):** Government 2.0 refers to Government policies that arm to harness interactive Internet tools to create an open source computing platform. Every year, more governments are using technology to become more user-friendly and transparent for citizens, and, ultimately, more effective moving from old-style patronage politics to performance politics. Government 2.0 is a great place to start for government leaders who want to make the right choices to have the biggest impact.

63. **(C)**

64. **(C): Woodrow Wilson** (1856-1924) was an American politician, academic, and university administrator who served as the 28th President of the United States from 1913 until 1921. Wilson's article argues that the increasing complexity of society and corresponding issues of public policy require administrative methods of government to deal with. He argues that questions of administration are of more practical importance to the function of American government than constitutional questions:

The weightier debates of constitutional principle are even yet by no means concluded; but they are no longer of more immediate practical moment than questions of administration. It is getting to be harder to run a constitution than to frame one.

65. **(B):** Water is currently a source of some tension between India and Nepal but could become the greatest asset to the relationship if a more confident, respectful and cooperative approach is engineered by the two governments.

The BASIC countries (also Basic countries or BASIC) are a bloc of four large newly industrialized countries – Brazil, South Africa, India and China – formed by an agreement on 28 November 2009. The four committed to act jointly at the Copenhagen climate summit, including a possible united walk-out if their common minimum position was not met by the developed nations.

66. **(C):** The great Greek philosopher, Aristotle, was one of the first. He thought that slavery was a natural thing and that human beings came in two types - slaves and non-slaves. Some people, he said, was born natural slaves and ought to be slaves under any circumstances. Other people were born to rule these slaves, could use these slaves as they pleased and could treat them as property. Natural slaves were slaves because their souls weren't complete - they lacked certain qualities, such as the ability to think properly, and so they needed to have masters to tell them what to do.

It's clear that Aristotle thinks that slavery was good for those who were born natural slaves, as without masters they wouldn't have known how to run their lives. In fact Aristotle seems to have thought that slaves were 'living tools' rather like domestic animals, fit only for physical labour. Slaves were not totally incapable of thought, but they only needed minimal amount of rational ability; just enough to understand and carry out their duties.

Similarly, slaves were not devoid of 'virtue', but once again, they only needed just enough to carry out their duties. But that 'virtue' was enough for them to be treated as human beings. Aristotle doesn't provide any sensible practical method of recognising natural slaves, and without that it's inevitable that some people will be made slaves who should not be. Aristotle also had a category of 'legal slaves'; they weren't natural slaves but through bad luck - perhaps being taken prisoner in war - they just happened to be slaves at a particular time. Aristotle argued that if the world was just, the legal slaves would be freed, and if any natural slaves were by chance free, they should be made slaves.

67. (C): Pressure groups are involved in politics and policy making process in India through direct and indirect means. In the democratic functioning of a polity, pressure groups play a vital role. They seek to promote, discuss, debate and mobilize public opinion on major public issues. In this process, they educate people and widen their vision, enhance their democratic participation and raise and articulate various issues. These groups try to bring changes in public policy. To achieve their objectives and goals, the pressure groups employ various techniques and methods. These include appeals, petitions, demonstrations, picketing, lobbying, and processions. They also write in the media, distribute pamphlets, issue press releases, organize discussions and debates, put up posters and chant slogans. They may carry out satyagraha, that is, a non-violent protest. At times, pressure groups resort to strikes in order to pressurize the legislators, the executive officials, the decision-makers. Often, they resort to boycott.

68. (A): Interest groups play an important role in decision-making—an indispensable part of the modem governmental process. It allows orderly expression of public opinion and increase political participation. The role played by pressure/interest groups has now been widely recognized by political scientists the world over.

These groups often try to influence the legislature to promote, withdraw or repeal legislation.

Gabriel Almond (1970) has categorized these groups in terms of structural forms as under:

1. Institutional interest groups.
2. Non-associational interest groups.
3. Associational interest groups.
4. Anomic interest groups.

69. (A): India's government is a hybrid system. The hybrid system combines two classical models: British traditions based on parliamentary sovereignty and conventions and American principles based on written constitutions, separation of powers, and judicial review. Because parliamentary sovereignty and constitutional supremacy are incompatible, the two models are incompatible. Both British and American principles have left their imprint on India's Constitution. In other words, India has evolved a completely different politico-constitutional arrangement since the adoption of the 1950 Constitution, with elements of both British and American constitutional practises. The oddity is that, despite being parliamentary, India's political system does not fully correspond to the British system simply because it has adopted federal principles as well; it will never be completely American because India's Parliament remains sovereign.

India, as a hybrid political system, has contributed to a completely unique politico-constitutional arrangement known as parliamentary-federalism, which has no precedent in the history of constitutional development. The Indian political system, which is based on both parliamentary practises and federal principles, is thus a conceptual puzzle that reveals previously unknown aspects of the socio-political history of nation-states imbued with British traditions and American principles.

70. (D): The term "Open Door" also describes the economic policy initiated by **Deng Xiaoping** in 1978 to open China to foreign businesses that wanted to invest in the country. The policy set into motion the economic transformation of China. In the 20th and 21st centuries, scholars such as Christopher Layne in the neorealist school have generalized the use of the term to applications in 'political' open door policies and 'economic' open door policies of nations in general, which interact on a global or international basis.

71. (C): Project 'Mausam' is a Ministry of Culture project to be implemented by Indira Gandhi National Centre for the Arts (IGNCA), New Delhi as the nodal coordinating agency with support of Archaeological Survey of India and National Museum as associate bodies.

Project 'Mausam' aims to understand how the knowledge and manipulation of the monsoon winds has shaped interactions across the **Indian Ocean** and led to the spread of shared knowledge systems, traditions, technologies and ideas along maritime routes.

72. (A): Recently, NITI Aayog has released the **Multidimensional Poverty Index (MPI).** Earlier, Global Multidimensional Poverty Index 2021 was released by the United Nations Development Programme (UNDP) and the Oxford Poverty & Human Development Initiative (OPHI).

The MPI seeks to measure poverty across its multiple dimensions and in effect complements existing poverty statistics based on per capita consumption expenditure. It has three equally weighted dimensions – health, education, and standard of living. These three dimensions are represented by 12 indicators such as nutrition, school attendance, years of schooling, drinking water, sanitation, housing, bank accounts among others.

73. (D)

74. (D): Kautilya's *saptanga* (seven organs) theory of state illustrates a novel dimension of state power that dialectically engages political rationality and normatively; *artha* and *dharma* respectively.

Drawing from a complex political life, Kautilya hand picks a set of seven key structural elements *(prakritis)* as 'state factors' which together constitute state power. The seven *prakritis* are constitutive of the state – *swamin,* the ruler; *amatya,* the ministers; *janapada,* territory and population; *durga,* fort/capital city; *kosa:* treasury; *danda,* coercive power of the state and *mitra,* ally.

75. (C)

76. (D): Maximilian Karl Emil Weber was a German sociologist, historian, jurist and political economist, who is regarded as among the most important theorists of the development of modern Western society. His ideas profoundly influence social theory and research. While Weber did not see himself as a sociologist, he is recognized as one of the fathers of sociology along with Auguste Comte, Karl Marx, and Émile Durkheim.

Max Weber's bibliography:

The Protestant Ethic and the Spirit of Capitalism.

The Theory of Social and Economic Organization.

Economy and Society : An Outline of Interpretive Sociology.

Basic Concepts in Sociology.

77. (C) **78. (B)**

79. (A): Indian Agrarian system: Ambedkar studied the problems of small holdings in India and suggested remedies which are quite relevant even today. His views on land holding were published in paper titled "Small Holdings in India and their Remedies" published in September 1918 by Journal of the Indian Economic Society, Vol. 1. In the said paper he pointed out that the average size of holdings varies from 25.9 acres in the Bombay Presidency to an acre or two in Pimpla Saudagar, near Pune.

80. (B)

81. (C): Self-Respect Movement was a dynamic social movement aimed at destroying the contemporary Hindu social order in its totality and creating a new, rational society without caste, religion and god.

It was started by E.V. Ramaswamy Naicker (also known as Periyar by his followers) in Tamil Nadu in 1925. It was an egalitarian movement that propagated the ideologies of breaking down of the Brahminical hegemony, equal rights for the backward classes and women in the society and revitalization of the Dravidian languages like Telugu, Tamil, Kannada, and Malayalam.

A number of political parties in Tamil Nadu, such as Dravida Munnetra Kazhagam (DMK) and All India Anna Dravida Munnetra Kazhagam (AIADMK) owe their origins to the Self-respect movement.

82. (B)

83. (C): The History of England (1754–61) is David Hume's great work on the history of England (also covering Wales, Scotland and Ireland), which he wrote in instalments while he was librarian to the Faculty of Advocates in Edinburgh.

84. (C): Jean-Jacques Rousseau was a French political theorist and philosopher. He is regarded to be very influential because of his impact on the leaders of the French Revolution and the Age of Enlightenment. One of his most notable works is his theory surrounding inequality, as put forth in his book *Discourse on Inequality*. This book is a criticism of the modern world and provides insights into how society could have evolved.

Rousseau mentioned the existence of 2 types of inequalities – Natural and Moral or Social or Conventional. The former refers to inequalities arising from one's health conditions, age, or physical features. On the other hand, moral inequality is the one that is established by man. Of these 2 social inequalities, natural inequalities are genetic and cannot be prevented while moral inequalities are unnatural and can be prevented.

85. (B): Samuel P. Huntington points out the following nine characteristics of modernization, which are also used as indices of development:

1. Modernization and development are radical processes of change in technology and culture. These may be identified with the change from nomadic to agrarian age and the current change from agrarian to urban-industrial culture.
2. These are complex and multidimensional processes linked with cognitive, behavioural and institutional reform and structural reformations in society.
3. These are grand processes which originate at a place and then encompass other parts of the world with their ideology and technology.
4. These are long-term processes and develop in due course.
5. Both the concepts are systematic and change in one dimension entails change in others.
6. These processes involve several stages of change.
7. These are homogenizing processes under which variations between societies are reduced.

8. Both are irreversible processes, with occasional inconsistencies and commotions.
9. These are progressive, indispensable and desirable processes and contribute in the long run to physical and cultural prosperity of human beings.

86. (B): Hegel published his *Philosophy of Right* in 1821. Georg Wilhelm Friedrich Hegel (1770 –1831) was a Germanic philosopher. He is one of the most important figures in German idealism and one of the founding figures of modern Western philosophy. His influence extends across the entire range of contemporary philosophical issues, from epistemology and metaphysics to the philosophy of art, philosophy of history, philosophy of religion, political philosophy, and the history of philosophy.

87. (B) **88. (D)**

89. (A): During the Cultural Revolution, millions of educated youths were sent to rural areas to work in the countryside and learn from the peasantry. Mao believed that this would ultimately create a new society where there was no gap between urban and rural, labourers and intellectuals.

To Mao the revolution had to be a permanent process, constantly kept alive through unending class struggle. Hidden enemies in the party and intellectual circles had to be identified and removed. Conceived of as a "revolution to touch people's souls," the aim of the Cultural Revolution was to attack the Four Olds— old ideas, old culture, old customs, and old habits—in order to bring the areas of education, art and literature in line with Communist ideology. Anything that was suspected of being feudal or bourgeois was to be destroyed.

90. (B)	**91. (B)**	**92. (D)**
93. (C)	**94. (D)**	**95. (C)**
96. (D)	**97. (A)**	**98. (C)**
99. (B)	**100. (C)**	

Previous Years' Paper (Solved)

National Testing Agency (NTA)

UGC-NET Junior Research Fellowship & Assistant Professor Eligibility Exam

POLITICAL SCIENCE, June–2021

(Online exam held on 22-11-2021)

PAPER-II

1. Which one of the following statements is true?
   A. No rights can be given to a man against the social interest
   B. Grant of Rights has no concern with social interest
   C. Rights can have anti-social character
   D. Rights are a selfish claim

2. In which aspect does Modern Liberalism NOT believe?
   A. Social liberalism
   B. Positive freedom
   C. Cradle to grave welfare
   D. Minimal state

3. "We are witnessing the end of history as such that is, the endpoint of mankind's ideological evolution and the universalisation of western liberal democracy as the final form of human government". Whose thesis is this?
   A. Francis Fukuyama B. Daniel Bell
   C. Milton Friedman D. A MacIntyre

4. How was early liberalism characterised by C.B. Macpherson?
   A. Possessive liberalism
   B. Welfaristic
   C. Altruistic
   D. Developmental

5. Which one of the following theories is NOT related to Marx?
   A. Theory of Alienalism
   B. Theory of Surplus Value
   C. Dictatorship of Proletariat
   D. Origin of the Family, Private Property and the State

6. Who amongst the following stated that life is "a perpetual and restless desire for power after power, that ceaseth only in death"?
   A. Aristotle B. Machiavelli
   C. Hobbes D. Rousseau

7. Who amongst the following wrote *The Art of War*?
   A. Machiavelli B. Mao
   C. Hobbes D. Rousseau

8. "Revolutionary violence is not just cathartic but it also allows the colonial subjects to recreate themselves". Whose statement is this?
   A. Hannah Arendt B. Frantz Fanon
   C. Machiavelli D. Hobbes

9. Which one of the following is NOT a part of the political philosophy of Pandit Deen Dayal Upadhyaya?
   A. Consideration of man as atoms
   B. Cultural nationalism
   C. Integral humanism
   D. Democratic governance

10. "We will get nothing by appealing to or shouting hoarse in the ears of the British Bureaucracy in India". Who said this?
    A. Lala Lajpat Rai
    B. Subhash Chandra Bose
    C. B.R. Ambedkar
    D. Bal Gangadhar Tilak

11. Which among the following statements regarding citizenship in India is NOT correct?
    A. Citizenship provisions came into force on 26 November 1949.

B. A person who voluntarily acquires the citizenship of a foreign country ceases to be an Indian citizen.
C. A citizen of India can simultaneously be the citizen of another country.
D. The Parliament has the power to make provisions pertaining to acquisition and termination of citizenship.

12. Periyar E. V. Ramaswamy argued in favour of:
A. Caste based social system
B. Human dignity
C. Varnaashram system
D. Enhancing the status of Hindi in India

13. Who considered bureaucracy as the 'State's consciousness'?
A. Marx B. Lenin
C. Miliband D. Poulantzas

14. Which one of the following is NOT a function of political parties?
A. Formation of public opinion
B. Formation of government and alternate government
C. Political education to public
D. To control the judiciary

15. Which one of the following is NOT a characteristic of constitutionalism?
A. Value based concept
B. Culture based concept
C. Party based concept
D. Dynamic concept

16. Who among the following distinguished between interest articulation function and other anomic group functions?
A. Almond and Powell
B. Almond and Coleman
C. Jean Blondel
D. Hugh Heclo

17. India is NOT a member of which multilateral export control regime?
A. Missile Technology Control Regime (MTCR)
B. Nuclear Suppliers Group (NSG)
C. Wassenaar Arrangement (WA)
D. Australia Group (AG)

18. Which one of the following is NOT the core issue related to the neo-realist theory of International Relations?
A. Actors react in an anarchical environment
B. Structure is a major determinant of actor's behavior
C. States are always engaged in the process of monopoly capitalism
D. Distrust and fear among actors creates problem of security dilemma

19. Which one of the following is NOT a feature of 'Sustainable Development'?
A. Unrestrained development
B. Based on principle of generational equity
C. Development without environmental degradation
D. Meeting present needs, without compromising needs for future

20. Who among the following dependency theorists added the concept of 'Semi-Periphery'?
A. Raul Prebisch
B. Andre Gunder Frank
C. Henrique Fernando Cardoso
D. Immanuel Wallerstein

21. Leaders of which organization were invited during Prime Minister Narendra Modi's swearing-in-ceremony in 2014?
A. ASEAN B. SAARC
C. BIMSTEC D. SCO

22. Which of the following is NOT provided to the Indian diaspora under the 'Overseas Citizenship of India (OCI) scheme'?
A. Right for economic activities
B. Political rights as citizens
C. Educational rights
D. To acquire life time visa

23. Which agreement of defence cooperation was signed by India with USA in 2020?
A. Basic Exchange and Cooperation Agreement (BECA)
B. General Security of Military Information Agreement (GSOMIA)
C. Logistic Exchange and Memorandum Agreement (LEMOA)

D. Communication and Information Security Memorandum Agreement (CISMOA)

24. Name the boundary line between India and China:

A. Durand Line B. Radcliffe Line
C. McMahon Line D. Palk Strait

25. How long can the Vice-President act as President, when the office of President falls vacant?

A. Six months B. One year
C. Two years D. Five years

26. The superintendence, direction and control of elections to be vested in an Election Comission (Article 324 of the Constitution of India) came into force on :

A. 26 January 1950
B. 15 August 1947
C. 26 November 1949
D. 25 January 1950

27. By which Constitutional Amendment the word 'Socialist, Secular' and 'Integrity' were incorporated in our Constitution?

A. 40th Amendment B. 42nd Amendment
C. 44th Amendment D. 46th Amendment

28. Which one of the following functions is NOT the concern of the local government?

A. Public health
B. Sanitation
C. Public utility services
D. Maintenance of public order

29. Which one of the following statements does NOT characterise a social action group?

A. They are partisan groups
B. They are non-institutional organisations
C. They are non-autonomous groups dependent on the support of the government
D. They are non-professional formations

30. Who among the following referred to the Constituent Assembly of India as 'Microcosm in action'?

A. B. R. Ambedkar B. Granville Austin
C. Rajni Kothari D. Rajendra Prasad

31. Which of the following does NOT characterise electoral politics in India today?

A. Multi-party system
B. Coalition formation
C. Stabilization of the Congress dominance system
D. Increase in the scope of electoral choices of voters

32. Atmanirbhar Bharat Abhiyan was launched on:

A. 12th May 2020
B. 12th October 2020
C. 12th November 2020
D. 12th December 2020

33. Who coined the famous acronym "POSDCORB"?

A. Henry Fayol
B. Mary P. Follett
C. Gulick and Urwick
D. Frederick Taylor

34. Who wrote Reinventing Government (1992)?

A. Robert Denhardt
B. Pfiffner and Presthus
C. Osborne and Gaebler
D. Gordon Tullock

35. Who is called the father of 'Comparative Public Administration'?

A. Edward Wiedner B. Fred Riggs
C. Ferrel Heady D. Chester Barnard

36. Which of the following statements is incorrect about the "Human Relations Theory"?

A. Organization is to be viewed as a social system
B. Workers are human beings with all humanly attributes
C. Informal elements do not play an important role in the overall organizational output
D. Organization has social ethics, instead of individual ethics

37. In 1989, the World Bank conceptualised "Governance" in the context of which of the following nations?

A. United Kingdom
B. Australia
C. Sub-Saharan Africa
D. New Zealand

38. Who said that "Public Administration is the accomplishment of politically determined objectives"?
A. Woodrow Wilson
B. L. D. White
C. Carson and Harris
D. Dimock and Dimock

39. "Budget is a document containing a preliminary approval plan of public revenue and expenditure". Whose definition is this?
A. Leroy Beaulieu B. Robert Walpole
C. Reno Storm D. Willoughby

40. Who has been the most prominent among the Chicago school economists?
A. Adam Smith B. Milton Friedman
C. Carl Menger D. Fredrick Hayek

41. Who among the following are not supporters of positive liberty?
(*a*) T. H. Green (*b*) John Locke
(*c*) Harold Laski (*d*) Jeremy Bentham

Choose the correct answer from the options given below:
A. (*a*) and (*b*) only B. (*b*) and (*d*) only
C. (*a*) and (*c*) only D. (*c*) and (*d*) only

42. What are the central beliefs of conservatism?
(*a*) Tradition
(*b*) Hierarchy and Authority
(*c*) Social Darwinism
(*d*) Social Liberalism

Choose the correct answer from the options given below:
A. (*a*) and (*c*) only B. (*a*) and (*b*) only
C. (*b*) and (*c*) only D. (*a*) and (*d*) only

43. Which of the following aspects have been defended by J. S. Mill?
(*a*) The rights of women
(*b*) Bentham's utilitarianism in toto
(*c*) Married woman's property bill
(*d*) Patriarchy

Choose the correct answer from the options given below:
A. (*a*) and (*c*) only B. (*b*) and (*d*) only
C. (*c*) and (*d*) only D. (*a*) and (*d*) only

44. Which of the following statements about Hegel are true?
(*a*) State is the march of God on Earth
(*b*) Hegel regarded women as inferior, with less reasoning abilities
(*c*) Hegel rejected the concept of civil society
(*d*) Hegel does not believe in war

Choose the correct answer from the options given below:
A. (*a*) and (*c*) only B. (*b*) and (*c*) only
C. (*c*) and (*d*) only D. (*a*) and (*b*) only

45. Which of the following about Raja Rammohan Roy are true?
(*a*) He was influenced by the Upanishads
(*b*) He was a rationalist and supporter of monotheism
(*c*) He was an atheist
(*d*) He was critical of the principle of trinitarianism advocated by Christianity

Choose the correct answer from the options given below:
A. (*a*), (*b*), (*c*) and (*d*)
B. (*a*), (*b*) and (*c*) only
C. (*a*), (*b*) and (*d*) only
D. (*b*), (*c*) and (*d*) only

46. Which of the following statements about Balgangadhar Tilak are true?
(*a*) He envisioned the formation of linguistic states
(*b*) He was both a restless nationalist and a realist
(*c*) He prefered political freedom over social reform
(*d*) For Tilak, political liberation and rights can be achieved through direct action and pressure

Choose the correct answer from the options given below:
A. (*a*), (*b*), (*c*) and (*d*)
B. (*b*), (*c*) and (*d*) only
C. (*a*) and (*b*) only
D. (*c*) and (*d*) only

47. Sri Aurobindo conceives nationalism as
(*a*) Spiritual nationalism, different from the western concept of nationalism

(*b*) A nation as an organism
(*c*) Nationalism as a religious aspiration and moral attitude
(*d*) Nation as a geographical entity

Choose the correct answer from the options given below:
A. (*a*), (*b*), (*c*) and (*d*)
B. (*a*), (*b*) and (*c*) only
C. (*b*) and (*c*) only
D. (*c*) and (*d*) only

48. Which of the following are prerequisites of the comparative method?
(*a*) Conceptual framework as a factor in unit selection
(*b*) Comparable conceptual issues as a focus of inquiry
(*c*) Definition of the focus of inquiry
(*d*) Theory building

Choose the correct answer from the options given below:
A. (*a*) and (*b*) only
B. (*a*), (*b*) and (*c*) only
C. (*a*), (*b*), (*c*) and (*d*)
D. (*a*) and (*d*) only

49. Which of the following are related to Karl W. Deutsch's approach of communication in Comparative Politics?
(*a*) Political system is like a machine working on the basis of information
(*b*) In his theory, homeostasis, instead of equilibrium, is used for dynamism
(*c*) Emphasis is given on structure and functionalism
(*d*) Output functions are given more importance

Choose the correct answer from the options given below:
A. (*b*) and (*c*) only B. (*c*) and (*d*) only
C. (*a*) and (*d*) only D. (*a*) and (*b*) only

50. Which amongst the following are reasons for the emergence of Neo-colonialism?
(*a*) Weakened position of European powers
(*b*) Rise of consciousness against imperialism
(*c*) India's foreign policy
(*d*) Japan's foreign policy

Choose the correct answer from the options given below:
A. (*a*) and (*b*) only B. (*b*) and (*c*) only
C. (*c*) and (*d*) only D. (*a*) and (*d*) only

51. Which of the following features are given in the UN Charter for preservation of peace?
(*a*) Peace-making procedure is given in Chapter-VI for the peaceful settlement of disputes
(*b*) Chapter-VIII deals with the peace-keeping activities
(*c*) Peace enforcement is given in Chapter-VII for coercive settlement of disputes
(*d*) Chapter-IX deals with economic cooperation among states

Choose the correct answer from the options given below:
A. (*a*) and (*b*) only B. (*a*) and (*c*) only
C. (*b*) and (*c*) only D. (*b*) and (*d*) only

52. Which of the following are true about the world system theory?
(*a*) It is influenced by the Marxian idea of accumulation of wealth
(*b*) On the basis of wealth accumulation, the world is divided between 'core', 'periphery' and 'semi-periphery'
(*c*) It involves important concepts like players, strategies, rules and outcomes
(*d*) It analyses the situation of conflict, competition and cooperation among states

Choose the correct answer from the options given below:
A. (*a*) and (*b*) only B. (*b*) and (*c*) only
C. (*c*) and (*d*) only D. (*a*) and (*d*) only

53. Which of the following are true about Regime Theory in International Politics?
(*a*) It is an attempt for the existence of rule-governed behavior in the anarchic international system
(*b*) They are to replace collective security system
(*c*) Major powers resolve conflicts through this mechanism
(*d*) They have been defined by principles, norms, rules and decision-making procedures

Choose the correct answer from the options given below:

A. (*a*) and (*b*) only B. (*b*) and (*c*) only

C. (*c*) and (*d*) only D. (*a*) and (*d*) only

54. Which of the following statements about India's foreign policy are true?

(*a*) India has signed the Land Boundary Agreement (LBA) with Bangladesh in 2015

(*b*) India has agreed to build Hambantota port in Sri Lanka in 2017

(*c*) India has signed a Strategic Partnership Agreement (SPA) with Afghanistan in 2011

(*d*) The regime of Abdulla Yameen (2013-2018) of Maldives was friendly with India

Choose the correct answer from the options given below:

A. (*a*) and (*b*) only B. (*b*) and (*c*) only

C. (*a*) and (*c*) only D. (*c*) and (*d*) only

55. Which of the following statements are incorrect with regard to the Finance Commission?

(*a*) The provision of Finance Commission has been mentioned in Article-280 of the Constitution.

(*b*) Finance Commission shall consist of Chairman and two members.

(*c*) Finance Commission submits its recommendations to the Parliament.

(*d*) The Parliament is authorized to determine the qualifications for appointment as member of the commission.

Choose the correct answer from the options given below:

A. (*a*) and (*b*) only B. (*b*) and (*c*) only

C. (*c*) and (*d*) only D. (*a*) and (*d*) only

56. In India's Foreign Policy, 'Indira Doctrine' is related to:

(*a*) It aims to make India a global power

(*b*) It is a policy to develop cooperation with neighbours

(*c*) It equates India's security with that of South Asia

(*d*) Any interference in the South Asian region will be considered a threat to India's security

Choose the correct answer from the options given below:

A. (*a*) and (*b*) only B. (*b*) and (*c*) only

C. (*c*) and (*d*) only D. (*a*) and (*d*) only

57. Which of the following are the exclusive powers of the Lok Sabha?

(*a*) Introduction of the money bill

(*b*) Ratification of the declaration of emergency

(*c*) To pass a motion of no-confidence against the council of ministers

(*d*) To impeach the President

Choose the correct answer from the options given below:

A. (*a*) and (*b*) only

B. (*a*) and (*c*) only

C. (*a*) and (*d*) only

D. (*a*), (*b*) and (*c*) only

58. The Supreme Court of India in its order dated 24th August 2017 in Justice. K.S. Puttaswamy (Retd) vs Union of India declared that:

(*a*) The right to privacy is protected as an intrinsic part of the right to life and personal liberty under Article 21 and as a part of the freedoms.

(*b*) The Union government must amend the Constitution and add a provision for the right to privacy.

(*c*) The right to privacy is protected by Article 14 (equality before the law), Article 19 (Right to freedom), Article 21 (Protection of life and personal liberty).

(*d*) Right to privacy is derived from Article 25 (Right to freedom of religion) and Article 14 (Protection of interests of minorities)

Choose the correct answer from the options given below:

A. (*a*) only B. (*b*) only

C. (*a*) and (*d*) only D. (*c*) and (*d*) only

59. Which of the following are the issues of debate in electoral politics?

(*a*) Electronic voting machine

(*b*) One nation, one election

(*c*) Single-member election commission

(*d*) Introduction of the two-children norm for eligibility to contest local elections

Choose the correct answer from the options given below:

A. (*a*) and (*b*) only

B. (*a*), (*b*) and (*c*) only

C. (*a*), (*b*) and (*d*) only

D. (*b*), (*c*) and (*d*) only

60. Labour movements in India suffers from

(*a*) Low membership

(*b*) Weak finances

(*c*) Multiplicity of union

(*d*) Presence of differentiated organizational structures for different classes of labor

Choose the correct answer from the options given below:

A. (*a*) and (*d*) only

B. (*b*) and (*c*) only

C. (*a*), (*b*) and (*c*) only

D. (*a*), (*b*), (*c*) and (*d*)

61. McGregor in his celebrated text, *The Human Side of the Enterprise* has given his famous "theoretical assumptions". Which of the following are the correct assumptions?

(*a*) The average human being, with relatively little ambition, prefers to be directed and wishes to avoid responsibility. Security is the main concern

(*b*) The average human being learns under proper conditions not only to accept but to seek responsibility

(*c*) The average human being has an innate antipathy to work, which he will avoid, if he can

(*d*) "Best management is a true science"

Choose the correct answer from the options given below:

A. (*a*) and (*b*) only

B. (*c*) and (*d*) only

C. (*a*) and (*d*) only

D. (*a*), (*b*) and (*c*) only

62. Performance-budget reflects how well a government entity is meeting its goals and objectives. Which of the following are the central point of Performance Budgeting?

(*a*) It requires the establishment of performance levels and the collection of information

(*b*) The amount of work that is done is measured

(*c*) The quality or the results of that work is measured

(*d*) This impacts how much money a department will receive in the future

Choose the correct answer from the options given below:

A. (*a*), (*b*) and (*c*) only

B. (*b*) and (*c*) only

C. (*a*), (*b*), (*c*) and (*d*) only

D. (*c*) and (*d*) only

63. Which of the following are the advanced ideas of Mary Follett?

(*a*) Functional Foremanship

(*b*) Constructive Conflict

(*c*) Zone of Acceptance

(*d*) Integration

Choose the correct answer from the options given below:

A. (*a*) and (*b*) only B. (*b*) and (*c*) only

C. (*c*) and (*d*) only D. (*b*) and (*d*) only

64. Which of the following are the schools of "New Right Ideology"?

(*a*) Austrian school

(*b*) Chicago school

(*c*) Frankfurt school

(*d*) New York school

Choose the correct answer from the options given below:

A. (*a*) and (*b*) only

B. (*a*) and (*d*) only

C. (*b*) and (*c*) only

D. (*a*) and (*c*) only

65. Which of the following were/are wage development and infrastructure development programmes?

(*a*) Crash Scheme of Rural Employment

(*b*) National Rural Employment Guarantee Programme

(*c*) Rural Landless Employment Guarantee Programme

(*d*) Changes in Agronomic Practices

Choose the correct answer from the options given below:

A. (*a*) and (*b*) only
B. (*a*) and (*d*) only
C. (*a*), (*b*) and (*c*) only
D. (*b*) and (*c*) only

66. Match List-I with List-II

List-I	List-II
(*a*) Catherine MacKinnon	(*i*) Feminism is for Everybody
(*b*) Susan Moller Okin	(*ii*) The Dialectic of Sex
(*c*) S. Firestone	(*iii*) Toward a Feminist Theory of State
(*d*) Bell Hook	(*iv*) Justice, Gender and the Family

Choose the correct answer from the options given below:

	(*a*)	(*b*)	(*c*)	(*d*)
A.	(*i*)	(*ii*)	(*iii*)	(*iv*)
B.	(*iii*)	(*iv*)	(*ii*)	(*i*)
C.	(*iv*)	(*iii*)	(*ii*)	(*i*)
D.	(*ii*)	(*i*)	(*iii*)	(*iv*)

67. Match List-I with List-II

List-I	List-II
(*a*) Bureaucratic Terror	(*i*) Frantz Fanon
(*b*) Cultural Revolution	(*ii*) Plato
(*c*) Apartheid	(*iii*) Mao Zedong
(*d*) Allegory of Caves	(*iv*) Hannah Arendt

Choose the correct answer from the options given below:

	(*a*)	(*b*)	(*c*)	(*d*)
A.	(*iv*)	(*iii*)	(*i*)	(*ii*)
B.	(*ii*)	(*i*)	(*iii*)	(*iv*)
C.	(*i*)	(*ii*)	(*iii*)	(*iv*)
D.	(*iii*)	(*iv*)	(*i*)	(*ii*)

68. Match List I with List II

List-I (*Books*)	List-II (*Author*)
(*a*) Fatawa-i-Jahandari	(*i*) Charles Bettelheim
(*b*) Thoughts on Linguistic States	(*ii*) M. N. Roy
(*c*) India Independent	(*iii*) Zia Barani
(*d*) The Future of Indian Policies	(*iv*) B.R. Ambedkar

Choose the correct answer from the options given below:

	(*a*)	(*b*)	(*c*)	(*d*)
A.	(*i*)	(*iii*)	(*ii*)	(*iv*)
B.	(*iii*)	(*iv*)	(*i*)	(*ii*)
C.	(*ii*)	(*i*)	(*iii*)	(*iv*)
D.	(*iv*)	(*ii*)	(*i*)	(*iii*)

69. Match List-I with List-II

List-I (*Authors*)	List-II (*Books*)
(*a*) Lord Bryce	(*i*) Comparative politics-A Developmental Approach
(*b*) Graham Wallace	(*ii*) New Aspects of Politics
(*c*) Gabriel Almond	(*iii*) Modern Democracies
(*d*) Charles E. Merriam	(*iv*) Human Nature in Politics

Choose the correct answer from the options given below:

	(*a*)	(*b*)	(*c*)	(*d*)
A.	(*i*)	(*ii*)	(*iii*)	(*iv*)
B.	(*iii*)	(*iv*)	(*i*)	(*ii*)
C.	(*iv*)	(*iii*)	(*ii*)	(*i*)
D.	(*ii*)	(*i*)	(*iv*)	(*iii*)

70. Match List-I with List-II

List-I	List-II
(*a*) SALT-I	(*i*) 1987
(*b*) SALT-II	(*ii*) 1990
(*c*) START-I	(*iii*) 1979
(*d*) INF Treaty	(*iv*) 1972

Choose the correct answer from the options given below:

	(a)	(b)	(c)	(d)
A.	(iv)	(iii)	(ii)	(i)
B.	(iii)	(ii)	(i)	(iv)
C.	(ii)	(iii)	(iv)	(i)
D.	(i)	(ii)	(iii)	(iv)

71. Match List-I with List-II

List-I	List-II
(a) Basic Exchange and Cooperation Agreement	(i) 2004
(b) Indo-US Civil Nuclear Deal	(ii) 2002
(c) High Technology Cooperation Groups	(iii) 2020
(d) Next Steps in Strategic Partnership	(iv) 2005

Choose the correct answer from the options given below:

	(a)	(b)	(c)	(d)
A.	(i)	(iii)	(iv)	(ii)
B.	(ii)	(i)	(iii)	(iv)
C.	(iv)	(ii)	(iii)	(i)
D.	(iii)	(iv)	(ii)	(i)

72. Match List-I with List-II:

List-I (Forms of Government)	List-II (Essential features)
(a) Cabinet Government	(i) Separation of powers
(b) Presidential Government	(ii) Collective responsibility
(c) Federal Government	(iii) Concentration of powers
(d) Unitary Government	(iv) Division of powers

Choose the correct answer from the options given below:

	(a)	(b)	(c)	(d)
A.	(iii)	(iv)	(i)	(ii)
B.	(ii)	(i)	(iv)	(iii)
C.	(i)	(ii)	(iii)	(iv)
D.	(iv)	(iii)	(ii)	(i)

73. Match List-I with List-II:

List-I (Author)	List-II (Books)
(a) Rabindra Ray	(i) The Naxalites and their Ideology
(b) Ashish Kumar Roy	(ii) The Spring Thunder and After
(c) Carole Spary	(iii) Gender, Development and the State in India
(d) Sanjay Kumar (ed)	(iv) Indian Youth and Educational Politics

Choose the correct answer from the options given below:

	(a)	(b)	(c)	(d)
A.	(i)	(ii)	(iii)	(iv)
B.	(ii)	(i)	(iv)	(iii)
C.	(iii)	(iv)	(ii)	(i)
D.	(iv)	(iii)	(i)	(ii)

74. Match List-I with List-II

List-I	List-II
(a) Decision Making	(i) Fred Riggs
(b) Ecological Approach	(ii) Edward Wiedner
(c) New Public Administration	(iii) Herbert Simon
(d) Development Administration	(iv) Minnowbrook Conference 1968

Choose the correct answer from the options given below:

	(a)	(b)	(c)	(d)
A.	(i)	(ii)	(iii)	(iv)
B.	(iii)	(i)	(iv)	(ii)
C.	(ii)	(iii)	(iv)	(i)
D.	(iv)	(iii)	(i)	(ii)

75. Match List-I with List-II

List-I	List-II
(a) Insurance Regulatory and Development Authority Act	(i) 1988
(b) Reserve Bank of India Act	(ii) 2003
(c) Fiscal Responsibility and Budget Management Act	(iii) 1999
(d) Prevention of Corruption (Amendment) Act	(iv) 1934

Choose the correct answer from the options given below:

	(a)	(b)	(c)	(d)
A.	(iii)	(iv)	(ii)	(i)
B.	(i)	(ii)	(iii)	(iv)
C.	(iv)	(iii)	(ii)	(i)
D.	(ii)	(iv)	(iii)	(i)

76. Arrange ideological focus of the Feminist movement under different stages in chronological order

(*a*) Focus on right to vote for women

(*b*) Focus on social and economic equality

(*c*) Focus on culture and context

(*d*) Focus on Ecofeminism

Choose the correct answer from the options given below:

A. (*a*), (*b*), (*c*), (*d*) B. (*d*), (*c*), (*b*), (*a*)

C. (*b*), (*c*), (*d*), (*a*) D. (*c*), (*b*), (*a*), (*d*)

77. Arrange the work of Hannah Arendt in ascending order

(*a*) The origin of totalitarianism

(*b*) The Human Condition

(*c*) On Revolution

(*d*) On Violence

Choose the correct answer from the options given below:

A. (*b*), (*c*), (*a*), (*d*) B. (*d*), (*b*), (*c*), (*a*)

C. (*a*), (*b*), (*c*), (*d*) D. (*c*), (*b*), (*a*), (*d*)

78. Arrange the following books written by B.R. Ambedkar in an ascending order

(*a*) Gandhi and Gandhism

(*b*) The problem of the Rupee: Its origin and its solution

(*c*) The Buddha and His Dhamma

(*d*) The Rise and Fall of Hindu Woman

Choose the correct answer from the options given below:

A. (*a*), (*b*), (*c*), (*d*) B. (*b*), (*d*), (*c*), (*a*)

C. (*d*), (*a*), (*b*), (*c*) D. (*c*), (*b*), (*d*), (*a*)

79. Arrange chronologically the following books in order of their publication:

(*a*) Contemporary Political Analysis by James C Charlesworth

(*b*) Modern Political Analysis by Robert A. Dahl

(*c*) The Process of Government by A.F. Bentley

(*d*) A System Analysis of Political life by David Easton

Choose the correct answer from the options given below:

A. (*a*), (*b*), (*c*), (*d*) B. (*b*), (*d*), (*c*), (*a*)

C. (*c*), (*b*), (*a*), (*d*) D. (*d*), (*c*), (*b*), (*a*)

80. Arrange the following international treaties in chronological order:

(*a*) Charter of the United Nations

(*b*) Treaty of Westphalia

(*c*) Treaty of Versailles

(*d*) Treaties of Utrecht

Choose the correct answer from the options given below:

A. (*a*), (*b*), (*c*), (*d*) B. (*c*), (*b*), (*d*), (*a*)

C. (*b*), (*d*), (*c*), (*a*) D. (*c*), (*a*), (*d*), (*b*)

81. Arrange the signing of the following agreements by India in order of their appearance:

(*a*) Land Boundary Agreement

(*b*) Tashkent Agreement

(*c*) Moscow Test Ban Treaty

(*d*) India-Russia Friendship Treaty

Choose the correct answer from the options given below:

A. (*c*), (*b*), (*d*), (*a*) B. (*b*), (*c*), (*a*), (*d*)

C. (*a*), (*c*), (*b*), (*d*) D. (*c*), (*d*), (*a*), (*b*)

82. Arrange the following in a chronological order:

(*a*) Communal Award

(*b*) Simon Commission

(*c*) First Round Table Conference

(*d*) Gandhi-Irwin Pact

Choose the correct answer from the options given below:

A. (*a*), (*b*), (*c*), (*d*) B. (*b*), (*c*), (*d*), (*a*)

C. (*c*), (*d*), (*a*), (*b*) D. (*d*), (*a*), (*b*), (*c*)

83. Arrange the following labour unions according to the year of their formation in descending order:

(*a*) INTUC
(*b*) Ahmedabad Textile Labour Association
(*c*) Bhartiya Mazdoor Sangh
(*d*) Bombay Mill Hands Association

Choose the correct answer from the options given below:

A. (*c*), (*a*), (*b*), (*d*) B. (*a*), (*b*), (*d*), (*c*)
C. (*d*), (*a*), (*c*), (*b*) D. (*b*), (*d*), (*a*), (*c*)

84. Rensis Likert has identified four systems of management on the basis of nature of authority and control of organization. Arrange in ascending order of efficiency

(*a*) Benevolent-Authority
(*b*) Consultative Leadership
(*c*) Participative
(*d*) Exploitative Authoritative

Choose the correct answer from the options given below:

A. (*a*), (*b*), (*c*), (*d*) B. (*d*), (*a*), (*b*), (*c*)
C. (*c*), (*b*), (*a*), (*d*) D. (*b*), (*a*), (*c*), (*d*)

85. Arrange the following books according to the years of their publication–

(*a*) Dror, *Yehezkel. Public Policy Making Re-examined*
(*b*) Dye, Thomas R. *Understanding Public Policy*
(*c*) Bhattacharya, Mohit. *New Horizons of Public Administration*
(*d*) Anderson, James E. *Public Policy Making*

Choose the correct answer from the options given below:

A. (*a*), (*b*), (*c*), (*d*) B. (*b*), (*d*), (*c*), (*a*)
C. (*b*), (*a*), (*d*), (*c*) D. (*d*), (*c*), (*a*), (*b*)

86. Given below are two statements, one is labelled as Assertion (A) and the other is labelled as Reason (R).

Assertion A: B.R. Ambedkar was critical of the existing federal structure.

Reason (R): The local self-governments neither have legislative power nor executive power in the real sense of the term, according to Ambedkar.

In light of the above statements, choose the correct answer from the options given below:

A. Both (A) and (R) are true and (R) is the correct explanation of (A)
B. Both (A) and (R) are true, but (R) is NOT the correct explanation of (A)
C. (A) is true, but (R) is false
D. (A) is false, but (R) is true

87. Given below are two statements, one is labelled as Assertion (A) and the other is labelled as Reason (R).

Assertion A: John Locke was portrayed as possessive individualist.

Reason (R): John Locke was not in favour of merely maximising interest.

In light of the above statements, choose the most appropriate answer from the options given below:

A. Both (A) and (R) are correct and (R) is the correct explanation of (A).
B. Both (A) and (R) are correct, but (R) is NOT the correct explanation of (A).
C. (A) is correct, but (R) is not correct
D. (A) is not correct, but (R) is correct

88. Given below are two statements

Statement I: Issues of peace and security are decided by 2/3 majority, including five permanent members, by the UN Security Council.

Statement II: UN Security Council represents all regions of the world in adequate manner.

In light of the above statements, choose the correct answer from the options given below:

A. Both Statement I and Statement II are true
B. Both Statement I and Statement II are false
C. Statement I is true, but Statement II is false
D. Statement I is false, but Statement II is true

89. Given below are two statements, one is labelled as Assertion (A) and the other is labelled as Reason (R).

Assertion (A): India supports global nuclear disarmament, but wishes to retain the option of "credible minimum deterrence".

Reason (R): Indian nuclear policy is rooted to meet, both its global and regional concerns.

In light of the above statements, choose the most appropriate answer from the options given below:

A. Both (A) and (R) are correct and (R) is the correct explanation of (A).

B. Both (A) and (R) are correct, but (R) is NOT the correct explanation of (A).

C. (A) is correct, but (R) is not correct.

D. (A) is not correct, but (R) is correct.

90. Given below are two statements, one is labelled as Assertion (A) and the other is labelled as Reason (R).

Assertion (A): India is illustrative of 'holding together' federation due to circumstances in which centre agreed to 'devolve' power for holding the federal units together.

Reason (R): This asymmetry of power division, along with era of coalitions and weaker governments at centre, let to assertion for demand of autonomy by states.

In light of the above statements, choose the correct answer from the options given below:

A. Both (A) and (R) are true and (R) is the correct explanation of (A)

B. Both (A) and (R) are true, but (R) is NOT the correct explanation of (A).

C. (A) is true, but (R) is false.

D. (A) is false, but (R) is true.

Directions (Qs. No. 91-95): *Read the following passage and answer the questions.*

Like in many other areas, even with regard to the question of women, Marx made Hegel the starting point. Hegel regarded women as inferior, with less reasoning abilities, seeing the natural differences between men and women as immutable.

Marx did not say much on the role and position of women. He took it for granted that Socialism would bring about their emancipation. In the German Ideology and the Capital, he spoke of the natural and spontaneous division of labour within the family. The natural relationship paved the way for social one, and the first property relationship was the one when the man regarded his wife and children as his slaves. The man had power over them, and could do with their labour as he chose, though Marx did not explain how this came about. Marx did not focus his attention on the position and role of women.

Engels, in the Origins, provided a materialist account of the origins of patriarchy, and linked women's subordination with the rise of private property. In the Holy Family, Marx and Engels observed that the degree of emancipation of women could be used as a standard bv which one could measure general emancipation. Marx reiterated this view in a letter to Dr. L. Kugelmann in 1868 that social progress could be assessed exactly by the social position of women. In 1845, Marx warned against treating the family regardless of its specific historic setting. In his criticism of Max Stirner (1805-1856), he observed that it was a misconception to speak of the family without qualification. Historically, the bourgeoisie endowed the family with the characteristics of the bourgeois family, whose ties were boredom and money.

91. According to Karl Marx, women emancipation can be judged from which of the following?

A. Division of Labour

B. Means of Production

C. Class Character

D. General Emancipation

92. Prior to Marx, which political thinker had a gender bias in his/her writings?

A. Hegel

B. J. S. Mill

C. Plato

D. Mary Wollstonecraft

93. Write the full name of Engels' book "Origins"?

A. *The Origins of Family and the State*

B. *The Origins of Family and Private Property*

C. *The Origins of the Family, Private Property and the State*

D. *The Origins of Family and State Property*

94. Social position of women vis-a-vis family can be judged by which nature of the family?
A. Educational background
B. Historical setting
C. Number of family members
D. Income of the family

95. What has been the general understanding about women's emancipation under Marxian philosophy?
A. Marx understood the women's position very correctly
B. Marx did not analyse women's condition beyond socialism
C. Due to class division, women got inferior status
D. Men and women had equal status

Directions (Qs. No. 96-100): *Read the following passage and answer the questions.*

Over the course of the 1990s, the question of the Indian state's relationship to the diaspora-formerly treated as more or less settled-once again came to the forefront of policy debates. Developments within diaspora communities, particularly in the United States served to facilitate this process. Chief among them was the creation of the 'Global Organization of People of Indian Origin' (GOPIO) in 1989, and the establishment of the 'India Caucus' within the US Congress in 1993. While the former served to provide a semblance of coherence to the interests of a variegated community, the latter suggested the potential for at least a section amongst the Indian diaspora to be conscious political actors in their adopted homeland. GOPIO members, for instance, kept alive the question of institutional recognition of the special place of the diaspora by proposing the idea of a 'Person of Indian Origin' card in their meetings with Indian government representatives in the mid-1990s.

Within the United States, politically active lobbyists of Indian origin became *de facto* spokespersons for the then Indian government, particularly in the aftermath of the nuclear tests of 1998. The support of these groups in mitigating the post-tests economic sanctions imposed by the United States, along with their enthusiastic response to the 'Resurgent India' bonds issued by the Indian government in the immediate aftermath of the nuclear tests as a measure to withstand the sanctions, was cited as an important indication of the continued commitment of the diaspora to the homeland. It was a commitment that according to the Indian government needed to be officially recognized in the new millennium.

96. Why debate on Indian diaspora got prominence for India's foreign policy makers?
A. Due to changed political milieu in the USA
B. India's economic thrust towards West Asia
C. Resurgence among the Indian Community
D. Compulsions of the Globalization process in India

97. What has been the task of 'Global Organization of People of Indian Origin' (GOPIO)?
A. Articulate the demands of NRIs
B. Representing articulated interests of various people of India origin
C. Increase in Indian cultural activities
D. Linkage between Bollywood and Holywood

98. What is the main task of 'India Caucus'?
A. To influence US policy making toward India
B. To form union of PIOs
C. To act as a linkage between PIOs and Government
D. To provide feedback to the Indian Government

99. Which organization gave the idea of issuing 'PIO Card' by Government of India?
A. GOPIO
B. India Caucus
C. Indo-US Association
D. NRIs Association

100. Why PIOs got significant attention during the end of 1990s?
A. Emerging Indo-US economic cooperation
B. Indo-US Nuclear civil deal
C. Pokhran-II and American sanctions
D. India-America defence deal

ANSWERS

1	2	3	4	5	6	7	8	9	10
A	D	A	A	D	C	A	B	A	D
11	**12**	**13**	**14**	**15**	**16**	**17**	**18**	**19**	**20**
C	B	A	D	C	B	B	C	A	D
21	**22**	**23**	**24**	**25**	**26**	**27**	**28**	**29**	**30**
B	B	A	C	A	C	B	D	C	B
31	**32**	**33**	**34**	**35**	**36**	**37**	**38**	**39**	**40**
C	A	C	C	B	C	C	A	C	B
41	**42**	**43**	**44**	**45**	**46**	**47**	**48**	**49**	**50**
B	B	A	D	C	A	B	B	D	A
51	**52**	**53**	**54**	**55**	**56**	**57**	**58**	**59**	**60**
B	A	D	C	B	C	B	A	C	C
61	**62**	**63**	**64**	**65**	**66**	**67**	**68**	**69**	**70**
D	C	D	A	C	B	A	B	B	A
71	**72**	**73**	**74**	**75**	**76**	**77**	**78**	**79**	**80**
D	B	A	B	A	A	C	B	*	C
81	**82**	**83**	**84**	**85**	**86**	**87**	**88**	**89**	**90**
A	B	A	B	*	A	B	C	A	B
91	**92**	**93**	**94**	**95**	**96**	**97**	**98**	**99**	**100**
D	A	C	B	B	D	B	A	A	C

EXPLANATORY ANSWERS

1. Universal Declaration of Human Rights:

Article 29

Everyone has duties to the community in which alone the free and full development of his personality is possible.

In the exercise of his rights and freedoms, everyone shall be subject only to such limitations as are determined by law solely for the purpose of securing due recognition and respect for the rights and freedoms of others and of meeting the just requirements of morality, public order and the general welfare in a democratic society.

On the basis of above mentioned principle no rights can be given to a man against the social interest.

2. Modern liberals differ from classical liberals in that they support an enabling state. This is where the state helps to protect individual freedoms by exercising a wider range of social and economic responsibilities than a minimal state. This involves reducing inequality, to help provide equality of opportunity for all, even the least well-off. Modern liberalism therefore supports welfarism. This was seen through the actions of the Liberal government of the early 1900s, which introduced old-age pensions and National Insurance. The Beveridge Report of 1942 reported that much of the British population were held back by the 'five giants': want (poverty), ignorance (lack of education), disease (ill health), squalor (poor living conditions) and idleness (unemployment).

Modern liberals suggest that the government had a responsibility to remove these, as they were barriers to freedom.

Modern liberalism also supports 'Keynesianism'—a rejection of classical liberal laissez-faire economics, based on the ideas of the economist John Maynard Keynes (1883-1946). Keynes rejected a self-regulating market and said that governments can influence 'aggregate demand' (the total amount people are spending in the economy) by spending its own money in the economy. The way to boost an economy would therefore be to increase spending OR cut taxes—to encourage people to spend more. Economic problems can be solved by government intervention, for example running a budget deficit (spending more than you have coming in). Keynes was not opposed to capitalism; he just acknowledged that an unrestricted market would not always be workable. His ideas became accepted practice for western countries by the mid-20th century, until the 1970s.

3. According to Francis Fukuyama, "We are witnessing the end of history as such that is, the endpoint of mankind's ideological evolution and the universalisation of western liberal democracy as the final form of human government".

Francis Fukuyama is a conservative political philosopher and economist. He was politically active during the Reagan administration, when he worked for the State Department, and also during the Clinton years, mainly through Washington think tanks. During the earlier years, Fukuyama was interested in US foreign policy, later becoming increasingly interested in broader, long-term political goals in the hope of providing solutions to problems on a global scale. He wrote *The End of History and the Last Man* in 1992 as an attempt to solve some of these problems. His contention in this book is that liberal democracy is the final form of government for the world, and the end of human ideological struggle.

4. C.B. Macpherson was a political philosopher who placed a genuinely novel interpretation on the history of political thought in The Political Theory of Possessive Individualism: Hobbes to Locke when the book appeared in 1962. Macpherson was a Canadian philosopher who influenced quite a few young scholars in the 1970s in North America and Great Britain. Macpherson offered the basis of a strong critique of a certain kind of liberalism — the liberalism that places essentially the whole normative weight on the value of the individual and his/her liberties, and essentially no emphasis on the social obligations we all have towards each other. A first wave of criticism of narrow liberalism took this form:

The repair that was needed [to liberal theory] was one that would bring back a sense of the moral worth of the individual, and combine it again with a sense of the moral value of community, which had been present in some measure in the Puritan and Lockean theory.

5. The Origin of the Family, Private Property and the State is not related to Marx. It is a work of Friedrich Engels. The Origin of the Family, Private Property and the State (1884), was a provocative and profoundly influential critique of the Victorian nuclear family. Engels argued that the traditional monogamous household was in fact a recent construct, closely bound up with capitalist societies. Under this patriarchal system, women were servants and, effectively, prostitutes. Only Communism would herald the dawn of communal living and a new sexual freedom and, in turn, the role of the state would become superfluous.

6. One of the most important political theorists of all time is Thomas Hobbes. The influence of Thomas Hobbes derives from the book 'Leviathan' and his creation of a social contract. As befits the grandiose title of his work, Leviathan truly is a landmark piece in the history of political theory. Hobbes could genuinely be termed a pioneer in terms of providing a philosophical construct for the Westphalian system and for a social contract with an authoritarian role for the state.

Thomas Hobbes was born in an era characterised by a search for stability in an inherently unstable world, and this undoubtedly shaped his world-view. It is not hard to see why anyone who experienced the destruction and havoc caused by the English Civil War traversed the intellectual path that Hobbes did. According to Hobbes, the relationships that govern human nature are characterised as "a perpetual and restless desire for power after power that ceaseth only in death." Whilst there are some things we would not do in the pursuit of power - perhaps because they are morally reprehensible or simply illegal - life is nothing more than a struggle for power.

In the absence of a social contract, Hobbes memorably described life in a state of nature as "solitary, poor, nasty, brutish and short" and characterised by "a war of all against all." In a state of nature no-one would be strong enough to live in total security. Social order therefore demands a decisive and coercive role for the state. As such, Hobbes prescribes a dominant role for the state (or Leviathan) to prevent anarchy and to ensure that contracts are upheld because "covenants, without the sword, are but words."

7. Niccolò Machiavelli's *Art of War* is one of the world's great classics of military and political theory. Praised by the finest military minds in history and said to have influenced no lesser lights than Frederick the Great and Napoleon, the Art of War is essential reading for anyone who wants to understand the history and theory of war in the West—and for readers of *The Prince and Discourse on Livy* who seek to explore more fully the connection between war and politics in Machiavelli's thought.

8. Frantz Fanon made this statement, "Revolutionary violence is not just cathartic but it also allows the colonial subjects to recreate themselves". Frantz Fanon's approach to violence and its effects on the individual is uniquely guided by his lived experience. Fanon's outlines both the potentialities and negative aspects of violence. His most famous and controversial remarks are those around the cathartic and self-actualising affect that violence can have on a colonial subject.

9. Pandit Deendayal Upadhyaya devised the political philosophy Integral Humanism, which advocates the simultaneous and integrated program of the body, mind and intellect and soul of each human being.

This philosophy of his is a synthesis of the material and the spiritual; the individual and the collective.

For India, he visualised a decentralised polity and self-reliant economy with the village being the core basis — which thought of India as an independent nation which cannot rely upon Western concepts like individualism, democracy, socialism, communism or capitalism.

Deendayal was of the view that India is in urgent need of a 'fresh breeze' to get rid of the post-independence westernisation.

He felt Indian intellect had been suffocated, and Indian polity was no more rooted in the traditions of our ancient culture.

This, as per Upadhyaya, left a 'roadblock' to the growth of Bharatiya thought.

When it came to modern technology, he wanted it to be adapted, but in such a way that it suits Indian requirements.

10. Tilak was the first political Leader to break through the routine of its somewhat academic methods, to bridge the gulf between the present and the past and to restore continuity to the political life of the nation. He developed a language and a spirit and used methods which indianized the movement and brought into the masses. Tilak had not faith in the constitutional method adopted by Gokhle and others to achieve their goal. He pointed out that the constitutional method might be very appropriate in a country like Britain where there is a constitution and a responsible government for the public. But it is totally inapplicable to a country like India where the penal code is the constitution and the people have no democratic means to change the government. He asserted that Indian could not base their agitation on law because the law could be changed by the irresponsible and autocratic government at any point of time and in any manner it like. About the ineffectiveness of the Constitutional method he wrote in Kesari, "We will get nothing by appealing to or shouting hoarse in the ears of the British bureaucracy in India. It is like breaking our heads against a stone wall. He was off the opinion that the British government is unresponsive to the demands of the Congress leaders, because it was convinced that they could 'only bark and had no teeth to bite.' Thus he adopted a method of agitation which must heart the Britist government.

12. E.V. Ramasamy (1879-1973), popularly known as EVR, is hailed as 'Periyar' by his followers. He was a demagogue who used the social evils which were then prevalent, or perceived, as a capital for his propaganda. He was neither a rationalist nor a humanist. He was anti-Hindu and pro-British.

Periyar was a prolific writer and orator, who could communicate with all sections of society effectively. He has argued that nationalism will make sense only when 'a nation's citizens could realise their ideal, without having to forgo or compromise on their dignity'. His complex idea of the free nation included ideals such as 'an all-round growth of knowledge, spread of education, the cultivation of rational thought, work, industry, equality, unity, initiative and honesty and the abolition of poverty, injustice and untouchability'.

13. According to Karl Marx,

The bureaucracy is the state formalism of civil society. It is the state's consciousness, the state's will, the state's power, as a Corporation. (The universal interest can ,behave vis-a-vis the particular only as a particular so long as the particular behaves vis-a-vis the universal as a universal. The bureaucracy must thus defend the imaginary universality of particular interest, *i.e.*, the Corporation mind, in order to defend the imaginary particularity of the universal interests, *i.e.*, its own mind. The state must be Corporation so long as the Corporation wishes to be state.) Being the state's consciousness, will, and power as a Corporation, the bureaucracy is thus a particular, closed society within the state. The bureaucracy wills the Corporation as an imaginary power. To be sure, the individual Corporation also has this will for its particular interest in opposition to the bureaucracy, but it wills the bureaucracy against the other Corporation, against the other particular interest. The bureaucracy as the completed Corporation therefore wins the day over the Corporation which is like incomplete bureaucracy. It reduces the Corporation to an appearance, or wishes to do so, but wishes this appearance to exist and to believe in its own existence. The Corporation is civil society's attempt to become state; but the bureaucracy is the state which has really made itself into civil society.

14. Functions of a Political Party:

- A political party contests elections by putting up candidates.
- In countries like the USA, the candidates are selected by members and supporters of a party.
- On the other hand, in countries like India, the candidates are chosen by top party leaders.
- Every party has different policies and programmes. Voters make a choice in

accordance with the policies and programmes liked by them.

- In a democratic country, a large group of people that has certain similar opinions group together and form a party. Then, give a direction to the policies adopted by the government.
- Those parties which lose elections form the opposition. They voice different views and criticise the government for their failures and mobilize opposition to the government.
- Political parties shape public opinion and Political education to public. With the help of the pressure groups, the parties launch movements for solving problems faced by the people.
- Parties even offer access to government machinery and welfare schemes. The local party leader serves as a link between the citizen and the government officer.

17. The Nuclear Suppliers Group (NSG) is a group of nuclear supplier countries that seeks to contribute to the non-proliferation of nuclear weapons through the implementation of two sets of Guidelines for nuclear exports and nuclear-related exports.

The NSG came into being as a response to the 1974 nuclear tests by India. There is a Trigger List and items from the list are forbidden to be exported to Non-NPT member countries.

It has 48 participating governments. China is a member of the NSG but not of the Wassenaar Arrangement or the MTCR.

India is not a member of the NSG because all its efforts were consistently blocked by China and some other members. India's bid for membership being blocked on the ground of India being a non-signatory to the nuclear non-proliferation treaty.

China demanded for a non-discriminatory procedures for entry of the countries that haven't signed NPT. China to further obstruct India's membership demand, had clubbed India's membership bid with that of Pakistan's. However, Pakistan's credentials for membership is extremely inaccurate.

19. Unrestrained development is not a feature of 'Sustainable Development'. Sustainable development is defined as the development that meets the present needs without compromising the ability of future generations to meet their own needs. The statement is reliable and provides a goal to which many people desire, though it provides no guidance or no assurance on how to assess progress towards sustainable development. The term sustainability is often referred to as "sustainable development". Development may be regarded as the defined growth and hence sustainable development means refining the problem caused by, but not challenging, continuous economic growth. The term "sustainable development" gained wide popularity in the international scientific community after the renowned report "Our Common Future" was published by the World Commission on Environment and Development in 1987.

20. World Systems Theory, like dependency theory, suggests that wealthy countries benefit from other countries and exploit those countries' citizens. In contrast to dependency theory, however, this model recognizes the minimal benefits that are enjoyed by low status countries in the world system. The theory originated with sociologist Immanuel Wallerstein, who suggests that the way a country is integrated into the capitalist world system determines how economic development takes place in that country.

According to Wallerstein, the world economic system is divided into a hierarchy of three types of countries: core, semi-peripheral, and peripheral. Core countries (e.g., U.S., Japan, Germany) are dominant, capitalist countries characterized by high levels of industrialization and urbanization.

Core countries are capital intensive, have high wages and high technology production patterns and lower amounts of labour exploitation and coercion. Peripheral countries (e.g., most African countries and low income countries in South America) are dependent on core countries for capital and are less industrialized and urbanized. Peripheral countries are usually agrarian, have low literacy rates and lack consistent Internet access. Semi-peripheral countries (e.g., South Korea, Taiwan, Mexico, Brazil, India, Nigeria, South Africa) are less developed than core nations but more developed than peripheral nations. They are the buffer between core and peripheral countries.

Core countries own most of the world's capital and technology and have great control over world trade and economic agreements. They are also the cultural centres which attract artists and intellectuals. Peripheral countries generally provide labour and materials to core countries. Semi-peripheral countries exploit peripheral countries, just as core countries exploit both semi-peripheral and peripheral countries. Core countries extract raw materials with little cost. They can also set the prices for the agricultural products that peripheral countries export regardless of market prices, forcing small farmers to abandon their fields because they can't afford to pay for labour and fertilizer. The wealthy in peripheral countries benefit from the labour of poor workers and from their own economic relations with core country capitalists.

23. India and the United States on October 27, 2020 signed the Basic Exchange and Cooperation Agreement (BECA), which, along with the two agreements signed earlier— the Logistics Exchange Memorandum of Agreement (LEMOA) and the Communications Compatibility and Security Agreement (COMCASA) - completes a troika of "foundational pacts" for deep military cooperation between the two countries.

BECA will help India get real-time access to American geospatial intelligence that will enhance the accuracy of automated systems and weapons like missiles and armed drones. Through the sharing of information on maps and satellite images, it will help India access topographical and aeronautical data, and advanced products that will aid in navigation and targeting.

24. The McMahon Line marks the boundary between the China-occupied territory of the East-Himalayan region and the Indian regions. This region is a mountainous place of high altitude. This line was determined by Sir Henry McMahon, then Foreign Secretary in the Government of British India, and it is called the McMahon Line after his name. The length of this line is 890 kilometers.

The McMahon line was the result of the Shimla Treaty of 1914 which took place between India and Tibet. But China does not accept this agreement and line.

The Shimla Treaty was signed between the representatives of India and Tibet for clear demarcation in 1914. China was not present in this agreement treaty because till this time Tibet was an independent region, that is why there was no requirement of the Chinese representation at the time of this Treaty.

25. Since the vacancy of the president should be filled with in six months according to article-62, so a vice president can be a president up to maximum six months.

The Vice-President acts as President, during casual vacancy in the office of the President by reason of death, resignation or removal or otherwise, until a new President is elected as soon as practicable and, in no case, later than six months from the date of occurrence of the vacancy. When the President is unable to discharge his functions owing to absence, illness or any other cause, the Vice-President discharges those functions till the President resumes office. During this period, the Vice-President has all the powers, immunities and privileges of the President and receives emoluments and allowances payable to the President.

27. The 'Preamble' of the Constitution of India is a brief introductory statement that sets out the guiding purpose and principles of the document, and it indicates the source from which the document which derives its authority, meaning, the people

- It was adopted on 26 November 1949 by the Constituent Assembly of India and came into effect on 26th January 1950.
- After the 42nd amendment, three new terms "Socialist, Secular, and Integrity" were added to the Preamble.
  - 42nd Amendment Act, 1976 is one of the most important amendments to the Indian Constitution.
  - It was enacted by the Indian National Congress headed by Indira Gandhi then.
  - Due to the large number of amendments this act has brought to the Indian Constitution, it is also known as the 'Mini-Constitution'.
- Only one time the Preamble was amended in 1976 till date.

30. 'Granville Austin referred to the Constituent Assembly of India as 'Microcosm in action'.

Prof. Austin in his scholarly analysis of the Indian constitution, which he described it as, "first and foremost a social document".

"The Indians' sense of their rich cultural heritage, their record of professional achievements in the arts and sciences of the modern world, and their faith in their ability to govern themselves, combined to give them a national maturity that allowed a reasoned approach to the creation and working of government."

Thus wrote Granville Austin, renowned scholar of the Indian constitution and constitutional assembly debates, in his seminal tome, 'The Indian Constitution: Cornerstone of a Nation.'

32. Atmanirbhar Bharat Abhiyaan or Self-reliant India campaign is the vision of new India envisaged by the Hon'ble Prime Minister Shri Narendra Modi. On 12 May 2020, our PM raised a clarion call to the nation giving a kick start to the Atmanirbhar Bharat Abhiyaan (Self-reliant India campaign) and announced the Special economic and comprehensive package of INR 20 lakh crores — equivalent to 10% of India's GDP — to fight COVID-19 pandemic in India.

The aim is to make the country and its citizens independent and self-reliant in all senses. He further outlined five pillars of Aatma Nirbhar Bharat—Economy, Infrastructure, Technology driven System, Vibrant Demography and Demand. Finance Minister further announces Government Reforms and Enablers across Seven Sectors under Aatmanirbhar Bharat Abhiyaan.

The government took several bold reforms such as Supply Chain Reforms for Agriculture, Rational Tax Systems, Simple & Clear Laws, Capable Human Resource and Strong Financial System.

33. POSDCORB is an acronym which means Planning, Organizing, Staffing, Directing, Coordinating, Reporting and Budgeting which was first coined in a paper on administrative management that was written for the Brownlow Committee by Luther Gulick and Lyndall Urwick. POSDCORB can be used as a systematic framework for efficiently executing business processes in a company or by an individual.

POSDCORB can be explained sequentially in detail below:

1. **Planning:** This essentially refers to establishing a broad sketch of the work to be completed and the procedures incorporated to implement them.

Planning is the first and most important step in POSDCORB as it sets the overall structure of the process with activities and timelines.

2. **Organizing:** Organizing involves formally classifying, defining and synchronizing the various sub-processes or subdivisions of the work to be done.

   It makes sure that the activities and timelines in the first step of planning are refined and organized further so that right people can be staffed to execute these tasks.

3. **Staffing:** This involves recruiting and selecting the right candidates for the job and facilitating their orientation and training while maintaining a favourable work environment.

4. **Directing:** This entails decision making and delegating structured instructions and orders to execute them.

   Directing is an important step in the POSDCORB cycle as it makes thing happen by giving clear objectives to teams and individuals.

5. **Coordinating:** This basically refers to orchestrating and interlinking the various components of the work.

6. **Reporting:** Reporting involves regularly updating the superior about the progress or the work related activities. The information dissemination can be through records or inspection.

7. **Budgeting:** Budgeting involves all the activities that under Auditing, Accounting, Fiscal Planning and Control.

34. The book, Reinventing Government which heralded the birth of new public management is written by David Osborne and Ted Gaebler in 1992.

35. Comparative public administration gained prominence in 1962 when the Ford Foundation received significant funding to run the Comparative Administrative Group (CAG) within the American Society for Public Administration. Throughout the sixties, the CAG organized many research, essays, experimental lectures, and special seminars with administrators. This CAG was led by Fred Riggs. He gave a theoretical form to comparative public administration.

He spreads the discussion of public administration outside the United States, especially in Third World countries. And facilitates the path of comparative analysis within the administrations of Third World countries. That is why Fred Riggs has been called the father of comparative public administration for his outstanding contributions. The other contributors to this field are Leonard White, Robert Dahl, Farrell Heady, Ramesh Arora, Paul Mayer, etc.

38. Woodrow Wiison states that "Public administration is the accomplishment of politically determined objectives". Public administration must be concerned with policy, searching for ways to solve problems and attain society's goals.

To them therefore public administration is mainly pre-occupied with the daily work of government (implementing public policies and not private or individual policies), therefore public interest is of paramount concern. Public Administration is the machinery for implementing government policy".

39. **Budget:** Important Definitions:

(1) According to Rene Stourn, "The budget is a document containing a preliminary approval plan of public revenue and expenditure."

(2) According to Findlay Shirras, "A budget in short includes a statement of the receipts and expenditure of the previous year, an estimate of the receipts and expenditure of the ensuring financial year and proposals as to meet ways and means for meeting a deficit or distributing a surplus, if any."

(3) According to P.F. Taylor, "Budget is a master financial plan of the government. It

brings together estimates of anticipated revenue and proposed expenditures for the budget year".

40. The Chicago school of economics is a neoclassical school of economic thought associated with the work of the faculty at the University of Chicago, some of whom have constructed and popularized its principles. Milton Friedman and George Stigler are considered the leading scholars of the Chicago school.

Chicago macroeconomic theory rejected Keynesianism in favour of monetarism until the mid-1970s, when it turned to new classical macroeconomics heavily based on the concept of rational expectations. The freshwater-saltwater distinction is largely antiquated today, as the two traditions have heavily incorporated ideas from each other. Specifically, new Keynesian economics was developed as a response to new classical economics, electing to incorporate the insight of rational expectations without giving up the traditional Keynesian focus on imperfect competition and sticky wages.

Chicago economists have also left their intellectual influence in other fields, notably in pioneering public choice theory and law and economics, which have led to revolutionary changes in the study of political science and law. Other economists affiliated with Chicago have made their impact in fields as diverse as social economics and economic history.

42. Conservatism, political doctrine that emphasizes the value of traditional institutions and practices.

Conservatism is a preference for the historically inherited rather than the abstract and ideal. This preference has traditionally rested on an organic conception of society-that is, on the belief that society is not merely a loose collection of individuals but a living organism comprising closely connected, interdependent members. Conservatives thus favour institutions and practices that have evolved gradually and are manifestations of continuity and stability. Government's responsibility is to be the servant, not the master, of existing ways of life, and politicians must therefore resist the temptation to transform society and politics. This suspicion of government activism distinguishes conservatism not only from radical forms of political thought but also from liberalism, which is a modernizing, anti-traditionalist movement dedicated to correcting the evils and abuses resulting from the misuse of social and political power.

43. The Subjection of Women is an essay by philosopher and political economist John Stuart Mill. Mill argues in favour of legal and social equality between men and women. He writes that 'the legal subordination of one sex to the other' is 'wrong in itself, and now one of the chief hindrances to human improvement'. The Subjection of Women was published in 1869.

At the time that Mill wrote The Subjection of Women, women could not vote. A married woman was not a separate legal entity from her husband, and any property or money she owned came under his governance.

A common justification for women's inferior legal status was that they were morally superior to men, and therefore better restricted to the home, where they would be protected from the polluting influence of public life and could shape the morals of the future generation. Mill argues that this is illogical: 'there is no other situation in life in which it is... considered quite natural and suitable, that the better should obey the worse'.

47. Sri Aurobindo was one of the most creative and significant figures in the history of the Indian renaissance and Indian nationalism. Romain Rolland regarded him as the highest synthesis of the genius of the East and the

West and the 'Prince among the Indian thinkers'. Dr. Radhakrishnan described Aurobindo as 'the most accomplished of modern Indian thinkers'. Tagore painted him as the 'Messiah of Indian culture and civilisation'. C.R. Das called Aurobindo as the 'poet of patriotism, the prophet of nationalism and the lover of humanity'. Aurobindo was indeed a versatile genius - a great poet, a profound thinker, a notable metaphysican, a great seer and an ardent patriot. His writings represent the crystallization of the new and rising soul of India and have a spiritual message for humanity.

The contribution of Sri Aurobindo to modern Indian political thought may conveniently be summarized under four headings : His concept of spiritual nationalism, a nation as an organism, nationalism as a religious aspiration and moral attitude and divinity of motherland; his exposition of the ideal of complete freedom from foreign rule; his contribution to the theory of boycott and passive resistance and finally his vision of the high role that India was destined to play in world affairs and his ideal of human unity.

52. The world systems theory, developed by sociologist Immanuel Wallerstein, is an approach to world history and social change that suggests there is a world economic system in which some countries benefit while others are exploited. Just like we cannot understand an individual's behaviour without reference to their surroundings, experiences, and culture, a nation's economic system cannot be understood without reference to the world system of which they are a part.

The main characteristics of this theory are:

- The world systems theory is established on a three-level hierarchy consisting of core, periphery, and semi-periphery areas.
- The core countries dominate and exploit the peripheral countries for labour and raw materials.
- The peripheral countries are dependent on core countries for capital.
- The semi-peripheral countries share characteristics of both core and peripheral countries.
- This theory emphasizes the social structure of global inequality.

55. Finance Commission is a constitutional body for the purpose of allocation of certain revenue resources between the Union and the State Governments. It was established under Article 280 of the Indian Constitution by the Indian President. It was created to define the financial relations between the Centre and the states. President after two years of the commencement of Indian Constitution and thereafter every 5 years, has to constitute a Finance Commission of India.

It shall be the duty of the Commission to make recommendations to the President in relation to the distribution between the Union and the States of the net proceeds of taxes which are to be, or maybe, divided between them and the allocation between the States of the respective shares of such proceeds; the principles which should govern the grants in aid of the revenues of the States out of the Consolidated Fund of India; any other matter referred to the Commission by the President in the interests of sound finance.

The Commission shall determine their procedure and shall have such powers in the performance of their functions as Parliament may by law confer on them.

Chairman: Heads the Commission and presides over the activities. He should have had public affairs experience. Along with chairman four members are associated with it.

The Parliament determines legally the qualifications of the members of the Commission and their selection methods.

57. Lok Sabha enjoys special powers in regard to the 'collective responsibility' of the Government and in financial matters. The Constitution provides that the Council of Ministers shall be collectively responsible to the House of the People (Lok Sabha). The power to control the purse also lies with Lok Sabha. A Money Bill has to be introduced only in Lok Sabha. Similarly, Demands for Grants of the various Ministries are also made to, discussed and voted in Lok Sabha.

Confidence or no-confidence motion can only be moved in Lok Sabha and passed by it.

58. Justice K.S. Puttaswamy (Retd.) & Anr. vs. Union of India & Ors. :

This case is the cornerstone of the 'Right to Privacy' jurisprudence in India. The nine Judge Bench in this case unanimously reaffirmed the right to privacy as a fundamental right under the Constitution of India. The Court held that the right to privacy was integral to freedoms guaranteed across fundamental rights, and was an intrinsic aspect of dignity, autonomy and liberty.

The case began with the question of whether the right to privacy was a fundamental right, which was raised in 2015 in the arguments concerning the legal validity of the Aadhaar database. The Attorney General appearing for the State argued that the existence of the right to privacy as a fundamental right was in doubt in view of the two decisions in the cases of M.P. Sharma vs. Satish Chandra, District Magistrate, Delhi ((1954) SCR 1077), rendered by an eight Judge Bench, and Kharak Singh vs. State of Uttar Pradesh ((1964) 1 SCR 332), rendered by a six Judge Bench. Both the cases, the State argued, contained observations that the Constitution did not specifically protect the right to privacy as a fundamental right. At the same time, several subsequent judgments over the years had recognised the right to privacy as a fundamental right. However, these subsequent decisions that affirmed the existence of the right to privacy were rendered by benches of a smaller strength than M.P. Sharma and Kharak Singh. Due to issues relating to the precedential value of judgments and noting the far-reaching importance of the right to privacy, this case was referred to a nine Judge Bench of the Supreme Court.

The Bench unanimously held that "the right to privacy is protected as an intrinsic part of the right to life and personal liberty under Article 21 and as a part of the freedoms guaranteed by Part III of the Constitution". In doing so, it overruled previous judgments of the Supreme Court in M.P. Sharma and Kharak Singh, insofar as the latter held that the right to privacy was not recognised under the Indian Constitution.

In addition to cementing the place of the right to privacy as a fundamental right, this case also laid down the need for the implementation of a new law relating to data privacy, expanded the scope of privacy in personal spaces, and discussed privacy as an intrinsic value.

61. In The Human Side of Enterprise, McGregor presents two ways of describing managers' thinking: Theory X and Theory Y. Theory X is traditional carrot-and-stick thinking, built on 'the assumption of the mediocrity of the masses'. This assumes that workers are inherently lazy, need to be supervised and motivated, and regard work as a necessary evil to provide money. The premises of Theory X, writes McGregor, are: '(1) that the average human has an inherent dislike of work and will avoid it if he can, (2) that people, therefore, need to be coerced, controlled, directed, and threatened with punishment to get them to put forward adequate effort toward the organization's ends and (3) that the typical human prefers to be directed, wants to avoid responsibility, has relatively little ambition, and wants security above all.'

McGregor lamented that Theory X 'materially influences managerial strategy in a wide sector of American industry,' and observed 'if there is a single assumption that pervades conventional organizational theory it is that authority is the central, indispensable means of managerial control.'

'The human side of enterprise today is fashioned from propositions and beliefs such as these,' writes McGregor, before going on to conclude that 'this behaviour is not a consequence of man's inherent nature. It is a consequence rather of the nature of industrial organizations, of management philosophy, policy, and practice.' It is not people who have made organizations, but organizations that have transformed the perspectives, aspirations, and behaviour of people.

The other extreme is described by McGregor as Theory Y, which is based on the principle that people want and need to work. If this is the case, then organizations need to develop the individuals commitment to its objectives, and then to liberate his abilities on behalf of those objectives. McGregor described the assumptions behind Theory Y: '(1) that the expenditure of physical and mental effort in work is as natural as in play or rest—the typical human doesn't inherently dislike work; (2) external control and threat of punishment are not the only means for bringing about effort toward a company's ends; (3) commitment to objectives is a function of the rewards associated with their achievement—the most important of such rewards is the satisfaction of ego and can be the direct product of effort directed toward an organizations purposes; (4) the average human being learns, under the right conditions, not only to accept but to seek responsibility; and (5) the capacity to exercise a relatively high degree of imagination, ingenuity, and creativity in the solution of organizational problems is widely, not narrowly, distributed in the population.

62. Each performance budget will in the first instance indicate the organisational structure and the broad objectives that govern the approaches and work of the administrative agency. This is followed by a Financial Requirements Table. This Table is the most important part of the performance budget and has three basic elements:

- a programme and activity classification indicating the range of work of the agency in meaningful categories
- object-wise classification showing the same amount distributed among the different objects of expenditure such as establishment charges; and
- sources of financing indicating the budgetary and account heads under which the funds are being provided in the budget.

Four basic steps are involved in the introduction of performance budgeting:

(*i*) Establishing a meaningful classification of public expenditure in terms of functions,

(*ii*) the establishment, improvement and extension of activity schedules for all measurable activities of the government;

(*iii*) the establishment of work output, employee utilisation, standard or unit costs by objective methods, *i.e.* bringing the system of accounting and financial management into accord with the classification; and

(*iv*) the creation of related cost and performance recording and reporting system.

63. Mary Parker Follett, or the "Mother of Modern Management," believed that management was "the art of getting things done through people."

Though she never managed a for-profit enterprise, she offered valuable insight on the importance of "powering with" rather than "powering over," and integrating with employees to solve conflicts.

"Leadership is not defined by the exercise of power but by the capacity to increase the sense of power among those led," Follett once said. "The most essential work of the leader is to create more leaders."

Follett practiced these principles of coordination that helped develop her theory of management:

- **Direct contact:** Direct contact between employees and managers helps organizations avoid conflict and misunderstandings. Holding regular meetings or discussing assignments in person is a simple way to practice this principle.

- **Early stages:** Coordination should be learned and mastered straight away. No employee should feel less important than the next; each has a significant role that compliments the roles of others.
- **Reciprocal relationship:** Every worker, regardless of their level in hierarchy, is responsible for pulling their weight and integrating with the rest of the organization. No one person should be trying less or more than another— it's a team effort.
- **Continuous process:** Coordination must be maintained. Don't just learn it and forget about it; channel it in everything you do.

64. The growing theoretical influence of the New Right reached its zenith in a sustained period of political hegemony for the Conservative Party during the 1980s, a development initially moulded by the dynamism of its own agenda, but further fuelled by the apparent failures of the post-war 'social-democratic' political settlement. The Thatcher government was evidently influenced and intellectually bolstered by the neoliberal theories of economists of the New Right such as Milton Friedman and F.A Hayek; Friedman being associated with the 'Chicago School' (University of Chicago), with Hayek attached in academic terms to the 'Austrian School'. While both Friedman and Hayek were highly critical of the Keynesian post-war economic settlement that had been consolidated across much of the western world for approximately three decades, they did not wholly agree on specific solutions. Hayek had initially expounded his warning of escalating 'statism' in his 1944 seminal text 'The Road to Serfdom', while Friedman was a more contemporary figure who became US President Ronald Reagan's economic adviser and who has been referred to as the founding father of monetarist theory; which primarily advocated that a government's key responsibility in terms of economic management 'was to ensure that the currency was sound', which practically entailed limiting the money supply, reducing state intervention/public spending, and also adhering to the 'monetarist axiom' of restricting borrowing. A further underlying influence on the moulding of New Right thought into practice was Maurice Cowling, a conservative Cambridge historian who emphasized the value of individual freedom (notably from the state) as one of the emerging strands of this ideological movement, notably 'the sort of freedom that will maintain existing inequalities or restore lost ones'. At a basic level, these varying key influences on New Right thought shared major concerns about the escalating 'statist' tendencies of many western liberal democracies, concluding that the post-war 'social-democratic' model of the state represented an unjustified 'source of coercion' regarding the autonomy of individual citizens.

76. The feminist movement (also known as the women's movement or feminism) refers to a series of Social movements and Political campaigns for reforms on women's issues created by the inequality between men and women. Such issues are women's liberation, reproductive rights, domestic violence, maternity leave, equal pay, women's suffrage, sexual harassment, and sexual violence. The movement's priorities have expanded since its beginning in the 1800s, and vary among nations and communities. Priorities range from opposition to female genital mutilation in one country, to opposition to the glass ceiling in another.

Feminism in parts of the Western world has been an ongoing movement since the turn of the century. During its inception, feminism has gone through a series of four high moments termed Waves. The First-wave feminism was oriented around the station of middle-or upper-class white women and involved suffrage and political equality, education, right to property, organizational leadership, and marital freedoms. The Second-wave feminism attempted to further combat social and cultural inequalities. Although the first wave of feminism involved mainly middle class white women, the second wave brought in women of different social classes, women of colour, and women from other developing nations that were seeking solidarity. The Third-wave feminism continued to address the financial, social, and cultural inequalities of women in business and in their home lives, and included renewed campaigning for greater influence of women in politics and media. In reaction to political activism, feminists have also had to maintain focus on women's reproductive rights, such as the right to abortion. The Fourth-wave feminism examines the interlocking systems of power that contribute to the social stratification of traditionally marginalized groups, as well as the world around them.

77. Works by Arendt :

Der Liebesbegriff bei Augustin: (1929).

Rahel Varnhagen: The Life of a Jewish Woman (1974).

The Origins of Totalitarianism (1951).

The Human Condition (1958).

Eichmann in Jerusalem: A Report on the Banality of Evil (1963).

On Revolution (1963).

Between Past and Future (1968).

Men in Dark Times (1968).

On Violence (1970).

82. Simon Commission:

- In 1927, the British Government appointed a commission under the chairmanship of Sir John Simon.
- The Commission was appointed to study the reforms of 1919 and suggest further measures for Constitutional reforms.
- The Commission had no Indian member in it.
- The Indians boycotted this all-White commission.

First Round Table Conference:

- The First Round Table Conference was held from 12 November 1930 to 19 January 1931.
- The Congress boycotted the conference as its demand for a discussion on Poorna Swaraj of India was rejected by the British Government.
- The representatives of the Princely states, minority communities, and depressed classes attended the conference.
- But without the congress, the conference failed to reach any settlement on Indian problems.

Gandhi Irwin Pact:

- After the failure of the First Round Table Conference efforts were made by the Government to make an agreement with the congress so that it would attend the next Round Table Conference.
- The Viceroy, Lord Irwin, was authorised to hold talks with Mahatma Gandhi.
- Finally, Gandhi and Irwin reached an agreement on 5 March 1931.
- The agreement is called the Gandhi-Irwin pact. By this pact, the Government agreed to release most of the civil disobedience volunteers, against whom there was no allegation of violence.
- The Congress suspended the Civil Disobedience Movement and agreed to participate in the Second Round Table Conference.

Communal Award:

- In August 1932, the Government announced the communal Award which provided separate electorates for Muslims, Sikhs, and depressed classes.

- Gandhi strongly opposed the order by undertaking a fast unto death in the Yeravada Jail. The nation was shocked at Gandhi's decision. The leaders immediately negotiated with the representatives of the backward castes and compromise was affected.

84. Rensis Likert established management styles called Likert's management systems in the 1960s. To characterize the interaction, engagement, and roles of managers and subordinates in industrial contexts, he proposed four management systems. He developed the procedures based on research conducted with highly productive managers and their teams at an American insurance company. Later, he and Jane G. Likert altered the methods so that they could be applied in educational contexts. They were created to define the duties of principals, students, and teachers; however, other stakeholders like superintendents, administrators, and parents were subsequently added. Rensis Likert and his colleagues at the University of Michigan in the United States studied the patterns and styles of managers for three decades and established a four-fold model of management systems. The model was developed using information from a poll of over 200 managers as well as research into the performance characteristics of various types of firms.

There are four management systems or four leadership styles, according to Likert:

System 1 : Exploitative Authoritative

System 2 : Benevolent Authoritative

System 3 : Consultative

System 4 : Participative

88. Issues of peace and security are decided by 2/3 majority, including five permanent members, by the UN Security Council. The Security Council has primary responsibility, under the UN Charter, for the maintenance of international peace and security. It has 15 Members (5 permanent and 10 non-permanent members). Each Member has one vote. Under the Charter, all Member States are obligated to comply with Council decisions. The Security Council takes the lead in determining the existence of a threat to the peace or act of aggression. It calls upon the parties to a dispute to settle it by peaceful means and recommends methods of adjustment or terms of settlement. In some cases, the Securitv Council can resort to imposing sanctions or even authorize the use of force to maintain or restore international peace and security.

89. India's "minimum credible nuclear deterrence" doctrine and "no first use" policy are based on the concept of deterrence by denial, rather than deterrence by punishment. Should deterrence ever break down, India will have to pay an enormous price for a nuclear first strike by an adversary before launching massive punitive retaliation. Nuclear doctrine has to be ultimately tested in the crucible of operational reality. Across the entire spectrum of conventional conflict, the first use of nuclear weapons by India does not make sound strategic sense. The real distinguishing feature of India's nuclear doctrine is that it is anchored in India's continued commitment to global, verifiable and non-discriminating nuclear disarmament.

The object of deterrence is to persuade an adversary that the costs to him of seeking a military solution to his political problems will far outweigh the benefits. The object of reassurance is to persuade one's own people, and those of one's allies, that the benefits of military action, or preparation for it, will outweigh the costs.

Previous Years' Paper (Solved)

National Testing Agency (NTA)

UGC-NET Junior Research Fellowship & Assistant Professor Eligibility Exam

POLITICAL SCIENCE, June–2020

(Online exam held on 09-10-2020)

PAPER-II

Note: *This paper contains* ***hundred (100)*** *objective type questions of* ***two (2)*** *marks each.* ***All*** *questions are* ***compulsory***.

1. 'All aspects of luck, including natural ability, should be irrelevant to distributive justice'— This statement refers to the concept of:
A. Meritocracy
B. Plutocracy
C. Luck egalitarianism
D. Aristocracy

2. Which among the following is NOT a salient feature of 'individualist anarchism'?
A. Private property
B. Ultra liberalism
C. Civil disobedience
D. Organicism

3. The theory that 'the Earth is best understood as a living entity that acts to maintain its own existence' is known as:
A. Tragedy of commons
B. Sustainability
C. Social ecology
D. Gaia hypothesis

4. Which among the following countries have no written constitution?
A. Australia B. New Zealand
C. Spain D. France

5. Which among the following forms of government is ideal for Machiavelli?
A. Republic
B. Aristocracy
C. Democracy
D. Hereditary Monarchy

6. Which of the following thinkers did not believe in women equality?
A. Plato and Mill
B. Aristotle and Hegel
C. Mill and Mary Wollstonecraft
D. Plato and Mary Wollstonecraft

7. In "The Considerations on Representative Government", J.S. Mill did not elaborate upon:
A. Ideal government based on proportional representation
B. Protection of minorities
C. Institutions of self-government
D. Political Economy

8. Aristotle's "ideal state is always Plato's second best:" Who said this?
A. G.H. Sabine B. W. Ebenstein
C. J.A. Dunning D. C.L Wayper

9. Which one of the following is not the function of State, according to Kautilya?
A. Acquisition of that which is not under its control and possession
B. Preservation of what has been acquired
C. Accentuation of what has been preserved
D. Empire building only

10. 'Agganasutta' is related with:
A. Hindu Philosophy
B. Buddhist Philosophy
C. Jain Philosophy
D. Vedanta Philosophy

11. Which one of the following party firstly joined by E.V. Ramasami Periyar?
A. Bharatiya Janata Party

B. Indian National Congress
C. Justice Party
D. Communist Party of India

12. The concept of 'credible minimum deterrent' relates to which of the following types of weapons?
A. Chemical B. Biological
C. Nuclear D. Space-based

13. Who gave the idea of 'the New Northern Concert of Power' (NNCP) to analyse the relevance of non-aligned movement in post-cold war era?
A. M.S. Rajan B. S.D. Muni
C. A.P. Rana D. Muchkund Dubey

14. In which of the following subjects, Rajya Sabha has got more power than Lok sabha?
A. Ratification of President's rule in a state
B. Creation of a new All India Service
C. Creation of Legislation Council in a state
D. Alteration in the boundary of a state

15. Which article of the Indian Constitution is associated with judicial activism?
A. 14 B. 18
C. 21 D. 25

16. Who among the following was strongly opposed to the idea of Panchayati Raj system in India?
A. B.R. Ambedkar
B. Jaya Prakash Narayan
C. Ram Manohar Lohia
D. Mahatma Gandhi

17. Which of the following statement is false about the Indian federalism?
A. it is a good example of 'holding together' federation
B. it has a tendency of strong Central Government
C. it reflects the spirit of 'coming together' federation
D. it has been referred to as 'quasi federal' system

18. Who has given originally the idea of 'Hindu Rashtra'?
A. V.D. Savarkar B. K.B. Hedgewar
C. B.S. Moonje D. M.S. Golwalkar

19. Who among the following characterized the Indian polity as being stable not in the sense of a stationary unresponsive state but in terms of a 'regulated movement'?
A. Myron Weiner
B. W.H. Morris Jones
C. James Manor
D. Atul Kohli

20. Who among the following was not a member of the 'Syndicate' group of the Congress party?
A. M.N. Nijalingappa
B. Morarji Desai
C. K. Kamaraj
D. Y.V. Chauvhan

21. A formal organization, according to Chester Bernard, comes into existence when:
A. There are persons who are willing to contribute action
B. There are persons with different goals and purpose
C. There are prsons willing to communicate through informal channels only
D. Executive is unwilling to handle the economy of incentives within an organisation

22. The concept of 'traditional' authority involves:
A. Use of authority by virtue of their inherited status by persons
B. The exercise of power subject to rules and regulations
C. The use of power based on the basis of magical qualities by a person
D. The use of power/authority as per inherited status as well as extraordinary contribution to the history of advanced business organisation

23. Which of the following factors did not contribute to the evolution of the scientific management theory?
A. lack of effective standards of work
B. lack of clear understanding of worker-management responsibilities
C. rule-of-thumb based decisions by the management
D. proper job design and economic incentives to workers

24. Which of the following statements about the 'Consumer Protection Act 2019' is NOT true?
A. It has widened the definition of consumer
B. It provides for E-filing of complaints
C. It establishes Central Consumer Protection Authority
D. It ignores mediation as an alternate disputes resolution mechanism

25. 'Consumer Protection Bill 2019' was passed by the Indian Parliament on:
A. 13th July 2019 B. 25th July 2019
C. 6th August 2019 D. 9th August 2019

26. 'Hegemony' refers to:
A. economic exploitation
B. structural inequality
C. the capacity of bourgeoisie to displace rival views and become, in effect, the common sense of the age
D. military domination

27. Who among the following rejected 'scientific determinism' and advocated political and intellectual struggle?
A. Antonio Gramsci B. Karl Marx
C. V.I. Lenin D. Friedrich Engels

28. Which of the following indicates the nature of planning in India in Contemporary times?
A. Annual Planning
B. Centralised Planning
C. Perspective Planning
D. Five year Planning

29. Who among the following was/is the first chairman of NITI Aayog in India?
A. Amitabh Kant B. Arvind Pangariya
C. Narendra Modi D. Manmohan Singh

30. Who among the following has presented the incremental model of public policy?
A. Henry Fayol
B. Charles E. Lindblom
C. Fred W. Riggs
D. David Easton

31. Which one of the following is not a theory or model of representation?
A. Trusteeship B. Delegation
C. The Mandate D. Consensus

32. According to Greek system of classification of regimes, the degenerative form of rule by many is known as:
A. Tyranny
B. Aristocracy
C. Anarchic democracy (mob rule)
D. Oligarchy

33. Who among the following is often portrayed as the 'father' of cultural nationalism?
A. Guisseppe Mazzini
B. Charles Maurras
C. Frantz Fanon
D. Johann Gottfried Herder

34. Which one of the following is NOT a cause of Democratic Shift in the context of Democratisation?
A. Crisis of import-substitution
B. Loss of popularity and legitimacy by military regimes
C. Social change
D. Media

35. Who among the following reformulated Hans Morgenthau's 'six principles of political realism' from a feminist perspective?
A. Judith Butler
B. J. Ann Tickner
C. Helen M. Kinsella
D. Betty Friden

36. 'The combination of liberal democracy and the market had drawn a finishing line in the history of political and social development'. Who made this statement?
A. Samuel P. Huntington
B. Benjamin Barber
C. Francis Fukuyama
D. Alexander Wendt

37. Which of the following is the executive-bureaucratic arm of the European Union?
A. The European Council
B. The European Commission
C. The Council
D. The European Parliament

38. Which of the following is not a principle of *jus ad bellum* (just recourse to war)?
A. just cause

B. legitimate authority
C. proportionality
D. humanity

39. Who among the following is NOT a key figure of 'Conservatism'?
A. T.H. Green
B. Edmund Burke
C. Michael Oakshott
D. Friedrich Von Hayek

40. In which one of the following countries, 'consociationalism' as a power-sharing mechanism is not practiced?
A. Germany B. Netherlands
C. Switzerland D. Belgium

41. Which among the following is not an element of G.A. Cohen's thought on the theory of socialism?
(*a*) Theory of maldistribution of freedom under capitalism
(*b*) Genuine fraternity promulgated by liberal egalitarianism
(*c*) Deep inegalitarian structure of John Rawl's theory
(*d*) Market socialism
Choose the ***correct*** answer from the options given below:
A. (*a*) and (*b*) Only
B. (*a*) and (*c*) Only
C. (*b*) and (*c*) Only
D. (*c*) and (*d*) Only

42. Which of the following statements are true about dependency theory?
(*a*) Dependency theory was strongly influenced by Marxists and Non-Leninists who were critical of Development theory
(*b*) Dependency theory stressed the peaceful, evolutionary process of modernisation
(*c*) Development in the third world was dependent on development in the already developed nations.
(*d*) The First World does not exploit the third world
Choose the ***most appropriate*** answer from the options given below:
A. (*a*) and (*b*) Only B. (*a*) and (*d*) Only
C. (*a*) and (*c*) Only D. (*c*) and (*d*) Only

43. Which of the following statements are true about the Authoritarianism and Totalitarianism?
(*a*) In authoritarian regime, government is not constitutionally responsible to the public
(*b*) Authoritarian regimes may be institutionalised and legitimate
(*c*) Totalitarian regimes seek to control and transform all aspects of the state, society and economy
(*d*) Totalitarian regimes do not have strong ideological goal and do not use violence as a tool for remaking institutions
Choose the most appropriate answer from the options given below:
A. (*b*), (*c*) and (*d*) Only
B. (*c*), (*d*) and (*a*) Only
C. (*d*), (*a*) and (*b*) Only
D. (*a*), (*b*) and (*c*) Only

44. According to Aristotle, which of the following statements are correct?
(*a*) Polis should be large enough to guarantee self sufficiency and small enough to ensure good government
(*b*) The Polis was natural and prior to the individual, not chronologically but teleologically
(*c*) Polis is the highest and most comprehensive of Human Associations
(*d*) Polis is man writ large
Choose the correct answer from the options given below:
A. (*a*) and (*d*) Only
B. (*b*) and (*d*) Only
C. (*c*) and (*d*) Only
D. (*a*), (*b*) and (*c*) Only

45. Marx's concept of alienated labour includes:
(*a*) Alienation from the Product
(*b*) Alienation from the Process
(*c*) Alienation from Species
(*d*) Alienation from Nature
Choose the correct answer from the options given below:
A. (*a*) and (*b*) Only
B. (*b*) and (*c*) Only
C. (*c*) and (*d*) Only
D. (*a*), (*b*), (*c*) and (*d*) Only

46. Given below are the statements about the difference between passive resistance and satyagraha. Which ones are true?

(*a*) Passive resistance is weapon of the weaker sections, satyagraha never desires to terrorise the opponent

(*b*) Passive Resistance is negative in practice, whereas satyagraha is positive morality

(*c*) Passive Resistance is equivalent to satyagraha

(*d*) Passive Resistance is not afraid of the physical strength while satyagraha is afraid of physical strength

Choose the correct answer from the options given below:

A. (*a*) and (*b*) Only B. (*c*) and (*d*) Only
C. (*b*) and (*c*) Only D. (*a*) and (*d*) Only

47. Jaya Prakash Narayan formed which of the following parties?

(*a*) Congress Socialist Party

(*b*) Bhoodan Aandolan Party

(*c*) Praja Socialist Party

(*d*) Democratic Praja Socialist Party

Choose the most appropriate answer from the options given below:

A. (*a*) and (*b*) Only B. (*b*) and (*c*) Only
C. (*c*) and (*d*) Only D. (*a*) and (*c*) Only

48. 'Fatwa-i-Jahandari' of Ziauddin Barani is related with:

(*a*) Advices for Muslim kings in order to earn religious merit and the gratitude of the subject

(*b*) Advices to all the kings

(*c*) Description of the origin of state

(*d*) Tenets of secularism

Choose the correct answer from the options given below:

A. (*a*) and (*b*) Only B. (*a*) Only
C. (*b*) and (*c*) Only D. (*c*) and (*d*) Only

49. Which of the following statements are true with regard to Pandita Ramabai?

(*a*) She was a staunch supporter of Hindu Philosophy

(*b*) She was a pioneer in the field of education and emancipation of women in India

(*c*) She was the writer of 'The High Caste Hindu Women'

(*d*) She was Anti-Christianity

Choose the correct answer from the options given below:

A. (*a*) and (*b*) B. (*b*) and (*c*)
C. (*c*) and (*d*) D. (*a*) and (*d*)

50. In which of the following countries, did India participate in the peace keeping operations?

(*a*) Korea (*b*) Gaza strip
(*c*) Cyprus (*d*) Lebanan

Choose the correct answer from the options given below:

A. (*a*) and (*b*) Only
B. (*a*), (*b*) and (*c*) Only
C. (*b*), (*c*) and (*d*) Only
D. (*a*), (*b*), (*c*) and (*d*) All

51. Which of the following features of the Indian political system are false?

(*a*) Dual government

(*b*) Supremacy of the Parliament

(*c*) Indestructability of the union

(*d*) Indestructability of the states

Choose the correct answer from the options give below:

A. (*a*) and (*b*) only B. (*b*) and (*c*) only
C. (*b*) and (*d*) only D. (*c*) and (*d*) only

52. Which of the following are civil society organizations?

(*a*) Bachpan Bachao Andolan

(*b*) India Against Corruption

(*c*) Vigyan Prasar

(*d*) Majdoor Kisan Sangharsh Samiti

Choose the correct answer from the options given below:

A. (*a*) and (*c*) only
B. (*a*) and (*b*) only
C. (*a*), (*b*), (*c*) and (*d*)
D. (*a*), (*b*) and (*d*) only

53. Which of the following statements regarding women's movement in India are true?

(*a*) Arya Samaj was not concerned about women's issues at all,

(*b*) All India Women's Conference was set up in 1924.

(*c*) Sarojini Naidu and Annie Besant raised the issue of right to vote for women.

(*d*) Tilak's 'Ganesh Utsavas' were mainly aimed at drawing women into national movement.

Choose the correct answer from the options given below :

A. (*a*) and (*b*) only B. (*b*) and (*c*) only
C. (*c*) and (*d*) only D. (*a*) and (*d*) only

54. Who among the following provide the structural - functional perspective on the nature of Indian State?

(*a*) W.H. Morris Jones
(*b*) Rajni Kothari
(*c*) Francine Frankel
(*d*) Llyod Rudolph

Choose the correct answer from the options given below:

A. (*a*) and (*b*) only B. (*b*) and (*c*) only
C. (*c*) and (*d*) only D. (*a*), (*b*), (*c*), (*d*)

55. Which of the following are the characteristics of prismatic model of F. W. Riggs?

(*a*) Formalism
(*b*) Heterogeneity
(*c*) Overlapping
(*d*) Bureau of office

Choose the correct answer from the options given below:

A. (*a*), (*b*) and (*c*) only
B. (*a*), (*b*), (*c*) and (*d*) only
C. (*b*) and (*d*) only
D. (*c*) and (*d*) only

56. Which of the following are associated with the notion of governance?

(*a*) Competitive democracies
(*b*) Participatory democracy
(*c*) Democratic administration
(*d*) Change - oriented democracy

Choose the correct answer from the options given below:

A. (*a*) and (*b*) only B. (*b*) and (*c*) only
C. (*c*) and (*d*) only D. (*b*) and (*d*) only

57. Which of the following statements are true about the concept of governance?

(*a*) It does not simply mean 'rule' or 'administration'
(*b*) It has a specific meaning in the context of globalisation
(*c*) It is the manner in which power is exercised
(*d*) Governance and government are the same thing

Choose the correct answer from the options given below:

A. (*a*) and (*b*) only
B. (*a*), (*b*) and (*c*) only
C. (*a*), (*b*), (*c*), (*d*)
D. (*b*), (*c*), (*d*) only

58. Which of the following terms is referred to as the 'software' of the state?

A. Capacity B. Accountability
C. Resilience D. Responsiveness

59. Who among the following regarded state as a 'necessary evil'?

A. Jeremy Bentham B. Thomas Paine
C. James Mill D. J.S. Mill

60. Who among the following is NOT a post modern thinker?

A. Jean Francois Lyotard
B. Michel Foucault
C. Richard Rorty
D. Herbert Marcuse

61. Match List-I with List-II

List-I	List-II
(*a*) The Age of Consent	(*i*) Jacques Derrida
(*b*) Parecon	(*ii*) Naomi Klein
(*c*) Spectres of Marx	(*iii*) George Monbiot
(*d*) No Logo	(*iv*) Michael Albert

Choose the correct answer from the options given below:

	(*a*)	(*b*)	(*c*)	(*d*)
A.	(*ii*)	(*i*)	(*iv*)	(*iii*)
B.	(*iv*)	(*iii*)	(*ii*)	(*i*)
C.	(*iii*)	(*iv*)	(*i*)	(*ii*)
D.	(*i*)	(*ii*)	(*iii*)	(*iv*)

62. Match List-I with List-II

List-I	List-II
(*a*) Security Complex	(*i*) Karl Deutsch
(*b*) Common Security	(*ii*) Robert Jervis
(*c*) Security Community	(*iii*) Barry Buzan
(*d*) Security Regimes	(*iv*) Palme Report, 1992

Choose the correct answer from the options given below:

	(*a*)	(*b*)	(*c*)	(*d*)
A.	(*i*)	(*ii*)	(*iii*)	(*iv*)
B.	(*iv*)	(*iii*)	(*ii*)	(*i*)
C.	(*iv*)	(*iii*)	(*i*)	(*ii*)
D.	(*iii*)	(*iv*)	(*i*)	(*ii*)

63. Match List-I with List-II

List-I	List-II
(*a*) Bipolarity is the most stable distribution of power	(*i*) Kenneth Waltz
(*b*) Interests are defined as power	(*ii*) John Mearsheimer
(*c*) States seek to maximize their relative power position	(*iii*) Hans Morgenthau
(*d*) Justice, law and society have no place or are circumscribed in international politics	(*iv*) Thucidides

Choose the correct answer from the options given below:

	(*a*)	(*b*)	(*c*)	(*d*)
A.	(*iv*)	(*ii*)	(*iii*)	(*i*)
B.	(*i*)	(*iii*)	(*ii*)	(*iv*)
C.	(*iii*)	(*i*)	(*iv*)	(*ii*)
D.	(*ii*)	(*iv*)	(*i*)	(*iii*)

64. Which of the following characterise International Criminal Court (ICC)?

(*a*) The Rome statute established ICC as 'Court of last resort'

(*b*) ICC can exercise jurisdiction only when national courts are unwilling or unable to investigate or prosecute

(*c*) It can not prosecute acts of war crimes

(*d*) ICC is not located in the Hague

Choose the correct answer from the options given below:

A. (*a*) and (*b*) only B. (*b*) and (*c*) only

C. (*c*) and (*d*) only D. (*a*) and (*d*) only

65. Which of the following characterise shallow or reformist ecology?

(*a*) Reformist ecology seeks to reconcile ecology with capitalist modernity

(*b*) It recognises 'limits to growth'

(*c*) It rejects all forms of anthropocentrism, embracing ecocentrisim

(*d*) It considers damage to environment as an externality or 'social cost'

Choose the correct answer from the options given below:

A. (*a*), (*b*) and (*c*) only

B. (*b*), (*c*) and (*d*) only

C. (*a*), (*b*) and (*d*) only

D. (*a*), (*c*) and (*d*) only

66. Which of the following statement is true about International Monetary Fund (IMF)?

(*a*) The IMF is not created by the Bretton Woods Agreement

(*b*) Its functions is to ensure exchange rate stability

(*c*) Critics see IMF as political arm of neoliberal globalization

(*d*) The IMF is not a specialized agency of the UN

Choose the correct answer from the options given below:

A. (*a*) and (*b*) only B. (*c*) and (*d*) only

C. (*b*) and (*c*) only D. (*a*) and (*d*) only

67. Match List-I with List-II:

List-I (Author)	List-II (Book)
(*a*) Hannah Arendt	(*i*) Little Red Book
(*b*) Frantz Fanen	(*ii*) The Wretched of the Earth
(*c*) Mao Tse Tung	(*iii*) Affluent Society
(*d*) John K. Galbraith	(*iv*) The Human Condition

Choose the correct answer from the options given below:

	(*a*)	(*b*)	(*c*)	(*d*)
A.	(*i*)	(*ii*)	(*iii*)	(*iv*)
B.	(*ii*)	(*iii*)	(*iv*)	(*i*)
C.	(*iv*)	(*ii*)	(*i*)	(*iii*)
D.	(*iii*)	(*ii*)	(*iv*)	(*i*)

68. Match List-I with List-II:

List-I (Works of Rabindranath Tagore)	List-II (Content of the work)
(*a*) Geetanjali	(*i*) The realization of life
(*b*) Gora	(*ii*) Devotion of God
(*c*) Sadhana	(*iii*) Deeper meaning of life in the backdrop of Swadeshi movement

(*d*) Ghare - Baire (The home and the world) — (*iv*) Analysis of the multifarious social life in colonial India

Choose the correct answer from the options given below:

	(*a*)	(*b*)	(*c*)	(*d*)
A.	(*iii*)	(*ii*)	(*i*)	(*iv*)
B.	(*iv*)	(*i*)	(*ii*)	(*iii*)
C.	(*ii*)	(*iv*)	(*i*)	(*iii*)
D.	(*ii*)	(*i*)	(*iv*)	(*iii*)

69. Match List-I with List-II:

List-I (Landmarks in Indian foreign policy)	List-II (Prime Ministers)
(*a*) Shimla Accord	(*i*) Rajiv Gandhi
(*b*) Act East Policy	(*ii*) Indira Gandhi
(*c*) India's Peace keeping in Sri Lanka	(*iii*) Atal Behari Vajpayee
(*d*) Lahore Declaration	(*iv*) Narendra Modi

Choose the correct answer from the options given below:

	(*a*)	(*b*)	(*c*)	(*d*)
A.	(*i*)	(*ii*)	(*iii*)	(*iv*)
B.	(*ii*)	(*iv*)	(*i*)	(*iii*)
C.	(*iv*)	(*iii*)	(*ii*)	(*i*)
D.	(*iii*)	(*ii*)	(*iv*)	(*i*)

70. Match List-I with List-II:

List-I (President)	List-II (Term of Office)
(*a*) Shankar Dayal Sharma	(*i*) 2012-2017
(*b*) R. Venkatraman	(*ii*) 2007-2012
(*c*) Pratibha Patil	(*iii*) 1992-1997
(*d*) Pranab Mukherjee	(*iv*) 1987-1992

Choose the correct answer from the options given below:

	(*a*)	(*b*)	(*c*)	(*d*)
A.	(*iii*)	(*iv*)	(*i*)	(*ii*)
B.	(*iii*)	(*iv*)	(*ii*)	(*i*)
C.	(*iv*)	(*ii*)	(*iii*)	(*i*)
D.	(*ii*)	(*i*)	(*iv*)	(*iii*)

71. Match List-I with List-II:

List-I (Environmental Movement)	List-II (State)
(*a*) Narmada Bachao Andolan	(*i*) Odisha
(*b*) Chipko movement	(*ii*) Karnataka
(*c*) Appiko movement	(*iii*) Uttarakhand
(*d*) Chilka movement	(*iv*) Madhya Pradesh

Choose the correct answer from the options given below:

	(*a*)	(*b*)	(*c*)	(*d*)
A.	(*i*)	(*ii*)	(*iii*)	(*iv*)
B.	(*iv*)	(*iii*)	(*ii*)	(*i*)
C.	(*iii*)	(*ii*)	(*i*)	(*iv*)
D.	(*iv*)	(*iii*)	(*i*)	(*ii*)

72. Match List-I with List-II:

List-I (Centres of Adi Dravid Movements)	List-II (Leaders)
(*a*) Madras	(*i*) Vithoba Raoji
(*b*) Hyderabad	(*ii*) Murugesh Pillai
(*c*) Mysore	(*iii*) B.R. Verma
(*d*) Nagpur	(*iv*) M.S. Raja

Choose the correct answer from the options given below:

	(*a*)	(*b*)	(*c*)	(*d*)
A.	(*i*)	(*ii*)	(*iii*)	(*iv*)
B.	(*ii*)	(*iii*)	(*i*)	(*iv*)
C.	(*iv*)	(*iii*)	(*ii*)	(*i*)
D.	(*iii*)	(*ii*)	(*i*)	(*iv*)

73. Match List-I with List-II:

List-I (Books)	List-II (Authors)
(*a*) Policy Science	(*i*) Robert Dahl
(*b*) Principles of Public Administration	(*ii*) Herbert Simon
(*c*) Administrative Behaviour : A Study of Decision Making Processes in Administrative Organisations	(*iii*) D. Lerner and Herald Larswele
(*d*) The Science of Public Administration : Three Problems	(*iv*) W.F. Willoughby

Choose the correct answer from the options given below:

	(a)	(b)	(c)	(d)
A.	(i)	(ii)	(iii)	(iv)
B.	(iii)	(iv)	(ii)	(i)
C.	(ii)	(i)	(iv)	(iii)
D.	(iv)	(iii)	(i)	(ii)

74. Arrange the following freedoms mentioned in Article 19 of the constitution in the order of their appearance:

(*a*) Form Associations or unions
(*b*) Practise any profession
(*c*) Move freely throughout the territory of India
(*d*) Assemble peaceably and without arms

Choose the correct answer from the options given below:

A. (*c*), (*b*), (*a*), (*d*) B. (*d*), (*a*), (*c*), (*b*)
C. (*a*), (*b*), (*c*), (*d*) D. (*b*), (*c*), (*d*), (*a*)

75. Arrange the following Parliamentary Committees in order of their formation:

(*a*) Estimates Committee
(*b*) Departmental Standing Committee
(*c*) Public Accounts Committee
(*d*) Committee on Public Undertakings

Choose the correct answer from the options given below:

A. (*a*), (*b*), (*c*), (*d*) B. (*d*), (*c*), (*b*), (*a*)
C. (*c*), (*a*), (*d*), (*b*) D. (*b*), (*c*), (*d*), (*a*)

76. Arrange the following foundational elements of Indian foreign policy in order of their appearance:

(*a*) Gujaral Doctrine
(*b*) Panchasheel
(*c*) Look East Policy
(*d*) Indo-Soviet Treaty of Friendship

Choose the correct answer from the options given below:

A. (*a*), (*b*), (*c*), (*d*) B. (*d*), (*c*), (*b*), (*a*)
C. (*c*), (*d*), (*a*), (*b*) D. (*b*), (*d*), (*a*), (*c*)

77. Arrange the works of Karl Marx in ascending order:

(*a*) The Capital (Das Capital)
(*b*) The Communist Manifesto
(*c*) The Critique of the Gotha Programme
(*d*) The Economic and Philosophical Manuscripts

Choose the correct answer from the options given below:

A. (*a*), (*b*), (*c*), (*d*) B. (*c*), (*a*), (*b*), (*d*)
C. (*b*), (*a*), (*c*), (*d*) D. (*d*), (*b*), (*c*), (*a*)

78. Match List-I with List-II:

List-I (Books)	List-II (Authors)
(*a*) Politics and Markets	(*i*) Robert Dahl
(*b*) The Power Elite	(*ii*) C. Wright Mills
(*c*) A Preface to Democratic Theory	(*iii*) Mancure Olson
(*d*) The Logic of Collective Action : Public Goods and the Theory of Groups	(*iv*) Charles Lindblom

Choose the correct answer from the options given below:

	(a)	(b)	(c)	(d)
A.	(iii)	(i)	(iv)	(ii)
B.	(iv)	(iii)	(ii)	(i)
C.	(i)	(ii)	(iii)	(iv)
D.	(iv)	(ii)	(i)	(iii)

79. Who called 1857 revolt as the First War of Independence?

A. V.D. Savarkar
B. Ram Manohar Lohia
C. Swami Vivekananda
D. Deendayal Upadhyaya

80. Given below are two statements : one is labelled as Assertion (A) and the other is labelled as Reason (R):

Assertion (A): Swadeshi, Boycott, National Education and Passive Resistane were the means of protest used by Bal Gangadhar Tilak.

Reasons (R): Boycott was accepted to be an effective weapon by Tilak.

In the light of the above statements, choose the most appropriate answer from the options given below:

A. Both (A) and (R) are correct and (R) is the correct explanation of (A)
B. Both (A) and (R) are correct, but (R) is not the correct explanation of (A)
C. (A) is correct, but (R) is not correct
D. (A) is not correct, but (R) is correct

81. Given below are two statements : one is labelled as Assertion (A) and the other is labelled as Reason (R):
Assertion (A): The idea of 'governance' gained in prominence by connoting a plurality of rules in place of the states' monopoly.
Reasons (R): The idea of governance owes its origin to the World Bank.
In the light of the above statements, choose the correct answer from the options given below:
A. Both (A) and (R) are true and (R) is the correct explanation of (A)
B. Both (A) and (R) are true, but (R) is not the correct explanation of (A)
C. (A) is true, but (R) is false
D. (A) is flase, but (R) is true

Directions (Qs. No. 82-90): *Given below are two statements. In the light of the given statements, choose the correct answer from the options given below:*
A. Both Statement I and Statement II are true
B. Both Statement I and Statement II are false
C. Statement I is correct but Statement II is false
D. Statement I is incorrect but Statement II is true

82. Statement I : Globalisation has helped in deepening of democracy in India.
Statement II : Globalisation has deeply impacted the Indian society.

83. Statement I : Chaudhary Charan Singh was the only Prime Minister in India who did not face the Parliament.
Statement II : Passage of a no–confidence motion in Lok Sabha leads to the ouster of a government from office.

84. Statement I : India has deliberately been christened as a 'Union of states' instead of a 'federation of states' by the Constitution.
Statement II : The word 'Union' does indicate a particular type of federation that Constitution makers envisaged for India.

85. Statement I : A country's foreign policy is the product of its history.
Statement II : Core values of Indian national movement constituted the building blocks of Indian foreign policy.

86. Statement I : M.N. Roy considered the economic interpretation of history propounded by Marx as misconceived and imperfect.
Statement II : M.N. Roy argued that the real form of social and economic process is not determined merely by types of material resources.

87. Statement I : Oligarchy is a government dominated by the few.
Statement II : Robert Mckenzie formulated the iron law of oligarchy.

88. Statement I : Social democracy combines elements of liberalism and socialism to reconcile freedom and equality.
Statement II : Social democratic regimes use the system of neo corporatism wherein policy-making involves the state, labour and the businesses.

89. Statement I : Every constitution has a philosophy of its own.
Statement II : For the philosophy underlying Indian Constitution, we must look back into the historic Objective Resolution moved by Pandit Nehru.

90. Statement I : Chester Bernard defined organization as a system of consciously coordinated activities of two or more persons.
Statement II : Chester Bernard supported the viewpoint that man is mainly motivated by economic incentives.

Directions (Qs. No. 91-95): *Read the passage and answer the questions.*

From this perspective of democracy, representation can help or hurt democracy, even if representation cannot be democratic since it cannot replicate the *demos*. But the phenomenon of representation reflects an emotional roller - coaster - great hopes during an election campaign, great disappointment from the work of governments in office. This problem stems in part from the fact that representative government and, the *demos* potentially operate at cross - purposes. The office of a representative results from elections, which elevate a set of political rulers above the ruled in order to make the laws. In office, they make compromises to get legislative business done. Representatives may feel proud of what they accomplished, because they made the decisions that led to the compromise. But citizens can't take pride in legislative work, and they mostly suffer the consequences required by the compromise. That doesn't mean representatives always will be scorned, as mentioned above, their office -enables them to undertake political initiatives not viable during an election campaign or to protect minorities whose needs may have been neglected. That said, the necessary activity of legislative compromise takes place above the heads and behind the backs of the people. As such, it contradicts the 'Athenian and Aristotelian understanding of democracies as political orders that depend on the deliberative and decisive power of citizens (i.e., the *demos*) acting with authoritative power. Citizens of the Athenian democracy were said to rule and be ruled in turn, but in every case their power required the political presence and deliberative action of citizens.

91. Which of the following is reflected in the phenomenon of representation?
A. Great hopes during an election campaign
B. Great appreciation for the work of government in office
C. Great promises from the representative democracy
D. Great challenges from liberalization, privatisation and globalisation

92. What is the obvious outcome of an election?
A. Career of a leader
B. Ministerial birth of a politician
C. Office of a representative
D. Future prospects of a budding activist

93. Athenian and Aristotelian understanding of democracies means:
A. Political orders depending on the deliberative powers of citizens
B. Political system rooted in grassroot politics
C. System of government prevalent in Greek city states
D. Western conceptualization of democracy

94. What takes place above the heads and behind the backs of the people?
A. Executive arrogance
B. Judicial activism
C. Parliamentary sovereignty
D. Legislative compromise

95. Why could have representatives felt proud of what they accomplished?
A. They made the decisions for their followers
B. They made the decisions that led to the compromise
C. They made a level jump in their career progression
D. They made their adversaries compromise with their core values

Directions (Qs. No. 96-100): *Read the passage and answer the questions.*

Ronald Dworkin's thesis is that some of the rights people have fundamental, but many are not. They are fundamental because they are 'the rights against the state'. Dworkin says that the notion of rights as trumps "marks the distinctive conept of an individual right against the state which is the heart ... of constitutional theory in the United States." In the special supplement, Dworkin argued that the concept of right against the government becomes most useful particularly when the society is divided on racial lines into majority and minority. The right to freedom of speech and religious freedom belong to this category. Therefore, they are strong rights. He asserts that these rights should be permitted and they should not be interfered or banned. These freedoms are to be allowed even if the welfare of the collectivity is infringed.

On the contrary, he also presupposes a large area of rights where the state can make legislations curtailing those rights to achieve common welfare. They can be called *weak rights.* Right to liberty for example becomes a weak right against right to equality, a strong right. This at the outset may look contradictory, but it is not. For example, restraining the movement on the roads for safety and smooth traffic movement does not mean restraining the rights, on the other hand, putting a restriction on publication or restraining the freedom of speech will infringe the rights even if it enhances general welfare. Thus, even though in both cases rights are involved, curtailment of one is justified, whereas the other is not.

96. The rights claimed against the state are considered as:
A. Fundamental rights
B. Human rights
C. Natural rights
D. Legal rights

97. The idea of right against the government becomes very useful when the society is divided into majority and minority on the basis of:
A. Caste B. Class
C. Race D. Religion

98. The strong rights need to be:
A. inferred B. permitted
C. borrowed D. ordained

99. Which of the following is a weak right?
A. Right to property
B. Right to equality
C. Right to liberty
D. Right to religious freedom

100. The rights that can be curtailed to achieve common welfare may be called as:
A. Strong rights
B. Fundamental rights
C. Human rights
D. Weak rights

ANSWERS

1	2	3	4	5	6	7	8	9	10
C	D	D	B	A	B	D	A	D	B
11	**12**	**13**	**14**	**15**	**16**	**17**	**18**	**19**	**20**
B	C	C	B	C	A	C	A	B	D
21	**22**	**23**	**24**	**25**	**26**	**27**	**28**	**29**	**30**
A	A	D	D	C	C	A	C	C	B
31	**32**	**33**	**34**	**35**	**36**	**37**	**38**	**39**	**40**
D	C	D	D	B	C	B	D	A	A
41	**42**	**43**	**44**	**45**	**46**	**47**	**48**	**49**	**50**
B	C	D	D	D	A	D	B	B	D
51	**52**	**53**	**54**	**55**	**56**	**57**	**58**	**59**	**60**
C	D	C	A	A	A	B	B	B	D
61	**62**	**63**	**64**	**65**	**66**	**67**	**68**	**69**	**70**
C	D	B	A	C	*	C	C	B	B
71	**72**	**73**	**74**	**75**	**76**	**77**	**78**	**79**	**80**
B	C	B	B	C	D	C	D	A	A
81	**82**	**83**	**84**	**85**	**86**	**87**	**88**	**89**	**90**
A	D	A	C	A	A	C	A	A	C
91	**92**	**93**	**94**	**95**	**96**	**97**	**98**	**99**	**100**
A	C	A	D	B	A	C	B	C	D

* *No option is correct or the question is wrong.*

EXPLANATORY ANSWERS

1. Luck egalitarianism is the name of a group of theories of justice that subscribes to the idea that a just society compensates for brute luck, but does not compensate for bad outcomes that fall under the responsibility of the agent himself. Notable defenders of versions of the theory are Dworkin (2000) and Cohen (1989).

3. The Gaia hypothesis advances the idea that the Earth is best understood as a living entity that acts to maintain its own existence (Gaia is the name of the Greek goddess of the Earth). The basis for the Gaia hypothesis is that the Earth's biosphere, atmosphere, oceans and soil exhibit precisely the same kind of self-regulating behaviour that characterises other forms of life. Gaia has maintained 'homeostasis', a state of dynamic balance, despite the major changes that have taken place in the solar system. The most dramatic evidence of this is the fact that although the sun has warmed up by more than 25 per cent since life began, the temperature on Earth and the composition of its atmosphere have remained virtually unchanged.

4. New Zealand's constitution is not found in one document. Instead, it has a number of sources, including crucial pieces of legislation, several legal documents, common law derived from court decisions as well as established constitutional practices known as conventions. Increasingly, New Zealand's constitution reflects the Treaty of Waitangi as a founding document of government in New Zealand.

The Constitution Act 1986 is a key formal statement of New Zealand's system of government, in particular the executive, legislature and the judiciary. The Act recognises the Queen as the Head of State of New Zealand and the Governor-General as her representative.

Other laws that outline the powers and functions of the three branches of government in more detail include the State Sector Act 1988, the Electoral Act 1993, the Judicature Act 1908 and the Senior Courts Act 2016 and the District Court Act 2016.

Other important legislation includes the Treaty of Waitangi Act 1975, Ombudsmen Act 1975, the Official Information Act 1982, the Public Finance Act 1989, the New Zealand Bill of Rights Act 1990, the Human Rights Act 1993. Some British laws, such as parts of Magna Carta 1297 and The Bill of Rights 1688, and the Act of Settlement 1701 and the Royal Marriages Act 1772, have been incorporated into New Zealand law by the Imperial Laws Application Act 1988.

5. Machiavelli has been wrongly criticized by many as an advocate of despotism. His preference for republican and popular government is clear in 'Discourses'. While it is true that in "Prince" he suggests a monarchical form of government in order to consolidate and create a strong state, he discusses republican government in 'Discourses'. A serious study of both these works shows that Machiavelli suggested monarchy only for those states where popular government would not be able to unite and form a strong state. For example, a state which faces corruption, strife and division, like Italy, the only solution is a monarchy with a strong ruler. On the other hand, peaceful states can establish republican government. He appreciated Rome and other republics which uphold the value of general good over individual prosperity. He believed that in republics, individuals are not selfish and corrupt, and they work towards achieving the common good. This is the reason behind the greatness and success of republics.

Machiavelli repudiates the belief that democratic states degenerate with time. He rather argues that if people and their representatives in legislatures are regulated by law, then self-governing societies tend to be most stable. It is only when individuals act superior to law that anarchy follows. His preference for republican states over monarchy is evident when he argues that people in general are more prudent and is a better judge of situations than a prince.

7. Mill's essays *On Liberty* published in 1859 and *The Subjection of Women* published in 1869 are classic elaborations of liberal thought on important issues like law, liberty and rights. *The Considerations on Representative Government* was published in 1861. It provides an outline of his ideal government which is to be based on proportional representation. The two other principles are the protection of minorities and institutions of self-government. His famous pamphlet, *Utilitarianism* was published in 1863, in this work though he endorsed the Benthamite principle of the greatest happiness of the greatest number, yet makes a significant departure from the Benthamite assumption by arguing that this principle can only be defended if only one distinguishes happiness from pleasure.

8. In the portrayal of his Ideal State, Aristotle clearly felt the impact of Plato, even though he was more practical and realistic than Plato. As a realist he goes more closer to Plato's Laws rather than his Republic. Hence, Sabine rightly says that what Aristotle calls the Ideal State is always Plato's second best state. Prof. Barker also says "It is curious and suggestive that when Aristotle depicts his best, he should copy Plato's Second Best. It was perhaps due to Aristotle's touch for realism that did not take him to the flights of imagination to which Plato had gone".

9. *Arthashasta* as Science of Political-Economy

'The substance of mankind is termed *Artha* (wealth), the earth that contains and is termed *Artha* (wealth)! the science, which deals with the means of acquiring and maintaining the Earth'

Politics (Dandaniti) deals with:

- "the acquisition of what has not been gained (*Alabdha Laabhaartha*);
- the preservation of what has been acquired (*labdha Parirakshani*);
- the accentuation or increase of what has been preserved *(Rakshit Vivardhani)*; and
- Due-apportionment or the bestowal of the surplus upon the deservers (*Vriddhasya Tirtheshu Pratipaadini*)."

10. Among thirty-four Suttas in the Digha Nikaya, or "Collection of Long Discourses", the first division of the Sutta Pitaka, the Aggañña Sutta has outstanding content revealing comprehensive account of social development or the origin of human society. It also informs how the kingship was formed.

12. Credible Minimum Deterrence (CMD) is one of the central pillars of India's nuclear policy. Nuclear policy makers after argue that India's nuclear weapons programme, has always been guided by the understanding of minimum deterrence—avoiding largest in terms of cost, pace or posture. Credibility came upon demonstration of weapons capability. The credible minimum posture was considered apt to justify India's nuclear weapons and missile capabilities after the 1998 tests. K. Subrahmanyam called it a doctrine adopted to suit India's requirements and thinking on nuclear weapons (Subrahmanyam 1999). Bharat Karnad (2008) defines it as a self-explanatory, moderate, limited, reasonable and legitimate posture. The CMD doctrine highlights that India does not seek an open-ended nuclear arsenal and pillars other postures like the second-strike capability and no first use. CMD has now become the over-arching feature of the Indian Nuclear Doctrine, advertising three aspects of a nuclear weapons-empowered India: security with a thrust on deterrence, a responsible nuclear weapons state and commitment to global nuclear disarmament.

The concept of "credible minimum deterrence" is used in conjunction with the concepts of "No First Use" and "Non Use" against nuclear weapon states.

14. **Special powers of the Rajya Sabha—**The Rajya Sabha has following special powers:
    (*a*) Under Article 249, the Rajya Sabha may be a resolution passed by not less than 2/3rd of its members present and voting declare a subject of State List to be of National importance. By the force of such resolution, the Parliament gets the power to legislate on such subject.
    (*b*) The Rajya Sabha is empowered under Article 312 to pass a resolution supported by not less than 2/3 members present and voting to create a new All India Service in the national interest. Only such resolution enables Parliament to create a new All India Service. This power is given to the Rajya Sabha because members of this service are appointed in the administration of the States.
    (*c*) The resolution to remove the Vice-President of India can be initiated in the Rajya Sabha only.

15. According to Black's Law Dictionary, judicial activism is a "philosophy of judicial decision making whereby judges allow their personal views about public policy, among other factors, to guide their decisions." Judicial activism can also be defined as when a Court takes some legislative power away from legislators. Judicial Activism to define broadly, is the assumption of an active role on the part of the judiciary. For example, giving a judgement that gay marriage is a constitutional right in India would be "judicial activism."

    Judicial activism means going beyond normal constraints of the judiciary. According to Justice J.S. Verma, judicial activism is an "active process of implementation of the rule of law, essential for the preservation of a functional democracy". However, in a vibrant democratic system, it can also been seen as a phenomenon to curb executive tyranny and legislative misuse of power. In India, Article 21 of the Constitution associated with Judicial Activism.

16. Dr. B.R. Ambedkar was critical of the Panchayati Raj system. He believed that local self-government meant giving extra power to the already dominating local elites and upper castes. Thus such a system would lead do further exploitation of the lower castes and the downtrodden.

17. Federalism is a system of government in which powers have been divided between the centre and its constituent parts such as provinces or states. Unlike a unitary state, sovereignty is constitutionally split between at least two territorial levels so that units at each level have final authority and can act independently of the others in some area. The constituent units possess certain level of autonomy depending on type of federation. There are two types of federations:
    1. **Holding together federation:** In this form of federation, the powers are shared among various social groups/constituent parts to accomodate the diversity present in the society. In this type of federation, the powers are somewhat tilted towards the central authority. India, Spain, Belgium etc. follow this form of federalism.
    2. **Coming together federation:** In this form of federation, the independent states come together to form a bigger unit and sacrifice some of their powers to be enjoyed by the central authority. The states here enjoy more autonomy as compared to the states in "holding together federation" system. Countries such as the USA, Switzerland, Australia follow this form of federalism.

18. Savarkar was the first systematic exponent of the Hindu nationalism. He elaborately described his theory of Hindutva in his book 'Hindutva' published in 1924. By that time, he had abandoned his concept of Indian

nationalism that he borrowed from Joseph Mazzini in favour of Hindu nationalism. In the process of developing his concept of Hindu nationalism, he rejected some of the arguments of territorial nationalism. He held that the existence of a mere territory did not make nation but nation was made by the people who constituted themselves as a political community, bound together by cultural affinities and traditions.

20. The AICC session held in Lalbagh, Bangalore, in 1969 was a historic session and paved the way for the split of the Congress Party. Mr. Nijalingappa was the leader of the Syndicate group consisting of Kamaraj Nadar, S.K. Patil, Atulia Ghosh and Morarji Desai. Mrs. Indira Gandhi was supported by a younger group called the 'Young Turks' in the party, consisting of Chandrashekhar, Krishna Kant, and Mohan Dharia. In the Bangalore session, the Syndicate group who were virtually ruling the country proposed Mr. Neelam Sanjeeva Reddy as candidate for the post of President of India, owing to the vacancy caused by the demise of Dr. Zakir Hussain. Mrs. Indira Gandhi and her supporters opposed this presidential candidate, Neelam Sanjeeva Reddy, and left the AICC session in Bangalore and flew to Delhi and announced Mr. V.V. Giri, the then Vice-President of India as the Presidential candidate. This led to the expulsion of Mrs. Indira Gandhi from the Congress by Mr. Nijalingappa. Then, Mrs. Indira Gandhi called a parallel AICC session in Mumbai in 1969 and expelled all the senior leaders who had expelled her. Thus, the Congress was split.

21. A formal organization for Barnard is a 'system of consciously coordinated activities or forces of two or more persons'. This definition, and the analysis based on it, can be applied to all forms of organization: the state, the church, the factory, the family. An organization comes into being when '(*i*) there are persons able to communicate with each other (*ii*) who are willing to contribute action (*iii*) to accomplish a common purpose'. Willingness to *contribute action* in this context means the surrender of the control of personal conduct in order to achieve coordination. Clearly the commitment of particular persons to do this will vary from maximum willingness through a neutral point to opposition or hatred. Indeed Barnard maintains that, in modern society, the commitment of the majority of possible contributors to any given organization will lie on the negative side. Equally important, the commitment of any individual will fluctuate, and thus the total willingness of all contributors to cooperate in any formal system is unstable—a fact which is evident from the history of all such organizations. Willingness to cooperate is the result of the satisfactions or dissatisfactions obtained, and every organization depends upon the essentially subjective assessment of these made by its members.

22. Traditional authority derives its legitimacy from the acceptance of it since hoary past. The persons exercising authority generally are called 'Masters' who enjoy personal authority by virtue of their inherited status. Their commands carry legitimacy because of the customs but they can also give orders based on their personal decision. Thus confirmity with customs and personal arbitrariness are two characteristics of traditional authority. The persons who obey the orders here are called 'Followers'. They carry out the commands of the master out of sheer personal loyalty and a pious regard for his time-honoured status. In this patrimonial regime the persons who carry out the orders are personal retainers, household officials, relatives, favourites of the master. In a feudal society they are the loyal allies of the master. Thus, in the system of traditional authority, the officials carrying out the orders, look like the 'household staff' of the master and their spheres of activity change according to his whims and fancies. However, all these actions are legitimized in the name of traditions and customs.

23. The fundamental concern of the scientific management school is to increase the efficiency of the worker through efficient job design and appropriate training. Fredrick Winslow Taylor, the father of the scientific management movement, developed many ideas to increase organisational efficiency. Taylor (1947) demonstrated that through proper handling of work, and worker selection and training, productivity could be increased. Henry Gantt, a colleague of Taylor's, developed charts, now familiar as the Gantt Chart, for the planning and scheduling of production activities to increase efficiency. Frank and Lillian Gilbreth, also proponents of scientific management, developed time and motion studies to measure, record and improve efficiency.

The scientific management school subscribes to the theory that efficiency could be attained by finding the right methods to get the job done, through specialisation, by planning and scheduling activities, by setting standard times to do the job, and by proper selection and training of workers and rewarding them through wage incentives for effective performance.

24. The Consumer Protection Act, 2019 was notified on August 9th, 2019. However, it came into effect from July 20th, 2020.

While retaining certain old provisions, the New Act has certain new provisions that tightens the existing rules to further safeguard consumer rights and create exhaustive consumer protection law.

New provisions under Consumer Protection Act, 2019:

- Inclusion of E-commerce, Direct selling Establishment of Central Consumer Protection Authority (CCPA).
- Strict Norms for Misleading Advertisement.
- Strict Norms for product liability.
- Changes in the Pecuniary Jurisdiction.
- Greater ease to dispute resolution Addition in the clause of "Unfair Trade Practice".
- Unfair Contract.
- Alternate Dispute Resolution through mediation.

25. The Parliament passed the Consumer Protection Bill, 2019 on 06.08.2019 to replace the Consumer Protection Act, 1986 ("1986 Act"). The President of India gave its assent to the Consumer Protection Act, 2019 ("2019 Act") on 09.08.2019 and the same will come into force on the date it is notified by the Central Government. The 2019 Act has been enacted for the purpose of providing timely and effective administration and settlement of consumer disputes and related matters.

26. The Marxist theory of ideology was perhaps developed furthest by Antonio Gramsci. Gramsci argued that the capitalist class system is upheld not simply by unequal economic and political power, but by what he termed the 'hegemony' of bourgeois ideas and theories. Hegemony means leadership or domination and, in the sense of ideological hegemony, it refers to the capacity of bourgeois ideas to displace rival views and become, in effect, the common sense of the age. Gramsci highlighted the degree to which ideology is embedded at every level in society: in its art and literature; in its education system and mass media; in everyday language; and in popular culture. This bourgeois hegemony, Gramsci insisted, could only be challenged at the political and intellectual level, which means through the establishment of a rival 'proletarian hegemony', based on socialist principles, values and theories.

27. An Italian Marxist and social theorist, Gramsci tried to redress the emphasis within orthodox Marxism on economic and material factors. He rejected any form of 'scientific' determinism by stressing, through the theory of hegemony (the dominance of bourgeois ideas and beliefs), the importance of the political and intellectual struggle. Gramsci highlighted the degree to which ideology is embedded at every level in society and called for the establishment of a rival 'proletarian hegemony', based on socialist principles and values. Gramsci's major work is *Prison Notebooks*.

29. About NITI Aayog: The Government, in January 2015, replaced Planning Commission with NITI Aayog (National Institution for Transforming India).

Aim: to achieve Sustainable Development Goals and to enhance cooperative federalism by fostering the involvement of State Governments of India in the economic policy-making process using a bottom-up approach.

Role of NITI Aayog: The institution has to provide governments at the central and state levels with relevant strategic and technical advice across the spectrum of key elements of policy. This includes matters of national and international import on the economic front, dissemination of best practices from within the country as well as from other nations, the infusion of new policy ideas and specific issue-based support. The institution has to be able to respond to the changing and more integrated world that India is part of.

Composition of NITI Aayog:

Chairperson: Prime Minister of India (Narendra Modi) as the Chairperson.

Governing Council comprising the Chief Ministers of all the States and Lt. Governors of Union Territories.

Regional Councils will be formed to address specific issues and contingencies impacting more than one state or a region. These will be formed for a specified tenure.

The Regional Councils will be convened by the Prime Minister and will comprise of the Chief Ministers of States and Lt. Governors of Union Territories in the region. These will be chaired by the Chairperson of the NITI Aayog or his nominee.

Experts, specialists and practitioners with relevant domain knowledge *as special invitees nominated by the Prime Minister.*

The full-time organizational framework will comprise of, in addition to the Prime Minister as the Chairperson:

Vice-Chairperson: To be appointed by the Prime Minister.

Members: Full-time.

Part-time members: Maximum of 2 from leading universities research organizations and other relevant institutions in an ex-officio capacity. Part time members will be on a rotational basis.

Ex Officio members: Maximum of 4 members of the Union Council of Ministers to be nominated by the Prime Minister.

Chief Executive Officer : To be appointed by the Prime Minister for a fixed tenure, in the rank of Secretary to the Government of India.

30. Charles L. Lindblom in his article *The Science of Muddling Through* (1959) advocated the 'incremental model' of decision-making. It is diametrically opposite to Herbert Simon's 'rational comprehensive model'.

Lindblom says that the actual decision-making in administration is different from the way it is generally described in theory. He recognises the practical problems in the rational comprehensive approach. He highlights the various limitations like money, time, information, politics, and others, which govern the actual decision-making process in the administration.

Lindblom opined that the decision-makers always continue the existing programmes and policies with some additions. Thus, he argues that what actually occurs in administrative decisions is 'incrementalism', that is, virtual continuation of the previous activities with few modifications. The incremental model is also known as 'branch technique' or 'model of successive limited comparisons' or 'step-by-step decision-making'.

Thus, Lindblom assumes that the past activities and experiences are used by the administrators to make future decisions. He applied two concepts to describe the actual decision-making process in administration—'marginal incrementalism' and 'partisan mutual adjustment'.

31. There are a number of models which are useful for looking at the nature of representing others. They are—trustee, delegate, politico, mandate and resemblance. The first two models—trustee and delegate—were developed prior to the advent of political parties so reflect the image of the independent representative (which the majority of our local government elected representatives are). Put simply, the trustee is a free agent who acts for others by exercising independent judgment, while the delegate acts for others by conveying their views on the basis of instructions. The politico tends to take a position midway between these two, being more flexible and sensitive than both, depending on the circumstances.

The other two models of representation-mandate and resemblance—have been the focus of more recent debate over policy directions in a time of much economic and societal change worldwide in which there has been growing disillusionment with politics and discussion on the merits of different electoral systems. The mandate model emerged as one of the most influential theories of representation associated with the development of political parties. Based on the premise that a party is elected to govern on a mandate containing policies and programmes promised during an election campaign, this model sees the party, rather than individual representatives, as the agency of representation. The mandate is thus authorised by voters who see it as a way of supporting particular policies and keeping politicians accountable. Finally, the resemblance model is one where more recent debate on electoral change has rested. This model centres on the notion that those elected should be representative of the society over which they will ultimately govern, with the result that government is proportionally representative of all groups in society (particularly in relation to gender, ethnicity, geograpy and socio-economic position).

32. The traditional classifications of governments follow the course set by Aristotle. Aristotle, however, was not original. He borrowed from Plato as Plato had borrowed from Socrates. Aristotle based his classification on two principles:

1. the number of persons who exercise supreme power; and
2. the ends they serve.

Applying the first principle, Aristotle said if the supreme power is vested in one single person it is a *monarchy.* If it is rule of the few, it is *aristocracy,* and if the supreme power is vested in many, it is a *polity.*

Aristotle, then, proceeds to distinguish between what he calls the "normal" and the "perverted" forms of government basing his conclusions on the ends which the rulers serve. A *normal* State is that which always aims at the good of the community as a whole. It becomes a *perverted* form when the ruler or rulers become selfish and he or they exercise power vested in him or them for his or their own benefits rather than for the benefits of the community as a whole. *Monarchy, aristocracy* and *polity* are the normal forms of government. In their perverted form they become *tyranny, oligarchy* and *democracy.* Tyranny, Aristotle said, was the degenerated form of monarchy, oligarchy as the degenerated shape of aristocracy and democracy as the degenerated form of polity. Tyranny placed in the hands of the monarch arbitrary control over the lives and fortunes of the citizens. In oligarchy, the wealthy few ruled for selfish ends and used their powers and privileges for the oppression of the common people. Democracy meant mere mob rule, wherein the interests of none were safe and there was confusion and chaos all round.

33. Johann Gottfried Herder : Father of Cultural Nationalism

- Johann Gottfried von Herder was a German poet, critic, theologian and philosopher.
- He is influenced by authors such as Goethe.
- The role he played in the development of the larger cultural movement known as romanticism.
- He is a father of Cultural Nationalism.

35. Broadly, classical realism indicates the evolution of the realist theory prior to the publication of Kenneth Waltz's book the *Theory of International Politics.* In the recent years, generalizations about state behaviour since ancient times ranging from Thucydides till Waltz's book is recognized as part of classical realism. However, realist theory was established as a means to study international politics through the publication of Hans Morgenthau's book *Politics among Nations.* His six principles are widely accepted as the principles of the theory of international relations. These principles are:

- Politics is governed by objective laws that have their roots in human nature.
- Interest is defined in terms of power.
- Interest defined as power is an objective category which is universally valid, but whose meaning can change.
- Universal moral principles cannot be applied to the actions of states in the abstract; the circumstances of time and place must be considered.
- The moral laws that govern the universe are distinct for the morals of any one nation.
- The difference between political realism and other schools is real and profound.

The political realist facilitates and maintains the autonomy of the political sphere by asking, 'How does this policy affect the power of the nation?' Political realism is based on a pluralistic concept of human nature. A man who is nothing but a 'political man' would be a beast, for he would be completely lacking in moral restraints. But, in order to develop an autonomous theory of political behaviours, a 'political man' must be abstracted from other aspects of human nature.

Despite being so popular, these principles of Morgenthau's realist theory are widely criticized. J. Ann Tickner, a feminist international relations theorist, has criticized these principles as nothing but a masculine interpretation of international politics. According to her, Morgenthau completely ignores the cooperative behaviour of states which is also equally significant along with the power politics. Besides, along with the 'real politics' there is also striving for justice, rule and peace in international politics, which Morgenthau tends to ignore.

In addition to the feminist critic, Kenneth Waltz also criticized Morgenthau's principles on the grounds that it does not take into account the impact of international structure on the state behaviour. Besides, Morgenthau's theory also fails to distinguish between the domestic policy and politics at the international level. To bridge this gap, Waltz gave a structural explanation of international politics. This variant of realism is also known as neo-realism.

37. The European Commission is the executive-bureaucratic arm of the EU, responsible for generating new laws and policies, overseeing their implementation, managing the EU budget, representing the EU in international negotiations, and promoting the interests of the EU as a whole. Headquartered in Brussels, the Commission consists of a college of appointed commissioners, who function collectively much like a national government cabinet in a parliamentary system, and several thousand full-time European bureaucrats, each assigned to one of the Commission's directorates-general (DGs), the functional equivalent of national government departments. There is a DG for each major policy area in which the EU is active, and each DG is supported by services that provide policy advice, research support, and legal expertise. Confusingly, both the commissioners and the European bureaucrats are separately and collectively described as "the Commission."

38. The principles of just war are divided into two sections. The first, *jus ad bellum,* refers to the justice of deciding to participate in a war; the second, *jus in bello,* refers to the rules of morality which govern the way any war may be conducted.

Jus Ad bellum (Just Recourse to War)

Just Cause

Legitimate Authority

Just Intentions

Public Declaration (Of Causes and Intents)

Proportionality

(More Good than Evil Results)

Last Resort

Reasonable Hope of Success

Jus In Bello (Just Conduct in War)

Discrimination

(Noncombatant Immunity)

Proportionality

(Amount and Type of Force Used)

Each of these principles merits elaboration.

- ***Just cause:*** Just cause means having right on your side. In general, just cause embraces four types of situations. First, and most important for this discussion, is self-defense against unjustified aggressive actions. Self-defense is the only just cause formally recognized in modern international law. Three other types of just cause are the right to intervene to protect one's "neighbour," the right to punish wrongdoers, and the right of the state to protect its fundamental ideology.

- ***Legitimate authority:*** Legitimate authority refers to the lawfully constituted government of a sovereign state. Only the primary authority of the state has the power to commit its citizens to war.

  In the nuclear age, the problem of legitimate authority has taken on a new dimension and may now be said to be more vitally concerned with the conduct of war than with the decision to participate at all. This is because the only slim hope mankind has for achieving some reasonable balance between the aims and consequences of a nuclear war is to keep it limited. But keeping it limited requires controlling it, which in turn requires effective command, control, communications, and intelligence systems on both sides of the conflict. This is incompatible with a decapitation targeting policy, which aims to remove a hostile nation's leadership at an early stage in hopes of curtailing its ability and willingness to continue the fight. Decapitation is not only of dubious validity in light of contemporary nuclear weapon control procedures but also gambles away any possibility of controlling escalation within a nuclear conflict.

- ***Just intentions:*** This element of *jus ad bellum* in Western thought was first articulated at length by St. Thomas Aquinas, who based it upon natural law. It may also be said to derive from the Judeo-Christian "love thy neighbor" ethic. This obligation does not cease in wartime. We are not permitted to forget that our enemy is also our neighbor, even though most neighborly obligations are suspended for the duration of hostilities. Revenge is not a morally acceptable basis for conducting war. Although it is permissible to intervene to prevent your neighbor's cheek from being struck, the war must be prosecuted with reluctance, restraint, and a willingness to accept peace when the security objectives which justified the war in the first place have been achieved. Although classified under the *jus ad bellum* section of the principles, "just intentions" has even greater significance for the individual soldier in the conduct of war, philosophically underlying the rules of war which protect noncombatants and require acceptance of rules of war which protect noncombatants and require acceptance of surrender and humane treatment of prisoners of war.

Aquinas also developed the theory of "double effect." This theory was originally formulated to reconcile an evil (killing) with a good (resisting aggression). So long as the killing itself was not desired, but was merely an unavoidable consequence of achieving the lawful objective, it was permitted. Later, "double effect" was extended to permit military actions which, while justified in themselves by necessity and the other principles of just war, caused collateral harm to civilians and their property. Basically, it is now a rationale for violating the principle of noncombatant immunity.' The principle has many safeguards, including that the evil effects not be intended, that all reasonable efforts be made to achieve the desired military goal without the undesired noncombatant effects, and that the good achieved outweigh the evil which incidentally occurs.

- ***Public declaration:*** The purpose of this requirement is to state clearly the casus belli and the terms under which peace might be restored. It also serves to inform a state's citizenry of the cause which requires resort to arms and the ensuing risk to life and limb of those who will participate in the conflict.
- ***Proportionality:*** In terms of *jus ad bellum,* or justification for going to war, proportionality means having a reasonable relationship between the goals and objectives to be achieved and the war means being used to achieve them.
- ***Last resort:*** This principle recognizes the destructive consequences of war and insists that it be avoided if at all possible, consistent with the legitimate interests of the state. It means that negotiations, compromise, economic sanctions, appeals to higher authority (the United Nations, for example), and the like must be pursued to redress grievances, if possible, before resort to war is justified.
- ***Reasonable hope of success:*** The state must not squander the lives and property of its citizens in a hopeless effort.

Nuclear weapons have had at least one positive effect in terms of just-war tradition. Their existence causes nations to be much more cautious about initiating hostilities against any nation that might employ them. In other words, they raise the threshold for war. This has resulted in a period of almost unprecedented peace between the major powers since the end of World War II. That is not to say that there have been no wars. There have obviously been many, some of which continue today. But the great powers have not been direct participants against each other, and consequently the level of death and destruction has been minuscule compared to the scale of the two World Wars.

Nuclear weapons have created serious complications for any reasonable prosecution of war, however. The two *jus in bello* principles, discrimination (or noncombatant immunity) and proportionality, are both casualties when megatonnage is exploded anywhere in the vicinity of large population centers. Thus, the swirl of debate since 1945 over acceptable war modes has focused on these two *jus in bello* principles.

- ***Discrimination:*** Army Chaplain Donald Davidson has written on this aspect:

Virtually every moral commentary on war since World War II, whether focused on the air battle or ground combat, has discussed the problem of noncombatant immunity. The issue is not whether noncombatants should be immune to attack; there has been general agreement on this point since classical times. Rather, the problem is deciding "who" is a noncombatant; that is, the problem of discrimination. The difficulty of differentiating between combatants and noncombatants has escalated with each stage in the development of modern warfare: the advent of conscript armies and large standing armies in Napoleon's era, new weaponry developed in the industrial revolution, the mobilization of whole societies in major wars, the large-scale employment of guerrilla or insurgency war and terrorism, and the invention of weapons of mass destruction.

Davidson goes on to explain that noncombatants have traditionally been divided into two groups, based on class and function. The "class" of noncombatants refers to persons who have been defined as not acceptable as military targets, including medical personnel and clergy, whether in uniform or not, infants and small children (normally all children), the infirm, aged , wounded, or sick, and those otherwise helpless to protect themselves. Those who are noncombatants by "function" include farmers, merchants, and others not directly involved in the war effort. Davidson continues:

> Among civilians, those who make war decisions or produce war materials are generally considered as direct contributors to the war effort and, thus, are combatants. Those who perform services or produce goods necessary for living are noncom-batants, even though their services or goods may be used by military personnel. This line of reasoning, for example, allows bombardment of munitions factories, but not canneries.

- ***Proportionality:*** Just as proportionality is one of the *jus ad bellum* principles, so does moral proportionality apply to the means by which war is waged. With respect to *jus in belloy,* proportionality means that the amount and type of force used must be such that the unjust consequences do not exceed the legitimate objectives. Compliance with this principle requires an affirmative answer to the question: "If I take this military action, will more good than harm result from it?" The problem, of course, is often in defining what is meant by "good" and what is meant by "harm." Are human lives to be regarded as equally valuable, for instance? How many villagers may be killed in an air strike to eliminate a sniper—or a machine gun emplacement? And is the policy to be evaluated by a single engagement or from the perspective of the whole war?

39. T.H. Green gave to idealism a new lease of life. He rejected the mechanistic theory of the state on the ground that it had made the state as an artificial institution and ignored the various factors which had contributed to state building. He rejected the force theory of the origin of the state and was convinced that will not force was the basis of state. Green is an idealist but he can also be hailed as an individualist. He gave the individual a far more effective protection against the undue exercise of the state's power than anything with which utilitarianism could provide him. Green revitalized the principle of liberty and instead of giving it a negative gave it a positive social meaning.

40. The Dutch political system was famously described by Lijphart as a form of consociational democracy. Consociationalism refers to the fragmented but surprisingly stable form of democracy that was traditionally found in countries such as the Netherlands, Belgium and Austria. It is fragmented, as numerous societal subgroups are represented in Parliament by a large number of political parties. The political institutions of consociationalism traditionally compel party elites to cooperate across party boundaries, and they have to be more sensitive and respectful towards their political opponents than is common in dualistic political systems. This basically lowers the levels of political antagonism in parliament, as most parties and politicians know that they are likely to be forced to cooperate with their opponents in the near future. The cooperation between elites ensures the stability of the democratic system but also leads to a spread of responsibilities and institutions, as the different parties to a coalition government carve up the 'benefits' of the office and divide the spoils among a large number of beneficiaries. In the past decades, this 'pillarised' system is in transformation and the old more or less corporatist style of politics is giving way. However, the corporatist style of governance remains a constant factor in the Dutch governance even though political rhetorics have become stronger.

42. Dependency theory arose in the late 1960s and achieved considerable popularity especially—but not exclusively—among students on the left of the political spectrum. Indeed, that was part of the problem with dependency theory right from the beginning: it was not clear if dependency was a new and serious approach in comparative politics or simply a political position.

Dependency theory arose from two major sources, which helps explain the confusion as to what it represented. One strong influence was Marxian thought. Marxism was a small minority current in comparative politics, and for a long time it had wielded no influence because of the over-whelming dominance of the political development approach. However, with the U.S. military intervention in the Dominican Republic in 1965, the Vietnam War, and the student protests of 1969-1970, the Marxian approach began to attract more attention. It focused on the contradictions between U.S. interests in the developing nations and the interests of the developing nations themselves, as well as on the contradictions and conflicts within these countries. In contrast, development theory had stressed the peaceful, evolutionary process of modernization and the harmony between U.S. interests and those of the developing nations. An early statement of the dependency alternative and approach to development was Andre Gunder Frank's book *Capitalism and Underdevelopment in Latin America,* a book published at the height of the Vietnam War protests in 1969 and one that, while often misrepresenting facts and making erroneous interpretations, nevertheless set forth a strong Marxian position.

43. Authoritarianism is a theory and a system of government customarily linked with dictatorship, in contrast to democracy. It is a principle based on obedience to authority, and opposes autonomy of individuals in thought and action. As a form of government, authoritarianism concentrates power in a leader or in a small elite not constitutionally accountable to the people. Unlike totalitarian systems, authoritarian governments usually lack a highly developed ideology. Also, the latter tends to tolerate a degree of pluralism in social organization, usually lacks the power to mobilize the nation for collective goals, and exercises its power within limits. Leaders in authoritarian systems often exercise their power arbitrarily and consider themselves above existing law. Modern authoritarian systems usually operate through single, dominant parties, which control government and other key parts of society, including the economy, media and education. They usually do not hold free elections, which could replace them with a competing party (see Political

Parties). It is either difficult or impossible for citizens to create opposition groups or parties.

44. Aristotle points out that the state evolves from lower associations. The first human association is the Household which includes three kinds of relationships. The first is that of husband and wife, the second that of parents and children and the third between the master and the slaves. A cluster of households form a village. The *polis* is a conglomeration of villages and households. The *polis* should be large enough to ensure self-sufficiency and small enough to ensure good government.

45. *The Economic and Philosophical Manuscripts of 1844,* was publish by Karl Marx. In it he described the course and methods due to which the workers' class was exploited by the capitalists. He also elaborated, how the Capitalists, by adopting such modes of production which can benefit them and cause exploitation of the wrorkers. Due to that exploitation the Capitalists and the Worker classes estranged.

He regarded that process and occurrence as *Alienation.* That means that working people put everything into their jobs but get little in return. That causes class conflict and estrangement between the both. So Marx claimed that under the capitalist rule or in a society of capitalism, the workers and the workers' class becomes alienated. This alienation is multi-dimensional and encompasses all areas of life—religion, politics, social and economic relations—but it particularly effects in labour.

Types of Alienation: This alienation in labour or earning, appears as the following types of that alienation *e.g.* alienation in the process of production, alienation from the produced objects which the workers produced by their labour and alienation from other workers, from the rest of humanity and even alienation from nature also.

47. Congress Socialist Party, or (CSP), was a left-wing group within the Congress. It was formed with Acharya Narendra Deva as President and Jay Prakash Narayan as General Secretary in 1934.

In 1948, J.P. Narayan along with some progressive elements in the Congress, left the party and worked relentlessly towards the creation of an anti-Congress platform. In 1952, they formed the Praja Socialist Party (PSP).

By forming the PSP, he gave voice to the marginalised and offered an alternative political platform. Two years later, he announced that he would devote his life to the Bhoodan Movement, founded by Acharya Vinobha Bhave, for the redistribution of land among the landless.

49. Pandita Ramabai Saraswati was an Indian social reformer who championed the cause of emancipation of women.

She was the first woman to be awarded the titles of Pandita and Saraswati, as a Sanskrit scholar, after being examined by University of Calcutta.

A social worker, scholar and a champion of women's rights, freedom and education; Pandita Ramabai also participated in the freedom movement.

A renowned social reformer of Maharashtra fought for the rights of women and spoke against the practice of child marriage. She promoted girls education and started the Arya Mahila Samaj in 1881, in Pune, to improve the condition of women, especially child widows. In 1889, she established the Mukti Mission, in Pune, a refuge for young widows who had been deserted and abused by their families.

She also started Sharda Sadan which provided housing, education, vocational training, and medical services to widows, orphans and the visually challenged. She also wrote many books showing the hard life of women, including child brides and child widows.

51. **Unitary Features of the Indian Constitution:** Unitary Features of constitution make a centralized government. It is a government in which all powers held by the government belong to a single, central agency. A unitary system is governed constitutionally as one single unit. All power is top down. A unitary state is a sovereign state governed as one single unit in which the central government is supreme.

Unitary government is known as a centralized government. In such government all powers held by the government belong to a single, central agency. The central government creates local units of government for its own convenience. A unitary system is governed constitutionally as one single unit, with one constitutionally created legislature. All power is top down. A unitary state is a sovereign state governed as one single unit in which the central government has the supreme power.

Besides the federal features, the Indian Constitution also possesses the following unitary or Nonfederal features:

1. Strong Centre
2. States Not Indestructible
3. Single Constitution
4. Flexibility of the Constitution
5. No Equality of State Representation
6. Emergency Provisions
7. Single Citizenship
8. Integrated Judiciary
9. All-India Services
10. Integrated Audit Machinery
11. Parliament's Authority Over State List
12. Appointment of Governor
13. Integrated Election Machinery
14. Veto Over State Bills

54. **Nature of Indian state:** The favourite theme of the scholars writing on India has been to unravel the true face of the state in India—a trend starting in the 1950s and 1960s and continuing to date. Thus. W.H. Morris-Jones, *The Government and Politics of India* (London : Hutchinson University Library, 1964) set the tone for the liberal-structural functional approach to the study of Indian politics. A precursor of even Morris-Jones happens to be Norman D. Palmer's *The Indian Political System* (Boston: Houghton Mifflin Co., 1961). Rajni Kothari's *Politics in India* (Boston: Little, Brown and Company, 1970), harped on the notion of dominant political centre to convey the autonomy of political processes in the country.

The liberal political economy approach providing a serious critique of development planning in India was evolved by Francine Frankel's *India's Political Economy 1947-2004* (Delhi : Oxford University Press, 2005). Lloyd Rudolph and Susanne Rudolph's *In Pursuit of Lakshmi: The Political Economy of the Indian State* (New Delhi: Orient Longman, 1987), exposes the paradoxical traits of the Indian state, *e.g.*, weak-strong centre, command and demand polity.

The Marxian perspective on the Indian state has been provided by A.R. Desai's *State and Society in India: Essays in Dissent* (Bombay: Popular Praksahan, 1975), which views state in India as an instrument of class-domination. Achin Vanaik's *The Painful Transition* (London: Verso, 1990) looks at the Indian state as a relatively autonomous entity. The economic critique of the state in India is provided by Pranab Bardhan's *Political Economy of Development in India* (London : Oxford University Press, 1984). Among others, Atul Kohli's *State and Poverty in India* (Cambridge: Cambridge University Press, 1987), adopts a state-oriented focus in his comparative study of politics of reform in the three Indian states of UP, Karnataka and West Bengal.

55. **Prismatic model of developing societies:** Riggs defines development administration as the combined process of both the 'administration of development' (implementation of

development policies and plans) and the 'development of administration' (improvement of administrative capabilities). Riggs eventually came up with a new analytical construct (known as the prismatic model) to explain these transitional nations. Riggs articulated this prismatic model based on the metaphor of prism—as the fused white sunlight (which represents the fusion of several colours) passes through a prism; it becomes diffracted into several separate colours.

Here the fused light signifies the fused structures of traditional society (single structure performing all necessary functions); the diffracted colours represent the specialized or differentiated structures of modern society (separate structures or institutions for major functions); and the situation within the prism (which is a transitional phase between the fused and diffracted stages) reflects the condition in developing nations, which Riggs began to define as prismatic societies (Riggs, 1964). In explaining the nature of administration in these transitional societies, Riggs syste-matically used an ecological approach to explore their non-administrative domains of society, politics, economy and culture.

In general, such prismatic societies are characterized by formalism (theory-practice gap), heterogeneity (co-existence of the traditional and the modern), and functional overlaps (similar functions are performed by different institutions). These features are reflected in the prevalence of poly-communalism in society (interaction among communities based on suspicion and distrust); the bazaar-canteen model economy and its price-indeterminacy (caused by the influence of social status, bargaining capacity, and official position on economic behaviour); and poly-normativism in decision process (representing the use of both rational and non rational criteria). These ecological or contextual factors, according to Riggs play significant role in shaping the nature of public administration in developing nations, which he presents as *sala* (complex and mixed) model administration characterized by the coexistence of universal official norms and respect for traditions, which is reflected in the influence of family and community on official decisions (*e.g.*, nepotism and favouritism); prevalence of both ascriptive and achievement criteria leading to the 'attainment' norms in public offices; and so on. However, Riggs refined this prismatic model with unique ecological and contextual forces in the process of developmental regimes.

57. In the 1992 report entitled "Governance and Development", the World Bank set out its definition of good governance. This term is defined as "the manner in which power is exercised in the management of a country's economic and social resources for development".

The World Bank identified three distinct aspects of governance:

(*a*) the form of the political regime;

(*b*) the process by which authority is exercised in the management of a country's economic and social resources for development; and

(*c*) the capacity of governments to design, formulate and implement policies and discharge functions.

60. A group of French thinkers in the 1970s associated with post-structuralism radicalized the critique of modern philosophy and became labelled as "postmodern" theorists. Derrida, Foucault, Lyotard, Baudrillard, and others developed original and challenging modes of thought and writing, driving philosophy into novel arenas and topics. In the 1980s, postmodern theory spread throughout the world and American thinker Richard Rorty also became associated with the postmodern turn in philosophy.

64. The International Criminal Court (ICC) was established in 2002 as the first permanent international criminal court for investigation and prosecution of individuals for genocide, crime against humanity, apartheid and war crimes. The court became operational when the signatory nations met in the Assembly of State Parties to appoint a prosecutor and 18 judges. It opened on March 11, 2003. The Rome Statute of the International Criminal Court (The ICC Statute or the Statute) is the most important of the international agreements that defined International Crimes. The jurisdictional relationship between the ICC and various national justice systems is based on the so-called complimentarily principle. Under this principle, national courts take precedence over the ICC in dealing with violations of international humanitarian law. The Court can only exercise its jurisdiction when national courts are unwilling or unable to investigate or prosecute such crimes, thus being a court of last resort.

65. **Reformist** ecology seeks to reconcile the principle of ecology with the central features of capitalist modernity (individual self-seeking, materialism, economic growth and so on), which is why it sometimes called 'modernist' ecology. It is clearly a form of humanist or **'shallow' ecology.** The key feature of reformist ecology is that recognition that there are 'limits to growth', in that environmental degradation (in the form of, for instance, pollution or the use of non-renewable resources) ultimately threatens prosperity and economic performance. The watchword of this form of ecologism is sustainable development, especially what is called 'weak' sustainability. In economic terms, this means 'getting rich more slowly'. From the reformist perspective, damage to the environment is an **externality,** or 'social cost'. By taking account of such costs, modernist ecologists attempted to develop a balance between modernization and **sustainability.**

The chief ideological influence on reformist ecology is **utilitarianism,** which is based on classical liberal thinking. In that sense, reformist ecology practises what can be called 'enlightened' anthropocentrism, encouraging individuals to take account of long-term, not merely short-term, interests. The British utilitarian philosopher and politician John Stuart Mill (1806–73) thus justified a steady-state economy (one without economic growth) on the grounds that the contemplation of nature is a 'higher' pleasure. Peter Singer (1993) justified animal rights on the grounds that all species, and not just humans, have a right to avoid suffering. More generally, utilitarian thinking acknowledges the impact on the quality of human life of environmental degradation by recognizing the interests of future generations. The most straightforward case for conserving resources is therefore that it maximises the welfare or happiness of people, taking account of both the living and of people who have yet to be born. Finally, reformist ecology is defined by the means through which it would deal with environmental problems, as typified by the mainstream environmental movement.

68. Following is a short description of the famous works of Rabindranath Tagore:

1. **Gitanjali:** *Subject:* Devotion to God; *Genre:* Poem; Also known as 'Song Offerings', Rabindranath's Gitanjali is a collection of poems, originally written in Bengali and later translated into English. It made him win him the Nobel Prize in Literature. His unfathomable pain and unshaken devotion to God are captured in the moving prose verses of Gitanjali. *'Where the mind is without fear and the head held high; Where knowledge is free; Where the world has not been broken up into fragments by narrow domestic walls'*
2. **Chokher bali:** *Subject:* Extra-marital affair; *Genre:* Novel; A Bengali novel written by Tagore, 'Chokher Bali' or 'A grain of sand' is a story which revolves

around an extra-marital affair. It is a story about passion, desires, relationships, unfulfilled dreams as well as honesty. The complexity of relationships and of human character are very well portrayed in this novel.

3. **The Postmaster:** *Subject:* Loneliness and the search for meaning in the world; This is a touching story of a city-bred young man working as a postmaster in a remote village to earn his bread and butter.
4. **Gora:** *Genre:* Novel; It is the largest and the most complex of the 12 novels written by Rabindranath Tagore. It raises a number of issues/concerns, which seem very contemporary and are easily applicable to current scenario of our country. This book is a reflection and analysis of the multi-farious social life in colonial India.
5. **Kabuliwallah** (*The Fruitseller from Kabul*), 1961: The Kabuliwala is a moving tale of an Afghan vendor trying to earn a living in faraway Calcutta and the emotional bond he develops with the narrator's five-year-old daughter.
6. **Sadhana:** *The realization of life;* It relates a theory of a few points of the teaching of Jesus Christ and Gautama Buddha. This narrative touches many bases dealing with the virtue of man, greed, love and compassion.
7. **Shesher Kabita:** *Genre:* Novel; The novel was serialised in 1928, from Bhadro to Choitro in the magazine Probashi, and was published in book form the following year. It has been translated into English as *The Last Poem and Farewell song.* The book is about a platonic love of a matured couple. It is a saga, an epic love story.
8. **Ghare Baire** (*The Home and the World*): *Genre:* Autobiographical novel; It is a psychological novel and reflects upon the deeper meaning of life through a portrayal of the struggles of three distinct individuals. The backdrop of this novel is Swadeshi Movement, which played an important role in the independence of India.
9. **Nastanirh** (*The Broken Nest*): *Genre:* Novel; It narrates stories of those times when men were the main breadwinners of their families which allowed them to move out of the house, for work, for education, while their women tended to families.

70. Presidents of India

Name	Tenure
Rajendra Prasad	26-Jan-1950 to 13-May-1962
Sarvepalli Radhakrishnan	13-May-1962 to 13-May-1967
Zakir Hussain	13-May-1967 to 3-May-1969
Varahagiri Venkata Giri (Acting)	3-May-1969 to 20-July-1969
Justice Muhammad Hidayatullah (Acting)	20-July-1969 to 24-August-1969
Varahagiri Venkata Giri	24-August-1969 to 24-August-1974
Fakhruddin Ali Ahmed	24-August-1974 to 11-February-1977
Basappa Danappa Jatti	11-February-1977 to 25-July-1977
Neelam Sanjiva Reddy	25-July-1977 to 25-July-1982
Giani Zail Singh	25-July-1982 to 25-July-1987
Ramaswamy Venkataraman	25-July-1987 to 25-July-1992

Name	Tenure
Shankar Dayal Sharma	25-July-1992 to 25-July-1997
Kocheril Raman Narayanan	25-July-1997 to 25-July-2002
A. P. J. Abdul Kalam	25-July-2002 to 25-July-2007
Pratibha Patil	25-July-2007 to 25-July-2012
Pranab Mukherjee	25-July-2012 to 25-July-2017
Ram Nath Kovind	25-July-2017- till date

71. **Chipko Movement:** A forest conservation movement which began in 1973 in Uttrakhand against uncontrolled commercial logging under the leadership of Chandi Prasad Bhatt and Sundar Lal Bahuguna. It was essentially non-violent and Gandhian in nature which also comes under eco-feminist trend. It was mainly against the illegal commercial logging in the area.

Appiko Movement: Similar in nature, scope and cause to the Chipko movement which began in 1983 in Uttara Kannada district in Karnataka under the leadership of Pandurang Hegde.

Narmada Bachao Andolan: A social movement against the number of large dams being built across the Narmada river under the leadership of Medha Patkar and Baba Amte in 1985. Their mode of the campaign includes court actions, hunger strikes, rallies and gathering support from notable film and art personalities. This movement was against the inequitable distribution of resources and challenged the dominant model of development.

74. Article 19(1) of the Constitution guarantees basic civil liberties to all citizens of India: "(1) All citizens shall have the right to

(*a*) freedom of speech and expression;

(*b*) assemble peaceably and without arms;

(*c*) form associations or unions;

(*d*) move freely throughout the territory of India;

(*e*) reside and settle in any part of the territory of India;

(*f*) hold property;

(*g*) practice any profession or carry on any occupation, trade, or business."

75. **Public Accounts Committee:** Historically, the Webly Commission of 1896 indicated the need for an accounts committee to highlight financial irregularities. The Montague Chelmsford reforms suggested the creation of such committees out of the provincial legislatures.

The first such committee on Public Accounts was created at the centre to deal with the appropriation of Accounts of the Governor General in Council and the report of the Auditor General thereon. The British Parliament acquired power to grant appropriation with the Revolution of 1688. The power to ascertain how the money had been spent was conferred only in 1861, when the House of Commons created the committee on Public Accounts.

In India, the Public Accounts Committee was first created at the centre in 1923 with the coming into force of the Montford reforms in 1921. It became a major force in the legislative control of Public expenditure. Despite the limitations of its constitution and the restrictions on its authority, it exercised enormous influence in bringing to bear upon government the need to enforce economy in the expenditure of public money.

Estimates Committee: The Estimates Committee was first created in April, 1950 and its functions were enlarged in 1953. There had been a predecessor or Estimates Committee, called the Standing Finance Committee, which was first constituted in 1921 and attached to the Finance Department of the Government of India. This committee depended on the will of the executive. It had no statutory status. Its functions were not clearly defined and its deliberations were not satisfying to the elected representatives of the legislative assembly.

Committee on Public Undertakings: Till April 1964 the affairs of Public Enterprises in India used to be looked after by the two Committees: namely the Estimates Committee and Public Accounts Committee. But in view of huge investments and manifold increase in the activities of public enterprises it was felt that there should be a separate agency which should look into the working of public enterprises in detail and report to the Parliament. In 1964, on the recommendation of the Krishna Menon Committee, a separate committee on Public Undertakings was constituted. This committee, which started functioning from May 1, 1964 took over the work relating to autonomous Public Enterprises from the other two Committees viz the Estimates Committee and the Public Accounts Committee.

76. Panchsheel: The guiding principles of India's Foreign Policy have been founded on Panchsheel, pragmatism and pursuit of national interest. The five principles of peaceful coexistence or Panchsheel was evolved during talks between India and the People's Republic of China in 1954. The five principles which formed the basis of the non-aligned movement were laid down by Jawaharlal Nehru.

The Gujral Doctrine: This doctrine was an expression of the foreign policy initiated by Inder Kumar Gujral, the Foreign Minister in Deve Gowda Government which assumed office in June 1996. The Gujral Doctrine is a set of five principles to guide the conduct of foreign relations with India's immediate neighbours as spelt out by I.K. Gujral, first as India's External Affairs Minister and later as the Prime Minister.

"Look East Policy" of India was launched by the former Prime Minister P.V. Narasimha Rao in 1991. The main focus of this policy was to shift the country's trading focus from the west and neighbours to the booming South East Asian countries. This policy continued till the formation of the NDA government in 2014 after which, the newly formed government under PM Narendra Modi upgraded it to "Act East Policy". The "Act East Policy" was launched at the East Asia Summit in Myanmar in November 2014.

77. The Capital (Das Capital) : 1867

The Communist Manifesto : 1848

The Critique of the Gotha Programme : 1875

The Economic and Philosophical Manuscripts : 1932

79. The term first War of Independence was first popularized by Vinayak Damodar Savarkar in his 1909 book. The History of the War of Indian Independence, which was originally written in Marathi.

83. Prime Minister Chaudhary Charan Singh did not face Parliament. His tenure was from 28.07.1979–14.01.1980. Chaudhary Charan Singh, Prime Minister of India, Deputy Prime Minister, Home Minister and was also the Chief Minister of UP twice.

84. The constitutional provisions regarding the territories of India and their alteration are given in Articles 1 to 4. Article 1 of the Constitution says, "India, that is Bharat, shall be Union of States." It means the official name of India is Bharat and it is constituted as 'Union of States'. The term 'Union of States' was deliberately opted in place of Federation of States by the Constituent Assembly. According to Dr. B.R. Ambedkar, the Chairman of Drafting Committee, it implied two things—First, the federal system in India was not the result of agreement among the constituent units e.g., States as happened in the USA. Secondly, the constituent units of the union have no freedom to secede from the union.

Article 1(2) of the Constitution provides that the States and the territories thereof shall be as specified in the first schedule. Thus the first schedule of the Constitution lists the names of states and the centrally administered union territories.

86. Roy strongly believed that the Marxian interpretation of history is defective because it allowed no role to mental activity in the social process. History can never be interpreted solely with reference to materialistic objectivism.

The intelligence of human beings and their cumulative actions are very powerful social forces. Further, consciousness is regarded as being posterior to reality. Though later Marxists have tried to replace the old theory of dominance of material and social reality with that of concept of interaction between ideas and social forces, the Marxist philosophy of history and the creative role of ideas were minimized.

At this juncture, M.N. Roy tried to restate Marxism and propounded a theory of two parallel processes—ideal and physical—for composing history. According to Roy, there is a reciprocal interaction between the dynamism of ideas and the progression of social process. The theory of the parallelism of ideas and the texture of the objective society implies that no direct specific correlation is possible between a system of ideas and a set of events.

87. Unlike his Italian counterparts, Robert Michels studied specific organisations. He propagated the famous "iron law of oligarchy. " Oligarchy meaning rule by the few. In path breaking studies Michels proved that his law was applicable to socialist parties, most organisations and even the Labour party in England.

88. Features of corporatism:

- State, society and the market under corporatism are viewed as a single organic body with each element cooperating and performing its own specific and limited role.
- By it an authoritarian system attempts to solidify its control over the public by creating or sanctioning a limited number of organisation to represent the interest of the public, and restricting those not set up or approved by the state.
- As opposed to overlapping memberships, competition and ever-changing nature of organisations and political parties in a pluralist society.

Features of Neo-corporatism.

- It is a system of policy making involving state, labour and business groups.
- It rejects limited role of state. Instead, it uses policy in order to build consensus over competition by creating a limited number of associations that represent a large segment of business and labour. Many decisions are left to the state alone.

90. Chester Barnard defines an organisation as a "System of consciously coordinated activities or forces of two or more persons". He says that organisation comes into being when:

(*a*) There are persons able to communicate with each other;

(*b*) Who are willing to contribute action; and

(*c*) To accomplish a common purpose.

Previous Paper (Solved)

National Testing Agency (NTA)

UGC-NET-Junior Research Fellowship & Assistant Professor Exam

Political Science, December-2019*

PAPER-II

1. Arrange the formation of following states in chronological order:

(*a*) Sikkim (*b*) Goa
(*c*) Gujarat (*d*) Telangana

Choose the correct option:
A. (*a*), (*b*), (*c*) and (*d*)
B. (*d*), (*b*), (*c*) and (*a*)
C. (*b*), (*c*), (*a*) and (*d*)
D. (*c*), (*a*), (*b*) and (*d*)

2. Which of the following types of policy evaluation lays emphasis on determining the success level in achieving its basic objectives?
A. Programme Strategy Evaluation
B. Programme Impact Evaluation
C. Project Monitoring
D. Cost-benefit analysis

3. Which of the following two are correct regarding the adoption of inductive method?
(*a*) Plato
(*b*) Machiavelli
(*c*) Thomas Aquinas
(*d*) Thomas Hobbes

Choose the correct options:
A. (*a*) and (*b*) B. (*a*) and (*c*)
C. (*b*) and (*d*) D. (*a*) and (*d*)

4. Arrange the following in an ascending chronological order:
(*a*) Right to Education Act
(*b*) Consumer Protection (Amendment) Act
(*c*) Food Security Act
(*d*) Prevention of Corruption (Amendment) Act

Choose the correct option from below:
A. (*b*), (*c*), (*d*) and (*a*)
B. (*b*), (*a*), (*c*) and (*d*)
C. (*a*), (*b*), (*c*) and (*d*)
D. (*c*), (*a*), (*d*) and (*b*)

5. Which of the following are the salient features of Draft National Water Policy 2012?
(*a*) Setting up of Water Regulatory Authority
(*b*) Incentivisation of recycle and re-use
(*c*) Community participation in managing the water resources projects
(*d*) Water users association should be given statutory powers

Choose the correct option from below:
A. (*a*), (*b*) and (*c*)
B. (*a*), (*b*), (*c*) and (*d*)
C. (*b*), (*c*) and (*d*)
D. (*a*), (*b*) and (*d*)

6. Agganna Sutta deals with:
(*a*) Origin of life
(*b*) Origin of social order and castes
(*c*) Origin of secularism
(*d*) Origin of six fold policy

Select the correct answer from the code given below:
A. (*a*) only B. (*b*) only
C. (*a*) and (*b*) D. (*a*), (*b*) and (*d*)

7. According to G.A. Almond comparatively "Homogenous culture" is found in:
A. Developed countries
B. Underdeveloped countries
C. Developing countries
D. Least developed countries

* *Online exam held on 05 December, 2019.*

8. Make a sequence of Decision-making approach:
(*a*) Search for information
(*b*) Problem recognition
(*c*) Selection of alternative
(*d*) Definition of alternative
Select the right option:
A. (*a*), (*c*), (*d*), (*b*) B. (*b*), (*d*), (*a*), (*c*)
C. (*b*), (*a*), (*c*), (*d*) D. (*b*), (*a*), (*d*), (*c*)

9. 73rd Amendment of the Constitution seeks to provide which of the following to the Panchayati Raj Institutions?
(*a*) Constitutional status
(*b*) Financial autonomy
(*c*) Empowerment of marginalized sections of the rural population
(*d*) Decentralised planning
Choose the correct option from below:
A. (*a*), (*b*) and (*c*)
B. (*a*), (*b*), (*c*) and (*d*)
C. (*b*), (*c*) and (*d*)
D. (*a*), (*b*) and (*d*)

10. Given below are the two statements. One labelled as Assertion (A) and the other labelled as Reason (R):
Assertion (A): According to Plato, human soul consists of three elements – Reason, spirit and aptitude.
Reason (R): The state is the individual writ large.
Code:
A. Both (A) and (R) are true and (R) is the correct explanation of (A)
B. Both (A) and (R) are true, but (R) is not correct explanation of (A)
C. (A) is true, but (R) is false
D. (A) is false, but (R) is true

11. Which of the following is not related to Kabir?
A. Begampura B. Bhakti
C. Panchvani D. Gender inequality

12. Name the editor of the book. "Towards a New Public Administration-Minnowbrook":
A. James Charlesworth
B. Frank Marini
C. W.F. Willoughby
D. Frank J. Goodnow

13. Arrange the following in their chronological order:
(*a*) Jallianwala Bagh Massacre
(*b*) Report Submission by Hunter Committee
(*c*) Chauri-Chaura incident
(*d*) Establishment of Swaraj Party
Choose the correct option:
A. (*a*), (*b*), (*c*), (*d*) B. (*d*), (*c*), (*b*), (*a*)
C. (*a*), (*b*), (*d*), (*c*) D. (*d*), (*b*), (*a*), (*c*)

14. The book "Aspects of Political Development" is written by:
A. Lucian Pye B. G.A. Almond
C. G.H. Sabine D. Maurice Duverger

15. Match the following:

A	B
(*a*) Two Factor Theory	(*i*) McClelland
(*b*) Hierarchy of needs theory	(*ii*) McGregor
(*c*) Theory of needs	(*iii*) Maslow
(*d*) Theory X and Y	(*iv*) Herzberg

Code:

	(*a*)	(*b*)	(*c*)	(*d*)
A.	(*ii*)	(*iv*)	(*iii*)	(*i*)
B.	(*iii*)	(*iv*)	(*ii*)	(*i*)
C.	(*iv*)	(*i*)	(*iii*)	(*ii*)
D.	(*iv*)	(*iii*)	(*i*)	(*ii*)

16. The author of the book "Nation and Nationalism" is:
A. Ernest Gellner
B. Hans J. Morganthau
C. J.S. Coleman
D. Rajni Kothari

17. Which of the following statements are true regarding the composition of Rajya Sabha?
(*a*) Not more than 238 members represent States and Union territories in Rajya Sabha
(*b*) Representatives of Puducherry in the Rajya Sabha are elected
(*c*) Third Schedule of the Constitution deals with the allocation of seats in Rajya Sabha to States

(*d*) Fourth Schedule of the Constitution deals with the allocation of seats in Rajya Sabha to States

Choose the correct answer from the options given below:

A. (*a*) and (*b*) B. (*b*) and (*c*)
C. (*a*) and (*c*) D. (*a*), (*b*) and (*d*)

18. Which Article of the Indian Constitution provides power to the President to promulgate ordinances?

A. Article 123 B. Article 221
C. Article 222 D. Article 223

19. Which of the following pairs are correctly matched?

(*a*) John Rawls – Egalitarian
(*b*) Plato – Idealist
(*c*) Mary Wollstonecraft – Communist
(*d*) Gramsci – Feminist

Choose the correct answer from the options given below:

A. (*a*) and (*b*) B. (*b*) and (*c*)
C. (*c*) and (*d*) D. (*c*) and (*a*)

20. Which of the following two statements regarding World Trade Organization are correct?

(*a*) It is the only international organization dealing with global trade rules between nations
(*b*) It was established in 1996
(*c*) Its Headquarters is in Geneva
(*d*) It employs some 680 staff

Choose the correct options:

A. (*a*) and (*b*) B. (*a*) and (*c*)
C. (*c*) and (*d*) D. (*a*) and (*d*)

21. Which of the following two are correct regarding Right to Development?

(*a*) The Declaration on the Right to Development was adopted by General Assembly in 1986
(*b*) This is an inalienable human right
(*c*) It found no place in the 1993 Vienna Declaration and Programme of action
(*d*) In 1990 the Commission on Human Rights established a working group to monitor its progress

Choose the correct options

A. (*a*) and (*b*) B. (*b*) and (*c*)
C. (*c*) and (*d*) D. (*a*) and (*d*)

22. Who had formed the "Society for right to die with dignity"?

A. Jai Prakash Narayan
B. Minoo Masani
C. Krishna Ayyar
D. Medha Patkar

23. Arrange the following four reports of Second Administrative Reforms Commission in their sequential order:

(*a*) Right to Information
(*b*) Unlocking Human capital
(*c*) Crisis Management
(*d*) Ethics in Governance

Choose the correct option:

A. (*a*), (*b*), (*c*), (*d*) B. (*d*), (*c*), (*b*), (*a*)
C. (*a*), (*d*), (*b*), (*c*) D. (*c*), (*a*), (*d*), (*b*)

24. Who is not a supporter of Libertarianism?

A. Robert Nozick B. Milton Friedman
C. Robert Dahl D. F.A. Hayek

25. Who defined leadership as "the ability of a manager to induce subordinates to work with zeal and confidence"?

A. Koontz and O'Donnell
B. Chester Bernard
C. M.P. Follet
D. Peter Drucker

26. When did International Labour Organization become a specialized agency of the United Nations Organization?

A. 1945 B. 1946
C. 1947 D. 1948

27. Two statements are given below. One is a Assertion (A) and the other is Reason (R):

Assertion (A): United Nations Organisation was established on 24 October 1945

Reason (R): Its main object is to establish world peace and security.

Choose the correct options:

A. (A) and (R) both are correct and (R) is correct explanation of (A)

B. Both (A) and (R) are correct, but (R) is not correct explanation of (A)
C. (A) is correct, but (R) is wrong
D. (A) is wrong, but (R) is correct

28. Under which constitutional provision, elections to Panchayati Raj Bodies are conducted in India?
A. Article 243 J
B. Article 243 K
C. Article 243 L
D. Article 243 M

29. Which constitutional provision provides for formation of a Gram Sabha?
A. Article 243 A
B. Article 243 B
C. Article 243 C
D. Article 243 D

30. Which of the following statements about the significance of public policy is correct?
(*a*) Public policies help in achieving socio-economic development
(*b*) Public policies help maintain national unity and integrity
(*c*) It's basic purpose is to serve individual interest and solve public problems
(*d*) Public policy aims at shaping the society for its betterment

Choose the correct option from below:
A. (*a*), (*b*), (*c*) and (*d*)
B. (*b*), (*c*) and (*d*)
C. (*a*), (*b*) and (*d*)
D. (*a*), (*b*) and (*c*)

31. Rigg's Fused model is based on:
(*a*) dependence on agriculture
(*b*) attainment value in society
(*c*) domination of royal family
(*d*) economic system based on barter system

Choose the right option:
A. (*a*), (*c*), (*d*) B. (*a*), (*b*)
C. (*b*), (*c*), (*d*) D. (*a*), (*b*), (*c*)

32. Which of the following writers are from Italy?
(*i*) Vilfredo Pareto
(*ii*) Gaetano Mosca
(*iii*) Robert Michels
(*iv*) C. Wright Mills

Code:
A. (*i*) and (*ii*) B. (*i*) and (*iii*)
C. (*i*) and (*iv*) D. (*iii*) and (*iv*)

33. Which of the following freedoms was not mentioned by Roosevelt?
A. Freedom of speech
B. Freedom of worship
C. Freedom from fear
D. Freedom against exploitation

34. In which year did Rabindranath Tagore surrender the knighthood as a protest against Jallianwala Bagh Massacre?
A. 1919 B. 1924
C. 1935 D. 1937

35. Match List-I with List-II :

List-I (Author)	***List-II (Book)***
(*a*) Paul H Appleby	(*i*) Principles of Public Administration
(*b*) John M Gaus, L.D. White and M.E. Dimock	(*ii*) Ideas and Issues in Public Administration
(*c*) W.F. Willoughby	(*iii*) Morality and Administration in Democratic Government
(*d*) Dwight Waldo	(*iv*) The Frontiers of Public Administration

Code:

	(*a*)	(*b*)	(*c*)	(*d*)
A.	(*i*)	(*ii*)	(*iii*)	(*iv*)
B.	(*iii*)	(*iv*)	(*i*)	(*ii*)
C.	(*iv*)	(*ii*)	(*iii*)	(*i*)
D.	(*ii*)	(*i*)	(*iv*)	(*iii*)

36. Match the following:

A	***B***
(*a*) Common High Court for two or more states	(*i*) Art. 229
(*b*) Transfer of certain cases to High Court	(*ii*) Art. 233
(*c*) Appointment of District Judges	(*iii*) Art. 231

(*d*) Administrative expenses of High Courts (*iv*) Art. 228

Choose the correct options:

	(*a*)	(*b*)	(*c*)	(*d*)
A.	(*iii*)	(*iv*)	(*ii*)	(*i*)
B.	(*ii*)	(*iv*)	(*i*)	(*iii*)
C.	(*iv*)	(*ii*)	(*i*)	(*iii*)
D.	(*iii*)	(*ii*)	(*iv*)	(*i*)

37. Match List I with List II:

List-I (School of Modernization)	***List-II (Thinkers)***
(*a*) Psychological School	(*i*) Daniel Lerner
(*b*) Normative School	(*ii*) Mahatma Gandhi
(*c*) Structural School	(*iii*) G.A. Almond
(*d*) Technological School	(*iv*) David Apter

Choose the correct answer from below:

	(*a*)	(*b*)	(*c*)	(*d*)
A.	(*i*)	(*ii*)	(*iii*)	(*iv*)
B.	(*ii*)	(*iii*)	(*iv*)	(*i*)
C.	(*iv*)	(*ii*)	(*i*)	(*iii*)
D.	(*iii*)	(*i*)	(*ii*)	(*iv*)

38. Kyoto Protocol was enforced in:

A. 1997 B. 2000

C. 2005 D. 2006

39. On which of the following date, India joined as a member of the United Nations Human Rights Council?

A. 1 August 2019

B. 1 June 2019

C. 1 January 2019

D. 1 July 2019

40. Which of the following statements about the powers of the President is correct?

A. He presides over the meetings of the Zonal Councils

B. He is the head of the Inter-State Council

C. He can disqualify a member of Parliament under Art. 102 on the recommendation of the Election Commission

D. He can declare national emergency at his discretion

41. Who said, "Every state is known by the rights that it maintains"?

A. Laski B. Green

C. Hegel D. Barker

42. Which incident made Periyar an Atheist?

A. Self Respect Movement

B. Kashi Pilgrimage Incident

C. Dravída National Movement

D. Discrimination in society

43. Which of the following two statements are correct regarding Chinese policy of "Theory of Palm and five fingers"?

(*a*) It includes Bhutan and Nepal

(*b*) It includes Arunachal Pradesh, Sikkim and Laddakh

(*c*) It includes Mizoram and Manipur

(*d*) It includes Tripura and Nagaland

Choose the correct options:

A. (*a*) and (*c*) B. (*a*) and (*d*)

C. (*a*) and (*b*) D. (*b*) and (*c*)

44. Which of the following are the arguments for women's equality?

(*a*) Inferiority of women to men is socially constructed and has no legal justification

(*b*) Non-application of the principles of liberty and equality to the conditions of women is paradoxical

(*c*) Women are naturally inferior to men

(*d*) Women's inequality survived because it was justifiable

Choose the correct option from below:

A. (*a*), (*b*) and (*c*)

B. (*a*), (*b*), (*c*) and (*d*)

C. (*a*) and (*b*)

D. (*c*) and (*d*)

45. Which one of the following is not a function of political parties?

A. Socialisation and Recruitment

B. Interest articulation

C. Interest aggregation

D. Rule adjudication

46. Which among the following is the full title of the book written by Mary Wollstonecraft?

A. A Vindication of the Rights of Women
B. A Vindication of the Rights of Women with strictures on political and moral subjects
C. Reflections on the French Revolution
D. A Vindication of the Rights of Human Beings

47. Arrange the following of UN system in their chronological order:
(*i*) International Bank for Reconstruction and Development
(*ii*) Multilateral Investment Guarantee Agency
(*iii*) International Finance Corporation
(*iv*) International Development Association

Choose the correct option:
A. (*iv*), (*iii*), (*ii*), (*i*)
B. (*i*), (*iii*), (*iv*), (*ii*)
C. (*ii*), (*iv*), (*i*), (*iii*)
D. (*iii*), (*iv*), (*i*), (*ii*)

48. Arrange the following books as per the year of their publication in chronological order:
(*a*) Modern Democracies
(*b*) Constitutional Government and Democracy
(*c*) Public Opinion and Popular Government
(*d*) The American Commonwealth

Choose the correct option from below:
A. (*a*), (*b*), (*c*) and (*d*)
B. (*d*), (*c*), (*a*) and (*b*)
C. (*d*), (*a*), (*b*) and (*c*)
D. (*a*), (*c*), (*d*) and (*b*)

49. Arthashastra is known as:
A. Shruti B. Smriti
C. Samhita D. Nitishastra

50. Arrange these in a chronological order:
(*a*) Benn and RS Peters' Social Principles and Democratic State
(*b*) John Rawls' A Theory of Justice
(*c*) Susan Mollerokin's Justice, Gender and Family
(*d*) Rousseau's Social Contract

Choose the correct option from below:
A. (*d*), (*b*), (*a*) and (*c*)
B. (*a*), (*d*), (*b*) and (*c*)
C. (*b*), (*a*), (*c*) and (*d*)
D. (*c*), (*b*), (*d*) and (*a*)

51. Two statements are given below. One is Assertion (A) and other is Reason (R):

Assertion (A): Shimla Pact was signed by India and Pakistan in 1972.

Reason (R): It provides that the two countries will solve their disputes through mediation of other countries.

Choose the correct options:
A. Both (A) and (R) are correct and (R) is correct explanation of (A)
B. Both (A) and (R) are correct, but (R) is not correct explanation of (A)
C. (A) is correct, but (R) is wrong
D. (A) is wrong, but (R) is correct

52. Which of the following two statements are true regarding Indo-Pak relations on Kashmir?
(*a*) The Security Council first discussed the issue of Jammu and Kashmir in 1948.
(*b*) A summit meeting took place in 2004 in Islamabad between A.B. Vajpayee and Pervez Muzharraf
(*c*) A bus service across the ceasefire line was inaugurated in 2006
(*d*) Terrorist attack on Samjhauta Express was made in 2007

Choose the correct options:
A. (*a*) and (*b*) B. (*a*) and (*c*)
C. (*a*) and (*d*) D. (*c*) and (*d*)

53. Arrange the following Institutions/Organizations in chronological order:
(*i*) BRICS Development Bank
(*ii*) IBSA
(*iii*) G-7
(*iv*) G-20

Choose the correct option:
A. (*iii*), (*iv*), (*ii*), (*i*) B. (*i*), (*ii*), (*iii*), (*iv*)
C. (*iv*), (*iii*), (*ii*), (*i*) D. (*iii*), (*ii*), (*iv*), (*i*)

54. In which year UNESCO was set up?
A. 1945 B. 1946
C. 1947 D. 1948

55. The book "Political Order in Changing Societies" is written by:
A. Lucian Pye B. G.A. Almond
C. Ernest Barker D. S.P. Huntington

56. Who is the author of the book "Escape from Freedom"?
A. Herbert Marcuse
B. Erich Fromm
C. Jurgen Habermas
D. Thomas Friedman

57. Which one of the following is incorrect statement?
A. Globalisation means internationalization of economy
B. Globalisation gives emphasis on market economy
C. Globalisation gives rise to international institutions to supervise economy
D. Globalisation tends to perpetuate parochial culture

58. Who had condemned utilitarianism in his Theory of justice?
A. Plato B. Hayek
C. Rawls D. Milton

59. Ram Manohar Lohia was opposed to:
(*a*) Capitalism
(*b*) Communism
(*c*) Socialism
(*d*) Decentralisation of powers
Select the correct answer from the options given below:
A. (*a*) and (*b*) B. (*c*) and (*d*)
C. (*a*), (*b*) and (*c*) D. (*b*), (*c*) and (*d*)

60. Which are the themes of New Public Management?
(*a*) Adoption of private sector practices
(*b*) Improved reporting and monitoring mechanism
(*c*) Performance targets
(*d*) Adoption of public sector practices
Choose the correct option:
A. (*a*), (*b*) B. (*a*), (*b*), (*c*)
C. (*b*), (*c*), (*d*) D. (*c*), (*d*)

61. Two statements are given below. One is Assertion (A) and other is Reason (R):
Assertion (A): Herbert Simon rejected Principles of Administration
Reason (R): For Simon, these are merely proverbs
Choose the correct options:
A. Both (A) and (R) are true and (R) is the correct explanation of (A)
B. Both (A) and (R) are true, but (R) is not correct explanation of (A)
C. (A) is true, but (R) is false
D. (A) is false, but (R) is true

62. "Distributive Justice is mainly concerned with distribution of honours or wealth". Who said it?
A. Plato
B. Aristotle
C. Marx
D. Gramsci

63. Which statements are true about an Election Commissioner?
(*a*) He is appointed by President
(*b*) He can be removed from office on same grounds as a Judge of Supreme Court
(*c*) He can be removed by the President only on recommendation of Chief Election Commissioner
(*d*) His term of office is six years or upto the age of 65 whichever is earlier
Choose the correct answer:
A. (*a*), (*b*) B. (*b*), (*d*)
C. (*a*), (*c*) D. (*a*), (*c*), (*d*)

64. Match List I with List II:

List-I (Thinker)	*List-II (Work)*
(*a*) Mary Wollstonecraft	(*i*) The Wretched of the Earth
(*b*) Gramsci	(*ii*) Political Liberalism
(*c*) Frantz Fanon	(*iii*) Vindication of the Rights of Women
(*d*) John Rawls	(*iv*) The Prison Notebook

Code:

	(a)	(b)	(c)	(d)
A.	(iii)	(ii)	(iv)	(i)
B.	(iii)	(iv)	(i)	(ii)
C.	(ii)	(iii)	(iv)	(i)
D.	(i)	(ii)	(iii)	(iv)

65. Match the following:

A	B
(a) Absolute Veto	(i) When a bill is returned for reconsideration
(b) Qualified Veto	(ii) President cannot withhold assent if Bill is adopted again by the Houses
(c) Suspensive Veto	(iii) President may either assent or refuse to give assent without any time limit
(d) Pocket Veto	(iv) Power to say "no" to a bill passed by both Houses

Select the right code:

	(a)	(b)	(c)	(d)
A.	(ii)	(i)	(iii)	(iv)
B.	(iv)	(iii)	(ii)	(i)
C.	(iv)	(ii)	(i)	(iii)
D.	(iii)	(ii)	(iv)	(i)

66. Which of the following statements about National Health Policy, 2017 are correct?

(a) It aims to ensure availability of 2 beds per 1000 population

(b) It proposes free drugs, free diagnostics and free emergency health care services in all public hospitals

(c) Reduction of total fertility rate to 2.1 at national and sub-national level by 2025

(d) Reduce mortality rate of children under 5 years of age to 23 (per 1000) by 2020

Choose the correct option from below:

A. (a), (b) and (c)

B. (a), (b), (c) and (d)

C. (a) and (b)

D. (c) and (d)

67. Who defined Public Administration as "the art and science of management applied to the affairs of the state"?

A. L.D. White

B. H. Simon

C. D. Waldo

D. Pfiffner and Presthus

68. Who had differentiated between natural and conventional inequality?

A. Hobbes B. Locke

C. Rousseau D. Bentham

69. Match List I with List II:

List-I (Thinker)	*List-II (Work)*
(a) Jai Prakash Narayan	(i) Salt Taxation in India
(b) Ram Manohar Lohia	(ii) The Reconstruction of religious thought in Islam
(c) Muhammad Iqbal	(iii) Why socialism
(d) Barani	(iv) Fatwa-*i*-Jahandari

Select the correct option from the given below:

	(a)	(b)	(c)	(d)
A.	(iii)	(i)	(ii)	(iv)
B.	(ii)	(iii)	(iv)	(i)
C.	(i)	(ii)	(iii)	(iv)
D.	(iv)	(i)	(ii)	(iii)

70. Which of the following two are correct?

(a) According to August Comte, the principal methods are observation, experiment and comparison

(b) According to Bluntshli, the true methods are philosophical and historical

(c) Very few thinkers are pragmatic and inductive methods in contemporary times

(d) John Rawls had used deductive and dogmatic methods

Choose the correct options:

A. (a) and (b) B. (a) and (c)

C. (a) and (d) D. (b) and (c)

71. Theory of form and allegory of caves is related with:

A. Plato B. Aristotle

C. Machiavelli D. Hobbes

72. The Comptroller and Auditor-General of India can undertake evaluation studies on the basis of which of the following?
(*a*) On its own initiative
(*b*) The request of financial committees
(*c*) Directive in legislation
(*d*) The request of the Organization and Methods division of a Ministry

Choose the correct option from below:
A. (*a*), (*b*), (*c*) and (*d*)
B. (*a*), (*b*) and (*d*)
C. (*b*), (*c*) and (*d*)
D. (*a*), (*b*) and (*c*)

73. From legal point of view which of the following is called a "soft law"?
A. Right to Environment
B. Right to Development
C. Right to Health
D. Right to Privacy

74. The sequencing of communication process in organisation is:
A. Sender, message, receiver, encoding
B. Message, channel, feedback, encoding
C. Sender, encoding, decoding, receiver
D. Sender, encoding, message, channel

75. Which of the following two are correct?
(*a*) Plato laid more emphasis on duties than rights
(*b*) His ideal state was merely an idea not reality
(*c*) He was not a feminist
(*d*) He did speak about class state

Choose the correct option:
A. (*a*) and (*b*) B. (*a*) and (*c*)
C. (*a*) and (*d*) D. (*b*) and (*c*)

76. In which year, Government of India decided to observe the birthday of Swami Vivekananda as the National Youth Day?
A. 1984 B. 1985
C. 1986 D. 1987

77. The term "Sanskritisation" was coined by:
A. M.N. Srinivas B. M.S. Golwalkar
C. S.P. Mukherjee D. Andre Beteille

78. Vandana Shiva is known as:
A. Post Modernist B. Marxist
C. Eco-feminist D. Conservatist

79. Which of the following is not correct?
A. Nation is psychological concept
B. State is legal concept
C. Nationalism is attribute of Nation
D. Nation and state are co-terminus

80. On which of the following grounds Writ of Certiorari can be issued by the Judiciary?
(*a*) Lack of jurisdiction
(*b*) Locus Standi
(*c*) Excess of jurisdiction
(*d*) Error of law

Choose the correct option from below:
A. (*a*), (*b*) and (*c*)
B. (*a*), (*b*) and (*d*)
C. (*a*) and (*b*)
D. (*a*) and (*c*)

81. The positive impact of Liberalisation are:
(*a*) Foreign investment
(*b*) Increased production
(*c*) Increased unemployment
(*d*) Technological advancement

Choose the right answer:
A. (*a*), (*b*), (*d*) B. (*b*), (*c*)
C. (*a*), (*c*) D. (*b*), (*c*), (*a*)

82. Given below are two statements, one labelled as Assertion (A) and the other labelled as Reason (R):

Assertion (A): Aristotle was the first thinker to adopt inductive method but it was accidental.

Reason (R): In case of Machiavelli use of Inductive method was intentional.

Choose the correct option:
A. Both (A) and (R) are correct and (R) is correct explanation of (A)
B. Both (A) and (R) are true, but (R) is not correct explanation of (A)
C. (A) is true, but (R) is false
D. (A) is false, but (R) is true

83. Match List-I with List-II:

List-I	List-II
(*a*) Marx's theory of Alienation	(*i*) Herbert Marcuse
(*b*) Alienation and objectification	(*ii*) Erich Fromm
(*c*) Contemporary theory of Alienation	(*iii*) George Lukacs
(*d*) One-dimensionalisation: studies in the ideology of advanced industrial society	(*iv*) Economic and Philosophic Manuscripts of 1844

Choose the correct answer:

	(*a*)	(*b*)	(*c*)	(*d*)
A.	(*i*)	(*ii*)	(*iii*)	(*iv*)
B.	(*i*)	(*iv*)	(*iii*)	(*ii*)
C.	(*iv*)	(*ii*)	(*i*)	(*iii*)
D.	(*iv*)	(*iii*)	(*ii*)	(*i*)

84. When was Jaiprakash Narayan awarded Bharat Ratna?

A. 1999 B. 1998
C. 1997 D. 1996

85. Match List-I with the List-II regarding terrorism:

List-I	List-II
(*a*) Convention on offences and certain other acts committed on Board Aircraft (Tokyo)	(*i*) 1999
(*b*) Convention for suppression of unlawful acts against the safety of Civil Aviation (Montreal)	(*ii*) 1997
(*c*) International Convention for suppression of Terrorist Bombing	(*iii*) 1971
(*d*) International Convention for Suppression of Financing of Terrorism	(*iv*) 1963

Code:

	(*a*)	(*b*)	(*c*)	(*d*)
A.	(*i*)	(*ii*)	(*iii*)	(*iv*)
B.	(*iv*)	(*iii*)	(*ii*)	(*i*)
C.	(*iv*)	(*ii*)	(*iii*)	(*i*)
D.	(*ii*)	(*iii*)	(*iv*)	(*i*)

86. Which of the following two statements are correct regarding Preamble of Indian Constitution?

(*a*) Justice-social, economic and political
(*b*) Liberty of thought, expression, belief, faith and worship
(*c*) Equality of status, character and of opportunity
(*d*) Fraternity assuring the dignity and respect of the individual

Choose the correct option:

A. (*a*) and (*c*) B. (*a*) and (*d*)
C. (*c*) and (*d*) D. (*a*) and (*b*)

87. Match List-I with List II:

List-I (Organization)	List-II (Number of member states)
(*a*) Economic Community of West African States	(*i*) 6
(*b*) South African Development Community	(*ii*) 12
(*c*) Economic Community of Central African States	(*iii*) 16
(*d*) Eastern African Community	(*iv*) 15

Choose the correct options:

	(*a*)	(*b*)	(*c*)	(*d*)
A.	(*i*)	(*ii*)	(*iii*)	(*iv*)
B.	(*iv*)	(*iii*)	(*ii*)	(*i*)
C.	(*i*)	(*iv*)	(*iii*)	(*ii*)
D.	(*iii*)	(*iv*)	(*ii*)	(*i*)

88. The best propounder of Pluralist Theory of Citizenship was:

A. T.H. Marshal B. Anthony Giddens
C. B.S. Turner D. David Held

89. Which of the following statements about the definition of Welfare State are correct?

(*a*) It is a state that provides for its citizens a wide range of social services
(*b*) It is a compromise between communism on the one side and unbridled individualism on the other
(*c*) Welfare state sets a pattern for any humane and progressive society

(*d*) Welfare state guarantees a minimum standard of subsistence without removing incentives to private sector

Choose the correct option from below:

A. (*a*), (*b*) and (*c*)
B. (*b*), (*c*) and (*d*)
C. (*a*), (*b*), (*c*) and (*d*)
D. (*a*), (*b*) and (*d*)

90. Arrange the following Ashrams/Institutions founded by Gandhi in chronological order:

(*a*) Phoenix Settlement
(*b*) Kochrab Ashram
(*c*) Sevagram Ashram
(*d*) Tolstoy Farm

Select the correct answer from the options as given below:

A. (*a*), (*b*), (*c*), (*d*)
B. (*a*), (*d*), (*b*), (*c*)
C. (*d*), (*c*), (*b*), (*a*)
D. (*a*), (*c*), (*d*), (*b*)

Directions (Qs. 91-95): *Read the passage and answer the questions.*

Post modernist thinkers hold the view that there cannot be objective knowledge of social issues. For the Post Modernist, knowledge is not simply a cognitive factor: knowledge is also normative and political Power and knowledge are mutually supportive and they directly imply one another. The Post Modernist are critical of classical liberals as well as contemporary positivist who believed in objectivity and superiority of science. Through deconstruction, the post modernist want to look at every accepted or settled idea with new lenses.

91. Who among the following is not a Post Modernist thinker?

A. Richard Ashly
B. Jenny Adkins
C. Michel Foucault
D. J. Burton

92. Which one of the following statement is incorrect according to Post Modernist thinkers?

A. Post Moderners challenged the notion that knowledge is eternal
B. Knowledge is linked to power
C. Knowledge leads to progress of world
D. No knowledge is impartial

93. Which of following term is not preferred by Post Modernist thinkers?

A. Post structuralism
B. Deconstruction
C. Modernism
D. Subjectivity

94. According to Post-Modernist thinker, which attribute of knowledge does not exist?

A. Normative
B. Cognitive
C. Political
D. Objectivity

95. Which of the following is Post Modernist thinker?

A. Jacques Derrida
B. Immanuel Kant
C. H.J. Laski
D. Karl Deutsch

Directions (Qs. 96-100): *Read the passage and answer the questions.*

The term "globalisation" primarily refers to economic activities like trade, movement of capital, goods, labour and communication system across boundaries facilitating higher levels of inter-connectedness in the world. These economic activities have greater impact on socio-political sectors nationally and internationally. The increasing strong presence of non-state actors like MNCs, the NGOs and IGOs has questioned the supremacy of state sovereignty. The rich states are benefited due to their superior control over the flow of capital, technology and communication system. A profit oriented global market can never think of benefit of all people of the world. The North-South divide has not been obliterated.

96. Which one of the following has not limited state sovereignty?

A. Multinational Corporations
B. Inter Governmental Organization
C. Non-Governmental Organisation
D. Anomic Pressure Groups

97. The globalisation has increased the demand for:
A. Laissez Faire state
B. Welfare state
C. Totalitarian state
D. Socialistic state

98. Which one of the following is incorrect?
The state has become weak in shaping the:
A. Flow of capital
B. International trade and labour
C. Finance
D. Collection of revenues

99. Globalisation has induces greater:
A. Urbanisation B. Tradition
C. Rural societies D. Parochial culture

100. Globalisation has benefited the countries of:
A. Europe and America
B. Asia
C. Africa
D. Latin America

ANSWERS

1	2	3	4	5	6	7	8	9	10
D	B	C	*	B	C	A	D	A	D
11	**12**	**13**	**14**	**15**	**16**	**17**	**18**	**19**	**20**
A	B	A	A	D	A	D	A	A	B
21	**22**	**23**	**24**	**25**	**26**	**27**	**28**	**29**	**30**
A	B	A	C	A	B	A	B	A	C
31	**32**	**33**	**34**	**35**	**36**	**37**	**38**	**39**	**40**
A	A	D	A	B	A	A	C	C	C
41	**42**	**43**	**44**	**45**	**46**	**47**	**48**	**49**	**50**
A	B	C	C	D	B	B	B	D	A
51	**52**	**53**	**54**	**55**	**56**	**57**	**58**	**59**	**60**
C	A	A	A&B	D	B	D	C	A	B
61	**62**	**63**	**64**	**65**	**66**	**67**	**68**	**69**	**70**
A	B	D	B	C	A	C	C	A	A
71	**72**	**73**	**74**	**75**	**76**	**77**	**78**	**79**	**80**
A	D	B	D	A	A	A	C	D	D
81	**82**	**83**	**84**	**85**	**86**	**87**	**88**	**89**	**90**
A	B	D	A	B	D	B	C	C	B
91	**92**	**93**	**94**	**95**	**96**	**97**	**98**	**99**	**100**
D	C	C	D	A	D	A	D	A	A

EXPLANATORY ANSWERS

2. Programme Impact Evaluation lays emphasis on determining the success level in achieving its basic objectives. An impact evaluation analyses the (positive or negative, intended or unintended) impact of a project, programme or policy on the target population, and quantifies how large that impact is. Impact evaluations establish the causal effect of a project, programme or policy on one or several outcome(s). It involves buildings of counter-factual.

Impact evaluations thus show whether measurable changes in people's live can be attributed to a particular development project or programme. Impact evaluations are not about quantifying the effect of a project or programme on big overarching development goals—such as climate change reduction or poverty alleviation—that are only indirectly related to a programme. When speaking about impact evalution, impact is synonymous with that direct causal effect of a project, programme or policy on an outcome of interest.

3. Machiavelli and Thomas Hobbes are correct regarding the adoption of inductive method. In his methodology, Machiavelli was greatly influenced by Aristotle. But like Plato his method was inductive rather than deductive and he borrowed a great deal from the historical method of Aristotle. Unlike the other medieval thinkers, Machiavelli did not appeal to the revealed will be God, instead he appealed to reasons and history. It has rightly been said that "The Prince was the first great work in which the two authorities—the divine and the human, were clearly seen in collision and in which the venerable axioms of earlier generation were rejected as practically misleading and theoretically unsound."

The scientific method is one of the greatest contributions of Hobbes to political theory. He applied it for the first time to social sciences and tried to draw deductions from the axioms, assumptions and already established truths. No doubt, Plato before him also applied scientific method to the study of political thought, but he was the first thinker who asserted that political theory was based on the existence of matter and motion.

5. National Water Policy is formulated by the Ministry of Water Resources of the Government of India to govern the planning and development of water resources and their optimum utilization. The first National Water Policy was adopted in September, 1987. It was reviewed and updated in 2002 and later in 2012.

Salient features of NWP-2012:

- Envisages to establish a standardized national information system with a network of data banks and data bases.
- Resource planning and recycling for providing maximum availability.
- To give importance to the impact of projects on human settlements and environment.
- Guidelines for the safety of storage dams and other water-related structures.
- Regulate exploitation of groundwater.
- Setting water allocation priorities in the following order: Drinking water, Irrigation, Hydropower, Navigation, Industrial and other uses.
- The water rates for surface water and ground water should be rationalized with due regard to the interests of small and marginal farmers.

The policy also deals with participation of farmers and voluntary agencies, water quality, water zoning, conservation of water, flood and drought management, erosion etc.

6. Agganna Sutta of Digha Nikaya clearly explains how human society comes into being and disappears. According to the Sutta, the appearance of society is called vivatthakappa or evolving time, opening or evolution. The disappearance of the society is called samvattakappa-devolving time or dissolution.

The Agganna Sutta of the Digha Nikaya begins by portraying an ideal world of natural effortless existence. Ethereal, self-luminescent beings live in bliss and know no discrimination between polar opposites such as male and female, good and evil, rich and poor. The earth itself is 25 made of a delightful soft edible substance that looks like butter and is as sweet as honey.

Gradually, however, because of karma remaining from a previous world cycle, this Golden Age comes to an end. On account of greed, those being began to eat the existing substance. The self-illumination disappeared. People began to live on plant, mushroom, creepers and rice. They started living on rice; their sex division came into existence. They had sex in the public and later they were criticized as immoral and were chased out. As a result, the shelter was built as hiding place for those who engaged in sex.

Later people began to store up rice for future consumption. This also led to the development. At this stage, greed, grasping, sex, theft, violence and murder are introduced. Finally, sheer anarchy prevails, and in order to put an end to it, the beings get together to select from among their ranks a king to rule over them and maintain order. This is the Mahasammata, the Great Elect, and in return for fulfilling his functions as a monarch, the beings each agree to pay him a portion of their rice. This is the development of human society.

7. Gabriel Almond and Sidney Verba in 'The Civic Culture' outlined three pure types of political culture based on level and type of political participation and the nature of people's attitudes towards politics—

Parochial: Where citizens are only remotely aware of the presence of central government, and live their lives near enough regardless of the decisions taken by the state, distant and unaware of political phenomena. They have neither knowledge nor interest in politics. This type of political culture is in general congruent with a traditional political structure.

Subject: Where citizens are aware of central government, and are heavily subjected to its decisions with little scope for dissent. The individual is aware of politics, its actors and institutions. It is affectively oriented towards politics, yet it is on the "downward flow" side of the politics. In general congruent with a centralized authoritarian structure.

Participant: Citizens are able to influence the government in various ways and they are affected by it. The individual is oriented toward the system as a whole, to both the political and administrative structures and processes (to both the input and output aspects). In general congruent with a democratic political structure.

8. The decision-making process involves the following steps:

1. Define the problem.
2. Identify limiting factors.
3. Develop potential alternatives.
4. Analyze the alternatives.
5. Select the best alternative.
6. Implement the decision.
7. Establish a control and evaluation system.

9. The Constitution (73rd Amendment) Act was passed in 1992 and it came into effect on 24 April 1993. The Act empowered state governments to take the necessary steps that would lead to the formalisation of the gram panchayats and help them operate as units of self-governance. This Act added a new chapter into the Constitution called 'Part IX: The Panchayats'.

- The chief features of the act are mentioned below:
  - This Act made the Panchayati Raj institutions in the country constitutional bodies.
  - Under Article 243-B, it has become compulsory for every state to establish panchayats in their territories.
  - Article 243-G makes it mandatory for the state governments to devolve powers, responsibilities and authority to the panchayats.
  - The gram panchayats have a fixed tenure of 5 years.
  - State election commissions have been provided with the mechanism to conduct independent elections to the village panchayats.
  - Article 243-D gives provisions for the due representation of women and SC/STs.
  - The State Finance Commission should also evaluate the financial position of the panchayats every five years.

The passing of the 73rd Amendment has improved local self-government in the country vastly.

In order to celebrate this and further give impetus to the institutions, the central government in 2010 decided to observe 24th April every year as National Panchayati Raj Day.

Today, the formalised panchayati raj functions in three levels namely, the Gram Panchayat (at the village level), the Mandal Parishad/ Panchayat Samiti/Block Samiti (at the Block level), and the Zila Parishad (at the district level).

10. Plato belong to the school of Idealism and was known as a father of political philosophy. According to Plato state is magnified version of individual (man), he suggested that state do not come out of oak or rock but it's present in the mind of the individual who lives in the state. He makes this statement on the contest of deriving the principle of Justice, since the state is a bigger form of an individual so the principles of Justice found at the level of individual can be applied at the level of state. According to Plato, if just (honest) man is one in whom 'Reason' dominates over 'Courage and Appetite'. Just state is where 'man of reason (philosopher king)' rules over 'man of courage and appetite'. It is to be noted that Plato suggested that justice is actually the quality of soul and just state can be created only when people living in the state are just. The principles that should govern life of the people is known as ethics and he suggested that ethics should be the basis of politics.

12. Toward a New Public Administration: The Minnowbrook Perspective is edited by Frank Marini in 1971. New Public Administration traces its origins to the first Minnowbrook Conference held in 1968 under the patronage of Dwight Waldo. This conference brought together the top scholars in public administration and management to discuss and reflect on the state of the field and its future.

The 1960s in the USA was a time of unusual social and political turbulence and upheaval. In this context, Waldo concluded that neither the study nor the practice of public administration was responding suitably to the escalating turmoil and the complications that arose from those conditions. Part of the reasoning for this Waldo argued, was the general mistrust that had become associated with public administration itself. A call to revamp the ethical obligations of the service sector was necessary in rebuilding the public's trust of government and bureaucracy in which had been plagued by corruption and the narrow self interests of others. Moving toward a more ethical public service, then, required attention to the underlying values that support public service-and public servants-in any sector.

13. The Jallianwala Bagh massacre, also known as the Amritsar massacre, took place on 13 April 1919, when Acting Brigadier-General Reginald Dyer ordered troops of the British Indian Army to fire their rifles into a crowd of unarmed Indian civilians in Jallianwala Bagh, Amritsar, Punjab, killing at least 400 people including men and women. Over 1,000 people were injured.

On 14 October 1919, after orders issued by the Secretary of State for India, Edwin Montagu, the Government of India announced the formation of a committee of inquiry into the events in Punjab. Referred to as the Disorders Inquiry Committee, it was later more widely known as the Hunter Commission. It was named after the chairman, William, Lord Hunter, former Solicitor-General for Scotland and Senator of the College of Justice in Scotland. Although the members of the Commission had been divided by racial tensions following Dyer's statement, and though the Indian members had written a separate, minority report, the final report, comprising six volumes of evidence and released on 8 March 1920, unanimously condemned Dyer's actions.

The Chauri Chaura incident took place at Chauri Chaura in the Gorakhpur district of the United Province, (modern Uttar Pradesh) in British India on 4 February 1922, when a large group of protesters, participating in the Non-cooperation movement, clashed with police, who opened fire. In retaliation the demonstrators attacked and set fire to a police station, killing all of its occupants. The incident led to the deaths of three civilians and 22 policemen. Mahatma Gandhi, who was strictly against violence, halted the non-co-operation movement on the national level on 12 February 1922, as a direct result of this incident.

The Swaraj Party was established as the Congress-Khilafat Swaraj Party. It was a political party formed in India in January 1923 after the Gaya annual conference in December 1922 of the National Congress, that sought greater self-government and political freedom for the Indian people from the British Raj. The two most important leaders were Chittaranjan Das, who was its president and Motilal Nehru, who was its secretary.

14. The book Aspects of Political Development is written by Lucian W. Pye. Lucian W. Pye (1921-2008) was an American political scientist, sinologist and comparative politics expert considered one of the leading China scholars in the United States. Educated at Carleton College and Yale University, Pye chose to focus on the characteristics of specific cultures in forming theories of political development of modernization of Third World nations, rather than seeking universal and overarching theories like most political scientists. As a result, he became regarded as one of the foremost contemporary practitioners and proponents of the concept of political culture and political psychology.

16. Nations and Nationalism is a 1983 book by the philosopher Ernest Gellner, in which the author expands on his theory of nationalism. Gellner's theory of nationalism was developed by Ernest Gellner over a number of publications from around the early 1960s to his 1995 death. Gellner discussed nationalism in a number of works, starting with Thought and Change (1964), and he most notably developed it in Nations and Nationalism (1983). Gellner analyzed nationalism by a historical perspective. He saw the history of humanity culminating in the discovery of modernity, nationalism being a key functional element. Modernity, by changes in political and economic system, is tied to the popularization of education, which, in turn, is tied to the unification of language. However, as modernization spread around the world, it did so slowly, and in numerous places, cultural elites were able to resist cultural assimilation and defend their own culture and language successfully.

17. Article 80 of the Indian Constitution deals with composition of the council of states (Rajya Sabha). Clause 1 of this article provides that the maximum strength of the Rajya Sabha is 250 out of which 12 members are nominated by the president and 238 are representatives of the states and the union territories. The present strength of Rajya Sabha, however, is 245, out of which 233 are representatives of the States and Union territories of Delhi, Puducherry and J&K and 12 are nominated by the president. The members nominated by the President are persons having special knowledge or practical experience in respect of such matters as literature, science, art and social service. The Rajya Sabha is not subject to dissolution; one third of its members retire every second year. 4th Schedule of the constitution deals with the allocation of seats in Rajya Sabha.

18. Article 123 deals with the power of the President to promulgate ordinances to enact new legislations/amend existing legislations. This power is executed in 2 scenarios—

1. If either one of houses of Parliament is not in session.
2. If both of the houses of Parliament are not in session.

The ordinances so promulgated has to be passed by both houses within 6 weeks of reassembly of the Parliament. *i.e.,* maximum duration of an ordinance is 6 months and 6 weeks.

Remember, even ordinance making power can't bypass judicial scrutiny. If found unconstitutional, it can well be scrapped.

20. World Trade Organization (WTO), international organization established to supervise and liberalize world trade. The WTO is the successor to the General Agreement on Tariffs and Trade (GATT), which was created in 1947 in the expectation that it would soon be replaced by a specialized agency of the United Nations (UN) to be called the International Trade Organization (ITO). Although the ITO never materialized, the GATT proved remarkably successful in liberalizing world trade over the next five decades. By the late 1980s there were calls for a stronger multilateral organization to monitor trade and resolve trade disputes. Following the completion of the Uruguay Round (1986-94) of multilateral trade negotiations, the WTO began operations on January 1, 1995. Its headquarter is in Geneva. As of 2019 the WTO has 164 member countries, with Liberia and Afghanistan the most recent members, having joined in July 2016, and 23 "observer" countries.

21. Everyone is "entitled to participate in, contribute to, and enjoy economic, social, cultural and political development, in which all human rights and fundamental freedoms can be fully realized," the groundbreaking UN Declaration on the Right to Development proclaimed in 1986 that development is a right that belongs to everyone.

The right to development is an inalienable human right by virtue of which every human person and all peoples are entitled to participate in, contribute to, and enjoy economic, social, cultural and political development, in which all human rights and fundamental freedoms can be fully realized.

The human right to development also implies the full realization of the right of peoples to self-determination, which includes, subject to the relevant provisions of both International Covenants on Human Rights, the exercise of their inalienable right to full sovereignty over all their natural wealth and resources.

22. Minoo Masani, an astute parliamentarian and liberal thinker, founded 'The Society for the Right to Die with Dignity' in May 1981, Mumbai, gracefully articulating the demand for voluntary euthanasia at a time when the topic was not much in vogue. In the following excerpt (from Freedom First, November 20, 1995), Masani eloquently presents his case for the right to choose between life and death.

24. Libertarian political thought is characterized by the strict priority given to liberty (understood in negative terms) over other values, such as authority, tradition and equality. Libertarians thus seek to maximize the realm of individual freedom and minimize the scope of public authority, typically seeing the state as the principal threat to liberty.

In the 1970s, Robert Nozick was responsible for popularizing this usage of the term in academic and philosophical circles outside the United States, especially with the publication of 'Anarchy, State and Utopia-1974', a response to social liberal John Rawls' 'A Theory of Justice-1971'. In this book, Nozick proposed a 'minimal state' on the grounds that it was an inevitable phenomenon which could arise without violating individual rights.

Other libertarians are F.A. Hayek, Milton Friedman, Randy Barnett, Murray Rothbard, etc.

25. The definitions given by some famous authors and management experts are given below:

Koontz and O'Donnel: Leadership is the ability of a manager to induce subordinates to work with confidence and zeal.

Peter Drucker: Leadership is not making friends and influencing people, i.e., salesmanship it is the lifting of man's visions to higher rights, the raising of man's personality beyond its normals limitations.

Chester Bernard: Leadership is the ability of a superior to influence the behaviour of a subordinate or group and persuade them to follow a particular course of action.

26. International Labour Organization (ILO), specialized agency of the United Nations (UN) dedicated to improving labour conditions and living standards throughout the world. Established in 1919 by the Treaty of Versailles as an affiliated agency of the League of Nations, the ILO became the first affiliated specialized agency of the United Nations in 1946. In recognition of its activities, the ILO was awarded the Nobel Prize for Peace in 1969.

The functions of the ILO include the development and promotion of standards for national legislation to protect and improve working conditions and standards of living. The ILO also provides technical assistance in social policy and administration and in workforce training; fosters cooperative organizations and rural industries; compiles labour statistics and conducts research on the social problems of international competition, unemployment and underemployment, labour and industrial relations, and technological change (including automation); and helps to protect the rights of international migrants and organized labour.

27. United Nations (UN), international organization established on October 24, 1945. The United Nations (UN) was the second multipurpose international organization established in the 20th century that was worldwide in scope and membership. Its predecessor, the League of Nations, was created by the Treaty of Versailles in 1919 and disbanded in 1946. Headquartered in New York City, the UN also has regional offices in Geneva, Vienna, and Nairobi. Its official languages are Arabic, Chinese, English, French, Russian, and Spanish.

In addition to maintaining peace and security, other important objectives include developing friendly relations among countries based on respect for the principles of equal rights and self-determination of peoples; achieving worldwide cooperation to solve international economic, social, cultural, and humanitarian problems; respecting and promoting human rights; and serving as a centre where countries can coordinate their actions and activities toward these various ends.

28. 243 K. Elections To The Panchayats:

(1) The superintendence, direction and control of the preparation of electoral rolls for, and the conduct of, all elections to the Panchayats shall be vested in a State Election Commission consisting of a State Election Commissioner to be appointed by the Governor.

(2) Subject to the provisions of any law made by the Legislature of a State, the conditions of service and tenure of office of the State Election Commissioner shall be such as the Governor may by rule determine:

Provided that the State Election Commissioner shall not be removed from his office except in like manner and on the like grounds as a Judge of a High Court and the conditions of service of the

State Election Commissioner shall not be varied to his disadvantage after his appointment.

(3) The Governor of a State shall, when so requested by the State Election Commission, make available to the State Election Commission such staff as may be necessary for the discharge of the functions conferred on the State Election Commission by clause (1).

(4) Subject to the provisions of this Constitution, the Legislature of a State may, by law, make provision with respect to all matters relating to, or in connection with, elections to the Panchayats.

29. Article-243 A— A Gram Sabha may exercise such powers and perform such functions at the village level as the Legislature of a State may, by law, provide. "Gram Sabha" means a body consisting of persons registered in the electoral rolls relating to a village comprised within the area of Panchayat at the village level.

31. Fred Riggs, who is known as the Father of Comparative Public Administration is propounder of ecological approach. He wrote the book "The Ecology of Public Administration" in 1962 in which he threw light on the relationship & interaction of an administration with its external surroundings. He analyzed that many factors like political, social, economic, administrative etc. are influenced by its environment & in turn influences the environment in which it works.

In his approach, he described two types of models:

[A] Agraria-Transita-Industria Model [1956-1957]

[B] Fused-Prismatic-Diffracted Model [1959] [Outcome of ATI MODEL]

Fused-Prismatic-Diffracted Model deals with underdeveloped, developing & developed societies. For this he used the example from Thailand [Underdeveloped Society] and contemporary U.S.A [*i.e.* developed society].

Between both of these extremes, there exists the PRISMATIC SOCIETY which has administrative sub-system known as "SALA" Model.

Riggs mainly focussed on Prismatic Society and its features by a diagram of PRISM.

Fused society performs multiple functions *i.e.* there is a large volume of work whereas in diffracted society there are specific and limited number of functions,

There are 3 basic features of Prismatic-Sala Models:

1. **Heterogeneity:** In this type of system, there are different kinds of patterns, rules, systems & viewpoints. This society is a blend of elements of "CHAMBER" [*i.e.* of fused society] & "BUREAU" [*i.e.* of diffracted society]. Thus heterogeneous group where the qualities are not alike are seen in this Model.
2. **Formalism:** This is the second most important feature which show a wide gap between theory and practice i.e. what is formally prescribed and effectively practiced. It shows a distinction between norms and realities.
3. **Overlapping:** This features shows that differentiated structures [clubs] co-exist with undifferentiated structures [Sects]. This denotes overlapping of administrative behaviour of both the societies.

Riggs called these elements as "CLECTS" (club + sects).

33. The Four Freedoms were goals articulated by United States President Franklin D. Roosevelt in 1941. In an address known as the Four Freedoms speech (technically the 1941 State of the Union address), he proposed four fundamental freedoms that people "everywhere in the world" ought to enjoy:

1. Freedom of speech
2. Freedom of worship
3. Freedom from want
4. Freedom from fear

34. Due to Jallianwala Bagh massacre (happened in 13th April 1919) incident, Rabindranath Tagore surrendered his title to British. Rabindranath Tagore got Knighthood from King George-V in 1915 for his contribution to literature. Later in 1919, he renounced knighthood for the inhuman act of British in Jallianwala Bagh. Due to same reason Gandhi returned the Kaiser-i-Hind Gold medal given to him by British government for his work during Boer war.

36. **Article 228:** If the High Court is satisfied that a case pending in a court subordinate to it involves a substantial question of law as to the interpretation of this constitution the determination of which is necessary for the disposal of the case, it shall withdraw the case and may.

(*i*) either dispose of the case itself, or

(*ii*) determine the said question of law and return the case to the court from which the case has been so withdrawn together with a copy of its judgement on such question, and the said court shall on receipt thereof proceed to dispose of the case in confirmity with such judgement.

Article 229: The administrative expenses of a High Court, including all salaries, allowances and pensions payable to or in respect of the officers and servants of the court, shall be charged upon the Consolidated Fund of the State, and any fees or other moneys taken by the Court shall form part of that Fund.

Article 231: It states that the Parliament may by law establish a common High Court for two or more states or for two or more states and a Union territory.

Article 233: Appointments of persons to be, and the posting and promotion of, district judges in any state shall be made by the Governor of the state in consultation with the High Court exercising jurisdiction in relation to such state.

38. The Kyoto Protocol is a protocol (update) to the United Nations Framework Convention on Climate Change. It was initially adopted on 11 December 1997 in Kyoto, Japan and entered into force on 16 February 2005.

This international treaty seeks to implement the objectives of the United Nations Framework Convention on Climate Change (UNFCCC) to combat global warming by decreasing greenhouse gas concentrations in the atmosphere.

The major greenhouse gases that are addressed are :

- Carbon dioxide (CO_2)
- Methane (CH_4)
- Nitrous oxide (N_2O)
- Hydrofluorocarbons (HFCs)
- Perfluorocarbons (PFCs)
- Sulphur hexafluoride (SF_6)

39. India was elected to the United Nations' top human rights body for a period of three years beginning January 1, 2019, getting 188 votes in the Asia-Pacific category, the highest number of votes among all candidates. The 193-member UN General Assembly held elections here for new members to the UN Human Rights Council. The 18 new members were elected by absolute majority through a secret ballot. Countries needed a minimum of 97 votes to get elected to the Council.

40. Article 102 of the Constitution of India "Disqualification's for membership":

(1) A person shall be disqualified for being chosen as, and for being, a member of either House of Parliament:

(*a*) if he holds any office of profit under the Government of India or the Government of any State, other than an office declared by Parliament by law not to disqualify its holder;

(*b*) if he is of unsound mind and stands so declared by a competent court;
(*c*) if he is an undischarged insolvent;
(*d*) if he is not a citizen of India, or has voluntarily acquired the citizenship of a foreign State, or is under any acknowledgement of allegiance or adherence to a foreign State;
(*e*) if he is so disqualified by or under any law made by Parliament.

Explanation:

(1) For the purposes of this clause a person shall not be deemed to hold an office of profit under the Government of India or the Government of any State by reason only that he is a Minister either for the Union or for such State.

(2) A person shall be disqualified for being a member of either House of Parliament if he is so disqualified under the Tenth Schedule.

Article 103 of the Constitution of India "Decision on questions as to disqualifications of members":

(1) If any question arises as to whether a member of either House of Parliament has become subject to any of the disqualifications mentioned in clause (1) of Article 102, the question shall be referred for the decision of the President and his decision shall be final.

(2) Before giving any decision on any such question, the President shall obtain the opinion of the Election Commission and shall act according to such opinion.

41. According to Laski, "rights are those conditions of social life without which no man can seek, in general to be himself at his best." Even though the rights aim at the development and enrichment of the individual they lead to the all-round development of social life because the development of the part automatically leads to the enrichment of the entire society. Therefore, it is in the interest of the state to maintain rights. Laski has rightly said that, "Every state is known by the rights that it maintains." According to the latest and the most current view, state is a welfare or social agency and strives to guarantee the rights of the individuals dwelling in it.

42. In 1904, E.V. Ramasamy went on a pilgrimage to Kasi to visit the revered Shiva temple of Kashi Vishwanath. Though regarded as one of the holiest sites of Hinduism, he witnessed immoral activities such as begging, and floating dead bodies. His frustrations extended to functional Hinduism in general when he experienced what he called Brahmanic exploitation.

However, one particular incident in Kasi had a profound impact on E.V. Ramasamy's ideology and future work. At the worship site there were free meals offered to guests. To E.V. Ramasamy's shock, he was refused meals at choultries, which exclusively fed Brahmins. Due to extreme hunger, E.V. Ramasamy felt compelled to enter one of the eateries disguised as a Brahmin with a sacred thread on his bare chest, but was betrayed by his moustache. The gatekeeper at the temple concluded that E.V. Ramasamy was not a Brahmin, as Brahmins were not permitted by the Hindu shastras to have moustaches. He not only prevented Periyar's entry but also pushed him rudely into the street.

As his hunger became intolerable, Periyar was forced to feed on leftovers from the streets. Around this time, he realised that the eatery which had refused him entry was built by a wealthy non-Brahmin from South India. This discriminatory attitude dealt a blow to Periyar's regard for Hinduism, for the events he had witnessed at Kasi were completely different from the picture of Kasi he had in mind, as a holy place which welcomed all. Ramasamy was a theist until his visit to Kasi, after which his views changed and he became an atheist.

43. India and China display a peculiar case of "constrained cooperation," in which the convergence of their economic interests tends to mask their prevailing strategic differences. Yet these divergences, of which the territorial and boundary dispute is foremost, still hold the potential of upstaging ties at any point. The boundary issue comes foremost in the list of problem areas. India's doubts emanate from China's aggressive policies as Mao's description of China's 'palm' (Tibet) and 'five fingers' (Nepal, Sikkim, Bhutan, NEFA and Ladakh). China also published maps showing India's Assam, even Andamans, as 'historically' parts of China. Chinese claims are based on its historical period which ended in 1912.

45. Every political party has a number of functions to perform. Here we have listed some of them:

(*i*) A political party contests elections by putting up candidates.

(*ii*) Representing groups of interests.

(*iii*) Every party has different policies and programmes. Voters make a choice in accordance with the policies and programmes liked by them.

(*iv*) Political parties shape public opinion. With the help of the pressure groups, the parties launch movements for solving problems faced by the people.

(*v*) Providing platform for socialisation and recruitment processes.

(*vi*) Parties even offer access to government machinery and welfare schemes.

46. A Vindication of the Rights of Woman: with Strictures on Political and Moral Subjects (1792), written by the 18th-century British proto-feminist Mary Wollstonecraft, is one of the earliest works of feminist philosophy. In it, Wollstonecraft responds to those educational and political theorists of the 18th century who did not believe women should receive a rational education. She argues that women ought to have an education commensurate with their position in society, claiming that women are essential to the nation because they educate its children and because they could be "companions" to their husbands, rather than mere wives. Instead of viewing women as ornaments to society or property to be traded in marriage, Wollstonecraft maintains that they are human beings deserving of the same fundamental rights as men.

47. The International Bank of Reconstruction and Development (IBRD) is one of the two major institutions that make up the World Bank, with the other being the International Development Association (IDA). The IBRD was founded in 1944 with the goal of helping war-torn European countries rebuild their infrastructure and their economies.

The International Finance Corporation (IFC) is an international financial institution that offers investment, advisory, and asset-management services to encourage private-sector development in less developed countries. The IFC is a member of the World Bank Group and is headquartered in Washington, D.C. in the United States. It was established in 1956, as the private-sector arm of the World Bank Group, to advance economic development by investing in for-profit and commercial projects for poverty reduction and promoting development.

The International Development Association (IDA) is an international financial institution which offers concessional loans and grants to the world's poorest developing countries. The IDA is a member of the World Bank Group and is headquartered in Washington, D.C. in the United States. It was established in 1960 to complement the existing International Bank for Reconstruction and Development by lending to developing countries which suffer from the lowest gross national income, from troubled creditworthiness, or from the lowest per capita income. Together, the International Development Association and International Bank for Reconstruction and Development are collectively generally known as the World

Bank, as they follow the same executive leadership and operate with the same staff.

The Multilateral Investment Guarantee Agency (MIGA) is an international financial institution which offers political risk insurance and credit enhancement guarantees. These guarantees help investors protect foreign direct investments against political and non-commercial risks in developing countries. MIGA is a member of the World Bank Group and is headquartered in Washington, D.C. in the United States. MIGA was established in 1988 as an investment insurance facility to encourage confident investment in developing countries.

49. *Arthashastra* is known as nitishastra. The title "Arthashastra" is often translated to "the science of politics", but the book Arthashastra has a broader scope. It includes books on the nature of government, law, civil and criminal court systems, ethics, economics, markets and trade, the methods for screening ministers, diplomacy, theories on war, nature of peace, and the duties and obligations of a king. The text incorporates Hindu philosophy, includes ancient economic and cultural details on agriculture, mineralogy, mining and metals, animal husbandry, medicine, forests and wildlife.

The *Arthashastra* explores issues of social welfare, the collective ethics that hold a society together, advising the king that in times and in areas devastated by famine, epidemic and such acts of nature, or by war, he should initiate public projects such as creating irrigation waterways and building forts around major strategic holdings and towns and exempt taxes on those affected.

51. The Shimla Agreement/Pact/Treaty signed by Prime Minister Indira Gandhi and President Zulfikar Ali Bhutto of Pakistan on 2nd July 1972 was much more than a peace treaty seeking to reverse the consequences of the 1971 war (*i.e.* to bring about withdrawals of troops and an exchange of PoWs). It was a comprehensive blueprint for good neighbourly relations between India and Pakistan. Under the Shimla Pact both countries undertook to abjure conflict and confrontation which has marred relations in the past, and to work towards the establishment of durable peace, friendship and cooperation.

The Shimla Agreement emphasize respect for each other's territorial integrity and sovereignty; non-interference in each other's internal affairs; respect for each other unity, political independence, sovereign equality and abjuring hostile propaganda. The following principles of the Agreement are, however, particularly noteworthy:

(*i*) A mutual commitment to the peaceful resolution of all issues through direct bilateral approaches.

(*ii*) To build the foundations of a cooperative relationship with special focus on people to people contacts.

(*iii*) To uphold the inviolability of the Line of Control in Jammu and Kashmir which is a most important CBM between India and Pakistan, and a key to durable peace.

54. UNESCO, acronym for United Nations Educational, Scientific and Cultural Organization, specialized agency of the United Nations (UN) that was outlined in a constitution signed November 16, 1945. The constitution, which entered into force in 1946, called for the promotion of international collaboration in education, science, and culture. The agency's permanent headquarters are in Paris, France.

UNESCO's initial emphasis was on rebuilding schools, libraries, and museums that had been destroyed in Europe during World War II. Since then its activities have been mainly facilitative, aimed at assisting, supporting, and complementing the national efforts of member states to eliminate illiteracy and to extend free education. UNESCO also seeks to encourage the free exchange of ideas and knowledge by organizing conferences and providing clearinghouse and exchange services.

55. Political Order in Changing Societies is a 1968 book by Samuel P. Huntington dealing with changes in political systems and political institutions. Huntington rejected the prevalent more optimistic modernization theories, arguing that order and stability themselves are crucial objectives in developing countries. As stated by Francis Fukuyama, Huntington argued that political decay was "at least as likely as political development", and that neither "economic nor social development" could proceed without political order, the actual experience of newly independent countries being "one of increasing social and political disorder".

56. "Escape from Freedom" is Erich Fromm's psychological history of the social conditions that developed in Europe between the Middle Ages and the mid-20th century which culminated in the rise of the Nazi Party to power in Germany under Adolf Hitler. Fromm is writing in 1941, after Hitler has come to power and begun his aggressive campaign to conquer Europe, but before the United States has entered what is to become the Second World War. The underlying question of Fromm's work is how the German people allowed Hitler's totalitarian regime to gain power seemingly willingly and with their enthusiastic support. A secondary question Fromm asks is whether or not democracy such as that found outside of Germany makes a people safe from similar developments. He identifies a basic psychological need which has led to the support for the Nazis in Germany and concludes by warning that this need is not necessarily filled in a democracy.

57. Globalization is now widely discussed, but the debates often focus on economic issues. A lucid and engaging writer, John Tomlinson goes far beyond traditional discussions to analyze the wide-ranging cultural, social, and moral aspects of globalization. Tomlinson begins this ambitious project by studying the relationship between globalization and contemporary culture, explaining the importance of time and space concerns, cultural imperialism, "deterritorialization," the impact of the media and communication technologies, and the possible growth of more cosmopolitan culture. We come to understand how someone may face unemployment as a result of downsizing decisions made at a company's head office on another continent, or how the food we find in our grocery stores is radically different today from twenty years ago. He discusses the uneven nature of the experience of global modernity in relation to first and third world countries, and concludes that a genuinely cosmopolitan culture is unlikely to emerge unless we respect cultural differences and share a common sense of commitment about the world.

58. Rawls described his theory of justice called "Justice as Fairness" in his book A Theory of Justice. Rawls agrees with Nozick that justice is quite separate from morality and he too rejects utilitarian forms of justice. He first suggests a new way to learn about principles of justice—the original position. The original position asks us to imagine that a group of people will get to decide the principles of justice. These people don't know who they are (what he calls a 'veil of ignorance'), they are self-interested, and they know everything science has to offer. He argues that in a veil of ignorance they couldn't be as biased towards their profession, race, gender, age, or social status because they wouldn't know which categories they belong to. As far as self-interest is concerned, Rawls argues that they will want principles of justice that will "fairly distribute" certain goods that everyone will value—what Rawls calls "primary social goods". Rawls argues that the people in the original position will discuss which principles of justice are best before voting on them, and the best principles worth having will reach a "reflective equilibrium"—the most intuitive principles will be favoured and incompatible less intuitive principles will have to be rejected in order to maintain coherence. He argues that two intuitive principles of justice in particular will reach reflective equilibrium:

- Each person is to have an equal right to the most extensive total system of equal basic liberties compatible with a similar system of liberty for all.
- Social and economic inequalities are to satisfy two conditions: first, they are to be attached to positions and offices open to all under conditions of fair equality of opportunity; and second, they are to be the greatest expected benefit of the least advantaged members of society.

59. Lohiya was deeply influenced by thinkers of the West. Prominent among them was Karl Marx. Gandhis' concept of Satyagraha had made a strong impact on India. Lohiya was impressed by the way in which millions of unarmed Indians fought the mighty British. He advocated the realization of socialist ideals through Satyagraha. He firmly believed that the differences between the haves and the havenots, the rich and the poor could be resolved by nonviolent means. Huge mechanization may be useful in advanced regions like Europe and America. India is a land of teeming, millions. The biggest problem is to provide jobs for millions. Hence using small machinery is the only solution. There are, of course, differences between Capitalism and Communism, but both rely on large-scale use of heavy machines. Mere change of ownership does not bring about equality. The very idea of mechanised industry should be changed. Such were Lohiya's views.

60. The core themes for the New Public Management were:

- A strong focus on financial control, value for money and increasing efficiency.
- A command and control mode of functioning, identifying and setting targets and continuance monitoring of performance, handing over the power to the senior management.
- Introducing audits at both financial and professional levels, using transparent means to review performances, setting benchmarks, using protocols to ameliorate professional behaviour.
- Greater customer orientation and responsiveness and increasing the scope of roles played by non public sector providers.
- Deregulating the labour market, replacing collective agreements to individual rewards packages at senior levels combined with short term contracts.
- Discouraging the self regulatory power of the professionals and handing over the power from individuals to management.
- Encouraging more entrepreneurial management than bureaucracy with high retrospective accountability requirements upwards.
- Introducing new forms of corporate governance, introducing a board model of functioning and concentrating the power to the strategic core of the organizations.

61. Simon on theory criticizes the classical theory of administration, "As being mere proverbs, or myths, so gains and pompous entities".

He says classical principles of administration is are unscientific. Classical principles of administration are in fact based on rule of thumb. The principle of classical theories of administration individually appear to be logical and nicely argued, but when applied to reality they are contradictory to each other. When these principles of administration confront evidence they fail.

62. Aristotle said that "distributive justice is mainly concerned with distribution of honour or wealth". Aristotle was of the opinion that this form of justice is the most powerful law to prevent any revolution, as this justice believes in proper and proportionate allocation of offices, honours, goods and services as per their requirement being a citizen of the state.

This justice is mostly concerned with political privileges. Aristotle advocated that every political organization must have its own distributive justice. He, however, rejected democratic as well as oligarchic criteria of justice and permitted the allocation of offices to the virtuous only owing to their highest contributions to the society, because the virtuous people are few. Aristotle believed that most of the offices should be allocated to those few only..

63. The Constitution has created an independent Election Commission of India in which vests the superintendence, direction and control of the preparation of electoral rolls for, and conduct of elections to, the offices of President and Vice-President of India and Parliament and State Legislatures (Article 324).

Article 324 to 329 of the constitution deals with powers, functions, tenure, eligibility, etc. of the commission and the member.

Originally the commission had only one election commissioner, but after the Election Commissioner Amendment Act 1989, it consists of one Chief Election Commissioner and two Election Commissioners.

The Chief Election Commissioner and Election Commissioners appointed by The President, have a fixed tenure of six years, or up to the age of 65 years, whichever is earlier.

The Chief Election Commissioner and Election Commissioners enjoy the same status and receive salary and perks as available to the Judges of the Supreme Court of India.

The Chief Election Commissioner can be removed from office only through a process of removal similar to that of a Supreme Court judge for by Parliament. But, the constitution is silent about the procedure for removal of the other Election Commissioners. It only provides that they cannot be removed from office except on the recommendation of the CEC.

The Chief Election Commissioner of India can be removed from office as can be a judge of the Supreme Court of India: a two-thirds majority resolution passed by the Parliament of India outlining the grounds of misbehaviour or incapacity. A Chief Election Commissioner has not yet to be impeached.

65. The power of Veto refers to the power of the executive to override any act of the legislature. This is a very special privilege. Veto power can of the following types :

1. Absolute Veto: Withholding of assent to the Bill passed by the legislature.
2. Qualified Veto: Which can be overridden by the legislature with a higher majority.
3. Suspensive Veto: Which can be overridden by the legislature with an ordinary majority.
4. Pocket Veto: Taking no action on the Bill passed by the legislature.

Article 111 in India's Constitution governs the Veto powers of the President. It states that "When a Bill has been passed by the Houses of Parliament, it shall be presented to the President, and the President shall declare either that he assents to the Bill, or that he withholds assent therefrom.

The subsequent provision moderates this discretion: The President may return the Bill "as soon as possible" to the Houses with a message to reconsider it.

However, if the Houses enact the Bill with or without amendments and present it to the President for assent, "the President shall not withhold assent therefrom"

The following observations can be made:

1. President may return the Bill to the Houses seeking reconsideration. This is

some sense is a public statement that the President disagrees with the preferences of the two Houses.

2. Article 111 sets no definite timeline. The President can withhold assent. In case he decides to return the Bill, the provision nudges him or her to do so "as soon as possible".
3. It is clearly stated that if a Bill is returned to the President for the 2nd time, the President "shall not withhold assent therefrom".

For a Bill to become an Act, the President must affirmatively assent. That naturally raises the possibility of "death" and not just delay by Presidential inaction. Unlike the US President, the Indian President can sit on a Bill indefinitely.

From the above discussion, it can be concluded that the President has Suspensive Veto, Pocket Veto and Absolute Veto (not discretionary). He/she does not have Qualified Veto.

67. According to D. Waldo "Public Administration is the art and science of management as applied to the affairs of the state." He further observes "The process of Public Administration consists of the actions involved in affecting the intent or desire of a government. It is thus the continuously, business part of a government, concerned with carrying the law as made by legislative bodies and interpreted by the course, through the process of organization and management.... of Public Administration focuses upon Public Administration as a process."

68. J.J. Rousseau had differentiated between natural and conventional inequality. He was an advocate of approximate social equality but not total equality. He was willing to permit two sorts of inequality. The first was the natural inequality between the young and old, the weak and strong, the wise and stupid; the second was the inequality that resulted from rewarding those who rendered special service to the community. Natural inequalities and those who made distinguished contributions to society were the only types of inequalities that he permitted. He maintained that existing social inequality did not belong to these types.

71. Plato described the working of the human mind and the way it acquired knowledge with the help of—(*i*) the allegory of the cave; (*ii*) the metaphor of the Divided Line; and (*iii*) the doctrine of Forms. He believed that individuals have different capacities for learning and attaining knowledge. He also asserted that most of us live in the darkness of the cave, which represented the realm of beliefs. At the mouth of the cave was daylight, symbolizing knowledge. This was akin to the Hindu belief. The teacher or the guru meant one who helped a person to attain enlightenment from darkness. Martin Heideggar pointed out that Plato, through the allegory of the cave, intended to state the essence of education and the meaning of being. Moreover, Plato was also the first to emphasize the problem of universals, when he stated that there was a form or Idea for everything that exists in the real world.

73. From legal point of view 'Right to Development' is called a "soft law". Soft law refers to rules that are neither strictly binding in nature nor completely lacking legal significance. In the context of international law, soft law refers to guidelines, policy declarations or codes of conduct which set standards of conduct. However, they are not directly enforceable.

The right to development is an inalienable human right by virtue of which every human person and all peoples are entitled to participate in, contribute to, and enjoy economic, social, cultural and political development, in which all human rights and fundamental freedoms can be fully realized.

74. Communications is a continuous process which mainly involves three elements viz. sender, message, and receiver. The elements involved in the communication process are explained below in detail:

1. **Sender:** The sender or the communicator generates the message and conveys it to the receiver. He is the source and the one who starts the communication.
2. **Message:** It is the idea, information, view, fact, feeling, etc. that is generated by the sender and is then intended to be communicated further.
3. **Encoding:** The message generated by the sender is encoded symbolically such as in the form of words, pictures, gestures, etc. before it is being conveyed.
4. **Media:** It is the manner in which the encoded message is transmitted. The message may be transmitted orally or in writing. The medium of communication includes telephone, internet, post, fax, e-mail, etc. The choice of medium is decided by the sender.
5. **Decoding:** It is the process of converting the symbols encoded by the sender. After decoding the message is received by the receiver.
6. **Receiver:** He is the person who is last in the chain and for whom the message was sent by the sender. Once the receiver receives the message and understands it in proper perspective and acts according to the message, only then the purpose of communication is successful.
7. **Feedback:** Once the receiver confirms to the sender that he has received the message and understood it, the process of communication is complete.
8. **Noise:** It refers to any obstruction that is caused by the sender, message or receiver during the process of communication. For example, bad telephone connection, faulty encoding, faulty decoding, inattentive receiver, poor understanding of message due to prejudice or inappropriate gestures, etc.

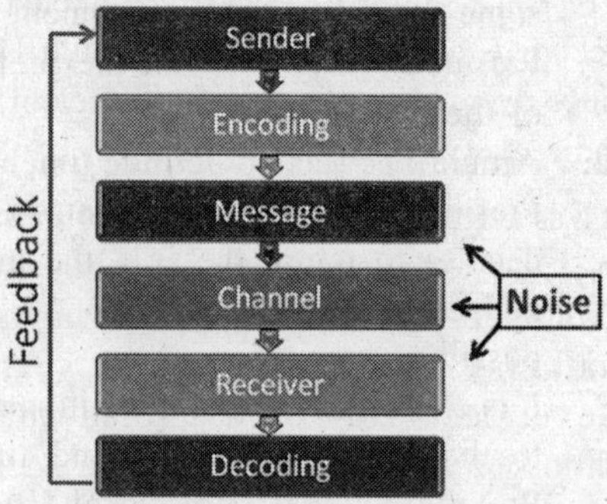

75. PLATO'S theory of justice is the concept of moral justice. He has therefore laid more emphasis upon the duties rather than the rights. Undeniably, emphasis on duties keeps the society united and in the state of solidarity, exclusive emphasis, however, leads to exploitation. Both rights and duties are important in an ideal society.

Plato's ideal state is just that—an ideal. It is as hollow as any other ideal, an idea that cannot be applied and only belongs in philosophy books.

- His concept of communism and justice collided with each other.
- Plato gave importance to Music, Logic, Games and Philosophy while ignoring other disciplines like Law, History, and Psychology.
- His concept of justice is unclear. He believes in non interference, but also stated that a person is a social animal with civilized existence and is therefore in need of interrelation and interference.
- Plato favoured absolute monarchy.
- His concept is against equality and liberty.
- There is no systematic structure of legislature, political parties, human rights, and local government.

Plato's idea is composed of a bit of reality but mostly Utopia. Despite that, it plays a critical role in politics and education even at this time and age.

76. National Youth Day is celebrated on 12 January being the birthday of Swami

Vivekananda. In 1984 the Government of India declared this day as National Youth Day and since from 1985 the event is celebrated in India every year.

It was a decision of Government of India taken in 1984 to celebrate the birthday of great Swami Vivekananda, *i.e.,* 12 January, as National Youth Day every year. The Government of India quoted that 'the philosophy of Swamiji and the ideals for which he lived and worked could be a great source of inspiration for the Indian Youth Day.'

77. The concept 'Sanskritization' was first introduced by Prof. M.N. Srinivas the famous Indian sociologist. He explained the concept of sanskritization in his book "Religion and society among the coorgs of South India" to describe the cultural mobility in the traditional caste structure of Indian society. In his study of the coorgs of Mysore, he came to know that the lower castes were trying to raise their status in their caste hierarchy by adopting some cultural ideals of the Brahmins. As a result they left some of their ideals which are considered to be impure by the Brahmins. To explain this process of mobility, Srinivas used the term 'Brahminization'. Later on he called it 'Sanskritization' in a broad sense.

Defining Sanskritization Srinivas writes, "Sanskritization is a process by which a lower caste or tribe or any other group changes its customs, rituals, ideology and way of life in the direction of a higher or more often twice-born caste."

78. Vandana Shiva is known as Eco-feminist. Vandana Shiva plays a major role in the global Eco-feminist movement. According to her 2004 article Empowering Women, Shiva suggests that a more sustainable and productive approach to agriculture can be achieved through reinstating the system of farming in India that is more centered on engaging women. She advocates against the prevalent "patriarchal logic of exclusion," claiming that a woman-focused system would change the current system in an extremely positive manner. She believes that ecological destruction and industrial catastrophes threaten daily life, and the maintenance of these problems have become the responsibility of women.

79. Although mostly used interchangeably, technically, state and nation are different, state is a government, or a territory governed by a single government. A nation is a group of people who have a shared cultural identity (can be shared ethnicity, language and history). A state can be composed of many "nations"... and a nation can also be separated into many states. For example, the Arab nation (the Arabs) are separated by different states: Jordan, UAE, Kuwait, etc.. Different states but they are all under one Arab Nation! And in contrast, there is the one state of China comprised of the Han nation and the non-Han minority nations of Hmongs, Miao, Hui, Tibetans, Mongolians, etc. Israel is also a great example: state of Israel with the nation of the Jews and the Arab Palestinian nation living under state of Israel. Ukraine has the Ukrainian nation, Russian nation, and the minority Jews and Polish nations within Ukraine.

80. Literally, Certiorari means to be certified. The writ of certiorari can be issued by the Supreme Court or any High Court for quashing the order already passed by an inferior court, tribunal or quasi judicial authority.

There are several conditions necessary for the issue of writ of Certiorari:

(*a*) There should be court, tribunal or an officer having legal authority to determine the question with a duty to act judicially.

(*b*) Such a court, tribunal or officer must have passed an order acting without jurisdiction or in excess of the judicial authority vested by law in such court, tribunal or officer.

(c) The order could also be against the principles of natural justice or the order could contain an error of judgment in appreciating the facts of the case.

81. The positive impact of Liberalisation are:

(i) Free flow of capital: Liberalisation has enhanced the flow of capital by making it affordable for businesses to reach the capital from investors and take a profitable project.

(ii) Diversity for investors: The investors will be benefitted by investing a portion of their business into a diversifying asset class.

(iii) Impact on agriculture: In this area, the cropping designs have experienced a huge change, but the impact of liberalisation cannot be accurately measured. Government restrictions and interventions can be seen from production to distribution of the crop.

(iv) Technological Impact: Rapid increase in technology forces many enterprises and small scale industries in India to either adapt to changes or close their businesses.

(v) Stock Market Performance: Generally, when a country retaxes its laws, taxes, the stock market values also rise. Stock Markets are platforms on which corporate securities can be traded in real time.

82. Deductions are one of two species of argument recognized by Aristotle. The other species is induction. He has far less to say about this than deduction, doing little more than characterize it as "argument from the particular to the universal". However, induction (or something very much like it) plays a crucial role in the theory of scientific knowledge in the Posterior Analytics: it is induction, or at any rate a cognitive process that moves from particulars to their generalizations, that is the basis of knowledge of the indemonstrable first principles of sciences.

Machiavelli's status as a political thinker rests in part on the novelty he claimed for his method of political enquiry. A common interpretation of Machiavelli hails him as the founder of modern political science and as a pioneer of empiricism and what is now known as the inductive method of reasoning—a process of inferring generalisations from the observation of particular examples.

84. Jayaprakash Narayan (1902-1979), popularly referred to as JP or Lok Nayak , was an Indian independence activist, theorist, socialist and political leader. He is also known as the "Hero of Quit India Movement" and he is remembered for leading the mid-1970s opposition against Prime Minister Indira Gandhi, for whose overthrow he had called for a "total revolution". His biography, Jayaprakash, was written by his nationalist friend and an eminent writer of Hindi literature, Rambriksh Benipuri. In 1999, he was posthumously awarded the Bharat Ratna, India's highest civilian award, in recognition of his social work. Other awards include the Magsaysay award for Public Service in 1965.

86. The Preamble states:

WE, THE PEOPLE OF INDIA , having solemnly resolved to constitute India into a SOVEREIGN SOCIALIST SECULAR DEMOCRATIC REPUBLIC and to secure to all its citizens:

JUSTICE, social, economic and political;

LIBERTY of thought, expression, belief, faith, and worship;

EQUALITY of status and of opportunity;

and to promote among them all

FRATERNITY assuring the dignity of the individual and the unity and integrity of the Nation;

IN OUR CONSTITUENT ASSEMBLY this twenty-sixth day of November 1949, do HEREBY ADOPT, ENACT AND GIVE TO OURSELVES THIS CONSTITUTION.

The Four Components of the Preamble are:

1. The Preamble indicates that the source of authority of the Constitution lies with the people of India.

2. It declares India to be a sovereign, socialist, secular, democratic and a republic nation.
3. It states its objectives to secure justice, liberty, equality to all citizens and promote fraternity to maintain unity and integrity of the nation.
4. It mentions the date (November 26, 1949) on which the constitution was adopted.

88. Bryan Turner explains that: at the heart of Marshall's account of citizenship lies the contradiction between the formal political equality of the franchise and the persistence of extensive social and economic inequality, ultimately rooted in the character of the capitalist market place and the existence of private property. Marshall proposed the extension of citizenship as the principal political means for resolving, or at least containing, those contradictions. (Turner 1990)

However, it is well known that Marshall's scheme focussed on a specific period in British history (from the middle of the seventeenth century to the middle of the twentieth century). This explains the main limitations of Marshall's approach, which has been criticised for being evolutionary, unitary and ethnocentric. Certainly, Marshall's theory of citizenship failed to emphasize "the notion of social struggles as the central motor of the drive for citizenship" (Turner 1990), and therefore it does not distinguish "between active and passive forms of citizenship, which arise from variations in the relationship between the subject and the state" (Turner 2000). The former expands citizenship rights through a process of political conflict; the latter is the effect of the political strategies of the dominant political elite.

Brian Turner (1993), among the first to revisit Marshall's theory, defines citizenship as a set of legal, economic, and cultural practices which define an individual as a competent member of society. Such practices shape the flow of resources to individuals and social groups. Turner's definition allows us to analyse how individuals and groups have differentiated opportunities of becoming competent members of society. From this point of view, citizenship identity, the sense of belonging and solidarity, is necessarily connected with the problem of unequal distribution of resources in society.

89. Welfare state, concept of government in which the state or a well-established network of social institutions plays a key role in the protection and promotion of the economic and social well-being of citizens. It is based on the principles of equality of opportunity, equitable distribution of wealth, and public responsibility for those unable to avail themselves of the minimal provisions for a good life. The general term may cover a variety of forms of economic and social organization.

A fundamental feature of the welfare state is social insurance, a provision common to most advanced industrialized countries (*e.g.*, National Insurance in the United Kingdom and Social Security in the United States). Such insurance is usually financed by compulsory contributions and is intended to provide benefits to persons and families during periods of greatest need. It is widely recognized, however, that in practice the cash benefits fall considerably short of the levels intended by the designers of the plans.

The welfare state also usually includes public provision of basic education, health services, and housing (in some cases at low cost or without charge). In these respects the welfare state is considerably more extensive in western European countries than in the United States, featuring in many cases comprehensive health coverage and provision of state-subsidized tertiary education.

Antipoverty programs and the system of personal taxation may also be regarded as aspects of the welfare state. Personal taxation falls into this category insofar as its progressivity is used to achieve greater justice in income distribution (rather than merely to raise revenue) and also insofar as it used to finance social insurance payments and other benefits not completely financed by compulsory contributions. In socialist countries the welfare state also covers employment and administration of consumer prices.

The modern use of the term is associated with the comprehensive measures of social insurance adopted in 1948 by Great Britain on the basis of the report Social Insurance and Allied Services (1942) by Sir William Beveridge.

90. The Phoenix Settlement was established by Gandhiji near Durban in 1904. The Phoenix Settlement comprised of 100 acres of land and was purchased by Gandhiji in 1904. It was on this Settlement that Gandhi started his journey of transforming from a successful Lawyer to a simple Peasant with a passion for liberation, non-violence and spirituality.

The Tolstoy Farm was named such by Herman Kallenbach, Gandhi's associate. It was founded in 1910 and disbanded in 1913 proved to be an ideal laboratory for Gandhi's educational experiments.

The Kochrab Ashram was the first ashram in India organized by Mohandas Gandhi, the leader of the Indian independence movement, and was gifted to him by his friend Barrister Jivanlal Desai. Founded on 25 May 1915, Gandhi's Kochrab Ashram was located near the city of Ahmedabad in the state of Gujarat.

Sevagram is the name of a town in the state of Maharashtra, India. It was the place of Mohandas Gandhi's ashram and his residence from 1936 to his death in 1948.

Previous Paper (Solved)

National Testing Agency (NTA)

UGC-NET Junior Research Fellowship & Assistant Professor Online Exam

Political Science, June-2019*

PAPER-II

Note: *This paper contains* **hundred (100)** *objective type questions of* **two (2)** *marks each.* **All** *questions are* **compulsory**.

1. Who authored the book, *Silent Spring*?

A. Frank Thone
B. Raymond L. Bryant
C. Rachel Carson
D. Roy Rappaport

2. Pandita Ramabai was accorded the title 'Pandita' for:

A. social reforms
B. emancipation of women
C. eradication of caste system
D. being a Sanskrit scholar

3. Karl Marx, the founder of Marxism, formally was the citizen of which one of the following countries?

A. Germany B. France
C. UK D. None of the above

4. Which of the following writings were associated with Muhammad Iqbal?

(*a*) *Tarana-e-Hind*
(*b*) *The Reconstruction of Religious Thought in India*
(*c*) *Historical Role of Islam*
(*d*) *The Bang-e-Dara*

Select the correct answer from the given options:

A. (*a*), (*b*) and (*c*)
B. (*a*), (*c*) and (*d*)
C. (*a*), (*b*) and (*d*)
D. (*b*), (*c*) and (*d*)

5. Which of the following newspapers are NOT related with Tilak?

(*a*) Kesari
(*b*) Maratha
(*c*) Sudharak
(*d*) Harijan

Select the correct answer from the given options:

A. (*a*) and (*b*) B. (*b*) and (*c*)
C. (*a*) and (*d*) D. (*c*) and (*d*)

6. Match List-I with List-II:

List-I (Books)	*List-II (Thinkers)*
(*a*) *Marx, Gandhi and Socialism*	(*i*) Aurobindo
(*b*) *Gandhi and Gandhism*	(*ii*) Rabindranath Tagore
(*c*) *Savitri : A Legend and a Symbol*	(*iii*) Ram Manohar Lohia
(*d*) *Gitanjali*	(*iv*) B.R. Ambedkar

Choose the correct option from those given below:

	(*a*)	(*b*)	(*c*)	(*d*)
A.	(*iii*)	(*iv*)	(*i*)	(*ii*)
B.	(*ii*)	(*i*)	(*iv*)	(*iii*)
C.	(*iv*)	(*iii*)	(*i*)	(*ii*)
D.	(*iii*)	(*i*)	(*ii*)	(*iv*)

7. Match List-I with List-II:

List-I	*List-II*
(*a*) Late Capitalism	(*i*) Michel Foucault
(*b*) Deconstructionism	(*ii*) Fredric Jameson
(*c*) Collapse of grand Narrative	(*iii*) Jacques Derrida
(*d*) Concept of knowledge and power	(*iv*) Lyotard

* Exam held on 25-06-2019.

Choose the correct option from those given below:

	(a)	(b)	(c)	(d)
A.	(ii)	(iii)	(iv)	(i)
B.	(i)	(iv)	(ii)	(iii)
C.	(ii)	(iv)	(i)	(iii)
D.	(iv)	(i)	(iii)	(ii)

8. How many prakrities of Mandal Theory of State are enumerated by Kautilya?
A. 60 B. 68
C. 70 D. 72

9. Who is the writer of the book, *A Great and Terrible World?*
A. Antonio Gramsci
B. Hannah Arendt
C. Hegel
D. John Rawls

10. Agganna Sutta is the:
A. 27th Sutta of the Digha Nikaya
B. 27th Sutta of the Majjhima Nikaya
C. 26th Sutta of Samyutta Nikaya
D. 27th Sutta of Anguttara Nikaya

11. 'Making someone better without making others worse' is associated with which one of the following?
A. Pareto' s principle of Optimality
B. Nozick's principle of Entitlement
C. Foucault's principle of Power
D. Rawls's principle of Distributive Justice

12. Who said that art, religion and philosophy differ only in form, their purpose is the same?
A. Georg Lukacs
B. Sartre
C. Hegel
D. Erik Olin Wright

13. Which one among the following is NOT related to Neo-Marxism?
A. Jurgen Habermas
B. Erich Fromm
C. Herbert Marcuse
D. Rosa Luxemburg

14. Integrated humanism means
(*a*) Human life is not isolated
(*b*) Harmony among individual, society and nation
(*c*) The essential unity of the man
(*d*) State is superior than Nation

Select the correct answer from the given options:
A. (*a*), (*b*) and (*c*) B. (*a*), (*b*) and (*d*)
C. (*b*), (*c*) and (*d*) D. (*a*), (*c*) and (*d*)

15. Feminists argue that women's values are based primarily on
A. Religious laws
B. Prescribed social roles
C. Biology and prescribed social roles
D. Biology

16. Which one of the following is NOT a correct match?

A. Fabianism	Peaceful Change
B. Guild Socialism	Professional Representation
C. Syndicalism	Trade Unionism
D. Democratic Socialism	Radical Change

17. Dialectic method was used for the first time in the writing of which one of the following thinkers?
A. Socrates B. Plato
C. Hegel D. Marx

18. The immigrating ethnic cultural groups which never get opportunity to become citizens under multiculturalism are called
A. Metics
B. National minorities
C. Immigrant groups
D. Isolationist ethno-religious groups

19. Who said that political work is the life blood of all economic work?
A. John Rawls B. Mao Zedong
C. Karl Marx D. Frantz Fanon

20. Given below are two statements, one labelled as Assertion (A) and the other labelled as Reason (R):

Assertion (A): According to Gandhi, politics divorced from religion is a deathtrap.

Reason (R): The entry of religion into politics is necessary because without religion it may take communal colour.

On the basis of the two statements choose the correct answer from the options given below:

A. Both (A) and (R) are true and (R) is the correct explanation of (A)

B. Both (A) and (R) are true, but (R) is not the correct explanation of (A)

C. (A) is true, but (R) is false

D. (A) is false, but (R) is true

21. Given below are two statements, one labelled as Assertion (A) and the other labelled as Reason (R):

Assertion (A): In Machiavellian thought end justifies the means.

Reason (R): The key objective of the Prince was to bring unity and integrity of the State.

On the basis of the two statements choose the correct answer from the options given below:

A. Both (A) and (R) are true and (R) is the correct explanation of (A)

B. Both (A) and (R) are true, but (R) is not the correct explanation of (A)

C. (A) is true, but (R) is false

D. (A) is false, but (R) is true

22. Gandhi believes in

A. End justifies Means

B. Means justifies End

C. Neither End justifies Means nor Means justifies End

D. End and Means both should be justified

23. Who stated that placing restrictions on freedom of expressions of human beings is like robbing off the present and the future races?

A. J.S. Mill B. John Locke

C. Isaiah Berlin D. F.A. Hayek

24. *Black Skin, White Masks* is written by

A. Gramsci B. Hannah Arendt

C. Frantz Fanon D. Wollstonecraft

25. "The English think they are free. They are free only during the election of members of parliament". Who said this?

A. J.S. Mill B. T.H. Green

C. Locke D. Rousseau

26. Who wrote the biography of Jayaprakash Narayan?

A. Jayaprakash Narayan himself

B. Ramvriksha Benipuri

C. Vinoba Bhave

D. Namboodiripad

27. The Idea of Justice as fairness in Rawlsian theory flows from

A. Individual B. Society

C. State D. Nation

28. Who wrote the book, *Multicultural Citizenship: A Liberal Theory of Minority Rights* (1995)?

A. T.H. Marshal B. B.S. Turner

C. Will Kymlica D. Bheekhu Parekh

29. Which one of the following is incorrect with regard to post modernism?

A. Primacy of consumption instead of knowledge

B. Deconstruction of totality

C. Commonality to greatness

D. Historical tendency

30. Who stated that the life of man is solitary, poor, nasty, brutish and short?

A. Machiavelli B. Hobbes

C. Locke D. Rousseau

Directions (Qs. No. 31 to 33): *Read the paragraph carefully and answer these questions.*

Democratic politics has undergone significant transformation in the last seven decades of post-independence India. While electoral participation has increased significantly over the decades, primordial identities as rooted primarily in caste have further strengthened 'politicization of castes' as well as 'casteization of politics'.

The 21st Century Market State in India has paved the way for a third democratic upsurge. However, instead of dismantling the primordial. Structures in its pursuit of development, the Market State seems to be oscillating between populism and governance.

31. Which of the following is NOT a component of primordialism?

A. Caste B. Class

C. Community D. Clan

32. Who among the following is/are the exponent(s) of three democratic upsurges in the democratic politics of India?
A. Atul Kohli
B. Lloyd and Susanne Rudolphs
C. Partha Chatterjee
D. None of the above

33. Who among the following used the term 'politicization of caste' in Indian politics for the first time?
A. Rajni Kothari B. Yogendra Yadav
C. Surinder Jodka D. M.N. Srinivas

34. Which of the following is incorrect with regard to the Plan Holidays?
A. These were short-term contingency plans.
B. The period of these plans was 1966-69.
C. The reasons for these plans were war, inflation and drought
D. Plan Holidays were introduced due to the failure of all three preceding Five Year Plans.

35. Given below are two statements one labelled as Assertion (A) and the other labelled as Reason (R):

Assertion (A): There is no ideal number of persons a supervisor can supervise.

Reason (R): Span of control varies depending on factors like function time, space and delegation of authority.

On the basic of the two statements choose the correct answer from the codes given below:
A. Both (A) and (R) are true and (R) is the correct explanation of (A)
B. Both (A) and (R) are true, and (R) is not the correct explanation of (A).
C. (A) is true, but (R) is false
D. (A) is false, but (R) is true

36. Which one of the following Commissions are statutory bodies?
(*a*) National Commission for Scheduled Tribes
(*b*) National Commission for Human Rights
(*c*) National Commission for Minorities
(*d*) National Commission for Scheduled Castes

Select the correct answer from the given options:
A. (*a*) and (*b*) B. (*b*), (*c*) and (*d*)
C. (*a*) and (*d*) D. (*b*) and (*c*)

37. NITI Aayog is:
A. a staff agency
B. a line agency
C. an auxiliary agency
D. neither staff nor line agency

38. Stasiology is the study of:
A. statistics B. elections
C. political parties D. movements

39. Who among the following summarizes the themes of New Public Administration under five heads - relevance, values, social equity, change and client-focus?
A. Frank Marini B. D. Waldo
C. F.W. Taylor D. M.P. Follett

40. Which of the following traits have been introduced by the right to information in the politico-administrative system?
(*a*) Caution
(*b*) Care
(*c*) Vigilance
(*d*) Red-tapism

Select the most suitable answer from the options given below:
A. (*a*), (*b*), (*c*) and (*d*)
B. (*a*), (*b*) and (*c*)
C. (*b*), (*c*) and (*d*)
D. (*b*) and (*d*)

41. Who is the largest G-20 invester country in India?
A. Japan B. USA
C. UK D. Brazil

42. "New Democracy' as hegemony of the workers, peasants and other marzinalized sections of the society is associated with which one of the following?
A. Subaltern School
B. Marxist School
C. Post-Behavioural School
D. Post-Modernist School

43. Which of the following does not form the basis of difference between voluntary organizations and NGOs?
A. Philanthropy
B. Membership
C. Funding
D. Commitment to the secular and democratic ideals

44. Given below are two statements, one labelled as Assertion (A) and the other labelled as Reason (R):

Assertion (A): Nation and nationalism can variedly be conceptualised and defined but without being generalized in common theorization.

Reason (R): There can be discourses, not common theories, on nation and nationalism.

On the basic of the two statements choose the correct answer from the options given below:
A. Both (A) and (R) are true and (R) is the correct explanation of (A)
B. Both (A) and (R) and true, but (R) is not the correct explanation of (A).
C. (A) is true, but (R) is false
D. (A) is false, but (R) is true

45. "When diplomacy ends, war begins." Who said this?
A. Adolf Hitler
B. Napolean Bonaparte
C. Hans Morgenthau
D. Mao Tse Tung

46. Look West Policy of India advocated expansion and extension of India's relations with
A. Western Countries
B. European Union
C. West Asian Countries
D. Africa and Latin America

47. The Anti-Satellite Missile Test conducted by India on 27th March 2019 is known as
A. Mission Antarriksh
B. Mission Bharat
C. Mission Shakti
D. Mission A-SAT

48. Who equated revolution with 'fever'?
A. Theda Skocpol
B. Barrington Moore
C. Crane Brinton
D. Francine R. Frankel

49. The demand for 'Harit Pradesh' is related to which one of the following regions in India?
A. Western Uttar Pradesh
B. Bundelkhand
C. Uttaranchal
D. Vidharbha

50. Which one of the following is an **incorrect** pair?

A. Melting pot	:	USA
B. Boiling pot	:	Israel
C. Salad bowl	:	India
D. Fruit bowl	:	UK

51. The fundamental difference between institutionalism and new institutionalism would primarily be located on the principle of:
A. deduction B. induction
C. experimentation D. investigation

52. 'Circulation of elites' most closely refers to which one of the following?
A. Rotation of elites
B. Replacement of elites
C. Retention of elites
D. Restoration of elites

53. Which of the following is NOT a Violent Non-State Actor (VNSA)?
A. ISIS B. Bokoharam
C. PLO D. Hezobollah

54. Which of the following ways are suggested by Mary Parker Follett for resolving conflict in an organization?
(*a*) Domination
(*b*) Compromise
(*c*) Surrender
(*d*) Integration

Select the most suitable answer from the options given below:
A. (*a*), (*b*) and (*c*) B. (*a*), (*b*) and (*d*)
C. (*b*), (*c*) and (*d*) D. (*a*), (*b*), (*c*) and (*d*)

55. Which of the following Indian traditions is declared recently as 'Intangible Cultural Heritage of Humanity'?

A. Kumbh B. Yoga
C. Nouraz D. Bihu

56. India is holding talks with ASEAN to extend which highway to Vietnam?

A. India-Myanmar-Thailand
B. India-Myanmar-Korea
C. India-Myanmar-Bangladesh
D. India-Myanmar-China

57. In Samuel P. Huntington's analysis, India is placed in which one of the 'waves of democratization'?

A. First wave B. Second wave
C. Third wave D. Fourth wave

58. Who among the following makes a distinction between public administration and private administration?

(*a*) Paul Appleby
(*b*) L.D. White
(*c*) Herbert Simon
(*d*) Sir Josia Stamp

Select the correct answer from the given option:

A. (*a*) and (*b*) only
B. (*b*) and (*c*) only
C. (*a*), (*c*) and (*d*) only
D. (*a*), (*b*), (*c*) and (*d*)

59. Arrange the following committees in chronological order:

(*a*) Satish Chandra Committee
(*b*) Hota Committee
(*c*) Kothari Committee
(*d*) Yoginder K. Alagh Committee

Select the correct answer from the options given below:

A. (*a*), (*b*), (*c*) and (*d*)
B. (*c*), (*a*), (*d*) and (*b*)
C. (*b*), (*d*), (*a*) and (*c*)
D. (*d*), (*c*), (*a*) and (*b*)

60. The Supreme Court of India has the power to adjudicate disputes between the Union and the States through

A. Appellate Jurisdiction
B. Original Jurisdiction
C. Advisory Jurisdiction
D. Writ Jurisdiction

61. Happiness index is the creation of which one of the following countries?

A. Bhutan B. Nepal
C. UK D. Switzerland

62. Internal communication can be

A. upward only
B. downward only
C. upward and downward only
D. upward, downward and across

63. The term 'flying bees' got associated with which of the following associations?

A. ASEAN
B. SAARC
C. Shanghai Cooperation Organisation
D. BRICS

64. Which of the following statements is true with regard to NPT and CTBT?

A. India has signed but not ratified NPT.
B. India has signed CTBT.
C. India has signed NPT.
D. India has neither signed nor ratified either NPT or CTBT.

65. Who among the following predicted that bureaucracy is likely to go out of use in the wake of new social systems better suited to the 20th century demands of industrialization?

A. Warren Bennis B. Max Weber
C. Peter Blau D. Martin Albrow

66. "The poor are poor ... not because of what they do not have, but because of what they cannot do." Who said this?

A. Hans Singer B. Amartya Sen
C. Mahboob ul Haq D. Harsh Mander

67. Arrange the introduction of the following development programmes in an ascending order:

(*a*) Pradhan Mantri Gram Sadak Yojana
(*b*) Indira Awas Yojana
(*c*) Deen Dayal Upadhyay Gram Jyoti Yojana
(*d*) Atal Pension Yojana

Select the correct answer from the codes given below:
A. (*b*), (*a*), (*d*) and (*c*)
B. (*a*), (*b*), (*c*) and (*d*)
C. (*b*), (*a*), (*c*) and (*d*)
D. (*a*), (*b*), (*d*) and (*c*)

68. Match List-I with List-II:

List-I (Systems)	*List-II (Articles)*
(*a*) Electoral system	(*i*) 243-243(O)
(*b*) Services under the Union and States	(*ii*) 124-147
(*c*) Panchayats	(*iii*) 324-329
(*d*) Judicial system at Union level	(*iv*) 308-323

Choose the correct option from those given below:

	(*a*)	(*b*)	(*c*)	(*d*)
A.	(*iii*)	(*iv*)	(*i*)	(*ii*)
B.	(*ii*)	(*i*)	(*iv*)	(*iii*)
C.	(*iii*)	(*i*)	(*iv*)	(*ii*)
D.	(*i*)	(*ii*)	(*iii*)	(*iv*)

69. What is meant by the term 'jus in bello'?
A. A just recourse to war
B. Restricted use of legitimate force
C. The just conduct of war
D. All of the above

70. Which one of the following services is not mentioned in the Constitution?
A. Indian Administrative Service (IAS)
B. Indian Police Service (IPS)
C. Indian Foreign Service (IFS)
D. Indian Judicial Service (IJS)

71. Madan Mohan Punchhi Commission was appointed to study
A. Centre-State Relations
B. State Reorganisation
C. Panchayati Raj
D. Delimitation of Constituencies

72. India and EU have established which mechanism for furthering trade ties?
A. International Facilitation Mechanism
B. Investment Facilitation Mechanism
C. Global Facilitation Mechanism
D. EU-India Facilitation Mechanism

73. Which one of the following theories is known as traditional theory?
A. Organisation theory
B. Human relations theory
C. Scientific management theory
D. Bureaucratic theory

74. The only tribal leader honoured by the Parliament of India through installation of his portrait in its Museum is
A. Bisoi
B. Birsa Munda
C. Kanho
D. Bhagiji Naik

75. Members of the Cabinet Mission Plan were:
A. Lord Pethick–Lawrence, Sir Stafford Cripps and A.V. Alexander
B. Sir Stafford Cripps, A.V. Alexander and Lord Wavell
C. Lord Pethick-Lawrence, A.V. Alexander and Lord Ripon
D. Sir Stafford Cripps., Lord Mountbatten and Lord Pethick–Lawrence

76. Which one of the following is NOT a classified category of political parties as defined by the Election Commission of Indian?
A. National Parties
B. State Parties
C. Regional Parties
D. Registered (Unrecognized) Parties

77. The 'Clash of Civilization' thesis means:
A. Religious clashes would be a core area of study
B. a rejection of the cultural and political inheritance of the West
C. widespread disagreement over moral issues
D. conflict would not be primarily ideological or economic but, rather cultural in character

78. Which of the following Commissions/ Committees has recommended the creation of a District Council in every district with representatives from both urban and rural areas?
A. Balwant Rai Mehta Committee
B. L.M. Singhvi Committee
C. Ashok Mehta Committee
D. Second Administrative Reforms Commission

79. Which International Agreement gave for the 'first time' legally binding targets on reducing Greenhouse Emissions to the countries?
A. Copenhagen 2009
B. Kyoto Protocol 1997
C. Durban Conference 2011
D. Rio de Janerio 1992

80. Match List-I with List-II:

List- I (Authors)	***List-II (Terms)***
(*a*) David Easton	(*i*) Development Syndrome
(*b*) Lucian Pye	(*ii*) Political Man
(*c*) Samuel P. Huntington	(*iii*) Black Box
(*d*) Seymour Martin Lipset	(*iv*) Waves of Democratization

Choose the correct option from those given below:

	(*a*)	(*b*)	(*c*)	(*d*)
A.	(*iii*)	(*i*)	(*ii*)	(*iv*)
B.	(*i*)	(*iii*)	(*iv*)	(*ii*)
C.	(*iii*)	(*i*)	(*iv*)	(*ii*)
D.	(*ii*)	(*iii*)	(*iv*)	(*i*)

81. Which of the following are the detrimental effects of corruption on development?
(*a*) Lower level of social services
(*b*) Lower economic growth
(*c*) Higher tax burden and fewer services
(*d*) Lower opportunities for fanners to sell their product

Select the correct answer from the options given below:
A. (*a*) and (*b*) only
B. (*b*) and (*d*) only
C. (*b*), (*c*) and (*d*)
D. (*a*), (*b*), (*c*) and (*d*)

82. Which one of the following is the Nodal Ministry for the National Human Rights Commission?
A. Ministry of Human Resource Development
B. Ministry of Social Justice and Empowerment
C. Ministry of Home Affairs
D. Ministry of Personnel, Public Grievances and Pensions

83. Which from the following is the full title of the book written by Hans J Morgenthau?
A. Politics Among Nations
B. Politics Within Nations
C. Politics Among Nations : The Struggle for Power and Peace
D. Politics Among Nations: The Struggle for Peace and Power

84. Under the Lokpal and Lokayukta Act a person can be appointed Chairperson of Lokpal if he or she
(*a*) is or has been the Chief Justice of India
(*b*) is or has been a Judge of the Supreme Court
(*c*) is or has been an eminent person
(*d*) is or has been an administrator with at least 10 years of experience

Select the most suitable answer from the options given below:
A. (*a*), (*b*), (*c*) and (*d*)
B. (*a*), (*b*) and (*d*)
C. (*a*), (*b*) and (*c*)
D. (*b*), (*c*) and (*d*)

85. With which country has India signed a long-term agreement for Sukhoi Su-30MKI combat aircraft fleet?
A. USA
B. Japan
C. Israel
D. Russia

86. Under the 'Indus Water Treaty' with Pakistan, India has the exclusive rights over the rivers
A. Chenab, Ravi, Beas
B. Ravi, Beas, Sutlej
C. Beas, Sutlej, Jhelum
D. Ravi, Chenab, Jhelum

87. Chronologically arrange the following parties in ascending order in terms of their entry in the democratic politics of India:
(*a*) Maharashtra Navnirman Sena
(*b*) Telangana Rashtra Samiti
(*c*) All India Trinamool Congress
(*d*) Nationalist Congress Party

Select the correct answer:
A. (*a*), (*b*), (*c*) and (*d*)
B. (*c*), (*d*), (*b*) and (*a*)

C. (*c*), (*d*), (*a*) and (*b*)
D. (*d*), (*c*), (*b*) and (*a*)

88. Match List-I with List-II:

List-I (Stages in the evolution of public administration)	***List-II (Period)***
(*a*) Crisis of identity	(*i*) 1938-1947
(*b*) Era of challenge	(*ii*) 1927- 1937
(*c*) Principles of administration	(*iii*) 1887- 1926
(*d*) Politics-administration dichotomy	(*iv*) 1948-1970

Choose the correct option from those given below:

	(*a*)	(*b*)	(*c*)	(*d*)
A.	(*ii*)	(*i*)	(*iii*)	(*iv*)
B.	(*iv*)	(*i*)	(*ii*)	(*iii*)
C.	(*iv*)	(*ii*)	(*i*)	(*iii*)
D.	(*iv*)	(*iii*)	(*ii*)	(*i*)

89. Which of the following taxes are levied by the Union but are collected and appropriated by the States?
(*a*) Stamp duties
(*b*) Excise duties on medical and toilet materials
(*c*) Sales tax
(*d*) Land revenue

Select the correct answer from the given options:
A. (*a*) and (*b*) only B. (*b*) and (*c*) only
C. (*a*), (*b*) and (*c*) D. (*c*) and (*d*) only

90. India has signed Comprehensive Economic Partnership Agreement (CEPA) with which of the following countries?
A. USA B. Russia
C. Japan D. Israel

91. Which of the following are the main features of scientific management?
(*a*) A single administrative science whose principles were applicable not only to business but also to government, religious and other organisations
(*b*) Functional foremanship
(*c*) Separation of planning and execution
(*d*) Differential piecework plan

Select the most suitable answer from the given options:
A. (*b*), (*c*) and (*d*)
B. (*a*), (*b*) and (*d*)
C. (*a*), (*b*), (*c*) and (*d*)
D. (*b*) and (*d*)

92. The book, *The Intellectual Crisis in American Public Administration* deals with:
A. public choice approach
B. new public administration
C. ecological approach
D. decision-making approach

93. India was re-elected on the executive board of which of the following UN bodies in 2017?
A. UNESCO B. UNDP
C. UNICEF D. UNAID

94. Which one of the following is NOT true with regard to BREXIT?
A. BREXIT refers to the UK leaving the European Union
B. Association with EU has incurred huge economic pressure leading to unemployment in UK
C. The issue of BREXIT led to the resignation of PM David Cameroon
D. The young voters have primarily voted in favour of BREXIT

95. Match List-I with List-II:

List-I (Authors)	***List-II (Books)***
(*a*) Granville Austin	(*i*) The Government and Politics of India
(*b*) Morris Jones	(*ii*) Some Characteristics of Indian Constitution
(*c*) M.V. Pylee	(*iii*) The Indian Constitution: Cornerstone of a Nation
(*d*) Ivor Jennings	(*iv*) Constitutional Government in India

Choose the correct option from those given below:

	(a)	(b)	(c)	(d)
A.	(iii)	(i)	(iv)	(ii)
B.	(ii)	(iv)	(i)	(iii)
C.	(iii)	(i)	(ii)	(iv)
D.	(iii)	(ii)	(i)	(iv)

96. The total number of Ministers including Prime Minister and Deputy Prime Minister shall not exceed:

A. 20% members of the Lok Sabha
B. 10% members of the Lok Sabha
C. 15% members of the Lok Sabha
D. 25% members of the Lok Sabha

97. In which case was it declared that the Preamble is NOT the part of the Constitution?

A. Kesavananda Bharati case
B. Maneka Gandhi case
C. Vishakha case
D. Berubari case

98. Match List-I with List-II:

***List-I* (*Writs*)**	***List-II* (*Meanings*)**
(a) Habeas corpus	(i) To command
(b) Mandamus	(ii) By what warrant
(c) Certiorari	(iii) You should have the body
(d) Quo warranto	(iv) To inform

Choose the correct option from those given below:

	(a)	(b)	(c)	(d)
A.	(ii)	(i)	(iv)	(iii)
B.	(iii)	(i)	(iv)	(ii)
C.	(iii)	(iv)	(i)	(ii)
D.	(ii)	(i)	(iii)	(iv)

99. Which of the following appointments are made by the President of India by warrant under his sign and seal?

(a) Judges of the Supreme Court of India
(b) Governor of a State
(c) Chairman of the Union Public Service Commission
(d) Attorney-General of India

Select the correct answer from the codes given below:

A. (a), (b), (c) and (d)
B. (a), (b) and (c)
C. (a), (b) and (d)
D. (a) and (b)

100. The term 'ABCD' is primarily associated with which one of the following?

A. Formation of States
B. Reorganization of States
C. Decentralization of States
D. Institutionalization of States

ANSWERS

1	2	3	4	5	6	7	8	9	10
C	D	D	C	D	A	A	D	A	A
11	**12**	**13**	**14**	**15**	**16**	**17**	**18**	**19**	**20**
A	C	D	A	B	D	B	A	B	A
21	**22**	**23**	**24**	**25**	**26**	**27**	**28**	**29**	**30**
A	D	A	C	D	B	A	C	D	B
31	**32**	**33**	**34**	**35**	**36**	**37**	**38**	**39**	**40**
B	D	A	D	A	D	A	C	A	B
41	**42**	**43**	**44**	**45**	**46**	**47**	**48**	**49**	**50**
C	A	D	A	A	C	C	C	A	D
51	**52**	**53**	**54**	**55**	**56**	**57**	**58**	**59**	**60**
C	A	C	B	A	A	B	C	B	B

61	62	63	64	65	66	67	68	69	70
A	D	A	D	A	B	A	A	C	*
71	**72**	**73**	**74**	**75**	**76**	**77**	**78**	**79**	**80**
A	B	A	B	A	C	D	D	B	C
81	**82**	**83**	**84**	**85**	**86**	**87**	**88**	**89**	**90**
D	C	C	C	D	B	B	B	A	C
91	**92**	**93**	**94**	**95**	**96**	**97**	**98**	**99**	**100**
A	A	A	D	A	C	D	B	D	A

* Error in Question/Option

EXPLANATORY ANSWERS

1. *Silent spring* is an environmental science book by *Rachel Carson.* The book was published on September 27, 1962 documenting the adverse environmental effects caused by the indiscriminate use of pesticides. Carson accused the chemical industry of spreading disinformation, and public officials of accepting the industry's marketing claims unquestioningly.

Starting in the late 1950s, prior to the book's publication, Carson had focused her attention on environmental conservation, especially environmental problems that she believed were caused by synthetic pesticides. The result of her research was *silent spring,* which brought environmental concerns to the American public. The book was met with fierce opposition by chemical companies, but, owing to public opinion, it brought about numerous changes. It spurred a reversal in the united states' national pesticide policy, led to a nationwide ban on DDT for agricultural uses, and helped to inspire an environmental movement that led to the creation of U.S. Environmental protection Agency.

Over there decades later, in 1996, a follow-up book, Beyond *silent spring,* co-written by H.F. Van Emden and David Peakall, was published. In 2006, *silent spring* was named one of the 25 greatest science books of all time by the editors of Discover Magazine.

2. Pandita Ramabai Sarasvati was an Indian social reformer, a pioneer in the education and emancipation of women in India. She was the first women to be accorded the titles of Pandita as a Sanskrit scholar and Sarasvati after being examined by the faculty of the university of Calcutta. She was one of the ten women delegates of the congress session of 1889 at Bombay. In the late 1890s, she founded Mukti Mission at Kedgaon village, 40 miles east of the city of Pune. The mission was later named Pandita Ramabai Mukti Mission. She is the ideal for women's and basically widow's.

3. Karl Marx (5 May 1818 – 14 March 1883) was a German philosopher, economist, historian, sociologist, political theorist, journalist and socialist revolutionary.

Born in Trier, Germany, Marx studied law and philosophy at university. He married Jenny von Westphalen in 1843. Due to his political publications, Marx became stateless and lived in exile with his wife and children in London for decades, where he continued to develop his thought in collaboration with German thinker Friedrich Engels and publish his writings, researching in the reading room of the British Museum. His best-known titles are the 1848 pamphlet, *The Communist Manifesto*, and the three-volume *Das Capital*. His political and philosophical thought had enormous influence on subsequent intellectual, economic and political history, and his name has been used as an adjective, a noun and a school of social theory.

4. Muhammad Iqbal also known as Allama Iqbal (1877-1938), was a Muslim philosopher, poet and politician of early 20th-century. He is particularly known in India, Pakistan, Bangladesh and Nepal for his Urdu philosophical poetry. Iqbal became prominence since 1899, when he recited *Nalay e Yatem* at the annual meeting of Anjuman-e-Himayat-e-Islam, Lahore. The poems he wrote up to 1905, imbibe patriotism that includes the *Tarana-e-Hind* (popularly known as *Saare Jahan Se Achcha*). The *Bang-e-Dara* is a collection of Urdu poetry written in three distinct phases of Iqbals life, In his early work he also wrote on most of the Indian iconic personalities such as *Rama Tirtha*, *Guru Nanak* and *Rama*.

Iqbal wrote two books on the topic of *The Development of Metaphysics in Persia* and *The Reconstruction of Religious Thought in Islam* and many letters in the English language. In these, he revealed his thoughts regarding Persian ideology and Islamic Sufism – in particular, his beliefs that Islamic Sufism activates the searching soul to a superior perception of life. He also discussed philosophy, God and the meaning of prayer, human spirit and Muslim culture, as well as other political, social and religious problems.

5. ***Sudharak***, meaning *Reformer*, was a newspaper in India. It was founded in 1888 by Gopal Ganesh Agarkar, who had previously edited *Kesari*. The Newspaper was an Anglo-Marathi-language work and was published in Poona, Maharashtra.

Gandhi started publishing a weekly journal called "Harijan" on 11 February 1933 from Yerwada Jail during British rule. He created three publications: *Harijan* in English (from 1933 to 1948), *Harijan Bandu* in Gujarati, and *Harijan Sevak* in Hindi. These newspapers found Gandhi concentrating on social and economic problems, much as his earlier English newspaper, *Young India*, had done from 1919 to 1932.

8. Kautilya in Arthashastra has detailed the notion of Raja Mandala or circle of states and Shadguna or six-fold diplomatic policy, which can amazingly encompass every aspect of modern foreign policy. The Rajmandala theory consists of four principal types of states viz. Vijigishu, Ari, Madhyama and Udasina. Each of them has an ally and ally's ally thus making 12 kings and 60 types of combinations called material constituents (for example, enemy's enemy, mitra's enemy, enemy's mitra, mitra's mitra and so on). This together combines into the total 72 elements of Raja Mandala.

This scheme is based on assumption that two neighbouring states which share their borders are hostile to each other; and the enemy of hostile neighbour is a naturally ally. The vijigishu is located at the centre of this circle.

9. Antonio Gramsci is the writer of the book A Great and Terrible World. A collection of letters is also essentially a biography – here of a man recognized as one of the twentieth century's leading thinkers. By translating and presenting for the first time many letters previously overlooked by other volumes, this collection greatly expands what the English-speaking world knows of him, both politically and personally. These extracts from his pre-prison correspondence—with his wife and her sister, international communist leaders, and fellow Italian revolutionaries—show his most important ideas at their beginnings, and give a well rounded picture of Gramsci's political, intellectual, and emotional development.

Antonio Gramsci (1891–1937) was a founding member of the Italian Communist Party, and among the twentieth century's most influential theorists.

10. **Agganna Sutta** is the 27th Sutta of the Digha Nikaya collection. The sutta describes a discourse imparted by the Buddha to two brahmins, Bharadvaja and Vasettha, who left their family and caste to become monks. The two brahmins are insulted and maligned by their own caste for their intention to become members of the Sangha. The Buddha explains that caste and lineage cannot be compared to the achievement of morality practice and the Dhamma, as anyone from the four castes can become a monk and reach the state of Arahant. Then, he explains about the beginning of the Earth and the birth of social order and its structure, including the castes. The Buddha emphasizes the message of universality in the Dhamma and how the Dhamma is the best of all things.

11. **Multi-criteria optimization**, or **multiobjective optimization** is a way of solving a mathematical or economic problem where many different parameters need to be changed to get one of the best possible solutions to the problem. The result of this is called **Pareto efficiency**, named after Vilfredo Pareto, who first used it in his studies.

    In economics, the idea of Pareto efficiency is very simple: If there is no way of improving the situation of one person, without making that of another person worse, the solution found is Pareto-efficient.

    If we look at what the economy produces, we might say it is on its **Pareto Frontier** or **Production Possibility Frontier**, meaning that it is making (or "producing") all it can with the things it has (such as machines, labour, land and ideas — all called **resources** or **factors of production**). If this is the case, making more of one thing would mean making less of another; the resources are already being used to full capacity, so making more of one thing will take resources away from making another.

    Just because something is Pareto efficient, it doesn't mean it is fair or "equitable". Even though no-one could be made better off without making someone else worse off, it is possible that one person owns all of the world's things. To make anyone else better off, some would have to be taken away from this person, making them worse off.

12. The philosophy of **Hegel** is the most complete of the history of philosophy. As a true architect, **Hegel** has built a cathedral, a complete system, totalling all knowledge of his time (art, religion, philosophy, history, ...). Even if Hegel appears as pretentious (**Kierkegaard**), funky for others (**Husserl**, **Sartre**), it remains that the work of **Hegel** is one of the most complex (it is often recommended reading *The Phenomenology of Mind* from five years of philosophy at the university ...)

    We bet, however, that we can somewhat explain his thinking in retaining its leading thoughts and quotes:

    "In the hierarchy of the means used to express the absolute, religion and culture in the wake of reason hold the highest degree, well above that of art"

    "Art, religion and philosophy differ only in form, their purpose is the same"

    "In saying that beauty is an idea, we want to say is that beauty and truth are one and the same thing"

    "There is no philosophical opinions".

13. **Rosa Luxemburg**, Polish-born German revolutionary and agitator who played a key role in the founding of the Polish Social Democratic Party and the Spartacus League, which grew into the Communist Party of Germany. As a political theoretician, Luxemburg developed a humanitarian theory of Marxism, stressing democracy and revolutionary mass action to achieve international socialism.

    Due to her pointed criticism of both the Leninist and the more moderate social democratic schools of socialism, Luxemburg has had a somewhat ambivalent reception among scholars and theorists of the political left. Nonetheless, Luxemburg and Liebknecht were extensively idolized as communist martyrs by the East German communist regime. The German Federal Office for the Protection of the Constitution notes that idolization of Luxemburg and Liebknecht is an important tradition of German far-left extremism.

14. **Integral humanism** was a set of concepts drafted by Deendayal Upadhyaya as a political program and adopted in 1965 as the official doctrine of the Jan Sangh. Upadhyaya borrowed the Gandhian principles such as sarvodaya (progress of all), swadeshi (domestic), and Gram Swaraj (village self rule) and these principles were appropriated selectively to give more importance to cultural-national values. These values were based on an individual's undisputed subservience to nation as a corporate entity. Richard Fox has characterised this as "ideological hijacking" and a "transplant" that was designed with a purpose to appropriate the authority that the Gandhian idioms had on Indian politics.

15. Feminists argue that women's values are based primarily on prescribed social roles. Feminism is characterized primarily by its political stance — the attempt to advance the social role of women. Feminists have highlighted what they see as a political relationship between the sexes, the supremacy of men and the subjection of women in most, if not all, societies. The 'first wave' of feminism was closely associated with the women's suffrage movement, which emerged in the 1840s and 1850s. The 'second wave' of feminism arose during the 1960s and expressed, in addition to the established concern with equal rights, the more radical and sometimes revolutionary demands of the growing women's liberation movement.

    The central concept in the feminist theory of sexual politics is patriarchy, a term that draws attention to the totality of oppression and exploitation to which women are subject. This, in turn, highlights the political importance of gender, understood to refer to socially imposed rather than biological differences between men and women. Most feminists view gender as a political construct, usually based upon stereotypes of 'feminine' and 'masculine' behaviour and social roles.

16. **Democratic socialism** is a term used to refer to the socialist political philosophy which advocates political democracy alongside a socially owned economy, with an emphasis on workers' self-management and democratic control of economic institutions within a market or some form of a decentralised planned socialist economy. Democratic socialists argue that capitalism is inherently incompatible with the values of freedom, equality and solidarity and that these ideals can be achieved only through the realisation of a socialist society. Democratic socialism can support either revolutionary or reformist politics as a means to establish socialism. In the term democratic socialism, the adjective democratic is added and used to distinguish democratic socialists from Marxist–Leninist inspired socialism which to many is viewed as being undemocratic or authoritarian in practice. Democratic socialists oppose the Stalinist political system and the Soviet-type economic system, rejecting the perceived authoritarian form of governance and highly centralised command economy that took form in the Soviet Union and other Marxist–Leninist states in the early 20th century. Democratic socialism is distinguished from meliorist and Third Way social democracy on the basis that democratic socialists are committed to systemic transformation of the economy from capitalism to socialism whereas Third Way social democrats are opposed to ultimately ending capitalism and are instead supportive of progressive reforms to capitalism.

17. Socrates (470-399BC) engaged his learners by asking questions (now known as the Socratic or dialectic method). He often insisted that he really knew nothing, but his questioning skills allowed others to learn by self-generated understanding.

Plato (428-348 BC), who was a student of Socrates and the teacher of Aristotle, wrote down the Dialogues, which have inspired thinkers for more than two thousand years. Plato called this process the *dialectic,* and considered it the pinnacle of learning. One of the significant features of the dialogical (dialectic) method is that it emphasizes collective, as against solitary activity. This is a question and answer form of arguing with an "expert" on one side and a "searcher" on the other. In the dialogues, the questioning of the expert by the searcher often exposes gaps in the reasoning. It is through this back and forth argument amongst friends (or adversaries) that understanding grows and becomes revealed to the learners. Such philosophical pursuit alongside and within a full education allows humans to transcend their desires and sense in order to attain true knowledge.

18. A Metic is a term that refers primarily to a non-citizen person permanently dwelling in Athens between 500 and 400 BC, a time in which foreigners were welcomed to settle in the city because of their positive impact on trade, culture and education. Most metics were either immigrants from other parts of Greece, freed slaves, or children of either of the two categories of people. Metics were found in most states except Sparta.

Because citizenship in ancient Athens was not based on where a person was born, but rather as a benefit of inheritance, many metic families had lived in Athens for generations and were likely physically indistinguishable from other local citizens. Based on the record of many tombstones, Metics retained the citizenship of their city of origin and preferred to list their home city on their tombs.

19. Mao Zedong-Political work is the life-blood of all economic work. This is particularly true at a time when the social and economic system is undergoing fundamental change.

20. The principles of Truth and Non-violence which forms the pivot of Gandhi's political activity are basically religious principles. He brought down these principles from the heights of spiritualization to the day to day life of common man. By this he wanted to show that there is nothing bad about politics if it was guided by moral and religious principles. Hence he stated that, "for me there is no politics devoid of religion. ... politics bereft of religion is a death trap because it kills the soul". He firmly held that success in politics should be achieved only by truthful means. Thus Gandhiji revolutionized politics by introducing the maxims of ethics and religion. Gandhi basically believed in the unity of religion and politics. Politics divorced from religion, according to him becomes debasing and is like a corpse only fit to be buried. He is firm in his opinion that the degeneration of modern civilization and particularly politics is only because it has been divorced from religion. Politics and religion are often seen degenerated because we are attempting to separate them.

21. In Machiavellian thought end justifies the means because the key objective of the Prince was to bring unity and integrity of the state. Machiavelli did condone the use of immoral or wicked ways. To him, the end was important, which could be attained by any means. He arrived at this understanding after observing the political game from close quarters in which ends justified the means. He contended that a ruler need not always adhere to conventional morality rather he should be willing to do so. He also insisted that a private individual would have to display impeccable moral values of the highest order. For Machiavelli, the home and family nurtured these moral values, teaching the individual the virtues of independence, simplicity, purity, loyalty and trust. He emphasizsed that an individual adhered to these values, whereas a statesman could be flexible as far as the conduct of state affairs was concerned, but not in private dealings.

In politics, fair was foul and foul was fair, depending on circumstances and situations. No general rule was valid, for everything became a matter of political expediency.

22. Gandhi seems to stand almost alone among social and political thinkers in his firm rejection of the rigid dichotomy between ends and means and in his extreme moral preoccupation with the means to the extent that they rather than the ends provide the standard of reference. He was led to this position by his early acceptance of satya and ahimsa, truth and nonviolence, as twin moral absolutes and his consistent view of their relationship. In Hind Swaraj he wrote that even great men who have been considered religious have committed grievous crimes through the mistaken belief that there is no moral connection or interdependence between the means and the end. We cannot get a rose through planting a noxious weed. "The means may be likened to a seed, the end to a tree; and there is just the same inviolable connection between the means and the end as there is between the seed and the tree." It is not as though violence and nonviolence are merely different means to secure the same end. As they are morally different in quality and essence, they must necessarily achieve different results. The customary dichotomy between means and ends originates in, and reinforces, the view that they are two entirely different categories of action and that their relationship is mainly a technical matter to be settled by considering what will be effective and what is possible in a given situation, that the ethical problem of choice requires an initial decision regarding the desired end and the obligatory acceptance of whatever steps seem necessary to secure it or are most likely to do so. Gandhi, however, was led by his metaphysical belief in the "law" of karma - the "law" of ethical causation or moral retribution that links all the acts of interdependent individuals - to the view that the relationship between means and ends is organic, the moral quality of the latter being causally dependent upon that of the former. The psychology of human action in a morally indivisible community of apparently isolated units demands that the means-end relationship must be seen in terms of the consistent growth in moral awareness of individuals and communities and not in relation to the mechanical division of time into arbitrary and discrete intervals. If for Gandhi there was no "wall of separation" between means and end, this was because of his basic belief that in politics as in all spheres of human action we reap exactly what we sow.

Gandhi's view of the means-end relationship may be put in the form of the following statements, which overlap and yet express several distinct ideas: "For me it is enough to know the means. Means and end are convertible terms in my philosophy of life." "We have always control over the means but not over the end." "I feel that our progress towards the goal will be in exact proportion to the purity of our means." "They say 'means are after all means'. I would say 'means are after all everything'. As the means so the end."

23. J.S. Mill stated that placing restrictions on freedom of expressions of human beings is like robbing off the present and the future races. He regarded liberty of conscience, liberty to express and publish one's opinions, liberty to live as one pleased and freedom of association as essential for a meaningful life and for the pursuit of one's own good. His defence of freedom of thought and expression was one of the most powerful and eloquent expositions in the western intellectual tradition. "If all mankind minus one were of one opinion, mankind would be no more justified in silencing that one person than he, if he had the power, would be justified in silencing mankind."

Mill's defence of freedom of thought and expression was linked to the persecution of error. Even if an opinion was incorrect, it ought to be articulated, for only through active interaction and dialogue could opinions evolve; otherwise they would lose their vitality and become dead dogmas. Ideas were to be subjected to critical scrutiny from other points of view for arriving at the truth.

24. Frantz Fanon (July 20, 1925–December 6, 1961) was a psychiatrist, intellectual, and revolutionary born in the French colony of Martinique. Fanon wrote about the effects of colonialism and oppression in books such as "Black Skin, White Masks" and "Wretched of the Earth." His writings, as well as his support of the Algerian War of Independence, have influenced anti-colonial movements across the world, including in South Africa, Palestine, and the United States.

25. "The people of England regards itself as free; but it is grossly mistaken; it is free only during the election of members of parliament. As soon as they are elected, slavery overtakes it, and it is nothing."

—Jean-Jacques Rousseau,
The Social Contract

27. The idea of justice as fairness flows from individual. The conception of justice as fairness was given by John Rawls in his book A Theory Of Justice 1971. He describes certain basic minimum principles on which any conception of justice has to be based. Such principles of justice have to arrived at from an original position under a veil of ignorance.

28. Multicultural Citizenship: A Liberal Theory of Minority Rights authored by Will Kymlicka. The increasingly multicultural fabric of modern societies has given rise to many new issues and conflicts, as ethnic and national minorities demand recognition and support for their cultural identity. This book presents a new conception of the rights and status of minority cultures. It argues that certain sorts of rights for minority cultures are consistent with liberal democratic principles, and that standard liberal objections to recognizing such rights on the grounds of individual freedom, social justice, and national unity can be answered. However, no single formula can be applied to all groups, and the needs and aspirations of immigrants are very different from those of indigenous peoples and national minorities. The book analyses some of the issues, which, though central to an understanding of multicultural politics (such as language rights, group representation, land rights, federalism, and secession), have been surprisingly neglected in contemporary liberal theory.

29. Postmodernism is an intellectual stance or a mode of discourse that rejects the possibility of reliable knowledge, denies the existence of a universal, stable reality, and frames aesthetics and beauty as arbitrary and subjective. It can be described as a reaction against scientific attempts to explain reality with objective certainty, recognizing that reality is constructed as the mind tries to understand its own personal circumstances. It is characterized by an attitude of skepticism, irony, or rejection toward the grand narratives and ideologies of modernism, often denying or challenging the validity of scientific inquiry, or declaiming the arbitrariness of the aesthetics of artistic works or other artifacts of cultural production, or questioning various assumptions of Enlightenment rationality. Initially, postmodernism was a mode of discourse on literature and literary criticism, commenting on the nature of literary text, meaning, author and reader, writing and reading. Postmodernism developed in the mid- to late-twentieth century across philosophy, the arts, architecture, and criticism as a departure or rejection of modernism.

Postmodernism relies on critical theory, an approach that confronts the ideological, social, and historical structures that shape and constrain cultural production. Common targets of postmodernism and critical theory include universalist notions of objective reality, morality, truth, human nature, reason, language, and social progress. Postmodernist approaches have been adopted in a variety of academic and theoretical disciplines, including political science, organization theory, cultural studies, philosophy of science, economics, linguistics, architecture, feminist theory, and literary criticism, as well as art movements in fields such as literature and music.

Postmodern thinkers frequently call attention to the contingent or socially-conditioned nature of knowledge claims and value systems, situating them as products of particular political, historical, or cultural discourses and hierarchies. Accordingly, postmodern thought is broadly characterized by tendencies to self-referentiality, epistemological and moral relativism, pluralism, and irreverence. Postmodernism is often associated with schools of thought such as deconstruction and post-structuralism, as well as philosophers such as Jean-François Lyotard, Jacques Derrida, and Fredric Jameson.

30. For Hobbes, the state of nature is characterized by the "war of every man against every man," a constant and violent condition of competition in which each individual has a natural right to everything, regardless of the interests of others. Existence in the state of nature is, as Hobbes famously states, "solitary, poor, nasty, brutish, and short." The only laws that exist in the state of nature (the laws of nature) are not covenants forged between people but principles based on self-preservation. What Hobbes calls the first law of nature, for instance, is that every man ought to endeavour peace, as far as he has hope of obtaining it; and when he cannot obtain it, that he may seek and use all helps and advantages of war.

In the absence of a higher authority to adjudicate disputes, everyone fears and mistrusts everyone else, and there can be no justice, commerce, or culture. That unsustainable condition comes to an end when individuals agree to relinquish their natural rights to everything and to transfer their self-sovereignty to a higher civil authority, or Leviathan. For Hobbes, the authority of the sovereign is absolute, in the sense that no authority is above the sovereign and that its will is law. That, however, does not mean that the power of the sovereign is all-encompassing: subjects remain free to act as they please in cases in which the sovereign is silent (in other words, when the law does not address the action concerned). The social contract allows individuals to leave the state of nature and enter civil society, but the former remains a threat and returns as soon as governmental power collapses. Because the power of Leviathan is uncontested, however, its collapse is very unlikely and occurs only when it is no longer able to protect its subjects.

34. Due to miserable failure of the Third Plan the government was forced to declare "plan holidays" (from 1966-67, 1967-68, and 1968-69). Three annual plans were drawn during this intervening period. During 1966-67 there was again the problem of drought. Equal priority was given to agriculture, its allied activities, and industrial sector. The government of India declared "Devaluation of Rupee" to increase the exports of the country. The main reasons for plan holidays were the war, lack of resources and increase in inflation.

36. NHRC of India is an independent statutory body established on **12 October, 1993** as per provisions of Protection of Human Rights Act, 1993, later amended in 2006. It is the watchdog of human rights in the country, i.e. the rights related to life, liberty, equality and dignity of the individual guaranteed by Indian Constitution or embodied in the international covenants and enforceable by courts in India. It was established in conformity with the **Paris Principles,** adopted for the promotion and protection of human rights in Paris (October, 1991) and endorsed by the General Assembly of the United Nations on 20 December, 1993.

The Union Government set up the **National Commission for Minorities** (NCM) under the

National Commission for Minorities Act, 1992. Six religious communities, viz; Muslims, Christians, Sikhs, Buddhists, Zoroastrians (Parsis) and Jains (6) have been notified in Gazette of India as minority communities by the Union Government all over India. Original notification of 1993 was for Five religious communities Sikhs, Buddhists, Parsis, Christians and Muslims.

38. The term 'stasiology' as it applies to the area of general science can be defined as 'the study of political parties'. Borrowing from French stasiologie, coined in 1951 by French jurist, sociologist and politician Maurice Duverger (1917-2014) from stase ("stasis") + ology (*indicating the study of a particular subject*), because of the way the opposition of political parties tends to prevent governments from making dramatic changes.

39. FRANK MARINI summarizes the themes of new public administration under five heads: RELEVANCE, VALUES, SOCIAL EQUITY, CHANGE, and CLIENT ORIENTATION.

1. **Relevance:** Advocate of new public administration opined that traditional public administration has been loaded with abstract. And comprehensively indefinable goals like efficiency and economy. And hence ignored the real life issue, which enable administrative effectiveness. Therefore they advocated that there is relevant knowledge of public administration whether it decides or not doesn't matter.
2. **Values:** According to the scholar of new public administration values cannot be ignored in administrative studies as public administrative what's in a political and social environment. Hence these both influence the administration & vice versa.
3. **Change:** Advocates of new public administration said that the approach of traditional public administration was status-quo. It was cultural bound, parochial and lack of mobility. While demand of new public administration is mobility and dynamism. Therefore public administration should strive for bringing the change in society.
4. **Social equity:** According to scholar of new public administration the ultimate purpose of public administration is social equity. In this context Frederickson has said that public administration which faith to work for the changes, try to regress the deprivation of minorities will likely be eventually use to regress those minorities.
5. **Client Orientation:** Administrator should treat the administration as client/customer.

42. 'New Democracy' as hegemony of the workers, peasants and other marginalized sections of the society is associated with Subaltern School. The term "subaltern" in this context is an allusion to the work of Italian Marxist Antonio Gramsci (1891-1937). The term's semantic range has evolved from its first usage by Ranjit Guha, following Gramsci, to refer solely to peasants who had not been integrated into the industrial capitalist system. It now refers to any person or group of inferior rank or station, whether because of race, class, gender sexual orientation, ethnicity or religion..

45. Adolf Hitler said that "when diplomacy ends, war begins". In international politics nations do not go to war without pursuing any diplomatic channels. So, first it will be negotiation through diplomatic means. They will try the best to solve the disputes and avoid conflict at all means. But if that fails, then the nations will have no other options than fighting it out in the battle. May be this could be the reason he meant. Of course, Hitler is not lunatic as the media projects. He went through the diplomatic channels, it worked with chamberlain and others. But after that he has to take the forced means to get back the territories Germany lost after the Treaty of Versailles. And he had the plan to get the most of Eastern Europe and probably Russia to make Germany Great again.

46. After successfully implementing a "Look East" policy to promote trade and investment with its Asian neighbours, India has adopted a similar policy toward West Asia.

The Gulf region has become a major economic partner, is a home to over 4 million Indians and a major source of oil and gas.

This has resulted in increased interaction, enhanced trade and economic relations and launch of negotiations towards FTA with the Gulf Cooperation Council (GCC) countries. The Government is keen to cooperate with the Gulf countries in the promotion of peace and stability in the region. It has appointed a Special Envoy for the Gulf and West Asia.

Indian stakes and interests in the Gulf region are as obvious as they are immense. Geographically, the Gulf is India's extended neighbourhood and the only link with the no less vital Central Asia, with Pakistan denying this country transit rights and Afghanistan having sunk into chaos. Historically, the relationship between the subcontinent and the Gulf goes back to ancient, pre-Islamic days. Britain controlled the Gulf littoral tightly because of its overwhelming strategic importance for the defense of India, the brightest jewel in the crown. The region has more to it than just being a centre of Israel-Arab confrontation. The geographical extent of what was West Asia has greatly expanded since the collapse of the USSR and is now called the "Greater Middle East". This region shares a long historical association with India. It is the source for India's ever-expanding needs of energy. It is also huge markets for Indian goods, services and skilled manpower.

47. On March 27, 2019 India conducted Mission Shakti, an anti-satellite missile test, from the Dr. A.P.J. Abdul Kalam Island launch complex. This was a technological mission carried out by DRDO. The satellite used in the mission was one of India's existing satellites operating in lower orbit. The test was fully successful and achieved all parameters as per plans. The test required an extremely high degree of precision and technical capability.

The significance of the test is that India has tested and successfully demonstrated its capability to interdict and intercept a satellite in outer space based on complete indigenous technology.

With this test, India joins an exclusive group of space faring nations consisting of USA, Russia and China.

48. In his book, Anatomy of Revolution, Crane Brinton compares revolution to a fever. In this respect, a revolution is not a positive phenomena, it is something to be avoided and cured, when and if, it occurs. This is due to the fact that *"nobody wants to have a fever"*. However, fever, and Revolution, *"in itself is a good thing .... for the organism that survives it. ... The revolution destroys wicked people and harmful and useless institutions"*. Brinton breaks down the revolution into three entities: the symptoms, the fever itself, which is the manipulation of revolution, and the break of the fever, when things more or less return to normal. Symptoms can take several different forms: economic problems, inefficiency of the government, the rise of the self-proclaimed revolutionaries, and the overthrow of the old regime, followed by the breakup of the revolutionaries' coalition. In the early stages of the revolution itself, Brinton sees the moderates seize power, but then the extremists take that power away from them. Then the fever breaks, Thermidor occurs and the revolution is over. In Brinton's view there is nothing much that can be done about revolutionaries, the fever has to burn out on its own. In his book, Crane Brinton uses the American Revolution as one of his examples. One assumes that he vies the American Revolution as a real Revolution, though the author states that it does not fit perfectly his conceptual schemes. Brinton sees the American Revolution as a territorial-nationalist one, in which the aim of the revolutionaries was not to overturn the existing *"social and economic system, but rather to set the English North American colonies up as an independent nation-state"*.

49. **Harit Pradesh** (also known as **Pashchim Pradesh & Pashchimanchal**) is a proposed new state of India comprising the western parts of Uttar Pradesh state. Harit means Green which signifies the agricultural prosperity of the region and Pradesh means state. The region has some demographic, economic and cultural patterns that are distinct from other parts of Uttar Pradesh, and more closely resemble those of Haryana, Punjab and Rajasthan states.

50. The melting pot theory of diversity propagates a construct of diversity as monoculturalism, where the various groups are assimilated into one culture, often with the minority groups rejected or hiding their differences and unique attributes, to take on the characteristics of the dominant culture.

Some countries are made of people who are almost all the same in terms of race, religion, and culture. Then there are places like the United States, where there are many different types of people. A place like that is a melting pot, because the people — despite their differences — manage to coexist and live together as one nation. Anywhere diverse people are assimilated could be called a melting pot. In a melting pot, differences become less important than unity.

The salad bowl (or fruit bowl) theory of diversity propagates a theory of pluralism, where differences between cultures are accepted, appreciated, celebrated and even utilized to create something stronger. There is still one entity (a salad) but the individual components (lettuce, tomatoes, carrots, cucumbers, etc.) are still distinguishable.

In reality, the melting pot theory of diversity is not a theory of inclusion; it is more about exclusion of unique strengths and attributes.

52. Pareto's thesis was that elites always rule. There is always the domination of the minority over the majority. And history is just the story of one elite replacing another. This is what he called the "circulation of elites". When the current elite starts to decline, it is challenged and makes way for another. Pareto thought that this came about in two ways: either through assimilation, the new elite merging with elements of the old, or through revolution, the new elite wiping out the old. He used the metaphor of a river to make his point. Most of the time, the river flows continuously, smoothly incorporating its tributaries, but sometimes, after a storm, it floods and breaks its banks.

53. The **Palestine Liberation Organization** is an organization founded in 1964 with the purpose of the "liberation of Palestine" through armed struggle, with much of its violence aimed at Israeli civilians. It is recognized as the "sole legitimate representative of the Palestinian people" by over 100 states with which it holds diplomatic relations, and has enjoyed observer status at the United Nations since 1974. The PLO was considered by the United States and Israel to be a terrorist organization until the Madrid Conference in 1991. In 1993, the PLO recognized Israel's right to exist in peace, accepted UN Security Council resolutions 242 and 338, and rejected "violence and terrorism". In response, Israel officially recognized the PLO as the representative of the Palestinian people.

55. The Intergovernmental Committee for the Safeguarding of the Intangible Cultural Heritage under UNESCO has inscribed 'Kumbh Mela' on the Representative List of Intangible Cultural Heritage of Humanity during its 12th session being held at Jeju, South Korea from 4-9 December 2017.

The inscription of 'Kumbh Mela' was recommended by the expert body which examines in detail the nominations submitted by Member States, according to a MEA note.

The Committee observed that 'Kumbh Mela' is the largest peaceful congregation of pilgrims on earth. The festival, held in Allahabad, Haridwar, Ujjain and Nasik, represents a syncretic set of rituals related to worship and ritual cleansing in holy rivers in India.

This inscription is the third in two years following the inscriptions of 'Yoga' and 'Nouroz'.

57. Samuel Huntington (1991) describes the pattern of global democratization as a series of three waves and reverse waves. The first wave of democratization started in the early 19th century and persisted until the 1920s, with many democracies backsliding at that time to autocracy (*i.e.*, the first reverse wave). With the end of World War Two came a second wave of democratization. This wave was however relatively brief, with a large proportion of countries succumbing to autocracy in the 1950s and the remainder of the second reverse-wave of democratization. In the mid-1970s the third wave of democratization began, continuing in force through the 1990s with the end of the Cold War. Huntington's analysis of these waves of democratization is based on the proportion of democratic regimes over time.

59. Kothari Committee (1976) Objective test to qualify for mains Written and interview test Post training test on completion of foundation course Attempt in any language mentioned under constitution With 3 attempts and 2 years age relaxation Based on 1st ARC.

Satish Chandra Committee (1989) Essay paper was introduced.

Y.K. Alagh Committee (2001) Continue optional for Prelims but recast GS comprising analytical ability questions Optionals to be replaced by 3 set of compulsory papers in Mains It favoured testing the candidates in a common subject rather than on optional subjects. Majority candidates opting subject based on scorability rather than specialization.

Bhatnagar Committee Preliminary examination with two objective type papers - Civil Services Aptitude Test (300 marks) and General Studies (300 marks). CSAT in prelims started since 2011 Hota Commission (2004) Recommended the use of ICT to spread awareness about government policies and programs. It advocated the use of eGovernance, code of ethics, public evaluation of services etc. to increase the efficiency of administration. Age – 21 to 24 years with relaxation to ST/SC.

SK Khanna Committee Preliminary stage reforms – Recommended CSAT format Reforms under 2nd ARC.

Nigavekar Committee (2011) Mains stage reforms Reforms under 2nd ARC Eligibility – 50% & more marks Prelims score should have 2 year validity 3 day interview Alternative career opportunities to those who fail Change exam system every 5 years 5 attempts irrespective of category Conduct CSAT online Combine prelims and mains.

60. The Supreme Court of India has the power to adjudicate disputes between the Union and the states through original jurisdiction. As a federal court, the Supreme court decides the disputes between different units of the Indian Federation. More elaborately, any dispute between—

1. The centre and one or more states; or
2. The centre and any state or states on one side and one or more states on the other; or
3. Between two or more states.

In the above federal disputes, the Supreme Court has exclusive original jurisdiction. Exclusive means, no other court can decide such disputes and original means, the power to hear such disputes in the first instance, not by way of appeal.

62. Internal communication can be upward, downward and across. **Internal communications (IC)** is the function responsible for effective communications among participants within an organization. The scope of the function varies by organization and practitioner, from producing and delivering messages and campaigns on behalf of management, to facilitating two-way dialogue and developing the communication skills of the organization's participants.

Modern understanding of internal communications is a field of its own and draws on the theory and practice of related professions, not least journalism, knowledge management, public relations (*e.g.*, media relations), marketing and human resources, as well as wider organizational studies, communication theory, social psychology, sociology and political science.

65. Warren Bennis predicted that bureaucracy is likely to go out of use in the wake of new social systems better suited to the 20th century demands of industrialization. **Warren Gamaliel Bennis** (March 8, 1925 – July 31, 2014) was an American scholar, organizational consultant and author, widely regarded as a pioneer of the contemporary field of Leadership studies. Bennis was University Professor and Distinguished Professor of Business Administration and Founding Chairman of The Leadership Institute at the University of Southern California.

66. According to Amartya Sen, "the poor are poor .... not because of what they do not have, but because of what they cannot do". Sen further said, "poverty is not just a lack of money; it is not having the capability to realize one's full potential as a human being".

Sen is an Indian economist and philosopher. He has made contributions to welfare economics, social choice theory, economic and social justice, economic theories of famines, and indices of the measure of well-being of citizens of developing countries.

67. Pradhan Mantri Gramin Awaas Yojana (PMGAY), previously **Indira Awaas Yojana (IAY)**, is a social welfare flagship programme, created by the Indian Government, to provide housing for the rural poor in India. Indira Awaas Yojana was launched in 1985 by Rajiv Gandhi, the then Prime Minister of India, as one of the major flagship programs of the Ministry of Rural Development to construct houses for BPL population in the villages.

The **Pradhan Mantri Gram Sadak Yojana (PMGSY)** was introduced in 2000 by the then-prime minister of India Late Shri Atal Bihari Vajpayee.

Atal Pension Yojana (or APY, previously known as **Swavalamban Yojana**) is a government-backed pension scheme in India, primarily targeted at the unorganised sector. It was mentioned in the 2015 Budget speech by the then Finance Minister Arun Jaitley. It was launched by Prime Minister Narendra Modi on 9 May in Kolkata.

The Government of India has launched the scheme "Deendayal Upadhyaya Gram Jyoti Yojana" for rural electrification in 2015. The erstwhile Rajiv Gandhi Grameen Vidyutikaran Yojana (RGGVY) scheme for village electrification and providing electricity distribution infrastructure in the rural areas has been subsumed in the DDUGJY scheme. Rural Electrification Corporation is the Nodal Agency for implementation of DDUGJY.

69. *Jus ad bellum* refers to the conditions under which States may resort to war or to the use of armed force in general. The prohibition against the use of force amongst States and the exceptions to it (self-defence and UN authorization for the use of force), set out in the United Nations Charter of 1945, are the core ingredients of jus ad bellum. *Jus in bello* regulates the conduct of parties engaged in an armed conflict. IHL(International humanitarian law) is synonymous with *jus in bello*; it seeks to minimize suffering in armed conflicts, notably by protecting and assisting all victims of armed conflict to the greatest extent possible.

IHL applies to the belligerent parties irrespective of the reasons for the conflict or the justness of the causes for which they are fighting. If it were otherwise, implementing the law would be impossible, since every party would claim to be a victim of aggression. Moreover, IHL is intended to protect victims of armed conflicts regardless of party affiliation. That is why *jus in bello* must remain independent of *jus ad bellum*.

71. The Punchhi Commission was constituted by the Government of India in 2007 as a commission on centre-state relations. It was chaired by Justice Madan Mohan Punchhi who was formerly the CJI. The commission came into effect on the 27th of April, 2007 to relook into the problems and issues in centre-State relations in India ever since these issues were earlier looked into by the Sarkaria Commission which had submitted its report in 1988.

Composition of the Punchhi Commission:

1. Madan Mohan Punchhi — Chairman
2. Dhirendra Singh — Member
3. Vinod Kumar Duggal — Member
4. N.R. Madhav Menon — Member
5. Vijay Shanker — Member Secretary
6. Amaresh Bagchi — Member till the death

The commission had submitted its report to the then Home Minister of India, P. Chidambaram in March 2010. The commission submitted its report in 7 volumes and 4 supplementary volumes.

72. European Union (EU) and India announced the establishment of an Investment Facilitation Mechanism (IFM) for EU Investments in India. The mechanism will allow for a close coordination between the European Union and the Government of India with an aim to promote and facilitate EU investment in India.

This agreement builds on the Joint Statement of the 13th EU-India Summit held in Brussels in March 2016, where the EU had welcomed India's readiness to establish such a mechanism and leaders from both sides had reaffirmed their shared commitment to oppose protectionism and to work in favour of a fair, transparent and rule-based trade and investment environment.

As part of the IFM, the EU Delegation to India and the Department of Industrial Policy & Promotion (DIPP), Ministry of Commerce & Industry, agreed to hold regular high level meetings to assess and facilitate "ease of doing business" for EU investors in India. This will include identifying and putting in place solutions to procedural impediments faced by EU companies and investors in establishing or running their operations in India.

75. On 22nd January 1946, the decision to send Cabinet Mission was taken and on 19th February 1946, the British PM C.R. Attlee Government announced in the House of Lords about the mission and the plan to quit India. A high-powered mission of three British Cabinet members- Lord Pethick-Lawrence, the Secretary of State for India, Sir Stafford Cripps, President of the Board of Trade, and A.V. Alexander, the First Lord of the Admiralty reached Delhi on 24th March 1946.

The main objective of **Cabinet Mission** was to find out ways and means for the peaceful transfer of power in India, to suggest measures for the formation of a Constitution making machinery and also to set up the Interim Government.

77. The **Clash of Civilizations** is a hypothesis that people's cultural and religious identities will be the primary source of conflict in the post-Cold War world. The American political scientist Samuel P. Huntington argued that future wars would be fought not between countries, but between cultures. It was proposed in a 1992 lecture at the American Enterprise Institute, which was then developed in a 1993 *Foreign Affairs* article titled "The Clash of Civilizations?", in response to his former student Francis Fukuyama's 1992 book, *The End of History and the Last Man*. Huntington later expanded his thesis in a 1996 book *The Clash of Civilizations and the Remaking of World Order.*

The phrase itself was earlier used by Albert Camus in 1946, by Girilal Jain in his analysis of the Ayodhya dispute in 1988, by Bernard Lewis in an article in the September 1990 issue of *The Atlantic Monthly* titled "The Roots of Muslim Rage" and by Mahdi El Mandjra in his book "La première guerre civilisationnelle" published in 1992. Even earlier, the phrase appears in a 1926 book regarding the Middle East by Basil Mathews: *Young Islam on Trek: A Study in the Clash of Civilizations*. This expression derives from "clash of cultures", already used during the colonial period and the Belle Epoque.

78. Second Administrative Reforms commission has recommended the creation of a District Council in every district with representatives from both urban and rural areas. The 2nd ARC was constituted on 31 August 2005, as a commission of Inquiry, under the chairmanship of Veerappa Moily of preparing a detailed blue-print for revamping the public administrative system.

79. The Kyoto Protocol is an international agreement linked to the United Nations Framework Convention on Climate Change, which **commits** its Parties by setting internationally binding emission reduction targets.

Recognizing that developed countries are principally responsible for the current high levels of GHG emissions in the atmosphere as a result of more than 150 years of industrial activity, the Protocol places a heavier burden on developed nations under the principle of "common but differentiated responsibilities."

The Kyoto Protocol was adopted in Kyoto, Japan, on 11 December 1997 and entered into force on 16 February 2005. The detailed rules for the implementation of the Protocol were adopted at COP 7 in Marrakesh, Morocco, in 2001, and are referred to as the "Marrakesh Accords."

82. Ministry of Home Affairs is the Nodal Ministry for the NHRC. The National Human Rights Commission (NHRC) of India was established on 12 October, 1993. The statute under which it is established is the Protection of Human Rights Act (PHRA), 1993 as amended by the Protection of Human Rights (Amendment) Act, 2006.

It is in conformity with the Paris Principles, adopted at the first international workshop on national institutions for the promotion and protection of human rights held in Paris in October 1991, and endorsed by the General Assembly of the United Nations by its Regulations 48/134 of 20 December, 1993.

The NHRC is an embodiment of India's concern for the promotion and protection of human rights.

Section 2(1)(d) of the PHRA defines Human Rights as the rights relating to life, liberty, equality and dignity of the individual guaranteed by the Constitution or embodied in the International Covenants and enforceable by courts in India.

83. Politics Among Nations: The Struggle for Power and Peace is a political science book by Hans J. Morgenthau published in 1948.

The book introduces the concept of political realism, presenting a realist view of power politics. This concept played a major role in the foreign policy of the United States, which made it exercise globe-spanning power in the Cold War period. The concept also called for a reconciliation of power politics with the idealistic ethics of earlier American discussions about foreign policy.

85. Indian has signed with Russia a long term agreement for Sukhoi Su-30MKI. India and Russia are set to sign a pact for quick delivery of spare parts for the Su-30MKI fleet that would ensure that the aircraft is available for more combat mission—a key focus area for Defence Minister Manohar Parrikar who has working on reducing the amount of time frontline fighters are grounded due to technical issues.

The longterm spares agreement will provide for an express process for the delivery of spares for the fleet for the next five years.

86. The water distribution treaty between India and Pakistan that was brokered by the World Bank in 1960 to use the water available in the Indus system of rivers originating in India. This treaty was signed in Karachi by the first Prime Minister of India Pandit Jawaharlal Nehru and then president of Pakistan Ayub Khan.

According to this agreement, control over the water flowing in three 'eastern' rivers of India—the Beas, the Ravi and the Sutlej — was given to India, while control over the water flowing in three 'western' rivers of India — the Indus, the Chenab and the Jhelum — was given to Pakistan.

87. After being a member of the Indian National Congress for over 26 years, Mamata Banerjee formed her own party of Bengal, the "Trinamool Congress", which was registered with the Election Commission of India during mid-December 1999. The Election Commission allotted to the party an exclusive symbol of *Jora Ghas Phul*. On 2 September 2016 election commission recognized AITC as a national political party.

The NCP was formed on 25 May 1999, by Sharad Pawar, P.A. Sangma, and Tariq Anwar after they were expelled from the Indian National Congress (INC) on 20 May 1999, for disputing the right of Italian-born Sonia Gandhi to lead the party.

Telangana Rashtra Samithi (abbreviated as **TRS**) is an Indian regional political party based in Telangana. It was founded on 27 April 2001 by K. Chandrashekar Rao, with a single-point agenda of creating a separate Telangana state with Hyderabad as its capital.

The **Maharashtra Navnirman Sena** is a nationalist far-right Indian political party based in the state of Maharashtra and operates on the motto of "Sons of the Soil". It was founded on 9 March 2006 in Mumbai by Raj Thackeray after he left the Shiv Sena party due to differences with his paternal cousin Uddhav Thackeray and to his sidelining by the Shiv Sena in major decisions like distribution of election tickets.

89. Article 268. Duties levied by the Union but collected and appropriated by the States.

1. Such stamp duties and such duties of excise on medicinal and toilet preparations as are mentioned in the Union List shall be levied by the Government of India but shall be collected:

   (*a*) in the case where such duties are leviable within any Union territory, by the Government of India, and

   (*b*) in other cases, by the States within which such duties are respectively leviable.

2. The proceeds in any financial year of any such duty leviable within any State shall not form part of the Consolidated Fund of India, but shall be assigned to that State.

90. CEPA stands for Comprehensive Economic Partnership Agreement and CECA stands for Comprehensive Economic Cooperation Agreement. Recently India signed a CEPA with Japan and CECA with Malaysia. India had also signed a Comprehensive Economic Partnership Agreement (CEPA) with South Korea. With Singapore signed CECA. The terms that make difference are "Cooperation" and "partnership". Both these terms are synonymous with each other but the major "technical" difference between a CECA and CEPA is that CECA involves only "tariff reduction/elimination in a phased manner on listed / all items except the negative list and tariff rate quota (TRQ) items" , CEPA also covers the trade in services and investment, and other areas of economic partnership. So CEPA is a wider term that CECA and has the widest coverage.

92. The Intellectual Crisis in American Public Administration has written By Vincent Ostrom and Barbara Allen. A classic book in the fields of public administration and political science since its publication in 1973, The Intellectual Crisis in American Public Administration examines various constitutional crises the nation has experienced since Watergate. This revised and expanded third edition extends the analysis to account for the most recent developments in American politics, up to and including the Clinton and Bush administrations.

94. Brexit is an abbreviation for "British exit," referring to the U.K.'s decision in a June 23, 2016 referendum to leave the European Union (EU). The vote's result defied expectations and roiled global markets, causing the British pound to fall to its lowest level against the dollar in 30 years. Former Prime Minister David Cameron, who called the referendum and campaigned for Britain to remain in the EU, announced his resignation the following day.

Britain is slated to leave the EU by October 31, 2019. The government has so far extended the negotiating period twice to avoid a "hard Brexit," or leaving without ratifying a deal with the EU.

96. Article 75 of the Constitution prescribes that the total number of Ministers, including the Prime Minister, in the Council of Ministers shall not exceed 15 per cent of the number of members of the House of the People.

Prior to January 1, 2004 (effective date of 91st Amendment of the Constitution) the Prime Minister had discretion to appoint any number in his council of ministers. But the Constitution (Ninety-first Amendment) Act in 2003 made a drastic change in curbing such power of the Prime Minister.

This Amendment added clause (1A) in this Article which made a specific provision that, the total number of Ministers, including Prime Minister, in no case can exceed 15 per cent of the total number of Lok Sabha members.

The Prime Minister can induct into his ministry a person who is not a member of either House of Parliament. However, a minister who for a period of six consecutive months is not a member of either House of Parliament shall at the expiration of that period cease to be one.

The amendment to the Constitution on the ceiling to the number of ministers was done as it was found that abnormally large councils of ministers were being constituted. However, in the case of smaller States like Sikkim, Mizoram and Goa having 32, 40 and 40 members in the Legislative Assemblies respectively, a minimum strength of seven ministers is proposed.

97. In the *Berubari Union* case (1960), the Supreme Court said that the Preamble shows the general purposes behind the several provisions in the Constitution, and is thus a key to the minds of the makers of the Constitution. Further, where the terms used in any article are ambiguous or capable of more than one meaning, some assistance at interpretation may be taken from the objective enshrined in the Preamble. Despite this recognition of the significance of the Preamble the supreme court specifically opined that preamble is *not* a part of the Constitution.

In the *Kesavananda Bharati* case (1973), the Supreme Court rejected the earlier opinion and held that Preamble is a part of the Constitution. It observed that the Preamble is of extreme importance and the Constitution should be read and interpreted in the light of the grand and noble vision expressed in the Preamble. In the *LIC of India* case (1995) also, the Supreme Court again held that the Preamble is an integral part of the Constitution.

98. **Habeas corpus**, an ancient common-law writ, issued by a court or judge directing one who holds another in custody to produce the person before the court for some specified purpose. Although there have been and are many varieties of the writ, the most important is that used to correct violations of personal liberty by directing judicial inquiry into the legality of a detention.

Mandamus is a writ which commands an individual, organization (*e.g.* government), administrative tribunal or court to perform a certain action, usually to correct a prior illegal action or a failure to act in the first place.

Certiorari is a Latin word meaning "to be informed of, or to be made certain in regard to". It is also the name given certain appellate proceedings for re-examination of actions of a trial court, or inferior appeals court.

Quo Warranto is a legal procedure taken to stop a person or organization from doing something for which it may not have the legal authority, by demanding to know by what right they exercise the controversial authority.

99. Comptroller and Audit-General, judges of Supreme court and governors are appointed by the President of India by warrant under his hand and seal. The words, "by warrant under his hand and seal" refers that the appointment letter bears the seal and signature of the president of India. This is enshrined in article 155 of the constitution of India.

100. After India became independent from the British Empire in 1947, the constituent units of India were classified under the following distinct categories:

Category	Description	Administrator	States
Part A states	Former British provinces	An elected governor and state legislature	9 states: Assam, Bihar, Bombay, East Punjab, Madhya Pradesh, Madras, Odisha, Uttar Pradesh, and West Bengal
Part B states	Former princely states or groups of Covenanting states	Rajpramukh (former princes)	9 states: Hyderabad, Jammu and Kashmir, Madhya Bharat, Mysore, Patiala and East Punjab States Union (PEPSU), Rajasthan, Saurashtra, Travancore-Cochin, and Vindhya Pradesh
Part C	Former princely states and provinces	Chief commi-ssioner	10 states: Ajmer, Coorg, Cooch-Behar, Bhopal, Bilaspur, Delhi, Himachal Pradesh, Kutch, Manipur, and Tripura
Part D	Union Territory	Governor appointed by the Indian president	Andaman and Nicobar Islands

Previous Paper (Solved)

National Testing Agency (NTA)

UGC-NET-Junior Research Fellowship & Assistant Professor Exam

Political Science, December-2018*

PAPER-II

Note: *This paper contains* ***hundred (100)*** *objective type questions of* ***two (2)*** *marks each.* ***All*** *questions are* ***compulsory***.

1. In the two lists given below. List-I provides the list of Kautilya's organs of the State, while List-II indicates the Organs of the human body. Match the two lists and choose the correct answer from the code given below:

***List-I* (Kautilya's organs of the State)**	***List-II* (Organs of the human body)**
(*a*) Amatya	(*i*) Mouth
(*b*) Suhrid	(*ii*) Eyes
(*c*) Durga	(*iii*) Arms
(*d*) Kosha	(*iv*) Ears

Code:

	(*a*)	(*b*)	(*c*)	(*d*)
A.	(*iv*)	(*iii*)	(*ii*)	(*i*)
B.	(*ii*)	(*iv*)	(*iii*)	(*i*)
C.	(*i*)	(*iii*)	(*ii*)	(*iv*)
D.	(*iii*)	(*ii*)	(*iv*)	(*i*)

2. Which of the following are the features of Plato's theory of education?

(*i*) It is a means of social righteousness and realisation of truth.

(*ii*) Elementary education begins at childhood up to the age of six.

(*iii*) The public test is held at the age of twenty.

(*iv*) At the age thirty, a second selective test is to take place.

Choose the correct answer from the code given below:

A. (*i*) and (*ii*) B. (*ii*) and (*iii*)

C. (*i*), (*iii*) and (*iv*) D. (*i*), (*ii*), (*iii*) and (*iv*)

3. Thomas Hobbes constructed his Political Philosophy on the basis of his postulates derived from:

A. Principles of Natural Science

B. Social Science

C. Theology

D. Metaphysics

4. Rousseau's General Will means:

A. Actual will B. Sum total of wills

C. Majority will D. Real will

5. Who among the following firmly believed that periodic communitarian correction is required because 'Liberalism is a self-subverting doctrine'?

A. John Rawals B. R. Nozick

C. R. Dworkin D. M. Walzer

6. Who among the following sought to establish the non-utilitarian proposition that some pleasures are of a higher quality than others?

A. Priestley B. Hutcheson

C. J. Bentham D. J.S.Mill

7. Who among the following described modern democracies as 'Polyarchy'?

A. David Easton

B. Robert Dahl

C. Joseph Schumpeter

D. S. Huntington

8. In the two lists given below, List-I provides the list of Authors, while List-II indicates their important concepts. Match the two lists and choose the correct answer from the code given below:

*Exam held on 21-12-2018.

List-I (Authors)	*List-II (Important concepts)*
(*a*) John Rawls	(*i*) Communitarian Perspective of Justice
(*b*) Robert Nozick	(*ii*) Global Justice
(*c*) Michael Walzer	(*iii*) Distributive Justice
(*d*) Thomas Pogge	(*iv*) Justice as Entitlement

Code:

	(*a*)	(*b*)	(*c*)	(*d*)
A.	(*iii*)	(*iv*)	(*i*)	(*ii*)
B.	(*i*)	(*ii*)	(*iii*)	(*iv*)
C.	(*ii*)	(*i*)	(*iv*)	(*iii*)
D.	(*iv*)	(*iii*)	(*ii*)	(*i*)

9. Arrange the following writings of Lenin in the order in which they appeared:
(*i*) Materialism and Empirio-Criticism
(*ii*) Socialism and War
(*iii*) What Is To Be Done?
(*iv*) The Development of Capitalism in Russia

Choose the correct answer from the code given below:
A. (*i*), (*ii*), (*iii*), (*iv*) B. (*iv*), (*iii*), (*i*), (*ii*)
C. (*iii*), (*i*), (*ii*), (*iv*) D. (*ii*), (*iv*), (*iii*), (*i*)

10. Who among the following said, "Political behaviour stands for both an intellectual tendency and a concrete academic movement?
A. R.A. Dahl B. G.A. Almond
C. Arthur Bentley D. David Easton

11. John Rawal's concept of 'veil of ignorance' does ***not*** imply to which of the following?
A. No one knows his place in society
B. No one knows his class position or social status
C. No one knows his fortune in the distribution of natural assets
D. Parties know their conception of good

12. Given below are two statements, one labelled as Assertion (A) and the other labelled as Reason (R). Read the statements and choose the correct answer from the code given below:

Assertion (A): Carlyle called Bentham's utilitarian doctrine as 'Pig philosophy'.

Reason (R): To him happiness is much more than pleasure.

Code:
A. Both (A) and (R) are true and (R) is the correct explanation of (A)
B. Both (A) and (R) are true, but (R) is not the correct explanation of (A)
C. (A) is true, but (R) is false
D. (A) is false, but (R) is true

13. Given below are two statements, one labelled as Assertion (A) and the other labelled as Reason (R). Read the statements and choose the correct answer from the code given below:

Assertion (A): For Gandhiji, enlightened anarchy refers to a form of society which functions without the coercive power of the State.

Reason (R): Individuals have full control of themselves.

Code:
A. Both (A) and (R) are true and (R) is the correct explanation of (A)
B. Both (A) and (R) are true, but (R) is not the correct explanation of (A)
C. (A) is true, but (R) is false
D. (A) is false, but (R) is true

14. Which of the following factors are responsible for the decline of political theory?
(*i*) Historicism
(*ii*) Positivism
(*iii*) Moral relativism
(*iv*) Hyperfactualism

Choose the correct answer from the code given below:
A. Only (*i*) and (*ii*)
B. Only (*ii*) and (*iii*)
C. Only (*i*), (*iii*) and (*iv*)
D. (*i*), (*ii*), (*iii*) and (*iv*)

15. For Aristotle, which of the following characteristics do ***not*** necessarily qualify to become an Athenian citizen?

(*i*) Residence in a particular place
(*ii*) The right of suing and being sued
(*iii*) Those who are disenfranchised or exiled
(*iv*) Descent from a citizen

Choose the correct answer from the code given below:

A. Only (*i*) and (*ii*)
B. Only (*ii*) and (*iv*)
C. Only (*ii*), (*iii*) and (*iv*)
D. (*i*), (*ii*), (*iii*) and (*iv*)

16. Arrange the following Ambedkar's writings in the order in which they appeared:

(*i*) The Untouchables.
(*ii*) Who Were the Shudras?
(*iii*) Annihilation of Caste
(*iv*) The Buddha and his Dharma

Choose the correct answer from the code given below:

A. (*iii*), (*ii*), (*i*), (*iv*)
B. (*iv*), (*iii*), (*ii*), (*i*)
C. (*ii*), (*i*), (*iii*), (*iv*)
D. (*i*), (*iii*), (*ii*), (*iv*)

17. M.N. Roy's Integral Scientific Humanism is also known as:

A. Marxism
B. Orthodox Marxism
C. Scientific Socialism
D. New Humanism

18. Which of the following features of Hegel's Theory of State are correct?

(*i*) State is a super-organism.
(*ii*) It is "The march of God on Earth".
(*iii*) It is an end in itself.
(*iv*) It is unchecked by any moral law, for it itself is the creator of morality.

Choose the correct answer from the code given below:

A. Only (*ii*) and (*iii*)
B. Only (*i*) and (*iv*)
C. Only (*ii*), (*iii*) and (*iv*)
D. (*i*), (*ii*), (*iii*) and (*iv*)

19. Which of the following statements on Gramsci are correct?

(*i*) The State cannot be understood without a thorough understanding of the Civil Society.
(*ii*) Civil Society is not the ensemble of organisms commonly called 'Private'.
(*iii*) It is in the Civil Society that the struggle for hegemony takes place.
(*iv*) He derived the terms Civil Society and Political Society from Hegel.

Choose the correct answer from the code given below:

A. Only (*i*) and (*iv*)
B. Only (*ii*) and (*iii*)
C. Only (*i*), (*iii*) and (*iv*)
D. (*i*), (*ii*), (*iii*) and (*iv*)

20. Which of the following features of Marx's dialectical materialism are correct?

(*i*) All the mass phenomena of history are determined by economic conditions.
(*ii*) Production is the most important of all human activities.
(*iii*) Men in association produce more than men in isolation.
(*iv*) Religion is the opium of the people.

Choose the correct answer from the code given below:

A. Only (*i*) and (*iv*)
B. Only (*ii*) and (*iv*)
C. Only (*i*), (*ii*) and (*iii*)
D. (*i*), (*ii*), (*iii*) and (*iv*)

21. Which of the following statements with regard to Almond's characterisation of political system are correct?

(*i*) All political systems have political structures.
(*ii*) All political systems do not perform the same functions.
(*iii*) All political systems are not multi-functional.
(*iv*) All political systems are mixed systems in the cultural sense.

Choose the correct answer from the code given below:

A. Only (*i*), (*ii*) and (*iii*)
B. Only (*i*) and (*iv*)
C. Only (*ii*) and (*iv*)
D. Only (*iii*) and (*iv*)

22. David Easton had identified four kinds of inputs in terms of demands. What are they?

A. Allocation of goods and services, Regulation of behaviour, Participation in the economic system, Communication and information
B. Regulation of behaviour, Participation in the political system, Allocation of goods and services, Communication and information
C. Communication and information, Participation in international system, Allocation of goods and services, Regulation of behaviour
D. Participation in social system, Allocation of goods and services, Communication and information, Regulation of behaviour

23. Who said, "A Government without a Constitution is a power without right"?

A. Thomas Paine B. Karl Deutsch
C. David Apter D. Walter Bagehot

24. Which of the following statements are correct?

(*i*) Federal Councillors in Switzerland can be impeached.
(*ii*) Vice-President presides over the joint sessions of American Congress.
(*iii*) The President of India sent a message to Indian Parliament once.
(*iv*) The Prime Minister of Britain oversees the operation of the Civil Services and Government Agencies.

Choose the correct answer from the code given below:

A. Only (*i*), (*iii*) and (*iv*)
B. Only (*ii*) and (*iv*)
C. Only (*iii*) and (*iv*)
D. Only (*i*) and (*iii*)

25. Which principle was established for the first time by the US Supreme Court in deciding McCulloch vs. Maryland Case?

A. Equality among States
B. Equality between the Federal Government and States
C. Supremacy of the States over the Federal Government
D. Supremacy of the Federal Government over the States

26. According to Powell, any nation's political culture may be mapped at three levels. Identify these levels.

A. The political system level, The people level, The process level
B. The people level, The process level, The policy level
C. The political system level, The process level, The policy level
D. The process level, The policy level, The power level

27. Lucian Pye had identified 'Crises' that new States in the Third World face in achieving political development. Which one of the following groups is correct?

A. Identity, Legitimacy, Penetration, Participation, Integration, Distribution
B. Identity, Penetration, Participation, Disintegration, Distribution, Economic instability
C. Penetration, Diffusion, Disintegration, Centralisation, Leadership, Governance
D. Participation, Representation, Penetration, Integration, Legitimacy, Centralisation

28. Given below are two statements, one labelled as Assertion (A) and the other labelled as Reason (R). Read the statements and choose the correct answer from the code given below:

Assertion (A): Most legislatures today do not make laws, rather they formally approve laws made elsewhere.

Reason (R): Legislature is the law making body of the State.

Code:

A. Both (A) and (R) are true and (R) is the correct explanation of (A)
B. Both (A) and (R) are true, but (R) is not the correct explanation of (A)
C. (A) is true, but (R) is false
D. (A) is false, but (R) is true

29. In the two lists given below, List-I provides the list of Proponents, while List-II indicates Concepts. Match the two lists and choose the correct answer from the code given below:

List-I (Proponent)	***List-II (Concept)***
(*a*) S.P. Huntington	(*i*) Associated-development-dependent
(*b*) R.A. Dahl	(*ii*) Political simulation
(*c*) Kenneth Boulding	(*iii*) Political decay
(*d*) Fernando H. Cardoso	(*iv*) Polyarchical democracy

Code:

	(*a*)	(*b*)	(*c*)	(*d*)
A.	(*iii*)	(*iv*)	(*ii*)	(*i*)
B.	(*iii*)	(*ii*)	(*iv*)	(*i*)
C.	(*i*)	(*iii*)	(*iv*)	(*ii*)
D.	(*ii*)	(*iv*)	(*iii*)	(*i*)

30. In the two lists given below, List-I provides the list of Books, while List-II indicates their Authors. Match the two lists and choose the correct answer from the code given below:

List-I (Books)	***List-II (Authors)***
(*a*) British Political Parties	(*i*) Robert Michels
(*b*) Political Parties	(*ii*) Robert Mckenzie
(*c*) Comparative Government : An Introduction	(*iii*) James A. Bill and Robert H. Hardgrave
(*d*) Comparative Policies: Quest for Theory	(*iv*) Jean Blondel

Code:

	(*a*)	(*b*)	(*c*)	(*d*)
A.	(*i*)	(*iv*)	(*iii*)	(*ii*)
B.	(*iii*)	(*ii*)	(*i*)	(*iv*)
C.	(*ii*)	(*iii*)	(*iv*)	(*i*)
D.	(*ii*)	(*i*)	(*iv*)	(*iii*)

31. In the two lists given below, List-I provides the list of Revolutions, while List-II indicates Countries. Match the two lists and choose the correct answer from the code given below:

List-I (Revolution)	***List-II (Country)***
(*a*) Velvet Revolution	(*i*) Uzbekistan
(*b*) Orange Revolution	(*ii*) Portugal
(*c*) Carnation Revolution	(*iii*) Vietnam
(*d*) August Revolution	(*iv*) Czechoslovakia

Code:

	(*a*)	(*b*)	(*c*)	(*d*)
A.	(*i*)	(*iii*)	(*ii*)	(*iv*)
B.	(*ii*)	(*iv*)	(*iii*)	(*i*)
C.	(*iii*)	(*ii*)	(*i*)	(*iv*)
D.	(*iv*)	(*i*)	(*ii*)	(*iii*)

32. Which of the following statement/s is/are correct with regard to theories of Elite?

(*i*) James Burnham proposed the concept of 'Circulation of elites'.
(*ii*) C. Wright Mills' triumvirate power group consists of political, economic and managerial classes.
(*iii*) G. Mosca emphasised on the personal characteristics of elite.
(*iv*) Elite theory supports pluralism.

Choose the correct answer from the code given below:

A. Only (*i*), (*iii*) and (*iv*)
B. Only (*iii*)
C. Only (*ii*)
D. Only (*iii*) and (*iv*)

33. Which of the following statements are correct?

(*i*) American Senate has the power to amend revenue bills.
(*ii*) House of Representatives has special power to originate revenue bills.

(*iii*) In Britain, executive and legislature relationship is based on diffusion of powers.

(*iv*) American President can dissolve the House of Representatives.

Choose the correct answer from the code given below:

A. Only (*i*) and (*ii*)
B. Only (*ii*) and (*iv*)
C. Only (*i*), (*iii*) and (*iv*)
D. Only (*i*) and (*iii*)

34. Given below are two statements, one labelled as Assertion (A) and the other labelled as Reason (R). Read the statements and choose the correct answer from the code given below:

Assertion (A): The essence of federalism lies not in the institutional or constitutional structure but in the society itself.

Reason (R): Coalition governments are the most suitable form of governments in a heterogeneous society.

Code:

A. Both (A) and (R) are true and (R) is the correct explanation of (A)
B. Both (A) and (R) are true, but (R) is not the correct explanation of (A)
C. (A) is true, but (R) is false
D. (A) is false, but (R) is true

35. The Bill of Rights (first ten amendments) in America includes in it among others:

A. Right to assembly, Right to bear arms, Right to speedy trial, Right to social security allowance
B. Right to security, Right to life, Right to assembly, Right to social security allowance
C. Right to assembly, Right to bear arms, Right to speedy trial, Right to security against unreasonable searches
D. Right to bear arms, Right to freedom of speech, Right to equality, Right to social security allowance

36. Lukes' description of three forms of power does ***not*** include:

A. Decision-making
B. Thought control
C. Capability enhancement
D. Agenda setting

37. The primary agents of political socialisation are:

A. Family and School
B. Family and Social class
C. School and Peer group
D. Peer group and Social class

38. In the two lists given below, List-I provides the list of Descriptions of political development, while List-II indicates Scholars. Match the two lists and choose the correct answer from the code given below:

List-I (Description of political development)	***List-II (Scholars)***
(*a*) Political Modernisation	(*i*) J. Ronald Pennock
(*b*) Building of Democracy	(*ii*) S.M. Lipset
(*c*) Operation of Nation State	(*iii*) Talcott Parsons
(*d*) Administrative and Legal Development	(*iv*) Edward A. Shils

Code:

	(*a*)	(*b*)	(*c*)	(*d*)
A.	(*ii*)	(*iv*)	(*iii*)	(*i*)
B.	(*ii*)	(*i*)	(*iv*)	(*iii*)
C.	(*iv*)	(*ii*)	(*iii*)	(*i*)
D.	(*i*)	(*iii*)	(*ii*)	(*iv*)

39. Which of the following are the kinds of party systems described by Arendt Lijphart?

A. Consensual party system, Conflictual party system and Accommodative party system
B. Conflictual party system, Democratic party system and Accommodative party system
C. Accommodative party system, Secular party system and Consensual party system
D. Secular party system, Consensual party system and Democratic party system

40. Which of the following are the variables of political culture suggested by S.E. Finer?

A. Mature political culture, Developed political culture and Secular political culture

B. Developed political culture, Low political culture and Democratic political culture

C. Mature political culture, Sectarian political culture and Orthogenic political culture

D. Mature political culture, Developed political culture and Low political culture

41. Who among the following described the nationalist movement before the arrival of Mohandas Karamchand Gandhi as "a movement representing the classes" as opposed to the masses?

A. Judith Brown B. Ravinder Kumar

C. Michael Brecher D. Bipin Chandra

42. Which of the following was ***not*** a feature of the Government of India Act of 1919?

A. Bicameral Legislature at the Centre

B. Legislative Assembly to have an elected majority

C. Legislative Council enabled to move resolutions on Budget

D. Communal representation extended to the Sikhs

43. Consider the following statements:

(*i*) The Fundamental Rights constitute limitations upon State action, the Directive Principles instruct the State to do certain things.

(*ii*) The Directive Principle are not enforceable in the courts.

(*iii*) If any law is made to implement any of the Directives mentioned in Part IV of the Constitution, it would be immune from unconstitutionality on the ground of violation of Fundamental Rights conferred by Articles 14 and 19.

(*iv*) The Directive Principles require to be implemented by legislation.

Choose the correct answer from the code given below:

A. (*i*) and (*ii*) are correct

B. (*ii*) and (*iv*) are correct

C. (*iii*) and (*iv*) are correct

D. (*i*), (*ii*) and (*iv*) are correct

44. Which of the following statement/s about Fundamental Duties is/are ***not*** correct?

(*i*) The Fundamental Duties are incorporated in Article 51A (Part IVA) of Constitution.

(*ii*) The Fundamental Duties were inserted in the Constitution by the 42nd Constitution Amendment Act, 1976.

(*iii*) The Fundamental Duties have to be fulfilled by every person living in India.

(*iv*) The eleventh Fundamental Duty was added by the 86th Constitution Amendment Act, 2006.

Choose the correct answer from the code given below:

A. (*i*) and (*ii*) are not correct

B. (*ii*) and (*iii*) are not correct

C. (*iii*) and (*iv*) are not correct

D. Only (*iii*) is not correct

45. By which Constitutional Amendment Act, was 'Forest and Protection of Wild Animals' shifted from State to Concurrent list?

A. 39th Constitutional Amendment

B. 40th Constitutional Amendment

C. 41st Constitutional Amendment

D. 42nd Constitutional Amendment

46. By which amendment of the Constitution can the same person be appointed as Governor of one or more States or Lt. Governor of the Union Territory?

A. Fourth Amendment Act, 1955

B. Fifth Amendment Act, 1955

C. Sixth Amendment Act, 1956

D. Seventh Amendment Act, 1956

47. In the two lists given below, List-I provides the list of Prime Ministers, while List-II indicates Governments. Match the two lists and choose the correct answer from the code given below:

List-I *(Prime Minister)*	*List-II* *(Government)*
(*a*) Chandra Shekhar	(*i*) United Front
(*b*) Deve Gowda	(*ii*) National Democratic Alliance
(*c*) Atal Bihari Vajpayee	(*iii*) United Progressive Alliance
(*d*) Manmohan Singh	(*iv*) National Front

Code:

	(*a*)	(*b*)	(*c*)	(*d*)
A.	(*iv*)	(*ii*)	(*i*)	(*iii*)
B.	(*iv*)	(*i*)	(*ii*)	(*iii*)
C.	(*ii*)	(*iii*)	(*i*)	(*iv*)
D.	(*iii*)	(*iv*)	(*i*)	(*ii*)

48. Arrange the following Speakers of the Lok Sabha in chronological order:

(*i*) Shivraj V. Patil
(*ii*) Somnath Chatterjee
(*iii*) Manohar Joshi
(*iv*) N. Sanjeeva Reddy

Choose the correct answer from the code given below:

A. (*iv*), (*iii*), (*i*), (*ii*) B. (*ii*), (*i*), (*iii*), (*iv*)
C. (*iii*), (*ii*), (*iv*), (*i*) D. (*iv*), (*i*), (*iii*), (*ii*)

49. Which of the following were the recommendations of the Sarkaria Commission about the appointment of the Governor?

(*i*) He should be eminent in some walk of life.
(*ii*) He should be a person from outside the State.
(*iii*) He should be a detached figure and not too intimately connected with local politics of the State.
(*iv*) He should be a person who has not taken too great a part in politics, in general, and in the recent past, in particular.

Choose the correct answer from the code given below:

A. Only (*i*) and (*ii*)
B. Only (*i*) and (*iii*)
C. Only (*i*), (*iii*) and (*iv*)
D. (*i*), (*ii*), (*iii*) and (*iv*)

50. Consider the following statements regarding the duration of Panchayat:

(*i*) The term of a Panchayat shall be for five years from the date of its being elected.
(*ii*) If it is dissolved earlier, then the elections must take place within six months of its dissolution.
(*iii*) A Panchayat reconstituted after premature dissolution shall have a fresh term of five years.
(*iv*) It shall not be necessary to hold elections if the remainder of the period is less than six months.

Choose the correct answer from the code given below:

A. Only (*i*) is correct
B. Only (*i*) and (*ii*) are correct
C. Only (*ii*) and (*iii*) are correct
D. Only (*i*), (*ii*) and (*iv*) are correct

51. Given below are two statements, one labelled as Assertion (A) and the other labelled as Reason (R). Read the statements and choose the correct answer from the code given below:

Assertion (A): Article 1 described India as a "Union of States".

Reason (R): The term "Union of States" was used to curb sub-nationalism and strengthening unity and integrity of the country.

Code:

A. Both (A) and (R) are true and (R) is the correct explanation of (A)
B. Both (A) and (R) are true, but (R) is not the correct explanation of (A)
C. (A) is true, but (R) is false
D. (A) is false, but (R) is true

52. Who among the following has criticized the Supreme Court as a 'deeply paradoxical institution' because it wields immense power with limited accountability?

A. Granville Austin
B. James Manor
C. Paratap B. Mehta
D. Niraja Gopal Jayal

53. Which Article of the Constitution enjoins/bounds all authorities to act in the aid of the Supreme Court of India?

A. Article 139 B. Article 141
C. Article 144 D. Article 142

54. In the two lists given below, List-I provides the list of names of Newspapers, while List-II indicates Editors-in-Chief, as on July, 2018. Match the two lists and choose the correct answer from the code given below:

List-I ***(Name of Newspaper)***	***List-II*** ***(Editors-in-Chief)***
(*a*) The Hindu	(*i*) Jaideep Bose
(*b*) The Times of India	(*ii*) Raj Kamal Jha
(*c*) The Hindustan Times	(*iii*) N. Ravi
(*d*) The Indian Express	(*iv*) Sukumar Ranganathan

Code:

	(*a*)	(*b*)	(*c*)	(*d*)
A.	(*iv*)	(*i*)	(*iii*)	(*ii*)
B.	(*iii*)	(*ii*)	(*iv*)	(*i*)
C.	(*iii*)	(*i*)	(*iv*)	(*ii*)
D.	(*ii*)	(*iii*)	(*i*)	(*iv*)

55. In which of the following groups of States, did the BJP win all the Lok Sabha seats in the 16th Lok Sabha elections?

A. Rajasthan, Delhi, Himachal Pradesh and Haryana
B. Gujarat, Delhi, Madhya Pradesh and Uttarakhand
C. Rajasthan, Gujarat, Uttarakhand and Himachal Pradesh
D. Uttarakhand, Himachal Pradesh, Delhi and Jharkhand

56. In the two lists given below, List-I provides the list of Electoral Problems, while List-II indicates Electoral Reforms. Match the two lists and choose the correct answer from the code given below:

List-I ***(Electoral Problem)***	***List-II*** ***(Electoral Reform)***
(*a*) Fake registration of voters	(*i*) Voting in phases
(*b*) Delay in counting of votes	(*ii*) Raising the security deposit of candidates
(*c*) Violence during elections	(*iii*) Electronic voting machines
(*d*) Excessive contestants	(*iv*) Photo identity cards

Code:

	(*a*)	(*b*)	(*c*)	(*d*)
A.	(*i*)	(*ii*)	(*iii*)	(*iv*)
B.	(*iv*)	(*iii*)	(*ii*)	(*i*)
C.	(*ii*)	(*i*)	(*iv*)	(*iii*)
D.	(*iv*)	(*iii*)	(*i*)	(*ii*)

57. Given below are two statements, one labelled as Assertion (A) and the other labelled as Reason (R). Read the statements and choose the correct answer from the code given below:

Assertion (A): In India, democracy had already been granted by the elite, but the elite had monopolized power for decades.

Reason (R): The revolution is now passing through the polling booth.

Code:

A. Both (A) and (R) are true and (R) is the correct explanation of (A)
B. Both (A) and (R) are true, but (R) is not the correct explanation of (A)
C. (A) is true, but (R) is false
D. (A) is false, but (R) is true

58. Which of the following pairs is correctly matched?

List-I	***List-II***
(*a*) Myron Weiner	(*i*) The Third Democratic Upsurge
(*b*) Rajni Kothari	(*ii*) The Indian Paradox
(*c*) Suhas Palshikar	(*iii*) The Congress System
(*d*) Yogendra Yadav	(*iv*) Post-Congress Polity

Code:

	(*a*)	(*b*)	(*c*)	(*d*)
A.	(*iv*)	(*ii*)	(*iii*)	(*i*)
B.	(*iii*)	(*ii*)	(*i*)	(*iv*)
C.	(*ii*)	(*iii*)	(*iv*)	(*i*)
D.	(*ii*)	(*iv*)	(*iii*)	(*i*)

59. In the two lists given below, List-I provides the list of Perspectives, while List-II indicates Criticisms of Indian Democracy. Match the two lists and choose the correct answer from the code given below:

List-I (Perspective)	***List-II (Criticism of Indian Democracy)***
(*a*) Hindu Nationalist	(*i*) Very limited space for direct and local democracy
(*b*) Gandhian	(*ii*) Not succeeded in ensuring individual dignity and freedom
(*c*) Marxist	(*iii*) Imitation of western democracy ignoring indigenous democratic traditions
(*d*) Liberal Democratic	(*iv*) Sham because it perpetuates the powers and privileges of the dominant interests

Code:

	(*a*)	(*b*)	(*c*)	(*d*)
A.	(*iii*)	(*ii*)	(*i*)	(*iv*)
B.	(*i*)	(*iii*)	(*iv*)	(*ii*)
C.	(*ii*)	(*i*)	(*iii*)	(*iv*)
D.	(*iii*)	(*i*)	(*iv*)	(*ii*)

60. Which was the first State in independent India where the government was formed after engineering splits and defections?

A. PEPSU B. Madras
C. Andhra D. Rajasthan

61. Who among the following said, "Like physics or chemistry, administration is governed by principles?

A. L.D. White B. H. Simon
C. Gullick D. Urwick

62. Henry Fayol mentioned the following functions of administration. Put them in correct order.

(*i*) Organising
(*ii*) Planning
(*iii*) Command
(*iv*) Control
(*v*) Coordination

Choose the correct answer from the code given below:

A. (*i*), (*ii*), (*iii*), (*iv*), (*v*)
B. (*ii*), (*i*), (*iii*), (*v*), (*iv*)
C. (*ii*), (*i*), (*v*), (*iii*), (*iv*)
D. (*ii*), (*i*), (*iv*), (*iii*), (*v*)

63. Which of the following statements are correct about development administration?

(*i*) It is change oriented.
(*ii*) Its objectives are simple.
(*iii*) It is dynamic and flexible.
(*iv*) It is concerned with new tasks.

Choose the correct answer from the code given below:

A. (*i*), (*ii*), (*iii*) and (*iv*)
B. Only (*i*), (*iii*) and (*iv*)
C. Only (*ii*), (*iii*) and (*iv*)
D. Only (*i*), (*ii*) and (*iv*)

64. Match List-I with List-II and select the correct answer from the code given below:

List-I	***List-II***
(*a*) Elton Mayo	(*i*) Classical Theory of Organisation
(*b*) Henry Fayol	(*ii*) Scientific Management
(*c*) Nicholas Henry	(*iii*) Human Relations Theory
(*d*) F.W. Taylor	(*iv*) New Public Management

Code:

	(*a*)	(*b*)	(*c*)	(*d*)
A.	(*iii*)	(*i*)	(*iv*)	(*ii*)
B.	(*i*)	(*iii*)	(*iv*)	(*ii*)
C.	(*i*)	(*ii*)	(*iii*)	(*iv*)
D.	(*iii*)	(*iv*)	(*ii*)	(*i*)

65. Match List-I with List-II and select the correct answer from the code given below:

List-I	***List-II***
(*a*) Barnard	(*i*) Delegation
(*b*) Fayol	(*ii*) Principles of Management
(*c*) Gullick	(*iii*) The Functions of the Executive
(*d*) Terry	(*iv*) Bases of Organisation

Code:

	(a)	(b)	(c)	(d)
A.	(iii)	(ii)	(iv)	(i)
B.	(ii)	(iii)	(iv)	(i)
C.	(iii)	(iv)	(i)	(ii)
D.	(ii)	(iv)	(iii)	(i)

66. Who among the following considered the concept of delegation as a mere myth of organisational (administrative) theory?

A. Follett B. Terry
C. Mooney D. Millet

67. Who among the following gave the Bounded Rationality model of decision-making?

A. Herbert Simon
B. Elton Mayo
C. D. Osborne
D. Edward Weidner

68. Which one of the following is the goal of Scientific Management?

A. Generating employment
B. Maximising social welfare
C. Higher industrial efficiency
D. Welfare of the workers

69. Which one of the following types of bureaucracy is found in the colonial rule?

A. Ruler-dominated bureaucracy
B. Ruling bureaucracy
C. Caste bureaucracy
D. Party-State bureaucracy

70. Who among the following said, "Bureaucracy is the price of parliamentary democracy"?

A. Ramsay Muir
B. H.J. Laski
C. Herbert Morrison
D. F.M. Marx

71. Which of the following Committees are helped by the CAG in exercising legislative control over the executive?

(*i*) Estimates Committee
(*ii*) Public Accounts Committee
(*iii*) Business Advisory Committee
(*iv*) Committee on Government Assurances

Choose the correct answer from the code given below:

A. Only (*i*) and (*ii*)
B. Only (*ii*) and (*iv*)
C. Only (*i*), (*ii*) and (*iv*)
D. (*i*), (*ii*) (*iii*) and (*iv*)

72. Who among the following suggested the abolition of the office of the Comptroller and Auditor-General of India?

A. Paul Appleby B. A.D. Gorwala
C. N.N. Vohra D. L.K. Jha

73. In which of the following countries can a person enter the public service at almost any level and at almost any age?

A. UK B. USA
C. India D. France

74. Which of the following factors hinder the observance of administrative ethics by the civil servants?

(*i*) Anonymity
(*ii*) Humbleness
(*iii*) Indifferentism
(*iv*) Officiousness

Choose the correct answer from the code given below:

A. Only (*ii*) and (*iv*)
B. Only (*iii*) and (*iv*)
C. Only (*ii*) and (*iii*)
D. Only (*ii*) (*iii*) and (*iv*)

75. Which of the following committees was appointed on 'Revitalisation of Panchayati Raj Institutions for Democracy and Development'?

A. Balwant Rai Mehta Committee
B. Ashok Mehta Committee
C. G.V.K. Rao Committee
D. L.M. Singhvi Committee

76. Which Committee recommended "United Grading Structure" for the British Civil Service?

A. Masterman B. Fulton
C. Asheton D. McGraw

77. Which of the following countries have dual citizenship—National citizenship and State citizenship?
A. India and USA
B. India and Switzerland
C. Switzerland and USA
D. USA and UK

78. Given below are two statements, one labelled as Assertion (A) and the other labelled as Reason (R). Read the statements and choose the correct answer from the code given below:

Assertion (A): An Election Commissioner cannot be removed from office except on the recommendation of the Chief Election Commissioner of India.

Reason (R): He/She is appointed on the recommendation of the Chief Election Commissioner.

Code:
A. Both (A) and (R) are true and (R) is the correct explanation of (A)
B. Both (A) and (R) are true, but (R) is not the correct explanation of (A)
C. (A) is true, but (R) is false
D. (A) is false, but (R) is true

79. Given below are two statements, one labelled as Assertion (A) and the other labelled as Reason (R). Read the statements and choose the correct answer from the code given below:

Assertion (A): The salary and conditions of service of the Comptroller and Auditor-General of India cannot be varied to his/her disadvantages after his/her appointment.

Reason (R): The office of the CAG is a constitutional office.

Code:
A. Both (A) and (R) are true and (R) is the correct explanation of (A)
B. Both (A) and (R) are true, but (R) is not the correct explanation of (A)
C. (A) is true, but (R) is false
D. (A) is false, but (R) is true

80. In the two lists given below, List-I provides the list of Approaches, while List-II indicates Characteristics. Match the two lists and choose the correct answer from the code given below:

List-I (Approach)	***List-II (Characteristics)***
(*a*) Ecological	(*i*) Legal-Rational
(*b*) Decision-making	(*ii*) Negative Feed-back
(*c*) Bureaucratic	(*iii*) Agraria-Industria
(*d*) General systems	(*iv*) Fact-value proposition

Code:

	(*a*)	(*b*)	(*c*)	(*d*)
A.	(*iv*)	(*ii*)	(*iii*)	(*i*)
B.	(*iii*)	(*iv*)	(*i*)	(*ii*)
C.	(*iii*)	(*i*)	(*iv*)	(*ii*)
D.	(*ii*)	(*iii*)	(*i*)	(*iv*)

81. Who among the following was the first thinker to use the term 'superpower'?
A. Hans J. Morgenthau
B. William Fox
C. E.H. Carr
D. Robert Cox

82. Which of the following statements is ***not*** correct?
A. Idealist approach stresses the role of moral values
B. Idealism is essentially a variant of liberal internationalism
C. Idealist approach aims at reforming international system through international law
D. Idealism is coextensive with liberalism

83. Arrange the following developments in chronological order:
(*i*) Nuremberg and Tokyo trials
(*ii*) Gorbachev's appointment as Secretary General of CPSU
(*iii*) Islamic Revolution in Iran
(*iv*) CSCE meeting for formally ending the Cold War

Choose the correct answer from the code given below:

A. (*i*), (*iii*), (*ii*), (*iv*)
B. (*iii*), (*ii*), (*iv*), (*i*)
C. (*ii*), (*iv*), (*i*), (*iii*)
D. (*iv*), (*i*), (*iii*), (*ii*)

84. Match List-I with List-II and choose the correct answer from the code given below:

List-I	*List-II*
(*a*) The Twenty Years Crisis, 1919-39	(*i*) Karl Deutsch
(*b*) The Analysis of International Relations	(*ii*) Kwame Nkrumah
(*c*) Imperialism : A Study	(*iii*) E.H. Carr
(*d*) Neo-Colonialism: The Last Stage of Imperialism	(*iv*) J.A. Hobson

Code:

	(*a*)	(*b*)	(*c*)	(*d*)
A.	(*iii*)	(*i*)	(*iv*)	(*ii*)
B.	(*i*)	(*ii*)	(*iii*)	(*iv*)
C.	(*iv*)	(*iii*)	(*ii*)	(*i*)
D.	(*ii*)	(*iv*)	(*iii*)	(*i*)

85. Which of the following statements ***not*** correct about US policy of containment?

A. The policy aimed at containing Soviet influence
B. The US used foreign aid as an instrument of containment
C. The policy was meant for countering Soviet influence in Eastern Europe only
D. Diplomacy and military intervention were also used for the purpose of containment

86. Who said that theories should be judged "not by some pre-occupied abstract principle or concept unrelated to reality. Its purpose is to bring order and meaning to a mass phenomena"?

A. E.H. Carr
B. Hans J. Morgenthau
C. Stephen Krasner
D. Kenneth Waltz

87. In the two lists given below, List-I provides the list of Treaties, while List-II indicates Years. Match the two lists and choose the correct answer from the code given below:

List-I (Treaties)	***List-II (Years)***
(*a*) Comprehensive Test-Ban Treaty (CTBT)	(*i*) 2002
(*b*) Anti-Ballistic Missile (ABM) Treaty	(*ii*) 1991
(*c*) Strategic Arms Reduction Treaty-I (START-I)	(*iii*) 1972
(*d*) Strategic Offensive Reduction Treaty (SORT)	(*iv*) 1996

Code:

	(*a*)	(*b*)	(*c*)	(*d*)
A.	(*i*)	(*ii*)	(*iv*)	(*iii*)
B.	(*ii*)	(*iv*)	(*iii*)	(*i*)
C.	(*iv*)	(*iii*)	(*ii*)	(*i*)
D.	(*iii*)	(*iv*)	(*i*)	(*ii*)

88. Which of the following statements is ***not*** correct about pre-emptive strategy?

A. The strategy was designed to prevent war
B. The strategy related to threats from rogue regimes
C. The strategy approved attack before a potential aggressor gets too strong
D. The strategy was in tune with UN Charter

89. Which of the following countries did ***not*** witness political violence in the aftermath of Arab Spring, 2011?

A. Tunisia
B. Egypt
C. Libya
D. Saudi Arabia

90. Which of the following statements is correct about the role of UN in the Syrian Civil War?

A. UN intervened in Syria in 2011 following Arab Spring
B. UN intervened again in 2003 following Hezbollah support for the Syrian army
C. After Sarin nerve gas attack in Damascus in 2013, UN voted for eliminating chemical weapons
D. UN wanted Syria's stockpile of chemical weapons eliminated but fixed no time limit for elimination

91. Who said that "We must deal wisely with the world's largest democracy... We need to work harder and more consistently to assist India... while not neglecting our friends in Pakistan"?

A. Nichola Burns
B. Colin Powell
C. David C. Mulford
D. Henry Kissinger

92. When did P.V. Narshima Rao unveil the 'Look East Policy'?

A. In Singapore, through his lecture in September 1994
B. In January 1992, when India became sectoral dialogue partner of ASEAN
C. In 1995, on the occasion of India's elevation as 'full dialogue partner' of ASEAN
D. Through MEA Annual Report for the year 1995-96

93. Who of the following considers self-defence, enforcing of rights, seeking reparations for injury and punishing wrong-doer, as the causes for a just war?

A. M. Koskenniemi B. Hugo Grotius
C. C. Gray D. J.G. Starke

94. Following India's nuclear explosions at Pokhran in 1998, which of the following were the responses?

(*i*) The US condemned nuclear tests of both India and Pakistan.
(*ii*) UN Security Council passed resolution condemning nuclear explosions.
(*iii*) The US and its strategic allies imposed economic sanctions on India.
(*iv*) Following US pressures India consented to sign NPT.

Choose the correct answer from the code given below:

A. Only (*i*), (*ii*) and (*iv*)
B. Only (*i*) and (*ii*)
C. Only (*i*), (*ii*) and (*iii*)
D. Only (*i*), (*iii*) and (*iv*)

95. Which of the following was ***not*** a part of the Millennium Development Goals approved by UN General Assembly in 2000?

A. Eradicating extreme poverty and hunger
B. Achieving universal primary education
C. Sharing of 2% of GDP by rich countries for developmental aid
D. Ensuring environment sustainability

96. Who among the following Prime Ministers propounded the notion of 'genuine non-alignment'?

A. Morarji Desai
B. Jawaharlal Nehru
C. Lal Bahadur Shastri
D. Inder Kumar Gujral

97. In January 2002, which of the following countries were described as 'axis of evil' by the US President?

A. Iran, Libya, North Korea
B. North Korea, Iran, Iraq
C. North Korea, Afghanistan, Syria
D. Syria, Iran, Iraq

98. When were post-Pokharan II sanctions imposed on India lifted by the US?

A. In the wake of 9/11 in October, 2001
B. At the time of US attack on Iraq in March, 2003
C. On the eve of inauguration of Bush in the second-term in January, 2005
D. In September, 2005 during 60th UN General Assembly meet

99. Who was Chairman of the UN Committee, meant for inspecting places in Iraq for finding nuclear weapons during Saddam Hussein's regime?

A. M.J. Miller B. Hans Blix
C. Mohamad Mahathir D. M. Bouazizi

100. Which of the following statements is ***not*** correct?

A. Following horrors of the First World War, liberal internationalists sought to end war
B. They held that right to self-determination and statehood was impermissible
C. They were convinced that system of balance of power would give way to collective security
D. They also held that diplomacy would be replaced by consent

ANSWERS

1	2	3	4	5	6	7	8	9	10
B	D	A	D	D	D	B	A	B	D
11	**12**	**13**	**14**	**15**	**16**	**17**	**18**	**19**	**20**
D	A	A	D	D	A	D	D	C	D
21	**22**	**23**	**24**	**25**	**26**	**27**	**28**	**29**	**30**
B	B	A	B	D	C	A	B	A	D
31	**32**	**33**	**34**	**35**	**36**	**37**	**38**	**39**	**40**
*	D	A	B	C	C	B	B	A	D
41	**42**	**43**	**44**	**45**	**46**	**47**	**48**	**49**	**50**
B	C	D	C	D	D	B	D	D	D
51	**52**	**53**	**54**	**55**	**56**	**57**	**58**	**59**	**60**
A	C	C	C	C	D	B	C	D	B
61	**62**	**63**	**64**	**65**	**66**	**67**	**68**	**69**	**70**
C	B	B	A	A	A	A	C	B	C
71	**72**	**73**	**74**	**75**	**76**	**77**	**78**	**79**	**80**
A	A	B	B	D	B	*	C	A	B
81	**82**	**83**	**84**	**85**	**86**	**87**	**88**	**89**	**90**
B	D	A	A	C	B	C	D	D	C
91	**92**	**93**	**94**	**95**	**96**	**97**	**98**	**99**	**100**
B	A	B	C	C	A	B	A	B	B

* Error in Question/Option

EXPLANATORY ANSWERS

1. According to Kautilya, a state has seven elements or constituents, namely Swamin (the King), Amatya (the minister), Janapada (the land and the people), Durga (the fortress), Kosha (the treasury), Danda (the army) and Mitra (the allies). This entire set-up of the kingdom was described as Saptanga theory in ancient India.

The state was regarded as a physical organism and its elements as the parts of the body. It was stated that king was considered the head, ministers as the eyes, treasury as the mouth or face, army as the mind, fort as the hands & arms and country as a whole as the legs of the human body.

2. Plato's educational curriculum consists of two stages, elementary and higher stages. The first stage starts from birth to the age of six years, during this stage both boys and girls were to be given education of languages, the children were to be given basic education on religion. The second stage from 6 to 18 years, and child should be given education on music and gymnastics. The music would give necessary development of soul and gymnastics would provide growth of body. The third stage was prolonged from 18 to 20 years, both of them must be given military education during this stage.

The stage of higher education starts from 20 to 35 years, by the end of 20 years was to be taught those who have interest in science and philosophy. The higher education again can be divided into two sub-stages, the first ranging from 20 to 30 years, second stage from 30 to 35. In the first stage subjects like mathematics, Astronomy, Logics and other Sciences and said that geometry must be taught. During the second stage stress must be given to dialectics, and this stage of education is required for the production of philosopher king. King was to rule from 35 to 50 years and after 50 years king had to retire and start study of God.

3. Thomas Hobbes constructed his political philosophy on the basis of his postulates derived from Principles of Natural Science. In developing his moral and political philosophy, Hobbes assumes the methodological approach of deductive reasoning, combining mathematics and the mechanics of science to formulate his ideas on human nature. Hobbes was critical of the assumptions of scholastic philosophers, whose evidence for human nature was based upon Aristotelian metaphysics and Cartesian observation, as opposed to reasoning and definition. Though Hobbes did not fully reject the value of observational or 'prudential' knowledge, he dismissed the view that this was at all scientific or philosophical in nature. To Hobbes, this type of knowledge was based on subjective and diverse experience, and was therefore only capable of producing speculative assumptions. This view predetermined Hobbes's method of deductive reasoning, which involved the application of geometry, Galilean scientific concepts and definition. This scientific method stresses the importance of first establishing well-defined principles of human nature and 'deducing' aspects of political life from this. Hobbes first used the mechanics of motion to define principles of human perception, behaviour and reasoning, which were then used to draw the conclusions of his political philosophy. In rejecting what he believed were 'conjectures' relating to intangible or supernatural objects or realities, Hobbes's philosophy is drawn from material and physical reality and experience.

4. The idea of the general will is at the heart of Rousseau's philosophy. The general will is not the will of the majority. Rather, it is the will of the political organism that he sees as an entity with a life of its own. The general will is an additional will, somehow distinct from and other than any individual will or group of individual wills. The general will is, by some means, endowed with goodness and wisdom surpassing the beneficence and wisdom of any person or collection of persons. Society is coordinated and unified by the general will.

   Rousseau believed that this general will actually exist and that it demands the unqualified obedience of every individual. He held that there is only one general will and, consequently, only one supreme good and a single overriding goal toward which a community must aim. The general will is always a force of the good and the just. It is independent, totally sovereign, infallible, and inviolable.

5. Michael Walter firmly believed that periodic communitarian correction is required because 'Liberalism is a self-subverting doctrine'. But it is not a particularly helpful form of correction to suggest that liberalism is literally incoherent or that it can be replaced by some preliberal or antiliberal community waiting somehow just beneath the surface or just beyond the horizon. Nothing is waiting; American communitarians have to recognize that there is no one out there but separated, rights-bearing, voluntarily associating, freely speaking, liberal selves. It would be a good thing, though, if we could teach those selves to know themselves as social beings, the historical products of, and in part the embodiments of, liberal values. For the communitarian correction of liberalism cannot be anything other than a selective reinforcement of those same values or, to appropriate the well-known phrase of Michael Oakeshott, a pursuit of the intimations of community within them.

6. Although pleasure is the ultimate test of moral value, J.S. Mill thought it essential to strengthen the utilitarian position by drawing a distinction between the different kinds of pleasure. He sought to establish the non-utilitarian proposition that some pleasures are of a higher quality than others. For Bentham and James Mill, pleasures differ only in quantity and one pleasure is as good in itself as another, as Bentham put it, "quantity of pleasure being equal, pushpin is as good as poetry". On the contrary, J.S. Mill regarded it as quite compatible with the principle of utility to introduce the distinction between quantity and quality of pleasure, and to lay emphasis on quality. Pleasures are in themselves intrinsically different—there are higher and lower among them. The proof of this is appeal to intelligent people who have had experience of both—they are judges and their testimony is decisive. In the words of J.S. Mill, "It is better to be a human being dissatisfied than a pig satisfied; better to be Socrates dissatisfied than a fool satisfied. And if the fool or the pig is of a different opinions, it is because they only know their own side of the question. The other party to the comparison knows both sides".

7. Polyarchy, concept coined by the American political scientist Robert Dahl to denote the acquisition of democratic institutions within a political system that leads to the participation of a plurality of actors. Polyarchy, which means "rule by many," describes the process of democratization, in contrast to democracy itself.

Central to any definition of democracy is electoral representation by means of free elections and representative government. The concept of polyarchy is Dahl's attempt to develop an empirical definition of democratization as well as to elaborate a set of normative criteria for deciding whether or not a political system can be counted as a democracy. Polyarchy, as presented by Dahl, should be understood as a process by which a set of institutions that comes close to what one could call the ideal type of democracy is developed.

10. David Easton said, "Political behaviour stands for both an intellectual tendency and a concrete academic movement". It has so many facets—a revolution, a reform movement, a mood, an approach and an attitude. It has been adopted because of its objectivity, observability, value-neutrality and verifiability. Behaviouralism maintains that there are certain fundamental units of analysis relating to human behaviour out of which generalisations can be formed. These generalisations offer a common base on which a 'science of man' can be appropriately built.

Behaviouralism in political science not only concerned with behaviour but also concerned with its perpetual, motivational, and attitudinal components making for man's political beliefs, values and goals. In sum, it involves external aspects of behaviour and the affective, contiguous, and evaluative processes engrossed through it.

11. In *A Theory of Justice*, Rawls devises a novel thought experiment. He asks us to imagine that we are tasked with coming up with the rules for the distribution and allocation of goods within a hypothetical society. We are to carry out this task behind a veil of ignorance. This means that we put aside such factors as race, gender, and social class and concentrate on which kind of society would best maximize liberty. It also means that we don't concern ourselves with what's best for us, but for society as a whole.

Rawls believes that by doing this we will arrive at the kind of liberal state and society that he strongly endorses. If we operate behind a veil of ignorance when determining the allocation of resources in society, then we'll inevitably choose a system which would be as just and fair as possible. Because we're behind a veil of ignorance, we don't know where we'd be in this hypothetical society;

we could be fantastically rich or dirt poor; we could be a member of the dominant class or part of the exploited class; we could be racially privileged or subject to bigotry and repression. We just don't know. So it's better to be on the safe side and devise a system based on maximizing equality, fairness, and justice.

12. Thomas Carlyle called Bentham's utilitarian doctrine as 'Pig philosophy' because to him happiness is much more than pleasure. He called Bentham's utilitarianism "a philosophy fit for swine", contending that it encouraged people to live like pigs, pursuing pleasure by any means possible. If the only good is feeling good, Carlyle had argued, human beings are no better than pigs.

13. According to Gandhi, political power of state is just a means not end itself. It is the means to regulate national life by the national representatives. For him life of nation would become perfect when power would be self regulated, wherein no representatives are necessary. There is then a state of "enlightened anarchy". In such a state sovereignty vests in every one who is his own ruler. Speaking of this ideal state Gandhi says "There is then a state of enlightened anarchy. In such a state everyone is his own ruler. He rules himself in such a manner that he is never a hindrance to his neighbour. In the ideal state, therefore, there is no political power because there is no state".

Gandhi visualized the goal of enlightened anarchy in three phases. In the first stage the goal is one of immediate swaraj based on nationalization and in the second stage the objective is to bring about a non-violent state through the evolution of village republics. In the final stage the purpose is to achieve Ram Raj.

14. S.P. Varma in his work "Modern Political Theory" identifies following causes for the decline of political theory which have been attributed by Easton. These include:

- **Historicism:** According to David Easton, writers such as Dunning, Sabine, Mcliwain, Lindsay, Carlyle, are more interested in describing the causes for rise of an ideology, system of values etc. They do not engage in stimulating their own thought to find solutions to contemporary social problems.
- **Moral Relativism:** Easton accuses Hume and Weber of having relativistic attitude towards 'values' and neglecting what consequences do they have for the 'facts.' However, a political scientist to be sensitive towards social problems, construct values and not transplant them.
- **Confusing Science and Theory:** Easton accuses the political theorists of using science and theory in a wrong way. In fact, he points out that mere use of scientific method cannot generate theories. The latter task involves identifying major variables and establishing a harmonious relationship between them.
- **Hyper factualism:** Easton accuses writers like Paul Bryce of using theory simply to accumulate facts. Such tendencies, in his opinion fail to relate themselves with the significant problems in a political system. He observes "theory without facts may be a well-piloted ship with an unsound keel. But where preoccupation with fact-gathering siphons away energy from seeing the facts in their theoretical significance then the ultimate value of factual research itself will be lost".

16. Dr. Bhimrao Ramji Ambedkar, popularly known as Babasaheb Ambedkar, was a jurist, social reformer and politician. He is also known as the Father of Indian Constitution. A well-known politician and an eminent jurist, his efforts to eradicate social evils like untouchability and caste restrictions were remarkable. Throughout his life, he fought for the rights of the dalits and other socially backward classes. Ambedkar was appointed as India's first Law Minister in the cabinet of J.L. Nehru. He was posthumously awarded the Bharat Ratna, India's highest civilian honour, in 1990. His notable works are as follows:

- Annihilation of Caste—1936
- Who Were the Shudras—1946
- The Untouchables—1948
- The Buddha and His Dharma—1957

17. During his last years, Roy became an exponent of a new theory called 'New Humanism'. However, there were other humanists like Protagoras, Erasmus, Buchanan and Herder who influenced Roy. Roy was of the opinion that there has been liberation in mans creative energies, especially after the advancement of science. It is science that emancipated him from the dominance of superstition and trans-terrestrial fears.

Roys humanist intellectual work is greatly influenced by philosophical radicals like Hutcheson, Shaftesbury and Bentham, who had a critical approach to the contemporary political, social and economic situations. These philosophical radicals advocated an individualistic approach towards moral problems.

18. For Hegel, State is a super-organism; it is "the march of God on earth", it is an end in itself and it is unchecked by any moral law, for it itself is the creator of morality. The state represented universal altruism. It synthesized dialectically the elements within the family and civil society. As in the case of the family, the state functioned in a manner that the interests of everyone were furthered and enhanced. It represented the universal tendencies within civil society, thus giving rise to the notion of citizenship. The state had "its reality in the particular self-consciousness raised to the place of the universal". The state was "absolutely rational" and had "substantive will" for realizing itself through history, and was therefore eternal. "This substantive unity is its own motive and absolute end. In this end freedom attains its highest right. This end has the highest right over the individual, whose highest duty in turn is to be a member of the state".

20. According tc Karl Marx, the features of dialectical materialism are:

- All the mass phenomena of history are determined by economic conditions.
- Production is the most important of all human activities.
- Men in association produce more than men in isolation.
- Religion is the opium of the people.

Dialectical materialism, a philosophical approach to reality derived from the teachings of Marx and Engels. For Marx and Engels, materialism meant that the material world perceptible to the senses, has objective reality independent of mind or spirit. They did not deny the reality of mental or spiritual processes but affirmed that ideas could arise, therefore, only as products and reflections of material conditions.

Marx and Engels understood materialism as the opposite of idealism, by which they meant any theory that treats matter as dependent on mind or spirit, or mind or spirit as capable of existing independently of matter. For them, the materialist and idealist views were irreconcilably opposed throughout the historical development of philosophy. They adopted a thoroughgoing materialist approach, holding that any attempt to combine or reconcile materialism with idealism must result in confusion and inconsistency.

21. Almond and his collaborators introduced new concepts of comparative politics. The concept of political system replaced the state and its legal apparatus. Structure replaced institution, role took the place of office and function substituted for power. Almond suggested that all political systems have four characteristics:

- All political systems have structures.
- The same political functions are performed in all political systems.
- All political structures are multifunctional.
- All political systems are mixed in the cultural sense.

22. David Easton considered that the political system receives inputs in the form of demands and support. Among competing demands, the demands which enjoy more support shape decisions and policies. Various organizations such as pressure/interest groups and political parties, individuals, politicians, administrators, opinion leaders, etc place demands. The demands which enjoy the most support shape the output policies and decisions. This process prevents the system from getting overloaded and breaking down. Also, the extent of support enjoyed by the authoritative decisions and policies reflect upon the fate of the political authorities (often elected governments) and the regime's nature (democratic or authoritarian) and the political community (open or close). Outputs are so produced so that they enjoy maximum support.

Easton has provided an elaborate classification of demands, supports and outputs to illustrate their nature.

Demands are sub-classified into four types:

- The demand for allocation of goods and services.
- The demand for regulation of behaviour.
- Demands for participation in the political system.
- Demands for communication and information.

Outputs are sub-classified into:

- Extraction (revenue for the state)
- Regulation of behaviour (to benefit of people and order)
- Allocation of goods and services
- Symbolic outputs such as affirmation, communication and display of values.

Feedback mechanism makes the system responsive and keeps the process in perpetual motion. It helps the political process to attain the goals of the community. It also guides the direction of the policy in such a manner that it reflects the will of the community.

Though the modal is an over simplification of the complex forces at play across the body politic, it provides a theoretical framework for comparative political analysis.

23. "A constitution is not the act of a government, but of a people constituting a government and a government without a constitution is a power without right" is the statement of Thomas Paine.

This is the fragility of all governments including autocracies. Without the "consent of the governed" governments are vulnerable to a revolt.

It recognizes that the ultimate repository of rights, is the individual. And the individual can limit his own rights, in return for something the individual finds useful; for instance protection against other hostile states, or hostile neighbours.

25. McCulloch vs Maryland, US Supreme Court case decided in 1891, in which chief justice John Marshall affirmed the constitutional doctrine of Congress "implied powers". It determined that Congress had not only the powers expressly conferred upon it by the constitution but also all authority "appropriate" to carry out such powers. In the specific case the court held that Congress had the power to incorporate a national bank, despite the constitution's silence on both the creation of corporations and the chartering of banks. It was concluded that since a national bank would facilitate the accomplishment of purposes expressly confided to the federal government, such as the collection of taxes and the maintenance of armed forces, Congress had a choice of means to achieve these proper ends. The doctrine of implied powers became a powerful force in the steady growth of federal power.

26. According to Powell, any nation's political culture may be mapped at three levels are:

- The political system
- The political and policy making process
- Policy outputs and outcomes

Political culture implies that the all individuals generally have the same level of awareness of their rights, duties and expectations from the government and society as citizens. All societies imparts their own specific set of norms and values to the members who develop their own perception about the functioning of political system and the responsibility of government towards the citizens. They also develop their own ideas about their own roles and responsibilities. This complete set of beliefs, symbols, and values associated with the political system comprises the political culture of a nation.

27. Pye in his *Aspects of Political Development* (1966) pointed out six crises in the development of England:

- Identity,
- Legitimacy,
- Penetration,
- Participation,
- Unification, and
- Distribution.

One can treat them as six stages of political development. Pye's first three crises can be equated with Organski's political unification. Rest are almost similar to the stages of Organski's process of political development. But, it must be reminded they are related to the developmental process of advanced countries. One cannot legitimately expect developing countries to follow the same order.

29. Political decay is a political theory, originally described by Samuel P. Huntington, which describes how chaos and disorder can arise from social modernization increasing more rapidly than political and institutional modernization.

In Western European political science, the term polyarchy was used by Robert Dahl to describe a form of government in which power is invested in multiple people. It takes the form of neither a dictatorship nor a democracy. This form of government was first implemented in the United States and France and was gradually adopted by many other countries.

Kenneth Boulding is proponent of political simulation.

Former Brazilian President Fernando Henrique Cardoso wrote extensively on dependency theory while in political exile during the 1960s, arguing that it was an approach to studying the economic disparities between the centre and periphery. He is proponent of associated development dependent.

32. In political science and sociology, elite theory is a theory of the state that seeks to describe and explain power relationships in contemporary society. The theory posits that a small minority, consisting of members of the economic elite and policy-planning networks, holds the most power—and this power is independent of democratic elections.

Gaetano Mosca emphasized the sociological and personal characteristics of elites. He said elites are an organized minority and that the masses are an unorganized majority. The ruling class is composed of the ruling elite and the sub-elites. He divides the world into two groups—Ruling class and Class that is ruled. Mosca asserts that elites have intellectual, moral, and material superiority that is highly esteemed and influential.

33. A revenue bill focuses on methods for raising money, *e.g.*, taxes, user fees, customs duties, and tariffs. Under the US Constitution, federal revenue bills are required to be initiated in the House of Representatives and the Senate has the power to amend revenue bills. Many state statutes have similar statutes, requiring revenue bills to originate in a particular house of the legislature, or that revenue bills must be passed before a certain number of days prior to the expiration of the legislative session.

35. The first 10 amendments to the Constitution make up the Bill of Rights. James Madison wrote the amendments, which list specific prohibitions on governmental power, in response to calls from several states for greater constitutional protection for individual liberties.

- **Amendment I:** Congress shall make no law respecting an establishment of religion, or prohibiting the free exercise thereof; or abridging the freedom of speech, or of the press; or the right of the people peaceably to assemble, and to petition the government for a redress of grievances.
- **Amendment II:** A well-regulated militia, being necessary to the security of a free state, the right of the people to keep and bear arms, shall not be infringed.
- **Amendment III:** No soldier shall, in time of peace be quartered in any house, without the consent of the owner, nor in time of war, but in a manner to be prescribed by law.
- **Amendment IV:** The right of the people to be secure in their persons, houses, papers, and effects, against unreasonable searches and seizures, shall not be violated, and no warrants shall issue, but upon probable cause, supported by oath or affirmation, and particularly describing the place to be searched, and the persons or things to be seized.
- **Amendment V:** No person shall be held to answer for a capital, or otherwise infamous crime, unless on a presentment or indictment of a grand jury, except in cases arising in the land or naval forces, or in the militia, when in actual service in time of war or public danger; nor shall any person be subject for the same offense to be twice put in jeopardy of life or limb; nor shall be compelled in any criminal case to be a witness against himself, nor be deprived of life, liberty, or property, without due process of law; nor shall private property be taken for public use, without just compensation.
- **Amendment VI:** In all criminal prosecutions, the accused shall enjoy the right to a speedy and public trial, by an impartial jury of the state and district wherein the crime shall have been committed, which district shall have been previously ascertained by law, and to be informed of the nature and cause of the accusation; to be confronted with the witnesses against him; to have compulsory process for obtaining witnesses in his favour, and to have the assistance of counsel for his defense.
- **Amendment VII:** In suits at common law, where the value in controversy shall exceed twenty dollars, the right of trial by jury shall be preserved, and no fact tried by a jury, shall be otherwise reexamined in any court of the United States, than according to the rules of the common law.
- **Amendment VIII:** Excessive bail shall not be required, nor excessive fines imposed, nor cruel and unusual punishments inflicted.
- **Amendment IX:** The enumeration in the Constitution, of certain rights, shall not be construed to deny or disparage others retained by the people.
- **Amendment X:** The powers not delegated to the United States by the Constitution, nor prohibited by it to the states, are reserved to the states respectively, or to the people.

36. Steven Lukes in his work "Power : A Radical View–1974" distinguishes between three 'faces' or 'dimensions' of power. In practice, a perfectly acceptable, if broad, definition of power can encompass all its various manifestations if A gets B to do something A wants but which B would not have chosen to do, power is being exercised. In other words, power is the ability to get someone to do what they would not otherwise have done. Lukes's distinctions are nevertheless of value in drawing attention to how power is exercised in the real world, to the various ways in which A can influence B's behaviour. In this light, power can be said to have three faces. First, it can involve the ability to influence the making of decisions; second, it may be reflected in the capacity to shape the political agenda and thus prevent decisions being made; and third, it may take the form of controlling people's thoughts by the manipulation of their perceptions and preferences.

37. Political socialization is a particular type of political learning whereby people develop the attitudes, values, beliefs, opinions, and behaviours that are conducive to becoming good citizens in their country. Socialization is largely a one-way process through which young people gain an understanding of the political world through their interaction with adults and the media.

The primary agents of political socialization are: Family, Social class, Media, Peers, Education, Religion, Faith, Race, Gender, Political system, etc.

40. Political cultures have many forms. They can be based on several factors. A political culture can have many sub-political cultures. These sub-political cultures, in the context of specific political institutions and their processes, generate different political attitudes and values. When sub-political cultures dominate political culture, a political culture suffers crises after crises.

Professor S.E. Finer suggests three variables of political culture:

- Mature political culture
- Developed political culture
- Low political culture.

41. The nationalist movement before the arrival of Mahatma Gandhi was characterised what Judith Brown call it as 'politics of studied limitations' and by Ravinder Kumar as 'a movement representing the classes' as opposed to the masses. Prior to his arrival, the national movement was limited to western educated professionals belonging to particular castes and communities, certain linguistic and economic groups, residing primarily in the Presidency towns of Calcutta, Bombay and Madras.

42. The Government of India Act of 1919 came into force in 1921. It is also known as Mantagu-Chemsford Reforms as Montagu was Secretary of State for India and Lord Chelmsford was Viceroy of India. It introduced bicameralism and direct elections in the country. The majority of members of both the Houses were chosen by direct election. It separated the central and provincial subjects thus relaxing central's hold over provinces. The central and provincial legislatures could make laws on subjects on their respective list of subjects, but the structure of government continued to be centralized and unitary. Provincial subjects had two parts—transferred and reserved. The transferred subjects were to be administered by the governor with the aid of ministers responsible to the legislative council. The reserved subjects were to be administered by the governor and his executive council without being responsible to the legislative council. It provided separate electorates for Sikhs, Indian Christians, Anglo-Indians and Europeans as per the principle of Communal representation.

43. The DPSPs provide the ideals which the Union and the State governments must keep in mind while formulating a policy or passing a law. The DPSPs constitute a comprehensive social and economic objective for a modern democratic state. While fundamental rights provide the political pillar of Indian democracy, its social and economic pillars are provided by DPSPs.

FRs are Justiciable rights but DPSPs are non-justiciable rights. Although DPSPs were no less important than fundamental rights yet they entailed financial back-up to implement them. Since the Indian state had and still has limited economic capacity, making DPSPs justiciable would have put the state in a tight situation. This fact explains why DPSPs were deliberately made non-justiciable. Despite being non-justiciable importance of DPSPs has been stated in Art. 37 which declares that although the DPSPs are non-justiciable, they should be considered fundamental in the governance of the country.

44. The Fundamental Duties enshrined in Part IVA of the Indian Constitution (Article 51A) were inserted by the 42nd Constitutional Amendment Act in 1976. In this article we will go through the list of Fundamental Duties, their background or need, legal position and suggestions of committees.

Article 51A states that - It shall be the duty of every citizen of India:

- to abide by the Constitution and respect its ideals and institutions, the national Flag and the National Anthem;
- to cherish and follow the noble ideals which inspired our national struggle for freedom;
- to uphold and protect the sovereignty, unity and integrity of India;
- to defend the country and render national service when called upon to do so;
- to promote harmony and the spirit of common brotherhood amongst all the people of India transcending religious, linguistic and regional or sectional diversities; to renounce practices derogatory to the dignity of women;
- to value and preserve the rich heritage of our composite culture;
- to protect and improve the natural environment including forests, lakes, rivers and wild life, and to have compassion for living creatures;
- to develop the scientific temper, humanism and the spirit of inquiry and reform;
- to safeguard public property and to abjure violence;
- to strive towards excellence in all spheres of individual and collective activity so that the nation constantly rises to higher levels of endeavour and achievement;
- Every parent or guardian to provide opportunities for education to his child or ward between the age of 6 and 14 years (86th Amendment Act, 2002).

45. The 42nd Amendments Act 1976 transferred five subjects to Concurrent list from state list that

- Education
- forests
- protection of wild Animals and birds
- weight and Measures
- administration of justice; constitution and organization of all courts except Supreme Court and High Courts.

48. The Speaker of the Lok Sabha is the presiding officer of the Lok Sabha. The speaker is elected in the very first meeting of the Lok Sabha following general elections. Serving for a term of five years, the Speaker chosen from amongst the members of the Lok Sabha, and is by convention a member of the ruling party or alliance.

Speakers of Lok Sabha and their tenure:

S.No	Name	Period
1	Ganesh Vasudev Mavalankar	1952-1956
2	M.A. Ayyangar	1956-1962
3	Sardar Hukam Singh	1962-1967
4	Neelam Sanjiva Reddy	1967-1969
5	Gurdial Singh Dhillon	1969-1975
6	Bali Ram Bhagat	1976-1977
7	Neelam Sanjiva Reddy	1977
8	K.S. Hegde	1977-1980
9	Balram Jakhar	1980-1989
10	Rabi Ray	1989-1991
11	Shivraj Patil	1991-1996
12	P.A. Sangma	1996-1998
13	G.M.C. Balayogi	1998-2002
14	Manohar Joshi	2002-2004
15	Somnath Chatterjee	2004-2009
16	Meira Kumar	2009-2014
17	Sumitra Mahajan	2014 - At Present

49. The Central government appointed a three-member commission in 1983 on centre-state relations under the chairmanship of R.S. Sarkaria, a retired judge of the Supreme Court. The Commission was asked to examine and review the working of existing arrangements between the centre and states in all spheres and recommend appropriate changes and measures.

The recommendations of the Sarkaria Commission about the appointment of the Governor are as follows:

- The governor's term of 5 years in a state should not be disturbed except for some extremely compelling reasons.
- He should be eminent in some walk of life.
- He should be a person from outside the state.
- He should be a detached figure and not too intimately connected with local politics of the state.
- He should be a person who has not taken too great a part in politics, in general, and in the recent past, in particular.

50. Duration of Panchayats:

- Every Panchayat, unless sooner dissolved under any law for the time being in force, shall continue for five years from the date appointed for its first meeting and no longer.
- No amendment of any law for the time being in force shall have the effect of causing dissolution of a Panchayat at any level, which is functioning immediately before such amendment, till the expiration of its duration specified in clause (1).
- An election to constitute a Panchayat shall be completed-
  - (*a*) before the expiry of its duration specified in clause (1);
  - (*b*) before the expiration of a period of six months from the date of its dissolution:

  Provided that where the remainder of the period for which the dissolved Panchayat would have continued is less than six months, it shall not be necessary to hold any election under this clause for constituting the Panchayat.
- A Panchayat constituted upon the dissolution of a Panchayat before the expiration of its duration shall continue only for the remainder of the period for which the dissolved Panchayat would have continued under clause (1) had it not been so dissolved.

53. Article 139: ***Conferment on the Supreme Court of powers to issue certain writs:*** Parliament may by law confer on the Supreme Court power to issue directions, orders or writs, including writs in the nature of habeas corpus, mandamus, prohibition, quo warranto and certiorari, or any of them, for any purposes other than those mentioned in clause (2) of Article 32.

Article 141: ***Law declared by Supreme Court to be binding on all courts :*** The law declared by the Supreme Court shall be binding on all courts within the territory of India.

Article 142: ***Enforcement of decrees and orders of Supreme Court and unless as to discovery, etc :*** (1) The Supreme Court in the exercise of its jurisdiction may pass such decree or make such order as is necessary for doing complete justice in any cause or matter pending before it, and any decree so passed or orders so made shall be enforceable throughout the territory of India in such manner as may be prescribed by or under any law made by Parliament and, until provision in that behalf is so made, in such manner as the President may by order prescribe; (2) Subject to the provisions of any law made in this behalf by Parliament, the Supreme Court shall, as respects the whole of the territory of India, have all and every power to make any order for the purpose of securing the attendance of any person, the discovery or production of any documents, or the investigation or punishment of any contempt of itself.

Article 144: ***Civil and judicial authorities to act in aid of the Supreme Court:*** All authorities, civil and judicial, in the territory of India shall act in aid of the Supreme Court.

61. Luther Gullick believed that the study of administration, guided by efficiency, could be made into a science equal to other scholarly disciplines. Like Physics or Chemistry, Gullick says, administration is governed by principles. The object of the administrative principles, is the accomplishment of the work at hand with the least expenditure of people and materials.

62. Henry Fayol, a French mining engineer and contemporary of F.W. Taylor, is called the 'Father of General Management'. His book 'General and Industrial Administration' was originally published in French in 1915 and its English translation was published in 1929. Most of the management writers agree on the classification of Henry Fayol regarding managerial functions : Planning, organizing, commanding, coordinating and controlling.

63. Development Administration is about projects, programs, policies and ideas which are focused at development of a nation, with the point of view of socio-economic and socio-political development of society in general, carried out by talented and skilled bureaucrats.

A model of Development Administration must contain the following points.

- It should reject status quo and be directed towards change and more so towards results. It is result oriented at its core and every development function should have a defined objective.
- Planning is essential to decide the framework of resources and time to be allotted for a development function.
- Innovation. It is dynamic in approach and encourages new and better ways to achieve objectives.
- It should focus on planning for the people as well as with the people. It is people-centered, must empower society as a whole and not product or profit-centered.

66. M.P. Follet considered the concept of delegation as a mere myth of organization (administrative) theory. She believed that authority belongs to the job and stays with the job. Hence, one who does the job, must have the authority whether his superior likes it or not. As authority belongs to the function (job), it cannot be delegated. The term delegation of authority is thus an absolute expression. She asserted, authority must be functional and functional authority carries with it responsibility.

67. Nobel Laureate Herbert A. Simon coined the concept of "bounded rationality" or limited rationality taking into account the human and environmental realities. There are two primary models or theories for decision-making: the Rational model and the Bounded rationality model. In the former, a decision-maker attempts to optimise the decision by selecting the best possible alternative. In the latter, rationality of individuals is limited by the information they have, cognitive limitations and time constraints.

68. The main aim of scientific management is to develop all men to their greatest efficiency and prosperity. The specific objectives are to enhance production and productivity, decrease cost of production and maximise prosperity both for employer and employees having common interests (not opposite to each other).

Scientific management lays importance on the human capital so as to maximise the advantage to both the management and the workers. It lays stress on a complete change of mental attitude on the part of management as well as labour.

The aims of scientific management are given below:

- To achieve higher production and acceleration in the rate of productivity by the use of standardized tools, equipment's and methods.
- Betterment in the quality of the products by research, quality control and effective inspection.
- Decrease in the cost of production by systematic planning, regulation and cost control techniques.
- Avoidance of wastage in the use of resources, time and method of production.
- Placement of the right person on the right job through scientific selection and training.
- Setting-up a sound system of wage payment so as to attain maximum efficiency.
- Ensuring a regular supply of goods to the consumers at reasonable prices.

70. Bureaucracy is looked upon with ridicule and the civil servants are contemptuously called 'Bureaucrats'. Harold Laski defined bureaucracy as "a system of government the control of which is so completely in the hands of the officials that their power jeopardizes the liberties of the ordinary citizens."

Ramsay Muir in his book *How Britain is Governed*, says, "Bureaucracy thrives under the cloak of Ministerial responsibility....It is ruinous when it becomes the master."

Morrison went to farther extreme when he suggested, "Bureaucracy is the price of parliamentary democracy." Hence it is wrong to suggest that in democracy, bureaucracy is misnomer. In fact, democracy cannot do without bureaucracy.

However, bureaucracy is to be efficient, non partisan and truly nationalistic. If love for their country is kept in the core of their heart, the civil services can prove a boon for a democratic country.

71. Estimates Committee and Public Accounts Committee are helped by the CAG in exercising legislative control over the executive. Comptroller and Auditor General of India is the constitutional body under the Article-148 provided an independent office. He is the head of the Indian account and audit department. He is the guardian of the public purse and controls the entire financial system of the company both state and union level. He is the one of the constitutional watchdog.

In the Article-149 of the constitution prescribe the duties and power of the CAG:

- He audit the account related to all expenditure from the consolidated fund of union government, state and union territory.
- He also audit all expenditure from the contingency fund of India and the public fund and the public account of the India as well as state fund.
- He audit all trading, manufacturing, profit and loss, balance sheet and other subsidiary account kept by any department of central and state government. There are so many financial audit done by the CAG. The CAG submit the three audit report to the president—audit report on appropriation account, audit report on finance accounts and audit report on public undertakings. The president lays these reports before both the Houses of parliament.

72. Paul H. Appleby in his two reports on Public Administration in India (1953) and re-examination of India's administrative system (1956), was very critical of the role of CAG and attacked the significance of his work. He also suggested that the CAG should be relieved of the responsibility of audit. In other words, he recommended the abolition of the office of CAG. His points of criticism of Indian Audit are—The function of the CAG in India, is in large measure, an inheritance from the colonial rule. The CAG is today, a primary cause of widespread and paralyzing unwillingness to decide and to act. Auditing has repressive and negative influence.

76. The pre-Fulton era, the British Civil Services divided into four major classes and each with its own internal grading structure—the administrative class, the executive class and clerical and specialist class. The Fulton Committee Report of 1968 recommended that the classes should be abolished and replaced by a single unified grading structure. To quote the Report "all civil servants should be organized in a single grading structure in which there are an appropriate number of different pay levels matching different levels of skills and responsibility, and the correct grading for each post is determined by an analysis of the job". In order to implement this recommendation, former classes were merged to form new entities known as "groups" and categories.

79. Article 148: Comptroller and Auditor-General of India

- There shall be a Comptroller and Auditor-General of India who shall be appointed by the President by warrant under his hand and seal and shall only be removed from office in like manner and on like grounds as a Judge of the Supreme Court.
- Every person appointed to be the Comptroller and Auditor-General of India shall, before he enters upon his office, make and subscribe before the President or some person appointed in that behalf by him, an oath or affirmation according to the form set out for the purpose in the Third Schedule.
- The salary and other conditions of service of the Comptroller and Auditor-General shall be such as may be determined by Parliament by law and, until they are so determined, shall be as specified in the Second Schedule.

  Provided that neither the salary of a Comptroller and Auditor-General nor his rights in respect of leave of absence, pension or age of retirement shall be varied to his disadvantage after his appointment.
- The Comptroller and Auditor-General shall not be eligible for further office either under the Government of India or under the Government of any State after he has ceased to hold his office.
- Subject to the provisions of this Constitution and of any law made by parliament, the conditions of service of persons serving in the Indian Audit and Accounts Department and the administrative powers of the Comptroller and Auditor-General shall be such as may be prescribed by rules made by the President after consultation with the Comptroller and Auditor-General.
- The administrative expenses of the office of the Comptroller and Auditor-General including all salaries, allowances and pensions payable to or in respect of persons serving in that office, shall be charged upon the Consolidated Fund of India.

81. In the modern geopolitical landscape, a number of terms are used to describe various types of powers, which include the following:

- **Superpower:** In 1944, William T.R. Fox defined superpower as "great power plus great mobility of power" and identified three states, the British Empire, the Soviet Union and the United States. With the decolonisation of the British Empire following World War II, and then the dissolution of the Soviet Union in 1991, the United States is currently the only country considered to be a superpower.
- **Great power:** In historical mentions, the term great power refers to the states that have strong political, cultural and economical influence over nations around them and across the world.
- **Middle power:** A subjective description of influential second-tier states that could not quite be described as great or small powers. A middle power has sufficient strength and authority to stand on its own without the need of help from others (particularly in

the realm of security) and takes diplomatic leads in regional and global affairs. Clearly not all middle powers are of equal status; some are members of forums such as the G20 and play important roles in the United Nations and other international organisations such as the WTO.

- **Small power:** The International System is for the most part made up by small powers. They are instruments of the other powers and may at times be dominated; but they cannot be ignored.

82. Main Features of Idealism:

- Human nature is essentially good and capable of good deeds in international relations.
- Human welfare and advancement of civilization are the concerns of all.
- Bad human behaviour is the product of bad environment and bad institutions.
- By reforming the environment, bad human behaviour can be eliminated.
- War represents the worst feature of relations.
- By reforming international relations, war can be and should be eliminated.
- Global efforts are needed to end war, violence and tyranny from international relations.
- International community should work for eliminating such global instruments, features and practices which lead to war.
- International institutions committed to preserve international peace, international law and order should be developed for securing peace, prosperity and development.

The main supporters of idealism have been Mahatma Gandhi, Bertrand Russell, Woodrow Wilson, Aldous Huxley, William Ladd, Richard Cobben, Margret Mead, and others. They strongly oppose the realist view of international politics as struggle for power and national interest and advocate the use of reason, education and science for securing reforms in relations and for eliminating war and other evils from international relations.

83. The Nuremberg Trial and the Tokyo War Crimes Trials (1945-1948): Following World War II, the victorious Allied governments established the first international criminal tribunals to prosecute high-level political officials and military authorities for war crimes and other wartime atrocities.

The Iranian Revolution (also known as the Islamic Revolution or the 1979 Revolution) was a series of events that involved the overthrow of the monarch of Iran, Mohammad Reza Shah Pahlavi, and the replacement of his government with an Islamic republic under the Grand Ayatollah Ruhollah Khomeini, a leader of one of the factions in the revolt. The movement against the United States-backed monarchy was supported by various leftist and Islamist organizations and student movements.

Mikhail Sergeyevich Gorbachev is a Russian and formerly Soviet politician. The eighth and last leader of the Soviet Union, he was General Secretary of the governing Communist Party of the Soviet Union from 1985 until 1991.

CSCE meeting held in 1991 for formally ending the cold war.

84. ***The Twenty Years Crisis: 1919-1939: An Introduction to the Study of International Relations*** is a book on international relations written by E. H. Carr. The book was written in the 1930s shortly before the outbreak of World War II in Europe and the first edition was published in September 1939, shortly after the war's outbreak; a second edition was published in 1945.

The Analysis of International Relations (1978) is the work of Karl Wolfgang Deutsch. His work focused on the study of war and peace, nationalism, co-operation, and communication.

Imperialism: A Study, by John A. Hobson, is a politico-economic discourse about the negative financial, economic, and moral aspects of imperialism as a nationalistic business enterprise.

Kwame Nkrumah was a Ghanaian politician and revolutionary. He was the first Prime Minister and President of Ghana, having led the Gold Coast to independence from Britain in 1957. An influential advocate of pan-Africanism, has written the book ***Neo-Colonialism, the Last Stage of Imperialism (1965)***.

86. Hans Morgenthau's work, *Politics Among Nations* (1948) was aimed at carving out the principles of realism. It was meant to provide intellectual support for the role of the United States in the post-war international political system. With a view to creating 'a science of international politics', Morgenthau posited the positivist methodology of the 'hard' or natural sciences to the study of international relations.

According to Morgenthau, theories should be judged 'not by some pre-conceived abstract principle or concept unrelated to reality', but by their purpose which is 'to bring order and meaning to a mass of phenomena which without it would remain disconnected and unintelligible'. They must be 'consistent with the facts and within itself'. In a nutshell, theories must be factual, independent and retrospective. Theories must satisfy strict empirical and logical criteria. As Morgenthau states, 'do the facts as they actually are lend themselves to the interpretation the theory has put on them, and do the conclusions at which the theory arrives follow with logical necessity from its premises?' He clearly believed that there is a 'knowable reality' or 'rational essence' of foreign policy which theories can reveal. This constitutes the methodological approach of positivism and it was applied to the study of international politics. He identifies with realism as a school of thought, which believes the world's imperfections are 'the result of forces inherent in human nature'. He lists 'six principles of political realism' which constitutes a theoretical approach to the study of international relations.

88. A strategy of addressing an emerging threat with a range of options including force was envisioned by the UN Charter. While traditional international law emphasized respect for state sovereignty by placing greater restrictions on the use of force, the literal language of the UN Charter has a more liberal standard when force is used under the auspices of the Security Council. For cases where force is used outside of the Security Council framework, it is not definitively clear whether under the UN Charter a state retains a traditional right of self-defense, including a right of anticipatory self-defense against an imminent threat, or if that right is curtailed to not include anticipatory self-defense. Some commentators argue that the UN Charter itself is no longer a valid source of international law, in which case a right of anticipatory self-defense would exist regardless and traditionally be limited to cases in which there is a threat of imminent attack.

Given the UN Charter's authorization of preemptive acts by the Security Council, ultimately the real division over preemption is not necessarily over preemption itself but over the multilateral framework under which it is carried out, who holds decision-making authority, and the extent to which those arrangements are codified and therefore rendered more stable and predictable. If the original concept of the Security Council was that the ad hoc coalition which won World War II would remain intact to stamp out future Hitlers before they reached a critical level of strength, historical changes such as the Cold War may have altered the course of that plan.

91. No wonder the Indian constituency felt reassured by Secretary of State Colin Powell's observation in his confirmation hearing before the Senate Foreign Relations Committee that India is "a country that should grow more and more focused in the lens of our foreign policy". "We must," Powell said, "deal more wisely with the world's largest democracy. Soon to be the most populous country in the world, India has the potential to help keep peace in the vast Indian Ocean and its periphery. We need to work harder and more consistently to assist India in this endeavour, while not neglecting our friends in Pakistan."

Perhaps the applause of Indians was premature, reflecting more their concern over the future of Indo-US relationship post-Clinton than any dramatic spelling out of the new administration's intent. The South Asia Bureau of the administration is still not in place, nor has Bush undertaken any policy initiative. Says Stephen Cohen, a leading Indian expert at Brookings Institution: "There could be some minor adjustments in Bush's India policy but no major changes will be made because the opening to India has already been made. Everything I've heard from Powell and Bush publicly indicates they are going to continue that policy."

93. Hugo Grotius considers self-defence, enforcing of rights, seeking reparations for injury and punishing wrong-doer as the causes for a just war. Grotius was a Dutch humanist and jurist whose philosophy of natural law had a major impact on the development of seventeenth century political thought and on the moral theories of the Enlightenment.

Valorized by contemporary international theorists as the father of international law, his work on sovereignty, international rights of commerce and the norms of just war continue to inform theories of the international legal order.

His major work, *De Jure Belli ac Pacis* (The Rights of War and Peace), is particularly notable in this respect, as well as *Mare Liberum*, a doctrine in favour of the freedom of the seas, which is considered an antecedent, inspiration and the backbone of the modern law of the sea.

Grotius was heavily influenced by classical philosophy, most prominently Aristotle and the Stoics, as well as by the contemporary humanist tradition and the late-medieval Scholastics. Caught up in the religious strife of the Reformation, Grotius promoted an irenic vision that would unite and reconcile the Christian Church on the principles of civil religion and toleration. He was well known in his time as much for his poetry and philosophy of religion as for his work on law and politics but is best remembered for his influence on theories of the social contract, natural rights and the laws of war.

94. on May 11, 1998, India took a leap into the unknown world of nuclear weapon powers with the tests at Pokhran. The five nuclear devices detonated during the Pokhran II Test were Shakti I, II, III, IV and V. It consisted of 5 detonations. First one was fusion and remaining 4 were fission bomb test. This test made India 6th nation to have tested a nuclear weapon..

A series of five nuclear explosions were conducted between May 11 and May 13, 1998.The second Pokhran Nuclear Test was conducted after Smiling Buddha in 1974.

The United States imposed sanctions on India, cutting off all aid except humanitarian assistance. The then President Bill Clinton signed official papers imposing the measures on India for carrying out nuclear tests.

The two new nuclear explosions drew further world condemnation. Pakistan had bitterly condemned the latest Indian tests.

- Pokhran-II nuclear tests resulted in a variety of sanctions against India by a number of major states, including Japan and the United States.
- The challenge to mitigate international opposition with US and eventually bridge the trust gap was a great concern.
- The test opened floodgates of trouble for India which include: economic and military and interactional isolation.

However, with those difficulties, Pokhran II has brought India to the nuclear mainstream and opened up the global nuclear market for development of nuclear power without signing the Treaty on the Non-Proliferation of Nuclear Weapons (NPT) or the Comprehensive Nuclear-Test Ban Treaty (CTBT) which further lead to The U.S.-India Nuclear Deal. The India-US civil nuclear deal was signed in 2008, after nearly 30 years of US-imposed sanctions since India tested its first nuclear weapon (1974).

95. In September 2000, building upon a decade of major United Nations conferences and summits, world leaders came together at the United Nations Headquarters in New York to adopt the United Nations Millennium Declaration.

The Declaration committed nations to a new global partnership to reduce extreme poverty, and set out a series of eight time-bound targets —with a deadline of 2015—that have become known as the Millennium Development Goals (MDGs).

The final MDG Report found that the 15-year effort has produced the most successful anti-poverty movement in history:

- Since 1990, the number of people living in extreme poverty has declined by more than half.
- The proportion of undernourished people in the developing regions has fallen by almost half.
- The primary school enrolment rate in the developing regions has reached 91 per cent, and many more girls are now in school compared to 15 years ago.
- Remarkable gains have also been made in the fight against HIV/AIDS, malaria and tuberculosis.
- The under-five mortality rate has declined by more than half, and maternal mortality is down 45 per cent worldwide.
- The target of halving the proportion of people who lack access to improved sources of water was also met.

The concerted efforts of national governments, the international community, civil society and the private sector have helped expand hope and opportunity for people around the world.

Yet the job is unfinished for millions of people—we need to go the last mile on ending hunger, achieving full gender equality, improving health services and getting every child into school. Now we must shift the world onto a sustainable path.

The global Sustainable Development Goals (SDGs), or Global Goals, will guide policy and funding for the next 15 years, beginning with a historic pledge on 25 September 2015, to end poverty, Everywhere, Permanently.

99. The Bush administration began a military buildup in the region, and after pushing hard gained passage of UN Security Council Resolution 1441. Led by Hans Blix, Head of the United Nations Monitoring, Verification and Inspection Commission (UNMOVIC) and Mohamed El Baradei Director General of the International Atomic Energy Agency (IAEA), the Resolution brought weapons inspectors back to Iraq in November 2002.

Inspectors began visiting sites where WMD production was suspected, but found no evidence of such activities, except for 18 undeclared empty 122 mm chemical rockets that were destroyed under UNMOVIC supervision. Inspectors also found that the Al-Samoud-2 and Al-fatah missiles violated the UN range restrictions, the former also being partially destroyed under UNMOVIC supervision.

Previous Paper (Solved)

UGC-NET-Junior Research Fellowship & Assistant Professor Exam

Political Science, July-2018*

PAPER-II

Note: *This paper contains* ***hundred (100)*** *objective type questions of* ***two (2)*** *marks each.* ***All*** *questions are* ***compulsory***.

1. Which one of the following statements is **not** correct in case of Kautilya?

A. He was the first to make political economy an independent subject

B. He propounded a theory of politics which dealt with immediate practical concerns of polity

C. He is credited with being the founder of nitisastra tradition

D. For the first time he emphasised the need for a strong political control in India

2. Who among the following said that the Republic pictures a utopia not because it is a romance but because plato intended it to be the start of a scientific attack upon the "idea of the good"?

A. G.H. Sabine B. Dunning

C. E. Barker D. Ebenstein

3. Who among the following said that in order of time state is latter than the family or the individual, but in order of nature, prior to them?

A. Cephalus B. Thrasymachus

C. Aristotle D. Lacophon

4. For Locke which of the following is **not** true in case of social contract?

A. Contract, once made, is irrevocable

B. Contract to which each generation must not consent

C. Contract in which men give up some of the rights they possessed in the state of nature

D. Contract does not put an end to the Law of Nature

5. For Rousseau which one of the following is **not** true?

A. For man's self-love, which satisfies his real needs, is only too apt to become pride

B. Pride becomes incompatible with sympathy

C. From pride all evil has grown

D. Pride does not seduce reason

6. Given below are two statements, one labelled as Assertion (A) and other labelled as Reason (R). Select the correct answer from the code given below:

Assertion (A): For J.S. Mill will is the basis of all institutions including the state.

Reason (R): Will is not only dependent on number, it has a qualitative foundation and the Will which makes the institutions takes on the form of a belief.

Code:

A. Both (A) and (R) are true and (R) is the correct explanation of (A)

B. Both (A) and (R) are true, but (R) is not the correct explanation of (A)

C. (A) is true, but (R) is false

D. (A) is false, but (R) is true

7. Match the List-I (Sources) and List-II (Ideas) which influenced Gandhi and select the correct answer from the code given below:

* *Exam held on 08 July, 2018.*

List-I *(Source)*	*List-II* *(Major Idea)*
(*a*) Jainism	(*i*) Catholicity of outlook
(*b*) Vaishnavism	(*ii*) Contempt for industrial civilization and ideas on passive resistance
(*c*) Ruskin and Tolstoy	(*iii*) Idealism and concern for moral values
(*d*) Plato	(*iv*) Emphasis on Non-violence

Code:

	(*a*)	(*b*)	(*c*)	(*d*)
A.	(*i*)	(*iii*)	(*ii*)	(*iv*)
B.	(*iv*)	(*i*)	(*ii*)	(*iii*)
C.	(*ii*)	(*iii*)	(*iv*)	(*i*)
D.	(*iii*)	(*ii*)	(*iv*)	(*i*)

8. Who among the following had started two weeklies, the Karmayogin and the Dharma?
A. Mahatma Gandhi B. Aurobindo
C. Ranade D. Tilak

9. Given below are two statements, one labelled as Assertion (A) and other as Reason (R): Select the correct answer from the code given below:

Assertion (A): M.N. Roy did not accept Marx's materialistic interpretation of history.

Reason (R): It had an element of determinism and idealism.

Code:
A. Both (A) and (R) are true and (R) is the correct explanation of (A)
B. Both (A) and (R) are true, but (R) is not the correct explanation of (A)
C. (A) is true, but (R) is false
D. (A) is false, but (R) is true

10. Who among the following said in the context of States Reorganisation Commission Report : "The Lambs are shorn of the wool" and "They are feeling the intensity of cold"?
A. J. Nehru B. B.R. Ambedkar
C. B.N. Rau D. K.T. Shah

11. Which of the following statements is **not** correct?
A. Traditional political theory is prescriptive and normative
B. Behavioural political theory concerned with uniformities and regularities
C. Post-behavioural political theory is tied to action and relevancy
D. Post-behavioural political theory is not holistic

12. Which one of the following contentions of Isaiah Berlin is not true in the context of resurgence of political theory (political philosophy)?
A. Politics exists in a society where ends collide. In a liberal order political theory can never see its end
B. The responsibility for causing decline of political theory should be laid on rank empiricists who have displaced classical tradition
C. Political theory shall continue to exist as a result of the inquisitive and rational inquiry of man
D. He is skeptical about the resurgence of political theory (philosophy)

13. Who among the following conceived society as a 'Cooperative venture for mutual advantage', more or less self-sufficient, and necessarily governed by rules?
A. Robert Nozick B. Friedrich Hayek
C. John Rawls D. Karl Marx

14. Who among the following has written the article "The Zigzag of Politics"?
A. John Rawls B. F.A. Hayek
C. R. Nozick D. J. Habermas

15. Who among the following is not a proponent of communitarianism?
A. Alasdair MacIntyre
B. Michael Sandel
C. Michael Walzer
D. Friedrich Hayek

16. Which of the following are the features of democracy?
(*a*) Democracy requires political equality.

(*b*) All citizens must be entitled to stand for election regardless of race, sex, colour or religion.

(*c*) All citizens must possess a vote (universal adult franchise).

(*d*) Political equality means 'one person one vote, one vote one value'.

Select the correct answer from the code given below:

A. (*a*) and (*c*) B. (*a*), (*c*) and (*d*)
C. (*a*), (*b*) and (*c*) D. (*a*), (*b*), (*c*) and (*d*)

17. Match the List-I with List-II and select the correct answer from the code given below:

List-I ***(Authors)***	***List-II*** ***(Books)***
(*a*) Brian Berry	(*i*) Justice
(*b*) Susan Moller Okin	(*ii*) Idea of Justice
(*c*) Amartya K. Sen	(*iii*) Justice, Gender and Family
(*d*) Tom Campbell	(*iv*) The Liberal Theory of Justice

Code:

	(*a*)	(*b*)	(*c*)	(*d*)
A.	(*iv*)	(*iii*)	(*ii*)	(*i*)
B.	(*iv*)	(*i*)	(*ii*)	(*iii*)
C.	(*iii*)	(*iv*)	(*ii*)	(*i*)
D.	(*i*)	(*iii*)	(*ii*)	(*iv*)

18. Which of the following are features of Marx's theory of surplus value?

(*a*) It is an extension of Ricardo's theory

(*b*) Labour power equals the brain, muscle and nerve of the labourer

(*c*) The value of every commodity is not proportional to the quantity or labour contained in it

(*d*) The worker must be paid a price proportional to the number of Labour hours that entered into its production

Select the correct answer from the code given below:

A. (*a*) and (*b*) B. (*b*) and (*d*)
C. (*a*), (*b*) and (*d*) D. (*a*), (*b*), (*c*) and (*d*)

19. Which of the following are Lenin's contribution to Marxist theory?

(*a*) His theory of the party as 'the vanguard of the proletariat' which guides the masses both before and after the revolution.

(*b*) His theory or capitalist imperialism, which he held to constitute the intermediary stage of capitalism.

(*c*) His version for the reconstruction of the world's first proletarian state.

(*d*) His theory of the strategy and tactics of revolution.

Select the correct answer from the code given below:

A. (*a*) and (*d*) B. (*a*), (*c*) and (*d*)
C. (*a*), (*b*) and (*c*) D. (*a*), (*b*), (*c*) and (*d*)

20. Which one of the following is not a feature of ideology?

A. A political belief system
B. An action-oriented set of political ideas
C. The world view of a particular social class or social group
D. The political ideas that do not embody or articulate class or social interests

21. Who among the following described comparative politics as primarily concerned with "parties, interests and leadership structure"?

A. Gabriel Almond
B. Sigmund Neuman
C. Roy C. Macridis and Ward
D. M.G. Smith

22. Who was the author of the book "The Presidential Republic"?

A. Jean Blondel B. Dorothy Pickles
C. Walter Bagehot D. E.H. Carr

23. Given below are two statements, one labelled as Assertion (A) and other labelled as Reason (R). Choose the correct answer from the code:

Assertion (A): Systems approach to comparative politics believes in the balance between the input structure and the output structure to maintain the equilibrium.

Reason (R): Systems approach is criticised as a 'status quoist' model.

Code:

A. Both (A) and (R) are true and (R) is the correct explanation of (A)
B. Both (A) and (R) are true, but (R) is not the correct explanation of (A)
C. (A) is true, but (R) is false
D. (A) is false, but (R) is true

24. Arrange the interest groups as given by Gabriel Almond in sequential order:

(*a*) Institutional groups
(*b*) Non-associational groups
(*c*) Associational groups
(*d*) Anomic groups

Code:

A. (*c*), (*b*), (*d*), (*a*) B. (*a*), (*c*), (*d*), (*b*)
C. (*b*), (*d*), (*a*), (*c*) D. (*d*), (*a*), (*c*), (*b*)

25. Which of the following pairs is not correctly matched?

A. Chartist Movement – Demand for Manhood suffrage in England
B. Philadelphia Convention – Declaration of independence and signing of the Constitution in US
C. Mayflower Compact – Abolition of Slavery in US
D. 1832 Reform Act – Changes in the electoral system of Britain

26. Given below are two statements, one labelled as Assertion (A) and other labelled as Reason (R). Select the correct answer from the code given below:

Assertion (A): Many Afro-Asian nations emerged independent after World War II.

Reason (R): Absence of economic developmental largely tended to make their independence more formal than substantive.

Code:

A. Both (A) and (R) are true and (R) is the correct explanation of (A)
B. Both (A) and (R) are true, but (R) is not the correct explanation of (A)
C. (A) is true, but (R) is false
D. (A) is false, but (R) is true

27. Which of the following pair is not correctly matched?

A. Political Continuity and change – Peter H. Merkil
B. Comparative Politics Today – S.P. Huntington
C. The Man on the Horseback – Samuel Finer
D. Modern Political Systems : Asia – R.C. Macridis

28. Which of the following are true regarding a revolution?

(*a*) Change of Constitution
(*b*) One ruling elite is replaced by another
(*c*) Transformation in Political Institutions
(*d*) Fundamental change in the Socio-economic and political structures

Code:

A. (*a*) and (*b*) B. (*b*) and (*c*)
C. (*a*) and (*d*) D. (*a*), (*b*), (*c*), (*d*)

29. Which of the following are true regarding a Unitary System of Government?

(*a*) It is most effective in protecting the unity and integrity of the nation.
(*b*) Power is delegated to the local units for administrative convenience.
(*c*) There is single law making body.
(*d*) The local administrative units do not derive their power from the Constitution.

Choose the correct answer:

A. (*a*) and (*c*) only
B. (*a*), (*b*), (*c*) and (*d*)
C. (*c*) and (*d*) only
D. (*b*), (*c*) and (*d*) only

30. Which of the following amendments of American Constitution laid down "Due process of law" relating to judicial scrutiny of legislative and executive actions:

(*a*) 4th Amendment
(*b*) 5th Amendment
(*c*) 14th Amendment
(*d*) 16th Amendment

Choose the correct answer from the below:

A. (*b*) and (*c*) B. (*a*) and (*b*)

C. (*a*) and (*d*) D. (*c*) and (*d*)

31. Which of the following pairs is not correctly matched?

A. Administrative Law – France

B. Appointment of Judges for life – Switzerland

C. Equal Representation of States in the House of Senate – USA

D. Rule of Law – England

32. Who among the following described political development as "administrative and legal development"?

A. Paul Baron B. James S. Coleman

C. Edward Shills D. Max Weber

33. Given below are two statements, one labelled as Assertion (A) and other labelled as Reason (R). Select the correct answer from the code given below:

Assertion (A): The system of democracy recognises the equality of all people and stands for the government of common people.

Reason (R): It is commonly believed that government is largely controlled and managed by 'power elite'.

Code:

A. Both (A) and (R) are true and (R) is the correct explanation of (A)

B. Both (A) and (R) are true, but (R) is not the correct explanation of (A)

C. (A) is true, but (R) is false

D. (A) is false, but (R) is true

34. Which of the following statements are correct regarding Max Weber's theory of bureaucracy?

(*a*) It is an iron cage of rule-based rational control.

(*b*) It is a key part of the "rational-legal authority."

(*c*) Bureaucracy means "domination through knowledge" in the form of merit.

(*d*) It enjoys popular acceptability in a democracy.

Choose the correct answer from the below:

A. (*a*) and (*d*) B. (*a*), (*b*) and (*c*)

C. (*c*) and (*d*) D. (*b*), (*c*) and (*d*)

35. Match the items of List-I with items of List-II by selecting the correct code:

List-I (Authors)	***List-II (Books)***
(*a*) Robert Dahl	(*i*) Legality and Legitimacy
(*b*) S.M. Lipset	(*ii*) Polyarchy : Participation And Opposition
(*c*) Schmittcarl	(*iii*) Political Man
(*d*) Roger Charlton	(*iv*) Political Realities : Comparative Government

Code:

	(*a*)	(*b*)	(*c*)	(*d*)
A.	(*ii*)	(*iii*)	(*i*)	(*iv*)
B.	(*iii*)	(*i*)	(*iv*)	(*ii*)
C.	(*i*)	(*iv*)	(*ii*)	(*iii*)
D.	(*iv*)	(*ii*)	(*iii*)	(*i*)

36. Given below are two statements, one labelled as Assertion (A) and other labelled as Reason (R). Select the correct answer from the code given below:

Assertion (A): Presidential system provides for a stable governance model for a full term.

Reason (R): Centralization of power is inherent in presidential system.

Code:

A. Both (A) and (R) are true and (R) is the correct explanation of (A)

B. Both (A) and (R) are true, but (R) is not the correct explanation of (A)

C. (A) is true, but (R) is false

D. (A) is false, but (R) is true

37. Match the items of List-I with items of List-II by selecting the correct answer from code:

List-I	List-II
(a) Islamic Revolution	(i) Led by Bolshevik Party
(b) Russian Revolution	(ii) Anti-Modernization Movement in Iran
(c) Glorious Revolution	(iii) 1649 Revolution to limit the arbitrary power of Charles II
(d) Puritan Revolution	(iv) Establishing Constitutional government in England

Code:

	(a)	(b)	(c)	(d)
A.	(ii)	(i)	(iv)	(iii)
B.	(i)	(iii)	(ii)	(iv)
C.	(iv)	(ii)	(iii)	(i)
D.	(iii)	(iv)	(i)	(ii)

38. Modernization is commonly understood as being analogous to:

(a) Westernization

(b) Europeanization

(c) Rise of Nation State System

(d) Industrialization

Choose the correct answer from the below:

A. (c), (d)

B. (b), (c)

C. (a), (b), (c)

D. (a), (b), (c), (d)

39. Examine the following statements regarding the media:

(a) Print media is witnessing a marginalised role in contemporary democracies.

(b) Electronic media assumes a decisive role.

(c) Media is dispassionate and objective in all political systems.

(d) Instruments of media are controlled by the industrial and corporate groups.

Choose the correct answer from the below:

A. (a), (b), (c), (d) B. (a) and (c)

C. (a), (b), (c) D. (a), (b) and (d)

40. Match the items of List-I with items of List-II by selecting the correct answer from the given code below:

List-I (Writers)	List-II (Concepts)
(a) Dicey	(i) Anomic interest groups
(b) S.P. Huntington	(ii) Judicial Review
(c) Almond	(iii) Political decay
(d) Marbury Vs Madison	(iv) Rule of law

Code:

	(a)	(b)	(c)	(d)
A.	(iv)	(iii)	(i)	(ii)
B.	(ii)	(iv)	(iii)	(i)
C.	(iii)	(i)	(ii)	(iv)
D.	(i)	(ii)	(iv)	(iii)

41. Which of the following was not a feature of the Government of India Act, 1919?

A. Provision for a bicameral legislature at the centre

B. The Legislative Assembly would have an elected majority and control over ministers

C. Communal representation was not only retained but extended

D. Enlarged the electorates both for provinces and emperial legislature

42. Who amongst the following provided a link between pre and post independence institutional framework to study Indian politics?

A. Rajni Kothari

B. Myron Weiner

C. Morris Jones

D. Paul R. Brass

43. Which of the following is true about the fundamental rights under Indian Constitution?

(a) It is protected and enforced by the Constitution.

(b) It can be changed by the common legislative process.

(c) Supreme Court is the guardian of fundamental rights.

(d) All Constitutional rights are fundamental rights.

Select the correct answer from the code given below:

A. (*a*) and (*c*) only
B. (*a*) and (*b*) only
C. (*a*), (*b*) and (*d*) only
D. (*a*), (*c*) and (*d*) only

44. Match List-I with List-II and select the correct answer from the code given below:

List-I (*Idea/Concept*)	*List-II* (*Person Associated*)
(*a*) Soft state	(*i*) Atul Kohli
(*b*) Politics of Scarcity	(*ii*) Subrata K. Mitra
(*c*) Crisis of Governability	(*iii*) Gunnar Myrdal
(*d*) Contentious Democracy	(*iv*) Myron Weiner

Code:

	(*a*)	(*b*)	(*c*)	(*d*)
A.	(*iii*)	(*iv*)	(*i*)	(*ii*)
B.	(*ii*)	(*iii*)	(*i*)	(*iv*)
C.	(*iv*)	(*ii*)	(*iii*)	(*i*)
D.	(*i*)	(*iv*)	(*ii*)	(*iii*)

45. Which of the following is not true about the amendment of the Constitution under Article 368?

A. The Bill may be introduced in either House of Parliament
B. The Bill must be passed by special majority (2/3rd present and voting and more than 50% of the total membership)
C. In case of disagreement between the Houses joint sitting may be called
D. The President is bound to give assent to the Bill duly passed and ratified

46. Put the following Presidents of India since 1989 in their chronological order and select the correct answer from the code given below:

K.R. Narayanan, A.P.J. Abdul Kalam, R. Venkatraman, Shankar Dayal Sharma, Pratibha Patil

Code:

A. K.R. Narayanan, R. Venkatraman, Pratibha Patil, A.P.J. Abdul Kalam, Shankar Dayal Sharma
B. R. Venkatraman, A.P.J. Abdul Kalam, Shankar Dayal Sharma, Pratibha Patil, K.R. Narayanan
C. Pratibha Patil, K.R. Narayanan, Shankar Dayal Sharma, R. Venkatraman, A.P.J. Abdul Kalam
D. R. Venkatraman, Shankar Dayal Sharma, K.R. Narayanan, A.P.J. Abdul Kalam, Pratibha Patil

47. Which article of the Indian Constitution empower the Parliament to make provisions for a contingency when the offices of both the President and the Vice-President fall vacant by reasons of death, resignation, removal or otherwise?

A. Article 123
B. Article 72
C. Article 70
D. Article 58

48. "India since 1989 has witnessed fewer abuses of power by Prime Ministers than the United Kingdom experienced under either Margaret Thatcher or Tony Blair". Whose statement is this?

A. Atul Kohli
B. Granville Austin
C. James Manor
D. Christophe Jafferlot

49. Who of the following regard the Supreme Court of India as having a dual personality—a legal institution and a public institution?

A. Granville Austin
B. Upendra Baxi
C. Madhav Khosla and Ananth Padmanabhan
D. N. Robinson

50. Who calls Election Commission of India as an effective 'bulwork of free and fair elections'?

A. Alistair McMillan
B. Lloyd and Susanne Rudolph
C. R.P. Bhalla
D. M. Katju

51. Match List-I with List-II and select the correct answer from the code given below:

List-I (Book)	List-II (Authors)
(a) An undocumented wonder: The Making of the Great Indian Election	(i) B.S. Rao
(b) The Framing of India's Constitution: A study	(ii) Granville Austin
(c) Working a Democratic Constitution: The Indian Experience	(iii) S.Y. Quraishi
(d) The politics of India since Independence	(iv) Paul R. Brass

Code:

	(a)	(b)	(c)	(d)
A.	(ii)	(iii)	(iv)	(i)
B.	(iii)	(i)	(ii)	(iv)
C.	(iv)	(ii)	(iii)	(i)
D.	(i)	(iv)	(ii)	(iii)

52. Match List-I with List-II and select the correct answer from the code given below:

List-I (State)	List-II (Chief Minister)
(a) Uttar Pradesh	(i) Jairam Thakur
(b) Assam	(ii) Sarbananda Sonowal
(c) Kerala	(iii) Yogi Adityanath
(d) Himachal Pradesh	(iv) Pinarayi Vijayan

Code:

	(a)	(b)	(c)	(d)
A.	(iii)	(iv)	(i)	(ii)
B.	(iii)	(ii)	(iv)	(i)
C.	(ii)	(iii)	(iv)	(i)
D.	(iv)	(i)	(iii)	(ii)

53. Who describes Indian federation as a "holding together federation and not a 'coming together federation"?

A. P. Bardhan B. R.L. Watts
C. Douglas Verney D. D.D. Basu

54. Which committee on Panchayati Raj in India takes of three phases : "The phase of ascendancy, The phase of stagnation and The phase of decline"?

A. Sadiq Ali B. L.M. Singhvi
C. Asoka Mehta D. B.R. Mehta

55. The grounds on which President's Rule has been imposed on the states in India are :

(a) If no stable government can be formed.
(b) If the Cabinet has lost majority and no other ministry commanding a majority in the Assembly can be formed at once.
(c) If the state government does not obey the directives given by the Union government or breakdown of federal structure.
(d) Corruption.

Select the correct answer from the codes given below:

A. (a) and (b) only
B. (a), (b) and (c) only
C. (a), (b) and (d) only
D. (a), (b), (c) and (d)

56. Match List-I with List-II and select the correct answer from the code given below:

List-I (Movement)	List-II (State)
(a) Tebhaga Movement	(i) Odisha
(b) Silent Valley Project	(ii) Uttar Pradesh
(c) Banwasi Seva Andolan	(iii) Kerala
(d) Chilka Bachao Andolan	(iv) West Bengal

Code:

	(a)	(b)	(c)	(d)
A.	(ii)	(iv)	(i)	(iii)
B.	(i)	(iii)	(ii)	(iv)
C.	(iv)	(iii)	(ii)	(i)
D.	(iii)	(ii)	(iv)	(i)

57. Which of the following have been discussed as crisis of India's national unity by Paul R. Brass in his book The Politics of India since Independence?

(a) Punjab
(b) The North East
(c) Casteism
(d) Kashmir

Select the correct answer from the code given below:

A. (*a*) and (*d*) only
B. (*b*) and (*c*) only
C. (*a*), (*b*) and (*c*) only
D. (*a*), (*b*) and (*d*) only

58. Consider the following statements and select the correct answer from the code given below:

Assertion (A): Lant Pritchett Calls India a "flailing state."

Reason (R): The state in India appears to undertake highly complex takes with relative efficiency—such as running atomic weapons programme or regulating monetary policy—while struggling to perform more ordinary governance tasks—such as delivering basic health and education.

Code:

A. Both (A) and (R) are true, and (R) is the correct explanation of (A)
B. Both (A) and (R) are true, but (R) is not the correct explanation of (A)
C. (A) is true, but (R) is false
D. (A) is false, but (R) is true

59. Which one of the following Commissions was not related to Backward Classes?

A. Bakshi Commission
B. Mandal Commission
C. Havnoor Commission
D. Shah Commission

60. "If Hume and other English liberals hoped to use Congress as a safety-valve, the Congress leaders hoped to use Hume as a lightening-conductor". Who said this?

A. S.R. Mehrotra
B. Sumit Sarkar
C. Bipin Chandra
D. Tapan Raychaudhuri

61. Who among the following was the first to advance the idea of worker's participation in management?

A. Henry Fayol B. Herbert Simon
C. F.W. Taylor D. Mary Parker Follet

62. Match List-I with List-II and select the correct answer from the code given below:

List-I	***List-II***
(*a*) Behavioural	(*i*) Administrative system as a sub-system of the society
(*b*) Bureaucratic	(*ii*) Agrarian - Transitia - Industria
(*c*) Ecological	(*iii*) Legal - Rational authority
(*d*) General system	(*iv*) Analysis of human behaviour in administrative settings

Code:

	(*a*)	(*b*)	(*c*)	(*d*)
A.	(*iv*)	(*iii*)	(*ii*)	(*i*)
B.	(*iii*)	(*iv*)	(*ii*)	(*i*)
C.	(*iv*)	(*i*)	(*iii*)	(*ii*)
D.	(*iii*)	(*ii*)	(*iv*)	(*i*)

63. Which of the following are the features of New Public Management?

(*a*) Contracting out
(*b*) Devolution of authority
(*c*) Focus on performance appraisal
(*d*) Focus on management

Select the correct answer from the code given below:

A. (*a*) and (*c*) B. (*a*) and (*b*)
C. (*a*), (*b*) and (*c*) D. (*a*), (*b*), (*c*) and (*d*)

64. Who among the following has criticized classical theory as 'homely proverbs, myths, slogans and pompous identities'?

A. W.F. Willougbhy
B. Luther Gulick
C. Henry Fayol
D. Herbert Simon

65. Who among the following said that behaviour in administration should be studied through psycho-analysis?

A. Alex Bavelas
B. Orway Tead
C. Abraham Maslow
D. Chester Banard

66. The Hawthorne experiments belong to the era of:

A. Mid 1930's B. Late 1930's
C. Early 1920's D. Late 1920's

67. Who among the following described bureaucracy as "The continental nuisance"?

A. Max Weber B. Thomas Carlyle
C. M. Crozier D. Karl Marx

68. 'Unity of Command' means:

A. That the subordinate will have only one supervisor
B. That the subordinate will have more than one supervisor
C. That all the units are put under one head
D. That the work is divided among all the subordinates

69. The Governor of a state in his capacity as Administrator of an adjoining Union Territory discharges his functions independently of:

A. The President of India
B. The Union Cabinet
C. The Union Home Minister
D. The State Council of Ministers

70. Which of the following are the factors determining the length of span of control?

(*a*) Age of the organisation
(*b*) Personality of the supervisor
(*c*) Calibre of the subordinates
(*d*) Organisational structure

Select the correct answer from the code given below:

A. (*b*) and (*c*)
B. (*a*) and (*c*)
C. (*b*), (*c*) and (*d*)
D. (*a*), (*b*), (*c*) and (*d*)

71. Which of the following are the benefits of E-governance?

(*a*) It makes government more accountable.
(*b*) It minimises people's participation in government affairs.
(*c*) It encourages bureaucratic tendencies.
(*d*) It lowers transaction costs.
(*e*) It helps in building trust between government and citizen.

Select the correct answer from the code given below:

A. (*a*), (*b*), (*c*), (*d*) and (*e*)
B. (*a*), (*b*), (*c*) and (*d*)
C. (*a*), (*b*), (*d*) and (*e*)
D. (*a*), (*d*) and (*e*)

72. Given below are two statements, one labelled as Assertion (A) and the other labelled as Reason (R). Select the correct answer from the code given below:

Assertion (A): According to Gleen Stahl, unless the recruitment is sound, there is very little hope for recruiting a first rate staff.

Reason (R): He considers recruitment as the cornerstone of the whole public personnel structure.

Code:

A. Both (A) and (R) are true and (R) is the correct explanation of (A)
B. Both (A) and (R) are true, but (R) is not the correct explanation of (A)
C. (A) is true, but (R) is false
D. (A) is false, but (R) is true

73. Given below are two statements, one labelled as Assertion (A) and other labelled as Reason (R). Select the correct answer from the code given below:

Assertion (A): Classical theory views organisation as a formal structure of authority based on Universal principles.

Reason (R): Classical theory views human beings who run an organisation as mere cogs in the machine.

Code:

A. Both (A) and (R) are true and (R) is the correct explanation of (A)
B. Both (A) and (R) are true, but (R) is not the correct explanation of (A)
C. (A) is true, but (R) is false
D. (A) is false, but (R) is true

74. Match List-I with List-II and select the correct answer from the code given below:

List-I	***List-II***
(*a*) Span of Control	(*i*) Supervision
(*b*) Hierarchy	(*ii*) One single boss
(*c*) Delegation	(*iii*) Through proper channel
(*d*) Unity of Command	(*iv*) Flow of authority

Code:

	(*a*)	(*b*)	(*c*)	(*d*)
A.	(*ii*)	(*i*)	(*iii*)	(*iv*)
B.	(*i*)	(*iii*)	(*iv*)	(*ii*)
C.	(*iii*)	(*i*)	(*iv*)	(*ii*)
D.	(*iii*)	(*ii*)	(*i*)	(*iv*)

75. The 73rd and 74th Amendment Acts have resulted in:

(*a*) Transparency in the governance
(*b*) Accountability in governance
(*c*) Gender empowerment
(*d*) Deepening of democracy

Select the correct answer from the code given below:

A. (*c*) and (*d*) B. (*a*) and (*c*)
C. (*b*), (*c*) and (*d*) D. (*a*), (*b*), (*c*) and (*d*)

76. After independence, the role of the District Magistrate has undergone a substantial change mainly due to:

A. Political awakening
B. The role of mass media
C. Democratic decentralisation
D. Periodical elections

77. The report 'Right to Information : Master key to Good Governance' was submitted by:

A. The Sarkaria Commission
B. Punchhi Commission
C. First Administrative Reforms Commission
D. Second Administrative Reforms Commission

78. Which one of the following Commissions/Committees/Thinkers has identified 27 modes of corruption?

A. Kautilya
B. Vohra Committee
C. Santhanam Committee
D. Central Vigilance Commission

79. The Joint Consultative Machinery in India was established on the recommendation of:

A. First Pay Commission
B. Second Pay Commission
C. First Administrative Reforms Commission
D. Paul Appleby Report

80. Which of the following Commissions/Committees has identified 'weak governance' as the main reason for corruption in India?

A. First Administrative Reforms Commission
B. Second Administrative Reforms Commission
C. Vohra Committee
D. Santhanam Committee

81. Which one of the following is the sequential order of the following states becoming acknowledged nuclear powers?

A. America, Britain, Soviet Union, France and China
B. America, Soviet Union, France, Britain and China
C. Soviet Union, America, Britain, China and France
D. America, Soviet Union, Britain, France and China

82. Which Chapter of the United Nations deals with the 'Pacific Settlement of Disputes'?

A. Chapter II B. Chapter III
C. Chapter IV D. Chapter I

83. Given below are two statements, one labelled as Assertion (A) and other labelled as Reason (R). Select the correct answer from the code given below:

Assertion (A): The Cold War and decolonisation process had discouraged more active involvement by United Nations within state.

Reason (R): States have national interest as its prime interest.

Code:

A. Both (A) and (R) are true and (R) is the correct explanation of (A)

B. Both (A) and (R) are true, but (R) is not the correct explanation of (A)
C. (A) is true, but (R) is false
D. (R) is true, but (A) is false

84. India has signed strategic partnership agreements with:
A. France, Russia, Iran and South Africa
B. China, America, Britain and Argentina
C. ASEAN, Japan, Australia and Tanzania
D. Vietnam, Seychelles, Mongolia and Singapore

85. Consider the following statements with regard to India and ASEAN.
(*a*) India became Sectoral partner of ASEAN in 1992.
(*b*) Delhi Dialogue is on Politico-economic issues between ASEAN and India.
(*c*) India became Dialogue partner of ASEAN in 1996.
(*d*) India became summit level partner of ASEAN in 2000.

Select the correct answer from the code given below:
A. (*a*) and (*d*) B. (*a*) and (*c*)
C. (*b*) and (*d*) D. (*a*) and (*b*)

86. Which of the following statements are true about SAARC?
(*a*) Australia, America, Japan and Russia are observers.
(*b*) Promote and strengthen collective defense among member states.
(*c*) Indian become Secretary General of SAARC twice.
(*d*) The Second Summit of SAARC was held in India.

Choose the correct statement from code given below:
A. (*a*), (*c*) and (*d*) B. (*b*) and (*c*)
C. (*c*) and (*d*) D. (*b*), (*c*) and (*d*)

87. Who have argued that far from an objective reality, international politics is a 'World of our making'?
A. Realists B. Feminists
C. Idealists D. Constructivists

88. Consider the following statements :
(*a*) India's 'Link West Policy' is an attempt to reconnect to the Western World.
(*b*) 'Project Mausam' is an Indian initiative for maritime cooperation in Indian ocean region.
(*c*) 'Operation Rahat' was conducted by India to rescue Indians from Libya.
(*d*) India has become member of Shanghai' cooperation organisation.

Choose the correct statements from the code given below:
A. (*c*), (*d*) and (*b*)
B. (*a*), (*b*) and (*c*)
C. (*a*), (*b*), (*c*) and (*d*)
D. (*b*) and (*d*)

89. Given below are two statements, one labelled as Assertion (A) and the other labelled as Reason (R). Select the correct answer from the code given below:

Assertion (A): Security is a Contested Concept.

Reason (R): Security is multidimensional in it's realization.

Code:
A. Both (A) and (R) are true, and (R) is the correct explanation of (A)
B. Both (A) and (R) are true, but (R) is not the correct explanation of (A)
C. (A) is true, but (R) is false
D. (A) is false, but (R) is true

90. Consider the following statements :
(*a*) OPEC was created at Riyadh conference in 1960.
(*b*) The charter of OAS was signed in 1948.
(*c*) Indonesia is a member of OPEC.
(*d*) Cuba is a member of OAS.

Choose the correct answer from the code given below:
A. (*b*) and (*c*) B. (*a*) and (*d*)
C. (*b*), (*c*) and (*d*) D. (*c*) and (*d*)

91. Neo Liberals, from their Lockean Universe Seek to create international regimes that optimize the:

A. Rational exploitation of nature
B. Rational functioning of the state system
C. Rational application of power
D. Rational utilisation of weapons

92. Democratic peace theory has been largely associated with the writings of:
A. Immanuel Kant and Voltaire
B. Michael Doyle and Bruce Russett
C. Thomas Christensen and Thomas Schelling
D. Mahatma Gandhi and Jawaharlal Nehru

93. Which one of the following is not part of the four main criteria set out by 1933 Montevideo Convention on the Rights and Duties of the state?
A. Capacity to enter into relations with other states
B. A defined territory
C. Strength to wage a war
D. A permanent population

94. Match List-I with List-II and select the correct answer from the code given below:

***List-I* (*Treaty*)**	***List-II* (*Purpose of agreement*)**
(*a*) Geneva protocol	(*i*) Bans multiple independent reentry vehicles
(*b*) START 2	(*ii*) Bans use of chemical weapons
(*c*) INF	(*iii*) Reduces strategic arms
(*d*) START 1	(*iv*) Bans two categories of land based missiles

Code:

	(*a*)	(*b*)	(*c*)	(*d*)
A.	(*i*)	(*iii*)	(*iv*)	(*ii*)
B.	(*iii*)	(*ii*)	(*iv*)	(*i*)
C.	(*iv*)	(*i*)	(*iii*)	(*ii*)
D.	(*ii*)	(*i*)	(*iv*)	(*iii*)

95. Which one of the following statement is **incorrect**?
A. Collective Security aims to defend the Status quo.
B. Collective Security Operates in an institutional framework.
C. The diffusion of Gulf crisis 1990-91 is a successful experiment of Collective Security.
D. Collective Security and balance of power policy are compatible under usual circumstances.

96. Morgenthau's classification of ideologies **doesn't** include:
A. Ideology of status quo
B. Ideology of imperialism
C. Ambiguous ideologies
D. Ideology of hegemony

97. Which one of the following is not part of five global commons?
A. The High Seas
B. The Climate System
C. The Deep Ocean floor
D. The Arctic region

98. Consider the following statements about arms control:
(*a*) It's meant to build the security dilemma.
(*b*) It's a defensive strategy in principle.
(*c*) It does take a peace without weapons stance.
(*d*) It aims at mutual security between partners and over stability.

Choose the correct statements from the code given below:
A. (*b*), (*c*) and (*d*) B. (*b*) and (*d*)
C. (*b*) and (*c*) D. (*a*), (*c*) and (*d*)

99. Which one of the pairs is **not** correctly matched?
A. Realism – States
B. Globalizm – Non state actors
C. Dependency – Economic interests
D. Feminism – Gender

100. Which one of the following pairs is mismatched?

	Books		**Author**
A.	The wretched of the earth	–	Frantz Fanon
B.	World order	–	Henry Kissinger
C.	Implosion of Capitalism	–	Samir Amin
D.	Neo-Colonialism: The last stage of Imperialism	–	Julius Nyerere

ANSWERS

1	2	3	4	5	6	7	8	9	10
C	B	C	B	D	A	B	B	A	B
11	**12**	**13**	**14**	**15**	**16**	**17**	**18**	**19**	**20**
D	D	C	C	D	D	A	C	B	D
21	**22**	**23**	**24**	**25**	**26**	**27**	**28**	**29**	**30**
C	A	B	*	C	B	B	D	B	A
31	**32**	**33**	**34**	**35**	**36**	**37**	**38**	**39**	**40**
B	D	B	B	A	B	A	D	D	A
41	**42**	**43**	**44**	**45**	**46**	**47**	**48**	**49**	**50**
B	C	A	A	C	D	C	C	C	B
51	**52**	**53**	**54**	**55**	**56**	**57**	**58**	**59**	**60**
B	B	A	C	D	C	D	A	D	C
61	**62**	**63**	**64**	**65**	**66**	**67**	**68**	**69**	**70**
D	A	D	D	C	D	B	*	D	D
71	**72**	**73**	**74**	**75**	**76**	**77**	**78**	**79**	**80**
D	B	B	B	D	C	D	D	B	B
81	**82**	**83**	**84**	**85**	**86**	**87**	**88**	**89**	**90**
D	*	A	D	B	C	D	D	A	*
91	**92**	**93**	**94**	**95**	**96**	**97**	**98**	**99**	**100**
A	B	C	D	D	D	D	B	B	D

* Error in Question/Option

EXPLANATORY ANSWERS

1. Kautilya is credited with being the founder of nitisastra tradition is not correct. The ancient Indian concepts of state and state-craft were derived from the concept of Dharma. It was the general philosophical position that the goal of each individual on earth is to move towards spiritual realisation or moksha and duties in one's day to day life or Karma was seen as a way of aiding that process. The branch of knowledge that prescribed how people in different positions in society should conduct their secular duties and carry out their roles were part of what was called Arthashastra as opposed to Dharmashastra that dealt with the realism of spiritual perfection. Arthashastra dealt with the science of prosperity and material gains, governance of a political unit or territory and promoting prosperity. Kautilya's Arthashastra deals with administration details more than with political theory. Kautilya in his work cover political and economic matters of administration as also morality, education, social problems, responsibilities of the king and subjects, international relations, army, spy system, etc.

2. To Plato when he wrote the Republic this determination to be scientific implied that his theory must sketch an ideal state and not merely describe an existing state. Though it may seem paradoxical, it is literally true that the Republic pictures a utopia not because it is a romance, as Dunning imagines, but because Plato intended it to be the start of a scientific attack upon the "idea of the good". The statesman was really to know what the good is and consequently what is required to make a good state. He must know also what the state is, not in its accidental variations but as it is intrinsically or essentially. Incidentally, the philosopher's right to rule could only be vindicated if this were shown to be implied by the nature of the state. Plato's state must be a 'state as such', a type or model of all states.

3. Aristotle said that in order of time state is latter than the family or the individual, but in order of nature, prior to them. The state is by nature clearly prior to the family and to the individual, since the whole is of necessity prior to the part, for example, if the whole body be destroyed, there will be no foot or hand, except in an equivocal sense, as we might speak of a stone hand; for when destroyed the hand will be no better than that. But things are defined by their working and power; and we ought not to say that they are the same name. The proof that the state is a creation of nature and prior to the individual is that the individual, is not self-sufficing; and therefore he is like a part in relation to the whole.

4. For Locke contract to which each generation must not consent is not true in case of social contract. According to Locke, it was for the purpose of protection of property that man entered into the 'social contract'. By property was meant life, liberty and estate. Locke says "every man has a property in his own person". Property was insecure because (*i*) there was no established law, nor (*ii*) an impartial judge and (*iii*) the natural power to execute natural law was not always commensurate with the claim. To remedy this flaw man entered into the social contract by which he fields to the sovereign, not all his rights, but only the power to preserve order and enforce the law of nature. People made two contracts, namely social and political contracts. The social contract was made between the people themselves. They surrendered only some of their rights—the right of interpreting and enforcing the law of nature. It was only a limited surrender and not a complete surrender of their rights. Moreover, they surrender their rights to the community as a whole and not to any particular individual. Thus, they established a civil society. The second contract, called the governmental contract was made between the people and the rule. It was made to enforce the first contract. By this the government came into existence. The state of nature was put to an end by means of these two contracts.

5. For Rousseau pride does not seduce reason is not true. For him man's self-love, which satisfies his real needs, is only too apt to become pride. Pride becomes incompatible with sympathy. From pride all evil has grown. Rousseau attributes to all creatures an instinctual drive towards self-preservation. Human beings therefore have such a drive, which he terms amour de soi (self-love). Amour de soi directs us first to attend to our most basic biological needs for things like food, shelter and warmth. Since, for Rousseau, humans, like other creatures, are part of the design of a benevolent creator, they are individually well-equipped with the means to satisfy their natural needs.

   In Emile, where Rousseau is concerned with the psychological development of an individual in a modern society, he also associates the genesis of amour propre (love of self, often rendered as pride or vanity in English translations) with sexual competition and the moment, puberty, when the male adolescent starts to think of himself as a sexual being with rivals for the favours of girls and women.

6. For J.S. Mill will is the basis of all institutions including the state because will is not only dependent on number, it has a qualitative foundation and the will which makes the institutions takes on the form of a belief. Mill's defence of freedom of thought and discussion was linked to the persecution of error. Even if an opinion was incorrect, it out to be articulated, for only through active interaction and dialogue could opinions evolve;

otherwise they would lose their vitality and become dead dogmas. Ideas were to be subjected to critical scrutiny from other points of view for arriving at the truth. He supported individuality, for great advances in society were made possible only by creative individuals. Creativity could be effective only if allowed to function freely. The early liberals defended liberty for the sake of efficient government, whereas for Mill, liberty was good in itself, for it helped in the development of a humane, civilized, moral person. It was "beneficial both to society that permits them and to the individual that enjoys them".

8. Sri Aurobindo had started two weeklies, the Karmayogin and the Dharma. The Karmayogi was in English and the Dharma in Bengali. Both weeklies had published in 1909. These were not completely political magazines, but could influence the instincts of man. In both weeklies he wrote articles on the deeper significance of Indian nationalism. The Karmayogin was to be a review of "National Religion, Literature, Science, Philosophy, etc." The weekly would emblazon the living Indian heritage in all its facets.

9. M.N. Roy did not accept Marx's materialistic interpretation of history because it had an element of determinism and idealism. According to Roy, the materialism of Marx was dogmatic and unscientific and neglected the creative role of the human subject. He opined that Marx under the influence of Hegel rejected the 18th Century materialism and also humanistic materialism propounded by Ludwig Feuerbach. This rejection of Feuerbachian humanist materialism by Marx is the most unfortunate event. Thus, Roy is critical of Marx's rejection of autonomy to the human being. Marx though glorified class struggle, did not lay emphasis on the empirical individual. Hence, Roy demanded for revolt against fatalism implicit in the prophetical sociology of Karl Marx.

Roy strongly believed that the Marxian interpretation of history is defective because it allowed no role to mental activity in the social process. History can never be interpreted solely with reference to materialistic objectivism.

10. The State Reorganisation Commission Report in Ambedkar's opinion had ignored the fact, or failed to realise that smaller states were a safeguard to the minorities. With the safeguards of separate electorates gone in the constitution of post-colonial India, "The lambs are shorn of the wool" and "they are feeling the intensity of the cold".

The solution to this problem was offered as follows: "It would be (simple) enough to have plural-member constituencies (of two or three) with cumulative voting in place the system of single-member constituency embodied in the present constitution. This will allay the fears which the minorities have about Linguistic states".

Ambedkar alleged that the SRCR conceded in agitating states that all people speaking one language should be brought within one state. Ambedkar's preference was that 'people speaking one language may be grouped under many sates, provided each state has under its jurisdiction people who are speaking one language'. To quote Ambedkar again: 'The formula one state; one language, must not be confused with the formula of one language, one state'.

Climatic conditions, feeling of the people of the South, and considerations of defence prompted Ambedkar to suggest two capitals for India, Delhi and Hyderabad.

11. After remaining popular for almost two decades (1940-60), the **Behavioural Approach** got transformed into Post-Behaviouralism. Twenty years of behavioural research brought to light its limitations and weaknesses.

The failure to make any real progress towards the objective of building a scientific political theory compelled the behaviouralists to admit reforms in the light of their experiences with behavioural research. They accepted several reforms and the exercise got the name Post-Behaviouralism.

Post-Behaviouralism did not constitute a return to the traditional approach. It accepted the merit of Behaviouralism but at the same time advocated the need to reform it. The Post-Behaviouralists were reformed behaviouralists. Post-Behaviouralism emerged as a reform movement within Behaviouralism.

Post-Behaviouralism accepted and advocated:

- The need to study all realities of Politics.
- The need to study social change.
- The need to end the obsession with methods and techniques and the need to study the substance of politics.
- The need to admit the study of values along with facts.
- The need to help the society to develop by the use of knowledge of politics.
- The need to put knowledge of politics into action by the political scientists.
- The need to serve the society by helping it to preserve and develop its values.

Post-Behaviouralists now advocated 'Relevance' and 'Action' as two guiding goals and accepted the need for the study of values in Politics.

12. Berlin was, for much of his life, an intellectually lonely figure, pursuing the history of ideas in an academic setting that was unreceptive to it, and advocating a moderate liberalism in a time dominated by ideological extremism. And yet this plea for moderation and advocacy of liberalism was shared and taken up by many others at the time. His interest in political philosophy and dedication to the defence of liberalism anticipated the work of John Rawls; yet the resurgence of political theory initiated by Rawls's work coincided with a period of eclipse in Berlin's reputation. Berlin's concern with the problem of culture anticipated the centrality in political theory of questions of identity and membership that began in the 1990s; his sympathy for the sentiments and needs underlying nationalism, which set him apart from many liberal theorists of his own time, presaged the revival of 'liberal nationalism' in the works of younger thinkers such as Michael Walzer, David Miller, Yael Tamir and Michael Ignatieff. His attack on monism, on the quest for certainty and the project of systematic knowledge, has led him to be embraced by some proponents of anti-foundationalism such as Richard Rorty. Yet Berlin's work remains difficult to assimilate to intellectual movements or projects such as postmodernism or multiculturalism, the excesses and obscurities of which provoked quizzical scepticism in him towards the end of his life.

13. John Rawls conceived society as a 'cooperative venture for mutual advantage', more or less self-sufficient, and necessarily governed by rules. In 'A theory of Justice', John Rawls envisions a society in which "men agree to share one another's fate." To satisfy their hopes and desires, not only will they learn to work together more or less efficiently and more or less without violence, but they will want to work together because they will understand that they can get more out of life working with each other than against.

Rawls also realizes that, just as people can shape their society, their society can shape them. Therefore, we want to be careful just what sort of society we build for ourselves. The social system we create, says Rawls, "shapes the wants and aspirations that its citizens come to have." What the system rewards, the people will become, and what it punishes, the people will cease to be, or as Rawls puts it, "how men work together now to satisfy their present desires affects the desires they will have later on, the kind of persons they will be." For Rawls, then, the goal is not necessarily to create the most efficient society, but the most noble.

14. Robert Nozick has written the article "The Zigzag of Politics". In his essay "The Zigzag of Politics", he wrote, quite clearly, "The libertarian position I once propounded now seems to me seriously inadequate", adding that joint action can only take on full symbolic coloration when undertaken on behalf of the social whole and concluding: "The point is not simply to accomplish the particular purpose—that might be done through private contributions alone—or to get the others to pay too—that could occur by stealing the necessary funds from them—but also to speak solemnly in everyone's name, in the name of the society, about what it holds dear".

15. Friedrich August Von Hayek is not a proponent of communitarianism. He is known as the father of neoliberalism. Alasdair MacIntyre, Michael Walzer and Michael Sandel are the proponent of communitarianism. The communitarian tradition has its origin in the 19th Century socialist utopianism of thinkers such as Robert Owen and Peter Kropotkin. Indeed, a concern with community can be seen as one of the enduring themes in modern political thought, expressed variously in the socialist stress upon fraternity and cooperation, the Marxist belief in a classless communist society, the conservative view of society as on organic whole, bound together by mutual obligations, and even in the fascist commitment to an indivisible national community. However, communitarianism as a school of thought articulating a particular political philosophy emerged only in the 1980s and 1990s. It developed specifically as a critique of liberalism, highlighting the damage done to the public culture of liberal societies by their emphasis upon individual rights and liberties over the needs of the community. This resulted in the so-called liberal-communitarian debate. 'High' and 'low' forms of communitarianism are sometimes identified : the former engages primarily in philosophical debate, while the latter, whose best-known figure is Amitai Etzioni, is more concerned with issues of public policy.

16. The following are the basic principles/ fundamental features of democracy:

- **Popular Sovereignty:** The principle of popular sovereignty, which means the people are the source of all power, is the very essence of a democracy. The government gets all its power from their people.
- **Principle of Equality:** The principle of equality is the foremost principle of democracy. In it all the people, without any discrimination, are treated as equal.
- **Equality of Opportunities:** Equality of opportunities is also a fundamental feature of democracy. It, however, does not stand for equal opportunities for all irrespective of their qualifications and abilities. It simply means that each individual should have a free and fair chance to compete and be selected on the basis of his/her qualifications and abilities.
- **Equal Opportunity for Participation in Polities:** Democracy is a government of the people and one of its principal features is that it ensures free and equal political participation for all. For this purpose uniform equal franchise *i.e.*, Universal Adult Franchise is granted to the people.
- **Civil and Political Equality:** In a democracy, equal political rights are granted to all the citizens. Society is free from discrimination.
- **Regular, Free and Fair Elections:** In a democratic system people are to elect their government. This requirement makes the holding of regular, free and fair elections an essential feature.

- **Rule of Law:** In a democratic system, the rule of law and not the rule of rulers is the rule. Everyone is under law.
- **Fundamental Rights and Freedom:** In a Democracy the people enjoy fundamental rights and freedoms including the right to secure the protection of their rights by the courts. An independent and powerful judicial system is provided for protecting the fundamental rights and freedoms of the people.
- **Independent, Impartial and Powerful Judiciary:** In a democracy, judiciary is always regarded as the guardian, interpreter and protector of the constitution and fundamental rights of the people.
- **Transparent, Responsive and Responsible Government:** A democratic government always works in an open and transparent way. It is responsive to the demands of public opinion. It always tries to act in accordance with the wishes of the people. It is always accountable for its acts.
- **Rule of Majority:** A sacred principle of democracy is the principle of taking all decisions by majority. The legislature passes laws by majority, the executive takes decisions by majority and the Supreme Court pronounces its judgements by majority.
- **Right to Freedom:** In a democratic system, the people enjoy the right to freedom as a fundamental right. It includes the right to freedom of speech and expression, freedom of press, freedom of peaceful assembly, freedom to form associations, freedom form arbitrary arrests and freedom to enjoy family life.
- **Freedom to form Political Parties, Interest Groups and Associations:** In a democratic system, the people have the freedom to form political parties and through these they get involved in the struggle for power *i.e.*, politics.
- **Decentralisation:** In a democratic system, power is not centralised in a few hands. It is kept decentralised in the hands of a large section of people.
- **Right of the People to Criticise and Change the Government:** In a representative democracy people can criticise the policies of the government. Right to oppose the government as well as to change the government through elections is a fundamental feature of representative democracy.

A democracy always upholds the ideology of liberalism. That is why in contemporary times, it is known as Liberal Democracy. Democracy is now conceptualised as Liberal Democracy. Social, political and economic liberalism is the hall mark of Democracy.

18. The theory of surplus value is one of the significant contributions of Karl Marx to political science. It is discussed in his monument work "Das Capital" which showed the opaque side of capitalism and is ample testimony of worker's exploitation in capitalist society.

His theory is based upon the labour theory of value as Sabine remarks "the theory of surplus value was professedly an extension of the labour theory of value already stated by Ricardo and the classical economists".

According to Marx, of the four elements of production viz., land, labour, capital and organization; only labour is the source of value. Every commodity was exchange value represented by price. However, workers get much less than what he produces.

Much of it is appropriated by the capitalist. This difference between the exchange value of the manufactured commodity and the price paid to the worker for his labour is called surplus value.

Under the socialist system the value of labour would be paid to the worker. Moreover, Marx emphasizes that "He who does not work, neither shall eat".

19. One of the greatest contributions of Lenin was that he adapted Marxism to Russia. Lenin was a Russian and being an arch revolutionary very soon realised that revolution was possible in Russia only under certain circumstances. The Czar must be defeated in war and there must be a group of highly disciplined and professional revolutionaries who must be in a position to take over the Government of the country. Lenin's theory of the party as 'the vanguard of the proletariat' which guides the masses both before and after the revolution. His version for the reconstruction of the world's first proletarian state.

20. The political ideas that do not embody or articulate class or social interests is not a feature of ideology. An ideology is a collection of normative beliefs and values that an individual or group holds for other than purely epistemic reasons. The term, and the system of ideas associated with it, was coined by Antoine Destutt de Tracy in 1796, and in contemporary philosophy is now narrower in scope than the original concept, or the ideas expressed in concepts such as wordview, imaginary and ontology. There are many well-known ideologies, which cover a wide range of humans activity. In the Althusserian sense, ideology is "the imagined existence (or idea) of things as it relates to the real conditions of existence."

21. Roy C. Macridis and Ward described comparative politics as primarily concerned with "parties, interests and leadership structure". The study of comparative politics involves conscious comparisons in studying political experience, institutions, behaviour and processes of the systems of government in a comprehensive manner. It includes the study of even extra-constitutional agencies having their immediate connection, open or tacit, with formal governmental organs.

It is, therefore, concerned with significant regularities, similarities and differences in the working of political institutions and in the patterns of political behaviour. In simple words, we can say, Comparative Politics involves a comparative study of various political systems either as a whole or through a comparative analysis of their structures and functions.

22. Jean Blondel was the author of the book "The Presidential Republic". Jean Blondel is a French political scientist specialising in comparative politics. He is currently Emeritus Professor at the European University Institute in Florence, and visiting professor at the University of Siena. His work has focused recently in a comparison of different presidential systems across the globe, with a particular emphasis on Latin America, Africa and the ex-Soviet republics. It seeks to be amongst the first comprehensive studies of different presidential systems.

25. The Mayflower Compact was the first governing document of Plymouth Colony. It was written by the male passengers of the *Mayflower*, consisting of separatist Puritans, adventurers, and tradesmen. The Puritans were fleeing from religious persecution by King James of England.

The Mayflower Compact was signed aboard ship on November 11, 1620. They used the Julian Calendar, also known as Old Style dates, which was ten days behind the Gregorian Calendar. Signing the covenant were 41 of the ship's 101 passengers while the *Mayflower* was anchored in Province town Harbor within the hook at the northern tip of Cape Cod.

27. 'Comparative Politics Today : A World View, 1974' has written by Gabriel A. Almond. Almond (1911-2002) was a political scientist from the United States best known for his pioneering work on comparative politics, political development and political culture.

Some notable publications of Almond are as follows:

- Aggressive Behaviour by Clients Toward Public Relief Administrations: A Configurative Analysis, 1934.

- The American People and Foreign Policy, 1950.
- The Appeals of Communism, 1954.
- The Civic Culture : Political Attitudes and Democracy in Five Nations, 1963.
- Political Theory and Political Science, 1966.
- Comparative Politics : A Development Approach, 1966.
- Crisis, Choice and Change : Historical Studies of Political Development, 1975.

28. In political science, a **revolution** (Latin: *revolutio*, "a turn around") is a fundamental and relatively sudden change in political power and political organization which occurs when the population revolt against the government, typically due to perceived oppression (political, social, economic). In his book *Politics*, the Ancient Greek philosopher Aristotle (384-322 BC) described two types of political revolution:

- Complete change from one constitution to another.
- Modification of an existing constitution.

Revolutions have occurred through human history and vary widely in terms of methods, duration and motivating ideology. Their results include major changes in culture, economy and socio-political institutions, usually in response to perceived overwhelming autocracy or plutocracy.

29. A unitary system of government, or unitary state, is a sovereign state governed as a single entity. The central government is supreme, and the administrative divisions exercise only powers that the central government has delegated to them. The subdivisional units are created and abolished, and their powers may be broadened and narrowed by the central government. It is most effective in protecting the unity and integrity of the nation. The local administrative units do not derive their power from the constitution. Britain, France, Japan, China, Italy, Belgium, Norway, Sweden, Spain and so on have the unitary model of government.

30. The 5th and 14th amendments of American constitution laid down "Due process of law" relating to judicial scrutiny of legislative and executive actions. The 5th and 14th amendments to the United States Constitution each contain a 'Due Process Clause'. Due process deals with the administration of justice and thus the 'Due Process Clause' acts as a safeguard from arbitrary denial of life, liberty or property by the government outside the sanction of law. The Supreme Court of the America interprets the clauses as providing four protections: procedural due process, substantive due process, a prohibition against vague laws and as the vehicle for the incorporation of the Bill of Rights.

32. The view of political development, as discussed by Lucian Pye, is the view which interprets political development as process of institution-building and citizenship development. This view has amongst its supporters such scholars as Max Weber and Joseph La Palombara.

This view associates political development, with the development of a legal order followed by an administrative order. In this view, administrative development is associated with the spread of rationality, the strengthening of secular, legal concepts and the elevation of technical and specialised knowledge in the direction of human affairs.

No one can deny that political development involves legal and administrative development; however, no one can equate the former with the latter.

33. The system of democracy recognizes the equality of all people and stands for the government of common people. It is commonly believed that government is largely controlled and managed by 'power elite'. **The Power Elite** is a 1956 book by sociologist

C. Wright Mills, in which Mills calls attention to the interwoven interests of the leaders of the military, corporate, and political elements of society and suggests that the ordinary citizen is a relatively powerless subject of manipulation by those entities.

34. "Bureaucracy is an organisational structure that is characterised by many rules, standardised processes, procedures and requirements, number of desks, meticulous division of labour and responsibility, clear hierarchies and professional, almost impersonal interactions between employees".

According to the bureaucratic theory of Max Weber, such a structure was indispensable in large organizations in structurally performing all tasks by a great number of employees. In addition, in a bureaucracy, selection and promotion only occur on the basis of technical qualifications. It is an iron cage of rule-based rational control and a key part of the "rational-legal authority".

36. Presidential system provides for a stable governance model for a full term and centralization of power is inherent in this system. In a Presidential government, the President is the Head of the State as well as of the government. There is a separation of powers in the presidential government. In this system the executive and legislature are separate from each other and they have equal status. In a presidential government, the President enjoys real powers of the administration and he exercises all those powers, which are given to him under the constitution and the law. At present Presidential government is seen in the United States of America, Brazil and in the some other countries of South America.

38. Modernization is commonly understood as being analogous to Westernization, Europeanization, rise of Nation-State system and Industrialization. Modernization theory emerged in the 1950s as an explanation of how the industrial societies of North America and Western Europe developed. The theory argues that societies develop in fairly predictable stages through which they become increasingly complex. Development depends primarily on the importation of technology as well as a number of other political and social changes believed to come about as a result.

39. The word 'media' is derived from the word medium, signifying mode or carrier. Media is intended to reach and address a large target group or audience. The word was first used in respect of books and newspapers *i.e.*, print media and with the advent of technology, media now encompasses television, movies, radio and internet. In today's world, media becomes as essential as our daily needs. Media of today is playing an outstanding role in creating and shaping of public opinion and strengthening of society. Media is the sword arm of democracy, but print media is witnessing a marginalised role in contemporary democracies while electronic media assumes a decisive role. Instruments of media are controlled by the industrial and corporate groups. Media acts as watchdog to protect public interest against malpractice and create public awareness.

41. The Legislative Assembly would have an elected majority and control over ministers was not a feature of the Government of India Act, 1919. Government of India Act, 1919 is also known as Montagu-Chelmsford Reforms (Montagu was the Secretary of State for India and Lord Chelmsford was the Viceroy of India). It introduced, for the first time, bicameralism and direct elections in the country. Thus, the Indian Legislative Council was replaced by a bicameral legislature consisting of an Upper House (Council of State) and a Lower House (Legislative Assembly). The majority of members both the Houses were chosen by direct election. It extended the principle of communal representation by providing separate electorates for Sikhs, Indian Christians, Anglo-

Indians and Europeans. It granted franchise to a limited number of people on the basis of property, tax or education.

43. The Fundamental Rights are named so because they are guaranteed and protected by the constitution, which is the fundamental law of the land. They are 'fundamental' also in the sense that they are most essential for the all-round development (material, intellectual, moral and spiritual) of the individuals. Supreme Court is the guardian of fundamental rights.

The Fundamental Rights are meant for promoting the ideal of political democracy. They prevent the establishment of an authoritarian and despotic rule in the country, and protect the liberties and freedoms of the people against the invasion by the state. They operate as limitations on the tyranny of the executive and arbitrary laws of the legislature. In short, they aim at establishing 'a government of laws and not of men'.

45. Part XX of Article 368 empowers the Parliament to amend Constitution by way of addition, variation or repeal of any provision according to the procedure laid down therein, which is different from the procedure for ordinary legislation. For amending the Constitution, the Bill may be introduced in either House of Parliament. The Bill must be passed by special majority (2/3rd present and voting and more than 50% of the total membership). If the amendment seeks to make any change in any of the provisions mentioned in the proviso to article 368, it must be ratified by the Legislatures of not less than one-half of the States. These provisions relate to certain matters concerning the federal structure or of common interest to both the Union and the States viz.

- the election of the President (articles 54 and 55);
- the extent of the executive power of the Union and the States (articles 73 and 162);
- the High Courts for Union territories (article 241);
- The Union Judiciary and the High Courts in the States (Chapter IV of Part V and Chapter V of Part VI);
- the distribution of legislative powers between the Union and the States (Chapter I of Part XI and Seventh Schedule);
- the representation of States in Parliament; and the provision for amendment of the Constitution laid down in article 368.

The Bill, passed by the required majority, is then presented to the President who is bound to give assent to the Bill.

48. Political institutions have passed through three phases since the establishment of the Republic of India, and thus the office of President, in 1950.

- **1950 to the late 1960s:** In this era, the Congress Party dominated politics at the national level and in almost every state. This had a paradoxical impact on formal institutions of state.
- **1971 to 1989:** During most of this era, power was radically centralized in the PMO. Whatever substance and autonomy most formal state institutions had acquired was systematically undermined, and this deinstitutionalization caused them to atrophy. Prime ministers often abused their power.
- **1989 to the present:** Between 1989 and 2014, a period in which no single party managed to win a majority in the Lok Sabha, massive powers have flowed away from the PMO to other formal institutions at the national level—the courts, Parliament and its committees, the Election Commission of India and the CAG's office, among others—and to state governments in the federal system and forces operating mainly at the state level. This redistribution of power has enabled many formal institutions to acquire greater substance and

autonomy than ever before—to regenerate and to play their assigned roles in the constitutional order more effectively, free of the subordination to a dominant party seen in Phase I, and to the overweening power of deinstitutionalizing Prime Ministers seen during most of Phase II. Newly empowered institutions have checked the power of the PMO. In this context, James Manor opined that India since 1989 has witnessed fewer abuses of power by Prime Ministers than the United Kingdom experienced under either Margaret Thatcher or Tony Blair".

50. While the Election Commission of India has overcome daunting challenges beginning with the first general election in 1952, its future course is by no means predetermined. Indeed, there remain serious concerns about the conduct of elections in India, namely the disconcerting influence of 'money' and 'muscle' power. Furthermore, while scholars Lloyd and Susanne Rudolph have rightly praised the commission for serving as an effective 'bulwork of free and fair elections', its status as regulator has not been free from controversy. As Alistair McMillan has pointed out, the commission has had to carefully balance the pressures of robust party politics with preserving. What it views to be in the national interest. Its role as a neutral 'referee' cannot so easily be disassociated from the normative implication of its decisions.

53. P. Bardhan describes Indian Federation as a 'holding together federation' and not a 'coming together federation'. Unlike the federal form of government in the United States, which is described as an indestructible union composed of Indestructible states, India is an indestructible Union of destructible states. The units of Indian federation have undergone multiple transformations since 1947. This is because Article-3 of the constitution empowers Parliament to create new states. While such a provision can be seen as giving the Union too much power, it has arguably been central to holding India together since it allows the federation to evolve and respond to sub-national aspirations.

Coming Together Federations:

- Under this the independent states come together on their own to form a bigger unit.
- Under this all the constituent states usually have equal powers.
- USA, Switzerland and Australia.

Holding Together Federations:

- Under this a large country decides to divide its power between the constituent states and the national government.
- Under this Central government tends to be more powerful.
- India, Spain and Belgium.

54. Asoka Mehta Committee on Panchayati Raj in India takes of three phases : "The phase of ascendancy, the phase of stagnation and the phase of decline". In December 1977, the Janata Government appointed this committee. It submitted its report in August 1978 and made 132 recommendations to revive and strengthen the declining Panchayati Raj system in the country. Its main recommendations were—

- The three-tier system of Panchayati Raj should be replaced by the two-tier system, that is, Zila Parishad at the district level, and below it, the Mandal Panchayat consisting of a group of villages with a total population of 15000 to 20000.
- There should be an official participation of political parties at all levels of panchayat elections.
- The Nyaya Panchayats should be kept as separate bodies from that of development panchayats. They should be presided over by a qualified judge.

Due to the collapse of the Janata Government before the completion of its term, no action could be taken on the recommendations of the Asoka Mehta Committee at the central level.

55. The grounds on which President's Rule has been imposed on the states in India are-

If no stable government can be formed. If the cabinet has lost majority and no other ministry commanding a majority in the Assembly can be formed at once. If the state government does not obey the directives given by the Union government or breakdown of federal structure and Corruption.

Article 355 imposes a duty on the Centre to ensure that the government of every state is carried on in accordance with the provisions of the Constitution. In performance of this duty, the Centre takes over,the government of a state under Article 356 in case of failure of constitutional machinery in state.

- This is popularly known as 'President's Rule'. It is also known as 'State Emergency' or 'Constitutional Emergency'.
- The President's Rule can be proclaimed under Article 356 on two grounds—one mentioned in Article 356 itself and another in Article 365.
- 356 empowers the President to issue a proclamation, if he is satisfied that a situation has arisen in which the government of a state cannot be carried on in accordance with the provisions of the Constitution.
- Notably, the president can act either on a report of the governor of the state or otherwise too (*i.e.*, even without the governor's report).
- Article 365 says that whenever a state fails to comply with or to give effect to any direction from the Centre, it will be lawful for the president to hold that a situation has arisen in which the government of the state cannot be carried on in accordance with the provisions of the Constitution.

58. Lant Pritchett calls India a "flailing state" because the state in India appears to undertake highly complex takes with relative efficiency such as running atomic weapons programme or regulating monetary policy—while struggling to perform more ordinary governance tasks—such as delivering basic health and education. India is an emerging global superpower as its rapid growth has transformed its economy and has maintained itself as the world's largest democracy. But at the same time India lags in many dimensions—its malnutrition rate is one of the highest in the world, its immunization rates are lower than most African countries, and Bangladesh has a better infant mortality rate. I argue that this is in part because the India state is "flailing"—its very capable head is not longer reliably connected to the arms and legs of implementation. In the four-fold transition of economy, polity, administration, and society the administrative capability of the state is lagging. I use examples from services like health, education, and routine transactions like issuing driver's licenses to show that the agents of the state routinely do not implement the tasks they are assigned—causing a massive divergence between de jure and de facto reality. The paper concludes with speculations about the causes of flailing and possible future trajectories.

59. Shah Commission was not related to Backward Classes. The Janata Party government headed by Morarji Desai constituted an enquiry commission to inquire into all the excesses committed in the Indian Emergency. It was headed by Justice J.C. Shah, a former chief Justice of India.

The commission published its report on the illegal events during the emergency and the persons responsible in three volumes totaling 525 pages. The first interim report was submitted on 11 March 1978, dealing with the lead-up to the declaration of the Emergency and the way in which the press was prevented from speaking out. The second interim report discussed police actions and the role of Sanjay Gandhi at the Turkman Gate incident in which police fired on a crowd of people protesting against demolition of their houses. The final report was issued on 6 August, 1978 and covered prison conditions, torture and forced mass-sterilisation atrocities.

60. Congress was founded by the cooperation of A.O. Humes and 72 political workers. It is undoubtedly true that Hume impressed the liberal and democratic contemporaries, including Lajpat Rai, as a man of high ideals with whom it was no dishonour to cooperate. Considering the size of subcontinent, there were very few political persons in the early 1880s and the tradition of open opposition to the rulers was not yet firmly entrenched.

Contagious and committed persons like Dadabhai Naoroji, justice Ranade, Ferozshah Mehta, G. Subramaniya Iyer and Surendranath Banerjee cooperated with Hume because they did not want to arouse official hostility at such an early stage of their work. Gokhale explicitly in 1913 said 'No Indian could have started the INC...if an Indian had...come forward to start such a movement embracing all India, the officials in India would not have allowed the movement to come into existence'.

In other words, according to Bipin Chandra, "if Hume and other English liberals hoped to use the Congress as a safety-valve, the Congress leaders hoped to use Hume as a lightning conductor". And as later developments show, it was the Congress leaders whose hopes were fulfilled.

61. Mary Parker Follet was the first advance the idea of worker's participation in management. She is known as the "Mother of Modern Management". Follet believed that management was "the art of getting things done through people". Though she never managed a for-profit enterprise, she offered valuable insight on the importance of "powering with" rather than "powering over", and integrating with employees to solve conflicts. "Leadership is not defined by the exercise of power but by the capacity to increase the sense of power among those led", Follet once said. "The most essential work of the leader is to create more leaders".

63. New Public Management (NPM) can be defined as a new set of experiments in public-sector management informed with the market principles of efficiency and economy to make ailing public sector effective.

Following are the features of the NPM:

- Revamping of organizational structure
- Empowerment of citizens
- Greater autonomy for public sector manager
- Application of performance measurement technique
- Disaggregation of public bureaucracy
- Cost-cutting
- Goal-orientation
- Use of quasi-markets and contracting out technique
- Emphasis on managerial support service
- Organizational and spatial decentralization

64. Herbert Simon, a nobel prize winner in Economics, has made significant contributions in the field of management particularly administrative behaviour and decision making.

His contributions cover both social systems and decision theory approaches, more particularly the latter. Simon examined the principles of management given by Urwick and Gulick and found them contradictory and ambiguous. He described these principles as 'homely proverbs, myths, slogans and pompous identities'. Simon looked at organisational problems in totality of socio-psychological context and viewed that decision making takes place in this context.

65. Abraham Maslow said that behaviour in administration should be studied through psychoanalysis. Maslow is one of the most influential psychologists of the twentieth century. His biggest contributions to psychology were his contributions to humanistic psychology as well as his development of the hierarchy of needs. Maslow's career in psychology greatly predated the modern positive psychology movement, but it might not look the same were it not for him.

Soon after Maslow began his career, he became frustrated with the two "forces" of psychology at the time, which were Freudian psychoanalysis and behavioural psychology. Maslow believed that psychoanalysis focused too much on "the sick half of psychology" and not enough on "the healthy half". On the other hand, he believed that behaviourism did not focus enough on how humans differ from the animals studied in behaviourism. He thus contributed to the third force of psychology that arose in response to this frustration.

66. The Hawthorne studies were conducted on workers at the Hawthorne plant of the Western Electric Company by Elton Mayo and Fritz Roethlisberger in the late 1920s. The Hawthorne studies were part of a refocus on managerial strategy incorporating the socio-psychological aspects of human behaviour in organizations.

The studies originally looked into whether workers were more responsive and worked more efficiently under certain environmental conditions, such as improved lighting. The results were surprising: Mayo and Roethlisberger found that workers were more responsive to social factors—such as the people they worked with on a team and the amount of interest their manager had in their work—than the factors (lighting, etc.) the researchers had gone into inspect.

The Hawthorne studies discovered that workers were highly responsive to additional attention from their managers and the feeling that their managers actually cared about, and were interested in, their work. The studies also found that although financial motives are important, social issues are equally important factors in worker productivity.

67. Thomas Carlyle (1795-1881) was a British literary, historian and political writer. Best known as the author of Sartor Resartus (1833) and on Heroes and Hero Worship (1841). He characterised the people as irrational and disorderly in Reminiscences of My Irish Journey (1882). For him, "The world is a republic of mediocrities, and always was". Carlyle attacked laissez-faire theory and parliamentary government and affirmed his belief in the necessity for strong, paternalistic government. Thomas Carlyle described the spread of the term bureaucracy as the "continental nuisance".

70. Span of control is the term now used more commonly in business management, particularly human resource management. Span of control refers to the number of subordinates a supervisor has.

The eight main factors to be considered when determining span of control or management. The factors are: 1. Capacity of Superior 2. Capacity of Subordinates 3. Nature of Work 4. Degree of Decentralisation 5. Degree of Planning 6. Communication Techniques 7. Use of Staff Assistance 8. Rate of Change.

71. The ultimate goal of the e-government is to be able to offer an increased portfolio of public services to citizens in an efficient and cost effective manner. It allows for government transparency because it allows the public to be informed about what the government is working on as well as the policies they are trying to implement.

The main advantage while implementing electronic government will be to improve the efficiency of the current system (Paper based system). That would in return save money and time. The introduction would also facilitate better communications between governments and businesses.

For example: E-procurement facilitates G2G and B2B communication; this will permit smaller business to compete for government contracts as well as larger business. Hence the advantage of creating an open market and stronger economy. Business and citizens can obtain information at a faster speed and it is possible at any time of the day.

The society is moving towards the mobile connections and the ability of an e-government service to be accessible to citizens irrespective of location throughout the country brings the next and potentially biggest benefit of an e-government service as we live in what is now termed as the Knowledge era.

The anticipated benefits of e-government include efficiency, improved services, better accessibility of public services, and more transparency and accountability.

75. The 73rd and 74th Amendment Acts have resulted in transparency in the governance, accountability in governance, gender empowerment and deepening of democracy.

The salient features of 73rd Amendment Act, 1992 are as follows:

- To provide 3-tier system of Panchayati Raj for all States having population of over 20 lakh.
- To hold Panchayat elections regularly every 5 years.
- To provide reservation of seats for Scheduled Castes, Scheduled Tribes and women (not less than 33%)
- To appoint State Finance Commission to make recommendations as regards the financial powers of the Panchayats.
- To constitute District Planning Committee to prepare draft development plan for the district as a whole.

The salient features of 74th Amendment Act, 1992 are as follows:

Three Types of Municipalities. The act provides for the constitution of the following three types of municipalities in every state.

- A nagar panchayat (by whatever name called) for a transitional area, that is, an area in transition from a rural area to an urban area.
- A municipal council for a smaller urban area.
- A municipal corporation for a larger urban area.

76. On the eve of independence, in 1947, the Collector had become something of a jack of all trades. He had no effective control over the activities of specialist departments in the district even though he was generally charged with the satisfactory functioning of each department. The old priorities were suddenly gone. The role of the administrative system changed in the context of three major factors, namely democracy, development and decentralization. The Community Development Programme was introduced in the early fifties and the early the three-tier Panchayati Raj in the late fifties and the early sixties. Administration was to carry out the policies and programmes for economic development and social change. This implied transformation not only in the aims of administration but also in its means. This together with a rapidly growing population and its rising expectations changed the entire nature of district administration. The district administration was no longer the rulers but the servants of the people.

78. Corruption need not necessarily be in the form of money. The Central Vigilance Commission has identified following twenty-seven modes of corruption.

- Acceptance of substandard stores/works.
- Misappropriation of public money and misappropriation of stores.
- Incurring pecuniary obligations of persons with whom the public servants have official dealings.
- Borrowings money from contractors/firms having official dealings with officers.
- Showing favours to contractors and firms.

- Claiming of false travelling allowance, house rent, etc.
- Possession of disproportionate assets.
- Causing loss to government by negligence or otherwise.
- Purchase of immovable property, etc. without prior permission or intimation.
- Abuse of official position/powers.
- Acceptance of illegal gratification in recruitments, postings, transfers and promotions.
- Misuse of government employees for personal work.
- Production of forged certificates of age, of birth of community, etc.
- Irregularities in the reservation of seats by Rail and by Air.
- Non-delivery of money orders, insured covers, value payable parcels, etc.
- Replacement of new postal stamps by used ones.
- Irregularity in grant of import and export licenses.
- Misuse of imported and allotted quotas by various firms with the connivance of the public servants.
- Irregularity in the grant of telephone connections.
- Moral turpitude.
- Acceptance of gifts.
- under assessments of income tax, estate duty, etc., for pecuniary gain.
- Misuse of advances sanctioned for purchase of scooters and cars.
- Abnormal delay in settlement of compensation claims to displaced persons.
- Wrong assessment of claims of displaced persons.
- Cheating in connection with the sale and purchase of plots for residential purposes.
- Unauthorized occupation and subletting of government quarters.

79. Joint Consultative Machinery or JCM as it is colloquially called, is a mechanism by which goal congruence is achieved in government departments through consultation with their employees. This helps in developing harmonious relation between government and its staff and improving the working environment so that the objectives of government department is achieved since a satisfied lot of employees enhances productivity and helps in achieving its aim.

The concept of the scheme is very simple *i.e., joint consultation* and it is similar to Whitley Council in Britain.

The scheme was proposed by Govt of India in 1960 following recommendation of IInd Pay Commission and employees demand thereafter. The scheme envisaged an arbitration council with limited compulsory arbitration alongwith three tier structure of joint consultation. However, employees expressed their doubts over some of the points of the scheme and only after a long discussion between staff union and government, the scheme was finally announced on 28 October, 1966 which opened a new chapter in the history of staff relation in public services.

80. Second Administrative Reforms Commission has identified 'weak governance' as the main reason for corruption in India.

The Administrative Reforms Commission or ARC is the committee constituted by the Government of India to prepare a detailed blueprint for revamping the public administration system. The Commission is given wide terms of reference covering all aspects of public administration. The first ARC was established by the Ministry of Home Affairs in 1966. The second Administrative Reforms Commission (ARC) was constituted in 2005. The first ARC was initially chaired by Morarji Desai, and later on K. Hanumanthaiah became its chairman when Desai became the Deputy Prime Minister of India. The Second Administrative Reforms Commission (ARC) was constituted under the Chairmanship of Veerappa Moily.

83. The cold war and decolonisation process had discouraged more active involvement by United Nations within state because states have national interest as its prime interest. By the mid-1990s the UN had become involved in maintaining international peace and security by resisting aggression between states, attempting to resolve disputes within states, and focussing on economic, social and political conditions within states. The United Nations does not have a monopoly on peace operations. While the UN often provides legitimation, operations are sometimes conducted by regional organizations, ad hoc coalitions or hybrid arrangements involving UN and non-UN actors, such as the African Union.

84. India has signed strategic partnership agreements with Vietnam, Seychelles, Mongolia and Singapore. Strategic partnership means, first, that both retain the flexibility to continue political engagement and economic cooperation with their common adversary. Second, they avoid "entrapment", or being dragged into a partner's disputes and potentially into conflict, which happened in the First World War. Third, regular high-level political and military interactions facilitate a collaborative approach to strategic policies over a range of economic and military activities. India and Japan, for instance, are not only moving forward on economic and defence cooperation but are also cooperating on other important issues such as civil nuclear energy and Security Council reform.

85. India and ASEAN nations share common colonial, historical and cultural linkages. India even supported some nations like Indonesia in their struggle for independence. During Nehru's era in India, various initiatives were taken to build closer ties with the countries of Southeast Asia. But the efforts did not materialized into developing full fledges economic, political or strategic partnership between India and ASEAN. This was partly due to China's dominance in south East Asian region, recognition of Kampuchea regime in Vietnam contrary to ASEAN interests, inclination of India towards Soviet Union etc.

However, the launch of India's 'Look East Policy' in 1992 was a turning point in India-ASEAN relations. By then ASEAN countries too realized the importance of India as the fastest growing economy in Asia and an emerging regional power. The realization of growing complementaries led to the establishment of sectoral dialogue partnership between two sides in 1992. This was elevated to a full-fledged dialogue partnership in 1996, and eventually in 2002 India started annual summits with ASEAN. Endeavours were made to establish robust economic relations by signing FTA in goods with ASEAN in 2009 and in services in 2014.

Currently, the growing synergies between two sides can be gauged from the fact that there are about 30 platforms for engagement, including an annual leaders' summit and ministerial dialogues. The engagement has evolved not only at economic but also at political, strategic, security and defence level ties.

87. Constructivists have argued that, far from an objective reality, international politics is a 'world of our making' (Onuf, 1989). In response to the over-determination of 'structure' in neorealist and neoliberal theory, constructivists introduced the possibility of agency and have emphasized processes of interaction. It is not that actors are totally free to choose their circumstances, but rather that they make choices in the process of interacting with others and, as a result, bring historically, culturally and politically distinct 'realities' into being. In this respect, international relations is a social construction rather than existing independently of human meaning and action. States and other actors do not merely react as rational individuals but interact in a meaningful world.

88. Project 'Mausam' is the initiative of Ministry of Culture to be implemented by the Archaeological Survey of India (ASI) as the nodal agency with research support of the Indira Gandhi National Centre for the Arts (IGNCA) and National Museum as associate bodies. This project aims to explore the multi-faceted Indian Ocean 'world'—collating archaeological and historical research in order to document the diversity of cultural, commercial and religious interactions in the Indian Ocean. It also aims to promote research on themes related to the study of Maritime Routes. Main objective of the project is to inscribe places and sites identified under Project Mausam as transnational nomination for inscription on UNESCO's World Heritage List.

The Shanghai Cooperation Organisation (SCO), or Shanghai Pact, is a Eurasian political, economic, and security alliance, the creation of which was announced on 15 June, 2001 in Shanghai, China by the leaders of China, Kazakhstan, Kyrgyzstan, Russia, Tajikistan, and Uzbekistan; the Shanghai Cooperation Organisation Charter, formally establishing the organisation, was signed in June, 2002 and entered into force on 19 September, 2003. The Heads of State Council (HSC) is the supreme decision-making body in the SCO, it meets once a year and adopts decisions and guidelines on all important matters of the organisation. Military exercises among members are also regularly conducted to promote coordination against terrorism, and to maintain regional peace and stability. India and Pakistan joined SCO as full members on 9 June, 2017 at a summit in Astana,

91. Neo liberals, from their Lockean Universe, seek to create international regimes that optimize the 'rational exploitation' of nature, both as a 'tap' (in providing energy and natural resources) and as a 'sink' (via the waste assimilation services of the earth, oceans and atmosphere) in ways that expand the menu of state development options. However, their rational choice framework implicity sanctions an instrumental orientation towards the non-human world and leaves little room for understanding or promoting alternative 'green identities' of particular states or non-state actors. Whereas neoliberals implicity accept capitalist markets and sovereign states as background 'givens' to international regime negotiations, green IR theorists are concerned to expose the ways in which these social structures serve to thwart the development of more effective environmental initiatives. They also seek to give voice to new forms of counter-hegemonic resistance to neoliberal economic globalization. Like all critical theorists, green IR theorists emphasize the role of agents in transforming social structures—in this case, to promote environmental justice and sustainability.

92. The idea that democracies do not fight each other can be traced back to the writings of Immanuel Kant over two hundred years ago in essay 'On Perpetual Peace', however, only in the early 1980s and with the writings of Michael Doyle was the idea consolidated. According to Doyle and other advocates of the democratic peace theory, liberal democratic states have been able to maintain peaceful relations amongst themselves, but are prone to wage war against non-democratic regimes. In order to prove this theory, vast databases have been constructed of historical dyadic relationships between states as well as detailed breakdowns of incidents of inter-state war. The conclusions reached are best shown in the work of Bruce Russett "A neo-Kantian perspective: democracy, interdependence, and international organizations in building security communities."

93. Montevideo Convention, in full Montevideo Convention on the Rights and Duties of States, agreement signed at Montevideo, Uruguay, on December 26, 1933 (and entering into force the following year), that established the standard definition of a state under international law. Adopted by the Seventh International Conference of American States, the convention stipulated that all states were equal sovereign units consisting of a permanent population, defined territorial boundaries, a government, and an ability to enter into agreements with other states. Among the convention's provisions were that signatories would not intervene in the domestic or foreign affairs of another state, that they would not recognize territorial gains made by force, and that all disputes should be settled peacefully. The agreement was signed by the United States, Argentina, Brazil, Chile, Colombia, Cuba, the Dominican Republic, Ecuador, El Salvador, Guatemala, Haiti, Honduras, Mexico, Nicaragua, Panama, Paraguay, Peru, Uruguay, and Venezuela. Bolivia was the only country attending the conference that refused to sign the agreement.

96. The role of ideology in international relations can be hardly over emphasized. It is an element of National Power. In fact, the true nature of a policy followed by a nation is always concealed under ideological justifications and rationalizations. U.S. President Nixon's New Peace Policy was in reality a policy of 'Divide and be Strong' between the erstwhile USSR and China.

Morgenthau refers to three such typical ideologies of the foreign policy:

- Ideology of Status Quo
- Ideology of Imperialism, and
- Ambiguous Ideologies.

97. The term global commons "denotes areas and natural resources that are not subject to the national jurisdiction of a particular state but are shared by other states, if not the international community as a whole."

He adds: "The high seas, the deep seabed, outer space, the Moon and other celestial bodies ... can be viewed as global commons because no national entity can claim sole jurisdiction over these physical areas."

Some who see the Arctic as a global commons take issue with the fact that "the current discourse on the Arctic is dominated by the Arctic Five countries and the Arctic Council." However, much of the region's ocean falls within the recognized national jurisdictions of the Arctic coastal states—Canada, Denmark, Norway, Russia and the U.S. They are sometimes referred to as the Arctic Five.

Those insisting that the Arctic is a global commons are conflating the high seas of the central Arctic Ocean with the entire Arctic region. The Arctic Five acknowledge that those waters qualify as a global commons, but the distinction between the high seas and whole Arctic region is not always clearly articulated.

98. Scholars and practitioners such as John Steinbruner, Jonathan Dean or Stuart Croft worked extensively on the theoretical backing of arms control. Arms control is meant to break the security dilemma. It aims at mutual security between partners and overall stability (be it in a crisis situation, a grand strategy, or stability to put an end to an arms race). Other than stability, arms control comes with cost reduction and damage limitation. It is different from disarmament since the maintenance of stability might allow for mutually controlled armament and does not take a peace-without-weapons-stance. Nevertheless, arms control is a defensive strategy in principle, since transparency, equality, and stability do not fit into an offensive strategy.

100. "Kwame Nkrumah's "Neo-Colonialism: The last stage of Imperialism" is the classic statement on the post-colonial condition. African, Caribbean and Third World nation-states after flag independence find they have achieved government or state power but still cannot control the political economies of their country as they appear to be directed from the outside by multinational corporations. Many African Americans use this analysis to suggest even when Black people win elections they really are not in charge and this is consistent with the theory found in this work."

Previous Paper (Solved)

UGC-NET-Junior Research Fellowship & Assistant Professor Exam

Political Science, November-2017*

PAPER-II

Note: *This paper contains **fifty (50)** objective type questions of **two (2)** marks each. **All** questions are compulsory.*

1. Who said "Kautilya's *Arthashastra* exemplified radical Machiavellianism, compared to it, Machiavelli's *Prince* is harmless"?
   A. Weber
   B. Morgenthau
   C. Waltz
   D. Kissinger

2. According to Plato, justice is:
   A. Distribution of goods and services
   B. Burdens and Benefits
   C. Punishment and retribution
   D. One man one work, one class one duty

3. Given below are two statements, one labelled as Assertion (A) and the other as Reason (R). Select the correct answer from the code given below:
   Assertion (A): Oakeshott says Hobbes is the greatest political thinker produced by the English speaking people.
   Reason (R) : No other thinker can match his philosophical foundations and clarity of thought.
   Code:
   A. Both (A) and (R) are true and (R) is the correct explanation of (A)
   B. Both (A) and (R) are true, but (R) is not the correct explanation of (A)
   C. (A) is true, but (R) is false
   D. (A) is false, but (R) is true

4. Hegel's dialectical method was:
   A. to build a science of politics
   B. to accept the Enlightenment's philosophical method
   C. to assert that the methods of natural sciences and those of social sciences were identical
   D. to solve the problem of contradiction

5. Who distinguished the Young Marx from the Old Marx?
   A. Althusser B. Lenin
   C. Miliband D. Luxemburg

6. Gramsci characterised Fascism as:
   A. Hegemonic revolution
   B. Passive revolution
   C. Bourgeois revolution
   D. Petit Bourgeois revolution

7. Given below are two statements, one labelled as Assertion (A) and the other as Reason (R). Select the correct answer from the code given below:
   Assertion (A): Gandhi was critical of the material civilisation and particularly detested the Industrial Revolution.
   Reason (R) : He believed that Industrial Revolution was destroying deeper values.
   Code:
   A. Both (A) and (R) are true and (R) is the correct explanation of (A).
   B. Both (A) and (R) are true, but (R) is not the correct explanation of (A).
   C. (A) is true, but (R) is false.
   D. (A) is false, but (R) is true.

* *Held on 5 November, 2017.*

8. Roy-Lenin debate centred around:
A. Dialectical Materialism
B. Marxist Theory of History
C. The Theory of Surplus Value
D. Colonial Question

9. Deliberative Democracy is:
A. A theory that champions exclusively Human Rights.
B. A theory that puts forward environment as the most important agenda.
C. A theory that concentrates on refining the familiar framework of liberal democracy.
D. A theory that wants to usher in socialism by democratic means.

10. Why was behaviouralism shortlived?
A. Inability to evolve consensus
B. Too much dogmatism
C. It was a localised event
D. Coloured by Cold War prejudices

11. Given below are two statements, one labelled as Assertion (A) and the other as Reason (R). Select the correct answer from the code given below:

Assertion (A): According to Weber, comparative politics could be comprehended within the larger framework of culture, which he did by demolishing Marx's theory of economic determinism.

Reason (R) : As without this rejection, his theory was totally untenable.

Code:
A. Both (A) and (R) are true and (R) is the correct explanation of (A).
B. Both (A) and (R) are true, but (R) is not the correct explanation of (A).
C. (A) is true, but (R) is false.
D. (A) is false, but (R) is true.

12. Given below are two statements, one labelled as Assertion (A) and the other as Reason (R). Select the correct answer from the code given below:

Assertion (A): Institutional approach can help in mapping the landscape of politics.

Reason (R) : The goal of institutional approach is to reconcile the competing values of individual freedom and collective equality.

Code:
A. Both (A) and (R) are true and (R) is the correct explanation of (A).
B. Both (A) and (R) are true, but (R) is not the correct explanation of (A).
C. (A) is true, but (R) is false.
D. (A) is false, but (R) is true.

13. Which century according to Easton is "The Age of Scientific Method"?
A. Seventeenth Century
B. Eighteenth Century
C. Nineteenth Century
D. Twentieth Century

14. Aristotle's classification of constitutions was based on the categories of:
A. who rules and who benefits from the rule
B. ways and means of perpetuating in power
C. accepting the basic formulations of Plato's *The Republic*
D. to ensure rule of the majority

15. Which one of the following countries follow a semi-presidential system?
A. Sri Lanka B. Germany
C. Italy D. France

16. Who challenged the established view that in Great Britain the Conservative party was elitist and leader dominated, while the Labour party was characterised by a high measure of internal democracy?
A. Robert Michels B. Robert Mekenzie
C. Tony Benn D. Mosei Ostrogonski

17. Bureaucratic authoritarianism is a variant of:
A. Military rule B. Fascism
C. Communism D. Despotism

18. Which theory held that as societies developed they would become capitalist democracies, converging around a shared set of values and characteristics?
A. Dependency Theory

B. Structural Functional Theory
C. Modernization Theory
D. Post-modernization Theory

19. Legitimation crisis as an alternative to Weberian approach to legitimacy was developed by:
A. Miliband and Sweezy
B. Plekhanov and Lenin
C. Camus and Sartre
D. Habermas and Offe

20. Who said Revolution meant a drastic sudden substitution of one group in charge of the running of a territorial political entity by another?
A. Hannah Arendt B. Theda Skocpol
C. Crane Brinton D. Hubert Johnson

21. Put the following events in their chronological order and select the correct answer from the code given below:
Poona Pact, Third Round Table Conference, Swaraj Party, Communal Award, Nehru Report.
Code:
A. Swaraj Party, Poona Pact, Third Round Table Conference, Nehru Report, Communal Award
B. Swaraj Party, Nehru Report, Communal Award, Poona Pact, Third Round Table Conference
C. Poona Pact, Swaraj Party, Communal Award, Nehru Report, Third Round Table Conference
D. Nehru Report, Third Round Table Conference, Swaraj Party, Poona Pact, Communal Award

22. Which of the following parties/groups the Cabinet Mission did not recognise?
A. The Muslim League
B. The Congress
C. The Sikhs
D. The Princes Guild

23. Which of the following come within the ambit of Article 21 of the Indian Constitution?
(*a*) Right to shelter
(*b*) Right to good roads
(*c*) Right to reputation
(*d*) Right to pure drinking water
Select the correct answer from the code given below:
Code:
A. (*a*) and (*b*) B. (*a*), (*c*) and (*d*)
C. (*a*), (*b*) and (*d*) D. (*a*), (*b*), (*c*) and (*d*)

24. Which of the following cases reflect on the elements of the basic structure of the Indian Constitution? Choose correct answer from the code given below:
(*a*) Indira Nehru Gandhi V. Raj Narain
(*b*) Kesavanand Bharti V. State of Kerala
(*c*) S.P. Gupta V. Union of India
(*d*) Minerva Mills V. Union of India
Code:
A. (*a*), (*b*) and (*d*) only
B. (*a*), (*b*), (*c*) and (*d*)
C. (*c*), (*d*) and (*b*) only
D. (*a*), (*b*) and (*c*) only

25. When were the rules regarding Department Related Parliamentary Standing Committees made in India?
A. 1977 B. 1981
C. 1989 D. 2010

26. Which of the following state has a seat reserved on the basis of religion in the Legislative Assembly?
A. Goa
B. Mizoram
C. Jammu and Kashmir
D. Sikkim

27. Which of the following pairs is not correctly matched?
A. Rolling Plan - National Front Government
B. 20 Point Programme - Congress Government
C. National Commission to Review the Working of the Constitution - NDA-I Government
D. National Rural Employment Guarantee Act - UPA-I Government

28. Who among the following was not a member of the Sarkaria Commission on Centre-State Relations?
A. Justice R.S. Sarkaria
B. G.V. Ramakrishna
C. B. Shivaraman
D. Dr. S.R. Sen

29. Since when the Election Commission of India has become a three member body?
A. 1989 B. 1990
C. 1993 D. 2001

30. Arrange the following peasant movements in their chronological order. Select the correct answer from the code given below:
(*a*) Tebhaga
(*b*) Champaran
(*c*) Singur
(*d*) Bardoli
Code:
A. (*b*), (*a*), (*c*), (*d*) B. (*b*), (*d*), (*a*), (*c*)
C. (*c*), (*a*), (*b*), (*d*) D. (*d*), (*b*), (*c*), (*a*)

31. Which of the following approaches is the precursor of the Ecological approach?
A. Classical approach
B. Human Relations approach
C. Systems approach
D. Behavioural approach

32. Match List-I with List-II and select the correct answer from the code given below:

List-I (Theory)	***List-II (Thinker)***
(*a*) Classical Theory	(*i*) Elton Mayo
(*b*) Human Relations Theory	(*ii*) Henry Fayol
(*c*) Decision-Making Theory	(*iii*) V. Ostrom
(*d*) Public Choice Theory	(*iv*) Herbert Simon

Code:

	(*a*)	(*b*)	(*c*)	(*d*)
A.	(*i*)	(*ii*)	(*iv*)	(*iii*)
B.	(*ii*)	(*iii*)	(*iv*)	(*i*)
C.	(*i*)	(*ii*)	(*iii*)	(*iv*)
D.	(*ii*)	(*i*)	(*iv*)	(*iii*)

33. Who among the following has specified six qualities of an administrator/manager - physical, mental, moral, general education, special knowledge and experience?
A. Fayol B. Gulick
C. Urwick D. Follet

34. Which of the following is an example of auxiliary agency?
A. Department of Defence
B. Department of Home
C. Prime Minister's Office (PMO)
D. Public Works Department

35. Which one of the following types of bureaucracy tend to exhibit a bias towards party interests?
A. Caste bureaucracy
B. Patronage bureaucracy
C. Guardian bureaucracy
D. Ruling bureaucracy

36. Which of the following are excluded from the RTI Act?
(*a*) Central Bureau of Investigation (CBI)
(*b*) Research and Analysis Wing (RAW)
(*c*) Central Reserve Police Force (CRPF)
(*d*) Prime Minister's Office (PMO)

Select the correct answer from the code given below:
A. (*a*) and (*d*) B. (*a*) and (*b*)
C. (*a*), (*b*) and (*c*) D. (*c*) and (*d*)

37. Which of the following commissions/ committees recommended that the financial year should be from January 1 to December 31?
A. L.K. Jha Committee
B. Sarkaria Commission
C. Sixth Pay Commission
D. Second Administrative Reforms Commission

38. Which one of the following types of training prepares future recruits for the public service?
A. Informal training
B. Formal training
C. Pre-entry training
D. Post-entry training

39. Which of the following statements are correct about the Central Vigilance Commission?

(*a*) It was set up on the recommendation of the Santhanam Committee

(*b*) It is a statutory body

(*c*) It is a multi-member commission

(*d*) It exercises superintendence over the working of the CBI

Select the correct answer from the code given below:

A. (*a*) and (*b*) only
B. (*b*) and (*c*) only
C. (*a*), (*b*) and (*c*)
D. (*a*), (*b*), (*c*) and (*d*)

40. Given below are two statements, one labelled as Assertion (A) and the other labelled as Reason (R). Select the correct answer from the code given below:

Assertion (A): The expenditure charged on the Consolidated Fund of India is not subject to the vote of Parliament.

Reason (R) : It is in the nature of obligatory payment.

Code:

A. Both (A) and (R) are true and (R) is the correct explanation of (A)
B. Both (A) and (R) are true, but (R) is not the correct explanation of (A)
C. (A) is true, but (R) is false
D. (A) is false, but (R) is true

41. Which of the following combination game theory utilizes to analyse strategic interaction among decision-makers?

A. Mathematics and Reason
B. Reason and Logic
C. Logic and Rationality
D. Mathematics and Logic

42. Consider the following statements with regard to MTCR:

(*a*) China is not a member of MTCR

(*b*) India is a member of MTCR

(*c*) Aims at restricting complete rocket systems

(*d*) Pakistan is a member of MTCR

Select the correct answer from the code given below:

A. (*a*), (*b*), (*c*)
B. (*b*), (*d*), (*c*)
C. (*b*), (*c*), (*d*)
D. (*d*), (*b*), (*a*)

43. Which one of the following is ***not*** a criteria of just war?

A. Be authorized by a sovereign prince
B. Be proportionate
C. Be pursued for just intent
D. be undeclared

44. Whose Presidency in America was marked by 'war on terrorism'?

A. George H W Bush
B. George W Bush Jr
C. Bill Clinton
D. Barack Obama

45. A unipolar condition to which George W Bush Jr referred as a balance of power that favours:

A. Security
B. Cooperation
C. Peace
D. Freedom

46. Match List-I with List-II and select the correct answers from the code given below:

List-I (Authors)	***List-II (Books)***
(*a*) Andrew Linklater	(*i*) Cooperation under Anarchy
(*b*) F. Clark	(*ii*) The transformation of political community
(*c*) Kenneth Oye	(*iii*) Gendering world politics
(*d*) J.A. Tickner	(*iv*) Hegemony in International Studies

Code:

	(*a*)	(*b*)	(*c*)	(*d*)
A.	(*ii*)	(*i*)	(*iv*)	(*iii*)
B.	(*iii*)	(*ii*)	(*i*)	(*iv*)
C.	(*ii*)	(*iv*)	(*i*)	(*iii*)
D.	(*iv*)	(*ii*)	(*i*)	(*iii*)

47. Given below are two statements, one labelled as Assertion (A) and the other labelled as Reason (R). Select the correct answer from the code given below:

Assertion (A): India is seeking permanent membership of Security Council of UNO.

Reason (R) : India is a nuclear power.

Code:

A. Both (A) and (R) are true, and (R) is the correct explanation of (A)

B. Both (A) and (R) are true, but (R) is not the correct explanation of (A)

C. (A) is true, but (R) is false

D. (A) is false, but (R) is true

48. Match the List-I with List-II and select the correct answer from the code given below:

List-I	***List-II***
(*a*) Nixon doctrine	(*i*) Support to anti-guerilla movements
(*b*) Kennedy doctrine	(*ii*) Pursuit of peace through a partnership with allies
(*c*) Reagan doctrine	(*iii*) Intervention to prevent genocide
(*d*) Clinton doctrine	(*iv*) Foreign policy initiatives towards Latin America

Code:

	(*a*)	(*b*)	(*c*)	(*d*)
A.	(*i*)	(*iii*)	(*iv*)	(*ii*)
B.	(*iii*)	(*ii*)	(*iv*)	(*i*)
C.	(*iv*)	(*ii*)	(*iii*)	(*i*)
D.	(*ii*)	(*iv*)	(*i*)	(*iii*)

49. Consider the following statements with regard to Non-aligned movement.

(*a*) Julius Nyerere was one of the founding members of NAM

(*b*) India hosted seventh NAM summit

(*c*) The seventeenth NAM summit was held in Venezuela

(*d*) The headquarters of NAM is in Belgrade

Select the correct answer from the code given below:

A. (*a*), (*b*) and (*c*)

B. (*a*), (*c*) and (*d*)

C. (*b*) and (*c*)

D. (*b*) and (*d*)

50. Which one of the following is ***not*** a part of 'Three Pillars' of R2P (Responsibility to Protect)?

A. If a state fails to protect its population, International community take collective action in accordance with the UN Charter

B. It is state's responsibility to protect its population from four mass atrocity crimes

C. It is the responsibility of International Community to protect people from crimes against humanity

D. International Community's responsibility to assist individual states in meeting the responsibility

ANSWERS

1	2	3	4	5	6	7	8	9	10
A	D	A	D	A	B	A	D	C	A
11	**12**	**13**	**14**	**15**	**16**	**17**	**18**	**19**	**20**
A	A	C	A	*	B	A	C	D	C
21	**22**	**23**	**24**	**25**	**26**	**27**	**28**	**29**	**30**
B	C	D	B	C	D	A	B	C	B
31	**32**	**33**	**34**	**35**	**36**	**37**	**38**	**39**	**40**
C	D	A	D	B	C	A	C	D	A
41	**42**	**43**	**44**	**45**	**46**	**47**	**48**	**49**	**50**
C	A	D	B	D	C	B	D	C	C

EXPLANATORY ANSWERS

1. Max Weber was the first to see that the writings of Machiavelli, when contrasted with the brutal realism of other cultural and political traditions, were not so extreme as they appear to some critics. "Trully radical 'Machiavellianism', in the popular sense of that word", Weber said in his famous lecture "Politics as a Vocation", "is classically expressed in Indian literature in the Arthashastra of Kautilya: compared to it, Machiavelli's The Prince is harmless". In this article, I contrast Machiavelli's writings to those of Kautilya and question why Machiavelli omitted the harsher aspects of political domination such as spies, assassination of enemies and torture. Could it be that he was afraid to tell a prince about the harsher characteristics of tyrannical rule? If so, why?

2. Justice in the state meant that the three social classes (rulers, warriors and producers) performed the deliberative and governing, defence, and production, without interfering with the functions of the others. Justice was "one class, one duty; one man, one work". Plato drew a parallel line between the three social classes and the three elements of the human soul.

   Each soul had a corresponding social class. A Just society recognized and educated every individual talent according to the dominant element in one's soul and ordered these elements into coherent classes.

4. Hegel's dialectical method played a crucial role in his political philosophy. By applying the categories of a thesis, an antithesis and a synthesis, Hegel's major thrust was to solve the problem of contradiction. It attempted to reconcile the many apparent contradictory positions and theories developed by earlier thought processes. As a method of interpretation, it attempted to reconcile the various different traits developed in the past. He never claimed to be its inventor, and even acknowledged that the ancient Greek philosopher Socrates used it.

5. Louis Althusser popularized the conception of an "epistemological break" between the Young Marx and the Mature Marx, that is the point where Marx broke with ideology to enter the domain of science, a point generally considered to consist in his break with Feuerbach. However, the epistemological break, a concept which Althusser drew out of Gaston Bachelard, is not to be conceived as a chronological point, but as a "process", thus making the question of the distinction between a "Young Marx" and a "Mature Marx" a problematic one.

6. Gramsci characterised Fascism as passive revolution. The increasingly accepted notion that Fascism was not merely reactionary but revolutionary, competing with Marxism, invites reassessment of Gramsci's interpretation of Fascism.

   With his emphasis on the relative autonomy of political and cultural factors, Gramsci might have recognized the scope for a competing revolution, even if only the better to counter it. But though his initial analysis of the Italian revolutionary situation was almost proto-Fascist in certain respects, he dismissed Fascist claims to constitute an alternative revolution, and, partly as a result, he consistently underestimated Fascism prior to 1926.

   After his imprisonment, however, he began seeking to devise the categories necessary to understand Fascism's unanticipated triumph. Although he continued to sidestep aspects of the Fascist challenge, his innovative way of analyzing Fascism as a form of caesarism, engaged in a war of attrition, enabled him to illuminate the peculiar combination of accomplishment, limitation and failure that characterized the Fascist regime.

7. Gandhi was critical of the material civilisation and particularly detested the Industrial Revolution because he believed that Industrial Revolution was destroying deeper values. As we know industrialisation, urbanisation and westernization are not essentially connected with modernity.

Modernity brings reason, universality, order, autonomy, equality, freedom and many other metanarratives. But Gandhi used modern civilisation, western civilisation and some time British civilisation as synonyms and for him all these words stand for industrialization and urbanization and they are associated with the modern virtues of rationality, equality and unversality.

They are applicable to the various institutions of modern life as well. Gandhi criticizes industrialization and urbanization because, as he says, he believes that, "the distinguishing characteristic of modern civilization is an indefinite multiplication of wants", As Ramchandra Guha observes, to satisfy these wants, one had to forage far and wide for raw materials and commodities and it is totally against and altogether contradictory to his idea of civilization. For him "Civilization in the real sense of the term consists not in the multiplication, but in the deliberate and voluntary reduction of wants".

8. Before the opening of the Second World Congress of the Communist International (1920), Lenin prepared a draft thesis on the national and colonial question. M.N. Roy, a young Bengali attending his first international communist gathering, eagerly responded to Lenin's request for criticisms. As a result, Lenin invited him to write an alternative thesis. Both these were modified as a result of discussions within the National and Colonial commission, and both were subsequently adopted by the Congress. After his encounter with Lenin, Roy rose rapidly in the comintern hierarchy. In 1922 he was elected a candidate member of the Executive Committee of the Communist International (ECCI), and a full voting member in 1924.

He became a member of the Presidium in 1924. It was in the year 1926, however, that Roy attained the peak of his influence in the Comintern. In February of that year he was appointed to the editorial staff of the Communist International, and in the following December he was reelected to the Presidium and joined the Political Secretariat of the ECCI.

9. Deliberative democracy or Discursive democracy is a form of democracy in which deliberation is central to decision-making. It adopts elements of both consensus decision-making and majority rule. Deliberative democracy differs from traditional democratic theory in that authentic deliberation, not mere voting, is the primary source of legitimacy for the law.

Deliberative democracy is compatible with both representative democracy and direct democracy. Some practitioners and theorists use the term to encompass representative bodies whose members authentically deliberate on legislation without unequal distributions of power, while others use the term exclusively to refer to decision-making directly by lay citizens, as in direct democracy.

The term "deliberative democracy" was originally coined by Joseph M. Bessette in his 1980 work Deliberative Democracy: The Majority Principle in Republican Government.

11. According to Weber, comparative politics could be comprehended within the larger framework of culture, which he did by demolishing Marx's theory of economic determinism because without this rejection, his theory was totally untenable. The historical, economic, and political analysis of Marx and Weber is largely structuralist. That is, they attempted to understand the large structures and institutions that affect the lives of people, and how these changed over time and space.

For Marx, these were primarily economic structures–involving factors such as the development of the productive forces and ownership or non-ownership of the means of production.

For Weber, "the economic order was of paramount importance in determining the precise position of different communities but other important structures such as religion, ideas, status, and bureaucracy" could influence people's actions in ways not directly derivative from purely 'economic' interests. In particular, for Weber "rational bureaucracy, rather than class struggle, was the most significant factor."

12. Institutional approach can help in mapping the landscape of politics because the goal of institutional approach is to reconcile the competing values of individual freedom and collective equality. This is a very old and important approach to the study of politics and political system. The institutional approach is concerned with the study of formal structures and institutions like legislature, executive, judiciary, political parties, etc. The advocates of this approach include both ancient and modern political thinkers. Among the ancient thinkers Aristotle is an important contributor to this approach while the modern thinkers include James Bryce, Bentley, Walter Bagehot, Harold Laski, etc.

13. Easton tries to reinforce his argument by invoking the scientific works of Copernicus, Kepler, Galileo and Newton and their cumulative impact on the development of a specific trend of scientific enquiry in Europe. Hobbes was the first product of the scientific revolution. However, his conclusions did not match the expectations of the basic verification of facts of a generalised theory.

Hobbes is important for his spirit and not for his result. The philosophers of the Enlightenment like Rousseau, Helvetius, Condorcet, Diderot and Montesquieu were more speculative than empirical. But they were also pioneers in emphasising "the necessity of scientific reason". In the 19th century, the overall temper was to be scientific and Easton calls it "the age of scientific method". The three examples of Comte, Marx and Spencer prove the sway of the scientific method on the century, with a great deal of optimism in their projections.

14. Aristotle's classification of constitutions was based on the categories of who rules and who benefits from the rule. Aristotle analyzed and compared 158 constitutious, thereby uniting the empirical and speculative modes of enquiry. He built on Plato's classification of constitutions in the statesman by taking into account the ends of a constitution and the number who wielded political power. Constitutions promoting general well-being of the governed were true or good, whereas those that fettered the interests of the ruler were bad or perverted. A government ruled by one, few or many in the self-interest of the community was monarchy, aristocracy and polity respectively.

Conversely, a government ruled by one, few or many in the self-interest of the ruler was tyranny, oligarchy and democracy respectively. In each of these true and perverted constitutions, merit within the system of distributive justice was defined in a particular way befitting the constitution.

16. Robert Mekenzie challenged the established view that in Great Britain the conservative party was elitist and leader dominated, while the Labour party was characterised by a high measure of internal democracy. Mekenzie was Canadian-born British political scientist and television commentator on electoral politics. In the latter role, Mekenzie popularized to the British public the word psephology (the study of votes) and the idea of "swing" votes, using a device he called a "Swingometer" to show the shifting fortunes of the major parties during the announcement of election results.

17. Bureaucratic authoritarianism is a type of authoritarian regime that feathres rule by an alliance of military leaders, civilians with technical expertise and leading business sectors.

These regimes are hypothesized to form under certain conditions where a nation is attempting to industrialized and faces popular agitation or unrest that makes it difficult for elites to maintain order.

The original paradigms of the bureaucratic-authoritarian regime were Latin American countries of the 1960s, Latin American regimes in the 1970s and 1980s, as well as East Asian countries that have provided the opportunity for political science to test the theories proposed their development.

Guillermo O'Donnell coined the term bureaucratic authoritarianism in Modernization and Bureaucratic-Authoritarianism (1973), which examined the military regimes of South America that made economic performance a key component of their legitimation formulae. O'Donnell argued that the modern authoritarian regimes that came to power in Brazil (1964) and Argentina (1966) were supported by a coalition of military officers, civilian technocrats, and big business that sought to move beyond the populist, distribution-oriented politics previously prevalent in those societies. The new regimes sought to replace distributional conflict with a more technocratic, bureaucratic approach to making economic policy.

18. Modernization theory held that as societies developed they would become capitalist democracies, converging around a shared set of values and characteristics. This theory is used to explain the process of modernization within societies. Modernization refers to a model of a progressive transition from a 'pre-modern' or 'traditional' to a 'modern' society. Modernization theory originated from the ideas of German Sociologist Max Weber, which provided the basis for the modernization paradigm developed by sociologist Talcott Parsons.

The theory looks at the internal factors of a country while assuming that with assistance, "traditional" countries can be brought to development in the same manner more developed countries have been. Modernization theory was a dominant paradigm in the social sciences in the 1950s and 1960s, then went into a deep eclipse. It made a comeback after 1990 but remains a controversial model.

19. Legitimation crisis as an alternative to Weberian approach to legitimacy was developed by Habermas and Offe. Max Weber simply analysed the concept of legitimacy. But the neo-Marxists departed from Weberian theory of legitimacy and focused their attention to the legitimation crisis. The champion of this new trend is Jurgen Habermas. This 'Legitimation Crisis' was published in 1973. Habermas and several other neo-Marxists have thoroughly studied the nature and functioning of capitalism and have concluded that "within liberal democracies there are crisis tendencies which challenge the stability of such regimes by undermining legitimacy. The core of this argument was the tension between a private enterprise or capitalist economy, on the one hand and a democratic political system, on the other hand, in effect, the system of capitalist democracy may be inherently unstable".

20. According to Crane Brinton, "Revolution is one of the looser words but our focus is on drastic, sudden substitution of one group in charge of the running of a territorial political entity by another group hitherto not running that government. There is one further implication: the revolutionary substitution of one group for another, if not made by actual violent uprising, is made by coup d'etat, putsch, or some other kind of skullduggery".

22. The Sikhs group did not recognise by the Cabinet Mission. Cabinet Mission was composed of three Cabinet Ministers of England—Sir Pethick Lawrence (Secretary of State for India), Sir Stafford Cripps (President of the Board of Trade) and Alexander.

The Mission arrived on March 24, 1946. The objective of this Mission was to devise a machinery to draw up the constitution of independent India, make arrangements for interim government and thus the Mission was like a declaration of India's independence.

The Mission spent some 3 weeks to discuss with the leaders of various political parties, but could not arrive at any agreed solution. So, finally it announced its own recommendations on May 16, 1946.

23. Article 21 declares that no person shall be deprived of his life or personal liberty except according to procedure established by law. The Supreme Court has declared the following rights as part of Article 21:

1. The right to go abroad.
2. The right to privacy.
3. The right against solitary confinement.
4. The right against hand cuffing.
5. The right against delayed execution.
6. The right to shelter.
7. The right against custodial death.
8. The right against public hanging.
9. Doctors assistance
10. The right to good roads
11. The right to reputations
12. The right to pure drinking water
13. The right to information
14. The right to free education up to 14 years of age
15. The right to information, etc.

25. In 1989, three standing committees were constituted which dealt with Agriculture, Science & Technology and Environment & Forests. On the recommendation of the Rules Committee of the Lok Sabha, 17 Departmentally–Related Standing Committees (DRSCs) were set up in the Parliament in 1993. In 2004, 7 more such committees were setup, thus increasing their number from 17 to 24. The main objective of the standing committees is to secure more accountability of the Executive to the Parliament, particularly financial accountability. They also assist the Parliament in debating the budget more effectively.

26. The Sikkim state has a seat reserved on the basis of religion in the Legislative Assembly. The Sikkim Legislative Assembly is the unicameral state legislature. There are 32 members in a legislative assembly. There are 2 seats reserved for SCs, 12 for STs out of 32 seats.

These scheduled tribes include ethnic tribes such as Bhutia, Lepcha, Sherpa communities as specified during the merger of the kingdom of Sikkim (Monarchy) into India making it the 22nd state of the Indian Republic in 1975, setting up a democracy within the state. One Sangha seat is reserved for 2900 monks of over 100 monasteries.

27. The Janta Government terminated the Fifth Five Year Plan in 1977-78 and launched its own Sixth Five Year Plan for period 1978-83 and called it a Rolling Plan. The meaning of the Rolling Plan was that now, every year the performance of the plan will be assessed and a new plan will be made next year based upon this assessment.

In the Rolling Plans there are three kind of plans. First is the plan for the current year which comprises the annual budget. Second is a plan for a fixed number of years, which may be 3, 4 or 5 years. This second plan is kept changing as per the requirements of the economy and politics. Third is a perspective plan which is for 10, 15 or 20 years. Thus, there is no fixation of dates in respect of commencements and end of the plan in the rolling plans.

28. Sarkaria Commission was set up in June 1983 by the central government of India. The Sarkaria Commission's charter was to examine the relationship and balance of power between state and central governments in the country and suggest changes within the framework of Constitution of India. The Commission was so named as it was headed by Justice Rajinder Singh Sarkaria, a retired judge of the Supreme Court of India. The other two members of the committee were Shri B Sivaraman and Dr SR Sen.

29. Since 1993 the Election Commission of India has become a three member body. Originally in 1950, the commission had only a Chief Election Commissioner. Two additional Commissioners were appointed to the commission for the first time on 16 October, 1989 but they had a very short tenure, ending on 1 January, 1990.

The CEC and the two Election Commissioners who are usually retired IAS officers draw salaries and allowances as par with those of the judges of the Supreme Court of India as par the Chief Election Commissioner and other Election Commissioners Rules, 1992.

31. Systems approach is the precursor of the Ecological approach. This approach belongs to the category of modern approach. This approach makes an attempt to explain the relationship of political life with other aspects of social life. The idea of a system was originally borrowed from biology by Talcott Parsons who first popularized the concept of social system. Later on David Easton further developed the concept of a political system. According to this approach, a political system operates within the social environment. Accordingly, it is not possible to analyze political events in isolation from other aspects of the society.

In other words, influences from the society, be it economic, religious or otherwise, do shape the political process.

33. The first expert of Administrative Management Theory was Henri Fayol (1841-1925). Fayol is called the "Father of Modern Management". Henri Fayol was a French industrialist and a management consultant. He started the functional approach to management.

The other management experts who contributed to the Administrative Management schools are Mary Parker Follett, Luther Gulick, Lyndall Urwick, James Mooney, Alan Reiley, Oliver Sheldon, Ernest Dale, etc.

According to Fayol, a manager requires the following qualities and skills:

Physical qualities,

Mental qualities,

Moral qualities,

General education,

Special knowledge, and

Work experience.

34. Public Works Department (PWD) is an example of auxiliary agency. In the interest of the efficiency and economy, it was considered desirable that the departmental organization should be broken into two new directions. These new directions were 'staff agencies' and 'auxiliary agencies' as distinct from 'line agencies'.

Pfiffner does not distinguish between staff and auxiliary agencies. He includes auxiliary agencies within the term 'staff'. According to him, there are three kinds of staff services general staff, technical staff and auxiliary staff. The general staff is the staff which helps the chief or other officer in his administrative work by advice, collection of information, research and shifting of important issues from the unimportant ones.

The technical staff consists of the technical officers such as engineers, doctors, financial experts, etc. The auxiliary staff consists of officers or units which perform certain duties and functions common to the various administrative departments but which are incidental in character.

35. In politics and government, a spoils system (also known as a patronage system) is a practice in which a political party, after winning an election, gives government civil service jobs to its supporters, friends and relatives as a reward for working toward victory, and as an incentive to keep working for the party—as opposed to a merit system, where offices are awarded on the basis of some measure of merit, independent of political activity.

The term was used particularly in politics of the United States, where the federal government operated on a spoils system until the Pendleton Act was passed in 1883 due to a civil service reform movement. Thereafter, the spoils system was largely replaced by a nonpartisan merit at the federal level of the United States.

The term was derived from the phrase "to the victor belongs to the spoils" by New York Senator William L. Marcy, referring to the victory of Andrew Jackson in the election of 1828, with the term spoils meaning goods or benefits taken from the loser in a competition, election or military victory.

Similar spoils systems are common in other nations that traditionally have been based on tribal organization or other kinship groups and localism in general.

37. The L.K. Jha Committee recommended that the financial year should be from January 1 to December 31. The present financial year in India (1st April to 31st March) was adopted by the Government of India in 1867 principally to align the Indian financial year with that of the British government. Prior to 1867, the financial year in India used to commence on 1st May of the current year to 30th April of the following calendar year. Interestingly, serious demands for changing the financial year seem to be, at times, preceded by drought years or years when the monsoon rains were bad.

The most comprehensive attempt to examine this matter was when the Government of India set up a committee on change in financial year under the chairmanship of Shri L. K. Jha in 1984. This committee was formed after the country experienced major droughts in 1979-80 and 1982-83.

39. Central Vigilance Commission (CVC) is an apex Indian governmental body created in 1964 to address governmental corruption. It is a statutory and an autonomous body, free of control from any executive authority, charged with monitoring all vigilance activity under the Central Government of India, advising various authorities in central Government organizations in planning, executing, reviewing and reforming their vigilance work.

It was set up by the Government of India in February, 1964 on the recommendations of the Committee on Prevention of Corruption, headed by Shri K. Santhanam, to advise and guide Central Government agencies in the field of vigilance.

The Annual Report of the CVC not only gives the details of the work done by it but also brings out the system failures which leads to corruption in various Departments/Organisations, system improvements, various preventive measures and cases in which the Commission's advises were ignored etc.

The Commission shall consist of:

- A Central Vigilance Commissioner - Chairperson;
- Not more than two Vigilance Commissioners - Members;

40. The expenditure charged on the Consolidated Fund of India is not subject to the vote of Parliament because it is in the nature of obligatory payment. This Fund was constituted under Article 266(1) of the Constitution of India.

All revenues received by the government by way of direct taxes and indirect taxes, money borrowed and receipts from loans given by the government flow into the Consolidated Fund of India.

All governmental expenditure is made from this fund, except exceptional items which are met from the Contingency Fund or the Public Account. Importantly, no money can be withdrawn from this fund without the Parliament's approval.

41. By the combination of Logic and Rationality game theory utilizes to analyse strategic interaction among decision-makers. Game theory, also known as interactive decision theory, studies the behaviour of decision makers in situations of strategic interdependence.

Its founders are John Von Neumann and Oskar Morgenstern who published the book 'The Theory of Games and Economic Behaviour in 1944'. The relevance of the theory for International Relations (IR) goes undisputed; it is a truism to assert that states interact by trying to predict other states' reactions to their decisions.

Yet one has to apply the theory to IR, because the tool of game theory cannot produce by itself insight about IR.

42. The 'Missile Technology Control Regime' (MTCR) is a multilateral export control regime. It is an informal and voluntary partnership among 35 countries to prevent the proliferation of missile and unmanned aeriel vehicle technology capable of carrying above 500 kg payload for more than 300 km. Among 35 members India is included but China and Pakistan are excluded.

The MTCR was established in April 1987 by the G-7 countries–Canada, France, Germany, Italy, Japan, the United Kingdom, and the USA.

43. The classic Just-War Theory has its origins in Christian theology. Saint Augustine is usually identified as the first individual to offer a theory on war and justice. The Saint referred to the Bible and regarded some wars as necessary to amend an evil.

Saint Thomas Aquinas revised Augustine's version, creating three criteria for a Just war: the war needed to be waged by a legitimate authority, have a just cause, and have the right intentions.

The moral justifications for a war are expressed in jus adbellum; whereas, the moral conduct of the war is expressed in jus in bello. The Just-war theory is a set of rules for military combat.

44. The 'War on Terrorism', also known as the 'Global War on Terrorism', is an international military campaign that was launched by the U.S. government after the 9/11 attacks in the U.S. in 2001. The naming of the campaign uses a metaphor of war to refer to a variety of actions that do not constitute a specific war as traditionally defined. U.S. President George W Bush Jr. first used the term "war on terrorism" on 16 September 2001, and then "war on terror" a few days later in a formal speech to Congress. In the latter speech, George Bush stated, "Our enemy is a radical network of terrorists and every government that supports them". The term was originally used with a particular focus on countries associated with al-Qaeda.

47. India is seeking permanent membership of Security Council of UNO but having nuclear weapons does not mean you should have a permanent seat on the security council. The permanent members of the UN security council were not the states that had nuclear weapons at the time, nor were they the states that were legally allowed to have nuclear weapons, nor is nuclear capability a requirement to be a permanent member on the Security Council. When the UN was formed in 1945, only the United States had nuclear weapons; the Soviet Union didn't explode their first bomb till 1949, the UK till 1952, France till 1960, and China till 1964.

Furthermore, the treaty that says these five countries are the only ones allowed to have nuclear weapons, the Nuclear Non-proliferation Treaty, wasn't signed until 1968.

49. The Non-Aligned Movement (NAM) was created and founded during the collapse of the colonial system and the independence struggles of the peoples of Africa, Asia, Latin America and other regions of the world and at the height of the cold war.

During the early days of the movement, its actions were a key factor in the decolonization process, which led later to the attainment of freedom and independence by many countries and peoples and to the founding of tens of new sovereign states. Throughout its history, the movement of Non-Aligned countries has played a fundamental role in the preservation of world peace and security.

In 1960, in the light of the results achieved in Bandung (Bandung Asian-African Conference 1955), the creation of the Movement of Non-Aligned countries was given a decisive boost during the Fifteenth ordinary session of the United Nations General Assembly, during which 17 new African and Asian countries were admitted. A key role was played in this process by the then Heads of State and Government Gamal Abdel Nasser of Egypt, Kwame Nkrumah of Ghana, Shri Jawaharlal Nehru of India, Ahmed Sukarno of Indonesia and Josip Broz Tito of Yugoslavia, who later became the founding fathers of the movement and its emblematic leaders. The 1st conference of NAM held in September 1961 in Belgrade and its headquarters is in Jakarta.

50. The Responsibility to Protect-known as R2P-refers to the obligation of states toward their populations and toward all populations at risk of genocide and other mass atrocity crimes. In 2009, the UN Secretary-General released a report on implementing the Responsibility to Protect. R2P stipulates three pillars of responsibility.

Pillar I: Every state has the responsibility to protect its populations from four mass atrocity crimes-genocide, war crimes, crimes against humanity and ethnic cleansing.

Pillar II: The wider international community has the responsibility to encourage and assist individual states in meeting that responsibility.

Pillar III: If a state is manifestly failing to protect its populations, the international community must be prepared to take appropriate collective action, in a timely and decisive manner and in accordance with the UN charter.

PAPER-III

Note: *This paper contains* ***seventy five (75)*** *objective type questions of* ***two (2)*** *marks each. All questions are* ***compulsory.***

1. The Classical Tradition in political theory is considered to be a common school of enquiry because:

A. Unity in style and manner of argument
B. Unity in themes and style
C. Unity in searching the same goal
D. Unity in having a common vision for humankind

2. Who described the classical tradition as "Epic theory"?

A. Isaiah Berlin
B. Karl Popper
C. Sheldon Wolin
D. Michael Oakeshott

3. Match List-I with List-II and select the correct answer from the code given below:

List-I (Concepts)	***List-II (Thinkers)***
(*a*) Tacit consent	(*i*) Rawls
(*b*) Self regarding and other regarding action	(*ii*) Berlin
(*c*) Negative and positive liberty	(*iii*) Locke
(*d*) Well ordered society	(*iv*) Bentham

Code:

	(*a*)	(*b*)	(*c*)	(*d*)
A.	(*ii*)	(*i*)	(*iv*)	(*iii*)
B.	(*iii*)	(*iv*)	(*ii*)	(*i*)
C.	(*i*)	(*ii*)	(*iii*)	(*iv*)
D.	(*iv*)	(*iii*)	(*i*)	(*ii*)

4. Who feared that Marx's dictatorship of the proletariat would become dictatorship on the proletariat?

A. Lassalle
B. Proudhon
C. Bakunin
D. Luxemberg

5. Given below are two statements, one labelled as Assertion (A) and the other as Reason (R). Select the correct answer from the code given below:

Assertion (A): In spite of the fact that Rawls theory has strong procedural features it can also be seen as a major contribution to social justice.

Reason (R): He is categorical that there is a need for rational justification of all departures from equality.

Code:

A. Both (A) and (R) are true and (R) is the correct explanation of (A).
B. Both (A) and (R) are true, but (R) is not the correct explanation of (A).
C. (A) is true, but (R) is false
D. (A) is false, but (R) is true

6. Convergence theory pointed out the convergence between:

A. advanced capitalism and developed socialism
B. manufacturing nations and raw material exporting countries
C. national interests in international organizations
D. need to have common policy to fight climate change

7. Given below are two statements, one labelled as Assertion (A) and the other as Reason (R). Select the correct answer from the code given below:

Assertion (A): Lenin's revolutionary seizure of power is like a coup and negation of Marxism.

Reason (R): Marx thought a communist party would capture power peacefully.

Code:

A. Both (A) and (R) are true and (R) is the correct explanation of (A).
B. Both (A) and (R) are true, but (R) is not the correct explanation of (A).
C. (A) is true, but (R) is false.
D. (A) is false, but (R) is true.

8. Mao's most original contribution was in emphasizing the revolutionary role of the:
A. Proletariat
B. Intelligentsia
C. Combination of the proletariat and the peasantry
D. Peasantry

9. Who questioned the view that Locke was a defender of the Glorious Revolution?
A. Tawney B. Sabine
C. Macpherson D. Ashcraft

10. Which political thinker rejects Aristotle completely?
A. Machiavelli B. Hobbes
C. Locke D. Rousseau

11. Who described Rousseau as a totalitarian democrat?
A. Karl Popper B. Carl Friedrich
C. Hannah Arendt D. Jacob Talmon

12. Power, not right is the focal point for Hobbes. Why?
A. Power is more important than right.
B. Rights will entail duties.
C. There is an inherent conflict between power and right.
D. Difficult to obtain agreement among individuals.

13. Match List-I with List-II and select the correct answer from the code given below:

List-I* *(Marx's writing)	***List-II* *(Themes)***
(*a*) Paris Manuscripts	(*i*) Relative Autonomy of the state
(*b*) Das Capital	(*ii*) Dictatorship of the proletariat
(*c*) 18th Brumaire of Louis Bonaparte	(*iii*) Surplus Value
(*d*) Critique of the Gotha Programme	(*iv*) Alienation

Code:

	(*a*)	(*b*)	(*c*)	(*d*)
A.	(*i*)	(*ii*)	(*iii*)	(*iv*)
B.	(*iv*)	(*iii*)	(*i*)	(*ii*)
C.	(*iii*)	(*iv*)	(*ii*)	(*i*)
D.	(*ii*)	(*i*)	(*iv*)	(*iii*)

14. Which of the following is true of Machiavelli's political theory?
(*a*) Idolized Ancient Rome
(*b*) Used History extensively to draw lessons for state-craft
(*c*) Private army needed for the success of a prince/ruler
(*d*) Blamed religion for Italy's moral regeneration
Choose the correct answer from the code given below:
A. (*a*) and (*b*)
B. (*b*) and (*d*)
C. (*c*) and (*d*)
D. (*a*) and (*c*)

15. How did Gandhi describe himself?
A. Philosophical Anarchist
B. Liberal Democrat
C. Social Democrat
D. Communist

16. Which of the following is true of Aristotle's contribution to comparative method?
(*a*) To study the then existing political systems
(*b*) To develop an empirical science of politics
(*c*) To arrive at the Ideal type
(*d*) To apply abstract ideas in practice
Code:
A. (*a*) and (*c*) B. (*a*) and (*b*)
C. (*b*) and (*d*) D. (*c*) and (*d*)

17. New Institutionalism emphasises on:
A. Institutions rather than individuals
B. A balance between institutions and individuals
C. A group theory in politics
D. Economics dominates over politics

18. Easton described his drastic revision in political science in 1969 as:
A. Counter Reformation
B. Genuine Revolution
C. Correction to earlier studies
D. Abandoning his own earlier research

19. The essential framework of liberal political economy was provided by:
A. Locke B. Hume
C. Montesquieu D. Smith

20. What has mainly accounted for the evolution of the unwritten constitution of Great Britain?
A. The British practice of following continuity and change peacefully
B. The British acceptance of conventions as sacred as law but not enforceable in courts
C. The British belief that the 'King can do no wrong'
D. The common law tradition in Britain

21. In which country the practice of 'once a speaker always a speaker' is followed?
A. USA B. UK
C. India D. Switzerland

22. The Supreme Court's right to judicial review was first established in:
A. USA B. India
C. France D. Switzerland

23. In which of the following countries individual citizen's rights have developed by the significant intervention of the judiciary?
A. Switzerland B. U.K.
C. U.S.A. D. France

24. Match List-I with List-II and select the correct answer from the code given below:

List-I (Electoral system)	***List-II (Countries)***
(*a*) First-Past-the-Post System	(*i*) France
(*b*) Second Ballot System	(*ii*) Germany
(*c*) Alternative Vote System	(*iii*) USA
(*d*) Additional Member System	(*iv*) Australia

Code:

	(*a*)	(*b*)	(*c*)	(*d*)
A.	(*iv*)	(*iii*)	(*ii*)	(*i*)
B.	(*ii*)	(*iv*)	(*i*)	(*iii*)
C.	(*i*)	(*ii*)	(*iii*)	(*iv*)
D.	(*iii*)	(*i*)	(*iv*)	(*ii*)

25. Given below are those statements, one labelled as Assertion (A) and the other as Reason (R). Select the correct answer from the code given below:
Assertion (A): The theories of development of the 1950's like behaviouralism, could never develop an universally accepted paradigm because they were locally dated.
Reason (R) : They originated during the Cold War period and consequently biased.
Code:
A. Both (A) and (R) are true and (R) is the correct explanation of (A).
B. Both (A) and (R) are true, but (R) is not the correct explanation of (A).
C. (A) is true, but (R) is false.
D. (A) is false, but (R) is true.

26. Political Socialization deals with:
A. Process of formulating political ideas
B. Career planning and political socialization
C. Elaborating the theories of Durkheim
D. Elaborating the theories of Weber

27. Subject - participatory culture was associated with:
A. Erstwhile communist regimes
B. Fascist regimes
C. Post Colonial Societies
D. Non Ideological dictatorships

28. Who has commented that politics is about diversity and conflict and the essential ingredient of its existence is scarcity?
A. Leftwich B. Lasswell
C. Crick D. Millett

29. Huntington criticizes the modernization theory for not taking into account:
A. Presence of several competing value systems or cultures in traditional society
B. The difference between base and superstructure
C. The question of leadership
D. Overdeveloped nature of modernizing nations

30. Who among the following provided an economic approach to elitism?
A. Pareto B. Mosca
C. Mills D. Burnham

31. According to whom the Indian Constitution aimed at the tripartite goal of national unity, democracy and social revolution as three distinct strands interwoven into a "seamless web"?

A. W.H. Morris Jones B. Rajni Kothari
C. Granville Austin D. Sunil Khilnani

32. Which of the following grounds come within the ambit of reasonable restrictions put by the state on the exercise of freedom under Article 19 of the Indian Constitution?
(*a*) Security of state
(*b*) Public order
(*c*) Decency or morality
(*d*) Contempt of court

Select the correct answer from the code given below:
A. (*a*) and (*b*) only
B. (*a*) and (*d*) only
C. (*a*), (*b*) and (*c*) only
D. (*a*), (*b*), (*c*) and (*d*)

33. Once approved by Parliament for how long can the proclamation of financial emergency remain in operation?
A. 2 months
B. 3 years
C. Till the term of that Parliament
D. Indefinitely

34. Consider the following statements about the Vice-President of India and select the correct answer from the code given below:
(*a*) Elected by the system of proportional representation by a single transferable vote
(*b*) Elected by all the members of the Lok Sabha and the Rajya Sabha
(*c*) Members of State Assemblies have no right to vote
(*d*) He is the Chairman of the Rajya Sabha

Code:
A. (*a*) and (*b*)
B. (*b*), (*c*) and (*d*)
C. (*a*), (*b*), (*c*) and (*d*)
D. (*a*), (*b*) and (*c*)

35. Arrange the chronological order of the following cases and select the correct answer from the code given below:
(*a*) Bandhua Mukti Morcha V. Union of India
(*b*) M.C. Mehta V. Union of India
(*c*) ADM Jabalpur V. Shiv Kant Shukla
(*d*) BALCO Employees Union V. Union of India

Code:
A. (*c*), (*a*), (*b*), (*d*) B. (*a*), (*d*), (*c*), (*b*)
C. (*d*), (*b*), (*a*), (*c*) D. (*b*), (*a*), (*d*), (*c*)

36. Which of the following principles evolved from the judgement delivered in Bommai case in relation to Article 356?

Choose correct answer from the code given below:
(*a*) The proclamation issued under Article 356 is subject to judicial review
(*b*) The state Assembly should not be dissolved immediately after issuing proclamation
(*c*) The Assembly should be dissolved only after the Parliament has approved the proclamation
(*d*) The court may require the Union Government to disclose the material on the basis of which it was decided to invoke Art. 356

Code:
A. (*b*) and (*c*) B. (*a*), (*c*) and (*d*)
C. (*a*), (*b*) and (*d*) D. (*a*), (*b*), (*c*) and (*d*)

37. Justice Punchhi Commission is related to:
A. Urban Governance
B. Union - State Relations
C. District Administration
D. Electoral Reforms

38. Match List-I with List-II and select the correct answer from the code given below:

List-I ***(Center's Accord with)***	***List-II*** ***(Year)***
(*a*) Assam	(*i*) 1988
(*b*) Mizoram	(*ii*) 1985
(*c*) Tripura	(*iii*) 1985
(*d*) Punjab	(*iv*) 1986

Code:

	(*a*)	(*b*)	(*c*)	(*d*)
A.	(*iv*)	(*ii*)	(*iii*)	(*i*)
B.	(*ii*)	(*iv*)	(*i*)	(*iii*)
C.	(*iii*)	(*i*)	(*iv*)	(*ii*)
D.	(*i*)	(*iii*)	(*ii*)	(*iv*)

39. Which committee felt that the Panchayati Raj institutions could have survived well if they had been encouraged well by entrusting responsibilities as a "vanguard of development in village India"?

A. Asoka Mehta B. L.M. Singhvi
C. G V K Rao D. P.K. Thungan

40. Who was the Chief Election Commissioner who wrote a letter to the President of India recommending the removal of Election Commissioner?

A. Navin Chawla B. N. Gopalaswami
C. T.N. Seshan D. M.S. Gill

41. Given below are two statements, one labelled as Assertion (A) and the other labelled as Reason (R). Select the correct answer from the code given below:

Assertion (A): Law and order is the responsibility of the District Magistrate.

Reason (R) : Law and order is still one of the major problems in India.

Code:

A. Both (A) and (R) are true and (R) is the correct explanation of (A).
B. Both (A) and (R) are true, but (R) is not the correct explanation of (A).
C. (A) is true, but (R) is false.
D. (A) is false, but (R) is true.

42. Match List-I with List-II and select the correct answer from the code given below:

List-I (State)	***List-II (State Parties)***
(*a*) Bihar	(*i*) Apna Dal
(*b*) West Bengal	(*ii*) Indian National Lok Dal
(*c*) Uttar Pradesh	(*iii*) Revolutionary Socialist Party
(*d*) Haryana	(*iv*) Lok Janshakti Party

Code:

	(*a*)	(*b*)	(*c*)	(*d*)
A.	(*iii*)	(*ii*)	(*i*)	(*iv*)
B.	(*iv*)	(*iii*)	(*i*)	(*ii*)
C.	(*ii*)	(*i*)	(*iii*)	(*iv*)
D.	(*i*)	(*iv*)	(*ii*)	(*iii*)

43. Who of the following was **not** a member of the *Towards Equality* report?

A. Lotika Sarkar B. Neera Dogra
C. Vina Mazumdar D. Sushila Nayar

44. Match List-I with List-II and select the correct answer from the code given below:

List-I (Type of Pressure Groups)	***List-II (Name of Pressure Groups)***
(*a*) Based on traditional social structure	(*i*) Associated Chamber of Commerce and Industry in India
(*b*) Based on labour interest	(*ii*) Nair Service Society
(*c*) Based on institutional interest	(*iii*) Delhi University Teacher's Association
(*d*) Based on business interest	(*iv*) Hind Mazdoor Parishad

Code:

	(*a*)	(*b*)	(*c*)	(*d*)
A.	(*i*)	(*iii*)	(*iv*)	(*ii*)
B.	(*ii*)	(*iv*)	(*iii*)	(*i*)
C.	(*iii*)	(*ii*)	(*i*)	(*iv*)
D.	(*iv*)	(*i*)	(*ii*)	(*iii*)

45. Which of the following are the main problems of nation building in India ? Select the correct answer from the code given below:

(*a*) Poverty
(*b*) Illiteracy
(*c*) Trade Unions
(*d*) Corruption
(*e*) Regional Political Parties
(*f*) Terrorism

Code:

A. (*a*), (*b*), (*e*), (*f*) B. (*a*), (*c*), (*d*), (*e*), (*f*)
C. (*a*), (*b*), (*d*), (*f*) D. (*b*), (*d*), (*e*), (*f*)

46. Which of the following are the models of reforms identified by Peters as alternatives to the traditional public administration?

(*a*) Market Model
(*b*) Participatory State Model
(*c*) Flexible Government Model
(*d*) Deregulated Government Model

Select the correct answer from the code given below:
A. (*a*) and (*b*)
B. (*a*) and (*c*)
C. (*a*), (*c*) and (*d*)
D. (*a*), (*b*), (*c*) and (*d*)

47. Arrange the following administrative thinkers in chronological order:
(*a*) Willoughby
(*b*) M.P. Follet
(*c*) F.W. Riggs
(*d*) Robert Dahl

Select the correct answer from the code given below:
A. (*b*), (*a*), (*d*) and (*c*)
B. (*a*), (*b*), (*c*) and (*d*)
C. (*b*), (*a*), (*c*) and (*d*)
D. (*a*), (*c*), (*b*) and (*d*)

48. Who among the following gave the 4P-Formula for departmental Organisation?
A. Fayol
B. Urwick
C. Gulick
D. Mooney

49. Given below are two statements, one labelled as Assertion (A) and other labelled as Reason (R). Select the correct answer from the code given below:

Assertion (A): Herbert Simon has ridiculed the classical theory of organisation as a machine model theory.

Reason (R) : Classicists are too much pre-occupied with the formal structural part of organisation and that too at the cost of human factors.

Code:
A. Both (A) and (R) are true and (R) is the correct explanation of (A).
B. Both (A) and (R) are true, but (R) is not the correct explanation of (A).
C. (A) is true, but (R) is false.
D. (A) is false, but (R) is true.

50. Which of the following statements is **not** correct about the Right to Information Act?
A. The Right to Information Act came into force on 12 October 2005.
B. The Freedom of Information Act, 2002 has been repealed.
C. The Official Secrets Act, 1923 has also been repealed.
D. Central Information Commission and State Information Commissions have been constituted.

51. 73rd Constitutional Amendment provided for:
(*a*) Constitutional status to rural and urban bodies
(*b*) Three-tier system for all Panchayati Raj Institutions
(*c*) Direct elections of Chairpersons and members of Panchayati Raj Institutions at all levels
(*d*) Audit of panchayat funds by CAG

Select the correct answer from the code given below:
A. (*b*) only
B. (*a*) and (*b*) only
C. (*a*), (*b*) and (*c*)
D. (*a*), (*b*) and (*d*)

52. The Central Information Commission consists of the Chief Information Commissioner and Information Commissioners:
A. not exceeding three in number
B. not exceeding five in number
C. not exceeding seven in number
D. not exceeding ten in number

53. Who among the following said, "Development administration is an action-oriented and goal-oriented administrative system"?
A. F.W. Riggs
B. Edward Weidner
C. Ferrel Heady
D. H. Walker

54. Which of the following are the voluntary provisions of the 73rd Constitutional Amendment Act 1992?
(*a*) Providing reservation for backward classes
(*b*) Setting up a State Finance Commission
(*c*) Making the Panchayats autonomous bodies
(*d*) Giving the Panchayats financial powers in relation to taxes, fees, etc.

Select the correct answer from the code given below:

A. *(a)* and *(b)* B. *(b)*, *(c)* and *(d)*
C. *(a)*, *(b)* and *(c)* D. *(a)*, *(c)* and *(d)*

55. Match List-I with List-II and select the correct answer from the code given below:

List-I	*List-II*
(a) Hota Committee	*(i)* Centre-State Relations
(b) Santhanam Committee	*(ii)* Civil-Service Reforms
(c) Sarkaria Commission	*(iii)* Prevention of Corruption
(d) Yashpal Committee	*(iv)* Higher Education Reforms

Code:

	(a)	*(b)*	*(c)*	*(d)*
A.	*(i)*	*(ii)*	*(iii)*	*(iv)*
B.	*(ii)*	*(iii)*	*(i)*	*(iv)*
C.	*(ii)*	*(i)*	*(iii)*	*(iv)*
D.	*(iv)*	*(ii)*	*(i)*	*(iii)*

56. Promotion to higher position involves:
(a) Change of title
(b) Change of pay
(c) Change of duties
(d) Change of responsibility

Select the correct answer from the code given below:

A. *(a)* and *(b)* only B. *(b)* and *(c)* only
C. *(a)*, *(c)* and *(d)* D. *(a)*, *(b)*, *(c)* and *(d)*

57. The process by which the selected candidate is sent for an appointment is known as:
A. Selection B. Appointment
C. Certification D. Placement

58. Defending policy is the function of:
A. Line agency
B. Staff agency
C. Auxiliary agency
D. Both Staff and Line agencies

59. Who among the following are the critics of the bureaucratic theory?
(a) Talcott Parsons
(b) Michel Crozier
(c) Robert Presthus
(d) F.W. Riggs

Select the correct answer from the code given below:
A. *(a)* and *(b)* only
B. *(b)* and *(d)* only
C. *(b)*, *(c)* and *(d)*
D. *(a)*, *(b)*, *(c)* and *(d)*

60. Who among the following rejected the politics-administration dichotomy?
A. Woodrow Wilson
B. Frank Goodnow
C. Herbert Simon
D. Robert Merton

61. Who was of the opinion that survival depends on a state's material capabilities and its alliances with other states?
A. John Mearsheimer B. Kenneth Waltz
C. Thucydides D. J. Snyder

62. Consider the following statements:
(a) Neo realism and neo liberalism are rationalist approaches
(b) Neo realism and feminism are reflectivist approaches
(c) Post-structuralism and neo liberalism are rationalist approaches
(d) Feminism and post-structuralism are reflectivist approaches

Select the correct answer from the code given below:
A. *(a)* and *(b)* B. *(a)*, *(c)* and *(d)*
C. *(a)*, *(b)* and *(d)* D. *(a)* and *(d)*

63. Which of the following statements are **true** about soft power?
(a) Soft power can be used by state actors
(b) Soft power can be used by non state actors
(c) Soft power is the second face of power
(d) Soft power is a form of idealism

Select the correct answer from the code given below:
A. *(a)*, *(b)* and *(d)* B. *(b)*, *(c)* and *(d)*
C. *(a)*, *(b)* and *(c)* D. *(c)*, *(d)* and *(a)*

64. Which one of the following is **not** a Kantian influence that acts as a constraint on War ?
A. Democracies will refrain from using force against other democracies

B. Economically important trade creates incentives to maintain peaceful relations
C. Global civil society exerts itself
D. International organisations can constrain decision makers by promoting peace

65. Find out the incorrect statement/s about Johan Galtung's models of conflict, violence and peace:
(*a*) He suggested that conflict could be viewed as triangle with contradiction, attitude and behaviour
(*b*) He talked of structural, cultural, direct and indirect violence
(*c*) He discussed about peace building, peace making and peace keeping
(*d*) He explained about direct war, proxy war and intrastate

Code:
A. (*a*) and (*d*) B. (*b*) and (*c*)
C. (*a*) and (*c*) D. (*a*), (*b*) and (*c*)

66. Match List-I with List-II and select the correct answer from the code given below:

List-I (Authors)	***List-II (Books)***
(*a*) Stephen Kraser	(*i*) Empire of Civil Society
(*b*) J. Rosenberg	(*ii*) From International to World Society
(*c*) E.M. Wood	(*iii*) International Regimes
(*d*) Barry Buzan	(*iv*) Empire of Capital

Code:

	(*a*)	(*b*)	(*c*)	(*d*)
A.	(*iii*)	(*ii*)	(*i*)	(*iv*)
B.	(*iii*)	(*i*)	(*iv*)	(*ii*)
C.	(*iv*)	(*ii*)	(*i*)	(*iii*)
D.	(*ii*)	(*i*)	(*iv*)	(*iii*)

67. Which one of the following pair is mismatched?
A. World or Global Security - World community or human kind
B. Societal Security - Societal needs
C. Economic Security - Welfare
D. Environmental Security - Resources

68. Which of the following have emphasis in India's nuclear deterrent:
A. Large numbers and deterrent force
B. Nuclear parity and capability to retaliate
C. Small numbers and capability to deter
D. Deterrent force and nuclear parity

69. Consider the following statements about National Security Council (NSCI) of India :
(*a*) It's a three tier organisation consisting of strategic policy group, joint intelligence committee and National Security Advisory Board.
(*b*) Ministers for External Affairs, Defence, Home, Finance and Commerce are its members
(*c*) It was formed in the year 1998
(*d*) The former National Security Advisers were Brajesh Mishra, J.N. Dixit, K.P. Singh.

Select the correct answer from the code given below?
A. (*d*), (*c*) and (*a*) B. (*a*) and (*b*)
C. (*c*), (*d*) and (*b*) D. (*a*) and (*d*)

70. Which one of the following is/are incorrect statement/s:
(*a*) The 'Neemrana Dialogue' is on India - China Relations
(*b*) The 'Ottawa Dialogue' is on India - Pakistan Relations
(*c*) Shangri-La Dialogue is on India - Singapore Relations
(*d*) Raisina Dialogue is India's flagship conference of geopolitics and geoeconomics

Code:
A. (*a*), (*b*) and (*c*) B. (*b*), (*c*) and (*d*)
C. (*a*) and (*c*) D. (*c*) and (*d*)

71. Consider the following statements about India's role in United Nations. Which of the statements are correct?
(*a*) India is a major contributor to UN Democracy Fund
(*b*) Indian delegation to San Francisco Conference of 1945 was led by Vijayalakshmi Pandit
(*c*) In 2001, India piloted a draft comprehensive convention on International Terrorism

(*d*) India submitted along with other countries an Action Plan for phased elimination of nuclear weapons 1996-2020

Select the correct answer from the code given below:

A. (*a*), (*c*) and (*d*) B. (*a*), (*b*) and (*c*)
C. (*a*) and (*d*) D. (*c*) and (*d*)

72. Given below are two statements, one labelled as Assertion (A) and the other labelled as Reason (R). Select the correct answer from the codes given below:

Assertion (A): States continue to exist as sovereign states.

Reason (R) : Globalization has weakened the Westphalian state system.

Code:

A. Both (A) and (R) are true and (R) is the correct explanation of (A).
B. Both (A) and (R) are true, but (R) is not the correct explanation of (A).
C. (A) is true, but (R) is false.
D. (R) is true, but (A) is false.

73. Match the List-I with List-II and select the correct answer from the code given below:

List-I	***List-II***
(*a*) Wassenaar Agreement	(*i*) Stopping spread of chemical and biological weapons
(*b*) Australia Group	(*ii*) Non-proliferation of nuclear weapons
(*c*) Nuclear Suppliers Group	(*iii*) Export control for conventional arms and dual use technologies
(*d*) Missile Technology Control Regime	(*iv*) Non-proliferation of systems intended for the delivery of WMD

Code:

	(*a*)	(*b*)	(*c*)	(*d*)
A.	(*iii*)	(*i*)	(*ii*)	(*iv*)
B.	(*iii*)	(*ii*)	(*i*)	(*iv*)
C.	(*iv*)	(*ii*)	(*iii*)	(*i*)
D.	(*ii*)	(*iii*)	(*iv*)	(*i*)

74. Which one of the following statements is incorrect?

A. New Development Bank is a multilateral development bank established by BRICS
B. Asian Intrastructure Investment Bank is an initiative of China
C. WTO recognises least developed countries as those which are designated as such by UNO
D. International Finance Corporation offers political risk insurance and encourages private sector development in developing countries

75. Consider the following statements with regard to Security Council:

(*a*) India became member of Security Council seven times
(*b*) Japan became a member of Security Council eleven times
(*c*) It appoints non-permanent members
(*d*) It appoints Secretary General

Select the correct answer from the code given below:

A. (*a*) and (*b*) B. (*b*) and (*c*)
C. (*b*) and (*d*) D. (*d*) and (*a*)

ANSWERS

1	2	3	4	5	6	7	8	9	10
A	C	B	C	A	A	C	D	D	B
11	**12**	**13**	**14**	**15**	**16**	**17**	**18**	**19**	**20**
D	D	B	A	A	B	A	B	D	D
21	**22**	**23**	**24**	**25**	**26**	**27**	**28**	**29**	**30**
B	A	C	D	A	A	A	B	A	D

31	32	33	34	35	36	37	38	39	40
C	D	D	C	A	D	B	B	A	B
41	**42**	**43**	**44**	**45**	**46**	**47**	**48**	**49**	**50**
A	B	D	B	C	D	A	C	A	C
51	**52**	**53**	**54**	**55**	**56**	**57**	**58**	**59**	**60**
A	D	B	D	B	D	C	A	D	C
61	**62**	**63**	**64**	**65**	**66**	**67**	**68**	**69**	**70**
B	D	C	C	B	B	B	C	B	C
71	**72**	**73**	**74**	**75**					
C	B	A	D	A					

EXPLANATORY ANSWERS

1. Courses in political theory normally offer detailed and elaborate study of books or particular political philosophies from Plato to contemporary times, from a historical perspective. These books are studied for their normative statements about the desirability of certain types of institutions, governments and laws, which are generally accompanied by rational arguments. The classics are portrayed as timeless in quality, permanent in relevance and universal in their significance. The classical tradition demonstrates a great deal of unity in style and manner of argument, which is why it constitutes a common school of enquiry. However, in spite of this intrinsic unity, the classic offer divergent interpretations of politics, and this makes their study useful for understanding contemporary politics.

2. Sheldon Wolin described the classical tradition as "Epic theory". One of Wolin's central arguments was that the western tradition of political philosophy was often antidemocratic and antipolitical in nature. Classical political philosophy and modern political economy emerged in moments of institutional crisis, when the reigning powers were becoming increasingly illegitimate and civil war was on the horizon. They sought, therefore, not to democratize politics but to close it off. Classical thought attempted to do this by substituting philosophy for public opinion, philosopher kings for participation. Liberal and Marxist theorists hoped to use economic policies in order to create societies that were no longer riven by social divisions. The constitutive features of democratic politics were neglected if not intentionally suppressed.

4. Mikhail Bakunin feared that Marx's dictatorship of the proletariat would become dictatorship on the proletariat. The dictatorship of the proletariat originally was conceived by Karl Marx as a dictatorship by the Majority class. Because Marx regarded all governments as class dictatorships, he viewed proletarian dictatorship as no worse than any other form of government. However, the Bolshevik Revolution in Russia in 1917 resulted in a dictatorship not of the majority class of proletarians but of a political party that claimed to represent proletarian interests. Contrary to Marx's vision and as George Orwell, Bakunin and others had foreseen, the proposed dictatorship of the proletariat eventually became a dictatorship of former proletarians.

6. Convergence theory pointed out the convergence between advanced capitalism and developed socialism. From the point of view of its class essence, the convergence theory is a refined form of apology for capitalism. Although it appears to place itself above capitalism and socialism and seems to advocate some undefined "integrated" economic system, it essentially proposes a synthesis of the two systems on a capitalist basis, on the basis of private ownership of the means of production. Since the convergence theory is above all a variant of contemporary bourgeois and reformist ideological doctrines, it also fulfills quite a specific practical function: its advocates attempt to provide the capitalist countries with ways to establish "social peace" and propose that the socialist countries enact measures toward a rapprochement of the socialist and capitalist economies via a so-called socialism.

8. Mao's most original contribution was in emphasizing the revolutionary role of the peasantry. The central mission of Maoist revolutionary strategies concerned mass mobilization. In particular, Mao emphasized the importance of taking the peasants as the main force of the Chinese revolution. This clearly distinguished Maoism from the urban, working-class-centered mobilization strategies favoured by orthodox Marxism-Leninism. Yet Mao's dependence on peasants drove him into a fundamental dilemma in furthering his "continuous revolution" after 1949. While adhering to the populist belief that the peasants' spontaneous "revolutionary initiatives" represented a natural source of the "revolution after revolution", Mao was simultaneously obsessed by the "petty bourgeois tendency" of the peasants in practical life. When the "socialist planning economy", which made industrial development the top priority, encountered resistance from the peasants, Mao argued that "a serious question is how to educate the peasants".

9. Locke has been interpreted very differently by Laslett, Macpherson and Ashcraft. Laslett convincingly demonstrated that Locke was neither a spokesman of Whig Orthodoxy nor a defender of the Glorious Revolution of 1688. Macpherson, in contrast, analyzed Locke as an apologist and a theorist of bourgeois society. Ashcraft drew attention to Locke's radicalism by his active involvement in the revolutionary process. Ashcraft interprets Locke as revolutionary and that has created problems for both the left and right. All along, the left and the Marxists interpreted Locke as an apologist of bourgeois society. The right found it equally discomfiting to accept that the Glorious Revolution had a revolutionary side to it. All along, they projected it as a symbol of the international and evolutionary process of change.

10. According to Hobbes, there is liberty where there is the possibility for physically unconstrained action. He rejects Aristotle's view of different levels of voluntary and involuntary actions, according to a variety of constraining circumstances by pointing to the possibility of unconstrained physical actions in all these circumstances. In particular he rejects Aristotle's famous claim that throwing goods off a ship during a storm is a largely involuntary action because it is done to preserve life. This has a political point, which is that physical liberty exists however many laws the sovereign passes constraining actions, so we should not criticise any government for constraining liberty.

Hobbes criticises any idea that a political community can be based on voluntary agreements, contracts and customs. A *polis*, political community, only exists where a sovereign can enforce obedience to laws. Hobbes believes that Aristotle regarded a *polis* as a purely voluntary arrangement between free citizens unconstrained by any sovereign.

Hobbes implicitly rejects Aristotle's account of the importance of friendship in a *polity*. For Aristotle, friendship is necessary to a happy life and while friendship can involve self-interest it can also rest on shared virtues and desire for the good. Friendship connects citizens into a *polity* and is the correct attitude of the ruler to citizens. Hobbes defines friendship as mutual self-interest only. Even if we think this is too strong, we could produce the more moderate statement that most friendship includes some shared self-interest. This would be enough to undermine any claim that a*polis* can be unified by virtuous friendship, or that the ruler could be god ruler by regarding everyone in the *polis* as friends. What Hobbes is moving towards is the idea that a community is unified by commerce and economic activity, which does not exclude virtue but certainly requires self-interest, as Hume and Smith will discuss in the following century.

Democracy does not guarantee more liberty despite Aristotle's claim that democracy is based on liberty. A point Hobbs supports with reference to the Ancient Athenian practice of exiling unpopular personalities purely on the basis of a vote, not because they were convicted of a crime.

11. Jacob Talmon described Rousseau as a totalitarian democrat.

Talmon's 1952 book '*The Origins of Totalitarian Democracy*' discusses the transformation of a state in which traditional values and articles of faith shape the role of government into one in which social utility takes absolute precedence. His work is a criticism of the ideas of Jean-Jacques Rousseau, a Swiss philosopher whose ideas influenced the French Revolution. In *The Social Contract*, Rousseau contends that the interests of the individual and the state are one and the same, and it is the state's responsibility to implement the "general will".

12. Power, not right is the focal point for Hobbes because difficult to obtain agreement among individuals. The question of power is central to the study of politics. Thomas Hobbes has been hailed as the author of the greatest political philosophy written in the English language, and indeed as the philosopher of power par excellence. Nonetheless, I argue that conceptualizing political power is a problem for Hobbes. He starts with a common sense view that understands the power of individuals as their natural faculties, and that then envisages these powers being compounded together by covenant to form the power of a commonwealth.

14. Idolized Ancient Rome and used History extensively to draw lessons for statecraft are true of Machiavelli's political theory. Many scholars have taken such evidence to indicate that Machiavelli was himself profoundly anti-Christian, preferring the pagan civil religions of ancient societies such as Rome, which he regarded to be more suitable for a city endowed with *virtù*.

Anthony Parel argues that Machiavelli's cosmos, governed by the movements of the stars and the balance of the humours, takes on an essentially pagan and pre-Christian cast. For others, Machiavelli may best be described as a man of conventional, if unenthusiastic, piety, prepared to bow to the externalities of worship but not deeply devoted in either soul or mind to the tenets of Christian faith.

15. Gandhi describes himself as philosophical anarchist. Philosophical anarchism is an anarchist school of thought which holds that the state lacks moral legitimacy while not supporting violence to eliminate it. Though philosophical anarchism does not necessarily imply any action or desire for the elimination of the state, philosophical anarchists do not believe that they have an obligation or duty to obey the state, or conversely, that the state has a right to command. Philosophical anarchism is a component especially of individualist anarchism.

Philosophical anarchists of historical note include Gandhi, William Godwin, Proudhon, Herbert Spencer, Henry David Thoreau, etc. Contemporary philosophical anarchists include A. John Simmons, Robert Paul Wolff and Michael Huemer.

Philosophical anarchists may accept the existence of a minimal state as an unfortunate, and usually temporary, "necessary evil" but argue that citizens do not have a moral obligation to obey the state when its laws conflict with individual autonomy.

16. To study the then existing political systems and to develop an empirical science of politics are true of Aristotle's contribution to comparative method. Though the comparative approach to politics is of recent origin, it was greatness of Aristotle to use it to study 158 constitutions. Aristotle remains the first to make an attempt to separate politics from ethics by use of scientific methods to analyze political issue. Unlike his master and predecessors, Aristotle engaged himself in analyzing a wide variety of political issues. What was more significant was his use of scientific method. Perhaps this explains the reason why he is hailed as more pragmatic political scientist.

17. New Institutionalism (Neoinstitutionalism) is a methodological approach in the study of political science, economics, organizational behaviour and sociology in the United States that explores how institutional structures, rules, norms and cultures constrain the choices and actions of individuals when they are part of a political institution. Such methodology became prominent in the 1980s among scholars of U.S. politics. That so-called new institutionalism combined the interests of traditionalist scholars, with behaviouralist scholars, who examined the actions of individual political actors.

The new institutionalist approach has its roots in the early to mid-1980s. Often considered two of the leading founders of the new institutionalism, American political scientist James G. March and Norwegian political scientist Johan P. Olsen published a very influential piece, "The New Institutionalism : Organizational Factors in Political Life – 1984", followed by a book, "Rediscovering Institutions : The Organizational Basis of Politics – 1989". They continued to argue for further institutional analysis in "Democratic Governance – 1995". In each piece, March and Olsen argued that political scientists needed to rediscover institutional analysis in order to better understand the behaviour of individual political actors within political institutions. In other words, according to those authors, studying individual political behaviour without examining institutional constraints on that behaviour was giving scholars a skewed understanding of political reality.

18. David Easton has enumerated some basic features of post-behaviouralism. In the first place, according to Easton, as behaviouralism was the outcome of dissatisfaction against traditionalism, post-behaviouralism also denotes "deep dissatisfaction with political research and teaching".

Post-behaviouralism strives to convert political science into a rigorous scientific discipline. It must be based on solid foundation so that it can cope with the emergent issues that were plaguing American society. While behaviouralism heavily emphasised the methods and techniques and neglected many burning questions of the present-day society.

In the second place, post-behavioural revolution chalks out a scheme for the future and in that sense it is future-oriented. The chief objective of this approach is to provide a new direction for political science. What the subject wants to do in the coming years post-behaviouralism wants to emphasise that.

It has no intention to go back to an imaginary golden age of political science and research. Dealing with post-behaviouralism as a revolution Easton makes the following observation: "Post-behaviouralism seeks to propel political science in new directions.... This new development is then a genuine revolution, not a reaction, a becoming, not a preservation, a reform and not a counter-reformation". So we find that post-behaviouralism never makes any attempt to look backwards, it is not willing to remain satisfied with what has happened. Its motto is to go ahead.

Thirdly, post-behaviouralism is both a movement and an intellectual tendency. We have already noted that post-behaviouralism is future-oriented; it has an ambition and wants to lead political science to a particular direction. In order to achieve this ambitious goal, post-behaviouralism must be converted into a movement. Here the word movement is a misnomer.

Movement does not mean agitation made by some political parties or groups. Continuous and serious efforts are to be made for the realisation of goals. Again, according to Easton, it is an intellectual tendency. Research methods, adopted by post-behaviouralists include rigorous scientific and statistical methods.

The appeal of post-behaviouralists is not to those persons who are disinterested in the subject or those who are the common people. Its appeal is to young graduated political scientists or old members of the profession. Ordinary people may not be interested in what we call post-behaviouralism or behaviouralism.

Even the members of other professions are not supposed to take interest in post-behaviouralism. Easton has further claimed that post-behaviouralism is a genuine revolution and not a reaction. It does not deny the importance of traditionalism or past heritage. It respectfully recollects the past, the contribution of past political scientists. It chiefly wants to say that society is undergoing constant changes and a suitable political research must comprehend them.

19. The essential framework of liberal political economy was provided by Adam Smith. Smith is best known as the author of "An Inquiry into the Nature and Causes of the Wealth of Nations–1776", one of the most influential books ever written. The Wealth of Nations deeply influenced the politicians of the time and provided the intellectual foundation of the great 19th century era of free trade and economic expansion. Even today the common sense of free trade is accepted worldwide, whatever the practical difficulties of achieving it.

20. The Common Law tradition in Britain has mainly accounted for the evolution of the unwritten constitution of Great Britain. Constitutions organise, distribute and regulate state power. They set out the structure of the state, the major state institutions, and the principles governing their relations with each other and with the state's citizens. Britain is unusual in that it has an 'unwritten' constitution: unlike the great majority of countries there is no single legal document which sets out in one place the fundamental laws outlining how the state works. Britain's lack of a 'written' constitution can be explained by its history. In other countries, many of whom have experienced revolution or regime change, it has been necessary to start from scratch or begin from first principles, constructing new state institutions and defining in detail their relations with each other and their citizens. By contrast, the British Constitution has evolved over a long period of time, reflecting the relative stability of the British polity. It has never been thought necessary to consolidate the basic building blocks of this order in Britain. What Britain has instead is an accumulation of various statutes, conventions, judicial decisions and treaties which collectively can be referred to as the British Constitution. It is thus more accurate to refer to Britain's constitution as an 'uncodified' constitution, rather than an 'unwritten' one.

21. In UK, the practice of 'once a speaker always a speaker' is followed. Speakers still stand in general elections. They are generally unopposed by the major political parties, who will not field a candidate in the speaker's constituency—this includes the original party they were a member of. During a general election, speakers do not campaign on any political issues but simply stand as 'the speaker seeking re-election'.

Speakers must be politically impartial. Therefore, on election the new speaker must resign from their political party and remain separate from political issues even in retirement. However, the speaker will deal with their constituents' problems like a normal MP.

22. The Supreme Court's right to judicial review was first established in USA. Judicial review is a process under which executive and legislative actions are subject to review by the judiciary. The power of courts to assess whether a law is in compliance with the constitution. A court with judicial review power may invalidate laws and decisions that are incompatible with a higher authority, an executive decision may be invalidated for being unlawful or a statute may be invalidated for violating the terms of a written constitution. Judicial review is one of the checks and balances in the separation of powers: the power of the judiciary to supervise the legislative and executive branches when the latter exceed their authority. The doctrine varies between jurisdictions, so the procedure and scope of judicial review may differ between and within countries.

23. Individuals in the United States enjoy a number of important civil liberties under the U.S. Constitution. When people talk about constitutional rights like freedom of speech or religion, they often refer to them as guarantees. But no rights are absolute. Government has the power to limit individuals' freedom under certain circumstances, like when they've committed a crime. And the First Amendment doesn't protect some speech, such as violent threats.

Still, the U.S. Supreme Court has held that certain rights are so "fundamental" that any law restricting them must have an especially strong purpose and be narrowly targeted to serve that purpose without unnecessary restrictions (the legal test known as "strict scrutiny"). Most of those rights are spelled out in the first ten amendments to the Constitution, known as the Bill of Rights, as well as the Fourteenth Amendment. The Supreme Court has also recognized other fundamental rights that aren't specifically mentioned in the Constitution or its amendments.

26. Political socialization is a lifelong process by which people form their ideas about politics and acquire political values. The family, educational systems, peer groups and the mass media all play a role. While family and school are important early in life, what our peers think and what we read in the newspaper and see on television have more influence on our political attitudes as adults.

27. Subject-participatory culture was associated with erstwhile communist regimes the term '**political culture**' is used in the field of social science. It refers to historically-based, widely-shared beliefs, feelings, and values about the nature of political systems, which can serve as a link between citizens and government. Different countries have different political cultures, which can help us understand how and why their governments are organized in a certain way, why democracies succeed or fail, or why some countries still have monarchies. Understanding our own political culture can also provide clues to political relationships, such as those we share with each other or our governments.

In 1963, two political scientists, **Gabriel Almond** and **Sydney Verba**, published a study of the political cultures associated with five democratic countries: Germany, Italy, Mexico, the United Kingdom, and the United States. According to Almond and Verba, there are three basic types of political culture, which can be used to explain why people do or do not participate in political processes.

In a **parochial political culture**, like Mexico, citizens are mostly uninformed and unaware of their government and take little interest in the political process. In a **subject political culture**, such as those found in Germany and Italy, citizens are somewhat informed and aware of their government and occasionally participate in the political process. In a **participant political culture**, like the United Kingdom and the United States, citizens are informed and actively participate in the political process.

28. **Politics as power:** This is the broadest and the most radical definition of politics. At its broadest, politics concerns the production, distribution and use of resources in the course of social existence. Politics is, in essence, power: the ability to achieve a desired outcome, through whatever means. This notion was neatly summed up in the title of Harold Lasswell's book Politics: Who Gets What, When, How? (1936). From this perspective, politics is about diversity and conflict, but the essential ingredient is the existence of scarcity: the simple fact that, while human needs and desires are infinite, the resources available to satisfy them are always limited. Politics can therefore be seen as a struggle over scarce resources, and power can be seen as the means through which this struggle is conducted. Politics, in this view, is everywhere; indeed, given the widespread potential for power-related conflict, politics may come to be seen as co-extensive with social existence itself.

29. ***Political Order in Changing Societies*** is a 1968 book by Samuel P. Huntington dealing with changes in political systems and political institutions. Huntington argues that those changes are caused by tensions within the political and social system, and criticizes modernization theory, contending that its argument for economic change and development being the prime factors responsible for the creation of stable, democratic political systems is flawed. Focusing on other factors like urbanization, increased literacy, social mobilization, and economic growth, he stresses that those factors are not significantly related to political development; in fact a major part of his argument is that those processes are related but distinct.

Huntington argues that order itself is a crucial objective in developing countries. The existence (or lack) of order should not be confused with the issue of the type of that order (both on political level - democratic, authoritarian, and on economic level - socialist, free-market, etc.) While modernity equals stability, modernization is actually a cause for instability, due to urbanization, rising expectations due to literacy, education and the spread of media, etc.

30. In explaining the theory of the elite, Burnham adopts the economic approach, which looks similar to the approach of Marx but it is not really so. According to him, the power of elite depends upon the degree of control he has over the principal means of production and distribution. Because of this control, the elite manage to get preferential treatment in the society and is able to prevent the rest of others to enjoy the same position in the society. Thus, the easiest way "to discover what the ruling group is in any society, is usually to see that the group gets the biggest income".

However, Burnham is not a Marxist on account of this reason but is to justify and defend the present capitalist system. He takes only the importance of the control of means of production from Marx but where Marx vests it in the hands of the labour class, he vests it in the hands of an elite.

31. Indian constitution as a document has generally been interpreted as a quintessential liberal document. Granville Austin, for example, is highly appreciative of India's choice of constitutional principles and values but also the method of making of the constitution through liberal democratic consensus and accommodation. According to Austin, the Indian constitution rejected the methods adopted by China and Russia and aimed at the tripartite goal of national unity, democracy and social revolution as three distinct strands interwoven into a "seamless web". This line of interpretation would appear to facilitate the emergence of the modern culture of constitutionalism in India.

32. Article-19 guarantees to all citizens the 6 rights. These are:

(*i*) Right to freedom of speech and expression.

(*ii*) Right to assemble peaceably and without arms.

(*iii*) Right to form associations or unions or cooperative societies.

(*iv*) Right to move freely throughout the territory of India.

(*v*) Right to reside and settle in any part of the territory of India.

(*vi*) Right to practice any profession or to carry on any occupation, trade or business.

Originally, Article 19 contained 7 rights. But, the right to acquire, hold and dispose of property was deleted by the 44th Amendment Act of 1978.

The State can impose 'reasonable' restrictions on the enjoyment of these 6 rights on the grounds, namely–security of state, public order, decency or morality, contempt of court, etc.

33. Once approved by Parliament, the proclamation of financial emergency continues indefinitely till it is revoked. This implies two things:

(*i*) There is no maximum period prescribed for its operation; and

(*ii*) repeated parliamentary approval is not required for its continuation.

A resolution approving the proclamation of financial emergency can be passed by either House of Parliament only by a simple majority, that is, a majority of the members of that house present and voting.

A proclamation of financial emergency may be revoked by the President at anytime by a subsequent proclamation. Such a proclamation does not require the parliamentary approval.

34. The **Vice-President of India** is the second-highest constitutional office in India after the President. Article 63 of Indian Constitution states that "there shall be a Vice-President of India". The Vice-President acts as President in the absence of the President due to death, resignation, impeachment, or other situations.

The Vice-President of India is also *ex officio* Chairperson of the Rajya Sabha. When a bill is introduced in Rajya Sabha, vice-president decides whether it is a financial bill or not. If he is of the opinion, a bill introduced in the Rajya Sabha is a money bill, he would refer the case to the Speaker of the Lok Sabha for deciding it.

Article 66 of the Indian Constitution states the manner of election of the Vice-President. The Vice-President is elected indirectly by members of an electoral college consisting of the members of both Houses of Parliament in accordance with the system of Proportional Representation by means of the Single transferable vote and the voting is by secret ballot conducted by election commission.

36. ***S. R. Bommai v. Union of India*** was a landmark judgement of the Supreme Court of India, where the Court discussed at length provisions of Article 356 of the Constitution of India and related issues. This case had huge impact on Centre-State Relations. The judgement attempted to curb blatant misuse of Article 356 of the Consti-tution of India, which allowed President's rule to be imposed over state governments.

The SC laid down certain guidelines so as to prevent the misuse of A356 of the constitution.

1. The majority enjoyed by the Council of Ministers shall be tested on the floor of the House.
2. Centre should give a warning to the state and a time period of one week to reply.
3. The court cannot question the advice tendered by the CoMs to the President but it can question the material behind the satisfaction of the President. Hence, Judicial Review will involve three questions only:

    (*a*) Is there any material behind the proclamation

    (*b*) Is the material relevant.

    (*c*) Was there any mala fide use of power.
4. If there is improper use of A356 then the court will provide remedy.
5. Under Article 356(3) it is the limitation on the powers of the President. Hence, the president shall not take any irreversible action until the proclamation is approved by the Parliament *i.e.,* he shall not dissolve the assembly.
6. Article 356 is justified only when there is a breakdown of constitutional machinery and not administrative machinery.

Article 356 shall be used sparingly by the center, otherwise it is likely to destroy the constitutional structure between the center and the states. Even Dr. Ambedkar envisaged it to remain a 'dead letter' in the constitution.

37. The Government of India constituted a Commission on Centre-State Relations under the chairmanship of Justice Madan Mohan Punchhi, former Chief Justice of India on 27th April 2007 to look into the new issues of Centre-State relations keeping in view the changes that have taken place in the polity and economy of India since the Sarkaria Commission had last looked at the issue of Centre-State relations over two decades ago.

Composition of the Commission

Justice Madan Mohan Punchhi, Dhirendra Singh, Vinod Kumar Duggal, Dr. N.R. Madhava Menon, Shri Vijay Shanker.

The Commission examined and reviewed the working of the existing arrangements between the Union and States, various pronouncements of the Courts in regard to powers, functions and responsibilities in all spheres including legislative relations, administrative relations, role of governors, emergency provisions, financial relations, economic and social planning, Panchayati Raj institutions, sharing of resources including inter-state river water etc. The Commission made 273 recommendations in its seven volume report presented to Government on 30 March 2010.

39. The Government accords highest priority to rural development so as to increase agricultural production, create employment, eradicate poverty and bring on all round improvement in the rural economy. The government considers that the maximum degree of decentralisation, both in planning and in implementation, is necessary for the attainment of these objectives. The Government of India, therefore, appointed a Committee, popularly known as Ashok Mehta Committee on Panchayati Raj Institutions in December 1977, with the main task assigned "To enquire into the working of Panchayati Raj Institutions and to suggest measures to strength them so as to enables a decentralised planning and development to be effective".

The terms of reference were so wide in scope that they covered almost all important aspects of Panchayati Raj, including development administration and decentralised planning. That is why the report of the Committee Submitted in August 1978. Covered the entire gamut of Panchayati Raj in as many as three hundred one pages covering one hundred thirty two recommendations. As the authors of the Report put it. "The story of Panchayti Raj has been a story of ups and downs. It seems to have passed through three phases; the phase of ascendancy (1959-64) the phase of stagnation (1965-69); and the phase of decline (1969-77)" but at the same time it added. "It would in fact, be wrong to conclude from the existing evidence that Panchayati Raj institutions have failed in the sphere of planning and development. The fact is that the Panchayati 33 Raj institutions have not been given the chance to serve as vanguard of development in village India. Where ever they have been the responsibility, to whatever limited extent as in Maharastra and Gujrat, they have done well".

However, the Ashok Mehta Committee has suggested a new approach towards Panchayati Raj which favours a two-tier system of these institutions, namely, the Zila Parishad at the district level and Mandal Panchayat (a unit of cluster of villages) at the grass root level. The recommendations of this Committee have not been implemented.

40. In a move guaranteed to stir up institutional and political controversy, Chief Election Commissioner N. Gopalaswami has Suo Motu sent a recommendation to the President that Election Commissioner Navin Chawla should be removed from office on the alleged ground of 'partisanship'. The President has forwarded the CEC's missive to the Prime Minister.

Mr. Gopalaswami's action has raised eyebrows within the government on account of its timing as well as its departure from well-settled readings of the relevant constitutional provisions. The 15th general election, along with Assembly elections in some states, will be held in April-May 2009; Mr. Gopalaswami himself will retire as CEC on April 20 and Mr. Chawla will succeed him.

43. ***Towards Equality*** was the title of the report of the Committee on the Status of Women in India (1974-75). This 1974 document is said to lay the foundation of women's movement in independent India, highlighting discriminatory socio-cultural practices, political and economic processes. The findings of the report reopened the women's question for government, academia and women's organisation. Its authors included Vina Mazumdar and Lotika Sarkar, who later founded the Centre for Women's Development Studies in Delhi.

The report proved to be an "eye opener" women's condition by talking about development and democracy from gender perspective. It brought to the forefront the issues of declining sex ratio (missing women). It led to women-sensitive policy-making in India and stress on girls' education.

45. The fundamental basis of any country lies on its unity and integrity. It is the national unity that acts a bulwark against forces of domination and exploitation. It also assures peace, prosperity and progress. Consequently, every country-state aims to strengthen its unity and attain leverage in enjoying the benefits of human civilization.

Major obstacles to the process of Nation building communalism continues to be a major stumbling block in achieving national integration. The policy of 'Divide and Rule' used by British to serve their interest, continues to plague Indian society in more robust forms.

Regionalism and sub-regionalism continue to affect India. It is true that a multicultural society like India cannot aspire to be a homogeneous one, but the fissiparous demands add to the woes of the polity.

Politics of populism exploits the inherent structural dimensions of Indian society. The use of caste, creed, colour or sex as a tool to mobilize votes continues to be a black spot on the political process.

Poverty and illiteracy have continuously created apathy among Indian nationals. They have shown disenchantment with the polity and remain preoccupied either with their conventional ethos and way of life or turn to violent methods. Story of Tribes and Naxals speak volumes about their either anti or non-Indian stands.

Politics of violence and movements centered on sectarian goals damages not only the political propriety but also a belief in the strength of the nation. Anarchy and political turmoil created by these forces hinder the pace of unity and integration.

48. Luther Gulick has given 4P-formula regard with the establishment of departments, universally—Purpose, Process, Person and Place.

According to him, the organization made on the basis of purpose, process, person or place. Purpose based organisations means the organisation which are formed for a particular purpose such as conducting coordination.

Process based organization refer the organization in which basically the processing is done like ministry of law, statistic department, accounting department etc.

Person based organizations are the organisation which are formed to serve any particular target group, community or society like department of scheduled caste, minorities etc.

Placed based organisation are basically formed to serve any particular territory.

49. Herbert Simon has ridiculed the classical theory of organisation as a machine model theory because classicists are too much preoccupied with the formal structural part of organization and that too at the cost of human factors. The classical writers viewed organisation as a machine and human beings as components of that machine. They were of the view that efficiency of the organization can be increased by making human beings efficient. Their emphasis was on specialization and coordination of activities. Most of the writers gave emphasis on efficiency at the top level and few at lower levels of organisation. That is why this theory has given streams; scientific management and administrative management. The Scientific management group was mainly concerned with the tasks to be performed at operative levels.

50. **Right to Information** (**RTI**) is an Act of the Parliament of India to provide for setting out the practical regime of right to information for citizens and replaces the erstwhile Freedom of Information Act, 2002. Under the provisions of the Act, any citizen of India may request information from a "public authority" (a body of Government or "instrumentality of State") which is required to reply expeditiously or within thirty days. The Act also requires every public authority to computerise their records for wide dissemination and to proactively certain categories of information so that the citizens need minimum recourse to request for information formally.

This law was passed by Parliament on 15 June 2005 and came fully into force on 12 October 2005. The first application was given to a Pune police station. Information disclosure in India was restricted by the Official Secrets Act 1923 and various other special laws, which the new RTI Act relaxes. It codifies a fundamental right of citizens.

51. The 73rd Amendment 1992 added a new Part IX to the constitution titled "The Panchayats" covering provisions from Article 243 to 243(O); and a new Eleventh Schedule covering 29 subjects within the functions of the Panchayats.

Significance of the amendment: This amendment implements the article 40 of the DPSP which says that "State shall take steps to organise village panchayats and endow them with such powers and authority as may be necessary to enable them to function as units of self-government" and have upgraded them from non-justifiable to justifiable part of the constitution and has put constitutional obligation upon states to enact the Panchayati Raj Acts as per provisions of the Part IX. However, states have been given enough freedom to take their geographical, politico-administrative and others conditions into account while adopting the Panchayati Raj System.

Part IX provides for a 3 tier Panchayat system, which would be constituted in every state at the village level, intermediate level and district level. This provision brought the uniformity in the Panchayati Raj structure in India. However, the states which were having population below 20 Lakh were given an option to not to have the intermediate level.

All the members of these three levels are elected. Further, the chairperson of panchayats at the intermediate and district levels are indirectly elected from amongst the elected members. But at the village level, the election of chairperson of Panchayat (Sarpanch) may be direct or indirect as provided by the state in its own Panchayati Raj Act.

52. The RTI Act 2005 provides for establishment of Central and State Information Commissioner as a designated authority to receive and inquire into a complaint from any person. The Central Information Commission consists of the Chief Information Commissioner and Information Commissioners not exceeding 10 in number. The CIC and Information Commissioners shall be appointed by the President on the recommendation of a committee comprising—Prime Minister as chairperson, the Leader of Opposition in the Lok Sabha; a Union Cabinet Minister to be nominated by the Prime Minister.

According to the RTI Act 2005, CIC/ Information Commissioner shall hold office for a term of 5 years or till he attains the age of 65 years. The CIC shall not be eligible for reappointment.

53. Development administration is related to desirable change brought by the government through various socio-economic programmes accompanied with appropriate mobilization of resource. It mainly emphasize on change in public administration from top down approach to bottom up decentralised approach. It basically aims at restructuring the public administration.

The colonial administration didn't cater to the needs of varied sections of the society. Hence to bring in speedy economic and social growth, development administration had to be action oriented. Therefore, after independence, the focus shifted on development enhancing the capability of government to carry out diverse functions.

Development administration is characterised by purpose, loyalties and its attitudes. The purpose is social and economic progress; for this administration needs loyal bureaucracy accountable to the people ; positive, persuasive and innovative attitude towards achieving the prescribed goal. This in a way calls for structural refashioning of established agencies. Hence, restructuring should be done with the pretext of action oriented nature.

The action oriented nature of the government aims at increasing the participation of people at local level, decentralisation of policy making, with enhanced focus of goals of the policies and efficient way of achieving the goals.

Efficiency would not only mean cost effectiveness but also in terms of achievement of results. Considerable investment may go into implementing the right to education program but the effectiveness of the program gets reflected only in the quality of education imparted. Family planning programmes could be effective only if success in reduction of birth rate is achieved. As wiedner has rightly said development administration has to be action oriented and goal oriented.

54. Voluntary provisions of the 73rd Constitutional Amendment Act 1992 are as follows:

1. Giving representation to members of the Parliament (both the Houses) and the state legislature (both the Houses) in the panchayats at different levels falling within their constituencies.
2. Providing reservation of seats (both members and chairpersons) for backward classes in panchayats at any level.
3. Granting powers and authority to the panchayats to enable them to function as institutions of self-government.
4. Devolution of powers and responsibilities upon panchayats to prepare plans for economic development and social justice; and to perform some or all of the 29 functions listed in the Eleventh Schedule of the Constitution.
5. Granting financial powers to the panchayats, *i.e.* authorizing them to levy, collect and appropriate taxes, duties, tolls and fees.

56. The advancement of an employee from one job position to another job position that has a higher salary range, a higher level job title, and, often, more and higher level job responsibilities in an organization, is called a promotion. Sometimes a promotion results in an employee taking on responsibility for managing or overseeing the work of other employees. Decision-making authority tends to rise with a promotion as well.

Unlike in a lateral move, the promotion can result in more status within the organization. But, along with the authority and status conveyed with the new position title, comes additional responsibility, accountability, and expanded expectations for contributions.

58. Defending policy is the function of Line agency.

There are four types of line agencies in public administration:

- Government departments
- Public corporations
- Government companies
- Independent regulatory commission, IRC.

The first three are found in all the countries of the world while the last one is a special feature of the administrative system of USA.

The line agencies have the following characteristic features:

(*i*) They directly carry out the function of accomplishing the sustentative of the organization.

(*ii*) They are given authority to make decisions and issue orders and directives.

(*iii*) They directly come in contact with the people and provide them various services, regulate conduct, and collect taxes.

Thus, the line agencies are executive in nature and are subordinate divisions of operating responsibility working under the direct control, direction, and supervision of the chief executive.

According to L. D. White, major functions of the line agencies include:

- Making decision
- Taking responsibility
- Interpreting and defending policy and operations
- Maintaining production and seeking efficiency and economy.

60. Herbert Simon rejected the politics–administration dichotomy. The politics-administration dichotomy is a theory that constructs the boundaries of public administration and asserts the normative relationship between elected officials and administrates in a democratic society. The phrase politics administration dichotomy itself does not appear to have a known inventor, even after exhaustive research, the combination of words that make up the phrase was first found in public administration literature from the 1940s with no clear originator.

61. Kenneth Waltz was of the opinion that survival depends on a state's material capabilities and its alliances with other states. Based on structural realism as advanced by Kenneth Waltz (Theory of International Politics–1979) the self-help anarchic system and shifts in the relative distribution of capabilities mean that balances of power recurrently form in the international system. How states balance will depend on the distribution of capabilities among the greater powers. In bipolar distributions of power (two great powers) states will balance through internal military build up. In multipolar distributions of power states will balance through the formation of counterbalancing alliances.

63. **Soft power** is the ability to attract and co-opt, rather than by coercion (hard power), which is using force or giving money as a means of persuasion. Soft power is the ability to shape the preferences of others through appeal and attraction. A defining feature of soft power is that it is non-coercive; the currency of soft power is culture, political values, and foreign policies. Recently, the term has also been used in changing and influencing social and public opinion through relatively less transparent channels and lobbying through powerful political and non-political organizations. In 2012, Nye explained that with soft power, "the best propaganda is not propaganda", further explaining that during the Information Age, "credibility is the scarcest resource".

Joseph Nye of Harvard University coined the term in a 1990 book, *Bound to Lead: The Changing Nature of American Power*. In this book, he wrote: "when one country gets other countries to want what it wants-might be called co-optive or soft power in contrast with the hard or command power of ordering others to do what it wants." He further developed the concept in his 2004 book, *Soft Power: The Means to Success in World Politics*. The term is now widely used in international affairs by analysts and statesmen. For example, the US Secretary of Defense Robert Gates spoke of the need to enhance American soft power by "a dramatic increase in spending on the civilian instruments of national security - diplomacy, strategic communications, foreign assistance, civic action and economic reconstruction and development." In 2011, as Xi Jinping was preparing to take power from General Secretary Hu Jintao, the 17th Central Committee of the Chinese Communist Party devoted a whole plenary session to the issue of culture, with the final Communiqué declaring that it was a national goal to "build our country into a socialist cultural superpower". And in 2014, Xi announced, "We should increase China's soft power, give a good Chinese narrative, and better communicate China's messages to the world".

64. It has been argued that the absence of war between democratic states 'comes as close as anything we have to an empirical law in international relations'. Although statistically the probability of war between any two states is considerably low, the absence of war among liberal democracies across a wide range of different historical, economic, and political factors suggests that there is a strong predisposition against the use of military violence between democratic states. This democratic peace proposition not only challenges the validity of other political systems (*i.e.*, fascism, communism, authoritarianism, totalitarianism), but also the prevailing realist account of international relations, which emphasises balance-of-power calculations and common strategic interests in order to explain the peace and stability that characterises relations between liberal democracies. This essay argues, however, that the structural and normative arguments of the democratic peace theory together offer a far more logical and convincing explanation for this seeming anomaly. Furthermore, in line with Immanuel Kant's theory of perpetual peace, I argue that the global spread of democracy will result in greater international peace if this occurs in parallel with the strengthening of economic interdependence and international organisations. The difficulty lies in the significant risk of instability inherent in the process of democratisation and the uncertainty that remains in an 'incomplete Kantian world' where the Hobbesian state of anarchy has not yet entirely disappeared from the international system.

65. Some of the major ideas put forwarded by world's eminent peace philosopher Johan Galtung are: Direct, Structural and Cultural Violence; Conflict Transformation by Peaceful Means (Transcend Method), Transcend Method in Conflict Mediation Across Levels, Mahatma Gandhi as the Master of Masters, Peace Journalism, and from a 20th Century of War to a 21st Century of Peace. Democracy for Peace and Development, Peace Studies and Conflict Resolution, the Six and Fifteen Contradictions of USSR and USA respectively, and reconciliation are some of the other key parts of Galtung's findings. Galtung frequently refers the negative vs. positive peace and peace-conflict lifecycle and their structural, institutional, individual, procedural, and political levels of relations.

67. "Societal security" is the umbrella term for efforts to cope with modern security threats to society. The concept of 'societal security' has been formulated to account for the phenomenon of societal identity and cohesion as sources of instability. The most influential idea to emerge from the conceptual widening of the Security Studies in the 90's by the Copenhagen School was that of the societal security. The concept is leading basically to non-military threats with non-military solutions when the subject is not the state (national security), neither the individuals in it (human security, safety), but the society. The Copenhagen School did a service to the concept of security by releasing the discipline related to this - security studies, strategic studies, international relations, conflict analysis - from the state-centric strait jacket. By this step, consideration was made to political killing of people by their own government or other sections of the society, as well as offering an explanation to the death of individuals due to social construction, however abstract and subjective they may be. "Societal security concerns the ability of a society to persist in its essential character under changing conditions and possible or actual threats". This security is threatened when "societies perceive a threat in identity terms".

"Societal security is the new dimension that is being constructed. It is meant to bridge the gap between state security and human safety." The term societal security was first used by Barry Buzan in the book "People, States and Fear". Societal security was just one of the five sectors in his five-dimensional approach to security theory, along with military, political, economic, and environmental security. Here, however, all of Buzan's dimensions, including the societal one, were still sectors of state security: Society, for example, was just one sector where the state could be threatened.

69. The National Security Council (NSC) of India is a three-tiered organization that oversees political, economic, energy and security issues of strategic concern. It operates within the executive office of the prime minister of India, liaising between the government's executive branch and the intelligence services, advising leadership on intelligence and security issues. The National Security Council comprises the Strategic Policy Group, the National Security Advisory Board and a secretariat from the Joint Intelligence Committee. The National Security Advisor presides over the NSC, and is also the primary advisor to the prime minister. The current National Security Advisor is Ajit Doval.

71. India is a major contributor to UN Democracy Fund and it submitted along with other countries an Action Plan for phased elimination of nuclear weapons 1996-2020. India was among the original members of the

United Nations that signed the Declaration by United Nations at Washington, D.C. on 1944 October and also participated in the United Nations Conference on International Organization at San Francisco from 25 April to 26 June 1945. As a founding member of the United Nations, India strongly supports the purposes and principles of the UN and has made significant contributions in implementing the goals of the Charter, and the evolution of the UN's specialised programmes and agencies.

72. States continue to exist as sovereign states and globalization has weakened the Westphalian state system. In general, globalization may ultimately reduce the importance of nation states. Supranational institutions such as the European Union, The WTO, The G8 or the International Criminal Court replace or extend national functions to facilitate international agreement.

The principle of state's sovereignty promoted in 1648 became soon the crucial pivot for the creation of the national-states, first across Europe and later around the world. The essence of modern national-state became the Westphalian idea that political legitimacy has to come from secular legal authority rather than from divine sanction as it was a practice in the Middle Ages.

74. **The International Finance Corporation (IFC)** is an international financial institution that offers investment, advisory, and asset-management services to encourage private-sector development in developing countries. The IFC is a member of the World Bank Group and is headquartered in Washington, D.C. It was established in 1956, as the private-sector arm of the World Bank Group, to advance economic development by investing in for-profit and commercial projects for poverty reduction and promoting development. The IFC's stated aim is to create opportunities for people to escape poverty and achieve better living standards by mobilizing financial resources for private enterprise, promoting accessible and competitive markets, supporting businesses and other private-sector entities, and creating jobs and delivering necessary services to those who are poverty stricken or otherwise vulnerable.

Since 2009, the IFC has focused on a set of development goals that its projects are expected to target. Its goals are to increase sustainable agriculture opportunities, improve healthcare and education, increase access to financing for microfinance and business clients, advance infrastructure, help small businesses grow revenues, and invest in climate health.

75. India and Japan became members of Security Council seven and eleven times respectively. Under the Charter, the Security Council has primary responsibility for the maintenance of international peace and security. It has 15 Members, and each Member has one vote. Under the Charter, all Member States are obligated to comply with Council decisions.

The Security Council takes the lead in determining the existence of a threat to the peace or act of aggression. It calls upon the parties to a dispute to settle it by peaceful means and recommends methods of adjustment or terms of settlement. In some cases, the Security Council can resort to imposing sanctions or even authorize the use of force to maintain or restore international peace and security.

The Security Council also recommends to the General Assembly the appointment of the Secretary-General and the admission of new Members to the United Nations. And, together with the General Assembly, it elects the judges of the International Court of Justice.

Previous Paper (Solved)

UGC-NET-Junior Research Fellowship & Assistant Professor Exam

Political Science, January-2017*

PAPER-II

Note: *This paper contains **fifty** (**50**) objective type questions of **two** (**2**) marks each. **All** questions are compulsory.*

1. Given below are two statements, one labelled as Assertion (A) and the other as Reason (R). Select the correct answer from the codes given below:

Assertion (A) : Kautilya emphasizes the need for a strong ruler.

Reason (R) : He was having acute awareness of the dangers of anarchy as well as the absolute necessity to establish order in society.

Codes:

A. Both (A) and (R) are true and (R) is the correct explanation of (A).

B. Both (A) and (R) are true, but (R) is not the correct explanation of (A).

C. (A) is true, but (R) is false.

D. (A) is false, but (R) is true.

2. Which one of the following is not a source of Plato's theory of Ideas?

A. Heracleitus-The notion of sphere of Becoming.

B. Antisthenes-The notion of absolute asceticism and rigorous self-mortification.

C. Socrates-The doctrine of concepts.

D. Eleatics-The idea of a sphere of absolute being.

3. Match List-I with List-II and select the correct answer from the codes given below:

List–I (Aristotle's theory of causation)	***List–II (Explanations)***
(*a*) The efficient cause	1. The substance and essence of the thing.
(*b*) The final cause	2. Matter of which it is composed.
(*c*) The material cause	3. The purpose towards which the movement is directed.
(*d*) The formal cause	4. The cause of motion.

Codes:

	(*a*)	(*b*)	(*c*)	(*d*)
A.	1	2	3	4
B.	4	3	2	1
C.	3	4	1	2
D.	2	1	4	3

4. Given below are the two statements, one labelled as Assertion (A) and the other labelled as Reason (R):

Select the correct answer from the codes given below:

Assertion (A) : For Locke, Labour is the source and justification of property.

Reason (R) : Its function is to turn the earth into consumable goods.

Codes:

A. Both (A) and (R) are true and (R) is the correct explanation of (A).

B. Both (A) and (R) are true, but (R) is not the correct explanation of (A).

C. (A) is true, but (R) is false.

D. (A) is false, but (R) is true.

* *Held on 22 January, 2017.*

5. Which one of the features of Rawls' concept of 'Veil of ignorance' is not true?
   A. No one knows his place in society, his class position or social status.
   B. No one knows his fortune in the distribution of natural assets and abilities.
   C. The parties know their special psychological propensities.
   D. The parties do not (even) know their conception of the good.

6. Who among the following described the welfare state as a kind of enslavement?
   A. Karl Popper B. F.A. Hayek
   C. R. Nozick D. Milton Friedman

7. E.M.S. Namboodiripad's book *Mahatma and Ism* is an analysis of Mahatma Gandhi from the point of view:
   A. Syndicalism B. Socialism
   C. Liberalism D. Marxism

8. Which of the following statements is not true in case of M.N. Roy?
   A. He prepared a model constitution for free India.
   B. Sovereign power was to be vested in the people.
   C. People's committees to be set up in villages, towns and cities.
   D. He did not concede the right of secession to its constituent units.

9. Which of the following statements is not true?
   A. Traditional political theory is qualitative.
   B. Behavioural political theory is quantitative.
   C. Post-behavioural political theory is both qualitative and quantitative.
   D. Post-behavioural political theory is ethnocentric; focuses especially on western democracies.

10. Who among the following emphasized 'procedural theory of democracy' highlighting three criteria?
    A. S.M. Lipset B. R.A. Dahl
    C. Joseph Schumpeter D. Sheldon Wolin

11. Which one of the following is not a formulation of Max Weber?
    A. Rationality, functional differentiation and specialization resulting in order, harmony and efficiency.
    B. Dominant authority based on beliefs and symbols in relation to ideal types.
    C. Dominant authority is hierarchical and related to state and ruling class.
    D. Rationalization and ideal typology method.

12. Who said that federalism requires people "Who desire union and must not desire unity"?
    A. James Bryce B. A.V. Diecy
    C. K.C. Wheare D. H. Finer

13. The assertion that there is no direct connection between the shape of a political culture and the stability of governance is made by
    A. Lijphart B. Wolin
    C. Kavanagh D. Blondel

14. The ability of the U.S. President to get their way depends on four crucial relationships (*a*) Congress, (*b*) The federal bureaucracy, (c) The Supreme Court and (*d*) The mass media. Which of the above is undoubtedly the most critical?
    A. The Congress
    B. The Federal bureaucracy
    C. The Supreme Court
    D. The mass media

15. C. Wright Mills' *The Power Elite* (1956) offered a general analysis of elites in:
    A. Entire capitalistic world.
    B. Developed capitalistic world of North America and Western Europe.
    C. Developed capitalistic nations of North America, Western Europe and Japan.
    D. Developed capitalism of the U.S.A.

16. Power is like money is formulated by
    A. C. Wright Mills B. Paul Sweezy
    C. Talcott Parsons D. Ralph Miliband

17. Catch all party describes the post second world war party system in
    A. Western Europe
    B. Eastern Europe
    C. The U.S. Party system
    D. All of the above

18. Who believed that the success of a revolution occurs when it is limited to the political and not extending to the social?

A. Crane Brinton B. V.I. Lenin
C. Hannah Arendt D. Mahatma Gandhi

19. The Capitalist world economy is made up of "Commodity Chains" of producers and consumers, sellers and buyers linking countries in the core of the world economy", is the basis of

A. Globalization and modernization theory
B. Lenin's theory of imperialism
C. Friedman's World is flat theory
D. World system theory

20. Given below are two statements, one labelled as Assertion (A) and the other labelled as Reason (R):

Select the correct answer from the codes given below:

Assertion (A) : Consociational democracy is an incomplete theory of democracy.

Reason (R) : As it blocks the way of a genuine alternative

In the context of the two statements, which one of the following is correct?

A. Both (A) and (R) are true and (R) is the correct explanation of (A).
B. Both (A) and (R) are true, but (R) is not the correct explanation of (A).
C. (A) is true, but (R) is false.
D. (A) is false, but (R) is true.

21. Who said, "The Constituent Assembly was a one party body in an essentially one party country. The Assembly was the congress and the congress was India"?

A. Morris Jones B. Paul R. Brass
C. Granville Austin D. Richard Sisson

22. Match List-I with List-II and select the correct answer from the codes given below:

List–I (Books)	*List–II (Authors)*
(*a*) The Child and the State in India	1. Atul Kohli
(*b*) The Hindu Nationalist Movement and Indian Politics	2. Pranab Bardhan
(*c*) The Political Economy of Development in India	3. Christopher Jafrelot
(*d*) Poverty Amid Plenty in the New India	4. Myron Weiner

Codes:

	(*a*)	(*b*)	(*c*)	(*d*)
A.	3	4	1	2
B.	4	3	2	1
C.	2	1	3	4
D.	1	2	4	3

23. Which of the following have been identified as the ground for judicial review in the exercise of power of pardon by the President of India or Governor of a state?

(*a*) that the order has been passed without application of mind.
(*b*) that the order is malafide.
(*c*) that the order is based on extraneous or wholly irrelevant considerations.
(*d*) that the order suffers from arbitrariness.

Select the correct answer from the codes given below:

Codes:

A. (*a*), (*c*) and (*d*) B. (*b*), (*c*) and (*d*)
C. (*a*), (*b*) and (*d*) D. (*a*), (*b*), (*c*) and (*d*)

24. Match List-I with List-II and select the correct answer from the codes given below:

List–I (Panchayati Raj Committee)	*List–II (Year)*
(*a*) C.H. Hanumantha Rao	1. 1978
(*b*) G.V.K. Rao	2. 1984
(*c*) Ashok Mehta	3. 1986
(*d*) L.M. Singhvi	4. 1985

Codes:

	(*a*)	(*b*)	(*c*)	(*d*)
A.	4	2	1	3
B.	2	4	1	3
C.	1	3	2	4
D.	3	1	4	2

25. Given below are two statements, one labelled as Assertion (A) and the other labelled as Reason (R):

Select the correct answer from the codes given below:

Assertion (A) : Fundamental Duties are non-justiciable.

Reason (R) : They are supposed to inculcate a sense of patriotic and sensible citizenship.

Codes:

A. Both (A) and (R) are true and (R) is the correct explanation of (A).
B. Both (A) and (R) are true, but (R) is not the correct explanation of (A).
C. (A) is true, but (R) is false.
D. (A) is false, but (R) is true.

26. Which of the following are the privileges of the Legislature in India?

(*a*) Right to publish debates and proceedings and the right to restrain others from publishing.
(*b*) The privilege of excluding strangers from the house.
(*c*) The right to regulate its internal matters.
(*d*) The right to punish members and outsiders for breach of privilege.

Select the correct answer from the codes given below:

Codes:

A. (*a*), (*c*) and (*d*) B. (*b*), (*c*) and (*d*)
C. (*a*), (*b*) and (*d*) D. (*a*), (*b*), (*c*) and (*d*)

27. Arrange the following peasant movements in India in chronological order and select the correct answer from the codes given below:

(*i*) Singur
(*ii*) Bardoli
(*iii*) Tebhaga
(*iv*) Champaran

Codes:

A. (*iv*), (*iii*), (*i*), (*ii*) B. (*iv*), (*ii*), (*iii*), (*i*)
C. (*ii*), (*iii*), (*iv*), (*i*) D. (*i*), (*ii*), (*iii*), (*iv*)

28. Identify the correct chronological order of the developments of events related to federalism in India.

A. Anandpur Sahib Resolution, Rajamannar Committee, Punchhi Commission, West Bengal Memorandum.
B. West Bengal Memorandum, Rajamannar Committee, Anandpur Sahib Resolution, Punchhi Commission
C. Rajamannar Committee, West Bengal Memorandum, Anandpur Sahib Resolution, Punchhi Commission
D. Rajamannar Committee, Anandpur Sahib Resolution, West Bengal Memorandum, Punchhi Commission

29. Who described Indian capitalism as "Dharmashala Capitalism"?

A. V.K.R.V. Rao B. J. Bhagwati
C. Amartya Sen D. Raj Krishna

30. Which of the following is not associated with electoral reforms in India?

A. Tarkunde Committee
B. Dinesh Goswami Committee
C. N.N. Vohra Committee
D. Indrajit Gupta Committee

31. Arrange the following approaches to the study of Public Administration in a sequential order:

(*a*) Behavioural approach
(*b*) Systems approach
(*c*) Institutional approach
(*d*) Public Policy approach

Select the correct answer from the codes given below:

Codes:

A. (*a*), (*b*), (*c*), (*d*) B. (*c*), (*b*), (*a*), (*d*)
C. (*a*), (*c*), (*d*), (*b*) D. (*c*), (*a*), (*b*), (*d*)

32. Given below are two statements, one labelled as Assertion (A) and the other labelled as Reason (R):

Select the correct answer from the codes given below:

Assertion (A) : Civil servants in India do not have any political rights.

Reason (R) : Neutrality is the hallmark of the civil services in India.

Codes:

A. Both (A) and (R) are true and (R) is the correct explanation of (A).
B. Both (A) and (R) are true, but (R) is not the correct explanation of (A).
C. (A) is true, but (R) is false.
D. (A) is false, but (R) is true.

33. Which of the following have been identified by the Second Administrative Reforms Commission as barriers to citizen-centric administration in India?

(*a*) Inflexible self-perpetuating and inward looking attitude of civil servants.

(*b*) Lack of accountability of civil servants.
(*c*) Absence of well educated political leadership.
(*d*) Low levels of awareness of the rights and duties of citizens.

Select the correct answer from the codes given below:

Codes:

A. (*a*), (*b*) and (*c*) B. (*a*), (*b*) and (*d*)
C. (*a*), (*c*) and (*d*) D. (*a*), (*b*), (*c*) and (*d*)

34. Which of the following is the nodal agency for budget implementation in India?
A. Parliament
B. Public Accounts Committee
C. Ministry of Finance
D. Comptroller and Auditor General of India

35. In India, the term deficit financing was first defined by
A. First Five Year Plan
B. Finance Commission
C. Administrative Reforms Commission
D. A.D. Gorwala Report

36. Which of the following types of bureaucracy regards itself as the custodian of public interest but is independent of and unresponsive to public opinion?
A. Merit bureaucracy
B. Caste bureaucracy
C. Patronage bureaucracy
D. Guardian bureaucracy

37. Which of the following are the common features between the 73rd Constitutional Amendment Act and the 74th Constitutional Amendment Act?
(*a*) Periodical elections.
(*b*) Empowerment of socially and economically weak groups.
(*c*) Constitution of State Election Commission.
(*d*) Constitution of Ward Committees.

Select the correct answer from the codes given below:

Codes:

A. (*a*) and (*c*) B. (*a*), (*b*) and (*c*)
C. (*a*), (*c*) and (*d*) D. (*a*), (*b*), (*c*) and (*d*)

38. Which of the following are statutory bodies?
(*a*) University Grants Commission
(*b*) Official Language Commission
(*c*) Railway Board
(*d*) Atomic Energy Commission

Select the correct answer from the codes given below:

Codes:

A. (*a*) and (*b*) B. (*a*), (*c*) and (*d*)
C. (*a*), (*b*) and (*d*) D. (*b*) and (*d*)

39. Which one of the following ministries is an example of ministry formed on the basis of clientele principle?
A. Ministry of Defence
B. Ministry of Human Resource Development
C. Ministry of Agriculture
D. Ministry of Law

40. Who among the following are of the view that the managerial techniques and skills of Planning, Organizing, Coordinating and Budgeting are same in both Public and Private Administration?
(*a*) Henry Fayol (*b*) M.P. Follet
(*c*) Luther Gulick (*d*) L. Urwick

Select the correct answer from the codes given below:

Codes:

A. (*a*) and (*c*) B. (*b*) and (*d*)
C. (*a*), (*b*) and (*c*) D. (*a*), (*b*), (*c*) and (*d*)

41. Who of the following belongs to British School of Realism?
A. Reinhold Niebuhr B. N.J. Spykman
C. Quincy Wright D. Hedley Bull

42. The notion of 'Balance of Terror' is related to
A. Global Terrorism
B. Counter Terrorist strategies
C. Terrorist activities of drug traffickers
D. Over-kill capacity emanating from nuclear weapons.

43. Which one of the following is not a major assumption of balance of power?
A. States are determined to protect vital national interests.
B. Vital national interests may be threatened.
C. Relative power positions of the states can be measured.
D. States apply moral parameters for assessing others' behaviour.

44. Which country/countries refused to accept legally binding emission cuts following Kyoto Protocol?
A. India
B. China
C. India and China both
D. Sweden

45. Which leader of the USSR introduced the policy of 'peaceful-coexistence'?
A. Mikhail Gorbachev
B. N. Khrushchev
C. L. Brezhnev
D. Joseph Stalin

46. At the end of cold war Francis Fukuyama constructed the thesis of 'end of history' which meant:
A. The world would no longer be unfolding events.
B. The tension and conflict would cease to exist at global level.
C. Ideological struggles had come to an end.
D. Ideological struggles would be waged with new vigour.

47. NATO's partnership for peace programme was aimed at
A. Incorporating ex-Eastern bloc states into the organisation.
B. Tackling problem of Serbs in Bosnia.
C. Implementing military action against Yugoslavia.
D. Taking action against Al Asad Regime in Syria.

48. Which of the events mentioned below is taken as signalling the end of Cold War?
A. Soviet Union's collapse in 1991
B. Breaching of Berlin Wall in 1989
C. Declaration of independence by Republic of Kazakhstan in 1991
D. Large scale revolt for freedom in Baltic States in 1989

49. The renaming of European Community (EC) to European Union resulted from the signing of
A. Maastricht Treaty B. Treaty of Rome
C. The Lisbon Treaty D. Treaty of Nice

50. Which of the following is not a specialized agency of the United Nations?
A. WHO B. IMF
C. FAO D. OPEC

ANSWERS

1	2	3	4	5	6	7	8	9	10
A	B	B	A	C	C	D	D	D	B
11	12	13	14	15	16	17	18	19	20
C	B	A	A	D	C	A	C	D	B
21	22	23	24	25	26	27	28	29	30
C	B	D	B	B	D	B	D	D	C
31	32	33	34	35	36	37	38	39	40
D	D	B	C	A	D	B	B	C	D
41	42	43	44	45	46	47	48	49	50
D	D	D	C	B	C	A	B	A	D

EXPLANATORY ANSWERS

1. Kautilya was convinced that society can never hope to be in peace without a strong state. Realizing the dangers of anarchy and necessity to transcend it by establishing order in society, Kautilya used the simile of Matsyanyaya depicting larger fish eating the smaller fish when anarchy prevails. It endangers both the social system as well as the individual's sense of security and his yearning for future. Kautilya finds remedy in strong ruler capable of creating order. Asserting for supremacy of the king, Kautilya warns against tyrannical tendencies, which may result in popular wrath and destroy the kingdom. He argues that "when people are impoverished, they become greedy; when they are greedy, they become disaffected; when disaffected, they voluntarily go to the side of the enemy and destroy their own master." Hence, no king should give room to such causes that may bring impoverishment, greed or disaffection among the people.

3. The "four causes" are elements of an influential principle in Aristotelian thought whereby explanations of change or movement are classified into four fundamental types of answer to the question "why?". Aristotle wrote that "we do not have knowledge of a thing until we have grasped its why, that is to say, its cause." While there are cases where identifying a "cause" is difficult, or in which "causes" might merge, Aristotle was convinced that his four "causes" provided an analytical scheme of general applicability. Aristotle held that there were four kinds of answers to "Why" questions–

   (*i*) **Matter:** a change or movement's material "cause", is the aspect of the change or movement which is determined by the material that composes the moving or changing things. For a table, that might be wood; for a statue, that might be bronze or marble.

   (*ii*) **Form:** a change or movement's formal "cause", is a change or movement caused by the arrangement, shape or appearance of the thing changing or moving. Aristotle says for example, that the ratio 2 : 1, and number in general, is the cause of the octave.

   (*iii*) **Agent:** a change or movement's efficient or moving "cause", consists of things apart from the thing being changed or moved, which interact so as to be an agency of the change or movement. For example, the efficient cause of a table is a carpenter, or a person working as one, and according to Aristotle the efficient cause of a boy is a father.

   (*iv*) **End or purpose:** a change or movement's final "cause", is that for the sake of which a thing is what it is. For a seed, it might be an adult plant.

4. Locke uses the word 'property' in both broad and narrow senses. In a broad sense, it covers a wide range of human interests and aspirations; more narrowly, it refers to material goods. He argues that property is a natural right and is derived from labour.

   In chapter V of his 'Second Treatise', Locke argues that the individual ownership of goods and property is justified by the labour exerted to produce those goods or utilise property to produce goods beneficial to human society. Locke stated his belief, in his 'Second Treatise', that nature on its own provides little of value to society, implying that the labour expended in the creation of goods gives them their value. This position can be seen as a labour theory of value.

   From this premise, Locke developed a labour theory of property, viz., the ownership of property is created by the application of labour. In addition, he believed that property precedes government and government cannot "dispose of the estates of the subjects arbitrarily". Karl Marx later critiqued Locke's theory of property in his own social theory.

5. The parties know their special psychological propensities feature is not true of Rawls' concept of 'veil of ignorance'. Rawls employed the device of the social contract to develop an ethical theory which represents an alternative to utilitarianism. His theory of 'justice as fairness' is based upon principles that he believed people would support if they were placed behind a veil of ignorance which deprived them of knowledge of their own social position and status. He proposed that social inequality is justified only if it works to the benefit to the least advantaged. This presumption in favour of equality is rooted in

the belief that people cooperating together for mutual advantage should have an equal claim to the fruits of their cooperation and should not be penalized as a result of factors, such as gender, race and genetic inheritance, over which they have no control. Redistribution and welfare are therefore 'just' because they conform to a widely held view of what is fair. Rawls developed a similar justification for the principles of equal liberty and equality of opportunity.

6. Robert Nozick described the welfare state as a kind of enslavement. In Nozick's view, it is the surprising and radical conclusion that *taxation,* of the redistributive sort in which modern states engage in order to fund the various programmes of the bureaucratic welfare state, is morally illegitimate. It amounts to a kind of *forced labour,* for the state so structures the tax system that any time you labour at all, a certain amount of your labour time — the amount that produces the wealth taken away from you forcibly via taxation — is time you involuntarily work, in effect, for the state. Indeed, such taxation amounts to partial *slavery,* for in giving every citizen an entitlement to certain benefits (welfare, social security, or whatever), the state in effect gives them an entitlement, a *right,* to a part of the proceeds of your labour, which produces the taxes that fund the benefits; every citizen, that is, becomes in such a system *a partial owner of you* (since they have a partial property right in part of you, *i.e.,* in your labour). But this is flatly inconsistent with the principle of self-ownership.

7. The first full-fledged attempt by a Marxist to evaluate Gandhi's role in India's freedom struggle.

E.M.S. Namboodiripad, who began his political life as an ardent Gandhian, was uniquely positioned to analyse the various phases of the national movement and the role of Gandhi. The key question he poses is: how did Gandhi become the undisputed leader of the anti-colonial national liberation movement? In answering this question, he looks at the individual role of Gandhi and the unique contribution he made to develop the national movement, while also simultaneously taking into account the social and historical forces that shaped Gandhi and his worldview.

First published in 1958, *The Mahatma and the Ism* remains important for its pioneering effort to assess Gandhism, for its rich content and sensitive handling of a great personality, and for subjecting the ideology and politics of that personality to incisive critical appraisal.

9. After remaining popular for almost two decades (1940-60), the Behavioural Approach got transformed into Post-Behaviouralism. Twenty years of behavioural research brought to light its limitations and weaknesses.

The failure to make any real progress towards the objective of building a scientific political theory compelled the behaviouralists to admit reforms in the light of their experiences with behavioural research. They accepted several reforms and the exercise got the name Post-Behaviouralism.

Post-Behaviouralism did not constitute a return to the traditional approach. It accepted the merit of Behaviouralism but at the same time advocated the need to reform it. The Post-Behaviouralists were reformed behaviouralists. Post-Behaviouralism emerged as a reform movement within Behaviouralism.

10. Robert A. Dahl emphasized 'Procedural theory of democracy' highlighting three criteria. The advocates of 'pluralist' theory of democracy like Karl Mannheim, Raymond Aron, A.F. Bentley, David Truman and Robert Dahl, etc., describes that the policy-making process is a highly decentralized process of bargaining among relatively autonomous 'groups'. They repudiate the claim of 'elitist' theory of democracy that policy making is not the will of an 'elite' or chosen few.

It is an outcome of the interaction of all groups who make claims upon particular issues. But the pluralist theory also projects that various pressure groups compete for political influence and politics are biased towards the corporate power. Because of the uneven distribution of socio-economic power it is only a few groups that have edge over the others.

The essential focus of these theories is on the mere procedural aspect of democracy whether it is through elites or groups competing in the mere process of selecting the incumbents through electoral process or in the contest of policy making. Both fail to divert their attention from the procedural framework.

11. Max Weber does not formulate that dominant authority is hierarchical and related to state and ruling class. Weber defined authority simply as a matter of people's belief about its rightfulness, regardless of where that belief came from and whether or not it is morally justified. Weber's approach treats authority as a form of power; authority is 'legitimate power', power clocked in legitimacy. According to this view, a government that is obeyed can be said to exercise authority, even though that obedience may have been brought about by systematic indoctrination and propaganda.

13. For Lijphart there is no direct connection between the shape of a political culture and the stability of its governance. Of course, Lijphart did not jettison the idea of culture altogether. Power-sharing in consociational democracies is reliant upon a coalescent elite political culture. But then we need to ask what role the institutional environment plays in the promotion of coalescent attitudes among political elites. If it does play a role, culture becomes a derivative of institutions.

14. The relationship between Congress and the President is dynamic, changing with every issue, every event. Sometimes it is cordial and cooperative. Sometimes it is hostile and polarized. And sometimes it is both things on the same day, shifting with the issue under consideration. It lies at the very core of system of government in U.S., and, under the U.S. Constitution, tension and struggle between these rivals for power is inevitable. A democracy without conflict is not a democracy. The framers did not set out to promote gridlock between President and Congress, but they did intend that conflicting opinions in society should be considered carefully before government takes action.

15. In the view of C. Wright Mills ('The Power Elite–1956'), however, industrialized societies like the USA are dominated by a 'power elite', a small cohesive group that commands 'the major hierarchies and organizations of modern society'. Such a theory suggests that power is institutional in character and largely vested in the non-elected bodies of the state system, including the military, the bureaucracy, the judiciary and the police. Mills argued, in fact, that the means for exercising power are more narrowly concentrated in a few hands in such societies than at any earlier time in history. From this perspective, the principle of political equality and the process of electoral competition upon which liberal democracy is founded are nothing more than a sham.

16. **Power is like money is formulated by Talcott Parsons.** Parsons was an American sociologist of the classical tradition, best known for his social action theory and structural functionalism. Parsons is considered one of the most influential figures in the development of sociology in the 20th century. After earning a PhD in economics, he served on the faculty at Harvard University from 1927 to 1979, and in 1930, was among the first professors in its newly created sociology department.

Based on empirical data, Parsons' social action theory was the first broad, systematic, and generalizable theory of social systems developed in the United States. Some of Parsons' largest contributions to sociology in the English-speaking world were his translations of Max Weber's work and his analyses of works by Weber, Émile Durkheim, and Vilfredo Pareto. Their work heavily influenced Parsons' view, and was the foundation for his social action theory, in which he viewed voluntaristic action through the lens of the cultural values and social structures that constrain choices and ultimately determine all social actions, as opposed to actions that are determined based on internal psychological processes. Although Parsons is generally considered a structural functionalist, towards the end of his career in 1975, he published an article in which he stated the terms "functional" and "structural functionalist" were inappropriate ways to describe the character of his theory.

19. The capitalist world economy is made up of "commodity chains" of producers and consumers, sellers and buyers linking countries in the core of the world economy", is the basis of world systems theory.

World-systems theory (also known as **world-systems analysis or the world-systems perspective**) is a multidisciplinary, macro-scale approach to world history and social change which emphasizes the world-system (and not nation states) as the primary (but not exclusive) unit of social analysis.

"World-system" refers to the inter-regional and transnational division of labour, which divides the world into core countries, semi-periphery countries, and the periphery countries. Core countries focus on higher skill, capital-intensive production, and the rest of the world focuses on low-skill, labour-intensive production and extraction of raw materials. This constantly reinforces the dominance of the core countries. Nonetheless, the system has dynamic characteristics, in part as a result of revolutions in transport technology, and individual states can gain or lose their core (semi-periphery, periphery) status over time. This structure is unified by the division of labour. It is a world-economy rooted in a capitalist economy. For a time, certain countries become the world hegemon; during the last few centuries, as the world-system has extended geographically and intensified economically, this status has passed from the Netherlands, to the United Kingdom and (most recently) to the United States of America.

20. Consociational democracy can be found in countries that are deeply divided into distinct religious, ethnic, racial, or regional segments—conditions usually considered unfavourable for stable democracy. The two central characteristics of consociationalism are government by grand coalition and segmental autonomy. Government by grand coalition is the institutional setting in which representatives of all significant segments participate in common decision making with regard to common concerns, whereas decision making remains autonomous for all other issues. In all respects, consociationalism contrasts profoundly with majority-rule democracy (majoritarianism). While the notion of consociationalism has been known since the 17th Century, it was conceptualized in the 1960s, in particular by Arend Lijphart, and is used today as both an analytical and a normative category. Based on a number of factors, it takes different forms in different countries, and it has been widely criticized.

21. Granville Austin said, "The Constituent Assembly was a one party body in an essentially one party country. The assembly was the Congress and the Congress was India." The above quote reflects the view point of Austin on the composition of constituent assembly. With the division of country into two and subsequent withdrawal of Muslim League from the Assembly, the body became largely a Congress dominated body. As a party which inherited the success of independence, Congress not only dominated the Constituent Assembly, but also the central and regional governments. It enjoyed an overwhelming support of the masses, largely due to the charisma of Gandhi and Nehru. Though there were other parties present at that time, their representation and influence was marginal.

23. The Constitution of India vests sovereign power in the President and Governors. The governance in the Centre and states are carried out in the name of President and Governor respectively. A President is empowered with the power to pardon under Article 72 of the Indian Constitution. Article 72 says that the President shall have the power to grant pardons, reprieves, respites or remissions of punishment or to suspend, remit or commute the sentence of any person convicted of any offence. Similarly, as per Article 161: Governor of a State has the power to grant pardons, reprieves, respites or remissions of punishment or to suspend, remit or commute the sentence of any person convicted of any offence against any law relating to a matter to which the executive power of the State extends. Please note that President can grant pardon to a person awarded death sentence. But Governor of State does not enjoy this power. The question is that whether this power to grant pardon is absolute or this power of pardon shall be exercised by the President on the advice of Council of Ministers. The pardoning power of President is NOT absolute. It is governed by the advice of the Council of Ministers. This has not been discussed by the Constitution but is the practical truth. Further, the Constitution does not provide for any mechanism to question the legality of decisions of President or Governors exercising mercy jurisdiction. But the SC in Epuru Sudhakar case has given a small window for judicial review of the pardon powers of President and Governors for the purpose of ruling out any arbitrariness. The court has earlier held that court has retained the power of judicial review even on a matter which has been vested by the Constitution solely in the Executive.

25. Fundamental Duties are non-justiciable and are supposed to inculcate a sense of patriotic and sensible citizenship. The Fundamental Duties of citizens were added to the Constitution by the 42nd Amendment in 1976, upon the recommendations of the Swaran Singh Committee that was constituted by the government earlier that year. Originally ten in number, the Fundamental Duties were increased to eleven by the 86th Amendment in 2002, which added a duty on every parent or guardian to ensure that their child or ward was provided opportunities for education between the ages of six and fourteen years. The other Fundamental Duties obligate all citizens to respect the national symbols of India, including the Constitution, to cherish its heritage, preserve its composite culture and assist in its defense. They also obligate all Indians to promote the spirit of common brotherhood, protect the environment and public property, develop scientific temper, abjure violence, and strive towards excellence in all spheres of life. Citizens are morally obligated by the Constitution to perform these duties. However, like the Directive Principles, these are non-justifiable, without any legal sanction in case of their violation or non-compliance. There is reference to such duties in international instruments such as the Universal Declaration of Human Rights and International Covenant on Civil and Political Rights, and Article 51A brings the Indian Constitution into conformity with these treaties.

The Fundamental Duties noted in the constitution are as follows:

It shall be the duty of every citizen of India

- To abide by the Constitution and respect its ideals and institutions, the National Flag and the National Anthem;
- To cherish and follow the noble ideals which inspired our national struggle for freedom;
- To uphold and protect the sovereignty, unity and integrity of India;
- To defend the country and render national service when called upon to do so;
- To promote harmony and the spirit of common brotherhood amongst all the people of India transcending religious,

linguistic and regional or sectional diversities; to renounce practices derogatory to the dignity of women;

- To value and preserve the rich heritage of our composite culture;
- To protect and improve the natural environment including forests, lakes, rivers, wildlife and to have compassion for living creatures;
- To develop the scientific temper, humanism and the spirit of inquiry and reform;
- To safeguard public property and to abjure violence;
- To strive towards excellence in all spheres of individual and collective activity, so that the nation constantly rises to higher levels of endeavour and achievement;
- Who is a parent or guardian, to provide opportunities for education to his child, or as the case may be, ward between the age of six and fourteen years.

26. **Article 105** of the Constitution provides for the privileges of the Houses of the Parliament, of the members and Committees thereof.

Article 194 underlines those of the Houses of the State Legislatures, and of the members and Committees thereof. The privileges are the same and are discussed hereunder:

1. **Freedom of Speech:** Subject to the Articles 118 and 120 (in case of Parliament), and 208 and 211 (in case of State Legislatures), which state that the conduct of judges cannot be questioned, there shall be freedom of speech in the legislature.
2. **Right of publication of proceedings:** The Constitution provides that no person shall be liable in respect of the publication, by order under the authority of a House of Parliament or State Legislature, of any report, paper, votes or proceedings.
3. **Other privileges:** Clause 3 of Articles 105 and 194 provides that the privileges of each House, its members and Committees shall be such as determined by the respective legislature from time to time and until it does so, which it has not done, shall be such as on 20th June, 1979. The privileges which were existing then include the freedom from arrest, right to exclude strangers (which can be regarded as a corollary of the freedom of speech), right to prohibit the publication of debates, right of the House to regulate its own constitution and internal proceedings, to punish members and outsiders and members for contempt, and the right to expel members.

Each House of the legislature has its Committee of Privileges, which considers the matters of the breach of privilege or contempt.

28. The correct chronological order of the developments of events related to federalism in India is as follows:

(*i*) A Centre-State Relations Enquiry Committee was set up by the then DMK Government of Tamil Nadu on 2nd September, 1969 under the Chairmanship of Dr. P.V. Rajamannar to consider the entire question regarding relationship that should subsist between the Centre and the States in a federal set up.

(*ii*) The Anandpur Sahib Resolution was a statement made by a Sikh political party, the Shiromani Akali Dal, in 1973.

(*iii*) West Bengal Memorandum published in 1977 with demand for state autonomy by West Bengal government.

(*iv*) In April 2007, a three member commission headed by the former Chief Justice of India M.M. Punchhi Set up to take a fresh look at relative roles and responsibilities of various levels of government and their inter-relations. This Commission had submitted its report in 2010 to then Home Minister P. Chidambaram.

30. Some of the key classic committees towards electoral reforms in the country include: Tarkunde Committee Report (1975), Goswami Committee Report (1990), Election Commission's recommendations (1998),

Indrajit Gupta Committee Report (1998). The important recommendations of the Tarkunde Committee are as follows:

The election commission should be a three member body. The minimum age of voting should be 18 years. The TV and radio should be placed under the control of autonomous statutory corporation. A voter's council should be formed in as many constituencies as possible which can help in free and fair election.

The major recommendations of Goswami committee are as follows:

Time limit for bye-elections. Increase in deposits from independents. A check on advertisements on new papers and strengthening of the election commission. A series of legislative measures should be set up to eradicate booth-capturing, rigging and intimidating. The committee also called for amendment of the anti-defection law to restrict disqualification. Indrajit Gupta was the chairman of the all-party parliamentary committee on state funding of elections. The 8-member committee that set up by the all-party conference in May, 1998, submitted its report in January, 1999 with the following recommendations:

State funding should be in kind, that is, no financial support is to be given to parties and also, part of the financial burden of the parties should be initially borne by the state. A ₹ 600 crore contribution from the centre and an equal amount by the states, annually, towards an election corpus fund for the purpose. Only EC-recognized political parties should be given the state support in terms of printing material and facilities; electronic media time; vehicles and fuel, etc. Political parties should compulsorily submit their annual accounts to the Income Tax Department, showing their receipts and expenditure failing which the party or the candidate foregoes the state support. Complete account of the election expenditure should be filled by the parties to the EC. All donations above ₹ 10,000 by the parties should be in the form of cheque/draft and the names of the donors should be disclosed in the accounts. Ban on donations by the government companies for political purposes will continue, but whether other companies can donate or not is to be determined by the parliament. The election commission has produced a comprehensive set of proposals regarding electoral reforms and implemented many of the recommendations of the above committees.

31. The approaches to the study of Public Administration can be categorized from many angles such as normative approach and empirical approach. Normative approach concentrates on what public administration should be. Empirical approach sets its eyes on description and analysis of actual administrative situations. Another classification of approaches is based upon the objects of study the individual scholar seeks to emphasize, such as;

(*i*) Philosophical approach

(*ii*) Legal approach

(*iii*) Historical approach

(*iv*) Scientific approach

(*v*) Case Method approach

(*vi*) Institutional and Structural approach

(*vii*) Behavioural approach.

33. The concept of good governance is not new. Kautilya in his treatise *Arthashastra* elaborated the traits of the king of a well governed State thus: "in the happiness of his subjects lies his happiness, in their welfare his welfare, whatever pleases himself, he does not consider as good, but whatever pleases his subjects he considers as good". Mahatma Gandhi had propounded the concept of 'Su-raj'.

The 2nd Administrative Reforms Commission identified as barriers to citizen-centric administration (good governance) in India are as follows:

(*i*) Indifferent attitude of public servants.

(*ii*) Lack of Accountability.

(*iii*) Red Tapism.

(*iv*) Low levels of awareness of the rights and duties of citizens.

(*v*) Ineffective implementation of laws and rules.

34. The Ministry of Finance is an important ministry within the Government of India concerned with the economy of India, serving as the Indian Treasury Department. In particular, it concerns itself with taxation, financial legislation, financial institutions, capital markets, centre and state finances, and the Union Budget.

The following Cadre Controlling Authority of the Civil Services (including Indian Revenue Service, Indian Economic Service, Indian Cost Accounts Service and Indian Civil Accounts Service) are under the administration and supervision of the Finance Ministry.

35. In India, the term 'deficit financing' was first defined by First Five Year Plan. Planning Commission has defined the term as "deficit financing is used to denote the direct addition to gross national expenditure through budget deficit whether the deficits are on the revenue account or on capital account.

The essence of such a policy lies therefore in government's spending; in excess of the revenue it receives in the shape of the taxes earnings of state enterprise, loans from public deposits and funds and other miscellaneous sources.

The government may cover the deficit either by running down its accumulated balances or by borrowing from the banking system". It includes borrowing from the central bank and withdrawal of cash balances, and excludes market borrowing.

36. Guardian bureaucracy regards itself as the custodian of public interest but is independent of and unresponsive to public opinion. Bureaucracy is a term that refers to both a body of non-elective government officials and an administrative policy-making group. Historically, a bureaucracy was a government administration managed by departments staffed with non-elected officials. Today, bureaucracy is the administrative system governing any large institution. The public administration in many countries is an example of a bureaucracy.

M. Marx defines Guardian bureaucracy as that which is dedicated to general welfare and acts as champion of justice and custodian of community's welfare. The Guardian Bureaucracy may be explained on 'a scholastic official doom trained in right conduct according to the classics'.

38. University Grants Commission, Railway Board and Atomic Energy Commission are statutory bodies whether Official Language Commission was constituted by the President of India in pursuance to the provision stated in the Article-344 of the Indian Constitution. This Commission was constituted on June 7, 1955 vide a notification of the Ministry of Home Affairs, Government of India.

As defined in Article-344 of the constitution, it shall be the duty of the Commission to make recommendations to the President as to:

(*i*) The progressive use of the Hindi language for the official purposes of the Union;

(*ii*) Restrictions on the use of the English language for all or any of the official purposes of the union;

(*iii*) The language to be used for all or any of the purposes mentioned in Article-348;

(*iv*) The form of numerals to be used for anyone or more specified purposes of the Union;

(*v*) Any other matter referred to the Commission by the President as regards the official language of the Union and the language for communication between the union and a state or between one state and another and their use.

40. Henry Fayol, M.P. Follet, Luther Gulick and L. Urwick are of the view that the managerial techniques and skills of planning, organizing, coordinating and budgeting are same in both

Public and Private Administration. Fayol said that all kinds of administration function on some general principle irrespective of them being public or private. The planning, organizing, commanding and controlling are similar for all administrations.

The above arguments and several other points suggested and illustrated by other authors as well clearly point out that there are more similarities between the two administrations than what we see and understand.

41. Hedely Bull belongs to British School of Realism. The English School of international relations theory (sometimes also referred to as Liberal Realism, the International Society School or the British institutionalists) maintains that there is a 'society of states' at the international level, despite the condition of anarchy (that is, the lack of a global ruler or world state). The English school stands for the conviction that ideas, rather than simply material capabilities, shape the conduct of international politics, and therefore deserve analysis and critique. In this sense it is similar to constructivism, though the English School has its roots more in world history, international law and political theory, and is more open to normative approaches than is generally the case with constructivism.

The classical English school starts with the realist assumption of an international system that forms as soon as two or more states have a sufficient amount of interaction. It underlines the English school tradition of realism and Machtpolitik (power politics) and puts international anarchy at the centre of International Relations Theory.

Hedley Bull, however, argued that states share a certain common interest (usually the "fear of unrestricted violence") that leads to the development of a certain set of "rules". He thus defined an international society as existent when:

...a group of states (or, more generally, a group of independent political communities) which not merely form a system, in the sense that the behaviour of each is a necessary factor in the calculations of the others, but also have established by dialogue and consent common rules and institutions for the conduct of their relations, and recognise their common interest in maintaining these arrangements.

In Bull's view, any type of society needed to have rules about restraints on the use of force, about the sanctity of agreements, and about property rights. Without elements of these three there would be no society.

42. The phrase "balance of terror" is usually, but not invariably, used in reference to the nuclear arms race between the United States and the erstwhile Soviet Union during the Cold War.

It describes the tenuous peace that existed between the two countries as a result of both governments being terrified at the prospect of a world-destroying nuclear war. The term is usually used for rhetorical purposes, and was probably coined by Lester Pearson in June 1955 at the 10th anniversary of the signing of the UN Charter: "the balance of terror has replaced the balance of power".

Some political scientists use this phrase as a means of differentiating the world situation that followed World War II from that which preceded it. Previously, empires had prevented war between each other by maintaining a relative balance of their ability (economic, military, and political) to wage war against each other—the phrase "balance of power" was often used to describe this kind of tentative peace.

The atomic bomb created a new political reality, in which two superpowers had the ability to destroy all of human civilization. The obstacle to war between the communists and the capitalists was no longer the fear that the other side was more powerful, but rather the realization that nuclear arsenals were now large enough and deadly enough that winning would still likely result in the destruction of one's country (and the rest of the world as well).

In this counterintuitive way, the existence of the most powerful weapons ever created actually supported a kind of peace: while many wars were fought around the world during the Cold War, the superpowers never fought each other directly, nor have atomic bombs been dropped in war since the atomic bombing of Nagasaki in 1945.

Lawrence Summers, after the financial meltdown of 2008, adopted the term as appropriate for the situation of a 'financial balance of terror' in global markets.

43. According to Hans. J. Morgenthau, "Whenever the term 'balance of power' is used without qualification, it refers to an actual state of affairs in which power is distributed among nations with approximately equality". The balance of power rests upon several fundamental postulates and assumptions–

(*i*) Balance of Power assumes that states are determined to protect their vital rights and interests by all means, including war.

(*ii*) Vital interests of the states are threatened.

(*iii*) The relative power position of states can be measured with a degree of accuracy.

(*iv*) Balance of Power assumes that 'balance' will either deter the threatening state from launching an attack or permit the victim to avoid defeat if an attack should occur.

(*v*) The statesmen can, and they do make foreign policy decisions intelligently on the basis of power considerations.

44. Both India and China refused to accept legally binding emission cuts following Kyoto Protocol.

The Kyoto Protocol is an international treaty which extends the 1992 United Nations Framework Convention on Climate Change (UNFCCC) that commits State Parties to reduce greenhouse gas emissions, based on the scientific consensus that (a) global warming is occurring and (b) it is extremely likely that human-made CO_2 emissions have predominantly caused it. The Kyoto Protocol was adopted in Kyoto, Japan, on December 11, 1997 and entered into force on February 16, 2005. There are currently 192 parties to the Protocol.

The Kyoto Protocol implemented the objective of the UNFCCC to fight global warming by reducing greenhouse gas concentrations in the atmosphere to "a level that would prevent dangerous anthropogenic interference with the climate system" (Art. 2). The Protocol is based on the principle of common but differentiated responsibilities: it puts the obligation to reduce current emissions on developed countries on the basis that they are historically responsible for the current levels of greenhouse gases in the atmosphere.

45. In a speech (text) at the Twentieth Party Congress in 1956, Khrushchev attacked Stalin, saying that Stalin was a murderer and a tyrant. Khrushchev began to 'de-stalinise' Russia — political prisoners were set free and Beria (Stalin's Chief of Secret Police) was executed. In 1961 Khrushchev declared that the period of 'the dictatorship of the proletariat' was at end, and that he would bring in instead: 'the state of the whole people'.

Khrushchev said that he wanted 'peaceful co-existence' with the West. Western leaders hoped this meant the end of the Cold War.

46. ***The End of History and the Last Man*** is a 1992 book by Francis Fukuyama, expanding on his 1989 essay "The End of History?" published in the international affairs journal *The National Interest*. In the book, Fukuyama argues that the advent of Western liberal democracy may signal the endpoint of humanity's sociocultural evolution and the final form of human government.

What we may be witnessing is not just the end of the Cold War, or the passing of a particular period of post-war history, but the end of history as such: that is, the end point of mankind's ideological evolution and the universalization of Western liberal democracy as the final form of human government.

Fukuyama's position contradicts that of Karl Marx, who predicted that communism would displace capitalism. Fukuyama himself identifies on some level with Marx, but more strongly with the German philosopher Georg Wilhelm Friedrich Hegel, by way of Alexandre Kojève. Kojève argued that the progress of history must lead toward the establishment of a "universal and homogeneous" state, most likely incorporating elements of liberal or social democracy; but Kojève's emphasis on the necessarily "post-political" character of such a state (and its citizens) makes such comparisons inadequate, and is irreducible to any mere "triumph" of capitalism.

48. On November 9, 1989, as the Cold War began to thaw across Eastern Europe, the spokesman for East Berlin's Communist Party announced a change in his city's relations with the West. Starting at midnight that day, he said, citizens of the GDR were free to cross the country's borders. East and West Berliners flocked to the wall, drinking beer and champagne and chanting "Tor auf!" ("Open the gate!"). At midnight, they flooded through the checkpoints.

More than 2 million people from East Berlin visited West Berlin that weekend to participate in a celebration that was, one journalist wrote, "the greatest street party in the history of the world." People used hammers and picks to knock away chunks of the wall-they became known as "mauerspechte," or "wall woodpeckers"—while cranes and bulldozers pulled down section after section. Soon the wall was gone and Berlin was united for the first time since 1945. "Only today," one Berliner spray-painted on a piece of the wall, "is the war really over."

The reunification of East and West Germany was made official on October 3, 1990, almost one year after the fall of the Berlin Wall.

49. The **Maastricht Treaty** (formally, the **Treaty on European Union** or **TEU**) undertaken to integrate Europe was signed on 7 February 1992 by the members of the European Community in Maastricht, Netherlands. On 9-10 December 1991, the same city hosted the European Council which drafted the treaty. Upon its entry into force on 1 November 1993 during the Delors Commission, it created the three pillars structure of the European Union and led to the creation of the single European currency, the euro.

50. OPEC is not a specialized agency of the United Nations. **Organization of the Petroleum Exporting Countries (OPEC)** is an inter-governmental organization of 14 nations as of May 2017, founded in 1960 in Baghdad by the first five members (Iran, Iraq, Kuwait, Saudi Arabia and Venezuela), and headquartered since 1965 in Vienna. As of 2016, the 14 countries accounted for an estimated 44 per cent of global oil production and 73 per cent of the world's "proven" oil reserves, giving OPEC a major influence on global oil prices that were previously determined by American-dominated multinational oil companies. OPEC's stated mission is "to coordinate and unify the petroleum policies of its member countries and ensure the stabilization of oil markets, in order to secure an efficient, economic and regular supply of petroleum to consumers, a steady income to producers, and a fair return on capital for those investing in the petroleum industry." The organization is also a significant provider of information about the international oil market. As of May 2017, OPEC's members are Algeria, Angola, Ecuador, Equatorial Guinea, Gabon, Iran, Iraq, Kuwait, Libya, Nigeria, Qatar, Saudi Arabia , United Arab Emirates, and Venezuela, while Indonesia is a former member. Two-thirds of OPEC's oil production and reserves are in its six Middle Eastern countries that surround the oil-rich Persian Gulf.

PAPER-III

Note: *This paper contains **seventy five (75)** objective type questions of **two (2)** marks each. All questions are compulsory.*

1. Who of the following said, "An important function of Political theory is not only to show what a political practice is but also to show what it means. In showing what a practice means, or what it ought to mean, Political theory can alter what it is"?

A. G.H. Sabine B. Leo Strauss
C. Michael Oakeshott D. Isaiah Berlin

2. Who among the following disputed the view that human behaviour could be adequately described without reference to the intentions, motives and reasons of the actors involved?

A. Peter Winch B. C. Hull
C. D. Hume D. R.A. Dahl

3. Match the List-I with List-II and select the correct answer from the codes given below:

List–I (Authors)	***List–II (Concepts)***
(*a*) John Rawls	1. Equality of What?
(*b*) John C. Harsanyi	2. Primary Goods Reconsidered
(*c*) Richard J. Arneson	3. Justice as Fairness
(*d*) Alex Callinicos	4. The Maximin Principle

Codes:

	(*a*)	(*b*)	(*c*)	(*d*)
A.	1	2	3	4
B.	3	2	1	4
C.	3	4	2	1
D.	4	3	1	2

4. Given below are two statements, one labelled as Assertion (A) and other labeled as Reason (R). Select the correct answer from the codes given below:

Assertion (A) : Lenin produced a new theory of the revolutionary function of the intellectuals.

Reason (R) : The ideas and not the material conditions of production are the effective causes of revolution.

Codes:

A. Both (A) and (R) are true and (R) is the correct explanation of (A).
B. Both (A) and (R) are true, but (R) is not the correct explanation of (A).
C. (A) is true, but (R) is false.
D. (A) is false, but (R) is true.

5. Who among the following declared: "For me morals, ethics, and religion are convertible terms. A moral life without reference to religion is like a house built upon sand"?

A. Aurobindo B. Savarkar
C. Mahatma Gandhi D. Jayaprakash

6. Match the List-I with List-II and select the correct answer from the codes given below.

List–I (Plato's Dialogues)	***List–II (Main Themes)***
(*a*) Symposium	1. The sphere of Physics
(*b*) Philebus	2. The sphere of Politics
(*c*) Timaeus	3. Application of the theory of ideas to the sphere of ethics
(*d*) Republic	4. The metaphysics of love

Codes:

	(*a*)	(*b*)	(*c*)	(*d*)
A.	4	3	1	2
B.	1	2	3	4
C.	3	4	2	1
D.	2	1	4	3

7. Given below are two statements, one labelled as Assertion (A) and other labelled as Reason (R): Select the correct answer from the codes given below:

Assertion (A) : No genuine understanding of Aristotle can endorse the opinion that his philosophical system was the opposite of Plato.

Reason (R) : Aristotle's system is an attempt to Philosophize on idealism free from the defects of Plato's system.

Codes:
A. Both (A) and (R) are true and (R) is the correct explanation of (A).
B. Both (A) and (R) are true, but (R) is not the correct explanation of (A).
C. (A) is true, but (R) is false.
D. (A) is false, but (R) is true.

8. Given below are two statements, one labelled as Assertion (A) and other labelled as Reason (R). Select the correct answer from the codes given below:

Assertion (A) : Machiavellism stands for double standard of morals, one for the ruler and another for the private citizen.

Reason (R) : The ruler, as the creator of the state, is not only outside the Law, and outside morality as well.

Codes:
A. Both (A) and (R) are true and (R) is the correct explanation of (A).
B. Both (A) and (R) are true, but (R) is not the correct explanation of (A).
C. (A) is true, but (R) is false.
D. (A) is false, but (R) is true.

9. Whose ideas of the following were incorporated in the Philosophical radicalism of utilitarianism?
A. Machiavelli B. Thomas Hobbes
C. John Locke D. Rousseau

10. Given below are two statements, one labelled as Assertion (A) and other labelled as Reason (R). Select the correct answer from the codes given below:

Assertion (A) : Karl Marx is interpreted by some as an economic determinist but by others as a humane socialist.

Reason (R) : The problem stems from the wide range and complex nature of his own writings.

Codes:
A. Both (A) and (R) are true and (R) is the correct explanation of (A).
B. Both (A) and (R) are true, but (R) is not the correct explanation of (A).
C. (A) is true, but (R) is false.
D. (A) is false, but (R) is true.

11. Who among the following defined Civil power as "the right of making laws with penalties... for the regulating and preserving of property, and of employing the force of the community, in the execution of such laws.... All this only for the public good."?
A. Machiavelli B. Thomas Hobbes
C. John Locke D. Rousseau

12. Who among the following said, 'Ideology is the most elusive concept in the whole of Social Science'?
A. Martin Seliger B. David McLellan
C. J.B. Thompson D. John Plamenatz

13. Arrange the following works of Sri Aurobindo in chronological order: Select the correct answer from the codes given below:
(*a*) Love and Death
(*b*) The Life Divine
(*c*) Essays on Gita
(*d*) Savitri : A Legend and a Symbol
Codes:
A. (*a*), (*b*), (*d*) and (*c*) B. (*a*), (*b*), (*c*) and (*d*)
C. (*b*), (*d*), (*a*) and (*c*) D. (*d*), (*a*), (*b*) and (*c*)

14. Which one of the following statements is not true in case of Liberalism?
A. Liberal thought focuses upon needs and interests of the 'individual,' rather than those of any group or 'collective'.
B. The liberals desire to create a society in which each individual is capable of developing and flourishing to the fullness of his or her potential.
C. Liberals do not believe in universalism that individuals are all of equal moral worth.
D. Individual liberty is for liberals the Supreme Political Value.

15. Who among the following argued that 'the only purpose for which power can be right fully exercised over any member of a civilized community against his will, is to prevent harm to others'?
A. James Mill B. Jeremy Bentham
C. J.S. Mill D. J.B. Priestley

16. In the year 1960, application of structural functionalism by Almond and Powell was an application of
A. Easton's Framework of Political System
B. Dahl's Polyarely
C. Lucian Pye's Modernization Theory
D. Rostow's Theory of Stapes of Growth

17. Economics is value free, but political economy orginates in the context of the ideological debate of the eighteenth century is a comment made by
A. Marx B. Keynes
C. Schumpeter D. Amartya Sen

18. Which of the following is not an integral part of liberal constitutionalism?
A. Individual freedom
B. Toleration and consent
C. Majoritanianism
D. Minority rights

19. The Presidential system operates most successfully in the U.S.A. because of
A. A strong two party system
B. A well demarcated constitution
C. Judicial review
D. Minor contradictions in society

20. The House of Lords in Great Britain is mainly retained because
A. It is as important as the House of Commons.
B. It plays an important role of checks and balances.
C. It acts as a judicial court.
D. It is maintained as an institution.

21. Given below are two statements, one labelled as Assertion (A) and other labelled as Reason (R). Select the correct answer from the codes given below:
Assertion (A) : Huntington is correct in asserting that the combination of the role of the state and government of the U.S. President is a medieval practice.
Reason (R) : It is because in other liberal democracies, the two roles are not combined.
Codes:
A. Both (A) and (R) are true and (R) is the correct explanation of (A).
B. Both (A) and (R) are true, but (R) is not the correct explanation of (A).
C. (A) is true, but (R) is the false.
D. (A) is false, but (R) is true.

22. The growth of judicial power over the last one hundred years in liberal democracies have taken place because
A. The constitutions have given the judiciary more powers.
B. Acceptance of the theory of separation of powers.
C. The U.N. Directives.
D. Protect Human Rights.

23. Environmental Green parties originated from
A. Breakaway from main stream political parties.
B. Pressure of public opinion
C. Emergence of a planetary consciousness
D. New social movements

24. Duverger's theory asserts that a two party system emerges in a
A. representational parliamentary system.
B. homogeneous political order.
C. welfare state
D. a majoritarian parliamentary system.

25. The first use of the concept of political culture was made by
A. Gabriel Almond
B. G. Bingham Powell, Jr.
C. Karl Deutseh
D. Lucian Pye

26. Which one of the following orientations is not a part of the basic types of political culture?
A. Cognitive orientations
B. Affective orientations
C. Evaluative orientations
D. Individual orientations

27. The progressive comparativists in political development do not emphasize in one of the following:
A. Under development B. Dependency
C. Imperialism D. Modernization

28. The Theory of Modernization and decay is formulated by
A. Rostow B. Pye
C. Huntington D. Lipset

29. Which of the following is not an essential prerequisite for making elitism compatible with democracy in Schumpeter?
A. The calibre of politicians must be high.
B. Competition is to take place within a relatively restricted range.
C. Presence of a well trained independent bureaucracy.
D. A well organised party system

30. Beliefs and symbols are the distinctive features of the notion of authority in
A. Marx B. Parsons
C. Verba D. Weber

31. Regarding the Interim Government of 1946, which of the following is not correct?
A. Jawaharlal Nehru was the Prime Minister/ Head of the Executive Council.
B. Jawaharlal Nehru was designated as the Vice-President of the Viceroy's Executive Council.
C. The Viceroy continued to be the Head of the Executive Council.
D. The members of the Interim Government were members of viceroy's Executive Council.

32. Which one of the following statements is not correct regarding Certiorari?
A. A High Court can issue a writ against itself in its administrative capacity.
B. A bench of a High Court can issue a writ to another bench of the same High Court.
C. A High Court cannot issue a writ to another High Court.
D. A High Court can issue certiorari to a tribunal situated within its jurisdiction.

33. In which one of the following cases the Supreme Court of India used the principle of "continuing mandamus"?
A. S.P. Gupta Vs. Union of India
B. Sunil Batra Vs. Delhi Administration
C. Vineet Narain Vs. Union of India
D. Sagir Ahmad Vs. State of U.P.

34. Who was the first President of India to make use of 'Pocket Veto'?
A. Zakir Hussain B. Sanjeeva Reddy
C. R. Venkatraman D. Gyani Zail Singh

35. Who said Indian federalism is "a new kind of federation to meet India's peculiar needs"?
A. Granville Austin B. Ivor Jenneigs
C. Alexandrowicz D. Ronald Wats

36. Adi Ambedkar Samaj movement is related to which State?
A. Maharashtra B. Punjab
C. Rajasthan D. Uttar Pradesh

37. Who was the Chairman of the Group of Interlocutors for Jammu and Kashmir?
A. T.S.R. Subramanian B. Dilip Padgaonkar
C. Radha Kumar D. Dr. Karan Singh

38. Which of the following statements is true about the constitution of P.K. Thungan Committee?
A. To consider the type of political and administrative structure needed in the District Planning.
B. To consider the administrative arrangements for rural Development.
C. To consider the need for decentralized planning.
D. For drawing guidelines for Block level planning.

39. When did the Communist Party of India (Marxist) emerge as a separate political party?
A. 1960 B. 1964
C. 1968 D. 1973

40. Match the List-I with List-II and give the correct answer from the codes given below:

List–I (Case)	***List–II (Subject)***
(*a*) Rudal Vs. State of Bihar	1. Right to Fly tricolour
(*b*) A.D.M. Jabalpur Vs. Shiv Kant Shukla	2. Right to know antecedents of candidates for election
(*c*) Union of India Vs. Naveen Jindal	3. Award of monetary compensation
(*d*) Union of India Vs. Association for Democratic Reforms	4. Right to life

Codes:

	(*a*)	(*b*)	(*c*)	(*d*)
A.	3	4	1	2
B.	2	3	4	1
C.	1	2	3	4
D.	4	1	2	3

41. Who described the critical and creative role of politics in India as "the Indian model of development"?
A. Rajni Kothari B. Amartya Sen
C. Jagdish Bhagwati D. James Maner

42. Match List-I with List-II and identify the correct answer from the codes given below:

List–I (Event)	List–II (Year)
(*a*) Millennium Development Goals Report	1. 2010
(*b*) National Commission for Women	2. 2006
(*c*) Ministry of Women and Child Development	3. 1992
(*d*) National Mission for Empowerment of Women	4. 2011

Codes:

	(*a*)	(*b*)	(*c*)	(*d*)
A.	1	2	4	3
B.	4	3	2	1
C.	1	4	3	2
D.	3	1	2	4

43. Who among the following made a significant contribution to theories of the Interaction between social dominance and state power in contemporary India?
A. Francine R. Frankel & M.S.A. Rao
B. Myron Weiner
C. Lloyd and Susane Rudolph
D. Partha Chatterjee

44. Which one of the following Committees opposed the state funding of elections in India?
A. Justice B.P. Jeevan Reddy
B. Indrajit Gupta
C. Tarkunde
D. Dinesh Goswami

45. Which of the following newspaper is managed by a trust in India?
A. Times of India B. Indian Express
C. Hindu D. Tribune

46. Who among the following hold the view that administration comprises of the work of only those persons who are engaged in performing managerial functions in an organization?
(*a*) Luther Gulick (*b*) Herbert Simon
(*c*) Victor Thomson (*d*) Henry Fayol

Select the correct answer from the codes given below:

Codes:
A. (*a*) and (*b*) B. (*b*) and (*c*)
C. (*b*), (*c*) and (*d*) D. (*a*), (*b*), (*c*) and (*d*)

47. Which one of the following stages of evolution of public administration is called the era of politics administration dichotomy?
A. First stage B. Second stage
C. Third stage D. Fourth stage

48. Which of the following are the salient features of the New Public Management?
(*a*) Empowerment of Citizens
(*b*) Disaggregation of Public Bureaucracy
(*c*) Cost-cutting
(*d*) Organizational Centralization

Select the correct answer from the codes given below:

Codes:
A. (*a*) and (*c*) B. (*a*), (*c*) and (*d*)
C. (*a*), (*b*) and (*c*) D. (*a*), (*b*), (*c*) and (*d*)

49. 'Squealer' in the Human Relations theory is
A. one who does too much work.
B. one who does too little work.
C. one who absents himself from work.
D. one who communicates detrimental information about others to the supervisor.

50. Match the List-I with List-II and select the correct answer from the codes given below:

List–I	List–II
(*a*) Proverbs of Administration	1. Henry Fayol
(*b*) Principles of Management	2. Herbert Simon
(*c*) Functions of Executive	3. Morestein Marx
(*d*) Elements of Public Administration	4. Chester Barnard

Codes:

	(*a*)	(*b*)	(*c*)	(*d*)
A.	2	1	4	3
B.	1	2	3	4
C.	2	3	4	1
D.	3	4	1	2

51. Who among the following has defined budget as "a series of goals with price tags attached"?

A. Wildavsky B. Paul Appleby
C. Chester Barnard D. John D. Millet

52. Who among the following is the creator of Zero-Based-Budgeting?
A. Hoover Commission
B. Peter A. Phyrr
C. Herbert Simon
D. Gug Peters

53. What is the correct sequence of Morstein Marx's classification of bureaucracy given below:
(*a*) Merit (*b*) Patronage
(*c*) Caste (*d*) Gurdian
Select the correct answer from the codes given below:
Codes:
A. (*d*), (*c*), (*b*) and (*a*) B. (*a*), (*b*), (*c*) and (*d*)
C. (*a*), (*d*), (*c*) and (*b*) D. (*d*), (*a*), (*b*) and (*c*)

54. Who among the former Prime Ministers had observed that "only a committed bureaucracy could bring about social transformation....."?
A. Jawaharlal Nehru B. Morarji Desai
C. Indira Gandhi D. V.P. Singh

55. The purpose of an adjournment motion is to
A. seek the leave of the House to introduce a bill.
B. censure the Government.
C. propose a reduction in the budget.
D. draw the attention of the House to a matter of urgent public importance.

56. The First attempt to confer constitutional status on rural local government was made by
A. the 64th Constitutional Amendment Bill
B. the 68th Constitutional Amendment Bill
C. the 72nd Constitutional Amendment Bill
D. the 73rd Constitutional Amendment Act

57. Match the List-I with List-II and select the correct answer from the codes given below:

List–I	***List–II***
(*a*) Finance Commission	1. Ashok Mehta Committee
(*b*) Nagar Panchayats	2. 73rd Constitutional Amendment Act
(*c*) Democratic Decentralisation	3. 74th Constitutional Amendment Act
(*d*) Mandal Panchayats	4. Balwantrai Mehta Committee

Codes:

	(*a*)	(*b*)	(*c*)	(*d*)
A.	2	3	4	1
B.	1	2	3	4
C.	3	4	2	1
D.	2	3	1	4

58. Given below are two statements, one labelled as Assertion (A) and other labelled as Reason (R). Select the correct answer from the codes given below:
Assertion (A) : The Principle of Unity of Command cannot always be strictly followed in organizations.
Reason (R) : Employees are quite often subject to dual control administrative and technical.
Codes:
A. Both (A) and (R) are true and (R) is the correct explanation of (A).
B. Both (A) and (R) are true, but (R) is not the correct explanation of (A).
C. (A) is true, but (R) is false.
D. (A) is false, but (R) is true.

59. e-governance is
(*a*) cost-efficient (*b*) transparent
(*c*) time-saving (*d*) responsive
Select the correct answer from the codes given below:
A. (*a*) and (*c*) B. (*a*), (*b*) and (*c*)
C. (*a*), (*c*) and (*d*) D. (*a*), (*b*), (*c*) and (*d*)

60. Which one of the following Commissions/ Committees has recommended legal protection to whistle blowers?
A. First Administrative Reforms Commission
B. Second Administrative Reforms Commission
C. Vohra Committee
D. Election Commission

61. Which one of the following arrangements was not visualized by Morton Kaplan?
A. Balance of Power
B. Tight bipolar system
C. Loose bipolar system
D. Unipolar system

62. Which one of the following is not the technique of the balance of power?
A. Amassing of weapons

B. Seizing of territory
C. Methods of persuasion
D. Creating of buffer states

63. In 1999 NATO acted against Serbia accusing of indulging in act of 'ethnic cleansing' in Kosovo. To this, other major powers such as Russia and China reacted as under:
A. Russia criticised NATO acting without UN approval.
B. China described NATO act as illegal
C. Both Russia and China criticised NATO acting without UN approval.
D. Russia and China remained non-committal on the issue.

64. Which one of the following was not the basis invoked by the US for attacking Iraq in March, 2003?
A. Iraq possessed weapons of mass destruction.
B. Saddam Hussain had links with Al Quaeda.
C. Regime Change in Iraq
D. Iraq had not withdrawn from Kuwait completely.

65. 'Common but differentiated' responsibility principle on climate mitigation agenda emerged from
A. Kyoto Protocol
B. Rio Earth Summit
C. Rio + 20
D. Paris Climate Conference

66. Which of the following Republic/Republics was/were supported by Russia in Georgian war of 2008?
A. South Ossettia
B. South Ossettia and Abkhazia both
C. Abkhazia
D. Nogorno Karabakh

67. As per United Nations Convention on the Law of Sea (UNCLOS) states are entitled for Jurisdiction over sea water as under:
A. three miles from sea shore as territorial waters.
B. twelve miles from the shore for shipping.
C. two hundred miles as Exclusive Economic Zone (EEZ)
D. all the three jurisdictions.

68. India's good neighbourhood policy based on the principle of non-reciprocity is attributed to
A. P.V. Narashima Rao
B. Inder Kumar Gujral
C. A.B. Vajpayee
D. Rajiv Gandhi

69. Sir John Chilcot Commission has indicated
A. U.K. for its conduct in US led NATO war in Afghanistan
B. U.K. for its conduct in Iraq war in 2003
C. US for its invasion in Iraq in 2003
D. Russia for its attacks in Syria

70. The Washington consensus did not stand for
A. Fiscal discipline
B. Tax reforms
C. Financial and Trade Liberlisation
D. State Controlled Market System

71. Under Bush Doctrine, the USA held states responsible for activities inside their territories and thus acquired the right to
A. act unilaterally against rogue and failed states.
B. act against states which were opposed to it ideologically.
C. move against states which refused to join in drive for NATO expansion.
D. intervene in situations of ethnic cleansing.

72. Match the List-I with List-II and select the correct answer from the codes given below:

List–I	*List–II*
(*a*) Uniting for Peace Resolution	1. 1999
(*b*) The Suez Crisis	2. 2002
(*c*) UN Security Council Resolution on Iraq weapons	3. 1956
(*d*) UN Mission in Kosovo	4. 1950

Codes:

	(*a*)	(*b*)	(*c*)	(*d*)
A.	3	2	1	4
B.	2	1	3	4
C.	4	3	2	1
D.	1	2	4	3

73. Match the List-I with List-II and select correct answer from the codes given below:

List–I	*List–II*
(*a*) Conventional Arms Cut Treaty	1. 1996
(*b*) Strategic Arms Reduction Treaty-I	2. 1993

(*c*) Strategic Arms Reduction Treaty-II		3. 1990
(*d*) Comprehensive Test Ban Treaty		4. 1991

Codes:

	(*a*)	(*b*)	(*c*)	(*d*)
A.	3	4	2	1
B.	2	3	1	4
C.	4	2	3	1
D.	1	3	4	2

74. The US stopped cultivating ties with Taliban regime in Afghanistan after

A. 9/11 attacks in the US
B. attacks on US embassies in Kenya and Tanzania
C. attack on US military mission headquarter in Riyadh
D. failures of talks on gas pipeline through Afghanisatan

75. Who among the following statesmen described USSR as an 'evil empire'?

A. John F. Kennedy B. Ronald Regan
C. Richard Nixon D. Henry Kissinger

ANSWERS

1	**2**	**3**	**4**	**5**	**6**	**7**	**8**	**9**	**10**
A	A	C	A	C	A	A	A	B	A
11	**12**	**13**	**14**	**15**	**16**	**17**	**18**	**19**	**20**
C	B	A	C	C	A	C	C	D	D
21	**22**	**23**	**24**	**25**	**26**	**27**	**28**	**29**	**30**
A	D	D	D	A	D	D	C	D	D
31	**32**	**33**	**34**	**35**	**36**	**37**	**38**	**39**	**40**
A	B	C	D	A	B	B	A	B	A
41	**42**	**43**	**44**	**45**	**46**	**47**	**48**	**49**	**50**
A	B	A	A	D	D	A	C	D	A
51	**52**	**53**	**54**	**55**	**56**	**57**	**58**	**59**	**60**
A	B	A	C	D	A	A	A	D	B
61	**62**	**63**	**64**	**65**	**66**	**67**	**68**	**69**	**70**
D	C	C	D	A	B	D	B	B	D
71	**72**	**73**	**74**	**75**					
A	C	A	B	B					

EXPLANATORY ANSWERS

1. G.H. Sabine said that "an important function of political theory is not only to show what a political practice is but also to show what it means. In showing what a practice means, or what it ought to mean, political theory can alter what it is". Political theory is a set of specified relationships encompassing political matters that focus and organize inquiry to describe, explain, and predict political events and behaviours. Political theory is considered as the basis and branch of political science which attempts to arrive at generalizations, inference, or conclusions to be drawn from the data gathered by other specialists, not only in political science, but throughout the whole range of human knowledge and experience.

2. Peter Winch and Charles Taylor questioned the adequacy of behaviouralism as an account of human action. They disputed the view that human behaviour could be adequately described without reference to the intentions, motives and reasons of the actors involved. Drawing on both the earlier hermeneutic critics of positivism and the later work of Ludwig Wittgenstein, they argued further that social practices embodied a 'form of life' involving certain rule-like norms and forms of rationality. A practice such as volting, therefore, could not be understood solely in terms of individual physical movements or even subjective desires, but rather made sense only against the backdrop of a complex set of social norms, values, concepts and practices.

4. Lenin produced a new theory of the revolutionary function of the intellectuals and persistently rejected the view that the working class was capable of achieving socialism without leaders. He argued that trade union consciousness represented the peak of working class consciousness. Socialism, he affirmed, would be achieved by a band of revolutionaries at the head of a discontented but non-socialist-conscious working class. The Bolshevik "revolution" was a classic example of Leninist thinking; in fact it was a coup d'état carried out by professional revolutionaries and based on the populist slogan, "Peace, Land and Bread". Socialism was not on offer, nor could it have been.

5. Mahatma Gandhi declared his view in the Harijan that "For me morals, ethics, and religion are convertible terms. A moral life without reference to religion is a like house built upon sand." And religion divorced from morality is like 'sounding brass' good only for making a noise and breaking heads. Morality includes truth, ahimsa and continence. Every virtue that mankind has ever practiced is referable to and derived from these three fundamental virtues. Nonviolence and continence are again derivable from Truth, which for me is God.

7. No genuine understanding of Aristotle can endorse the opinion that his philosophical system was the opposite of Plato because Aristotle's system is an attempt to philosophize on idealism free from the defects of Plato's system. Despite Aristotle's Criticism of Plato, there were many similarities which could not be overlooked. Like Plato, Aristotle ensured the sovereignty of law with the rulers as its guardian, "its servant". Aristotle's description of the state as evolving from the family, the patriarchal nature of early states, the need for a state by everyone except an angel or a beast, war as a means for peace and not as an end in itself, the role of education, mixed constitutions, the rols of agriculture and retail trade, were some of the common points. Aristotle retained and redefined many of Plato's ideas, but his contribution was in building a philosophical system based on empiricism.

8. Machiavelli separated the private from the public sphere of morality. While the state (ruler) had a morality of its own—the morality of success the private individual was at all times to display qualities that were in consonance with the highest moral standards. He spoke of the raison d'etat of the state. In politics, fair was foul and foul was fair, depending on circumstances and situations. No general rule was valid, for everything became a matter of political expediency. A prince had to be compassionate, humane, loyal, and honest, while simultaneously willing to use force, fraud, deception and treachery. Machiavelli argued that political actions were to conform to high moral standards, namely compassion, good faith, trustworthiness and honesty in times of stability. However, in times of strife, chaos and disorder, principled politics would spell ruin. He asserted that power was anything but divine, and to think that states came into existence by the will of God was absurd. He also rejected the divine rights theory of kings.

9. Ideas of Thomas Hobbes were incorporated in the philosophical radicalism of utilitarianism. Hobbes saw the state as a conciliator of interests, a point of view that the utilitarians developed in great detail. Hobbes created an all-powerful state, but it was no totalitarian monster. It had to guarantee peace, order and security, and was not interested in self-glorification. The state did not control or regiment areas that were politically irrelevant. Hobbes accepted the fact that there were many types of human activities that had to be left to the reales of the non-political.

11. John Locke defined Civil power as "the right of making laws with penalties ..... for the regulating and preserving of property, and of employing the force of the community, in the execution of such laws ..... All this only for the public good". Through the discussions on property, Locke stated that it represented human entitlements and in fact "the great and chief and of men's uniting into commonwealth and putting themselves under government is the preservation" and protection of their property. The purpose of government was to secure human entitlements and ensure lives, liberties and the material possessions of all human beings. Even if the commonwealth was based on freely elected representatives, it could not dispose of the property of its subjects arbitrarily.

12. Ideology is difficult to define and probably therefore dangerous. David McLellan said "Ideology is the most elusive concept in the whole of social sciences". An ideology is one's collective set of beliefs or ideas, perhaps a philosophy. Ideology is rarely questioned by trusting devoted followers.

Ideology dictates the unconscious orientation, habits and social practices which may them have a strong influence on politics and government. An ideology is generally more strongly held than just an opinion, although the usage of the word "ideology" in the mainstream is loose about this.

Ideology assists those interested in visionary theory. Understanding people's belief systems allow another to more easily discuss and push an agenda of with the heavy use of the social engineering, psychology, propaganda, the mass media and other communication and cultural mechanisms to help create a specific society. Terrorists have very strongly held ideologies, which incline some of them to die, or encourage other to die for their ideological cause.

14. Liberal thought is characterized by a commitment to individualism, a belief in the supreme importance of the human individual, implying strong support for individual freedom. The liberals desire to create a society in which each individual is capable of developing and flourishing to the fullness of his or her potential. As a result, liberals look towards the creation of a meritocratic society in which rewards are distributed according to individual talent and hard work. As an economic doctrine, classical liberalism extols the merits of a self-regulating market in which government intervention is both unnecessary and damaging.

15. The belief "that no one should be forcibly prevented from acting in any way he chooses provided his acts are not invasive of the free acts of others" has become one of the basic principles of libertarian politics.

While the phrase "harm principle" was not itself used until 1969, the harm principle itself was first fully articulated by the English thinker John Stuart Mill in his book *On Liberty* (1859), where he argued that:

The object of this Essay is to assert one very simple principle, as entitled to govern absolutely the dealings of society with the individual in the way of compulsion and control, whether the means used be physical force in the form of legal penalties, or the moral coercion of public opinion. That principle is, that the sole end for which mankind are warranted, individually or collectively, in interfering with the liberty of action of any of their number, is self-protection. That the only purpose for which power can be rightfully exercised over any member of a civilized community, against his will, is to prevent harm to others. His own good, either physical or moral, is not a sufficient warrant. He cannot rightfully be compelled to do or forbear because it will be better for him to do so, because it will make him happier, because, in the opinion of others, to do so would be wise, or even right... The only part of the conduct of anyone, for which he is amenable to society, is that which concerns others. In the part which merely concerns himself, his independence is, of right, absolute. Over himself, over his own body and mind, the individual is sovereign.

16. In the year 1960, application of structural functionalism by Almond and Powell was an application of Easton's framework of political system. The Structural-Functional analysis originated in the biological and mechanical sciences. In the social sciences, it was first used in Anthropology. Later on it was developed and refined as a mode of sociological analysis, predominantly by Talcott Parsons and Marion Levy.

It has been under the influence of the sociologists, particularly these two, that the Structural-Functional Approach has come to be developed by political scientists, particularly by Gabriel A. Almond and his associates.

In 1960, Almond and Coleman, in their work 'The Politics of Developing Areas,' used this approach for the study of non-Western political systems. Six years later, Almond and Bingham Powell published their work 'Comparative Politics: A Development Approach'.

In this, they came out with the Structural-Functional Approach designed to study and classify political systems in terms of the levels of their political development.

The Structural-Functional Approach has several strong exponents and supporters, but more them, a place of primacy belong to Almond and his co-authors.

18. Individual freedom, minority rights, toleration and consent are the integral parts of liberal constitutionalism whether Majoritarianism is a traditional political philosophy or agenda that asserts that a majority of the population is entitled to a certain degree of primacy in society, and has the right to make decisions that affect the society. This traditional view has come under growing criticism and democracies have increasingly included constraints in what the parliamentary majority can do, in order to protect citizens' fundamental rights. Under a democratic majoritarian political structure, the majority would not exclude any minority from future participation in the democratic process. Majoritarianism is sometimes pejoratively referred to by its opponents as "ochlocracy" or "tyranny of the majority". Majoritarianism is often referred to as majority rule, which may be referring to a majority class ruling over a minority class, while not referring to the decision process called majority rule. It simply means majority people will govern or make all in the the country without taking care of the need of minority.

19. The Presidential system operates most successfully in the U.S.A because of minor contradictions in society. A presidential system is a democratic and republican system of government where a head of government leads an executive branch that is separate from the legislative branch. This head of government is in most cases also the head of state, which is called president.

In presidential countries, the executive is elected and is not responsible to the legislature, which cannot in normal circumstances dismiss it. Such dismissal is possible, however, in uncommon cases, often through impeachment.

A presidential system contrasts with a parliamentary system, where the head of government is elected to power through the legislative. There is an intermediary system called semi-presidentialism.

Presidentialism is the dominant form of government in the continental Americas, with 20 of its 23 sovereign states being presidential republics. It is also prevalent in Central and West Africa and in Central Asia.

20. The House of Lords in Great Britain is mainly retained because it is maintained as an institution. The House of Lords of Great Britain, referred to ceremonially as the House of Peers, is the upper house of the parliament of the United Kingdom. Like the House of Commons, it meets in the palace of Westminster. While the House of Commons (lower house) has a defined 650-seat membership, the number of members in the House of Lords is not fixed. There are currently 808 sitting Lords. The House of Lords is the only upper house of any bicameral parliament to be larger than its respective lower house.

23. Environmental Green parties originated from New social movements. Political parties campaigning on a predominantly environmental platform arose in the early 1970s in various parts of the world. The world's first political parties to campaign on a predominantly environmental platform were the United Tasmania Group contested the April 1972 state election in Tasmania, Australia and the values Party of New Zealand, which contested the November 1972 New Zealand general election.

A Green Party is a formally organized political party based on the principles of green politics, such as social justice, environmentalism and non-violence. Greens believe that these issues are inherently related to one another as a foundation for world peace. Green party platforms typically embrance social-democratic economic policies and forming coalitions with leftists. Green parties exists in nearly 90 countries around the world; many are members of Global Greens.

24. A two-party system often develops in a plurality voting system. In this system, voters have a single vote, which they can cast for a single candidate in their district, in which only one legislative seat is available. In plurality voting (i.e. first past the post), in which the winner of the seat is determined purely by the candidate with the most votes, several characteristics can serve to discourage the development of third parties and reward the two major parties.

Duverger suggests two reasons this voting system favours a two-party system. One is the result of the "fusion" of the weak parties, and the other is the "elimination" of weak parties by the voters, by which he means that voters gradually desert the weak parties on the grounds that they have no chance of winning.

Duverger's law suggests a nexus or synthesis between a party system and an electoral system: a proportional representation (PR) system creates the electoral conditions necessary to foster party development while a plurality system marginalizes many smaller political parties, resulting in what is known as a two-party system.

25. The first use of the concept of political culture was made by Gabriel Almond. In 1963, two political scientists, Gabriel Almond and Sydney Verba, published a study of the political cultures associated with five democratic countries: Germany, Italy, Mexico, the United Kingdom, and the United States. According to Almond and Verba, there are three basic types of political culture, which can be used to explain why people do or do not participate in political processes.

In a parochial political culture, like Mexico, citizens are mostly uninformed and unaware of their government and take little interest in the political process. In a subject political culture, such as those found in Germany and Italy, citizens are somewhat informed and aware of their government and occasionally participate in the political process. In a participant political culture, like the United Kingdom and the United States, citizens are informed and actively participate in the political process.

Other theories of political culture address how political culture takes root and is transferred from generation to generation through political socialization and include Seymour Martin Lipset's formative events theory, which describes the long-lasting effects of key events that took place when a country was founded; Louis Hartz's fragment theory, which explains the long-lasting effects of European colonization on countries and societies; and Roger Inglehart's post-materialism theory, which explains the long-lasting effects of childhood economic and social conditions.

26. Cognitive orientations, Affective orientations and Evaluative orientations are the parts of the basic types of political culture but Individual orientations are not the part. Political culture is defined by the International Encyclopedia of the Social Sciences as the "set of attitudes, beliefs and sentiments that give order and meaning to a political process and which provide the underlying assumptions and rules that govern behaviour in the political system". It encompasses both the political ideals and operating norms of a polity. Political culture is thus the manifestation of the psychological and subjective dimensions of politics. A political culture is the product of both the history of a political system and the histories of the members. Thus it is rooted equally in public events and private experience.

28. The theory of Modernization and decay is formulated by Samuel P. Huntington. Huntington explores the conflict between political mobilization and institutionalization and the importance of institutional development concerning democratization. A common occurrence in much of the developing world is the fact that political participation is growing much more rapidly than formal political institutions. In many of the developing societies, the conflict between mobilization and institutionalization is an area of chief concern in politics. Despite the growing importance of political institutionalism, much of the literature written about the developing world tends to ignore the idea for the most part. Instead, political scientists tend to emphasize the processes of modernization and the idea of social mobilization and increasing political participation. Huntington argues that a more balanced view of contemporary politics in the developing world instead requires more attention to the growth of political institutions and that it is useful to distinguish political development from modernization and to instead identify political development with the institutionalization of political organizations and procedures. Additionally, Huntington states that rapid increases in political mobilization and participation instead undermine political institutions and lead to political decay.

30. Beliefs and symbols are the distinctive features of the notion of authority in Max Weber. Weber categorized three types of authority are traditional, charismatic and legal-rational authority. Weber suggested that in traditional societies authority is based upon respect for long-established customs and traditions.

Weber's second form of legitimate domination was charismatic authority. This form of authority is based entirely upon the power of an individual's personality, his or her charisma.

The third form of domination Weber identified was what he called legal-rational authority. This was the most important kind of authority since, in Weber's view, it had almost entirely displaced traditional authority and become the dominant mode of organization within modern industrial societies.

31. On 2nd September 1946 the Interim Government of India was formed. This temporary government was formed from the Constituent Assembly of India.

This government was entrusted the task of helping the transition of India and Pakistan from British rule to Independence as two separate nations. The Interim Government was in place till 15th August 1947, when the nations of Indian and Pakistan received Independence from colonial rule.

Clement Attlee, the then Prime Minister of the United Kingdom sent across the 1946 Cabinet Mission to help the formation of a government which would lead to an Independent India. The Executive branch of this Interim Government was the Viceroy's Executive Council. Initially, headed by the Viceroy of India, it was changed to a council of ministers. Jawaharlal Nehru was the Vice President of the council and he held powers of a Prime Minister.

32. A bench of a High Court can issue a writ to another bench of the same High Court is not correct regarding certiorari. Certiorari is a Latin word meaning "to be informed of, or to be made certain in regard to". It is issued by a higher court to a lower court or tribunal either to transfer a case pending with the latter to itself or to equash the order of the latter in a case. It is issued on the grounds of excess of jurisdiction or lack of jurisdiction or error of law. Thus, unlike prohibition, which is only preventive, certiorari is both preventive as well as curative. Like prohibition, certiorari is also not available against legislative bodies and private individuals or bodies.

33. Continuing Mandamus is a writ of Mandamus issued to a lower authority by the higher authority in general public interest asking the officer or the authority to perform its task expeditiously for an unstipulated period of time for preventing miscarriage of justice.

The concept of Continuing Mandamus has been discussed and dealt with in the respective cases of Vineet Narain v. Union of India and Bandhua Mukti Morcha v. Union of India & Ors.

When a petition is filed under Article 32 or Article 226 of the Constitution of India in the Supreme Court or the High Court respectively, the court can issue the writ of Mandamus in the interest of general public welfare. The facts and circumstances of the cases were of utmost public importance, and the increasing need for preservation of democracy and equality in this society. The investigation into every accusation made against each person on a reasonable basis, irrespective of the position and status of that person, must be conducted and completed expeditiously. This is imperative to retain public confidence in the impartial working of the Government agencies.

34. The power of the President not to take any action on the boll is known as the 'Pocket Veto'. In 1986, president Zail Singh becomes the first president of India to make use of 'Pocket Veto'. Zail Singh exercised this Veto with respect o the Indian Post Office (Amendment) Bill. The bill, passed by the Rajiv Gandhi Government, imposed restrictions on the freedom of press and hence, was widely criticised.

It should be noted here that the president has no Veto power in respect of a Constitutional Amendment Bill. The 24th Constitutional Amendment Act–1971 made it obligatory for the president to give his assent to a constitutional amendment bill.

35. Granville Austin said Indian federalism is "a new kind of federation to meet India's peculiar needs". He also called the Indian federalism as a "cooperative federalism". He said that the constitution of India has created a strong central government, it has not made the state governments weak has not reduced them to the level administrative agencies for the execution of policies of the central government.

K.C. Wheare described the constitution of India as "quasi-federal". He remarked that "Indian union is unitary State with subsidiary federal features rather than a federal state with subsidiary unitary features.

Paul Appleby characterizes the Indian system as "extremely federal."

Morris Jones termed it is a "bargaining federalism."

Ivor Jennings has described it as a "federation with a strong centralising tendency". He observed that "the Indian Constitution is mainly federal with unique safeguards for enforcing national unity and growth".

37. Dilip Padgaonkar was the chairman of the group of interlocutors for Jammu and Kashmir. In October 2010, Government of India had appointed a group of three interlocutors to hold sustained dialogue with all sections of the people in Jammu and Kashmir. They were as follows:

- **Dr. Dileep Padgaonkar:** Padgaonkar is a journalist, editor and author. He worked in various capacities in journalistic field including Executive Editor and Editor of the Times of India.
- **Prof. M.M. Ansari:** Ansari was Information Commissioner in the Central Information Commission, New Delhi. He has the background of an Economist and Education Specialist and has served several institutions in senior positions and provided research and consultancy service to national and international organizations.
- **Prof. (Mrs) Radha Kumar:** Radha Kumar is Director of the Mandela Centre for Peace and Conflict Resolution at Jamia Millia Islamia University and trustee of the Delhi Policy Group.

39. The Communist Party of India has officially stated that it was formed on 25 December 1925 at the first party conference in Kanpur.

But as per the version of CPI(M), the Communist Party of India was founded in Tashkent on 17 October 1920, soon after the Second Congress of the Communist International. Ideological differences lead to the split in the party in 1964 when two different party conferences were held, one of CPI and one of the Communist Party of India (Marxist). There is a common misconception that the rift during Sino-Indian war lead to the 1962 split. In fact, the split was leftists versus rightists, rather than internationalists versus nationalists.

41. Rajni Kothari has described the critical and creative role of politics in India as "the Indian model of development".

Kothari in his first book, Politics in India, examined the politicisation process. Differing from the European case, where political participation, he claimed, was confined to the upper classes of society and political activity was not a significant engine of change, India was also unlike the 'revolutionary experiments' of China and Russia where, for example, parochial identities were suppressed and competition disallowed. Instead, he described the Indian model of development as the 'politicisation of a fragmented social structure through a penetration of political forms, values and ideologies.......operating against the background of an essentially a political condition of society'. By this Kothari was referring to India's long past of failed attempts at constructing a viable political authority, the building of a political-centre.

43. Francine R. Frankel & M.S.A. Rao made a significant contribution to theories of the interaction between social dominance and state power in contemporary India... Politics in each state has its own internal dynamics, and it is different from others, multifacetedly. It has undergone significant transformation over the decades since the formation of states in terms of social structure, their power relations, electoral participation on the one hand and political governance and economic development on the other. This course attempts to examine the commonalities, diversities and perspectives to study state politics in India. It also seeks to examine the changing role of caste, class and community and their impact on state politics, particularly in the context of global market economy.

44. Justice B.P. Jeevan Reddy committee opposed the state funding of elections in india. This Committee recommends following provisions:

(*a*) The Commission advocated a total ban on splits and mergers of political parties during the term of the Lok Sabha or Legislative Assembly.

(*b*) Once a member has been elected on a ticket of a particular recognized party, then he should remain in that party till the dissolution of the House or till the end of his membership by resignation or otherwise.

(*c*) The Commission has recommended an adequate representation.

(*d*) To discourage non-serious persons from contesting elections, the Commission has recommended a steep ten-fold hike in the deposits of independent and non-recognized party candidates.

(*e*) To curb criminalisation of politics, the Commission has suggested that a person should be disqualified from contesting elections to the Lok Sabha or an Assembly if a court has ordered framing of charges in respect of offences listed in the Representation of the People Act, 1951.

45. The Tribune is an Indian English-language daily newspaper published from Chandigarh, New Delhi, Jalandhar, Dehradun and Bathinda. It was founded on 2 February 1881, in Lahore (now in Pakistan), by Sardar Dyal Singh Majithia, a philanthropist, and is run by a trust comprising five persons as trustees. It is a major Indian newspaper with a worldwide circulation in India, it is among the leading English daily for Punjab, Haryana, Himachal Pradesh, and the Union Territory of Chandigarh.

Aside from The Tribune in English, it has two sister publications: Dainik Tribune (in Hindi) and Punjabi Tribune. Santosh Tewari is the Editor of Dainik Tribune and Surinder Singh

Tej is the Officiating Editor of the Punjabi Tribune. Harish Khare is the Editor-in-Chief of The Tribune Group of Newspapers. The Internet Edition of The Tribune was launched in July 1998. The Internet editions of the Punjabi Tribune and Dainik Tribune were launched on 16 August 2010. All the three newspapers are published by 'The Tribune Trust'.

The Tribune had Prem Bhatia, Hari Jai Singh, H.K. Dua, AJ Phillip and Raj Chengappa among others as its Editors-in-chief in the past. Present Jammu and Kashmir Governor N N Vohra is on its board of trustees.

47. The evolution of first stage of public administration is called the era of politics administration dichotomy. Historically, Woodrow Wilson was considered as the author of the separation of politics and administration in government (*i.e.*, the politics–administration dichotomy). In his opinion, politics is dealt with questions of policy formulation; administration is dealt with carrying them out. He defined Public Administration as "detailed and systematic execution of public law". To Wilson, Public Administration was much more than technical detail and it was to be conducted in a political context. Thus he treated "politics and public administration as two sides of a coin."

48. Some of the salient features of New Public Management are as follows:

- Public agencies should employ the private sector techniques to provide quality services to citizens with managerial autonomy to the public management.
- Emphasis should be on performance evaluation indicators to measure actual achievements and the quality of services.
- Central departments should be relieved from the operational activities which should be shifted to the field agencies. In order to make use of more expertise and employee creativity working conditions must be made flexible and contractual appointments must be promoted.
- Public agencies should publicize their results and performance on regular basis.
- Steps should be taken to create conducive environment for more effective and productive managerial leadership. To achieve this, hierarchical structure of organization should be abandoned. Recruitment and training of personnel should be based on merit and performance. Attractive salary structures and diverse roles should be offered to maintain the moral of the managerial force.
- Personal accountability and responsibility should be ensured by linking up rewards like pay structures with fulfillment of performance targets.
- Managerial decisions should reflect cost consciousness.

49. In the Human Relations Theory 'Squealer' communicates detrimental information about others to the supervisor. This theory is a concept regarding the principles and goals of management in organizations, especially in industry, that developed in bourgeoise social science. The theory arose in the 1920's in the USA as the attitudinal and methodological basis of the industrial sociology of labour. Its leading advocates were F. J. Roethlisberger, W. E. Moore, and E. Mayo in the USA and G. Friedmann in France.

The term "human relations theory" reflects an attempt by bourgeois ideologists to pass off a program of measures as the humanization of labour that are of practical value for increasing profits. In fact, the human relations theory attempts to conceal or rationalize the profound social conflicts of capitalist society.

51. Aaron Wildavsky has defined budget as "a series of goals with price tags attached". Wildavsky in his The Politics of Budgeting Process has analysed the budgeting of various countries along with problems and complexities. He says that the final structure of a budget is decided by various bargains. In liberal democratic states there are many groups and associations who put pressures upon the government or civil servants to meet their demands. This is the nature of polycentric character of liberal democracies.

52. Peter A. Phyrr is the creater of Zero-Based-Budgeting. Zero-Based-Budgeting (ZBB) is a tool that was invented in the 1970s by Texas Instruments' Peter Phyrr, as a way to develop and control a more austere and effective budgeting system. ZBB is "a method of budgeting in which all expenses must be justified for each new period. It starts from a 'zero base' and every function within an organization is analysed for its needs and costs. Budgets are then built around what is needed for the upcoming period, regardless of whether the budget is higher or lower than the previous one". ZBB has gained a lot of popularity recently, both in the corporate world and the public sector.

53. According to Morstein Marx, the correct sequence of the classification of bureaucracy is given below:

(*i*) The Guardian Bureaucracy
(*ii*) The Caste Bureaucracy
(*iii*) The Patronage Bureaucracy and
(*iv*) The Merit Bureaucracy

(*i*) **Guardian Bureaucracy:** Marx defines Guardian Bureaucracy as that which is dedicated to general welfare and acts as champion of justice and custodian of community's welfare. The Guardian Bureaucracy may be explained on a scholastic official doom trained in right conduct according to the classics.

Ancient Chinese administrative personnel who were influenced by the teachings of Confucius is the example. These bureaucrats led an exemplary life.

(*ii*) **Caste Bureaucracy:** The British Civil Service which was drawn from Oxford and Cambridge graduates who mostly belonged to aristocratic families affording exorbitant fees belongs to this category. In ancient India Brahmins and Kshatriyas could hold the pivotal offices because of their labelling as two upper classes.

(*iii*) **Patronage Bureaucracy:** If public appointments are made on the basis of personal favour or as political rewards it is termed as Patronage Bureaucracy. The spoils system prevalent in USA provides for such a type of bureaucracy. To the critics the spoils was the well accepted theory in USA prior to the passage of Pendaltion Act 1883.

It had a great corrupting influences on the socio-economic life of the country. It was denounced as an anachronism due to its lack of competence concealed avariciousness and careless discipline.

(*iv*) **Merit Bureaucracy:** If the Civil Services are appointed on the basis of merit through competitive examination it is termed as Merit Bureaucracy.

54. The former Prime Minister Indira Gandhi had observed that "only a committed bureaucracy could bring about social transformation". During 1969 to 1974 personality cult was promoted. The officers were not expected to be as loyal to the Constitution, as they had to be to their ministers. Mrs Gandhi desired the bureaucracy to be completely committed to the ruling party. On a sustained and systematic basis, the process of committed bureaucracy flourished, thus undermining the integrity, values, ethos and confidence of the service. Officers were supposed to be the servicemen to carry out the orders of political bosses.

55. Adjournment Motion is introduced in the parliament to draw attention of the House to a definite matter of urgent public importance, and needs the support of 50 members to be admitted. As it interrupts the normal business of the House, it is regarded as an extraordinary device. It involves an element of censure against the government and hence Rajya Sabha is not permitted to make use of this device. The discussion on an adjournment motion should last for not less than two hours and thirty minutes.

56. The first attempt to confer constitutional status on rural local government was made by the 64th Constitutional Amendment Bill. This bill was introduced by the Rajiv Gandhi Government in the Lok Sabha in 1989 to constitutionalise

Panchayati Raj institutions and make them more powerful and broad based. Although, the Lok Sabha passed the bill in August 1989, it was not approved by the Rajya Sabha. The bill was vehemently opposed by the Opposition on the ground that it sought to strengthen centralisation in the federal system.

59. Electronic governance or e-governance is the application of information and communication technology (ICT) for delivering government services, exchange of information, communication transactions, integration of various stand-alone systems and services between government-to-customer (G2C), government-to-business (G2B), government-to-government (G2G) as well as back office processes and interactions within the entire government framework. Through e-governance, government services will be made available to citizens in a convenient, efficient and transparent manner. The three main target groups that can be distinguished in governance concepts are government, citizens and businesses/interest groups. In e-governance there are no distinct boundaries.

Generally four basic models are available - government-to-citizen (customer), government-to-employees, government-to-government and government-to-business.

61. Morton Kaplan has been the chief exponent of the Systems Approach in international relations. He advocates that international politics offers the best sphere for the application of the concept of 'system' as a tool for investigating all its phenomena. International System is most inclusive as it is constituted by those interactions among international actors which are neither fully cooperative nor totally conflictual. It has its sub-systems and a set of actors, both international and supra-national actors. It is constituted by interactions among the international actors.

Morton Kaplan's Six Models of International System:

1. The Balance of Power System
2. The Loose Bi-polar System
3. The Tight Bi-polar System
4. The Universal System
5. The Hierarchical System
6. The Unit Veto System.

62. Balance of Power is not automatic; it has to be secured by the states following this policy. In fact, there are several methods by which states try to secure and maintain balance of power. "Balance of Power is a game which is played by actors with the help of several devices."

Major Methods of Balance of Power:

I. Compensation
II. Alliances and Counter Alliances
III. Intervention and Non-intervention
IV. Divide and Rule
V. Buffer States or Zones
VI. Armaments and Disarmaments
VII. The Holder of the Balance or the Balancer.

65. 'Common but differentiated' responsibility principle on climate mitigation agenda emerged from Kyoto Protocol. The Kyoto protocol is an international agreement linked to the United Nations Framework Convention on Climate Change (UNFCCC), which commits its parties by setting internationally binding emission reduction targets.

Recognizing that developed countries are principally responsible for the current high levels of Green House Gas emissions in the atmosphere as a result of more than 150 years of industrial activity, the Protocol places a heavier burden on developed nations under the principle of "Common but differentiated responsibilities".

67. As per United Nations Convention on the Law of Sea (UNCLOS) states are entitled for jurisdiction over sea water as under:

(*i*) Three miles from sea shore as territorial waters.
(*ii*) Twelve miles from the shore for shipping.
(*iii*) Two hundred miles as Exclusive Economic zone.

The 'United Nations Convention on the Law of the Sea' is also called the 'Law of the Sea Convention' or the 'Law of the Sea Treaty'. It is the international agreement that resulted from the third United Nations Conference on the Law of the Sea (UNCLOS III), which took place between 1973 and 1982. The Law of the Sea Convention defines the rights and responsibilities of nations with respect to their use of the world's oceans, establishing guidelines for businesses, the environment, and the management of marine natural resources.

68. India's good neighbourhood policy based on the principle of non-reciprocity is attributed to Inder Kumar Gujral. The Gujral Doctrine is a milestone in India's foreign policy. It was propounded and initiated in 1996 by I.K. Gujral, the then Foreign Minister in the Deve Gowda Government.

The Doctrine advocates that India, being the biggest country in South Asia, should extend unilateral concessions to the smaller neighbours. In other words, the doctrine is formulated on India's accommodating approach towards its smaller neighbours on the basis of the principle of non-reciprocity. It recognises the supreme importance of friendly and cordial relations with India's neighbours.

69. Sir John Chilcot Commission has indicated U.K. for its conduct in Iraq war in 2003. This commission was appointed for the inquiry of British conduct in Iraq war, due to which it is called Iraq Inquiry or Chilcot Inquiry. The inquiry was announced in 2009 by Prime Minister Gordon Brown. The Chilcot report stated that Saddam Hussein did not pose an urgent threat to British interests, that intelligence regarding weapons of mass destruction was presented with unwarranted certainty, that peaceful alternatives to war had not been exhausted, that the UK and USA had undermined the authority of the United Nations Security Council, that the process of identifying the legal basis was "far from satisfactory", and that a war in 2003 was unnecessary.

70. The Washington Consensus refers to a set of broadly free market economic ideas, supported by prominent economists and international organisations, such as the IMF, the World Bank, the EU and the US.

Essentially, the Washington consensus advocates, free trade, floating exchange rates, free markets and macroeconomic stability. The ten principles originally stated by John Williamson in 1989, includes ten sets of relatively specific policy recommendations.

1. Low government borrowing. Avoidance of large fiscal deficits relative to GDP;
2. Redirection of public spending from subsidies toward broad-based provision of key pro-growth, pro-poor services like primary education, primary health care and infrastructure investment;
3. Tax reform, broadening the tax base and adopting moderate marginal tax rates;
4. Interest rates that are market determined and positive (but moderate) in real terms;
5. Competitive exchange rates;
6. Trade liberalization: liberalization of imports, with particular emphasis on elimination of quantitative restrictions (licensing, etc.); any trade protection to be provided by low and relatively uniform tariffs;
7. Liberalization of inward foreign direct investment;
8. Privatization of state enterprises;
9. Deregulation: abolition of regulations that impede market entry or restrict competition, except for those justified on safety, environmental and consumer protection grounds, and prudential oversight of financial institutions;
10. Legal security for property rights.

The Washington consensus was important for determining policy towards economic development in Latin America, South East Asia and other countries.

75. The phrase 'evil empire' was first applied to the USSR in 1983 by U.S. President Ronald Reagan, who took an aggressive, hard-line stance that favoured matching and exceeding the Soviet Union's strategic and global military capabilities, in calling for a roll-back strategy that would, in his words, "write the final pages of the history of the Soviet Union". The characterization demeaned the Soviet Union and angered Soviet leaders.

Previous Paper (Solved)

UGC-NET-Junior Research Fellowship & Assistant Professor Exam

Political Science, July 2016*

PAPER–II

Note: *This paper contains **fifty (50)** objective type questions of **two (2)** marks each. **All** questions are **compulsory**.*

1. For Plato which of the following statements is not true?

(*a*) Ideas are substances.
(*b*) Ideas are essences of all things.
(*c*) Ideas are reflections of things.
(*d*) Ideas are universal.

Choose the correct answer from the codes given below:

Codes:

A. (*a*) and (*b*) B. (*b*) and (*d*)
C. (*b*) only D. (*c*) only

2. Who among the following called Machiavelli's "Prince" the great and true conception of a real political genius with the highest and noblest purpose?

A. Bentham B. J.S. Mill
C. Hegel D. Karl Marx

3. Match List-I with List-II and select the correct answer from the codes given below:

List-I (*Authors*)	**List-II (*Books*)**
(*a*) Quentin Skinner	1. Philosophy and Human Sciences
(*b*) Michael Sandel	2. The Foundations of Modern Political Thought
(*c*) Giovanni Sartori	3. Liberalism and the Limits of Justice
(*d*) Charles Taylor	4. Democratic Theory

Codes:

	(*a*)	(*b*)	(*c*)	(*d*)
A.	2	3	4	1
B.	1	2	3	4
C.	3	4	2	1
D.	4	1	3	2

4. Who among the following considers Marxism to be an ideology rather than a political theory?

A. Germino B. David Held
C. R.A. Dahl D. G.H. Sabine

5. Arrange the following works of Isaiah Berlin in chronological order of his publications. Select the correct answer from the codes given below:

(*a*) Concepts and Categories : Philosophical Essays
(*b*) Four Essays on Liberty
(*c*) Vico and Herder : Two Studies in the History of Ideas
(*d*) Karl Marx : His Life and Environment

Codes:

A. (*a*), (*b*), (*c*) and (*d*)
B. (*c*), (*b*), (*a*) and (*d*)
C. (*d*), (*b*), (*c*) and (*a*)
D. (*b*), (*d*), (*a*) and (*c*)

6. Who among the following conceived the society as 'a cooperative venture for mutual advantage'?

A. Rawls B. Nozick
C. Hayek D. Gramsci

7. Given below are two statements, one labelled as Assertion (A) and the other labelled as Reason (R). Select the correct answer from the codes given below:

Assertion (A): For Rousseau a thinking man is a depraved animal.

Reason (R): Common emotions give value to life.

Codes:

A. Both (A) and (R) are true, and (R) is the correct explanation of (A).

* Exam held on 10/07/2016

B. Both (A) and (R) are true, but (R) is not the correct explanation of (A).
C. (A) is true, but (R) is false.
D. (A) is false, but (R) is true.

8. Who among the following rejected the idea that caste status was the result of divine reward or punishment?
A. Bipin Chandra Pal
B. M.A. Jinnah
C. Jawaharlal Nehru
D. M.K. Gandhi

9. Who among the following said : "Research untutored by theory may prove trivial, and theory unsupported by data, futile"?
A. B. Crick B. Charles Merriam
C. David Easton D. R.A. Dahl

10. Given below are two statements, one labelled as Assertion (A) and the other labelled as Reason (R). Select the correct answer from the codes given below:
Assertion (A): For Fukuyama, liberal democracy may constitute the end point of mankind's ideological evolution.
Reason (R): The earlier forms of government were characterised by grave defects and irrationalities that led to their eventual collapse.
Codes:
A. Both (A) and (R) are true, and (R) is the correct explanation of (A).
B. Both (A) and (R) are true, but (R) is not the correct explanation of (A).
C. (A) is true, but (R) is false.
D. (A) is false, but (R) is true.

11. Which of the following constitutes the political elite?
A. Subalterns and marginalized leaders
B. Rulers and subjects
C. Leader and the followers
D. Oligarchy and Aristocracy

12. Who among the following is associated with the initial stages in the growth of comparative politics?
A. Karl Popper B. Arthur Bentley
C. E.H. Carr D. Graham Wallas

13. Which branch of comparative politics seeks to examine the formal and informal mechanisms by which political attitudes are inculcated?
A. Political socialization
B. Political communication
C. Political modernization
D. Political development

14. Who among the following contended that political development is administrative and legal development?
Choose the correct answer from the codes given below:
(*a*) R.R. Rostow (*b*) Talcott Parsons
(*c*) Sorokin (*d*) Max Waber
Codes:
A. (*a*) and (*d*) B. (*b*) and (*d*)
C. (*a*) and (*c*) D. (*b*) and (*c*)

15. Who became the first ever Prime Minister in a Parliamentary government?
A. William Pitt, the Elder
B. Henry Pelham
C. William Putenny
D. Robert Walpole

16. Who among the following were associated with institutional approach?
(*a*) Carew Hunt (*b*) Herman Finer
(*c*) Roy C. Macridis (*d*) Carl Friedrich
Choose the correct answer from the codes given below:
Codes:
A. (*a*) and (*c*) B. (*b*) and (*d*)
C. (*b*) and (*c*) D. (*a*) and (*d*)

17. Arrange the following revolutions in the sequence in which they took place:
(*a*) Chinese Revolution
(*b*) Cuban Revolution
(*c*) Bolshevik Revolution
(*d*) Puritan Revolution

Choose the correct answer from the codes given below:
Codes:
A. (*a*), (*b*), (*d*), (*c*) B. (*b*), (*a*), (*c*), (*d*)
C. (*d*), (*c*), (*a*), (*b*) D. (*c*), (*d*), (*b*), (*a*)

18. Identify the correct sequence of the following input functions?

(*i*) Political communication
(*ii*) Political socialization and recruitment
(*iii*) Interest aggregation
(*iv*) Interest articulation

Select the correct answer from the codes given below:

Codes:

A. (*i*), (*ii*), (*iii*) and (*iv*)
B. (*iv*), (*i*), (*iii*) and (*ii*)
C. (*ii*), (*iv*), (*iii*) and (*i*)
D. (*ii*), (*iii*), (*iv*) and (*i*)

19. Given below are two statements, one labelled as Assertion (A) and the other labelled as Reason (R). Select the correct answer from the codes given below:

Assertion (A): Iron law of oligarchy established that ultimate decision-making in all democratic organizations including the political parties is done by few leaders or a small elite group.

Reason (R): Decision making is very complex process which necessarily involves the role of few who function on behalf of many.

Codes:

A. Both (A) and (R) are true, and (R) is the correct explanation of (A).
B. Both (A) and (R) are true, but (R) is not the correct explanation of (A).
C. (A) is true, but (R) is false.
D. (A) is false, but (R) is true.

20. Given below are two statements, one labelled as Assertion (A) and the other labelled as Reason (R). Select the correct answer from the codes given below:

Assertion (A): Military is predominant in non-western democracies.

Reason (R): Social fragmentation and cleavages largely contribute to political instability.

Codes:

A. Both (A) and (R) are true, and (R) is the correct explanation of (A).
B. Both (A) and (R) are true, but (R) is not the correct explanation of (A).
C. (A) is true, but (R) is false.
D. (A) is false, but (R) is true.

21. Identify the correct chronological order of the formation of the following political parties in India:

A. Justice Party, Hindu Maha Sabha, National Conference, Shiromani Akali Dal
B. National conference, Shiromani Akali Dal, Hindu Maha Sabha, Justice Party
C. Hindu Maha Sabha, Shiromani Akali Dal, National Conference, Justice Party
D. Justice Party, Shiromani Akali Dal, Hindu Maha Sabha, National Conference

22. Which one of the following pairs is not correctly matched?

A. Conditions of eligibility of a Governor : Article 158
B. Dismissal of a Governor by the President : Article 156 (2)
C. Nomination of members of Legislative Council by the Governor : Article 171 (5)
D. Power of the Governor to recommend 'Money Bill' : Article 207

23. Consider the following statements and select the correct answer from the codes given below:

Statement I: The only mode of initiating a proposal for amendment is to introduce a bill in either house of the Union Parliament.

Statement II: If there is a disagreement between the two Houses of Parliament regarding the passage of a bill, the deadlock may be resolved by a joint session of the two Houses.

Codes:

A. Only Statement I is true.
B. Only Statement II is true.
C. Both Statements I and II are true.
D. Both Statements I and II are false.

24. Match List-I with List-II and select the correct answer from the codes given below:

List-I	List-II
(*a*) 36th Constitutional Amendment Act	1. Transparency in judicial appointments

(*b*) 61st Constitutional Amendment Act	2. Declaration of Sikkim as a full fledged state
(*c*) 97th Constitutional Amendment Act	3. Lowering of voting age from 21 to 18 years
(*d*) 99th Constitutional Amendment Act	4. Formation and functioning of cooperative societies

Codes:

	(*a*)	(*b*)	(*c*)	(*d*)
A.	3	2	4	1
B.	2	4	1	3
C.	3	2	1	4
D.	2	3	4	1

25. Match List-I with List-II and select the correct answer from the codes given below:

List-I	**List-II**
(*a*) Granville Austin	1. 'Quasi federal'
(*b*) K.C. Wheare	2. 'Federation with strong centralising tendency'
(*c*) Appleby	3. 'Cooperative federalism'
(*d*) Ivor Jennings	4. 'Extremely federal'

Codes:

	(*a*)	(*b*)	(*c*)	(*d*)
A.	2	1	3	4
B.	3	2	4	1
C.	3	1	2	4
D.	2	3	1	4

26. Match List-I with List-II and identify the correct answer from the codes given below:

List-I (*Acts*)	**List-II (*Provision*)**
(*a*) Government of India Act, 1858	1. Introduction of bi-cameral legislature for the first time
(*b*) Indian Councils Act, 1861	2. Complete imperial control by Secretary of State for India
(*c*) Indian Councils Act, 1909	3. Inclusion of non-official members in the Executive Council of Governor General for the first time
(*d*) Government of India Act, 1919	4. Separate representation of the Muslim community

Codes:

	(*a*)	(*b*)	(*c*)	(*d*)
A.	2	3	4	1
B.	3	2	1	4
C.	2	4	3	1
D.	3	4	1	2

27. Which of the following statements about the Writ of Habeas Corpus is correct?

A. It can be issued to secure the release of a person who has been imprisoned by a court of law on a criminal charge.

B. It can be issued to interfere with the proceeding for contempt by a Court of record or by Parliament.

C. The writ is a very powerful safeguard to the subject against arbitrary acts not only of private individuals but also of the executive.

D. By this writ, the Court can obtain knowledge of the reason a person has been imprisoned but cannot set her/him free if the imprisonment is unlawful.

28. Assertion (A): In the first three general elections, India produced a 'one party dominance' model, which is different from one party system.

Reason (R): Till 1967, the Congress party had exclusive control over governmental power both at the Centre and also in most of the states of India.

Codes:

A. Both (A) and (R) are true, and (R) is the correct explanation of (A).

B. Both (A) and (R) are true but (R) is not the correct explanation of (A).

C. (A) is true, but (R) is false.
D. (A) is false, but (R) is true.

29. Arrange the following Speakers of Lok Sabha of India in chronological order and select the correct answer from the codes given below:

I. Dr. Balram Jakhar
II. Dr. Gurdial Singh Dhillon
III. Neelam Sanjiva Reddy
IV. Bali Ram Bhagat

Codes:

A. I, II, III, IV B. II, III, I, IV
C. III, II, IV, I D. III, IV, II, I

30. Which of the following High Courts have Bench/Benches?

A. Allahabad, Bombay, Jabalpur
B. Jodhpur, Bombay, Hyderabad
C. Calcutta, Guwahati, Bangalore
D. Jabalpur, Madras, Guwahati

31. According to Peter Self, the study of public administration developed as an offshoot of which one of the following?

A. Political Science or Public law
B. Politics or Ethics
C. Public Policy or Policy making
D. Political system or interest aggregation

32. Which one of the following is not a part of the underlying ideas of traditional or mechanistic theory of organization?

A. It takes an administrative view of human relationship.
B. It considers economic incentives to be the sole motivating factor.
C. It ignores the dynamics of organizational behaviour.
D. It gives more importance to informal relationship.

33. Which one of the following key components of 'governance' was not identified by OECD, while laying down conditions for receiving economic assistance?

A. Participatory development
B. Strict auditing
C. Human rights
D. Democratisation

34. Cybernetics means:

A. Science of communicating
B. Communication methods
C. Artificial intelligence
D. Science of control and communication

35. Who among the following thinkers advocated 'effective communication' as a basic prerequisite for the attainment of organizational goals?

A. Herbert Simon B. Peter Self
C. Chester Barnard D. Woodrow Wilson

36. Taking an extreme view of the distinction between public and private administration, who said that all organizations share public and private features?

A. Dwight Waldo B. E.S. Savas
C. Barry Bozeman D. James W. Fesler

37. Given below are two statements, one labelled as Assertion (A) and the other labelled as Reason (R). Select the correct answer from the codes given below:

Assertion (A): Some departments are concerned not only with purely administrative work but some authority to make rules and regulations is also delegated to them by the legislature.

Reason (R): John M. Pfiffner prefers single head of the department under certain circumstances.

Codes:

A. Both (A) and (R) are true, and (R) is the correct explanation of (A).
B. Both (A) and (R) are true, but (R) is not the correct explanation of (A).
C. (A) is true, but (R) is false.
D. (A) is false, but (R) is true.

38. What is common among Duncan Black, Anthony Downs, James Buchanan, and Kenneth Arrow?

A. They are all advocates of Public Choice Theory in public administration.
B. They are all ex-Cabinet Secretaries of UK.
C. They are all supporters of Whitley Councils in UK.
D. They are all exponents of classical theories of administration.

39. Match List-I with List-II and select the correct answer from the codes given below:

List-I (*Books*)	List-II (*Authors*)
(*a*) An Introduction to Administrative Law	1. Frank J. Goodnow
(*b*) Justice and Administrative Law	2. A.V. Dicey
(*c*) Comparative Administrative Law	3. James Hart
(*d*) Introduction to the Study of the Law of the Constitution	4. W.A. Robson

Codes:

	(*a*)	(*b*)	(*c*)	(*d*)
A.	4	1	3	2
B.	2	3	4	1
C.	3	4	1	2
D.	1	2	3	4

40. Which one of the following is the correct chronological order of the Committees/Commissions/Reports?

A. Masterman Committee – Brownlow Committee – Gladstone Committee – Aitchison Commission
B. Aitchison Commission – Gladstone Committee – Brownlow Committee – Masterman Committee
C. Aitchison Commission – Masterman Committee – Brownlow Committee – Gladstone Committee
D. Gladstone Committee – Aitchison Commission – Masterman Committee – Brownlow Committee

41. Who among the following declared that the state is retreating in the face of the superior power of globalization?

A. McLean and McMillan
B. George Schwarzenberger
C. Kenneth Waltz
D. Susan Strange

42. Who among the following argued that 'realism is likely to remain the single most useful instrument in our intellectual toolbox'?

A. Holsti B. E.H. Carr
C. Hans Margenthau D. Stephen Walt

43. Which of the following is not the basic norm of the balance of power system that are clear to each of the state actors engaged in the process of balancing:

A. Any actor or coalition that tries to assume dominance must be constrained.
B. States want to increase their capabilities by acquiring territory, increasing their population or developing economically.
C. Negotiating is better than fighting.
D. Other states are viewed as potential enemies.

44. Match List-I with List-II and select the correct answer from the codes given below:

List-I (*Scholar*)	List-II (*Statement*)
(*a*) McLean and McMillan	1. It is not so much the absolute power of a state as its power position in relation to other states that counts.
(*b*) Morgenthau	2. Defined power as the capacity to impose one's will on others by reliance on effective sanctions in the case of non-compliance.
(*c*) George Schwarzerberger	3. Defined power as man's control over the minds and actions of other men.
(*d*) Van Dyke	4. Power is the ability to make people do what they would not otherwise have done.

Codes:

	(*a*)	(*b*)	(*c*)	(*d*)
A.	4	3	2	1
B.	4	3	1	2
C.	4	1	2	3
D.	1	2	3	4

45. Article 25 of the Charter of the United Nations provides that :

A. Use of force is allowed for self-defence.
B. Only peace loving states can become members of UN.

C. All UN members agree to accept and carry-out the decisions of the Security Council.
D. The Security Council has primary responsibility under the Charter for the maintenance of international peace and security.

46. Which of the following has not been incorporated into Indian law, either fully or partially?
A. The Tokyo Convention Act 1975
B. The Rome Statute of the International Criminal Court.
C. The Anti-Apartheid (United Nations Convention) Act, 1981
D. The Geneva Convention Act, 1960

47. Which of the following statements is not correct regarding International Criminal Court?
A. The statute of International Criminal Court was adopted by United Nations Conference on 18th July, 1998.
B. The International Criminal Court is not an organ of United Nations but it is an independent organization.
C. Its statute came into force on 1st July, 2002.
D. The four organs of International Criminal Court are the Presidency, the Judicial Division, the office of the Prosecutor and the Registry.

48. In which year the UN General Assembly adopted the Convention on the Rights of Persons with Disabilities?
A. 2006 B. 2007
C. 2008 D. 2009

49. Match List-I with List-II and select the correct answer from the codes given below:
List-I
(Committee of General Assembly of UN)
(*a*) First Committee
(*b*) Second Committee
(*c*) Third Committee
(*d*) Fourth Committee
List-II
(Issues related to Committee)
1. Economic and financial
2. Disarmament and international security
3. Special political and decolonisation
4. Social, humanitarian and cultural

Codes:

	(*a*)	(*b*)	(*c*)	(*d*)
A.	2	1	4	3
B.	1	2	3	4
C.	1	3	4	2
D.	4	3	2	1

50. Given below are two statements, one labelled as Assertion (A) and the other labelled as Reason (R). Select the correct answer from the codes given below:
Assertion (A): End of Cold War signified a shift from ideological politics in International relations.
Reason (R): Religious fundamentalism is posing a threat to security.
Codes:
A. Both (A) and (R) are true, and (R) is the correct explanation of (A).
B. Both (A) and (R) are true, but (R) is not the correct explanation of (A).
C. (A) is true, but (R) is false.
D. (A) is false, but (R) is true.

ANSWERS

1	2	3	4	5	6	7	8	9	10
D	C	A	A	C	A	A	D	C	A
11	**12**	**13**	**14**	**15**	**16**	**17**	**18**	**19**	**20**
D	B	A	A	D	B	C	C	A	B
21	**22**	**23**	**24**	**25**	**26**	**27**	**28**	**29**	**30**
D	B	C	D	C	A	C	A	C	A
31	**32**	**33**	**34**	**35**	**36**	**37**	**38**	**39**	**40**
A	D	B	D	C	C	B	A	C	B
41	**42**	**43**	**44**	**45**	**46**	**47**	**48**	**49**	**50**
D	D	D	A	C	B	A	A	A	B

EXPLANATORY ANSWERS

1. For Plato Ideas are substances, Ideas are essence of all things and also Ideas are universal. He was Greek philosopher and was born of an aristocratic family. He became a follower of Socrates, who's the principal figure in his ethical and philosophical dialogues. After Socrate's death in 399 BC, Plato founded his Academy in order to train the new Athenian ruling class, which might be considered the first 'university'.

Plato taught that the material world consists of imperfect copies of abstract and eternal 'Ideas'. His political philosophy, as expounded in the Republic, is an attempt to describe the 'Ideal State' in terms of a theory of justice.

2. Hegel called Machiavelli's "Prince" the great and true conception of a real political genius with the highest and noblest purpose. Machiavelli's major work, the Prince, written in 1513 and published in 1531, was intended to provide guidance for the ruler of a future united Italy, and drew heavily upon his first-hand observations of the statecraft of Cesare Borgia and the power politics that dominated his period. His 'scientific method' portrayed politics in strictly realistic terms and highlighted the use by the political leaders of cunning, cruelty and manipulation. This emphasis, and attacks upon him that led to his excommunication, meant that the term 'Machiavellian' subsequently came to mean scheming and duplicitous.

4. Dante Germino considers Marxism to be an ideology rather than a political theory. Marxism as a theoretical system developed out of, and drew inspiration from, the writings of Karl Marx. However, 'Marxism' as a codified body of thought came into existence only after Marx's death. It was the product of the attempt by later Marxists to condense Marx's ideas and theories into a systematic and comprehensive world view that suited the needs of the growing socialist movement.

However, a variety of Marxist traditions can be identified, including 'Classical' Marxism, 'Orthodox' Marxism or 'dialectical materialism', the mechanistic form of Marxism that served as the basis for Soviet Communism, and 'western', 'modern' or 'neo' Marxism, which tend to view Marxism as a humanist philosophy and are sceptical about its scientistic and determinist pretensions.

6. Rawls conceived the society as 'a cooperative venture for mutual advantage'. Rawls was the most important liberal philosopher of the second half of the 20th century. His theory of 'justice as fairness' not only condemns racial, sexual and religious discrimination, but also rejects many forms of social and economic inequality. Rawl's egalitarian form of liberalism has had a profound effect upon political philosophy generally, and has made a significant contribution to both the modern liberal and social-democratic political traditions.

8. In 1922 the Congress Working Committee, at Gandhi's instance, decided that the removal of untouchability was part of the congress programme. Again, in 1928 Gandhi told the congress, 'to postpone social reforms is not to know the meaning of Swaraj'. How could Indians demand Swaraj when they condemned vast number of their own countrymen as untouchables? 'What crimes', asked Gandhi, 'for which we condemn the government as satanic, have not we been guilty of towards our own untouchable brethren? We make them crawl on their bellies, we have made them rub their noses on the ground with eyes red with anger, we push them out of railway compartments. What more than this has British rule done? What charge that we bring against Dyer and O'Dwyer may not others, and even our own people, lay at our doors? We are not better than brutes until we have purged ourselves of the sins we have committed against our weaker brethren'.

But then Gandhi yet claimed that he was a sanatanist and did not want to destroy castes altogether. He accepted the functional division of society into four major castes of Brahmin, Kshatriya, Vaishya and Sudra, but he was opposed to the proliferation of castes. He rejected all caste sub-divisions that existed as also the theory that caste status was the result of divine reward or punishment, and he made it clear that in Varnashram Dharma, as he understood it, 'there is absolutely no idea of superiority or inferiority' so that 'all the bhangis, doctors, lawyers, merchants and others would get the same wages for an honest day's work.'

9. American political thinker David Easton said, "Research untutored by theory may prove trivial, and theory unsupported by data, futile". Behaviouralists seek to bring the rigour of empirical and scientific techniques to research in political science. But research should not be an end in itself; it should be linked to theory. Behaviouralists seek to relate research and theory, because, 'research, untutored by theory, may prove trivial and theory unsupported by data, futile.' In traditional political enquiry, theory tends to be become speculative and normative. Behaviouralists, unlike traditionalists who emphasize the value theory, give importance to the causal theory.

A value theory, for example, Plato's proposition that only a person who personifies the Idea of Good can be a philosopher king, is based on the deductive method, on normative and prescriptive principles; a causal theory, on the other hand, seeks a functional relationship between variables. For example, the social and economic background of a group of voters and their voting preferences are all variable that are linked to each other. For behaviouralists, only causal theory is important.

10. 'The End of History and the Last Man' is a 1992 book by Francis Fukuyama, expanding on his 1989 essay "The End of History", published in the international affairs journal. 'The National Interest'. In the book, Fukuyama argues that the advent of western liberal democracy may signal the end point of humanity's sociocultural evolution and the final form of human government.

What we may be witnessing is not just the end of the cold war, or the passing of a particular period of post-war history, but the end of history as such : that is, the end point of mankind's ideological evolution and the universalization of western liberal democracy as the final form of human government.

11. Oligarchy and Aristocracy constitutes the political elite. Elitist thinkers such as Gaetano Mosca, Vilfredo Pareto and Robert Michels were concerned to demonstrate that political power always lies in the hands of a small elite and that egalitarian ideas, such as socialism and democracy, are a myth.

Modern elitists, by contrast, have put forward strictly empirical theories about the distribution of power in particular societies, but have nevertheless drawn the conclusion that political power is concentrated in the hands of the few. An example of this was Joseph Schumpeter, whose 'capitalism, socialism and Democracy' suggested the theory of democratic elitism. Schumpeter described democracy as 'that institutional arrangement for arriving at political decisions in which individuals acquire the power to decide by means of a competitive struggle for the people's vote'. The electorate can decide which elite rules, but cannot change the fact that the power is always exercised by an elite.

Perhaps the most influential of modern elite theorists, C.Wright Mills, argued in 'The Power Elite' that US politics is dominated by big business and the military, commonly referred to as the 'military-industrial complex', which dictated government policy, largely immune from electoral pressure.

12. Arthur Bentley is associated with the initial stages in the growth of comparative politics. The study of comparative politics became highly significant in the 1950s when a good number of leading American political scientists sought to 'transform the field of politics' by taking the study of this subject from foreign to comparative political phenomenon and 'from the study of the governments to the study of the political systems'. However, the historical development of this subject may be roughly put into three phases unsophisticated, sophisticated, and increasingly sophisticated.

13. Political socialization is the "Study of the developmental processes by which people of all ages and adolescents acquire political cognition, attitudes, and behaviours". It refers to a learning process by which norms and behaviour acceptable to a well running system are transmitted from one generation to another. It is through the performance of this function that individuals are inducted into the political culture and their orientations towards political objects are formed.

These agents of socialization influence to different degrees an individual's political opinions : family, media, peers, education, religion, faith, race, gender, age and geography. These factors and many others that people are introduced to as they grow up will affect their political views throughout the rest of their lives. Political beliefs are often formed during childhood, as parents pass down their ideologies to their children and so on.

14. R.R. Rostow and Max Waber contended that political development is administrative and legal development. The origin of the term 'Political Development' can be traced to 1950's when a large number of American political scientists were attempting to study the political dynamics of the newly emerging countries of Asia, Africa and Latin America. Huge amounts of statistical and quantitative data on the social, political, economic and demographic aspects of these nations were collected to analyze their attitudes, values and behaviour patterns.

However, the term is still in the process of evolution and there is hardly any unanimity among the scholars on the constituent of political development. Such inconsistency is partly on account of interdisciplinary focus and partly a manifestation of ethnocentric bases.

15. Robert Walpole became the first ever prime minister in a parliamentary government. Walpole was a British Statesman who is generally regarded as the de facto first prime minister of Great Britain. Although the exact dates of his dominance are a matter of scholarly debate, 1721-42 are often used. He was a Whig from the gentry class, who was first elected to Parliament in 1701, and held many senior positions. He was a country squire and looked to country gentlemen for his political base. Historian Frank O'Gorman says his leadership in Parliament reflected his "reasonable and persuasive oratory, his ability to move both the emotions as well as the minds of men, and, above all, his extraordinary self-confidence". Hoppit says Walpole's policies sought moderation: he worked for peace, lower taxes, growing exports, and allowed a little more tolerance for protestant dissenters. He avoided controversy and high-intensity disputes, as his middle way attracted moderates from both the Whig and Tory Camps,

18. Correct sequence of the input functions are — Political socialization and recruitment, Interest articulation, Interest aggregation and Political communication. A political system consists of a linkage between what Easton called 'inputs' and 'outputs'. Inputs into the political system consist of both demands and supports. Demands can take the form of the desire for higher living standards, improved employment prospects or welfare benefits, greater participation in politics, protection for minority and individual rights and so forth. Supports, on the other hand, are the ways in which the public contributes to the political system by paying taxes, offering compliance and being willing to participate in public life. Outputs consist of the decisions and actions of government, including the making of policy, the passing of laws, the imposition of taxes and the allocation of public funds. Clearly, these outputs generate 'feedback' which in turn will shape further demands and supports. As Easton conceived it, the political system is thus a dynamic process, within which stability is achieved only if outputs bear some relationship to inputs. In other words, if policy outputs do not satisfy popular demands these will progressively increase until the point when 'systematic breakdown' will occur. The capacity to achieve such stability is based upon how the flow of inputs into the political system is regulated by 'gatekeepers', such as interest groups and political parties, and the success of government itself in converting inputs into outputs.

19. Iron law of oligarchy established that ultimate decision-making in all democratic organizations including the political parties is done by few leaders or a small elite group because decision-making is very complex process which necessarily involves the role of few who function on behalf of many. Michels proposed that elite rule followed from what he called 'The iron law of oligarchy'. This states that it is in the nature of all organizations, however democratic they may appear, for power to concentrate in the hands of a small group of dominant figures, who can organize and make decisions, rather than in the hands of the apathetic rank and file.

22. Article 156(2) of the Indian Constitution mentions that the Governor may, by writing under his hand addressed to the president, resign his office.

According to Article 158, the Governor shall not be a member of either House of Parliament or of a House of the Legislature of any State specified in the first schedule, and if a member of either House of Parliament or of a House of the Legislature of any such state be appointed Governor, he shall be deemed to have vacated his seat in that House on the date on which he enters upon his office as Governor.

Article 171(5) provides that the members to be nominated by the Governor under sub-clause (e) of clause (3) shall consist of persons having special knowledge or practical experience in respect of such matters as the following, namely—Literature, Science, Art, Co-operative movement and social service.

Article 207 provides that power of the Governor to recommend 'Money bill'.

23. The only mode of initiating a proposal for amendment is to introduce a bill in either house of the Parliament. If there is a disagreement between the two Houses of Parliament regarding the passes of a bill, the deadlock may be resolved by a joint session of the two Houses. Article 108 provides the provision of joint session of the two Houses. Article 368 provides for two types of amendments, that is, by a special majority of Parliament and also through the ratification of half of the States by a simple majority. But, some other articles provide for the amendment of certain provisions of the constitution by a simple majority of Parliament, that is, a majority of the members of each House present and voting (similar to the ordinary legislative process). Notably, these amendments are not deemed to be amendments of the constitution for the purposes of article 368.

Therefore, the constitution can be amended in three ways :

(*a*) Amendment by simple majority of the Parliament.

(*b*) Amendment by special majority of the Parliament, and

(*c*) Amendment by special majority of the Parliament and the ratification of half of the State legislatures.

25. It is clear that the Constitution of India has deviated from the traditional federal systems like US, Switzerland and Australia and incorporated a large number of unitary or non-federal features, tilting the balance of power in favour of the centre. This has promoted the constitutional experts to challenge the federal character of the Indian Constitution. Granville Austin called the Indian federalism as a "Cooperative Federalism". He said that though the constitution of India has created a strong Central government, it has not made the State governments weak and has not reduced them to the level of administrative agencies for the execution of policies of the Central government. He described the Indian federation as "a new kind of federation to meet India's peculiar needs".

K.C. Wheare described the Constitution of India as "quasi-federal".

Paul Appleby characterises the Indian system as a "federation with a strong centralising tendency", and Ivor Jennings has described it as a "extremely federal".

27. Habeas Corpus is a Latin term which literally means 'to have the body of'. It is an order issued by the court to a person who has detained another person, to produce the body of the latter before it. The court then examines the cause and legality of detention. It would set the detained person free, if the detention is found to be illegal. Thus, this Writ is a bulwark of individual liberty against arbitrary detention.

The Writ of Habeas Corpus can be issued against both public authorities as well as private individuals. The Writ, on the other hand, is not issued where the (*a*) detention is lawful, (*b*) The proceeding is for contempt of a legislature or a court, (*c*) detention is by a competent court and (*d*) detention is outside the jurisdiction of the court.

29. The Speaker is the head of the Lok Sabha, and its representative. He is the guardian of powers and privileges of the members, the House as a whole and its committees. He is the principal spokesman of the House, and his decision in all parliamentary matters is final. He is thus much more than merely the presiding officer of the Lok Sabha. In these capacities, he is vested with vast, varied and vital responsibilities and enjoys great honour, high dignity and supreme authority within the House.

The Speaker of the Lok Sabha derives his powers and duties from three sources, that is, the constitution of India, the rules of procedure and conduct of business of Lok Sabha, and Parliamentary conventions (residuary powers that are unwritten or unspecified in the rules). The chronological order of the speakers are:

(*i*) Neelam Sanjiva Reddy (17 March, 1967 — 19 July, 1967)

(*ii*) Dr. Gurdial Singh Dhillon (8 Aug., 1969 — 19 March, 1971 & 22 March, 1971 — 1 Dec., 1975)

(*iii*) Bali Ram Bhagat (15 January, 1976 — 25 March, 1977)

(*iv*) Dr. Balram Jakhar (22 January, 1980 — 27 October, 1984)

30. The article – 214 of the Indian Constitution provides for a High Court for each state, but the 7th Amendment Act of 1956 authorised the Parliament to establish a Common High Court for two or more states or for two or more states and a union territory. The territorial jurisdiction of a High Court is co-terminus with the territory of a state. Similarly, the territorial jurisdiction of a common High Court is co-terminus with the territories of the concerned states and union territory.

At present, there are 24 High Courts in the country. Out of them, three are common High Courts. Allahabad, Bombay and Jabalpur High Courts have Benches. Allahabad High Court Bench is situated at Lucknow, Bombay High Court Bench is situated at Nagpur, Panaji and Aurangabad. Jabalpur High Court Bench is situated at Gwalior and Indore.

33. Strict auditing is the key components of 'governance' was not identified by OECD, while laying down conditions for receiving economic assistance. The 'Organization for Economic Co-operation and Development (OECD)' is an intergovernmental economic organization with 35 member countries, founded in 1961 to stimulate economic progress and world trade. It is a forum of countries describing themselves as committed to democracy and the market economy, providing a platform to compare policy experiences, seeking answers to common problems, identify good practices and coordinate domestic and international policies of its members.

In 1948, the OECD originated as the 'Organization for European Economic Co-operation (OEEC)', led by Robert Marjolin of France, to help administer the Marshall Plan (which was rejected by the Soviet Union and its satellite states). This would be achieved by allocating American financial aid and implementing economic programs for the reconstruction of Europe after World War II. In 1961, the OEEC was reformed into the OECD by the convention on the organisation for Economic Co-operation and Development and Membership was extended to non-European states. Most OECD members are high-income economies with a very high Human Development Index (HDI) and are regarded as developed countries.

34. Cybernetics is a transdisciplinary approach for exploring regulatory systems—their structures, constraints and possibilities. Norbert Weiner defined cybernetics in 1948 as "the scientific study of control and communication in the animal and the machine." In the 21st century, the term is often used in a rather loose way to imply "control of any system using technology."

Cybernetics is applicable when a system being analyzed incorporates a closed signaling loop–originally referred to as a "circular causal" relationship—that is, where action by the system generates some change in its environment and that change is reflected in the system in some manner (feedback) that triggers a system change. Cybernetics is relevant to, for example, mechanical, physical, biological, cognitive and social systems. The essential goal of the broad field of cybernetics is to understand and define the functions and processes of systems that have goals and that participate in circular, causal chains that move from action to sensing to comparison with desired goal, and again to action. Its focus is how anything (digital, mechanical or biological) processes information, reacts to information and changes or can be changed to better accomplish the first two tasks. Cybernetics includes the study of feedback, black boxes and derived concepts such as communicaton and control in living organisms, machines and organizations including self-organization.

35. Chester Barnard advocated 'Effective communication' as a basic pre-requisite for the attainment of organizational goals. No organization, no group can exist without communication. Co-ordination of work is impossible and the organisation will collapse for lack of communication. Co-operation also becomes impossible because people cannot communicate their needs and feelings to others.

Every act of communication influences the organisation in some way or other. It is a thread that holds the various interdependent parts of an organization together. When it stops, organisation activity ceases to exist. An idea, however great it is, is useless until it is transmitted and understood by others. When communication is effective, it tends to encourage better performance and job satisfaction. People understand their jobs better and feel more involved in them.

38. The common among Duncan Black, Anthony Downs, James Buchanan and Kenneth Arrow is that they are all advocates of Public Choice Theory in Public Administration. Public Choice Theory refers to "the use of economic tools to deal with traditional problems of Political Science". Its content includes the study of political behaviour. In political science, it is the subset of positive political theory that studies self-interested agents (voters, politicians, bureaucrats) and their interactions, which can be represented in a number of ways—using standard constrained utility maximization, game theory or decision theory. Public choice analysis has roots in positive analysis but is often used for normative purposes in order to identify a problem or to suggest improvements to constitutional rules (*i.e.*, constitutional economics).

41. The phenomenon of economic globalisation, broadly defined as the increase in the magnitude and extent to which economic relations transcend national boundaries, has underpinned many important developments in the global economy in recent decades. This carries significant implications to the management of economic affairs, not least with regards to the ability of states to maintain control of economic relations within their borders. While some scholars, most notably Susan Strange, advance the thesis that there has been an erosion of State power—a "retreat of the state"—in the face of globalising forces, other contend that the state remain the central force in the global economy. This essay examines this debate by critically engaging with existing literature on globalisation and State power.

42. How important is domestic politics in understanding a nation's foreign policy? According to one of the most prominent theories of international relations, structural realism, domestic politics is not very important. For structural realists, the systemic forces of the international power distribution drive a state's foreign policy behaviour. Foreign policy, in this view, is primarily a function of the external environment. One prominent scholar (Stephen Walt) has written that even in the post-cold war period, "realism is likely to remain the single most useful instrument in our intellectual toolbox" for understanding world politics. Nevertheless, in recent years the finding of a democratic peace has led many international relation scholars to conclude that, infact, domestic politics does play a central role in foreign policy.

43. Other states are viewed as potential enemies is not the basic norm of the balance of power system that are clear to each of the state actors engaged in the process of balancing. The balance of power theory in international relations suggests that national security is enhanced when military capability is distributed so that no one state is strong enough to dominate all others. If one state becomes much stronger than others, the theory predicts that it will take advantage of its strength and attack weaker neighbours, thereby providing an incentive for those threatened to unite in a defensive coalition. Some realists maintain that this would be more stable as aggression would appear unattractive and would be averted if there was equilibrium of power between the rival coalitions.

45. Article 25 of the Charter of the United Nations provides that the members of the United Nations agree to accept and carry out the decisions of the security council in accordance with the present charter. In order to ensure prompt and effective action by the UN, its members confer on the Security Council primary responsibility for the maintenance of international peace and security, and agree that in carrying out its duties under this responsibility the SC acts on their bahalf. In discharging these duties the SC shall act in accordance with the purposes and principles of the UN. The specific powers granted to the SC for the discharge of these duties are laid down in chapters VI, VII, VIII and XII. The Security council shall submit annual and, when necessary, special reports to the General Assembly for its consideration.

47. The International Criminal Court is an intergovernmental organization and international tribunal that sits in the Hague in the Netherlands. The ICC has the jurisdiction to prosecute individuals for the international crimes of genocide, crimes against humanity and war crimes. The ICC is intended to complement existing national judicial systems and it may therefore only exercise its jurisdiction when certain conditions are met, such as when national courts are unwilling or unable to prosecute criminals or when the United Nations Security Council or individual states refer investigations to the court. The ICC began functioning on 1 July, 2002, the date that the Rome Statute entered into force. The Rome Statute is a multilateral treaty which serves as the ICC's foundational and governing document. States which become party to the Rome Statue, for example by ratifying it, become member states of the ICC. Currently, there are 124 states which are party to the Rome Statute and therefore members of the ICC.

48. The Convention on the Rights of Persons with Disabilities is an international human rights treaty of the United Nations intended to protect the rights and dignity of persons with disabilities. Parties to the convention are required to promote, protect and ensure the full enjoyment of human rights by persons with disabilities and ensure that they enjoy full equality under the law. The convention has served as the major catalyst in the global movement from viewing persons with disabilities as objects of charity, medical treatment and social protection towards viewing them as full and equal members of society, with human rights. It is also the only UN human rights instrument with an explicit sustainable development dimension. The convention was the first human rights treaty of the third millennium.

The text was adopted by the UN General Assembly on 13 December 2006, and opened for signature on 30 March 2007. Following ratification by the 20th party, it came into force on 3 May, 2008.

PAPER–III

Note: *This paper contains **seventy five** (75) objective type questions of **two** (2) marks each. **All** questions are **compulsory**.*

1. Who among the following said that political theory stands for an abstract model of the political order?

A. T.P. Jenkin B. R.A. Dahl
C. W.T. Bluhm D. Weinstein

2. Which one of the following statements is not true?

A. Classical political theory is qualitative.
B. Behavioural political theory is quantitative.
C. Post-behavioural political theory is both qualitative and quantitative.
D. Behavioural theory is not specially concerned with Anglo-American model.

3. Which one of the following statements is not true?

A. Neo-liberalism refers to significant revival of interest in classical liberalism.
B. Neo-liberal ideas were taken up by the political parties of the New Right in Britain.
C. The revival of classical liberalism occurred as a reaction against the onset of a world recession in the 1970s.
D. T.H. Green accepted the classical liberal notion of liberty only.

4. Who among the following dismissed John Rawl's concept of social justice as a 'mirage'?

A. Macpherson B. Friedrich Hayek
C. Isaiah Berlin D. Robert Nozick

5. Who among the following said that ideology should neither be thought of as liberating or oppressive, nor as true or false. It can be any these things?

A. Andrew Heywood
B. John Rawls
C. Andrew Gamble
D. Bill Coxall

6. Match List-I with List-II and select the correct answer from the codes given below:

List-I (*Year*)	List-II (*Event*)
(*a*) 1917	1. Mao started his historic 'Long March'.
(*b*) 1918	2. Mao participated in the first Congress of the CCP.
(*c*) 1921	3. Mao became a Library Assistant in Peking University
(*d*) 1934	4. Mao met Liu Shao-Chi

Codes:

	(*a*)	(*b*)	(*c*)	(*d*)
A.	2	1	3	4
B.	4	3	2	1
C.	1	2	3	4
D.	3	4	1	2

7. Match List-I with List-II and select the correct answer from the codes given below:

List-I (*Philosopher*)	List-II (*Idea*)
(*a*) Machiavelli	1. Revolt against Reason
(*b*) Hobbes	2. Moral indifference
(*c*) Locke	3. Instinct of self-preservation
(*d*) Rousseau	4. Natural Right to Property

Codes:

	(*a*)	(*b*)	(*c*)	(*d*)
A.	2	3	4	1
B.	1	2	3	4
C.	3	1	4	2
D.	4	3	2	1

8. Who among the following said : "Most religious men I have met are politicians in disguise. I, however, who wear the guise of a politician in disguise, am at heart a religious man"?

A. Bipin Chandra Pal
B. C.R. Das
C. M.K. Gandhi
D. M.A. Jinnah

9. Given below are two statements, one labelled as Assertion (A) and the other labelled as Reason (R). Select the correct answer from the codes given below:

Assertion (A): Platonic theory of ideas is based upon the theory of knowledge.

Reason (R): For him, knowledge is perception.

Codes:

A. Both (A) and (R) are true, and (R) is the correct explanation of (A).

B. Both (A) and (R) are true, but (R) is not the correct explanation of (A).

C. (A) is true, but (R) is false.

D. (A) is false, but (R) is true.

10. Who among the following said : "Aristotle's new general science of politics was not only empirical and descriptive, but even in some respects independent of any ethical purpose, since a statesman might need to be expert in governing even a bad state."?

A. E. Barker B. G.H. Sabine

C. E.B. England D. G.C. Field

11. For Locke, which of the following statements is not true?

(*a*) The state must be a constitutional state.

(*b*) Government must posses discretionary power.

(*c*) It is a tolerant state.

(*d*) The right to property is not a natural right.

Select the correct answer from the codes given below:

A. (*a*) and (*c*) B. (*a*) and (*b*)

C. (*b*) only D. (*d*) only

12. For Rousseau, which of the following statements is not true?

(*a*) Two original instincts *i.e.*, self-love and sympathy make up man's nature.

(*b*) A thinking man is a depraved animal.

(*c*) Family is the only natural society.

(*d*) General will is not a group mind.

Select the correct answer from the codes given below:

A. (*a*) and (*b*) B. (*b*) and (*c*)

C. (*c*) only D. (*d*) only

13. For J.S. Mill, which of the following statements is not true?

(*a*) Pleasures differ in quality as well as in quantity.

(*b*) Mill makes use of the non-utilitarian arguments.

(*c*) The felicific calculus is absurd.

(*d*) Pleasures can be objectively measured.

Select the correct answer from the codes given below:

A. (*b*) and (*c*) B. (*a*) and (*b*)

C. (*a*), (*b*) and (*c*) D. (*d*) only

14. Arrange the following works of Amartya Sen in chronological order of his publications. Select the correct answer from the codes given below:

(*a*) Idea of Justice

(*b*) Inequality Re-examined

(*c*) Development as Freedom

(*d*) Choice, Welfare and Measurement

Codes:

A. (*d*), (*b*), (*c*), (*a*) B. (*a*), (*b*), (*c*), (*d*)

C. (*c*), (*d*), (*a*), (*b*) D. (*b*), (*a*), (*d*), (*c*)

15. Given below are two statements, one labelled as Assertion (A) and the other labelled as Reason (R). Select the correct answer from the codes given below:

Assertion (A): There was great deal of similarity between the ideas of Mazzini and those of Aurobindo.

Reason (R): Both believed that faith in God was the basis of morality, that politics could not be separated from morality.

Codes:

A. Both (A) and (R) are true, and (R) is the correct explanation of (A).

B. Both (A) and (R) are true, but (R) is not the correct explanation of (A).

C. (A) is true, but (R) is false.

D. (A) is false, but (R) is true.

16. Identify the correct sequence in which general systems theory has been adopted in social sciences?

1. Psychology 2. Sociology

3. Anthropology 4. Political Science

Select the correct answer from the codes given below:

Codes:

A. 1, 2, 3 and 4 B. 3, 2, 1 and 4
C. 2, 3, 4 and 1 D. 3, 1, 2 and 4

17. The term 'legitimation crisis', in terms of erosion of confidence in public institutions resulting in coercive apparatus of states, was developed by:

A. David Apter B. S.P. Huntington
C. Edward Shills D. Habermas

18. Which of the following is not true of a Constitution?

A. It safequards the political institutions.
B. It is the source of all authority of the organs of the government.
C. It promotes trans-national security.
D. It incorporates fundamental laws.

19. Who among the following are European thinkers associated with the theory of political elites?

(*a*) Pareto (*b*) Mosca
(*c*) Schumpeter (*d*) Lasswell

Select the correct answer from the codes given below:

A. (*a*) and (*b*) B. (*a*), (*b*) and (*c*)
C. (*a*), (*b*) and (*d*) D. (*a*), (*b*), (*c*) and (*d*)

20. Who among the following do not make any distinction between interest groups and pressure groups?

(*a*) Jean Blondel (*b*) Myron Weiner
(*c*) Robert C. Bone (*d*) James Coleman

Select the correct answer from the codes given below:

A. (*a*) and (*b*) B. (*b*) and (*c*)
C. (*a*) and (*d*) D. (*d*) only

21. Identify the basic contentions of Dependency theory. Select the correct answer from the code given below:

(*a*) Development of colonies is viewed as Whiteman's burden.
(*b*) Third world nations provide natural resources and cheap labour.
(*c*) Industrialization and market economy are conducive for development.
(*d*) Advanced western nations perpetuate a state of dependency by various means.

Codes:

A. (*b*) and (*c*) B. (*b*) and (*d*)
C. (*a*) and (*c*) D. (*a*) and (*d*)

22. Which of the following is/are the common feature(s) between the Indian political system and the US political system?

(*a*) Residuary powers belong to the centre.
(*b*) Residuary powers are with the states.
(*c*) Presidents have the power of pocket veto.
(*d*) Upper houses have some nominated members.

Select the correct answer from the codes given below:

A. (*a*), (*c*) and (*d*) B. (*b*), (*c*) and (*d*)
C. (*c*) and (*d*) D. (*c*) only

23. Which one of the following types of bureaucracy exhibits a bias towards party interests?

A. Guardian bureaucracy
B. Caste bureaucracy
C. Patronage bureaucracy
D. Merit bureaucracy

24. In a single transferable vote system, each voter is required to:

A. Indicate one preference more than the seats to be filled up.
B. Indicate one preference less than the total seats to be filled up.
C. Indicate as many preferences as there are candidates to be elected.
D. Indicate only a single preference.

25. Which of the following are true of presidential system of government?

(*a*) President is both Head of the State and Head of the Government.
(*b*) It is based on separation of powers.
(*c*) President's term of office is fixed.
(*d*) Secretaries are responsible to the president as well as to the Senate.

Select the correct answer from the codes given below:

A. (*a*), (*b*) and (*c*) B. (*a*), (*b*), (*c*), (*d*)
C. (*a*), (*b*) and (*d*) D. (*a*), (*c*) and (*d*)

26. Which of the following Houses has had the longest speeches by the members?

A. House of Lords
B. Lok Sabha
C. US Senate
D. Swiss Council of States

27. Which of the following statements are correct about the Vice-Presidents of India and America?

(*a*) Both the Vice-Presidents are elected for a fixed term.
(*b*) They are the presiding officers of the upper house.
(*c*) They appoint the committees of the house.
(*d*) They have a casting vote in case of a tie.

Select the correct answer from the codes given below:

Codes:

A. (*a*), (*b*) and (*d*) B. (*b*) and (*c*)
C. (*a*), (*b*) and (*c*) D. (*a*), (*b*), (*c*) and (*d*)

28. Which one of the following characteristics is not true of Anomic interest groups?

A. They are spontaneous groups that are formed suddenly.
B. They are formed on the basis of prior organisation and planning.
C. Eruption of violent behaviour at times to ventilate the discontentment.
D. They are short lived and transitory as they cease to operate once the purpose is achieved.

29. Given below are two statements, one labelled as Assertion (A) and the other labelled as Reason (R). Select the correct answer from the codes given below:

Assertion (A): In the advanced liberal democracies of the western nations, military is subordinate to the civilian authority.

Reason (R): Military plays a key role in countries where democracy has not been institutionalized.

Codes:

A. Both (A) and (R) are correct, and (R) is the correct explanation of (A).
B. Both (A) and (R) are correct, but (R) is not the correct explanation of (A).
C. (A) is correct, but (R) is false.
D. (A) is false, but (R) is correct.

30. Match List–I with List–II and select the correct answer from the codes given below :

List-I (***Writer***)	**List-II** (***Concept/Model***)
(*a*) Robert Mitchels	1. Communication Model
(*b*) James Burnham	2. Power Elites
(*c*) C.Wright Mills	3. Managerial Revolution
(*d*) Harolds Lasswell	4. Iron Law of oligarchy

Codes:

	(*a*)	(*b*)	(*c*)	(*d*)
A.	2	4	1	3
B.	1	2	3	4
C.	4	3	2	1
D.	3	2	1	4

31. Which of the following statement/s about the Right to negative vote is/are correct? Select the correct answer from the codes given below:

I. The Election Commission of India wanted that 'None of the above' button on Electronic voting machine should be offered to voters.
II. The public interest litigation, in the Supreme Court for NOTA option was filed by the Association for Democratic Reforms.
III. Elections in a constituency will be held again if NOTA gets the highest votes.
IV. The candidate with highest number of votes will be declared elected even if she/he receives less than the NOTA votes.

Codes:

A. Only I and II are correct.
B. Only II and III are correct.
C. Only III and IV are correct.
D. Only I and IV are correct.

32. Given below are two statements, one labelled as Assertion (A) and the other labelled as Reason (R). Select the correct answer from the codes given below:

Assertion (A): Federalism is not dead in India.

Reason (R): New regions are constantly demanding statehood.

Codes:

A. Both (A) and (R) are true, and (R) is the correct explanation of (A).

B. Both (A) and (R) are true, but (R) is not the correct explanation of (A).

C. (A) is true, but (R) is false.

D. (R) is true, but (A) is false.

33. Which one of the following pairs is not correctly matched?

A. Laxmi Kant Pandey v/s Union of India : Inter-country adoption of Indian babies.

B. S.P. Gupta v/s President of India and others : Enabling citizens to file public interest litigation for social cause.

C. Mohini Jain v/s State of Karnataka : Enjoyment of pollution-free water and air.

D. Olga Tellis v/s Bombay Municipal Corporation : Right to livelihood.

34. Match List-I with List-II and select the correct answer from the codes given below :

List-I (***Presidents of India***)	**List-II** (***Tenure***)
(a) Varahgiri Venkatgiri	1. July 1987- July 1992
(b) Dr. Zakir Hussain	2. July 1977-July 1982
(c) R. Venkatraman	3. Aug.1969-Aug. 1974
(d) Neelam Sanjiva Reddy	4. May 1967-May 1969

Codes:

	(a)	*(b)*	*(c)*	*(d)*
A.	3	1	4	2
B.	3	4	1	2
C.	2	3	4	1
D.	1	2	3	4

35. Which one of the following is the correct break-up of the composition of Lok Sabha Constituencies?

	Total Constituencies	General Constituencies	SC Constituencies	ST Constituencies
A.	545	423	80	42
B.	543	423	79	41
C.	543	425	78	40
D.	545	427	79	39

36. According to the Supreme Court of India, the foundation of 'composite culture', as mentioned in clause (f) of Article 51 A, is:

A. the diverse culture of India

B. the Sanskrit language and literature

C. the secular fabric of India

D. the values evolved during the freedom movement

37. Which of the following Fundamental Rights are granted only to citizens of India? Select the correct answer from the code given below:

I. Cultural and educational rights.

II. Equality before the law.

III. Right against exploitation.

IV. Protection from discrimination on grounds only of religion, race, caste, sex or place of birth.

Codes:

A. I and II only B. II and IV only

C. III and IV only D. I and IV only

38. Which of the following statement/s about the Government of India Act, 1935 is/are not true? Select the correct answer from the code given below:

I. In six of the provinces, the legislature was bi-cameral.

II. The Governor-General had the power to make permanent acts but not ordinances.

III. The residuary powers of legislation were vested in the Central Legislature.

IV. Education as a subject was with Central Legislature.

V. Separate representation was provided only to the Muslim community.

Codes:

A. I, II, III and V B. II, IV and V

C. II, III, IV and V D. I, III, IV and V

39. Match List-I with List-II and select the correct answer from the codes given below:

List-I (*Farmer's Organization*)	List-II (*State*)
(*a*) Shetkari Sangathana	1. Gujarat
(*b*) Bhartiya Kisan Sangh	2. Maharashtra
(*c*) Samata Sangathan	3. Rajasthan
(*d*) Kisan Mazdoor Sangathan	4. Odisha
	5. West Bengal

Codes:

	(*a*)	(*b*)	(*c*)	(*d*)
A.	1	2	3	5
B.	3	2	1	4
C.	2	1	4	3
D.	2	1	4	5

40. Consider the following statements and select the correct answer from the codes given below:

I. Subject to legislation by Parliament, the power to declare any area as a 'Scheduled area' is given to the President.

II. The 5th Schedule of the Constitution deals with administration of 'Scheduled Areas' in Assam, Meghalaya and Tripura.

III. The Government of the states having 'Scheduled Areas' have to submit reports to the President regarding the administration of such 'Areas'.

IV. The executive power of the Union shall extend to giving directions to the respective states regarding administration of the 'Scheduled Areas'.

Which of the above statements are correct ?

Codes:

A. Only I and III B. Only I and IV
C. Only I and II D. Only II and III

41. Which one of the following is correctly matched about the outcome of the XVI Lok Sabha elections?

A. National Democratic Alliance : 336 seats and 35 per cent vote share.
B. United Progressive Alliance : 54 seats and 23 per cent vote share.
C. Left Front : 10 seats and 4.8 per cent vote share.
D. Congress : 44 seats and 17 per cent vote share.

42. Match List-I with List-II and give the correct answer from the codes given below:

List-I (*Author*)	List-II (*Book*)
(*a*) R.M. Jenkins	1. State Politics in India
(*b*) Myron Weiner(ed)	2. Language Religion and Politics in North India
(*c*) Christophe Jafferlot	3. Regional Reflections Comparing Politics Across India's States
(*d*) Paul R. Brass	4. India's Silent Revolution : The rise of the Low Castes in North Indian Politics

Codes:

	(*a*)	(*b*)	(*c*)	(*d*)
A.	3	1	4	2
B.	1	3	4	2
C.	2	1	4	3
D.	4	1	3	2

43. Which of the following pairs is not correctly matched?

A. Rajni Kothari – Congress system
B. Yogendra Yadav – Third Electoral System
C. Paul Brass – Disintegration of Congress organisation
D. James Manor – Post-Congress polity

44. Who among the following wrote, "In the context of society today, the caste system and much that goes with it are wholly incompatible, reactionary, restrictive, and barriers to progress."?

A. B.R. Ambedkar
B. Jawaharlal Nehru
C. M.K. Gandhi
D. R.M. Lohia

45. Consider the following statements about lower courts and identify the false statements from the codes given below:

(*a*) The Panchayat Courts have only civil jurisdiction.

(*b*) The Munsiff Courts are lower in hierarchy to the court of Subordinate Judges.

(*c*) The Sessions cases are the more serious civil cases in the Court of the District Judge.

Codes:

A. (*a*) only B. (*a*) and (*b*)

C. (*a*) and (*c*) D. (*a*), (*b*) and (*c*)

46. Match List-I with List-II and select the correct answer from the codes given below:

List-I (*Books*)

(*a*) The Art of Judgment : A Study of Policy Making

(*b*) Understanding Public Policy

(*c*) The New Science of Management Decision

(*d*) Personality and Organization

List-II (*Authors*)

1. Thomas R. Dye
2. Herbert Simon
3. Sir Geoffrey Vickers
4. Chris Argyris

Codes:

	(*a*)	(*b*)	(*c*)	(*d*)
A.	2	4	3	1
B.	3	1	2	4
C.	1	3	2	4
D.	4	2	3	1

47. At present, Public Account Committee consists of 22 members:

A. 15 from Lok Sabha and 7 from Rajya Sabha.

B. 14 from Lok Sabha and 8 from Rajya Sabha.

C. 12 from Lok Sabha and 10 from Rajya Sabha.

D. 11 from Lok Sabha and 11 from Rajya Sabha.

48. A horizontal grouping of specialized activities is attained in an organization that is:

A. Centralized B. Integrated

C. Decentralized D. Disintegrated

49. Which of the following statements about the Right to Information Act 2005 is/are correct?

(*a*) The Act came into force in October 2005.

(*b*) It repealed the Official Secrets Act, 1923.

(*c*) It has not repealed the Freedom of Information Act, 2002.

(*d*) It is available to Indian citizens only.

Choose the correct answer from the codes given below:

A. (*a*) and (*c*) B. (*b*) and (*d*)

C. (*c*) and (*d*) D. (*a*) and (*d*)

50. Which one of the following is not included as a cause for disciplinary action against public servants by L.D. White ?

A. Inefficiency

B. Long absence from duty

C. Immorality

D. Intoxication

51. The names associated with behavioural theory of organization are:

(*a*) Chester Barnard (*b*) J.L. Moreno

(*c*) Thomas Carlyle (*d*) A.H. Maslow

Select the correct answer from the codes given below:

A. (*a*), (*c*) and (*d*)

B. (*a*), (*b*), (*c*) and (*d*)

C. (*b*) and (*d*)

D. (*a*), (*b*) and (*d*)

52. Given below are two statements, one labelled as Assertion (A) and the other labelled as Reason (R). Select the correct answer from the codes given below:

Assertion (A): Decision making is a process of selection and the aim is to select the best alternative.

Reason (R): Decision making involves rationality.

Codes:

A. Both (A) and (R) are true, and (R) is the correct explanation of (A).

B. Both (A) and (R) are true, but (R) is not the correct explanation of (A).

C. (A) is true, but (R) is false.

D. (A) is false, but (R) is true.

53. Riggsian Agraria model is characterized by which of the following?

(*a*) Clan-based organization
(*b*) Communalistic value
(*c*) Impersonal human actions
(*d*) Divine authority source

Select the correct answer using the codes given below:

A. (*a*), (*b*) and (*c*)
B. (*b*), (*c*) and (*d*)
C. (*a*), (*b*) and (*d*)
D. (*a*), (*b*), (*c*) and (*d*)

54. Given below are two statements, one labelled as Assertion (A) and the other labelled as Reason (R). Select the correct answer from the codes given below :

Assertion (A): "The issue of decentralisation is more complex in concept and practice than is generally acknowledged".

Reason (R): 'The dual role approach to decentralisation is a kind of rehearsal of the area function dichotomy in a new setting.'

Codes:

A. Both (A) and (R) are true, and (R) is the correct explanation of (A).
B. Both (A) and (R) are true, but (R) is not the correct explanation of (A).
C. (A) is true, but (R) is false.
D. (A) is false, but (R) is true.

55. Which one of the following was not supported by Taylor in his Scientific Management theory?

A. Efficiency evaluation experts
B. Concept of 'Economic Man'
C. Functional foremanship
D. Standardization of tools

56. Chester Barnard developed a concept in respect of acceptance of authority by a subordinate from his manager. Identify it.

A. Motivation matrix
B. Decision making authority
C. Zone of indifference
D. Zone of coercive authority

57. Summarising the defects of bureaucracy, W.A. Robson did not include:

A. Excessive sense of self-importance.
B. Generalist dominated administrative system.
C. Indifference towards the feelings of individual citizens.
D. A failure to recognize the relations between the governors and the governed.

58. Max Weber and Fred W. Riggs have a commonality between them in the context of:

A. They constructed ideal type models.
B. They studied administrative systems in their environmental settings.
C. They concentrated on the problems of change.
D. They used deductive approach.

59. Upward communication is basically unconventional, but can be improved by:

(*a*) Management to give evidence that it is really interested in the opinions of employees.
(*b*) Superior should state his own position before he listens to subordinates.
(*c*) Chief should act upon the ideas and problems reported to him.
(*d*) Superior should ask his subordinates for reactions to his own ideas.

Select the correct answer from the codes given below:

A. (*a*), (*c*) and (*d*) B. (*a*) and (*c*)
C. (*b*), (*c*) and (*d*) D. (*a*), (*b*) and (*d*)

60. How many ways to embezzlement of government money have been mentioned by Kautilya in his Arthasastra?

A. 75 B. 40
C. 50 D. 30

61. Match List-I with List-II and select the correct answer from the codes given below:

List-I (***Secretary General of UN***)	**List-II** (***Tenure***)
(*a*) Kofi Annan	1. January 1972 to December 1981
(*b*) Boutros-Boutros Ghali	2. January 1982 to December 1991
(*c*) Javier Perez de Cuellar	3. January 1997 to December 2006

(*d*) Kurt Waldheim — 4. January 1992 to December 1996

Codes:

	(*a*)	(*b*)	(*c*)	(*d*)
A.	3	4	2	1
B.	3	4	1	2
C.	1	2	4	3
D.	4	3	2	1

62. Which of the following rights is not included in the second generation human rights?

A. Right to education
B. Right to health
C. Right to be free from torture and slavery
D. Right to housing

63. Which one of the following peace keeping operations of the United Nations is not an example of first generation peacekeeping operations?

A. UN Transitional Authority in Cambodia
B. UN Truce Supervision Organization
C. UN Emergency Force
D. UN Disengagement Observer Force

64. Match List-I with List-II and select the correct answer from the codes given below:

List-I (*Writer*)	List-II (*Idea*)
(*a*) Immanual Wallerstein	1. Game theory
(*b*) Von Newmann	2. End of history
(*c*) Morgenthau	3. Realism
(*d*) Francis Fukuyama	4. Dependency theory

Codes:

	(*a*)	(*b*)	(*c*)	(*d*)
A.	2	3	1	4
B.	3	2	4	1
C.	4	1	3	2
D.	1	4	2	3

65. Given below are two statements, one labelled as Assertion (A) and the other labelled as Reason (R). Select the correct answer from the codes given below :

Assertion (A): Non-alignment policy was more relevant during cold war period.

Reason (R): Non-aligned countries are divided on ethnic and religious differences.

Codes:

A. Both (A) and (R) are true, and (R) is the correct explanation of (A).
B. Both (A) and (R) are true but (R) is not the correct explanation of (A).
C. (A) is true, but (R) is false.
D. (A) is false, but (R) is true.

66. Given below are two statements, one labelled as Assertion (A) and the other labelled as Reason (R). Select the correct answer from the codes given below :

Assertion (A): American foreign policy supported the democratic regimes.

Reason (R): At times the military systems were also supported by America.

Codes:

A. Both (A) and (R) are true, and (R) is the correct explanation of (A).
B. Both (A) and (R) are true, but (R) is not the correct explanation of (A).
C. (A) is true, but (R) is false.
D. (A) is false, but (R) is true.

67. Which of the following statements is/are not true of dependency theory?

(*a*) Unequal relation between core and periphery.
(*b*) Developmental process in the third world nations reinforces underdevelopment.
(*c*) Industrialization leads to new forms of democratization and equity in global order.
(*d*) Strengthening of neo-colonialism.

Choose the correct answer from the codes given below:

A. (*a*) and (*d*)
B. (*b*) and (*c*)
C. (*a*), (*b*), (*c*) and (*d*)
D. (c) only

68. "Uniting for Peace Resolution" is also called as:

A. Truman plan
B. American plan
C. Achieson plan
D. Eisenhower plan

69. 'Balance of Power' is an important principle of:
A. Liberal thought in international politics.
B. Marxist thought in international politics.
C. Traditional thought in international politics.
D. Realist thought in international politics.

70. According to Iris L Calude Jr. which of the following is not a device for the management of power?
A. Arms control
B. Collective security
C. Balance of power
D. World Government

71. How many Asian countries are members of G-20?
A. 5 B. 6
C. 7 D. 8

72. The modern state system with its territorial sovereignty came into existence first in Europe in the wake of the
A. Treaty of Versailles
B. Congress of Vienna
C. Treaty of Westphalia
D. Congress of Berlin

73. Which of the following statements are correct regarding Economic and Social Council of U.N.? Choose your answer from the codes given below:
(*i*) The Council has 54 members.
(*ii*) The Council generally hold several short sessions and many preparatory meetings, and panel discussions with the members of civil society throughout the year.
(*iii*) It also holds a three-week substantive session in July.
(*iv*) Voting in the Council is by simple majority, each member has one vote.

Codes:
A. (*i*), (*ii*), (*iii*)
B. (*ii*), (*iii*), (*iv*)
C. (*i*), (*ii*), (*iv*)
D. (*i*), (*ii*), (*iii*), (*iv*)

74. According to Karen A. Mingrt, which of the following conditions is not essential to make first generation peacekeeping operations most effective?
A. A clear and practical mandate or purpose for the operation.
B. U.S. forces must also be present in the peace-keeping operations.
C. Consent of the parties involved as to the mandate and composition of the force.
D. Strong financial and logistical support of the members of the UN Security Council.

75. Match List-I with List-II and select the correct answer from the codes given below:

List-I (Term)	**List-II (Contents)**
(*a*) Preventive diplomacy	1. It is like classical peace-keeping. It refers to the deployment of a UN force in the field with the consent of all parties.
(*b*) Peace making	2. It involves developing social, political and economic infrastructure to prevent further violence and consolidate peace.
(*c*) Peace keeping	3. It involves confidence-building measures, fact finding and preventive deployment of UN authorised forces.
(*d*) Post-conflict peace building	4. It is designed to bring hostile parties to agreement essentially through peaceful means.

Codes:

	(*a*)	(*b*)	(*c*)	(*d*)
A.	3	4	1	2
B.	3	4	2	1
C.	1	2	3	4
D.	4	3	2	1

ANSWERS

1	2	3	4	5	6	7	8	9	10
C	D	D	B	A	B	A	C	C	B
11	**12**	**13**	**14**	**15**	**16**	**17**	**18**	**19**	**20**
D	D	D	A	A	B	D	C	A	D
21	**22**	**23**	**24**	**25**	**26**	**27**	**28**	**29**	**30**
B	D	C	C	A	C	A	B	B	C
31	**32**	**33**	**34**	**35**	**36**	**37**	**38**	**39**	**40**
D	B	C	B	B	B	D	C	D	B
41	**42**	**43**	**44**	**45**	**46**	**47**	**48**	**49**	**50**
B	A	D	B	C	B	A	C	D	B
51	**52**	**53**	**54**	**55**	**56**	**57**	**58**	**59**	**60**
D	A	C	B	A	C	B	B	B	B
61	**62**	**63**	**64**	**65**	**66**	**67**	**68**	**69**	**70**
A	C	A	C	B	B	D	C	D	A
71	**72**	**73**	**74**	**75**					
C	C	C	B	A					

EXPLANATORY ANSWERS

1. Political theory is not only a theory of politics, it is also the science of politics, the philosophy of politics at that. As a theory W.T. Bluhm explains, political theory "stands for an abstract model of the political order, a guide to the systematic collection and analysis of political data". Andrew Hacker, enlarging the point of view, says that political theory as a "theory, in ideal terms, is dispassionate and disinterested. As science, it will describe political reality without trying to pass judgement on what is being depicted, either implicity or explicity. As philosophy, it will describe rules of conduct which will secure good life for all of society". Political theory is not fantasy, though it may contain an element of political vision. It is not politicking, though it does take into account political realities for its study and analysis. It is not all scientism, though it seeks to reach the roots of all political activity analytically and systematically. It is not ideology, though it attempts to justify a political system and condemns another. It is theoretical, scientific, philosophical and at the same time dynamic with a clear objective of attaining a better social order. It thus, has in varying degrees, elements of 'theory', 'science', 'philosophy', and 'ideology'.

2. Behaviouralism is an approach in political science, which emerged in the 1930s in the US. It represents a sharp break from previous political science. This is because it emphasized an objective, quantified approach to explain and predict political behaviour. It is associated with the rise of the behavioural sciences, modeled after the natural sciences. This means that behaviouralism claims it can explain political behaviour from an unbiased, neutral point of view.

Behaviouralism seeks to examine the behaviour, actions and acts of individuals—rather than the characteristics of institutions such as legislatures, executive and judiciaries —and groups in different social settings and explain this behaviour as it relates to the political system.

3. A UK philosopher and social theorist, T.H. Green highlighted the limitations of early liberal doctrines and particularly laissez-faire. By drawing upon Kant and Hegel, he highlighted the limitations of the doctrine of 'negative' freedom, and developed a pioneering defence of 'positive' freedom, which helped liberalism to reach on accommodation with welfarism and social justice. Green was an important influence upon the development in Britain of 'new liberalism'. His chief works include 'Lectures on the Principles of Political Obligation' and 'Prolegomena to Ethics'.

4. F.A. Hayek dismissed John Rawl's concept of social justice as a 'mirage'. Hayek worked in the areas of philosophy of science, political philosophy, the free will problem and epistemology. For all that, Hayek was more hedgehog than fox. His life's work, for which he won a Nobel Prize in 1974, illuminated the nature and significance of spontaneous order. The concept seems simple, yet Hayek spent six decades refining his idea, evidently finding elusive the goal of being as clear about it as he aspired to be.

This essay concentrates on this enduring theme of Hayek's work, and a question : why would the scholar who did more than anyone in the 20th century to advance our understanding of price signals and the emergence of spontaneous orders also be driven to claim that social justice is a mirage?

5. Andrew Heywood said that ideology should neither be thought of as liberating or oppressive, nor as true or false. It can be any these things. Karl Mannheim elaborated further on the idea of the complex relation between reality and ideology by pointing to the human need for ideology. Ideologies are neither true nor false but are a set of socially conditioned ideas that provide a truth that people, both the advantaged and the disadvantaged, want to hear.

Ideology is simply a means by which a social group or an entire society achieves a measure of self-consciousness, by establishing a common identity or a set of collective goals. As such, ideology should not be thought of as liberating or oppressive, nor as true or false. It can be any of these things. The character of ideology is shaped by the historical forces from which it emerges and is fashioned by the social and political needs it serve ideology has therefore come to be indispensable feature of human condition.

8. Mahatma Gandhi said: "Most religious men I have met are politicians in disguise, I, however, who wear the guise of a politician in disguise, am at heart a religious man". Gandhi advanced a political philosophy based upon a religious ethic of non-violence and self-sacrifice, ultimately rooted in Hinduism. In his view, violence, 'the doctrine of the sword', was a western imposition upon India. His notion of non-violent, non-cooperation, satyagraha was intended both to manifest national strength and to constitute a new form of spiritual freedom.

10. G.H. Sabine said that "Aristotle's new general science of politics was not only empirical and descriptive, but even in some respects independent of any ethical purpose, since a statesman might need to be expert in governing even a bad state."

The whole science of politics, according to this new idea, included the knowledge both of the political good, relative as well as absolute, and also of political mechanics employed perhaps for an inferior or even a bad end. This enlargement of the definition of political philosophy is Aristotle's most characteristic conception.

11. A contribution of John Locke which signifies rights that individuals have by virtue of human beings. It includes right to life, liberty and property. Perhaps the whole philosophy of Locke revolves round his scheme of natural rights.

Locke, a great individualist advocated a negative conception of the state. Its role is limited to prevent the subjects from infringing one another's rights. The moment it fails to live upto its expectations, it forfeit the right to rule and can be legitimately over thrown. The state is limited to no more than a limited liability company.

According to Locke, law of nature has primacy over laws of state. In fact all laws made by the state must commensurate with law of nature.

12. In the social contract, Rousseau defined the 'general will' as that 'which tends always to the preservation and welfare of the whole'. The general will therefore represents the collective interests of society; it will benefit all citizens, rather than merely private individuals. Rousseau thus drew a clear distinction between the general will and the selfish, private will of each citizen. The general will is, in effect, what the people would wish if they were to act selflessly. The problem with such a notion of the public interest is that, so long as they persist in being selfish, it cannot be constructed on the basis of the revealed preferences of individual citizens. It is possible, in other words, that citizens may not recognize the general will as their own, even though Rousseau clearly believed that it reflected the 'higher' interests of each and every member of society.

13. J.S. Mill at the age of 16 founded the utilitarian society and sought to propagate Benthamite principle of utility. However, in view of scathing critiques, he started writing in defence of utilitarianism. Knowingly or unknowingly as Wayper says, "in his doctrine to safeguard utilitarianism from the reapproaches levelled against it, Mill goes towards overthrowing the whole utilitarian position".

This defence of utilitarianism marked following changes in Benthamite utilitarianism—

(*a*) Mill made qualitative as well as quantitative difference between different kinds of pleasure. He modifies Bentham's thesis that quantity being more important and holds that poetry is superior and preferable to pushpin or any other game.

(*b*) He abandoned the hedonistic "felicitous calculus". To him, pleasure or pain is only a subjective sensation that can not be objectively measured.

14. Amartya Sen is an Indian economist and philosopher of Bengali ethnicity, who since 1972 has taught and worked in the UK and the USA. Sen has made contributions to welfare economics, social choice theory, economic and social justice, economic theories of famines and indexes of the measure of well-being of citizens of developing countries. He was awarded the Nobel Prize in Economic sciences in 1998 and Bharat Ratna in 1999 for his work in welfare economics. He is currently the Thomas W. Lamont University Professor and Professor of Economics and Philosophy at Harvard University. He served as the chancellor of Nalanda University.

The chronological order of his publications are as follows—(*i*) Inequality Re-examined-1992 (*ii*) Choice, Welfare and Measurement-1999. (*iii*) Development as Freedom-1999 (*iv*) Idea of Justice-2009.

16. Classifications of government are clearly linked to what are called 'political systems'. However, the notion that politics is a 'system' is relatively new, only emerging in the 1950s, influenced by the development of systems theory and its application in works like Talcott Parson's 'The Social System (1951)'. It has, nevertheless, brought about a significant shift in the understanding of governmental processes. Traditional approaches to government focused upon the machinery of the state and examined the constitutional rules and institutional structure of a particular system of government. Systems analysis has, however, broadened the understanding of government by highlighting the complex interaction between it and the larger society. A 'system' is an organized or complex whole, a set of interrelated and interdependent parts that form a collective entity. Systems analysis therefore rejects a piecemeal approach to politics in favour of an overall approach : The whole is more important than its individual parts. Moreover, it emphasizes the importance of relationships, implying that each part only has meaning in terms of its function within the whole. A political system therefore extends far beyond the instructions of government themselves and encompasses all those processes, relationships and institutions through which government is linked to the governed. This theory has been adopted in Anthropology, Sociology, Psychology and Political science consecutively.

17. In 'Legitimation crisis-1975' the neo-marxist Jurgen Habermas argued that within liberal democracies there are 'crisis tendencies' which challenge the stability of such regimes by undermining legitimacy. The core of this argument was the tension between a private-enterprise or capitalist economy, on one hand, and a democratic political system, on the other; in effect, the system of capitalist democracy may be inherently unstable.

18. A Constitution is a set of fundamental principles or established precedents according to which a state or other organization is governed. These rules together make up, *i.e.* constitute, what the entity is. When these principles are written down into a single document or set of legal documents, those documents may be said to embody a written constitution; if they are written down in a single comprehensive document, it is said to embody a codified constitution. Some constitutions are uncodified, but written in numerous fundamental acts of a legislature, court cases or treaties.

19. Vilfredo Pareto and Gaetano Mosca associated with the theory of political elites. Pareto emphasized the psychological and intellectual superiority of elites, delieving that they were the highest accomplishers in any field. He discussed the existence of two types of elites: (*i*) Governing elites (*ii*) Non-governing elites. He also extended the idea that a whole elite can be replaced by a new one and how one can circulate from being elite to non-elite.

Mosca emphasized the sociological and personal characteristics of elites. He said elites are an organized minority and that the masses are an unorganized majority. The ruling class is composed of the ruling elite and the sub-elites. He divides the world into two groups : (*i*) Ruling class (*ii*) Class that is ruled. Mosca asserts that elites have intellectual, moral and material superiority that is highly esteemed and influential.

20. James Samuel Coleman was an American sociologist, theorist and empirical researcher do not make any distinction between interest groups and pressure groups. He was elected president of the American Sociological Association. He studied the sociology of education and public policy, and was one of the earliest users of the term 'social capital'. His foundations of social theory influenced sociological theory. His 'The Adolescent society' and 'Coleman Report' were two of the most cited books in educational sociology. The landmark Coleman Report helped transform educational theory, reshape national education policies, and it influenced public and scholarly opinion regarding the role of schooling in determining equality and productivity in the United States.

21. The Dependency theory was developed from a Marxian perspective by Paul A. Baran in 1957 with the publication of his 'The Political Economy of Growth'. Dependency theory shares many points with earlier Marxist theories of imperialism by Rosa Luxemburg and Vladimir Lenin, and has attracted continued interest from Marxists. Matias Vernengo identifies two main streams in dependency : the Latin American Structuralist, typified by the work of Prebisch, Celso Furtado and Anibal Pinto at the United Nations Economic Commission for Latin America (ECLAC); and the American Marxist, developed by Paul A. Baran, Paul Sweezy and Andre Gunder Frank.

Both groups would agree that at the core of the dependency relation between centre and periphery lays the inability of the periphery to develop an autonomous and dynamic process of technological.

22. Presidents have the power of pocket veto is the common feature between the Indian political system and the US political system. This power of the President not to take any action on the bill is known as the pocket veto. The president can exercise this veto power as the constitution does not prescribe any time-limit within which he has to take the decision with respect to a bill presented to him for his assent. In USA, on the other hand, the President has to return the bill for reconsideration within 10 days. Hence, it is remarked that the pocket of the Indian President is bigger than that of the American President.

23. Patronage bureaucracy exhibits a bias towards party interests. The growth of bureaucracy is a major social trend of modern society. It is found in both public and private organizations. Literally, the term bureaucracy means administration by bureaus.

In the politics of the United States, a spoils system (also known as a patronage system) is a practice in which a political party, after winning an election, gives government jobs to its supporters, friends and relatives as a reward for working toward victory, and as an incentive to keep working for the party—as opposed to a merit system, where offices are awarded on the basis of some measure of merit, independent of political activity.

24. In a single transferable vote system, each voter is required to indicate as many preferences as there are candidates to be elected. This system ensures that the successful candidate is returned by the absolute majority of votes. Each member of the electoral college is given only one ballot paper. The voter, while casting his vote, is required to indicate his preference by marking 1, 2, 3, 4 etc. against the names of candidates. This means that the voter can indicate as many preferences as there are candidates in the fray.

25. The features of the Presidential system of government are as follows:

President is both Head of the State and Head of the Government. This system is based on separation of powers and check and balance. President's term of office is fixed. He cannot be removed by the congress except by impeachment for a grave unconstitutional act. The President and his secretaries are not responsible to the congress for their acts. They neither possess membership in the congress nor attend its sessions. The President governs with the help of a cabinet or a smaller body called 'Kitchen Cabinet'. It is only an advisory body and consists of non-elected departmental secretaries. They are selected and appointed by him, are responsible only to him, and can be removed by him any time.

28. Pressure groups/interest groups are voluntary associations of individuals who have common goals and who work together to achieve their goals by attempting to influence government policy. They don't seek to win elections and form government. They are also known as NGOS. Pressure groups can be classified into four broad categories as follows—(*i*) Anomic (*ii*) Associational (*iii*) Non-Associational and (*iv*) Institutional.

Anomic groups are ad hoc (unplanned) groups which come into existence as a result of turmoil and excitement, a crisis, a specific event or issue. Anomic groups do not have a formal structure or leaders and their actions are often violent. They act spontaneously and in an uncoordinated fashion and are short-lived. They express their grievances through violent riots, demonstrations and street protests. Anomic groups may attract temporary publicity but they are usually of little importance to the political system except as indicators of current public opinion. Some examples of anomic groups—Disaffected (dissatisfied) youths in poor urban areas in France protesting against discrimination. Protests and demonstrations in several countries against the American invasion of Iraq.

33. Mohini Jain v/s State of Karnataka, a 1989 Supreme Court of India case, occured when the government of Karnataka issued a notification that permitted the private medical colleges in the state of Karnataka to charge exorbitant tuition fees from the students admitted other than the 'Government Seat quota'. Miss Mohini Jain, a medical aspirant student filed a petition in Supreme Court challenging this notification. The Apex Court raised an important question that 'whether right to education is guaranteed to the Indian citizen under the constitution of India'?

The Supreme Court of India observed that mention of 'Life and personal liberty' in article 21 of the constitution automatically implies some other rights, those are necessary for the full development of the personality, though they are not enumerated in Part III of the constitution. Education is one such factor responsible for overall development of an individual and therefore, right to education is integrated in Article 21 of the constitution.

37. The Fundamental Rights are enshrined in Part III of the constitution from Article 12 to 35. In this regard, the framers of the constitution derived inspiration from the constitution of USA (*i.e.,* Bill of Rights).

Part III of the constitution is rightly described as the Magna Carta of India. It contains a very long and comprehensive list of 'justiciable' Fundamental Rights. In fact, the Fundamental Rights in our constitution are more elaborate than those found in the constitution of any other country in the world, including the USA. FR available only to citizens and not to foreigners are following—

(*i*) Prohibition of discrimination on grounds of religion, race, caste, sex or place of birth (A-15).

(*ii*) Equality of opportunity in matters of public employment (A-16).

(*iii*) Protection of six rights regarding freedom of : (*a*) speech of expression (*b*) assembly (*c*) association (*d*) movement (*e*) residence and (*f*) profession (A-19).

(*iv*) Protection of language, script and culture of minorities (A-29).

(*v*) Right of minorities to establish and administer educational institutions (A-30).

38. The Government of India Act, 1935 was a lengthy and detailed document having 321 Sections and 10 Schedules. The features of this Act are as follows—

In six of the provinces out of eleven, the legislature was bi-cameral. These provinces are Bengal, Bombay, Madras, Bihar, Assam and the United province. Upper house is

Legislative council and lower house is Legislative Assembly. However, many restrictions were placed on them. It further extended the principle of communal representation by providing separate electrorates for depressed classes, women and labour. Residuary powers were given to the Viceroy.

41. The 16th Lok Sabha general election held in 2014. The elections were conducted in 9 phases from 7 April to 12 May 2014 by the Election Commission of India. The results of the election were declared on 16 May, 2014. The BJP (of the NDA) achieved an absolute majority with 282 seats out of 543. Its PM candidate Narendra Modi took office on 26 May 2014 as the 15th PM of independent India. The UPA got 54 seats and 23% vote while the INC could only manage 44 seats. There is no leader of the opposition in the 16th Lok Sabha as the Indian Parliament rules state that a party in the Lok Sabha must have at least 10% of total seats (545) in order to be considered the opposition party. Mallikarjun Kharge has been declared the leader of the INC in the Lok Sabha.

44. Communalism and Caste system constitutes a formidable obstacle to the realization of the ideal of secular state. According to Jawaharlal Nehru, caste has been largely responsible for weakening India's Civilization throughout her long history. The caste system in the early centuries had a certain flexibility. But later "along with the growth of rigidity in the caste system, grew rigidity of mind and the creative energy faded away," says Nehru. So he vehemently revolted against caste behaviour patterns. Thus Panditji observed, "in the context of society today, the caste system and much that goes with it are wholly incompatible, reactionary, restrictive and barriers to progress. These can be no equality in status and opportunity within its framework, nor can there be political democracy and much less, economic democracy".

45. A Nyaya Panchayat is a system of dispute resolution at village level in India. Nyaya Panchayats can be endowed with functions based on broad principles of natural justice and can tend to remain procedurally as simple as possible. They can be given civil and minor criminal jurisdiction. But they should never follow civil and criminal procedure code in toto.

District court is referred to as Sessions court when it exercises its jurisdiction on criminal matters under code of criminal procedure (CrPc). As per section 9 of CrPc, the court is established by the State Government for every session division. The court is presided over by a Judge, appointed by the High Court of that particular state. The High Court may also appoint Additional Sessions Judges and Assistant Sessions Judges in this court. In Indian cities, the Session court is responsible for adjudicating matters related to criminal cases. The court is responsible for cases relating to murders, theft, pick-pocketing and other such cases.

47. The Public Account Committee is a committee of selected members of Parliament, constituted by the Parliament of India, for the auditing of the revenue and the expenditure of the Government of India. This committee is formed every year with a strength of not more than 22 members of which 15 are from Lok Sabha, the lower house of the Parliament, and 7 from Rajya Sabha, the upper house of the Parliament. The term of office of the members is one year. The chairman is appointed by the speaker of Lok Sabha. Since 1967, the chairman of the committee is selected from the opposition. Earlier, it was headed by a member of the ruling party. Its chief function is to examine the audit report of Comptroller and Auditor General (CAG) after it is laid in the Parliament. CAG assists the committee during the course of investigation. None of the 22 members shall be a minister in the government.

49. Right to Information (RTI) is an act of the Parliament of India "to provide for setting out the practical regime of right to information for citizens" and replaces the erstwhile Freedom of Information Act, 2002. Under the provisions of the act, any citizen of India may request information from a "Public authority" which is required to reply expeditiously or within thirty days. The act also requires every public authority to computerise their records for wide dissemination and to proactively certain categories of information so that the citizens need minimum recourse to request for information formally.

This law was passed by Parliament on 15 June 2005 and came fully into force on 12 October 2005. The first application was given to a Pune police station. Information disclosure in India was restricted by the Official Secret Act 1923 and various other special laws, which the new RTI Act relaxes. It codifies a fundamental right to citizens.

52. Decision-making means choosing one alternative from among various alternatives. It is essentially problem-solving in nature. Decision-making is closely related to policy-making, but they are not the same. Terry has clarified the difference between decision and policy as follows, "a decision is usually made within the guidelines established by policy. A policy is relatively extensive, affects many problems, and is used again and again. In contrast, a decision applies to a particular problem and has a non-continuous type of usage." The first comprehensive analysis of the decision-making process is given by Chester Barnard. He observed, "the processes of decision are largely techniques for narrowing choice".

53. Riggsian Agraria model is characterized by Clan-based organization, communalistic value and divine authority source. Riggs made a significant contribution to the field of development administration. He defined development administration as "organized efforts to carry out programmes or projects through by those involved to serve developmental objectives.

Riggs identified the following as the structural features of Agraria model—(*i*) Ascriptive values (*ii*) Particularistic (*iii*) Diffuse pattern (*iv*) Simple and stable occupational differences (*v*) Existence of differential stratification system (*vi*) Limited social and spatial mobility.

55. Efficiency evaluation experts was not supported by Taylor in his Scientific Management Theory. Scientific management, also called Taylorism, is a theory of management that analyzes and synthesizes work flows. Its main objective is improving economic efficiency, especially labour productivity. It was one of the earliest attempts to apply science to the engineering of processes and to management.

Its development began in the USA with F.W. Taylor in the 1880s and 90s within the manufacturing industries. Its peak of influence came in the 1910s; by the 1920s, it was still influential but had entered into competition and syncretism with opposing or complementary ideas.

56. Chester Barnard developed a zone of indifference in respect of acceptance of authority by a subordinate from his manager. Barnard does not agree with traditional concept of authority and introduces 'acceptance' as the basis of his theory of authority. He defines the authority as "the character of a communication in a formal organization by virtue of which it is accepted by a contributor or 'member' of the organisations as governing or determining what he does or is not to do so far as the organisation is concerned". This definition has both subjective and objective aspects. The former implies acceptance of a communication as authority. The latter is concerned with the character in the communication by virtue of which it is accepted.

57. Prof. W.A. Robson has summarized its defects in the following words: "The maladies from which bureaucracy most frequently suffers are an excessive sense of self-importance on the part of officials or an undue idea of the importance of their office; an indifference towards the feeling or the convenience of individual citizens; an obsession with the binding and inflexible authority of departmental decisions, precedents, arrangements or forms, regardless of how badly or with what injustice they may work in individual cases; a mania for regulations and formal procedure; a pre-occupation with the activities of particular units of administration and an inability to consider the Government as a whole; a failure to recognize the relations between the governors and the governed as an essential part of democratic process."

59. Upward communication is basically unconventional, but can be improved by management to give evidence that it is really interested in the opinions of employees and also it can be improved by chief should act upon the ideas and problems reported to him. Upward communication is the process of information flowing from the lower levels of a hierarchy to the upper levels. This type of communication is becoming more popular in organizations as traditional forms of communication are becoming less popular. The more traditional organization types such as a hierarchy, places people into separate ranks.

Upward communication helps employees to express their requirements, ideas and feelings. For the top management, upward communication is an important source of information for business decisions. It helps in alerting top management about the requirement of changes in an organisations. Upward contribution is the core contributor of business process re-engineering in many organisations.

60. There are 40 ways to embezzlement of government money have been mentioned by Kautilya in his Arthasastra. Corruption in India is has been a problem ever since the country had been having a multilayered administration by officers, ministers and other administrative chiefs. The corruption problem in ancient India, coupled with bribery, kept infesting the society more and more in an increasing rate. This is quite clear from the way the contemporary writers like Kautilya, Ksemendra and Kalhana have condemned the government officials, as well as other employees of different levels, in their celebrated works.

62. The Second generation of human rights are based on the principles of social justice and public obligation—they tend to be 'positive' rights, based on continental European conceptions of liberty as equality. This generation of human rights developed through those who had a strong desire for the state to provide protection for its neediest inhabitants via providing relief to the less fortunate. This second generation of rights has since evolved into what are now known as 'social' or 'economic' rights.

Important examples of second generation rights are as follows:

(*i*) Right to education

(*ii*) Right to health

(*iii*) Right to housing

(*iv*) Right to just and favourable conditions of work.

(*v*) Right of protection against unemployment, etc.

63. UN transitional authority in Cambodia is a peace keeping operations of the United

Nations is not an example of first generation peacekeeping operation. First-generation forces typically possess a mandate under chapter VI of the UN charter, are lightly armed, and operate under strictly limiting rules of engagement. The interpretation of state sovereignty prevalent during the Cold War era, which created a 'vertical relationship' between states' rights and human rights, emphasizing the former, placed tight restrictions on the nature of peace operations; these crystallized into three basic principles which guide peace operations to this day.

(*i*) The consent of the host nations.

(*ii*) Impartiality between the conflict factions.

(*iii*) The non-use of force by United Nations troops.

67. Industrialization leads to new forms of democratization and equity in global order is not true about dependency theory. Dependency theory is the notion that resources flow from a 'periphery' of poor and underdeveloped states to a 'core' of wealthy states, enriching the latter at the expense of the former. It is a central contention of dependency theory that poor states are impoverished and rich ones enriched by the way poor states are integrated into the 'world system'.

The theory aroses as a reaction to modernization theory, an earlier theory of development which held that all societies progress through similar stages of development, that today's underdeveloped areas are thus in a similar situation to that of today's developed areas at some time in the past, and that, therefore, the task of helping the underdeveloped areas out of proverty is to accelerate them along this supposed common path of development, by various means such as investment, technology transfers, and closer integration into the world market. Dependency theory rejected this view, arguing that underdeveloped countries are not merely primitive versions of developed countries, but have unique features and structure of their own; and, importantly, are in the situation of being the weaker members in a world market economy.

68. "Uniting for Peace Resolution" is also called as Achieson Plan. Uniting for peace has been implemented 11 or 12 times since the adoption of General Assembly resolution 377(v) on 3 November 1950, depending on how one characterises the first case. The Security council has referred a majority of the cases, but has not done so since 1982, while the General Assembly has done so most recently albeit not since 1997.

The first request from the General Assembly interestingly came from a permanent member of the Security Council, the USSR and all General Assembly requests have dealt with situations that place one or more of the P3 (France, UK, USA) on the spot.

69. 'Balance of Power' is an important principle of Realist thought in international politics. The International relations among the states are often accompanied by the mechanics of power. But, the nations power are not absolute. They are limited by a number of factors.

By this principle, sizeable restriction is placed on the power of a state. The existence of a number of powers in the international arena automatically limits the power.

71. The Group of Twenty (G-20) was established in 1999 to bring together Finance Minister and Central Bank Governors of systemically important industrialized and developing economies to discuss key issues relating to the global economy and financial stability. By contributing to the strengthening of the international financial architecture and providing opportunities for dialogue on national policies, international co-operation and international financial institutions, the

G-20 helps to support growth, financial stability and development across the globe. The G-20 comprises 20 countries namely—Argentina, Australia, Brazil, Canada, China, European Union, France, Germany, India, Indonesia, Italy, Japan, Mexico, Russia, Saudi Arabia, South Africa, South Korea, Turkey, Britain, America. It represents 90 per cent of the global gross national product, 80% of the world's trade and two-third of the world's population.

72. The modern state system with its territorial sovereignty came into existence first in Europe in the wake of the treaty of Westphalia. The Westphalia area of north-western Germany gave its name to the treaty that ended the 30 year's war (1618-1648), one of the most destructive conflicts in the history of Europe. The treaty gave the Swiss independence of Austria and the Netherlands independence of Spain. The German principalities secured their autonomy. Sweden gained territory and a payment in cash, Brandenburg and Bavaria made gains too, and France acquired most of Alsace-Lorraine. Prospect of a Roman catholic reconquest of Europe vanished forever. Protestantism was in the world to stay.

73. The United Nations Economic and Social Council (ECOSOC) is one of the six principal organs of the UN, responsible for coordinating the economic, social and related work of 15 UN specialised agencies, their functional commissions and five regional commissions. The ECOSOC has 54 members. It holds a four-week session each year in July, and since 1998, it has also held a meeting of April with finance ministers heading key committees of the World Bank and the International Monetary Fund (IMF). The council generally hold several short sessions and many preparatory meetings, and panel discussions with the members of civil society throughout the year.

Previous Paper (Solved)

UGC-NET JRF & Assistant Professor Exam Political Science, December 2015

PAPER–II

Note: *This paper contains* ***fifty (50)*** *objective type questions of* ***two (2)*** *marks each.* ***All*** *questions are* ***compulsory***.

1. Which of the following is **not** an organ of Kautilya's state?

A. Swami B. Amatya
C. Varna system D. Danda

2. Plato's communism of family and property was largely derived from the experience of :

(*a*) Stagira (*b*) Sparta
(*c*) Athens (*d*) Venice

Choose the **correct** answer:

A. (*a*) and (*b*) B. (*a*) and (*c*)
C. (*c*) only D. (*b*) only

3. Scholasticism of middle ages sought to establish :

(*a*) Supremacy of political domain over the spiritual.
(*b*) The autonomy of intellectual freedom over the political regimes.
(*c*) The ascendancy of theology over the philosophy.
(*d*) The subordination of rational element to the theological element of the church.

Select the **correct** answer from the codes given below :

A. (*c*) and (*d*) B. (*a*) and (*d*)
C. (*a*) and (*c*) D. (*b*) and (*d*)

4. Match the following:

List-I	List-II
(*a*) Modern political thinker	(*i*) Plato
(*b*) Positivist school	(*ii*) Machiavelli
(*c*) Normative political theory	(*iii*) August Comte
(*d*) Scientific/inductive method	(*iv*) Aristotle

Codes:

	(*a*)	(*b*)	(*c*)	(*d*)
A.	(*ii*)	(*iii*)	(*i*)	(*iv*)
B.	(*ii*)	(*iv*)	(*i*)	(*iii*)
C.	(*i*)	(*ii*)	(*iv*)	(*iii*)
D.	(*iv*)	(*i*)	(*iii*)	(*ii*)

5. Given below are two statements, one labelled as Assertion (A) and the other labelled as Reason (R).

Assertion (A): Power corrupts and absolute power corrupts absolutely.

Reason (R): Democracy is the best check against the misuse of power as the power is distributed among various groups.

In the context of the above two statements which one of the following is **correct**?

A. Both (A) and (R) are true and (R) is the correct explanation of (A).
B. Both (A) and (R) are true but (R) is not correct explanation of (A).
C. (A) is true, but (R) is false.
D. (A) is false, but (R) is true.

6. Match the following:

List-I (Thinker)	List-II (Idea)
(*a*) John Locke	(*i*) Partyless democracy
(*b*) Hobbes	(*ii*) Consent theory
(*c*) Jaya Prakash Narain	(*iii*) Neo-liberalism
(*d*) Robert Nozick	(*iv*) Absolute sovereignty

Codes:

	(*a*)	(*b*)	(*c*)	(*d*)
A.	(*ii*)	(*iv*)	(*i*)	(*iii*)
B.	(*i*)	(*iii*)	(*iv*)	(*ii*)
C.	(*ii*)	(*i*)	(*iii*)	(*iv*)
D.	(*iv*)	(*ii*)	(*i*)	(*iii*)

7. Match the items of List-I with items of List-II by selecting the **correct** answer from the codes :

List-I (Thinkers)	**List-II (Theories)**
(*a*) Mao Tse Tung	(*i*) Proletarian Dictatorship
(*b*) Lenin	(*ii*) Cultural Revolution
(*c*) Marx	(*iii*) One Country Socialism
(*d*) Stalin	(*iv*) Communist Party as the Vanguard of the proletariat

Codes:

	(*a*)	(*b*)	(*c*)	(*d*)
A.	(*ii*)	(*iv*)	(*i*)	(*iii*)
B.	(*iii*)	(*i*)	(*iv*)	(*ii*)
C.	(*iv*)	(*ii*)	(*i*)	(*iii*)
D.	(*ii*)	(*iv*)	(*iii*)	(*i*)

8. Rearrange the following works of Karl Marx in sequential order in terms of Publication Year.

(*a*) Critique of Political Economy
(*b*) Poverty of Philosophy
(*c*) Communist Manifesto
(*d*) The Holy Family

Codes:

A. (*d*), (*b*), (*c*) and (*a*)
B. (*a*), (*c*), (*d*) and (*b*)
C. (*b*), (*a*), (*d*) and (*c*)
D. (*d*), (*c*), (*b*) and (*a*)

9. Communitarian theory lays emphasis on:

A. Community as an inescapable ideal
B. Unlimited freedom of the individual
C. Limited role of the state
D. Partial regulation of market economy

10. Given below are the two statements, one labelled as Assertion (A) and the other labelled as Reason (R). Select the **correct** answer from the codes given below.

Assertion (A): Behavioural political theory sought to eliminate the role of values and make Political Science a pure science and quantitative.

Reason (R): Political Science, being a social science, can never be value-free as it deals with human beings who are value-bound.

A. Both (A) and (R) are true and (R) is the correct explanation of (A).
B. Both (A) and (R) are true and (R) is not the correct explanation of (A).
C. (A) is true, but (R) is false.
D. (A) is false, but (R) is true.

11. In whose description Maulana Azad, Jawaharlal Nehru, Vallabhbhai Patel and Rajendra Prasad formed 'an oligarchy within the (Constituent) Assembly'?

A. Granville Austin B. Morris Jones
C. V.P. Menon D. Richard Sisson

12. Which one of the following Acts has not been passed under article 34 of the Indian Constitution?

A. The Border Security Force Act
B. The Police Forces (Restriction of Rights) Act
C. Armed Forces Special Power Act
D. The Army Act

13. "The Supreme Court of India is at long last becoming, after thirty two years of the Republic, the Supreme Court for Indians". Who said this?

A. Justice V.R. Krishna Aiyyer
B. Justice P.N. Bhagwati
C. Upendra Baxi
D. Nani Palkhiwala

14. "India has a hallowed place in discussions of democracy...... But it has become less tolerant, less secular, less law-abiding, less liberal. And these two trends—democratization and illiberalism are directly related". Who wrote this?

A. Atul Kohli B. Sunil Khilnani
C. Fareed Zakaria D. Paul R. Brass

15. In which one of the following cases the Supreme Court of India has laid down exhaustive guidelines for preventing sexual harassment of working women in place of their work?

A. Hussainara Khatoon V. State of Bihar
B. Delhi Domestic Working Women's Forum V. Union of India
C. Olga Tellis V. Bombay Municipal Corporation
D. Vishakha V. State of Rajasthan and others.

16. Match List-I with List-II and select the correct answer from the codes given below:

List-I (Leaders)	**List-II (Political Parties)**
(*a*) Ram Vilas Paswan	(*i*) Samajwadi Party
(*b*) H.D. Kumarswamy	(*ii*) Nationalist Congress Party
(*c*) Praful Patel	(*iii*) Janata Dal (Secular)
(*d*) Akhilesh Yadav	(*iv*) Lok Janshakti Party

Codes:

	(*a*)	(*b*)	(*c*)	(*d*)
A.	(*iii*)	(*ii*)	(*iv*)	(*i*)
B.	(*iv*)	(*iii*)	(*ii*)	(*i*)
C.	(*ii*)	(*i*)	(*iv*)	(*iii*)
D.	(*i*)	(*ii*)	(*iii*)	(*iv*)

17. How many functional items have been placed within the purview of municipalities by the Twelfth Schedule to the Constitution?

A. 18 B. 30
C. 35 D. 40

18. Rearrange the following in chronological order:

(*a*) Punchhi Commission
(*b*) Anandpur Sahib Resolution
(*c*) Administrative Reforms Commission
(*d*) Rajamannar Committee

Choose the **correct** code:

A. (d), (a), (b) and (c)
B. (b), (d), (a) and (c)
C. (a), (b), (d) and (c)
D. (c), (d), (b) and (a)

19. Who among the following was not the speaker of the Lok Sabha?

A. Rabi Ray
B. Hukum Singh
C. Baliram Bhagat
D. Gopal Swarup Pathak

20. Match the following and select the correct pairs:

List-I (Authors)	**List-II (Books)**
(*a*) Norman D. Palmer	(*i*) The success of India's Democracy.
(*b*) Granvelli Austin	(*ii*) Elections and Political Development: South Asian Experience
(*c*) Myron Weiner	(*iii*) Indian Constitution: The cornerstone of A Nation
(*d*) Atul Kohli	(*iv*) Politics of Scarcity

Codes:

	(*a*)	(*b*)	(*c*)	(*d*)
A.	(*ii*)	(*iii*)	(*iv*)	(*i*)
B.	(*iii*)	(*ii*)	(*i*)	(*iv*)
C.	(*i*)	(*ii*)	(*iii*)	(*iv*)
D.	(*iv*)	(*i*)	(*ii*)	(*iii*)

21. Which of the following were described by David Easton as intellectual foundations of the System Analysis? Give the correct answer from the codes given below:

(*a*) Regularities (*b*) Verification
(*c*) Techniques (*d*) Quantification

Codes:

A. (*a*) B. (*a*), (*b*)
C. (*a*), (*b*), (*c*) D. (*a*), (*b*), (*c*), (*d*)

22. The study of comparative politics became significant after the:

(*a*) World War I
(*b*) World War II
(*c*) Emergence of new nations
(*d*) Rise of middle eastern nations

Choose the **correct** answer:

A. (*a*) and (*b*) B. (*b*) and (*c*)
C. (*a*) and (*d*) D. (*b*) and (*d*)

23. Who among the following is regarded as the Father of Comparative Politics?

A. Plato B. Aristotle
C. Lucian Pye D. G.A. Almond

24. Match List-I with List-II and select the correct answer by using the codes given below:

List-I (Author)	**List-II (Title)**
(*a*) C.W. Mills	(*i*) The ruling class
(*b*) Vilfredo Pareto	(*ii*) Iron Law of Oligarchy
(*c*) Gaetano Mosca	(*iii*) The Power Elite
(*d*) Roberto Michels	(*iv*) Circulation of Elites

Codes:

	(*a*)	(*b*)	(*c*)	(*d*)
A.	(*iv*)	(*iii*)	(*ii*)	(*i*)
B.	(*i*)	(*iii*)	(*iv*)	(*ii*)
C.	(*ii*)	(*iii*)	(*iv*)	(*i*)
D.	(*iii*)	(*iv*)	(*i*)	(*ii*)

25. Which of the following is **not** true of pressure groups?

(*a*) interest articulation
(*b*) funding the political parties
(*c*) influencing the policies of the government
(*d*) implementation of policies

Choose the **correct** answer from the below:

A. (*a*) and (*b*) B. (*b*) and (*c*)
C. (*d*) only D. (*c*) only

26. Match List-I with List-II and select the correct answer from the codes given below:

List-I	**List-II**
(*a*) India	(*i*) Rule of Law
(*b*) U.S.A.	(*ii*) Judicial Review
(*c*) U.K.	(*iii*) Two sets of courts
(*d*) France	(*iv*) Due process of law

Codes:

	(*a*)	(*b*)	(*c*)	(*d*)
A.	(*i*)	(*ii*)	(*iii*)	(*iv*)
B.	(*ii*)	(*iv*)	(*i*)	(*iii*)
C.	(*ii*)	(*i*)	(*iv*)	(*iii*)
D.	(*iv*)	(*ii*)	(*i*)	(*iii*)

27. Which one of the following statements is **not** correct in regard to Aristotle's classification of governments?

A. The classification of governments was on the basis of number of people involved in the task of governing.
B. Whether rulers governed in common interest (the genuine form) or in their own (perverted form)
C. The government is more effective and stable when rulers govern in the long interest
D. The government is captured by shared interest and remains insensitive to shared interests of the whole community.

28. The crises described by Leonard Binder *et* all. In their book "crises and sequences in Political Development" are:

(*a*) Identity crises
(*b*) Integration crises
(*c*) Legitimacy crises
(*d*) Resource Mobilisation crises

Codes:

A. (*a*) B. (*a*), (*b*)
C. (*a*), (*b*), (*c*) D. (*a*), (*b*), (*c*), (*d*)

29. Which of the following factors are related to load capacity in the communications theory?

(*a*) responsiveness
(*b*) fidelity
(*c*) background noise
(*d*) distortion

Select the **correct** answer from the codes given below:

A. (*a*) and (*b*) B. (*b*) and (*c*)
C. (*a*), (*b*) and (*c*) D. (*a*), (*b*), (*c*) and (*d*)

30. Which one of the following said, "the power is a matter of getting people to do what they would not have otherwise done"?

A. Hannah Arendt B. Robert Dahl
C. Max Weber D. Hans Morgenthau

31. Who among the following is not associated with evolving the principles of organisation?

A. Henri Fayol B. L.D. White
C. L.F. Urwick D. Luther Gulick

32. Who among the following remained chairman of the Comparative Administrative Group in the United States of America for 10 years?
A. Woodrow Wilson
B. D. Waldo
C. Fred Riggs
D. Herbert Simon

33. The 'one best way' in scientific management means:
A. Equal division of work
B. Intensive analysis of work processes
C. Mental revolution on the part of workers and management
D. Standardisation of work methods

34. Which one of the following is not a staff agency in U.S.A.?
A. State Department
B. Office of Budget and Management
C. National Security Council
D. The White House

35. What is the **correct** sequence of F.M. Marx's classification of bureaucracy?
(*a*) Merit (*b*) Guardian
(*c*) Patronage (*d*) Caste

Select the **correct** answer from the codes given below:
A. (a), (b), (c) and (d)
B. (b), (c), (d) and (a)
C. (b), (d), (c) and (a)
D. (c), (d), (a) and (b)

36. Performance Budgeting was introduced in India on the recommendation of:
A. Paul Appleby Report
B. Gorwala Report
C. First Administrative Reforms Commission Report
D. Santhanam Committee Report

37. Domicile qualification for public appointments was first used in:
A. the U.K. B. the U.S.A.
C. India D. Australia

38. The Chief Information Commissioner and Information Commissioners in India are appointed for a term of:
A. 3 years B. 4 years
C. 5 years D. 6 years

39. Given below are two statements, one labelled as Assertion (A) and the other labelled as Reason (R). Select the **correct** answer from the codes given below:

Assertion (A): The practical application of the principle of unity of command is not always feasible.

Reason (R): Administrative and technical tasks generally need different kinds of supervision.

Codes:
A. Both (A) and (R) are true and (R) is the correct explanation of (A)
B. Both (A) and (R) are true but (R) is not the correct explanation of (A)
C. (A) is true, but (R) is false
D. (A) is false, but (R) is true

40. The aim of E-Government is to make the interaction between government and citizens.
(*a*) more friendly (*b*) convenient
(*c*) transparent (*d*) inexpensive

Select the **correct** answer from the codes given below:
A. (a) and (c) B. (a), (b) and (c)
C. (b), (c) and (d) D. (a), (b), (c) and (d)

41. Economic diplomacy is also termed as:
A. cultural diplomacy
B. oil diplomacy
C. crisis diplomacy
D. development diplomacy

42. Which of the following is not a characteristic feature of non-alignment?
A. Non-alignment stands for plurality and democratic equality among community of nations.
B. It opposes all forms of racialism and discrimination and it champions the cause of fundamental freedoms. Economic and social justice is the motto of non-alignment.

C. Non-alignment rests on the presumption that national security is linked with national strength of individual nations.
D. Non-alignment asserts that international peace is an alienable prerequisite for attaining national aspirations and for the exercise of sovereign independence.

43. Which of the following is not a technique to exercise National Power?
A. Diplomacy
B. Economic state craft
C. Use of military force
D. To join a world organisation

44. Match List - I with List - II and select the correct answer from the codes given below :

List-I (Book)	List-II (Author)
(*a*) International Relations Theory: The Three Traditions	(*i*) Gerhard Wahlers
(*b*) The North South Divide and the International System	(*ii*) Tadjbaksh Shakbanon and Anuradha Chenoy
(*c*) Human security	(*iii*) N.B. Adams
(*d*) India and the European Union	(*iv*) Martin Wight

Codes:

	(*a*)	(*b*)	(*c*)	(*d*)
A.	(*iv*)	(*iii*)	(*ii*)	(*i*)
B.	(*ii*)	(*iv*)	(*i*)	(*iii*)
C.	(*iii*)	(*i*)	(*iv*)	(*ii*)
D.	(*i*)	(*iii*)	(*ii*)	(*iv*)

45. Which one of the following can be regarded as the currency of power?
A. Food
B. Nuclear Weapons
C. Industrial Capacity
D. Military Preparedness

46. Which of the following statements are correct?
(*a*) According to Article 3 of the charter, the countries that attended the San Francisco conference, June 1945 and those who signed the United Nations Declaration on 1st January 1942 became original members of United Nations.
(*b*) Switzerland became a member of United Nations in 2003.
(*c*) The regular session of General Assembly commences in September and usually goes on till the end of the year.
(*d*) The retiring members of economic and social council are eligible for immediate re-election also.

Select the **correct** answer from the codes given below:
A. (*a*), (*b*) and (*c*)
B. (*b*), (*c*) and (*d*)
C. (*a*), (*b*) and (*d*)
D. (*a*), (*c*) and (*d*)

47. Who was of opinion that, "the end of cold war represented the victory of ideal state", and liberal capitalism?
A. Michael Doyle
B. Thomas Dunne
C. Francis Fukuyama
D. Samuel Huntington

48. Match List - I with List - II and select the correct answer from the codes given below:

List-I	List-II
(*a*) Soviet Union - German non-aggression pact	(*i*) September, 1939
(*b*) Germany invaded soviet union	(*ii*) March, 1939
(*c*) Germany occupied Czechoslovakia	(*iii*) June, 1941
(*d*) Germany invaded Poland	(*iv*) April, 1941

Codes:

	(*a*)	(*b*)	(*c*)	(*d*)
A.	(*iv*)	(*iii*)	(*ii*)	(*i*)
B.	(*ii*)	(*iv*)	(*i*)	(*iii*)
C.	(*iii*)	(*i*)	(*iv*)	(*ii*)
D.	(*i*)	(*iii*)	(*ii*)	(*iv*)

49. Which of the following statements are **correct**?
(*a*) The convening of Bandung conference, 1955 was suggested by Sri Lanka.

(*b*) The immediate provocation to convene this conference was conclusion of a treaty between Taiwan and the United States, and creation of SEATO and Baghdad Pact.

(*c*) The idea of holding this conference was welcomed by USSR and China.

(*d*) Bandung is a city of Indonesia.

Select the **correct** answer from the codes given below:

A. (*a*), (*b*) and (*c*) B. (*b*), (*c*) and (*d*)
C. (*a*), (*b*) and (*d*) D. (*a*), (*c*) and (*d*)

50. Which of the following article of charter of United Nations provides that "all the members of the UN undertake to make available to the security council, on its call and in accordance with special agreements, armed forces, assistance and facilities, including rights of passage, necessary for the purpose of maintaining international peace and security".

A. Article 41 B. Article 42
C. Article 43 D. Article 44

ANSWERS

1	2	3	4	5	6	7	8	9	10
C	D	A	A	A	A	A	A	A	B
11	**12**	**13**	**14**	**15**	**16**	**17**	**18**	**19**	**20**
A	C	C	C	D	B	A	D	D	A
21	**22**	**23**	**24**	**25**	**26**	**27**	**28**	**29**	**30**
D	B	B	D	C	B	D	D	D	B
31	**32**	**33**	**34**	**35**	**36**	**37**	**38**	**39**	**40**
B	C	D	A	C	C	B	C	A	D
41	**42**	**43**	**44**	**45**	**46**	**47**	**48**	**49**	**50**
D	D	D	A	B	D	C	A	A	C

EXPLANATORY ANSWERS

1. Varna system is not an organ of Kautilya's state. The Mauryan era of ancient India gave the world a significant treatise, the Arthashastra of Kautilya. It offers deep insights into political statecraft. Kautilya is known as the Indian Machiavelli because of his ruthless and shrewd tactics and policies reflecting an approach to state craft including warfare. Kautilya's Saptang theory of state enumerated seven prakritis or essential organs of the state. They are as follows—

(*i*) Swami (The Ruler)
(*ii*) Amatya (The Minister)
(*iii*) Janapada (The Population)
(*iv*) Durga (The Fortified Capital)
(*v*) Kosha (The Treasury)
(*vi*) Danda (The Army)
(*vii*) Mitra (Ally and Friend)

2. Plato's communism of family and property was largely derived from the experience of Sparta. Plato taught that the material world consists of imperfect copies of abstract and eternal 'ideas'. His political philosophy, as expounded in the Republic is an attempt to describe the 'ideal state' in terms of a theory of justice. Plato's just state was decidedly authoritarian and was based upon a strict division of labour that supposedly reflected different character-types and human attributes. He argued that government should be exercised exclusively by a small collection of philosopher-kings, supported by the auxiliaries (collectively termed the 'Guardians'), whose education and communistic way of life would ensure that they ruled on the basis of wisdom. In his view, knowledge and virtue are one.

3. Scholasticism is a method of critical thought which dominated teaching by the academics (scholastics) of medieval universities in Europe from about 1100 to 1700, and a program of employing that method in articulating and defending dogma in an increasingly pluralistic context. It originated as an outgrowth of, and a departure from, christian monastic schools at the earliest European universities. Some of the main figures of scholasticism include Anselm of Canterbury, Albertus Magnus, William of Ockham and Thomas Aquinas. Aquinas's masterwork Summa Theologica, considered to be the pinnacle of scholastic, medieval and christian philosophy.

Scholasticism of middle ages sought to establish the ascendency of theology over the philosophy and the subordination of rational element to the theological element of the church.

5. Lord Acton's famous aphorism, 'power corrupts and absolute power corrupts absolutely', but in democratic political system, there is provision to check against the misuse of power because in this system power is distributed among various groups. The term democracy and the classical conception of democratic rule are firmly rooted in ancient Greece.

Concept of power links it to the ability to achieve a desired outcome, sometimes referred to as power to. This could include the accomplishment of actions as simple as walking across a room or buying a newspaper. In most cases, however, power is thought of as a relationship, as the exercise of control by one person over another, or as power over.

9. Communitarianism is a philosophy that emphasizes the connection between the individual and the community. Although the community might be a family unit, communitarianism usually is understood, in the wider, philosophical sense, as a collection of interactions, among a community of people in a given place, or among a community who share an interest or who share a history. Communitarian philosophy is based upon the belief that a person's social identity and personality are largely moulded by community relationships : with a smaller degree of development being placed on individualism.

10. Although political science was a child of the 20th century, it drew upon roots which dated back to the empiricism of the 17th century. 'Science' refers to a means of acquiring knowledge through observation, experiment and measurement. Its central feature, the 'scientific method', involves verifying or falsifying hypotheses by testing them against empirical evidence, preferably using repeatable experiments. The almost unquestioned status which science has come to enjoy in the modern world is based upon its claim to be objective and value-free, and so to be the only reliable means of disclosing truth. Political science is therefore essentially empirical, claiming to describe, analyse and explain government and other political institutions in a rigorous and impartial manner. The high point of enthusiasm for a 'Science of politics' came in the 1950s and 1960s with the emergence, most strongly in the USA, of a form of political analysis that drew heavily upon behaviouralism. Behaviouralism developed as a school of psychology (known as behaviourism) which, as the name implies, studies only the observable and measurable behaviour of human beings. This encouraged political analysts such as David Easton to believe that political science could adopt the methodology of the natural sciences, leading to a proliferation of studies in areas like voting behaviour where systematic and quantifiable data were readily available.

13. Upendra Baxi said that "the Supreme Court of India is at long last becoming, after 32 years of the Republic, the Supreme Court for Indians." For too long, the apex constitutional court had become "an arena of legal quibbling for men with long purses." Now, increasingly, the court is being identified by justices as well as people as the "last resort for the oppressed and the bewildered." The transition from a traditional captive agency with a low social visibility into a liberated agency with a high socio-political visibility is a remarkable development in the career of the Indian appellate judiciary. A post-emergency phenomenon, the transformation is characterized chiefly by judicial populism. The court is augmenting its support base and moral authority in the nation at a time when other institutions of governance are facing a legitimation crisis. In the process, like all political institutions, the court promises more than it can deliver and is severely exposed to the dynamics of disenchantment.

15. Vishakha V. state of Rajasthan and others was a 1997 Indian Supreme court case where Vishakha and other women groups filed Public Interest Litigation (PIL) against state of Rajasthan and Union of India to enforce the fundamental rights of working woman under Articles 14, 19 and 21 of the Constitution of India. The petition was filed after Bhanwari Devi, a social worker in Rajsthan was brutally gangraped for stopping a child marriage. The court decided that the consideration of "International Conventions and norms are significant for the purpose of interpretation of the guarantee of gender equality, right to work with human dignity in Article 14, 15, 19 (1)g and 21 of the Constitution and the safeguards against sexual harassment implicit therein." The petition, resulted in what are popularly known as the Vishakha Guidelines. The judgement of August 1997 given by a bench of Justices J.S. Verma (then C.J.I.), Sujata Manohar and B.N. Kirpal, provided the basic definitions of sexual harassment at the workplace and provided guidelines to deal with it. It is seen as a significant legal victory for women's groups in India.

17. 18 functional items have been placed within the purview of Municipalities by the 12th Schedule to the Constitution. 74th amendment act of 1992 has added a new part IX-A to the constitution of India. It is entitled 'The Municipalities' and consists of provisions from Articles 243P to 243ZG. In addition, the act has also added a new 12th schedule to the constitution. This schedule contains eighteen functional items of municipalities. It deals with Article 243W.

The act gave constitutional status to the Municipalities. It has brought them under the purview of justiciable part of the Constitution. In other words, state governments are under constitutional obligation to adopt the new system of Municipalities in accordance with the provisions of the act.

The act aims at revitalising and strengthening the urban government so that they function effectively as units of local government.

19. Gopal Swarup Pathak was not the Speaker of the Lok Sabha. The Speaker is elected by the Lok Sabha from amongst its members (as soon as may be, after its first sitting). Whenever the office of the Speaker falls vacant, the Lok Sabha elects another member to fill the vacancy. The date of election of the Speaker is fixed by the President.

Usually, the speaker remains in office during the life of the Lok Sabha. However, he has to vacate his office earlier in any of the following three cases—

(*i*) If he ceases to be a member of the Lok Sabha;

(*ii*) If he resigns by writing to the Deputy Speaker, and

(*iii*) If he is removed by a resolution passed by a majority of all the members of the Lok Sabha. Such a resolution can be moved only after giving 14 days advance notice.

It should be noted here that, whenever the Lok Sabha is dissolved, the Speaker does not vacate his office and continues till the newly-elected Lok Sabha meets.

21. David Easton has identified 8 major tenets which he regarded as 'intellectual foundation stones' on which movement is constructed. These intellectual foundations of the system Analysis are as follows—

(*i*) **Regularities—**Discoverable uniformities that can be expressed in theory like statements for expectation and prediction.

(*ii*) **Verification—**Each generalisation must be testable by observation.

(*iii*) **Techniques—**Self-conscious selection, refined and validated means. For observing, recording and analysing pet behaviour.

(*iv*) **Quantification—**Unless it is done, it would be impossible to obtain precise and accurate knowledge.

(*v*) **Values—**Objective scientific enquiry has to be value-free or value-neutral.

(*vi*) **Systematization—**Research must be theory-oriented and theory-directed.

(*vii*) **Pure Science—**Knowledge would be utilized in the solution of urgent practical problems of society. and

(*viii*) **Integration—**Since the man is a social animal, so political research was to take into account the findings of other disciplines.

22. The study of comparative politics became significant after the World War II and emergence of new nations. It is a systematic outcome of realization within the circle of political scientists to study political reality with the use of new methods and techniques to evolve what may be called a science of politics. Moreover, widespread scepticism and disenchantment with the traditional approaches provided impetus to this trend.

23. Aristotle is regarded as the father of comparative politics. He was a student of Plato and the tutor of the young Alexander the Great. He established his own school of philosophy in Athens in 335 BC and studied 158 constitutions of different states. Aristotle's twenty-two surviving treatises were compiled as lecture notes and range over logic, physics, metaphysics, astronomy, biology, ethics and politics. His best known political work is politics, a comprehensive study of the nature of political life and the forms it might take. In describing politics as the 'master science', he emphasized that it is in the public not private domain that human beings strive for justice and live the 'good life'. Aristotle's taxonomy of forms of government led him to prefer those that aim at the common good over those that benefit sectional interests, and to recommend a mixture of democracy and oligarchy, in the form of what he called polity.

25. Implementation of policies is not true of pressure groups. The pressure groups influence the policy-making and policy-implementation in the government through legal and legitimate methods like lobbying, correspondence, publicity, propagandising, petitioning, public debating, maintaining contacts with their legislators and so forth. However, sometimes they resort to illegitimate and illegal methods like strikes, violent activities and corruption which damages public interest and administrative integrity.

According to Odegard, pressure groups resort to three different techniques in securing their purposes. First, they can try to place in public office persons who are favourably disposed towards the interests they seeks to promote. This technique may be labelled electioneering. Second, they can try to persuade public officers, whether they are initially favourably disposed toward them or not, to adopt and enforce the policies that they think will prove most beneficial to their interests. This technique may be labelled lobbying. Third, they can try to influence public opinion and thereby gain an indirect influence over government, since the government in a democracy is substantially affected by public opinion. This technique may be labelled as propagandizing.

27. One of the earliest attempts to classify forms of government was undertaken by Aristotle. In his view, governments can be categorized on the basis of 'who rules' and 'who benefits from rule'. Government can be placed in the hands of a single individual, a small group as the many. In each case, however, government can be conducted either in the selfish interests of the rulers or for the benefit of the entire community. As a result, Aristotle identified six forms of government. Tyranny, oligarchy and democracy are all, he suggested, debased or perverted forms of rule in which, respectively, a single person, a small group and the masses govern in their own interests and therefore at the expense of others. By contrast, monarchy, aristocracy and polity are to be preferred because the single individual, small group or the masses govern in the interests of all.

29. Responsiveness, fidelity, background noise and distortion factors are related to load capacity in the communication theory. The communication theory of International relation emphasize the role played by communication. It visualizes politics as a process of steering, coordination and control. The focus is on the decision-making apparatus which itself is a bundle of numerous information networks. As such, it is itself a 'self-adjusting and self-regulating mechanism'.

Karl Deutsch in his works 'The Nerves of Government' and 'Nationalism and social Communication' puts forward his communication theory. Charles McClelland is another exponent of this theory.

30. Robert Dahl said that "The power is a matter of getting people to do what they would not have otherwise done". According to his view, power is a question of who gets their way, how often they get their way and over what issues they get their way. The attraction of this treatment of power is that it corresponds to the common sense belief that power is somehow about getting things done, and is therefore most clearly reflected in decisions and how they are made. It also has the advantage, as Dahl pointed out, that it makes possible an empirical, even scientific, study of the distribution of power within any group, community or society.

35. Fritz Morstein Marx was a German-American political and administrative scientist. He was born in Hamburg in 1900. Marx studied law after a short military service in the First World War. In 1992 he was awarded his doctorate at the University of Hamburg and then entered in the administration service of the Free and Hanseatic city of Hamburg. In 1930-31 he had done research with the scholarship of the Rockefeller Foundation in the USA and in 1933 emigrated to USA after the transfer of power to the National Socialists. He worked in academic teaching and also in administration. From 1942 to 1960 he was a member of the Bureau of the budget of the US-president. In addition, he was research professor at Princeton University. From 1960 to 1962 he was dean at Hunter College in New York city.

In 1962 Marx returned to Germany and became professor of Comparative Public Administration and Public Law at the University of Administrative Sciences in Speyer. He classified the bureaucracy as—Guardian, Caste, Patronage and Merit.

36. The type of Performance Budgeting (earlier called as Functional Budgeting or Activity Budgeting) originated in the USA. The term 'Performance budget' was coined by the first Hoover Commission (1949). This commission recommended the adoption of performance budgeting in the USA to make effective management approach to budgeting. Accordingly, it was introduced in 1950 by President Truman.

In India, the adoption of performance budget was recommended first by the Estimates Committee of Parliament in 1956. In 1964, the government invited Frank W. Krause, an American expert, to study the suitability and feasibility of this system of budgeting in India. Finally, the central government introduced performance budgeting in 1968 on the recommendation of the Administrative Reforms Commission Report.

38. The Chief Information Commissioner and an Information Commissioner hold office for a term of 5 years or until they attain the age of 65 years, whichever is earlier. They are not eligible for reappointment.

The President can remove the Chief Information Commissioner or any Information Commissioner from the office under the following circumstances:

(*i*) If he is adjudged an insolvent; or

(*ii*) If he has been convicted of an offence which (in the opinion of the President) involves a moral turpitude; or

(*iii*) If he engages during his term of office in any paid employment outside the duties of his office; or

(*iv*) If he is (in the opinion of the President) unfit to continue in office due to infirmity of mind or body; or

(*v*) If he has acquired such financial or other interest as is likely to affect prejudicially his official functions.

In addition to these, the President can also remove the Chief Information Commissioner or any Information Commissioner on the ground of proved misbehaviour or incapacity. However, in these cases, the President has to refer the matter to the Supreme Court for an enquiry. If the Supreme Court, after the enquiry, upholds the cause of removal and advises so, then the President can remove him.

40. Electronic governance or e-governance is the application of information and communication technology for delivering government services, exchange of information communication transactions, integration of various stand-alone systems and services between government-to-customer, government-to-business, government-to-government as well as back office processes and interactions within the entire government framework. Through e-governance, government services will be made available to citizens in a convenient, efficient and transparent manner. The three main target groups that can be distinguished in governance concepts are government, citizens and businesses/interest groups. In e-governance there are no distinct boundaries.

41. Economic diplomacy is also termed as Development diplomacy. It is a form of diplomacy. Economic diplomacy is the use of the full spectrum economic tools of the state to achieve its national interest. It includes all the economic activities, including but not limited to export, import, investment, lending, aid, free trade agreements etc.

Economic diplomacy is concerned with economic policy issues, *e.g.*, work of delegations at standards setting organizations such as World Trade Organization (WTO). Economic diplomats also monitor and report on economic policies in foreign countries and give the home government advice on how to best influence them. Economic diplomacy employs economic resources, either as rewards or sanctions, in pursuit of a particular foreign policy objective. This is sometimes called 'economic statecraft'.

42. Non-alignment stands for plurality and democratic equality among community of nations, it opposes all forms of racialism and discrimination and it champions the cause of fundamental freedoms. Economic and social justice is the motto of non-alignment. Non-alignment rests on the presumption that national security is linked with national strength of individual nations. But, NAM asserts that international peace is an alienable prerequisite for attaining national aspirations and for the exercise of sovereign independence is not a characteristic feature of non-alignment.

When the world was divided into two blocs on ideological basis, namely, the capitalist bloc headed by USA and the communist bloc headed by the former USSR. In such a situation of 'cold war', India, Egypt, Indonesia, Yugoslavia, etc. refused to join any of these two blocs and adopted a policy of non-alignment.

43. Diplomacy, Economic state craft and use of military force are the techniques to exercise National Power. The concept of power is one of the crucial ingredient of international politics. As it plays a vital role in the conduct of relations among nations, its study remains a significant aspect of international relations. However, the flexibility with which the term is used remains a problematic task in the study of power. Nevertheless, 'the problem of power', writes Frankel, "enters into all types of international relations—wars, competition and cooperation, all involve power .... a state which is devoid of resources and organization can neither complete nor cooperate successfully with other states".

47. Bernard Crick has pointed out that democracy is the most promiscuous of political terms. In the sense that the word means different things to different people, democracy is an example of an 'essentially contested' concept. No settled model of democracy exists, but only a number of competing models. Nevertheless, a particular model or form of democracy has come to dominate thinking on the matter, to the extent that many in the West treat it as the only feasible or meaningful form of democracy. This is liberal democracy. It is found in almost all advanced capitalist societies and now extends, in one form or another, into parts of the former communist world and the developing world. Indeed, in the light of the collapse of communism, the US New Right theorist, **Francis Fukuyama,** proclaimed the worldwide triumph of liberal democracy, describing it as the 'end of history', by which he meant the struggle between political ideas.

Such triumphalism, however, should not obscure the fact that, despite its attractions, liberal democracy is not the only model of democratic government, and, like all concepts of democracy, it has its critics and detractors.

50. Article-43 of the UN Charter provides that "all the members of the UN undertake to make available to the security council, on its call and in accordance with special agreements, armed forces, assistance and facilities, including rights of passage, necessary for the purpose of maintaining international peace and security." Such agreement or agreements shall govern the numbers and types of forces, their degree of readiness and general location, and the nature of the facilities and assistance to be provided. The agreement or agreements shall be negotiated as soon as possible on the initiative of the security council. They shall be concluded between the security council and members or between the security council and groups of members and shall be subject to ratification by the signatory states in accordance with their respective constitutional processes.

PAPER–III

Note: *This paper contains* ***seventy five*** *(75) objective type questions of* ***two*** *(2) marks each.* ***All questions*** *are* ***compulsory****.*

1. Who among the following referred to the 'decline' of political theory?
   (*a*) David Easton and Alfred Cobbon
   (*b*) Lasslett and Robert Dahl
   (*c*) Will Durant
   (*d*) Nathenial Hawthorn
   A. (*b*) and (*c*) B. (*c*) and (*d*)
   C. (*a*) and (*c*) D. (*a*) and (*b*)
2. Which of the following statements are **true** regarding Political theory?
   (*a*) It accepts scientism and repudiates the normativism.
   (*b*) It synthesises political philosophy and scientific enquiry of political phenomenon.
   (*c*) It is structural and institutional and examines the logic and basis of political institutions and organizations.
   (*d*) Political theory is philosophical as well as scientific, normative as well as empirical, evaluative as well as explanatory; historical as well as analytical.

   Choose the **correct** answers from the below:
   A. (*a*) and (*d*) B. (*b*) and (*c*)
   C. (*d*) only D. (*c*) and (*d*)
3. Which of the following is **true** of modern liberalism?
   (*a*) Freedom of the individual as against the authority of the state.
   (*b*) Recognise the importance of 'group'.
   (*c*) Supports the limited role of the state.
   (*d*) Supports the state regulation to safeguard the weak.

   Choose the **correct** answer.
   A. (*a*) and (*c*) B. (*b*) and (*d*)
   C. (*a*) and (*d*) D. (*c*) and (*d*)
4. Which of the following statements relating to Mao's theory of contradictions are **true?**
   (*a*) Contradictions are universal in all times and in all societies.
   (*b*) Antagonistic contradictions exist among the hostile classes in terms of ownership of productive forces.
   (*c*) Non-antagonistic contradictions could exist among people which could be resolved without resorting to violence.
   (*d*) Contradictions have no place in a socialist system.

   Choose the **correct** answer from the below:
   A. (*d*) and (*a*) B. (*b*) and (*d*)
   C. (*a*), (*b*) and (*c*) D. (*a*), (*b*), (*c*) and(*d*)
5. Given below are two statements one labelled as Assertion (A) and the other labelled as Reason (R).

   Assertion (A): For John Locke, Natural Rights are a product of nature.

   Reason (R): State has to protect and safeguard these rights.

   A. Both (A) and (R) are true and (R) is the right explanation of (A)
   B. Both (A) and (R) are true, but (R) is not the right explanation of (A)
   C. (A) is true, but (R) is false
   D. (A) is false, but (R) is true
6. Which of the following is **not** true of Aristotle's theory of state?
   (*a*) Organic conception of State.
   (*b*) State as a magnified individual.
   (*c*) Rights of the individual can exist only as a member of the state.
   (*d*) There is no conflict between the end of the individual and end of the state.

   Choose the **correct** answer:
   A. (*a*) and (*b*) B. (*d*) and (*c*)
   C. (*c*) only D. (*d*) only
7. Machiavelli is regarded as the first modern political thinker because of:
   A. Separation of ethics and religion from politics.

B. Forerunner of nation state.
C. Represented the spirit of renaissance.
D. Subordination of Church to state.

8. Which one of the following statements of Hobbes was **wrong**?
A. State of Nature was pre-political and pre-social.
B. Sovereign was a party to the contract.
C. Human nature was dominated by acquisitive instinct, possessive instinct and love of glory.
D. Man in the state of Nature was 'solitary, nasty, brutish and short'.

9. John Locke's contribution chiefly lies in his:
(*a*) Consent theory.
(*b*) Limited Government.
(*c*) Theory of state as a corporate body.
(*d*) Organic conception of state.

Select the **correct** answer from the codes given below:
A. (*a*) and (*d*) B. (*a*) and (*c*)
C. (*b*) and (*c*) D. (*a*) and (*b*)

10. Match List-I with List-II and select the **correct** answer from the codes given below:

List-I (Concepts)	List-II (Thinker's)
(*a*) Veil of Ignorance	(*i*) Karl Popper
(*b*) Alienation	(*ii*) Robert Nozic
(*c*) Piecemeal Social engineering	(*iii*) John Rawls
(*d*) Night Watchman State	(*iv*) Karl Marx

Codes:

	(*a*)	(*b*)	(*c*)	(*d*)
A.	(*i*)	(*iv*)	(*ii*)	(*iii*)
B.	(*ii*)	(*i*)	(*iii*)	(*iv*)
C.	(*iii*)	(*iv*)	(*i*)	(*ii*)
D.	(*iv*)	(*iii*)	(*ii*)	(*i*)

11. "Man must eat before he thinks. To eat he must produce. Production is a basic activity". Who said this?
A. Mao
B. Rosa Luxumburg
C. Luis Althusser
D. Karl Marx

12. Which of the following thinkers held the view that "the probable mischiefs of obedience are less than the probable mischiefs of resistence".
A. J.S. Mill B. James Mill
C. Bentham D. Blackstone

13. Dialectical materialism of Karl Marx postulates that:
(*a*) Matter is in a state of motion.
(*b*) Motion in the matter is due to the pressure of environment.
(*c*) Law of transformation is both quantitative and qualitative.
(*d*) Conflict in matter is continuous and endless.

Identify the **correct** answer:
A. (*a*), (*b*) and (*d*) B. (*a*) and (*c*)
C. (*b*) and (*d*) D. (*c*) and (*d*)

14. Which of the following statement is **correct** regarding J.S. Mill?
(*a*) State is justified in confirming itself to limited functions
(*b*) Welfare policies are more important.
(*c*) State intervention into 'self-regarding' action.
(*d*) State intervention into 'other regarding action' is justified.

Choose the **correct** answer:
A. (*b*) and (*c*) B. (*a*) and (*b*)
C. (*a*) only D. (*d*) only

15. Which of the following is **true** regarding Gandhian concept of 'Sarvodaya'?
(*a*) Welfare of the majority of people
(*b*) Government by the majority party
(*c*) Protection of the minorities
(*d*) Welfare of all sections of the society

Choose the **correct** answer from the below:
A. (*a*) and (*c*) B. (*a*) and (*b*)
C. (*d*) only D. (*b*) only

16. Match List-I with List-II and select the **correct** answer from the codes given below:

List-I	List-II
(*a*) Charter Act of 1813	(*i*) Separate electorate
(*b*) Charter Act of 1833	(*ii*) Abolition of the trade monopoly of East India Company
(*c*) The Government of India Act, 1858	(*iii*) Complete abolition of monopoly in trade by East India Company
(*d*) Government of India Act, 1909	(*iv*) Secretary of State for India

Codes:

	(*a*)	(*b*)	(*c*)	(*d*)
A.	(*ii*)	(*i*)	(*iii*)	(*iv*)
B.	(*ii*)	(*iii*)	(*iv*)	(*i*)
C.	(*i*)	(*iv*)	(*iii*)	(*ii*)
D.	(*iv*)	(*ii*)	(*iii*)	(*i*)

17. Who presided over the All Party Conference (1928)?

A. Pt. Motilal Nehru
B. Dr. M.A. Ansari
C. Madan Mohan Malviya
D. C.R. Das

18. Which of the following statements are **correct**?

Select your answer from codes given below:

(*a*) The Union of India has power to issue directions to a state to ensure compliance with the laws.
(*b*) In case of failure, the President may assume to himself all the functions of the Government of that state.
(*c*) The Governor of a state is appointed by the President and holds office during his pleasure.
(*d*) The Governor is not responsible to state.

Codes:

A. (*a*), (*c*) and (*d*)
B. (*b*), (*c*) and (*d*)
C. (*a*), (*b*) and (*c*)
D. (*a*), (*b*), (*c*) and (*d*)

19. Which of the following is **not** recognised as a 'tension' area in Indian federation?

(*a*) Inter-State Council
(*b*) Article 356
(*c*) Role of the Governor
(*d*) Union-State Financial Relations

Choose the **correct** answer:

A. (*a*) and (*d*) B. (*d*) only
C. (*a*) only D. (*c*) and (*d*)

20. 74th Constitutional Amendment Act of 1992 does not apply to the scheduled areas in the states of:

(*a*) Rajasthan (*b*) Haryana
(*c*) Uttar Pradesh (*d*) Odisha

Select the **correct** answer from the codes given below:

A. (*b*) and (*c*)
B. (*c*) and (*d*)
C. (*a*), (*c*) and (*d*)
D. (*a*), (*b*), (*c*) and (*d*)

21. Match List-I with List-II and select the **correct** answer from the codes given below:

List-I (Movements)	List-II (Personalities)
(*a*) Chipko movement	(*i*) Medha Patker
(*b*) Narmada Bachao Andolan	(*ii*) K. Chandrasekhar Rao
(*c*) Right to Information movement	(*iii*) Sunder Lal Bahuguna
(*d*) Telangana movement	(*iv*) Aruna Roy

Codes:

	(*a*)	(*b*)	(*c*)	(*d*)
A.	(*iv*)	(*i*)	(*ii*)	(*iii*)
B.	(*iii*)	(*i*)	(*iv*)	(*ii*)
C.	(*ii*)	(*iii*)	(*i*)	(*iv*)
D.	(*i*)	(*ii*)	(*iv*)	(*iii*)

22. Arrange the following Vice-Presidents of India in chronological order and select the **correct** answer from the codes given below:

(*a*) K.R. Narayanan
(*b*) Gopal Swarup Pathak
(*c*) Krishan Kant
(*d*) Justice Mohammad Hidayatullah

Codes:

A. (*d*), (*b*), (*a*), (*c*)
B. (*b*), (*d*), (*c*), (*a*)
C. (*d*), (*b*), (*c*), (*a*)
D. (*b*), (*d*), (*a*), (*c*)

23. Which of the following pairs showing the state and dominant caste is **not correct**?

A. Punjab – Jat Sikh
B. Rajasthan – Rajput
C. Kerala – Velma
D. Karnataka – Lingayat

24. Who among following classifies regional movements in India in terms of "ethnic" and "nativist" movements?

A. Sajal Basu
B. Myron Weiner
C. James Manor
D. Rob Jenkivs

25. When was Inter-State Council under Article 263 of the constitution of India set up in India?

A. 1961
B. 1972
C. 1990
D. 1998

26. Match List-I with List-II and select the **correct** answer from the codes given below:

List-I (Student Organization)	List-II (Party Affiliation)
(*a*) Akhil Bharatiya Vidyarthi Parishad	(*i*) CPI
(*b*) All Indian Students Federation	(*ii*) CPIM
(*c*) National Students Union of India	(*iii*) BJP
(*d*) Students Federation of India	(*iv*) Congress (I)

Codes:

	(*a*)	(*b*)	(*c*)	(*d*)
A.	(*i*)	(*iii*)	(*iv*)	(*ii*)
B.	(*iv*)	(*iii*)	(*ii*)	(*i*)
C.	(*iii*)	(*i*)	(*iv*)	(*ii*)
D.	(*ii*)	(*iv*)	(*i*)	(*iii*)

27. Since when consensus has emerged in India that the post of Deputy Speaker should go to opposition party?

A. 1984
B. 1989
C. 1996
D. 2001

28. Match the following and select the **correct** pairs:

List-I (Authors)	List-II (Books)
(*a*) Selig G. Harrison	(*i*) Green Revolution in India
(*b*) Rudolf and Rudolf	(*ii*) Indian Paradox
(*c*) Frankline Frankel	(*iii*) In Pursuit of Laxmi: The Political Economy of the Indian State
(*d*) Myron Weiner	(*iv*) India: The Most Dangerous Decades

Codes:

	(*a*)	(*b*)	(*c*)	(*d*)
A.	(*ii*)	(*i*)	(*iii*)	(*iv*)
B.	(*i*)	(*ii*)	(*iv*)	(*iii*)
C.	(*iv*)	(*iii*)	(*i*)	(*ii*)
D.	(*iii*)	(*iv*)	(*ii*)	(*i*)

29. Match List-I with List-II and select the **correct** answer from the codes given below:

List-I	List-II
(*a*) S.P. Gupta Vs Union of India	(*i*) Taj Pollution
(*b*) M.C. Mehta Vs Union of India	(*ii*) Basic Structure
(*c*) Keshavanand Bharti Vs The State of Kerala	(*iii*) Judges Transfer
(*d*) Common Cause Vs Union of India	(*iv*) Petrol Pump Allotment

Codes:

	(*a*)	(*b*)	(*c*)	(*d*)
A.	(*iii*)	(*i*)	(*ii*)	(*iv*)
B.	(*iv*)	(*ii*)	(*i*)	(*iii*)
C.	(*ii*)	(*iv*)	(*iii*)	(*i*)
D.	(*i*)	(*iii*)	(*iv*)	(*ii*)

30. Which one of the following Acts has been made under Article 34 of the Indian Constitution?

A. The Army Act
B. The Armed Forces Special Power Act (AFSPA)
C. The Border Security Force Act
D. The Navy Act

31. Which of the following statements is **not** correct?

A. The U.S. House of Representatives is weaker than the British House of Commons.

B. The House of Representatives is weaker than Senate.

C. U.S. Executive is not accountable to U.S. Legislature.

D. The House of Representatives has overshadowed the American senate.

32. Which one of the following statements is **not** correct?

A. Swiss federal legislature is bicameral.

B. The Lower House is called the National Council.

C. The Upper House is called Council of states.

D. The qualification of voters and candidate is decided by National Council.

33. Which one of the following is **not** a feature of United Kingdom judiciary?

A. Based on common law tradition.

B. Devolution to Scotland have given more scope to a traditionally restrained Judiciary.

C. Devolution to Wales have given more scope to a traditionally restrained Judiciary.

D. Judges of Higher Courts are appointed by the Crown on the recommendations of the House of Commons.

34. The Magna Carta, the Glorious Revolution and the writings of John Locke all contributed to the strengthening of Great Britain:

A. Absolute Monarchy

B. Ethnic Rivalaries

C. Parliamentary Democracy

D. Imperialist Policies

35. Which one of following is **correct**?

A. K.C. Wheare: The English Constitution

B. Robert Michel: Iron Law of Oligarchy

C. G.Sartori: Moderate and Extreme Multi Party System

D. Bagehot: Party Politics

36. Match List-I with List-II and select the **correct** answer from the codes given below:

List-I	**List-II**
(*a*) Pareto	(*i*) Circulation of Elites
(*b*) Mosca	(*ii*) History is a Graveyard of Aristocracies
(*c*) Michels	(*iii*) Theory of the Masses
(*d*) Gasset	(*iv*) Iron Law of Oligarchy

Codes:

	(*a*)	(*b*)	(*c*)	(*d*)
A.	(*i*)	(*ii*)	(*iii*)	(*iv*)
B.	(*ii*)	(*i*)	(*iv*)	(*iii*)
C.	(*i*)	(*ii*)	(*iv*)	(*iii*)
D.	(*i*)	(*iii*)	(*iv*)	(*ii*)

37. Political institutionalisation involves:

(*a*) Political mobilisation

(*b*) Political integration

(*c*) Political representation

(*d*) Political Fragmentation

Select the **correct** answer from the codes given below:

A. (*a*), (*b*), (*c*)　　B. (*a*), (*b*), (*c*), (*d*)

C. (*a*), (*d*)　　D. (*c*), (*d*)

38. Which countries were the basis of the study of Almond and Verba's 'Civic Culture'?

A. Chile, US, UK, France, Spain

B. US, France, Mexico, Italy, Germany

C. Mexico, Germany, Italy, US, UK

D. US, UK, Chile, Mexico, Spain

39. The five stages of economic growth proposed by W.W. Rostow are:

A. Traditional society, mercantile capitalism, industrial capitalism, financial capitalism, globalisation.

B. Preconditions for take-off, take-off, maturing of industry, industrial capitalism, full employment.

C. Traditional society, preconditions for take-off, take-off, drive to maturity, the epoch of high mass consumption.

D. Preconditions for take-off, mechanisation, industrialisation, take-off, financial capitalism.

40. Which world leader gave a special concept of 'Development' after the Second World War?

A. Franklin Delano Roosevelt
B. Harry Truman
C. Jawaharlal Nehru
D. Winston Churchill

41. What are the three types of political culture according to Almond and Verba's study 'Civic Culture'?

A. Parochial, subject, participant
B. Citizen, communal, democratic
C. Associative, adjudicative, parochial
D. Feudal, semi-feudal, democratic

42. Choose the **correct** answer from the codes given below:

Arrange the steps in the working of the general system of Proportional Representation in the **correct** sequence:

(*a*) the candidates are arranged in order of the votes they receive.
(*b*) each party puts up a list of candidates equal to the number of seats being fought.
(*c*) the leftover votes, or remainder votes are divided up between the candidates.
(*d*) Lists can be closed or open, open lists allow votes to indicate individual candidate preferences and vote for individual candidates.

A. (*a*), (*b*), (*c*), (*d*) B. (*c*), (*b*), (*d*), (*a*)
C. (*b*), (*d*), (*a*), (*c*) D. (*d*), (*b*), (*c*), (*a*)

43. Given below are two statements, one labelled as Assertion (A) and the other labelled as Reasoning (R).

Choose the **correct** answer using the codes given below:

Assertion (A): Only when power is combined with authority does it have legitimacy.

Reasoning (R): Power is the use of force over others.

A. Both (A) and (R) are true and (R) is the correct explanation of (A)
B. Both (A) and (R) are true, but (R) is not the correct explanation of (A)
C. (A) is true, but (R) is false
D. (A) is false, but (R) is true

44. Match List-I with List-II and select the **correct** answer from the codes given below:

List-I (Author)	**List-II (Title of book)**
(*a*) Gane Beinton	(*i*) Europe in Revolutions
(*b*) Ted Gurr	(*ii*) Anatomy of a Revolution
(*c*) Charles Tilly	(*iii*) States and Revolutions
(*d*) Theda Skocpol	(*iv*) Why Men Rebel

Codes:

	(*a*)	(*b*)	(*c*)	(*d*)
A.	(*i*)	(*ii*)	(*iii*)	(*iv*)
B.	(*ii*)	(*iv*)	(*i*)	(*iii*)
C.	(*iv*)	(*ii*)	(*i*)	(*iii*)
D.	(*iii*)	(*ii*)	(*iv*)	(*i*)

45. Tick the **correct** option from the codes given below:

The theories of modernisation were criticised by:

(*a*) dependency theories
(*b*) liberal theories
(*c*) under development theories
(*d*) world-systems theories

Codes:

A. (*a*), (*b*), (*c*), (*d*) B. (*a*), (*b*), (*c*)
C. (*a*), (*c*), (*d*) D. (*b*), (*d*)

46. Who among the following do **not** make a distinction between public and private administration?

(*a*) Henri Fayol (*b*) M.P. Follet
(*c*) Luther Gulick (*d*) L. Urwick

Select the **correct** answer from the codes given below:

A. (*a*) and (*c*)
B. (*b*), (*c*) and (*d*)
C. (*a*), (*b*) and (*c*)
D. (*a*), (*b*), (*c*) and (*d*)

47. Who among the following laid down 'Seven principles of organisation'?
A. Gulick and Urwick
B. Mary P. Follet
C. Henri Fayol
D. F.W. Taylor

48. Which one of the following is **not** a principle of organisation?
A. Hierarchy
B. Span of Control
C. Unity of command
D. Staffing

49. The literature on new public administration lays emphasis on:
(*a*) Relevance (*b*) Values
(*c*) Equity (*d*) Change

Select the **correct** answer from the codes given below:
A. (*a*) and (*b*)
B. (*b*), (*c*) and (*d*)
C. (*a*), (*b*) and (*d*)
D. (*a*), (*b*), (*c*) and (*d*)

50. In an informal organisation, authority always flows:
A. upwards
B. downwards
C. upwards and across
D. across and downwards

51. 'Garbage Can Model' was developed by:
(*a*) Michael D. Cohen
(*b*) James G. March
(*c*) Peter Drucker
(*d*) Johan P. Olsen

Select the **correct** answer from the codes given below:
A. (*a*) and (*d*) B. (*a*), (*b*) and (*d*)
C. (*a*), (*b*) and (*c*) D. (*b*), (*c*) and (*d*)

52. The traditional home of patronage bureaucracy is:
A. U.K. B. U.S.A.
C. China D. France

53. Who among the following coined the term 'representative bureaucracy'?
A. Donald Kingsley
B. Peter Blau
C. Max Weber
D. Martin Albrow

54. Which one of the following was the first country to enact a Law—Freedom of the Press Act—as early as in 1766?
A. U.K. B. U.S.A.
C. Sweden D. Denmark

55. Which of the following statements about Gender Budgeting are **correct**?
(*a*) It is a separate budget.
(*b*) It is passed along with the general budget.
(*c*) It seeks to translate gender commitments into budget commitments.
(*d*) It addresses the needs of women in the areas of education, health, employment, etc.

Select the **correct** answer from the codes given below:
A. (*a*) and (*c*) B. (*b*) and (*d*)
C. (*a*) and (*d*) D. (*c*) and (*d*)

56. Which of the following are the compulsory provisions of the 73rd Constitutional Amendment Act (1992)?
(*a*) Indirect election to the post of Chairperson of Panchayats at the intermediate level.
(*b*) Reservation of one-third seats for women.
(*c*) Reservation of seats for backward classes.
(*d*) Constitution of a state Finance Commission.

Select the **correct** answer from the codes given below:
A. (*a*) and (*c*)
B. (*a*), (*b*) and (*c*)
C. (*a*), (*b*) and (*d*)
D. (*a*), (*b*), (*c*) and (*d*)

57. Which of the following statements is **not** correct?
A. India is a signatory to the UN Convention against corruption.
B. India ranked 95th out of 178 countries according to the Transparency International's Index.

C. Lokpal and Lokayukta Bill was first introduced in Parliament in 1968.

D. Central Vigilance Commission was set up on the recommendation of Santhanam Committee.

58. Given below are two statements, one labelled as Assertion (A) and the other labelled as Reason (R).

Select the **correct** answer from the codes given below:

Assertion (A): The ambit of RTI Act needs to be widened.

Reason (R): At present, there is trend toward privatisation and outsourcing of many erstwhile government activities.

Codes:

A. Both (A) and (R) are true and (R) is the correct explanation of (A)
B. Both (A) and (R) are true but (R) is not the correct explanation of (A)
C. (A) is true, but (R) is false
D. (A) is false, but (R) is true

59. Given below are two statements, one labelled as Assertion (A) and the other labelled as Reason (R).

Select the **correct** answer from the codes given below:

Assertion (A) : Authority and responsibility are the two sides of the same coin.

Reason (R): Authority is divisible, responsibility is not.

Codes:

A. Both (A) and (R) are true and (R) is the correct explanation of (A)
B. Both (A) and (R) are correct but (R) is not the correct explanation of (A)
C. (A) is true, but (R) is false
D. (A) is false, but (R) is true

60. Given below are two statements, one labelled as Assertion (A) and the other labelled as Reason (R).

Select the **correct** answer from the codes given below:

Assertion (A): The concept of development administration is of recent origin.

Reason (R): Many countries became independent after World War II.

Codes:

A. Both (A) and (R) are true and (R) is the correct explanation of (A)
B. Both (A) and (R) are true but (R) is not the correct explanation of (A)
C. (A) is true, but (R) is false
D. (A) is false, but (R) is true

61. Which of the following terms of International Relationships was coined by Nicholas Onuf in his book - World of Our Making?

A. Realism B. Neo-realism
C. Neo-liberalism D. Constructivism

62. Match List-I with List-II and select the **correct** answer from the codes given below:

List-I (Authors)	**List-II (Books)**
(a) B. Buzan	*(i)* Man, the State and War
(b) I. Hansen	*(ii)* Social Theory of International Politics
(c) K.N. Waltz	*(iii)* The Evolution of International Security Studies
(d) A. Wendt	*(iv)* People, States and Fear

Codes:

	(a)	*(b)*	*(c)*	*(d)*
A.	*(iv)*	*(iii)*	*(i)*	*(ii)*
B.	*(iv)*	*(iii)*	*(ii)*	*(i)*
C.	*(i)*	*(ii)*	*(iii)*	*(iv)*
D.	*(iv)*	*(i)*	*(ii)*	*(iii)*

63. Which of the following is **not correct** regarding W.T.O?

A. It administers W.T.O. trade agreements.
B. It acts as a forum for trade negotiations.
C. It monitors national trade policies.
D. It supplies technical assistance and training for developing and developed countries.

64. Which country is the example of Latent Nuclear Capacity?

A. India
B. Japan
C. China
D. North Korea

65. Match List I with List II and select the **correct** answer from the codes given below:

List-I	List-II
(*a*) Counter force strategy	(*i*) Types of nuclear strategy that threatens assets that are valuable to an adversary, such as cities with industrial assets and large populations.
(*b*) Counter-proliferation	(*ii*) International lawyers who argue that there is a legal right of humanitarian intervention in both UN charter law and customary international law.
(*c*) Counter-restrictionist	(*iii*) Term used to describe a variety of efforts to obstruct slow, or roll back nuclear weapons programmes and nuclear proliferation.
(*d*) Counter value strategy	(*iv*) Type of nuclear strategy that targets an adversary's military and nuclear capabilities.

Codes:

	(*a*)	(*b*)	(*c*)	(*d*)
A.	(*iv*)	(*iii*)	(*ii*)	(*i*)
B.	(*iv*)	(*iii*)	(*i*)	(*ii*)
C.	(*ii*)	(*i*)	(*iii*)	(*iv*)
D.	(*iii*)	(*iv*)	(*i*)	(*ii*)

66. Who is given credit to coin the term—Soft Power?

A. Joseph Nye
B. N. Alarcon
C. A. J. Bellamy
D. S. Chesterman

67. Marshall Plan, 1947 was also formally known as:

A. European Reconstruction Programme
B. European Revival Plan
C. European Recovery Programme
D. European Restrengthening Plan

68. According to K.J. Holsti, which one of the following is **not** a feature of the contemporary state system?

A. The rise in the number and type of states.
B. The great potential for destruction by those who possess nuclear weapons and modern delivery systems.
C. The predominant position of influences that has been achieved by the three essentially non-European states : Russia, China and the United States.
D. The large number of states are keen to join political and economic alliances.

69. The Principal purpose of India's foreign policy vis-a-vis the UN is to pursue three closely related goals.

Which of the following is **not** included among them?

A. A significant role in the shaping of international relations in the 21st century.
B. A movement towards a non-violent and humane international system.
C. The promotion of conditions for a sustainable and relatively equitable pattern of international development.
D. To help UN to develop its own financial resources.

70. Which of the following is **not** included in the Doctrine of Panchsheel, 1954?

A. Mutual respect for each other's territorial integrity and sovereignty.
B. Not to develop nuclear weapons.
C. Equality and mutual benefit.
D. Peaceful Co-existence.

71. Match List-I with List-II and select the **correct** answer from the codes given below:

List-I (Regional Organisations)	**List-II (Region)**
(*a*) OSCE	(*i*) Europe
(*b*) V4	(*ii*) Eurasia
(*c*) BSEC	(*iii*) Euro-Atlantic
(*d*) NAFTA	(*iv*) North America

Codes:

	(*a*)	(*b*)	(*c*)	(*d*)
A.	(*iii*)	(*i*)	(*ii*)	(*iv*)
B.	(*iv*)	(*iii*)	(*ii*)	(*i*)
C.	(*i*)	(*ii*)	(*iii*)	(*iv*)
D.	(*ii*)	(*i*)	(*iv*)	(*iii*)

72. The roots of newly emerging forces of globalisation have been traced in specific economic and political developments in the late 1980s or early 1990s. Which of the following can not be included in this category?

A. The end of Cold War.

B. Testing of nuclear devices by India and Pakistan in 1998.

C. Dismantling of state socialism in the USSR.

D. The collapse of the Berlin wall.

73. Who among the following is associated with Democratic Peace Theory?

A. Kenneth Waltz

B. Michael Doyle

C. Jackson and Sorenson

D. John Mearsheimer

74. In which country did Saudi Arabia militarily intervene in March, 2015?

A. United Arab Emirates

B. Yemen

C. Egypt

D. Kuwait

75. Which of the following are organs of organisation of American States?

(*a*) Secretariat

(*b*) The Inter-American Conference

(*c*) The treaty of consultation of Ministers of Foreign Affairs

(*d*) The Council

Select the **correct** answer from the codes given below:

A. (*a*), (*b*) and (*c*) B. (*b*), (*c*) and (*d*)

C. (*a*), (*b*) and (*d*) D. (*a*), (*c*) and (*d*)

ANSWERS

1	2	3	4	5	6	7	8	9	10
D	C	B	C	A	C	A	B	D	C
11	**12**	**13**	**14**	**15**	**16**	**17**	**18**	**19**	**20**
D	C	A	D	C	B	B	D	C	A
21	**22**	**23**	**24**	**25**	**26**	**27**	**28**	**29**	**30**
B	D	C	B	C	C	C	C	A	B
31	**32**	**33**	**34**	**35**	**36**	**37**	**38**	**39**	**40**
D	D	D	C	B	B	A	C	C	B
41	**42**	**43**	**44**	**45**	**46**	**47**	**48**	**49**	**50**
A	C	B	B	C	D	A	D	D	D
51	**52**	**53**	**54**	**55**	**56**	**57**	**58**	**59**	**60**
B	B	A	C	D	C	C	A	B	A
61	**62**	**63**	**64**	**65**	**66**	**67**	**68**	**69**	**70**
D	A	D	B	A	A	C	D	D	B
71	**72**	**73**	**74**	**75**					
A	B	B	B	B					

EXPLANATORY ANSWERS

1. Barely a decade after Sabine proclaimed in his article "What is Political Theory–1939", 'political theory has remained a subject of perennial concern', that writers such as Easton and Cobbon declared it to be declining. Peter Lasslett and Robert Dahl declared it as already dead. While Neal Riemer saw it to be in the doghouse. The main thrust of their argument was that they associated political theory with political philosophy as Easton points out "lives parasitically on ideas a century old and what is more discouraging, we see little prospect of the development of new political synthesis. Its genesis had been synthesised in the background of a school called logical positivism known as Vienna Circle. The prominent figures were Rudolf Carnap, O.V. Neurath, etc. and they laid stress on experience as a mode of knowledge construction. However, there is hardly any unanimity among the proponent of 'decline' as regards the causes."

2. Political theory is philosophical as well as scientific, normative as well as empirical, evaluative as well as explanatory, historical as well as analytical. The study of politics is usually seen to encompass two, and some would say three, distinct subdivisions. On the one hand, there is what is called political science and, on the other, political theory and political philosophy—terms that are often used interchangeably but between which distinctions are sometimes drawn. Political theory is, however, usually regarded as a distinctive approach to the subject, even though, particularly in the USA, it is seen as a subfield of political science. Political theory involves the analytical study of ideas and doctrines that have been central to political thought.

4. According to Mao's theory of contradictions, contradictions are universal in all times and in all societies. Antagonistic contradictions exist among the hostile classes in terms of ownership of productive forces. Non-antagonistic contradictions could exist among people which could be resolved without resorting to violence.

   Mao Zedong (1893-1976) was a Chinese Marxist theorist and leader of the people's Republic of China. He adapted Marxism-Leninism to the needs of an overwhelmingly agricultural and still traditional society. His ideological legacy is often associated with the Cultural Revolution (1966-70), a radical egalitarian movement that denounced elitism and 'capitalist roaders'. Maoism emphasizes the importance of politics in the form of the radical zeal of the masses, acknowledges the necessity of opposition and conflict, and stresses community rather than hierarchic state organization.

5. John Locke championed the cornerstone liberal idea that government arises out of the agreement, or consent, of the governed, outlined in social-contract theory. In this view, the purpose of government is to protect natural rights (for Locke, the rights to life, liberty and property), but when the government breaks the terms of its contract its legitimacy evaporates and the people have the right of rebellion. Lockian liberalism laid down the basis for limited government, representation and constitutionalism, and greatly influenced the American Revolution.

7. Machiavelli is regarded as the first modern political thinker because of separation of ethics and religion from politics. Machiavelli's major work, 'The Prince', written in 1513 and published in 1531, was intended to provide

guidance for the ruler of a future united Italy, and drew heavily upon his first-hand observations of the statecraft of Cesare Borgia and the power politics that dominated his period. His 'scientific method' portrayed politics in strictly realistic terms and highlighted the use by the political leaders of cunning, cruelty and manipulation. This emphasis, and attacks upon him that led to his excommunication, meant that the term 'Machiavellion' subsequently came to mean scheming and duplicitous. His 'Discourses', written in 1513-17 and published in 1531, provides a fuller account of Machiavelli's republicanism, but commentators have disagreed about whether it should be considered as an elaboration of or a departure from the ideas outlined in 'The Prince'.

8. According to Hobbes, sovereign was not a party to the contract. In 'Leviathan–1651', Hobbes advanced the view that rational human beings should respect and obey their government because without it society would descend into a civil war 'of every man against every man'. Social-contract theorists develop their argument with reference to an assumed or hypothetical society without government, a so-called 'state of nature'. Hobbes graphically described life in the state of nature as being 'solitary, poor, nasty, brutish and short'. In his view, human beings were essentially power-seeking and selfish creatures, who would, if unrestrained by law, seek to advance their own interests at the expense of fellow humans. Even the strongest would never be strong enough to live in security and without fear : the weak would unite against them before turning upon one another. Quite simply, without government to restrain selfish impulses, order and stability would be impossible. Hobbes suggested that, recognising this, rational individuals would seek to escape from chaos and disorder by entering into an agreement with one another, a 'social contract', through which a system of government could be established.

9. John Locke's contribution chiefly lies in his consent theory and limited government. Constitutional governments may nevertheless fail to establish legitimacy if they do not, in some way, ensure that government rests upon the consent or agreement of the people. Locke, for instance, was perfectly aware that government had not in practice developed out of a social contract, but argued, rather, that citizens ought to behave as if it had. He therefore developed the notion of 'tacit consent', an implied agreement among citizens to obey the law and respect government. However, for consent to confer legitimacy upon a regime it must take the form not of an implied agreement but of voluntary and active participation in the political life of the community. Political participation is thus the active expression of consent..

13. Marx's concept of dialectical materialism constitutes the foundation on which entire Marxist thought is based. He borrowed the concept 'Dialectic' from Hegal and gave it a materialist twist.

Karl Marx appreciated Hegelian conception but he replaced dialectical idealism with dialectical materialism. Unlike Hegel, he believed that the social institutions are shaped by material conditions of life, which are determined by the economic mode of production.

According to Marx, the world by its very nature is material and the various phenomenon of the world constitute different forms of matter in motion. In his own words, "it is not the consciousness of men that determines their being, but on the contrary their social being that determines their consciousness."

14. J.S. Mill's work was crucial to the development of liberalism because it straddled the divide between classical and modern theories. In 'On Liberty–1859' he advanced an eloquent defence of freedom based upon the principle that the only justification for restricting individual freedom is to prevent 'harm to others'. His opposition to collectivist tendencies and traditions, including those embodied in majoritarian democracy, was rooted in a commitment to 'individuality'. His essay, 'Utilitarianism–1861', was designed to outline the basic themes of the utilitarian tradition, but departed from them in emphasising the difference between 'higher' and 'lower' pleasures. In 'Consideration on Representative Government–1861', Mill discussed the representative and electoral mechanisms, he believed, would balance broader participation against the need for an intellectual and moral elite. 'The Subjection of Women–1869', written in collaboration with his wife Harriet Taylor, proposed that women should enjoy the same rights and liberties as men, including the right to vote.

15. 'Sarvodaya' is a Sanskrit term meaning 'universal lift' or 'progress of all' or welfare of all sections of the society the term was used by Mahatma Gandhi as the title of his 1908 translation of John Ruskin's tract of political economy, 'Unto This Last', and Gandhi came to use the term for the ideal of his own political philosophy. Later Gandhians like the Indian non-violence activist Vinoba Bhave, embraced the term as a name for the social movement in post-independence India which strove to ensure that self-determination and equality reached all strata of Indian society.

17. Dr. M.A. Ansari was an Indian nationalist and political leader, and former president of the Indian National Congress and the Muslim League during the Indian independence movement. One of the founders of the Jamia Millia Islamia University, he remained its chancellor form 1928 to 1936.

Dr. Ansari served several terms as the AICC General secretary, as well as the President of the Indian National Congress during its 1927 session. He also presided over the All Party Conference held in 1928.

19. Inter-State council is not recognised as a 'tension' area in Indian federation. Article-263 contemplates the establishment of this council to effect coordination between the states and between centre and states. Thus, the President can establish such a council if at anytime it appears to him that the public interest would be served by its establishment. He can define the nature of duties to be performed by such a council and its organization and procedure.

20. 74th Constitutional Amendment Act of 1992 does not apply to the schedule areas in the states of Haryana and U.P. This Act has added a new part IX-A to the Constitution of India. It is entitled 'The Municipalities' and consists of provisions from Article 243P to 243ZG. In addition, the Act has also added a new 12th schedule to the constitution. This schedule contains 18 functional items of Municipalities.

The Act aims at revitalising and strengthening the urban governments so that they function effectively as units of local government.

25. The Sarkaria Commission on Centre-State Relations (1983-87) made a strong case for the establishment of a permanent Inter-State council under Article 263 of the Constitution. It recommended that in order to differentiate the Inter-State council from other bodies established under the same Article 263, it must be called as the Inter-Governmental Council. The Commission recommended that the Council should be charged with the duties laid down in clauses (b) and (c) of Article 263.

In pursuance of the above recommendations of the Sarkaria Commission, the Janata Dal Government headed by V.P. Singh established the Inter-State Council in 1990.

27. Like the Speaker, the Deputy Speaker is also elected by the Lok Sabha itself from amongst its members. He is elected after the election of the Speaker has taken place. The date of election of the Deputy Speaker is fixed by the Speaker. Whenever the office of the Deputy Speaker falls vacant, the Lok Sabha elects another member to fill the vacancy.

Upto the 10th Lok Sabha, both the Speaker and the Deputy Speaker were usually from the ruling party. Since the 11th Lok Sabha (1996), there has been a consensus that the Speaker comes from the ruling party and the post of Deputy Speaker goes to the main opposition party.

30. The Armed Forces Special Power Act (AFSPA) has been made under Article 34 of the Indian Constitution while the Army Act, The Border Security Force Act and the Navy Act have been made under Article 33 of the constitution. AFSPA are acts of the Parliament of India that grant special powers to the Indian Armed Forces in what each act terms 'disturbed areas'. One such act passed on September 11, 1958 was applicable to the 'Seven Sister States' in India's northeast. Another passed in 1983 and applicable to 'Punjab and Chandigarh' was withdrawn in 1997. An act passed in 1990 was applied to J&K and has been in force since.

The acts have received criticism from several sections for alleged concerns about human rights violations in the regions of its enforcement alleged to have happened. Irom Chanu Sharmila who is also known as the 'Iron Lady of Manipur' is a civil rights activist, who had been in a hunger strike for nearly 15 years. Her primary demand to the Indian government has been the repeal of the AFSPA.

31. The House of Representatives has overshadowed the American Senate is not a correct statement because American Senate is the most powerful second chamber of the world.

The US Congress is the bicameral legislature of the federal government of the United States consisting of two houses : The Senate and the House of Representatives. The Congress meets in the capital in Washington D.C. Both senators and representatives are chosen through direct election, though vacancies in the senate may be filled by a gubernatorial appointment. Members are usually affiliated to the Republican party or to the Democratic Party, and only rarely to a third party or as independents. Congress has 535 voting members : 435 representatives and 100 senators.

34. The Magna Carta (1215), the Glorious Revolution (1688) and the Writings of John Locke, all contributed to the strengthening of Parliamentary Democracy of Great Britain. The Parliament of England was the legislature of the Kingdom of England. In 1055 William of Normandy introduced what, in later centuries, became referred to as a feudal system, by which he sought the advice of a council of tenants-in-chief and ecclesiastics before making laws. In 1215, the tenants-in-chief secured Magna Carta from king John, which established that the king may not levy or collect any taxes (except the feudal taxes to which they were hitherto accustomed), save with the consent of his royal council, which gradually developed into a Parliament.

38. The civic culture or The civic culture : Political Attitudes and Democracy in Five Nations is a 1963 non-fiction political science book by Gabriel Almond and Sidney Verba. The book is credited with popularizing the political culture sub-field and is considered to be the first systematic study in this field.

In the text Almond and Verba examine the democratic systems in five countries, the United States, Germany, Mexico, Italy and the UK. They interviewed several individuals about how they viewed the government as it pertained to the person. Through the book Almond and Verba identify three political structures, participant, subject and Parochial. They considered political culture to be the element that connects individual attitudes with the overall political system structure.

39. The Rostow's stages of economic growth model is one of the major historical models of economic growth. It was published by American economist Walt Whitman Rostow in 1960. The model postulates that economic growth occurs in five basic stages, of varying length—

(*i*) Traditional society

(*ii*) Preconditions for take-off

(*iii*) Take-off

(*iv*) Drive to maturity

(*v*) The epoch of high mass consumption.

Rastow's model is one of the more structuralist models of economic growth, particularly in comparison with the 'backwardness' model developed by Alexander Gerschenkron, although the two models are not mutually exclusive.

41. Parochial, subject and participant are the three types of political culture according to Almond and Verba's study 'Civic Culture'. Parochial culture exists in simple to additional societies in which there is very little specialization. People are backward and ignorant about their political system.

Subject culture is found in Eastern European countries where people are oriented to the system as a whole and to its outputs. Orientations towards the other two aspects viz., inputs and the self is absent. Individuals accept the system and its output passively. The people do not participate in policy decisions processes.

And finally, participant culture exists in highly developed societies where people take active part in the political sphere by considering themselves as active members of the polity.

43. The notion that power is a form of domination or control that forces one person to obey another, runs into the problem that in political life power is very commonly exercised through the acceptance and willing obedience of the public. Those 'in power' do not merely possess the ability to enforce compliance, but are usually thought to have the right to do so as well this highlights the distinction between power and authority. What is it, however, that transforms power into authority, and on what basis can authority be rightfully exercised? This leads, finally, to question about legitimacy, the perception that power is exercised in a manner that is rightful, justified or acceptable. Legitimacy is usually seen as the basis of stable government, being linked to the capacity of a regime to command the allegiance and support of its citizens.

45. The theories of modernisation were criticised by dependency, underdevelopment and world-systems theories. Modernisation theory is used to explain the process of modernization within societies. Modernization refers to a model of a progressive transition from a 'pre-modern' or 'traditional' to a 'modern' society. The theory looks at the internal factors of a country while assuming that with assistance, "traditional" countries can be brought to development in the same manner more developed countries have been.

Modernization theory both attempts to identify the social variables that contribute to social progress and development of societies and seeks to explain the process of social evolution. Modernisation theory is subject to criticism originating among socialist and free-market ideologies, world-systems theorists, globalization theorists and dependency theorists among others. Modernization theory stresses not only the process of change but also the responses to that change. It also looks at internal dynamics while referring to social and cultural structures and the adaptation of new technologies.

49. New Public Administration is an anti-positivist, anti-technical and anti-hierarchical reaction against traditional public administration. A practical theory in response to the ever changing needs of the public and how institutions and administrations go about solving them. Focus is on the role of governments and how they can provide these services to citizens in which are a part of public interest, by means, but not limited to public policy. The literature on new public administration lays emphasis on Relevance, values, social equity, change, client focus and management-worker relations. New Public administration provides solutions for achieving these goals, popularly called 4 D's *i.e.* Decentralisation, Debureaucratisation, Delegation and Democratisation.

52. In the politics of the United States, a spoil system (also known as a Patronage system) is a practice in which a political party, after winning an election, gives government jobs to its supporters, friends and relatives as a reward for working toward victory, and as an incentive to keep working for the party—as apposed to a Merit System, where offices are awarded on the basis of some measure of merit, independent of political activity.

The term was derived from the phrase "to the victor belong the spoils" by New York Senator William L. Marcy, referring to the victory of the Jackson Democrats in the election of 1828, with the term spoils meaning goods or benefits taken from the loser in a competition, election or military victory.

53. The term representative bureaucracy is generally attributed to J. Donald Kingsley's book titled 'Representative Bureaucracy' that was published in 1944. In his book Kingsley calls for a "liberalisation of social class selection for the English bureaucracy", due to the "Dominance of social, political and economic elites within the British bureaucracy" which he claimed resulted in programs and political policy that did not meet the needs or interests of all social classes. To solve this issue, Kingsley states that "representative bureaucracy is necessary because there must be at least some administrators sympathetic to the programmatic concerns of the dominant political party". Despite criticism at the time of publication, years later, political scientist Samuel Krislov echoed Kingsley's sentiment in his book also called 'Representative Bureaucracy' and this has been expanded upon since then by a number of scholars all over the world.

56. 73rd Constitutional Amendment Act-1992 has added a new Part-IX to the Constitution of India. It is entitled as 'The Panchayats' and consists of provisions from Articles 243 to 2430. In addition, the act has also added a new 11th Schedule to the Constitution. This schedule contains 29 functional items of the Panchayats. Compulsory provisions of this act are as follows—

(*i*) Indirect election to the post of chairperson of Panchayats at the intermediate level.

(*ii*) Reservation of one-third seats for women.

(*iii*) Constitution of a state Finance Commission.

(*iv*) Establishment of a State Election Commission for conducting elections to the Panchayats.

(*v*) 21 years to be the minimum age for contesting elections to Panchayats.

57. The Administrative Reforms Commission (ARC) of India (1966-70) recommended the setting up of two special authorities designated as 'Lokpal' and 'Lokayukta' for the redressal of citizens grievances. These institutions were to be set up on the pattern of the institution of Ombudsman in Scandinavian Countries and the Parliamentary Commissioner for investigation in New Zealand. The Lokpal would deal with complaints against ministers and secretaries at central and state levels, and the Lokayukta would deal with complaints against other specified higher officials. The government of India accepted the recommendations of ARC and firstly introduce 'Lokpal and Lokayukta bill' in May 1968.

60. The term 'development administration' came into use in the 1950s to represent those aspects of public administration and those changes in public administration, which are needed to carry out policies, projects and programs to improve social and economic conditions. During a period of 15 years following the end of World War II, in 1945, colony after colony threw off the imperial yoke. Country after country achieved independence and political autonomy. This new status gave promise of freedom and liberty and self-determination in political systems of representative democracy. It gave hope of greater individual freedom and equality of treatment in the society. And independence created hopes of higher national and per capita income, a rapid rise in standards of living, and an increase in individual opportunity. Even in countries which had not been colonies but had been administered by some other form of authoritarian government, this was a generation of rising and insistent expectations pressing for rapid political, social and economic change. New governments and their bureaucracies, their administrative agencies and processes, were expected to give reality to these anticipated fruits of independence and liberty. These new functions, these demands upon the administration system, were not only enormous in size and weight, they were novel and complex in character.

63. WTO was created in 1995 at the Uruguay round of GATT negotiations. It implements 28 treaties related with the international trade. It is the 'watch dog' of world trade. The purpose of WTO is to promote free trade by reducing barriers like duties and quotas. Its headquarters is at Geneva. Objectives of WTO are as follows—

(*i*) It administers WTO trade agreements.

(*ii*) It acts as a forum for trade negotiations.

(*iii*) It monitors national trade policies.

(*iv*) It accepts the concept of sustainable development.

(*v*) It ensures optimum utilisation of world resources, etc.

66. Soft power is a concept developed by Joseph Nye of Harvard University to describe the ability to attract and co-opt rather than by coercion (hard power), using force or giving money as a means of persuasion. Soft power is the ability to shape the preferences of others through appeal and attraction. A defining feature of soft power is that it is non-coercive; the currency of soft power is culture, political values and foreign policies. Recently, the term has also been used in changing and influencing social and public opinion through relatively less transparent channels and lobbying through powerful political and non-political organizations. In 2012, Nye explained that with soft power, "The best propaganda is not propaganda", further explaining that during the Information Age, "credibility is the scarcest resource".

Joseph Nye coined the term in a 1990 book, 'Bound to Lead : The Changing Nature of American Power'. In this book, he wrote "When one country gets other countries to want what it wants—right be called co-optive or soft power in contrast with the hard or command power of ordering others to do what it wants." He further developed the concept in his 2004 book, "Soft Power : The Means to Success in World Politics". The term is now widely used in international affairs by analysts and statesmen. For example, the US secretary of Defence Robert Gates spoke of the need to enhance American soft power by "a dramatic increase in spending on the civilian instruments of national security—diplomacy, strategic communications, foreign assistance, civic action and economic reconstruction and development.

67. The Marshall Plan (officially the European Recovery Program, ERP) was an American initiative to aid Western Europe, in which the United States gave 13 billion dollar in economic support to help rebuild Western European economies after the end of World War II. The plan was in operation for four years beginning in April 1948. The goals of the USA were to rebuild war-devastated regions, remove trade barriers, modernize industry, make Europe prosperous again and prevent the spread of communism. The Marshall Plan required a lessening of interstate barriers, a dropping of many regulations and encouraged an increase in productivity, labour union membership, as well as the adoption of modern business procedures.

70. Panchsheel is an agreement signed between Nehru and Chou-en-Lai in 1954 that sought to govern the relationship between India and China on the basis of five principles—

(*i*) Mutual respect for each other's territorial integrity and sovereignty.

(*ii*) Mutual non-aggression.

(*iii*) Mutual non-interference in each other's internal affairs.

(*iv*) Equality and mutual benefits, and

(*v*) Peaceful co-existence.

72. The roots of newly emerging forces of globalisation however, have been traced in specific economic and political developments in the late 1980s or early 1990s. These events include the end of cold war, dismantling of state socialism in the USSR and the collapse of the Berlin Wall : all of which marked the victory of the Western liberal economic thoughts. As a result argues G Thompson, "in the early 1990s, everyone wanted to imitate the West, adopt its institutions and its philosophy, privatise state industries, deregulate and reduce government expenditures. In the 10 years from 1988 to 1998 almost all governments in the world, regardless of ideology, downsized their activities while private sector expanded them, thus gradually replacing governments as major economic players on the world scene."

73. Democratic Peace theory is a theory which posits that democracies are hesitant to engage in armed conflict with other identified democracies. In contrast to theories explaining war engagement, it is a "theory of peace" outlining motives that dissuade state-sponsored violence.

Some theorists prefer terms such as "mutual democratic pacifism" or "Inter-democracy non-aggression hypothesis" so as to clarify that a state of peace is not singular to democracies, but rather that it is easily sustained between democratic nations.

Among proponents of the democratic peace theory, several factors are held as motivating peace between liberal states—

(*i*) Democratic leaders are forced to accept culpability for war losses to a voting public;

(*ii*) Publicly accountable states' people are more inclined to establish diplomatic institutions for resolving international tensions;

(*iii*) Democracies are less inclined to view countries with adjacent policy and governing doctrine as hostile;

(*iv*) Democracies tend to possess greater public wealth than other states, and therefore eschew war to preserve infrastructure and resources.

Melvin Small and J. David Singer responded; they found an absence of wars between democratic states with two "marginal exceptions", but denied that this pattern had statistical significance. This paper was published in the Jerusalem Journal of International Relations which finally brought more widespread attention to the theory, and started the academic debate. A 1983 paper by political scientist **Michael W. Doyle** contributed further to popularizing the theory. Rudolf J. Rummel was another early researcher and drew considerable lay attention to the subject in his later works.

Previous Paper (Solved)

UGC-NET Political Science, June 2015

PAPER–II

Note: *This paper contains* ***fifty (50)*** *objective type questions of* ***two (2)*** *marks each.* ***All questions are compulsory.***

1. In Arthashastra, how many departments of the government find mention?

A. 32 B. 33
C. 34 D. 35

2. Who of the following fled Athens for Calchis, 'in order that the Athenians might not commit a second crime against philosophy'?

A. Socrates B. Plato
C. Aristotle D. Euclid

3. Who among the following said of Rousseau, "Ardent apostle of Reason, he has done more than most to prepare the way for the age of unreason in which he live"?

A. Maxey B. Sabine
C. Wayper D. Karl Popper

4. Match List-I with List-II and select the correct answer from the codes given below:

List-I	List-II
(*a*) Hobbes	(*i*) Defence of sovereignty and assertion of the claims of political authority over religion
(*b*) Locke	(*ii*) Defence of Individual freedom of thought and expression
(*c*) Rousseau	(*iii*) Limited form of constitutional government
(*d*) J.S. Mill	(*iv*) Claim that sovereignty has its origin in the people and remains with the people

Codes:

	(*a*)	(*b*)	(*c*)	(*d*)
A.	(*i*)	(*iii*)	(*ii*)	(*iv*)
B.	(*ii*)	(*iv*)	(*iii*)	(*i*)
C.	(*ii*)	(*iii*)	(*i*)	(*iv*)
D.	(*i*)	(*iii*)	(*iv*)	(*ii*)

5. Who among the following compares the organisations of civil society to a powerful system of 'Fortresses and earthworks' standing behind the state?

A. McLellan B. Bernstein
C. Lenin D. Gramsci

6. Which one of the following social contract traditions has not been revitalised by John Rawls in his book *A Theory of Justice*?

A. Hobbes B. John Locke
C. J.J. Rousseau D. Immanuel Kant

7. Who among the following said that Bhakti in religion may be a road to the salvation of the soul. But in politics, Bhakti or hero worship is a sure road to degradation and eventual dictatorship?

A. Jayaprakash Narayan
B. M.N. Roy
C. B.R. Ambedkar
D. Savarkar

8. Who said, 'therefore, the sword of Brutus is holy. Therefore, the Baghanakha of Shivaji is of fair fame. Therefore, the beheading of Charles I is a just deed. Therefore, the arrow of William Tell is divine?

A. M. N. Roy
B. Subhas Chandra Bose
C. Aurobindo Ghose
D. V.D. Savarkar

9. Which one of the following is **not** a feature of Easton's intellectual foundation stones of behaviouralism?

A. Regularities B. Values
C. Pure Science D. Stratification

10. Which one of the following is **not** a factor, for Fukuyama, leading to the triumph of liberal democracy?

A. The struggle for 'recognition'.

B. The logic of science's mastery over nature.

C. The absence of major contradictions in liberal democracy.

D. The triumph of liberalism is more in terms of economics than ideologies.

11. Since mid-1950s, the major trends in comparative politics have been in the areas of:

(*a*) systems theories
(*b*) culture theories
(*c*) development theories
(*d*) class theories

Select the correct answer from the codes given below:

Codes:

A. (*a*) and (*c*) B. (*a*), (*b*) and (*c*)
C. (*a*), (*c*) and (*d*) D. (*a*), (*b*), (*c*) and (*d*)

12. Match List-I with List-II and select the correct answer from the codes given below:

List-I (Thinkers)	**List-II (Concepts)**
(*a*) Karl Deutsch	(*i*) Modernisation - a multifaceted process
(*b*) Huntington	(*ii*) Circulation of elites
(*c*) Pareto	(*iii*) The gate-keepers
(*d*) David Easton	(*iv*) Receptors

Codes:

	(*a*)	(*b*)	(*c*)	(*d*)
A.	(*iii*)	(*i*)	(*ii*)	(*iv*)
B.	(*i*)	(*iii*)	(*iv*)	(*ii*)
C.	(*iv*)	(*i*)	(*ii*)	(*iii*)
D.	(*ii*)	(*iv*)	(*iii*)	(*i*)

13. Who among the following makes a distinction between system maintenance and system persistence?

A. Gabriel Almond B. David Easton
C. Lucian Pye D. F.W. Riggs

14. Arrange the following books in order in which they appeared. Use the code given below:

(*a*) Comparative Federalism
(*b*) Democratisation : Theory and Practice
(*c*) The End of History and the last man
(*d*) The Civic culture : Political attitude and Democracy in five nations

Codes:

A. (*c*), (*d*), (*b*), (*a*) B. (*b*), (*a*), (*c*), (*d*)
C. (*a*), (*c*), (*d*), (*b*) D. (*d*), (*c*), (*b*), (*a*)

15. Arrange the following concepts in order to in which they appeared. Use the code given below:

(*a*) Democratic Centralism
(*b*) Feed-Back System
(*c*) New Democracy
(*d*) Due Process of Law

Codes:

A. (*d*), (*b*), (*a*), (*c*) B. (*b*), (*d*), (*c*), (*a*)
C. (*d*), (*a*), (*c*), (*b*) D. (*a*), (*c*), (*d*), (*b*)

16. "We are under the Constitution, but the constitution is what the Judges say it is". Besides U.S.A. to which one of the following countries can this be applicable?

A. Switzerland B. India
C. U.K. D. Russia

17. Who among the following has written "The Federalist Papers"?

A. B. Anderson B. C. Reynoldes
C. James Madison D. Theodor Andorno

18. Who among the following argued, "The belief in the principle of authority is the only reliable means of securing order"?

A. Joseph de Maistre
B. Max Weber
C. Friedrich Nietzsche
D. Giovanni Gentile

19. Who among the following has argued that the electoral system determines the nature of the party system?

A. Duverger B. Mitchels
C. Schumpeter D. Weber

20. Given below are two statements, one labelled as Assertion (A) and the other labelled as Reason (R). Select the correct answer from the codes given below:

Assertion (A): Political development approach came under criticism in the mid - 1960s.

Reason (R): The approach based on the experiences of the United States and Western Europe had limited relevance in the Third world.

Codes:

A. Both (A) and (R) are true and (R) is the correct explanation of (A)

B. Both (A) and (R) are true, but (R) is not the correct explanation of (A)

C. (A) is true but (R) is false

D. (A) is false but (R) is true

21. What is the correct order in which the following terms are enshrined in the Preamble to the Constitution of India?

(*a*) Equality (*b*) Liberty

(*c*) Justice (*d*) Fraternity

Select the correct answer from the codes given below:

Codes:

A. (*a*), (*b*), (*c*) and (*d*)

B. (*c*), (*b*), (*a*) and (*d*)

C. (*b*), (*a*), (*c*) and (*d*)

D. (*c*), (*a*), (*b*) and (*d*)

22. Which of the following rights are available to foreigners living in India ?

(*a*) Equality before law

(*b*) Right to education

(*c*) Freedom of speech

(*d*) Freedom of movement

Select the correct answer from the codes given below:

A. (*b*) only B. (*a*) and (*b*)

C. (*b*) and (*d*) D. (*a*), (*b*) and (*c*)

23. Who is the First Law Officer of the Government of India?

A. Chief Justice of India

B. Law Secretary

C. Solicitor-General of India

D. Attorney-General of India

24. Which one of the following cannot be dissolved but can be abolished?

A. Lok Sabha

B. Rajya Sabha

C. State Legislative Council

D. State Legislative Assembly

25. Who among the following Governor - appointees can be removed only by the Governor?

(*a*) Advocate-General

(*b*) Members of the State Finance Commission

(*c*) Members of the State Public Service Commission

(*d*) Vice-Chancellor of a State University

Select the correct answer from the codes given below:

Codes:

A. (*a*), (*b*) and (*c*)

B. (*a*), (*b*) and (*d*)

C. (*b*), (*c*) and (*d*)

D. (*a*), (*b*), (*c*) and (*d*)

26. The maximum period of the President's Rule in a state under Article 356 can be:

A. One year B. Two year

C. Three year D. Four year

27. Which of the following statements are not true about the process of constitutional Amendment in India?

(*a*) The Parliament can amend the Constitution with a special majority.

(*b*) State Assemblies can propose amendment in the Constitution.

(*c*) A Bill for Constitutional Amendment can be introduced only in the Lower House of the Parliament.

(*d*) Deadlock between the two Houses of Parliament over a Bill for Constitutional Amendment can be removed by a joint session of the Parliament.

(*e*) The President of India enjoys the veto power over Constitutional Amendment Bills passed by the Parliament.

Select the correct answer from the codes given below:

A. (*a*), (*c*) and (*d*)
B. (*b*), (*c*), (*d*) and (*e*)
C. (*a*), (*d*) and (*e*)
D. (*a*), (*b*), (*c*) and (*d*)

28. Which of the following is not a condition for Parliament to legislate on the subjects mentioned in the State List?

A. If Lok Sabha decides that a subject mentioned in state list is of national importances
B. If two or more states assemblies pass a resolution to such an effect
C. If a state of Emergency is declared
D. If a treaty with a foreign country has to be put into effect

29. Any resolution passed by the Parliament for removing a Judge of the Supreme Court has to be investigated by a Committee comprising of:

A. Two judges of Supreme Court
B. Two Judges of Supreme Court and Attorney General of India
C. Two Judges of Supreme Court and a legal luminary
D. Chief Justice of Supreme Court and two Judges of the Supreme Court

30. Match List-I with List-II and select the correct answer from the codes given below:

List-I Movements	List-II Leader
(*a*) India Against Corruption	(*i*) Aruna Roy
(*b*) Narmada Bachao Andolan	(*ii*) Mahendra Singh Tikait
(*c*) Right to Information Movement	(*iii*) Anna Hazare
(*d*) Bhartiya Kisan Union	(*iv*) Medha Patkar

Codes:

	(*a*)	(*b*)	(*c*)	(*d*)
A.	(*iii*)	(*i*)	(*iv*)	(*ii*)
B.	(*iii*)	(*iv*)	(*i*)	(*ii*)
C.	(*iii*)	(*iv*)	(*ii*)	(*i*)
D.	(*iii*)	(*ii*)	(*i*)	(*iv*)

31. Match List-I with List-II and select the correct answer by using the codes given below:

List-I (Administrative Thinker)	List-II (Administrative Approach)
(*a*) M.P. Follett	(*i*) Garbage can Model
(*b*) Herbert Simon	(*ii*) Mixed scanning
(*c*) Michael D. Cohen	(*iii*) Psychological approach
(*d*) Amitai Etzioni	(*iv*) Rational approach

Codes:

	(*a*)	(*b*)	(*c*)	(*d*)
A.	(*iii*)	(*ii*)	(*i*)	(*iv*)
B.	(*ii*)	(*iv*)	(*iii*)	(*i*)
C.	(*iii*)	(*iv*)	(*i*)	(*ii*)
D.	(*iii*)	(*ii*)	(*iv*)	(*i*)

32. What was the name of the section which replaced Comparative Administration Group of the American Society of Public Administration?

A. Section of American Public Administration (SAP)
B. Section on Comparative Administration (SCA)
C. Section on International Public Administration (SIP)
D. Section on International and Comparative Public Administration (SICA)

33. Arrange MasLow's perceived human needs in correct chronological order:

A. Self esteem - physiological - security - self actualization - belongingness
B. Self actualization - security - belongingness - physiological - self esteem.
C. Security - self actualization - belongingness - physiological - self esteem.
D. Physiological - security - belongingness - self esteem - self actualization.

34. Given below are two statements, one labelled as Assertion (A) and the other labelled as Reason (R). Choose the correct answer by using the codes given below:

Assertion (A): "Both staff and auxiliary agencies assist the line agencies but are distinct from each other".

Reason (R): "Auxiliary agencies have no operating responsibilities"

Codes:

A. Both (A) and (R) are true and (R) is the correct explanation of (A)
B. Both (A) and (R) are true and (R) is not the correct explanation of (A)
C. (A) is true but (R) is false
D. (A) is false but (R) is true

35. Which one of the following types of leaders does not figure in Mooney and Reiley's classification of leaders?
A. Formal leaders
B. Titular leaders
C. Controllers
D. True organizers

36. Which one of the following is not included in the elements of Public Policy by Austin Rammey?
A. A set of objectives
B. A selected line of action
C. An implementation of intent
D. Reconsideration of objectives

37. Assheton committee (1944) did not include one of the following in the objects of training of civil servants:
A. To produce reliable work-skill
B. Flexibility
C. To broaden the mind of the trainee
D. To develop leadership qualities

38. Which one among the following is the correct ascending order of Commission/Committees appointed in the USA?
A. Hoover Commission, Taft Commission, The Grace Commission, Brownlow Committee.
B. The Grace Commission, Hoover Commission, Taft Commission, Brownlow Committee.
C. Taft Commission, Brownlow Committee, Hoover Commission, The Grace Commission.
D. Brownlow Committee, Taft Commission, The Grace Commission, Hoover Commission.

39. Who called bureaucrats as 'ruling servants'?
A. F.M. Marx
B. Martin Krygier
C. Robert K. Merton
D. Joseph La Palombara

40. Which constitutional amendment provided for the setting up of Administrative Tribunals in India?
A. 24th Amendment
B. 59th Amendment
C. 42nd Amendment
D. 44th Amendment

41. Who among the following regards International Politics as an autonomous discipline?
(*a*) C.A.W. Manning
(*b*) Karlin M. Copper
(*c*) Martin Wright
(*d*) Hoffson

Select the correct answer from the codes given below:

A. (*a*), (*b*) and (*c*) B. (*b*), (*c*) and (*d*)
C. (*c*), (*d*) and (*a*) D. (*a*), (*b*) and (*d*)

42. Which of the following pairs correctly match. Choose your answer from the codes given below:

(*a*) The control of the Arms Race – Hedley Bull
(*b*) Some Economic Aspects of Disarmament – L. Gromoo and V. Strigachow
(*c*) The challenge of the Nineteen sixties – James P. Warbarg
(*d*) Winning without war – Emile Benoit

Codes:

A. (*a*), (*b*) and (*c*)
B. (*b*), (*c*) and (*d*)
C. (*d*), (*c*) and (*a*)
D. (*b*), (*d*) and (*a*)

43. Who among the following is not related to Bargaining Theory?
A. Kenneth Waltz
B. J.F. Nash
C. Thomas Schelling
D. Roger Fisher

44. Which one of the following was not feature of Old Diplomacy?
A. Limited
B. Aristocratic
C. Transparency
D. Freedom of Action for Ambassadors

45. In which year Brezhnev had propounded the concept of Asian Collective Security System?
A. 1967 B. 1968
C. 1969 D. 1970

46. Which of the following Articles of the charter of United Nations Organisation are related to Regional Organisations?
(*a*) Article 51 (*b*) Article 52
(*c*) Article 53 (*d*) Article 54

Select the correct answer from the codes given below:

Codes:
A. (*b*), (*c*) and (*d*)
B. (*a*), (*c*) and (*d*)
C. (*a*), (*b*) and (*d*)
D. (*a*), (*b*) and (*c*)

47. Which of the following country is not a member of ASEAN:
A. Laos B. Combodia
C. Vietnam D. North Korea

48. Originally what was the total strength of security council of United Nations?
A. 9 B. 10
C. 11 D. 15

49. Recently France has agreed to set up atomic power plant in India at:
A. Kudankulam B. Tarapur
C. Kakarapar D. Jaitapur

50. Match List-I with List-II and select the correct answer from the codes given below:

List-I	List-II
(*a*) Second summit of Non-alignment	(*i*) Colombo
(*b*) Third summit of Non-alignment	(*ii*) Algiers
(*c*) Fourth summit of Non-alignment	(*iii*) Lusaka
(*d*) Fifth summit of Non-alignment	(*iv*) Cairo

Codes:

	(*a*)	(*b*)	(*c*)	(*d*)
A.	(*i*)	(*ii*)	(*iii*)	(*iv*)
B.	(*iv*)	(*iii*)	(*ii*)	(*i*)
C.	(*ii*)	(*i*)	(*iii*)	(*iv*)
D.	(*iv*)	(*i*)	(*iii*)	(*ii*)

ANSWERS

1	2	3	4	5	6	7	8	9	10
C	C	C	D	D	A	C	D	D	D
11	**12**	**13**	**14**	**15**	**16**	**17**	**18**	**19**	**20**
D	C	B	D	C	B	C	A	C	A
21	**22**	**23**	**24**	**25**	**26**	**27**	**28**	**29**	**30**
B	B	D	C	B	C	B	A	C	B
31	**32**	**33**	**34**	**35**	**36**	**37**	**38**	**39**	**40**
C	D	D	C	A	D	D	C	C	C
41	**42**	**43**	**44**	**45**	**46**	**47**	**48**	**49**	**50**
D	A	A	C	C	A	D	C	D	B

SOME SELECTED EXPLANATORY ANSWERS

1. Kautilya's Arthashastra mentioned 34 departments of the government. In 'Manav Dharmshastra' Acharya Manu mentioned 7 or 8 departments, in 'Shukraniti Sar' Shukracharya mentioned 10 departments and the Mahabharata mentioned 37 departments. Kautilya's Arthashastra contains fifteen books (Adhikaranas). The first five deals with tantra or the internal administration of the state, the next eight books deal with avapa or the state's relations with the neighbouring states. The last two are miscellaneous in character.

2. Aristotle's father was a physician to the king of Macedon. This provides him an opportunity to acquire knowledge about the Royal Court. It also provides him understanding to work with the state. It helped Aristotle to develop an analytical and scientific approach. At the age of 18, he came to Athens and joined Plato's 'Academy', where he stayed twenty years till the death of Plato in 347 B.C. He was called to Macedonia to became the tutor of the young Alexander. After the death of Alexander, Aristotle fled Athens for Calchis, in order that the Athenians might not commit a second crime against philosophy, because they had already committed crime against Socrates.

3. J.J. Rousseau postulated the 'contract theory' of the evolution of the state. His most famous book is the 'Social Contract'. C.L. Wayper said about the Rousseau, "Ardent apostle of reason, he has done more than most to prepare the way for the age of unreason in which he live"? Wayper, further stated, "Like Hobbes, Rousseau is an absolutist but is more democratic than Locke." He also said, "Rousseau has left moral influences on politics, education, religion and literature".

4. An overview of Hobbes's theory of sovereignty put forward in his work, 'Leviathan' might defence of sovereignty and assertion of the claims of political authority over religion. Locke's view on state are outcome of his concept of human nature. According to Prof. Vaughan, "Every thing in Locke's system revolves round the individual; everything is disposed so as to ensure the sovereignty of the individual." He expounded a state whose prime work is to protect the natural rights to life, liberty and property, It means the state is limited form of constitutional government.

Rousseau claims that sovereignty has its origin in the people and remains with the people. Utilitarianist J.S. Mill defended of individual freedom of thought and expression.

5. Antonio Gramsci emphasised on the role of the civil society in generating beliefs and thought conducive to the existence of capitalist state. He explained in terms of conception of ideological Hegemony. Gramsci compares the organisations of civil society to a powerful system of 'Fortresses and earthworks' standing behind the state'.

6. In 'A Theory of Justice', Rawls argues for a principled reconciliation of liberty and equality, it is meant to apply to the basic structure of a well-ordered society. Central to this effort is an account of the circumstances of justice, inspired by David Hume, and a fair choice situation for parties facing such circumstances, similar to some of Immanual Kant's views. Rawls belongs to the social contract tradition. However, Rawls' social contract takes a different view from that of previous thinkers. Rawls in his book, 'A Theory of Justice' has not been revitalised the Hobbes social contract traditions.

7. B.R. Ambedkar said that Bhakti in religion may be a road to the salvation of the soul. But in politics, Bhakti or hero worship is a sure road to degradation and eventual dictatorship. In the history of modern Indian political thoughts, Ambedkar will have a significant place because through his scholarly writings, speeches, leadership and constructive works, he has made significant awareness of the political, economic and social problems of the untouchable community.

8. V.D. Savarkar justified the actions of the leaders and heroes who had adopted violence for the vindication of justice. He wrote, "We do not hold the justice which gives the death sentence responsible for bloodshed but rather than the injustice which is taken to the gallows." Therefore, the sword of Brutus is holy. Therefore, the Baghnakha of Shivaji is sacred. Therefore, the bloodshed in the revolutions in Italy is of fair fame. Therefore, the beheading of Charles-I is a just deed. Therefore, the arrow of William Tell is divine. He had full faith that justice must triumph in the end. But because every Hiranyakashipu has his Narasimha, because every Dusshashan has his Bheema, because every evil-doer has his avenger, there is still some hope in the heart of the world that injustice cannot last.

9. Easton has identified eight major tenets which he regarded as 'Intellectual foundation stones' of behaviouralism. These major tenets are Regularities, verification, techniques, quantification, values, systematization, pure science & integration.

10. The triumph of liberalism is more in terms of economics than ideologies is not a factor, for Fukuyama, leading to the triumph of liberal democracy; whether the struggle for 'recognition', the logic of science's mastery over nature and the absence of major contradictions in liberal democracy are the factors of Fukuyama leading to the triumph of liberal democracy. The triumph of liberal democracy as a final form of government may be decried in some quarters, but as Stephen Eric Bronner argues, "A replacement to liberal democratic state no longer exists." However, it will have to be sensitive as regards contradictions of economic relations in the society. It will have to buttress itself with Egalitarian elements of socialism and cultural connectiveness of multiculturalism.

11. Since the mid-1950s, the major theoretical trends in the comparative politics field have tended to cluster into four general areas: systems theories, culture theories, development theories and class theories. It may be instructive to identify briefly the major contributions that shaped each area to become a central thrust in the field of comparative politics.

13. David Easton makes a clear distinction between system maintenance and system persistence. His method, being directed towards the study of the systems persistence rather than to its maintenance only, Easton claims, is definitely oriented towards exploring change as well as stability. He is aware of the continuous exchange going on between the political system and its environments, and of the fact that the system is constantly engaged in a conversion process, producing outputs and altering the environment. Easton's analysis claims to take note of the system's adaptive process, as well as of redirection in the form of goals-seeking feedback, though one cannot forget at the same time that the objective of the change is merely to modify or streamline the system with a view to its survival. Though persistence, rather than goal attainment, is claimed to be the primary objective of the system, survival and the preservation of essential variables within their critical range still continue to be its primary goals. An approach of this kind is not likely to take much note of patterns of control, power and influence, or of the politics of decline, disruption and breakdown in political systems, or of the analysis of mass political phenomena.

16. "We are under the constitution, but the constitution is what the Judges say it is" are applicable for USA and India. The power of Judicial Review is implicit in the American constitution but in the Indian constitution it is not explicitly stated. According to Article-13 of the Indian constitution, "Any action of the legislature or the executive in contravention of the provisions of the chapter of fundamental rights shall be declared void." While the courts in USA proceed on 'due process of law', India follows 'procedure established by law'. While procedure established by law enquires into the legality of any legislative or executive action, the phrase 'due process' also examines the malafide intention of the law maker.

17. The Federalist (later known as 'The Federalist Papers') is a collection of 85 articles and essays written by Alexander Hamilton, James Madison and John Jay promoting the ratification of the United States Constitution. 77 were published serially in the Independent Journal and the New York Packet between October 1787 and August 1788. A compilation of these and eight others, called the Federalist or the New Constitution, was published in two volumes in 1788 by J&A Mclean. The collection's original title was the Federalist, the title the Federalist Papers did not emerge until the 20th century.

21. The preamble to the constitution of India is as follows—We, the people of India, having solemnly resolved to constitute India into a Sovereign Socialist Secular Democratic Republic and to secure to all its citizens—Justice, social, economic and political, liberty of thought, expression, belief, faith and worship, equality of status and of opportunity; and to promote among them all.

Fraternity assuring the dignity of the individual and the unity and integrity of the Nation;

In our Constituent Assembly, this twenty-sixth day of November, 1949, do hereby adopt, enact and give to ourselves this constitution.

19. According to Schumpeter electoral system determines the nature of the party system. Schumpeter says that whenever universal suffrage was delayed the political party on its most advanced democratic forms was late in the appearing. Further, he said the first and foremost aim of each political party is to prevail over the others in order to get into power or to stay in it.

22. Rights available to foreigners living in India are as follows—

(*i*) Equality before law and equal protection of laws (Article-14).

(*ii*) Protection in respect of conviction for offences (A-20).

(*iii*) Protection of life and personal liberty (A-21).

(*iv*) Right to elementary education (A-21A).

(*v*) Protection against arrest and detention in certain cases (A-22).

(*vi*) Prohibition of traffic in human beings and forced labour (A-23).

(*vii*) Prohibition of employment of children in factories, etc. (A-24).

(*viii*) Freedom of conscience and free profession, practice and propagation of religion (A-25).

(*ix*) Freedom to manage religious affairs (A-26).

(*x*) Freedom from payment of taxes for promotion of any religion (A-27) and

(*xi*) Freedom from attending religious instruction or worship in certain educational institutions (A-28).

23. Article-76 of the Indian constitution has provided for the office of the Attorney General for India. He is the highest or the first law officer in the country. The Attorney General is appointed by the President. He must be a person who is qualified to be appointed a judge of the Supreme Court. In other words, he must be a citizen of India and he must have been a judge of some High court for five years or an advocate of some High court for ten years or an eminent jurist, in the opinion of the President.

24. According to the Article-169 "State Legislative Council" cannot be dissolved but can be abolished. Like the Rajya Sabha, the legislative council is a continuing chamber, that is, it is a permanent body and is not subject to dissolution. But, one-third of its members retire on the expiration of every second year. So, a member continues as such for six years.

25. Although the chairman and members of the State Public Service Commission are appointed by the Governor, they can be removed only by the President. Except members of the State Public Service Commission, the Governor can appoint and remove Advocate-General, members of the State Finance Commission and Vice-Chancellor of a State University.

26. Article-355 imposes a duty on the centre to ensure that the government of every state is carried on in accordance with the provisions of the constitution. It is this duty in the performance of which the centre takes over the government of a state under Article-356 in case of failure of constitutional machinery in the state. A proclamation imposing President's Rule must be approved by both the Houses of Parliament within two months from the date of its issue. If approved by both the Houses of Parliament, the President's Rule continues for 6 months. It can be extended for a maximum period of 3 years with the approval of the parliament, every 6 months.

27. The procedure for the amendment of the constitution as laid down in Article-368 is as follows—

(*i*) An amendment of the constitution can be initiated only by the introduction of a bill for the purpose in either House of Parliament and not in the state legislatures.

(*ii*) The bill must be passed in each House by a special majority, that is, a majority of the total membership of the House and a majority of two-thirds of the members of the House present and voting.

(*iii*) Each House must pass the bill separately. In case of a disagreement between the two Houses, there is no provisions for holding a joint sitting of the two Houses for the purpose of deliberation and passage of the bill.

(*iv*) If the bill seeks to amend the federal provisions of the constitution, it must also be ratified by the legislatures of half of the states by a simple majority, that is, a majority of the members of the House present and voting.

(*v*) After duly passed by both the Houses of Parliament and ratified by the state legislatures, where necessary, the bill is presented to the president for assent.

(*vi*) The President must give his assent to the bill. He an neither without his assent to the bill nor return the bill for reconsideration of the Parliament.

28. The constitution empowers the parliament to make laws on the subjects enumerated in the state list under the following conditions—

(*i*) When Rajya Sabha passes a resolution to that effect.

(*ii*) When a proclamation of National Emergency is in operation.

(*iii*) When two or more states make a joint request to the Parliament.

(*iv*) When necessary to give effect to international agreements, treaties and conventions.

(*v*) When President's Rule is in operation in the state.

29. The Judges Enquiry Act (1968) regulates the procedure relating to the removal of a judge of the supreme court by the process of impeachment—A removal motion signed by 100 members (in the case of Lok Sabha) or 50 members (in the case of Rajya Sabha) is to be given to the Speaker/Chairman. The Speaker/Chairman may admit the motion or refuse to admit it. If it is admitted, then the speaker/chairman is to constitute a three-members committee to investigate into the charges. The committee should consist of two judges of supreme court and a legal luminary.

33. Abraham Maslow in his classic paper 'A theory of Human Motivation—1943' propounded the 'Need Hierarchy' theory of human motivation. His popular book 'Motivation and Personality' was published in 1954.

Maslow's Need Hierarchy is the first systematic conceptual model of human motivation. He explained that human needs influence human behaviour. he, being a psychologist, understood human behaviour through psycho-analysis.

Maslow's Need Hierarchy concept consists of five levels of human needs. These human needs are in correct chronological order, as follows—Physiological—security—social or belongingness—Self esteem—self actualization.

36. A Public policy comprises certain elements. According to Austin Rammey, these are five—

(*i*) A particular object or set of objects—some designated part of the environment (an aspect of the society of physical world) which is intended to be affected.

(*ii*) A desired course of events—a particular sequence of behaviour desired in the particular object or set of objects.

(*iii*) A selected line of action—a particular set of actions chosen to bring about the desired course of event.

(*iv*) A declaration of intent—whether broadcast publicly to all who will listen, or communicated secretly to a special few, some statement by the policy-makers as to what they intend to do, how and why.

(*v*) An implementation of intent—the actions actually undertaken vis-a-vis the particular set of objectives in pursuance of the choices and declaration.

39. Robert K. Merton called bureaucrats as 'ruling servants'. A bureaucrat is a member of a bureaucracy and can compose the administration of any organization of any size although the term usually connotes someone within an institution of government. Some usages restrict the term so that it only embraces lower-ranked staff members in an agency, excluding higher-ranked managers, or so that it only signifies officials who perform certain functions such as those who work 'desk jobs' (the French Word for 'desk' being bureau, though bureau can also be translated as 'office').

40. The original constitution did not contain provisions with respect to tribunals. The 42nd Amendment Act of 1976 added a new part XIV-A to the constitution. This part is entitled as 'Tribunals' and consists of only two Articles—Article-323A dealing with administrative tribunals and Article-323B dealing with tribunals for other matters.

43. Kenneth Waltz is related to New Realist approach whether J.F. Nash, Thomas Schelling, Roger Fisher, etc. are related to Bargaining theory. The Bargaining theory is an extension of the Game theory. As Joseph Frankel observes, "Theory of bargaining is an application of the theory of game for international negotiations, or to put it in the terminology of the theory of game, the analysis of threats and deterrence and promises in mixed-motive-game-strategies."

47. The ASEAN was created in 1967 through Bangkok declaration by Indonesia, Malaysia, the Philippines, Singapore and Thailand. At the present time, the members of ASEAN are 10, such as Indonesia, Malaysia, the Philippines, Singapore, Thailand, Myanmar, Combodia, Laos, Vietnam and Brunei. The main objectives of the ASEAN are to accelerate the economic growth, social progress and cultural development in the region, to promote regional peace and stability, to promote active collaboration and mutual assistance on matters of common interest in the economic, social, cultural, technical, scientific and administrative fields, etc.

48. The security council is mainly an 'action agency' of the UN and thus is akin to the executive organ of government. Unlike the General Assembly it is much smaller but a continuous body, capable of meeting on any given day. Originally it consisted of 11 members. The first amendment of the charter in 1965 expanded its strength to 15 members. Now it has five permanent members USA, UK, Russia, France and the China and ten non-permanent members elected by the General Assembly for two years term.

50. The Non-Aligned Movement (NAM) is a group of states which are not formally aligned with or against any major power bloc. As of 2015, the movement has 120 members and 17 observer countries.

The organization was founded in Belgrade in 1961, and was largely conceived by India's first Prime Minister J.L. Nehru, Indonesia's first President Sukarno, Egyptian President A.G. Nasser, Ghana's President Kwame Nkruma and Yugoslavia's President J.B. Tito. Its different summits are as follows—2nd NAM Summit (1964) at Cairo, 3rd NAM Summit (1970) at Lusaka, 4th (1973) at Algiers and 5th (1976) at Colombo.

PAPER–III

Note: *This paper contains* ***seventy five (75)*** *objective type questions of* ***two (2)*** *marks each.* ***All*** *questions are* ***compulsory.***

1. Who among the following said, "Post-behaviouralism was a genuine revolution, not a reaction; a becoming, not a preservation; a reform, not a counter reformation"?

A. James Bryce
B. Charles E. Merriam
C. David Easton
D. G. A. Almond

2. Who among the following said, 'We can not shed our values in the way we remove our coats'?

A. Leo Strauss B. Alfred Cobban
C. Jean Blondel D. David Easton

3. Who among the following characterised early liberalism as 'possessive individualism'?

A. F. A. Hayek
B. Robert Nozick
C. C. B. MacPherson
D. Rawls

4. Given below are two statements, one labelled as Assertion (A) and the other labelled as Reason (R). Identify the correct answer.

Assertion (A): F. A. Hayek portrayed state intervention and collectivism, even in their moderate forms, as inevitably leading to an erosion of Liberty.

Reason (R): He is a supporter of laissez faire and opponent of Keynesian economics and the welfare state.

Codes:

A. Both (A) and (R) are true and (R) is the correct explanation of (A).
B. Both (A) and (R) are true, but (R) is not the correct explanation of (A)
C. (A) is true, but (R) is false
D. (A) is false, but (R) is true

5. Which one of the following statements is not true?
A. Marx drew distinction between 'ideology' and 'science'.
B. Napoleon denounced ideology as cloudy metaphysics that ignored history and reality.
C. de Tracy coined the term ideology.
D. Daniel Bell talked of 'ideology without an end'.

6. For whom, "ideas" and not the "material conditions of production" are the effective causes of revolution?
A. Karl Marx B. Lenin
C. Engels D. Stalin

7. Which of the following statements is false with respect to Plato's ideas?
A. Division of functions does not rest on difference of aptitude.
B. State is assumed to be merely individual writ large.
C. Athenian women were not allowed to participate in politics.
D. Ignorance and incompetence of politicians is the cause of democracy.

8. Which of the following is not an expression of the constitutional rule of Aristotle?
A. Rule in public interest
B. A lawful rule
C. A Government of willing subjects
D. Inconsistent with the dignity of the subjects

9. Who of the following said that felicity is "continued success in obtaining those things which a man from time to time desires"?
A. Bentham B. J.S. Mill
C. Hobbes D. Rousseau

10. Who of the following notes the existence of legislative, executive and federative powers of the state?
A. Hobbes B. Locke
C. Rousseau D. J. Bentham

11. Which of the following is not an idea of Rousseau?
A. A thinking man is a depraved animal
B. Science is the fruit of idle curiosity
C. Philosophy is mere intellectual frippery
D. General will is the sum total of wills

12. For J.S. Mill which one of the following is not true?
A. Pleasures differ in quality
B. The felicific calculus is absurd
C. The principle of utility is the final end of life
D. Liberty consists in doing what one desires

13. For Karl Marx, who among the following is not a Utopian socialist?
A. St. Simon B. Proudhon
C. .Fourier D. Engels

14. Given below are two statements, one labelled as Assertion (A) and other labelled as Reason (R). Select the correct answer from the codes given below:

Assertion (A): For Gandhiji, satyagraha is not identical to passive resistance.

Reason (R): Satyagraha denoted a legitimate, moral and truthful form of political action by the people against the Brutal state power.

Codes:
A. Both (A) and (R) are true and (R) is the correct explanation of (A)
B. Both (A) and (R) are true, but (R) is not the correct explanation of (A)
C. (A) is true, but (R) is false
D. (A) is false, but (R) is true

15. Who coined the slogan "No control, no co-operation"?
A. Mahatma Gandhi
B. J. Nehru
C. Aurobindo
D. Subhash Bose

16. What is the correct sequence of the following characteristics of political development ?
(*a*) Capacity
(*b*) Equality
(*c*) Differentiation

Select the correct answer from the codes given below:

Codes:

A. (*a*), (*b*) and (*c*) B. (*b*), (*a*) and (*c*)
C. (*c*), (*a*) and (*b*) D. (*c*), (*b*) and (*a*)

17. What is according to David Easton, the correct sequence of the following regulatory mechanisms?

(*a*) Socio-cultural norms
(*b*) Communication channels
(*c*) Gate-keeping at the boundary
(*d*) Reduction processes

Select the correct answer from the codes given below:

A. (*a*), (*c*), (*b*) and (*d*)
B. (*c*), (*a*), (*b*) and (*d*)
C. (*a*), (*b*), (*c*) and (*d*)
D. (*d*), (*b*), (*a*) and (*c*)

18. Match the following and select the correct pairs:

List-I (Authors)	List-II (Books)
(*a*) Arend Lijphart	(*i*) Comparative Federalism
(*b*) Thomas Hueglin	(*ii*) Comparing Federal System
(*c*) Giovanni Sartori	(*iii*) Patterns of Democracy : Government forms and performance in thirty-six countries
(*d*) Ronald L. Watts	(*iv*) Comparative constitutional Engineering : An Inquiry into structures, incentives and outcomes

Codes:

	(*a*)	(*b*)	(*c*)	(*d*)
A.	(*ii*)	(*iv*)	(*i*)	(*iii*)
B.	(*iv*)	(*ii*)	(*iii*)	(*i*)
C.	(*iii*)	(*i*)	(*iv*)	(*ii*)
D.	(*i*)	(*iii*)	(*ii*)	(*iv*)

19. Which of the following statements is not correct?

A. Political culture is a set of basic political attitudes.
B. Political culture cannot be empirically studied.
C. The study of political culture focuses on attitude of people and their likely effects on politics.
D. Political culture has a companion approach i.e. political socialisation.

20. In which of the following countries the residuary powers rest with the states/units?

(*a*) U.S.A.
(*b*) India
(*c*) Switzerland
(*d*) Australia

Select the correct answer from the codes given below:

Codes:

A. (*a*) and (*c*) B. (*c*) and (*d*)
C. (*a*) and (*d*) D. (*a*), (*c*) and (*d*)

21. Which of the following statements are correct?

(*a*) Cabinet is an extra-constitution institution in the United States of America.
(*b*) It is simply an advisory body.
(*c*) It is collectively responsible to the congress.
(*d*) The members of the cabinet quite often take part in the congress debates to defend the policy of the Government.

Select the correct answer from the codes of given below:

A. (*a*) and (*c*) B. (*a*) and (*b*)
C. (*b*) and (*d*) D. (*a*), (*b*) and (*d*)

22. Direct democracy is not possible in the modern times because:

A. People are indifferent towards the affairs of state.
B. Political parties are opposed to it.
C. Propertied classes oppose it.
D. Of the practical difficulties posed by the size and population of modern state.

23. Who among the following has given 'sleeping dogs' theory of democratic culture?

A. Lucian Pye and Robert E. Ward
B. James S. Coleman and Myron Weiner
C. James C. Charlesworth and F.W. Riggs
D. Almond and Verba

24. Who among the following has coined the terms 'The stick', 'The deal', 'The kiss', for influencing the decisions?

A. E.E. Schattschneider
B. Keith Boulding
C. Robert Dahl
D. Kate Millet

25. Which one of the following is a character of "Co-operative Federalism"?

A. A spirit of competition and rivalry between the centre and the state.
B. Co-operation secured on the basis of strong centre.
C. Decentralization and more state responsibility.
D. A spirit of co-operation among states.

26. Which one of the following practices is employed in the American legislative process in order to delay a particular legislation?

A. Gerrymandering B. Filibustering
C. Log Rolling D. Spoils system

27. The power that makes the Supreme Court of America the third Chamber of the legislative is:

A. Original B. Appellate
C. Advisory D. Judicial review

28. Who among the following has defined "political power" as the "relationship in which one person or a group is able to determine the actions of another in the direction of the former's own end"?

A. Bertrand Russel B. Habermas
C. Morgenthau D. David Easton

29. Given below are two statements, one labelled as Assertion (A) and the other labelled as Reason (R). Select the correct answer from the codes given below:

Assertion (A): Bureaucracy is an important feature of all democratic governments.

Reason (R): Bureaucracy is an ancient institution.

Codes:

A. Both (A) and (R) are true and (R) is the correct explanation of (A)
B. Both (A) and (R) are true, but (R) is not the correct explanation of (A)
C. (A) is true, but (R) is false
D. (A) is false, but (R) is true

30. Given below are two statements, one is labelled as Assertion (A) and the other labelled as Reason (R). Identify the correct answer.

Assertion (A): Comparative politics is a science of politics.

Reason (R): Comparative politics relies on empirical method of study.

Codes:

A. Both (A) and (R) are true and (R) is the correct explanation of (A)
B. Both (A) and (R) are true, but (R) is not the correct explanation of (A)
C. (A) is true, but (R) is false
D. (A) is false, but (R) is true

31. Match List-I with List-II and identify the correct answer from the codes given below:

List-I (Approach to study Indian Politics)	List-II (Name of Book and Author)
(*a*) Historical Approach	(*i*) Parliament in India, Morris Jones
(*b*) Institutional Approach	(*ii*) The Integration of Indian States, V.P. Menon
(*c*) Legal Approach	(*iii*) The modernity of Tradition, Rudolph and Rudolph
(*d*) Politico-sociological Approach	(*iv*) The Republic of India, Allen Gledhill

Codes:

	(*a*)	(*b*)	(*c*)	(*d*)
A.	(*i*)	(*iii*)	(*ii*)	(*iv*)
B.	(*ii*)	(*i*)	(*iv*)	(*iii*)
C.	(*i*)	(*ii*)	(*iv*)	(*iii*)
D.	(*iii*)	(*ii*)	(*i*)	(*iv*)

32. The Constituent Assembly of India comprised of:

A. 292 members from British provinces, 4 from Chief Commissionaires and 93 from Princely States

B. 294 members from British provinces, 4 from Chief Commissionaires and 91 from Princely States

C. 291 members from British provinces, 3 from Chief Commissionaires and 95 from Princely States

D. 292 members from British provinces, 5 from Chief Commissionaires and 92 from Princely States

33. Match List-I with List-II and identify the correct answer from the codes given below:

List-I (Name of Philosophy)	**List-II (Directive Principle)**
(*a*) Welfarism	(*i*) Promotion of cottage industry
(*b*) Socialism	(*ii*) Better health and living standard
(*c*) Gandhian philosophy	(*iii*) Promotion of international peace and security
(*d*) Internationalism	(*iv*) Equal pay for equal work

Codes:

	(*a*)	(*b*)	(*c*)	(*d*)
A.	(*i*)	(*iii*)	(*ii*)	(*iv*)
B.	(*ii*)	(*iii*)	(*i*)	(*iv*)
C.	(*i*)	(*ii*)	(*iv*)	(*iii*)
D.	(*ii*)	(*iv*)	(*i*)	(*iii*)

34. In which part and article of the Constitution of India, Fundamental Duties have been mentioned:

A. Part IV, Article 51

B. Part III, Article 51

C. Part IV (A), Article 51 (A)

D. Part III (A), Article 51 (A)

35. Given below are two statements, one labelled as Assertion (A) and the other labelled as Reason (R). Choose the correct answer using the codes given below:

Assertion (A): Ordinances provide minority governments with a useful device, but one that is now increasingly difficult to convert into legislation once parliament has covered.

Reason (R): Recent coalition governments have used ordinances to avoid debating legislation with their partners as much as with the opposition.

Codes:

A. Both (A) and (R) are correct and (R) is the correct explanation of (A)

B. Both (A) and (R) are correct, but (R) is not the correct explanation of (A)

C. (A) is true, but (R) is false

D. (A) is false, but (R) is true

36. Under which article/articles, the High Courts and the Supreme Court can issue writs?

A. Articles 44 and 45

B. Articles 123 and 213

C. Articles 32 and 226

D. Articles 53 and 153

37. Identify the incorrect pair.

(Name of State)		**(Demand for New State)**
A. Gujarat	:	Saurashtra
B. Uttar Pradesh	:	Gorkhaland
C. Rajasthan	:	Marupradesh
D. Maharashtra	:	Vidarbha

38. Which of the following Committee voiced concern about 'Criminalization of politics and politicization of criminals'?

A. Tarakunde Committee

B. Sachhar Committee

C. Vohra Committee

D. Indrajeet Gupta Committee

39. The study of state politics as an autonomous discipline has been primarily an outcome of:

A. Rise of regional parties

B. Rise of voter's turn out

C. New local governance system
D. Non-party political movements

40. Match List-I with List-II and select the correct answer from codes given below:

List-I (Concept)	List-II (Thinkers)
(*a*) Multi-culturalism	(*i*) Friedrik A. Hayek
(*b*) Post-modernism	(*ii*) Bhikhu Parekh
(*c*) Libertariansim	(*iii*) Amitai Etzioni
(*d*) Communitarianism	(*iv*) Michel Foucault

Codes:

	(*a*)	(*b*)	(*c*)	(*d*)
A.	(*i*)	(*ii*)	(*iv*)	(*iii*)
B.	(*ii*)	(*iv*)	(*i*)	(*iii*)
C.	(*iii*)	(*i*)	(*ii*)	(*iv*)
D.	(*iv*)	(*iii*)	(*i*)	(*ii*)

41. Which one of the following pairs is not correctly matched:

(Authors)		(Books)
A. S.M. Lipset	:	Political man : The Social Bases of politics
B. Lenin	:	Neo-colonialism : The highest stage of Imperialism
C. L. Anderson	:	Transitions to Democracy
D. Charles Tilly	:	From Mobilisation to Revolution

42. Who was the Chairman of the inaugural session of constituent assembly?
A. Dr. B.R. Ambedkar
B. Dr. Rajendra Prasad
C. Dr. Sacchidanand
D. Sardar Patel

43. Which of the following are statutory bodies?
(*a*) University Grants Commission
(*b*) Union Public Service Commission
(*c*) National Commission for Human Rights
(*d*) National Commission for Minorities

Select the correct answer from the codes given below:
A. (*a*) and (*b*)
B. (*b*) and (*c*)
C. (*c*) and (*d*)
D. (*a*), (*c*) and (*d*)

44. For the First time the communist party of India came into power in the state of:
A. West Bengal B. Tripura
C. Kerala D. Goa

45. Which one of the following rights was recognized by the Supreme Court in the Selvy Case Judgement (2010)?
A. Right to Mental Privacy
B. Right to purchase property in Jammu and Kashmir
C. Right to form pressure groups
D. NOTA (None of the above)

46. Arrange the following phases in the evolution of public administration as a discipline in chronological order using the codes given below:
(*a*) Ecological approach
(*b*) Principles approach
(*c*) Politics-Administration dichotomy
(*d*) Public Policy approach

Codes:
A. (*c*), (*a*), (*d*), (*b*)
B. (*c*), (*b*), (*d*), (*a*)
C. (*b*), (*c*), (*a*), (*d*)
D. (*c*), (*b*), (*a*), (*d*)

47. Match List-I with List-II and select the correct answer from codes given below :

List-I (Books)	List-II (Authors)
(*a*) Frontiers of Development Administration	(i) Braibanti
(*b*) Political and Administrative Development	(*ii*) Ferrel Heady
(*c*) Bureaucracy and Political Development	(*iii*) Fred W. Riggs
(*d*) Public Administration: A Comparative Perspective	(*iv*) J. La Palombara

Codes:

	(*a*)	(*b*)	(*c*)	(*d*)
A.	(*ii*)	(*iv*)	(*i*)	(*iii*)
B.	(*iii*)	(*i*)	(*iv*)	(*ii*)
C.	(*i*)	(*iii*)	(*ii*)	(*iv*)
D.	(*iv*)	(*ii*)	(*iii*)	(*i*)

48. Which one of the following statements about systems approach to organisation is not correct?

A. It is derived from one general systems theory

B. It leads to certain fundamental principles of organisation

C. It studies the organisation as a whole in relation to its environment

D. It views the organisation and its environment as interdependent for inputs and resources

49. In his 'Principles of administration', Pfiffner did not include:

A. Material and supply

B. Functions and powers of local authorities

C. Methods and procedure

D. Administrative accountability

50. 'Public Choice Approach' to public administration came into existence in the:

A. 1890s B. 1920s

C. 1940s D. 1960s

51. Who has analyzed leadership in terms of 'circular response'?

A. L. Urwick

B. H. Simon

C. C.I. Barnard

D. M.P. Follett

52. Which one of the following is not a feature of Barnard's theory of formal organisation?

A. General incentives

B. Common purpose

C. Communications

D. Willingness to cooperate

53. Which one of the following committees dealt with political activities of civil servants in Britain?

A. Mastermann Committee

B. Plowden Committee

C. Assheton Committee

D. Northcote-Trevelyan Committee

54. Consider the following statements and choose the correct answer using the codes given below:

The Civil Service Reform Act 1978 of the United States of America introduced:

(*a*) Performance budgeting system

(*b*) Merit pay provision for middle managerial personnel

(*c*) Performance appraisal system

(*d*) Office of Personnel Management

Codes:

A. (*a*), (*c*) and (*d*)

B. (*b*) and (*d*)

C. (*b*), (*c*) and (*d*)

D. (*a*) and (*d*)

55. Given below are two statements, one labelled as Assertion (A) and the other as Reason (R). Choose the correct answer using the codes given below:

Assertion (A): "Henri Fayol identified five elements as the primary functions of management activity."

Reason (R): According to Henri Fayol, "knowledge of administration is needed at higher levels of an organisation, rather than technical knowledge."

Codes:

A. Both (A) and (R) are true and (R) is the correct explanation of (A)

B. Both (A) and (R) are true, but (R) is not the correct explanation of (A)

C. (A) is true, but (R) is false

D. (A) is false, but (R) is true

56. Functional specialization in the Indian Administrative service was recommended by:

A. First Administrative Reforms Commission

B. Satish Chandra Committee

C. Appleby Report

D. Sarkaria Commission

57. 'Delegated legislation' is not:

A. Subordinate legislation

B. Executive legislation

C. Ordinance making power

D. Rule making power

58. Match List-I with List-II and choose the correct answer using the codes given below:

List-I (Citizen's grievance redressal)	List-II (Countries)
(*a*) Procurator system	(*i*) France
(*b*) Administrative Courts	(*ii*) Russia
(*c*) Ombudsman	(*iii*) Britain
(*d*) Parliamentary commissioner	(*iv*) Sweden.

Codes:

	(*a*)	(*b*)	(*c*)	(*d*)
A.	(*iii*)	(*ii*)	(*iv*)	(*i*)
B.	(*ii*)	(*i*)	(*iv*)	(*iii*)
C.	(*i*)	(*iii*)	(*iv*)	(*ii*)
D.	(*i*)	(*ii*)	(*iv*)	(*iii*)

59. The system of Efficiency Rating for scientifically assessing the performance of public officials for promotion first originated in:

A. China B. Japan
C. U.S.A. D. U.K.

60. Ashok Mehta Committee in 1977 recommended for the establishment of:

A. Nagar Panchayat
B. Panchayat Samiti
C. Maha Panchayat
D. Mandal Panchayat

61. Who among the following is associated with the concept of Realistic Liberalism?

A. E.H. Carr
B. Robert Byrd
C. George Kennan
D. John Herz

62. Bachract and Baratz have mentioned about the three classes of International Relations to control the conduct of states. Which of the following are the three classes?

(*a*) Influence Relationship
(*b*) Force Relationship
(*c*) Legitimate Relationship
(*d*) Power Relationship

Select the correct answer from the codes given below:

A. (*b*), (*c*) and (*d*) B. (*a*), (*c*) and (*d*)
C. (*d*), (*c*) and (*b*) D. (*b*), (*c*) and (*a*)

63. Which one of the following books was written by E.H. Carr?

A. The open society and its enemies
B. Twenty years crisis
C. Political Realism and Political Idealism
D. The Realities of American Foreign Policy

64. Frants Faron was the first scholar to use the term "Third World". To which country he belonged?

A. France B. England
C. Algeria D. Egypt

65. Which of the following pairs is not correctly matched?

Author		Book
A. William C. Olson	:	The Growth of a Discipline
B. G.F. Kennan	:	American Diplomacy
C. Russel H. Fifield	:	The Introductory Course in International Relations
D. Robert Strausz-Hupe and Stefan Possony	:	Intenational Relations : A General Theory

66. Who condemned Non-alignment as a selfish policy?

A. Morgenthau
B. William Johnstone
C. Schwarzenberger
D. Edward Crankshaw

67. Who among the following are supporters of Realistic Approach in International Politics ?

(*a*) Couloumbis and Wolfe
(*b*) Fredrick Schuman
(*c*) Nicholas Spykman
(*d*) E.H. Carr

Select the correct answer from the codes given below:

A. (*b*), (*c*) and (*d*)
B. (*a*), (*c*) and (*d*)
C. (*a*), (*b*) and (*d*)
D. (*a*), (*b*) and (*c*)

68. Who among the following had declared that arms race in itself is experience of terror?

A. Hadley Bull
B. Arnold Toynbee
C. Kenneth Boulding
D. Lynn Miller

69. Which of the following countries was a part of recently concluded P5+1 Nuclear Argument?

A. Japan
B. Australia
C. India
D. Germany

70. Which of the following is not a form of National Power?

A. Social Power
B. Military Power
C. Psychological Power
D. Economic Power

71. Which of the following countries is not a member of SAARC?

A. Maldives
B. Myanmar
C. Nepal
D. Afghanistan

72. Which of the following scholars of International Politics did not subscribe to this view that no social science can survive without idealistic aspects?

A. Herbert Butterfield
B. E.H. Carr
C. Reinhold Niebuhr
D. Arnold Wolters

73. Which of the following is also called as Total Disarmament?

A. Qualitative Disarmament
B. Quantitative Disarmament
C. General Disarmament
D. Comprehensive Disarmament

74. Who stated, "International Politics includes analysis of political relations and problems of peace among nations"?

A. Charles Scheichar
B. Norman Padelford
C. Harold Sprout
D. H.J. Morgenthau

75. Which member State of ASEAN had joined this regional organisation in 1999?

A. Laos
B. Myanmar
C. Combodia
D. Vietnam

ANSWERS

1	2	3	4	5	6	7	8	9	10
C	D	C	A	D	B	A	D	C	B
11	**12**	**13**	**14**	**15**	**16**	**17**	**18**	**19**	**20**
D	C	D	A	C	B	B	C	B	D
21	**22**	**23**	**24**	**25**	**26**	**27**	**28**	**29**	**30**
B	D	D	B	C	B	D	D	B	A
31	**32**	**33**	**34**	**35**	**36**	**37**	**38**	**39**	**40**
B	A	D	C	B	C	B	C	A	B
41	**42**	**43**	**44**	**45**	**46**	**47**	**48**	**49**	**50**
B	C	D	C	B	D	B	B	B	D
51	**52**	**53**	**54**	**55**	**56**	**57**	**58**	**59**	**60**
D	A	A	B	B	A	C	B	C	D
61	**62**	**63**	**64**	**65**	**66**	**67**	**68**	**69**	**70**
D	B	B	C	D	C	A	A	D	A
71	**72**	**73**	**74**	**75**					
B	D	D	D	C					

SOME SELECTED EXPLANATORY ANSWERS

1. In 1969 David Easton announced a new revolution that represented a shift of focus from strict methodological issues to a greater concern with public responsibilities. It stood for no complete departure from behaviourism rather it stood for consolidating it gains and applying them for problem solving and crisis management. Further he said, "Post-behaviouralism was a genuine revolution, not a reaction; a becoming, not a preservation; a reform, not a counter reformation."

2. The purpose here is not to discard the informative and the normative approaches, but rather to draw from both to build a formative approach wherein the student of political science is exposed, as far as possible, to rational and plausible perspectives. We say "as far as possible" because even conscious objectivity is not free from value judgements. As Easton says, "Whatever effort is exerted, in undertaking research we cannot shed our values in the way we remove our coats."

3. C.B. Macpherson's best-known contribution to political philosophy is the theory of "Possessive Individualism", in which an individual is conceived as the sole proprietor of his or her skills and owes nothing to society for them. These skills (and those of others) are a commodity to be bought and sold on the open market, and in such a society is demonstrated a selfish and unending thirst for consumption which is considered the crucial core of human nature. Macpherson spent most of his career battling these premises, but perhaps the greatest single exposition of this view can be found in The Political Theory of Possessive Individualism, where Macpherson examines the function of this particular kind of individualism in Hobbes, Harrington and Locke (and several writers in between, including the Levellers) and its resulting pervasiveness throughout most liberal literature of the period. An avowed socialist, he believed that this culture of possessive individualism prevented individuals from developing their powers of rationality, moral judgment, contemplation and even friendship and love. These were the "truly human powers," Macpherson claimed.

5. Daniel Bell argued that ideologies are exhausted and we have reached a post industrial society. They are prone to similar developments. Whatever differences and problems exist between them are purely of technical nature and do not require remedies in the doses of ideologies. Hence, Daniel Bell talked of 'ideology without an end' is not true.

6. According to V.I. Lenin, 'ideas' and not the 'material conditions of production' are the effective causes of revolution. Lenin was the most influential Marxist theorist of the twentieth century. He was primarily concerned with the issues of organisation and revolution, emphasising the central importance of a tightly-organized 'vanguard' party to lead and guide the proletarian class. He also emphasized on the necessity of ideology for proletarian class.

7. Plato taught that the material world consists of imperfect copies of abstract and eternal 'ideas'. His political philosophy, as expounded in the Republic, is an attempt to describe the 'ideal state' in terms of a theory of justice. Plato's just state was decidedly authoritarian and was based upon a strict division of labour that supposedly reflected different character-types and human attributes. He argued that government should be exercised exclusively by a small collection of philosopher-kings, supported by the auxiliaries (collectively termed the 'Guardians'), whose education and communistic way of life would ensure that

ruled on the basis of wisdom. In his view, knowledge and virtue are one.

8. According to Aristotle an expression of the constitutional rule are as follows—There is supremacy of law in his ideal state. He favours impersonal rule of law which represents the wisdom of community since the ages. It is an ethical institution to develop the moral qualities of the citizens to promote good and happy life of everyone. A government of willing subjects and consistent with the dignity of the subjects.

9. Thomas Hobbes said about human nature, "The end of every man is continued success in obtaining those things which he desires time to time". In life there exists a perpetual and restless desire of power because it helps in getting pleasure and avoiding pain.

Since all men desire more or less the same thing and they are roughly equal in strength and cunning, there is bound to be what, he calls "war of every man against every man". Thus, man is essentially selfish, altruistic, non-rational, impulsive and self-centred. Such a nature is transformed while entering into contract and forming state.

10. John Locke notes the existence of legislative, executive and federative powers of the state. Locke's view on state are outcome of his concept of human nature. According to Prof. Vaughan "everything in Locke's system revolves round the individual; everything is disposed so as to ensure the sovereignty of the individual." He expounds a mechanical state whose prime raison-de-etre is to protect the natural rights to life, liberty and property. In fact the state is secondary and natural rights are of primary importance in his scheme.

11. In his book 'The Social Contract–1762', Rousseau defined the General Will as that "which tends always to the preservation and welfare of the whole. The general will, therefore, represents the collective interests of society; it will benefit all citizens, rather than merely private individuals". Rousseau thus drew a clear distinction between the general will and the selfish, private will of each citizen, the general will is, in effect, what the people would wish if they were to act selflessly. The problem with such a notion of the public interest is that, so long as they persist in being selfish, it cannot be constructed on the basis of the revealed preferences of individual citizens. It is possible, in other words, that citizens may not recognize the general will as their own, even though Rousseau clearly believed that it reflected the 'higher' interests of each and every member of society.

12. J.S. Mill, one of the respected political thinker in British political circle was the last of the utilitarians and foremost of the individualists. His defence of utilitarianism marked following changes in Benthamite utilitarianism—

Mill made qualitative difference between different kinds of pleasures. He modified Bentham's thesis on quality being more important and holds that poetry is superior and preferable to pushpin or any other game. He abandoned the hedonistic 'felicitous calculus'. To him, pleasure or pain is only a subjective sensation that can not be objectively measured. Instead of pleasure, he makes dignity as final end of human life. To him, a sense of dignity is natural for human beings. Liberty consists in doing what one desires.

13. Engels is not a utopian socialist for Karl Marx. A utopia is literally an ideal or perfect society. The term was first used in utopia by Thomas More. Utopianism is a style of social theorising that develops a critique of the existing order by constructing a model of an ideal or perfect alternative. However, utopianism is not a political philosophy nor an ideological tradition. Substantive utopias differ from one another, and utopian thinkers have not advanced a common conception of the good life. Nevertheless, most utopias are characterized by the abolition of want, the absence of conflict, and the avoidance of violence and oppression. Socialism in general, and anarchism and Marxism in particular, have a marked disposition towards utopianism, reflecting their belief in the human potential for sociable, cooperative and gregarious behaviour. Socialist utopias, as a result, are strongly egalitarian and typically characterized by collective property ownership and a reduction in, or eradication of, political authority. Other utopias have been based upon faith in the benign influence of government and political authority.

15. Sri Aurobindo Ghosh coined the slogan "No control, no co-operation". In the context of modern Indian political theory and practice, Aurobindo presented an exalted, purified and sanctified nationalism. He was bold and had a straight vision and that was to achieve absolute Swaraj. He never interpreted nationalism as a narrow creed. He believed that five Indian values, namely, Dharma, Tapasya, Jganam, Bhramacharya and Shakti as dynamic galvanizing forces that rejuvenate the entire movement as well as the leaders and their followers.

20. The system of the United states, Switzerland and Australia are that their central governments have been given enumerated powers whereas the residuary powers are left with their state governments.

For the United States this point is covered by the tenth Amendment which provides that "the powers not delegated to the United States by the constitution nor prohibited by it to the states, are reserved to the states respectively, or to the people."

The Swiss constitution expressly declares that the Cantons "are sovereign in so far as their sovereignty is not limited by the Federal constitution, and, as such they exercise all rights which are not transferred to the Federal power."

21. The U.S. cabinet was created by Article-2, Section-2 of the U.S. constitution in 1787. The cabinet members, called secretaries, are appointed by the president to provide advice in matters related to their areas of expertise. In addition, cabinet members lead national and international policy creation and execution for their departments.

22. Direct democracy is not possible in the modern times because of the practical difficulties posed by the size and population of modern state. Modern democratic theories are closely abound to the idea of representation. When citizens no longer rule directly, democracy is based upon the claim that politicians serve as the people's representative. In politics, representation suggests that an individual or group somehow stands for, or on behalf of, a larger collection of people. Political representation therefore acknowledges a link between two otherwise separate entities—government and the governed—and implies that though this link the people's views are articulated or their interests are secured.

23. Almond and Verba's 'sleeping dogs' theory of democratic culture, which emphasizes the importance of passivity and deference, has been rejected by those who argue that political participation is the very stuff of democracy. Low electoral turnouts, for example, may reflect widespread alienation and ingrained disadvantage, rather than political contentment. Second, a civic culture may be more a consequence of democracy rather than its cause. In other words, the assumption that political attitudes and values shape behaviour, and not the reverse, is unproven. Third, this approach tends to treat political culture as being homogeneous; that is; as little more than a cipher for national culture or national character.

24. Keith Boulding has coined the terms 'The stick', 'The deal', 'The kiss' for influencing the decisions. Decision-making associated with liberal and pluralist perceptions focussing on who actually makes the decision. Boulding argues decision-making influenced in three ways—The stick (coercion), The deal (mutual benefit through negotiation) and The Kiss (sense of loyalty and commitment to individual, thus he has power).

25. Federalism involves the division of law-making power between a central body and a number of territorial units. Each level of government is allocated a range of duties, powers and functions, specified by some kind of constitutional document. Sovereignty is therefore divided between the centre and the periphery as, at least in theory, neither level of government may encroach upon the powers of the other.

'Co-operative Federalism' has character of decentralization and more state responsibility. Granville Austin called the Indian Federalism as a 'cooperative federalism'.

26. Filibustering is a senatorial device in the American legislative process by which a particular legislation are delayed by members through participating in debate for longer period. Senate enjoys co-equal power with House of Representative in the matter of legislation. Senate has wide ranging investigative functions and the strongest second chamber of the world.

27. The power that makes the Supreme Court of America the third chamber of the legislative is judicial review. Judicial review is the power of the Supreme Court to examine the constitutionality of legislative enactments and executive orders of both the central and state governments. On examination, if they are found to be violative of the constitution (ultra-vires), they can be declared as illegal, unconstitutional and invalid (null and void) by the supreme court. Consequently, they cannot be enforced by the governments.

32. The constituent Assembly was constituted in November 1946 under the scheme formulated by the Cabinet Mission Plan. The features of the scheme were—

The total strength of the constituent Assembly was to be 389. Of these, 296 seats were to be allotted to British India and 93 seats to the Princely states. Out of 296 seats allotted to the British India, 292 members were to be drawn from the eleven governors' provinces and 4 from the four chief commissioners' provinces, one from each.

34. In 1976, the Congress party set up the Sardar Swarn Singh Committee to make recommendations about Fundamental duties, the need and necessity of which was felt during the operation of the internal emergency (1975-77). The committee recommended the inclusion of a separate chapter on fundamental duties in the constitution. It stressed that the citizens should become conscious that in addition to the enjoyment of rights, they also have certain duties to perform as well. The Congress Government at centre accepted these recommendations and enacted the 42nd Constitutional Amendment Act in 1976. This amendment added a new part, namely, part IVA to the constitution. This new part consists of only one Article, that is, Article-51A. At present time, there are 11 Fundamental duties for the citizens of India.

36. Under the Articles-32 & 226, the Supreme court and the High courts can issue writs. The Supreme Court (under Article-32) and the High Courts (under Article-226) can issue the writs of Habeas corpus, Mandamus, Prohibition, Certiorari and Quo-Warranto. Further, the parliament (under Article-32) can empower any other court to issue these writs. Since no such provision has been made so far, only the supreme court and the high court can issue the writs and not any other courts. Before 1950, only the High Courts of Calcutta, Bombay and Madras had the power to issue the writs. Article-226 now empowers all the High Courts to issue the writs.

38. Vohra committee voiced concern about 'criminalization of politics and politicization of criminals'. The Vohra Committee Report was submitted by the former Indian Union Home Secretary, N.N. Vohra, in October 1993. It studied the problem of the criminalisation of politics and of the nexus among criminals, politicians and bureaucrats in India.

The report contained several observations made by official agencies on the criminal network which was virtually running a parallel government. It also discussed criminal gangs who enjoyed the patronage of politicians, of all parties, and the protection of government functionaries. It revealed that political leaders had become the leaders of gangs. They were connected to the military over the years criminals had been elected to local bodies, State Assemblies and Parliament. The unpublished annexures to the Vohra Report were believed to contain highly explosive material.

39. The study of state politics as an autonomous discipline has been primarily an outcome of rise of regional parties. Clearly, when we talk about the autonomy of state politics, we are talking about autonomy from national politics. In the last two decades, state politics has broken free of the logic of national politics and has acquired a rhythm and logic of its own. This manifests itself in many ways related to one another.

'Regional parties' or state-wide parties, have become more salient than ever before. One cannot even begin to play the favourite national sports of 'Kaun banega PM' without factoring in the prospects and the proclivities of the AIADMK, TDP, SP, BSP, JD(U), RJD and the TMC, even if one overlooks the regional parties that are now somewhat stable allies of the UPA or the NDA. The state units of national parties too are more independent, at least in terms of the issues, strategies and styles, if not leadership, than used to be the case. In some non-trivial ways, the CPM units in West Bengal, Kerala and Tripura are three different parties.

42. The inaugural session of constituent assembly on December 9, 1946. The Muslim League boycotted the meeting and insisted on a separate state of Pakistan. The meeting was thus attended by only 211 members. Dr. Sachchidanand Sinha, the oldest member, was elected as the temporary president of the assembly.

Later, on December 11, 1946, Dr. Rajendra Prasad and H.C. Mukherjee were elected as the President and Vice-president of the assembly respectively. Sir B.N. Rau was appointed as the constitutional advisor to the assembly.

43. University Grants Commission, National Commission for Human Rights and National Commission for Minorities are the statutory bodies. These commissions are established under legislation enacted by the parliament. Whether Union Public Service Commission (UPSC) is an independent constitutional body in the sense that it has been directly created by the constitution. Articles 315 to 323 in part XIV of the constitution contain elaborate provisions regarding the composition, appointment and removal of members along with the independence, powers and functions of the UPSC.

44. For the first time the communist party of India came into power in Kerala. EMS Namboodripad was an Indian communist politician and theorist, who served as the first chief minister of Kerala state in 1957-59 and then again in 1967-69. As a member of the CPI, he became the first non-Indian National Congress chief minister in the Indian republic. In 1964, he led a faction of the CPI that broke away to form the Communist Party of India (Marxist) (CPM).

46. As an academic discipline Public Administration has its origin in the work of Dr. Woodrow Wilson of U.S.A. who published an article entitled "The Study of Administration–1887". However, soon after a tortuous and unending debate started on its disciplinary character. It has taken several strides in the form of scientific management movement followed by Human Relations Approach of Elton Mayo, Decision Making Approach of Herbert Simon as well as system and structural Functional Approaches.

There are six phases of its development. Politics-Administration dichotomy, principles approach, Ecological approach, Public policy approach, scientific or logical positivist approach and New Public Management.

50. The most unique quality of Public Choice Approach Theory is that it was propounded by the scholars of the decade of 1960's of economic discipline.

Public Choice Approach Theory strictly opposes the bureaucratic model of administration. Vincent Ostrom is a supporter and protagonist of the Public Choice Approach Theory.

56. Functional specialization in the Indian Administrative Service was recommended by first Administrative Reforms Commission. The first ARC was established on 5 January 1966. The ARC was initially chaired by Morarji Desai and later on K. Hanumanthaiah became its chairman when Desai became the Deputy Prime minister of India. The commission submitted the 20 reports before winding up in mid-1970s.

57. 'Delegated legislation' is not ordinance making power. Often, a legislature passes statutes that set out broad outlines and principles, and delegated authority to an executive branch official to issue delegated legislation that flesh out the details (Substantive regulation) and provide procedures for implementing the substantive provisions of the statute and substantive regulations (procedural regulations). Delegated legislation can also be changed faster than primary legislation, so legislatures can delegate issues that may need to be fine-turned through experience.

60. In December 1977, The Janata Government appointed a committee on Panchayati Raj institutions under the chairmanship of Ashok Mehta. It submitted its report in August 1978 and made 132 recommendations to revive and strengthen the declining Panchayati Raj System in the country. It recommended that the three-tier system of Panchayati Raj should be replaced by the two-tier system, that is, Zila Parishad at the district level, and below it, the Mandal Panchayat consisting of a group of villages with a total population of 15000 to 20000.

63. The Twenty years crisis (1919-1939) is a book on international relations written by E.H. Carr. The book was written in the 1930s shortly before the outbreak of World War II in Europe and the first edition was published in September 1939, shortly after the war's outbreak, a second edition was published in 1945. In the revised edition, Carr did not "re-write every passage which has been in someway modified by the subsequent course of events", but rather decided "to modify a few sentences" and undertake other small efforts to improve the clarity of the work.

69. The P5+1 is a group of six world powers which, in 2006, joined together in diplomatic efforts with Iran with regard to its nuclear programme. The term refers to the UN Security Council's five permanent members (the P5); namely China, France, Russia, the United Kingdom and the United States; plus Germany.

70. National Power is the ability or capability of a nation to secure the goals and objectives of its national interests in relation with other nations. It involves the capacity to use force or threat of use of force or influence over others for securing the goals of national interest.

The three forms of national power are inseparable from each other. Without economic power no nation can develop her military power, and without the latter no nation can play an active role in international relations. Psychological power can be enduringly and really effective only when it is backed by economic and military power.

71. Myanmar is not a member of SAARC. SAARC (South Asian Association for Regional Co-operation) was formed in December, 1985 at Dhaka. India, Pakistan, Nepal, Bhutan, Bangladesh, Sri Lanka and Maldives are its founding members. Afghanistan became its 8th member in 2007. The original idea of this organisation was put forward by the president Zia-ur-Rahman of Bangladesh.

74. Morgenthau stated that, "International Politics includes analysis of political relations and problems of peace among nations". Morgenthau is a realist thinker. Realism focuses on state security and power above all else. Early realists such as E.H. Carr and Hans Morgenthau argued that states are self-interested, power-seeking rational actors, who seek to maximize their security and chances of survival. Cooperation between states is a way to maximize each individual state's security. Similarly, any act of war must be based on self-interest, rather than on idealism.

75. ASEAN (Association of South East Asian Nations) was formed in 1967 by Indonesia, Malaysia, Philippines, Singapore and Thailand with the main aim of guiding economic progress and promote economic stability in the region. Later on, Brunei (1984), Vietnam (1995), Laos and Myanmar (1997) and Cambodia (1999) became its member. The main objectives of this organisation are to accelerate the economic growth, social progress and cultural development in the region.

Previous Paper (Solved)

UGC-NET Political Science, December 2014

PAPER–II

Note: *This paper contains **fifty (50)** objective type questions of **two (2)** marks each. **All** questions are compulsory.*

1. Who among the following defined civil power as "the right of making laws with penalties... for the regulating and preserving of property, and of employing the force of the community, in the execution of such laws... all this only for the public good."?

A. Rousseau B. Karl Marx
C. John Locke D. J.S. Mill

2. Who of the following said that, "the emancipation of the working class is the work of the working class itself"?

A. Mao Tse Tung B. V.I. Lenin
C. Engels D. Karl Marx

3. Who of the following gave the slogan "Turn the imperialist war into a civil war, that is, into to a proletarian revolution."?

A. Kautsky B. Trotsky
C. Engels D. Lenin

4. Which of the following is not a feature of liberal communitarian debate?

A. Conception of self : 'encumbered' *vs.* 'unencumbered'
B. 'Universalism' *vs.* 'Particularism'
C. 'State neutrality' *vs.* 'non-neutrality of State'
D. Totalitarianism : 'procedural' *vs.* 'communitarian'

5. Given below are two statements, one labelled as Assertion (A) and the other labelled as Reason (R):

Assertion (A) : For Plato great diversity of wealth was inconsistent with good government.

Reason (R): He saw no way to abolish the evil except by abolishing wealth itself, so far as soldiers and rulers are concerned.

Codes:

A. Both (A) and (R) are true and (R) is the correct explanation of (A)
B. Both (A) and (R) are true, but (R) is not the correct explanation of (A)
C. (A) is true, but (R) is false
D. (A) is false, but (R) is true

6. Identify the correct sequence of the books written on Mahatma Gandhi on ascending order:

(*i*) Richard Attenborough	– *In Search of Gandhi*
(*ii*) C.F. Andrews	– *Mahatma Gandhi's Ideas*
(*iii*) B. Bhattacharya	– *Evolution of the Political Philosophy of Mahatma Gandhi*
(*iv*) J.B. Kripalani	– *Gandhian Thought*

Select the correct answer from the codes given below:

A. (*ii*), (*iv*), (*iii*), (*i*) B. (*i*), (*ii*), (*iii*), (*iv*)
C. (*iii*), (*i*), (*iv*), (*ii*) D. (*iv*), (*iii*), (*i*), (*ii*)

7. St. Augustine's *De Civitate Dei* is divided into

A. 19 books B. 20 books
C. 21 books D. 22 books

8. Which of the following is not a reason for the decline of political theory of David Easton?

A. Historicism
B. Moral Relativism
C. Ideological Reductionism
D. Hyperfactualism

9. Which of the following is not a feature of Jayaprakash Narayan's partyless democracy?
A. Dispersal of political power
B. Constant watch of the representatives by the electing bodies
C. Maximum propaganda
D. Comparatively less expensive elections

10. Who of the following advocated economic theory of democracy?
A. J. Lively B. C.B. Macpherson
C. Anthony Downs D. D. Held

11. Comparative politics as an autonomous discipline emerged
A. in the 1970s B. in the 1960s
C. in the 1950s D. in the 1930s

12. Which of the following are the characteristics of a system, according to Almond?
1. Comprehensiveness
2. Inter-dependence
3. Existence of boundaries
4. Availability of resources

Select the correct answer from the codes given below:

Codes:
A. 2, 3 and 4 B. 1, 3 and 4
C. 1, 2 and 4 D. 1, 2 and 3

13. Who among the following has used the concepts of goal changing, feedback and learning ?
A. David Easton B. Karl Deutsch
C. Gabriel Almond D. Lucian Pye

14. Match List-I with List-II and select the correct answer from the codes given below:

List-I	**List-II**
(*a*) Positive feedback	(*i*) Edward Shils
(*b*) The development of underdevelopment	(*ii*) Karl Deutsch
(*c*) Modernising Oligarchy	(*iii*) Ortega Gasset
(*d*) Nation–an organised human mass	(*iv*) Andre Gunder Frank

Codes:

	(*a*)	(*b*)	(*c*)	(*d*)
A.	(*ii*)	(*iv*)	(*i*)	(*iii*)
B.	(*i*)	(*iv*)	(*iii*)	(*ii*)
C.	(*i*)	(*ii*)	(*iii*)	(*iv*)
D.	(*ii*)	(*iv*)	(*iii*)	(*i*)

15. The cultural thrust in comparative politics became prominent during
A. the 1950s
B. the 1960s
C. the early 1970s
D. the late 1970s

16. Riots and demonstrations are the examples of
A. Institutional interest groups
B. Associational interest groups
C. Non-associational interest groups
D. Anomic interest groups

17. Who among the following has defined legitimacy as "conviction on the part of the member that it is right and proper to accept and obey the authorities"?
A. David Easton B. Seymour Lipset
C. Mark Suchman D. Karl Friedrich

18. Who among the following has classified dependency into 'Colonial dependency', 'Financial-industrial dependency' and 'Technological-industrial dependency'?
A. Andre Gunder Frank
B. Dos Santos
C. Maurice Wallerstein
D. Samir Amin

19. Who said, "Revolutions are the festivals of the oppressed and the exploited"?
A. Karl Marx B. Lenin
C. Mao D. Skocpol

20. Which of the following are the characteristics of Weber's bureaucracy?
1. Selection on the basis of professional qualifications
2. Appointment on contract basis
3. Staff members personally free
4. Officials free to leave the post

Select the correct answer from the codes given below:
A. 1 and 3 B. 1 and 4
C. 1, 2 and 3 D. 1, 2, 3 and 4

21. Khilafat Movement in India was started to show solidarity with the Sultan of
A. Saudi Arabia B. Turkey
C. Iran D. Iraq

22. Which one of the following writs is issued against an inferior tribunal which has declined to exercise its jurisdiction?

A. Certiorari B. Prohibition
C. Quo Warranto D. Mandamus

23. Who was the *protem* speaker of the 16th Lok Sabha?

A. Sumitra Mahajan B. Meira Kumar
C. Kamal Nath D. L.K. Advani

24. Match List-I with List-II and select the correct answer from the codes given below:

List-I *(Authors)*	**List-II** *(Books)*
(*a*) S. Khilnani	(*i*) India After Gandhi : The History of the World's Largest Democracy
(*b*) Rajni Kothari	(*ii*) The Idea of India
(*c*) R. Guha	(*iii*) The State Against Democracy : In Search of Human Governance
(*d*) Atul Kohli	(*iv*) The Success of India's Democracy

Codes:

	(*a*)	(*b*)	(*c*)	(*d*)
A.	(*ii*)	(*iii*)	(*i*)	(*iv*)
B.	(*i*)	(*iv*)	(*iii*)	(*ii*)
C.	(*iii*)	(*iv*)	(*ii*)	(*i*)
D.	(*iv*)	(*ii*)	(*i*)	(*iii*)

25. Who of the following is associated with the concept "Congress System"?

A. Morris Jones B. Paul R. Brass
C. Rajni Kothari D. Subrata K. Mitra

26. In India, 'Collegium System' was first introduced in relation to

A. Executive
B. Legislature
C. Judiciary
D. Union-State Relations

27. Which one of the following does not qualify for curtailing the freedom of speech and expression under Indian Constitution?

A. Security of the state
B. Public order, decency, morality
C. Demand for autonomy
D. Contempt of Court

28. Given below are two statements, one labelled as Assertion (A) and the other labelled as Reason (R):

Assertion (A): The transformation of the party system in India has centralized power at tier two of the government, namely at the State level.

Reason (R): Regional parties have less willingness to decentralize power.

Codes:

A. Both (A) and (R) are true and (R) is correct explanation of (A).
B. Both (A) and (R) are true, but (R) is not the correct explanation of (A).
C. (A) is true, but (R) is false.
D. (A) is false, but (R) is true.

29. Which one of the following, bearing names of Chief Election Commissioners of India, is arranged in chronological order?

A. S.P. Sen Verma, Sukumar Sen, J.M. Lyngdoh, T.N. Seshan
B. Sukumar Sen, S.P. Sen Verma, T.N. Seshan, J.M. Lyngdoh
C. S.P. Sen Verma, T.N. Seshan, Sukumar Sen, J.M. Lyngdoh
D. Sukumar Sen, T.N. Seshan, S.P. Sen Verma, J.M. Lyngdoh

30. Which of the following kinds of special provisions are made for the Scheduled Tribes in India?

1. Reservation of seats in Lok Sabha and State Legislative Assemblies.
2. Central Government to give special grants for welfare.
3. Reservation of seats in public services and in employment.
4. Reservation of seats in educational institutions.

Select the correct answer from the codes given below:

Codes:

A. 1, 2 and 3 B. 1, 3 and 4
C. 2, 3 and 4 D. 1, 2, 3 and 4

31. Which one of the following statements about the disadvantages of territorial principle of administrative organization is wrong?
A. Not suitable for large areas
B. Uniformity of administration becomes difficult
C. Encourages localism
D. Dominated by regional interests

32. Which one of the following was not a substitute of Merit System found earlier?
A. Exchange System B. Spoils System
C. Sale of Offices D. Patronage System

33. What is the bill called that contains all the demands voted by the Lok Sabha and the consolidated fund charges?
A. The Appropriation Bill
B. Voting of Demands Bill
C. Fiscal Policy Bill
D. The Finance Bill

34. Money received by the government of India under the State Provident Fund is credited to
A. Consolidated Fund
B. Treasury
C. Public Account
D. Contingency Fund

35. Arrange the following in correct chronological order of the hierarchy of human needs given by Maslow:
A. Security – Social – Self-esteem – Biological – Self-actualization
B. Self-esteem – Social – Biological – Self-actualization – Security
C. Self-actualization – Self-esteem – Social – Security – Biological
D. Biological – Security – Social – Self-esteem – Self-actualization

36. In UK, merit-based recruitment was adopted on the recommendation of which report?
A. Fulton Committee Report
B. Northcote – Trevelyan Report
C. Redcliff – Maud Commission Report
D. Tomlin Commission Report

37. Which one of the following was not included in the minimum criteria for ensuring good national governance by Nayef Al-Rodhan in his book 'Sustainable History and Dignity of Man'?
A. Equity and Inclusiveness
B. Rule of Law
C. A system of checks and balances
D. Transparency

38. Regarding the liability of holders of public office, when an official fails to perform a legal duty, it is known as
A. Malfeasance B. Nonfeasance
C. Disfeasance D. Misfeasance

39. Ombudsman in Sweden can take the following actions:
1. Can act against the judiciary
2. Can act on individual complaints
3. Can act against members of Parliament
4. Can act suo moto
Choose the correct answer from the code below:
Codes:
A. 2, 3, 4 B. 1, 2, 4
C. 1, 2, 3 D. 2, 4

40. Match List-I with List-II and choose the correct answer with the help of the code given below:

List-I *(Committees/ Commissions)*	**List-II** *(Year of appointment)*
(*a*) Ashok Mehta Committee	(*i*) 1953-54
(*b*) The Taxation Enquiry Committee	(*ii*) 1949-51
(*c*) The Local Finance Enquiry Committee	(*iii*) 1978
(*d*) G.V.K. Rao Committee	(*iv*) 1985

Codes:

	(*a*)	(*b*)	(*c*)	(*d*)
A.	(*iii*)	(*ii*)	(*iv*)	(*i*)
B.	(*ii*)	(*i*)	(*iii*)	(*iv*)
C.	(*iii*)	(*i*)	(*ii*)	(*iv*)
D.	(*iv*)	(*iii*)	(*i*)	(*ii*)

41. Game theory owes a heavy debt to the seminal work entitled, "The Theory of Games and Economic Behaviour". It has been written by
A. Mortan Kaplan
B. John Von Neumann and Oskar Morgenstern
C. Karl Deutsch
D. Michael Hass

42. Who among the following has remarked that, power in a political context means "the power of man over the minds and actions of other men"?

A. George Schwarzenberger
B. Herman Heller
C. Hans Morgenthau
D. Bertrand Russell

43. Match List-I with List-II and select the correct answer from the codes given below:

List-I *(Treaties/Proposals)*	List-II *(Year)*
(*a*) SALT II (Strategic Arms Limitation Talks)	(*i*) 1987
(*b*) PTBT (Partial Test Ban Treaty)	(*ii*) 1979
(*c*) Atom for Peace Proposal	(*iii*) 1963
(*d*) INF Treaty (Intermediate Nuclear Force Treaty)	(*iv*) 1953

Codes:

	(*a*)	(*b*)	(*c*)	(*d*)
A.	(*i*)	(*ii*)	(*iii*)	(*iv*)
B.	(*ii*)	(*iii*)	(*iv*)	(*i*)
C.	(*iv*)	(*ii*)	(*i*)	(*iii*)
D.	(*iii*)	(*ii*)	(*i*)	(*iv*)

44. Which one of the following factors contributed to the emergence of 'New Detente' after Cold War?

A. Pressure by the Non-aligned Movement
B. The signing of INF Treaty by Reagan and Gorbachev.
C. Emergence of Namibia as a free African Nation
D. Deployment of RDF (Rapid Deployment Force) in Persian Gulf

45. Given below are two statements, one labelled as Assertion (A) and the other labelled as Reason (R):

Assertion (A): India chose Non-alignment as a foreign policy choice in the post independence period.

Reason (R): NAM was an assertion of independence, equality and sovereignty.

Codes:

A. Both (A) and (R) are true and (R) is correct explanation of (A).
B. Both (A) and (R) are true, but (R) is not the correct explanation of (A).
C. (A) is true, but (R) is false.
D. (R) is true, but (A) is false.

46. The demand for New International Economic Order was first made at

A. Tehran Summit
B. Durban Summit
C. Kuala Lumpur Summit
D. Algiers Summit

47. Which one of the following is not correct about Association of South East Asian Nations (ASEAN)?

A. First India ASEAN Summit was held in November, 2002.
B. ASEAN declared South East Asian Nuclear Weapon free zone in 1995.
C. ASEAN is working to remove trade barriers and develop economic relationship with China, Japan and South Korea.
D. India became full dialogue partner of ASEAN in 1991.

48. Who among the following used the phrase – The United Nations is 'sharing in the name of solidarity' for underlining the necessity of the U.N.?

A. Winston Churchill
B. Dag Hammarskjold
C. Trygve Lie
D. Woodrow Wilson

49. Which one of the following is not a feature of 'Shopkeeper diplomacy'?

A. It is based on peaceful approach
B. It is a means of diplomacy for maintaining peace through compromise
C. It is based on the sound business principles of moderation
D. It tries to safeguard national interest through war only

50. Positive peace implies

A. a ceasefire
B. stopping the formation of death squads
C. transformation of relationship
D. social construction of war

ANSWERS

1	2	3	4	5	6	7	8	9	10
C	D	D	D	A	A	D	C	C	C
11	**12**	**13**	**14**	**15**	**16**	**17**	**18**	**19**	**20**
D	D	B	A	B	D	A	B	B	D
21	**22**	**23**	**24**	**25**	**26**	**27**	**28**	**29**	**30**
B	D	C	A	C	C	C	A	B	D
31	**32**	**33**	**34**	**35**	**36**	**37**	**38**	**39**	**40**
A	A	A	C	D	B	C	B	B	C
41	**42**	**43**	**44**	**45**	**46**	**47**	**48**	**49**	**50**
B	C	B	B	A	D	D	B	D	C

SOME SELECTED EXPLANATORY ANSWERS

1. John Locke is the father of 'Liberalism'. Liberalism is associated with 'Individualism'. Locke propounded the doctrine of natural right that includes life, liberty and property. Locke also contributed the principle of limited government and constitutionalism. Locke defined the civil power as 'the right of making laws with penalties.....for the regulating and preserving of property, and of employing the force of the community, in the execution of such laws.........all this only for the public good."

2. "In emancipation of the working class is the work of the working class itself," said by Karl Marx. Marx said the above statement in the context of class struggle. Marx and Friedrich Engles formulated the original ideas, concepts and theories of Marxism (scientific socialism).

3. The slogan "Turn the imperialist war into a civil war, that is, into a proletarian revolution," has given by Lenin. The doctrine of V.I. Lenin, especially his core contributions—on the party, the state, Imperialism and Revolution—to Marxist theory.

5. Plato, the disciple of Socrates and the teacher of Aristotle is one of the greatest political thinker produced by ancient Greece. Plato's concept of ideal state depicted a model of what state ought to be. The elements which constituted his ideal state are identified as Justice, Education, Philosopher King and Communism of wives and property. Communism of wives and property abolish the two evils wealth and private family but only soldiers and rulers are deprived from it.

7. St. Augustine's *De Civitate Dei* (The City of God) is divided into 22 books. This book had written in response to those who attributed the fall of Rome (410 AD) to the abolition of Pagan worship. This occasioned a sweeping account of the historical roles of church and state, and a philosophico-theological discussion of the relationship between them.

Augustine postulates two symbolic cities, "Jerusalem" (The City of God) and 'Babylon'. These are primarily moral and spiritual symbols : The celestial or spiritual, and the terrestrial or worldly.

8. American political scientist David Easton was one of the leading advocates of the behavioural movement. This movement studies facts and uses scientific methods like the quantitative and statistical methods but ignored values. Reasons for the declination of political theory of David Easton are historicism, moral relativism and hyper factualism.

9. The features of Jayaprakash Narayan's partyless democracy are dispersal of political power; constant watch of the representatives by the electing bodies; comparatively less expensive elections and the people can be the determinate sovereign. Maximum propaganda is associated with fascist ideology.

11. Comparative politics as an autonomous discipline emerged in the 1930s. It is characterized by an empirical approach based on the comparative method. In other words, comparative politics is the study of the domestic politics, political institutions, and conflicts of countries.

16. Riots and demonstrations are the act of Anomic interest groups. Anomic interest groups often resort to voilence and strikes/hartals to achieve their objectives. There are many types of pressure groups, such as Institutional pressure groups, Associational interest groups, social or Identity based groups, Non-associational interest groups, Ad-hoc groups and Anomic Interest groups, etc.

18. Marxist thinker 'Dos Santos' has classified dependency into 'colonial dependency', 'Financial-Industrial Dependency' and 'Technological-industrial Dependency'. Theory of Dependency is a concept of comparative analysis of third world countries in Asia, Africa and Latin America. This theory firstly evolved in Latin America during the late 1960s and early 1970s. According to 'Santos' dependence is a situation in which the economy of a certain country is conditioned by the development and expansion of another economy to which the former is subjugated.

19. Father of Soviet Revolution (1917) Bladimir Lenin stated that "Revolutions are the festivals of the oppressed and the exploited." Lenin's book 'State and Revolution' is the ideological defence of Russian revolution. Except the prior statement, Lenin also stated, "Imperialism is the highest stage of capitalism" and communist party is the vanguard of revolutionaries.

20. According to Max Weber, Bureaucracy Simply refers to "an administrative body of appointed officials." Weber described the characteristics of bureaucracy as follows– Selection on the basis of professional qualifications; appointment on contract basis; staff members personally free; officials free to leave the post and higher officials or offices supervise while lower official or offices have the right to appeal.

21. Khilafat Movement in India was started to show solidarity with the Sultan of Turkey. Khilafat Movement (1919-1924) was a significant Islamic movement in India during the British rule. This was an attempt by the Indian Muslim community to unite together in support of the Turkish Empire ruled by the Khalifa, which was attacked by European powers. The Muslims considered Khalifa as the custodian of Islam.

22. In India Article 32 and 226 of the constitution gives power to the Supreme Court and High Courts to issue writs in case of breach of Fundamental Rights of any citizen by the state. By such writs the judiciary can control the administrative actions and prevent any kind of arbitrary use of power and discretion. There are five kinds of writs - Mandamus, Certiorari, Prohibition, Quo warranto and Habeas Corpus.

A writ of mandamus is the name of one of the prerogative writs in the common law, and is issued by a superior court to compel a lower court or a government officer to perform mandatory or purely ministerial duties correctly.

23. After a general election and the formation of a new government, a list of senior Lok Sabha members prepared by the Legislative section is submitted to the Minister of Parliamentary Affairs, who selects a protem speaker. The appointment has to be approved by the President of India. Kamal Nath of the Indian National Congress (INC) party was the protem speaker of the 16th Lok Sabha. Kamal Nath has elected from Chhindwara (M.P.).

25. The eminent political thinker Rajni Kothari is associated with the concept "Congress system" or "one party dominant system". During the Nehru and Indira Period centre and state ruled by one party. From 1947 to 1967 congress ruled over India. In that context Kothari said this system is as like congress system or one party dominant system.

26. In India 'Collegium System' was first introduced in relation to the Judiciary, in the year 1993. In the 'Supreme Court Advocates-on Record Association *vs* Union of India', the Supreme Court said that in the appointment of Judges of the Supreme Court and High Courts, the President shall consult the Chief Justice of India and four senior-most judges of the Supreme Court (collegium).

27. Freedom of speech and expression under Indian constitutions is a fundamental right, provided by Article–19(1)(a). In spite, Article 19(2) imposes reasonable restrictions on the exercise of this right in the interests of the security of the state, friendly relations with foreign states, public order, decency or morality, or in relation to contempt of court.

29. Sukumar Sen was the first Chief Election Commissioner (CEC) of India from 21 March 1950 till 19 September 1958. S.P. Sen Verma was the third CEC of India from 1 October 1967 to 30 September 1972. T.N. Sheshan was the tenth CEC of India from 12 December 1990 till 11 December 1996. J.M. Lyngdoh was the twelfth CEC of India from 14 June 2001 till 7 February 2004.

The President of India appoints the Chief Election Commissioner and other Election Commissioners (Article 324). The CEC has tenure of six years, or up to the age of 65 years, whichever is earlier. The CEC can be removed only through impeachment by the Parliament.

30. The following kinds of special provisions are made for the Scheduled Tribes in India: (*a*) reservation of Seats in Lok Sabha and State Legislative Assemblies; (*b*) Central government to give special grants for welfare; (*c*) Reservation of seats in public services and in employment; (*d*) Reservation of seats in education institutions.

Article 330 of the Constitution of India provides for reservation of seats for Scheduled Castes (SCs) and Scheduled Tribes (STs) in the House of the People. Article 332 provides for reservation of seats for SCs and STs in the Legislative Assemblies of the States. Reservation of seats in public services and in employment is provided under Article 16. Article 15 provides for reservation of seats in educational institutions.

33. After the general discussion on the budget proposals and voting on Demand for grants have been completed, government introduces the Appropriation Bill. The Appropriation Bill is intended to give authority to government to incur expenditure from and out of the Consolidated Fund of India.

34. In the Public Account constituted under Article 266 (2) of the Constitution of India, the transactions relate to debt other than those included in the Consolidated Fund of India. The receipts under Public Accounts donot constitute normal receipts of government. Parliamentary authorization for payments from the Public Account is therefore not required.

35. The Hierarchy of Needs is a theory proposed by Abraham Maslow in his 1943 paper "A Theory of Human Motivation". The Correct Chronological order of the hierarchy of human needs is Biological – Security – Social – Self-esteem – Self-actualization.

36. The Northcote – Trevelyan Report was a document prepared by Stattford H. Northcote and C.E. Trevelyan. Published in February 1854, the report catalysed the development of Her Majesty's Civil Service in the United Kingdom. The report took nine months to draft and publish. It had four major conclusions:

(*a*) Recruitment into the Civil Service should be by open competition, conducted by an independent Civil Service.

(*b*) Entrants should be recruited into a 'Home Civil Service' as a whole, rather than to a specific Department.

(*c*) Recruits would be segregated at entry into a hierarchy of grades, ranging from clerical officers who would conduct routine tasks, though to those who would provide policy advice to ministers.

(*d*) Promotion would be on merit, not preferment, patronage, purchase or length of service.

39. The institution of Ombudsman was created in Sweden in 1809. A complaint to the Parliamentary Ombudsman can be made by anybody who feels that he or she or someone else has been treated wrongly or unjustly by a public authority or an official employed by the civil service or local government. A person need not be a Swedish citizen or have reached a certain age to be able to lodge a complaint. An Ombudsman in Sweden can act against the judiciary; can act on individual complaints and can act suo moto. However, he cannot act against Members of Parliament.

40. The Local Finance Enquiry Committee was established in 1949 under the chairmanship of P.K. Wattal. The Local Finance Enquiry Committee (1949-51) mainly suggested the widening of the sphere of taxation of urban bodies. The Taxation Enquiry Commission was established in 1953 under the chairmanship of P.K. Wattal. The Taxation Enquiry Commission (1953-54) recommended the segregation of certain taxes for exclusive utilisation by or for local government.

Ashok Mehta Committee was appointed in 1977 to study the Panchayati Raj System in the Country. It submitted its report in 1978 and made 132 recommendations to revive and strengthen the declining Panchayati Raj System in the country, some of its main recommendations were (*a*) The three tier system of Panchayati Raj should be replaced by the two-tier system; (*b*) There should be an official participation of political parties at all levels of panchayat elections; (*c*) The nyaya panchayats should be kept as separate bodies from that of development panchayats; (*d*) A constitutional recognition should be accorded to the Panchayati Raj institutions.

The Committee on Administrative Arrangement for Rural Development and Poverty Alleviation Programmes under the chairmanship of G.V.K. Rao was appointed by the Planning Commission in 1985. The committee came to conclusion that the development process was gradually bureaucratised and divorced from the Panchayati Raj. The Committee made the following recommendations: (*a*) The district level body, that is, the Zila Parishad should be of pivotal importance in the scheme of democratic decentralisation; (*b*) A post of District Development Commissioner should be created; (*c*) Elections to the Panchayati Raj institutions should be held regularly.

41. "The theory of games and economic behaviour" has been written by John Von Neumann & Oskar Morgenstern. Basically this theory was developed in the realm of Mathematics and Economics. Further it has come to occupy significant place in the sphere of International relations. Game theory provides models for studying behaviour of politics among nations.

42. The American Realist thinker 'Hans Morgenthau' has remarked that, Power in a political context means "The power of man over the minds and actions of other men." According to Morgenthau 'Power is most fundamental of all political activity'. Realistic approach emphasizes the importance of national interest and power as a means to attain or further those interest. Each nation is continuously involved in a struggle for power with other nations. The objective always is to secure national interest by means of power.

45. NAM (Non-Alignment Movement) was an assertion of independence, equality and sovereignty due to which India chose Non-alignment as a foreign policy choice in the post independence period. NAM was established in 1961 by J.L. Nehru, A.G. Nasir, Tito and Sukarno.

46. The demand for a New International Economic Order was first made at Algiers Summit in 1973. The New International Economic Order (NIEO) was a set of proposals put forward during the 1970s by some developing countries through the United Nations Conference on Trade and Development to promote their interests by improving their terms of trade, increasing development assistance, developed – country tariff reductions, and other means. The main tenets of NIEO are:

(*a*) Developing countries must be entitled to regulate and control the activities of multinational corporations operating within their territory.

(*b*) They must be free to rationalize or expropriate foreign property on conditions favourable to them.

(*c*) They must be free to set up associations of primary commodities producers similar to the OPEC; all other states must recognize this right and refrain from taking economic, military or political measures calculated to restrict it.

(*d*) International trade should be based on the need to ensure stable, equitable and remunerative prices for raw materials, tariff preferences, as well as transfer of technology to developing countries and should provide economic and technical assistance without any strings attached.

47. The Association of Southeast Asian Nations is a political and economic organisation of ten Southeast Asian countries. It was formed on 8 August 1967 by Indonesia, Malaysia, the Phillippines, Singapore and Thailand. Since then, membership has expanded to include Brunei, Cambodia, Laos, Myanmar (Burma) and Vietnam. Its aims include accelerating economic growth, social progress and sociocultural evolution among its members, protection of regional peace and stability, and opportunities for member countries to discuss differences peacefully. First ASEAN-India Summit was held in Phnom Penh on 5 November 2002. ASEAN declared South East Asian Nuclear weapon free zone in 1995 by the Bangkok treaty signed in 1995. ASEAN is working to remove trade barriers and develop economic relationship with China, Japan and South Korea. India became full dialogue partner of ASEAN in 1996.

48. Dag Hammarskjold was the General Secretary of the United Nations (UNO) during the period 1953 to 1961. He was Swedish person. Dag used the phrase that the UNO is 'sharing in the name of solidarity' for underlining the necessity of the UNO.

49. 'Shopkeeper diplomacy' don't try to safeguard national interest through war only rather it is based on peacful approach. It is a means of diplomacy for maintaining peace through compromise, also it is based on the sound business principles of moderation.

PAPER–III

Note: *This paper contains* ***seventy five (75)*** *objective type questions of* ***two (2)*** *marks each.* ***All*** *questions are compulsory.*

1. Who among the following said that "Political theory is, quite simply, man's attempt to consciously understand and solve the problems of his group life and organization"?

A. Ernest Barker B. G.H. Sabine
C. Leo Strauss D. David Easton

2. Who of the following lamented the 'death' of political philosophy?

A. Robert Dahl B. Peter Laslett
C. Peter Winch D. David Easton

3. Which one of the following answers is incorrect regarding neo-liberalism?

A. Neo-liberal vision largely evolved during the governments of Ronald Reagan and Margaret Thatcher.
B. It attacked the Keynesian notion of the international economic order.
C. It emerged as a total negation of Laissez-faire economics.
D. Its emphasis is on free markets and liberal reforms.

4. Which one of the following answers is correct regarding Post-Marxism?

A. The working class has not evolved into a revolutionary movement.
B. Economic class interests are relatively autonomous from ideology and politics.
C. The working class holds no basic position within socialism.
D. All the above

5. Match List-I with List-II and select the correct answer from the codes given below:

List-I (Authors)	List-II (Dominant Concept)
(*a*) Thomas Pogge	(*i*) Distributive Justice
(*b*) Michael Walzer	(*ii*) Communitarian Perspective of Justice
(*c*) Susan Moller Okin	(*iii*) Feminist Conception of Justice
(*d*) John Rawls	(*iv*) Global Justice

Codes:

	(*a*)	(*b*)	(*c*)	(*d*)
A.	(*i*)	(*ii*)	(*iii*)	(*iv*)
B.	(*iv*)	(*ii*)	(*iii*)	(*i*)
C.	(*ii*)	(*iii*)	(*i*)	(*iv*)
D.	(*i*)	(*ii*)	(*iv*)	(*iii*)

6. Which one of the following statements is incorrect regarding political ideology?

A. It is a belief system which helps to structure how the world is understood and explained.
B. It is a set of ideas which provides the basis for some kind of political action.
C. It is an action-oriented belief system.
D. Political ideology is not the same thing as political theory.

7. Who of the following said "Lenin's party was designed to be an elite, a minority chosen for intellectual and moral superiority, the most advanced part of the working class and so its vanguard"?

A. C.B. MacPherson B. D. McLellan
C. G.H. Sabine D. R. Miliband

8. Nocturnal Council finds a mention in Plato's

A. The Republic B. The Statesman
C. The Laws D. None of the above

9. Given below are two statements, one labelled as Assertion (A) and the other labelled as Reason (R):

Assertion (A): For Aristotle the authority of a constitutional ruler over his subjects is quite different from that of a master over his slaves.

Reason (R): Because the slave is inferior from birth and incapable of ruling himself.

Codes:

A. Both (A) and (R) are true and (R) is the correct explanation of (A)
B. Both (A) and (R) are true, but (R) is not the correct explanation of (A)

C. (A) is true, but (R) is false
D. (A) is false, but (R) is true

10. Match List-I with List-II and select the correct answer from the codes given below:

List-I *(Authors)*	List-II *(Books)*
(*a*) Willmoore Kendall	(*i*) John Locke, A Biography
(*b*) J.W. Gough	(*ii*) John Locke and the Doctrine of Majority-rule
(*c*) M.W. Cranston	(*iii*) John Locke's Political Philosophy
(*d*) Richard Cox	(*iv*) Locke on Peace and War

Codes:

	(*a*)	(*b*)	(*c*)	(*d*)
A.	(*ii*)	(*iii*)	(*i*)	(*iv*)
B.	(*i*)	(*ii*)	(*iv*)	(*iii*)
C.	(*iii*)	(*iv*)	(*ii*)	(*i*)
D.	(*iv*)	(*i*)	(*iii*)	(*ii*)

11. For whom of the following, science is the fruit of idle curiosity; philosophy is mere intellectual frippery; the amenities of polite life is tinsel?
A. Thomas Hobbes B. John Locke
C. J.J. Rousseau D. Karl Marx

12. Which one of the following is not correct regarding Marx's theory of alienation ?
A. Alienation from the product
B. Alienation from the activity of labour
C. Disalienation from species-being
D. Alienation of man from man

13. Who of the following is of the view that it is not Gandhi who made Satyagraha but it is Satyagraha which made Gandhi the Mahatma?
A. R.R. Diwakar B. C.F. Andrews
C. G.N. Dhawan D. Louis Fisher

14. In which of the following countries Narendranath Bhattacharya settled under the name of Manabendra Nath Roy?
A. Java
B. United States of America
C. Germany
D. Mexico

15. Who of the following said that God had appeared to him in prison, placed the Gita in his hands and made him realize the simple truths of the Sanatana Dharma?
A. Vivekananda B. Mahatma Gandhi
C. Aurobindo Ghose D. Savarkar

16. Comparative Politics is the study of
A. institutions and functions
B. all forms of political activity-governmental as well as non-governmental and all political phenomena
C. political processes
D. techniques and tools of comparative inquiry

17. What is the correct sequence in which the following approaches to the study of 'Comparative Politics' emerged?
1. Philosophical Approach
2. Systems Approach
3. New Institutional Approach
4. Behavioural Approach

Select the correct answer from the codes given below:

Codes:
A. 1, 3, 4 and 2 B. 1, 4, 2 and 3
C. 1, 2, 4 and 3 D. 3, 1, 2 and 4

18. Identify the correct sequence of the following input functions and select the correct answer from the codes given below:
1. Interest-aggregation
2. Interest-articulation
3. Political communication
4. Political socialization and recruitment

Codes:
A. 1, 2, 3 and 4 B. 1, 2, 4 and 3
C. 2, 1, 4 and 3 D. 4, 2, 1 and 3

19. The sociologists who influenced Gabriel Almond in his structural functionalism were
1. Max Weber 2. Talcott Parsons
3. David Truman 4. Karl Deutsch

Select the correct answer from the codes given below:

Codes:
A. 1, 2 and 3 B. 1 and 2
C. 1 and 3 D. 2 and 3

20. Which of the following statements about the Vice-President of India and Vice-President of America are true?

1. Both the Vice-Presidents are elected.
2. Both of them are the presiding officers of their respective upper Houses.
3. Both the Vice-Presidents are not the members of their respective Houses.
4. Both of them do not have a casting vote in case of a tie.

Select the correct answer from the codes given below:

Codes:

A. 1, 3 and 4 B. 1, 2 and 3
C. 1, 2 and 4 D. 1, 2, 3 and 4

21. Which one of the following governmental systems is considered to be the off-spring and successor of the theory of separation of powers?

A. Swiss B. American
C. Indian D. French

22. According to Riggs, lack of balance between equality and capacity is

A. Developmental syndrome
B. Developmental trap
C. Political decay
D. Goal-changing

23. Arrange the following books in order in which they appeared:

1. Political Order in Changing Societies
2. The Politics of Modernization
3. How Europe Underdeveloped Africa
4. Capitalism and Underdevelopment in Latin America

Select the correct answer from the codes given below:

Codes:

A. 2, 1, 4 and 3 B. 1, 2, 3 and 4
C. 2, 1, 3 and 4 D. 1, 2, 4 and 3

24. Which one of the following articles of the US Constitution vests the executive powers in the President?

A. Article 1 B. Article 2
C. Article 3 D. Article 4

25. Match List-I with List-II and select the correct answer from the codes given below:

List-I	List-II
(*a*) Both Houses have equal powers	(*i*) America
(*b*) Upper House is more powerful than Lower House	(*ii*) India
(*c*) Lower House is more powerful than Upper House	(*iii*) France
(*d*) National Assembly can overthrow the government	(*iv*) Switzerland

Codes:

	(*a*)	(*b*)	(*c*)	(*d*)
A.	(*iv*)	(*i*)	(*ii*)	(*iii*)
B.	(*iii*)	(*ii*)	(*i*)	(*iv*)
C.	(*iv*)	(*iii*)	(*ii*)	(*i*)
D.	(*i*)	(*ii*)	(*iii*)	(*iv*)

26. Consider the following:

1. Pocket Veto
2. President message to federal legislature
3. Caucus system
4. Pigeon hole-a bill

These are the parts of constitutional practice of

A. Indian Political System
B. American Political System
C. The Swiss Political System
D. The British Political System

27. Who among the following former British Prime Ministers belonged to the Labour Party?

1. Harold Wilson 2. Edward Heath
3. John Major 4. Tony Blair

Select the correct answer from the codes given below:

Codes:

A. 1 and 4 B. 1, 3 and 4
C. 1, 2 and 3 D. 1 and 3

28. The Judges of the US Supreme Court hold office

A. upto the age of 65 years
B. upto the age of 70 years
C. upto the age of 75 years
D. until death or resignation or removal by the Congress

29. Which one of the following Federal Courts has the power to declare laws passed by the state or the constituent unit of the federation invalid but not the federal laws?

A. The Supreme Court of America
B. The Supreme Court of India
C. The Swiss Federal Tribunal
D. The French Superior Courts

30. Given below are two statements, one labelled as Assertion (A) and the other labelled as Reason (R). Choose the correct answer from the codes given below:

Assertion (A): The British Parliament is sovereign.

Reason (R): The Queen in England is a nominal head of the State.

Codes:

A. Both (A) and (R) are true and (R) is the correct explanation of (A)
B. Both (A) and (R) are true, but (R) is not the correct explanation of (A)
C. (A) is true, but (R) is false
D. (A) is false, but (R) is true

31. "Since Indians wish to unite and develop a common culture, it is the bounden duty of all Indians to own up Hindi as their language... Any Indian who does not accept this proposal..., has no right to be Indian." Who among the following said this?

A. B.R. Ambedkar B. Bala Saheb Deoras
C. Dr. K.M. Munshi D. Seth Govind Das

32. Who has described Indian society as 'Apolitical Society'?

A. Rajni Kothari
B. Morris Jones
C. Stanley Kochanak
D. Paul R. Brass

33. Match List-I with List-II and select the correct answer from the codes given below:

List-I *(States)*	**List-II** *(Chief Ministers [2014])*
(*a*) Arunachal Pradesh	(*i*) T.R. Zeliang
(*b*) Mizoram	(*ii*) Lal Thanhawla
(*c*) Nagaland	(*iii*) Manik Sarkar
(*d*) Tripura	(*iv*) Nabam Tuke

Codes:

	(*a*)	(*b*)	(*c*)	(*d*)
A.	(*ii*)	(*i*)	(*iv*)	(*iii*)
B.	(*iv*)	(*ii*)	(*i*)	(*iii*)
C.	(*iii*)	(*iv*)	(*ii*)	(*i*)
D.	(*i*)	(*iii*)	(*iv*)	(*ii*)

34. Match List-I with List-II and select the correct answer from the codes given below:

List-I *(Features of Indian Constitution)*	**List-II** *(Sources)*
(*a*) Judicial Review, Fundamental Rights	(*i*) British
(*b*) Single Citizenship	(*ii*) Irish
(*c*) Nomination of Members to Rajya Sabha	(*iii*) Canadian
(*d*) Residuary Powers	(*iv*) American

Codes:

	(*a*)	(*b*)	(*c*)	(*d*)
A.	(*iv*)	(*i*)	(*ii*)	(*iii*)
B.	(*iii*)	(*ii*)	(*i*)	(*iv*)
C.	(*ii*)	(*iii*)	(*iv*)	(*i*)
D.	(*i*)	(*iv*)	(*iii*)	(*ii*)

35. In which of the following Acts the provincial subjects were divided into transferred and reserved subjects?

A. Indian Council's Act, 1892
B. Indian Council's Act, 1909
C. Montague Chelmsford Reforms Act, 1919
D. Government of India Act, 1935

36. Who of the following gave the idea of 'Saintly Idiom' in Indian politics?

A. Jayaprakash Narayan
B. Rajni Kothari
C. Morris Jones
D. James Manor

37. Arrange the following in chronological order:

(*i*) Navnirvan Movement in Gujarat
(*ii*) Formation of Maharashtra as a State
(*iii*) Split of the Communist Party of India
(*iv*) Formation of Janata Party

Codes:

A. (*i*), (*iii*), (*ii*), (*iv*) B. (*iii*), (*ii*), (*i*), (*iv*)
C. (*ii*), (*iii*), (*iv*), (*i*) D. (*ii*), (*iii*), (*i*), (*iv*)

38. Who describes social movements as 'non-party political formations'?

A. Ramchandra Guha
B. Rajni Kothari
C. Partha Chatterjee
D. T.K. Oommen

39. Arrange the following in chronological sequence:

(*i*) Naxalite Movement
(*ii*) Sarvodaya Movement
(*iii*) Narmada Bachao Andolan
(*iv*) Chipko Movement

Codes:

A. (*i*), (*iii*), (*ii*), (*iv*) B. (*ii*), (*i*), (*iv*), (*iii*)
C. (*iv*), (*ii*), (*i*), (*iii*) D. (*i*), (*iv*), (*iii*), (*i*)

40. Who among the following was a member of the Justice J.S. Verma Committee constituted following Nirbhaya case?

A. Justice Fatima Beevi
B. Justice Leila Seth
C. Justice Gyan Sudha Mishra
D. Justice G. Rohini

41. Which one of the following is not the function of the Election Commission of India?

A. Conduct of election to Parliament, State Legislatures, President and Vice-President
B. Preparation of electoral rolls
C. Counting of votes and declaration of results
D. Declaring an election void

42. On which date National Integration Day is celebrated in India ?

A. 14th November B. 19th November
C. 10th December D. 30th October

43. Which one of the following principles did not emerge out of Bommai case in relation to Article 356?

A. Proclamation issued under Art. 356 is subject to judicial review.
B. State Assembly should be dissolved only after the approval of proclamation by Parliament.
C. If a new political party assumes power at the Centre, it has the authority to dismiss Ministries formed by other parties in the States.
D. The Court may require the Union Government to disclose the materials on the basis of which Art. 356 was invoked.

44. Match List-I with List-II and select the correct answer from the codes given below:

List-I *(Committees of Parliament)*	**List-II** *(Number of Members)*
(*a*) Public Accounts Committee	(*i*) 45
(*b*) Estimates Committee	(*ii*) 22
(*c*) Department related Parliamentary Standing Committee	(*iii*) 15
(*d*) Rules Committee of Lok Sabha	(*iv*) 30

Codes:

	(*a*)	(*b*)	(*c*)	(*d*)
A.	(*iii*)	(*ii*)	(*iv*)	(*i*)
B.	(*ii*)	(*iv*)	(*i*)	(*iii*)
C.	(*i*)	(*iii*)	(*ii*)	(*iv*)
D.	(*iv*)	(*i*)	(*iii*)	(*ii*)

45. Given below are two statements, one labelled as Assertion (A) and the other labelled as Reason (R).

Assertion (A): The Courts follow the principle of natural justice while deciding cases.

Reason (R): Justice should not only be done but should manifestly and undoubtedly be seen to be done.

Codes:

A. Both (A) and (R) are true and (R) is the correct explanation of (A)
B. Both (A) and (R) are true, but (R) is not the correct explanation of (A)
C. (A) is true, but (R) is false
D. (A) is false, but (R) is true

46. The post 1970 phase in the development of Public Administration was characterized by

A. Status-quoism
B. Stability
C. Development theory
D. Value orientation

47. What was he referring to when Mooney said 'conferring of specified authority by a higher authority'?
A. Division of powers B. Responsibility
C. Conferring authority D. Delegation

48. Which one of the following was not in the list of functional requisites for any society, given by Fred W. Riggs?
A. Economic B. Administrative
C. Political D. Communicational

49. Which one of the following is not a stage in decision-making process given by Herbert Simon?
A. Intelligence activity
B. Speculative activity
C. Choice activity
D. Design activity

50. Which one of the following is not one of the styles of leadership given by Likert?
A. Exploitative authoritative
B. Benevolent authoritative
C. Cooperative authoritative
D. Participative

51. Choose the correct code for the Assertion (A) and Reason (R) as given below:
Assertion (A): To be valid and part of a science of public administration, hypothesis developed in the American cultural context should be tested in cross-cultural settings.
Reason (R): Comparative study has brought Politics and Public Administration closer to each other.
Codes:
A. Both (A) and (R) are true and (R) is the correct explanation of (A).
B. Both (A) and (R) are true, but (R) is not the correct explanation of (A).
C. (A) is true, but (R) is false.
D. (A) is false, but (R) is true.

52. What is the name of the Committee in Britain that takes up voting of demands and of taxes (revenue part)?
A. Appropriation Committee
B. Committee of Ways and Means
C. Committee of Supply
D. Estimates Committee

53. Match List-I with List-II and select the correct answer from the codes given below:

List-I *(Books)*	**List-II** *(Authors)*
(*a*) The Administrative State	(*i*) Ordway Tead
(*b*) The Art of Administration	(*ii*) Piffner and Presthus
(*c*) Public Administration	(*iii*) Dwight Waldo
(*d*) Organization and Management	(*iv*) Seckler-Hudson

Codes:

	(*a*)	(*b*)	(*c*)	(*d*)
A.	(*i*)	(*iii*)	(*iv*)	(*ii*)
B.	(*iv*)	(*ii*)	(*iii*)	(*i*)
C.	(*iii*)	(*i*)	(*ii*)	(*iv*)
D.	(*ii*)	(*iv*)	(*i*)	(*iii*)

54. 'Rule of Lapse' is essential for the effective financial control by the
A. Estimates Committee
B. Parliament
C. Department of Expenditure
D. Public Accounts Committee

55. Desk Officer System in the ministries of government of India had the following advantages:
1. Speedy disposal of cases
2. Dual records were available
3. Reduced expenditure
4. Qualitative improvement
Choose the correct answer from the code given below:
A. 1, 2, 4 B. 1, 2, 3
C. 1, 3, 4 D. 2, 3, 4

56. Which one of the following institutions was established in India on the recommendations of Paul A. Appleby?
A. L.B.S. Academy of Administration
B. Indian Institute of Public Administration
C. Indian Council of Social Science Research
D. Indian Police Academy

57. Arrange the following in correct chronological sequence in the stages of performance budgeting:
A. Objectives – Classification – Analysis – Evaluation

B. Analysis – Objectives – Evaluation – Classification
C. Classification – Analysis – Objectives – Evaluation
D. Objectives – Analysis – Classification – Evaluation

58. Public Service Commissions for the Union and States in India are created under which Article of the Constitution?

A. 268 B. 315
C. 312 D. 371(A)

59. Which one of the following was not recommended for Panchayatiraj by Thungon Committee?

A. Constitutional Status
B. Planning at Zila Parishad level
C. Dist. Collector to be Chief Executive of Zila Parishad
D. Three year term

60. Match List-I with List-II and select the correct answer with the help of the code given below:

List-I (Acts/Agencies)	List-II (Year)
(a) All-India Services (Conduct) Rules	(i) 1941
(b) Central Bureau of Investigation	(ii) 1860
(c) Indian Penal Code	(iii) 1963
(d) Special Police Establishment	(iv) 1954

Codes:

	(a)	(b)	(c)	(d)
A.	(i)	(ii)	(iii)	(iv)
B.	(iv)	(iii)	(ii)	(i)
C.	(iii)	(i)	(iv)	(ii)
D.	(i)	(iv)	(ii)	(iii)

61. Match List-I with List-II and select the answer from the codes given below:

List-I (Statements)	List-II (Scholar)
(a) "There is no possibility of drawing a sharp line between the will to live and the will to power."	(i) Haushofer
(b) "In its essence power is an indivisible whole."	(ii) Hans Morgenthau
(c) "For military reasons a state should be economically self sufficient."	(iii) Reinhold Neibuhr
(d) "The struggle for power is universal in time and space and is an undeniable fact of experience."	(iv) E.H. Carr

Codes:

	(a)	(b)	(c)	(d)
A.	(i)	(iii)	(iv)	(ii)
B.	(iii)	(iv)	(i)	(ii)
C.	(ii)	(iii)	(i)	(iv)
D.	(i)	(ii)	(iv)	(iii)

62. Arrange the following in their chronological sequence and choose your answer from the codes given below:

(i) Churchill's Fulton Speech
(ii) Launching of the African Union
(iii) A treaty to create South East Asian Nuclear weapon free zone
(iv) Recognition of South Sudan as a sovereign State and 193rd member of the U.N.

Codes:

A. (i), (ii), (iii), (iv) B. (i), (iii), (ii), (iv)
C. (i), (iv), (ii), (iii) D. (iv), (iii), (i), (ii)

63. Which one of the following statements regarding realism are true?

(i) Thucydides is called the first classical realist.
(ii) Power is the key to international politics.
(iii) The main goal of states is survival.
(iv) All states do not posses power to inflict some harm on its neighbour.

Choose your answer from the codes given below:

Codes:

A. (i), (iv), (ii) B. (i), (iii), (iv)
C. (ii), (iii), (iv) D. (i), (ii), (iii)

64. Who defined Non-alignment as a "Policy of keeping out of alliances"?
A. K.M. Pannikar
B. George Schwarzenberger
C. Marshall Tito
D. John Burton

65. The North American Free Trade Agreement 1994 (NAFTA) includes:
A. U.S.A., Canadă and Mexico
B. Mexico, Japan and South Korea
C. Brazil, Mexico and New Zealand
D. Canada, New Zealand and U.S.A.

66. Who among the following realist thinkers identifies 'three images of politics'?
A. Hans Morgenthau
B. Kenneth Waltz
C. Thucydides
D. E.H. Carr

67. Read the following statements about South-South Co-operation:
1. South-South Co-operation is an alternative to North-South Aid.
2. It refers to co-operative mutually beneficial activities in the field of trade, service and technology.
3. UN General Assembly declared 19 December the annual UN Day for South-South Co-operation.
4. W.T.O. came into existence for facilitating South-South Co-operation.

Select your answer from the codes given below:
Codes:
A. 1, 3, 4 B. 2 and 4
C. 1, 2, 3 D. Only 4

68. Operation Enduring Freedom 2001 is related to
A. Eviction of terrorists from Iraq
B. Eviction of Taliban regime from Afghanistan
C. Eviction of Cremean forces from Russia
D. Eviction of Arabs from Gaza strip

69. Which one of the following countries is not a member of BIMSTEC that started in 1997?
A. Bangladesh B. India
C. Thailand D. China

70. What is not true about ASEAN (Association of South East Asian Nations)?
A. Its declared objectives is regional peace and stability.
B. It stands for strategic co-operation at regional level.
C. It is intended to promote co-operation in social, economic, cultural, scientific and administrative spheres.
D. Malaysian Prime Minister Abdul Razak announced that ASEAN was not committed to any political ideology.

71. Which one of the following is the report that triggered the process of U.N. reform?
A. Secretary General Kofi Annan's Report 2005 entitled 'In Larger Freedom'
B. Secretary General Boutros Boutros Ghali Report 1992 'An Agenda for Peace'
C. Secretary General Kofi Annan's Report 2005 entitled, Investing in the UN : For a Stronger Organisation World Wide.
D. Amnesty International Report 1997 entitled, 'Refugees' : Human Rights have no Borders'.

72. Which one of the following Reports cites the unjust global trade regime as primary cause in increasing global inequality?
A. Doha Round (of GATT) Resolution, 2003
B. Development Assistance Committee Report, 2003
C. Human Development Report (HDR) of 2005
D. World Bank Report of 1989

73. Read the following statements and choose your answer from the codes given below:
1. "While all politics is necessarily pursuit of power, ideologies render involvement in that contest for power, psychologically and morally acceptable to the actors and their audience".
2. The Ideals of Peace and of International law are eminently qualified to serve as Ideologies for a policy of status quo.
3. The Ideology of Peace has a tremendous role in attaining the objectives of the U.N.
4. Ideology has always an edge over National Interest.

Codes:

A. All statements 1, 2, 3 and 4 are correct
B. Only 1 is correct
C. 1, 2 and 3 are correct
D. Only 4 is correct

74. Match List-I with List-II and choose your answer from the codes given below:

List-I *(Authors)*	**List-II** *(Books)*
(*a*) Walden Bello	(*i*) A Globalizing World? Culture, Economics, Politics
(*b*) Jagadish Bhagwati	(*ii*) Globalization and its Discontents
(*c*) D. Held	(*iii*) In Defence of Globalization
(*d*) Joseph E. Stiglitz	(*iv*) Deglobalization : Ideas for a New Economy

Codes:

	(*a*)	(*b*)	(*c*)	(*d*)
A.	(*iv*)	(*iii*)	(*i*)	(*ii*)
B.	(*iii*)	(*i*)	(*iv*)	(*ii*)
C.	(*ii*)	(*iv*)	(*iii*)	(*i*)
D.	(*i*)	(*ii*)	(*iii*)	(*iv*)

75. Which one of the following is not an IGO (Intergovernmental Organization) ?

A. United Nations
B. Amnesty International
C. Arab League
D. African Union

ANSWERS

1	**2**	**3**	**4**	**5**	**6**	**7**	**8**	**9**	**10**
B	B	C	D	B	D	C	C	A	A
11	**12**	**13**	**14**	**15**	**16**	**17**	**18**	**19**	**20**
C	C	A	D	C	B	B	D	B	B
21	**22**	**23**	**24**	**25**	**26**	**27**	**28**	**29**	**30**
B	B	A	B	A	B	A	D	C	B
31	**32**	**33**	**34**	**35**	**36**	**37**	**38**	**39**	**40**
A	A	B	A	C	C	D	B	B	B
41	**42**	**43**	**44**	**45**	**46**	**47**	**48**	**49**	**50**
D	B	C	B	A	D	D	B	B	C
51	**52**	**53**	**54**	**55**	**56**	**57**	**58**	**59**	**60**
B	B	C	B	C	B	D	B	D	B
61	**62**	**63**	**64**	**65**	**66**	**67**	**68**	**69**	**70**
B	B	D	B	A	B	C	B	D	B
71	**72**	**73**	**74**	**75**					
B	C	C	A	B					

SOME SELECTED EXPLANATORY ANSWERS

1. According to G.H. Sabine, "Political theory is, quite simply, man's attempt to consciously understand and solve the problems of his group life and organization." Political theory is, however, usually regarded as a distinctive approach to the subject, even though, particularly in the USA, it is seen as a subfield of political science. Political theory involves the analytical study of ideas and doctrines that have been central to political thought.

2. Peter Laslett in his introduction to philosophy, politics and society (1956) famously declared that 'political philosophy is dead' its 'death' was largely a consequence of important shifts in philosophy, notably the rise of logical positivism. Logical positivism, originally advanced by a group of philosophers collectively known as the Vienna circle, reflected a deep faith in scientific understanding and suggested that propositions that are not empirically verifiable are simply meaningless.

3. Neo-liberalism refers to a set of market-liberal economic policies. In the developed world Neo-liberalism is often coupled with Thalcherism and grew up in opposition to Keynesianism. In the developing world it emerged in opposition to the development strategies based on import-substitution industrialization which had dominated the period 1945 to the early 1980s. Here it is often linked to the so called 'Washington consensus' (Privatization and deregulation; trade and financial liberalization; shrinking the role of the state; encouraging foreign direct investment) and to the structural adjustment programmes promoted by the IMF and World Bank. More recently, it has been used (for example by the anti-globalization movement) to characterize the economic ideology behind capitalist globalization.

4. Post-Marxism is a ideology that improves the classical theory of Marxism. This ideology stated that the working class has not evolved into a revolutionary movement. Economic class interests are relatively autonomous from ideology and politics. The working class holds no basic position within socialism.

5. Justice has been of central importance to political philosophy for over two thousand years. Though the ages, political thinkers have protrayed the 'Good Society' as a 'just' society. However, there has been far less agreement about what justice stands for. In every day language, infact, justice is used so imprecisely that it is taken to mean 'fairness', 'rightness' or simply, that which is 'morally correct'.

Different thinkers focused on different types of justice. Thomas Pogge referring about global justice, Michael Walzer focusing on communitarian perspective of justice, Susan Moller Okin favoured to Feminist conception of justice and John Rawls advocating for Distributive or pure procedural justice.

6. Political ideology is a belief system which helps to structure how the world is understood and explained. Also it is a set of ideas which provides the basis for some kind of political action. Political ideology is an action-oriented belief system.

7. According to G.H. Sabine, "Lenin's party was designed to be an elite, a minority chosen for intellectual and moral superiority, the most advanced part of the working class and so its vanguard." A Russian revolutionary and leader of the Soviet Union, 1917-24, Lenin was the most influential Marxist theorist of the 20th century. He was primarily concerned with the issues of organisation and revolution, emphasising the central importance of a tightly-organized 'vanguard' party to lead and guide the proletarian class.

8. Nocturnal council finds a mention in Plato's 'The Laws'. Plato's political philosophy, as expounded in the Republic, is an attempt to describe the 'ideal state' in terms of a theory of justice. Plato's just state was decidedly authoritarian and was based upon a strict division of labour that supposedly reflected different character-types and human attributes. He argued that government should be exercised exclusively by a small collection of. philosopher-kings, supported by the auxiliaries (collectively termed the 'Guardians'), whose education and communistic way of life would ensure that ruled on the basis of wisdom.

In his view, knowledge and virtue are one. In The Laws, he advocated a system of mixed government, but continued to emphasize the subordination of the individual to the state and law.

9. According to Aristotle the authority of a constitutional ruler over his subjects is quite different from that of a master over his slaves because the slave is inferior from birth and incapable of ruling himself. Aristotle justify the slavery system. Aristotle's twenty-two surviving treatises were compiled as lecture notes and range over logic, physics, metaphysics, astronomy, meteorology, biology, ethics and politics. His best known political work is 'politics', a comprehensive study of the nature of political life and the forms it might take. In describing politics as the 'Master Science', he emphasized that it is in the public not private domain that human beings strive for justice and live the 'good life'. Aristotle's taxomony of forms of government led him to prefer those that aim at the common good over those that benefit sectional interests and to recommend a mixture of democracy and oligarchy, in the form of what he called polity.

10. British political thinker John Locke is the father of Liberalism. Locke was the first to base the government on the consent of the governed to protect their right. It is the individual endowed with the tool of reason who are source of all political power. Many thinkers are commented on Locke's theory and his life. Willmoore Kendall has written John Locke and the doctrine of Majority rule; J.W. Gough has written the book John Locke's political philosophy; M.W Cranston wrote John Locke, A Biography and Richard Cox wrote the book Locke on peace and war.

11. According to J.J. Rousseau, 'Science is the fruit of idle curiosity; philosophy is mere intellectual frippery; the amenities of polite life is tinsel'. In 1749, inspired by the title set by the 'Academy of Dijon' for an essay competition, Rousseau wrote his 'Discourse on the Sciences and Arts', and was awarded first prize. Published in 1750, this established his reputation as a writer. He wrote the 'Discoure on Inequality' in 1755, again for the 'Academy of Dijon', but did not win. In both discourses, Rousseau contrasted the simplicity and innocence of solitary man in a state of nature, living in terms of his own being, with the dishonesty of man in society who see himself, and hence lives, only in terms of the opinions of others. Sciences and Arts, on the one hand, and the Inequality on the other, are manifestations of this corruption. In between the state of nature and corrupt society, he puts the primitive family which is so small that no dishonesty can exist between its members, and which therefore provides a context for morality.

12. Marx's 'theory of alienation' is mentioned in his work 'Paris manuscripts' (economic-philosophical manuscripts of 1844). By theory of alienation Marx shows the drawbacks of capitalism. Under capitalism, for instance, factory work (through the division of labour) turns labour from a social activity into an individuated process, alienating workers from each other. Factory work dehumanizes workers by giving them repetitive tasks which require no free, creative input. Thus workers are alienated from their human potential. The products one produces fail any longer to express one's personality. For Marx, then, the superseding of capitalism is a necessary prerequisite for ridding alienation of its distorted elements.

13. R.R. Diwaker opined the view that it is not Gandhi who made Satyagraha but it is Satyagraha which made Gandhi the Mahatma. Gandhi's ethic of non-violent resistance, Satyagraha, reinforced by his ascetic lifestyle, gave the movement for Indian independence enormous moral authority and provided a model for later civil rights activists. First outlined in Hind Swaraj (Home Rule) (1909), it was based upon a philosophy ultimately derived from Hinduism in which the universe is regulated by the primacy of truth or Satya.

14. Manavendra Nath Roy was born on 6 Feb. 1886. His original name was Narendranath Bhattacharya. He had been a revolutionary since his college days. He was greatly influenced by Swami Vivekananda, Bankim Chandra, Swami Ramthirtha, Dayanand Saraswati and other stalwarts. It was during the Swadeshi movement in Bengal that Roy got carried away with the revolutionary fervor and began to take an active part in revolutionary activities. Roy was a founder of the 'Mexican Communist Party' and the 'Communist Party of India'.

15. Aurobindo Ghose said that God has appeared to him in prison, placed the Gita in his hands and made him realize the simple truths of the Sanatana Dharma. Sri Aurobindo (Aravinda Akroyd Ghose) born on 15 August 1872, was an Indian nationalist, scholar, poet, mystic, philosopher, yogi and guru, who developed concepts of human progress and spiritual revolution with the help of his spiritual collaborator, Mirra Alfassa, he founded the 'Sri Aurobindo Ashram'.

16. Comparative politics is the study of all forms of political activity-governmental as well as non-governmental and all political phenomena. There have been three trends in the development of comparative politics. In the earliest phase, Aristotle employed comparative method with the aim of evolving a better political order.

In the second phase comes the works of writers like Samuel Beer, Macridies, etc. It represents more sophistication in the realm of political enquiry.

In the third phase comes the works of David Easton, Almond, Karl Deutsch, Lasswell etc. with the help of interdisciplinary focus in their enquiry they evolved a number of tools and techniques for the analysis of politics.

17. There are two types of the approaches to the study of comparative politics—Traditional and Modern approaches. Philosophical, Historical, Legal-Institutional are traditional approaches and Behaviouralism, Post-Behaviouralism, system, structural-functionalism are modern approaches.

Philosophical approach is the most ancient study of politics and deals with basic problems of the nature and functions of the state, citizenship, rights and duties and political ideas.

Behavioural approach takes into account the behaviour of persons and groups in society and not institution's structure or ideologies. System approach emphasises on integration of all knowledge and treats all systems as inter-related. David Easton developed the concept of a political system.

18. The input-output mehtod developed by David Easton. According to Easton the political system receives inputs from the environment in the form of demands and supports and then it produces outputs in the form of policies and decisions. The outputs again flow back into the environment through a feedback mechanism, giving rise to fresh demands etc. The sequences of the input functions are political socialization and recruitment, interest-articulation, interest-aggregation and political communication.

19. Max Weber and Talcott Parsons influenced Gabriel Almond in his structural-functionalism approach. According to Almond, a political system has four characteristics that may be called 'legitimate patterns of interaction'.

Every political system has its structures, some of which may be more specialized, performing more functions, while others may be less specialized, performing less functions in it.

Whatever differences may be between the system and its structures, the same political functions are performed in all political system.

Political structures are multifunctional. All political system beings parts of the society as a whole, have a culture of their own fact is always a mixture of the traditional and the modern.

20. The provision of the Vice-President of India has taken from United State's constitution. So, too much similarities between both the Vice-presidents. Both the Vice-presidents are elected. Both of them are the presiding officers of their respective upper houses Rajya Sabha and Senate. Both the Vice-presidents are not the members of their respective houses but both of them have right to casting vote in case of a tie.

21. The 'theory of separation of powers' was propounded by the French political philosopher Montesquieu; and the American governmental system is considered to be the off-spring and successor of this theory. The American constitution is that of checks and balances throughout. Complete separation of powers is not provided in the constitution as it was neither practicable nor desirable. The theory of separation of powers is supplemented by the principles of checks and balances, which mean that a branch of government should neither be able to work without the co-operation of the other branches nor it should be in a position to become independent and establish its dictatorship.

22. According to W.F. Riggs, lack of balance between equality and capacity is called development trap. Political development involves a system's capacity to absorb and utilise more and more information from its environment. Its goal is to respond to this information and to bring about change to satisfy its needs, and to enhance the range and diversity of goals that can be satisfied.

23. 'The politics of modernization' has written by David E. Apter in 1967; 'Political order in changing societies' has written by Samuel P. Huntington in 1968; 'Capitalism and under development in Latin America' has written by Andre Gunder Frank in 1967 and Walter Rodney wrote the book 'How Europe underdeveloped Africa' in 1972.

24. United States constitution consists only 7 Articles, in which Article-2 vests the executive powers in the President. American President have too much executive powers, such as; ensures the observance, enforcement of laws, treaties and decisions of court and acts as chief administrator. Nominates and appoints the ambassadors, ministers, consuls, Judges of the Supreme Court and other officers. He is the Commander-in-Chief of Army, Navy and the Air Force. He can grant reprieves and pardons for offences against the USA. Also he is the chief foreign policy maker and accredited official spokesman of USA in international relations.

25. The Federal assembly of Switzerland is a bicameral legislature known as 'Council of states' and 'National Council'. Both houses have equal powers.

Upper house is more powerful than lower house, is the feature of United States constitution. Senate is the most powerful second chamber in the world.

Lower house is more powerful than upper house, is the feature of Indian constitution. In Indian constitution 'Lok Sabha' is lower house and 'Rajya Sabha' is upper house.

According to French Vth Republic, National Assembly can overthrow the government.

26. Pocket Veto, president message to federal legislature, Caucus system, pigeon hole-a bill are the parts of constitutional practice of American political system.

In the United States, before a bill that has passed the House of representative and the Senate becomes a law the president must sign it. If he declines to sign a particular bill it automatically becomes law after 10 congressional working days. However, if congress adjourns before the required 10 days have elapsed the bill is deemed not to have passed. The president has, in a sense, placed the bill in his pocket.

President message to federal legislature on the beginning of the session. Caucus is an exclusive meeting of the members of a party or faction for organizational and/or strategic purposes. In the United States there are nominating caucuses and congressional caucuses. Pigeon hole-bill related to the United States political system.

27. There are many political parties in UK. Such as Conservative, Labour, Liberal, Scottland, National Party, Green Party, etc. But the two main parties are Labour and Conservative. The former Prime ministers Harold Wilson and Tony Blair belonged to the Labour party. This party was established as the 'Labour Representation Committee' in 1900, becoming the Labour party in 1906.

After 1918 the party traditionally presented its policies as 'socialist', emphasizing the importance of a large state-controlled sector of the economy, relatively high levels of taxation and comprehensive state-organized welfare provision.

28. The Judges of the US Supreme Court hold office until death or resignation or removal by the congress. While the constitution of India has not fixed the tenure of a judge of the Supreme Court. However, it makes the following three provisions in this regard: He holds office until he attains the age of 65 years. He can resign his office by writing to the president. He can be removed from his office by the president on the recommendation of the parliament.

29. The Swiss Federal Tribunal was created in 1874 and its members are elected by the Federal Assembly. Swiss Court is a single court. It does not have subordinate courts. This Federal court has power to declare laws passed by the State or the Constituent unit of the federation invalid but not the federal laws.

30. The British Political system is based on the doctrine of the sovereignty of parliament, while the parliament is not supreme in India and enjoys limited and restricted powers due to a written constitution, federal system, judicial review and fundamental rights. De Lolme, a British political analyst, said, 'The British parliament can do every thing except make a woman a man and a man a woman'. The head of the state in England (that is, king or queen) is a nominal head of the state. He enjoys a hereditary position.

31. Maker of Indian Constitution and chairman of the Drafting Committee of the constitution Dr. B.R. Ambedkar said, in the constituent Assembly of India, that "Since Indians wish to write and develop a common culture, it is the bounden duty of all Indians to own up Hindi as their language ....Any Indian who does not accept this proposal....., has no right to be Indian."

34. Many features borrowed by Indian constitution from foreign countries, such as; Fundamental Rights and Judicial Review borrowed from USA; Single citizenship from UK; Nomination of members of Rajya Sabha from Ireland; federation with a strong centre, vesting of residuary powers in the centre, appointment of state governors by the centre, advisory jurisdiction of the Supreme Court from Canada. Except it, federal scheme, office of governor, judiciary, public service commissions, emergency provisions and administrative details borrowed from government of India Act-1935.

35. The Government of India Act of 1919 is also known as Montague-Chelmsford reforms. Montague was the secretary of state for India and Lord Chelmsford was the viceroy of India. This Act relaxed the central control over the provinces by demarcating and separating the central and provincial subjects. The central and provincial legislatures were authorised to make laws on their respective list of subjects. However, the structure of government continued to be centralised and unitary. It further divided the provincial subjects into two parts—transferred & reserved. The transferred subjects were to be administered by the Governor with the aid of ministers responsible to the legislative council. The reserved subjects, on the other hand, were to be administered by the governor and his executive council without being responsible to the legislative council. This dual scheme of governance was known as 'Dyarchy'.

36. Back in the 1950s, the British scholar W.H. Morris Jones identified three idioms of Indian politics. These were the modern, the traditional and the Saintly. Thus, he wrote, "The modern language of politics is the language of the Indian constitution and the courts; of parliamentary debates; of the higher administration."

On the other hand, the traditional idiom was local and sectarian. It "knows little or nothing of the problems of anything as big as India". Here, "Caste (or sub-caste or community) is the core of traditional politics." Finally, there was the saintly idiom, illustrated at the time Morris Jones was writing, by the land-donation movement of Acharya Vinobha Bhave, "the 'Saint on the March', who tourerd India on foot preaching the path of self-sacrifice and love and polity without power."

37. Navnirman movement of Gujarat was led by students in 1974. It has started with the call of J.P. Narayan. In 1960 Maharashtra and Gujarat comes in existence as separate states. After the Indo-China war (1962) communist party of India divided into two parts, namely CPI & CPI(M). This division occured in 1964. Formation of Janata Party was took place in 1977.

38. Rajni Kothari, an eminent political analyst, describes Social movement as 'non-party political formations'. Kothari also call the Indian party system as 'one party dominance system' or the 'Congress system'. The dominant position enjoyed by the Congress has been declining since 1967 with the rise of regional parties and other national parties.

39. In 1950s later Gandhians, like the Indian non-violence activist Vinoba Bhave, embraced the term as a name for the social movement in post-independence India which strove to ensure that self-determination and equality reached all strata of Indian society. Bhave started the Sarvodaya movement from Andhra Pradesh.

Naxalite movement started in India by Charu Majumdar and Kanu Sanyal in May, 1967. Communist leader Charu Majumdar wrote various articles based on Marx-Lenin-Mao thought, which later came to be known as 'Historic eight documents' and formed the basis of naxalite movement.

In the 1970s, an organized resistance led by Sundar Lal Bahuguna to the destruction of forests spread throughout India and came to be known as the Chipko Movement, the name of the movement comes from the word 'embrace', as the villagers hugged the trees and prevented the contractors from felling them.

Narm la Bachao Andolan is a social movement consisting of Adivasis, farmers, environmentalists and human rights activists against a number of large dams being built across the Narmada river. leading spokes-persons of this movement are Medha Patkar and Baba Amte.

40. Justice Verma Committee was constituted following Nirbhaya case to recommend amendments to the criminal law so as to provide for quicker trial and enhanced punishment for criminals accused of committing sexual assault against women. On December 23, 2012 a three member committee headed by Justice J.S. Verma, former chief Justice of the S.C. the other members of the committee were justice Leila Seth, former judge of the H.C. and Gopal Subramanium, former Soliciter General of India.

41. Under the Article-324(1) of Indian Constitution, the superintendence, direction and control of the preparation of the electoral rolls for, and the conduct of, all elections to parliament and to the legislature of every state and of elections to the offices of president and vice president held under this constitution shall be vested in the Election Commission of India.

42. The National Integration Day is celebrated in India on 19th November every year on birth memoire of Smt. Indira Gandhi. India is a land of widespread diversities in terms of religion, language, caste, tribe, race, region and so on. Hence, the achievement of national integration becomes very essential for the all-round development and prosperity of the country.

43. In Bommai case (1994), the following propositions have been laid down by the Supreme Court on imposition of president's rule in a state under A-356:

The presidential proclamation imposing president's rule is subject to judicial review. The satisfaction of the president must be based on relevant material. The action of the president can be struck down by the court if it is based on irrelevant or extraneous grounds or if it was found to be malafide or perverse. Burden lies on the centre to prove that relevant material exist to justify the imposition of the President's Rule. The court cannot go into the correctness of the material or its adequacy but it can see whether it is relevant to the action. If the court holds the presidential proclamation to be unconstitutional and invalid, it has power to restore the dismissed state government and revive the state legislative assembly if it was suspended or dissolved.

The state legislative assembly should be dissolved only after the parliament has approved the presidential proclamation, until such approval is given, the president can only suspend the assembly. In case the parliament fails to approve the proclamation, the assembly would get reactivated. The question of the state government losing the confidence of the legislative assembly should be decided on the floor of the legislative house and until that is done the ministry should not be unseated.

Finally, the power under Article 356 is an exceptional power and should be used only occassionally to meet the requirements of special situations.

44. Public Accounts Committee was set up first in 1921 under the provisions of the government of India Act of 1919. At present, it consists of 22 members (15 from the Lok Sabha and 7 from the Rajya Sabha).

The first estimates committee in the post-independence era was constituted in 1950 on the recommendation of John Mathai, the then Finance minister. Originally, it has 25 members but in 1956 its membership was raised to 30. All the 30 members are from Lok Sabha only.

Rules Committee of Lok Sabha considers the matters of procedure and conduct of business in the House and recommends necessary amendments or additions to the rules of the house. The Lok Sabha committee consists of 15 members including the speaker as its ex-officio chairman. In the Rajya Sabha, it consists of 16 members including the chairman as its ex-officio chairman.

58. Subject to the provisions of the Article–315, there shall be a public service commission for the union and for each state. Two or more states may agree that there shall be one public service commission for that group of states, and if a resolution to that effect is passed by the House or, where there are two houses, by each house of the legislature of each of those states, parliament may be law provide for the appointment of a Joint State Public Service Commission to serve the needs of those states.

59. Consultative committee of parliament appoints a sub-committee under chairpersonship of P.K. Thungon to consider constitutional Amendment. Thungon committee formed in 1988 during the Rajiv Gandhi government. This committee recommends constitutional status for panchayats. On the basis of recommendation 73rd & 74th Amendment Act of 1992 was adopted. Recommendations of this committee are constitutional status for the Panchayats, planning at Zila Parishad level and District collector to be Chief executive of Zila Parishad.

60. 'All-India Services (conduct) Rules' Act made in 1968 for civil servants. The Central 'Bureau of Investigation (CBI)' was set up in 1963 by a resolution of the ministry of Home Affairs. Later, it was transferred to the Ministry of Personnel and now it comes under the administrative control of the 'Department of Personnel and Training (DoPT)'. 'Indian Penal Code (IPC)' drafting by Lord Macallay enacted in 1860. The 'Special Police Establishment' (which looked into vigilance cases) set up in 1941 was also merged with the CBI.

The establishment of the CBI was recommended by the 'Santhanam Committee' on prevention of corruption (1962-64). The CBI is not a statutory body. It drives its power from the Delhi Special Police Establishment Act-1946.

61. Haushofer, Hans Morgenthau, Reinhold Neibuhr and E.H. Carr are international political thinkers. Haushofer stated that, A state should be economically self sufficient for military reasons.

Realist thinker Hans Morgenthau was the first to develop a realist theory in 'Politics Among Nations'. He stated that the struggle for power is universal in time and space and is an undeniable fact of experience.

Reinhold Neibuhr said that there is no possibility of drawing a sharp line between the will to live and the will to power.

According to E.H. Carr, every act of the state, in its power aspect, is directed towards war, not as a desirable weapon but as a weapon which it may require in the last resort. Carr also said that, in its essence power is an indivisible whole.

62. Churchill's Fulton Speech held in USA in May 1946. Churchill was the Prime minister of England. Originally the 'Organisation of African Unity' (OAU), restyled the African Union in July 2002. The OAU was established in 1963 at Addis Ababa, with a continent wide membership. Recognition of South Sudan as a sovereign state and 193rd member of the U.N. was in 2011.

63. Realism is a theory to understanding International relations. It is conventional to counterpose realist thinking to Idealism. Realism dominated the discipline in the decades following the 2nd world war. It claims an intellectual heritage going back to Thucydides, Machiavelli, Hobbes and Rousseau. Post-war realism was dominated by the writting of E.H. Carr, Hans Morgenthau and John Herz. A revival under the label neorealism started in the late 1970s led by the work of Kenneth N. Waltz.

In realistic approach, Thucydides is called the first classical realist. Realism believe that power is the key to international politics and the main goal of states is survival.

64. George Schwarzenberger defined non-alignment as a 'policy of keeping out of alliances'. Schwarzenberger carry six concepts, that is oftenly regarded as the concept of non-alignment. These six concepts are Isolationism, Non-commitment, Neutrality, Neutralisation, Unilateralism and Non-envolvement.

65. The North American Free Trade Agreement was negotiated between the USA, Canada and Mexico between 1991 and 1993. It is the largest free trade area in the world, with a GNP of almost $5 trillion, and encompassing a population of over 360 million. Building on earlier US-Canada free trade accords, the final agreement establishes the progressive elimination of most tariff and non-tariff barriers to trade between these two countries and Mexico. The agreement also facilitates cross-border investment, and includes side-agreements addressing cooperation on labour and the environment.

66. Neorealists Kenneth N. Waltz identifies 'three images of politics'. Realism in all of its forms emphasizes the continuities of the human condition, particularly at the international level. Classical realists tended to find the source of these continuities in the permanence of human nature as reflected in the political construction of states. Neorealists find them in the anarchic structure of the international system, which they see as a historically enduring force that shapes the behaviour and construction of states.

67. The origin of the South-South co-operation lies in the failure of the North-South dialogue or co-operation. As the North did not respond favourably to the demand of the South for reduction in tariff liberalisation, international commodity agreements to stabilise prices, official aid at concessional rates and reforms in the International Monetary System, the countries of the south were convinced that there was no common ground between North and South. United Nation confirmed this co-operation and declare 19th December the annual UN Day for South-South co-operation.

68. September 11th, 2001 terrorist attacks launched by the Al-Qaida network on targets in the USA, which caused thousands of deaths. Four passenger airlines were hijacked; two were flown into the twin towers of the World Trade Centre in New York and one into the Pentagon building near Washington. One plane crashed in Pennsylvania. The US President George W. Bush, described the attacks as an act of war and responded by launching a military campaign in Afghanistan, where the Taliban government was seen to be harbouring terrorists and the leader of Al-Qaida, Osama Bin Laden. This Military Campaign is called 'Operation Endurin Freedom 2001'.

69. BIMSTEC (Bangladesh, India, Myanmar, Sri Lanka, Thailand Economic Cooperation) is a regional organisation formed in June, 1997. In 2004, Nepal & Bhutan also became its members. The organisation seeks to promote the socio-economic development and create an environment of cooperation in various fields so as to enhance the livelihood of people in the region. The members of BIMSTEC agree on 'Free Trade Area' in Phuke (Thailand) on 8 Feb. 2004. The BIMSTEC was renamed as 'Bay of Bengal Initiative for Multisectoral Technical and Economic Cooperation'.

70. ASEAN (Association of South-East Asian Nations) was formed in 1967 by Indonesia, Malaysia, Philippine, Singapore and Thailand with the main objective of guiding economic progress and promote economic stability in the region. Later on, Brunei, Vietnam, Laos, Myanmar and Combodia became its members. ASEAN's declared objectives are regional peace & stability, it is intended to promote co-operation in social, economic, scientific, cultural and administrative spheres.

71. Secretary General Boutros Boutros Ghali (Egypt) Report 1992 'An agenda for peace' triggered the process of U.N. reforms though the talks for reform have remained dormant from 1992 onwards; there has emerged a renewed interests in it. Except the secretary general, many other countries suggested for the reformation of UNO. In these countries India is most vocal member. India want to increase the no. of members of the security council and more democratization of this institute.

75. Amnesty International is not an Inter-governmental organization. It is an international non-governmental organization, formed in 1961, which campaigns against violations of human rights. Widely respected and awarded the Nobel peace prize in 1977, its monitoring of human rights issues through Amnesty International Reports has provided information widely used by policy makers and political scientists.

Previous Paper (Solved)

UGC-NET POLITICAL SCIENCE, JUNE 2014

PAPER–II

Note: *This paper contains fifty (50) objective type questions of two (2) marks each. All questions are compulsory.*

1. To Kautilya, the concept "rupadarshaka" means :
   A. Beautician
   B. Magistrate
   C. Inspector of coins
   D. Zamindar

2. Plato appropriated the ideas of
   A. Heraclitus B. Parmenides
   C. Socrates D. All the above

3. For whom "All existence is simply a matter in motion."?
   A. Plato
   B. Hobbes
   C. T.H. Green
   D. Rousseau

4. Rousseau won the prize in an essay contest sponsored by the Academy of Dijon in 1749 on the subject
   A. "Has the progress of the sciences and the Arts contributed to corrupt or purify morals?"
   B. "Has the progress of the sciences contributed to corrupt morals?"
   C. "Has the development of the sciences contributed to corrupt or purify morals?"
   D. None of the above

5. Given below are two statements, one labelled as Assertion (A) and the other labelled as Reason (R) :

   Assertion (A) : For Plato, knowledge is neither perception nor opinion.

   Reason (R) : Right opinion is knowledge.

   Codes :
   A. Both (A) and (R) are true and (R) is the correct explanation of (A).
   B. Both (A) and (R) are true and (R) is not the correct explanation of (A).
   C. (A) is true and (R) is false.
   D. (A) is false, but (R) is true.

6. The laws of the dialectic of Marx does not include
   A. The law of transformation of quantity into quality and vice-versa.
   B. The law of the unity of opposites.
   C. The law of the negation of the negation.
   D. Dialectic is confined to its operation to the understanding of the past only.

7. Who said "Leninism is Marxism of the era of imperialism and of the proletarian revolution"?
   A. Marx B. Lenin
   C. Stalin D. Mao

8. Identify the correct sequence of the tenets of Behaviouralism as advocated by David Easton.
   (*i*) Regularities (*ii*) Techniques
   (*iii*) Quantification (*iv*) Verification

   Select the correct answer from the codes given below :
   A. (*i*), (*ii*), (*iii*), (*iv*)
   B. (*i*), (*iv*), (*ii*), (*iii*)
   C. (*i*), (*iii*), (*iv*), (*ii*)
   D. (*i*), (*ii*), (*iv*), (*iii*)

9. In which place of South Africa did Gandhiji for the first time organize mass protest?
   A. Cape Town B. Johannesburg
   C. Soweto D. Pretoria

10. Match List-I with List-II and select the correct answer from the codes given below :

List-I	List-II
(*a*) Charles. E. Merriam	(*i*) The Governmental process
(*b*) Heinz Eulan	(*ii*) What is political philosophy? and other studies
(*c*) Leo Strauss	(*iii*) New aspects of politics
(*d*) D. Truman	(*iv*) The behavioural persuasion in politics

Codes :

	(*a*)	(*b*)	(*c*)	(*d*)
A.	(*iii*)	(*iv*)	(*ii*)	(*i*)
B.	(*ii*)	(*iii*)	(*i*)	(*iv*)
C.	(*i*)	(*ii*)	(*iii*)	(*iv*)
D.	(*iv*)	(*i*)	(*iii*)	(*ii*)

11. Who among the following political thinkers are generally regarded as founders of philosophical approach?

A. Plato and Aristotle
B. Hobbes, Locke, Rousseau
C. Jeremy Bentham and J.S. Mill
D. Kant, Hegel

12. Which of the following are the characteristics of Weber's ideal bureaucracy?

1. Staff and line
2. Impersonality
3. Hierarchy
4. Informal organization

Select the correct answer from the codes given below :

A. 1 and 2 B. 2 and 3
C. 3 and 4 D. 1 and 4

13. Which of the following does not figure in Almond and Verba's classification of political cultures?

A. Cognitive orientation
B. Affective orientation
C. Evaluative orientation
D. Empirical orientation

14. Given below are two statements, one labelled as Assertion (A) and the other labelled as Reason (R):

Assertion (A) : Dependency is a relationship between the groups of economies those, who condition others and those, who are conditioned by others.

Reason (R) : Dependency is dependent on the core periphery relationship of the international political economy.

Codes :

A. Both (A) and (R) are true and (R) is the correct explanation of (A).
B. Both (A) and (R) are true and (R) is not the correct explanation of (A).
C. (A) is true, but (R) is false.
D. (A) is false, but (R) is true.

15. Who said "A state is human activity that successfully claims the monopoly of the legitimate use of physical force within a given territory"?

A. David Easton B. G.A. Almond
C. Karl Marx D. Max Weber

16. The traditional approaches to the comparative politics neglected the

A. Study of Government
B. Institutional studies
C. Comparison of the constitutions
D. Empirical investigations

17. Match List-I with List-II and select the correct answer from the codes given below:

List-I (Electoral System)	List-II (Countries)
(*a*) First-Past-the-post system	(*i*) India
(*b*) Two Rounds of system	(*ii*) Egypt
(*c*) List System	(*iii*) Brazil
(*d*) Single Transferable vote system	(*iv*) Ireland

Codes :

	(*a*)	(*b*)	(*c*)	(*d*)
A.	(*i*)	(*ii*)	(*iii*)	(*iv*)
B.	(*iv*)	(*iii*)	(*ii*)	(*i*)

C. (*iii*) (*iv*) (*i*) (*ii*)
D. (*ii*) (*i*) (*iv*) (*iii*)

18. Match List-I with List-II and select the correct answer from the codes given below :

List-I (Books)	List-II (Authors)
(*a*) Interest groups in American Society	(*i*) H.W. Ehrmann
(*b*) Interest groups of four Continents	(*ii*) H. Zeigler
(*c*) Anonymous Empire	(*iii*) Graham Wallas
(*d*) Human Nature in Politics	(*iv*) Samuel Finer

Codes :

	(*a*)	(*b*)	(*c*)	(*d*)
A.	(*i*)	(*ii*)	(*iii*)	(*iv*)
B.	(*ii*)	(*iii*)	(*i*)	(*iv*)
C.	(*iii*)	(*iv*)	(*ii*)	(*i*)
D.	(*ii*)	(*i*)	(*iv*)	(*iii*)

19. Which one of the following approaches studies, among others, public opinion and people's political choices?
A. Political Philosophical Approach
B. Institutional Approach
C. Behavioural Approach
D. Legal Approach

20. Match List-I with List-II and select the correct answer from the codes given below:

List-I (Political Culture)	List-II (Countries)
(*a*) Homogeneous culture	(*i*) Uganda
(*b*) Elite mass culture	(*ii*) U.K.
(*c*) Subject political culture	(*iii*) India
(*d*) Parochial culture	(*iv*) China

Codes :

	(*a*)	(*b*)	(*c*)	(*d*)
A.	(*i*)	(*ii*)	(*iii*)	(*iv*)
B.	(*ii*)	(*iii*)	(*iv*)	(*i*)
C.	(*iii*)	(*iv*)	(*ii*)	(*i*)
D.	(*iv*)	(*iii*)	(*i*)	(*ii*)

21. Which one of the following pairs are not correctly matched?

	List-I (President)		List-II (Vice-President)
A.	Dr. Rajendra Prasad	–	Dr. S. Radha Krishnan
B.	Dr. Zakir Hussain	–	V.V. Giri
C.	Sanjeeva Reddy	–	B.D. Jatti
D.	Dr. S. Radha Krishnan	–	Dr. Zakir Hussain

22. What is the percentage fixed by the constitution regarding the strength of the Ministers including the chief minister in a state?
A. 10% B. 12%
C. 15% D. 16%

23. Which one of the following is mainly associated with Panchayati Raj in tribal areas?
A. P.K. Thungan Committee
B. Dilip Singh Bhuria Committee
C. Sadiq Ali Committee
D. Doomarlal Baitha Committee

24. Arrange the following writs in the correct sequence as given in the Indian Constitution:
(*i*) Certiorari
(*ii*) Habeas Corpus
(*iii*) Quo Warranto
(*iv*) Prohibition
(*v*) Mandamus

Codes :
A. (*i*), (*iii*), (*v*), (*ii*), (*iv*)
B. (*ii*), (*iv*), (*iii*), (*i*), (*v*)
C. (*ii*), (*v*), (*iv*), (*i*), (*iii*)
D. (*iii*), (*i*), (*ii*), (*iv*), (*v*)

25. Arrange the following in their chronological sequence:
(*i*) Cripps Mission
(*ii*) Montague Chelmsford Report
(*iii*) Simon Commission
(*iv*) Morley-Minto Reforms

Codes :
A. (*ii*), (*iii*), (*i*), (*iv*)
B. (*iv*), (*ii*), (*iii*), (*i*)
C. (*iii*), (*i*), (*ii*), (*iv*)
D. (*i*), (*iv*), (*iii*), (*ii*)

26. Match List-I with List-II and select the correct answer from the codes given below :

List-I (Parties)	**List-II (Characteristic)**
(*a*) Indian National Congress	(*i*) National Party
(*b*) Telugu Desam Party	(*ii*) State Party
(*c*) Kerala Congress	(*iii*) Umbrella Party
(*d*) Communist Party of India (marxist)	(*iv*) Regional Party

Codes :

	(*a*)	(*b*)	(*c*)	(*d*)
A.	(*ii*)	(*i*)	(*iv*)	(*iii*)
B.	(*i*)	(*iii*)	(*iv*)	(*ii*)
C.	(*iii*)	(*iv*)	(*ii*)	(*i*)
D.	(*iv*)	(*ii*)	(*i*)	(*iii*)

27. Which one of the following was denounced by congress as "inadequate, unsatisfactory and disappointing"?

A. Indian Councils Act, 1909
B. Montague Chelmsford Report, 1918
C. Simon Commission Report, 1930
D. Communal Award, 1932

28. Given below are two statements, one labelled as Assertion (A) and the other labelled as Reason (R):

Assertion (A) : A federal arrangement aims at reconciling freedom with unity and diversity of political cultures and identities with effective collective action.

Reason (R) : India opted for a pluralistic model of nation building.

Codes :

A. Both (A) and (R) are correct and (R) is the correct explanation of (A).
B. Both (A) and (R) are correct, but (R) is not the correct explanation of (A).
C. (A) is correct, but (R) is not correct.
D. (R) is correct, but (A) is not correct.

29. Given below are two statements, one labelled as Assertion (A) and the other labelled as Reason (R) :

Assertion (A) : Bulk of the provisions of the Constitution of India were adopted from the Government of India Act of 1935.

Reason (R) : The Congress party passed a resolution adopting the government of India Act of 1935 as the basis of the constitution.

Codes :

A. Both (A) and (R) are true and (R) is the correct explanation of (A).
B. Both (A) and (R) are true, but (R) is not the correct explanation of (A).
C. (A) is true, but (R) is false.
D. (R) is true, but (A) is false.

30. Match List-I with List-II and select the correct answer from the codes given below :

List-I (Articles)	**List-II (Provisions)**
(*a*) 359	(*i*) Financial Emergency
(*b*) 312	(*ii*) Finance Commission
(*c*) 280	(*iii*) Suspension of Fundamental Rights
(*d*) 360	(*iv*) All India Services

Codes :

	(*a*)	(*b*)	(*c*)	(*d*)
A.	(*iii*)	(*iv*)	(*ii*)	(*i*)
B.	(*ii*)	(*iii*)	(*i*)	(*iv*)
C.	(*i*)	(*ii*)	(*iv*)	(*iii*)
D.	(*iv*)	(*i*)	(*iii*)	(*ii*)

31. Who among the following has created eighteen definitions of public administration and put them in four categories of political, legal, occupational and managerial?

A. Gulick and Urwick
B. Shafritz and Russell
C. David H. Rosenbloom
D. Paul H. Appleby

32. Who among the following has not made a distinction between public and private administration?

A. Henry Fayol B. Herbert Simon
C. Paul H. Appleby D. John Gaus

33. What is the correct chronological sequence of the following reports?

1. A.D. Gorwala Report

2. Paul H. Appleby Report
3. Santhanam Committee Report
4. First Administrative Reforms Commission Report.

Select the correct answer from the codes given below :

A. 1, 2, 3, 4 B. 2, 1, 4, 3
C. 1, 3, 2, 4 D. 1, 3, 4, 2

34. Max Weber used the Greek word 'Charisma' to refer to

1. qualities acquired by experience
2. inherited qualities
3. supernatural qualities
4. super human qualities

Select the correct answer from the codes given below :

A. 2, 3 and 4 B. 1, 3 and 4
C. 1 and 3 D. 3 and 4

35. Which one of the following is not a base of organization?

A. Function B. Budgeting
C. Process D. Clientele

36. Which of the following statement is not correct in respect of India?

A. Tax can be levied except by authority of law
B. No expenditure can be incurred from public funds except in the manner provided in the constitution and in accordance with law
C. Executive is bound to spend money in the manner as sanctioned by Parliament
D. None of the above

37. Match List-I with List-II and select the correct answer from the codes given below:

List-I	List-II
(*a*) Hierarchy	(*i*) Dr. K.S. Kothari
(*b*) Report on Public Administration (1951)	(*ii*) House keeping
(*c*) Preliminary screening examination in Indian civil service	(*iii*) Scalar process
(*d*) Auxilliary Agency	(*iv*) A.D. Gorwala

Codes :

	(*a*)	(*b*)	(*c*)	(*d*)
A.	(*i*)	(*iii*)	(*ii*)	(*iv*)
B.	(*iv*)	(*ii*)	(*iii*)	(*i*)
C.	(*iii*)	(*iv*)	(*i*)	(*ii*)
D.	(*ii*)	(*i*)	(*iv*)	(*iii*)

38. Which one of the following was the first state to establish the institution of the Lokayukta in India?

A. Rajasthan B. Bihar
C. Uttar Pradesh D. Maharashtra

39. Given below are two statements, one labelled as Assertion (A) and the other labelled as Reason (R) :

Assertion (A) : Under the spoils system the public offices are distributed to the members of the party victorious at the polls.

Reason (R) : The public offices are considered spoils to be enjoyed by the victors.

Codes :

A. Both (A) and (R) are true and (R) is the correct explanation of (A).
B. Both (A) and (R) are true, but (R) is not the correct explanation of (A).
C. (A) is true, but (R) is false.
D. (A) is false, but (R) is true.

40. Who among the following are the protagonists of the integral view of public administration?

1. Henry Fayol
2. Marshall Dimock
3. Simon
4. Gulick

Select the correct answer from the codes given below :

Codes :

A. 1 and 4 B. 1 and 3
C. 1 and 2 D. 2 and 3

41. Match List-I with List-II and select the correct answer from the codes given below :

List-I (Authors)	List-II (Books)
(*a*) E.H. Carr	(*i*) Neorealism and Its Critics

(*b*) R. Keohane	(*ii*) From Wealth to Power
(*c*) J. Mearsheimer	(*iii*) The Twenty Year Crisis
(*d*) F. Zakaria	(*iv*) The Tragedy of Great Power Politics

Codes :

	(*a*)	(*b*)	(*c*)	(*d*)
A.	(*i*)	(*ii*)	(*iii*)	(*iv*)
B.	(*iv*)	(*iii*)	(*i*)	(*ii*)
C.	(*iii*)	(*i*)	(*iv*)	(*ii*)
D.	(*ii*)	(*iv*)	(*i*)	(*iii*)

42. Given below are two statements, one labelled as Assertion (A) and the other labelled as Reason (R) :

Assertion (A) : Globalization is a multidimensional process.

Reason (R) : It involves economic, political, social and cultural globalizations.

Codes :

A. Both (A) and (R) are true and (R) is the right explanation of (A).
B. Both (A) and (R) are true but (R) is not the right explanation of (A).
C. (A) is true, but (R) is false.
D. (A) is false, but (R) is true.

43. When two combatants are so different in their characters, and in their areas of comparative strategic advantage, that a confrontation between them comes to turn one side's ability to force, the other side to fight on their own terms. Name the type of war?

A. Unequal war
B. Asymmetric war
C. New war
D. Post-westphalian war

44. Name the UN fact finding mission on the Gaza Conflict 2009 Report

A. Golding Report
B. Goldstone Report
C. Goldman Sachs Report
D. Gaza Report

45. Under which chapter and article does the UN security council consider a threat to international peace; first explores ways to settle the dispute peacefully

A. Chapter VI, Article 36
B. Chapter VI, Article 33
C. Chapter VII, Article 47
D. Chapter VII, Article 42

46. Which of the following are correct features of the modern institution of international law?

(i) Unilateral legislation
(ii) Consent and legal obligation
(iii) Language and practice of justification
(iv) Discourse of institutional antonomy

Select the correct answer from the codes given below :

A. (i), (ii) and (iii) are correct.
B. (i), (iii) and (iv) are correct.
C. (i), (ii) and (iv) are correct.
D. (ii), (iii) and (iv) are correct.

47. The United Nations Conference well known as Copenhagen, COP 15 dealt with the issue of

A. Global Warming
B. Climate Change
C. Environment
D. Population Explosion

48. Match List-I with List-II and select the correct answer from the codes given below:

List-I (Regional Organization)	**List-II (Year of Origin)**
(*a*) Organization of American States (OAS)	(*i*) 1989
(*b*) North Atlantic Free Trade Agreement (NAFTA)	(*ii*) 1948
(*c*) Arab Maghreb Union (AMU)	(*iii*) 1954
(*d*) South East Asian Treaty Organization (SEATO)	(*iv*) 1994

Codes :

	(*a*)	(*b*)	(*c*)	(*d*)
A.	(*i*)	(*iii*)	(*ii*)	(*iv*)
B.	(*ii*)	(*iv*)	(*i*)	(*iii*)
C.	(*iv*)	(*ii*)	(*iii*)	(*i*)
D.	(*iii*)	(*i*)	(*iv*)	(*ii*)

49. Given below are two statements, one labelled as Assertion (A) and the other labelled as Reason (R) :

Assertion (A) : India is pursuing a positive asymmetry in South Asia.

Reason (R) : India is strategically contained by China-Pakistan partnership.

Codes :

A. Both (A) and (R) are true and (R) is the right explanation of (A).

B. Both (A) and (R) are true, but (R) is not the right explanation of (A).

C. (A) is true, but (R) is false.

D. (A) is false, but (R) is true.

50. Who is the author of the book "Pakistan's Arms Procurement and Military build-up 1979-99 : In search of a policy"?

A. Ahmed Rashid

B. Ayesha Jalal

C. Ayesha Siddiqa Ada

D. Stephen Cohen

ANSWERS

1	2	3	4	5	6	7	8	9	10
C	D	B	A	C	D	C	B	B	A
11	**12**	**13**	**14**	**15**	**16**	**17**	**18**	**19**	**20**
A	B	D	A	D	D	A	D	C	B
21	**22**	**23**	**24**	**25**	**26**	**27**	**28**	**29**	**30**
C	C	B	C	B	C	B	A	C	A
31	**32**	**33**	**34**	**35**	**36**	**37**	**38**	**39**	**40**
B	A	A	D	B	A	C	D	A	C
41	**42**	**43**	**44**	**45**	**46**	**47**	**48**	**49**	**50**
C	A	B	B	D	D	B	B	B	C

SOME SELECTED EXPLANATORY ANSWERS

1. Kautilya talks of strict control over markets and trade. An officer called the *panyadhyaksha* was in charge of trade, including the price fixation and sale of goods produced by state-run manufacturing units. The *sansthadhyaksha* was the superintendent of markets, the *rupadarshaka* the inspector of coins, and the *pautavadhyaksha* was in charge of ensuring the use of standardized weights and measures. The *Arthashastra* advocates strict state control over artisans' guilds. It prescribes a scale of wages for different types of artisans and lays down punishments for artisans failing to deliver proper goods. The Kautilyan state was also an entrepreneur. State run textile workshops were to be placed under a *sutradhayaksha* and chariot workshops under a *rathadhyaksha*.

2. Plato can help us to get some idea of Heraclitus' real question. For him, it is a question of the paradox of sudden change and, along with it, the being-one of being. What is life and what is death; what are the creation and the extinction of life? This is the riddle that Heraclitus ponders. He seeks the one in all oppositionality, and, in the one, he finds what is oppositional—in fire, the flame; in the *logos,* the soul; in the one, the true. Plato depict the great Parmenides leading the bewildered young Socrates in some bold games—that the one is in everything, and that even the ideas themselves are oppositional, they pass over into one another, and they are the one. This is how Plato can appropriate Heraclitus.

3. Hobbes's strategy was to show that there is a basic mental activitiy, perception, or, as he called it, "sense," from which all other mental phenomena are derived and that perception itself reduces to matter in motion.

   Perception, he maintained, occurs as follows: Motion in the external world causes motion within us. This motion within (which Hobbes called a "phantasm") is experienced by us as an external object (or group of objects) having certain properties. The properties do not *really* exist in the objects, Hobbes said; they are just the way the objects *seem* to us.

4. Rousseau wrote *Discourse* in response to an advertisement that appeared in a 1749 issue of *Mercure de France*, in which the Academy of Dijon set a prize for an essay responding to the question: "Has the progress of the sciences and arts contributed to the purification of morals?" According to Rousseau, "Within an instant of reading this, I saw another universe and became another man." Rousseau found the idea to which he would passionately dedicate the rest of his intellectual life: the destructive influence of civilization on human beings. Rousseau went on to win first prize in the contest in July 1750 and—in an otherwise mediocre career as composer and playwright, among other things—he had newfound fame as a philosopher.

7. Stalin summed it up most eloquently that: "The whole truth about Leninism is that Leninism not only restored Marxism, but also took it a step forward, developing Marxism further under the new conditions of capitalism and of the class struggle of the proletariat."

   We are in a new era of imperialism that is being rapidly advanced by the continuing technology that makes capitalism even more parasitic on the economic level as well as on the militaristic level.

9. At the beginning of the South African War, Gandhi thought that Indians must support the war effort in order to legitimize their claims to full citizenship. He helped organize a volunteer ambulance corps of 300 free Indians and 800 indentured labourers. At the end of the war, however, conditions for Indians did not improve. In 1906 the Transvaal government passed a new act compelling the colony's Indian population to register. In Johannesburg that year Gandhi held a mass protest. For the first time he articulated his philosophy of *satyagraha* or "Truth Force," asking his fellow Indians to defy the new law nonviolently. In seven years of difficult struggle, Gandhi was imprisoned several times, and many other Indians were jailed, shot, or beaten for refusing to register. Finally, however, the government was forced to negotiate a compromise with Gandhi because of the negative publicity the campaign had generated.

11. Philosophical Approach: The philosophical approach, as the name suggests, treats political issues as philosophical concerns. Its main concern is to find out *what should be* or *ought to be* the principles, ideals and organizing criteria of political and human society.

   The Greek thinkers espoused, and enquired into, philosophical issues. In the writings of Plato and Aristotle we find philosophical concerns, such as the proposition of an ideal State/society, principle of justice, and so on. From this concern for the ideal, the philosophical approach becomes prescriptive and normative, and reflects ethical concerns.

13. Empirical orientation does not figure in Almond and Verba's classification of Political cultures.

15. Max Weber famously argued that 'A state is a human community that successfully claims the monopoly of the legitimate use of physical force within a given territory'. This definition reaches back to Hobbes' account of *Leviathan*.

It confers legitimacy on a human institution that imposes order on a society that otherwise tends to anarchy or a brutal state of nature. Weber believed, however, that what made the modern state distinctive was its sense of service to the nation or the public. The emerging states of northern Europe were meant to respond efficiently to the demands of what Foucault would later call 'populations': to the needs of urbanites for clean water and sanitation, for example, or of children for state-provided education.

19. Behavioural research in politics is not, in fact, concerned with the individual actor as such. It more often seeks to describe and explain the political behaviour of a group, an organization, a community, an elite, a mass movement, or a nation, but also assumes that such collectivities do not exist apart from the conduct of their individual members.

22. The Constitution (91st Amendment) Act, 2003, which limits the size of all ministries in India, comes into force on July 7. This Act stipulates that the strength of a council of ministers should not exceed 15 per cent of the total number of members in the Lok Sabha (in case of the central government) or the relevant state assembly. An exception has been made only for smaller states such as Sikkim, Mizoram and Goa where the strength of the assembly is 40 or less. There, the state government can have a maximum of 12 ministers.

23. To examine issues arising out of the extension of Part IX of the Constitution to Scheduled Areas, the government of India appointed a committee of parliamentarians and experts under the chairmanship of Dileep Singh Bhuria in June, 1994. Based on the recommendations of the committee, the Panchayat (Extension to Scheduled Areas) Act, 1996 (PESA) was enacted. The basic provisions of the PESA were aimed at facilitating participatory democracy in tribal areas by empowering the Gram Sabha to manage and control its own resources. The Gram Sabhas were given special functional powers and responsibilities to ensure effective participation of tribal communities in their own development in harmony with their culture so as to preserve/conserve their traditional rights over natural resources. The Act restored primary control over natural resources including land, water, forest and minerals and bestowed ownership rights over minor forest produces to the Gram Sabha.

27. It is with a view to prepare a scheme of reforms Montague came to India in 1917. He met the Indian leaders and tried to understand their aspirations. In consultation with the governor general Lord Chelmsford he prepared 'The Report on Constitutional Reforms' which came to be known as 'Montford Report'. It was published in July 1918 and became the basis for the Government of India Act, 1919. But the Extremists who then dominated the Congress did not favourably receive the Montague-Chelmsford Report. Annie Besant described it as "unworthy to be offered by England or to be accepted by India". A special session of the Congress, held at Bombay in August 1918 denounced the Montague-Chelmsford Report as, inadequate, unsatisfactory and disappointing. It is interesting to note that at the outset Mahatma Gandhi himself welcomed the act of 1919 and not only that he in his speech to the Amritsar session of the Congress on 1st January 1920 urged the Congress to grasp the extended hand of the king emperor and take the fullest advantage of the Reforms.

31. Shafritz and Russell have created eighteen definitions clustered in four categories, namely political, legal, occupational and managerial.

Analyzing the Definitions of Public Administration: *Political* — Public administration is what government does. It exists within a political environment, and it is this political context that makes it "public".

Public administration is about implementation of the public interest. It is also about doing collectively what cannot be done as well individually. ***Legal***—The foundations of public administration in the United States are legal ones and are bound by instruments of law. Public administrations is law in action in the form of statutes, regulations, ordinances, codes, etc. ***Managerial***—The executive nature of public administration enables the public will to be translated into action by the people responsible for running the public bureaucracy. ***Occupational*** — Public administration includes many occupational fields—medicine, engineering, social welfare, economics, etc. It is within the framework of each of these fields that the political, legal and managerial aspects of public administration are transformed by public administrators into the work of government.

32. Scholars like Henry Fayol, Mary P. Follet and L. Urwick do not make a distinction between public and private administration. The classical writers held the view that public and private administrations are the undifferentiated members of the genus administration. Henri Foyal, for example, says that there is only one administrative science, which can be applied equally well to public and private sectors.

35. Budgeting is not a base of organization, whereas function, process and clientele are the base of organization.

38. The ***Lokayukta*** is an anti-*corruption ombudsman* organization in the Indian states. The Lokayukta, along with the Income Tax Department and the Anti Corruption Bureau, mainly helps people publicize corruption among the Politicians and Government Officials. Many acts of Lokayukta have resulted in criminal or other consequences for those charged.

Maharashtra was the first state to introduce the institution of Lokayukta through The *Lokayukta and Upa-Lokayuktas Act in 1970.* This was followed by similar acts being enacted by states of Rajasthan, Bihar, Uttar Pradesh, Karnataka, Madhya Pradesh, Andhra Pradesh, Gujarat and Delhi.

Maharashtra Lokayukta is considered as week due to lack of powers, adequate staff, funds and no independent investigating agency. Karnataka Lokayukta is considered as the most powerful Lokayukta in the country.

40. **Integral View:** According to Integral view, public administration is sum total of all the activities undertaken in pursuit of and in fulfillment of public policy. These activities include not only managerial and technical but also manual and clerical. Thus the activities of all persons from top to bottom constitute administration, although they are of varying significance to the operational dynamics of administrative machinery. In this view, all the acts of the officials of the government, right from the attendant up to the secretaries to the government and the head of the state constitute public administration. L.D. White, Marshall Dimock, Henry Fayol, etc. have contributed to this view of public administration.

43. **Asymmetric war** is war between belligerents whose relative military power differs significantly, or whose strategy or tactics differ significantly.

Asymmetric war can describe a conflict in which the resources of two belligerents differ in essence and in the struggle, interact and attempt to exploit each other's characteristic weaknesses. Such struggles often involve strategies and tactics of unconventional warfare, the weaker combatants attempting to use strategy to offset deficiencies in quantity or quality. Such strategies may not necessarily be militarized. This is in contrast to symmetric warfare, where two powers have similar military power and resources and rely on tactics that are similar overall, differing only in details and execution.

44. His Report of the United Nations Fact-Finding Mission on the Gaza Conflict, also known as the "Goldstone Report," was published on September 15, 2009, and has been highly controversial, with potentially important implications for the laws of armed conflict, particularly with respect to the ability of states to fight terrorist groups.

47. Various bodies under the umbrella of the UNFCCC met several times to prepare the ground for a new agreement regarding climate change issues. Owing to their unremitting endeavors, the Bali Conference as the thirteenth Conference of the Parties (COP 13) of the UNFCCC and the Copenhagen Conference as the fifteenth Conference of the Parties (COP 15) of the UNFCCC were held to deal with the new climate change framework beyond 2012.

50. This book is written by Ayesha Siddiqa Ada. It presents a fundamental departure in presenting an analysis of the internal dynamics of defense management and decision making in Pakistan—a new nuclear weapon state. This is an in-depth study of Pakistan's security link with its arms suppliers and defense industrial capacity, and the influence of Pakistan's army on conventional and unconventional defense decisions. The analysis is backed with numerous case studies of defense decisions carried out from 1979-99.

PAPER–III

Note: *This paper contains **seventy five** (75) objective type questions of **two** (2) marks each. **All** questions are compulsory.*

1. Who described political theory as 'the systematic thinking about the purpose of the government'?

A. Leacock B. Garner
C. Plamenatz D. Berlin

2. Who is the author of the book 'The Philosophy of J.S. Mill'?

A. M. Cowling B. J. Gray
C. R.P. Anschutz D. J.W. Mueller

3. Who is the author of 'Savitri'?

A. M.N. Roy
B. Mahatma Gandhi
C. Aurobindo
D. R. Tagore

4. "Once God is let in, there is an end to the sovereignty of man." Who said this?

A. B.R. Ambedkar
B. Vivekananda
C. M.N. Roy
D. J. Nehru

5. Who said "Man is what he eats"?

A. Marx B. Engels
C. Lenin D. Feuerbach

6. Who is the propounder of labour theory of value?

A. Hobbes B. Locke
C. Rousseau D. Bentham

7. Which one of the following is correct regarding the writings of Machiavelli?

A. Discourses
B. The Golden Ass
C. The Art of War
D. All the above

8. Match List-I with List-II and select the correct answer form the codes given below:

List-I (Thinker)	List-II (Dominent Concept)
(*a*) Beitz	(*i*) Justice as mutual advantage
(*b*) Gauthier	(*ii*) Entitlement Theory of Justice
(*c*) Dworkin	(*iii*) On Global Justice
(*d*) Nozick	(*iv*) On equality

Codes :

	(a)	(b)	(c)	(d)
A.	(i)	(ii)	(iii)	(iv)
B.	(iii)	(i)	(iv)	(ii)
C.	(ii)	(iii)	(i)	(iv)
D.	(iv)	(i)	(ii)	(iii)

9. Plato developed his theory of the nature of the ultimate reality explaining the actual world in

A. The Republic B. The Politics
C. The Laws D. The Timaeus

10. Given below are two statements one labelled as Assertion (A) and the other labelled as Reason (R):

Assertion (A): For Rawls the Right is prior to good.

Reason (R): The loss of freedom for some is made right by greater good shared by others.

Codes :

A. Both (A) and (R) are true and (R) is the right explanation of (A).
B. Both (A) and (R) are true, but (R) is not the right explanation of (A).
C. (A) is true, but (R) is false.
D. (A) is false, but (R) is true.

11. Identify the correct sequence in ascending order of Lenin's writings :

(i) Left Wing Communism
(ii) The State and Revolution
(iii) the Proletarian Revolution and the Renegade Kautsky
(iv) The War and the Second International

Select the correct answer from the codes given below:

A. (iv) (ii) (iii) (i)
B. (i) (ii) (iii) (iv)
C. (iii) (iv) (ii) (i)
D. (ii) (iii) (iv) (i)

12. Which one of the following is not included in the well known sayings of Mao?

A. Weapons are an important factor in war but not the decisive one.
B. Politics is war without bloodshed.
C. The party commands the gun and the gun must never be allowed to command the party.
D. Let a hundred flowers blossom and a hundred schools of thought contend.

13. Which one of the following books is not written by Tilak?

A. The Orion
B. Arctic Home in Vedas
C. Gita Rahasya
D. Life Divine

14. Marx's theory of the state and revolution is taken from

A. German classical philosophy
B. British political economy
C. French revolutionary tradition
D. American war of independence

15. Aristotle devoted himself to a critical study of the ideal states projected by

A. Phaleas B. Hippodamus
C. Plato D. All the above

16. Given below are two statements, one labelled as Assertion (A) and the other labelled as Reason (R):

Assertion (A): According to Lucian W. Pye political development is characterized by equality, capacity and differentiation.

Reason (R): A state should attempt to strengthen these aspects.

Codes:

A. Both (A) and (R) are true and (R) is the correct explanation of (A)
B. Both (A) and (R) are true, but (R) is not the correct explanation of (A)
C. (A) is true, but (R) is false
D. (A) is false, but (R) is true

17. The process of socialization in Traditional Society is

1. diffuse 2. particularistic
3. ascriptive 4. instrumental

Select the correct answer from the codes given below:

Codes:

A. 1, 2, 3 B. 2, 3, 4
C. 4, 3, 1 D. 1, 2, 4

18. Which one of the following is not a kind of power mentioned by Alvin Tofler in his book Powershift?

A. Violence B. Social structure
C. Wealth D. Knowledge

19. Match List-I with List-II and select the correct answer from the codes given below:

List-I (Schools of Modernization)	**List-II (Authors)**
(*a*) Structural School	(*i*) Daniel Lerner
(*b*) Normative School	(*ii*) G.A. Almond
(*c*) Technological School	(*iii*) Mahatma Gandhi
(*d*) Psychological School	(*iv*) David Apter

Codes :

	(*a*)	(*b*)	(*c*)	(*d*)
A.	(*ii*)	(*iii*)	(*iv*)	(*i*)
B.	(*ii*)	(*i*)	(*iii*)	(*iv*)
C.	(*iii*)	(*ii*)	(*iv*)	(*i*)
D.	(*i*)	(*iii*)	(*ii*)	(*iv*)

20. The Presidents and Vice-presidents of the following countries can not seek re-election for a third term.

1. The US President
2. The French President
3. Indian President
4. Indian Vice-President

Select the correct answer from the codes given below :

A. 1 B. 1 and 2
C. 1 and 4 D. 1, 2 and 3

21. Which one is not the feature of the Presidential form of government of U.S.A.?

A. Direct election of the President
B. Fixed terms of offices for the president and legislature
C. Fusion of power between legislature and executive
D. President serves as head of the state

22. Which one among the following countries, according to Almond and Verba, came closest to their conception of civic culture?

A. U.S.A. B. West Germany
C. Mexico D. Great Britain

23. "Efficiency Record" method for determining the merit for promotion is practised in

A. The USA B. Switzerland
C. The U.K. D. India

24. In which of the following countries judges are elected by the people?

Select the correct answer from the codes given below:

(*i*) U.S.A. (*ii*) Switzerland
(*iii*) India (*iv*) U.K.

Codes:

A. (*i*), (*ii*) B. (*i*), (*ii*), (*iii*)
C. (*ii*), (*iii*) D. (*ii*), (*iii*), (*iv*)

25. In which of the following countries the courts do not have the power of Judicial Review?

(*i*) USA (*ii*) UK
(*iii*) France (*iv*) India

Codes :

A. (*iii*) B. (*ii*) and (*iii*)
C. (*i*) and (*iii*) D. (*ii*)

26. Who among the following said "Federalism is obsolescent, it is essentially negative in its effect. It is not suitable for positive action, it is financially expensive due to duplication of work."?

A. David Easton B. S.P. Huntington
C. K.C. Wheare D. H.J. Laski

27. Who among the following has argued that modernization could be associated with a highly differentiated political structure and the diffusion of political power and authority into all spheres of society?

A. Max Weber
B. Talcott Parson
C. S.N. Eisenstadt
D. Walt W. Rostow

28. Consider the following statements about a constitutional government. A constitutional government is

1. a form of limited government
2. one where authority is derived from the constitution
3. one where the constitution and the laws limit the exercise of power
4. where the head of the state enjoys nominal powers

Select the correct answer from the codes given below :

A. 1, 2 and 3 B. 2, 3 and 4
C. 1, 3 and 4 D. 1, 2 and 4

29. Who among the following thinkers gave the concept of "lions" and "foxes"?

A. Robert Michaels
B. C. Wright Mill
C. Vilfred Pareto
D. Burham

30. Given below are two statements one labelled as Assertion (A) and the other labelled as Reason (R) :

Assertion (A) : Parliamentary form of government is the most acceptable system in the entire world today.

Reason (R) : In the parliamentary system, ministers get their democratic legitimacy from the legislature and are accountable to it.

Codes:

A. Both (A) and (R) are true and (R) is the correct explanation of (A).
B. Both (A) and (R) are true, but (R) is not the correct explanation of (A).
C. (A) is true, but (R) is false.
D. (A) is false, but (R) is true.

31. Which of the following is not related to electoral reforms in India?

A. Santhanam Committee
B. Tarkunde Committee
C. Indrajeet Gupta Committee
D. Dinesh Goswami Committee

32. Who of the following gave the idea of a dominant caste?

A. Rajni Kothari
B. Paul R. Brass
C. M.N. Srinivas
D. Lloyd I. Rudolph

33. Which one of the following states in India has instituted Ombudsman for local governments until 2013?

A. Bihar B. Kerala
C. Karnataka D. Uttar Pradesh

34. Who is the author of "Factional politics in an Indian State"?

A. Paul R. Brass B. Myron Weiner
C. James Manor D. S.K. Mitra

35. Which one of the following pairs are not correctly matched?

	List-I (Political Parties)	List-II (Leaders)
A.	Telangana Rastriya Samiti	– Chandra Shekhar Rao
B.	Peoples Democratic Party	– Mahbooba Mufti
C.	Bhartiya Janata Party	– Kalyan Singh
D.	Shiromani Akali Dal	– Navjot Singh Siddhu

36. In which one of the following cases the Supreme Court of India held that both Fundamental Rights and Directive Principles of state policy are equally important and one cannot be sacrificed for the other?

A. S.R. Bommai *v/s* Union of India
B. Balaji *v/s* State of Mysore
C. Minerva Mills *v/s* Union of India
D. A.K.Gopalan *v/s* State of Madras

37. Which one of the following is arranged in chronological order?

A. Anandpur Sahib Resolution, Rajamannar Committee Report, West Bengal Government Memorandum, Sarkaria Commission report.

B. Rajamannar Committee report, West Bengal Government Memorandum, Anandpur Sahib Resolution, Sarkaria Commission Report.

C. Sarkaria Commission Report, West Bengal Government Memorandum, Anandpur Sahib resolution, Rajamannar Committee Report.

D. Rajamannar Committee Report, Anandpur Sahib Resolution, West Bengal government memorandum, Sarkaria Commission Report.

38. Match List-I with List-II and select the correct answer from the codes given below :

List-I (Deputy Prime Ministers)	**List-II (Government)**
(*a*) Morarji Desai	(*i*) Janata Party
(*b*) Jagjivan Ram	(*ii*) Congress
(*c*) Devilal	(*iii*) National Democratic Alliance
(*d*) L.K. Advani	(*iv*) United Front

Codes :

	(*a*)	(*b*)	(*c*)	(*d*)
A.	(*i*)	(*iii*)	(*ii*)	(*iv*)
B.	(*ii*)	(*iv*)	(*iii*)	(*i*)
C.	(*ii*)	(*i*)	(*iv*)	(*iii*)
D.	(*iii*)	(*ii*)	(*i*)	(*iv*)

39. Who one of the following was not a member of States Reorganization commission, 1953?

A. Fazl Ali B. H.N. Kunzru
C. V.P. Menon D. K.N. Panikkar

40. The governor of a state has the power to dismiss a chief minister.
Which of the following pairs are not correctly matched?

	Governor		**Chief Minsiter Dismissed**
A.	Dharma Vira	–	Ajoy Mukherjee
B.	Gopal Reddy	–	Charan Singh
C.	Kumud Joshi	–	N.T. Rama Rao
D.	Romesh Bhandari	–	Kalyan Singh

41. Who among the following talked about the politics of scarcity in India?

A. Paul R. Brass B. Paul Wallace
C. Myron Weiner D. Morris Jones

42. In which case the Supreme Court decided that the confidence of the house in the ministry should be tested on the floor of the house itself?

A. B.R. Kapoor *v/s* State of Tamil Nadu
B. S.R. Bommai *v/s* Union of India
C. Jagdambika Pal *v/s* Union of India
D. Shamsher Singh *v/s* State of Punjab

43. Different parts of the Constitution will act and react on each other and the (supreme) court will have to decide questions arising from such a situation...discharging its duties as perhaps no other court has so far been called upon to do. Whose statement is this?

A. Justice Patanjali Sastri
B. Justice Harilal Kania
C. Justice P.B. Gajendragadkar
D. Dr. B.R. Ambedkar

44. Which one among the following authorities has the power to declare a caste, race or tribe or part of group within the caste as scheduled castes in relation to a state or union territory?

A. Prime Minister
B. Parliament
C. Judiciary
D. President of India

45. Which one of the following is the chief function of the inter-state council?

A. To settle inter-state river water disputes
B. To settle disputes relating to the movement of good between states
C. To debate on reforming centre state relations
D. To act as a forum for settling inter-state boundary disputes

46. Which one among the following is considered as the first coherent theory of organization?

A. The Human Relations Theory
B. Scientific Management Theory
C. The Systems Theory
D. The Bureaucracy Theory

47. Which one of the following was the first committee to demand constitutional recognition for Panchayats?

A. Balwantrai Mehta Committee
B. Ashok Mehta Committee
C. Santhanam Committee
D. G.V.K. Rao Committee

48. Given below are two statements, one labelled as Assertion (A) and the other labelled as Reason (R) :

Assertion (A) : The Central service officers are not All India service officers, but the nature of their job and postings make them truly All India in character.

Reason (R) : Unlike officers of the All India services, central service officer's do not work under the state governments while working in the states.

Codes :

A. Both (A) and (R) are true and (R) is the correct explanation of (A).
B. Both (A) and (R) are true, but (R) is not the correct explanation of (A).
C. (A) is true, but (R) is false.
D. (A) is false, but (R) is true.

49. Which one of the following is not a function of the UPSC?

A. Advise the union government on all matters relating to the method of recruitment and principles to be followed in making appointments to civil service.
B. Advise the government on the suitability of candidates for promotion.
C. Advise the government on disciplinary matters affecting civil servants.
D. Advise the government on all matters relating to the transfer of civil servants.

50. Name the country which was the first to evolve a sound recruitment system?

A. Prussia B. India
C. China D. USA

51. Which one among the following is described as the 'corner-stone' of the whole public personnel structure?

A. Promotion
B. Recruitment and selection
C. Discipline
D. Morale

52. The term 'spoil system' applies to :

A. Guardian bureaucracy
B. Caste bureaucracy
C. Patronage bureaucracy
D. Merit bureaucracy

53. Chronologically arrange the correct sequence of the following landmarks in the growth and emergence of New Public Administration :

1. The minnowbrook conference
2. The honey report on higher education for public service
3. The Philadelphia conference on the theory & practices of public administration
4. Publication of 'Towards a new public administration : The Minnowbrook perspective'

Codes:

A. 4, 3, 1, 2 B. 2, 3, 1, 4
C. 2, 4, 1, 3 D. 1, 2, 3, 4

54. Who amongst the following emphasized development administration as an approach?

1. Riggs 2. Fainsod
3. Heady 4. Weidner

Select the correct answer from the codes given below :

A. 1, 2 and 4 B. 2, 3 and 4
C. 1, 2 and 3 D. 1, 2, 3 and 4

55. Which of the following political rights are not available to a civil servant in India?

1. Expressing a political view
2. Supporting a political movement
3. Contributing financially to a political party
4. Voting in state and national elections

Select the correct answer from the codes given below :

A. 1, 3 and 4 B. 2, 3 and 4
C. 1, 2 and 3 D. 2 and 3

56. Which among the following is not a principle of organization?
A. Collective Responsibility
B. Hierarchy
C. Span of Control
D. Integration

57. Who among the following has divided the scope of public administration into administration theory and applied theory?
A. H. Walker
B. Ferral Heady
C. F.A. Nigro
D. Nicholas Henry

58. "Officials make work for each other". This is said by:
A. Peter Drucker B. Ramsay Muir
C. Parkinson D. H. Finer

59. The first country in the world to introduce the right to information was :
A. Norway B. USA
C. Sweden D. Finland

60. Which one among the following statements is false?
A. The first hour of every parliament day is reserved for questions.
B. Zero hour is a typical Indian innovation in the field of parliamentary practice.
C. New public administration is an uniquely American phenomenon.
D. Judicial control over administrative acts stems from natural law.

61. Match List-I with List-II and select the correct answer from the codes given below :

List-I (Approaches-Feminism)	List-II (Feminist thinkers)
(a) Critical Theory	(i) Elisabeth Prugl
(b) Social Constructivism	(ii) Chandra Mohanty
(c) Post Structuralism	(iii) Sandra Whiteworth
(d) Post Colonialism	(iv) Charlotte Hooper

Codes :

	(a)	(b)	(c)	(d)
A.	(iv)	(iii)	(ii)	(i)
B.	(i)	(ii)	(iii)	(iv)
C.	(ii)	(iv)	(i)	(iii)
D.	(iii)	(i)	(iv)	(ii)

62. Globalization signifies which of the following:
A. Time-space compression
B. The integration of the world-economy
C. The growth of supra-territorial relations between people
D. All the above

63. Who said the following "In crucial situations, however the ultimate concern of states is not for power but for security"?
A. Thomas Schelling
B. Kenneth Waltz
C. Barry Buzan
D. John Mearshemier

64. Institutionalist approach of international political economy draws on theories from
A. Incentive structures
B. Delegation and agency
C. Historical factors
D. Sociological factors

65. Who has proposed a three tiered conception of international law based on Moravsik's new liberalism?
A. M. Byers B. A.M. Slaughter
C. Koskenniemi D. A. Guzman

66. Identify the correct sequence of the process as recommended by the seminal report, 'An Agenda for Peace' (1992)
(i) Peace keeping
(ii) Preventive diplomacy
(iii) Peace building
(iv) Peace making

Codes :
A. (ii) (iv) (i) (iii)
B. (i) (ii) (iii) (iv)
C. (iii) (i) (iv) (ii)
D. (iv) (iii) (ii) (i)

67. Who said that 'The United States is not simply a superpower; it is a hyper power'?

A. Hubart Vedrine
B. Robert Gates
C. Richard Haas
D. Paul Kennedy

68. Match List-I with List-II and select the correct answer from the codes given below :

List-I (UN conference place)	List-II (Issues)
(a) Rio de Janeiro (1992)	(i) Population
(b) Vienna (1993)	(ii) Women
(c) Cairo (1994)	(iii) Human Rights
(d) Beijing (1995)	(iv) Environment

Codes :

	(a)	(b)	(c)	(d)
A.	(i)	(iv)	(ii)	(iii)
B.	(ii)	(i)	(iii)	(iv)
C.	(iii)	(ii)	(iv)	(i)
D.	(iv)	(iii)	(i)	(ii)

69. Bay of pigs is associated with which crisis during the cold war?

A. Cuban Missile B. Hungary
C. Korea D. Suez Canal

70. Black widows are women terrorists. To which country do they belongs?

A. Palestine B. Chechenya
C. Sri Lanka D. Lebanon

71. Chronologically arrange the following treaties on environment in the correct ascending order.

(i) UN Law of the Sea
(ii) Kyoto Protocol
(iii) Antarctic Treaty
(iv) Cartogena protocol on Biosafety

Codes:

A. (iii), (i), (ii), (iv)
B. (ii), (iv), (i), (iii)
C. (iv), (ii), (iii), (i)
D. (i), (iii), (iv), (ii)

72. Match List-I with List-II and select the correct answer from the codes given below :

List-I (Authors)	List-II (Books)
(a) S.D. Muni	(i) Crossing the Rubicon
(b) C. Rajamohan	(ii) Anatomy of a flawed Inheritance/Indo Pak relations
(c) Urmila Phadnis	(iii) Pangs of proximity
(d) J.N. Dixit	(iv) Ethnicity and nation-building in South Asia

Codes :

	(a)	(b)	(c)	(d)
A.	(iii)	(i)	(iv)	(ii)
B.	(ii)	(i)	(iii)	(iv)
C.	(i)	(ii)	(iv)	(iii)
D.	(iv)	(iii)	(ii)	(i)

73. India's tryst with Asia was enunciated in the vision of engagement which was articulated by:

A. Indira Gandhi
B. Sardar Patel
C. Mahatma Gandhi
D. Jawaharlal Nehru

74. Given below are two statements, one labelled as Assertion (A) and the other labelled as Reason (R) :

Assertion (A) : The factors and forces that constrained Nehru's India from playing its legitimate role in Asia have either been mitigated to an extent, or redefined.

Reason (R) : The end of the cold war and expansion of the strategic space for India to pursue its national interests has widened.

Codes :

A. Both (A) and (R) are true and (R) is the correct explanation of (A).
B. Both (A) and (R) are true, but (R) is not the correct explanation of (A).
C. (A) is true, but (R) is false.
D. (A) is false, but (R) is true.

75. When did the United Nations general assembly resolution 2832 on the declaration of the Indian Ocean as a zone of peace, adopt?

A. 1970 B. 1971

C. 1972 D. 1973

ANSWERS

1	2	3	4	5	6	7	8	9	10
C	C	C	C	D	B	D	B	D	C
11	**12**	**13**	**14**	**15**	**16**	**17**	**18**	**19**	**20**
A	B	D	C	D	B	A	B	A	B
21	**22**	**23**	**24**	**25**	**26**	**27**	**28**	**29**	**30**
C	D	A	A	D	D	C	A	C	A
31	**32**	**33**	**34**	**35**	**36**	**37**	**38**	**39**	**40**
A	C	B	A	D	C	D	C	C	C
41	**42**	**43**	**44**	**45**	**46**	**47**	**48**	**49**	**50**
C	B	B	D	C	B	A	B	D	A
51	**52**	**53**	**54**	**55**	**56**	**57**	**58**	**59**	**60**
B	C	B	D	C	A	A	C	C	C
61	**62**	**63**	**64**	**65**	**66**	**67**	**68**	**69**	**70**
D	D	B	B	B	A	A	D	A	B
71	**72**	**73**	**74**	**75**					
A	A	D	A	B					

SOME SELECTED EXPLANATORY ANSWERS

1. "By political theory," John Plamenatz wrote, "I do not mean explanations of how governments function; I mean systematic thinking about the purposes of government." Political theory is a normative discipline, designed to let us evaluate rather than explain; in this it resembles moral or ethical theory. What distinguishes it among normative disciplines is that it is designed to facilitate in particular the evaluation of government or, if that is something more general, the state. We are to identify the purposes of government—more strictly, the *proper* purposes of government—so that we can decide on the best political arrangements for society.

2. The author of the book 'The Philosophy of J.S. Mill' is R.P. Anschutz. This book attempts to unravel the tangled skein of Mill's speculative thinking by stressing the ideal of scientific knowledge which he derived from the study of Newton's physics.

3. *Savitri: A Legend and a Symbol* is an epic poem in blank verse by Sri Aurobindo, based upon the theology from the *Mahabharata*. Its central theme revolves around the transcendence of man as the consummation of terrestrial evolution, and the emergence of an immortal supramental gnostic race upon earth.

5. Feuerbach said, "Man is what he eats." Yes indeed, but what he eats has just died; he eats in order to live, but instead he began living in order to eat, and in this senseless and vicious circle lies the horrible determinism of human life.

6. John was an English philosopher and physician regarded as one of the most influential of Enlightenment thinkers and known as the "Father of Classical Liberalism". Considered one of the first of the British empiricists, following the tradition of Francis Bacon, he is equally important to social contract theory.

John Locke came close to a labour theory of the origin of value when he explained how nearly all the value of commodities today is due to labour. He thought that the value of a commodity includes the labour that was immediately necessary to produce it plus all the labour that went into the materials, supplies, machinery, buildings and other capital goods that were used up producing it; and so on back to the state of nature. This is a retrospective view of value like a pure labour theory of value. Locke concluded, however, that labour constituted no more than 99 per cent of the value of commodities, because even the free gifts of nature were worth something. He had a land-plus-labour theory of the origin value, like Petty.

7. Machiavelli wrote many of his literary works: the *Discourses,* the satirical poem *The Golden Ass,* the *Dialogue on our Language,* the short story *Balfagor,* the ribald play *Mandragola* and *The Art of War,* based on discussions set in the gardens.

9. In the *Timaeus* Plato presents an elaborately wrought account of the formation of the universe. Plato is deeply impressed with the order and beauty he observes in the universe, and his project in the dialogue is to explain that order and beauty. The universe, he proposes, is the product of rational, purposive, and beneficent agency. It is the handiwork of a divine Craftsman who, imitating an unchanging and eternal model, imposes mathematical order on a preexistent chaos to generate the ordered universe. The governing explanatory principle of the account is teleological: the universe as a whole as well as its various parts are so arranged as to produce a vast array of good effects. It strikes Plato strongly that this arrangement is not fortuitous, but the outcome of the deliberate intent of Intellect.

13. "Life divine" book is written by Aurobindo Ghosh. His main literary works are *The Life Divine*, which deals with theoretical aspects of Integral Yoga; *Synthesis of Yoga*, which deals with practical guidance to Integral Yoga; and *Savitri*, an epic poem which refers to a passage in the *Mahabharata*, where its characters actualise Integral Yoga in their lives.

14. The idea of revolution as expressed by the French Revolution appealed because of its simplicity and universality. "Liberty, Equality, and Fraternity" could inspire populations from Brussels to Beijing, from Poland to Peru. This was the contribution of the nineteenth-century socialists, supremely in the thinking of Karl Marx. For Marx, the French Revolution remained to be completed. It had freed the capitalists, the bourgeoisie, but at the cost of turning the mass of workers into exploited and propertyless proletarians. The liberal gains of the French Revolution—and Marx never denied that they were gains—had to be converted into the emancipation of the people as a whole. This would be accomplished by a socialist or communist revolution that would abolish private property and bring about the "free association of producers."

17. The process of socialisation differs in different kinds of political systems. In traditional political system, it is particularistic, diffuse and ascriptive, that is to say, it is influenced by kinship relations of castes and tribes, and other traditional groups. In a modern political system, socialisation is more universalistic, manifest, rational, secular, and achievement-oriented.

21. **The Presidential System (USA):** The United States Constitution provides for an institutional *separation* between the legislature and the top executive authority. The legislature (Congress) and the chief executive (the President) are *separate and largely independent* branches or organs of government. Under the U.S. Constitution, each of the separated branches or institutions of government has its own set of powers. However, the executive and the legislature also share certain powers.

22. **Civic culture:** The term used by Almond and Verba to signify the balance of subject and participant political cultures that best supports democracy. In the civic culture, subject and participant cultures are mixed to produce neither too much nor too little participation. Citizens are active and elites respond to their demands, but citizens also trust their political leaders and give them a degree of independence. Almond and Verba found that the UK in the late 1950s came closest to the civic culture.

23. "Efficiency Record" method for determining the merit for promotion is practised in the USA.

27. Modernization usually associated with capitalist development, Eisenstadt understood modernization as highly differentiated political structure and diffusion of political power and authority into all spheres of society. In his early work Apter considered modernization as a particular form of development, involving a stable social system, differentiated social structures, and social skills and knowledge adaptable to a technologically advanced world. Later he described this from of modernization as the attempt of traditional societies to replicate the institutions and values of advanced industrial societies. Parallel to this was another form of modernization that takes conflict and inequality rather than integration into account.

29. Pareto's law of income distribution derived from British data on income which showed a linear relationship between each income level and the number of people who received more than that income. He found similar results for Prussia, Saxony, Paris, and some Italian cities. Pareto thought his law should be "provisionally accepted as universal," but realised that exceptions were possible.

His work on elites is of great interest and a more concrete view than Marxism as it examines human nature rather than constructing abstract ideology. "The circulation of the elites" examines differences in the temper and style of the rulers. His most profoundest insights are Lions and Foxes which give a better understanding into how we are ruled and misruled. They are grounded in how people behave rather than vague and dated abstractions about class behaviour.

31. In 1962, the Santhanam Committee was set up to make recommendations on Prevention of Corruption. One of the principal recommendations of this Committee was that company donations be banned. The Committee's report observed: "...in Indian conditions, companies should not be allowed to participate in politics through their donations".

32. **Mysore Narasimhachar Srinivas** was an Indian sociologist. He is mostly known for his work on caste and caste systems, social stratification, Sanskritisation and Westernisation in southern India and the concept of 'Dominant Caste'.

33. **Ombudsman for Local Governments** in the Indian state of Kerala is an independent quasi judicial authority which investigates the complaints against local governments in

Kerala or the functionaries working under them. The Ombudsman is functioning at the State level with its headquarters in the State Capital. Possibly no other State in India has such an institution to oversee the functioning of Local Self Government Institutions.

34. The author of "Factional politics in an Indian State" is Paul R. Brass. Professor Paul Brass has given us, in this work, the best study so far published of how the Congress Party is organized and actually operates today in a major Indian state. The chosen arena for this comprehensive analysis is Uttar Pradesh, the most populous, one of the most complex, and certainly one of the most crucial political entities comprising the Indian Union.

35. Mr. Navjot Singh Sidhu is a veteran Indian leader associated with Bharatiya Janata Party (B.J.P.)

37. Rajamannar committee report – 1971
Anandpur Sahib Resolution – 1973
West Bengal Memorandum – 1977
Sarkaria Commission – 1983

39. State reorganization commission – 1953
Chairman : Shri S. Fazl Ali.
Members : Shri H.N. Kunzru; Shri K.M. Panikkar.
Secretary : Shri P.C. Chaudhuri.
The States Reorganization Commission was constituted under the Ministry of Home Affairs. The Commission will investigate the conditions of the problem, the historical background, the existing situation and the bearing of all important and relevant factors thereon.

43. The Indian constitution conferred the power of judicial review on its courts in order to protect and preserve the fundamental rights of individuals within the state. At the inaugural sitting of the Supreme Court on 28 January 1950, Chief Justice Harilal Kania stated, "Different parts of the Constitution will act and react on each other and the [Supreme] Court will have to decide questions arising from such a situation…discharging its duties as perhaps no other court has so far been called upon to do".

44. The president of India has the power to declare a caste, race or tribe or part of group within the caste as scheduled castes in relation to a state or union territory.

46. Frederick Taylor (1917) developed scientific management theory at the beginning of this century. His theory had four basic principles: (1) find the one "best way" to perform each task, (2) carefully match each worker to each task, (3) closely supervise workers, and use reward and punishment as motivators, and (4) the task of management is planning and control.

While Taylor's *scientific management theory* proved successful in the simple industrialized companies at the turn of the century, it has not faired well in modern companies. The philosophy of "production first, people second" has left a legacy of declining production and quality, dissatisfaction with work, loss of pride in workmanship, and a near complete loss of organizational pride.

47. The Balwant Rai Mehta Committee (1957) was the first of its kind that looked into the bureaucratic framework of these local institutions. Despite its claim that community development could endure when the community was involved, not much was gained. There are various reasons for this, such as, the political and bureaucratic resistance at the state level to a sharing of power and resources with local level institutions and a takeover of these institutions by the rural elite.

50. The first country in modern times to have evolved a sound recruitment system is Prussia.

51. Recruitment is that process through which suitable candidates are induced to compete for appointments to the public service. It is thus an integral part of a more inclusive process of selection which also includes the process of examination and certification.

According to Stahl O. Glenn, "Recruitment is the cornerstone of the whole public personnel structure."

In the second Century China started a definite and scientific method of recruitment on the basis of competitions. In the modern age Prussia is the first country which started a system of recruitment by abolishing the patronage system. During the British Rule in 1853, the principle of merit was recognised and adopted in Indian Civil Service.

52. In the politics of the United States, a spoil system (also known as a patronage system) is a practice where a political party, after winning an election, gives government jobs to its voters as a reward for working toward victory. Jobs are also awarded as an incentive to keep working for the party. This is opposed to a merit system, where offices are awarded on the basis of some measure of merit, independent of political activity.

54. The term 'development administration' was first coined by U.L. Goswami, an Indian Scholar. He used this term in his article entitled 'The Structure of Development Administration in India', published in 1955. However, it is George Gant, an American Scholar, who is regarded as the father of development administration. He too started using the term during the same period. His book *Development Administration: Concepts, Goals and Methods* was first published in 1979.

Edward Wiedner is the foremost proponent of development administration. He is also the first to conceptually explain the definition of development administration.

58. C. Northcote Parkinson in his well-known work 'Parkinson's Law' published in the year 1957 said that work expands to occupy the time made available for its completion. According to Parkinson this phenomenon is motivated by two forces: (*i*) 'An official wants to multiply subordinates, not rivals' and (*ii*) 'Officials make work for each other.' He says that bureaucracy is self-perpetuating in the sense that the civil servants have a tendency to increase day by day in number, irrespective of the work load because officials make work for each other.

59. Sweden was the first country in the world to introduce "Right to Information".

62. Globalization is variously defined in the literature as:

1. 'The intensification of worldwide social relations which link distant localities in such a way that local happenings are shaped by events occurring many miles away and vice versa'.
2. 'The integration of the world-economy.'
3. 'De-territorialization–or ... the growth of supraterritorial relations between people.'
4. 'time-space compression'.

63. "The desire to attain a maximum of power is universal" and it is "one of objective laws that have their roots in human nature". Waltz, however, argues that power is a means to an end, and that end is security, and as Waltz notes, "Because power is a possibly useful means, sensible statesmen try to have an appropriate amount of it. In crucial situations, however, the ultimate concern of states is not for power but for security".

64. A different application of rational choice lies in the institutionalist approach to IPE. This approach applies the assumptions of rational choice to states in their interaction with other states. Drawing on theories of delegation and agency, it offers an explanation as to why institutions exist and for what purposes. The core assumption is that states create international institutions and delegate power to them in order to maximize utility within the constraints of world markets and world politics. Frequently, this comes down to the need to resolve collective-action problems.

67. Among the 193 countries in the world today, one constitutes a category all by itself, notwithstanding the formal equality of states of the United Nations. I'm talking about the United States, the world's only "hyperpower." The United States is predominant in all areas: economic, technological, military, monetary, linguistic, cultural.

69. Bay of pigs is associated with cuban missile crisis during the cold war.

70. Murphy points out that called for international jihadists to flock to Chechenya to begin an Islamic revolution. With this in mind, their tactics went far beyond guerrilla warfare. They introduced the tactics of terrorism and suicide bombings. Given the Russian tendency to ravage areas where they were attacked, the jihadists sought a new weapon, female suicide bombers called the Black Widows. The Black Widows were women who had suffered at the hands of the Russians and who gained a reputation for effectiveness.

75. The United Nations general assembly resolution 2832 on the declaration of the Indian Ocean as a zone of peace, adopt 1971.

Previous Paper (Solved)

UGC-NET POLITICAL SCIENCE, DECEMBER 2013

PAPER–II

Note: *This paper contains* ***fifty*** *(50) multiple-choice questions, each question carrying* ***two*** *(2) marks. Attempt* ***all*** *of them.*

1. Who among the following is not a principal character in Plato's *Republic*?

A. Polemarchus B. Adeimantus
C. Protagoras D. Glaucon

2. Match List-I with List-II and select the correct answer from the codes given below the lists:

List–I ***(Authors)***	***List–II*** ***(Books)***
(*a*) A. Arblaster	1. Participation and Democratic Theory
(*b*) C.B. Mac Pherson	2. Models of Democracy
(*c*) C. Pateman	3. The Real World of Democracy
(*d*) D. Held	4. Democracy

Codes:

	(*a*)	(*b*)	(*c*)	(*d*)
A.	1	2	3	4
B.	4	3	1	2
C.	2	1	4	3
D.	3	4	2	1

3. Identify the correct sequence of Marx's Writings in ascending order :

(*i*) Contribution to the Critique of Political Economy
(*ii*) Poverty of Philosophy
(*iii*) Thesis on Feuerbach
(*iv*) Communist Manifesto

Select the correct answer from the codes given below:

Codes :

A. (*i*), (*ii*), (*iii*), (*iv*) B. (*ii*), (*iii*), (*iv*), (*i*)
C. (*iii*), (*ii*), (*iv*), (*i*) D. (*iv*), (*i*), (*ii*), (*iii*)

4. Given below are two statements, one labelled as Assertion (A) and the other labelled as Reason (R):

Assertion (A) : For behaviouralists, it was better to be wrong than vague.

Reason (R) : It was better to be vague than non-relevantly precise.

Codes :

A. Both (A) and (R) are true and (R) is the right explanation of (A).
B. Both (A) and (R) are true, but (R) is not the correct explanation of (A).
C. (A) is false, but (R) is true.
D. (A) is true, but (R) is false.

5. Who said, "Each person possesses an inviolability founded on justice that even the welfare of society as a whole cannot override"?

A. John Rawls B. Robert Nozick
C. Friedrich Hayek D. Habermas

6. Who was the founder of Utilitarianism?

A. Bentham B. James Mill
C. David Hume D. Priestley

7. Which one of the following writings is not written by Mao?

A. On New Democracy
B. On Coalition Government
C. People's War
D. On People's Democratic Dictatorship

8. Why did Gandhiji go to South Africa?

A. On invitation by the Indians in South Africa.
B. To study Bar-at-Law.
C. To fight a case of a Gujarati Business-man.
D. To visit South Africa with family.

9. Who founded the 'Mexican Socialist Workers' Party' which was later named as 'Mexican Communist Party'?
A. Jaya Prakash Narayan
B. B.R. Ambedkar
C. M.N. Roy
D. Lenin

10. Whom did Lord Minto describe as the most 'dangerous man'?
A. B.G. Tilak B. Aurobindo Ghosh
C. Gandhiji D. Sardar Patel

11. Arrange in ascending order the following stages of Political Development as enunciated by A.F.K. Organski. Select the correct answer from codes given below :
(*i*) Primitive National Unification
(*ii*) Abundance
(*iii*) Industrialisation
(*iv*) National Welfare

Codes :
A. (*i*), (*ii*), (*iii*), (*iv*)
B. (*i*), (*iii*), (*ii*), (*iv*)
C. (*i*), (*iii*), (*iv*), (*ii*)
D. (*iv*), (*ii*), (*iii*), (*i*)

12. Who among the following talks of pseudo-pressure groups?
A. Jean Blondel
B. Almond
C. Maurice Duverger
D. V.O. Key

13. Match List-I with List-II and select the correct answer from the codes given below :

***List–I* (*Thinkers*)**	***List–II* (*Ideas*)**
(*a*) Karl Marx	1. State of paternalistic bond between peasantry and property owners
(*b*) Chalmers Johnson	2. Aggregate psychological perspective
(*c*) Ted Gurr	3. Revolution as a process through which structural inequalities could be eliminated
(*d*) Barrington Moore	4. Value co-ordinated social system model

Codes:

	(*a*)	(*b*)	(*c*)	(*d*)
A.	1	3	2	4
B.	2	1	3	4
C.	3	4	2	1
D.	4	1	3	2

14. Match List-I with List-II and select the correct answer from the codes given below the list.

***List–I* (*Type of Government*)**	***List–II* (*Principal Attributes*)**
(*a*) Military Regime	1. Based on deference
(*b*) Dynastic Regime	2. Based on coercion
(*c*) Psuedo Democracy	3. Trappings of a liberal democracy like periodic elections but power rests in the hands of oligarchy.
(*d*) Liberal Democracy	4. Voluntary participation in government process is extensive

Codes:

	(*a*)	(*b*)	(*c*)	(*d*)
A.	1	2	3	4
B.	2	1	3	4
C.	4	3	2	1
D.	3	1	4	2

15. The process of Socialisation in Modern Society is
1. Specific
2. Universalistic
3. Instrumental
4. Ascriptive

Select the correct answer from the codes given below:

Codes :
A. 1, 2, 3 B. 2, 3, 4
C. 3, 4, 1 D. 4, 2, 1

16. Which one of the following is not a totalitarian form of Government?
A. Military Government
B. Fascist Government
C. Communist Government
D. Parliamentary form of Government

17. Who among the following writers classified Elites into broad types?
(*i*) Organising and directing elites.
(*ii*) Informally organised and diffused elites
A. Vilfredo Pareto B. Robert Michaels
C. Gaetano Mosca D. Karl Mannheim

18. Who among the following classified parties under competitive system into two major categories?
(*i*) Turnover and Hegemonic
(*ii*) Ideological and Pragmatic
A. Myron Weiner and Lapalombara
B. G.A. Almond and Verba
C. Neil A. Mcdonald
D. Peter H. Merkel

19. The concept of dependency evolved in the 1960s in
A. Europe B. Africa
C. Asia D. Latin America

20. Match List-I with List-II and select the correct answer from codes given below :

List–I (Books)	***List–II (Authors)***
(*a*) Approaches to the Study of Politics	1. R. Young
(*b*) Dynamics of Modernization	2. C.E. Black
(*c*) Influencing Voters	3. R. Rose
(*d*) Studies in Political Development	4. J.S. Coleman

Codes:

	(*a*)	(*b*)	(*c*)	(*d*)
A.	1	2	3	4
B.	2	3	4	1
C.	4	3	2	1
D.	3	4	2	1

21. Given below are two statements, one labelled as Assertion (A) and the other labelled as Reason (R). Choose the correct answer from the codes :

Assertion (A) : Secularization does not necessarily imply that people have become anti-religious, or that religion has disappeared from both the public domain and the domain of personal belief.

Reason (R) : Religion is not just one, and not necessarily the most important way in which people understand themselves and their relationships.

Codes :
A. Both (A) and (R) are correct and (R) is the correct explanation of (A).
B. Both (A) and (R) are correct, but (R) is not the correct explanation of (A).
C. (A) is correct, but (R) is false.
D. (R) is correct, but (A) is false.

22. Given below are two statements, one labelled as Assertion (A) and the other labelled as Reason (R).

Assertion (A) : The 1980s, a period of great turbulence in Indian Politics, marked the appearance of several new political parties.

Reason (R) : National Parties got marginalized or became adjuncts to State Parties in many States.

Codes :
A. Both (A) and (R) are true, and (R) is the correct explanation of (A).
B. Both (A) and (R) are true, but (R) is not the correct explanation of (A).
C. (A) is true, but (R) is false.
D. (R) is true, but (A) is false.

23. Arrange the following in their chronological sequence:
(*i*) Nehru Committee Report
(*ii*) Quit India Movement
(*iii*) Civil Disobedience Movement
(*iv*) Declaration of Complete Independence

Codes :
A. (*ii*), (*i*), (*iv*), (*iii*)
B. (*iii*), (*ii*), (*iv*), (*i*)
C. (*i*), (*iv*), (*iii*), (*ii*)
D. (*iv*), (*ii*), (*i*), (*iii*)

24. In which of the following case the Supreme Court of India held that, the power of amendment belonged to the Parliament, and this power was an unlimited one?
A. Sankari Prasad V. Union of India
B. Bela Banerjee and Others V. State of West Bengal

C. Kesavananda Bharati V. State of Kerala
D. Romesh Thapar V. State of Madras

25. Which one of the following States does not have a Bicameral Legislature?
A. Uttar Pradesh B. Bihar
C. Maharashtra D. Kerala

26. Identify the correct chronological order of the following Prime Minister/Chief Minister of J & K :
A. Sheikh Abdullah, Bakshi Ghulam Mohammad, Farooq Abdullah, Omar Abdullah.
B. Sheikh Abdullah, G.M. Sadiq, Mir Qasim, Farooq Abdullah.
C. Sheikh Abdullah, G.M. Sadiq Shamsuddin, Mufti Mohammad Sayeed.
D. Sheikh Abdulla, Bakshi Ghulam Mohammad, Shamsuddin, G.M. Sadiq.

27. Match List-I with List-II and select the correct answer from the codes given below :

List–I (Conspiracy Cases)	***List–II (Revolutionaries Punished)***
(*a*) Nasik case (1909-10)	1. Sachindranath Sanyal
(*b*) Benares case (1916)	2. Ram Prasad Bismil
(*c*) Kakori case (1924)	3. Bhagat Singh
(*d*) Lahore case (1929-30)	4. Vinayak Savarkar

Codes:

	(*a*)	(*b*)	(*c*)	(*d*)
A.	1	3	4	2
B.	1	2	3	4
C.	4	1	2	3
D.	3	4	1	2

28. Which one of the following is not a sufficient ground for convening a joint sitting of both Houses of Parliament?
A. Rejection of a bill by one House of the Parliament when the other House has passed it.
B. Both Houses have finally disagreed as to the amendments to be made in a bill.
C. More than six months has elapsed from the date of the reception of the Bill by the other House without the Bill being passed by it.
D. President has refused to give his assent to the Bill.

29. Who is the author of *Federal India : A Design for Change*?
A. Balveer Arora
B. K.C. Wheare
C. Rasheeduddin Khan
D. Ronald Watts

30. Who among the following has made pioneering contribution in the area of subaltern studies?
A. Ramachandra Guha
B. Ranjit Guha
C. Rajni Kothari
D. James Manor

31. Who among the following questioned the claim that Public Administration is a Science?
A. Robert Dahl B. Luther Gulick
C. L. Urwick D. Frank Goodnou

32. F.W. Taylor, the founding father of Scientific Management Movement, propounded the theory which was conceived to be a scientific methodology of
A. Careful observation
B. Managerial techniques
C. Generalization
D. All of the above

33. Who among the following is not a protagonist of the managerial view of Public Administration?
A. Simon B. Smithburg
C. Gulick D. Henry Fayol

34. Match List-I with List-II l select the correct answer from the codes en below :

List–I	***ıst–II***
(*a*) Line Agency	1. :ollection of data and its analysis.
(*b*) General Staff	2. Maintenance of diary of different engagements of line officials.

(*c*) Specialised Staff	3. Functions directly contributing to goal achievement
(*d*) Personal Staff	4. Looking after Personnel Administration

Codes:

	(*a*)	(*b*)	(*c*)	(*d*)
A.	3	4	1	2
B.	2	3	4	1
C.	1	2	3	4
D.	4	1	2	3

35. The role of the Finance Commission in Centre-State fiscal relations has been undermined by the

A. The State Governments
B. The Zonal Councils
C. The Planning Commission
D. The Election Commission

36. To which of the following classes of job in the public service in India, merit-cum-seniority principle is adopted in promotion?

A. Class-I
B. Class-II
C. Class-III
D. Class-I and II

37. Which of the following, according to Kautilya, are the principles of good governance for a king?

1. Merging individuality with duties.
2. Leading a disciplined life with a code of conduct.
3. Maintaining law and order.
4. Replacing bad ministers by lekhaks (writers).

Select the correct answer from the codes given below:

Codes :

A. 1, 2 and 4
B. 1, 2 and 3
C. 2, 3 and 4
D. 1, 2, 3 and 4

38. Given below are two statements, one labelled as Assertion (A) and the other labelled as Reason (R):

Assertion (A) : Position–classification is the foundation of modern personnel administration.

Reason (R) : Position–classification allows rationalization in Civil Services.

Codes :

A. Both (A) and (R) are true and (R) is the correct explanation of (A).
B. Both (A) and (R) are true, but (R) is not the correct explanation of (A).
C. (A) is true, but (R) is false.
D. (A) is false, but (R) is true.

39. Given below are two statements, one labelled as Assertion (A) and the other labelled as Reason (R).

Assertion (A) : The relation between a generalist and a specialist is one of a senior and a subordinate.

Reason (R) : A specialist is required to assist the generalist in the formulation and implementation of public policy.

Codes :

A. Both (A) and (R) are true and (R) is the correct explanation of (A).
B. Both (A) and (R) are true, but (R) is not the correct explanation of (A).
C. (A) is true, but (R) is false.
D. (A) is false, but (R) is true.

40. Given below are two statements, one labelled as Assertion (A) and the other labelled as Reason (R).

Assertion (A) : Public Administration is generally characterised by an absence of profit motive.

Reason (R) : Governmental activities are not undertaken simply to maximize profit but to promote societal welfare.

Codes :

A. Both (A) and (R) are true and (R) is the correct explanation of (A).
B. Both (A) and (R) are true, but (R) is not the correct explanation of (A).
C. (A) is true, but (R) is false.
D. (A) is false, but (R) is true.

41. Given below are two statements, one labelled as Assertion (A) and the other labelled as Reason (R).

Assertion (A) : In the Post Soviet era, Nuclear armed states are likely to have military run or weak civilian governments.

Reason (R) : They will lack the positive constraining mechanisms of civilian control.

Codes :

A. Both (A) and (R) are true and (R) is the correct explanation of (A).
B. Both (A) and (R) are true, but (R) is not the correct explanation of (A).
C. (A) is true, but (R) is false.
D. (A) is false, but (R) is true.

42. Where is India's Hi-Tech Naval Base "Project Varsha" located?
A. Rambilli
B. Ezhimalai
C. Araku Valley
D. Kochi

43. "Atoms for Peace" was a disarmament plan put forward by which world leader?
A. J. Nehru B. Krushchev
C. Eisenhower D. Kennedy

44. Match List-I with List-II and select the correct answer from the codes given below :

List–I (Thinkers)	*List–II (Concepts)*
(*a*) William Cohen	1. New Wars
(*b*) Martin Shaw	2. Revolution in Military Affairs
(*c*) Raymond Aron	3. Degenerate Wars
(*d*) Mary Kaldor	4. Hyperbolic Wars

Codes:

	(*a*)	(*b*)	(*c*)	(*d*)
A.	2	3	4	1
B.	1	2	3	4
C.	3	4	1	2
D.	4	1	2	3

45. Who created the Global Environmental Facility (GEF) as an international mechanism specifically for funding environmental projects in developing countries?
A. IMF B. UNDP
C. UNEP D. World Bank

46. Chronologically arrange the following treaties in the correct ascending order :
(*i*) The Charter of the UN
(*ii*) The Treaty of Westphalia
(*iii*) Treaties of Utrecht
(*iv*) Treaty of Paris

Select the correct answer from the codes given below:

Codes :

A. (*iv*), (*i*), (*ii*), (*iii*)
B. (*iii*), (*iv*), (*i*), (*ii*)
C. (*ii*), (*iii*), (*iv*), (*i*)
D. (*i*), (*ii*), (*iii*), (*iv*)

47. What are the four defining elements of a regime?
A. Principles, Norms, Rules, Decision making procedures.
B. Principles, Rules, Regulations, Procedures.
C. Norms, Rules, Regulations, Precedents.
D. Principles, Precedents, Procedures, Practices.

48. Chronologically arrange the following milestones in the Women's movement in the correct ascending order.
(*i*) Mexico City – UN Conference
(*ii*) Copenhagen – UN Conference
(*iii*) Beijing
(*iv*) Nairobi

Select the correct answer from the codes given below:

Codes :

A. (*iv*), (*i*), (*iii*), (*ii*)
B. (*i*), (*ii*), (*iv*), (*iii*)
C. (*ii*), (*iii*), (*i*), (*iv*)
D. (*iii*), (*iv*), (*ii*), (*i*)

49. When did India and Nepal sign the revised Double Taxation Avoidance Agreement (DTAA)?
A. 2011
B. 2012
C. 2010
D. 2009

50. Which of the following countries are included in ASEAN Plus Three?
A. China, India, Japan
B. China, South Korea, Russia
C. China, Russia, Japan
D. China, Japan, South Korea

ANSWERS

1	2	3	4	5	6	7	8	9	10
C	B	C	*	A	A	C	C	C	B
11	**12**	**13**	**14**	**15**	**16**	**17**	**18**	**19**	**20**
C	A	C	B	A	D	D	A	D	A
21	**22**	**23**	**24**	**25**	**26**	**27**	**28**	**29**	**30**
A	A	C	A	D	D	C	D	C	B
31	**32**	**33**	**34**	**35**	**36**	**37**	**38**	**39**	**40**
A	D	A	A	C	D	B	A	D	A
41	**42**	**43**	**44**	**45**	**46**	**47**	**48**	**49**	**50**
*	A	C	A	D	C	A	B	A	D

SOME SELECTED EXPLANATORY ANSWERS

1. The principal characters in the Republic are Cephalus, Polemarchus, Thrasymachus, Socrates, Glaucon, and Adeimantus. Cephalus appears in the introduction only, Polemarchus drops at the end of the first argument, and Thrasymachus is reduced to silence at the close of the first book. The main discussion is carried on by Socrates, Glaucon, and Adeimantus.

3. Marx wrote several books, viz., *Critique of Hegel's Philosophy of Right* (1844), *The Holy Family* (1844) (with Fredrick Engels), *Theses on Feuerbach* (1845), *The German Ideology* (with Engels), *The Poverty of Philosophy* (1847), *The Communist Manifesto* (1848), *Wage, Labour and Capital* (1849), *The Class Struggles in France* (1850), *The Eighteenth Brunaire of Louis Bonaparte* (1850), *A Contribution to the Critique of Political Economy* (1859).

5. The concept of social justice has been associated with the moral and political philosopher, John Rawls, particularly in his works *A Theory of Social Justice* (1971) and *Political Liberalism* (1993). He draws on the utilitarian principles of Bentham and Mill, the social contract ideas of Locke, and the categorical imperative ideas of Kant. His reference to social justice was made in *A Theory of Justice* (1971), where he proposed that "Each person possesses an inviolability founded on justice that even the welfare of society as a whole cannot override. For this reason justice denies that the loss of freedom for some is made right by a greater good shared by others" (Rawls 1971). Social justice, as defined by Rawls, is an abstraction, which is humanistic in essence.

6. John Stuart Mill was an English philosopher and economist. He wrote one of his most famous essays, Utilitarianism, in 1861. Utilitarianism is a moral and legal theory, with origins in classical philosophy, that was famously propagated in the 18th and 19th centuries by Jeremy Bentham.

7. Mao's Writings:

- On New Democracy – 1940
- On Coalition Government – 1945
- On People's Democratic Dictatorship – 1949

8. Gandhiji got an offer from Dada Abdulla, a South African businessman of Gujarati origin and who knew the Gandhi family to help him fight his court cases in South Africa. He accepted the offer and in April 1893 he left for Durban.

9. The Communist Party of India was founded by M.N. Roy in 1920. A Marxist political theorist from Bengal, Roy was one of the founders of the Communist Party of Mexico in 1919.

11. In his *Stages of Political Development* (1965), Organski examined four developmental stages: (1) primitive national unification, (2) industrialization, (3) national welfare, and (4) abundance. He viewed development as the increasing government efficiency in mobilizing human and material resources toward national ends.

15. In the early stages, the process of socialisation is said to be diffuse, particularistic, ascriptive and affective. As the society develops, it becomes specific, universalistic and instrumental.

16. Totalitarianism: A form of government in which all political, economic, social, cultural and religious aspects of society are under the control of a small group, often headed by a dictator. Its most famous examples are the fascist government in Germany under Adolf Hitler (1933-45) and the communist regime under Joseph Stalin (1928-53) in the Soviet Union.

18. A combination of regime and ideology is employed by LaPalombara and Weiner in their classification of parties in developing countries. They distinguish firstly between competitive and non-competitive systems and then two dimensions along which parties differ within each system. *Competitive systems* are associated with large and/or ethnically fragmented countries such as India, Nigeria, Malaysia and Sri Lanka. One dimension of such a system ranges from 'hegemonic', where one party dominates for a long period, to 'turnover', where change in the party of government is frequent. The other dimension refers to parties themselves rather than regimes, and distinguishes between ideological and pragmatic parties. The typology was also useful if one was interested in the ability of parties to manage conflict effectively: 'in competitive systems the ideological–hegemonic and the ideological–turnover systems are less able to cope (short of repressive measures) with conflicts than either pragmatic–turnover or pragmatic–hegemonic systems'. Another hypothesis offered is that any drive for hegemonic control is likely to be made by parties with a strong ideological position.

Party control in a *non-competitive system* is by definition likely to be hegemonic rather than 'turnover'. Combinations of hegemonic party systems and the ideological variable produce three main types of single-party system. The one-party authoritarian system (such as Mali, Ghana and South Vietnam in the 1960s) treats opposition as a threat to revolutionary or nationalistic objectives. The one-party pluralist system is characterized by a pluralistic party organization and a pragmatic ideology, as in Mexico's Institutional Revolutionary Party. The one-party totalitarian system has the state itself as an instrument of the party whose objective is social and economic transformation, as in China, Vietnam and North Korea.

19. Dependency Theory was a reaction to modernization theory. It represents Marxism on an international scale. It asserts that some nations could not develop economically because they were dependent on the wealthy nations. Dependency theory also implies that traditional modernization theory is patronizing and ethnocentric, that is, Western centric. It accuses the West of cultural and economic imperialism. Dependency Theory developed in 1950s and 1960s and became popular as an explanation for poverty continuing in Latin America generation after generation (and for the rest of the underdeveloped world as well) through to the late 1970s when Dependency Theory began to take hold in academic circles.

29. Khan, Rasheeduddin, *Federal India: A Design for Change:* This book places the problem of federalism in the global context and focuses attention on the problems of federal polity in India. It is a policy-oriented study covering themes such as the sociocultural dimensions of India's federal polity, political federalism, and the pattern of federal nation building in India.

30. Subaltern, meaning 'of inferior rank', is a term adopted by Antonio Gramsci to refer to those group in society who are subject to the *hegemony* of the ruling classes. Subaltern classes may include peasants, workers and other groups denied access to 'hegemonic' power.

31. Many modern writers do not accept the view of classical writers that there is a science of Public administration. They give the following arguments to prove that Public administration has not yet become a science.

1. In his "Administrative Behaviour" Herbert Simon has dismissed the so called principles of administration as mere proverbs. He questioned their scientific basis and found them to be mutually contradictory. Robert Dahl, another modern writer, said that the principles enunciated by classical writers were limited to a few examples in a few national and historical settings. Hence, it is said that such unscientific principles without universal validity cannot make Public administration a science.
2. In his "The Science of Public administration: three problems" Robert Dahl points out the impossibility of excluding normative considerations from the problems of Public administration. Public administration is not value free, since Public administrators often face the ethical considerations in doing their duties. As a result of the influence of values, the researcher in Public administration cannot be completely objective. Since Public administration is value-laden, it cannot be regarded as an exact science.
3. Rober Dahl also points out that Public administration is not a science because it deals with certain aspects of human behaviour in organizations. Human behaviour cannot be examined in controlled experiments in a laboratory setting.
4. Public administration is not a science because, it is largely influenced by cultural factors. The influence of culture on Public administration makes it vary from country to country. In the opinion of Dahl, Public administration cannot claim the status of science, unless it is studied on a comparative basis.

35. The Constitution of India envisages the Finance Commission as the balancing wheel of Fiscal Federalism in India. However, its role in the centre-state fiscal relations has been undermined by the emergence of the planning commission, a non-constitutional and a non-statutory body.

37. Development of Good Governance: Governance has existed since ancient times, Kautilya in the *Arthashastra* emphasises that in the pursuit of good governance, the king need to govern for the welfare of the people. Kautilya mentions the following ten imperatives of good governance for a king:

1. Merge his individuality with his duties
2. Guide administration
3. Avoid extremes without missing the goal
4. Lead a disciplined life with a code of conduct
5. Pay fixed salaries and allowances
6. Maintain law and order
7. Stress the role of *lekhaks* (writers)
8. Carry out preventive/punitive measures against corrupt officials
9. Replace bad ministers by good ones
10. Emulate positive administrative qualities.

42. INS Varsha is a new naval base being developed under Project Varsha for the Indian Navy. This base will be the home of the navy's new fleet of nuclear submarines and ships. It was planned to be located within a radius of approximately 200 kilometers from Visakhapatnam, the headquarters of the navy's Eastern Naval Command.

43. On December 8, 1953, President Eisenhower delivered an address on peaceful uses of atomic energy to the U.N. General Assembly. The ideas outlined in this speech and its follow-on policies became known as the Atoms for Peace initiative.

45. The Global Environment Facility is a pilot program to assist developing countries contribute toward solving global environmental problems. A global environment facility was proposed in September 1989 by the French representative at a meeting of the Development Committee—a joint World Bank-IMF ministerial advisory group. Germany put forward a similar proposal. Fourteen months later, in November 1990, the GEF was formally established by a group of developing and industrialized countries meeting in Paris.

47. Regimes can be defined as sets of implicit or explicit principles, norms, rules, and decision-making procedures around which actors' expectations converge in a given area of international relations. Principles are beliefs of fact, causation, and rectitude. Norms are standards of behaviour defined in terms of rights and obligations. Rules are specific prescriptions or proscriptions for action. Decision-making procedures are prevailing practices for making and implementing collective choice.

48. Four major UN world conferences on women—the Mexico City conference in 1975, the Copenhagen conference in 1980, the Nairobi conference in 1985, and the Beijing conference in 1995—have played a vital role in mobilizing public opinion on gender issues; promoting dialogue among governments, international agencies, women's organizations, and specialists; and influencing global and national policies through declarations of principles and programs of action.

49. India and Nepal signed a revised Double Taxation Avoidance Agreement (DTAA) on 27 November 2011, to improve Indian investment in Nepal and ease procedures for stakeholders with commercial interest in both countries.

50. The ASEAN Plus Three forum comprises the ASEAN nations together with China, Japan, and South Korea. ASEAN Plus Three is an attempt to build a regional association that is more limited in its geographic membership than APEC or the ARF.

PAPER–III

Note: *This paper contains* ***seventy five*** *(75) objective type questions of* ***two*** *(2) marks each.* ***All*** *questions are compulsory.*

1. Which one of the following factors is not responsible for the decline of Political Theory?

A. Positivism
B. Historicism
C. Moral Relativism
D. Ideological Pluralism

2. Neo-liberalism does not believe in

A. Deregulation
B. Debureaucratisation
C. Disinvestment
D. Statisation

3. Who said, 'Taxation equals forced labour'?

A. John Rawls B. Hayek
C. Nozick D. Berlin

4. Match List-I with List-II and select the correct answer from the codes given below :

List–I (Authors)	***List–II (Books)***
(*a*) Richard Lowenthal	1. Red China Today
(*b*) Benjamin L. Schwartz	2. Mao's Revolution and the Chinese Political Culture
(*c*) Edgar Snow	3. World Communism
(*d*) Richard H.Solomon	4. Communism and Chinese Ideology in Flux

Codes:

	(*a*)	(*b*)	(*c*)	(*d*)
A.	3	4	1	2
B.	4	3	2	1
C.	2	1	3	4
D.	1	2	4	3

5. Who defined an ideology as 'a set of ideas by which men posit, explain and justify the ends and means of organized social action, irrespective of whether such action aims to preserve, amend, uproot or rebuild a given social order'?

A. de Tracy
B. Martin Seliger
C. D. McLellan
D. J. Larrain

6. Given below are two statements, one is labelled as Assertion (A) and the other labelled as Reason (R):

Assertion (A) : All Political Philosophers are political theorists.

Reason (R) : All Political Theorists are not necessarily Political Philosophers.

Select the correct answer from the codes given below:

Codes :

A. Both (A) and (R) are true and (R) is the right explanation of (A)
B. Both (A) and (R) are true, but (R) is not the correct explanation of (A)
C. (A) is true, but (R) is false
D. (A) is false, but (R) is true

7. Who said that Labour power equals the brain, muscle, and nerve of the Labourer?

A. Lenin
B. M.N. Roy
C. Marx
D. Jayaprakash Narayan

8. The reappearance of Plato is found in the

A. *Utopia* of Sir Thomas More
B. *City of the Sun* of Campanella
C. *New Atlantis* of Bacon
D. All the above

9. Which one of the statements is not correct in respect of Aristotle?

A. Men are by nature unequal.
B. There is subordination of inferior to superior.
C. Women are, by nature, subordinated to men.
D. Slavery is justified because it does not secure the best conditions for the slave.

10. Who did help to humanize J.S. Mill's revised version of Utilitarianism?

A. James Mill
B. Mrs. Harriet Taylor
C. Priestley
D. Hutcheson

11. For Hobbes, 'Felicity' means

A. Pleasure
B. A continued success in obtaining those things which a man from time to time desires.
C. Empathy
D. None of the above

12. 'The "natural" man will be one in whom strong conscience and stead fast reason have successfully harmonized self-love and sympathy'. Who advocated this?

A. Hobbes B. Rousseau
C. Bentham D. Locke

13. Locke's *Essay Concerning Human Understanding* was a refutation of

A. Hobbes' *Leviathan*
B. Priestley's *Essay on Government*
C. Bentham's *Fragment on Government*
D. Sir Robert Filmer's *Patriarcha.*

14. The Politics of Society must be based on two principles as (*i*) 'Treat others as self' and (*ii*) 'help the other persons in need'. Whose saying is this?

A. Rammohan Roy B. B.R. Ambedkar
C. Aurobindo D. Savarkar

15. Identify the correct sequence of M.N. Roy's activities/events in ascending order :

(*i*) Formed "The League of Radical Congressman'.
(*ii*) Founded "The Indian Renaissance Movement".
(*iii*) Expelled from "Comintern"
(*iv*) Founded a weekly, "The Independent India".

Select the correct answer from the codes given below:

Codes :

A. (*iii*), (*iv*), (*i*), (*ii*)
B. (*iv*), (*iii*), (*ii*), (*i*)
C. (*ii*), (*i*), (*iii*), (*iv*)
D. (*i*), (*ii*), (*iv*), (*iii*)

16. Who among the following was elected as U.S. President for the fourth term?

A. George Washington
B. Franklin D. Roosevelt
C. Theodore Roosevelt
D. Andrew Jackson

17. Given below are two statements, one labelled as Assertion (A) and the other labelled as Reason (R). Choose the correct answer from the codes :

Assertion (A) : Democratic values command widespread acceptance within liberal democracies as an ideal, but at the same time citizens have become more critical of the working of the core institutions of representative democracy.

Reason (R) : The declining faith in government represents a deflation of the political culture, reducing the capacity of the political system to achieve shared goals.

Codes :

A. Both (A) and (R) are correct, and (R) is the correct explanation of (R).
B. Both (A) and (R) are correct, but (R) is not the correct explanation of (A).
C. (A) is false, but (R) is correct.
D. (A) is correct, but (R) is false.

18. Which of the following countries has a simple constitution-amending procedure?

A. U.S.A. B. U.K.
C. India D. France

19. In reference to Presidential system which President of U.S.A. said, "for the folly of just one man may spell disaster for the whole nation."?

A. Jimmy Carter
B. Barrack Obama
C. George W. Bush
D. Woodrow Wilson

20. Which one of the following statements about the U.S. President is not correct?

A. No U.S. President has ever been impeached.
B. Richard Nixon's impeachment failed by one vote.
C. The House of Representatives has the power to initiate impeachment proceedings.
D. The case is tried by the Senate with the Chief Justice presiding.

21. Match List-I with List-II and select the correct answer from the codes given below :

List–I ***(Model of Development)***	**List–II** ***(Features)***
(*a*) Bourgeoisie model	1. Urban Economic growth development of Legislature and Electoral process.
(*b*) Autocratic model	2. Suppress middle class.
(*c*) Technocratic model	3. Low political participation and high foreign investment.
(*d*) Populist model	4. Stresses high political participation as well as economic inequality.

Codes:

	(a)	(b)	(c)	(d)
A.	1	2	3	4
B.	4	3	2	1
C.	3	2	1	4
D.	2	3	4	1

22. Match List-I with List-II and select the correct answer from the codes given below :

List–I (Authors)	*List–II (Books)*
(a) Robert Michaels	1. Democracy and its critics
(b) Samuel Huntington	2. State Building : Governance and World order in the Twenty First Century
(c) Robert Dahll	3. Political Parties
(d) Francis Fukuyama	4. The Third Wave : Democratization in the Late Twentieth Century.

Codes:

	(a)	(b)	(c)	(d)
A.	1	3	4	2
B.	3	4	1	2
C.	4	2	3	1
D.	2	1	3	4

23. Who among the following has adopted the 'Political-conflict approach' in the analysis of revolution?

A. Thdeda Skocpol
B. Alexis de Tocqueville
C. Charles Tilly
D. Emile Durkheim

24. Match List-I with List-II and select the correct answer from the given codes below :

List–I (Books)	*List–II (Authors)*
(a) The Politics of Modernization	1. Amartya Sen
(b) Development as Freedoms	2. Samuel P. Huntington
(c) Political order in Changing Societies	3. Celso Furtado
(d) Development and Underdevelopment	4. David E. Apter

Codes:

	(a)	(b)	(c)	(d)
A.	1	2	3	4
B.	4	1	2	3
C.	2	3	4	1
D.	4	1	3	2

25. Which of the following thinkers defined modernization in terms of three conditions :

(i) An innovative social system
(ii) Differentiated, flexible social structure
(iii) Social basis for skill and knowledge, in technologically advanced world.

A. C.E. Black
B. David E. Apter
C. Samuel P. Huntington
D. S.N. Eisenstadt

26. Which of the following statements are correct about the Swiss Political System?

1. The Centre in Switzerland is more powerful than that of the U.S.A.
2. Swiss Government has right to military intervention in case of secession.
3. The residuary powers belong to the units.
4. Swiss political system is unitary.

Codes :

A. 1, 2, 4 B. 2, 3, 4
C. 1, 2, 3 D. 1, 2, 3, 4

27. Match List-I with List-II and select the correct answer from the codes given below :

List–I (Thinkers)	*List–II (Concepts)*
(a) M. Focault	1. Will to power
(b) Steven Lukes	2. Bio power
(c) Stewart Clegg	3. Radical view of power
(d) F. Nietzche	4. Circuits of power

Codes:

	(a)	(b)	(c)	(d)
A.	4	1	2	3
B.	3	2	1	4
C.	1	4	3	2
D.	2	3	4	1

28. Which one is not the attribute of one party system?

A. Sectarian (Exclusive, regional, class, ideological) support.

B. Closed, Authoritarian, Direct action, Repressive organization.
C. Diffused, National integration, Community building, Mobilisation.
D. Comprehensive, Clientele oriented, Pragmatic support.

29. Which of the following, according to Lucian Pye, are the crises of Political development?
1. Crisis of Identity
2. Crisis of Legitimacy
3. Crisis of Leadership
4. Crisis of Integrity

Select the correct answer from the codes given below:

Codes :

A. 1, 2 B. 2, 3
C. 3, 4 D. 1, 4

30. Match List-I with List-II. Select correct answer from the codes given below :

List–I *(Elites)*	*List–II* *(Functions)*
(*a*) Current Political Elites	1. Goal attainment
(*b*) Economic Military, Scientific, Diplomatic Elites	2. Adaptation
(*c*) Priest, Philosophers, Educators	3. Integration
(*d*) Artists, Writers, top Actors	4. Pattern Maintenance

Codes:

	(*a*)	(*b*)	(*c*)	(*d*)
A.	1	2	3	4
B.	4	3	2	1
C.	3	2	1	4
D.	2	1	4	3

31. Who made the following statement in the Constituent Assembly in connection with the Amendment Procedure of the Constitution of India?

'That while we want this Constitution to be solid and as permanent as a structure we can make it, nevertheless there is no permanence in Constitutions. ... If you make anything rigid and permanent, you stop the Nation's growth, the growth of a living, vital organic people'.

A. Dr. B.R. Ambedkar
B. Jawaharlal Nehru
C. Sardar Vallabhbhai Patel
D. Dr. Rajendra Prasad

32. Which of the following Articles cannot be suspended during National Emergency?

A. Articles 14 and 15
B. Articles 19 and 20
C. Articles 21 and 22
D. Articles 20 and 21

33. Who among the following called Jayaprakash Narain, Ram Manohar Lohia and other Socialists as Japanese agents during 1942 movement?

A. Communist Party of India
B. Akali Dal
C. Rashtriya Swayam Sevak Sangh
D. Muslim League

34. Given below are two statements, one labelled as Assertion (A) and the other labelled as Reason (R). Choose the correct answer from the codes.

Assertion (A) : Caste system was an epitome of the traditional society, a 'closed system', where generation after generation of individuals did similar kinds of work and lived more or less similar kinds of lives.

Reason (R) : Caste system encapsulated within it the features of a social structure and normative religious behaviour, and even provided a fairly comprehensive idea about the personal lives of individuals living in the Hindu Caste Society.

Codes :

A. Both (A) and (R) are correct, and (R) is the correct explanation of (A).
B. Both (A) and (R) are correct, but (R) is not the correct explanation of (A).
C. (A) is correct, but (R) is false.
D. (R) is correct, but (A) is false.

35. Given below are two statements, one labelled as Assertion (A) and the other labelled as Reason (R). Choose the correct answer from the codes.

Assertion (A) : Over the years, the Supreme Court of India has failed to demonstrate a commitment to preserving constitutional liberty, and expanding and protecting human rights.

Reason (R) : The Supreme Court has played and continues to play a critical role in shaping India's constitutional democracy far beyond that which the drafters of the Constitution envisaged or what courts in other countries play.

Codes :

A. Both (A) and (R) are correct and (R) is the correct explanation of (A).
B. Both (A) and (R) are correct, but (R) is not the correct explanation of (A).
C. (A) is correct, but (R) is false.
D. (A) is false, but (R) is correct.

36. Which one of the following is not applicable to Public Interest Litigation?

A. Constitutional obligation of the Judiciary towards the marginalised sections of society.
B. *Locus standi.*
C. Public spirited citizens can move the court on behalf of the poor.
D. Judiciary overlooks a strict construction of procedural formalities in entertaining petitions.

37. Which among the following pertains to the sixty first Constitutional Amendment?

A. Ninth Schedule
B. Defection
C. Amendment of Article 368
D. Lowering of voting age

38. The Sikhs got special electorates in which of the following Acts?

A. Indian Councils Act, 1892
B. Indian Councils Act, 1909
C. Government of India Act, 1919
D. Government of India Act, 1935

39. Which of the following Committees of the Constituent Assembly was chaired by Jawaharlal Nehru?

A. Steering Committee
B. Union Powers Committee
C. Committee on Fundamental Rights and Minorities
D. Provincial Constitution Committee

40. Who among the following developed the concept, 'derivative discourse'?

A. Ashish Nandy
B. Partha Chatterjee
C. Ashutosh Varshney
D. Sudipta Kaviraj

41. MNREGA is not associated with which of the following?

A. Providing Employment Opportunities
B. Reduction of poverty
C. Preventing Distress Migration
D. Agrarian crises

42. Match List-I with List-II and select the correct answer from the codes given below :

List–I Commission/ Committee	***List–II Issues***
(*a*) Mahajan Commission	1. Maharashtra-Karnataka Boundary Dispute
(*b*) Sri Krishna Commission	2. Muslim Minority
(*c*) Punchi Commission	3. Telengana/A.P.
(*d*) Sachar Committee	4. Centre-State Relations

Codes:

	(*a*)	(*b*)	(*c*)	(*d*)
A.	2	4	1	3
B.	1	3	4	2
C.	3	2	1	4
D.	4	1	3	2

43. Who among the following first initiated the study of State Politics in India?

A. Iqbal Narain
B. Paul R. Brass
C. Stanley Kochanak
D. Myron Weiner

44. Which one of the following was the largest Opposition party in the Eighth Lok Sabha (1984)?

A. Bhartiya Janata Party
B. Communist Party of India

C. Telugu Desam Party
D. National Lok Dal

45. With which of the following States, was the Programme, Janmabhoomi associated?

A. Kerala B. Karnataka
C. Tamil Nadu D. Andhra Pradesh

46. Match List-I with List-II and select the correct answer from the codes given below :

List–I (Approach)	*List–II (Characteristics)*
(*a*) Behavioural	1. Agrarian-Transition Industrialization
(*b*) Bureaucratic	2. Administrative system as a subsystem of the society
(*c*) Ecological	3. Analyses of human behaviour in administrative settings
(*d*) General Systems	4. Legal-Rational Authority

Codes:

	(*a*)	(*b*)	(*c*)	(*d*)
A.	2	3	4	1
B.	3	4	1	2
C.	1	2	3	4
D.	4	1	2	3

47. Which of the following is concerned with the substantive functions of the Government?

A. Staff Agency
B. Line Agency
C. Auxiliary Agency
D. Staff and Auxiliary Agencies

48. Who among the following termed the four different bases of organization as four Ps?

A. Luther Gulick
B. L.D. White
C. Henry Fayol
D. Herbert Simon

49. The chief reason for delegation of authority from headquarters to field officers is to

A. facilitate decision-making at the local level.
B. inculcate skills in the field officers.
C. control the field office.
D. decongest the headquarters.

50. Which of the following are the characteristics of development administration?

1. Change-orientation
2. Client orientation
3. Citizen-participative orientation
4. Ecological perspective

Select the correct answer from the codes given below:

Codes :

A. 1 and 2 B. 2 and 3
C. 1, 2 and 4 D. 1, 2, 3 and 4

51. Domicile qualification for public services was first prescribed by

A. The United States of America
B. U.K.
C. India
D. France

52. Which one of the following is the Cadre-controlling authority for the Indian Police Service?

A. The Ministry of Personnel, Public Grievances and Pensions
B. The Ministry of Home Affairs
C. Prime Minister's Office (PMO)
D. Cabinet Secretary

53. The process of transferring funds from one budget head to another of the same department where there is a need for more expenditure is called

A. transfer
B. re-allocation
C. re-appropriation
D. sectoral allocation

54. Promotion generally means

1. Change in position
2. Change in duties
3. Change in title
4. Change in pay

Select the correct answer from the codes given below:

Codes :

A. 1 and 2 B. 1, 2 and 3
C. 1, 3 and 4 D. 1, 2, 3 and 4

55. Which of the following statements are correct?

1. Panchayati Raj is mentioned in the Constitution as a Directive Principle.
2. Sadiq Ali Committee was appointed to report on the working of the Panchayat system in India.
3. G.V.K. Rao Committee was appointed by the Planning Commission.
4. Local Government figures in State List.

Select the correct answer from the codes given below:

Codes :

A. 1, 3 and 4 B. 2, 3 and 4
C. 1, 2 and 3 D. 1, 2, 3 and 4

56. Who among the following has termed bureaucracy as "an organization that cannot correct its behaviour by learning from its errors"?

A. R.K. Merton B. M. Crozer
C. Max Weber D. C.N. Parkinson

57. Who is the Chairperson of the National Council of Joint Consultative Machinery (JCM)?

A. Cabinet Secretary
B. Secretary for Home Affairs
C. Personnel Secretary
D. Finance Secretary

58. Of all the controls over Public Administration the one which is more continuous and self-corrective is

A. controlled by the Legislature
B. controlled by the Executive
C. controlled by the Judiciary
D. controlled by the Media

59. Given below are two statements, one labelled as Assertion (A) and the other as Reason (R).

Assertion (A) : A few years back, the Government of India started what is known as "file-jumping experiment".

Reason (R) : Hierarchical structure causes inordinate delay in the disposal of work.

Codes :

A. Both (A) and (R) are true and (R) is the correct explanation of (A).
B. Both (A) and (R) are true, but (R) is not the correct explanation of (A).
C. (A) is true, but (R) is false.
D. (A) is false, but (R) is true.

60. Given below are two statements, one labelled as Assertion (A) and the other as Reason (R).

Assertion (A) : Planning Commission in India is neither a Statutory Body nor a Constitutional Body.

Reason (R) : It was established by an Act of Parliament.

Codes :

A. Both (A) and (R) are true and (R) is the correct explanation of (A).
B. Both (A) and (R) are true, but (R) is not the correct explanation of (A).
C. (A) is true, but (R) is false.
D. (A) is false, but (R) is true.

61. With which liberal thinker would you associate "Democratic Peace Theory"?

A. Michael Doyle
B. James Rosenau
C. Richard Falk
D. Michael Walzer

62. Given below are two statements, one labelled as Assertion (A) and the other labelled as Reason (R).

Assertion (A) : Regimes represent an important feature of globalization.

Reason (R) : The onset of détente, the loss of hegemonic status by the USA and the growing awareness of environmental problems sensitized social scientists.

Codes :

A. Both (A) and (R) are true and (R) is the right explanation of (A).
B. Both (A) and (R) are true, but (R) is not the correct explanation of (A).
C. (A) is true, but (R) is false.
D. (A) is false, but (R) is true.

63. Who said, "Power in International Politics is like the weather. Everyone talks about it, but few understand it"?

A. Hans J.Morganthau
B. Henry Kissinger
C. Joseph Nye
D. Susan Strange

64. Match List-I with List-II and select the correct answer from the codes given below :

List–I (Reasons of failure)	*List–II (States)*
(*a*) Tribal conflict	1. Rwanda
(*b*) Endless violence for nonpolitical purposes	2. Somalia
(*c*) Ethnic genocide	3. Congo
(*d*) Transnational war	4. Liberia

Codes:

	(*a*)	(*b*)	(*c*)	(*d*)
A.	2	4	1	3
B.	1	3	4	2
C.	4	2	3	1
D.	3	1	2	4

65. Chronologically arrange the arms control and disarmament agreements in an ascending order.

1. Strategic Offensive Reduction Treaty (SORT) - 2002
2. Chemical Weapons Convention - 1993
3. Open Skies Treaty - 1992
4. Ottawa Landmine Convention–1997

Codes :

A. 4, 1, 3, 2 B. 1, 4, 2, 3
C. 3, 2, 4, 1 D. 2, 3, 1, 4

66. Given below are two statements one labelled as Assertion (A) and the other labelled as Reason (R).

Assertion (A) : The Post-Cold War period is a multi polar moment in an uni polar world.

Reason (R) : America remains the world's pre eminent actor, but it is also stretched militarily, in debt financially, divided domestically and unpopular internationally.

Codes :

A. Both (A) and (R) are true and (R) is the correct explanation of (A).
B. Both (A) and (R) are true, but (R) is not the correct explanation of (A).
C. (A) is true, but (R) is false.
D. (A) is false, but (R) is true.

67. With which Doctrine is "Containment" associated?

A. Dulles Doctrine
B. Truman Doctrine
C. Nixon Doctrine
D. Roosevelt Doctrine

68. Which country has the world's largest reserves of natural gas, the second largest coal reserves, and the eighth largest oil reserves?

A. Iran B. USA
C. Saudi Arabia D. Russia

69. Match List-I with List-II and select the correct answer from the codes given below the lists:

List–I (Books)	*List–II (Authors)*
(*a*) A Hundred Horizons : The Indian Ocean in the Age of Global Empire.	1. C. Raja Mohan
(*b*) Global Swing States : Brazil, India, Indonesia, Turkey and the Future of International Order.	2. Sugato Bose
(*c*) War in the Indian Ocean	3. David Kliman & Richard Fontaine
(*d*) Samundra Manthan : Sino Indian Rivalry in the Indo-Pacific	4. Vice-Admiral Mihir Kumar Roy

Codes:

	(*a*)	(*b*)	(*c*)	(*d*)
A.	4	1	2	3
B.	3	4	1	2
C.	2	3	4	1
D.	1	2	3	4

70. Which countries were identified as the "Axis of Evil" by President Bush in his State of Union Speech in 2002?

A. Russia, China, Iran
B. Iran, Iraq, Syria
C. Cuba, Venezuela, Russia
D. Iraq, Iran, North Korea

71. When was the UN Peace building Commission established?

A. January 2003
B. December 2004
C. December 2005
D. January 2006

72. As part of a regional initiative, India initiated the 2004 Tokyo Agreement. Name the organization which emerged as a result.
A. BRICS
B. ARF
C. ReCAAP
D. IOR-ARC

73. Name the military strategist who stated that all war is based on deception and praised it as the 'divine art of subtlety and secrecy'.
A. Clausewitz B. Kautilya
C. Sun Tzu D. Machiavelli

74. Name the person who headed the United Nations Monitoring, Verification and Inspection Commission (UNMOVIC) to Iraq in 2002?
A. Kofi Annan B. Hans Blix
C. David Petraeus D. Colin Powell

75. Which among the following States least influences India's Foreign Policy?
A. Jammu and Kashmir
B. West Bengal
C. Madhya Pradesh
D. Tamil Nadu

ANSWERS

1	2	3	4	5	6	7	8	9	10
D	D	C	A	B	B	C	D	D	B
11	**12**	**13**	**14**	**15**	**16**	**17**	**18**	**19**	**20**
B	B	*	C	A	B	B	B	A	B
21	**22**	**23**	**24**	**25**	**26**	**27**	**28**	**29**	**30**
A	B	C	B	B	C	D	D	A	A
31	**32**	**33**	**34**	**35**	**36**	**37**	**38**	**39**	**40**
B	D	A	B	D	B	D	C	B	B
41	**42**	**43**	**44**	**45**	**46**	**47**	**48**	**49**	**50**
D	B	D	C	D	B	B	A	A, D	D
51	**52**	**53**	**54**	**55**	**56**	**57**	**58**	**59**	**60**
A	A	C	D	A	B	A	B	A	C
61	**62**	**63**	**64**	**65**	**66**	**67**	**68**	**69**	**70**
A	B	C	A	C	D	B	D	C	D
71	**72**	**73**	**74**	**75**					
C	C	C	B	C					

SOME SELECTED EXPLANATORY ANSWERS

3. The libertarian philosopher Robert Nozick comments in his influential book, *Anarchy, State and Utopia,* that: 'Taxation of labour incomes is on a par with forced labour.'

5. The world 'ideology' was coined by the French writer Destutt De Tracy to mean 'the science of ideas': literally an idea-ology—a positive usage which emerged at a time when many academics were seeking to create or espouse a social 'science'—psychology, sociology, ecology and so on.

The most common usage today is a purely descriptive and neutral one (as suggested by Martin Seliger, *Politics and Ideology,* 1976): an 'ideology' as a set or system of related ideas, beliefs and values which may be used to understand and interpret events, and to guide and direct actions towards specified aims. According to this usage, the concept of ideology will have four elements: first, a concept of human nature; second, a theory about how human history has developed and why; third, an analysis of the role of the state as it is and should be; and, finally some broad philosophical and policy prescriptions. By this usage, any '-ism'—communism, fascism, conservatism, liberalism, anarchism—is an ideology, and no value judgements are being made about whether it is good or bad.

11. The idea of felicity, which Hobbes in the sixth chapter of *Leviathan* defines as 'continual success in obtaining those things which a man from time to time desireth.'

18. Constitutions can be categorized on the basis of the ease with which they may be changed. "Flexible" constitutions, such as those of the United Kingdom and New Zealand, may be altered by a simple majority vote in the legislature. "Rigid" constitutions, as in the United States and Russia, have amendment procedures that require more than a simple majority vote of the legislature; how rigid they are depends on the degree of difficulty of the amending process, such as requiring supermajorities of the legislature and ratification by referendum or political subdivisions of the nation-state.

23. The political conflict perspective has developed mainly in critical response to discontent and societal disintegration explanations of political violence. According to Tilly, theorists such as Gurr and Davies and Johnson and Smelser have failed to see that political violence is essentially a by-product of omnipresent processes of political conflict among mobilized—that is, organized and resource-controlling—groups and governments.

Tilly places "political conflict" at the center of attention. And he proposes to analyze it with the aid of a general model whose major elements are government ("organizations which control the principal means of coercion") and contenders for power, including both polity members and challengers (Tilly).

29. On the basis of historical understanding of growth and evolution of western political systems, Lucian Pye has identified certain stages or crises which each political system has to pass through on the path of political development. These crises occur in definite sequences as given below:

1. Identity crisis
2. Legitimacy crisis
3. Penetration crisis
4. Participation crisis
5. Integration crisis
6. Distribution crisis

32. While the proclamation of National Emergency under Article 352 comes into effect, the fundamental rights given under Art. 19 (right to freedom of speech, association etc.) are automatically suspended. Other fundamental rights may be suspended by the President by issuing a separate notification to the effect under Art. 359. However, after the 44th Amendment, 1978; the two fundamental rights namely rights relating to protection in respect of conviction of offences (Art. 20) and right to protection of life and personal liberty (Art. 21) cannot be suspended even during the operation of national emergency.

37. The sixty-first amendment of 1988 has lowered the voting age from 21 years to 18 years for the Lok Sabha and Assembly elections.

38. As a result of the August Declaration, the Government of India Act, 1919 or Montagu-Chelmsford of Reforms were introduced in 1919. Its main feature was diarchy, a kind of double government in the provinces. Separate electorates were further extend to the Sikhs in the Punjab.

39. The prominent members of the Constituent Assembly were assigned various tasks allocated under various committees. These committees were: Provincial Constitution Committee, Union Constitution Committee, Steering Committee, Rules Committee, etc. Following were the prominent committees with the name of the chairs:

1. States Committee: Jawaharlal Nehru
2. Advisory Committee on Fundamental Rights, Minorities and Tribal and Excluded Areas: Ballabhbhai Patel
3. Union Powers Committee: Jawaharlal Nehru
4. Union Constitution Committee: Jawaharlal Nehru
5. Provincial Constitution Committee: Ballabhbhai Patel
6. Drafting Committee: B.R. Ambedkar

40. The phrase 'derivative discourse' is the subtitle of Partha Chatterjee's book *Nationalist Thought and the Colonial World* (1986) which challenges Anderson's model, suggesting that the relationship between anti-colonial and metropolitian nationalisms is structured by an intricate relationship of both borrowing and difference.

43. The fourth General Elections held in 1967 occupy a unique place in the history of electoral politics in India for a number of reasons. The Indian citizens saw governments of different political parties in the various states, although the Congress party 'with a much reduced majority' continued in office at the Centre. For some political observers it was the beginning of real democracy and true form of federalism in the country and leading the era of state politics in India. Ever since Myron Weiner took steps in 1965 for the study of state politics in India, there had been considerable enthusiasm on the part of Indian scholars also to probe into this area of study. Myron Weiner's book *State Politics in India* purports to analyse and compare the political processes of a few carefully selected states within the Indian Union by the application of the comparative method. After a review of the studies of the eight authors in the book, Myron Weiner examines to some extent, in the light of these, a number of important themes bearing on state politics in India such as the history and nature of Indian federalism, the role of the Congress party, the pattern of administrative system, political integration and political participation in the state, state party systems, the social and economic basis of the conflicts and conditions for political stability.

45. The Janmabhoomi Program was launched in the state of Andhra Pradesh on 1 January 1997. This people-centered participatory development process reportedly evolved out of the experience gained in the implementation of the Prajala Vaddaku Palana (taking administration to the people) and Sharmadan (volunteer labour for development) programs and micro-level planning in the state from November 1995 to December 1996.

48. There are four bases of organising—purpose, process, clientele and area. Luther Gulick called these—purpose, process, person and place—the four Ps.

Principles of Departmentalisation: The following four principles underlie departmentalisation or simply, departmentation:

1. The *purpose* one is serving, such as supplying electricity, controlling crime, or conducting education;
2. The *process* he is using, such as engineering, medicine, law, statistics, accounting;
3. The *persons* or things dealt with or served, such as scheduled tribes, ex-servicemen, forests, mines, automobilies, or the poor;
4. The *place* where he renders his service.

50. The development administration has the following characteristics:

1. Change-orientation, that is, bringing about socio-economic change rather than maintenance of status-quo.
2. Goal-orientation that is, achieving progress in social, economic, political and cultural goals (result-orientation).
3. Commitment, that is, high morale and motivation in work situation to achieve the developmental goals.
4. Client orientation, that is, meeting the needs of the specific target groups like small farmers, children and so on.
5. Temporal dimension, that is, completing development programmes within a time limit (time-orientation).
6. Citizen-participative orientation, that is, enlisting popular support and involvement in the formulation and implementation of development programmes.
7. Innovativeness, that is, replacing or improving the administrative structures, methods and procedures for the effective realisation of developmental goals.
8. Ecological perspective, that is, interaction between developmental bureaucracy and its social, economic and political environment.
9. Effective coordination, that is, achieving coordination between the multiple specialised units and programmes involved in the developmental tasks (high degree of integration).
10. Responsiveness, that is, responding to popular needs and demands.

51. The countries opting for federal system of government lay down domicile qualification. This qualification was first introduced in the United States of America to give due representation to each federating unit in the national services.

54. Following are the elements (components) of promotion:

1. Change of position, that is, from lower position to higher position.
2. Change of duties, that is, from less difficult type of work to more difficult type of work.
3. Change of responsibility, that is, from lesser responsibility to greater responsibility.
4. Change of title, that is, from lower designation to higher designation.
5. Change of pay, that is, from lower salary to higher salary scale.

56. Michel Crozier in his book 'The Bureaucratic Phenomena's (1964) has described bureaucracy as "a rigid organization that cannot correct its behaviour by learning from its errors".

61. **Democratic Peace Theory:** In recent years, the concept of democracy has sufraced in a debate, which had occupied attention of several scholars of international studies. Known as the "Democratic Peace Theory", it is based on the assumption that liberal and democratic states do not go to war against each other. The idea in itself is explosive and has the powerful suggestion that democracy might be the panacea for world politics. Ideationally, the theory has been traced and attributed to the Prussian philosopher Immanuel Kant. In his book, *Perpetual Peace,* Kant argued that liberal and republican states have created a political space, distinct from others. The theory borrows three elements outlined by Kant—republican democratic representation, the importance of human rights and transnational relations. In the twenty-first century, Michael Doyle and Bruce Russet are amongst the well-known proponents of this theory. It would be incorrect to conclude however, that democratic peace theorists are convinced that democratic states are benign and committed to peace. Doyle points out that democratic states are just as aggressive towards authoritarian states, but two democratic states would not go to war. Several scholars have argued that the US foreign policy is guided by this conviction in the democratic peace theory.

67. The Truman Doctrine was the first practical application of the 'Policy of Containment'. This meant "Keeping Russia's power or area of control within acceptable limits or boundaries"

71. The UN Peacebuilding Commission was established in December 2005 as an intergovernmental advisory subsidiary body of the General Assembly and the Security Council.

72. The Regional Cooperation Agreement on Combating Piracy and Armed Robery against Ships in Asia (ReCAAP) is the first regional government-to-government agreement to promote and enhance cooperation against piracy and armed robbery in Asia. ReCAAP was adopted in 2004 and entered into force in 2006. To date, 19 States have become Contracting Parties to ReCAAP. The ReCAAP information Sharing Centre (ISC) was established under the ReCAAP Agreement. The roles of ReCAAP ISC include exchanging information among Contracting Parties on incidents of piracy and armed robbery, supports capacity building efforts of Contracting Parties, and for cooperative arrangements.

Previous Paper (Solved)

UGC-NET POLITICAL SCIENCE, JUNE 2013

PAPER–II

Note: *This paper contains fifty (50) multiple-choice questions, each question carrying two (2) marks. Attempt all of them.*

1. What constitutes the mean in Aristotle's social structure?

A. Wealthy class B. Poor citizen
C. Middle class D. Artisan class

2. Whom did Machiavelli blame for the moral degradation of Italy?

A. The Prince B. The Church
C. The Aristocracy D. Corrupt People

3. For Hegel which one of the following is correct?

A. Family is the thesis, Bourgeois society is the anti-thesis and the State represents synthesis
B. The rational is real and the real is rational.
C. Contradictions are not obstacles preventing us reaching truth
D. All of the above

4. Who among the following criticised Bentham's Philosophy as "Pig Philosophy"?

A. Leslie Stephen B. Karl Marx
C. Carlyle D. J.S. Mill

5. Which of the following is correct so far as John Rawls' writings are concerned?

A. A theory of Justice
B. Political Liberalism
C. The Law of Peoples
D. All of the above

6. Which one of the following Mao has not said?

A. Political power grows out of barrel of gun.
B. Three years of hard work : ten thousand years of happiness.
C. Atom bombs are real tigers.
D. A revolution is not a dinner party.

7. Which one among the following statements is true?

A. Behaviouralism is based on Stimulus-Response paradigm
B. Post-behaviouralism consists of seven tenets
C. Post-behaviouralism wholly negates behaviouralism
D. There are no differences between behaviourism and behaviouralism

8. Given below are two statements, one labelled as Assertion (A) and the other labelled as Reason (R):

Assertion (A): Karl Marx termed early socialists as Utopian socialists.

Reason (R): They attacked the capitalist system itself.

Codes:

A. Both (A) and (R) are true and (R) is the right explanation of (A)
B. Both (A) and (R) are true but (R) is not the correct explanation of (A)
C. (A) is true but (R) is false
D. (A) is false but (R) is true

9. Identify the correct sequence of the Plato's four components of virtue:

1. Justice
2. Courage
3. Temperance
4. Wisdom

Select the correct answer from the codes given below:

A. 1, 2, 3, 4 B. 2, 3, 4, 1
C. 4, 2, 3, 1 D. 3, 2, 1, 4

10. Match List-I with List-II and select the correct answer from the codes given below:

List-I	*List-II*
(*a*) Savarkar	1. Associated with a secret society "Lotus and Daggers."
(*b*) M.N. Roy	2. Author of the book *A Plea for Reconstruction of Indian Polity*
(*c*) Aurobindo Ghose	3. Convicted in the Kanpur conspiracy case
(*d*) Jayaprakash Narayan	4. Hinduize all politics and militarize Hinduism

Codes :

	(*a*)	(*b*)	(*c*)	(*d*)
A.	4	3	1	2
B.	3	2	4	1
C.	2	1	3	4
D.	1	2	4	3

11. Notion of uneven development was a response to the 19th century ideas of

A. Capitalism
B. Evolution and gradualism
C. Positivism
D. Anarchism

12. Match List-I with List-II and select the correct answer from the codes given below :

List-I (Dependency Theorists)	*List-II (Books)*
(*a*) Samir Amin	1. Dependency and Development
(*b*) A.G. Frank	2. Accumulation on a world scale
(*c*) F. Henrique cardoso	3. Capitalism and under development in Latin America
(*d*) Paul Swezey	4. Monopoly Capital

Codes :

	(*a*)	(*b*)	(*c*)	(*d*)
A.	4	1	3	2
B.	3	4	2	1
C.	1	2	4	3
D.	2	3	1	4

13. Who among the following is associated with Institutional Approach?

A. James Bryce B. Merriam
C. Arthur Bentley D. Lasswell

14. Who among the following challenged the idea of political development as an unilinear process?

A. Shils B. Huntington
C. Almond D. Halpren

15. Which of the following pairs are not correctly matched?

List-I (Thinkers)		*List-II (Concepts)*
1. Easton	—	Regulatory mechanisms
2. Deutsch	—	Modernising oligarchy
3. Shils	—	Structural differentiation
4. Lucian Pye	—	Negative Feedback

Select the correct answer from the codes given below:

A. 2 and 3 B. 1 and 2
C. 1, 3 and 4 D. 2, 3 and 4

16. What is 'Cultural Dualism'?

A. The existence of two religious cultures
B. Newly emerging nations have two languages
C. A small elite is modernized while the vast majority remains in rigid ascriptive patterns of tradition
D. It is separation of the sacred from the secular

17. Identify the correct sequence of the following input functions of Almond's Political System:

1. Interest aggregation
2. Interest articulation
3. Political socialisation and recruitment
4. Political communication

Select the correct answer from the codes given below:

A. 2, 3, 1 and 4 B. 3, 2, 1 and 4
C. 3, 1, 2 and 4 D. 1, 2, 3 and 4

18. The classical theory of administration is also known as

A. Locational theory
B. Historical theory

C. Mechanistic theory
D. Human Relations theory

19. Pareto's description of elites as 'speculators' and 'rentiers' resembles the characterisation of governing cliques of

A. Plato B. Aristotle
C. Machiavelli D. Marx

20. The difference between order and disorder is more important than the difference between communism and liberal democracy is advocated by

A. Lipset B. Lijphart
C. Dahl D. Huntington

21. Which of the following statements are not correct?

1. As per the provisions of the Constitution, the Council of Ministers is both collectively and individually responsible to the Lok Sabha.
2. A motion expressing lack of confidence in an individual minister is not admissible.
3. A no-confidence motion must set out the grounds on which it is based.
4. If a no-confidence motion is passed by the Lok Sabha, the Council of Ministers is bound to resign.

Select the correct answer from the codes given below:

A. 1 and 2 B. 1 and 3
C. 1, 2 and 3 D. 2 and 3

22. The Avadi Session of the Congress (1956) accepted the policy of

A. Cooperative Farming
B. Import Substitution
C. Garibi Hatao
D. Socialistic pattern of society

23. What was the main findings of the Union Government administrative committee headed by Home Secretary N.N. Vohra in 1993?

A. Electoral Reforms
B. Minimum qualification for politicians
C. Nexus between politicians, criminals and bureaucrats.
D. Internal security priorities

24. Partha Chatterjee has commented that the latest phase of the globalization of capital will witness an emerging opposition between

A. Modernity and Democracy
B. Feudalism and Democracy
C. Inclusion and Democracy
D. Elitism and Mass cultures

25. The President can make a proclamation of Financial Emergency under Art. 360

A. for the whole of India or any part of India
B. for the whole of India except Nagaland, Tripura, Manipur, Meghalaya, Mizoram and Arunachal Pradesh
C. for the whole of India except Jammu and Kashmir
D. for the whole of India except Andaman and Nicobar Islands

26. Given below are two statements, one labelled as Assertion (A) and the other labelled as Reason (R).

Assertion (A): The secular ideology of the Indian State appears to be paradox in view of the deeply religious orientation of the Indian society.

Reason (R): India's secularism was invented for integrating the multicultural plurality of the society into a common nation-state as well as for containing potentialities of the imperial 'divide and rule' and Muslim Leagues' 'two-nation' theory in British India.

Codes:

A. Both (A) and (R) are true and (R) is the correct explanation of (A)
B. Both (A) and (R) are true but (R) is not the correct explanation of (A)
C. (A) is true but (R) is false
D. (R) is true but (A) is false

27. Dharamsala model of Indian capitalism was propounded by

A. Dandekar and Rath
B. Arjun Sengupta
C. Raj Krishna
D. Amartya Sen

28. The 1963 Kamraj Plan was initiated by Nehru
A. to revive Congress party commitments
B. to attract the youth to the party
C. to plan and execute succession procedure in the party
D. to plan gender parity in the party

29. Which of the following statements about the Central Vigilance Commissioner is not true?
A. The Central Vigilance Commissioner is appointed by the President of India
B. The post of Central Vigilance Commissioner is a statutory post
C. He holds office for a term of five years
D. He is empowered to exercise superintendence over the functioning of CBI

30. Which of the following statements are not true?
1. The Election Commission of India has created a Special Election Expenditure Monitoring Division in the Commission.
2. The accounts of political parties are audited annually.
3. Paid news in connection with elections is an electoral offence
4. Videography of the poll proceedings inside the polling stations is permissible

Select the correct answer from the codes given below:

Codes:

A. 1, 3 and 4 B. 2, 3 and 4
C. 1 and 3 D. 2 and 3

31. Assertion (A): The arguments of C. Wright Mill's power elites are based on the classical elitist framework.

Reason (R): Elitist formulation is not possible without reference to classical elitism.

Codes:

A. Both (A) and (R) are true and (R) is the correct explanation of (A)
B. Both (A) and (R) are true but (R) is not the correct explanation of (A)
C. (A) is true but (R) is false
D. (A) is false but (R) is true

32. The theory of "Prismatic Society" is based on
A. Historical studies of public administration in different societies
B. Study of public services in developed and developing countries
C. Institutional comparison of public administration in developed countries
D. Structural-functional analysis of public administration in developing countries

33. Job loading means
A. Deliberate upgrading of responsibility, scope and challenges
B. Shifting of an employee from one job to another
C. Making the job more interesting
D. All of the above

34. Negative motivation is based on
A. Anxiety B. Threat
C. Money D. Fear

35. Simon was positively influenced by the ideas of
A. L.D. White B. Terry
C. Barnard D. Henry Fayol

36. Assertion (A): Classical theory of organisation is based on formal principles.

Reason (R): Classicists lacked behavioural analysis.

A. (A) and (R) are true and (R) is the correct explanation of (A)
B. (A) and (R) true but (R) is not the correct explanation of (A)
C. (A) is true but (R) is false
D. (R) is true but (A) is false

37. What is the methodology proposed by Herbert Simon?
A. Bounded Rationality
B. Logical Positivism
C. Decision making
D. Satisfying

38. Who among the following thinkers rejected the principles of administration as myths and proverbs?
A. Herbert Simon B. W.F. Willoughby
C. L.D. White D. Chester Bernard

39. The concept of the "zone of indifference" is associated with
A. Power B. Decision making
C. Authority D. Leadership

40. Name the scholar who analysed leadership as "circular response".
A. Taylor B. Millet
C. M.P. Follett D. C.I. Barnard

41. Non-state dimension of warfare is also called
A. Westphalian warfare
B. Post-westphalian warfare
C. New war
D. Pre-westphalian warfare

42. Tehran Declaration of 1 December 1943 drew a plan for
A. Trusteeship
B. New-membership
C. Peace-keeping
D. Conflict resolution

43. Who coined the term "Functionalist theory of Integration"?
A. David Mittarany B. Ernst Haas
C. Joseph Nye D. Andrew Linklater

44. The CEPA (Comprehensive Economic Partnership Agreement) was officially endorsed in October 2010 between
A. India and Japan
B. India and China
C. India and Russia
D. India and South Korea

45. What is the correct sequence of Morton Kaplan's models of systems analysis?
1. Balance of Power
2. Loose Bipolarity
3. Tight Bipolarity
4. Universal International System

Codes:
A. 4, 3, 2, 1 B. 3, 4, 2, 1
C. 4, 2, 3, 1 D. 1, 2, 3, 4

46. Who wrote the book "Stable Peace"?
A. Johan Galtung
B. Gunnar Myrdal
C. Kenneth Boulding
D. Peter Wallerstein

47. Security Council Resolution No. 1441 of Nov. 2002 deals with
A. U.N. involvement in Somalia
B. Enforced the no fly zone in Bosnia
C. Sanctioned intervention at the end of the Gulf War to protect the Kurds in Northern Iraq
D. Resolution on Iraq, which threatned serious consequences, if Saddam Hussain failed to reveal his weapons of mass destruction to team of U.N. Inspectors

48. Who enunciated International society theory as a combination of three schools of thought – Realism, Rationalism and Revolutionism?
A. Martin Wight B. Kenneth Waltz
C. Hedley Bull D. Raymond Aron

49. **Assertion (A):** The decisions of the security council are binding, and must only be passed by the majority of nine out of the 15 members, as well as each of the five permanent members.

Reason (R): These five permanent members have veto power over all Security Council decisions.

Codes:
A. Both (A) and (R) are true and (R) is the correct explanation of (A)
B. Both (A) and (R) are true but (R) is not the correct explanation of (A)
C. (A) is true but (R) is false
D. (A) is false but (R) is true

50. Which of the following are part of Morganthau's realist principles?
1. Politics is rooted in a permanent and unchanging human nature.
2. Self-interest is a basic fact of the human condition.
3. Coercion is only part of foreign policy.
4. National interest defined in terms of power.

Codes:
A. All are correct
B. 1, 2 and 4 are correct
C. 1, 3 and 2 are correct
D. 1, 3 and 4 are correct

ANSWERS

1	2	3	4	5	6	7	8	9	10
C	B	D	C	D	C	B	C	C	A
11	12	13	14	15	16	17	18	19	20
A	D	A	B	D	C	B	C	D	D
21	22	23	24	25	26	27	28	29	30
B	D	C	A	C	A	C	A	C	D
31	32	33	34	35	36	37	38	39	40
C	D	A	D	C	B	B	A	C	C
41	42	43	44	45	46	47	48	49	50
B	C	A	A	D	C	D	A	A	B

SOME SELECTED EXPLANATORY ANSWERS

1. For Aristotle, democracy is the 'least bad' among perverted forms of government – tyranny and oligarchy – because the many, 'when they meet together may very likely be better than the few good, if regarded not individually but collectively, just as a feast to do which many contribute is better than a dinner provided out of a single purse'. Though a vigorous critic of democracy, he still offers a fair assessment of its advantages. To enumerate some, collective opinions and judgements are more satisfying than individual ones and that many rather than few should rule. Its disadvantage is the way it treats the extraordinary. However, he does not, like Plato, fear the mass of people, and has more faith like Pericles, in their ability to collectively articulate their judgement on the effects of policies and the ability of rulers. The polity, which to Aristotle represents the best practicable state, is in accordance with his principle of golden mean, obviating the extreme tendencies between oligarchic and democratic systems. Democracy is a constitution with a majority government, which the free born and poor control, while oligarchy is controlled by a minority, namely the rich and well placed. From the standpoint of political stability, it is necessary to enlarge a group that is neither rich nor poor, the middle class. This is because the rich enjoy great benefits and privileges, but are unwilling to accept discipline. The poor, because of their deprivation, lack spirit and enthusiasm. Therefore, the middle class constitutes the mean in the social structure, not only balancing the oligarchic with democratic elements but also mixing them in the right proportion so as to ensure stability. The larger the middle class, the greater the possibility of tranquillity and stability, for it steers clear between the insolence of the rich and the unruly behaviour of the bitterly poor. The middle class state a 'save' state, a term that he borrows from Euripides, fulfils two important political ideals: equality and consensus.

4. Because of Bentham's failure to consider quality as well as quantity in his assessment of pleasures, and his treatment of animal pleasures as equal to those of human beings, his philosophy was referred to as "pig philosophy" (by Thomas Carlyle). The pleasures of a pig and a person were not considered any different in value if they were the same in degree. Bentham's concern was with more or less pleasure, not with better or worse, and this implies that he would approve

the mode of life of a happy pig for numan beings as well.

5. **Rawls's major writings:** 'Justice as fairness', *Philosophical Review* (1959). *Theory of Justice,* Combridge, Massachusetts, Harvard University Press, 1971. *Political Liberalism,* New York, Columbia University Press, 1993. 'Reply to Habermas', *Journal of Philosophy* (1995). *The Law of Peoples,* Cambridge, Massachusetts, Harvard University Press, 1999.

7. Post-behaviouralism stands for a set of principles and intellectual direction, which includes relevant, purposive and value-laden research, and change- and action-oriented political enquiry, and demands that political scientists be critical intellectuals and guardian of human values instead of being mere methodologists. David Easton who had propounded the intellectual foundation stones of behaviouralism, now set forth seven major traits or features of post-behaviouralism, which he called 'Credo of Relevance'.

'Credo of Relevance': David Easton

Substance over technique: The primacy of substance and purposive research is emphasized over mere techniques. We may recall the charge made against behaviouralism that for the sake of applying sophisticated tools of research it chose only those areas of research that were amenable to these tools. This way many areas of political enquiry suffered. Post-behaviouralism reverses the behaviouralist slogan. *it is better to be wrong than vague,* and declares that *it is better to be vague than non-relevantly precise.*

Change orientation: Behaviouralism was charged with being an 'ideology of social conservatism tempered by modest incremental change'. Post-behaviouralism advocates change orientation and reform over preservation.

Relevant research: In the name of detached research, keeping away from the 'brute realities of politics' has made behaviouralism irrelevant. In an era of social upheavals and conflicts, fear and anxiety, if the political scientist was aloof and carrying out detached research and analysis, what use was political science to society? Post-behaviouralism insists on socially and politically relevant research.

Value-laden research: The fact-value dichotomy and insistence on value-free research advocated by behaviouralists has taken away the value premise on which all knowledge stands. Values must be the guiding force for all knowledge and values are necessary for setting up goals. The behavioural emphasis on fact-value dichotomy, value neutrality and scientism has led political science in the wrong direction.

Political scientist as critical intellectual: Post-behaviouralism asks the political scientist to be a 'critical intellectual'. As such, it is his/her duty to protect human values. According to Easton, 'Post-behaviouralism returns to the humanist conception of intellectual as the guardian of those civilized, human values known to most men'. By keeping themselves aloof and detached from political and social problems in the name of objectivity and pure science, political scientists would become mere technicians and mechanics tinkering with society and could not claim the freedom of enquiry.

Action-oriented research: According to Easton, 'to know is to bear the responsibility for acting and to act is to engage in reshaping society'. Post-behaviouralism demands that a sense of commitment and action must permeate all research in political science.

Politicization of the profession: Having recognized that intellectuals have a positive role in society to determine the proper goals for society and make it move in this direction, the politicization of the profession is inevitable and desirable.

9. Plato developed a categorization of positive character traits, four "cardinal virtues." These

are wisdom, fortitude, temperance, and justice. Aristotle and much later Thomas Aquinas took up this same classification of virtue. Fortitude is often equated with courage, but fortitude is a somewhat broader category, including elements such as perseverance and patience.

13. The institutional or structural approach may be visualised in the works of several English and American writers. We may refer to the wades of Walter Bagehot, F.A. Ogg, W.B. Munro, Herman Finer, H.J. Laski, Richard Neustadt, C.F. Strong, Bernard Crick, James Bryce, Harold Zink, Maurice Duverger and Giovanni Sartori. The striking feature of their works is that the study of politics has been confined to the formal, as well as informal, institutional structures of a political system.

14. In the past few decades, the most productive work on the concept of political development has been accomplished by those who challenge the inevitability of political development. In fact, one group of writers has taken a giant step by encouraging a more fruitful analysis of the concept: S.N. Eisenstadt, Samuel P. Huntington, and Mancur Olson have challenged the notion that political change inevitably leads to political development. They suggest that rapid and pervasive changes occurring in societies can result in political breakdowns, political decay, or political instability. Political change can lead to turmoil rather than to order and stability. Huntington makes this clear when he separates the processes of political change and political development. He notes that political change is manifested in the mobilizing and politicizing of individuals in a society, but increased participation does not automatically lead to the development of a system of government capable of managing conflict.

This argument represents a landmark in the analysis of the process of political development. Huntington and others suggest that the process of political change is not deterministic – that it is not a unilinear but a multilinear process. Political change may lead to political development, but it also may lead to political decay. The two different modes of analysis can be expressed as follows:

unilinear analysis: → political change → political development

multilinear analysis: → political change ↗ political development
↘ political decay

18. **Classical theory (Fayol, Urwick, Gulick and others)**

The classical theory of administration was developed during the first half of the twentieth century. The major exponents of this theory are Henry Fayol, Luther Gulick, Lyndall Urwick, J.D. Mooney, A.C. Reiley, Mary Parker Follet and R. Shelton. This theory reached its zenith in 1937 when the *Papers on the Science of Administration,* by Gulick and Urwick was published. This book is the most pursuasive exposition of the classical approach to administration.

Classical theory is also known by various other names, like, the 'traditional theory', the 'formal organisation theory', the 'mechanistic theory', the 'structural theory' and the 'management process school'. It is also called as 'administrative management theory' by March and Simon.

22. The Avadi session of the Congress in January 1955 significance for two reasons. First was that Nehru stepped down as Congress president at Avadi. U.N. Dhebar was elected president at the session. Dhebar was, in fact, Nehru's nominee. He continued to preside over the party until Indira Gandhi was elected president at the Nagpur session in February 1959. The second significant aspect of the Avadi session was in the realm of the reassertion made by the Congress party of its commitment to building a socialistic pattern of the society. The immediate context was that it was time, by then, to set the direction for the second five-year plan. At Avadi, the Congress session laid out that the objective

for the plan shall be the creation of a society where the means of production are brought under social ownership and the national wealth is distributed equitably.

23. The Vohra Committee, headed by the then Home Secretary, Mr. N.N. Vohra was set up on 9 July 1993 "to take stock about the activities of crime syndicates and mafia organisations which had evolved links and were being protected by Government functionaries and political personalities". It submitted its report on 5 October 1993, but the Government shelved it for 18 months claiming that it was an internal administrative report till it was cornered by the opposition and directed by the Speaker to lay the report on the table of the House. The Report of the Vohra Committee was laid on the table of both Houses of Parliament on 1 August 1995 after consistent pressure from the opposition to expose the criminalisation of politics.

The report says, "that there has been a rapid spread and growth of criminal gangs, armed senas, drug mafias, smuggling gangs, drug peddlers and economic lobbies in the country, which have over the years, developed an extensive network of contacts with the bureaucrats/Government functionaries at the local levels, politicians, media-persons, and strategically located individuals in the non-state sector. Some of these syndicates have also international linkages including the foreign intelligence agencies.

27. Private capitalism in India is dependent capitalism. It relies on the patronage and protection of the third actor, the state, for its profits and security. Private capitalism is protected from the rigors of competition by government-licensed production and by protectionist trade policies that continue from the import substitution development strategy. In the absence of private finance capital, private producers must rely on the policies and discretion of government-owned banks and long-term lending institutions. Private-sector boards are heavily infiltrated by government representatives. Under what Raj Krishna called the *dharmshala* model (a shelter for the pious poor), government guarantees capital against failure by taking over "sick" industries.

28. Kamaraj Plan was a political plan formulated in 1963 by K. Kamaraj, a senior leader of Indian National Congress party. At that time he was in the third term as the Chief Minister of Tamil Nadu. He proposed that all senior Congress leaders should resign from their ministerial posts and devote all their energy to the revitalization of the Congress. The plan had support of Jawaharlal Nehru, the then Prime Minister of India. Six Union Ministers and six Chief Ministers including Lal Bahadur Shastri, Jagjivan Ram, Morarji Desai, Biju Patnaik and S.K. Patil followed suit and resigned from their posts. In 1964, Kamaraj was elected the President of the All India Congress and he successfully navigated the nation through the stormy years following Nehru's death.

32. To develop his concept of ecology, Riggs borrows from sociology the tools of structural functional analysis (such as, interdependent sub-systems, pattern variables and latent and manifest functions). He then identifies three 'ideal types' of society for which he uses the attractive labels of 'fused society', 'prismatic society' and 'diffracted society'. Using the metaphor of light passing through a prism, there is, on one side, the fused society and, on the other side, the diffracted society. There is, finally, the society between the fused and the diffracted called the prismatic society.

33. **Job Loading:** Job loading refers to a process of assigning greater and/or more varied duties and responsibilities to a particular job so as to enhance employee's on-the-job knowledge, skills, and abilities, and to provide greater motivation. Job loading can be of two types:

(*a*) horizontal job loading and (*b*) vertical job loading. Job loading is *horizontal loading* when the newly assigned tasks are at the same level of interest and responsibility as the job's original tasks. Employee's scope of work is increased but does not include higher responsibilities. It is used as a job-enlargement technique. It provides employees the scope to be doing different tasks than what they would normally be doing, and this could serve as a good training ground for future career growth. Job loading is *vertical loading* when the newly assigned tasks allow for increased responsibility, recognition and personal achievement. Herzberg suggested vertical job loading for job enrichment.

34. Types of Motivation

Motivation is generally considered to be of two types—Positive and Negative motivation.

Positive Motivation: Positive motivation or incentive motivation is based on rewards. The workers are offered incentives for achieving the desired goals. The incentives may be in the form of more pay, promotion, recognition of work, etc. Employees are motivated when they are offered incentives and they try to improve their performance, willingly. Real and positive motivators are responsible for the achievement of a high standard of performance and the participation of the worker as a responsible citizen in the community. Positive motivation is achieved by the cooperation of employees as then they have a feeling of belongingness and happiness. Some positive motivation techniques which improve standards of performance and lead to good team spirit and pride are:

1. Praise and credit for work done well
2. A sincere interest in the welfare of the subordinates
3. Delegation of authority and responsibility to subordinates
4. Participation of subordinates in the decision-making process

Negative Motivation: Negative or fear motivation is based on fear or the use of force, power or threats. Fear causes employees to act in certain ways. In case, they do not act in accordance with what is desired of them, then they may be punished with demotions or lay-offs. This fear acts as a push mechanism. The employees do not willingly cooperate, but rather they work to avoid punishment. Through fear employees work up to a level where punishment is avoided, but this type of motivation causes anger and frustration and may generally, become a cause of industrial unrest. However, it has been found that the fear of punishment and the actual punishment result in controlling individual misbehaviour and has contributed towards positive performance in many situations, but it is not recommended as a viable alternative in the current business and industrial environment.

35. In developing his behavioural approach to administration Simon was greatly influenced by M.P. Follott's ideas on group dynamics in organizations, Elton Mayo's Human Relations approach, and especially the writings of Chester Barnard. Barnard's "Functions of the Executive" had positive influence of Simon's thinking about administration. In fact, many of Barnard's ideas are found in Simon's early work, namely, "Administrative Behaviour".

37. Logical positivism (also called *logical empiricism* and *neo-positivism*) is a school of philosophy that combines empiricism with rationalism. It is a doctrine according to which scientific knowledge is the only kind of factual knowledge. Its main criteria for any statement are verifiability, which comes from two different sources: *empirical statements,* which come from science, and *analytic truth,* statements which are true or false by definition.

Since the 1950s, the unifying perspective in public administration has been logical positivism, most notably as defined and promoted by Herbert Simon. Simon's concept of administration has two basic elements. viz.

(*i*) The emphasis upon decision-making approach as the alternative to the classical thinkers' principles approach (i.e. structural approach); and (*ii*) the advocacy of empirical approach (value-free approach) as against the normative approach to the study of administration. Herbert Simon proposed a new concept of administration based on theories and methodology of logical positivism with the focus on decision-making.

39. Zone of Indifference: *Barnard* has presented a concept: Zone of indifference for achieving cooperation in accepting authority. The 'zone of indifference' indicates the specific limits that are set by individuals themselves within which they will respond willingly to the exercise of authority over them. In fact, not all orders are obeyed with equal enthusiasm. The zeal or reluctance with which a subordinate carries out an order is the result of his weighing, often subconscious the effect while trying to carry out the order will have upon his personal career. When all the orders can be arranged reasonably in order of their acceptability to the person on whom the authority is exercised, then an employee can conceive: (*i*) actions which are clearly unacceptable, and which will not be carried out (*e.g.*, washing clothes, cleaning utensils in a professor's house); (*ii*) actions that are borderline cases either barely acceptable or barely unacceptable (for *e.g.* getting a cinema ticket or railway ticket for the professor); and (*iii*) actions that are unquestionably acceptable (*e.g.*, completing an assignment, preparing for a seminar, etc.). This third group constitutes a zone of indifference. These actions are acceptable to the individual and will be carried out by him without questioning the authority. Outside this zone, superiors must earn the acceptance of their subordinates. The subordinates now begins to weigh whether to accept the order or not. According to *Simon,* there are four important motivations for accepting authority at this stage:

1. Rewards: A superior can obtain compliance by offering rewards in the form of promotion, pay increases or by enforcing sanctions in the form of reprimands, suspensions.
2. Legitimacy: If the subordinates think that what they do is right, they will do it. However, when they think in an opposite manner, commands will not be followed.
3. Social Approval: Authority is generally accepted by subordinates when they feel the rejection would be disapproved by their 'group'.
4. Confidence: Authority is accepted by subordinates because they (subordinates) have confidence in the manager that he (manager) is technically and professionally competent. A patient, for example, reposes confidence in a doctor and accepts the doctor's advice (authority) out of confidence.

40. Leadership: According to Follett, a leader is not the head of the department or president of the organisation, but one "who can see all around a situation, who sees it as related to certain purposes and policies, who sees it evolving into the next situation, who understands how to pass from one situation to another." He is "the man who can show that the order is integral to the situation." Follett stated that such people are found not only at the top but throughout the organisation.

Follett opined that the leader not only influences his group but is also influenced by it. She called this reciprocal relationship as 'circular response'.

41. From (state-centric) geopolitics to (geocentric) global politics

As globalization has intensified over the last five decades, it has become increasingly difficult to maintain the popular fiction of the 'great divide': that is, treating political life as having two quite separate spheres of action, the domestic and the international, which operate according to different logics with different rules, actors, and agendas. There is a growing recognition that, as former President Clinton described it:

"the once bright line between domestic and foreign policy is blurring. If I could do anything to change the speech patterns of those of us in public life, I would like almost to stop hearing people talk about foreign policy and domestic policy, and instead start discussing economic policy, security policy, environmental policy."

As the substantive issues of political life consistently ignore the artificial foreign/domestic divide, from the worldwide coordination of anti-globalization protests to national courts enforcing the rulings of the World Trade Organization, the Westphalian Constitution appears increasingly anachronistic. A post-Westphalian world order is emerging and with it a distinctive form of global politics.

To talk of global politics is to recognize that politics itself has been globalized and that as a consequence there is much more to the study of world politics than conflict and cooperation between states, even if this remains crucial. In other words, globalization challenges the one-dimensionality of orthodox accounts of world politics which conceive it purely in terms of geopolitics and the struggle for power between states. By contrast, the concept of global politics focuses our attention upon the global structures and processes of rule-making, problem-solving, and the maintenance of security and order in the world system.

43. The functionalist theory of integration put forward by David Mitrany (1966) as a means of promoting international conflict. Mitrany was, in fact, opposed to regional government, believing that it would merely reproduce national rivalries on a larger scale. Instead, he advocated the linking of authority to a specific function, thereby breaking the traditional link between authority and territory.

45. Morton Kaplan has developed the most elaborate discussion on international system. In his argument, he does not define international systems in particular, but describes the state of an international system or of its subsystems, assigning values to the following variables: the essential rules of the system, the transformation rules, the actor classificatory variables, capabilities variables, and the information variables.

Utilizing the five variables, he specifies six international systems, (*a*) the "balance of power" system, (*b*) the loose bipolar system, (*c*) the tight bipolar system, (*d*) the universal system, (*e*) the hierarchical system in its directive and non-directive forms, and (*f*) the unit veto system.

48. Martin Wight identified three main historical approaches to thinking about international relations: realism, rationalism, and revolutionism.

PAPER–III

Note: *This paper contains* ***seventy five*** *(75) objective type questions of* ***two*** *(2) marks each.* ***All*** *questions are compulsory.*

1. Who among the following said that Political theory contains factors of three kinds—the factual, the causal and the valuational?

A. Leo Strauss B. Dunning
C. G.H. Sabine D. Ebenstein

2. Who among the following said that political theory is in the doghouse in the 1950's?

A. Easton B. Laslett
C. R.A. Dahl D. Riemer

3. Who among the following said, "We can not shed our values in the way we remove our coats"?
A. Peter Laslett B. David Easton
C. Isiah Berlin D. Robert Dahl

4. Who among the following is associated with the resurgence of political theory?
A. David Easton B. Alfred Cobban
C. Vogelin D. Laslett

5. Which one of the following statements is false?
A. The term 'Liberal' has referred to a class of free men who are neither serfs nor slaves
B. The term 'liberalism' was first employed in Spain in 1812
C. Classical liberalism and modern liberalism have differences
D. The moral minuses of the anti-marketeers are the moral minuses of the pro-marketeers

6. Whose ideas are sometimes referred as 'Manchester Liberalism'?
A. Adam Smith and David Ricardo
B. Richard Cobden and John Bright
C. John Locke and J.S. Mill
D. Berlin and McPherson

7. Who said, "My own existence is a social activity and activity and mind are social in their context as well as in their origin, they are social activity and social mind"?
A. Robert Owen B. Karl Marx
C. Hegel D. J.S. Mill

8. From whom did Hobbes borrow the principle of resolutive composite?
A. Galileo B. Euclid
C. Descartes D. Aristotle

9. Who said, "J.J. Rousseau is the Father of Jacobin despotism, of Caesarian dictatorship and the inspirer of the absolute doctrines of Kant and of Hegel"?
A. H.J. Laski B. Duguit
C. Berlin D. Karl Popper

10. Who among the following made the State a moral institution with a moral end?
A. Bentham B. Machiavelli
C. James Mill D. J.S. Mill

11. Who among the following formed "The League of Radical Congressmen"?
A. M.K. Gandhi B. M.N. Roy
C. Aurobindo D. B.R. Ambedkar

12. Which one among the following is not written by Aurobindo?
A. Life Divine
B. Essays on the Gita
C. Yoga : Concept and Practice
D. The Ideals of Human Unity

13. Identify the correct sequence of the events undertaken by Mahatma Gandhi.
1. Organised the industrial workers in Ahmedabad for higher wages.
2. Protest against the Indigo planters at Champaran.
3. Satyagraha movement in Kaira against the collection of land revenue.
4. Protest against the Asiatic Registration Act.

Select the correct answer from the codes given below:

Codes:
A. 3, 4, 2, 1 B. 4, 2, 3, 1
C. 2, 3, 4, 1 D. 1, 2, 3, 4

14. Match the List-I with List-II and select the correct answer from the codes given below :

List-I (Authors)	List-II (Books)
(*a*) R.J. Bernstein	1. Spheres of Justice : A Defence of Pluralism and Equality
(*b*) M. Sandel	2. The Restructuring of Social and Political theory
(*c*) M. Waltzer	3. Contemporary Political philosophy
(*d*) W. Kymlicka	4. Liberalism and the Limits of Justice

Codes :

	(*a*)	(*b*)	(*c*)	(*d*)
A.	1	2	3	4
B.	3	4	1	2
C.	2	4	1	3
D.	4	1	3	2

15. Given below are two statements, one labelled as Assertion (A) and the other labelled as Reason (R).

Assertion (A): For Daniel Bell there is the 'end of ideology'.

Reason (R) : This is to validate a single ideology and to discredit every their ideology.

Select the correct answer from the codes given below:

A. Both (A) and (R) are true and (R) is the correct explanation of (A).
B. Both (A) and (R) are true, but (R) is not the correct explanation of (A).
C. (A) is true, but (R) is false.
D. (A) is false, but (R) is true.

16. Structuration as a concept is a way of analyzing the relationship between structures and actors was suggested by

A. Talcott Parsons   B. Anthony Giddens
C. Robert Nisbet   D. Michael Focault

17. Match List-I with List-II and select the correct answer from the codes given below :

List-I (Theories of Political Parties)	**List-II (Propounders)**
(*a*) Development Theory	1. Giovomin Sartori
(*b*) Spatial theory	2. Joseph la Palombara
(*c*) Re-alignment theory	3. Maurice Duverger
(*d*) Permeation theory	4. Bunham and Sandquist

Codes :

	(*a*)	(*b*)	(*c*)	(*d*)
A.	1	2	3	4
B.	2	1	4	3
C.	3	4	2	1
D.	4	2	1	3

18. According to Almond, which one is not a condition for political development?

A. Availability of resources
B. Adequate response to challenges
C. Overlapping of stages of development
D. Congruent development of the other social systems

19. Corporatism is an approach that is centrally concerned about

A. Structures of the public sector
B. Functions of the political system
C. Class conflict is interest based
D. Stresses the state and society interactions, especially the role of social interests influencing policy

20. Match the List-I with List-II and select the correct answer from the codes given below :

List-I (Thinkers)	**List-II (Books)**
(*a*) Anthony Downs	1. An Economic theory of Democracy
(*b*) Gabrial Almond and Sidney Verba	2. The Three Worlds of Welfare Capitalism
(*c*) Stein Rokkan	3. The Civic Culture
(*d*) Gosta Esping Anderson	4. Citizens, Elections, Parties

Codes :

	(*a*)	(*b*)	(*c*)	(*d*)
A.	1	3	4	2
B.	2	1	3	4
C.	3	4	2	1
D.	4	2	1	3

21. The term "Cooperative Federalism" emerged after

A. The First World War
B. At the time of New Deal Legislations in the USA
C. As part of the Soviet Constitution of 1937
D. After the Second World War

22. Which one of the following is not a feature of the Bipolar Party System?

A. Elements of both multi and two party systems
B. Coalition government
C. Alternation of power between parties
D. Two large coalitions composed of several parties

23. In the electoral studies, rational choice models have been the most popular which developed by

A. Elinor Ostrom   B. Hardin
C. Karl Deutsch   D. Anthony Downs

24. Conveyance theory between advanced capitalism and developed socialism was propounded by

A. Huntington B. Putman
C. Miliband D. Marcuge

25. Who among the following elite theorists said, "A man is effective in society as a whole, not so much because of his individual qualities as because of the social energies which have been deposited in him by the mass"?

A. Pareto B. Gasset
C. Michels D. Mosca

26. What is the correct chronological sequence of Edward Shils' categories of political system?

1. Political Democracy
2. Tutelary Democracy
3. Modernizing Oligarchy
4. Totalitarian Oligarchy
5. Traditional Oligarchy

Select the correct answer from the codes given below:

A. 1, 2, 3, 4 and 5 B. 1, 2, 4, 3 and 5
C. 1, 2, 4, 5 and 3 D. 2, 1, 3, 5 and 4

27. Assertion (A) : Samir amin argued that Marx foresaw that no colonial power would be able to continue for long the local development of capitalism.

Reason (R) : This was because of a dearth of knowledge of non-European societies.

Select the correct answer from the codes given below:

A. Both (A) and (R) are true and (R) is the correct explanation of (A).
B. Both (A) and (R) are true, but (R) is not the correct explanation of (A).
C. (A) is true, but (R) is false.
D. (A) is false, but (R) is true.

28. Which of the following statements about the US President are true?

1. The US President can seek re-election only once.
2. He can be impeached for treason, bribery and other crimes.
3. At the impeachment trials the Chief Justice of the Supreme Court presides.
4. Both the President and the Vice-President can be from the same state.

Select the correct answer from the codes given below:

Codes:

A. 1, 2 and 3 B. 1, 3 and 4
C. 2, 3 and 4 D. 1, 2 and 4

29. The politics of sex is no longer on the fringe of politics, but it is a central concern for policy and law makers. Which category will this issue be placed under?

A. Political Development
B. Political Modernization
C. Political Culture
D. Political Elites

30. Who holds the view that bureaucracy as an organisation cannot correct its behaviour by learning from its errors?

A. M. Crozier B. H.J. Laski
C. F.M. Marx D. Max Weber

31. Who said the following:

"New light has been poured on us, teaching us the new lesson that Kings are made for the people and not the people for the Kings."

A. Mahatma Gandhi
B. Raja Ram Mohan Roy
C. Dadabhai Naoroji
D. Bal Gangadhar Tilak

32. Who among the following had favoured Panchayati Raj System by giving the following statement in the India Constitutent Assembly? "....in the interest of democracy, the villages may be trained in the art of self-government... We must be able to reform the villages and introduce democratic principles of government there..."

A. Ananthasayanam Ayyangar
B. Dr. B.R. Ambedkar
C. B.N. Rao
D. Jawaharlal Nehru

33. Which of the following is not within the jurisdiction of the State High Court?

A. It can hear appeals from lower courts
B. It can issue writs for restoring Fundamental Rights

C. It can decide the river water dispute between the two states

D. It exercises superitendance and control over courts below it.

34. Match List-I with List-II and choose the correct answer from the codes given below :

List-I (Lok Sabha)	List-II (Speaker)
(*a*) 3rd Lok Sabha	1. Shivraj Patil
(*b*) 5th Lok Sabha	2. Balram Jakhar
(*c*) 7th Lok Sabha	3. G.S. Dhillon, Bali Ram Bhagat
(*d*) 10th Lok Sabha	4. Hukum Singh

Codes :

	(*a*)	(*b*)	(*c*)	(*d*)
A.	4	3	2	1
B.	4	1	2	3
C.	1	2	3	4
D.	3	4	2	1

35. Who characterized India as "A million mutinies" in 1990?

A. V.S. Naipaul B. M.S.A. Rao

C. Ghanshyam Shah D. Tedd Gurr

36. "Roses in December" is the autobiography of

A. Maulana Abul Kalam Azad

B. Khan Abdul Gaffar Khan

C. Hakim Ajmal Khan

D. Mohammad Karim Chhagala

37. Match List-I with List-II and select the correct answer from the codes given below:

List-I (Regional Political Party)	List-II (State of Origin)
(*a*) Rashtriya Lok Dal	1. Bihar
(*b*) Indian National Lok Dal	2. Karnataka
(*c*) Janta Dal (Secular)	3. Uttar Pradesh
(*d*) Rashtriya Janta Dal	4. Haryana

Codes :

	(*a*)	(*b*)	(*c*)	(*d*)
A.	3	4	2	1
B.	1	2	3	4
C.	4	3	2	1
D.	4	1	3	2

38. Who among the following is Editor/Author of the book "The New Regional Politics of Development".

A. Reinhard Bendix

B. Arie M.M. Kacowiez

C. Anthony Payne

D. Partha Chatterjee

39. Who among the following has described India as "weak-strong state"?

A. Lloyd and Susan Rudolph

B. Gunnar Myrdal

C. Rajni Kothari

D. K.C. Wheare

40. Who has called India a Democratic Developmental State?

A. Paul Brass

B. James Manor

C. Christopher Jefferlot

D. Atul Kohli

41. Match List-I with List-II and select the correct answer from the codes given below:

List-I (States)	List-II (No. of Lok Sabha seats reserved for the Scheduled tribes)
(*a*) Andhra Pradesh	1. 4
(*b*) Chhattisgarh	2. 5
(*c*) Jharkhand	3. 6
(*d*) Madhya Pradesh	4. 3

Codes :

	(*a*)	(*b*)	(*c*)	(*d*)
A.	1	2	3	4
B.	4	1	2	3
C.	4	3	2	1
D.	2	4	1	3

42. Match the List-I with List-II and select the correct answer from the codes given below:

List-I (Types)	List-II (Pressure groups)
(*a*) Institutional pressure groups	1. Association of Indian Universities
(*b*) Associational Pressure groups	2. All India Schedule Caste Federation

(*c*) Non-Associational pressure groups	3. All India Federation of University Teachers Association
(*d*) Anomic pressure groups	4. Gopalgarh communal riots in Rajasthan

Codes :

	(*a*)	(*b*)	(*c*)	(*d*)
A.	1	2	3	4
B.	1	3	2	4
C.	3	2	4	1
D.	4	1	2	3

43. Who has termed India as an example of "Polycentric Nationalism"?

A. Partha Chatterji B. Anthony D. Smith
C. Will Kymlicka D. Benedict Anderson

44. Who is the author of the book "India after Gandhi : The History of the World's Largest Democracy"?

A. Ramchandran Guha
B. Akhil Gupta
C. Achin Vanaik
D. Ashutosh Varshney

45. Which of the following was the first all Indian women's organization which came into force in 1926?

A. All India Women's Conference
B. National Council for Women in India
C. National Federation of Indian Women in India
D. Self-Employed Women's Association

46. Which one of the following Gullick has not covered under administrative functions of the Chief Executive?

A. Staffing B. Adjudicating
C. Directing D. Coordinating

47. Which of the following principles figure in the list of fourteen principles propounded by Henry Fayol?

1. Subordination of individual interest to general interest.
2. Appointment on the basis of a contract.
3. Espirit de corps.
4. Equity

Codes:

A. 1, 2 and 3 B. 1, 3 and 4
C. 2, 3 and 4 D. 1, 2 and 4

48. Under the code developed by workers at the Western Electric Company, one who passes unfavourable information about his colleagues to his superior is called

A. A squealer B. A puzzler
C. A rate-buster D. A chiseller

49. According to Herbert Simon, a decision is usually compounded of

A. one fact statement and one value statement
B. one value statement and several fact statement
C. several value statements and one fact statement
D. several value statements and several fact statements

50. Which one of the following principles of organisation has not been enunciated by Mooney and Reiley?

A. Equity principle
B. Scalar principle
C. Staff/Line principle
D. Functional principle

51. Which one of the following books contains the most comprehensive enunciation of the classical theory?

A. Introduction to the study of Public Administration
B. Public Administration
C. Papers on the Science of Administration
D. Policy and Administration

52. According to Max Weber which one of the following is not a feature of bureaucracy?

A. Separation of office from its incumbent
B. Rigid adherence to rules
C. Selection by Patronage
D. Fix remuneration of officials

53. Which one of the following is not an element of decision making?

A. It is an unconscious activity
B. It is not one time process

C. It is an environment linked activity
D. It needs studying and finding alternatives before taking final decisions

54. Who among the following are called staff officials?
A. Field workers
B. Advisory staff
C. Those who help the chief executive in the performance of his primary functions
D. Those who help the chief executive in the implementation of his functions

55. Which of the following concepts of administration is action oriented rather than structure oriented?
A. Democratic Administration
B. Autocratic Administration
C. Development Administration
D. All of the above

56. Point out from the following the uncommon factor between public and private administrations
A. Accounting
B. Filling
C. Managerial techniques
D. Scope and complexity

57. The Fiscal Five Year Plan was started in India after independence in the year
A. 1950-1951 B. 1951-1952
C. 1952-1953 D. 1953-1954

58. **Assertion (A):** The District Collector is the most important functionary at the apex of the district administration.

Reason (R): After independence, his role has become increasingly multi-dimensional.

Codes:
A. Both (A) and (R) are true and (R) is the correct explanation of (A)
B. Both (A) and (R) are true, but (R) is not the correct explanation of (A)
C. (A) is true, but (R) is false
D. (R) is true, but (A) is false

59. Match List-I with List-II and select the correct answer from the codes given below:

List-I (Authors)	List-II (Books)
(*a*) Chester Barnard	1. Philosophy of administration
(*b*) Herbert Simon	2. Ideas and Issues in Public Administration
(*c*) Dwight Waldo (ed).	3. Administrative Behaviour
(*d*) Marshall Dimock	4. The Functions of the Executive

Codes :

	(*a*)	(*b*)	(*c*)	(*d*)
A.	3	4	2	1
B.	4	3	2	1
C.	1	4	2	3
D.	2	1	3	4

60. Performance Budgeting became popular in the
A. 1950s B. 1960s
C. 1970s D. 1980s

61. Who builts on Kenneth Waltz's argument concerning the stability of bipolar system as compared to multipolar system?
A. Stanley Hoffmann
B. Charles Kindelberger
C. John Mearshemier
D. John Gaddis

62. Democratic Peace Theory is placed under which theoretical approach of International relations?
A. Structural Realism
B. Republican Realism
C. Neo-Realism
D. Institutional Liberalism

63. Which of the following statements are *not* true?
1. Security dilemma is an important paradox of the state system.
2. Arms race increases insecurity of states.
3. Arms control is a solution.
4. Standing armies contribute to security of all.

Codes :
A. 1, 2 and 4 B. 1 and 3
C. 3 and 4 D. 1 and 4

64. The "Clash of Civilizations and New World Order" predict an ideological shift in the Post-Cold War period from

A. Political ideology to economic liberalism
B. Geopolitics to geo-economics
C. Nation-state to the civilizations area
D. Political ideology to culture and religion

65. Assertion (A): Modern technology enhances the importance of war and threates of war.

Reason (R): War no longer is just a contest of strength. It is more a contest of nerve and risk taking.

Codes:

A. Both (A) and (R) are true and (R) is the correct explanation of (A)
B. Both (A) and (R) are true, but (R) is not the correct explanation of (A)
C. (A) is true, but (R) is false
D. (A) is false, but (R) is true

66. What is a "Quasi-State"?

A. A State that possess juridical statehood but severely deficient in empirical statehood
B. A State that possesses empirical statehood
C. A State that possesses neither juridical statehood nor empirical statehood
D. A State that has divided loyalties

67. With which approach would one associate the following statement?

Economic globalization is an uneven, hierarchical process and benefits only a tiny minority?

A. Economic Liberalism
B. Economic Realists
C. Mercantilism
D. Neo-Marxism

68. Match the List-I with List-II and select the correct answer from the codes given below :

List-I (Foreign Policy think tank)	**List-II (Country)**
(*a*) Foreign Policy Institute	1. USA
(*b*) Institute for Defense & Strategic Analysis	2. UK
(*c*) Carnegie Endowment	3. Turkey
(*d*) International Institute for strategic studies	4. India

Codes :

	(*a*)	(*b*)	(*c*)	(*d*)
A.	1	2	3	4
B.	2	3	4	1
C.	3	4	1	2
D.	4	2	3	1

69. Match List-I with List-II and select the correct answer from the codes given below:

List-I (Terrorist Organisations)	**List-II (Countries)**
(*a*) LTTE	1. Peru
(*b*) Hizbullah	2. Nigeria
(*c*) Bako Haram	3. Iran
(*d*) Shining Path	4. Sri Lanka

Codes :

	(*a*)	(*b*)	(*c*)	(*d*)
A.	1	2	3	4
B.	4	3	2	1
C.	2	1	4	3
D.	3	4	1	2

70. The Panel on United Nations Peace Operations was set up by the earlier Secretary General Kofi Annan. Name the report

A. Hammarskjold Report
B. Rajeshwar Dayal Report
C. Brahimi Report
D. Kofi Annan Report

71. Indian troops, military observers and civilian police personnel served in U.N.O. peace keeping operation in

A. Western Sahara B. Bosnia
C. Herzegovina D. All of the above

72. Match the List-I with List-II and select the correct answer from the code given below:

List-I (Countries)	**List-II (Problems)**
(*a*) Sri Lanka	1. Kachativu
(*b*) Pakistan	2. Wular Barrage

(*c*) Nepal 3. Susta Border
(*d*) Bangladesh 4. New Moore Island

Codes:

	(*a*)	(*b*)	(*c*)	(*d*)
A.	1	2	3	4
B.	4	3	2	1
C.	3	4	1	2
D.	2	3	4	1

73. Which one of the following is not a Indo-Pak dispute?

A. Siachin dispute
B. Sir Creek dispute
C. Cross Border terrorism
D. Dahagram dispute

74. Match List-I with List-II and select the correct answer from the code given below:

List-I (State)	**List-II (Minorities)**
(*a*) Myanmar	1. Hindus
(*b*) Malaysia	2. Rohingas
(*c*) Indonesia	3. Tamils
(*d*) Laos	4. Vietnamese

Codes:

	(*a*)	(*b*)	(*c*)	(*d*)
A.	4	3	2	1
B.	3	2	1	4
C.	2	3	1	4
D.	1	2	3	4

75. Recently there were tensions between Cambodia and Thailand. What is the issue in conflict?

A. Illegal migrations B. Prachvihar
C. Emerald Buddha D. Minorities

ANSWERS

1	**2**	**3**	**4**	**5**	**6**	**7**	**8**	**9**	**10**
C	D	B	C	D	B	B	A	B	D
11	**12**	**13**	**14**	**15**	**16**	**17**	**18**	**19**	**20**
B	C	B	C	C	B	B	C	D	A
21	**22**	**23**	**24**	**25**	**26**	**27**	**28**	**29**	**30**
D	*	D	D	B	A	A	A	C	A
31	**32**	**33**	**34**	**35**	**36**	**37**	**38**	**39**	**40**
C	A	C	A	A	D	A	C	A	B
41	**42**	**43**	**44**	**45**	**46**	**47**	**48**	**49**	**50**
B	B	B	A	B	B	B	A	B	A
51	**52**	**53**	**54**	**55**	**56**	**57**	**58**	**59**	**60**
C	C	A	C	C	D	A	A	B	A
61	**62**	**63**	**64**	**65**	**66**	**67**	**68**	**69**	**70**
C	D	C	D	B	A	D	C	B	C
71	**72**	**73**	**74**	**75**					
D	A	D	C	B					

SOME SELECTED EXPLANATORY ANSWERS

1. A typical political theory includes, according to Sabine, (*a*) "factual statements about the postures of affairs that gave rise to it", (*b*) statements of "what may be roughly called a causal nature", and (*c*) statements that "something ought to happen or is the right and desirable thing to have happened". Political theories, thus, constitute, according to Sabine, three elements – the factual, the causal and the valuationary.

2. In the middle of the twentieth century, many observers were ready to write an obituary on political theory. Some spoke of its decline (Cobban 1953 and 1960a; Easton 1953). Others proclaimed its death (Laslett 1957; Dahl 1958). One referred to political theory being in the doghouse (Riemer 1962: 1). The major reason for such a dismal views was that the classical tradition in political theory was by and large loaded with value judgements beyond the control of empirical testing. The criticism of normative theory came from the logical positivists in the 1930s, and subsequently from behaviouralists.

   Easton contends that since political theory is concerned with some kind of historical form, it had lost its constructive role. Political theory as practised by William Dunning, Charles H. McIlwain and George Holland Sabine had declined into "historicism", for it dissuaded students from a serious study of value theory.

3. The *logical* separation of 'facts' and 'values' does not imply that in *practice* they can always be separated; nor does it imply the possibility of any kind of 'value-free' social science. It is impossible for a political scientist to free himself from the value system which underpins and shapes the way he thinks. In the words of David Easton, 'we cannot shed our values in the way we remove our coats. Values are an integral part of personality, and as long as we are human, we can assume that these mental sets and preferences will be with us'.

6. The Manchester School liberalism of John Bright (1811-89) and Richard Cobden (1804-65) gave way in the 1880s and 1890s to the more interventionist liberalism of the British idealists, which was inspired by the writings of Thomas Hill Green (1836-82). This movement gave birth to the New Liberalism whose main theoreticians were Leonard Trelawny Hobhouse (1864-1929) and Hobson himself.

7. Marx's way of thinking is often referred to as *dialectical materialism*. Materialism is a philosophical position based on the axiom that all events in the phenomenal world can be explained adequately in terms of other events, or causes, in the world. A major influence in the development of materialism was Locke's view that all our ideas are caused by the perceptions of the external world which reach us via our five senses, and by our reflections on these. In asserting this, he was rebutting Descartes' claim that people were born with innate ideas of God and other absolute truths, such as those of geometry, from which their knowledge was constructed. For Marx, as for Locke, ideas can have no existence without prior causes in the external world, but while Locke was asserting this doctrine against those who maintained that knowledge was ultimately produced by divine intervention or other metaphysical (literally 'beyond the physical') influences, Marx used it against the eighteenth-century philosophers who had used such fictions as 'human nature' and 'pure reason' in their explanations of society. Most of all, he disputed the German idealists' claim that ideas can arise independently of social context and act as causes within society. He held that all social phenomena and human consciousness itself are produced by material causes, and that these causes lie finally in the economic arrangements of society, which he called *the mode of production*. 'Man', his thoughts and his activities, are therefore determined by society — an axiom which deliberately strikes at the liberal assumption of individual autonomy and free will. 'My own existence is a social activity', Marx said and 'activity and mind are social in their context as well as in their origin; they are *social* activity and *social* mind'.

10. J.S. Mill decided to modify some of the basic tenets of utilitarianism to defend the same from the anti hedonist movement led by Carlyle. He opined that some pleasures are of

a higher quality than others. For Bentham and James Mill pleasures differ only in quantity. Bentham has put it as "quantity of pleasure being equal, pushpin is as good as poetry". Mill offers a singular proof that Bentham is wrong. But Mill truly reflects human experience when he says that it is better to be a human being dissatisfied than a pig satisfied better to be Socrats dissatisfied than a fool satisfied. And if the fool or the pig is of a different opinion, it is because they only know their own side of their question. The other party to the comparison knows both sides. It is surely non-utilitarian view.

According to Mill pleasures cannot be measured in an objective manner. The specific cause is, he said absurd and men have always relied upon the testimony of those most competent to judge. According to C.L. Wayper "what means are there of determining which is the acutest of two pains or the intensest of two pleasurable sensations except the general suffrage of those who are familiar with both?" This argument clearly indicates the hollowness of utilitarianism.

Mill maintained the further non-utilitarian position by holding the view that not principle of utility but the dignity of man is the final end of life. Here J.S. Mill approved of Humboldt's doctrine of "self-realisation." He asked that what more or better can be said of any condition of human beings than that it brings human beings themselves near to the best thing they can be." This doctrine of "self-realisation" had already been attacked by Bentham and James Mill. Their main aim was the achievement of pleasure and the avoidance of pain. To him state was a moral institution with a moral ends *i.e.* the promotion of virtue in the individual. Utilitarians have always subordinated liberty to the principle of utility; but to Mill, Liberty is a more fundamental end than utility.

11. Roy joined the Indian National Congress in November 1936. In December 1936, he attended the Annual Session of the Indian National Congress at Faizpur. He became a member of the A.I.C.C. He launched a weekly journal, *Independent India* on 4 April, 1937 from Bombay and in 1949 it was changed to *Radical Humanist.* He wanted to transform the Congress into a mass, political party. He was a staunch critic of Gandhian leadership. He was not satisfied with the Gandhian group and so he established the League of Radical Congressmen to carry forward the word of activising and democraticing the Congress in May 1939.

16. In sociology, Anthony Giddens (1984) proposed the concept of structuration as a way of analysing the relationship between structures and actors. According to Giddens, structures (i.e., the rules and conditions that guide social action) do not determine what actors do in any mechanical way; an impression one might get from the neorealist view of how the structure of anarchy constrains state actors. The relationship between structures and actors involves intersubjective understanding and meaning. Structures do constrain actors, but actors can also transform structures by thinking about them and acting on them in new ways. The notion of structuration therefore leads to a less rigid and more dynamic view of the relationship between structure and actors.

18. Conditions of Political Modernization

The conditions which facilitate political modernization in the new states could be treated as both (a) general, which are applicable to all political modernization, and (b) concrete, which are necessary in specific cases. Writers like Almond and Eisenstadt have given us some idea of some of the requirements which help in the process.

Almond's five conditions for political modernization are—(1) successiveness in the stages of development, (2) availability of resources, (3) congruent development of the other social systems, (4) intrinsic sufficient capability of the political system, and (5) adequate response to challenges by the elite. Almond believes that the various stages in political modernization should succeed one another and not overlap with each other. It is also necessary, according to Almond, that the society should have adequate resources for development. To him political system is a sub-system of society and believes that one of the necessary conditions of successful political modernization is the simultaneous development of the cultural, economic and participational sub-systems. The political system should have sufficient intrinsic capability to meet the challenges as they come up from time to time. Finally, the elite should be able to react positively and constructively to the challenges which come from society.

19. **Corporatism:** This approach stresses the central role of state and society interactions is governing, and especially the legitimate role of social interests in influencing policy.

21. The expression "cooperative federalism" arose in the United States in the 1930s and spread to Canada after the Second World War, attaining the peak of its popularity in the 1960s. The concept of cooperative federalism emphasizes the growing prominence of intergovernmental relations as a result of the expanding role of the state and the resulting difficulty of maintaining a rigid distinction between the two levels of government.

23. **Rational choice:** The rational-choice theory of voting originates with Anthony Downs (1957), a work which starts with the assumption that citizens are rational and vote on the basis of a calculation of which party most closely gives them all the political information they need; they then act on the basis of their own self-interest. Voting decisions are similar to those of consumers (voters) in the economic market who calculate the costs and benefits of choosing one commercial product (political party) rather than another. Voting for a party is rather like choosing a basket of goods in a supermarket, in that voters select the 'package' of party policies that best fits their preferences. Similarly, parties are like business competing for customers in the market place. They try to locate themselves and their policies as closely as they can to the median voter. Rational choice, in short, can explain the behaviour of individual voters and it can explain the strategies and policies of political parties in terms of an economic theory of *consumers* (voters) and the *producers* of public policies (parties).

25. Gasset Ortega in his study "The Revolt of the Masses" has tried to study the elite. His theory of elite is based on his superficial respect to the dogma of the masses. He says that a man is effective in society as a whole not so much because of his individual qualities but because of the social energies which have been deposed in him by the masses and a nation is an organised human mass, given structure by a minority of select individuals. He further observed that it is the people who create the elites by reposing their faith in and by rendering their support to this choosen element. It shows the capacity of leading in very few and the capacity of being led in many. The masses revolt when aristocracy becomes corrupt and inefficient and the motive behind the revolt is not that they have objection, to being ruled by aristocracy but they would like to be ruled by a more competent aristocracy. The main theme of his theory of elite is that "when the masses in a country believe that they can do without aristocracy, the nation inevitably declines. In their disillusionment the masses again turn to the new leadership and a new aristocracy emerges.

26. Shils outlines a model where the criteria of political development are based on the Western value system, but he also offers a typology or political-systems that accommodate the non-Western types. These

criteria lie in Shils' conception of political development as 'the model regime of civilian rule through representative institutions in the matrix of public liberties'. Shils offers five types of political systems as indicating different courses of political development.

1. **Political Democracy,** which is characterized by (*a*) the stability, coherence and effectiveness of the ruling elite; (*b*) the practice and acceptance of opposition; (*c*) adequate machinery of authority for the protection of the constitutional order; (*d*) the institutions of public opinion; and (*e*) the civil order, which based on civility, would embrace a sense of nationality, interest in public affairs, legitimacy of the political order, a sense of dignity and of obligations, and a consensus regarding values, institutions and practices.
2. **Tutelary Democracy,** the traits of which are (*a*) a stronger and more authoritative executive than that in political democracy; (*b*) identity of the party with the government; (*c*) discipline through the influence of personality; (*d*) a diminishing of the powers of the opposition; and (*e*) that the rule of law, however, continues.
3. **Modernizing Oligarchy,** implying (*a*) an urge to modernity and to unity; (*b*) apprehensions regarding the overwhelming power of traditional elements; (*c*) a higher concentration of authority; (*d*) an organized ruling elite and an elaborate bureaucracy; and (*e*) the lack of an ideology in particular.
4. **Totalitarian Oligarchy,** constituting (*a*) an ideology as the state doctrine; (*b*) an organized small clique; (*c*) the absence of an opposition; and (*d*) total government control.
5. **Traditional Oligarchy,** characterized by (*a*) a dynastic constitution and palace rule; (*b*) kinship and a personal choice of advisors; and (*c*) traditional beliefs and institutions.

30. Michel Crozier in his book 'The Bureaucratic Phenomena' (1964) has described bureaucracy as "a rigid organization that cannot correct its behaviour by learning from its errors".

39. Some Indian and Western scholars have tried to understand the nature of the Indian state in a rather objective and ideologically detached manner. Gunnar Myrdal, in his voluminous study entitled *Asian Drama: An Inquiry into the Poverty of Nations,* has called it a 'soft state', as it was unwilling and hesitant to take radical and drastic steps to destroy old religious attitudes, cultural patterns and social structures. Francine R. Frankel has tried to understand its nature as a 'paradox of accommodative politics and radical social change'. To her, the Indian state has always tried to debilitate the aspirations of and energy for radical socio-economic changes through a fabricated consensus and accommodative politics. Lloyd and Susanne Rudolph have read the nature of the Indian state as a paradox of a 'weak-strong' state.

43. The Indian subcontinent has developed three major nation-states. The largest, India, to borrow the terms of Anthony D. Smith, is an example of "polycentric nationalism" and Pakistan and Bangladesh are "ethnocentric" nations founded primarily on religion (Islam) and language (Bengali). All these three kinds of nation-states in our neighbourhood have their own problems in all the three dimensions of democracy, development, and culture—communal and national.

46. Chief Executive: All the apex of the administrative hierarchy of a government is the chief executive who is known by different names in different countries. Chief Executive is head of an organisation and is responsible for its planning, direction, coordination and budgeting etc. Gullick has described functions of the chief executive as POSDCORB (Planning, Organising, Staffing, Directing, Coordinating, Reporting and Budgeting). Cadre management is the primary function of the chief executive.

48. The Human Relations Theory of Organisation

Hawthorne Experiments were carried out in the U.S.A., in the late 1920s and early 1930s.

The experiments were carried out at the Western Electric Company (owned by the Bell Telephone Company) at Hawthorne (near Chicago), under the leadership of Elton Mayo and his colleagues of the Harvard Business School. They are ably discussed in *Management and the Worker* (by F.J. Roethlisberger and William J. Dickson), published in 1939.

In one 'experiment', the activities of a group of workers engaged in making telephone switches were observed. These workers were operating under a piece-rate system, and the management believed that this would stimulate the workers to earn more. Contrary to management's expectations, they worked to a level which ensured them what they considered to be adequate earnings, and, thus, refused to work more to earn more. They feared that if they produced more, some of them may face retrenchment or even the wages may be reduced. It was discovered by the researchers that these workers constituted a small, well-knit social group which was governed by a code which effectively discouraged a 'rate-buster' (who does too much work), a 'chiseller' (who does too little), and a 'squealer' (who passes unfavourable information about his colleagues to his superior).

49. According to Simon, every decision consists of a logical combination of fact and value propositions. A fact is a statement indicating what the product is, was, or has been. A statement of fact may be proved or disproved. Value is an expression of preference. Every decision, as Simon explains, is made up of several fact statements and one or more value statements or usually a decision is compounded of one value statement and several fact statements.

50. In the USA the comprehensive attempt to formulate the classical theory really began in 1931 when Mooney and Reiley (two General Motors executives) published their work *Onward Industry.* This book was re-published under the title of *The Principles of Organisation* in 1939. Mooney and Reiley were concerned with certain universal principles and contributed four principles of organisation, namely, the coordinative principle, the scalar principle, the functional principle, and staff-line principle. Both of them believed that coordination is the determining principle of organisation. They insisted that the structure of an organisation should follow the scalar principle. To them, the scalar chain constitutes the universal process of coordination. Mooney and Reiley contended that an efficient organisation should be based on certain principles. They set forth some fundamentals of organisation, which are to be regarded as their contribution to the development of early organisation theory.

51. Gulick and Urwick were great systematisers of the classical approach to administration. Gulick was a well-known American administrative expert and reformer. He was one of the trail blazers in American administrative theory. He was a professor at Columbia University when he co-authored "Papers on the Science of Administration". Urwick was a management consultant and historian.

Both Gulick and Urwick were greatly involved in the problems of American Public administration. They were confidantes of President Franklin D. Roosevelt, and they advised him on a variety of administrative problems and managerial matters. They wrote many reports on administrative reform and efficiency.

Gulick and Urwick adited their noted landmark volume called "Papers on the Science of Administration" in 1937. The principles of orthodox Public administration wre more or less condified in it. It contained the most comprehensive enunciation of the classical theory and marked the highnoon of orthodoxy and prestige for Public administration. Gulick's own article in this work, "Notes on the Theory of organization" has been of particular importance in the classical tradition of administration. It examines the concepts of structure, departmentalization etc.

55. The term 'development administration' was first coined by U.L. Goswami, an Indian Scholar. He used this term in his article entitled 'The Structure of Development Administration in India', published in 1955. However, it is George Gant, an American Scholar, who is regarded as the father of development administration. He too started using the term during the same period. His book *Development Administration: Concepts, Goals and Methods* was first published in 1979.

Edward W. Weidner, Fred W. Riggs, Joseph La Polombara, John D. Montogomery, Ferrel Heady, Milton J. Esman, Albert Waterson, Lucian Pye, Merle Fainsod, Alfred Diamant, Irving Swerdlow, William J. Saffin, and Han been Lee have contributed to the popularisation and growth of the concept of development administration in the field of public administration.

Edward Wiedner is the foremost proponent of development administration. He is also the first to conceptually explain the definition of development administration.

Development administration is essentially a concept of administration which is action oriented rather than structure oriented. It involves not only the study of a traditional and routine type of administrative system but is more directed towards the dynamics of an administrative system with a view to judging its capacities as an instrument of programme planning and execution.

60. Performance Budgeting: The system of performance budgeting (earlier called as functional budgeting or activity budgeting) originated in the USA. The term 'performance budget' was coined by the First Hoover Commission (1949). This commission recommended the adoption of performance budgeting in the USA to make effective management approach to budgeting. Accordingly, it was introduced in 1950 by President Truman.

Unlike the line-item budgeting, the performance budgeting emphasises on the purpose of expenditure rather than the expenditure itself. It presents budget in terms of functions, programmes, activities and projects. It establishes a correlation between the physical (performance or output) and financial (input) aspects of each programme and activity. Hence, it necessitates a functional classification of the budget.

In India, the adoption of performance budget was recommended first by the Estimates Committee of Parliament in 1956. In 1964, the Government invited Frank W. Krause, an American expert, to study the suitability and feasibility of this system of budgeting in India. Finally the Central Government introduced performance budgeting in 1968 on the recommendation of the Administrative Reforms Commission. According to this commission, the advantages (benefits/ objectives) of the performance budgeting are as follows:

(*i*) It presents more clearly, the purposes and objectives for which the funds are sought by the executive from the parliament.

(*ii*) It brings out the programmes and accomplishments in financial and physical terms.

(*iii*) It facilitates a better understanding and better review of the budget by the Parliament.

(*iv*) It improves the formulation of the budget.

(*v*) It facilitates the process of decision-making at all levels of government.

(*vi*) It increases the accountability of the management.

(*vii*) It provides an extra tool of management control of financial operations.

(*viii*) It renders performance audit more purposeful and effective.

In 1968, the performance budgeting was introduced in four ministries of the Government of India. Later in 1977-78, it was extended to about 32 developmental departments.

61. Different scholars define differently the polarity of the international system. For some, pre-World War I Europe was bipolar, in the eyes of others it was multipolar. Following Kenneth Waltz, John Mearsheimer argues that bipolar systems are more stable than multipolar ones; this provides the foundation for his pessimistic predictions about the future of Europe.

62. Democratic Peace Theory: This theory holds that although liberal democracies may go to war with non-democratic states, they typically do not fight each other. A key issue is the extent to which democracy has been consolidated in a country. History shows that new or transitional democracies can be war-prone in their international politics. In addition, democratic peace theory does not explain the impact of democratization on internal conflict.

66. Quasi-state: A state that possesses juridical statehood but is severely deficient in empirical statehood. A large number of states in the Third World can be defined this way: they are recognized as states and participate in the state system, but they have weak or corrupt political institutions, underdeveloped economies, and little or no national unity.

Previous Paper (Solved)

UGC-NET POLITICAL SCIENCE, DECEMBER 2012

PAPER–II

Note: *This paper contains fifty (50) multiple-choice questions, each carrying two (2) marks. Attempt **all** of them.*

1. In Hegel's notion the highest possible achievement of Mind as expressed in social life was in

A. The Contemporary Prussian State
B. Rome
C. Athens
D. Contemporary Great Britain

2. Machiavelli advised the Prince to pursue

A. Moderate behaviour
B. Extreme generosity
C. Perfect strictness
D. Great kindness

3. Which is not a part of Rawls' well ordered society?

A. Stable B. Efficient
C. Justice D. Equal

4. Who among the following wrote,

"Laws are the rules of just and unjust; nothing being reputed unjust that is not contrary to some law"?

A. Bentham B. Hegel
C. Hobbes D. Rousseau

5. Arrange the following works of Rousseau chronologically, using the codes given below:

(*a*) The Social Contract
(*b*) A discourse on the Arts and Sciences
(*c*) Emile
(*d*) A Discourse on the Origin of Inequality

Codes:

A. (*d*), (*c*), (*b*), (*a*) B. (*a*), (*c*), (*d*), (*b*)
C. (*c*), (*a*), (*b*), (*d*) D. (*b*), (*d*), (*c*), (*a*)

6. Match List-I with List-II and select the correct answer from the codes given below :

List-I	*List-II*
(*a*) On Liberty	1. Amartya Sen
(*b*) Lectures on the Principles of Political Obligation	2. T.H. Green
(*c*) Idea of Justice	3. Robert Nozick
(*d*) Anarchy, State and Utopia	4. J. S. Mill

Codes :

	(*a*)	(*b*)	(*c*)	(*d*)
A.	3	1	2	4
B.	1	3	2	4
C.	2	4	3	1
D.	4	2	1	3

7. Match List-I with List-II and select the correct answer from the codes given below :

List-I	**List-II**
(*a*) Justice as one person, one duty, one class one work	1. Plato
(*b*) Justice as fairness	2. Aristotle
(*c*) Justice as proportionate equality	3. Rawls
(*d*) Justice as the interest of the strong	4. Thrasymachas

Codes :

	(*a*)	(*b*)	(*c*)	(*d*)
A.	1	2	3	4
B.	2	1	3	4
C.	2	1	4	3
D.	1	3	2	4

8. Match List-I with List-II and select the correct answer from the codes given below :

List-I	**List-II**
(*a*) Perpetual peace	1. Plato

(*b*) Golden Mean 2. Kant
(*c*) Analogy of the cave 3. Aristotle
(*d*) Fortune as a woman 4. Machiavelli

Codes :

	(*a*)	(*b*)	(*c*)	(*d*)
A.	1	2	3	4
B.	2	3	1	4
C.	2	1	4	3
D.	4	3	2	1

Directions: *Given below are two statements, one labelled as Assertion (A) and the other labelled as Reason (R). Select the correct answer from the codes given below :*

9. Assertion (A): Marx was a revolutionary.
Reason (R): Marx was not concerned about the processes of history.
Codes :
A. Both (A) and (R) are true and (R) is the correct explanation of (A).
B. Both (A) and (R) are true, but (R) is not the correct explanation of (A).
C. (A) is true, but (R) is false.
D. (A) is false, but (R) is true.

10. Assertion (A): Aristotle is justifiably called the Father of Political Science.
Reason (R): His criticism of Plato's idealism justifies this claim.
Codes :
A. Both (A) and (R) are true and (R) is the correct explanation of (A).
B. Both (A) and (R) are true, but (R) is not the correct explanation of (A).
C. (A) is true, but (R) is false.
D. (A) is false, but (R) is true.

11. The operational part of the general systems theory in social sciences has been developed first in
A. Psychology B. Sociology
C. Political Science D. Anthropology

12. Who said, "Functionalism can indeed be interpreted as a conscious alternative to Marxism"?
A. W.G. Runciman
B. Robert K. Merton
C. Oran Young
D. David Easton

13. Who among the following stated that a developing society in order to reach the goals of development would have to pass through the stages of political unification, industrialization, national welfare and abundance ?
A. Rustow B. Organski
C. Lucian Pye D. David Apter

14. Which one of the following pairs is not correctly matched ?
A. Lucian Pye : Modernisation Theory
B. Wallerstein : World System Theory
C. Theda Skocpol : New Institutionalism
D. Karl Deutsch : Communications Theory

15. Which one of the following pairs is not correctly matched ?
A. Pareto : The concept of residues
B. Michels : The concept of mass mind
C. Mills : The concept of political formula
D. Gasset : The theory of the masses

16. The concept of civic culture developed out of a survey of
A. Mexico, India, Pakistan, U.S.A. and U.K.
B. U.S.A., U.K., Mexico, Germany and Italy.
C. U.S.A., U.K., Australia, Pakistan and India.
D. Australia, Canada, U.S.A., U.K. and France.

17. Unequal exchange is the formulation of
A. Samir Amin
B. Amartya Sen
C. Paul Sweezy
D. Andre Gunder Frank

18. Duverger's classification of the party system is derived from the experience of political parties in
A. Western Europe
B. All the democracies of the world
C. Party system in the developing world
D. Political party system in the communist world

19. Which of the following statements are correct about the President of America ?

1. He is the head of the State and also the head of the Government.
2. All executive powers are vested in him.
3. He is bound by the advice of his Cabinet.
4. He has the power to dissolve the legislature.

Codes :

A. 1 and 3 are correct.
B. 2, 3 and 4 are correct.
C. 1, 3 and 4 are correct.
D. 1 and 2 are correct.

20. Which one of the following is not a feature of F.M. Marx's guardian bureaucracy ?

A. Custodian of Public interest
B. Competent
C. Authoritarian
D. Corrupt

21. Which of the following Committee was appointed by the Government of India to Identify the creamy layer among Backward Classes in India ?

A. Justice R.N. Mishra Committee
B. Justice R.N. Madholkar Committee
C. Justice Ram Nandan Committee
D. Justice Rajender Sachar Committee

22. Who described Indian Politics as "Politics of Scarcity"?

A. Myron Weiner B. Paul R. Brass
C. Atul Kohli D. Morris-Jones

23. Which Congress President during British Raj initiated the idea of a Planning Commission?

A. Jawaharlal Nehru
B. Mahatma Gandhi
C. Maulana Azad
D. Subhash Chandra Bose

24. Which of the following statements are correct about Indian Government?

1. Rajya Sabha represents the local interests of the States.
2. A member of Rajya Sabha must be a resident of the State from which he is elected.
3. Number of seats allotted to a State has to be proportionate to its population.
4. The term of a member of Rajya Sabha is same as that of Senator in the US.

Codes :

A. 2, 3 and 4
B. 1, 2 and 3
C. 1, 3 and 4
D. 1 and 2

25. Who of the following was the first Satyagrahi of the Individual Civil Disobedience Movement started by Gandhiji in October 1940 ?

A. Dr. Rajendra Prasad
B. J.B. Kripalani
C. Sardar Vallabhbhai Patel
D. Acharya Vinoba Bhave

26. Who prefers to characterize the Indian federalism as "bargaining federalism"?

A. A.K. Chanda B. Morris Jones
C. K.C.Wheare D. D.D. Basu

27. Who was the Chairman of Mandal Commission ?

A. B.N. Mandal B. B.P. Mandal
C. D.L. Mandal D. R.N. Mandal

28. When was the Inter-State Council set up in India ?

A. 1987 B. 1989
C. 1990 D. 1992

29. When were the Lok Sabha rules amended to provide for Department Related Parliamentary Standing Committees ?

A. 1988 B. 1989
C. 1991 D. 1995

30. Which one of the following Acts/Reports created the Federal Court in India ?

A. Government of India Act, 1909.
B. Government of India Act, 1919.
C. Montague-Chelmsford Report
D. Government of India Act, 1935

31. The Book 'Introduction to Public Administration' was authored by

A. W.F. Willoughby
B. Woodrow Wilson

C. M.P. Follet
D. Leonard D. White

32. The concept of 'Informal Organisation' was profounded by
A. F.W. Taylor
B. Herbert Simon
C. Elton Mayo
D. F.M. Marx

33. 'Clect' is the sub-system of Riggs' Prismatic society
A. Social system
B. Administrative system
C. Economic system
D. Political system

34. 'Jacksonian Theory' is also called
A. Merit system B. Outsource theory
C. Spoils system D. Contract system

35. Which of the four major issues of Public Administration were debated in the Minnowbrooke Conference, 1968?
A. Relevance, values, equity and change.
B. History, qualities, values and development.
C. Text, context, relevance and status.
D. Norms, values, context and progress.

36. Who said, 'Successful Management involves Management by Objectives'?
A. F.W. Taylor
B. Peter F. Drucker
C. Kothari Committee
D. Edwin B. Flippo

37. In which book of the following, Robert Dahl explained the Theory of Decision Making?
A. Democracy, Liberty and Equality
B. Democracy at Cross Roads
C. Who Governs?
D. Modern Political Analysis

38. Which Committee recommended "Unified Grading Structure" for the British Civil Service?
A. Masterman
B. Fulton
C. Asheton
D. McGraw

39. Given below are two statements, one labelled as Assertion (A) and the other labelled as Reason (R). Find the correct answer using the codes given below :

Assertion (A): Adequate measures must be taken by the Government to ensure the stoppage of the practice of corruption.
Reason (R) : Corruption leads to decline of democratic process.

Codes :
A. Both (A) and (R) are true, but (R) is not correct explanation of (A).
B. (A) is true, but (R) is false.
C. Both (A) and (R) are true and (R) is correct explanation of (A).
D. (A) is false, but (R) is true.

40. Match the following :

The Office of Ombudsman was set up in these countries in the following years :

(Countries)	(Years)
(*a*) Sweden	1. 1967
(*b*) Finland	2. 1809
(*c*) New Zealand	3. 1978
(*d*) United Kingdom	4. 1919
	5. 1962

Select the correct answer :

Codes :

	(*a*)	(*b*)	(*c*)	(*d*)
A.	2	4	5	1
B.	1	5	3	4
C.	3	2	1	5
D.	4	3	5	1

41. In the post Soviet era Russia's outlook at global level is marked by
A. Rigid Ideological positions
B. Enhanced role for Soviet era legacies.
C. Pragmatic de-ideologised worldview.
D. Rigidities of cold war era.

42. Who of the following has coined the term under-development?
A. Antonio Gramsci
B. Rosa Luxemburg
C. Emmanual Wallerstein
D. Kenneth Waltz

43. The policy of containment formulated by the U.S. aimed at
- A. Checking globally the influence of the Soviet Union.
- B. Checking the nuclear proliferation of Iran.
- C. Containing defiant North Korea.
- D. Countering the expansionist policies of People's Republic of China.

44. The Kyoto Protocol of 1997 adopted the programme for
- A. ending global poverty
- B. the democratisation of U.N. system
- C. broadening the participation within I.M.F. and World Bank.
- D. reducing greenhouse emissions.

45. Match List-I with List-II and select correct answer from the codes given below :

List-I	List-II
(*a*) Morton Kaplan	1. Perestroika and Glasnost
(*b*) Andre Gunder Frank	2. Theory of Realism
(*c*) Hans J. Morgenthau	3. Systems Theory
(*d*) Mikhail Gorbachev	4. Dependency Theory

Codes :

	(*a*)	(*b*)	(*c*)	(*d*)
A.	3	4	2	1
B.	4	2	3	1
C.	2	4	1	3
D.	2	1	3	4

46. The principle of reciprocity within WTO framework envisages
- A. lowering of trade barriers by a State to be matched in return.
- B. creation of trade barriers on uniform basis.
- C. protection of intellectual property rights.
- D. enhanced role for State controls on trade.

47. What is the correct chronological order of the events listed below ?
1. U.S. Policy of Containment of the Soviet Union.
2. Dissolution of the former Soviet Union.
3. Iran-Iraq War.
4. US War on terrorism in Afghanistan.

Choose the right answer from the codes given below :

Codes :
- A. 4, 2, 3, 1
- B. 2, 4, 1, 3
- C. 3, 2, 4, 1
- D. 1, 3, 2, 4

48. The dictum, 'Imperialism is the highest stage of Capitalism' was propounded by
- A. Karl Marx
- B. V.I. Lenin
- C. Andre Gunder Frank
- D. Emmanual Wallerstein

49. Hans Blix was head of U.N. body for
- A. Peace-keeping operations in Somalia.
- B. Inspecting places in Iraq for verification of Weapons of Mass Destruction.
- C. Working modalities for the creation of NIEO.
- D. Rebuilding war-torn Afghanistan

50. Nagorno Karabakh is a disputed territory between
- A. Armenia and Azerbaizan
- B. Georgia and Ukraine
- C. Uzbekistan and Turkmenistan
- D. Russian Federation and China

ANSWERS

1	2	3	4	5	6	7	8	9	10
A	A	D	C	D	D	D	B	C	A
11	**12**	**13**	**14**	**15**	**16**	**17**	**18**	**19**	**20**
D	A	B	A	C	B	A	A	D	D
21	**22**	**23**	**24**	**25**	**26**	**27**	**28**	**29**	**30**
C	A	D	*	D	B	B	C	B	D

31	32	33	34	35	36	37	38	39	40
D	C	A	C	A	B	C	B	A	A
41	**42**	**43**	**44**	**45**	**46**	**47**	**48**	**49**	**50**
C	C	A	D	A	A	D	B	B	A

SOME SELECTED EXPLANATORY ANSWERS

1. The entire historical/cosmological process reached its climax and conclusion, according to Hegel, in the Germany of his own day: the contemporary Prussian state was the highest possible achievement of Mind as expressed in social life, Protestantism the highest expression of religion, Romanticism the highest perfection of art—all of which, in their different ways, expressed the full maturity of Spirit. But over and above all was philosophy, the crowning achievement of any age. In this case it was his philosophy that summed up his age; much more than that: he saw his philosophy as summing up the whole process, including the whole of history, the whole development of the universe and the whole evolution of Mind since before the universe was formed. It all culminates in Hegel's philosophy, because it is through his philosophy that Mind finally comes to understand itself and comes to realise that reality is its own creation, is itself (that is, an objectification of itself).

2. Machiavelli's "The Prince" is in the form of advice given to a ruler on the state craft. Some significant Machiavelli's "The Prince" is in the form of advice given to a ruler on the state craft. Some significant aspects of the advise to the ruler are as follows:

1. Machiavelli elaborates the doctrine of 'Raison D 'Etat'.
2. End justifies the Means.
3. State is sovereign, autonomous and non-religious.
4. A prince must combine the qualities of a lion and a fox.
5. Use a double standard of morality.
6. Favour despotic rule.
7. Maintain strong army.
8. Human nature is low and ungrateful, so Prince must consider this nature of man.
9. He should win the popularity of his people must not touch the property of the people.
10. A prince must have council of wise men and not of flatterers.
11. Separate politics from religion.
12. Remain free from emotions.

4. The first possible source of laws that define what one has a right to do is the civil sovereign. There is some textual evidence that this is Hobbes's view. He claims several times that the civil laws define what justice and injustice consist in. For example, he defines civil law as rules 'for the distinction of right and wrong' and argues for this definition on the grounds that it is self-evident, 'that laws are the rules of just, and unjust; nothing being reputed unjust, that is not contrary to some law'.

5. **Major Works of Rousseau:** A discourse on the Arts and Sciences (1750), A Discourse on the Origin of Inequality (1755), Emile (1762), The Social Contract (1762), Letters Written from the Mount (1764), Confessions (1770).

6. (*a*) On Liberty—J. S. Mill
(*b*) Lectures on the Principles of Political Obligation—T.H. Green
(*c*) Idea of Justice—Amartya Sen
(*d*) Anarchy, State and Utopia—Robert Nozick

7. (*a*) Justice as one person, one duty, one class one work—Plato
(*b*) Justice as fairness—Rawls

(c) Justice as proportionate equality—Aristotle
(d) Justice as the interest of the strong—Thrasymachas

8. (a) Perpetual peace—Kant
(b) Golden Mean—Aristotle
(c) Analogy of the cave—Plato
(d) Fortune as a woman—Machiavelli

12. A critical examination of the structural-functional approach from a strictly ideological point of view shows that it is all nothing else than an exercise to defend and justify the *status quo*. The real pursuit of the functionalists is to save a political system from changing towards socialism. A serious endeavour to maintain a system or its change, by all means, peaceful and gradual, in the direction of 'modernisation' aims at nothing else than an imitation or emulation of the 'western' model that presents an anti-thesis of a communist system. The functionalists are, therefore, accused of being the 'defenders of the bourgeoisie at home and of imperialism abroad'. A critic like W.G. Runciman has thus said that functionalism "can, indeed, be interpreted as a conscious alternative to Marxism.

16. The best political culture for a democracy is: Civic culture, the term used by Almond and Verba to signify the balance of subject and participant political cultures that best supports democracy. The civic culture, in which subject and participant cultures are mixed to produce neither too much nor too little participation. Citizens are active and elites respond to their demands but citizens also trust their political leaders and give them a degree of independence. Almond and Verba found that the UK in the late 1950s came closest to the civic culture.

The Civic Culture argued that political culture was a crucial theoretical concept that mediated between the micro- and subjective properties of a political system, and its macro-institutional features. Culture is shared by individuals, so aggregate individual statistics (i.e. national averages) describe the properties of the system as a whole. Cultures and structures are also mutually inter-dependent, so they must 'fit' each other.

17. Theories of unequal exchange have been formulated both by neo-Marxists such as Samir Amin and Arghiri Emmanuel and by non-Marxist theorists such as Raul Prebisch and Hans Singer. Theories of unequal exchange reject the orthodox economic proposition that differences in factor endowments in different regions result in mutually advantageous patterns of international trade based on comparative advantage. According to orthodox views, free trade and specialisation in those lines of production in which a country is relatively most efficient will increase all countries' welfare. In the long run free movements of factors of production will also result in a gradual equalisation of returns to the factors of production in rich and poor countries. Theories of unequal exchange, however, state that participation of developing countries in the international division of labour is detrimental to their chances of economic development. Only the rich countries profit from international trade.

18. Traditionally political scientists have been very much preoccupied with the number of parties, because this number was considered important for the mechanics of the party system. Since the late 1960s it has become customary to describe the format of a party system in terms of the number of parties as well as the distribution of party strength within it. Duverger (1964) is famous for his classification scheme of the single-party, the Anglo-Saxon two-party and the multi-party system. In the same vein Blondel (1968) talks of two-party systems, two-and-a-half-party systems and multi-party systems with or without dominant parties. More recently, Sartori's (1976) analysis also begins with numbers—'the number of parties immediately

indicates, albeit roughly, an important feature of the political system'—building a distinction between two-party systems, and systems of moderate and extreme pluralism, before going on to also incorporate the notion of ideological distance between the parties as an intervening variable.

20. Guardian bureaucracy may be defined as that civil service which regards itself as custodian or guardian of public interest, and is independent of and unresponsive to public opinion. It is righteous, incorruptible, efficient, competent and benevolent but authoritarian and unresponsive. The bureaucracy comprised guardians who were selected on the basis of their education and were then trained in right conduct. They were considered the custodians of justice and welfare of the community. Marx defined this type as "a scholastic officialdom trained in right conduct according to the classics". Guardian bureaucracy is one of the types of bureaucracy described by F. M. Marx. The other three are: Caste bureaucracy, Patronage bureaucracy and Merit bureaucracy. The Guardian bureaucracy was prevalent in China upto the advent of the Sung period (960 A.D.) and in Prussian during 1640 and 1740.

22. Myron Weiner was one of the American political scientists whose professional life and writings consisted of work he did in and on India from the early 1960s until his death in 1999. He used his intimate grasp of politics in India to make comparative studies of politics and democratic processes in developing countries and to make seminal contributions to political theory as well. It was his book based on his Ph.D. dissertation, Politics of Scarcity: Public Pressure and Political Response in India (1962) that brought him to the notice of scholars in India and in the United States. Fairly soon after came Party Building in a New Nation: The Indian National Congress (1967). Other books on India and on more general themes came out subsequently. Two books in the 1990s, one on a specific Indian problem, The Child and the State in India: Child Labour and Educational Policy in Comparative Perspective (1991) and the other on a global issue, The Global Migration Crisis (1995) were widely acclaimed.

23. Bose became the president of the Haripura Indian National Congress in 1938, against Gandhi's wishes. Gandhi commented "Subhas' victory is my defeat". Gandhi's continued opposition led to the latter's resignation from the Working Committee, and the possibility that the rest of the CWC would resign. In the face of this gesture of no-confidence, Bose himself resigned, and was left with no alternative but to form an independent party, the All India Forward Bloc. Bose also initiated the concept of the National Planning Committee in 1938.

25. Gandhi launched an individual civil disobedience movement on 17 October 1940 when Vinoba Bhave, the first satyagrahi chosen by him, made in anti-war speech at Paunar near Wardha. Four days later, Bhave was arrested. The second satyagrahi chosen by Gandhi was Nehru, who was arrested in November 1940 and was sentenced to four year's imprisonment.

26. In 1964 Morris-Jones described the centre-state relation in India as a form of co-operative federalism. He however characterized it as bargaining federalism. The term bargaining federalism, Morris-Jones argued described the character of Indian federalism throughout it referred to a pattern of centre-state relations in which neither centre nor states can impose decisions on the others in which hard compelative bargaining takes place in such institution as the Planning Commission, the Finance Commission and the Zonal Councils. In these institutions bargaining occurs between the centre and the states and among, the several states for the allocation of resources and patronage and for the solution of such divisive problems as the rights of linguistic minorities in the linguistically recognized states.

28. The Inter-State Council (ISC) was set up under Article 263 of the Constitution of India by the President in 1990. Prime Minister is the head of the ISC and the composition includes:

- six Ministers of Cabinet rank in the Union Council of Ministers to be nominated by the Prime Minister
- two Ministers of Cabinet rank in the Union Council of Ministers to be nominated by the Prime Minister as permanent invitees.
- Chief Ministers of all States
- Chief Ministers of Union territories having Legislative Assemblies
- Administrators of Union territories not having Legislative Assemblies
- Governors of States under President's Rule.

The following issues, as far as may be expedient, may not be brought up before the Council:

- Any issue which can be resolved by discussion at the official level or at the level of Ministers between the Central Government and the State Governments concerned.
- Any issue which has to be considered or dealt with by the National Development Council, the National Integration Council, the Finance Commission, the Planning Commission or such other body or authority of a like nature as may be set up from time to time to deal with specific subjects relating to Centre-State relations.
- Any issue which is currently under consideration or discussion in either House of Parliament or which is sub-judice.

30. Government of India Act, 1919 failed to satisfy Indians. After the three round table conferences held in London, the Government of India Act, 1935 was posed. The Act had 451 articles, 15 schedules and 450 written pages. The Act of 1935 had the following provisions—Under this art, 11 states under the governors, 6 states under the chief commissioners and the other princely states were to join. The subjects were divided into three lists i.e., : (i) Federal list (59 subjects), (i) State list (54 subjects), (iii) Concurrent list had 36 subjects. Dyarchy was established at the centre. The Act of 1935 also made provision of the federal court for India with one Chief Justice and a few other judges. This was the Supreme Court of India. The federal legislature now had two chambers: (i) The upper house (council of states-260 members), (ii) The lower house legislative council-250 members). The Act made the provision for the establishment of a separate federal railway authority to manage and administrator railway in India.

32. It was Elton Mayo who contributed to the concept of informal organisation. Informal organisation are nor reflected in the organisation charts. But, the informal relationships are dynamic in nature. They are capable of affecting the relationships in the formal setting. A manager can lead and direct the subordinates better, to the advantage of the organisation, if he is aware of the importance of these interpersonal relationships.

35. The Minnowbrook Conference, 1968: It was also called Youth Conference on Public Administration, born partly out of a paper published in Public Administration Review in 1968 by Waldo on 'Public Administration in a Time of Revolution' and partly by the restlessness of young scholars and practitioners of the New Discipline. This gave birth to what is known as 'New Public Administration'. The Conference debated on four major issues—relevance, values, equity and change. The participants of the conference wanted that public administration should be value-loaded to take care of social justice or equity and thus help the underprivileged. Organisation should be designed to promote client loyalty and programme loyalty. It was stressed that public administration must attend to societal problems.

37. Polyarchy of Robert Dahl

- Robert Dahl explained the theory of Democracy in his book 'A preface to democratic Theory and Polyarchy'. In his democratic theory, Dahl has combined the elite concept of government and the electoral competition with the pluralist stress on the dispersal of power.
- The plurality of elites is regarded in the same light as plurality of groups.
- To him, People act both through the electoral system and through the group process.
- In this type of democracy, which he calls **Polyarchy,** there are several actors who make decisions merchants, consumers, politicians and voters.
- According to Dahl, the formulation of elites is natural in the industrial democratic societies but he rejects both the notion of the power elite and the ruling class.
- In his book, 'Who Governs', he came to the conclusion that the city was governed by a combination of elites in the cultural and economics fields but none of them was in the position to dominate political power on its own. It could be described as a democratically competing pluralist elite leadership drawn from a large number of elites in different fields of society.
- He examines the power structures (both formal and information) of the society in his work who governs? (1961).

38. The Fulton Report (1968): In 1966, the British government appointed the Fulton Committee on the civil service to examine the structure, recruitment, training and management—of the Home Civil Service. The committee submitted its report in 1968 and observed that the home civil service is still fundamentally the product of 19th century philosophy of North Cote-Trevelyan Report. The report highlights the basic 158 recommendations and the significant ones related to civil services are mentioned. A new civil service department should be created to manage the civil service. All classes should be abolished and replaced by a single unified grading structure covering all civil servants from top to bottom. The civil service should encourage greater professionalism both among specialists in a particular area of financial administration or social administration.

40. The Office of Ombudsman was set up in these countries in the following years :

(*a*) Sweden (1809)
(*b*) Finland (1919)
(*c*) New Zealand (1962)
(*d*) United Kingdom (1967)

44. The first global environmental conference was held in Stockholm, Sweden, in June 1972. The conference resulted in the Declaration of the United Nations Conference on the Human Environment, addressing population growth, sustainable development, and the preservation of natural resources, and created the United Nations Environment Programme (UNEP). The United Nations Framework Convention for Climate Change (UNFCCC) was adopted in June 1992 at the United Nations Conference on Environment and Development in Rio de Janeiro, Brazil. The Kyoto Protocol was adopted on December 11, 1997, in Kyoto, Japan, setting GHG emission reduction target for 37 industrialized countries and the European Union. The Kyoto Protocol received sufficient national ratification and entered into force on February 16, 2005.

45. (a) Morton Kaplan—Systems Theory
(b) Andre Gunder Frank—Dependency Theory
(c) Hans J. Morgenthau—Theory of Realism
(d) Mikhail Gorbachev—Perestroika and Glasnost

46. The WTO framework is based on the principle of reciprocity—that one state's lowering of trade barriers to another should be matched in return. It also uses the concept of non-discrimination, embodied in the most-favoured nation (MFN) concept, which says that trade restrictions imposed by a WTO member on its most favoured trading partner must be applied equally to all WTO members.

48. Imperialism, the Highest Stage of Capitalism (1917), by Lenin, describes the function of financial capital in generating profits from imperial colonialism, as the final stage of capitalist development to ensure greater profits. The essay is a synthesis of Lenin's modifications and developments of economic theories that Karl Marx formulated in Das Kapital (1867).

49. Hans Martin Blix is a Swedish diplomat and politician for the Liberal People's Party. He was Swedish Minister for Foreign Affairs (1978-1979) and later became the head of the International Atomic Energy Agency. As such, Blix was the first Western representative to inspect the consequences of the Chernobyl disaster in the Soviet Union on site, and lead the agency response to them. Blix was also the head of the United Nations Monitoring, Verification and Inspection Commission from March 2000 to June 2003, when he was succeeded by Dimitris Perrikos. In 2002, the commission began searching Iraq for weapons of mass destruction, ultimately finding none.

50. The landlocked mountainous region of Nagorno-Karabakh is a subject of an unresolved dispute between Azerbaijan, in which it lies, and its ethnic Armenian majority, backed by neighbouring Armenia.

PAPER–III

Note: *This paper contains seventy five (75) objective type questions of two (2) marks each. All questions are compulsory.*

1. The word 'theory', derived from the Greek word 'Theoria' means

A. A well organized political system

B. A well focused mental look

C. A well articulated economic structure

D. A system of physical arrangement

2. Who, among the following, is not associated with decline of political theory?

A. Peter Laslett B. David Easton

C. Jean Blondel D. Alfred Cobban

3. Who said 'negative liberty is superior to positive liberty'?

A. J.S. Mill B. Isaiah Berlin

C. T.H. Green D. Ernest Barker

4. Which one among the following statements is true ?

A. Social Justice violates the principles of equality.

B. Social Justice is derived from moral reasonableness.

C. Social justice is a negation of justice

D. Social justice is an instrument of political manipulation.

5. Which one among the following was the first mass movement Mao led?

A. The Cultural Revolution

B. The Great Leap Forward

C. Let hundred flowers blossom and hundred schools of thought contend.

D. None of the above

6. The term 'Leninism' was coined by

A. Trotsky B. Stalin

C. Marx D. Mao

7. Who is the author of the book *The Good Boatman*?

A. Erikson

B. Rajmohan Gandhi

C. Romain Rolland

D. Noema

8. Which one among the following statements is true?

A. Plato's Republic is a book on ethics
B. It is a book on politics
C. It is both on ethics and politics
D. It is a book on education

9. Which one among the following is not written by M.N. Roy?

A. The Future of Indian Politics
B. Gandhism, Nationalism and Socialism
C. New Humanism
D. Nationalism, Rationality and Revolution

10. Who among the following has compared fortune with a woman?

A. M.N. Roy B. Rousseau
C. Hobbes D. Machiavelli

11. Which one among the following is not a work about alienation?

A. Paris Manuscripts
B. Theses on Feuerbach
C. Poverty of Philosophy
D. The German Ideology

12. General Will means

A. Actual Will
B. Majority Will
C. Sum total of Wills
D. Real Will

13. **Assertion (A):** Social Contract established a sovereign Government.

Reason (R): Citizens do have an absolute obligation to obey all laws or accept any form of Government.

In the context of the two statements, which one of the following is correct?

A. Both (A) and (R) are true and (R) is correct explanation of (A).
B. Both (A) and (R) are true but (R) is not the correct explanation of (A).
C. (A) is true, but (R) is false.
D. (A) is false, but (R) is true.

14. Match the List-I with List-II and select the correct answer from the codes given below with reference to Aristotle and Plato :

List-I (Pure form)	**List-II (Degenerated form)**
(*a*) Monarchy	1. Democracy
(*b*) Aristocracy	2. Tyranny
(*c*) Polity	3. Oligarchy
(*d*) Ideal State	4. Timocracy (First stage)

Codes :

	(*a*)	(*b*)	(*c*)	(*d*)
A.	4	1	2	3
B.	2	3	1	4
C.	3	2	4	1
D.	1	4	3	2

15. What is the chronological correct sequence of the following books?

1. Richard Attenborough	*In Search of Gandhi.*
2. Louis Fisher	*The Life of Mahatma Gandhi*
3. E.H. Erikson	*Gandhi's Truth*
4. J. Eaton	*Gandhi : Fighter Without a Sword*

Select the correct answer from the codes given below :

Codes :

A. 4, 2, 3, 1
B. 3, 1, 2, 4
C. 2, 4, 3, 1
D. 1, 2, 4, 3

16. Match List-I with List-II and select the correct answer from the codes given below :

List-I (System Theorists)	**List-II (System)**
(*a*) Bertallanfy	1. a set of elements standing in interaction
(*b*) Hall and Fagen	2. a whole which is compounded of many parts
(*c*) Easton	3. a set of objects together with relationships between the objects and their attributes
(*d*) Colin Cherry	4. a set of interactions

Codes :

	(a)	(b)	(c)	(d)
A.	1	4	2	3
B.	2	3	1	4
C.	4	1	2	3
D.	3	2	4	1

17. Who among the following presents a 'flow model' of political system?

A. Gabriel Almond B. David Easton
C. Morton Kaplan D. Oran Young

18. Almond borrowed most of the terminology of his approach from

A. Robert K. Merton
B. Talcott Parsons
C. Malinowski
D. Arthur Bentley

19. Who among the following attached great importance to a balance between the principles of equality and capacity in political development?

A. Lucian Pye B. Huntington
C. Fred Riggs D. Danil Lerner

20. Who among the following is associated with the "will and capacity" approach to the study of political development?

A. Lucian Pye B. Organski
C. Halpern D. David Apter

21. Who among the following has connected cultures with civilizations?

A. Almond and Verba
B. Huntington
C. Lucian Pye
D. Edward Shils

22. "We are under the Constitution but the Constitution is what the judges say it is". Which of the following countries can this be applicable to?

1. India 2. America
3. Switzerland 4. Australia

Select the correct answer from the codes given below :

Codes :

A. 1 and 3 B. 1 and 2
C. 2 and 3 D. 3 and 4

23. Who among the following has associated the origins of political parties with three theories– institutional theories, historical crisis theories and development theories?

A. La Palombara and Myron Weiner
B. Peter K. Merkl
C. Harry Eckstein
D. Jean Blondel

24. Which of the following statements are not correct ?

1. The Swiss Federal Tribunal has the power to declare unconstitutional a law passed by the Federal Legislature.
2. The Communist Party is banned in the U.S.A.
3. The Constitution of India on the date of its commencement did have a provision that the advice of the Council of Ministers would be binding on the President.
4. Tories in England are known as Conservatives.

Select the correct answer from the codes given below :

Codes :

A. 1 and 2 B. 2 and 3
C. 2 and 4 D. 1 and 3

25. "There can be no comparison between the positions of number one and numbers two, three or four." Who said this about the British Prime Minister?

A. Harold Laski
B. Margaret Thatcher
C. Harold Wilson
D. Winston Churchill

26. Given below are two statements, one labelled as Assertion (A) and the other labelled as Reason (R) :

Assertion (A): Once the leaders reach the pinnacle of power, nothing can bring them down.

Reason (R) : The majority of human beings, according to Michels, are apathetic, indolent and slavish.

A. Both (A) and (R) are true and (R) is the correct explanation of (A).

B. Both (A) and (R) are true but (R) is not the correct explanation of (A).
C. (A) is true, but (R) is false.
D. (A) is false, but (R) is true.

27. Which of the following pairs are not correctly matched?

1. Pareto — Circulation of elites
2. Mosca — Theory of the masses
3. Michels — Concept of mass mind
4. Gasset — Political formula

Select the correct answer from the codes given below :

Codes :

A. 2 and 4   B. 1 and 2
C. 3 and 4   D. 2 and 3

28. Which of the following countries have dual citizenship–National citizenship and State citizenship?

A. India and U.S.A.
B. India and Switzerland
C. Switzerland and U.S.A.
D. U.S.A. and U.K.

29. Which of the following statements are not correct?

1. The U.S. President can seek election to the office of President for any number of times.
2. The President of India has been sending messages to Parliament.
3. Two-thirds members of Rajya Sabha retire every two years.
4. The residuary powers rest with the States in the United States of America.

Select the correct answer from the codes given below:

Codes :

A. 1, 2 and 4   B. 1, 2 and 3
C. 2, 3 and 4   D. 1, 3 and 4

30. The elite theory was first started in

A. the United States of America
B. the United Kingdom
C. Central and Western European Countries
D. Australia

31. The Preamble of the Constitution of India enshrines the ideals of liberty, equality and fraternity – ideals mainly inspired by the

A. Russian Revolution
B. Irish Revolution
C. French Revolution
D. Cultural Revolution

32. The name of a candidate for the Office of President of India is proposed by

A. any five citizens of India
B. any five Members of the Parliament
C. any fifty Members of the Electoral College
D. any ten members of the Electoral College

33. Which of the following Articles were not part of the original Constitution of India?

1. Art. 52A   2. Art. 51A
3. Art. 14   4. Art. 300A

Select the correct answer from the codes given below :

A. 1 and 2   B. 1 and 3
C. 2 and 3   D. 2 and 4

34. Who among the following former Presidents of India kept the 'Indian Post Office Amendment Bill' pending ?

A. Zakir Hussain
B. V.V. Giri
C. Zail Singh
D. Dr. Shanker Dayal Sharma

35. Who said 'All Communalism is harmful'? The logic of minority Communalism is separatism, and majority communalism culminates in Fascism?

A. Bhikhu Parekh   B. T.N. Madan
C. Bipin Chandra   D. Ashish Nandy

36. Who wrote the book, "Democracy and Discontent" ?

A. James Manor   B. Atul Kohli
C. Zoya Hasan   D. MSA Rao

37. Who emphasized the emergence of "a market polity" in India ?

A. Stanley A. Kochanek
B. James Manor
C. Morris-Jones
D. Paul Brass

38. Who described the nature of Indian State as 'incremental democratic modernization'?

A. Morris John
B. Rajni Kothari
C. Francine Frankel
D. Susan and Lloyd Rudolph

39. An alliance of national elites and the entrepreneurial class as a basis of development at the Centre does not preclude re-distributive concessions automatically.' Who said?

A. Partha Chatterjee
B. Atul Kohli
C. Yogendra Yadav
D. Paul Brass

40. Match List-I with List-II and choose the correct answer from the codes given below :

List-I Books	List-II Authors
(*a*) Language, Religion and Politics	1. Jagdish Bhagwati
(*b*) Party building in a New Nation	2. Paul Brass
(*c*) The Painful Transition: Bourgeois Democracy in India	3. Myron Weiner
(*d*) India in Transition: Freeing the Economy	4. Achin Vanaik

Codes :

	(*a*)	(*b*)	(*c*)	(*d*)
A.	2	3	4	1
B.	3	2	1	4
C.	1	4	3	2
D.	4	1	2	3

41. Identify the correct sequence in which the following Committees were appointed. Use the code given below :

1. Balwant Rai Mehta Committee
2. L.M. Singhvi Committee
3. G.V.K. Rao Committee
4. Ashok Mehta Committee

Codes :

A. 1, 4, 3, 2
B. 2, 3, 1, 4
C. 3, 2, 4, 1
D. 4, 1, 2, 3

42. Assertion (A) : Political parties in India have expanded their reach but their legitimacy has been deeply eroded.

Reason (R) : The consolidation of the party system at the State level cannot be aggregated at the National level.

A. Both (A) and (R) are true and (R) is the correct explanation of (A).
B. Both (A) and (R) are true and (R) is not the correct explanation of (A).
C. (A) is true, but (R) is false.
D. (A) is false, but (R) is true.

43. Which among the following Articles of the Constitution of India has ensured through legislation the participation of workers in management?

A. Article 42
B. Article 43
C. Article 43A
D. Article 49A

44. Who among the following termed Art. 356 as a "safety valve"?

A. Dr. Rajendra Prasad
B. Dr. B.R. Ambedkar
C. Jawaharlal Nehru
D. Sardar Vallabhbhai Patel

45. Match List-I with List-II and choose the correct answer from the codes given below :

List-I Books	List-II Authors
(*a*) Dalit Visions : The Anti-Caste Movement and the Construction of Indian Identity	1. Zoya Hasan
(*b*) Peasant Movements in India	2. V. Venkatesan
(*c*) Foreign Identities, Gender Communities and the State (Ed.)	3. Gail Omvedt
(*d*) Institutionalising Panchayati Raj in India	4. D.N. Dhanagre

Codes :

	(*a*)	(*b*)	(*c*)	(*d*)
A.	2	3	4	1
B.	3	4	1	2
C.	1	2	3	4
D.	4	1	2	3

46. Consider the following statements about Civil Service in a developing society :
1. It should act as an instrument of change.
2. It should have concern for social equity.
3. It should have common concern for vested interests.
4. It should be politically neutral.

Select the correct statements from the codes given below :

A. 1, 2, 3 and 4 B. 1, 3 and 4
C. 1, 2 and 4 D. 2, 3 and 4

47. Match List-I with List-II and choose the correct answer from the codes given below :

List-I	List-II
(*a*) Span of attention	1. Mooney and Reiley
(*b*) Scalar process	2. F.W. Taylor
(*c*) Human Relations Theory	3. V.A. Graicunas
(*d*) Functional Foremanship	4. Elton Mayo

Codes :

	(*a*)	(*b*)	(*c*)	(*d*)
A.	3	4	1	2
B.	3	1	4	2
C.	2	1	4	3
D.	1	3	2	4

48. Which one of the following was not included as a principle of administration by Willoughby in his 'Principles of Public Administration'?

A. General and overhead administration
B. Coordination
C. Finance
D. Personnel administration

49. The principle of unity of command mainly ensures

A. Accountability B. Specialization
C. Acceptability D. Coordination

50. Which one of the following is not one of the main characteristics of Taylor's scientific management?

A. Time and motion studies
B. Participation in decision making
C. Differential piece-rate system
D. Functional foremanship

51. Who among the following has called Weber's ideal type of bureaucracy as unsuitable for developing societies?

A. H. Simon
B. Chester I. Barnard
C. Fred W. Riggs
D. Dwight Waldo

52. The Committee on Assurances of the Parliament of India is an instrument of

A. Executive Control
B. Judicial Control
C. Civil-Society Control
D. Legislative Control

53. According to Herbert Simon, if a decision is directed towards individual's goal, it is

A. Organizationally rational
B. Personally rational
C. Objectively rational
D. Subjectively rational

54. The most logical criterion to distinguish a line function from staff is

A. the functional relationship
B. the authority relationship
C. the grouping of functions
D. the departmentalization

55. Central Vigilance Commission was set up on the recommendations of

A. First Administrative Reforms Commission
B. Gorwala Committee Report
C. Kripalani Committee Report
D. Santhanam Committee Report

56. The Lokpal and Lokayukta Bill 1968 passed by the Lok Sabha lapsed because

A. Rajya Sabha rejected the Bill
B. President withheld the Bill
C. Joint Committee of the two Houses rejected the Bill
D. of early Dissolution of Fourth Lok Sabha

57. Which one of the following committee's report said that Community Development Programme and National Extension Service had failed to evoke popular enthusiasm?

A. Sarkaria Committee Report
B. L.M. Singhvi Committee Report

C. G.V.K. Rao Committee Report
D. Balwant Rai Mehta Committee Report

58. Which one of the following was not included by C. Rajagopalachari in the list of six fundamental requirements of a good administrator?
A. Character
B. Capacity to judge matters
C. Expertise in technical matters
D. Firmness in decision making

59. Santhanam Committee on Prevention of Corruption was appointed in
A. 1961 B. 1962
C. 1963 D. 1964

60. Given below are two statements, one labelled as Assertion (A) and the other labelled as Reason (R).

Assertion (A) : Practical application of unity of command is not always possible.

Reason (R) : Technical and administrative tasks require different kinds of supervision.

Select the correct answer from the codes given below :
A. Both (A) and (R) are individually true and (R) is the correct explanation of (A).
B. Both (A) and (R) are individually true, but (R) is not the correct explanation of (A).
C. (A) is true, but (R) is false.
D. (A) is false, but (R) is true.

61. What is neo-realism?
A. An attempt to ignore the unpleasant realities of the world.
B. An attempt to restate the basic ideas of realism in a more 'scientific' form.
C. A claim that international society is basically orderly and peaceful.
D. A claim that individual human nature is central to an understanding of international politics.

62. Match List-I with List-II and select the correct answer from the codes below :

List-I (Author)	List-II (Book)
(*a*) Hedley Bull	1. Failed States
(*b*) Noam Chomsky	2. Conflict and Defense
(*c*) Robert Kaplan	3. Anarchial Society
(*d*) Kenneth Boulding	4. Monsoon

Codes :

	(*a*)	(*b*)	(*c*)	(*d*)
A.	3	1	4	2
B.	2	3	1	4
C.	1	4	3	2
D.	4	2	1	3

63. Arrange the following international politics theorists in a chronological order from the codes given below :
1. Reinhold Niebuhr
2. Immanuel Kant
3. Antonio Gramsci
4. Robert W. Cox

Codes :
A. 3, 4, 1, 2
B. 4, 1, 2, 3
C. 1, 2, 3, 4
D. 2, 3, 1, 4

64. What does RMA stand for?
A. Revolution in Martial Affairs
B. Revolution in Military Affairs
C. Referendum in Military Affairs
D. Raison d'etat in Mass Administration

65. What does Raison d'etat mean?
A. The national interest
B. The State ought to act reasonably at all times.
C. Citizens need to be given very good reasons for obeying the State.
D. Citizens should consume as many raisins as possible for a good and healthy life.

66. Why is reform of the Security Council problematic?
A. Enlarging the permanent membership could impair decision making.
B. None of the existing permanent members are keen to give up their seats.
C. It is difficult to make an uncontroversial case for any of the potential new permanent members.
D. All of the above.

67. Structural adjustment programmes require that
   A. Governments of poor countries should adopt privatization and other 'liberalizing' measures.
   B. States with weak economies should redistribute more resources to the poor.
   C. Governments of poor countries should knock down all ugly or dilapidated buildings.
   D. Ministers in under-performing countries should go on diets and keep fit.

68. Bandung Conference held in 1955 had the participation of representatives from
   A. Twenty two Asian countries
   B. Eighty Afro-Asian countries
   C. Twenty six African countries
   D. Twenty nine Afro-Asian countries

69. Who said, "Thus far the chief purpose of our military establishment has been to win wars. From now on its chief purpose must be to avert them."?
   A. Paul Nitze   B. George Kennan
   C. Bernard Brodie   D. Robert Jervis

70. Arrange the following treaties and agreements in a chronological order. Select the answer from the codes given below :
   1. Indo-US Nuclear Treaty
   2. Indo-Soviet Friendship Treaty
   3. Tashkent Agreement
   4. Shimla Agreement

   Codes :
   A. 3, 2, 4, 1
   B. 2, 3, 1, 4
   C. 1, 4, 2, 3
   D. 4, 1, 3, 2

71. Expand SORT.
   A. Strategic Offensive Reduction Treaty
   B. State Organization Replan Treaty
   C. Strategic Order Reorganization Treaty
   D. Security Organization Replan Treaty

72. Which of the following statements are correct?
   1. India has signed the NPT.
   2. China has not signed the NPT.
   3. India and Pakistan have not signed the NPT.
   4. NPT has been signed by Iran, North Korea.
   A. All are correct.
   B. All are false.
   C. 3 & 4 are correct.
   D. 1 & 2 are correct.

73. Identify which of the following are correct statements :
   1. India is a member of the Indian Ocean Rim Association for Regional Cooperation [IOR-ARC].
   2. [IOR-ARC] helps better relations with Pakistan.
   3. It defines the Exclusive Economic Zones.
   4. Indian Ocean has no sea piracy.

   Codes :
   A. 1 and 2 are correct.
   B. 3 and 4 are correct.
   C. 1 and 3 are correct.
   D. 2 and 4 are correct.

74. The Axis of evil is a phrase deliberately used by President George W. Bush in January 2002 to characterize
   A. Iran, North Korea and Iraq
   B. Taliban, Al-Queda and LeT
   C. Cuba, Venezuela, Nicaragua
   D. Pakistan, Afghanistan, Sri Lanka

75. Martin Wight emphasized three philosophical traditions of International politics, they are
   A. Realism, Liberalism, Marxism
   B. Realism, Rationalism, Revolutionism
   C. Radicalism, Realism, Religion
   D. Neo-Realism, Neo-Liberalism, Constructivism

ANSWERS

1	2	3	4	5	6	7	8	9	10
B	C	B	B	C	B	B	C	D	D

11	12	13	14	15	16	17	18	19	20
C	D	C	B	A	A	B	B	C	C
21	**22**	**23**	**24**	**25**	**26**	**27**	**28**	**29**	**30**
B	B	A	D	D	A	A	C	B	C
31	**32**	**33**	**34**	**35**	**36**	**37**	**38**	**39**	**40**
C	D	D	C	C	B	C	B	B	A
41	**42**	**43**	**44**	**45**	**46**	**47**	**48**	**49**	**50**
A	B	C	B	B	C	B	B	A	B
51	**52**	**53**	**54**	**55**	**56**	**57**	**58**	**59**	**60**
C	D	B	B	D	D	D	C	B	A
61	**62**	**63**	**64**	**65**	**66**	**67**	**68**	**69**	**70**
B	A	D	B	A	D	A	D	C	A
71	**72**	**73**	**74**	**75**					
A	C	C	A	B					

SOME SELECTED EXPLANATORY ANSWERS

1. Originating from the Greek workd 'Theoria', theory means a well-focused mental look taken at something in a state of contemplation with the intent to grasp or understand it.

3. In his famous essay *Two Concepts of Liberty,* written in 1958, Berlin distinguishes between two kinds of liberty, negative and positive. Negative liberty he defines as the absence of obstacles to someone's actions, positive liberty as personal autonomy, opportunity and capacity to act. While Berlin grants that both concepts of liberty represent valid human ideals, he points out that historically, the positive concept of liberty has been more susceptible to political abuse. In Berlin's view, negative liberty, the principle of non-interference, is superior to positive liberty in guaranteeing the freedom of individuals within a society.

5. In 1956, Mao personally launched a mass movement under the classical slogan "Let a hundred flowers bloom, let the hundred schools of thought contend".

6. The term Marxism-Leninism, invented by Stalin, was not used until after Lenin's death in 1924. It soon came to be used in Stalin's Soviet Union to refer to what he described as 'orthodox Marxism', which increasingly came to mean what Stalin himself to say about political and economic issues. Essentially, Marxism-Leninism was the 'official' ideology of the Soviet state and of all communist parties loyal to Stalin and his successors.

8. *The Republic* is a Socratic dialogue written by Plato around 380 BC concerning the definition of justice and the order and character of the just city-state and the just man. It is Plato's best-known work and has proven to be one of the most intellectually and historically influential works of philosophy and political theory.

10. In Machiavelli's *Prince* (1515) men dominate a world of violence, action and uncertainty. Successful Princes need to be strong and wily, like the lion and the fox, both metaphors for male prowess, intelligence and strength. Boldness, strength, 'reason' are qualities that seventeenth- and eighteenth-century political theory associates with male prowess. Machiavelli writes: 'It is better to be impetuous than cautious because Fortune is a woman and it is necessary, in order to keep her under, to cuff and maul her.' Women favour strong men and desire to submit to the bold. Men therefore know their strength through their ability in battle and through their impact on women.

12. The conception of the "general will" plays a very important part in Rousseau's system. What is the General will? It is the will of all the citizens when they are willing not their own private interests but the general good. According to Rousseau, the will of the sovereign which is always right is the "general will." Every individual is allowed to will his own will and the majority will is formed. The general will is for the general welfare. The social contract involves that whoever refuses to obey the general will shall be forced to do so. This means nothing less than that he will be forced to be free. This idea of being forced to be free is very metaphysical in nature. Rousseau says that the General will is not identical with the will of the majority. He distinguishes between our will for our selfish ends and our will for the general good. For common interest everybody is allowed to convey his will and thus the majority will is found, when we demand something not for us but for everyone, our will is general.

14. (*a*) Monarchy—Tyranny
(*b*) Aristocracy—Oligarchy
(*c*) Polity—Democracy
(*d*) Ideal State—Timocracy (First stage)

16. 1. Bertallanfy—a set of elements standing in interaction
2. Hall and Fagen—a set of interactions
3. Easton—a whole which is compounded of many parts
4. Colin—a set of objects together with relationships between the objects and their attributes

17. Flow Model of System Analysis: System analysis is described as a "flow model" of the political system as it is a cyclic process. It involves production of outputs by authorities, response by the members of the society to these outputs, communication of information about the response to the authorities in the form of new demands or inputs and possible succeeding action by the authorities.

18. Structural-functional analysis is an off shoot of systems analysis and it is based on the concept of the political system. As the name suggests, this analysis revolves around two key components-structures and functions. This model was developed by Gabriel Almond and J. Coleman on the basis of Talcott Parson's system analysis in the field of sociology.

20. Writing in the second half of the sixties, the thinkers clearly shifted from the infrastructural studies to an analysis of the will and capacity of political actors and institutions. Political modernization was not an end-product but a continuing process—"a persistent capacity", in the words of Halpern, "for coping with a permanent revolution". A whole group of writers—Eisenstadt, Halpern, Huntington, Diamont, Holt and Turner, Nye and others—developed this new approach to the study of political modernization variously known as "will and capacity" approach, "problem-solving capacity", "institutionalisation", "ability to sustain new goals", etc.

21. The Clash of Civilizations: In 1996, Samuel Huntington published his controversial book *The Clash of Civilizations,* in which he argues that we have reached a phase in history, following the end of the Cold War, when the clash of ideologies has ended. In his view cultural identity will become more important in determining friendships within and conflicts between "civilizations." With the decline in the influence of Western nations the world will be dominated by six "civilizations": the West, Islam, a Confucian bloc, a Hindu bloc, Latin America and eastern Orthodox Christianity. The "central focus of conflict for the immediate future will be between the West and several Islamic-Confucian states."

25. Some important statements about British Prime Minister by leading authors:

- **Benemy—**The Prime Minister is an elected monarch.
- **Winston Churchill—**There can be no comparison between the position of number one and numbers two, three or four.
- **John Marriot—**The PM is the pivot around which the whole political machinery revolves.
- **Lowell—**The PM is the core of the British constitutional system.
- **Gladstone—**Nowhere in the world, has so small a substance, cast so large a shadow.
- **John Morley—**The PM occupies a position which as long as it lasts, is one of exceptional and peculiar authority.
- **Asquith—**The office is what its holder chooses and is able to make of it.
- **Jennings—**All roads of the constitution, lead to the Prime Minister.
- **Greaves—**The government is the master of the country and the PM is the master of the government.

28. In spite of a dual polity, the Constitution of India, like that of Canada, adopted the system of single citizenship. There is only Indian Citizenship and no separate state citizenship. All citizens irrespective of the state in which they are born or reside enjoy the same rights all over the country. The other federal states like US, Switzerland and Australia have dual citizenship, that is, national citizenship as well as state citizenship.

30. The theory of political elites originated in Europe. Renowned European thinkers like Vilfred Pareto and Gactano Mosca, Roberto Michels and Ortega Y. Gasset discussed the relationship of the theory with fascism and democracy. They also applied the theory to ruling classes. Later the theory was widely discussed by the social scientists in the U.S.A. American economists like J.A. Schumpeter, political scientists like Harold D. Lasswell and sociologists like C. Wright Mills added much to the discussion of the theory.

31. Our Constitution was influenced by the ideas of Equality, Liberty and Fraternity, the three slogans released by the French Revolution (1789), the American Declaration of Independence (1776) and Gandhian thoughts.

32. *The Presidential and Vice-Presidential Election Act* provides that the nomination of each Presidential candidate should be proposed by at least ten electors and seconded by another ten electors of the electoral college. In the Vice-Presidential election, the nomination should be proposed and seconded by five members each of Parliament.

33. **Article 51A:** The Fundamental duties were added by 42nd Amendment, 1976 by inserting Art. 51A and IVA under the Directive Principles of State Policy. This means these Duties are not enforceable by court in case of non-fulfilment by citizens. However, the State can enforce them through appropriate laws, enacted by legislatures.

The Status of Right to Property : The right to property has been taken away as a Fundamental right and made a legal right under Art. 300A by 44th Amendment, 1978. This means that, now in case of violation of this right, a person can have a legal remedy only through ordinary courts, whereas in case of violation of fundamental right a person can directly seek remedy either in the High Courts or in the Supreme Court.

40. (*a*) Language, Religion and Politics—Paul Brass

(*b*) Party building in a New Nation—Myron Weiner

(*c*) The Painful Transition: Bourgeois Democracy in India—Achin Vanaik

(*d*) India in Transition: Freeing the Economy—Jagdish Bhagwati

41. 1. Balwant Rai Mehta Committee—1957
2. Ashok Mehta Committee—1977
3. G.V.K. Rao Committee—1985
4. L.M. Singhvi Committee—1986

43. Article 43A which has been inserted in the Constitution by the Constitution (Forty-second Amendment) Act, 1976 is a firm step towards transformation of our national economy into socialism. This will receive further support from addition of the word 'Socialist' in the Preamble to the Constitution of India by the Forty-second Amendment of the Constitution. Article 43A of the Constitution envisages that steps should be taken either by suitable legislative measure or in any other way to secure the participation of workers in the management of undertakings, establishments or other organisations engaged in any industry. No discrimination is to be made whether the undertaking, establishment or organisation in the industry belongs to a private individual, a company or a State.

44. The emergency powers in the Indian Constitution enable India, under certain circumstances, to transform itself into a unitary state. There are three types of constitutional emergency powers that combine to create this centralized pattern of federalism: (1) an emergency, under Article 356, arising out of a failure of the constitutional machinery in a state; (2) a national emergency, under Article 352, involving the security of India or of any part threatened by war, external aggression, or internal disturbances; and (3) a special emergency, under Article 360, involving a threat to financial security, stability, or credit.

45. (*a*) Dalit Visions : The Anti-Caste Movement and the Construction of Indian Identity—Gail Omvedt
(*b*) Peasant Movements in India—D.N. Dhanagre
(*c*) Foreign Identities, Gender Communities and the State (Ed.)—Zoya Hasan
(*d*) Institutionalising Panchayati Raj in India—V. Venkatesan

47. (*a*) Span of attention—V.A. Graicunas
(*b*) Scalar process—Money and Reiley
(*c*) Human Relations Theory—Elton Mayo
(*d*) Functional Foremanship—F.W. Taylor

48. Earlier American writers on public administration were much influenced by business thought and organisation but they found the categories enumerated by Fayol and his followers too abstract and narrow to encompass the significant processes of public administration and tried to modify them suitably. The earliest of such attempts was that of Willoughby who divided his well-known work *Principles of Public Administration* into five major sections or topics, namely, (1) general or overhead administration (including allocation of functions, direction, supervision and control), (2) organisation, *i.e.*, building up of the administrative structure, (3) personnel management, (4) materials and supply and (5) finance.

49. **Unit of Command:** The principle of unity of command states that a subordinate should report to only one manager. Without unity of command, conflicting demands and priorities from multiple managers can create problems.

50. F.W. Taylor (1856-1915) was an American engineer who invented work study and founded the scientific management approach to the world of work (sometimes known as Taylorism) at the beginning of the twentieth century. In 1878, he takes up an unskilled job at Midvale Steel Works where he does his first experiments. In 1881, he gains a masters degree in Mechanical Engineering. He placed great emphasis on analysing the constituent operations of a task down to the finer details. He advocated the concept of functional foremanship, time and motion study, differential piece rate plan, and exception principle. His main books are: (i) A Piece Rate System (1895), (ii) Shop management (1903), (iii) Art of Cutting Metals (1906) and (iv) Principles of Scientific Management (1911).

51. Fred W. Riggs: He observed the Wiber's ideal model of bureaucracy is not particularly relevant to the study of developing countries as it assumes a relatively autonomous administrative system. In the developed countries like USA, UK & France, the administrative structures enjoy sufficient autonomy from other social structures. In contrast, in the developing countries, they are less autonomous. Thus, Riggs said that Weber's ideal model does not facilitate the study of interaction between organisation and its environment. Accordingly, he advocated the 'ecological approach' to the study of public administration.

53. Simon explains that there are six different types of rationality, viz, objective, subjective, conscious, deliberate, organisational and personal. Simon differentiates between different types of rationality. A decision is:

1. Objectively rational where it is correct behaviour for maximising given values in a given situation;
2. Subjectively rational if the decision maximises attainment relative to knowledge of the subject;
3. Consciously rational where adjustment of means to ends is a conscious process;
4. Deliberately rational to the degree that the adjustment of means of ends has been deliberately sought;
5. Organisationally rational to the extent that it is aimed at the organisation's goals; and
6. Personally rational if the decision is directed to individual's goals.

54. Principal Distinctions between Line and Staff Authority

Line Manager	Staff Manager
Generalist	A myopic provincial fellow
Directs others	Assists
Delegates	Serves
Trains subordinates	Investigates
Exerts control	Plans
Uses sanctions	Solves special problems
Has veto powers	Supports line effort
Makes operating decisions	Provides ideas
Bears final responsibility	Has special expertise

55. The Central Vigilance Commission (CVC) was set up in 1964 in pursuance of the recommendation of the Santhanam Committee for the prevention of corruption. The CVC is a non-statutory body whose jurisdiction and functions can be amended not by parliament but by a government order. It deals with cases of corruption against gazetted officers of central government, union territories, officers of PSUs, and nationalized banks. It is independent of government control and works as an autonomous body like the union public service commission. Its role is merely advisory.

57. Balwant Rai Mehta Committee: In 1957, the government appointed a committee to review the laws passed by several states to implement Panchayati Raj. The Committee gave its report in 1958 recommending a three tier structure of local rural government.

These included:

1. Village Panchayat at Village level.
2. Panchayati Samiti at Block Level.
3. Zila Parishad at District level.

59. In 1962, the Central Government appointed a Committee on Prevention of Corruption under the chairmanship of K. Santhanam to review the existing arrangements for checking corruption in the public services and to advise on practical steps to be taken to make anti-corruption measures more effective. The Santhanam Committee recommended the setting up of a Central Vigilance Commission. The Government accepted this recommendation in February 1964, and as a result the Central Vigilance Commission was set up, headed by a Central Vigilance Commissioner.

62. (*a*) Hedley Bull—Anarchial Society
(*b*) Noam Chomsky—Failed States
(*c*) Robert Kaplan—Monsoon
(*d*) Kenneth Boulding—Conflict and Defence

65. The national interest, often referred to by the French expression raison d'Etat (English: reason of the State), is a country's goals and ambitions whether economic, military, or cultural. The concept is an important one in international relations where pursuit of the national interest is the foundation of the realist school.

68. The Bandung Conference was a meeting of representatives from twenty-nine African and Asian nations, held in Bandung (Indonesia) in 1955. Its aim was to promote economic and political cooperation and to oppose colonialism. The Conference was sponsored by Burma (Myanmar), India, Indonesia, Ceylon (Sri Lanka) and Pakistan.

70. (i) Tashkent Agreement—1966
(ii) Indo-Soviet Friendship Treaty—1971
(iii) Shimla Agreement—1972
(iv) Indo-US Nuclear Treaty—2005

71. The Treaty between the United States of America and the Russian Federation on Strategic Offensive Reductions (SORT), also known as the Treaty of Moscow, was a strategic arms reduction treaty between the United States and Russia that was in force from June 2003 until February 2011 when it was superseded by the New START treaty.

73. The Indian Ocean Rim Association for Regional Cooperation was launched in Mauritius in 1997. The Association comprises 19 member states: Australia, Bangladesh, India, Indonesia, Iran, Kenya, Madagascar, Malaysia, Mauritius, Mozambique, Oman, Seychelles, Singapore, South Africa, Sri Lanka, Tanzania, Thailand, UAE and Yemen. Egypt, Japan, China, France, and the United Kingdom are dialogue partners. The Association aims to facilitate trade and investment.

74. The "Axis of Evil" is a term used to describe the countries Iraq, Iran and North Korea. The phrase was introduced by President George W. Bush in his 29 January, 2002 State of the Union address. The three countries were grouped as threats to the United States capable of terrorism and nuclear attack.

Previous Paper (Solved)

UGC-NET POLITICAL SCIENCE, JUNE 2012

PAPER–II

Note: *This paper contains* ***fifty*** *(50) multiple-choice questions, each question carrying* ***two*** *(2) marks. Attempt* ***all*** *of them.*

1. Which of the following book is not authored by Karl Marx?
A. German Ideology
B. Critique of the Gotha Programme
C. Paris Manuscripts
D. Science of Logic

2. Who wrote "Over himself, over his own body and mind, the individual is sovereign"?
A. J.S. Mill
B. M.K. Gandhi
C. Jeremy Bentham
D. Robert Nozick

3. Rajni Kothari's book 'Politics in India' is written on the basis of the methodology of:
A. Structural functionalism
B. Normative theory
C. Marxism
D. Utilitarianism

4. Who is the first modern political thinker who deliberately ignores Aristotle?
A. Machiavelli B. Bodin
C. Hobbes D. Locke

5. Match List-I with List-II and select the correct answer from the codes given below :

List-I	*List-II*
(*a*) Dictatorship of the proletariat	(*i*) Gramsci
(*b*) Communist Party	(*ii*) Marx
(*c*) Hegemony	(*iii*) Lenin
(*d*) Polycentricism	(*iv*) Togliatti

Codes :

	(*a*)	(*b*)	(*c*)	(*d*)
A.	(*ii*)	(*iii*)	(*i*)	(*iv*)
B.	(*i*)	(*ii*)	(*iii*)	(*iv*)
C.	(*iii*)	(*i*)	(*ii*)	(*iv*)
D.	(*ii*)	(*i*)	(*iii*)	(*iv*)

6. Match List-I with List-II and select the correct answer from the codes given below:

List-I	*List-II*
(*a*) Twentieth century Jacobinism	(*i*) Gandhi
(*b*) Voluntary Poverty	(*ii*) Aurobindo
(*c*) I was born a Hindu but will not die as one	(*iii*) Ambedkar
(*d*) Integrated theory of evolution	(iv) M.N. Roy

Codes :

	(*a*)	(*b*)	(*c*)	(*d*)
A.	(*i*)	(*ii*)	(*iii*)	(*iv*)
B.	(*iv*)	(*i*)	(*iii*)	(*ii*)
C.	(*ii*)	(*iii*)	(*i*)	(*iv*)
D.	(*iii*)	(*i*)	(*ii*)	(*iv*)

7. Gandhi described himself as a:
A. Liberal
B. Socialist
C. Social Democrat
D. Philosophical Anarchist

8. The doctrine of overlapping consensus is advocated by:
A. Berlin B. Barry
C. Nozick D. Rawls

9. Who among the following first developed the concept of general systems theory?
A. Ludwig Von Bertallanfy
B. Colin Cherry
C. Robert K. Merton
D. Talcott Parsons

10. Structural functionalism as a method was developed to study the politics of:
A. Advanced capitalism
B. Developed socialism
C. Modern totalitarianism
D. Politics of developing countries

11. C. Wright Mill's 'The Power Elite' is a study of the contemporary politics of:
A. China
B. The United States of America
C. The Soviet Union
D. Great Britain

12. Who among the following identified the crises in political development on the basis of his study of England?
A. A.F.K. Organski
B. Lucian W. Pyea
C. Edward Shils
D. David Apter

13. Which one of the following pairs is not correctly matched?

A. C.W. Mills	The Power Elite
B. T.B. Bottomore	Elites and Society
C. Pareto	The Ruling Class
D. Ortega Y Gasset	The Revolt of the Masses

14. Who among the following postulated the law "officials make work for each other"?
A. Max Weber B. F.M. Marx
C. H. Finer D. N. Parkinson

15. Which of the following pairs is not correct?

A. U.S.A.	Double citizenship
B. India	Procedure established by law
C. Australia	Unitary form of Govt.
D. Switzerland	Plural Executive

16. Michels' Iron law of oligarchy was formulated on the basis of the study of:
A. German Social Democratic Party
B. British Labour Party
C. Democratic Party of the U.S.A.
D. Communist Party of the Soviet Union

17. Montesquieu's theory of separation of powers emphasises primarily on:
A. Accountability
B. Efficiency
C. Transparency
D. Liberty

Directions (Qs. 18-21): Each of the following four items consist of two statements, one labelled as Assertion (A) and the other labelled as Reason (R).
A. Both (A) and (R) are true and (R) is the correct explanation of (A).
B. Both (A) and (R) are true and (R) is not the correct explanation of (A).
C. (A) is true, but (R) is false.
D. (A) is false, but (R) is true.

18. **Assertion (A):** The Information Technology has made Staff Agency indispensable.

Reason (R): Staff Agency assists the Line Agency in decision-making.

19. **Assertion (A):** While declaring war on terrorism the US asserted that the states which were not on the side of the US were against it.

Reason (R): In the wake of war on terrorism the US denied states the liberty to be neutral.

20. **Assertion (A):** Ambedkar was in favour of separate electorate for depressed classes.

Reason (R): He was in agreement with Gandhi.

21. **Assertion (A):** The presidential system is successful only in the U.S.A.

Reason (R): The United States of America is the only nation with minor contradictions that ensures the success of the presidential system.

22. Which one of the following was not associated with the Hindustan Republic Association?
A. Chandrashekhar Azad
B. Jogesh Chandra Chatterjee
C. Aurobindo Ghosh
D. Bhagat Singh

23. Who gave the Indian National Congress the Constitution and made it a mass and cadre party?
A. Tilak B. Gokhale
C. Motilal Nehru D. Gandhi

24. Who appoints the Inter-State Council?
A. The President of India
B. The Union Cabinet
C. The Prime Minister
D. The Union Home Minister

25. Identify the States whose State Assemblies are meet at places other than the State capital:
A. Jammu-Kashmir and Madhya Pradesh
B. Madhya Pradesh and Karnataka
C. Maharashtra and Andhra Pradesh
D. Jammu-Kashmir and Maharashtra

26. Which amendment of the Constitution of India limits the number of Ministers?
A. 73rd B. 86th
C. 87th D. 91st

27. Which one of the following committees is not associated with Panchayati Raj in India?
A. Sadiq Ali Committee
B. Dinesh Goswami Committee
C. L.M. Singhvi Committee
D. P.K. Thungan Committee

28. Identify the correct sequence in which the following Deputy Prime Ministers were appointed in India?
(*i*) Sardar Vallabhbhai Patel
(*ii*) Ch. Devi Lal
(*iii*) Ch. Charan Singh
(*iv*) Morarji Desai
Codes:
A. (*i*), (*iii*), (*iv*), (*ii*)
B. (*i*), (*iv*), (*ii*), (*iii*)
C. (*iv*), (*i*), (*ii*), (*iii*)
D. (*i*), (*iv*), (*iii*), (*iv*)

29. Who of the following constituted an oligrachy within the Constituent Assembly of India?
A. Nehru, Patel, Prasad, Azad
B. Ambedkar, B.N. Rao, K.M. Munshi, Nehru
C. Patel, Azad, Munshi, Ambedkar
D. Krishnamachari, Pannikar, Nehru, Patel

30. Who describes Indian economy as "Bullock Cart Capitalism"?
A. Rajni Kothari
B. Atul Kohli
C. Granville Austin
D. Lloyd and Sussane Rudolph

31. Who among the following defines Public Administration as "the activities of the Executive Branches of the National, State and Local Government"?
A. Morstein Marx
B. Luther Gullick
C. Herbert A. Simon
D. Marshal E. Dimock

32. Public Accounts Committee has the following Members. Tick the correct answer :

	Lok Sabha	Rajya Sabha	Total
A.	10	5	15
B.	15	7	22
C.	11	5	16
D.	17	10	27

33. 'Span of Control' is also known as:
A. The Repair Boss
B. The Gang Boss
C. Military Type of Foreman
D. Business Frontline

34. The word 'Bureaucracy' was first coined by:
A. Max Weber
B. Alexander Pope
C. M. Crozier
D. Vincent de Gournay

35. Which one of the following is the correct function of Staff Agency?
A. Issuing orders to the subordinates
B. Controlling the activities of the subordinates
C. Advising the Chief Executive
D. Providing Institutional Services

36. Which one of the following statements is not correct with regard to Riggs' Perspective of Societies?
A. Fused societies are traditional.
B. Developed societies are diffracted societies.
C. Ascriptive values are found in diffracted societies.
D. Traditional societies have ascriptive values.

37. The Informal Channel of Communication is also known as:
A. Feedback B. Grapevine
C. Loopline D. Nerveline

38. Match the thinkers with the concepts:

Thinker	*Concept*
(*a*) F.W. Taylor	(*i*) Scalar
(*b*) Chester Bernard	(*ii*) Dissatisfier
(*c*) Henry Fayol	(*iii*) Zone of Acceptance
(*d*) Frederic Herzberg	(*iv*) Incentive system

Select the correct order :

Codes:

	(*a*)	(*b*)	(*c*)	(*d*)
A.	(*ii*)	(*iii*)	(*i*)	(*iv*)
B.	(*iii*)	(*ii*)	(*iv*)	(*i*)
C.	(*iv*)	(*ii*)	(*iii*)	(*i*)
D.	(*iv*)	(*iii*)	(*i*)	(*ii*)

39. Who stated that "Budget is a series of Goals with price tags attached"?

A. Wildavsky B. Walpole

C. Betram Gross D. Allen Schick

40. Which one of the following articles of the Constitution empowers Parliament to create an All India Service?

A. Article 300 B. Article 312

C. Article 320 D. Article 410

41. Which of the following resulted from Bretton Woods Conference?

A. United Nations

B. League of Nations

C. Institutions meant for checking nuclear proliferation

D. World Bank and IMF

42. Which of the following is not the basic principle of Hans J. Morgenthou's realism?

A. Politics is rooted in the human nature

B. Politics is autonomous

C. National interest is defined in terms of power

D. Politics is governed by Universal moral values

43. Marshall Plan was meant for:

A. Building the economics of the third world

B. Rebuilding Western European economics

C. Rebuilding the economics of the North-American countries

D. Building the economics of African countries

44. Russia has been given permanent seat on the UN Security Council by virtue of its being:

A. Second most powerful country in the world.

B. Successor State to the former Soviet Union.

C. Largest country in the world in terms of area.

D. One of the oldest civilisations in the world.

45. The major argument of Neo-realism of Kenneth Waltz is that:

A. Structures are more important than actors.

B. Actors play more crucial role than structures.

C. Human nature is crucial element in politics.

D. The states override the constraints imposed by international structures.

46. Non-reciprocity principle of India's policy towards neighbouring countries envisages:

A. hegemonic designs towards neighbouring countries.

B. efforts for improving ties with the neighbouring countries without reciprocity.

C. non-aligned policy posture in the South Asian context.

D. the disciplining of the neighbouring countries.

47. What is the correct chronological order of the developments listed below?

(*i*) Indo-Soviet Treaty of Friendship

(*ii*) India's first Nuclear Explosion at Pokhran

(*iii*) Cuban Missile Crises

(*iv*) Adoption of structural adjustment programme of India

Select the correct answer from the following codes :

A. (*ii*), (*iv*), (*iii*), (*i*)

B. (*iii*), (*i*), (*ii*), (*iv*)

C. (*iv*), (*ii*), (*i*), (*iii*)

D. (*i*), (*iv*), (*iii*), (*ii*)

48. **Assertion (A):** WTO pleads that free trade brings prosperity for all and therefore should be promoted.

Reason (R): Integration of the countries with global economy through the system of trade helps them to export goods abroad as also import goods which they need.

A. (A) and (R) are true and (R) is a correct explanation of (A).
B. Both (A) and (R) are true, but (R) is not the correct explanation of (A).
C. (A) is true, but (R) is false.
D. (A) is false, but (R) is true.

49. 14th SAARC Summit held in New Delhi in 2007, stressed:

A. Improving intra-regional connectivity
B. Commitment to bilateralism within SAARC
C. Connecting SAARC with other regional organisations
D. Not to extend SAARC membership

50. Collective Security System of the UN is based on the principle of:

A. All for one, one for all
B. Imposing sanctions against the belligerent state unilaterally
C. Maintenance of security by the major powers
D. Balance of power to be maintained by state of equilibrium.

ANSWERS

1	2	3	4	5	6	7	8	9	10
D	A	A	C	A	B	D	D	A	D
11	**12**	**13**	**14**	**15**	**16**	**17**	**18**	**19**	**20**
B	B	C	D	C	A	D	B	A	C
21	**22**	**23**	**24**	**25**	**26**	**27**	**28**	**29**	**30**
A	C	D	A	D	D	B	D	A	D
31	**32**	**33**	**34**	**35**	**36**	**37**	**38**	**39**	**40**
C	B	C	D	C	C	B	D	A	B
41	**42**	**43**	**44**	**45**	**46**	**47**	**48**	**49**	**50**
D	D	B	B	A	B	B	A	A	A

PAPER–III

Note: *This paper contains **seventy five** (75) objective type questions of **two** (2) marks each. **All** questions are compulsory.*

1. Which among the following statements is not correct?

A. Post-behavioural political theory interrelates value and fact.
B. Post-behavioural political theory is ethnocentric.
C. Post-behavioural political theory is tied to action and relevancy.
D. Post-behavioural political theory is change oriented.

2. Positive liberalism does not believe in

A. Welfare State
B. Nanny State
C. State as a moral agency
D. Minimal State

3. Marx does not believe in

A. Human consciousness determines social existence
B. Ideas are the reflections of the interplay of material forces
C. The base determines the superstructure
D. Matter is active and dynamic

4. Rawlsian concept of justice is based on
   A. Distributive principle
   B. Agreement principle
   C. Difference principle
   D. Joint method principle

5. The term 'Ideology' was first used in the year
   A. 1789 B. 1792
   C. 1795 D. 1797

6. Satyavir Ki Katha, translated into Gujarati by Gandhiji was from
   A. The Prince
   B. Dialogues of Plato
   C. The Social Contract
   D. War and Peace

7. Who adopted communism to Asiatic form?
   A. M.N. Roy
   B. Mao-Tse-Tung
   C. Lenin
   D. Trotsky

8. Which one among the following statements is correct?
   A. Platonic justice is a legal concept.
   B. The Greek word for Justice is dikaisune.
   C. Platonic justice meant true in word and deed and paying one's debts to Gods and men.
   D. Platonic Justice consists in conformity to the laws and institutions laid down by the Sovereign for his benefit and enforced by his power.

9. Locke's view on 'state of nature' is
   A. Pre-social
   B. Pre-political
   C. Both A and B
   D. Social and Political

10. Which one among the following statements is true?
    A. The Prince deals with providing requirements for the maintenance of political instability in the Republics.
    B. The Discourses expounds the requirements for the maintenance of political instability in principalities.
    C. The Prince is concerned with the qualities of Princes, the Discourses place a greater emphasis on the civic demands on citizens.
    D. None of the above

11. Who said : "Human nature is an ensemble of social relations"?
    A. Gandhiji B. M.N. Roy
    C. Aurobindo D. Mao

12. Aurobindo is mainly famous because of his
    A. Political Ideology
    B. Revolutionary Activities
    C. Life Divine
    D. Association with Mother

13. Given below are two statements, one labelled as Assertion (A) and the other labelled as Reason (R) :

    Assertion (A): Platonic justice represents a disposition to do the right thing.

    Reason (R): It is good to be unjust but bad to suffer injustice.

    Codes :
    A. Both (A) and (R) are true and (R) is the right explanation of (A).
    B. Both (A) and (R) are true but (R) is not the correct explanation of (A).
    C. (A) is true but (R) is false.
    D. (A) is false but (R) is true.

14. Match the List-I with List-II and select the correct answer from the codes given below :

List-I (Authors)	***List-II (Books)***
(*a*) Friedrich Hayek	(*i*) The Politics
(*b*) John Rawls	(*ii*) Idea of Justice
(*c*) Amartya Sen	(*iii*) The Road to Serfdom
(*d*) Plato	(*iv*) A Theory of Justice

Codes:

	(*a*)	(*b*)	(*c*)	(*d*)
A.	(*iv*)	(*i*)	(*iii*)	(*ii*)
B.	(*iii*)	(*iv*)	(*ii*)	(*i*)
C.	(*i*)	(*ii*)	(*iv*)	(*iii*)
D.	(*ii*)	(*iii*)	(*i*)	(*iv*)

15. What is the correct sequence of the following in the Aristotle's Theory of Causation?

(*i*) Material cause
(*ii*) Formal cause
(*iii*) Final cause
(*iv*) Efficient cause

Select the correct answer from the codes given below :

A. (*ii*) (*iv*) (*iii*) (*i*)
B. (*iv*) (*iii*) (*i*) (*ii*)
C. (*iii*) (*i*) (*ii*) (*iv*)
D. (*i*) (*iv*) (*ii*) (*iii*)

16. Who said that the structural-functional approach was weak in change, the social process approach was weak in politics and the comparative history approach was weak in theory?

A. Huntington
B. Paul F. Kress
C. Jean Blondel
D. Samir Amin

17. Who among the following interpreted functionalism as an alternative approach to Marxism?

A. Paul F. Kress
B. Nicholson and Reynolds
C. W.G. Runciman
D. Morton Kaplan

18. Which one of the following has tried to give an essentially engineering orientation to human behaviour?

A. Input-output analysis
B. Structural-functional approach
C. Communications theory
D. Behavioural approach

19. The characteristics of Almond's political system mostly resemble those of the political system(s) of

A. United States of America
B. Scandinavian countries
C. Developing countries
D. Latin American countries

20. Who among the following identifies political development with the "institutionalisation of political organisations and procedures"?

A. Huntington
B. Lucian Pye
C. Organski
D. Almond

21. Which one of the following approaches/ theories was first started as a critique of democracy and socialism?

A. Elite theory
B. Structural-functional approach
C. Communications theory
D. Game theory

22. Who among the following divided the non-competitive party system into one-party authoritarian, one-party pluralistic and one-party totalitarian?

A. Alan Ball
B. La Palombara and Myron Weiner
C. Harry Eckstein
D. James Jupp

23. In which of the following forms of Government is the second chamber as indispensable part of legislature?

A. Presidential
B. Parliamentary
C. Unitary
D. Federal

24. Which one of the following books has a chapter on 'Politics in India'?

A. The Civic Culture Revisited
B. Politics and Government
C. Political Development and Social Change
D. Comparative Politics Today

25. Match List-I with List-II and select the correct answer from the codes given below the lists:

List-I (*Form of Government*)	*List-II* (*Name of the Country*)
(*a*) Parliamentary, Federal, Republican	(*i*) The United Kingdom
(*b*) Presidential, Federal, Republican	(*ii*) India
(*c*) Parliamentary, Unitary, Monarchical	(*iii*) France
(*d*) Parliamentary-cum-Presidential, Unitary, Republican	(*iv*) The United States of America

Codes :

	(*a*)	(*b*)	(*c*)	(*d*)
A.	(*i*)	(*ii*)	(*iii*)	(*iv*)
B.	(*ii*)	(*iii*)	(*iv*)	(*i*)
C.	(*iii*)	(*ii*)	(*i*)	(*iv*)
D.	(*ii*)	(*iv*)	(*i*)	(*iii*)

26. In which country all courts including all levels of the State Courts have the power of Judicial review?

A. India B. Switzerland
C. America D. Australia

27. The Indian Federal System differs from the American Federal System in respect of the following :

1. Representation of the States in the Upper House of the Federal Legislature.
2. Existence of a Written Constitution.
3. Vesting of Residuary Powers.
4. Dual Citizenship.

Select the correct answer from the codes given below :

Codes :

A. 1 and 2 B. 3 and 4
C. 1, 2 and 3 D. 4 only

28. Which one of the following is the most important characteristic of a Parliamentary Government?

A. Majority Rule
B. Rule of Law
C. Direct election of Member of Parliament
D. Collective responsibility of the Executive to the Legislature

29. Which one of the following federal systems was taken as a model by K.C. Wheare for judging other federal systems?

A. Australian federal system
B. American federal system
C. Swiss federal system
D. Canadian federal system

30. Given below are two statements, one labelled as Assertion (A) and the other labelled as Reason (R). Choose the correct answer from the codes.

Assertion (A): Presidential system is suitable for meeting crises.

Reason (R): The President has a fixed tenure.

Codes :

A. Both (A) and (R) are true and (R) is the correct explanation of (A).
B. Both (A) and (R) are correct but (R) is not the correct explanation of (A).
C. (A) is true but (R) is false.
D. (A) is false but (R) is true.

31. The Constituent Assembly was set-up under the

A. Cripp Mission
B. Cabinet Mission Plan
C. Wavell Plan
D. Nehru Report

32. Who said the following? 'India's Constitution was born more in fear and trepidation than in hope and inspiration'

A. Paul Brass B. Myron Weiner
C. K.C. Wheare D. Jennings

33. Which of the following Articles of the Constitution shields legislation from being declared unconstitutional and void?

A. Art. 15 B B. Art. 51 A
C. Art. 31 B D. Art. 29 A

34. Which of the following Amendments to the Indian Constitution has made Right to Education a Fundamental Right?

A. 92nd B. 94th
C. 93rd D. 91st

35. Which of the following statements is not correct?

A. First Proclamation of Emergency was declared in 1962.
B. Second Proclamation of Emergency was declared in 1971.
C. Third Proclamation of Emergency was declared in 1975.
D. Second and Third Proclamations of Emergency were revoked in 1978.

36. The power of Supreme Court of India to decide the dispute between the Centre and the States falls under its

A. Advisory Jurisdiction

B. Appellate Jurisdiction
C. Original Jurisdiction
D. Advisory and Appellate Jurisdiction

37. Who tried to period Indian politics in terms of the tussle between a "demand polity" and a "command polity"?
A. Rajni Kothari
B. Partha Chatterjee
C. Lloyd and Susanne Rudolph
D. Myron Weiner

38. Caste based reservations are labelled as
A. Affirmative Action
B. Positive Discrimination
C. State Intervention
D. Society Egalitarianism

39. Which of the following was headed by Raja Dhare and Nam Devdhasal?
A. Dalit Tiger
B. Bheem Shakti
C. Dalit Panther
D. Dalit Elephant

40. Lloyd and Susanne Rudolph saw the State in India as 'Polymorphous'. What does it mean?
A. Creature of manifold forms and orientation
B. Creature of multiple layers
C. Hybrid creature
D. Constantly changing creature

41. Who is the author of 'Political Economy of Development in India'?
A. Amartya Sen B. Subipta Kaviraj
C. Pranab Bardhan D. Hanza Allavi

42. In order to ensure free and fair elections and to conduct all elections to the Panchayats, the power is vested with
A. Chief Election Commissioner of India
B. Chief Minister of the State
C. State Election Commission
D. Chief Secretary of the State

43. **Assertion (A):** The President of India is the Constitutional Head of the State.

Reason (R): All powers are vested in the Council of Ministers headed by the Prime Minister.

Select the correct answer from the codes given below :

Codes :

A. Both (A) and (R) are true and (R) is the correct explanation of (A).
B. Both (A) and (R) are true, but (R) is not the correct explanation of (A).
C. (A) is true, but (R) is false
D. (A) is false, but (R) is true.

44. Match List-I with List-II and select the correct answer from the codes given below :

List-I	***List-II***
(*a*) Emergence of Muslim League	(*i*) 1940
(*b*) Lucknow Pact	(*ii*) 1906
(*c*) Motilal Nehru Report	(*iii*) 1916
(*d*) Two-Nation Theory	(*iv*) 1928

Codes :

	(*a*)	(*b*)	(*c*)	(*d*)
A.	(*iii*)	(*ii*)	(*iv*)	(*i*)
B.	(*ii*)	(*iii*)	(*iv*)	(*i*)
C.	(*iv*)	(*iii*)	(*i*)	(*ii*)
D.	(*i*)	(*iii*)	(*iv*)	(*ii*)

45. What is the correct sequence of the following Presidents of India? Use the codes given below:

(*i*) Dr. Zakir Hussain
(*ii*) Dr. Rajendra Prasad
(*iii*) Dr. Shankar Dayal Sharma
(*iv*) R. Venkataraman

A. (*i*) (*ii*) (*iv*) (*iii*)
B. (*ii*) (*i*) (*iv*) (*iii*)
C. (*iv*) (*iii*) (*i*) (*ii*)
D. (*iii*) (*iv*) (*ii*) (*i*)

46. Consider the following statements : In the area of organizational principles

1. In working out organizational principles, Gulick was influenced by Fayol's fourteen principles.

2. Urwick warns against the 'use of committees for the purpose of administration'.
3. Gulick gives no regard to the bases on which work may be divided.
4. Fayol believed in the principle of 'unity of command'.

Which of these statements is/are correct?

A. 1, 2, 3 and 4
B. 1, 2 and 3
C. 1 and 4
D. 1, 2 and 4

47. Match List-I with List-II and select the correct answer from the codes given below :

List-I	***List-II***
(*a*) Frederick Herzberg	(*i*) The Need Hierarchy
(*b*) Abraham Maslow	(*ii*) The existence of 'Clects'
(*c*) Fred W. Riggs	(*iii*) Motivator-Hygiene Approach
(*d*) M.P. Follett	(*iv*) Concept of Partnership

Codes :

	(*a*)	(*b*)	(*c*)	(*d*)
A.	(*iii*)	(*i*)	(*ii*)	(*iv*)
B.	(*ii*)	(*iii*)	(*iv*)	(*i*)
C.	(*i*)	(*iv*)	(*ii*)	(*iii*)
D.	(*iv*)	(*iii*)	(*ii*)	(*i*)

48. According to Chester I. Barnard, which one of the following is not correct about an order to be authoritative?

A. It should conform to the purpose of the organization.
B. It should be intelligible.
C. It should be motivating monetarily.
D. It should be feasible.

49. According to Mooney, conferring of specified authority by a higher authority is

A. Decentralization
B. Delegation
C. Deconcentration
D. Disintegration

50. Who defined development administration as 'Action-oriented, goal-oriented administrative system'?

A. Fred W. Riggs B. Dwight Waldo
C. Robert Dahl D. Edward Weidner

51. According to David Nachmias and D.H. Rosenbloom, which one of the following is not a feature of participatory bureaucracy?

A. Civil Service Associations to protect them from political tyranny.
B. High level of social representativeness in a national bureaucracy.
C. Participation of bureaucratic employees in decisions.
D. Citizen participation in bureaucratic policy making

52. Who among the following introduced the concept of 'Zone of Indifference' in an organization?

A. Herbert Simon
B. Douglas McGregor
C. Chester I. Barnard
D. Chris Argyris

53. Taylor's concept of Mental Revolution stands for

A. Cooperation, Harmony and Restricted output
B. Restricted output and Cooperation
C. Harmony and Cooperation
D. Economy, Cooperation and restricted output.

54. Which of the following committee recommended two-tier Panchayati raj institutions?

A. Ashok Mehta Committee
B. G.V.K. Rao Committee
C. R.R. Diwakar Committee
D. L.M. Singhvi Committee

55. When was the Central Vigilance Commission set up by the Government of India?

A. 1961 B. 1964
C. 1967 D. 1971

56. Arrange the following committees in chronological order and choose the correct answer from the codes given below:

(*i*) Kripalani Committee
(*ii*) Santhanam Committee
(*iii*) Tek Chand Committee
(*iv*) Vivian Bose Committee

Codes :

A. (*iii*), (*iv*), (*i*), (*ii*)
B. (*i*), (*iv*), (*iii*), (*ii*)
C. (*iv*), (*i*), (*iii*), (*ii*)
D. (*iii*), (*i*), (*iv*), (*ii*)

57. Which of the following committees recommended Block Level Planning?
A. Hanumantha Rao Committee
B. G.V.K. Rao Committee
C. L.M. Singhvi Committee
D. Dantwala Committee

58. Which among the following is not a feature of Liberalisation?
A. Deregulation
B. Debureaucratisation
C. Disinvestment
D. Statisation

59. The institution of 'Ombudsman' was first introduced in
A. Denmark B. UK
C. Sweden D. Switzerland

60. Given below are two statements, one labelled as Assertion (A) and the other labelled as Reason (R).

Assertion (A): Talking about responsibility, Follett maintains that "the distinction between those who manage and those who are managed is somewhat fading."

Reason (R): 'Each individual function must be seen in terms of its interdependence with other functions' in the organization.

Select the correct answer from the codes given below :

Codes :

A. Both (A) and (R) are individually true and (R) is the correct explanation of (A).
B. Both (A) and (R) are individually true, but (R) is not the correct explanation of (A).
C. (A) is true, but (R) is false.
D. (A) is false, but (R) is true.

61. Which of the following was an important figure in the development of liberal perspectives on international politics?
A. Thomas Hobbes
B. Woodrow Wilson
C. Hans J. Morganthan
D. Henry Kissinger

62. Match List-I with List-II and select the correct answer from the codes given below :

List-I	***List-II***
(*a*) Samuel P. Huntington	(*i*) Retreat of the State
(*b*) Joseph Nye	(*ii*) World Systems
(*c*) Susan Strange	(*iii*) Clash of Civilizations
(*d*) Immanuel Wallerstein	(*iv*) Soft Power

Codes :

	(*a*)	(*b*)	(*c*)	(*d*)
A.	(*iii*)	(*iv*)	(*i*)	(*ii*)
B.	(*ii*)	(*iii*)	(*iv*)	(*i*)
C.	(*iv*)	(*ii*)	(*iii*)	(*i*)
D.	(*iii*)	(*i*)	(*ii*)	(*iv*)

63. The Bretton Woods Agreement
A. led to a campaign to save the rainforest
B. argues that the Soviet Union was a success of the unmixed economy
C. led to the establishment of the International Monetary Fund (IMF)
D. led to the establishment of the World Wildlife Fund (WWF)

64. According to many realists, how is international peace best secured?
A. Concessions by peaceful States to powerful ones.
B. A balance of power between States.
C. Trying to spread democratic values throughout the world.
D. A worldwide federation of States.

65. In the field of nuclear strategy what does MAD stand for?
A. Missiles Are Dangerous
B. Mammals Are Doomed
C. Make America Die
D. Mutually Assured Destruction

66. Who said the following, "War is Foreign Policy by other means"?

A. Carl von Clausewitz
B. Napoleon Bonaparte
C. Quincy Wright
D. Hugo Clausewitz

67. Non-alignment as India's foreign policy meant

A. neutrality
B. equidistance between the three blocs during the cold war
C. independence and judging each issue on its relevance to our national interest
D. interference into the internal affairs of other States

68. Given below are two statements, one labelled as Assertion (A) and the other labelled as Reason (R) :

Assertion (A): India is for nuclear disarmament at the global level and for a credible minimum deterrence at the regional level.

Reason (R): India's nuclear policy has dual objectives.

Codes :

A. Both (A) and (R) are true and (R) is the correct explanation of (A).
B. Both (A) and (R) are true, but (R) is not the correct explanation of (A).
C. (A) is true but (R) is false.
D. Both (A) and (R) are false.

69. What is the correct sequence of the following Ministers of External Affairs of India?

(*i*) S.M. Krishna
(*ii*) Atal. B. Vajpayee
(*iii*) Pranab Mukherjee
(*iv*) Swarna Singh

Arrange the following chronologically from who came first :

A. (*iv*) (*ii*) (*iii*) (*i*) B. (*ii*) (*iv*) (*i*) (*iii*)
C. (*iv*) (*iii*) (*ii*) (*i*) D. (*i*) (*iii*) (*iv*) (*ii*)

70. "Indira Doctrine" is considered an important aspect of India's foreign policy for it defines

A. The objectives of India's foreign policy.
B. It equates India's security with that of the region and the predominance of India.
C. India's security is coterminous with the region and any interference of external powers is taken as a threat to India's security.
D. Doctrine enunciated by Prime Minister Indira Gandhi which was for the neighbours.

71. The United Nations Charter is mainly

A. largely concerned with individual human rights.
B. wholly concerned with the relationship between States.
C. devoted to a wide range of subjects including peace, justice, freedom and economic and social rights.
D. devoted to duties and rights of great, medium and small powers.

72. International society tradition is also known as the

A. Anglo-American School of International Relations.
B. English School of International Relations.
C. European School of International Relations.
D. Alternative School of International Relations.

73. The main purpose of the Indo-Sri Lanka Accord was

A. India's war against Tamils.
B. India's intention to partition Sri Lanka.
C. To end the ethnic strife between the Sinhalese and Tamils.
D. To legalise Tamil Militant groups.

74. The Asia-Pacific Economic Cooperation (APEC) forum

A. is part of a more general trend towards regional blocs.

B. accounts for over half the world's GDP.
C. has member states which include authoritarian regimes as well as democracies.
D. All of the above are true

75. The US approach to the Cold War was originally set out in
A. The Nixon Doctrine
B. The Marshall Plan
C. The Monroe Doctrine
D. The Truman Doctrine

ANSWERS

1	2	3	4	5	6	7	8	9	10
B	D	A	C	D	B	B	B	B	C
11	12	13	14	15	16	17	18	19	20
B	C	C	B	D	A	C	C	A	A
21	22	23	24	25	26	27	28	29	30
A	B	D	D	D	C	B	D	B	B
31	32	33	34	35	36	37	38	39	40
B	A	C	C	D	C	C	B	C	A
41	42	43	44	45	46	47	48	49	50
C	C	A	B	B	D	A	C	B	D
51	52	53	54	55	56	57	58	59	60
A	C	C	A	B	D	D	D	C	B
61	62	63	64	65	66	67	68	69	70
B	A	C	B	D	A	C	A	A	C
71	72	73	74	75					
C	B	C	D	D					

YOUR SPACE

YOUR SPACE